Symbiosis, Symbolism, and the Power of the Past

Participants in the Albright/ASOR Centennial Symposium,
held May 29–31, 2000, at the Israel Museum in Jerusalem

From left

Front row: Osnat Misch-Brandl, Aren M. Maeir, Shalom Paul, Trude Dothan, William G. Dever, Lydie Shufro, Seymour Gitin, Sarah P. Morris, Susan Sherratt, Ziony Zevit.

2nd row: Peter Machinist, Baruch Halpern, Carol Meyers, Eilat Mazar, Vassos Karageorghis, David Stronach, H. G. M. Williamson, Avraham Faust.

3rd row: Edouard Lipiński, David Ussishkin, Manfred Bietak, Joseph Aviram, Susan Ackerman, Charles U. Harris, Sidnie White Crawford, Holly Pittman, Karel van der Toorn, Annie Caubet.

4th row: Mordechai Cogan, Joe Seger, Eliezer Oren, Simo Parpola, Anson F. Rainey.

Back row: Eric M. Meyers, J. Edward Wright, Amihai Mazar, Kenneth A. Kitchen, Dan Masters, Israel Finkelstein, James D. Muhly, John J. Collins, Mark S. Smith.

Absent: Michal Artzy, Dan Bahat, Amnon Ben-Tor, Avraham Biran, Shlomo Bunimovitz, Moshe Kochavi, Amy-Jill Levine, Baruch A. Levine, Jodi Magness, Abraham Malamat, Doron Mendels, Jerome Murphy-O'Connor, Sari Nusseibeh, James Snyder, Lawrence E. Stager, Ephraim Stern, Daniel Wolk.   [*Photo courtesy of the Israel Museum*]

Symbiosis, Symbolism, and the Power of the Past

Canaan, Ancient Israel, and Their Neighbors
from the Late Bronze Age through Roman Palaestina

Proceedings of the Centennial Symposium
W. F. Albright Institute of Archaeological Research and
American Schools of Oriental Research
Jerusalem, May 29–31, 2000

edited by
WILLIAM G. DEVER AND SEYMOUR GITIN

Winona Lake, Indiana
EISENBRAUNS
2003

Library of Congress Cataloging-in-Publication Data

Centennial Symposium, W. F. Albright Institute of Archaeological Research and
American Schools of Oriental Research (2000 : Jerusalem)
Symbiosis, symbolism, and the power of the past : Canaan, ancient Israel, and their
neighbors from the Late Bronze Age through Roman Palaestina : proceedings of
the Centennial Symposium, W. F. Albright Institute of Archaeological Research
and American Schools of Oriental Research, Jerusalem, May 29/31, 2000 / edited
by William G. Dever and Seymour Gitin.
       p. cm.
Includes bibliographical references and index.
ISBN 1-57506-081-7 (hc)
    1. Mediterranean Region—Civilization—Congresses.   2. Iron age—
Mediterranean Region—Congresses.   3. Palestine—Civilization—Congresses.
4. Iron age—Palestine—Congresses.   5. Mediterranean Region—Politics and
government—History—Congresses.   6. Palestine—Religious life and customs—
History—Congresses.   7. Social structure—Palestine—History—Congresses.
8. Family—Palestine—History—Congresses.   9. Mediterranean Region—
Antiquities. I. Dever, William G. II. Gitin, Seymour. III. W. F. Albright
Institute of Archaeological Research. IV. American Schools of Oriental
Research. V. Title.
DE59.C46 2000
930.1—dc22

                       2003021117

This volume is dedicated to the memory of

Joy Ungerleider-Mayerson

who for many years served as Chair of the Board of Trustees of the W. F. Albright Institute of Archaeological Research. Her love of archaeology and her commitment to uncovering the history of ancient Israel have had a profound effect on the Albright's role in advancing the goals of archaeological research.

The American Schools of Oriental Research

celebrate with

The W. F. Albright Institute of Archaeological Research

the Centennial of

their presence in Jerusalem (1900–2000)

LARRY G. HERR, Chair
ASOR Committee on Publications

Contents

Part I
Historical and Political Landscape:
The Levant and Beyond

Palace Economies in the Late Bronze Age and
The Dark Age That Never Was (Iron Age I)

The Dynamics of Statehood (Iron Age II)

Imperial Interventions
(The Persian, Hellenistic, and Roman Periods)

Part II
Religion and Distinction

Shadow-Boxing the Canaanites (The Late Bronze Age)

Emerging Forms and Practices (Iron Age I)

The Formative Period of State Religion (Iron Age II)

Cult—Coast and Interior (The Persian Period)

Romans, Jews, and Christians

Part III
The History of the Family: Continuity and Change

Units and Cultural Unities (Iron Age I)

Household Economy (Iron Age II)

Families, Houses, and Homes
(The Persian, Hellenistic, and Roman Periods)

Part IV
Closing Remarks

Special Public Lecture

Discussions

Appendix I

Appendix II

Indexes

Preface

More than 100 years have passed since the modern era of exploration of the ancient Near East began. Throughout this period, American archaeological research in the "Holy Land," including Turkish and British Palestine, Transjordan, Israel, Jordan, and the Palestinian Authority, has significantly advanced our knowledge of ancient Israel and its neighbors. From the outset, the issues of the historical and political landscape, religion and ritual practices, and development of family and kinship relationships described in the Bible and ancient Near Eastern texts have been a major interest of the American Schools of Oriental Research (ASOR) and the W. F. Albright Institute of Archaeological Research.[1] It was, therefore, only natural that these subjects would be the main focus of discussion at the Albright/ASOR Centennial Symposium, celebrating 100 years of the Institute's presence in Jerusalem and the culmination of a century of productive research in the field of ancient Near Eastern studies. At the same time, the centennial celebration marked the beginning of a new period of commitment to advancing the disciplines of the archaeology, languages, literature, and history of Canaan, ancient Israel, Palestine, and their neighbors, from prehistory through the Islamic period.

Throughout the 20th century, Albright/ASOR has had a profound impact on ancient Near Eastern, biblical, and Judaic studies programs in North America, Europe, and the Middle East. From its very inception, it has also been at the forefront of archaeological research and a major force in developing successive generations of America's leading Near Eastern archaeologists. Today, the Albright is recognized for its world-renowned international fellowship and archaeological research programs and for its unique intellectual environment, in which Americans and other foreign students and scholars from five continents, Israelis, and Palestinians meet freely to share ideas and exchange information. This role is further enhanced by the Institute's support of the newly established archaeological program at Al-Quds University; the ongoing American/Israeli Tel Miqne–Ekron excavation and publications project jointly sponsored with Hebrew University; and the Albright's international project, *The Neo-Assyrian Empire: A Study of Center and Periphery*, under the aegis of the Council of American Overseas Research Centers, Washington, D.C.

The idea of the Centennial Symposium was initially conceived by the Albright Director, Seymour (Sy) Gitin, and Trustee Lydie Shufro, the Albright Centennial Committee Chair, with the support of then Albright President Patty Gerstenblith and ASOR President Joe D. Seger. Subsequently, a concept and general plan were developed by the Officers and Trustees who served on the Albright Centennial Committee: Walter Aufrecht, Sidnie White Crawford, Barry Gittlen, Jodi Magness, Lawrence Stager, Jane Waldbaum,

---

1. The American School of Oriental Research in Jerusalem, established in 1900, was renamed in 1970 in honor of its most distinguished director, W. F. Albright, the father of Biblical Archaeology. William Foxwell Albright (1891–1971) served as director in Jerusalem from 1920 to 1929 and from 1933 to 1936.

and Edward Wright, as well as Sy Gitin. Albright Trustee Mark Smith and Sy Gitin formulated the Symposium title, *Symbiosis, Symbolism, and the Power of the Past: Canaan, Ancient Israel, and Their Neighbors from the Late Bronze Age through Roman Palaestina,* and the specific topic of each session. The program was organized by Symposium Program Committee Chair William G. Dever, Sy Gitin, and Lydie Shufro. Sy Gitin, Lydie Shufro, and Helene Roumani, then Assistant to the Albright Director, were responsible for the logistical arrangements.

The officers, trustees, and members of the Albright and ASOR wish to extend their thanks to James Snyder, Director of the Israel Museum, for providing the venue for the Symposium; to Osnat Misch-Brandl, Curator for the Bronze Age, for her guidance and support and for preparing the Israel Museum's special exhibit in honor of the Albright/ASOR Centennial—*Thundering on High: Images of the Canaanite Storm God*; and to Joseph Aviram, Director of the Israel Exploration Society, for his excellent counsel and for organizing the reception at the Israel Museum sponsored by the Israel Exploration Society on behalf of the archaeological institutions in Israel. Special thanks also go to the Albright Institute Manager, Nadia Bandak, and Chef, Hisham M'ffareh, for organizing the lavish closing dinner reception held in the Institute's Kershaw Garden.

The Symposium would not have been possible without the generous support of ASOR, a grant to the Albright from the United States Information Agency, and the Horace W. Goldsmith, Samuel H. Kress, and Lucius N. Littauer Foundations, together with special gifts from Eugene and Emily Grant, Austin and Norma Ritterspach, Jonathan and Jeannette Rosen, Joe D. Seger, Herschel Shanks, the Stuart A. Shikiar Family Foundation, Lydie Shufro, and Daniel Wolk.

We also wish to acknowledge the Centennial Symposium's honorary sponsoring institutions, without whose participation the Symposium would not have been the success it was: Al-Quds University, Institute of Islamic Archaeology; Bar-Ilan University, Department of Land of Israel Studies; Ben-Gurion University of the Negev, Department of Bible and the Ancient Near East; Bible Lands Museum, Jerusalem; Birzeit University, Palestinian Institute of Archaeology; British School of Archaeology in Jerusalem; Council for British Research in the Levant; École Biblique et Archéologique Française de Jerusalem; Eretz-Israel Museum, Tel Aviv; German Protestant Institute of Archaeology; Hebrew University of Jerusalem, Institute of Archaeology; Israel Antiquities Authority; Israel Exploration Society; Israel Museum, Jerusalem; Jerusalem Center for Near Eastern Studies; Jerusalem University College; L. A. Meyer Museum for Islamic Art, Jerusalem; Nelson Glueck School of Biblical Archaeology; Palestine Department of Antiquities; Pontifical Biblical Institute; Reuben and Edith Hecht Museum, Haifa; Studium Biblicum Franciscanum; Swedish Theological Institute; Tel Aviv University, Sonia and Marco Nadler Institute of Archaeology; University of Haifa, Zinman Institute of Archaeology.

For the preparation of the Symposium volume, we wish to express our thanks to the editors, W. G. Dever and Sy Gitin, and to Walter Aufrecht for his editorial assistance, as well as to Edna Sachar, former Assistant to the Albright Director, for her indefatigable efforts in copy-editing the volume. Special thanks also go to Norma Dever for her help in word-processing the manuscripts. The format of the volume follows the order of the Symposium for the most part. Due to unforeseen circumstance, the papers given by E. Oren and

H. Pittman are not included, necessitating that the first two sessions be combined under the title *Palace Economies in the Late Bronze Age and the Dark Age That Never Was (Iron Age I)*. The public lecture given by W. G. Dever also is not included. The texts of the discussion that took place after each session appear at the end of the volume, together with two appendixes: the remarks made at the opening of the Israel Museum's exhibit in honor of the Albright/ASOR Centennial and at the Israel Exploration Society's reception.

While many individuals and institutions contributed to the success of the Symposium and the publication of its proceedings, without the vision, unrelenting commitment, and persistent efforts of Lydie Shufro, the dream of the Centennial Symposium and this volume would not have become a reality. It is to her, therefore, that we owe our deepest gratitude and thanks.

Sidnie White Crawford, President, Albright
Lawrence T. Geraty, President, ASOR

Opening Remarks: Greetings

Joe D. Seger, President, American Schools of Oriental Research

It is my pleasure to extend special greetings to everyone on behalf of the American Schools of Oriental Research and its Board Chair, P. E. MacAllister, along with all of its trustees, officers, and members.

To celebrate a century seems quite modest in a city like Jerusalem—now honoring its own 3,000 (and more) years' anniversary—and even more so in a region like the Middle East, where one can so readily view and, indeed, touch the very stepping-stones of civilization's long climb through a dozen or more millennia. ASOR is nonetheless very proud of its 100 years of accomplishments; proud of its participation in the advances of disciplines related to archaeological and historical research; proud of its partnerships with other kindred professional societies and institutions in the Middle East and throughout the world; and proud of its involvement in numerous great discoveries through the century.

ASOR's first footprint in the Middle East was in Jerusalem, and through the first seven decades of the century, the American School served not only as a vital base for American research in the region but also as a catalyst for cooperation and exchange with other local and foreign institutes and societies with similar interests and objectives. Among the many scholar-heroes in the Jerusalem School's history, the name of W. F. Albright stands out as the most prominent. It was thus only fitting that, when the Jerusalem institute was separately incorporated in 1970, it was renamed in his honor. ASOR is thus especially pleased to share with the Albright Institute in this centennial symposium, celebrating these 100 years of our mission together in this great city. I want to underscore particularly the great debt of appreciation due to the various Albright Institute trustees and staff members—and most especially Lydie Shufro, Bill Dever, and Sy Gitin—for their good and deliberate work in organizing and preparing for this event.

From ASOR—to all of you—the very best of wishes, as we look forward together to an enjoyable and stimulating few days ahead and to the initiation of another vital century of archaeological research and discovery.

Sidnie White Crawford, President-Elect, W. F. Albright Institute of Archaeological Research

On behalf of President Patty Gerstenblith and the Trustees of the W. F. Albright Institute of Archaeological Research, it is my pleasure to welcome you to this Centennial Symposium celebrating the 100th anniversary of the founding of the American Schools of Oriental Research and the Albright Institute.

Such symposia do not come into being without much "blood, sweat, and tears" behind the scenes, and my first duty is to acknowledge the people who made it possible. First and foremost, I would like to thank Dr. Sy Gitin, the Director of the Albright, whose tireless efforts over the past year caused the program to take shape, the venues to appear, and brought our distinguished guests here to Jerusalem from all over the globe. This is Sy's 20th year as Director of the Albright, and the academic stature of the Institute and its position as the premier overseas institution for the study of archaeology and biblical literature is largely the result of his sweeping vision, hard work, and personal stature as one of the foremost Syro-Palestinian archaeologists in the world today. Sy, congratulations and thank you.

My thanks next go to Lydie Shufro, a long-term Albright Trustee and the Chair of our Centennial and Symposium Committees. Lydie put in innumerable hours—raising funds, helping to contact participants, and arranging publicity, lodging, and transportation. Without her energy and perspicacity, this Symposium would not have taken place. We also owe a large debt of thanks to Professor William Dever, former Director of the Institute, former Trustee and currently Honorary Trustee, who as Chair of the Program Committee helped to put together the distinguished program we are all looking forward to attending over the next few days. The Albright Institute is honored by the presence of so many scholars and students from Europe, the United States, Canada, Israel, and the Palestinian Entity, and we thank Sy, Lydie, and Bill for making this possible.

I would also like to acknowledge the hard work of the staff of the Albright Institute, especially Nadia Bandak, the Institute Manager, and Helene Roumani, the Assistant to the Director. Although they remain behind the scenes, their efforts will be evident throughout the Symposium.

Finally, I would like to thank the Israel Museum for providing us with this marvelous venue at which to hold our Symposium. I hope you all enjoy the Symposium, and I hope to see all of you at the closing reception at the Albright Institute on Wednesday evening!

Ernest S. Frerichs, Executive Director, Dorot Foundation (read by AIAR Trustee Lydie Shufro, Chair, Centennial and Symposium Committees)

On behalf of the Dorot Foundation and its Board of Directors, I am delighted to bring congratulations to the W. F. Albright Institute of Archaeological Research on the occasion of this symposium celebrating 100 years of archaeological scholarship in excavation, research, and publication. Many of you listening to these words have been assisted in your work by the informed benefactions of the late founder of the Dorot Foundation, Joy Ungerleider-Mayerson, of blessed memory. From the early days of her involvement, together with her father, in the purchase of the Dead Sea Scrolls in the United States and their return to Israel, Joy was an enthusiastic participant in the archaeology of ancient Israel and early Judaism. She used her resources to further important projects in the recovery of the ancient heritage of Israel, of which her most recent major support was in making possible the Tel Miqne–Ekron project over the past 20 years. As Chair of the Albright Board of Trustees, she always represented the cause of archaeology in the land of Israel with vigor and enthusiasm.

Across the 40 years of my friendship with Joy, we shared her commitment, and I found myself for the last 25 years serving the Albright Institute as a Trustee and Officer. Those of you who know me well will know the lament in my heart that these words are being read to you rather than spoken by me. Among the landmarks of my life is my association with the Albright Institute and with all of you, and I cannot convey the regret I am experiencing in being unable to be with you on this occasion.

Given the traditions of the United States and its understanding of the ways to support archaeology, the continuing steps forward in archaeological scholarship are bound together with the active support of persons like Joy Ungerleider-Mayerson. Her life in this regard is an example to be treasured and hopefully to inspire others to emulate her style, more concerned with the importance of the project than with the issue of personal identification. The Dorot Foundation salutes the Albright Institute and all of you, focusing your vision less on the achievements of the past century and more on the challenges of the new century. The recovery of artifacts from the past is our most important clue to understanding the lives led by ancient peoples. May the archaeology of the land of Israel flourish in the 21st century and may the leadership of the Albright Institute play a continuing role of significance in the archaeological investigations of the historic land of Israel.

Part I

Historical and Political Landscape:
The Levant and Beyond

Islands in the Sea:
Aegean Polities as Levantine Neighbors

Sarah P. Morris
Cotsen Institute of Archaeology, Department of Classics
University of California, Los Angeles

It is a privilege to have been invited to represent the Aegean at such a distinguished gathering in Israel, where I received my first archaeological field training more than 25 years ago. Knowing Jerusalem before Athens directed my own research toward contact between the Aegean and the Near East, and I welcome the chance to present an overview and a review of new directions.

In my contribution to the Albright/ASOR centennial symposium, I would like to transcend the usual focus on Aegean ceramics in the east and Keftiu in Egyptian records that has dominated the modern study of Aegean relations with the Near East. (I also choose to avoid the topic of chronology, which keeps the two regions forever codependent.) Instead, I propose to revisit Aegean culture from the social-science perspective, now widely applied to cultures of the Levant and recently epitomized in the conference and volume entitled *The Archaeology of Society in the Holy Land* (Levy 1998). For, if history and geography make the Aegean a neighbor and partner to Near Eastern enterprises, its recent scholarship shares research goals across the eastern Mediterranean among a new generation of archaeologists. In this paper, I view the Aegean from the eastern perspective, as a set of autonomous palatial polities of the second millennium, the developed industries of luxury goods of which provided their main link to eastern neighbors with an appetite for them.

This relationship is more vivid in archaeology than in texts in which Near Eastern terms such as "Keftiu" and "Caphtor" remain imprecise or variable, or in native texts in Mycenaean Greek that focus on the internal economy and geography of a single year, with infrequent references abroad. Foreign relations in "Linear B" texts are largely limited to Semitic names of commodities (sesame, linen, spices), personal names such as Misraios and Aigyptios borrowed from foreign locales (possibly by natives; Palaima 1991), or foreign ethnicities of women bought or captured on the western coast of Asia Minor (Chadwick 1989). This leaves our task largely to archaeology and the major events outside most epigraphic horizons.

I. Minoan Crete

In the early second millennium, centralized power emerged on Crete in the first monumental complexes still called palaces. New to the picture are not only fresh intellectual

Author's note: I am grateful to Eric and Carol Meyers for my first field experience at Meiron in 1975 and for supporting my development in archaeology.

approaches, but new sites under modern excavation: in eastern Crete at Petras (directed by Metaxia Tsipopoulou); in central Crete at Galatas (directed by Giorgos Rethemnio-takis); and in western Crete at Monastiraki (Athanasia Kanta), as well as Chania (directed by Erik Hallager and Iannis Tzedakis). Can we compare the dramatic scale and impact of this phenomenon with the rise of new citadels, cities, and palaces in the Near Eastern Levant, which has been termed the "dawn of internationalism" (Ilan 1998)? Both areas witness a revival of the kind of fortified urbanism already visible in the mid–third millennium. Given the role of maritime trade and international connections now recognized in that process in Canaan, what role did the Near East play in the emergence and activity of the first state-level societies on Crete? Is there a process of "secondary-state" formation or a core-periphery relationship involved in the rise of the first Minoan palaces?

By the time of the Ulu Burun shipwreck, built of timbers cut after 1306 B.C.E. (Bass 1998), certain key commodities controlled relations with the east, notably copper and tin. How did Aegean communities compete and pay/exchange for them? It has recently been argued that luxury industries such as purple dye extracted from mollusks and the textiles it colored offered mechanisms by which Minoan Crete established essential relations as a trading partner with the east (Burke 1999). Such labor-intensive, specialized industries demonstrate how a region poorer in resources than Cyprus was in copper, Egypt in gold, or the Near East in tin and lapis lazuli, intensified its output of commodities. With secondary products (wool, dyed cloth) or those made of local materials (stone), the Aegean islands could compete for more costly raw materials from the east.

Thus the humble Minoan loomweight and the image of a loom with suspended weights identified by Burke (1997) on Middle Minoan prism seal stones may herald a revolution in Aegean technology and economy. It may be no accident that the first Minoan scenes of ships with sails also appear on these prismatic seals, along with the first imports to Crete of ostrich eggs and scarabs from Egypt (Cherry 1986: 41). An ideogram for a loom in Crete's earliest syllabic ("Linear A") writing system succeeding these seals carries this in-dustry into the earliest palatial system, along with its organized administration. The ver-tical, warp-weighted loom facilitates the production of larger expanses of woven wool cloth, and the exploitation of murex "adds value" to such products in bright colors. In this way, once-modest communities on Crete contributed to the circulation of prestige goods in the eastern Mediterranean, and the Aegean joined the Near East as a major partner. Here may lie the very "revolution" sought by scholars such as Cherry (1986) in their quest for a significant catalyst to explain the rise of Cretan palaces. Such specialization allowed Minoan polities to compete for raw materials, in turn transformed into luxury goods (stone and metal vases, faience, cloth) for local elite consumption and export for profit. Did an acceleration in revenues, access to exotic goods, and centralized production stimulate an organizational transformation necessary for the emergence of state-level societies such as the early "palaces"?

Scholars have at times revived the notion that the Minoan palatial system owes its de-sign or inspiration to similar monumental complexes in the east—Beycesultan in Anatolia or Mari on the Euphrates (Hiller 1987; Watrous 1987; Militello 1999). But the real debt of Minoan palatial Crete to the east may be the economic ties between its luxury industries and the elite network of the Levant (Sherratt and Sherratt 1991a). Indeed, recent scholarship has even tied dramatic changes in native industries, such as Minoan pottery, to signif-icant events among foreign powers (MacGillivray 1998: 106). As has been pointed out, changes in trade and markets, rather than in rulers, are more likely to have affected craft production at home (Van der Moortel 2000: 609). Whatever the effect of foreign events, these industries enabled Minoan Crete to insert itself successfully into the international market of elite goods and services, and the Aegean became a major player through its manufactured goods, merchants, and craftsmen abroad.

Mobility abroad was a natural extension of village-based industries on Crete that com-plemented an economy based on the palaces. New excavations at smaller settlements on the north coast of Crete (Mochlos, Poros, Chrysokamino, Gounes) reveal active indus-tries in metallurgy, lithics, ceramics, and stone-carving of vases and gems. Intensive pro-duction sites were located near transport (the sea), thus proximate to the delivery of raw materials from and the shipment of finished products to overseas destinations (see the es-says by Betancourt, Dimopoulou, Soles, and Vlahaki, in Laffineur and Betancourt 1997). These sites supported "palatial" workshops of the second millennium with semiautono-mous industries off-site, which might be compared to the "regional subcenters" of a more complex rural hinterland recognized in Middle Bronze Age Canaan (Ilan 1998: 305–6). On Crete, these satellite centers for industry further enhanced the singular nature of the complexes called "palaces" by analogy to the Near East (as well as to the European monar-chies dominant during the exploration of prehistoric Crete). Their function as ceremonial centers of power and as consumers rather than producers of luxury goods may have sur-passed their identity as urban sites or seats of centralized authority (see below; and Hägg and Marinatos 1987).

This newly appreciated independence of Cretan luxury industries from the "palaces" supports the view of extrapalatial entrepreneurship central to current views on the Bronze Age Mediterranean political economy (Sherratt and Sherratt 1991a), with its itin-erant craftsmen. For it is clear that not just goods but those who produced them had jour-neyed abroad since the second millennium. As early as the Middle Kingdom, textile technologies (such as "spinning bowls" or bowls for soaking flax) found in Egypt and the Levant indicate the circulation of techniques first witnessed on Crete for processing wool or fibers into cloth (Barber 1991: 70–77; Burke 1999). In the first half of the second millen-nium, the continuum of "Hyksos" (Canaanite) activity along the Via Maris, from the Egyptian Delta to northern coastal Palestine (Kabri), with Syrian centers farther north (Alalakh), developed a network of partners who welcomed Aegean specialties, including wall painting (W.-D. Niemeier and B. Niemeier 1998). From the "Hyksos" period on, and from the Delta of Egypt along the maritime highway that led all the way to Cilicia, deco-rated residence walls as well as artifacts and specialized products in their ceramic contain-ers illustrate an eastern appetite for Aegean images and products. While the discussion of the new frescoes from Egypt and Israel (and those from the northern Levant newly re-stored, e.g., from Alalakh) has concentrated on the identities of the fresco painters, more important may be their demonstration of a wide circulation of tastes and themes (W.-D. Niemeier and B. Niemeier 1998; Bietak, Marinatos, and Palyvou 2000). By the Middle Bronze Age, this coastal network of the eastern Mediterranean enjoyed Aegean goods (and, by 2000 B.C.E., the term "Keftiu" was first used for people and products from the

Aegean, if not Crete). These phenomena link cultures separated by distance, language, and social organization at the level of an international elite with shared values in luxury arts and commodities, and engaged in producing, procuring, and exchanging them.

Despite classical legends recalling a Minoan "thalassocracy," however, this prosperous maritime diaspora never displayed a corresponding political identity, even at home in the Aegean. In fact, one crucial function that Minoan palaces apparently did not share with their eastern counterparts (see the essays in Hägg and Marinatos 1987) was the presence of the ruler who would make them palaces, and whose absence forces us to seek further explanation for these complexes (Rehak 1991). Throughout the Cyclades, the Dodecanese, and coastal Asia Minor, local settlements of affluent Aegean merchants, manufacturers, and ship-owners emulated Cretan taste in wall paintings, ceramics, and life-style (including Minoan language and script, now attested at both Miletus and Thera). Some of these, such as prehistoric Miletus (Millawanda in Hittite texts), qualify as Minoan settlements on the basis of their dominant proportions of Cretan compared to Anatolian material, resident potters manufacturing Minoan ceramics in Cretan style, and foundation legends linking them to Crete (Milatos; W.-D. Niemeier and B. Niemeier 1999). But, beyond the empire of Minos and the theme of this centennial symposium session ("Empire and Palace Economies"), the Aegean remains an anomaly among prehistoric cultures of the eastern Mediterranean. Although exercising territorial control over its own island (Crete) and being an implicit sponsor of overseas enterprises, the palatial system stopped short of the imperial expansion known in Egypt, Assyria, or Anatolia in the Bronze Age. Nor did it become a political partner to these entities. Thus the Aegean, through the Late Bronze Age, remained ever "on the edge of empires" (Bunimovitz 1998).

II. The Mycenaean World: The Edge of Empires?

In the last phase of the Late Bronze Age (1500–1200 B.C.E.), mainland successors of the Minoan hegemony occupied Knossos on Crete, retaining many features of its internal operations, including script and administration. At some point, the figure of the *wanax* entered mainland and Cretan hierarchies, as part of a "palatial" system representing a unique fusion of mainland chiefdoms and Minoan ceremonial central places. But records in "Linear B," a Greek version of Minoan syllabic writing, are late and limited in place and time.

Recent studies have revised views on how these palaces operated as economic entities and therefore as trading partners with the east. In a panel at the Society for American Archaeology, published by the Cotsen Institute of Archaeology at UCLA as a volume entitled *Rethinking Mycenaean Palaces* (Galaty and Parkinson 1999), anthropologists, archaeologists, and epigraphers applied current theories of early states to palaces such as Pylos in the Peloponnese. Much speculation has been directed to the question of "wealth" versus "staple" finance as driving forces in these prehistoric economies. Once viewed as centers of capture, storage, and redistribution of resources, Mycenaean palaces are now seen as more aggressive mobilizers of resources directed toward elite consumption and exchange for prestige goods. For such largely exploitative rather than redistributive centers, producing perfumed oil and textiles in quantity for export, requirements in human labor must be addressed.

Documents from Pylos offer specific demographics in the personnel tablets. Women and their children from cities in Asia Minor and neighboring islands, such as Miletus, Chios, Lemnos, Halicarnassus, and Knidos, are listed by the rations issued to them. They were employed at Pylos and outlying centers in the production (spinning and weaving) and finishing (embroidering, dying, fulling, and perfuming) of textiles (Hiller 1975; Chadwick 1989). This has raised a related question regarding Mycenaean campaigns in Asia Minor, familiar from Homeric poetry but also from Hittite records of raids by "Aḫḫiyawa" on the western boundaries of the empire. Bryce has asked whether the primary motive for such campaigns could have been the capture of women for labor (1998: 62). Rather than the romantic recovery of native women like Helen, the enslavement of fresh laborers (as Cassandra and other Trojan women became the prize of Greek warriors in the epic tradition) was a serious objective. This makes the early exploits of Aegean warriors overseas, as depicted marching toward a city on the miniature fresco from Thera (Morris 2000: pl. 1), more than an adventure, if they sought human booty, like the women carrying water in the background, not just weapons and glory. Nearly three centuries separate Aegean tablets and frescoes, and caution must be exercised in incorporating both into a normative, narrative account. But an integrated analysis of visual and epigraphic sources from the Aegean and Anatolia offers a more complex picture of interaction and social organization during the Late Bronze Age.

A second issue raised by the rehabilitation of Mycenaean palaces as centers of production, consumption, and exploitation involves distribution. Maritime matters and foreign places are nearly invisible in "Linear B" tablets, largely devoted to internal administration of a single kingdom (Palaima 1991), and limited to a single year, in a time of crisis. Here we transcend the epigraphic horizons of both the Near East and the Aegean to consider other invisible but indispensable operators in this system. The discovery of the shipwreck off Ulu Burun on the southern coast of Lycia in Turkey has brought to life for scholars of the eastern Mediterranean the contents of a merchant ship that sank after 1306 B.C.E. (Bass 1998). Amid much speculation as to the origin, destination, and crew of this important ship, many find its mixed cargo and contents a welcome illustration of independent, collaborative enterprise in the Mediterranean. Its contents have been compared to representations in Egyptian tomb paintings of Syrian and other Near Eastern ships being unloaded, but they do not duplicate precisely lists of merchandise or gifts exchanged in diplomatic transactions. The ultimate lesson of the Ulu Burun wreck is the international flavor of ancient maritime enterprise, the realia of sub-elite transport behind formal diplomatic documents of "prestige and interest" (Liverani 1990).

This complicates the question of foreign relations between the Aegean and its eastern neighbors. Beyond Hittite references to the king of Aḫḫiyawa as an equal ("my brother") to the Great King of Ḫatti (Cline 1991), few Aegean authorities played a role in the network of Near Eastern alliances, enmities, treaties, and marriages that governed lives ruled by "prestige and interest." The Aegean never gained the kind of political clout wielded by the Mitanni, the Kassite kings of Babylon, the Hittites, Alašiya (?), or Egypt. To rephrase this in terms of contemporary Ugaritic mythology, the craftsman-god Kothar wa-Ḫasis may have had a "throne" at Caphtor as well as Memphis, but we know of no political powers in the Aegean outside of those implied in Hittite sources. One reason for the absence of a single centralized power in the Aegean may have been the autonomy of individual kingdoms, the heterarchy that survived as individual city-states, the archaic *poleis*, only to be united under a foreign power (first Macedon, then Rome).

Here I admit that I subscribe to the "minimalist" position espoused, for example, and eloquently defended by Merrillees (1998: 150; see also S. Sherratt 2001). One possible connection links an Aegean trail of official, commemorative scarabs issued by Amenophis III with an itinerary inscribed on statues at his mortuary temple at Kom el-Hetan. We have been too eager to parlay these place-names, and the scarabs, into an historical event, such as a diplomatic mission to the Aegean on behalf of the Egyptian pharaoh (also argued for the cache of cylinder seals found at Thebes [Porada 1981]). But they are no more persuasive than the images of "Keftiu" in elite Theban tombs for official, historical relations at the top. All of this evidence forces archaeologists of the Aegean to work outside of historical scenarios available in the Levant. This has distracted many from the testimony of Homer, Greece's earliest literary source, just as Syro-Palestinian archaeologists have sought to distance themselves from the tyranny of the Hebrew Bible. But as Mazar points out (in this volume), there is room for the baby and the bathwater, in selective use, in reconstructing the Bronze and Iron Age prehistories of the Levant. In the Aegean, a similar solution allows archaeologists and historians to apply Homeric testimony critically.

Among the significant discoveries to recast relations between the Aegean and the Near East, the phenomenon of the "palace" has moved east and much closer to the Levant, and it should be considered a possible export to the east. Building X at Ayios Dhimitrios on Cyprus (fig. 1), with its large orthogonal plan, central courtyard, ashlar masonry, and extensive storage facilities (able to accommodate at least 50,000 liters of olive oil), simulates an Aegean palace, with Aegean-derived scripts and individuals, inserted into a native community (South 1995: 192–97; Preziosi and Hitchcock 1999: 203–4). This also places "Aegean" monumental architecture and its concomitant social organization in closer proximity to its siblings in the east, for example, at Alalakh, Ugarit, and Minet el-Beidha on the Syrian coast, Kabri farther south, and other Late Bronze Age monumental complexes in the Levant (Fiandra 1997). A similar social organization behind this palatial structure needed the labor to produce, process, store, and distribute the olive oil that was a chief commodity in the palatial structure at Ayios Dhimitrios, perhaps in partnership with metallurgy. Did Cyprus attract Aegean entrepreneurs thanks to its human as well as mineral resources?

III. *The End of the Bronze Age and Beyond*

Understanding the scale of the human factor driving these palatial systems helps to explain their dramatic collapse at the end of the Late Bronze Age, a phenomenon now increasingly viewed as a related process throughout the eastern Mediterranean. In all the various scenarios and explanations offered for this widespread catastrophe—including natural causes such as drought and famine—the most consistent element involves the relocation of people in large numbers and the re-formation of social groups in new locales and new forms of communities. Monarchy survived in some locales: Iron Age Cyprus, for example, continued to support royal residences (the palace at Vouni), Homeric status items (the ivory throne from Salamis), and Bronze Age titles (both *wanax* and *basileus*),

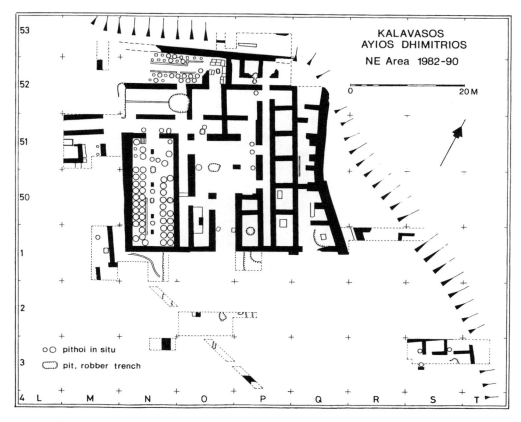

Fig. 1. Plan of NE area excavated at Kalavasos-Ayios Dhimitrios, Cyprus: Building X, with storage magazine, pithoi (after South 1995: 193, fig. 2).

but a new peer-polity model prevailed (Buitron-Oliver and Herscher 1997). This reconstitution describes the situation in the Levant as well as Anatolia and the Aegean, where centralized empires and monarchies yielded to smaller communities and autonomous city-states under charismatic, chiefly leadership. Once we have recognized the silent players in the Late Bronze Age—merchants and manufacturers, mercenaries and slaves—as a mobile army of diverse opportunists or victims of circumstances, it becomes much easier to envision how they overwhelmed the system in the end. And it does not require them to have acted in as organized a way as the Egyptian records portray (united as "Peoples of the Sea") or, as Drews sees them, as a new infantry force that overran the empires that originally recruited them (1993). Nor do we need to imagine the mass migrations that once dominated modern reconstructions of this period, over-determined by more recent phenomena (Drews 1993: 53–61, on Maspero). I share the view of this demographic turmoil as a symptom rather than a cause of Late Bronze Age collapse; its vivid historical events cannot be reduced to a social or economic upheaval alone. The perspective of the social sciences (Sherratt and Sherratt 1991b), focused on process, and that of the textual historian (Drews 1993), governed by "events," must balance each other for a total picture.

Fig. 2. Advertisement for Greek handicrafts in Athens News, *July 1999.*

A more holistic vision of the Late Bronze Age crisis facilitates a more global understanding of phenomena such as the Philistines, a favorite topic in Israel, thanks to so
many fresh discoveries and interpretations. As I have pleaded in the past (Morris 1998:
286–87), identifying the Philistines as an Aegean phenomenon on the basis of their Caph-
torite origin in the Bible and associations in material culture does not fully satisfy the evidence (Vanschoonwinckel 1999). As the figures on the Warrior krater from Mycenae

remind us, the situation in the Aegean, where palaces and citadels are refortified, then destroyed or abandoned, and reoccupied by realigned social groups, calls for its own explanation, as in the southern Levant. Elsewhere in the Mediterranean, the Hittite capital of Ḫattusas is abandoned outside the core settlement and eventually overrun by the Phrygians (Muhly 1999); Building X at Ayios Dhimitrios on Cyprus is burned and the settlement abandoned after 1200 (South 1995: 197). Those who settled as "Philistines" in the southern Levant could have relocated from closer at hand: Cyprus and Cilicia, as S. Sherratt (1992) and Killebrew (1998) have argued (or could even have been "acculturated" Canaanites [Drews 1998]). The Aegean is a fellow victim of these circumstances rather than an ultimate cause, with the specter of the Dorians, like the Philistines, equally inadequate to the evidence. Approaches to this phenomenon have either pursued an ethnic identity, supported by fieldwork in Philistia (most recently Barako 2000), or eschewed historical evidence for the sake of economic and social processes (S. Sherratt 1998). Surely a thorough understanding requires both methods, not a competition between disciplines.

These are some of the lessons I believe the discipline of Aegean archaeology can bring to the Levant, but also learn from it, and these shared lessons continue into the next millennium. A. and S. Sherratt have traced the Mediterranean economy in the Iron Age to the survivors and opportunists of these catastrophes of the Late Bronze Age, in their next incarnation (1991b). In concluding my paper, I would like to dwell on this continuity from the Bronze Age, to emphasize the shared legacy of the second millennium as it helped to shape early Iron Age communities in Greece and the Levant. The prehistory of the circumstances that brought the alphabet and Near Eastern literary traditions to Greece is crucial for understanding the rise of Iron Age cultures and social arrangements (Morris 1992). In time and continuity, the two eras are moving closer together: the next session in this symposium was called "The Dark Age That Never Was." The traditions behind the Bible and Homer both bequeathed to Western culture a unique legacy, and one that shared much.

I conclude with an illustration meant to edify as much as to amuse an AIAR/ASOR audience: an advertisement that appeared in Greek newspapers in 1999 and that was also widely distributed in tourist shops and public places (fig. 2). With an image selected and reproduced by the Greek Ministry of Development, Greek products are promoted by the National Authority on Handicrafts with a seal of authenticity, and I quote from the accompanying text (emphasis mine):

> The collection's distinctive mark, inspired by a mosaic created in the holy island of Delos more than 2,000 years ago, stands for exceptional quality in authentic handmade products. Unique craftsmanship, timeless aesthetic values, and *Hellenic origin* are the characteristics that define products bearing this mark of approval. If you are interested in handicrafts that are representative of the *Hellenic culture and heritage*, make sure that your choices are worthy.

Near Eastern archaeologists need no reminder that the motif chosen from an early Roman mosaic is in fact the sign of Tanit, perhaps the most ubiquitous symbol of the Punic (western Phoenician) presence in the classical Mediterranean. I offer this ironic symbol of "Hellenic origin" as a reminder that our cultures are perhaps today as interpenetrated as they were in antiquity, and that only our disciplines and our attitudes divide modern and ancient experience. I conclude with this symbol as an accidental ambassador, to build a bridge across centuries and continents, and as a signpost toward a future of international collaboration.

References

Barako, T.
  2000   The Philistine Settlement as Mercantile Phenomenon? *American Journal of Archaeology* 104: 513–30.
Barber, E.
  1991   *Prehistoric Textiles*. Princeton: Princeton University Press.
Bass, G.
  1998   Sailing between the Aegean and the Orient in the Second Millennium B.C. Pp. 183–91 in *The Aegean and the Orient in the Second Millennium: Proceedings of the 50th Anniversary Symposium, Cincinnati, 18–20 April, 1997*, ed. E. Cline and D. Harris-Cline. Aegaeum 18. Liège: Université de Liège.
Bietak, M.; Marinatos, N.; and Palyvou, C.
  2000   *The Maze Tableau from Tell el Dabʿa*. Pp. 77–90 in vol. 1 of *The Wall Paintings of Thera: Proceedings of the First International Symposium*, ed. S. Sherratt. Athens: Thera Foundation.
Bryce, T. R.
  1998   *The Kingdom of the Hittites*. Oxford: Clarendon.
Buitron-Oliver, D., and Herscher, E.
  1997   The City-Kingdoms of Early Iron Age Cyprus in Their Eastern Mediterranean Context. *Bulletin of the American Schools of Oriental Research* 308: 5–7.
Bunimovitz, S.
  1998   On the Edge of Empires: Late Bronze Age (1500–1200 B.C.E.). Pp. 320–31 in *The Archaeology of Society in the Holy Land*, ed. T. E. Levy. 2nd ed. London: Leicester University Press.
Burke, R. B.
  1997   The Organization of Textile Production on Bronze Age Crete. Pp. 413–22 in *TEXNH: Craftsmen, Craftswomen and Craftsmanship in the Aegean Bronze Age. Proceedings of the 6th International Aegean Conference / 6ᵉ Rencontre égéenne internationale, Philadelphia, Temple University, 18–21 April, 1996*, ed. R. Laffineur and P. Betancourt. Aegaeum 16. Liège: Université de Liège.
  1999   Purple and Aegean Textile Trade in the Early Second Millennium B.C. Pp. 75–82 in vol. 2 of *Meletemata: Studies in Aegean Archaeology Presented to Malcolm H. Wiener as He Enters His 65th Year*, ed. P. Betancourt et al. Aegaeum 20. Liège: Université de Liège.
Chadwick, J.
  1989   The Women of Pylos. Pp 43–96 in *Texts, Tablets and Scribes: Studies in Mycenaean Epigraphy Offered to Emmett L. Bennett, Jr.*, ed. J.-P. Olivier and T. G. Palaima. Minos 10. Salamanca: Universidad de Salamanca.
Cherry, J.
  1986   Evolution, Revolution and the Origins of Complex Society in Crete. Pp. 33–45 in *Minoan Society: Proceedings of the Cambridge Colloquium 1981*, ed. O. Krzyszowska and L. Nixon. Bristol: Bristol Classical Press.
Cline, E.
  1991   "My Brother, My Son": Rulership and Trade between the Late Bronze Age Aegean, Egypt, and the Near East. Pp. 143–50 in *The Role of the Ruler in the Prehistoric Aegean*, ed. P. Rehak. Aegaeum 11. Liège: Université de Liège.

Drews, R.
1993   *The End of the Bronze Age: Changes in Warfare and the Catastrophe ca. 1200 B.C.* Princeton: Princeton University Press.
1998   Canaanites and Philistines. *Journal for the Study of the Old Testament* 81: 39–61.

Fiandra, E.
1997   Similarities and Differences in the Architectural Structures of the Palaces in Crete and Ugarit. *Studi Micenei ed Egeo-Anatolici* 39/1: 49–73.

Galaty, M., and Parkinson, W. (eds.)
1999   *Rethinking Mycenaean Palaces: New Interpretations of an Old Idea.* Cotsen Institute of Archaeology Monograph 41. Los Angeles: Cotsen Institute of Archaeology.

Hägg, R., and Marinatos, N. (eds.)
1987   *The Function of the Minoan Palaces: Proceedings of the Fourth International Symposium at the Swedish Institute in Athens, 10–16 June, 1984.* Stockholm: Åströms.

Hiller, S.
1975   *Ra-mi-ni-ja.* Mykenisch-kleinasiatische Beziehungen und die Linear B-Texte. *Ziva Antika* 25: 388–411.
1987   Palast und Tempel im Alten Orient und im minoischen Kreta. Pp. 52–64 in *The Function of the Minoan Palaces: Proceedings of the Fourth International Symposium at the Swedish Institute in Athens, 10–16 June, 1984,* ed. R. Hägg and N. Marinatos. Stockholm: Åströms.

Ilan, D.
1998   The Dawn of Internationalism: The Middle Bronze Age. Pp. 297–319 in *The Archaeology of Society in the Holy Land,* ed. T. E. Levy. 2nd ed. London: Leicester University Press.

Killebrew, A.
1998   Mycenaean and Aegean-Style Pottery in Canaan during the 14th–12th Centuries B.C. Pp. 159–69 in *The Aegean and the Orient in the Second Millennium: Proceedings of the 50th Anniversary Symposium, Cincinnati, 18–20 April, 1997,* ed. E. Cline and D. Harris-Cline. Aegaeum 18. Liège: Université de Liège.

Laffineur, R., and Betancourt, P. (eds.)
1997   *TEXNH: Craftsmen, Craftswomen and Craftsmanship in the Aegean Bronze Age. Proceedings of the 6th International Aegean Conference / 6ᵉ Rencontre égéenne internationale, Philadelphia, Temple University, 18–21 April, 1996,* ed. R. Laffineur and P. Betancourt. Aegaeum 16. Liège: Université de Liège.

Levy, T. E. (ed.)
1998   *The Archaeology of Society in the Holy Land.* 2nd ed. London: Leicester University Press.

Liverani, M.
1990   *Prestige and Interest: International Relations in the Ancient Near East, ca. 1600–1100 B.C.* Padua: Sargon.

MacGillivray, J. A.
1998   *Knossos: Pottery Groups of the Old Palace Period.* British School at Athens Studies 5. London: British School at Athens.

Merrillees, R.
1998   Egypt and the Aegean. Pp. 149–58 in *The Aegean and the Orient in the Second Millennium: Proceedings of the 50th Anniversary Symposium, Cincinnati, 18–20 April, 1997,* ed. E. Cline and D. Harris-Cline. Aegaeum 18. Liège: Université de Liège.

Militello, P.
1999   Influenza orientale sui palazzi minoici? Il caso delle decorazioni parietale. Pp. 91–108 in *ΕΠΙ ΠΟΝΤΟΝ ΠΛΑΖΟΜΕΝΟΙ: Simposio italiano di studi egei dedicato a Luigi Bernabò Brea e Giovanni Pugliese Caratelli,* ed. V. La Rosa, D. Palermo, and L. Vagnetti. Rome: Scuola Archeologica Italiana di Atene.

Morris, S. P.
1992   *Daidalos and the Origins of Greek Art.* Princeton: Princeton University Press.

1998   Daidalos and Kothar: The Future of Their Relationship. Pp. 281–89 in *The Aegean and the Orient in the Second Millennium: Proceedings of the 50th Anniversary Symposium, Cincinnati, 18–20 April, 1997,* ed. E. Cline and D. Harris-Cline. Aegaeum 18. Liège: Université de Liège.

2000   From Thera to Scheria: Aegean Art and Narrative. Pp. 317–33 in vol. 1 of *The Wall Paintings of Thera: Proceedings of the First International Symposium,* ed. S. Sherratt. Athens: Thera Foundation.

Muhly, J.

1999   The Phoenicians in the Aegean. Pp. 517–26 in vol. 2 of *Meletemata: Studies in Aegean Archaeology Presented to Malcolm H. Wiener as He Enters His 65th Year,* ed. P. Betancourt et al. Aegaeum 20. Liège: Université de Liège.

Niemeier, B., and Niemeier, W.-D.

2000   Aegean Frescoes in Syria–Palestine. Pp. 763–800 in vol. 2 of *The Wall Paintings of Thera: Proceedings of the First International Symposium,* ed. S. Sherratt. Athens: Thera Foundation.

Niemeier, W.-D., and Niemeier, B.

1998   Minoan Frescoes in the Eastern Mediterranean. Pp. 69–98 in *The Aegean and the Orient in the Second Millennium: Proceedings of the 50th Anniversary Symposium, Cincinnati, 18–20 April, 1997,* ed. E. Cline and D. Harris-Cline. Aegaeum 18. Liège: Université de Liège.

1999   The Minoans of Miletus. Pp. 543–54 in vol. 2 of *Meletemata: Studies in Aegean Archaeology Presented to Malcolm H. Wiener as He Enters His 65th Year,* ed. P. Betancourt et al. Aegaeum 20. Liège: Université de Liège.

Palaima, T.

1991   Maritime Matters in the Linear B Tablets. Pp. 273–309 in *Thalassa: L'Egée Préhistorique et la Mer: Actes de la Troisième Rencontre égéenne internationale de l'Université de Liège, Calvi, Corse (23–25 Avril 1990),* ed. R. Laffineur and L. Basch. Aegaeum 7. Liège: Université de Liège.

Porada, E.

1981   The Cylinder Seals Found at Thebes in Boeotia. *Archiv für Orientforschung* 28: 1–70.

Preziosi, D., and Hitchcock, L.

1999   *Aegean Art and Architecture.* Oxford: Oxford University Press.

Rehak, P. (ed.)

1991   *The Role of the Ruler in the Prehistoric Aegean.* Aegaeum 11. Liège: Université de Liège.

Sherratt, A., and Sherratt, S.

1991a   From Luxuries to Commodities: The Nature of Mediterranean Bronze Age Trading Systems. Pp. 351–86 in *Bronze Age Trade in the Mediterranean,* ed. N. H. Gale. Studies in Mediterranean Archaeology 90. Jonsered: Åströms.

1991b   The Growth of the Mediterranean Economy in the Early First Millennium B.C. *Ancient Trade: New Perspectives. World Archaeology* 24/3: 361–78.

Sherratt, S.

1992   Immigration and Archaeology: Some Indirect Reflections. Pp. 316–47 in vol. 2 of *Acta Cypria: Acts of an International Congress on Cypriote Antiquities Held in Göteborg on 22–24 August 1991,* ed. P. Åström. Jonsered: Åströms.

1998   "Sea Peoples" and the Economic Structure of the Late Second Millennium in the Eastern Mediterranean. Pp. 292–313 in *Mediterranean Peoples in Transition: Thirteenth to Early Tenth Centuries B.C.E.,* ed. S. Gitin, A. Mazar, and E. Stern. Jerusalem: Israel Exploration Society.

2001   Potemkin Palaces and Route-Based Economies. Pp. 214–38 in *Economy and Politics in the Mycenaean Palace States: Proceedings of a Conference Held on 1–3 July 1999 in the Faculty of Classics, Cambridge,* ed. S. Voutsaki and J. Killen. Cambridge: Cambridge Philological Society.

South, A. K.

1995   Urbanism and Trade in the Vasilikos Valley Project in the Late Bronze Age. Pp. 187–97 in *Trade, Contact and the Movement of Peoples in the Eastern Mediterranean: Studies in Honour of*

J. Basil Hennessy, ed. S. Bourke and J.-P. Descoeudres. Mediterranean Archaeology Supplement 3. Sydney: Meditarch.

Van der Moortel, A.

2000   Review of J. A. MacGillivray, *Knossos: Pottery Groups of the Old Palace Period* (London: British School at Athens, 1998) in *American Journal of Archaeology* 104: 607–9.

Vanschoonwinckel, J.

1999   Between the Aegean and the Levant: The Philistines. Pp. 85–107 in *Ancient Greeks East and West*, ed. G. Tsetsekhladze. Mnemosyne Supplement 196. Leiden: Brill.

Watrous, L. V.

1987   The Role of the Near East in the Rise of the Cretan Palaces. Pp. 65–74 in *The Function of the Minoan Palaces: Proceedings of the Fourth International Symposium at the Swedish Institute in Athens, 10–16 June, 1984*, ed. R. Hägg and N. Marinatos. Stockholm: Åströms.

The Case of Ugarit and Carchemish: A Contrast

Annie Caubet

Département des Antiquités Orientales
Musée du Louvre, Paris

Our understanding of the chronology of the end of the Bronze Age in Syria relies on textual and archaeological evidence connected to Egypt and to the Hittite Kingdom. The evidence in most cases is restricted to one or the other of the two, and the main links between Egypt and the Hittites is provided by the archives from Ugarit. Until recently, most of the evidence attesting to the very end of the existence of Ugarit was believed to come from an "oven" in a courtyard of the royal palace containing the last batch of cuneiform tablets, including a letter of the Sun King to Ammurapi of Ugarit, which was being baked when the city was destroyed. This dramatic picture had to be revised (Calvet 1990: 40; Yon 1992; for a summary in English, see Millard 1995: 119 n. 2), and it is now believed that these tablets do not date to the very end of the city, although they cannot be dated much earlier. But the information will take a long time to be recognized by all, and seminal works on the end of the Bronze Age still refer to "the tablets from the oven" (e.g., Hawkins 1995: 58). On the other hand, the implications of new evidence for the reconstruction of the dynastic lines ruling over north Syria after 1200 B.C.E. (Hawkins 1988; 1993; 1995) have not always been fully recognized by historians interested in the chronology of Ugarit or of Egypt (Warburton 2000). It seems useful to present a summary of the recent chronological information linking Ḫatti, north Syria, and Egypt, and to compare the respective fates of Ugarit and Carchemish at the end of the second millennium B.C.E.

North Syria was politically connected to the Ḫatti about 1352 B.C.E. (the year of the death of King Tut Ankh Amun), when Hittite King Shuppiluliuma I conquered the Syrian states, from Halab (Aleppo) to Kadesh. Shuppiluliuma then established his son Sharri Kusuh as ruler over Carchemish, which became a vice royalty. The throne of Carchemish thereafter passed from father to son. While eight kings succeeded each other on the throne of Ḫattušas for five generations between Shuppiluliuma I and Shuppiluliuma II (Beckman 2000), only four kings of Carchemish covered the same time-span: Sharri Kusuh, son of Shuppiluliuma I; the son of Shahurunuwa, Ini Teshub, who by approximately 1230 B.C.E. seems to have established authority over most of the Syrian states (jointly with Tudhaliya IV, he signed the divorce settlement of Ammistamru II of Ugarit); Ini Teshub's son, Talmi Teshub, who must have been a contemporary of Ammurapi, the last king of Ugarit (see below); and one more king of Carchemish, Ku(n)zi Teshub, who has

---

Author's note: Marguerite Yon, Yves Calvet, and Dennis Pardee were, as always, of great help.

recently been added to the list (Sürenhagen 1986; Hawkins 1988). He appears to have survived the collapse of the Hittite Empire, claiming for himself the title of "Great King," previously reserved solely for the king of Ḫattušas. It seems, therefore, that Carchemish remained in control of a part of the Hittite Empire southeast of the Taurus, stretching at least from Malatya to Emar on the Euphrates. Subsequent kings of Carchemish during the Dark Ages, approximately 1150–1000 B.C.E., retained the title "Great King" and perhaps even held on to the territory, although they soon lost ground to the Arameans in the south. The renaissance of the Neo-Hittite kingdoms may now be dated to no later than the second half of the 12th century B.C.E., more than a century earlier than had previously been assessed. The direct dynastic ancestry between the rulers of these new city-states and the old line from Carchemish helps to explain the survival of many Hittite traditions in the early first millennium B.C.E., such as the use of circular royal seals. Victory stelae continued to be carved on rocks on the mountainous borders, and stone reliefs were placed in the walls of palaces and temples. The Neo-Hittite reliefs recently uncovered at Aleppo (Kohlmeyer 2000) are a good example.

Ugarit, on the other hand, suffered the same fate as Ḫattušas and did not survive the collapse of the Hittite Empire. Most of the data come from the archives of the royal palace (Nougayrol 1955; 1956) and from a few private houses of officials closely linked by family ties to the royal dynasty (Nougayrol 1968). They provide a synchronism between Ammurapi of Ugarit and Talmi Teshub of Carchemish, himself a third cousin of Shuppiluliuma II, the last king of Ḫattušas. On the Egyptian side, they shed some light on the very disturbed period between the reigns of Ramesses II and Ramesses III. Not all these texts, however, give the name of the current king, allowing for some ambiguity. The "Letter from the General," for instance, discovered in 1956 in the "House of Rapanu" (Nougayrol 1968: 69–79; Yon 1997), and other letters from the same archives mentioning "menacing boats" off the shore of Ugarit lack any names of officials or kings. They may not necessarily be dated to the end of the city and the reign of its last king, Ammurapi; Singer (1987), for instance, understands them as pertaining to the situation described by the Amarna letters during the reign of Amenophis III in the 15th century B.C.E. However, with the international archives from the "House of Urtenu," we have a series of documents that can be dated within a plausibly short time-span—that is, the early years of the reign of Ammurapi. The first batch of tablets was discovered by accident in 1973 by the military while digging a concrete blockhouse. Long off-limits, the site was evacuated by the army in 1986, thus allowing the scientific excavation to begin, and the remains of a house and its private archives were discovered (Lombard 1995). Publication of the texts followed the progress of the excavations (Bordreuil 1991 for the series uncovered in 1973 by the military; Yon and Arnaud 2001, for the series excavated between 1986 and 1992; Yon, Bordreuil, and Malbran 1995 for the discoveries of 1994). It must be stressed that, although the various texts from this location have been known for a long time, it is only now beginning to be accepted that their archaeological context strongly indicates that they belong to a coherent, contemporary corpus. The archives contained a number of letters written by and to a high-ranking official by the name of Urtenu, perhaps the same individual designated *sakinu*, "governor," of the queen; international letters from Egypt, Carchemish, and other Syrian states were addressed to the governor "while the king [Ammurapi] was young," and

Urtenu may have gained some international importance, and may have acted as regent to Ammurapi.

Letter RS 34.139 recounts the "battle at Nihriya" between Tudhaliya IV and an Assyrian king who could be either Shalmaneser I or Tukulti Ninurta (Lackenbacher 1991: 46). The name of the Ugaritic king to whom this text was addressed is missing. It has been reconstructed as Ibiranu (Lackenbacher 1991), possibly Ibiranu VI in Arnaud's list (1999: 163). In light of what we now know of the consistent character of Urtenu's archives, there is a problem concerning why this international letter would have been kept for three generations in a private house.

Several letters were written by "the king" (Malbran-Labat 2001). The title refers to the king of Carchemish (Yamada 1992), and we believe this unnamed king is Talmi Teshub.

Two letters are of special Egyptian interest. In letter RS 88.21581, sent by an Egyptian official to a sculptor, he refers to the material necessary for the erection of an image or statue of Merneptah in the Temple of Baal at Ugarit. It is unclear whether this was the image of the living pharaoh or whether it was commissioned in his memory, immediately following his death (Lackenbacher 1995: 77–83; 2001). In any case, this document is a welcome addition to the already rich dossier of this pharaoh at Ugarit and Ḫattušas (Liverani 1979: col. 1213). Estimates of the dates of the reign of Merneptah, which lasted 20 years, vary according to the high, middle, or low chronology (Lesko 1992). On the same principle as was the case for the above-mentioned "battle at Nihriya" text, we propose to link letter RS 88.21581 to the reign of Ammurapi.

The much-discussed fragment RS 86.2230 belongs to the same archive and must consequently be attributed to the same time period. It is most unsatisfactory, as only the name and title of the expeditor remains: "Beia, chief of the guards of the great king, the king of the land of Egypt" (Freu 1988; de Moor 1990; Hoffner 1992: 49; Arnaud 1993; Yon 1997: 136, no. 4). There is little doubt that this Beia is the same as Bay, an official of Asiatic (Syrian) descent and a dominant figure on the Egyptian political scene at the end of the 19th Dynasty, who was to become a usurper (Lesko 1992: 152). Freu (1988) dates the letter to Siptah's fifth year, 1193 B.C.E.

The international letters from the "House of Urtenu," all or most of which belong to a single generation, together with the archives from the royal palace, thus provide the basis for a tentative synchronism: in Egypt from Merneptah to Beia; Talmi Teshub at Carchemish; and at Ḫattušas, from the very end of the reign of Tudhaliya IV to the short, ill-fated reign of his successor, Shuppiluliuma II, all may be framed within the reign of Ammurapi of Ugarit. After his reign, all texts disappear from Ugarit and the archaeological evidence at the site shows that the city was violently destroyed and looted (Yon 1992). There may be a case for the presence of Mycenaean IIIC sherds at Ugarit (Montchambert 1996), with a brief reoccupation and rearrangement within the ruins by squatters, before a long abandonment that lasted until the Persian period.

While the southern Levant experienced a complete renewal of their population and political organization with the arrival of new settlers, northern Syria knew a contrasting destiny. In the west, next to the sea, village life continued for a long time, free from the control and financial demands of the ruling power from the city-states. The continuity in the toponyms of the kingdom of Ugarit from the Late Bronze Age to modern times is a witness to a continuity in population. In the hinterland, the crumbs of the Hittite Empire were collected and retained by the kingdom of Carchemish and other city-states, such as Milid-Malatya, and the appearance of the Neo-Hittite city-states seems to have occurred quite early.

References

Arnaud, D.
>1993   Lettre de Beya. Pp. 248–49 in *Syrie: Mémoire d'une civilisation*. Institut du Monde Arabe Exhibition Catalogue 222. Paris: Institut du Monde Arabe.
>1999   Prolégomènes à la rédaction d'une histoire d'Ougarit II: Les bordereaux de rois divinisés. *Studi Micenei ed Egeo-Anatolici* 41/2: 153–73.

Beckman, G.
>2000   Hittite Chronology. *Akkadica* 119–20: 19–32.

Bordreuil, P. (ed.)
>1991   *Une bibliothèque au sud de la ville*. Ras Shamra Ougarit 7. Paris: Éditions Recherche sur les Civilisations—Association pour la Diffusion de la Pensée Française.

Calvet, Y.
>1990   Les bassins du Palais Royal d'Ougarit. *Syria* 67: 31–42.

Freu, J.
>1988   La tablette RS 86.2230 et la phase finale du royaume d'Ugarit. *Syria* 65: 395–98.

Hawkins, D.
>1988   Kuzi-Tešub and the "Great Kings" of Karkamiš. *Anatolian Studies* 38: 99–108.
>1993   The New Inscription from the Südburg of Bagazköy Hattusa. *Archäologischer Anzeiger* 3: 305–14.
>1995   The Hieroglyphic Inscription of the Sacred Pool Complex at Hattusa *(Südburg)*. Studien zu den Bogazköy Texten 3. Wiesbaden: Harassowitz.

Hoffner, H. A.
>1992   The Last Days of Khattusha. Pp. 46–52 in *The Crisis Years: The 12th Century BC*, ed. W. A. Ward and M. Sharp Joukowsky. Dubuque, Ia.: Kendall/Hunt.

Kohlmeyer, K.
>2000   *Der Tempel des Wettergottes von Aleppo*. Münster: Rhema.

Lackenbacher, S.
>1991   Lettres et fragments. Pp. 83–104 in *Une bibliothèque au sud de la ville*, ed. P. Bordreuil. Ras Shamra Ougarit 7. Paris: Éditions Recherche sur les Civilisations.
>1995   Une correspondance entre l'administration du pharaon Merneptah et le roi d'Ougarit. Pp. 77–83 in *Les Pays d'Ougarit autour de 1200 av. J.C.*, ed. M. Yon, M. Sznycer, and P. Bordreuil. Ras Shamra Ougarit 11. Paris: Éditions Recherche sur les Civilisations.
>2001   Une lettre d'Égypte. Pp. 239–48 in vol. 1 of *Études ougaritiques*, ed. M. Yon and D. Arnaud. Ras Shamra Ougarit 14. Paris: Éditions Recherche sur les Civilisations.

Lesko, L. H.
>1992   Egypt in the 12th Century. Pp. 151–56 in *The Crisis Years: The 12th Century BC*, ed. W. A. Ward and M. Sharp Joukowsky. Dubuque, Ia.: Kendall/Hunt.

Liverani, M.
>1979   Ras Shamra: Histoire. Cols. 1295–347 in vol. 9 of *Supplément au Dictionnaire de la Bible*. Paris: Letouzay-Ané.

Lombard, P.
>1995   Contexte archéologique et données épigraphiques. Quelques reflexions sur l'interprétation du gisement de 1973–1992. Pp. 227–37 in *Les Pays d'Ougarit autour de 1200 av. J.C.*, ed. M. Yon, M. Sznycer, and P. Bordreuil. Ras Shamra Ougarit 11. Paris: Éditions Recherche sur les Civilisations.

Malbran-Labat, F.
    2001   Lettres. Pp. 249–55 in vol. 1 of *Études ougaritiques*, ed. M. Yon and D. Arnaud. Ras Shamra Ougarit 14. Paris: Éditions Recherche sur les Civilisations.

Millard, A.
    1995   The Last Tablets of Ugarit. Pp. 119–24 in *Les Pays d'Ougarit autour de 1200 av. J.C.*, ed. M. Yon, M. Sznycer, and P. Bordreuil. Ras Shamra Ougarit 11. Paris: Éditions Recherche sur les Civilisations.

Montchambert, J.-A.
    1996   Du Mycénien IIIC à Ougarit. *Orient Express* 1996/2: 45–46.

Moor, J. de
    1990   *The Rise of Yahwism: The Roots of Israelite Monotheism.* Leuven: Peeters.

Nougayrol, J.
    1955   Textes accadiens et hourrites des archives est, ouest et centrales. Pp. 1–308 in vol. 3 of *Le Palais Royal d'Ugarit*, ed. C. Schaeffer. Paris: Klincksieck.
    1956   Textes accadiens des archives sud. Pp. 1–300 in vol. 4 of *Le Palais Royal d'Ugarit*, ed. C. Schaeffer. Paris: Klincksieck.
    1968   Textes suméro-accadiens des archives et bibliothèques privées d'Ugarit. Pp. 1–446 in vol. 5 of *Ugaritica*, ed. C. Schaeffer. Paris: Geuthner.

Singer, I.
    1987   Dating the End of the Hittite Empire. *Hethitica* 8: 413–22.

Sürenhagen, D.
    1986   Ein Königsiegel aus Kargamis. *Mitteilungen des deutschen Orient Gesellschaft* 118: 184–90.

Warburton, D.
    2000   Synchronizing the Chronology of Bronze Age Western Asia with Egypt. *Akkadica* 119–20: 33–76.

Yamada, M.
    2000   Reconsidering the Letters from the "King" in the Ugarit Texts: Royal Correspondence of Carchemish. *Ugarit-Forschungen* 24: 431–46.

Yon, M.
    1992   The End of the Kingdom of Ugarit. Pp. 111–22 in *The Crisis Years: The 12th Century* BC, ed. W. A. Ward and M. Sharp Joukowsky. Dubuque, Ia.: Kendall/Hunt.
    1997   *La cité d'Ougarit sur le tell de Ras Shamra.* Paris: Éditions Recherche sur les Civilisations.

Yon, M., and Arnaud, D. (eds.)
    2001   *Études ougaritiques* 1. Ras Shamra Ougarit 14. Paris: Éditions Recherche sur les Civilisations.

Yon, M.; Bordreuil, P.; and Malbran-Labat, F.
    1995   Ras Shamra: Campagne 1994. *Comptes rendus de l'Académie des Inscriptions* 1995: 427–56.

Greece and Anatolia in the Early Iron Age:
The Archaeological Evidence and the Literary Tradition

James D. Muhly
American School of Classical Studies at Athens
Athens

The concept of a "Dark Age" (or "Ages") in Greek prehistory is still very much with us. The past 30 years have seen such publications as *The Dark Age of Greece* (Snodgrass 1971); *The Greek Dark Ages* (Desborough 1972); the *Zwettl Symposium* on the "Dark Ages" (held in 1980; published in 1983); *New Light on a Dark Age*, a collection of essays (Langdon 1997); and the Nineteenth Myres Memorial Lecture on *Light from Cyprus on the Greek "Dark Age"?* (Coldstream 1998).

On the first page of the printed version of his lecture, Coldstream states that:

> In Greece, in spite of recent discoveries, this is still an age that can be called "dark"; an age of total illiteracy and, in most Aegean regions, an age of poverty, poor communications, and isolation from the outside world. (1998; see also 1992–93: 8)

Such sentiments can be found in most works on Greek history covering the 300 years from 1100 to 800 B.C.E. Boardman (1999: 40) even expands the geographical horizon, stating that:

> To pretend that only the Greeks had a Dark Age does little justice to the almost impenetrable gloom that surrounds the archaeology of Canaanite/Phoenician cities in the same years, while even their historical record is still extremely thin until the 9th century. The Greek record might have been no worse had they been literate.

Tandy, in his recent book *Warriors into Traders: The Power of the Market in Early Greece* (1997: 1 n. 1), a most provocative work to which I shall return later, has it that:

> The collapse may not have been as rapid as once thought . . . but its precipitousness is still certain, and by 1050 the Aegean world had hit rock bottom.

But "rock bottom" coincides, in fact, with the earliest (and richest) burials in the North Cemetery at Knossos (Tombs 186, 200–202), the earliest (and richest) burials in the *Skales* cemetery at Palaepaphos (Tombs 49, 58, 76, 89), at Salamis (Tomb 1), Kourion *Kaloriziki* (Tombs 39–40), Amathus (Tombs 521, 523), Lapithos *Kastros*, Tiryns (Tomb 28). The mid–11th century B.C.E. also marks the beginning of Euboean expansion to the east, to Cyprus, Tyre, Tel Dor, and Tel Hadar; and of Phoenician expansion to the west, to Cyprus, Lefkandi, and Kommos (for site references, see Crielaard 1998). This is quite a spectacular "rock bottom," I would say.

Clearly, something has gone wrong. How can such a period possibly be seen as the nadir of Greek fortunes in the post–Bronze Age world? Clearly, what scholars are talking about is a special sort of collapse: the collapse of the palace structures and the regulated palace economies, and the total disappearance of the Late Bronze Age palaces and all the special features of life associated with these palaces, most notably the art of writing. After 1200 B.C.E., the entire palace structure disappears, never to be seen again in any subsequent chapter of Greek history. This collapse brought on the "Dark Age," but was it really so dark?

In the course of the Late Bronze Age, especially in the 14th and 13th centuries B.C.E., palatial administrations dominated the world of the eastern Mediterranean and the Near East. Centered at sites such as Mycenae, Tiryns, Pylos and Thebes, at Knossos, Ayia Triadha, and Hania, at Boğazköy, Maşat Höyük, and Alaca Höyük, at Ugarit and Emar, Megiddo and Hazor, these administrations worked together to create a system of intellectual and commercial exchange on a scale unlike anything that had ever existed before. We still do not know how this was accomplished. The bits and pieces of surviving evidence, the seals and sealings, stamps, and pot marks, have yet to be put together in any convincing fashion. But the conditions they created are unmistakable: a Mycenaean ceramic koine; common traditions in metal, glass, faience, and ivory working; freedom of the seas; and a sense of order and security. The mythicohistorical tradition of ancient Greece knew this entire period as a world brought about by "The Thalassocracy of Minos" (for palace organization, see Voutsaki and Killen 2001).

At some time after 1200 B.C.E., it all came to an end. The breakup of this Late Bronze Age world is still very poorly understood. Modern scholars blame it all on the "Sea Peoples." The ancient mythicohistorical tradition saw a great "Trojan War" as the dividing point between a golden age culminating in the Age of Heroes, when gods and demigods still walked on earth and intervened in the affairs of mankind, and the grim Age of Iron that came afterward (for Hesiod's "Ages," see Koenen 1994).

From our historical perspective, what came after the collapse of the Bronze Age palaces was the so-called "Dark Age," the defining feature of which was the very absence of those palaces. What was missing, however, was not really the palace itself, but the sense of order and security that had been the gift of palace administrations. What was missing in the "Dark Age" was state organization—the framework and the structure that palace or state administration had bestowed upon everyday life.

What followed the breakup of palace structures? Into the vacuum stepped a number of ruthless warlords, warrior princes determined to create something new out of the wreckage of the old: warriors with the drive, energy, and ambition to seize everything they could and fashion some sort of power base for themselves. There was no one to stop them. Opportunities for plunder were everywhere, and they apparently acted as quickly as possible.

These are the warrior princes buried in the rich tombs mentioned above, in Greece, Crete, and Cyprus. They are H. W. Catling's wandering heroes, his grandees (1994; 1995; 1996: 645–49). But I would see them not as wandering heroes, looking back to the Trojan War and what had gone before. It is better to see these burials in terms of what was to come. By seizing the best lands for themselves, claiming as their due the riches of the region, they laid the foundations for what were to become the aristocratic clans of Archaic

Greece. These warrior princes of the 11th and 10th centuries B.C.E. created the basis for the aristocratic world that was to dominate Greece for centuries to come.

Their world, I would argue, is the world of Homer, especially the world of the *Odyssey*. Odysseus is a warrior prince of the "Dark Age," a Homeric *Basileus*, a pirate as well as a farmer, a king who is really an adventurer. He rules a prosperous, wealthy kingdom, but only he can maintain order, by the strength of his own personality, his charisma. In his absence, chaos reigns. This lack of any real state organization is exactly the 11th–10th-century world of the warrior princes. In the absence of any real political structure, of anything that would perpetuate an office above and beyond the incumbent office-holder, everything depends upon the one dynamic individual. When he goes, everything goes with him.

This is what seems to have happened in the Toumba at Lefkandi. One man succeeded in creating for himself something of a kingdom, perhaps involving no more than about 50 individuals, during the first half of the 10th century B.C.E. (Middle Protogeometric; Snodgrass 1983: 169; J. R. Lenz 1993: 127). He built himself a grand dwelling or ruler's house, the largest, most monumental building in Greece following the Bronze Age collapse (Coulton 1993; Popham 1993; Mazarakis Ainian 1997: 48–58). Yet, when he died, it all seems to have fallen apart. His ostentatious dwelling was torn down and demolished, he and his concubine were buried, in splendor, amidst the ruins of his house, and a tumulus was heaped over the shaft burial dug into what had been the floor of the dwelling. Such, at any rate, is one possible reading of the archaeological evidence (following Crielaard and Driessen 1994; de Waele 1998; Morris 2000: 237). The wanton destruction of the central part of the building by bulldozer in August 1980 has ensured that there will never be a certain reading of the archaeological evidence (Calligas and Popham 1993).

And, like all Homeric heroes, our man of the Toumba was cremated, although the woman buried next to him was given an inhumation burial. Almost all of these warrior burials in Greece and on Cyprus are cremation burials. Crielaard has already done an excellent job of setting out all of the features that these burials have in common, of which the common rite of cremation is certainly one of the most important (1998: 187–90).

The parallels between the world of these warrior princes and the world presented in the Homeric poems, especially the *Odyssey*, are too obvious to be ignored. They have been ignored, however, because very few Homeric scholars today are prepared to accept the fact that the warrior princes of Crete, Cyprus, and Euboea in the 11th and 10th centuries B.C.E. were familiar with some version of the stories contained within the *Iliad* and the *Odyssey*, not necessarily the text as we know it today, and almost certainly not in written form. But, as Lowenstam (1997) has shown, contrary to the arguments advanced by Snodgrass (1998), there is every reason to believe that, prior to ca. 500 B.C.E., many versions of the "Homeric" stories were in circulation. Such stories almost certainly were already being recited at the princely courts of Crete and Cyprus in the 11th century B.C.E. And the choice of cremation at a time when inhumation was the norm was almost certainly a deliberate attempt to be associated with the Homeric heroes cremated before the walls of Troy.

It is reasonable to assume that the wealthy warrior princes buried in the North Cemetery at Knossos and the *Skales* cemetery at Palaepaphos had dwellings of some sort, at the courts of which 11th-century bards could have recited some version of the Trojan sagas; but, it has to be admitted, there is little evidence to support such a suggestion. Our evidence for Crete and Cyprus in this period comes entirely from cemeteries. The lack of settlements, of course, is the major weakness in all the arguments presented in this paper. The situation, however, is not hopeless. We know from the archaeological evidence that these warrior princes (or "travelling 'samurai,'" as Coldstream calls them [1998: 8]) went in for a great deal of ritual or convivial feasting and drinking. They imported not only pottery, but complete drinking sets and dining equipment. We find tripod stands and four-sided stands of bronze, as well as bronze roasting spits (or *obeloi*) in the tombs, and the great amphoroid bronze kraters used as ash urns in the cremation burial rite must have originally been used to hold wine (Crielaard 1998: 189). And this feasting must have occurred in a princely dwelling.

We do have the actual dwelling of the early-10th-century ruler at Lefkandi. In the southeastern corner of the building there was a stone circle, identical to those that appear in Geometric cemeteries and thought to have been used for ritual feasting (Hägg 1983; J. R. Lenz 1993: 140). Such a stone circle was also found in Unit IV-1 at Nichoria, another example of a "Dark Age" ruler's dwelling (Mazarakis Ainian 1997: 74–80).

This emphasis on feasting and wine-drinking suggests a possible parallel with bronze wine sets from the Levant, from Beth-shean Tomb 90, Tell es-Saʿidiyeh Grave 101, and Deir el-Balah Tomb 118, all to be dated to the early 12th century B.C.E. (Moorey 1980: 188). The Levantine wine set consisting of a cauldron or laver, bowl, strainer, and jug, represents a metallurgical tradition that has been connected with the "Sea Peoples" (Tubb 1988). Actually, this tradition of warrior burials associated with drinking sets, metal vessels, weapons, and horses is widespread throughout the ancient Near East at the end of the second millennium B.C.E. Excellent examples are found in the burials at Marlik on the southern shore of the Caspian Sea (Negahban 1996; Muscarella 2000). Ritual feasting and communal dining also has a Mycenaean background, as we know from Killen's work on the Linear B tablets (1994).

So where are we in terms of Bronze Age–Iron Age continuity and a "Dark Age" that was perhaps not so dark but only dusky (or subfusc, as Coldstream would have it [1998: 5])? For the ubiquitous "common man," life was probably much better in the 14th than it was in the 11th century B.C.E. Yet sites such as Perati, Ialysos (Benzi 1992: 222–23), and Koukounaries (on Paros) show us that things were not so bad in the 12th century (Schilardi 1992; Morris 2000: 198) and prosperity came back with remarkable celerity in the 11th century. The gloom and doom that past generations of scholars foisted upon the 11th and 10th centuries B.C.E. has been dispelled by recent archaeological discoveries, never to return. Negbi has argued forcibly and convincingly for metallurgical continuity in the Levant (1991; see already 1974; Muhly 1980). I believe that the same case can be made for Cyprus and the Aegean, certainly for bronze and iron working and, I would argue, for gold working as well. Benson argued more than 30 years ago that "Dark Age" Aegean craftsmen could have learned a great deal from the study of only a small number of surviving Bronze Age works of art (1970: 109–23). The Old Babylonian gold pendant found with the female burial in the Toumba at Lefkandi, an antique some 800 years old when it was deposited as *agalmata* (for Mesopotamian parallels with pendants from Dilbat and Larsa, see Lilyquist

1994), would have been enough for a clever Aegean craftsman to regain knowledge of granulation and filigree techniques.

The remarkable earrings from the "Tomb of the Rich Athenian Lady," dating to ca. 850 B.C.E., certainly do seem in advance of anything known in the Aegean world for hundreds of years (Smithson 1968; Coldstream 1996), but that could be nothing more than an accident of archaeological discovery. I once thought them to be Phoenician (Muhly 1985: 183). I would now claim them for the Aegean world; they have no parallel in anything known from the Near East (Smithson 1968: 112), as Coldstream himself has had to admit (1992–93: 11).

The same is true for the famous bronze "shields" from the Idaean Cave on Crete. These appear to be vaguely "Oriental," but, in fact, nothing like them has ever been found in the Near East. There are no "Oriental" parallels. Kunze, the author of what is still the most detailed art historical study of these objects, concluded that they were wholly the product of Greek artists (1931: 73–74).

There is extensive literature on immigrant craftsmen in the Greek world, going back at least to the 1950s. Hoffman, in her recent book on *Imports and Immigrants*, devotes an entire chapter to this subject (1997: 153–89). In spite of the fact that many now take their existence for granted, there is no good evidence to support the presence of such craftsmen in Greek lands, and this holds true for work in all materials.

If the Greek "Dark Age" seems to become more illusory with every passing year, what of the situation in Anatolia, where the "Dark Age" seemed even darker than in Greece? It was claimed that between the fall of the Hittite Empire and the destruction of Homeric Troy at one end of the spectrum and the Phrygian occupation of Gordion and Boğazköy at the other, there was nothing, an archaeological void extending over some 400 years, ca. 1200–800 B.C.E. (Bittel 1970: 132–42; 1983: 34–36). Given the space limitations of this essay, I will discuss only a few recent developments, but in sufficient detail, I hope, to make clear the profound changes that these developments have brought about.

The most important thing to realize is that our evidence from Anatolia is the exact opposite of that from Greece. In Greece, all the evidence for conditions during the "Dark Age" comes from graves; as mentioned above, we have only cemeteries, no settlements. In Anatolia, there are only settlements, no cemeteries. Consequently, the relevant archaeological evidence from Anatolia tends to be of poorer quality; there is none of the spectacular gold jewelry, bronze and iron weapons, and bronze metalwork such as has come to light in Euboea, Crete, and Cyprus over the past 20 years. The burials of the warrior princes of Anatolia have yet to be discovered. They must exist, and the recent discoveries at Panaztepe on the Aegean coast of Turkey give us some idea of their immediate Bronze Age predecessors, but the "Dark Age" cemeteries of Anatolia still await their future discoverers (for Panaztepe, see Cline 1996: 142 n. 37, with full publications bibliography).

Starting with Troy, since all archaeology in Anatolia began with Troy, we face a curious situation. In his preliminary analysis of the results of his work at Troy, Blegen was sure that the site had been continuously occupied from the Bronze Age to the Roman period. In the course of preparing the material for final publication, he changed his mind, as he became convinced of the existence of a major hiatus following the destruction of Troy

VIIa, his "Homeric" Troy. This hiatus represented, of course, the period of the Anatolian "Dark Age" (for all the above, see Koppenhöfer 1997).

Renewed excavations at Troy (Korfmann 2001) have confirmed the accuracy of Blegen's initial impressions. Work in 1994 and 1995 established the stratigraphic reality of a sequence of at least three phases following the destruction of Troy VIIa, designated Troy VIIb1, b2, and b3. Troy VIIb1 produced the characteristic handmade Barbarian Ware known from sites in eastern Europe, Greece, and Cyprus. Troy VIIb2 yielded the distinctive "Knobbed Ware," or *Buckelkeramik*, often associated with a proto-Phrygian invasion of Anatolia, as it is known from southeastern Europe, Macedonia, and Gordion, the Phrygian capital (Koppenhöfer 1997).

Most surprising of all is the Troy VIIb3 phase, for it produced significant amounts of Greek Protogeometric pottery (R. W. V. Catling 1998; D. Lenz et al. 1998). This pottery consists for the most part of neck-handled amphoras with a decorative motif of vertical or wavy lines separating two sets of concentric circles (R. W. V. Catling 1998: 163). Such amphoras are known from quite a few sites in the Greek world, including Elateia, Kalapodi, Agnanti, Kastanas, Mende, and the Toumba at Lefkandi. They seem to have been produced somewhere in central Greece, in central Lokris or southern Thessaly (R. W. V. Catling 1998: 162), but what are they doing at Troy?

Their presence should not be all that surprising, for such an amphora from Troy was published by Brückner in 1894 (D. Lenz et al. 1998: 190–91, frag. 1). No attention was paid to this isolated find. Now, suddenly, Troy has become part of the Aegean world, at some time subsequent to ca. 1125 B.C.E. The precise dating of this pottery is, in fact, most difficult to determine. At many of the sites listed above, such Protogeometric pottery was found together with Late Helladic IIIC or Submycenaean wares. This is thought to represent a Late Helladic IIIC survival into the Early Iron Age at what are seen as rather remote, backward areas (R. W. V. Catling 1998: 163).

The results of the excavations at the site of Kilise Tepe (Postgate 1998) in the southeastern part of the country, in Konya and south of Karaman, are of special interest in any reevaluation of the Anatolian "Dark Age" and the Bronze Age–Iron Age transition. Level III, the period of Late Bronze Age occupation at the site, produced fragments of Hittite Red Burnished Ware, including examples of the long type of libation arm vessel (Baker et al. 1995: 181, frag. 17). Following two Bronze Age destructions, there is an early Iron Age occupation in Level II, with the stone foundations of the Level IIa building resting directly on top of the Level IIId destruction debris (Hansen and Postgate 1999: 111). From Level IIb deposits came two Hittite seals with hieroglyphic Luwian inscriptions, one bearing the name of "Tarhunta-piya the charioteer" (Hansen and Postgate 1999: 111).

Level IIc had the most complete version of the early Iron Age building, designated the "Stele Building" because of the presence of a painted stela (Hansen and Postgate 1999: 112). In other words, following the destruction of the Hittite period level at Kilise Tepe, during which the settlement must have been part of the kingdom of Tarhuntassa, the site was reoccupied by inhabitants still using hieroglyphic Luwian seals (as well as the state administration that went with those seals) and painted architectural decoration. All of this comes in the aftermath of the destruction of the Hittite Empire. Tarhuntassa seems to have survived the Hittite collapse, as did Ahhiyawa, if we accept Mountjoy's association of that state with an "East Aegean Koine" (1998).

The destruction of Level IId by fire is put by the excavators at ca. 1150 B.C.E. (Hansen and Postgate 1999: 112), but must certainly be later, in spite of the presence of Late Helladic IIIC sherds. This is the same problem we encountered with the early Protogeometric pottery from Troy and elsewhere, as discussed above. After the destruction of Level IId and an ephemeral Level IIe, there seems to be a hiatus in occupation, although the excavators do not mention such a possibility. In Level IIf, a stone-lined pottery kiln was found filled with white ash and approximately 5,000 potsherds. Many of these sherds were identified as being of the Cypriot types designated White Painted IV and Plain White IV Wares (Hansen and Postgate 1999: 112–13). Such pottery, however, can be dated no earlier than ca. 750 B.C.E. (Postgate 1998: 132). But these sherds cannot represent Cypriot imports: they were found in a pottery kiln at Kilise Tepe and were made of local clay (Hansen and Postgate 1999: 117). They must represent local imitations of Cypriot pottery, but where are the originals? How did the potters of Kilise Tepe know what to imitate?

Obviously we still have much to learn, but it is clear that the post-Hittite history of Anatolia is far more complex than previously realized. Hawkins, in several recent articles, has made clear the ongoing 12th- and 11th-century history documented in texts from Carchemish and Malatya (1999 and references there); and this neo-Hittite continuity, in terms of architecture and relief sculpture, is also documented by recent finds from the excavations of the citadel at Aleppo (Khayyata and Kohlmeyer 1998; Kohlmeyer 1999). The new excavations at Gordion (Voigt and Henrickson 2000) have exposed the first architecture preserved from the early Iron Age at the site in the form of a complex of rooms making up at least two, if not three, independent structures dating to ca. 1100 B.C.E. This is Phase 7B, the earliest Iron Age occupation following a short hiatus after the end of Hittite occupation (Phase 8). Yet the pottery of Phase 7B is entirely different from that of the preceding Middle and Late Bronze Age phases (10–8). And not only the pottery; everything else is different as well: architecture, domestic features, and animal remains (Henrickson and Voigt 1998: 101). How does one account for these changes, quite different from the seeming continuity documented at other Anatolian early Iron Age sites? Henrickson and Voigt argue that "the archaeological evidence strongly suggests a population change at this time, rather than simply a shift in political and economic organization" (1998: 101).

The current excavators of Troy strongly agree, arguing for an invasion from the Balkans that resulted in the destruction of Troy VIIa and the complete Balkanization of the Troad (Koppenhöfer 1997: 340). Yet Sams, codirector of the new excavations at Gordion, while believing in the existence of newcomers, also argues that "We have no indications that these newcomers played a role in the collapse of the Hittite Empire; nor that they took the site by force" (Sams 1997: 244). What actually is going on here?

I am very much afraid that, by suggesting that a particular type of pottery, that is, Barbarian Wares, especially *Buckelkeramik*, can be associated with the arrival of a particular group of people, that is, the Phrygians, Henrickson and Voigt (1998) have opened up a

Pandora's Box of ills and abuses. They have done this even though the archaeological evidence for the equation, especially the total lack of this pottery in the southern and eastern Marmara, as well as in the broad expanse between Troy and Gordion, is very problematic, as Özdoğan has pointed out (1993: 162).

What is involved is obviously something much more than a simple pots = people equation, but the danger is a real one nevertheless. And it is precisely this obsession with ethnicity and making connections between bodies of archaeological evidence and ethnic groups that has bedevilled scholarship on the early Iron Age for the past 150 years, ever since Stark (1852) argued that the so-called "Sea Peoples" should be identified with the Phoenicians. It has to be admitted that all too often the interest of modern scholars has been directed not toward "what was being done" but rather toward "who was doing it." It has never been thought sufficient in the study of pottery to understand how it was made, where it was made, where it was exported, and so on. All scholars have also attempted to identify the ethnic group that made the pottery: Minoan, Mycenaean, Egyptian, Hittite, Cypriot, Israelite, Phoenician, Philistine, Euboean, and so on.

In some cases, these identifications are obvious. There is no real question regarding who made Minoan or Mycenaean or Hittite pottery, although we do have to contend with local imitations. The problem has arisen for the early Iron Age, involving the basic developments that are the subject of this paper. In the course of working on the pottery from the *Skales* cemetery on Cyprus, Bikai pointed to the frequent difficulty of deciding whether a particular vase was Cypriot or Phoenician, and went on to note that she had encountered similar problems in distinguishing between Cypriot and Philistine pottery and between Philistine and Phoenician wares (Bikai 1994: 31).

Bikai knew the problems inherent in working with the objects themselves. Like many other scholars, however, she could not bring herself to question the methodological assumptions underlying the way she had been taught to do research. Had she done so, she might have concluded that perhaps making such distinctions was not all that important. Perhaps there were more important questions to be asked, and hopefully answered, than questions of ethnicity. In what sense is the "Phoenician" pottery from Cyprus actually Phoenician? And what about the "Phoenician" pottery from the Cretan site of Kommos? What about the "Mycenaean" pottery from Tel Miqne–Ekron in Philistia? All of these identifications are based on what Hall calls the fallacy "that an ethnic group must necessarily be identifiable in the archaeological record" (1997: 128–29).

In this regard, clay analysis has come to play a major role in modern ceramic studies. But it is not just a question of where the clay came from or where the kilns were located. Identifying styles of pottery or of ivory carving or of metalwork with distinct ethnic groups raises far more fundamental questions about research methodology. We have yet to deal in any fundamental way with what references to "Mycenaean" at Miqne or "Phoenician" at Kommos actually mean.

The current excavations at Bronze Age Miletus help to put these questions in proper perspective. There we have real Minoan and Mycenaean settlements, and I would insist upon the use of the term "settlement," not "colony." We should refer to the Greek/Achaean settlement of Cyprus, not the colonization of Cyprus. The archaeological evidence for settlement at Miletus should be compared with the sort of evidence we are using to document Phoenician, Cypriot, and Euboean settlement in the early Iron Age (Niemeier and Niemeier 1997).

So what do I think was actually going on in the early Iron Age, in the 12th and 11th centuries B.C.E.? It seems to me that Greece, Anatolia, and Cyprus all experienced a collapse of the centers that had dominated their respective Late Bronze Age worlds. Mycenae, Pylos and Thebes, Boğazköy and Maşat Höyük, Enkomi and Hala Sultan Tekke all collapsed in the early 12th century. But this collapse did not bring things to an end. Rather, the 12th and 11th centuries saw an expansion out of the centers into the peripheries. This expansion was led by warrior princes, all out to seize what they could for themselves.

Much of the evidence for this from Greece is still unpublished. One has to go to the Lamia Museum to see on display all the recently excavated warrior graves from the 12th and 11th centuries B.C.E., and to the Chios Museum for the exhibit of material from the warrior graves excavated on the tiny island of Psara, off the northwest coast of the island of Chios.

In Anatolia, the main focus of activity shifted from the central part of the country to the southeast, from Hattusa to Tarhuntassa, to Malatya, Carchemish, and Kilise Tepe, and farther south into Syria, at sites such as Aleppo. On Cyprus, the most dramatic shift in site location was certainly that from Enkomi to Salamis. In some parts of the island, the archaeological evidence tells a story of historical continuity, a lack of destruction at the end of the Late Bronze Age, and continuity of settlement in the same general area, as at Gordion in central Turkey. Our best evidence for this at present comes from southwestern Cyprus, from the area of Paphos. The current excavator of Palaipaphos argues for a scenario in which "the end of the Late Bronze Age is not marked by a violent break in the life of the settlement, but by a gradual (and possibly peaceful) transition into the Geometric period" (Maier 1999: 82). The situation is complex, but it is becoming increasingly obvious that we are not looking at a "Dark Age," only a shift in settlement patterns and the development of new life-styles.

Coldstream himself would now regard the term "Dark Age" as somewhat tendentious, and recognizes an early Greek period "when the Aegean world now proves to have been never wholly isolated from the eastern Mediterranean" (2000: 16). The palaces were gone for good. In the Aegean world they seem to have represented a Near Eastern aberration. The warrior princes of the "Dark Age" must be seen, in my opinion, as the founders of the aristocratic clans that dominated Greece from ca. 1100 to 600 B.C.E.

Since this paper was first prepared for presentation at a symposium in Jerusalem celebrating the centennial of the Albright Institute and ASOR, it is perhaps appropriate to conclude by putting the arguments presented above in their Palestinian perspective. When W. F. Albright (1956) argued for a continuity in monumental art and architecture in Syria and Palestine from the 12th–9th centuries B.C.E., rejecting the influential ideas presented by Frankfort (1954), he was arguing against the concept of a "Dark Age." In doing so he presented arguments very similar to those presented above for the Aegean and Anatolia. Subsequently, Albright presented his point of view in the form of a rhetorical question: "Was the Age of Solomon without Monumental Art?" (1958). The anticipated answer is, of course, no. I would agree, even though we find it difficult these days to agree upon just what constitutes the archaeology of the "Age of Solomon."

References

Albright, W. F.
  1956   Northeast-Mediterranean Dark Ages and the Early Iron Age Art of Syria. Pp. 144–64 in
          The Aegean and the Near East: Studies Presented to Hetty Goldman, ed. S. S. Weinberg. Locust
          Valley, N.Y.: Augustin.
  1958   Was the Age of Solomon without Monumental Art? Pp. 1*–9* in *Eretz-Israel 5* (B. Mazar
          volume), ed. M. Avi-Yonah et al. Jerusalem: Israel Exploration Society.
Baker, H. D., et al.
  1995   Kilise Tepe 1994: The Seventh Preliminary Report. *Anatolian Studies* 45: 139–91.
Benson, J. L.
  1970   *Horse, Bird, and Man: The Origins of Greek Painting.* Amherst: University of Massachusetts
          Press.
Benzi, M.
  1992   *Rodi e la civiltà micenea.* 2 vols. Incunabula Graeca 94. Rome: Gruppo editoriale interna-
          zionale.
Bikai, P.
  1994   The Phoenicians and Cyprus. Pp. 31–36 in *Cyprus in the 11th Century B.C.*, ed. V. Kara-
          georghis. Nicosia: University of Cyprus Press.
Bittel, K.
  1970   *Hattusha: The Capital of the Hittites.* Oxford: Oxford University Press.
  1983   Die archäologische Situation in Kleinasien um 1200 v. Chr. und während der nachfol-
          genden vier Jahrhunderte. Pp. 25–47 (47–65 Diskussion) in *Griechenland: Die Ägäis und die
          Levante während der "Dark Ages" vom 12. bis zum 9 Jh.v.Chr.*, ed. S. Deger-Jalkotzy. Vienna:
          Österreichischen Akademie der Wissenschaften.
Boardman, J.
  1999   Greek Colonization: The Eastern Contribution. Pp. 39–50 in *Conference à Georges Vallet.*
          Rome: Ecole Française de Rome.
Calligas, P. G., and Popham, M. R.
  1993   The Site and the Course of Its Partial Destruction and Excavation. Pp. 1–4 in *Lefkandi
          II/2: The Protogeometric Building at Toumba: The Excavation, Architecture and Finds*, ed.
          M. R. Popham, P. G. Calligas, and L. H. Sackett. Athens: British School at Athens.
Catling, H. W.
  1994   Cyprus in the 11th Century B.C.: An End or a Beginning? Pp. 133–40 in *Cyprus in the 11th
          Century B.C.*, ed. V. Karageorghis. Nicosia: University of Cyprus Press.
  1995   Heroes Returned? Subminoan Burials from Crete. Pp. 123–30 in *The Ages of Homer: A
          Tribute to Emily Townsend Vermeule*, ed. J. B. Carter and S. P. Morris. Austin: University of
          Texas Press.
  1996   The Subminoan Phase in the North Cemetery. Pp. 639–49 in *Knossos North Cemetery:
          Early Greek Tombs II. Discussion*, ed. J. N. Coldstream and H. W. Catling. Athens: British
          School at Athens.
Catling, R. W. V.
  1998   The Typology of the Protogeometric and Subprotogeometric Pottery from Troia and Its
          Aegean Context. *Studia Troica* 8: 151–87.
Cline, E. H.
  1996   Assuwa and the Achaeans: The "Mycenaean" Sword at Hattušas and Its Possible Implica-
          tions. *Annual of the British School at Athens* 91: 137–51.
Coldstream, J. N.
  1992–93 Early Greek Visitors to Egypt and the Levant. *Journal of the Ancient Chronology Foundation*
          6: 6–18.
  1996   The Rich Lady of the Areiopagos and Her Contemporaries: A Tribute to Evelyn Lord
          Smithson. *Hesperia* 64: 391–403.

1998   *Light from Cyprus on the Greek "Dark Age"?* Nineteenth J. L. Myres Memorial Lecture. Oxford: Leopard's Head.

2000   Exchanges between Phoenicians and Early Greeks. *National Museum News, Beirut* 11: 15–32.

Coulton, J.

1993   The Toumba Building: Description and Analysis of the Architecture. Pp. 33–70 in *Lefkandi II/2: The Protogeometric Building at Toumba—The Excavation, Architecture and Finds*, ed. M. R. Popham et al. Athens: British School at Athens.

Crielaard, J. P.

1998   Surfing on the Mediterranean Web: Cypriot Long-Distance Communications during the Eleventh and Tenth Centuries B.C. Pp. 187–207 in *Eastern Mediterranean: Cyprus-Dodecanese-Crete 16th–6th Centuries B.C.*, ed. N. C. Stampolidis, A. Karetsou, and A. Kanta. Heraklion: University of Crete Press.

Crielaard, J. P., and Driessen, J.

1994   The Hero's Home: Some Reflections on the Building at Toumba, Lefkandi. *Topoi* 4: 251–70.

Desborough, V. R. d'A.

1972   *The Greek Dark Ages.* London: Benn.

Frankfort, H.

1954   *The Art and Architecture of the Ancient Orient.* Baltimore, Md.: Penguin.

Hägg, R.

1983   Funerary Meals in the Geometric Necropolis at Asine? Pp. 189–93 in *The Greek Renaissance of the Eighth Century B.C.: Tradition and Innovation*, ed. R. Hägg. Stockholm: Åströms.

Hall, J.

1997   *Ethnic Identity in Greek Antiquity.* Cambridge: Cambridge University Press.

Hansen, C. K., and Postgate, J. N.

1999   The Bronze to Iron Age Transition at Kilise Tepe. *Anatolian Studies* 49: 111–21.

Hawkins, J. D.

1999   Tarkasnawa King of Mira "Tarkondemos," Boğazköy Sealings and Karabel. *Anatolian Studies* 48: 1–31.

Henrickson, R. C., and Voigt, M. M.

1998   The Early Iron Age at Gordion: The Evidence from the Yassihöyük Stratigraphic Sequence. Pp. 79–106 in *Thracians and Phrygians: Problems of Parallelism*, ed. N. Tuna, Z. Aktüre, and M. Lynch. Ankara: Centre for Research and Assessment of the Historic Environment.

Hoffman, G. L.

1997   *Imports and Immigrants: Near Eastern Contacts with Iron Age Crete.* Ann Arbor: University of Michigan Press.

Khayyata, W., and Kohlmeyer, K.

1998   Die Zitadelle von Aleppo: Vorläufiger Bericht über die Untersuchungen 1996 und 1997. *Damaszener Mitteilungen* 10: 69–95.

Killen, J. T.

1994   Thebes Sealings, Knossos Tablets and Mycenaean State Banquets. *Bulletin of the Institute of Classical Studies* 39: 67–84.

Koenen, L.

1994   Greece, the Near East, and Egypt: Cyclic Destruction in Hesiod and the Catalogue of Women. *Transactions of the American Philological Soicety* 124: 1–34.

Kohlmeyer, K.

1999   *Der Tempel des Wettergottes von Aleppo* (Gerda Henkel Vorlesung). Düsseldorf.

Koppenhöfer, D.

1997   Troia VII: Versuch einer Zusammenschau einschliesslich der Ergebnisse des Jahres 1995. *Studia Troica* 7: 295–353.

Korfmann, M. (ed.)
 2001 *Troia: Traum und Wirklichkeit*. Stuttgart: Theiss.
Kunze, E.
 1931 *Kretische Bronzereliefs*. 2 vols. Stuttgart: Kohlhammer.
Langdon, S. (ed.)
 1997 *New Light on a Dark Age: Exploring the Culture of Geometric Greece*. Columbia, Mo.: University of Missouri Press.
Lenz, D., et al.
 1998 Protogeometric Pottery at Troia. *Studia Troica* 8: 189–222.
Lenz, J. R.
 1993 *Kings and the Ideology of Kingship in Early Greece (c. 1200–700 B.C.): Epic, Archaeology and History*. Ph.D. Dissertation, Columbia University.
Lilyquist, C.
 1994 The Dilbat Hoard. *Metropolitan Museum Journal* 29: 5–36.
Lowenstam, S.
 1998 Talking Vases: The Relationship between the Homeric Poems and Archaic Representations of Epic Myth. *Transactions of the American Philological Association* 127: 21–76.
Maier, F. G.
 1999 Palaipaphos and the Transition to the Early Iron Age: Continuities, Discontinuities and Location Shifts. Pp. 79–93 in *Cyprus: The Historicity of the Geometric Horizon*, ed. M. Iacovou and D. Michaelides. Nicosia: University of Cyprus Press.
Mazarakis Ainian, A.
 1997 *From Rulers' Dwellings to Temples: Architecture, Religion and Society in Early Iron Age Greece (1100–700 B.C.)*. Studies in Mediterranean Archaeology 121. Jonsered: Åströms.
Moorey, P. R. S.
 1980 Metal Wine-Sets in the Ancient Near East. *Iranica Antiqua* 15: 181–97.
Morris, I.
 2000 *Archaeology as Cultural History: Words and Things in Iron Age Greece*. Oxford: Blackwell.
Mountjoy, P. A.
 1998 The East Aegean–West Anatolian Interface in the Late Bronze Age: Mycenaeans and the Kingdom of Ahhiyawa. *Anatolian Studies* 48: 33–67.
Muhly, J. D.
 1980 Bronze Figurines and Near Eastern Metalwork. *Israel Exploration Journal* 30: 148–61.
 1985 Phoenicia and the Phoenicians. Pp. 177–91 in *Biblical Archaeology Today: Proceedings of the International Congress on Biblical Archaeology, Jerusalem, April 1984*, ed. J. Amitai. Jerusalem: Israel Exploration Society.
Muscarella, O. W.
 2000 Review of U. Löw, *Figürlich verzierte Metallgefässe aus Nord-und Nortwestiran* (Münster: Ugarit-Verlag, 1998). *Bibliotheca Orientalis* 57: 187–95.
Negahban, E. O.
 1996 *Marlik: The Complete Excavation Report*. 2 vols. Philadelphia: University Museum.
Negbi, O.
 1974 The Continuity of the Canaanite Bronzework of the Late Bronze Age into the Early Iron Age. *Tel Aviv* 1: 159–72.
 1991 Were There Sea Peoples in the Central Jordan Valley at the Transition from the Bronze Age to the Iron Age? *Tel Aviv* 18: 205–43.
Niemeier, B., and Niemeier, W.-D.
 1997 Milet 1994–1995. Projekt "Minoisch-mykenisches bis protogeometrisches Milet": Zielsetzung und Grabungen auf dem Stadionhügel und am Athenatempel. *Archäologischer Anzeiger* 1997: 189–248.

Özdoğan, M.
1993　The Second Millennium of the Marmara Region: The Perspective of a Prehistorian on a Controversial Historical Issue. *Istanbuler Mitteilungen* 43: 151–63.

Popham, M. R.
1993　The Main Excavation of the Building (1981–83). Pp. 7–31 in *Lefkandi II/2: The Protogeometric Building at Toumba—The Excavation, Architecture and Finds*, ed. M. R. Popham, P. G. Calligas, and L. H. Sackett. Athens: British School at Athens.

Postgate, J. N.
1998　Between the Plateau and the Sea: Kilise Tepe 1994–97. Pp. 127–41 in *Ancient Anatolia: Fifty Years' Work by the British Institute of Archaeology at Ankara*, ed. R. Matthews. Ankara: British Institute of Archaeology.

Sams, G. K.
1997　Gordion and the Kingdom of Phrygia. Pp. 239–48 in *Frigi e Frigio*, ed. R. Gusmani, M. Salvini, and P. Vanniecelli. Rome: Consiglio Nazionale delle Richerche.

Schilardi, D. U.
1992　Paros and the Cyclades after the Fall of the Mycenaean Palaces. Pp. 621–39 in *Mykenaïka: Actes du IXᵉ Colloque international sur les textes mycéniens et égéens organisé par le Centre de l'Antiquité Grecque et Romaine de la Fondation Hellénique des recherche scientifiques et l'École française d'Athènes*, ed. J.-P. Olivier. Bulletin de Correspondence Hellénique Supplément 25. Paris: Boccard.

Smithson, E. L.
1968　The Tomb of a Rich Athenian Lady, *ca.* 850 B.C. *Hesperia* 37: 77–116.

Snodgrass, A.
1971　*The Dark Age of Greece: An Archaeological Survey of the Eleventh to the Eighth Centuries B.C.* Edinburgh: University of Edinburgh Press.
1983　Two Demographic Notes. Pp. 167–71 in *The Greek Renaissance of the Eighth Century B.C.: Tradition and Innovation*, ed. R. Hägg. Stockholm: Åströms.
1998　*Homer and the Artists: Text and Picture in Early Greek Art*. Cambridge: Cambridge University Press.

Stark, K. B.
1852　*Gaza und die Philistäische Küste*. Jena: Mauke.

Tandy, D. W.
1997　*Warriors into Traders: The Power of the Market in Early Greece*. Berkeley: University of California Press.

Tubb, J. N.
1988　The Role of the Sea Peoples in the Bronze Industry of Palestine/Transjordan in the Late Bronze–Early Iron Age Transition. Pp. 251–70 in *Bronze Working Centres of Western Asia*, ed. J. E. Curtis. London: Kegan Paul.

Voigt, M. M., and Henrickson, R. C.
2000　Formation of the Phrygian State: The Early Iron Age at Gordian. *Anatolian Studies* 50: 37–54.

Voutsaki, S., and Killen, J. (eds.)
2001　*Economy and Politics in the Mycenaean Palace States*. Cambridge Philosophical Society Supplement 27. Cambridge: Cambridge Philosophical Society.

Waele, J. A. K. E. de
1998　The Layout of the Lefkandi "Heroon." *Annual of the British School at Athens* 93: 380–84.

Zwettl Symposium
1983　*Griechenland, die Ägäis und die Levante während der "Dark Ages" vom 12. bis zum 9. Jh.v.Chr. Akten des Symposions von Stift Zwettl, 11–14 October 1980*, ed. S. Deger-Jalkotzy. Vienna: Österreichischen Akademie der Wissenschaften.

The Mediterranean Economy:
"Globalization" at the End of the Second Millennium B.C.E.

Susan Sherratt

Ashmolean Museum
University of Oxford

Introduction

For much of the last one and one-half centuries, we have been accustomed to thinking of the years around 1200 B.C.E.[1] as the beginning of a "dark age," conceived analogously to the post-Roman "Dark Age" of Western Europe in sweeping terms of the breakup of empires and widespread depopulation, the destruction and disappearance of established political and economic centers, the retreat of literacy or loss of historical records, the disruption or forced cessation of interregional trade, and cultural or artistic decline—all ultimately brought about by the encroachment of mass migratory movements from the wilds of barbariandom into the centers of civilization of the eastern half of the Mediterranean. It has also been the convention to think of these same years as ushering in the Iron Age—a technological development once intimately linked with the "dark age" in the sense that iron was seen as introduced to Greece by invading Dorians and to the Levant by migratory Philistines, or at the very least let loose on the eastern Mediterranean world by the catastrophic events that destroyed the Hittite Empire and led to the liberation of its closely-guarded technological secrets.

Few probably would nowadays subscribe to quite such a dramatic, millennial vision of the onset of a dark age characterized by generalized invasion or migration followed by a descent into a comparative loss of civilization over a wide area ranging from Greece in the west to Assyria in the east, from Anatolia in the north to the borders of Egypt in the south. Each region of increasingly specialized archaeological endeavor now has its own version of what happened in this period, some distinctly less "dark" than others, each conceived and presented independently in different ways according to the current regional archaeological record and its interpretation. Examples of views of how things now

---

Author's note: I am most grateful to the participants in the Albright/ASOR Centennial Symposium for much stimulating discussion of some of the issues with which this paper is concerned. I am particularly indebted to Nicola Schreiber for information about patterns of Cypriot ceramic imports to the Levant in the later Iron Age, and to Sabine Laemmel for discussion of various contextual and other aspects of Philistine Monochrome ("Mycenaean IIIC:1") and Bichrome pottery.

1. Throughout this paper, 1200 B.C.E. should be treated, in accordance with the principles of archaeological chronology, as a purely notional date (as its convenient roundness suggests) and not as a single, precise point in a historical scale of time. Allowance should be made for flexibility within a period of roughly two–three decades on either side of this notional point.

look in Syria, Greece, and Anatolia can be found elsewhere in this volume (Caubet; Muhly; see also, e.g., Liverani 1987; and various papers in Ward and Joukowsky 1992, including the essays by Caubet, Güterbock, McClellan, Muhly, Rutter, and Sader). In the Cypriot coastal centers, much of the 12th century now begins to look like a more-concentrated continuation of Negbi's 13th-century "climax of urban development" (1986; cf., e.g., Muhly 1992: 19; Cadogan 1998: 13). In the southern Levant, the current consensus (insofar as there is one) seems to offer a picture of a gradual but uneven retreat of Egyptian imperial control during the two centuries or so following the battle of Kadesh (Dever 1992; for a range of varying perspectives, cf. Weinstein 1992; Joffe 1997: 216; Mazar 1997a: 218), accompanied in the decades around 1200 B.C.E. by the invasion and migration (via Cyprus) of the so-called "Sea Peoples," some of whom settled there as the Philistines of the Bible or the Sherden and Tjeker of Egyptian texts. The Philistines, we are reassured, are far from agents of "darkness," as a combination of biblical propaganda, German colloquial metaphor, and the rhetorical conceits of Matthew Arnold might once have misled us into believing (Dothan and Dothan 1992: 3–6, 259). Under their current guise as bearers of Aegean (or, logically, since the decipherment of Linear B, "Greek") civilization, they can hardly be tarred with that particular brush.[2] On the contrary, they are now seen as responsible for imposing a full-blown exotic urban tradition on the smoldering ruins of the generally smaller Egypto-Canaanite centers that they destroyed on their arrival (Stager 1995; Barako 2000). Nevertheless, at least one element that has traditionally formed part of the attributes of a generalized "dark age" is still seen as present in the early Iron Age of the southern Levant: in particular, the apparent cessation of trade between the Levant, Cyprus, and the Aegean after 1200 B.C.E. Indeed, it is the seemingly abrupt and complete cessation of trade between these areas, in comparison with the plentiful evidence for it during the preceding Late Bronze Age, that provides one of the main archaeological pillars on which the belief in a sudden, once-and-for-all, mass immigration from the west continues to rest among Levantine archaeologists (Barako 2000; cf. Sharon 2001).

At the same time that the "dark age" has been modified and regionally individualized, it has gradually been decoupled from the onset of an Iron Age, at least in terms of a simple simultaneous package. Iron-sword-bearing Dorians have been irrevocably demolished in Greece; a Philistine monopoly on iron (if not a particular association with it) has been demoted in the Levant; and even the idea of a sudden liberation of secret Hittite technology

---

2. See the remarks of Evans (1909), who was in large part responsible for early propagation of the idea that the Philistines were of Aegean origin and, as such, bearers eastward of the Minoan linear script, which (he believed) was subsequently transformed into the Phoenician alphabet. From this, he went on to draw the conclusion that the Phoenicians themselves were well leavened by Aegean stock: "It must certainly be said that the character of the Phoenician maritime enterprise, their eclectic religion, and the cosmopolitan colonial spirit generated by their great cities somewhat belies a purely Semitic origin" (Evans 1909: 94). To this he adds in a self-consciously name-dropping footnote: "In an interesting conversation that I had with Mr. Gladstone at Hawarden in 1896, during which some of these possibilities were discussed, he enlarged on the maritime spirit of the Phoenicians and on other characteristics, and concluded with the remarkable expression of opinion, 'I have always believed that the Phoenicians were at bottom of non-Semitic stock'" (Evans 1909: 94). If ever a historical reconstruction could be said clearly to display its origins in the international agenda and domestic prejudices of late-19th-century British Liberalism, then this is surely it. It is a pity that its influence still seems so persistent.

no longer seems quite as compelling as it may once have been.[3] In terms of the labeling of periods, this has led in some places to a postponement of when the Iron Age is said to have begun. In Greece, where the once-neat package of invading Dorians, the destruction of Mycenaean palaces, iron, cremation, and Geometric pots[4] has long since fallen apart, the beginning of the Iron Age is notionally set around the middle of the 11th century, at the beginning of the Protogeometric period, when (at least in some places) iron weapons start to make their presence evident in graves (Snodgrass 1971: 222; Hooker 1976: 174; Osborne 1996: 27; cf. McDonald and Thomas 1990: 450).[5] On Cyprus, where Schaeffer's attempts to introduce a Levantine chronology were rejected in favor of a chronology that runs more explicitly parallel to that of Greece, the official beginning of the Iron Age is also set in the mid–11th century, at the beginning of Cypro-Geometric (Schaeffer 1948: 392ff.; Gjerstad et al. 1934: xvi; Karageorghis 1982: 10, 114). It is only in the Levant, where 12th-century iron objects of a practical nature are certainly no more numerous than on contemporary Cyprus (and arguably distinctly less so [cf. E. S. Sherratt 1994]), that the years around 1200 B.C.E. are still conventionally reckoned as marking the beginning of Iron Age I. While the effects (if any) of this terminological decoupling elsewhere on explanations of the introduction of utilitarian iron use in the Levant remain to be seen,[6] in other parts of the eastern Mediterranean (above all in Greece), it has resulted in the development of a more indirect cause-and-effect explanation: in particular, that the disruption or cessation of international trade from around 1200 B.C.E. on led to regional shortages of bronze (or more specifically tin), which stimulated the development of local iron technology (Snodgrass 1971).

---

3. In support of this last explanation, however, see most recently Moorey 1995: 53–68; but contra Muhly 1997: 14.

4. As summarized, for example, in the entry headed "Dorians" in the first edition of the *Oxford Classical Dictionary* (ed. M. Cary et al.; 1948).

5. Despite the fact that iron technology has long been decoupled from the collapse of the Mycenaean palaces in Greece, the realignment of the beginning of the Iron Age with the appearance of Attic Protogeometric has continued to preserve a general sense of the notion of a historical "watershed." This is partly because of the traditional division of labor (and to some extent of prejudices) in this part of the world between Aegean prehistorians on the one hand and ancient historians and Classical archaeologists on the other. The latter, in particular, tend to trace the earliest origins of historical Greek "civilization" from the point at which the last debased vestiges of Mycenaean culture, as typified particularly by ceramic style, give way (at least in Attica) to something that is often regarded as both technically and esthetically more elevated, a point also seen as the start of a newly cleaned slate (Starr 1961; cf. Osborne 1996: 23–24, 28, 41). It is not thought of as having anything (at least directly) to do with iron itself, which merely provides a coincidentally convenient (and ostensibly major) change of label within the traditional three-age system. An element of something similar can be seen in the arguments of Hallo (1992) for the retention of the Bronze Age/Iron Age transition at the beginning of the 12th century in the Levant. It is not so much a question of iron as such, but the idea of a significant break with various features of the past that justifies the change of label.

While I am in considerable sympathy with the second of these examples (in which iron is indeed part of the story), the hijacking in general of technologically derived labels for use as surrogates to mark more general historical "eras"—although convenient in terms of traditional terminologies—seems to me unhelpful. Although it is very hard to see how over a century of conventional usage can be undone easily, we should perhaps find some system of separating the two in the way we label chronological distinctions that are concerned with different classes of phenomena.

6. It seems unlikely at any rate that it was brought to the Levant by Philistines from the Aegean.

My aim in this paper is to suggest that it is indeed no coincidence that the changes that we associate with the disintegration of empires and the collapse of established second-millennium political and economic structures on the one hand, and the gradual adoption of utilitarian uses for iron (particularly on Cyprus) on the other, should have taken place together in the decades immediately surrounding 1200 B.C.E. Indeed, both can be seen as the outcome of economic processes that were already well underway in the 13th century. In this view, the gradual introduction of utilitarian iron has nothing to do with a shortage of bronze or its constituents, or with any regional difficulties in obtaining these.[7] On the contrary, it has much more to do with a significant *increase* in the net quantity of bronze entering the eastern Mediterranean economic system and in the pervasiveness and velocity of its subsequent circulation. Similarly, I would argue that interregional maritime trade, far from grinding to a halt at the end of the 13th century, continued into the 12th century, although the extent and nature of this trade and the way in which it operated had undergone a radical change. Finally, I want to propose that what we see is a further stage in the linking up of the Mediterranean, which brought about a form of "globalization," the effects of which were in certain ways analogous to some of those that we have been experiencing at the end of our own second millennium C.E.

I. Bronze and Iron

For the sake of convenience, we may begin the story at some notional point in the second half of the 13th century (although it actually starts about a century earlier, in the Amarna period). This corresponds to Late Bronze (LB) IIB in the southern Levant, Late Cypriot (LC) IIC on Cyprus, Late Helladic (LH) / Minoan IIIB in the Aegean, and the "Urnfield" period (more specifically, the transition from Reinecke Bronze D to Hallstatt A1) in Europe, north of the Alps. It is a time when several quite interesting (and, I believe, relevant) phenomena were either already well established or beginning to have a noticeable effect. One of these is the local production of Aegean (and in some cases also Cypriot) types of pottery in areas as far apart as the eastern and central Mediterranean.[8] In the central Mediterranean, this can be seen in southern Italy (where it seems to have started early in the 13th century), and possibly also in Sicily and Sardinia (Jones and Vagnetti 1991: 131–35; Vagnetti 1999a; Karageorghis 1995: 94–95; Graziadio 1997: 696; Leighton 1999: 172). It is accompanied by signs of increasing administrative complexity and economic specialization (including the manufacture of processed agricultural products such as olive oil and wine) at sites such as Broglio di Trebisacce in Calabria and Thapsos in Sicily, and it is best seen as a process of import substitution of "luxuries" originally introduced as imported exotica from farther east, and as a sign of the integration of local elites into the cultural and economic values of the eastern half of the Mediterranean (D'Agata 1997; Leighton 1999: 180–84; Vagnetti 1999a; cf. E. S. Sherratt 1999: 192–95).

Meanwhile in the 13th century, farther north on either side of the Alps, there is evidence of bronze-working activity on a surprisingly large and specialized scale, using local

---

7. See, e.g., Muhly 1992: 17–18; Pickles and Peltenburg 1998: 80–81.

8. For Troy, see, e.g., Blegen, Caskey, and Rawson 1953: 14, 16, 38; Mountjoy 1997; for Cyprus, see, e.g., Kling 1989; E. S. Sherratt 1992: 192; Knapp and Cherry 1994: 62.

and wider regional resources of copper and tin (Wells 1992: 35–36; Kristiansen 1994: 21–22; Pearce 2000). It is from some time around our notional point in the second half of the 13th century that the products of this circum-Alpine bronze industry (the so-called "Urnfield" bronzes) begin to make their way in significant quantities into the Aegean and eastern Mediterranean, where they turn up particularly on Cyprus (Bouzek 1985: 119–67; E. S. Sherratt 2000: 84–87). I see no reason to associate these with "Urnfield" invaders from the north or even with northern mercenaries, as has been commonly suggested in the past (Catling 1961; Sandars 1983; Bouzek 1985: 242–43; cf. Wells 1992: 38). The types represented fall overwhelmingly into the status-defining categories of personal ornaments and weapons—fibulae, pins, knives, and weapons, such as flange-hilted cut-and-thrust swords, Peschiera daggers, and a variety of relatively short forms of spearheads with circular-cast sockets—and their attractions are evident both in their typological (and functional) novelty and, in several cases, their obviously extravagant use of bronze. Both their distribution in the eastern half of the Mediterranean and the contexts in which they are found strongly suggest that they initially traveled eastward as finished bronze goods along predominantly maritime routes, picked up in the Tyrrhenian area or in the Adriatic. By the early 12th century, many of these types had become "naturalized" in the eastern half of the Mediterranean, a process undoubtedly facilitated by seaborne metalworkers, such as those indicated by the Gelidonya wreck or by the appearance of a single winged-axe mold at 13th century Mycenae (respectively, Bass 1967; Wace 1953: 15; cf. Borgna 1995). Current evidence suggests that these "naturalized" versions, along with others that continued to travel eastwards from the central Mediterranean, also circulated primarily along the main maritime routes (Matthäus 1980: 137–38; cf. E. S. Sherratt 2000: 87).

This development, which should also be seen against the more general background of a marked expansion of bronze industries in an arc around the northern fringes of the "civilized" world, from the Alps in the west to Luristan in the east (A. Sherratt 1993: 36, fig. 10; cf. Muhly 1997: 14), quite certainly represents a significant input into the total amount of bronze in circulation in the eastern half of the Mediterranean at the end of the 13th century. In that sense, it is undoubtedly related to another contemporary phenomenon: the increasing evidence in this period for the circulation of bronze in scrap form (Bass 1967; Knapp, Muhly, and Muhly 1988; Artzy 1994; Karageorghis and Kassianidou 1999; cf. E. S. Sherratt 2000: 87–88). Although traditionally interpreted as a sign of bronze (or tin) shortage, this is perhaps better seen as a manifestation of a further step in the commodification of alloyed bronze, which was at this stage circulating in increasingly small quantities and increasingly informally as a commodity in itself. The point is not recycling as such (which had been going on in one form or another since metalworking was first introduced in the late Neolithic), but the processes involved in the decentralized circulation and handling of bronze itself in relatively small units by independent individuals or small groups of traders and metalworkers (Pickles and Peltenburg 1998: 87–90). There was more bronze around and it was circulating more widely, reaching social groups whose access to it had previously been restricted or relatively tightly controlled. It is these individuals or small groups, working on a scale at which every scrap of bronze was economically worth using and conserving and in an environment of increasing commercial competition and resultant insecurity, who were probably responsible for the deliberately deposited hoards that are such a novel feature of the late 13th century in the eastern Mediterranean and Aegean (Pickles and Peltenburg 1998: 90; cf. Artzy 1998: 443 n. 13).

Cyprus was central to these developments in a number of ways. The distribution of "Urnfield" bronze types, with Cyprus as an apparent focal point in the eastern Mediterranean, suggests that these were moving primarily along the main maritime routes that connected the eastern with the central Mediterranean (E. S. Sherratt 2000). From some time around the middle of the 13th century, when the port of Kommos on the central–south coast of Crete fell out of use,[9] we begin for the first time to glimpse the direct activity of relatively small-scale Cypriot traders within western Aegean coastal waters: in the Iria wreck (Phelps, Lolos, and Vichos 1999) and in small quantities of recognizable Cypriot ceramics at sites such as Tiryns, Chania, and Lefkandi (Cline 1994: nos. 399–400, 446–48, 632, 788–96; cf. E. S. Sherratt 1994: 70 n. 16). The Cypro-syllabic marks found incised after firing on Mycenaean pottery at Tiryns appear to belong particularly to this period and suggest that Cypriot traders were now traveling as far as the Argolid to pick up Argive pots directly, instead of obtaining them at more easterly transshipment points such as Rhodes, as they seem to have done earlier (Hirschfeld 1996). Farther west, there is growing evidence for specifically Cypriot links in the 13th and 12th centuries in southern Italy, Sicily, and Sardinia, and in the 12th century at Frattesina in the Po Valley, at the head of the Adriatic, where materials such as locally-made glass and imported unworked ivory and ostrich eggs are found (Bietti Sestieri 1982; Vagnetti 1986; 1999b; Vagnetti and Lo Schiavo 1989; Jones and Vagnetti 1991; Ridgway and Serra Ridgway 1992; Karageorghis 1995; Pearce 2000: 111). The particular involvement of Cypriots in a long-distance trade in bronze goods and materials is suggested, not only by the largely similar distributions of Cypriot and "Urnfield" metal types in the eastern half of the Mediterranean,[10] but also by the frequent association of these within the same hoards or other depositional contexts (E. S. Sherratt 2000: 88).

It is in this context of a more direct long-distance linkage between the eastern and central Mediterranean that I believe we should see the demise, around 1200 b.c.e., of the Mycenaean palaces. These essentially rather unimpressive centers (at least in eastern Mediterranean terms) owed their brief 14th–13th-century floruit to a temporary domination of coherent sections of maritime trading routes at a time when these were more rigidly segmented between local political centers. These comparatively primitive "nodal control centers" were increasingly bypassed by Cyprus-based traders operating in the Aegean and farther west in the later 13th and 12th centuries. These were the traders who were responsible in the 14th and 13th centuries for marketing vast quantities of their own pottery and lesser (but still large) quantities of Mycenaean (particularly Argive) pottery to a fairly wide social spectrum of consumers in the eastern Mediterranean (E. S. Sherratt

---

9. For the impressive haul of Cypriot and other eastern ceramic imports at Kommos in the 14th and early 13th centuries, see most recently Rutter 1999.

10. For the east–west distribution of Cypriot rod tripods and other stands from the 12th century on, which largely replicates the distribution of "Urnfield" bronzes within the Aegean, see, e.g., Mederos and Harrison 1996: fig. 5; Matthäus 1988: figs. 6–7. The Aegean distributions of 12th–11th-century amber and iron objects further suggest that the same networks were also responsible for these (Harding and Hughes-Brock 1974: fig. 3; Harding 1984: 86–87; E. S. Sherratt 1994: figs. 1–2).

1999). Their prosperity was thus built on a relatively informal type of commercial trade in pottery, which they subsequently applied to a wider range of goods. The ships they used were small and versatile, equipped with a boomless brail rig that enhanced maneuverability, often double-prowed and capable of navigating the lower reaches of rivers as well as the open sea.[11] That there was a general shift toward a preference for isthmus routes rather than long hauls around dangerous capes or across the open sea seems to be indicated by the fate of Messenia in the southwest Peloponnese, which, after the disappearance of the palace at Pylos around 1200 B.C.E., reverted to something of an underpopulated backwater,[12] and by a contrasting increase in the 12th century in the number of apparently prospering sites around the Argolic, Euboean, Saronic, and Corinthian gulfs, many of them showing evidence of eastward connections.[13]

The beginnings of iron use should be seen against the general background outlined above, and in particular against the devaluation of bronze as a result of the increase in the

11. For the Gelidonya ship, see Bass 1967: 44–51; Pulak 1999: 220; and for a hypothetical reconstruction of the Iria ship (based on estimations of the weight of the cargo), see Vichos 1999: 83, fig. 16; cf. the discussion in Phelps, Lolos, and Vichos 1999: 118–19. The former ship is envisaged as around 10–12 m in length; the latter no more than 9 m, shell-built with a curving hull. Both are thus considerably smaller than the earlier Uluburun ship and perhaps approximately the size of a small sponge-fishing boat (Bass 1967: 50). These are supplemented by a range of late-13th–12th-century representational evidence from the eastern Mediterranean and the Aegean showing ships of varying forms and possibly also sizes, e.g., on the Medinet Habu reliefs, on graffiti at Akko, in the Nahal Meʿarot above Tel Nami on the Carmel coast, and at Kition, as well as on contemporary and later ceramics from the Aegean (Basch 1987: 66–69; Artzy 1998: 444–45; Wachsmann 1998: figs. 7.8, 7.16–17, 7.19, 7.21–28). Although these include ships traditionally associated (as at Medinet Habu) with the "Sea Peoples," any attempt to pin them down geographically or impose distinct "ethnicities" on them is clearly problematic and does not seem very helpful. Most regard the Medinet Habu "Sea Peoples'" ships (although perhaps somewhat smaller) as little different in general design from Syrian or later Phoenician merchantmen (Sandars 1978: 130–31; Basch 1987: 68, 304–6; 1991: 52–53 [and cf. especially the double-prowed Phoenician inshore or river boats shown on various Assyrian reliefs: Basch 1987: figs. 648, 652; cf. also fig. 641]). Even if one accepts Wachsmann's arguments (1998: 163–97) for particular similarities to ship representations in the Aegean, there is nothing to suggest that representations of such ships appear any earlier there than in the eastern Mediterranean, and there is certainly no evidence that the boomless brail rig has priority in the Aegean. (The krater from Kynos [Dakoronia 1987: fig. 2], adorned with a ship representation that Wachsmann [1998: 172] compares most closely with the Medinet Habu ships, belongs to a relatively advanced stage of LH IIIC, and is thus likely to postdate the Medinet Habu reliefs by several decades.) The widespread and varied ship representations of the late 13th–12th centuries (some associated with shipboard fighting) are, to my mind, primarily indicative of a newly pervasive maritime emphasis in the culture of the whole eastern half of the Mediterranean, which is also reflected in the distributions of goods and materials and in changes in coastal and route-determined settlement patterns around this time, and which was characterized by the exploitation of new maritime economic and other opportunities. The significance of the adoption of the loose-footed brail rig, almost certainly initially in the eastern Mediterranean (Roberts 1991; Wachsmann 1998: 251–54; 2000: 809–10; cf. Liverani 1987: 70; it first appears in Aegean representations no earlier than mid-LH IIIC), lies in the greater versatility it allowed, both in marine and estuarine environments.

12. It remained as such well into the first millennium (Davis et al. 1997: 455–56).

13. The extent to which portage over isthmus routes was used by individual ships and crews almost certainly varied. In the case of the Corinthian isthmus, it is very likely that the ships themselves were hauled across with their cargoes, as they were in the first millennium, with or without the help of some primitive forerunner of the *diolkos*. In other cases—for example, the Mycenae corridor linking the Argive, Saronic, and Corinthian gulfs—we probably have to envisage goods traveling separately overland. Nonetheless, the high degree of consistent directionality visible in distributions of both eastern and central Mediterranean materials and goods over the entire length of the distance between the central Mediterranean and Cyprus suggests that much of this network was Cypriot-coordinated and Cypriot-capitalized, even if not operated exclusively by Cypriot ships and traders.

quantity of this material circulating more widely and at more diverse levels of society by the end of the 13th century. By contrast, the value of iron in the later second millennium was still perceived as very high—the preserve of kings and other super-elites—its status maintained through a combination of technologically-determined rarity and the kind of ideological hype that bestowed on it an extraterrestrial origin. Although blade-sized pieces of iron had previously probably been obtained adventitiously as a by-product of copper-smelting using iron-rich fluxes, what seems to have changed around 1200 B.C.E., particularly on Cyprus, was the regular exploitation of this process (Pickles and Peltenburg 1998). The motivation is not hard to see. If a trade in bronze and finished bronze goods could be supplemented by a relatively regular supply of iron knives or daggers injected into a cultural system that still regarded iron as immensely valuable, this would compensate for some of the downside of progressive bronze devaluation. It is, I believe, no coincidence that many of the iron types found on Cyprus and elsewhere in the 12th and 11th centuries closely echo the shapes of the "Urnfield" types imported into, or naturalized in, the eastern half of the Mediterranean from the later 13th century onward. Both were designed to appeal to the same sensibilities: the desire for exotic or novel personal ornaments and other status-enhancing objects of an ostentatiously extravagant nature that were only then becoming available comparatively cheaply. Similar to the role of Apple and Microsoft in taking computers from rare mainframe machines to a ubiquitous desktop facility and making them cheaper and more accessible, Cypriot commercial enterprise fueled the forces of globalization.

II. The 12th Century:
The Role of Cyprus in the Eastern Mediterranean

Despite conventional wisdom, it has long seemed evident to me that close economic connections between Cyprus and the Levantine coast continued well into the 12th century, just as they did between Cyprus and the Aegean and, indeed, areas still farther west. Even those scholars who are most closely wedded to the once-and-for-all mass migration scenario (which brings Philistines from the Aegean via Cyprus to Philistia in year 8 of Ramses III) emphasize the maritime outlook and aspects of Philistine settlement (Stager 1995: 338–39; 344–45, and passim) and are the first to admit the very close similarities between Philistia and Cyprus in several aspects of material culture (e.g., Barako 2000: 515). Yet, despite the fact that the immigrant Philistines immediately built their seaport at Ashkelon (Stager 1995: 342) and probably had other seaports at Ashdod, Gaza, and later Tell Qasile, on their arrival in Philistia the shutters are supposed to have come down and overseas trading ceased for well over a century (Barako 2000). The urbanism they imposed on Canaan, with its sophisticated lifestyle and intensive manufacturing capacities, was (we are asked to believe) a manifestation of some innate cultural inheritance rather than the product of economic interaction. Therefore, one can only assume that this urbanism depended on (and arose mysteriously quickly from) a wholly self-sufficient agricultural base, which there is little sign that they established in the first instance, and on their own account, in the surrounding countryside.[14]

---

14. This is the inference to be drawn from Barako's somewhat startling conclusion that the fully urbanized character of the Philistine sites and the socially and economically diverse communities inhabiting

It is easy to see why this idea arose. It depends primarily on the disappearance of the large quantities of White Slip, Base Ring, and other characteristic Cypriot wares and accompanying Mycenaean painted ware that had reached the Levant during much of the LB II period, and it is a symptom of a long-standing positivist (not to say ceramo-centric) archaeological tradition that tends to dictate that the presence or absence of trade between regions is seen primarily (and sometimes solely) in terms of the presence or absence of a trade in easily identifiable pots. There is more than one reason why trade in pottery between Cyprus and the Levant should no longer be immediately evident in Iron Age I. In the first place, the characteristic Cypriot handmade fine export wares of LC II were steadily fading out by the end of the 13th century, to be replaced by a catchall wheel-made painted ware of Aegean type (White Painted Wheelmade III). This ware incorporated a number of Aegean-looking shapes and decorations, which began as a form of import substitution in the coastal urban centers quite early in LC IIC and progressively increased in quantity in LC IIIA at the beginning of the 12th century. The growth of this Cypriot import substitution in turn gradually undermined the Cypriot market for specially produced fine wares from the Aegean (especially the Argolid), so that by the end of the 13th century the number of these reaching Cyprus and the eastern Mediterranean had diminished virtually to nothing, presumably along with whatever substances had traveled in the small decorated stirrup jars and piriform jars that had formed a substantial proportion of this trade.

In the second place, the Levant, too, subsequently embarked on its own manufacture of a functionally determined selection of the Cypriot White Painted Wheelmade III repertoire. This manufacture began in LB IIB with stirrup jars (and presumably their contents), such as those from Tel Nami, Deir ʿAlla, and possibly also Ugarit (respectively Artzy 1994: 130; Hankey 1981: 113–14; Monchambert 1983: 27–28; cf. E. S. Sherratt 1998: 302 n. 19), and continued with the wholly Cypriot-looking "Mycenaean IIIC:1" (White Painted Wheelmade III) repertoire of Ashdod XIIIB and other Philistine (and non-Philistine) sites (cf. Caubet 1992: 124–27, 130). An implication of this is that the scope for trade in what was effectively the same pottery on both sides of the water was probably extremely limited.[15] A second possibility, equally likely in my view, is that an economically significant trade in pots for their own sake, such as is undoubtedly represented by a large proportion of Cypriot and Aegean imports in the preceding centuries (E. S. Sherratt 1999), was simply no longer an important consideration, now that both traders and

them actively count against trade as having any role in their foundation or prosperity (2000). For the emphasis on the almost exclusively urban nature of Philistine settlement with little sign of accompanying (let alone preparatory) rural colonization, see also Stager 1995; for the implications of this emphasis, see Bauer 1998. As it is, Barako's conclusions seem at odds with Stager's observation that, since the Philistines lacked good supplies of timber and had no metal resources, they were obviously receiving both through their trading activities (1995: 344).

15. In this connection, it is worth noting that the repertoire of locally-produced "Mycenaean IIIC:1" ceramic types found at sites such as Tel Miqne-Ekron and Ashdod appears to consist of drinking and pouring vessels (bowls, kraters, and jugs of various sorts), with the addition of stirrup jars (Killebrew 1998: 397). Local manufacture of the former types, which are virtually identical in form and decorative style to their contemporary Cypriot-produced counterparts, would have rendered importation from Cyprus redundant, particularly since these would have been imported only for their own sake and not for their contents. By the same token, the local production of stirrup jars also implies import substitution of their typical contents, again reducing the scope of an import market for such vessels.

customers were free to deal in more valuable goods and materials that had once been more closely controlled or monopolized by regional elites. At any rate, it is interesting that, among the few White Painted Wheelmade III ("Mycenaean IIIC:1") pots that are generally agreed to be 12th-century Cypriot imports (for instance, from Tell Keisan and Beth-shean,[16] where there is no evidence of local production of such pottery; Warren and Hankey 1989: 163; Hankey 1993: 104; Stager 1995: 334; cf. Barako 2000: table 1), there is an overwhelming preponderance of closed-container shapes—mainly stirrup jars—which were presumably imported primarily for their contents, rather than as pots in their own right. As it is, even when Cypriot (Cypro-Geometric) ceramic imports to the Levant become readily recognizable again from the late 11th and 10th centuries onward (coinciding with Phoenician expansion), both the quantity and the distributional range seem to remain severely limited by comparison with their Late Bronze Age counterparts (Schreiber 2000).[17]

Continuing with the subject of pottery, that there was at least regular and substantial contact between Cyprus and the Levantine coast (including the Philistine area) after 1200 B.C.E. seems to be indicated by the observation (for instance, by the excavators of Tel Miqne-Ekron) that stylistic development during the Monochrome "Mycenaean IIIC:1" phase of early Iron Age IA parallels stylistic development on Cyprus during the earlier part of LC IIIA (Dothan 1989: 4–6; 1998: 152; cf. Kling 1989: 173; E. S. Sherratt 1998: 304). Indeed, one may go as far as to argue that, between them, Ashdod XIIIB, Ashkelon Grid 38, and Tel Miqne-Ekron VII–VIC represent the entire sequence of earlier stylistic development of White Painted Wheelmade III on Cyprus, from the end of LC IIC or the transition to LC IIIA to the end of Enkomi Level IIIA or Kition Floor III (Killebrew 1998: figs. 6–7, 10; E. S. Sherratt 1998: 302–3 n. 20; cf. E. S. Sherratt 1990: 156–63; Stager 1995: fig. 3). Similar considerations apply to the question of contact between Cyprus and the Aegean. Here, too, actual imports of Mycenaean pottery seem to tail off by the end of the 13th century, and I can think of only one certain example in the 12th century of an Aegean LH IIIC import found on Cyprus (possibly a Naxian stirrup jar, now in the City of Birmingham Museum [Catling 1972]). Yet, although the detailed styles are different, Cyprus shares with the Aegean a parallelism in the broad trends of development of its White Painted Wheelmade III ("Mycenaean IIIC:1") pottery during the 12th century, and it is even possible to trace specifically Cypriot developments traveling westward in the course

---

16. Among other things, the fragments from Beth-shean lack the frequently gritty surface texture characteristic of Monochrome ("Mycenaean IIIC:1") and Bichrome Philistine pottery from Ashkelon and possibly also Tel Miqne-Ekron and Ashdod (cf., e.g., Dothan 1990: 20–21; Stager 1991: 33–34; and sherds from Ashkelon in the Ashmolean Museum, Oxford [1927.2100]).

17. Indeed, there is probably a good argument to be made for the point of view that the unprecedented quantities of Cypriot (and lesser quantities of Mycenaean) ceramics that reached the Levant in the 14th and early 13th centuries, a considerable proportion of which traveled for their own sake rather than as containers for goods, are indicative of the specific politicoeconomic organization prevalent at the time rather than of the normal course of affairs. As long as the bulk movement of powerful materials such as metals was tightly controlled as far as possible by elites, the incentive to create and supply economically significant sub-elite or substitute-elite markets in attractive but politically and socially innocuous pottery was considerable, from the point of view of producers, carriers, and consumers (E. S. Sherratt 1999). Once these controls were removed, however, pottery reverted to its normal status as a typical "sailor's trade," in which profits were made strictly at the margin.

of the century to influence LH IIIC pottery (Catling 1972: 61; Kling 1989: 170–76; cf. E. S. Sherratt 1992: 195; Deger-Jalkotzy 1994: 19). We can hardly dismiss this as purely the result of some form of mystical, inherited cultural telepathy. Whatever the media by which such parallelism was effected (and both textiles and metalwork seem plausible possibilities), regular intercourse between Cyprus and areas to the west was demonstrably maintained, despite the lack of any obvious evidence of trade in pottery itself.

When we look at objects other than fine pottery, the picture of an absence of trade between Cyprus and the Levant in the 12th century rapidly disappears. At the LC IIIA site of Maa-Palaeokastro, 5,022 fragments of Canaanite jars were found, representing a minimum of 84 complete jars. Analysis of 26 samples of these, using a combination of petrographic and chemical techniques, suggests that the majority were made in centers in southern Palestine and the central Levant, while others were made on Cyprus (Hadjicosti 1988; Jones and Vaughan 1988). Equally large (if not larger) numbers of Canaanite jars spanning the LC IIC–IIIA periods are known from other Cypriot sites, including Hala Sultan Tekke, and these, too, seem to include a range of eastern Mediterranean origins (Åström 1991).[18] Ivory also continues to appear quite frequently in LC IIIA contexts on Cyprus (Karageorghis 1982: 108–9; Courtois, Lagarce, and Lagarce 1986: 127–38),[19] and it must have been imported from Egypt via the Levant, or from the Levant itself.[20]

Evidence for other types of goods and artifacts that crossed the water between the eastern Mediterranean mainland and Cyprus comes to us in less-direct forms. While we cannot prove that the iron knives found at Philistine and other southern Levantine sites originated on Cyprus, it seems a reasonable supposition that they did, given the considerably larger numbers of these found in contemporary contexts in Cyprus and their typological similarities (E. S. Sherratt 1994: 69, fig. 1). Even less direct is the evidence suggesting a trade in textiles, which not only arises from the prominence of artifacts connected with textile (and possibly also sail) manufacture at sites on both sides of the water (Karageorghis 2000: 257), but may also possibly be glimpsed second-hand in the type of decorations found on 12th-century (White Painted Wheelmade III/"Mycenaean IIIC:1" and Philistine Bichrome) pots. I find it particularly interesting that in the later part of the century, after the development of Philistine Bichrome that is characterized by the even-more-strikingly "textile" appearance of its decoration, Cypriot pottery (for example, in Enkomi Level IIIC and in some aspects of the subsequent Proto–White-Painted Ware of the early 11th century) introduces additional features of shape and/or decorative style that look much more convincingly "metallic" (e.g., Dikaios 1969: pls. 83–85; Karageorghis 1975: pls. 14, 34, 36, 40–41, 43; cf. Steel 1994: 243). These features continue and become even

---

18. Olive oil (perhaps carried in some of the Canaanite jars) seems to have been produced on a large scale at a number of 13th- and 12th-century sites on Cyprus (Hadjisavvas 1992; 1996: 133) and was probably also produced at the same time in Philistia. It may well have moved in both directions, either on account of differing specialized qualities or additives, or in response to fluctuations in supply and demand.

19. Ivory also appears in contemporary contexts farther west, for example, at Perati in eastern Attica, Patras and Teichos Dymaion in Achaea, Torre Mordillo in southern Italy, and Frattesina in the Po Valley (Poursat 1977: 171–72; Papadopoulos 1979: 147; Vagnetti 1999b: 191–92).

20. For hippopotamuses living in and around the Yarkon River in Iron Age I, see Mazar 1997b: 373. It seems likely that the hippopotamus bones found at the nearby site of Tell Qasile represent the exploitation of these animals primarily as a source of ivory, rather than a local gastronomic speciality.

more pronounced in some Cypro-Geometric wares of the late 11th–8th centuries. This hints at the development of an element of regional specialization within what had previously been an area of comparatively undifferentiated (and to that extent "irrational") trading activity, with parts of the southern Levant perhaps continuing to specialize in the textiles for which the region as a whole was to remain famous in the earlier first millennium. Meanwhile, Cyprus—with its own copper resources and access to other metals (including silver) in the Aegean and even farther west—concentrated increasingly on the supply and production of metal goods (cf. Bikai 1994: 34–35).

What I am arguing for (as I have done elsewhere) is an active maritime trading and manufacturing core in the eastern Mediterranean, at least for most of the 12th century, with its epicenter in the sea between Cyprus and certain areas of the mainland littoral, from Cilicia in the north to Philistia in the south. This maritime-centered core was set within a wider sphere of activity both in the east and much farther to the west. In the east, although our current knowledge is patchy due to the vagaries of excavation and the overburden of later population centers, the apparently somewhat differing repertoires of locally-made pottery of Cypriot "Mycenaean IIIC:1" type that may be observed in different parts of the eastern Mediterranean mainland (including differing emphases on the range of types produced) seem consistent with the idea of a series of independent participants, each linked separately into this core primarily through contact with Cyprus as a focal center, and probably engaged in trading varying ranges of goods and commodities, depending on local circumstances.

Moreover, there is a general impression of interstitial (not to say opportunistic) growth—of something that flowed like water in the cracks and crevices surrounding existing (and previously perhaps more tightly controlled) systems of trade and communication. Many of the 12th-century coastal sites that show the closest ceramic or other cultural relationships with Cyprus are situated broadly in areas where Egyptian or Hittite imperial or subimperial control[21] was strongest in the late 13th century, and where this was often accompanied by a relatively sparse network of urban centers with little sign of intensive occupation of intervening areas by settled populations (Liverani 1987: 70; McClellan 1992; Falconer 1994: 326–29; Bunimovitz 1995; 1998: 108; Joffe 1997: 216; Yener et al. 2000: 187). Increasing imperial demands sucked resources into this largely center-focused system, creating economic vacuums by distorting whole areas of independent local enterprise and discouraging many forms of diversified or decentralized activity—particularly where "powerful" or valuable materials or goods (i.e., other than pottery) were concerned.

In the context of the 12th century, the newly revived sites we are concerned with can generally be seen as located around the edges of reduced Egyptian and Hittite (or Neo-Hittite) spheres of activity, many of them well positioned, not only in relation to maritime activity, but also to take advantage of a proliferating series of inland-route networks that allowed them to siphon off goods and materials still traveling along "official" long-distance supply networks.[22] This can certainly be argued for the Philistine cities, which are well placed in relation to historical routes across the southern Judean Hills and the

---

21. Liverani's "great kings" and "small kings" (1987: 66–67).
22. As Artzy (1994; 1998) has argued for the slightly earlier Late Bronze IIB site of Tel Nami on the Carmel coast.

northern fringes of the Negev, such as the routes that gave rise to the centers of Beer-sheba,[23] Hebron, Bethlehem, and Jerusalem itself. Moreover, the significance of their situation immediately on the edge of the remaining area of most intense Egyptian influence and control, and close to the east–west corridor that linked the Ways of Horus with the King's Highway and the Arabah (along which goods desired by Egypt and others, such as copper from Timnah and Feinan and incense from Arabia, would naturally travel to the southern Mediterranean coast) has not been lost on others (Liverani 1987: 71; Finkelstein 1988; Bauer 1998: 162). The trickle of Midianite pottery that can be seen traveling northwestward to sites such as Gezer, Lachish, and Tell Farʿah around this time would at least appear to confirm the use of these trade routes in general (Barako 2000: 517–19; cf. Bauer 1998: 162), while the evident prosperity and apparently heterogeneous population of Tel Masos, together with the renewed upsurge of small sites in the Negev Highlands and the Transjordanian plateau, strongly suggest the involvement of greater numbers and a greater diversity of local and regional groups in the trade along them (Finkelstein 1988; Herr 1998).

Just who were the main beneficiaries of this trade—Egyptians or others—is hard to tell, but there is no reason why it should not have been both, with others perhaps progressively tapping into, and profiting from, what had originally started as supply lines predominantly for Egyptian-run centers and Egypt itself, at the same time adding increasingly diversified goods and creating and feeding new markets, both on land and overseas.[24] Equally, it is hard to gauge whether the growth of independent manufacturing and trading activities at centers such as Ashkelon and Ashdod was regarded by the Egyptian authorities on their borders as a subversive threat or a symbiotic convenience—but again the answer may be: both, at different times. At any rate, there is clear evidence of some quite close connections between Egypt and the Philistine cities, at least from the later 12th century onward (Weinstein 1998: 191–92; cf. Dothan 1990: 32, 34–35).[25]

Farther north, the site of Akko would appear to have occupied a similar niche in relation to Tell Abu Hawam, an important port for Egyptian traffic via the Jezreel Valley for much of the Late Bronze Age, and may indeed have displaced it for a time in the 12th century (cf. Artzy 1998: 442–43; Bauer 1998: 155–56). Farther north still, in an area that once came under Hittite imperial suzerainty, there is evidence that Ras ibn Hani, where both Cypriot-looking "Mycenaean IIIC:1" pottery (at least some of it locally made) and pottery that resembles Philistine Bichrome have been found, continued to fulfill at least some of

---

23. Cf. Gen 21:22–34 for the suggestive interaction of Abraham and Philistines at Beersheba. For Tel Masos as a 12th–11th-century structural predecessor of Beersheba, see Finkelstein 1988.

24. The fact that the chief period of prosperity at Tel Masos (associated with Philistine Bichrome pottery) and the efflorescence of sedentary sites in the Negev Highlands seem to belong mainly to the second half of the 12th century (Finkelstein 1988) suggests that—as Bauer (1998) has indicated—direct involvement in (as opposed to indirect and opportunistic pickings from) overland trade was a secondary development, at least on the part of the Philistine cities of the Coastal Plain.

25. By the time we reach the beginning of the 21st Dynasty in the early 11th century there is, of course, the question of whether by *Egypt* in this context we mean (Theban) Upper Egypt or the (Tanite) Delta. Although it is not clear that we could actually tell from the kinds of material remains involved (Weinstein 1998: 191–92), it seems reasonable to suppose that it was predominantly the latter (cf. also the tale of Wen-Amun, below). Indeed, it is quite possible that it was the increasing involvement of the Delta in the commercial and trading activities of the southern Levant that precipitated the Third Intermediate split in the first place.

the coastally oriented functions of its Ugaritic predecessor, perhaps along with the nearby site of Ras Bassit (Caubet 1992).[26] In the ʿAmuq, a particularly important crossroads linking the Mediterranean coast with major inland routes (some straddled by possibly continuing Neo-Hittite kingdoms such as Carchemish), "locally made imitations of Aegean pottery" from the period between 1200 and 1000 B.C.E. (ʿAmuq N) are also reported (Yener et al. 2000: 188–89). Although the precise nature (and probable date) of this pottery remains to be seen, it suggests that this region was also part of the same sort of Cypriot-linked phenomenon.

Cilicia, following the decline of direct Hittite imperial control, also seems to have been drawn into a Cypriot-centered maritime orbit (Sherratt and Crouwel 1987). There the appearance in the 12th century of a number of sites on the narrow coastal plain to the west of Mersin, at the coastal end of a number of small routes into and through the Taurus (and where there are scant traces of occupation during the period of Hittite domination [Sherratt and Crouwel 1987: 341]), suggests that these sites too may have been tapping into sources of goods and materials farther inland, probably in a largely opportunistic and small-scale manner.

The one puzzle in all of this—if only we knew more about them—is the position of the Phoenician cities. Unlike some of the areas discussed above, these cities appear to have lain midway between the spheres of direct Hittite and Egyptian political influence at least after the death of Ramses II (Bikai 1992: 136; Weinstein 1992: 142–43) and thus might be said to have occupied an interstitial position on a large scale, and probably for some decades, by the early 12th century. Although there is no clear evidence that these cities produced their own versions of Cypriot White Painted Wheelmade III in the 12th century, it seems inconceivable that they should not have continued to engage in maritime trade of some sort during this period—and indeed Sarepta Strata G–F, in which evidence of metalworking and textile-dying seems to continue without a break from the 13th to 12th centuries, produced a number of "Mycenaean IIIC:1" deep bowls apparently imported from Cyprus or elsewhere in the Levant (Pritchard 1975: 90–91, fig. 52:1, 3; 1978: 78–79, 117–23; Koehl 1985: 119–22, fig. 8).[27] Given the probably uninterrupted growth in the strength of their own trading position from at least the later part of the 13th century (Bikai 1992; Gilboa 1998), it is possible that the Phoenician cities (unlike other, more newly "interstitial," areas of the Levantine coast) were able to keep direct Cypriot interest in their own economic activities somewhat at bay and firmly under their own terms. If so, there would be little scope for the kind of intense Cypriot involvement and stimulation (including elements of Cypriot acculturation) of the kind that we seem to see elsewhere. An explanation of this sort might also have the ability to cast some light on the question of what happened to the Cypriot coastal urban centers at the end of the 12th century (see below).

26. It may have been via Ras ibn Hani that an iron knife and sword of probable Cypriot manufacture reached Hama in the 12th century (E. S. Sherratt 1994: 87).

27. These bowls include types that have parallels in various stages of LC IIIA on Cyprus, including some (e.g., Koehl 1985: 44, 121, no. 198, fig. 21) particularly characteristic of the later 12th century that are not replicated in the Philistine repertoire. Against this, a few of the Sarepta sherds look as though they may share the gritty surface texture characteristic of pottery produced at Philistine sites (cf. Koehl 1985: 44). The 12th-century strata at Sarepta also produced an iron knife with bronze rivets, most likely imported from Cyprus (Pritchard 1988: 107, no. 5).

In the 12th century, Cypriot-based (or Cypriot-capitalized) traders linked the eastern with the central Mediterranean via the Aegean. This western activity is not only seen in such phenomena as the orientalia found at sites such as Perati on the eastern Attic coast (Iakovides 1969–70: 2.454–57, 469–70), but the routes and nature of much of it can be traced in the essentially maritime-based distribution of such objects and materials as iron knives, Cypriot and "Urnfield" bronzes, amber, and ivory, and probably also the spread (both geographically and socially) of incense use in the Mediterranean (Mederos and Harrison 1996). The dominant role played by Cyprus in this westward activity is evident not only at the eastern end of these distributions and by the strong Cypriot links visible in places such as Frattesina and Sardinia, but also less directly in the conjunction of Adriatic and Cypriot objects on Thasos, for instance (E. S. Sherratt 1994: 75 n. 24; cf. Muhly 1996: 54), or in the indications that from around 1200 B.C.E. the area at the head of the Adriatic and the southeast Alpine region adopted a new weight system based on an eastern Mediterranean shekel unit (Pare 1999: 506–8).

III.　The 11th Century:
The Tyrian Challenge

It would almost certainly be a mistake to imagine, however, that this eastern Mediterranean maritime trading network ever operated in a wholly peaceful, stable, and harmonious setting. The stabilizing influences once exerted by the balance of Hittite and Egyptian imperial supervision had been written out of the picture, and the potentially high degree of competitiveness built into the kinds of opportunistic and decentralized trading activities involved is quite likely to have resulted in an environment in which rivalry existed at several levels (including interurban and in some cases possibly interregional), and in which armed aggression, possibly accompanied by privateering and coastal- and land-based raiding, was endemic. The periodic destructions observed at sites on Cyprus and the Levantine mainland during the course of the 12th and 11th centuries probably reflect this. This brings me to the question of what happened toward the end of the 12th century and in the early 11th century, a period of little more than 50 years that in some regions at least—although not in others—appears as the darkest remaining patch in our rapidly receding vision of a dark age once characterized by several centuries of economic decline and regional isolation. While there is plenty of light still in the southern Levant, where the Philistine area continued to flourish into the later 11th century, apparently with increasingly close Egyptian (or Tanite) connections (Dothan 1990: 32, 34–35; cf. Weinstein 1998: 192), across the water on Cyprus things do not look quite so good. There the disappearance or decline of 12th-century installations at centers such as Hala Sultan Tekke, Enkomi, and Kition is accompanied by the silting up of harbors by the end of the century, probably due more to a marked decline in their regular use than to any independent natural factors. A similar patch seems to have affected the western Aegean area, where coastal sites such as Tiryns and Asine appear to have decreased in size around the end of the 12th century or early in the 11th century, and Lefkandi disappears from sight for a short period (probably no more than 50 years) between the end of the LH IIIC settlement and the earliest graves of the Skoubris cemetery (Popham and Sackett 1968: 5, 23). Farther west in the central

Mediterranean our chronology is much fuzzier, and it is impossible to tell at present whether that region also experienced a similar patch.[28]

This is the period of Wen-Amun's epic journey, during which, after being given the run-around by the openly contemptuous princes of Dor and Byblos, he ends up somewhere on Cyprus, where the inhabitants are apparently either so unused to the arrival of foreign ships or so suspicious of their intentions that they are ready to kill him and his Byblite crew without first asking questions (Pritchard [ed.] 1958: 16–24). This is also the period of Tiglath-pileser I's opportunistic march to the Mediterranean as far as Arvad, as a result of which he received "tribute" from Arvad, Sidon, and Byblos. It is also the period in which, according to much later traditions, the ships of Ashkelon destroyed Sidon (Bikai 1992: 132–33; Aubet 1993: 21, 26). The conjunction of all the above factors suggests that what lies behind them is not in any sense a decline in maritime economic activity in the eastern Mediterranean as a whole as much as shifts of temporary dominance within it. The story of Wen-Amun tells us of 20 Byblite ships in regular commercial partnership with the by-then independent ruler of Tanis in the Delta, and of another 50 ships at Sidon in commercial partnership with Werket-el, variously identified as a resident of Ashkelon or (perhaps more likely in the context) of Tanis. We also hear of the quantity and variety of goods — including gold, silver, textiles, papyrus, hides, ropes, and foodstuffs (most of them destined to be invisible in the archaeological record, and without a pot in sight) — traded between Tanis and Byblos (Bikai 1992: 132 n. 6; Aubet 1993: 92–94). And Tiglath-pileser I would hardly have been drawn all the way to the Phoenician coast unless the "tribute" extracted from Arvad, Sidon, and Byblos were something well known to be worth pursuing. Rather, what we are probably seeing are the effects of the working out of new configurations and alignments as the central part played by the Cypriot coastal centers in setting up and maintaining decentralized maritime trading networks in the eastern Mediterranean at the beginning of the 12th century was progressively challenged and eventually displaced by one or more Phoenician cities, themselves subject to increasing competition from each other (Bikai 1992; 1994).

Be that as it may, by the later part of the 11th century we begin to glimpse the aggressively expanding star of Tyre emerging above the heads of its competitors and reinvigorating commercial links with Cyprus and beyond.[29] Within another 50 years, Hiram of Tyre, on the strength of his city's commercial maritime success and his own political position within the region, was able to form a mutually advantageous alliance with Solomon that not only guaranteed Tyre large quantities of Israelite wheat and oil and access to the Red Sea incense route, but also ensured that his old rivals in the Philistine Pentapolis, already

---

28. If it did, it is likely to have been experienced primarily at the level of a brief disruption in direct eastern contacts. That the west continued its own momentum of development, seen particularly in the continued expansion and homogenization of metalworking in the western and central Mediterranean and the increased integration of regional circulation patterns (Giardino 1992), seems clear.

29. It is to this period that the conjunction of a Levantine juglet and an iron dagger in Early Proto-geometric Tomb 46 in the Skoubris cemetery at Lefkandi in southwestern Euboea belongs (Popham, Sackett, and Themelis 1980: 126, 252–53, 347–48). This forms the prelude to an increasing quantity and variety of manufactured oriental trinkets in the Lefkandi cemeteries over the following two centuries. A Tyrian link is strongly hinted at by the fact that by far the greatest number of early southwestern Euboean ceramic exports to the eastern Mediterranean in the early 10th century seem to have headed straight for Tyre (Coldstream 1989: fig. 1:a; 1998).

under pressure from the rising power of Israel on the landward side, were effectively squeezed out of the competition.

Conclusion:
The Analogy of Globalization

In using the term *globalization* to refer to the processes outlined on the preceding pages, I am fully aware of being open to the charge of constructing the economic history of three millennia ago in terms of the contemporary *Zeitgeist* and its currently fashionable concepts, values, and anxieties. There are two reasons that I am nevertheless quite unrepentant about doing so. The first is that this is just what successive generations of archaeologists and ancient historians have done before us; and, as each new generation contributes its own interpretation of the archaeological and textual relics of the closing centuries of the second millennium B.C.E., conceived in the spirit and language of its own time, it adds to a rich accumulation of alternative approaches to choose from, most of which—in varying combinations—can probably offer something toward the sort of effectively uncommunicably complex model that we might be willing to accept as approximating historical "reality."

The second reason is that I believe there to be some genuinely useful analogies between the world of the eastern half of the Mediterranean at the end of the second millennium B.C.E. and the much larger world affected by changes at the end of the second millennium C.E. Both saw the demise of large, established, politico-economic systems characterized by ideals of central control, the decline of which resulted in an increase in political, social, and economic fragmentation and fluidity both inside and outside their former borders. In both cases this was also accompanied by mechanisms that led to the opening up and encouragement of direct exchange at hitherto unprecedented social levels and over unprecedented distances, to increasingly wide and ungovernable flows of hitherto more restricted materials and goods (whether in the form of bronze weapons, black market nuclear materials, or simply "information"), and to increasing incentives to invent new types of goods and stimulate new types of markets. The opening up of the Mediterranean, initially by the decentralized activities of Cypriot maritime traders who, from the 13th century onward, cut through the segmented route structure of earlier centuries to forge a direct link with the central Mediterranean, undermined the positions of existing established powers, with their ideals of elite political control over the more important aspects of interregional exchange, and ultimately paved the way for the Phoenician commercial expansion that succeeded it. It also created new interstitial opportunities along a ramifying system of maritime and overland route networks that led to the rise of new settlement patterns and new patterns of first activity-based, and ultimately regional, "identities" in the eastern half of the Mediterranean (Finkelstein 1988; Bauer 1998).

The opening up of the Mediterranean at the end of the second millennium B.C.E. also provides an analogy (albeit chronologically distant and geographically more limited) for our own increasingly homogeneous yet uncontrollable global economy and culture, in which stock-market movements or political uncertainties on one side of the world can drastically affect the economies of regions thousands of miles away, and in which free flows of goods or ideas make the notion of conventional fiscal or ideological control begin to appear increasingly irrelevant. Finally, it is no coincidence that as our own world becomes smaller and cultures and economies increasingly converge, new senses of local and regional identity emerge and become proportionately stronger, so that the kind of overarching politico-economic entities that seemed such a good idea a few decades ago recede into utopian impossibility. The restructuring of power-relationships, economic roles, and patterns of identity that took place at the end of the second millennium B.C.E. may have taken place on a different scale and been facilitated by different mechanisms, but the results were no less far-reaching.

References

Åström, P.
  1991   Canaanite Jars from Hala Sultan Tekke. Pp. 149–51 in *Bronze Age Trade in the Mediterranean*, ed. N. H. Gale. Studies in Mediterranean Archaeology 90. Jonsered: Åströms.
Artzy, M.
  1994   Incense, Camels and Collared Rim Jars: Desert Trade Routes and Maritime Outlets in the Second Millennium. *Oxford Journal of Archaeology* 13: 121–47.
  1998   Routes, Trade, Boats and "Nomads of the Sea." Pp. 439–48 in *Mediterranean Peoples in Transition: Thirteenth to Early Tenth Centuries BCE*, ed. S. Gitin, A. Mazar, and E. Stern. Jerusalem: Israel Exploration Society.
Aubet, M. E.
  1993   *The Phoenicians and the West: Politics, Colonies and Trade*, trans. M. Turton. Cambridge: Cambridge University Press.
Barako, T. J.
  2000   The Philistine Settlement as Mercantile Phenomenon? *American Journal of Archaeology* 104: 513–30.
Basch, L.
  1987   *Le musée imaginaire de la Marine antique*. Athens: Institut Hellénique pour la préservation de la tradition nautique.
  1991   Carènes égéennes à l'Age du Bronze. Pp. 43–54 in *Thalassa: L'Egée préhistorique et la mer*, ed. R. Laffineur and L. Basch. Aegaeum 7. Liège: Université de Liège.
Bass, G.
  1967   *Cape Gelidonya: A Bronze Age Shipwreck*. Philadelphia: American Philosophical Society.
Bauer, A. A.
  1998   Cities of the Sea: Maritime Trade and the Origin of Philistine Settlement in the Early Iron Age Southern Levant. *Oxford Journal of Archaeology* 17: 149–68.
Bietti Sestieri, A.
  1982   Frattesina. Pp. 201–7 in *Magna Grecia e Mondo Miceneo: Nuovi documenti*, ed. L. Vagnetti. Naples: Istituto per la Storia e l'archeologia della Magna Grecia.
Bikai, P. M.
  1992   The Phoenicians. Pp. 132–41 in *The Crisis Years: The 12th Century B.C. from beyond the Danube to the Tigris*, ed. W. A. Ward and M. S. Joukowsky. Dubuque, Ia.: Kendall/Hunt.
  1994   The Phoenicians and Cyprus. Pp. 31–37 in *Cyprus in the 11th Century B.C.*, ed. V. Karageorghis. Nicosia: Leventis Foundation/University of Cyprus.
Blegen, C. W.; Caskey, J. L.; and Rawson, M.
  1953   *Troy III: The Sixth Settlement*. Princeton: Princeton University Press.
Borgna, E.
  1995   I ripostigli delle acropoli micenee e la circolazione del bronzo alla fine dell'età palaziale. *Studi Micenei ed Egeo-anatolici* 35: 7–55.

Bouzek, J.

1985   *The Aegean, Anatolia and Europe: Cultural Interrelations in the Second Millennium* B.C. Prague: Academia.

Bunimovitz, S.

1995   On the Edge of Empires: Late Bronze Age (1500–1200 BCE). Pp. 320–31 in *The Archaeology of Society in the Holy Land*, ed. T. E. Levy. London: Leicester University Press.

1998   Sea Peoples in Cyprus and Israel: A Comparative Study of Immigration Processes. Pp. 103–13 in *Mediterranean Peoples in Transition: Thirteenth to Early Tenth Centuries BCE*, ed. S. Gitin, A. Mazar, and E. Stern. Jerusalem: Israel Exploration Society.

Cadogan, G.

1998   The Thirteenth Century Changes in Cyprus in Their East Mediterranean Context. Pp. 6–16 in *Mediterranean Peoples in Transition: Thirteenth to Early Tenth Centuries BCE*, ed. S. Gitin, A. Mazar, and E. Stern. Jerusalem: Israel Exploration Society.

Catling, H.

1961   A New Bronze Sword from Cyprus. *Antiquity* 35: 115–22.

1972   A Late Helladic IIIC Vase in Birmingham. *Annual of the British School at Athens* 67: 59–62.

Caubet, A.

1992   Reoccupation of the Syrian Coast after the Destruction of the "Crisis Years." Pp. 123–31 in *The Crisis Years: The 12th Century B.C. from beyond the Danube to the Tigris*, ed. W. A. Ward and M. S. Joukowsky. Dubuque, Ia.: Kendall/Hunt.

Cline, E. H.

1994   *Sailing the Wine-Dark Sea: International Trade and the Late Bronze Age Aegean*. BAR International Series 591. Oxford: British Archaeological Reports.

Coldstream, J. N.

1989   Early Greek Visitors to Cyprus and the Eastern Mediterranean. Pp. 90–96 in *Cyprus and the East Mediterranean in the Iron Age*, ed. V. Tatton-Brown. London: British Museum.

1998   The First Exchanges between Euboeans and Phoenicians: Who Took the Initiative? Pp. 353–60 in *Mediterranean Peoples in Transition: Thirteenth to Early Tenth Centuries BCE*, ed. S. Gitin, A. Mazar, and E. Stern. Jerusalem: Israel Exploration Society.

Courtois, J.-C.; Lagarce, J.; and Lagarce, E.

1986   *Enkomi et le Bronze récent à Chypre*. Nicosia: Leventis Foundation.

D'Agata, A. L.

1997   L'unità culturale e i fenomeni di acculturazione: La media età del bronzo. Pp. 447–57 in *Prima Sicilia alle origini della società siciliana*, ed. S. Tusa. Palermo: Regione siciliana, Assessorato al turismo.

Dakoronia, F.

1987   War-Ships on Sherds of LH IIIC Kraters from Kynos. Pp. 117–22 in *Tropis II: 2nd International Symposium on Ship Construction in Antiquity*, ed. H. Tzalas. Delphi: Hellenic Institute for the Preservation of Nautical Tradition.

Davis, J. L., et al.

1997   The Pylos Regional Archaeological Project, Part I: Overview and the Archaeological Survey. *Hesperia* 66: 391–494.

Deger-Jalkotzy, S.

1994   The Post-Palatial Period of Greece: An Aegean Prelude to the 11th Century B.C. in Cyprus. Pp. 11–30 in *Cyprus in the 11th Century B.C.*, ed. V. Karageorghis. Nicosia: Leventis Foundation/University of Cyprus.

Dever, W. G.

1992   The Late Bronze–Early Iron I Horizon in Syria–Palestine: Egyptians, Canaanites, "Sea Peoples," and Proto-Israelites. Pp. 99–110 in *The Crisis Years: The 12th Century B.C. from beyond the Danube to the Tigris,* ed. W. A. Ward and M. S. Joukowsky. Dubuque, Ia.: Kendall/Hunt.

Dikaios, P.
 1969   *Enkomi Excavations 1948–1958.* Mainz: von Zabern.
Dothan, T.
 1989   The Arrival of the Sea Peoples: Cultural Diversity in Early Iron Age Canaan. Pp. 1–14 in
         Recent Excavations in Israel: Studies in Iron Age Archaeology, ed. S. Gitin and W. G. Dever.
         Annual of the American Schools of Oriental Research 49. Winona Lake, Ind.: Eisen-
         brauns.
 1990   Ekron of the Philistines, Part I: Where They Came From, How They Settled Down and
         the Place They Worshiped In. *Biblical Archaeology Review* 16/1: 26–36.
 1998   Initial Philistine Settlement: From Migration to Coexistence. Pp. 148–61 in *Mediterra-
         nean Peoples in Transition: Thirteenth to Early Tenth Centuries* BCE, ed. S. Gitin, A. Mazar, and
         E. Stern. Jerusalem: Israel Exploration Society.
Dothan, T., and Dothan, M.
 1992   *People of the Sea: The Search for the Philistines.* New York: Macmillan.
Evans, A. J.
 1909   *Scripta Minoa I.* Oxford: Clarendon.
Falconer, S.
 1994   The Development and Decline of Bronze Age Civilization in the Southern Levant: A
         Reassessment of Urbanism and Ruralism. Pp. 305–33 in *Development and Decline in the
         Bronze Age Mediterranean,* ed. C. Mathers and S. Stoddart. Sheffield: Collis.
Finkelstein, I.
 1988   Arabian Trade and Socio-Political Conditions in the Negev in the Twelfth–Eleventh
         Centuries B.C.E. *Journal of Near Eastern Studies* 47: 241–52.
Giardino, C.
 1992   Nuragic Sardinia and the Mediterranean: Metallurgy and Maritime Traffic. Pp. 304–16 in
         *Sardinia in the Mediterranean: A Footprint in the Sea. Studies in Sardinian Archaeology Pre-
         sented to Miriam S. Balmuth,* ed. R. Tykot and T. Andrews. Sheffield: Sheffield Academic
         Press.
Gilboa, A.
 1998   Iron I–IIA Pottery Evolution at Dor: Regional Contexts and the Cypriot Connection.
         Pp. 413–25 in *Mediterranean Peoples in Transition: Thirteenth to Early Tenth Centuries* BCE,
         ed. S. Gitin, A. Mazar, and E. Stern. Jerusalem: Israel Exploration Society.
Gjerstad, E., et al.
 1934   *The Swedish Cyprus Expedition I.* Stockholm: The Swedish Cyprus Expedition.
Graziadio, G.
 1997   Le presenze Cipriote in Italia nel quadro del commercio Mediterraneo dei secoli XIV e
         XIII A.C. *Studi Classici e Orientali* 46/2: 681–719.
Güterbock, H. G.
 1992   Survival of the Hittite Dynasty. Pp. 53–55 in *The Crisis Years: The 12th Century B.C. from be-
         yond the Danube to the Tigris,* ed. W. A. Ward and M. S. Joukowsky. Dubuque, Ia.: Kendall/
         Hunt.
Hadjicosti, M.
 1988   "Canaanite" Jars from Maa-Palaeokastro. Pp. 340–85 in *Excavations at Maa-Palaeokastro
         1979–1986* by V. Karageorghis and M. Demas. Nicosia: Department of Antiquities,
         Cyprus.
Hadjisavvas, S.
 1992   *Olive Oil Processing in Cyprus from the Bronze Age to the Byzantine Period.* Studies in Medi-
         terranean Archaeology 99. Nicosia: Åström.
 1996   The Economy of the Olive. Pp. 127–37 in *The Development of the Cypriot Economy from the
         Prehistoric Period to the Present Day,* ed. V. Karageorghis and D. Michaelides. Nicosia: Uni-
         versity of Cyprus/Bank of Cyprus.

Hallo, W. W.

1992   From Bronze Age to Iron Age in Western Asia: Defining the Problem. Pp. 1–9 in *The Crisis Years: The 12th Century B.C. from beyond the Danube to the Tigris*, ed. W. A. Ward and M. S. Joukowsky. Dubuque, Ia.: Kendall/Hunt.

Hankey, V.

1981   Imported Vessels of the Late Bronze Age at High Places. Pp. 108–17 in *Temples and High Places in Biblical Times*, ed. A. Biran. Jerusalem: Nelson Glueck School of Biblical Archaeology.

1993   Pottery as Evidence for Trade: The Levant from the Mouth of the River Orontes to the Egyptian Border. Pp. 101–8 in *Wace and Blegen: Pottery as Evidence for Trade in the Aegean Bronze Age 1939–1989*, ed. C. Zerner. Amsterdam: Gieben.

Harding, A.

1984   *The Mycenaeans and Europe*. London: Academic Press.

Harding, A., and Hughes-Brock, H.

1974   Amber in the Mycenaean World. *Annual of the British School at Athens* 69: 145–72.

Herr, L. G.

1998   Tell el-ʿUmayri and the Madaba Plains Region during the Late Bronze–Iron Age I Transition. Pp. 251–64 in *Mediterranean Peoples in Transition: Thirteenth to Early Tenth Centuries BCE*, ed. S. Gitin, A. Mazar, and E. Stern. Jerusalem: Israel Exploration Society.

Hirschfeld, N.

1996   Cypriots in the Mycenaean Aegean. Pp. 289–97 in vol. 1 of *Atti e memorie del secondo Congresso internazionale de micenologia, 1991*, ed. E. De Miro, L. Godart, and A. Sacconi. Incunabula Graeca 98. Rome: Gruppo editoriale internazionale.

Hooker, J. T.

1976   *Mycenaean Greece*. London: Routledge & Kegan Paul.

Iakovides, S. E.

1969–70   *Peratē: To nekrotapheion*. 2 vols. Athens: Arkhaiologikē Hetaireia.

Joffe, A. H.

1997   Palestine in the Bronze Age. Pp. 212–17 in vol. 4 of *The Oxford Encyclopedia of Archaeology in the Near East*, ed. E. M. Meyers. New York: Oxford University Press.

Jones, R. E., and Vagnetti, L.

1991   Traders and Craftsmen in the Central Mediterranean: Archaeological Evidence and Archaeometric Research. Pp. 127–47 in *Bronze Age Trade in the Mediterranean*, ed. N. H. Gale. Studies in Mediterranean Archaeology 90. Jonsered: Åström.

Jones, R. E., and Vaughan, S. J.

1988   A Study of Some "Canaanite" Jar Fragments from Maa-Palaeokastro by Petrographic and Chemical Analysis. Pp. 386–98 in *Excavations at Maa-Palaeokastro 1979–1986* by V. Karageorghis and M. Demas. Nicosia: Department of Antiquities, Cyprus.

Karageorghis, V.

1975   *Alaas: A Protogeometric Necropolis in Cyprus*. Nicosia: Department of Antiquities, Cyprus.

1982   *Cyprus from the Stone Age to the Romans*. London: Thames and Hudson.

1995   Cyprus and the Western Mediterranean: Some New Evidence for Interrelations. Pp. 93–97 in *The Ages of Homer: A Tribute to Emily Townsend Vermeule*, ed. J. Carter and S. Morris. Austin: University of Texas.

2000   Cultural Innovations in Cyprus Relating to the "Sea Peoples." Pp. 249–73 in *The Sea Peoples and Their World: A Reassessment*, ed. E. D. Oren. Philadelphia: University Museum.

Karageorghis, V., and Kassianidou, V.

1999   Metalworking and Recycling in Late Bronze Age Cyprus: The Evidence from Kition. *Oxford Journal of Archaeology* 18: 171–88.

Killebrew, A. E.
    1998   Ceramic Typology and Technology of Late Bronze II and Iron I Assemblages from Tel
            Miqne-Ekron: The Transition from Canaanite to Philistine Culture. Pp. 379–405 in
            Mediterranean Peoples in Transition: Thirteenth to Early Tenth Centuries BCE, ed. S. Gitin,
            A. Mazar, and E. Stern. Jerusalem: Israel Exploration Society.

Kling, B.
    1989   *Mycenaean IIIC:1b and Related Pottery in Cyprus.* Studies in Mediterranean Archaeology 87.
            Gothenburg: Åström.

Knapp, A. B., and Cherry, J. F.
    1994   *Provenience Studies and Bronze Age Cyprus: Production, Exchange and Politico-economic
            Change.* Madison, Wisc.: Prehistory Press.

Knapp, A. B.; Muhly, J.; and Muhly, P.
    1988   To Hoard Is Human: Late Bronze Age Metal Deposits in Cyprus and the Aegean. *Report
            of the Department of Antiquities, Cyprus* 1988/1: 233–62.

Koehl, R.
    1985   *Sarepta III: The Imported Bronze and Iron Age Wares from Area II, X.* Beirut: Librairie ori-
            entale.

Kristiansen, K.
    1994   The Emergence of the European World System in the Bronze Age: Divergence, Conver-
            gence and Social Evolution during the First and Second Millennia BC in Europe. Pp. 7–30
            in *Europe in the First Millennium B.C.*, ed. K. Kristiansen and J. Jensen. Sheffield: Collis.

Leighton, R.
    1999   *Sicily before History: An Archaeological Survey from the Palaeolithic to the Iron Age.* Bristol:
            Bristol Classical Press.

Liverani, M.
    1987   The Collapse of the Near Eastern Regional System at the End of the Bronze Age: The
            Case of Syria. Pp. 66–73 in *Centre and Periphery in the Ancient World*, ed. M. Rowlands,
            M. Larsen, and K. Kristiansen. Cambridge: Cambridge University Press.

Matthäus, H.
    1980   Italien und Griechenland in ausgehende Bronzezeit: Studien zu einigen Formen der
            Metallindustrie beider Gebiete. *Jahrbuch des Deutschen Archäologischen Instituts* 95: 109–
            39.
    1988   Heirloom or Tradition? Bronze Stands of the Second and First Millennium B.C. in Cy-
            prus, Greece and Italy. Pp. 285–300 in *Problems in Greek Prehistory*, ed. E. B. French and
            K. A. Wardle. Bristol: Bristol Classical Press.

Mazar, A.
    1997a   Palestine in the Iron Age. Pp. 217–22 in vol. 4 of *The Oxford Encyclopedia of Archaeology in
            the Near East*, ed. E. M. Meyers. New York: Oxford University Press.
    1997b   Tell Qasile. Pp. 373–76 in vol. 4 of *The Oxford Encyclopedia of Archaeology in the Near East*,
            ed. E. M. Meyers. New York: Oxford University Press.

McClellan, T. L.
    1992   Twelfth Century B.C. Syria: Comments on H. Sader's Paper. Pp. 164–73 in *The Crisis Years:
            The 12th Century B.C. from beyond the Danube to the Tigris*, ed. W. A. Ward and M. S.
            Joukowsky. Dubuque, Ia.: Kendall/Hunt.

McDonald, W. A., and Thomas, C. G.
    1990   *Progress into the Past: The Rediscovery of Mycenaean Civilization.* Bloomington: Indiana Uni-
            versity Press.

Mederos, A., and Harrison, R.
    1996   "Placer de Dioses": Incensarios en soportes con ruedas del Bronce Final de la Peninsula
            Ibérica. *Complutum Extra* 6: 237–53.

Monchambert, J.-Y.
    1983   La céramique de fabrication locale à Ougarit à la fin du Bronze récent. *Syria* 60: 25–45.

Moorey, P. R. S.
  1995   *From Gulf to Delta and Beyond*, ed. E. D. Oren. Beer-Sheva 8. Beer-Sheva: Ben-Gurion University of the Negev.

Mountjoy, P. A.
  1997   Local Mycenaean Pottery at Troia. *Studia Troica* 7: 259–67.

Muhly, J. D.
  1992   The Crisis Years in the Mediterranean World: Transition or Cultural Disintegration? Pp. 10–26 in *The Crisis Years: The 12th Century B.C. from beyond the Danube to the Tigris*, ed. W. A. Ward and M. S. Joukowsky. Dubuque, Ia.: Kendall/Hunt.
  1996   The Significance of Metals in the Late Bronze Age Economy of Cyprus. Pp. 45–60 in *The Development of the Cypriot Economy from the Prehistoric Period to the Present Day*, ed. V. Karageorghis and D. Michaelides. Nicosia: University of Cyprus/Bank of Cyprus.
  1997   Metals: Artifacts of the Neolithic, Bronze, and Iron Ages. Pp. 5–15 in vol. 4 of *The Oxford Encyclopedia of Archaeology in the Near East*, ed. E. M. Meyers. New York: Oxford University Press.

Negbi, O.
  1986   The Climax of Urban Development in Bronze Age Cyprus. *Report of the Department of Antiquities, Cyprus* 1986: 97–121.

Osborne, R.
  1996   *Greece in the Making, 1200–479 BC*. London: Routledge.

Papadopoulos, T. J.
  1979   *Mycenaean Achaea*. Vol. 1. Studies in Mediterranean Archaeology 55/1. Gothenburg: Åström.

Pare, C. F. E.
  1999   Weights and Weighing in Bronze Age Central Europe. Pp. 421–514 in *Eliten in der Bronzezeit: Ergebnisse zweier Kolloquien in Mainz und Athen*. Mainz: von Zabern.

Pearce, M.
  2000   Metals Make the World Go Round: The Supply and Circulation of Metals in Bronze Age Northern Italy. Pp. 108–15 in *Metals Make the World Go Round: Supply and Circulation of Metals in Bronze Age Europe*, ed. C. Pare. Oxford: Oxbow.

Phelps, W.; Lolos, Y.; and Vichos, Y. (eds.)
  1999   *The Point Iria Wreck: Interconnections in the Mediterranean ca. 1200 BC*. Athens: Hellenic Institute of Marine Archaeology.

Pickles, S., and Peltenburg, E.
  1998   Metallurgy, Society and the Bronze/Iron Transition in the East Mediterranean and the Near East. *Report of the Department of Antiquities, Cyprus* 1998: 67–100.

Popham, M. R., and Sackett, L. H.
  1968   *Excavations at Lefkandi, Euboea 1964–66*. London: British School of Archaeology at Athens.

Popham, M. R.; Sackett, L. H.; and Themelis, P. G. (eds.)
  1980   *Lefkandi I: The Iron Age*. London: British School of Archaeology at Athens.

Poursat, J.-C.
  1977   *Catalogue des ivoires mycéniens du Musée national d'Athènes*. Athens: École française d'Athènes.

Pritchard, J. B.
  1975   *Sarepta: A Preliminary Report on the Iron Age*. Philadelphia: University Museum.
  1978   *Recovering Sarepta, a Phoenician City*. Princeton: Princeton University Press.
  1988   *Sarepta IV: The Objects from Area II, X*. Beirut: Université libanaise.

Pritchard, J. B. (ed.)
  1958   *The Ancient Near East: An Anthology of Texts and Pictures*. Princeton: Princeton University Press.

Pulak, C.
1999   The Late Bronze Age Shipwreck at Uluburun: Aspects of Hull Construction. Pp. 209–38 in *The Point Iria Wreck: Investigations in the Mediterranean ca. 1200 BC*, ed. W. Phelps, Y. Lolos, and Y. Vichos. Athens: Hellenic Institute of Marine Archaeology.

Ridgway, D., and Serra Ridgway, F.
1992   Sardinia and History. Pp. 355–63 in *Sardinia in the Mediterranean: A Footprint in the Sea. Studies in Sardinian Archaeology Presented to Miriam S. Balmuth*, ed. R. Tykot and T. Andrews. Sheffield: Sheffield Academic Press.

Roberts, O. T. P.
1991   The Development of the Brail into a Viable Sail Control for Aegean Boats of the Bronze Age. Pp. 55–60 in *Thalassa: L'Egée préhistorique et la mer*, ed. R. Laffineur and L. Basch. Aegaeum 7. Liège: Université de Liège.

Rutter, J. B.
1992   Cultural Novelties in the Post-Palatial Aegean World: Indices of Vitality or Decline? Pp. 61–78 in *The Crisis Years: The 12th Century B.C. from beyond the Danube to the Tigris*, ed. W. A. Ward and M. S. Joukowsky. Dubuque, Ia.: Kendall/Hunt.
1999   Cretan External Relations during Late Minoan IIIA2–B (ca. 1370–1200): A View from the Mesara. Pp. 139–85 in *The Point Iria Wreck: Interconnections in the Mediterranean ca. 1200 BC*, ed. W. Phelps, Y. Lolos, and Y. Vichos. Athens: Hellenic Institute of Marine Archaeology.

Sader, H.
1992   The 12th Century B.C. in Syria: The Problem of the Rise of the Aramaeans. Pp. 157–63 in *The Crisis Years: The 12th Century B.C. from beyond the Danube to the Tigris*, ed. W. A. Ward and M. S. Joukowsky. Dubuque, Ia.: Kendall/Hunt.

Sandars, N. K.
1978   *The Sea Peoples: Warriors of the Ancient Mediterranean*. London: Thames and Hudson.
1983   North and South at the End of the Mycenaean Age: Aspects of an Old Problem. *Oxford Journal of Archaeology* 2: 43–68.

Schaeffer, C.
1948   *Stratigraphie comparée et chronologie de l'Asie occidentale*. Oxford: Oxford University Press.

Schreiber, N.
2000   *An Archaeological and Historical Investigation into the "Cypro-Phoenician" Pottery of the Iron Age Levant*. Ph.D. dissertation, New College, Oxford.

Sharon, I.
2001   Philistine Bichrome Painted Pottery: Scholarly Ideology and Ceramic Typology. Pp. 555–609 in *Studies in the Archaeology of Israel and Neighboring Lands in Memory of Douglas L. Esse*, ed. S. R. Wolff. Studies in Ancient Oriental Civilization 59. Chicago: Oriental Institute, University of Chicago.

Sherratt, A.
1993   What Would a Bronze-Age World System Look Like? Relations between Temperate Europe and the Mediterranean in Later Prehistory. *Journal of European Archaeology* 1/2: 1–57.

Sherratt, E. S.
1990   Note on Two Pots from Palaepaphos-Eliomylia Tomb 119. Pp. 156–63 in *Tombs at Palaepaphos*, by V. Karageorghis. Nicosia: Leventis Foundation.
1992   Cypriot Pottery of Aegean Type in LC II–III: Problems of Classification, Chronology and Interpretation. Pp. 185–98 in *Cypriot Ceramics: Reading the Prehistoric Record*, ed. J. Barlow, D. Bolger, and B. Kling. Philadelphia: University Museum of Archaeology and Anthropology.
1994   Commerce, Iron and Ideology: Metallurgical Innovation in 12th–11th Century Cyprus. Pp. 59–107 in *Cyprus in the 11th Century B.C.*, ed. V. Karageorghis. Nicosia: Leventis Foundation/University of Cyprus.

1998   "Sea Peoples" and the Economic Structure of the Late Second Millennium in the Eastern Mediterranean. Pp. 292–313 in *Mediterranean Peoples in Transition: Thirteenth to Early Tenth Centuries BCE*, ed. S. Gitin, A. Mazar, and E. Stern. Jerusalem: Israel Exploration Society.

1999   *E pur si muove*: Pots, Markets and Values in the Second Millennium Mediterranean. Pp. 163–211 in *The Complex Past of Pottery: Production, Circulation and Consumption of Mycenaean and Greek Pottery (Sixteenth to Early Fifth Centuries BC)*, ed. J. P. Crielaard, V. Stissi, and G. J. van Wijngaarden. Amsterdam: Gieben.

2000   Circulation of Metals and the End of the Bronze Age in the Eastern Mediterranean. Pp. 82–98 in *Metals Make the World Go Round: Supply and Circulation of Metals in Bronze Age Europe*, ed. C. Pare. Oxford: Oxbow.

Sherratt, E. S., and Crouwel, J. H.

1987   Mycenaean Pottery from Cilicia in Oxford. *Oxford Journal of Archaeology* 6: 325–52.

Snodgrass, A. M.

1971   *The Dark Age of Greece*. Edinburgh: Edinburgh University Press.

Stager, L. E.

1991   When Canaanites and Philistines Ruled Ashkelon. *Biblical Archaeology Review* 17/2: 24–43.

1995   The Impact of the Sea Peoples in Canaan (1185–1050 BCE). Pp. 332–48 in *The Archaeology of Society in the Holy Land*, ed. T. E. Levy. London: Leicester University Press.

Starr, C. G.

1961   *The Origins of Greek Civilization: 1100–650 B.C.* New York: Knopf.

Steel, L.

1994   Pottery Production in Cyprus in the Eleventh Century B.C. Pp. 239–47 in *Cyprus in the 11th Century B.C.*, ed. V. Karageorghis. Nicosia: Leventis Foundation/University of Cyprus.

Vagnetti, L.

1986   Cypriot Elements beyond the Aegean in the Bronze Age. Pp. 201–16 in *Acts of the International Archaeological Symposium "Cyprus between the Orient and the Occident,"* ed. V. Karageorghis. Nicosia: Department of Antiquities, Cyprus.

1999a   Mycenaean Pottery in the Central Mediterranean: Imports and Local Production in Their Context. Pp. 137–61 in *The Complex Past of Pottery: Production, Circulation and Consumption of Mycenaean and Greek Pottery (Sixteenth to Early Fifth Centuries BC)*, ed. J. P. Crielaard, V. Stissi, and G. J. van Wijngaarden. Amsterdam: Gieben.

1999b   Mycenaeans and Cypriots in the Central Mediterranean before and after 1200 BC. Pp. 187–208 in *The Point Iria Wreck: Interconnections in the Mediterranean ca. 1200 BC*, ed. W. Phelps, Y. Lolos, and Y. Vichos. Athens: Hellenic Institute of Marine Archaeology.

Vagnetti, L., and Lo Schiavo, F.

1989   Late Bronze Age Long Distance Trade in the Mediterranean: The Role of the Cypriots. Pp. 217–43 in *Early Society in Cyprus*, ed. E. Peltenburg. Edinburgh: Edinburgh University Press.

Vichos, Y.

1999   The Point Iria Wreck: The Nautical Dimension. Pp. 77–98 in *The Point Iria Wreck: Interconnections in the Mediterranean ca. 1200 BC*, ed. W. Phelps, Y. Lolos, and Y. Vichos. Athens: Hellenic Institute of Marine Archaeology.

Wace, A.

1953   Mycenae 1939–1952. *Annual of the British School at Athens* 48: 3–93.

Wachsmann, S.

1998   *Seagoing Ships and Seamanship in the Bronze Age Levant*. College Station: Texas A. & M. University Press.

2000   Some Notes on Mediterranean Seafaring during the Second Millennium BC. Pp. 803–25 in *Proceedings of the First International Symposium: The Wall Paintings of Thera*, ed. S. Sherratt. Athens: Thera Foundation—Petros M. Nomikos.

Ward, W. A., and Joukowsky, M. S. (eds.)
    1992   *The Crisis Years: The 12th Century* B.C. *from beyond the Danube to the Tigris.* Dubuque, Ia.:
            Kendall/Hunt.
Warren, P., and Hankey, V.
    1989   *Aegean Bronze Age Chronology.* Bristol: Bristol Classical Press.
Weinstein, J.
    1992   The Collapse of the Egyptian Empire in the Southern Levant. Pp. 142–50 in *The Crisis
            Years: The 12th Century* B.C. *from beyond the Danube to the Tigris*, ed. W. A. Ward and M. S.
            Joukowsky. Dubuque, Ia.: Kendall/Hunt.
    1998   Egyptian Relations with the Eastern Mediterranean World at the End of the Second Mil-
            lennium BCE. Pp. 188–96 in *Mediterranean Peoples in Transition: Thirteenth to Early Tenth
            Centuries BCE*, ed. S. Gitin, A. Mazar, and E. Stern. Jerusalem: Israel Exploration Society.
Wells, P.
    1992   Crisis Years? The 12th Century B.C. in Central and Southeastern Europe. Pp. 31–9 in *The
            Crisis Years: The 12th Century* B.C. *from beyond the Danube to the Tigris*, ed. W. A. Ward and
            M. S. Joukowsky. Dubuque, Ia.: Kendall/Hunt.
Yener, K. A., et al.
    2000   The Amuq Valley Regional Project, 1995–1998. *American Journal of Archaeology* 104: 163–
            220.

The Patrimonial Kingdom of Solomon

Lawrence E. Stager
Department of Near Eastern Languages and Civilizations
Harvard University

Recently David and Solomon have been pummeled from two different quarters. One comprises a few archaeologists from Tel Aviv University (for example, Israel Finkelstein, David Ussishkin, and lately Zeev Herzog), who have tried to pull the material culture rug from under these 10th-century B.C.E. kings and relocate it a century later in the Northern Kingdom of Israel. Accordingly, Judah does not become a "full-fledged state" until much later, in the last quarter of the 8th century B.C.E., during the reign of Hezekiah (Finkelstein and Silberman 2001: 245; see also Jamieson-Drake 1991; Thompson 1992). Jerusalem, the capital of this nonexistent "United Monarchy," remains little more than a cow town before the reign of Hezekiah, when it expands to ten times its former size. The other quarter comprises radical revisionists from the University of Copenhagen led by Thomas Thompson and Niels Lemche. From their perspective the Hebrew Bible is largely irrelevant for recovering aspects of the political and cultural history of Iron Age Israel, since it is a novel composed in the Hellenistic era. Thompson (1999: 207) declares that the "stories of the golden age of the United Monarchy reflect the fantasy and ambitions of Jerusalem of the Maccabees." David and Solomon are fictional characters patterned after John Hyrcanus and Alexander the Great, respectively.[1]

The revisionists, in particular, castigate biblical historians and archaeologists, who, they claim, are caught up in the subjective web of solipsism. Lacking the self-referential qualities of other scholars, the revisionists would have us believe that their storytelling about the past is "objective history" (Provan 1995: 599). By misdating the bulk of the biblical sources to the Hellenistic era, however, they ignore a great deal of evidence for understanding ancient Israelites and the "state" that they created.[2]

It matters little to us whether the biblical accounts are "true" in the positivistic sense. We can gain insight into the minds of the ancient Israelites by understanding what they believed to be true. If properly dated and judiciously used, the testimony of preexilic sources constitutes part of the evidence by which historians construct their case; it should be emphasized, however, that they "do not construct the evidence for that case; rather, they *discover* it" (Windschuttle 1996: 219). As historians we are obliged to take seriously the intentionality of many of the biblical writers who make reference to the past (Provan 1995: 599–600) and their attempts at self-representation.

---

1. See also Davies 1992 and Lemche 1998. For telling critiques of the revisionists, see Barr 2000 and Dever 2001. Halpern (2001) makes a gallant and largely successful attempt to recover the historical David.

2. For the convergence of many biblical sources with archaeological and inscriptional evidence from the Iron Age, see Dever 2001: chapter 5; King and Stager 2001.

Of course, if scholars begin their inquiry into the sources—whether biblical, inscriptional, or archaeological—convinced that the period of the United Monarchy is a complete fiction and its kings did not exist, this eliminates a priori such evidence as the list of Solomonic officials and the provinces of his kingdom, a document that every great biblical scholar has considered, in part or in full, authentic (Cogan 2000). Revisionists expose themselves as nothing more than ideologues when confronted with extrabiblical evidence such as the Tel Dan stela, which attests to the "House of David" (*byt dwd*, referring to the kingdom of Judah) already in the mid–9th century B.C.E. (Biran and Naveh 1993; 1995; Halpern 1994; Puech 1994; Na'aman 1995; Schniedewind 1996). After unsuccessful attempts to convince epigraphists and philologists that *byt dwd* means something other than "House of David," some of the revisionists retreated to the last resort of the scoundrel by declaring the Tel Dan stela to be a forgery and a hoax, even though the stela was found in a carefully supervised excavation (Shanks 1997).

I. *Shishak and Solomon*

Let us consider a list from Egypt and an archival report from Jerusalem, both of which date to shortly after the reign of Solomon and pertain to Shishak's, or Sheshonq's, military campaign against Israel ca. 925 B.C.E. According to 1 Kgs 14:25 and 2 Chronicles 12, the invasion took place in the fifth year of Rehoboam, who paid tribute to the Egyptian pharaoh by turning over the Temple and palace treasures, thereby sparing Jerusalem from destruction. By correlating synchronous destructions at the excavated sites mentioned in the "hit list" of Shishak recorded in the Temple of Amun at Karnak, in which the names of scores of fortresses and towns in Palestine are listed, we should be able to establish an anchor point of absolute chronology, which, in turn, should give us a view of the towns that were standing a few years before Shishak's devastation, that is, during the years when Solomon purportedly reigned.

The method sounds simple but it is not. The problem is that there are too many sites with synchronous destruction levels in the period of 1000–840 B.C.E. from which to choose. What archaeologists who accept the traditional chronology would assign to Shishak in the 10th century, Finkelstein (1999: 38–39) and a few others, including Na'aman (1995), would attribute to the predations of the Aramean ruler Haza'el, ca. 840 B.C.E. What we traditionalists would consider a destruction dated ca. 1000/980 B.C.E., Finkelstein would attribute to Shishak in 925 B.C.E. All would seem to agree, however, that Arad XII represents the settlement known as "Great Arad" in Shishak's list of *ḥagarim*, or "fortresses," in the Negev. This correlation of pottery typology and absolute chronology becomes important later on when we discuss the transformations of Beth-Shemesh from Stratum III to Stratum II, which has pottery comparable to Arad XII.

Several names on the Shishak list have been erased or blurred. Missing from the list but probably not from his campaign in Palestine were Gezer and several towns in Judah. That he cut a swath through the Beth-Shean and Jezreel Valleys seems even clearer from the names of Megiddo, Taanach, Shunem, Beth-Shean, and Rehob on the "hit list" (Kitchen 1973: 432–47). All of these towns except Shunem have been or are being excavated.

At Megiddo Shishak even left a victory stela. Unfortunately, the fragment from the three-meter-high stela was not found in situ. Both Megiddo VIA and VA–IVB were great towns and both were destroyed in part by widespread conflagrations. The traditionalists would attribute to Shishak the partial destruction of Megiddo VA–IVB. It is a magnificent town with monumental ashlar buildings, including palaces and other impressive public buildings, as well as a six-chambered gate, very similar to gates at Hazor and Gezer.[3] Finkelstein (1996) and other low chronologists prefer to date the destruction of Megiddo VIA to 925 B.C.E. (rather than to 1000 B.C.E.) and put the end of Megiddo VA–IVB at ca. 840 B.C.E., synchronizing it with the demise of Jezreel (Na'aman 1997b).

In their most recent assessment, Finkelstein, Zimhoni, and Kafri (2000: 265) write that Megiddo VIB, "which features Philistine bichrome pottery and collared-rim pithoi, should be placed in the 11th century, while Stratum VIA, which lacks these types, should be placed in the 10th," which, in turn, they equate with Yoqne'am Stratum XVII (after Zarzecki-Peleg 1997). In his summary of Yoqne'am XVII, Ben-Tor (1993: 808) writes that "the majority of the pottery comprises local types characteristic of the Late Bronze Age. The second group is made of clay whose origin is clearly Phoenician. The third group is related to 'Philistine' pottery and resembles 'Philistine' vessels that have been found in southern Israel and on the Coastal Plain." Note, however, that Finkelstein, Zimhoni, and Kafri (2000: 265) make a point of discounting Philistine bichrome or "degraded" Philistine pottery at Megiddo VIA, apparently because this would deter them from bringing that and collared-rim pithoi down into the 10th century, even though both categories are present at Yoqne'am XVII, which Finkelstein down-dates as late as Shishak (Finkelstein and Ussishkin 2000: 598–600). More recently, Harrison (in press) has prepared for publication the University of Chicago's excavations of Megiddo VI. In the destruction level of Stratum VIA in Area CC, he finds abundant evidence of collared-rim pithoi and Philistine bichrome and "debased" wares. Like Yoqne'am, Megiddo VIA on this part of the mound has local Late Bronze Age wares persisting along with Phoenician and Philistine potting traditions. According to Harrison (in press), almost "the entire repertoire of vessel types typical of Philistine Bichrome Ware occur, including bell-shaped bowls, bell-shaped kraters, strainer-spouted jugs, stirrup jars, pyxides, cylindrical bottles, and horned vessels." Given the number of complete forms, there can be no doubt that these come from the Stratum VIA destruction layer, not from the slightly earlier Stratum VIB. This means that, if Finkelstein dates the Megiddo VIA destruction to Shishak, he must also lower the dates of the later phases of Philistine pottery to ca. 925 B.C.E., which he seems unwilling to do.

If we were to find a *bīt ḫilani* palace similar to those of Megiddo VA–IVB in a Syrian city, we would most likely find a temple beside it. Not so at Megiddo or in other provincial capitals of the 10th century. The reason is simple: the only place during the United

---

3. Ussishkin (1980) has argued that the foundations of the so-called "Solomonic" city gate at Megiddo were originally buried below street level and should, therefore, be assigned to Stratum IVA (contra Yadin 1980). This means that the beautiful ashlar foundations were never exposed. Unfortunately, little or nothing remains of this gate to be excavated. Recent partial excavation and restoration of the Late Bronze Age city gate of Megiddo by the Tel Aviv University team under the direction of Ussishkin, Finkelstein, and Halpern would seem to undermine the notion that city gate foundations were submerged (Ussishkin 2000: 116). The Late Bronze Age gate foundations are on, not below, street level. If such an above-ground foundation could be built in the Late Bronze Age, what was to prevent Iron Age builders from doing likewise?

Monarchy with a palace and temple complex was the capital, Jerusalem—the regal-ritual symbolic "center" of the kingdom and the cosmos.

The regal-ritual city provided the theater in which daily rituals, seasonal festivals, and other ceremonies could be enacted to insure participation of the divine in human and of human in divine affairs, thus creating order and harmony throughout the kingdom. Jerusalem before the 8th century B.C.E. was quite small in terms of spatial and demographic size, encompassing no more than 12 hectares (30 acres), with a population of under 3000. By the quantitative measure of social-evolutionary models, Jerusalem would not qualify as an urban center. But as the symbolic center, the capital of the cosmion (see n. 7 below), it was the "embodiment of the sacred in society—a city upon a hill" (Stager 1985: 25).[4]

With the discovery of the ʿAin Dara temple in Syria, it seems clear "that Solomon's Temple, as described in 1 Kings 6–7, is neither an anachronistic account based on later temple archetypes nor a literary creation. The plan, size, date, and architectural details of Solomon's Temple fit squarely into the traditions of sacred architecture known in north Syria (and probably in Phoenicia) from the 10th–8th centuries B.C.E." (Stager 1999: 187*). The Temple-Palace complex in Jerusalem, however, did not preclude smaller cultic installations (or "cult corners," as Shiloh [1979: 150] called them), such as the remarkable, virtually identical examples found inside the gate at Megiddo VA–IVB and in the "Cultic Structure" at Taanach IIB, rooms filled with incense altars, cult stands, and bowls full of sheep/goat astragali (King and Stager 2001: 341).

Both Megiddo and Taanach were on Shishak's "hit list." In addition to the identical cultic assemblages, there are many other ceramic links between Megiddo VA–IVB and Taanach IIB, the only destruction level at Taanach that could be attributed to Shishak. There is no Philistine pottery at the site. In fact, there is nothing at Taanach that corresponds to Megiddo VIA, only a gap in occupation during that period. The other major destruction at Taanach appears much earlier, in Stratum IB, which was destroyed, according to the traditional chronology, ca. 1100 B.C.E. Realizing that Taanach is a major thorn in his side, Finkelstein (1998) has desperately and futilely tried to compare Megiddo VIA (with Philistine pottery) with Taanach IB (with pre-Philistine pottery) and to lower the date of both destructions to the time of Shishak. As Rast (1978) demonstrated in his publication of the Taanach Iron Age pottery, Taanach IIB is contemporary with Megiddo VA–IVB. Both were destroyed by Shishak. What is true for Taanach and Megiddo is also true for Beth-Shean S1 = Lower V, as the recent excavations directed by A. Mazar (1997) have clarified. At Rehob, also on the Shishak list, there are three conflagration levels (Strata VII–V), one of which will certainly be attributable to Shishak when the details of the sequence have been studied further. Although no longer read as one of the cities on Shishak's list, Gezer VIII, with its six-chambered gate and nearby administrative buildings, suffered destruction at about the same time. So did Yoqneʿam XIV. And from there, comparisons with Hazor X–IX and its many subphases can be added to the roster of sites that underwent a major transformation in the 10th century (Ben-Tor and Ben-Ami 1998).

---

4. To counter the notion that Jerusalem was a "cow town," too small to support regal-ritual institutions, including a scribal elite, see Goldwasser 1991; Naʾaman 1997a; Cahill 1998; as well as Master 2001. For the continuity and maintenance of the fortified waterworks of Jerusalem from MB II through the Iron Age, see Reich and Shukron 1999; 2000; Shanks 1999; King and Stager 2001: 213–23.

A sizable portion of Shishak's list deals with settlements in the Negev Desert. These were mainly fortresses, known as *ḥagarim* (B. Mazar 1986a: 148–49). In response to enemy threats, a system of fortresses was established in the Negev Highlands during the 10th century (ca. 975–925 B.C.E., according to Haiman 1994: 61). After Shishak's campaign and the division of the United Monarchy, the border of Judah retracted to the Beersheba Valley.

With the chronological help derived from Shishak's activities in the Jezreel Valley and in the Negev Highlands, as well as links with contemporary 10th-century sites elsewhere, we have no qualms about invoking the brief but important notice in 1 Kgs 9:15, in which Solomon is said to have conscripted forced labor to build the Temple (*bêt yhwh*), his palace (*bêtô*), the Millo, and the wall of Jerusalem, of Hazor, of Megiddo, and of Gezer. The comparison that Yadin (1958; 1980) made long ago among the six-chambered gates of Hazor, Megiddo, and Gezer and their assignment to the 10th century has stood the test of time. The omission from the notice in 1 Kgs 9:15 of a 10th-century exemplar from Philistine Ashdod and another from 9th-century Lachish makes it all the more likely to be accurate. Of course Solomon would not have used forced labor to build a Phoenician-style gate in Philistia; and he was dead long before the foundations were laid for the city gate at Lachish, if the dating of that gate is correct.

II. The Provinces of Solomon

The archival list in 1 Kings 4, in full or in part, has been attributed to the reign of Solomon by a roster of prominent biblical historians (Alt 1913; Albright 1925; Noth 1960: 213–16; de Vaux 1961: 133–35; Wright 1967; B. Mazar 1986b: 128). It comes as no surprise that biblicists and archaeologists who deny the existence of the United Monarchy have difficulty in accepting this assignation. Nevertheless, if one is not wedded to a quantitative definition of state and its attendant "bureaucracy," this small list of government officials fits perfectly with Weber's patrimonial state, an ideal type based on comparative cultures (1978: chapter 12).

Solomon's officials included priests, scribes, a recorder, commander over the army, seneschal (i.e., one who is over the king's household), one who is over corvée, an official known as "friend of the king," and an official in charge of province or district officials (*niṣṣābîm*). In a patrimonial state, these are not "bureaucratic" offices with clearly defined duties and qualified civil servants to carry them out. These are officials whose main duty it is to serve the king in a loyal manner. It is a highly personal domain built on personal loyalties.

Next 1 Kings 4 states, "Solomon had twelve officials over all Israel, who provided food for the king and his household: each one had to make provision for one month in the year," and continues to list the 12 districts or provinces. Many of these provincial centers—Taanach, Megiddo, Beth-Shean, Jezreel, Dor, Beth-Shemesh, and Yokneʿam (reading Yokneʿam, not Yokmeʿam)—are mentioned in the Shishak list. Before Shishak's campaign in 925 B.C.E. (according to the traditional chronology), each site had undergone a radical transformation as it was converted into a regal center with monumental showpiece architecture, many of these transformations occurring during the reign of Solomon.

According to the traditional chronology, we see great fortifications, palaces, and other public buildings at Megiddo VA–IVB, Taanach IIB, Hazor X, Gezer VIII, Yokneʿam XIV, Beth-Shean S1 = Lower V, and Beth-Shemesh II (for details of this archaeological sequence, see Halpern 2001: 427–78; Master 2001).

Recent excavations at Beth-Shemesh under the direction of Bunimovitz and Lederman have revealed a major transformation of settlement type from Stratum III to Stratum II, the latter a well-planned provincial capital of Solomon's Second Province (1 Kgs 4:9), replete with governor's palace, fortifications, and an underground reservoir with a capacity of over 210,000 gallons to collect water for the whole community. This installation exemplifies a royal hydrology project known as ʾšwḥ in the Mesha Stela or Moabite Stone (King and Stager 2001: 128). The pottery of Beth-Shemesh II correlates with Arad XII, ascribed by all archaeologists to the 10th century B.C.E. (Bunimovitz and Lederman 1997; 2001).

Zertal (1992) has delineated the proper geography of the Third Province in Solomon's list by identifying its capital of Arubboth (1 Kgs 4:10) with Khirbet el-Hamam in the Samaria region and "all the land of Hepher" (ʾereṣ ḥēper), with its center at Tell Muḥaffar. This, then, puts the Third Province in the old tribal territory of Manasseh; and once again shows that these provinces, with the exception of newly conquered territories such as Dor in the Fourth Province and the Jezreel Valley in the Fifth Province, conformed pretty much with the lines of the older tribal territories.

Wright (1967) thought that Solomon's provincial system led to cross-cutting kin-groups, thereby gerrymandering tribal territories in the interest of breaking up old sodalities forged through common descent (whether real or fictive). This, in turn, led to a radical reassignment based on production and service to the king and his royal household. According to Wright, this reorganization of the countryside by Solomon (1 Kings 4) had the beneficial effect of replacing former kin loyalties with new royal ones and of distributing equally the tax burdens of each province according to the regional GNP, whereby each of the 12 units was required to provide for one month's living expenses during the year to support royal and ritual life in the cosmic center of this cosmion— Jerusalem (Stager 1985: 25; 1999).

That such a rational "bureaucratic" system never existed in ancient Israel and that the premonarchic clan and tribal allocations remained intact are partially demonstrated by the Samaria ostraca, receipts dated to the 8th century B.C.E. found in the Northern capital. They refer to the collection of in-kind taxes of olive oil and vintage wine, which were presented to the king by the notables or clan leaders—the local elite—who commanded enough loyalty and honor to represent clan districts before the king. These ostraca come from the tribal territory of Manasseh and represent the various clan districts in that territory still intact in the Third Province, more than two and one-half centuries after the establishment of the monarchy. This would seem to be most unlikely had the reorganization of Solomon's kingdom been as radical as suggested by those who believe that tribes and state cannot coexist.[5]

---

5. For the interactions between and oscillations within "tribes" and "states" of the Middle East, see Khoury and Kostiner 1990; Tapper 1990.

Wright, like almost every other biblical historian, has taken for granted the notion that the Israelite monarchy was some kind of alien (meaning "Canaanite") institution grafted onto a reluctant, egalitarian, kin-based society, which later became a class-riven society dominated by an oppressive, exploitative elite. This chimera of kingship that stamps out kinship as a basis of solidarity and gives rise to class consciousness is little more than the Marxist dialectic by which society changes from "primitive communalism" into a "slave society" with masters holding the means of production (Engels [1884] 1972). The progression of society through a series of evolutionary or revolutionary stages underpins many of the models of state formation (Fried 1967; Service 1971; Claessen and Skalnik 1978). A common scheme takes societies through a linear progression from clan to tribe to chiefdom to state. This evolutionary sequence has been imposed on the archaeological data relating to ancient Israel, as it is considered to have evolved from an egalitarian, kin-based tribal society to a chiefdom and finally to a state, in which class divisions and patronage displaced kinship relationships. This "objective" approach to the material remains has led to a variety of quantitative thresholds for each stage of the evolution. This, in turn, has resulted in disagreement about when that threshold was reached in the case of Israel and Judah. From archaeology alone, how does one distinguish a "big chief" from a "little king"?[6]

In the Israelite cosmion, however, it must be understood that the inhabitants had no concept of social stratification along class lines and that class consciousness did not exist. The vertical, dyadic relationships of superior to inferior were of a different order and were far more variegated than class concepts allow. For example, the term *ʿebed*, commonly translated "slave," has a variety of meanings that extend from the highest rung of the social ladder to the lowest. At its lowest level, *ʿebed* can mean slave, and at its highest, the right-hand man of the king, as in *ʿebed hammelek*. The social context of these referents must be known in order to understand the terminology. In a society such as that of ancient Israel, in which countless relationships within the patrimonial pecking order could thrive, it is not so difficult to imagine that a soldier-farmer such as Saul could become the first king or that a shepherd such as David could succeed him.

III. Patrimonial Kingdom

The political philosopher Voegelin understood that human society

is not merely a fact, or an event, in the external world to be studied by an observer like a natural phenomenon. Though it has externality as one of its important components, it is as a whole a little world, a cosmion, illuminated with meaning from within by the human

---

6. Even if a quantitative threshold for statehood is granted, when the regions of the provinces are taken together and the surface survey data are totaled from the thorough surveys conducted by Finkelstein (1988), Zertal (1988), Gal (1992), and others, the tally for the 10th century B.C.E. is quite adequate to support a United Monarchy with its capital in Jerusalem. Since much of the surface survey data is presented in blocks of Iron I and Iron II, we have taken only sites (40–50%), that continue from the Iron I to the Iron II as likely 10th-century candidates. This yields for the kingdom some 270 sites, for which we could estimate a total population of 50,000 or more—well above most minimal "state" levels (often put at ca. 20,000 individuals) suggested by anthropologists using modern models (e.g., Service 1971; Renfrew and Bahn 1991: 154–57; Holladay 1998: 372–75).

beings who continuously create and bear it as the mode and condition of their self-realization. It is illuminated through an elaborate symbolism, in various degrees of compact-
ness and differentiation—from rite, through myth, to theory—and this symbolism
illuminates it with meaning in so far as the symbols make the internal structure of such a
cosmion, the relations between its members and groups of members, as well as its existence as a whole, transparent for the mystery of human existence. The self-illumination
of society through symbols is an integral part of social reality, and one may even say its
essential part, for through such symbolization the members of a society experience it as
more than an accident or a convenience; they experience it as of their human essence.
(Voegelin 1952: 27)[7]

For such a cosmion, a little world of order, to exist and provide a world of meaning for its
inhabitants, they must assent to convergent legitimating beliefs. Community is then created within the cosmion by assent to imaginative symbols representing the relationship
between the ruler and the ruled. Although the cosmion is a product of human imagination, it appears in history as a real society with institutions, and becomes a force that
leaves a trail of symbols, ideas, and material residues in its wake.

From this perspective, it is obvious why an "archaeology of the state" cannot be based
on a comparison of material remains alone. The same configuration of these residues can
have very different meanings from one cosmion to another. Texts must then be used
alongside archaeology in order to understand the meaning of the symbols by which societies represent themselves and the trail of physical residues they leave behind.

In terms of Weber's (1978: 212–45) three types of legitimating authority—charismatic,
traditional, and legal-rational—the traditional type expressed in terms of patrimonial
domination seems most appropriate for the primary symbols of the Israelite cosmion.
Their creative analogue of the cosmos, which mediates between the finite and the infinite, is expressed through the central symbols of family and household (Master 2001;
Schloen 2001).

The Israelite cosmion is a three-tiered cosmos based on a series of nested households.
At the base of this hierarchy of order is the ancestral, or patriarchal, household known in
the Hebrew Bible as *bêt 'āb*, literally "house of the father." Physical remains of this symbol
can be found in the layout of pillared houses and their clusters throughout the Iron Age
(Stager 1985). At the level of the "state," or tribal kingdom, the king too functions as pater-
familias, with his subjects dependent on personal relationships and loyalty to the sovereign, in return for which allegiance they expect protection and succor. The king, then,
presides over his house (*bayit*), which includes families and households under his domain.
It is to this level of symbolism that the Arameans and the Moabites in the Tel Dan and
Mesha stelas, respectively (Puech 1994), allude when they refer to the Southern Kingdom
of Judah as the "House of David" (*byt dwd*), just as the Assyrians refer to the Northern
Kingdom as the "House of Omri" (*bīt ḫumri*). These two 9th-century references to Judah
are enough evidence in themselves to demonstrate that Judah was a "full-fledged state" in
the eyes of its neighbors long before the end of the 8th century.

---

7. Voegelin adopted the term *cosmion* from the Austrian philosopher Adolf Stöhr and his book *Wege des
Glaubens* (Vienna and Leipzig, 1921). According to Voegelin, *cosmion* is the equivalent of *subuniverse*, a term
coined by William James.

The king, however, does not represent the apex of authority in this three-tiered cosmion. This position is occupied by Yahweh (in the case of Israel), who reigns as supreme patrimonial lord, the ultimate authority over the king and the "children of Israel," bound to him by covenant as his kindred (*'am*) or kindred-in-law. Human kingship and divine kingship, then, are more-inclusive forms of patrimonial domination. Households are nested within households up the tiers of the cosmion, each tier becoming more overarching as one moves from domestic to royal to divine levels (King and Stager 2001: 4–5).

Summary

We find a wealth of converging evidence from texts both biblical and inscriptional, from archaeology, and from political theory, that supports the notion of an Israelite cosmion in which members of the community participated in the transformation from tribal confederation to tribal kingdom in the 10th century B.C.E. With an accurate chronology established by Egyptian sources through Shishak's campaign in Palestine in 925 B.C.E., an adequate understanding of what statehood entails through historically generated typologies, rich symbols from biblical and inscriptional sources, and a ripe field of archaeological remains from these symbols, we can declare with some confidence that the United Monarchy of Israel already existed by the 10th century B.C.E. and flourished even after its division.

References

Albright, W. F.
  1925   The Administrative Divisions of Israel and Judah. *Journal of the Palestine Oriental Society* 5: 17–54.

Alt, A.
  1913   Israels Gaue unter Salomo. Pp. 1–19 in *Alttestamentliche Studien Rudolf Kittel zum 60 Geburtstag*, ed. A. Alt. Leipzig: Hinrichs.

Barr, J.
  2000   *History and Ideology in the Old Testament: Biblical Studies at the End of a Millennium.* New York: Oxford University Press.

Ben-Tor, A.
  1993   Jokneam. Pp. 805–11 in *The New Encyclopedia of Archaeological Excavations in the Holy Land*, ed. E. Stern. Jerusalem: Israel Exploration Society.

Ben-Tor, A., and Ben-Ami, D.
  1998   Hazor and the Archaeology of the Tenth Century BCE. *Israel Exploration Journal* 48: 1–37.

Biran, A., and Naveh, J.
  1993   An Aramaic Stele Fragment from Tel Dan. *Israel Exploration Journal* 43: 81–98.
  1995   The Tel Dan Inscription: A New Fragment. *Israel Exploration Journal* 45: 1–18.

Bunimovitz, S., and Lederman, Z.
  1997   Beth-Shemesh: Culture Conflict on Judah's Frontier. *Biblical Archaeology Review* 23/1: 42–49, 75–77.
  2001   The Iron Age Fortifications of Tel Beth Shemesh: A 1990–2000 Perspective. *Israel Exploration Journal* 51: 121–47.

Cahill, J. M.
  1998   It Is There: The Archaeological Evidence Proves It. *Biblical Archaeology Review* 24/4: 34–41, 63.

Claessen, H. J. M., and Skalnik, P.
 1978 The Early State: Theories and Hypotheses. Pp. 3–30 in *The Early State,* ed. H. J. M. Claessen and P. Skalnik. New York: Mouton.
Cogan, M.
 2000 *I Kings.* Anchor Bible 10. New York: Doubleday.
Davies, P. R.
 1992 *In Search of "Ancient Israel."* Journal for the Study of the Old Testament Supplement Series 148. Sheffield: Sheffield Academic Press.
Dever, W. G.
 2001 *What Did the Biblical Writers Know and When Did They Know It?* Grand Rapids, Mich.: Eerdmans.
Engels, F.
 [1884] *The Origin of the Family, Private Property and the State*, trans. A. West. Reprinted, New York: International Publishers, 1972.
Finkelstein, I.
 1988 *The Archaeology of the Israelite Settlement.* Jerusalem: Israel Exploration Society.
 1996 The Archaeology of the United Monarchy: An Alternative View. *Levant* 28: 177–87.
 1998 Notes on the Stratigraphy and Chronology of Iron Age Taʿanach. *Tel Aviv* 25: 209–17.
 1999 State Formation in Israel and Judah: A Contrast in Context, A Contrast in Trajectory. *Near Eastern Archaeology* 62/1: 35–52.
Finkelstein, I., and Silberman, N. A.
 2001 *The Bible Unearthed.* New York: Free Press.
Finkelstein, I., and Ussishkin, D.
 2000 Archaeological and Historical Conclusions. Pp. 576–605 in *Megiddo III: The 1992–1996 Seasons,* ed. I. Finkelstein, D. Ussishkin, and B. Halpern. Tel Aviv: Tel Aviv University Press.
Finkelstein, I.; Zimhoni, O.; and Kafri, A.
 2000 The Iron Age Pottery Assemblages from Areas F, K and H and Their Stratigraphic and Chronological Implications. Pp. 244–324 in *Megiddo III: The 1992–1996 Seasons,* ed. I. Finkelstein, D. Ussishkin, and B. Halpern. Tel Aviv: Tel Aviv University Press.
Fried, M. H.
 1967 *The Evolution of Political Society.* New York: Random House.
Gal, Z.
 1992 *Lower Galilee during the Iron Age.* American Schools of Oriental Research Dissertation Series 8. Winona Lake, Ind.: Eisenbrauns.
Goldwasser, O.
 1991 An Egyptian Scribe from Lachish and the Hieratic Tradition of the Hebrew Kingdoms. *Tel Aviv* 18: 248–53.
Haiman, M.
 1994 The Iron Age II Sites of the Western Negev Highlands. *Israel Exploration Journal* 44: 36–61.
Halpern, B.
 1994 The Stela from Dan: Epigraphic and Historical Considerations. *Bulletin of the American Schools of Oriental Research* 296: 63–80.
 2001 *David's Secret Demons: Messiah, Murderer, Traitor, King.* Grand Rapids, Mich.: Eerdmans.
Harrison, T. P.
 In press *Megiddo III: Final Report of the Stratum VI Excavations.* Oriental Institute Publications. Chicago: University of Chicago Press.
Holladay, J. S.
 1998 The Kingdoms of Israel and Judah: Political and Economic Centralization in the Iron IIA–B (ca. 1000–750 BCE). Pp. 368–98 in *The Archaeology of Society in the Holy Land,* ed. T. E. Levy. London: Leicester University Press.

Jamieson-Drake, D. W.
  1991   *Scribes and Schools in Monarchic Judah: A Socio-Archaeological Approach.* Sheffield: Almond.
Khoury, P. S., and Kostiner, J.
  1990   Introduction: Tribes and the Complexities of State Formation in the Middle East. Pp. 1–22 in *Tribe and State Formation in the Middle East*, ed. P. S. Khoury and J. Kostiner. Berkeley: University of California Press.
King, P. J., and Stager, L. E.
  2001   *Life in Biblical Israel.* Library of Ancient Israel. Louisville: Westminster/John Knox.
Kitchen, K. A.
  1973   *The Third Intermediate Period in Egypt (1100–650 B.C.).* Warminster: Aris & Phillips.
Lemche, N. P.
  1998   *The Israelites in History and Tradition.* Louisville: Westminster/John Knox.
Master, D.
  2001   State Formation Theory and the Kingdom of Ancient Israel. *Journal of Near Eastern Studies* 60: 117–31.
Mazar, A.
  1997   Iron Age Chronology: A Reply to I. Finkelstein. *Levant* 29: 157–67.
Mazar, B.
  1986a   Pharaoh Shishak's Campaign to the Land of Israel. Pp. 139–50 in *The Early Biblical Period: Historical Essays*, ed. S. Aḥituv and B. A. Levine. Jerusalem: Israel Exploration Society.
  1986b   King David's Scribe and the High Officialdom of the United Monarchy of Israel. Pp. 126–38 in *The Early Biblical Period: Historical Essays*, ed. S. Aḥituv and B. A. Levine. Jerusalem: Israel Exploration Society.
Naʾaman, N.
  1995   Beth David in the Aramaic Stela from Tel Dan. *Biblische Notizen* 79: 17–24.
  1997a   Cow Town or Royal Capital?: Evidence for Iron Age Jerusalem. *Biblical Archaeology Review* 23/4: 43–74, 67.
  1997b   Historical and Literary Notes on the Excavation of Tel Jezreel. *Tel Aviv* 24: 122–28.
Noth, M.
  1960   *The History of Israel.* 2nd ed. New York: Harper & Row.
Provan, I. W.
  1995   Ideologies, Literary and Critical: Reflections on Recent Writing on the History of Israel. *Journal of Biblical Literature* 114: 585–606.
Puech, E.
  1994   La stèle araméenne de Dan: Bar Hadad II et la coalition des Omrides et de la maison de David. *Revue biblique* 101: 215–41.
Rast, W. E.
  1978   *Taanach I: Studies in the Iron Age Pottery.* Cambridge, Mass.: American Schools of Oriental Research.
Reich, R., and Shukron, E.
  1999   The Light at the End of the Tunnel. *Biblical Archaeology Review* 25/1: 22–23, 72.
  2000   The System of Rock-Cut Tunnels near Gihon in Jerusalem Reconsidered. *Revue biblique* 107: 5–17.
Renfrew, C., and Bahn, P.
  1991   *Archaeology: Theories, Methods, and Practice.* New York: Thames & Hudson.
Schloen, J. D.
  2001   *The House of the Father as Fact and Symbol: Patrimonialism in Ugarit and the Ancient Near East.* Studies in the Archaeology and History of the Levant 2. Cambridge: Harvard Semitic Museum / Winona Lake, Ind.: Eisenbrauns.
Schniedewind, W. M.
  1996   Tel Dan Stela: New Light on Aramaic and Jehu's Revolt. *Bulletin of the American Schools of Oriental Research* 302: 75–90.

Service, E. R.
 1971 *Primitive Social Organization.* New York: Random House.
Shanks, H.
 1997 Face to Face: Biblical Minimalists Meet Their Challengers. *Biblical Archaeology Review* 23/4: 26–42, 66.
 1999 Everything You Ever Knew about Jerusalem Is Wrong (Well, Almost). *Biblical Archaeology Review* 25/6: 20–29.
Shiloh, Y.
 1979 Iron Age Sanctuaries and Cult Elements in Palestine. Pp. 147–57 in *Symposia Celebrating the Seventy-Fifth Anniversary of the Founding of the American Schools of Oriental Research (1900–1975)*, ed. F. M. Cross. Cambridge, Mass.: American Schools of Oriental Research.
Stager, L. E.
 1985 The Archaeology of the Family in Ancient Israel. *Bulletin of the American Schools of Oriental Research* 260: 1–35.
 1999 Jerusalem and the Garden of Eden. Pp. 183*–94* in *Eretz-Israel* 26 (Frank Moore Cross Volume), ed. B. A. Levine et al. Jerusalem: Israel Exploration Society.
Tapper, R.
 1990 Anthropologists, Historians and Tribespeople on Tribe and State Formation in the Middle East. Pp. 48–73 in *Tribe and State Formation in the Middle East*, ed. P. S. Khoury and J. Kostiner. Berkeley: University of California Press.
Thompson, T.
 1992 *Early History of the Israelite People: From the Written and Archaeological Sources.* Leiden: Brill.
 1999 *The Mythic Past: Biblical Archaeology and the Myth of Israel.* New York: Basic Books.
Ussishkin, D.
 1980 Was the "Solomonic" City Gate at Megiddo Built by King Solomon? *Bulletin of the American Schools of Oriental Research* 239: 1–18.
 2000 Area G: Soundings in the Late Bronze Age Gate. Pp. 104–22 in *Megiddo III: The 1992–1996 Seasons*, ed. I. Finkelstein, D. Ussishkin, and B. Halpern. Tel Aviv: Tel Aviv University Press.
Vaux, R. de
 1961 *Ancient Israel: Its Life and Institutions.* New York: McGraw-Hill.
Voegelin, E.
 1952 *The New Science of Politics.* Chicago: University of Chicago Press.
Weber, M.
 1978 *Economy and Society*, ed. G. Roth and C. Wittick. 2 vols. Berkeley: University of California Press.
Windschuttle, K.
 1996 *The Killing of History: How Literary Critics and Social Theorists Are Murdering Our Past.* New York: Free Press.
Wright, G. E.
 1967 The Provinces of Solomon. Pp. 58*–68* in *Eretz-Israel* 8 (E. L. Sukenik Volume), ed. N. Avigad et al. Jerusalem: Israel Exploration Society.
Yadin, Y.
 1958 Solomon's City Wall and Gate at Gezer. *Israel Exploration Journal* 8: 80–86.
 1980 A Rejoinder. *Bulletin of the American Schools of Oriental Research* 239: 19–23.
Zarzecki-Peleg, A.
 1997 Hazor, Jokneam and Megiddo in the Tenth Century B.C.E. *Tel Aviv* 24: 258–88.
Zertal, A.
 1988 *The Israelite Settlement in the Hill Country of Manasseh.* Haifa: Haifa University (Hebrew).
 1992 Arubboth. Pp. 465–67 in vol. 1 of *Anchor Bible Dictionary*, ed. D. N. Freedman. New York: Doubleday.

City-States to States:
Polity Dynamics in the 10th–9th Centuries B.C.E.

Israel Finkelstein
Institute of Archaeology, Tel Aviv University
Ramat Aviv, Israel

It is conventional wisdom that the Late Bronze Age Egypto-Canaanite system of city-states came to an end in the second half of the 12th century B.C.E. (e.g., Ussishkin 1985; Singer 1988–89). But what happened next? Was this the *final* collapse of second-millennium Canaan? After all, both the Early Bronze and Middle Bronze Age urban systems suffered major shocks and recovered after a relatively short period of time. In other words, do we know when and how the city-state system of Canaan came to an end?

In the early days of research, cultural lines were not drawn by archaeology but, rather, according to two "historical" considerations: the biblical account of the conquest of Canaan and the "Israelite Settlement" that followed; and the Egyptian texts concerning the invasion of the "Sea Peoples" (e.g., Albright 1949: 109; A. Mazar 1990: 295). Theoretically, one might argue that the culture of Canaan could have recovered from the "Sea Peoples'" migrations. So the only reason for marking the year 1200 B.C.E. as the critical point in the history of Canaan would be textual—that is, biblical. But, with the progress in archaeological research, it has become abundantly clear that Canaan was not wiped out in a single military campaign and that early Israel (and its neighbors) emerged from the autochthonous population of the southern Levant. Still, the images of the devastated cities of Canaan, the eradication of the indigenous population, and young Israel's emergence from the ruins have not faded away.

On the textual side, there is wide agreement among scholars that the biblical narratives in question were not put into writing before the 7th century B.C.E. (e.g., Cross 1973: 274–88; Nelson 1981; Halpern and Vanderhooft 1991). And even if the texts preserve some earlier materials, in most cases these are beyond recovery, because the Deuteronomistic historian enmeshed them in his ideology and presented them in such a way that they could be used to advance his political goals. Therefore, anyone reading the biblical description of the conquest must be aware that he/she is in the ideological world of late Monarchic Judah, not in Late Bronze Age or Iron Age I realities. Hence, the description of the conquest of Galilee, which may have been based on an authentic folk-tale, was intended to show that Judah was the only legitimate heir to the territories of the then-vanquished Northern Kingdom. The report on the land that still remained to be taken aims to delineate what could not be fulfilled, even of the dreams of the late Davidic kings. The list of cities that were not conquered—all in the territories of the North—is no more than a theological fable on the failure of the Northern Kingdom to eradicate Canaanite

culture from its midst. And the tale of the great conquests of David is an ideological construct that declares the rise of the new, ultimate David (Josiah) and sets the agenda for the
"reconstruction" of a mythical, past golden age (on all these, see Finkelstein and Silberman 2001). To make a long story short, the basis for the historical reconstruction of the
end of Bronze Age Canaan that was built up in the 1920s and 1930s is no longer valid, and
therefore we are at liberty to look at the finds in a new light.

Studying the fall of Late Bronze Canaan, one should acknowledge that the finds at
sites such as Megiddo, Beth-shean, Lachish, and Ashdod reflect the events in the main
centers—city-states, ports, and Egyptian strongholds. Recent archaeological fieldwork
has indicated that the picture in the countryside was very different. Excavations at sites
such as Tel Menorah in the Beth-shean Valley (Gal 1979) and Tell el-Wawiyat and 'Ein
Zippori (Sepphoris) in the Lower Galilee (Dessel 1999) show that the rural sector was not
damaged. On the contrary, these sites indicate a clear demographic and cultural continuity during the Late Bronze–Iron I transition. This is also seen in settlement patterns. The
northern valleys were densely settled in both the Late Bronze and Iron I, with no sign of
a major crisis. In the western Jezreel Valley, for instance, the number of settlements, their
location, and the total built-up area did not change in the transition between these
periods.[1] According to A. Mazar (in a lecture at Tel Aviv University, March 2000), the
same holds true for the Beth-shean Valley farther to the east (for the northern Jordan Valley, see Ilan 1999: 162–71). Hence, the peasants of Canaan continued their age-old routine
only a few miles away from the ruined cities.

No wonder then that a short while after their destruction, even the main centers were
reoccupied. The best case-study is Megiddo. In the 11th century ("Low Chronology";
Finkelstein 1996a), after an occupational gap of a few decades, Megiddo was resettled in
Stratum VIB. This was a poor, small village that in the course of a few decades gradually
and uninterruptedly developed into the prosperous city of Stratum VIA, dating to the
10th century B.C.E.

The city of Stratum VIA is strikingly similar to that of Stratum VIIA (of the 12th century). And, no less importantly, the subsequent city at Megiddo is totally different. First,
the size of the two cities (VIIA and VIA) is similar, encompassing both the upper tel and
the lower terrace, an area of about 11 hectares (27 acres). The Iron II city occupied the
upper tel only. Second, both cities had a palace in the north, near the gate; the Stratum V
palaces are located elsewhere. Third, the pottery indicates clear cultural continuity (see
already Engberg 1940); the pottery of Stratum V begins the Iron II traditions. Fourth, the
bronze objects of Stratum VIA represent a continuity of Late Bronze traditions (Negbi
1974). Fifth, a typical open courtyard house in the second-millennium tradition has
recently been excavated in Area K of the renewed excavations. Sixth, the pottery assemblage from the last (and only) floor of the "Migdal" temple indicates that it continued to
function until the destruction of Stratum VIA (A. Mazar 1985: 97; Kempinski 1989: 77–83;
Ussishkin 1995: 256).

The identity of the inhabitants of this city has been fiercely debated, with some scholars pointing to "Philistine" or "Israelite" characteristics in its culture (e.g., respectively,

---

1. According to a survey conducted in the region in 1995, on behalf of the Megiddo Expedition. The
survey was headed by B. Halpern, A. Joffe, Michael Niemann, and the author.

Kempinski 1989: 82–83; Aharoni 1970). But, as demonstrated above, there is hardly any doubt that Megiddo VIA was a Canaanite city (see already Engberg 1940). The inhabitants probably came from the nearby villages, which gradually recovered from the blow that shook their centers of power in the 12th century. And that is not all; it seems to me that Megiddo VIA functioned as the center of a city-state, controlling the rural territories around it. With no written sources at hand, I can hardly prove this assumption. But the analysis of the finds—which points to a large prosperous city engaged in long-distance trade, with clear indications of social stratification, located in the center of a rural territory in which the old population was not crushed, a region with a tradition of city-state systems—leaves us with no alternative interpretation. At least in the north, Late Bronze Canaan, which suffered a severe blow in the mid–12th century, rose from the ashes in the late 11th and early 10th century B.C.E.

Megiddo was not the only link in this "New Canaan."[2] Other city-states can be identified at Tel Kinneret and Tel Reḥov in the Jordan Valley, and at Tel Dor and possibly Tell Keisan on the coast.

Iron I Kinneret replaced Late Bronze Ḥazor as the center of the upper Jordan Valley. A heavily fortified city, about 10 hectares (25 acres) in size, developed at Tel Kinneret within a short period of time, reaching its peak of prosperity in the Megiddo VIA horizon, and then was destroyed (Fritz 1999). The city was never again as large and prosperous as in the Iron I.

The excavations at Tel Reḥov indicate that the city contemporary with Megiddo VIA covered the entire mound, the upper tel and lower terrace alike, an area of about 10 hectares (25 acres; A. Mazar 1999). Considering that Reḥov was a major city-state in the Late Bronze Age (A. Mazar 1999: 42; Goren, Finkelstein, and Na'aman 2002), that it was the main city of the Beth-shean Valley in the Iron I, and that Beth-shean at the time was a relatively small settlement (A. Mazar 1993), one may suggest that Iron I Reḥov functioned as the center of a territorial entity that covered the Beth-shean and eastern Jezreel Valleys.

Acco declined at the end of the Late Bronze Age, but Tell Keisan, probably Late Bronze Achshaph, continued to prosper (Humbert 1993). It seems that it served as the main center of the northern coastal plain, with its port located at Tell Abu Hawam (Stratum IVA). Its territory probably included that of Late Bronze Acco.

Dor also prospered at that time, encompassing an area of 7–8 hectares (15–20 acres). Its inhabitants traded with Phoenicia and Cyprus (Gilboa 1999). The monumental building excavated on the south of the mound (Stern et al. 1997: 41–44) attests to the wealth and urban nature of the Iron I city, which must have dominated the coastal plain of the Carmel Ridge. It is possible that Dor replaced Late Bronze Gath (the village of Jatt) as the main center in this region, but the Iron I finds from Gath (Porath, Yannai, and Kasher 1999) are too scant to allow us to draw firm conclusions.

In order to complete this tour of "New Canaan," we need to look at Philistia. During the Late Bronze/Iron I transition, this area exhibited traits of both continuity and change. Recent studies have shown that the supposed migration of thousands from the west (Stager 1995) is highly unlikely and that the population of Iron I Philistia had a significant

---

2. I prefer this to the more accurate "Revived Canaan."

local component (Bunimovitz 1990). It seems therefore that an elite minority dictated cultural traits in a mixed population. From a demographic-territorial point of view, the main changes were the total elimination of the Late Bronze city-state of Lachish and its villages, the rise of Iron I Ekron, the significant growth of the central cities, and the dwindling of the rural sector (Finkelstein 1996b). Continuity is indicated in the undisturbed development of many villages and in the continuing domination of Gaza, Ashkelon, Ashdod, and Gath.

Hence, many if not most of the main city-states of Late Bronze Canaan recovered in the 11th century. In fact, only two dominant Late Bronze cities in the lowlands—Ḥazor and Lachish—were annihilated and replaced by nearby cities—Kinneret in the north and Ekron in the south.[3] A major change took place at that time only in the highlands, where a strong wave of settlement occurred, but even there, we do not know enough about the status of the two "old" Late Bronze centers, Jerusalem and Shechem.

In the north the prosperity of "New Canaan" stemmed from the stability of the rural sector and from the vibrant trade with Phoenicia, Cyprus, and beyond. The northern cities probably traded in secondary products of the horticultural niches in the highlands, serving as gateway communities for these products; according to Stern (in a lecture at Tel Aviv University, March 2000), some of the pithoi at Dor originated in the highlands. Metallurgical activity is evident at many of the major sites in the Jezreel and Jordan Valleys. It seems that the copper originated in the south. Knauf (1991: 185) suggested that local, ʿArabah Valley copper replaced the Cypriot ores following the collapse of the Late Bronze economy and until the recovery of Cyprus in the 9th century (for copper production at Wadi Feinan in the Iron I, see Hauptmann 2000).

Then, with no warning, "New Canaan" collapsed, its centers put to the torch. Violent destructions have been documented in all the main centers. At Megiddo, the entire city was burned to the ground; Kinneret never recovered from the blow. Although this time the fall of the Canaanite system was final, the rural sector was once again not disrupted. Assuming that the main centers were destroyed contemporaneously (only a thorough study of the pottery can substantiate this claim), who did it? In order to identify the destroyers, we need first to date the destruction. I have no intention of repeating in this paper my arguments for dating the Megiddo VIA horizon to the 10th century. I only wish to mention that recent radio-carbon samples from Megiddo, Dor, Tel Hadar, and Kinneret all point to a 10th century date of this phase in the history of Canaan (for Megiddo, I. Carmi, unpublished preliminary report; for Dor, Gilboa and Sharon 2001; for Tel Hadar, M. Kochavi, personal communication; for Kinneret, Fritz 1999: 112).

To the best of my knowledge, there are only two alternatives for explaining this 10th-century destruction of the Canaanite centers in the north. According to the first, the expanding settlement system of the highlands struck a blow against the cities of the lowlands and took them over. But it is not clear to me whether the early highlands polity had the power to destroy the lowland city-states, and one may rightly question the logic behind the idea that the highlanders would annihilate their economic ally. According to the

---

3. Acco declined, as well. Archaeology has not provided enough information on the fate of two other major Late Bronze centers in the lowlands, Gezer and Jatt.

second alternative, "New Canaan" was struck by Pharaoh Sheshonq I in the second half of the 10th century B.C.E. Reḥov and Megiddo are mentioned in Sheshonq I's list; and a fragment of a stela of Sheshonq I was found at Megiddo, unfortunately in an unstratified context. According to this alternative, Egypt dealt Canaan a devastating blow. But this time, it did not mean to stay (or did not succeed in staying) for long. Egypt's retreat after the annihilation of the old system created a vacuum that opened the way for the rulers of the northern hill country—the Northern Kingdom in its early days—to expand to the lowlands and to establish a large territorial, multiethnic state. I am well aware of the arguments against this idea. Why would Sheshonq I destroy these cities if he meant to continue dominating Canaan; and why would he erect a stela in a destroyed city (Ussishkin 1990: 73–74)? These questions call for a thorough discussion of the goals of Sheshonq I's campaign and the practice of erecting victory stelae in the ancient Near East, a discussion beyond the scope of this paper. I would only say that the latter alternative is no less attractive and no more problematic than the former.

Where is the biblical United Monarchy in this story? Considering the new interpretation I have offered above for the finds in the north; the redating of the Megiddo palaces and other 10th-century strata to the 9th century (Finkelstein 1996a); the meager 10th-century finds in Jerusalem (Ussishkin in press); the scant 10th-century finds in the highlands of Judah; and the general picture indicating that, throughout the southern Levant, territorial states did not emerge before the 9th century; considering all this, we are left with no archaeological evidence for a prosperous United Monarchy extending over much of the territory of Palestine. And, in light of the late and highly theological character of the Deuteronomistic history, we are left with no real textual evidence for its existence (on the Solomonic era see, for instance, Knauf 1991; Miller 1997; Niemann 1997; 2000). Ironically, the only "evidence" for a United Monarchy is the appeal of the Deuteronomistic historian to the collective memory of the people of Judah in his own time, promising them the recovery of a past golden age. In other words, the most one can maintain is that 7th-century Judah preserved a vague memory that the founders of the Davidic dynasty ruled over a territory in the highlands that was larger than the traditional territory of late Monarchic Judah, and that this territory included areas that were later incorporated into the Northern Kingdom. The nature of the evidence from both Jerusalem and the hill country to the south suggests that until the 9th century B.C.E., the southern hill country still featured a typical Amarna-like formation. Most likely, a "king" and his court ruled from a highland stronghold, which did not include much more than a modest palace and a shrine, over extensive, sparsely settled territory with a few sedentary villages and a large pastoral population.

Did the fall of "New Canaan" revolutionize the course of history and cultural developments in the southern Levant? In order to answer this question we need to examine the Northern Kingdom of Israel. After all, Judah did not emerge as a full-blown state until the 8th century (Jamieson-Drake 1991); Edom did not emerge until the Assyrian takeover; and Moab and Ammon were still small tribal entities (Knauf 1992; Younker 1997).

The monumental building activities of the Omrides at Samaria, Jezreel, and Ḥazor tell us a lot about the nature of their state. Omride architecture (Finkelstein 2000) at these sites is characterized by large-scale leveling and filling operations that created platforms for palaces and elaborate gates. The best demonstration of this method is found at Samaria, where a casemate wall was built as a retaining system for fills that were laid in order to extend the area of the hill and to support an exceptionally large and beautiful ashlar palace. Samaria probably represents the most impressive single building effort in Iron Age Israel. The huge stone and earth construction can only be compared to the work that Herod the Great carried out in the Temple compound in Jerusalem almost a thousand years later. Whoever approached the site faced a towering platform on top of a hill, surrounded by high support walls, and a palace rising on top of the platform. This must have been a majestic symbol of wealth and power.

Jezreel revealed similar features, including a large casemate compound laid on an immense fill; and somewhat similar characteristics can be identified at Ḥazor (Stratum X). The layout at Megiddo is different, but no less elaborate: the Omrides constructed two beautiful ashlar palaces, one of them similar in building method to the palace at Samaria (Fisher 1929: 16; Crowfoot 1940).

Some of the elements of the innovative Omride concept of a royal compound are known in Palestine in previous centuries. Most significantly, the concept of a commanding stronghold for a limited ruling class that controlled large highland territories is reminiscent of the elevated Middle Bronze elite strongholds at highland sites such as Shechem and Shiloh (Finkelstein 1992).

In order to understand this phenomenon, we need to remember that the Northern Kingdom was a multifaceted state, comprising a heterogeneous population. The highlands of Samaria—the core territory of the state and the seat of the capital—was inhabited by Israelites, that is, the descendants of the second-millennium highlands population, pastoral and sedentary alike. In the Northern lowlands, the rural population comprised mainly local indigenous elements, that is, Canaanites. The architecture of these small villages did not change much over the centuries, and as recently shown by Faust (2000), it did not absorb "Israelite" architectural features from the highlands. Even the major Israelite administrative centers in the valleys look very much like Late Bronze city-states. From the conceptual and functional points of view, the layout of 9th-century Megiddo was not very different from its layout in the Late Bronze Age. Large parts of the mound were devoted to public buildings and open areas, with only limited areas set aside for domestic quarters. The population consisted mainly of the ruling elite, who controlled the rural hinterland.

In the northeast, Israel bordered on the territories of Aram-Damascus. The population in this region was at least partially Aramaic. This is demonstrated in the meager albeit significant number of Aramaic inscriptions found at many Iron II sites in the region (e.g., B. Mazar et al. 1964: 27–29; Arav 1995: 17–18). Finally, the highlands of the Galilee and the northern coastal plain were inhabited by groups related to the Phoenician coastal cities (e.g., Gal 1995 for Ḥorvat Rosh Zayit; E. Mazar 1996 for the Achzib cemetery).

This ethnic and cultural diversity of the Northern Kingdom seems to provide the background for the monumental architecture of the Omrides. State-establishing dynasties that engage in territorial expansion into neighboring "foreign" lands are in urgent need of legitimacy. Their propaganda is directed toward both their own people and the inhabitants of the new territories. In the latter, the Omrides needed to pacify the population and to secure its loyalty. This was especially crucial since a strong competing state emerged in neighboring Damascus at the same time. The construction of fortified compounds, some with palatial quarters, in the Jezreel Valley (Jezreel) and on the border with the Aramean state of Damascus (Ḥazor X) should therefore be seen in the light of two objectives. First, they were built as administrative centers to control the "non-Israelite" areas of the newly established state. Second, they served the propaganda and legitimacy needs of a dynasty ruling from the highlands. Williamson (1996) has suggested that at Jezreel, in the midst of the Canaanite valley, the idea was to overawe, even intimidate, the local population, and that at Samaria, in the Israelite heartland, the aim was to impress. The monumental building activity was complemented by a moderate policy vis-à-vis the rural population in the valleys. The remarkable settlement stability in the Jezreel Valley throughout the Iron Age is a clear indication that the Israelite monarchs did not shake the "Canaanite" rural system in the northern lowlands.

The Omride state therefore also demonstrates both change and continuity. There was *change* in the sense that the Omrides succeeded in creating a territorial state covering large areas of both highlands and lowlands. There was *continuity* in the sense that this was an age-old dream of hill country rulers. Indeed, 9th-century Samaria was not very different, conceptually or architecturally, from Labayu's Shechem.

The real revolution in political dynamics came only in the 8th century, with the integration of the Northern Kingdom into the Assyrian economic hegemony and the rise of a true national state in Judah. And here we come full circle. That national state produced a historical saga so powerful that it led biblical historians and archaeologist alike to recreate its mythical past—from stones and potsherds.

References

Aharoni, Y.
  1970   New Aspects of the Israelite Occupation in the North. Pp. 254–65 in *Near Eastern Archaeology in the Twentieth Century: Essays in Honor of Nelson Glueck*, ed. J. A. Sanders. New York: Doubleday.

Albright, W. F.
  1949   *The Archaeology of Palestine*. Harmondsworth: Penguin.

Arav, R.
  1995   Bethsaida Excavations: Preliminary Report, 1987–1993. Pp. 3–63 in *Bethsaida: A City by the North Shore of the Sea of Galilee*, ed. R. Arav and R. A. Freund. Kirksville, Mo.: Thomas Jefferson University Press.

Bunimovitz, S.
  1990   Problems in the "Ethnic" Identification of the Philistine Culture. *Tel Aviv* 17: 210–22.

Cross, F. M.
  1973   *Canaanite Myth and Hebrew Epic*. Cambridge: Harvard University Press.

Crowfoot, J. W.
  1940   Megiddo: A Review. *Palestine Exploration Quarterly* 72: 132–47.

Dessel, J. P.
  1999   Tell ʿEin Zippori and the Lower Galilee in the Late Bronze and Iron Ages: A Village Perspective. Pp. 1–32 in *Galilee through the Centuries: Confluence of Cultures*, ed. E. M. Meyers. Duke Judaic Studies Series 1. Winona Lake, Ind.: Eisenbrauns.

Engberg, R. M.
   1940   Historical Analysis of Archaeological Evidence: Megiddo and the Song of Deborah. *Bulletin of the American Schools of Oriental Research* 78: 4–7.

Faust, A.
   2000   Ethnic Complexity in Northern Israel during Iron Age II. *Palestine Exploration Quarterly* 132: 2–27.

Finkelstein, I.
   1992   Middle Bronze Age "Fortifications": A Reflection of Social Organization and Political Formations. *Tel Aviv* 19: 201–20.
   1996a   The Archaeology of the United Monarchy: An Alternative View. *Levant* 28: 177–87.
   1996b   The Philistine Countryside. *Israel Exploration Journal* 46: 225–42.
   2000   Omride Architecture. *Zeitschrift des deutschen Palästina-Vereins* 116: 114–38.

Finkelstein, I., and Silberman, N.
   2001   *The Bible Unearthed: Archaeology's New Vision of Ancient Israel and the Origin of Its Sacred Texts*. New York: Free Press.

Fisher, C. S.
   1929   *The Excavation of Armageddon*. Chicago: University of Chicago Press.

Fritz, V.
   1999   Kinneret: Excavations at Tell el-Oreimeh (Tel Kinrot). Preliminary Report on the 1994–1997 Seasons. *Tel Aviv* 26: 92–115.

Gal, Z.
   1979   An Early Iron Age Site near Tel Menorah in the Beth-shean Valley. *Tel Aviv* 6: 138–45.
   1995   The Diffusion of Phoenician Cultural Influence in Light of the Excavations at Hurvat Rosh Zayit. *Tel Aviv* 22: 89–93.

Gilboa, A.
   1999   The Dynamics of Phoenician Bichrome Pottery: A View from Tel Dor. *Bulletin of the American Schools of Oriental Research* 316: 1–22.

Gilboa, A., and Sharon, I.
   2001   Early Iron Age Radiometric Dates from Tel Dor: Preliminary Implications for Phoenicia and Beyond. *Radiocarbon* 43 (3): 1343–51.

Goren, Y.; Finkelstein, I.; and Na'aman, N.
   2002   The Seat of Three Disputed Canaanite Rulers according to Petrographic Investigation of the Amarna Tablets. *Tel Aviv* 29: 221–37.

Halpern, B., and Vanderhooft, D.
   1991   The Editions of Kings in the 7th–6th Centuries B.C.E. *Hebrew Union College Annual* 62: 179–244.

Hauptmann, A.
   2000   *Zur frühen Metallurgie des Kupfers in Fenan/Jordanien (Der Anschnitt* 11). Bochum: Deutsches Bergbaumuseum.

Humbert, J.-B.
   1993   Keisan, Tell. Pp. 862–67 in vol. 3 of *The New Encyclopedia of Archaeological Excavations in the Holy Land*, ed. E. Stern. Jerusalem: Israel Exploration Society.

Ilan, D.
   1999   Northeastern Israel in the Iron Age I: Cultural, Socioeconomic and Political Perspectives. Ph.D. dissertation, Tel Aviv University.

Jamieson-Drake, D. W.
   1991   *Scribes and Schools in Monarchic Judah*. Sheffield: Almond.

Kempinski, A.
   1989   *Megiddo: A City-State and Royal Centre in North Israel*. Munich: Beck.

Knauf, E. A.
   1991   King Solomon's Copper Supply. Pp. 167–86 in *Phoenicia and the Bible*, ed. E. Lipiński. Leuven: Peeters.

1992   The Cultural Impact of Secondary State Formation: The Cases of the Edomites and Moabites. Pp. 47–54 in *Early Edom and Moab. The Beginning of the Iron Age in Southern Jordan*, ed. P. Bienkowski. Sheffield: J. R. Collis.

Mazar, A.

1985   The Emergence of the Philistine Material Culture. *Israel Exploration Journal* 35: 95–107.

1990   *Archaeology of the Land of the Bible 10,000–586 B.C.E.* New York: Doubleday.

1993   Beth Shean in the Iron Age: Preliminary Report and Conclusions of the 1990–1991 Excavations. *Israel Exploration Journal* 43: 201–29.

1999   The 1997–1998 Excavations at Tel Reḥov: Preliminary Report. *Israel Exploration Journal* 49: 1–42.

Mazar, B., et al.

1964   ʿEin Gev Excavations in 1961. *Israel Exploration Journal* 14: 1–49.

Mazar, E.

1996   *The Achzib Burials: A Test Case for Phoenician-Punic Burial Customs.* Ph.D. dissertation, Hebrew University (Hebrew).

Miller, J. M.

1997   Separating the Solomon of History from the Solomon of Legend. Pp. 1–24 in *The Age of Solomon: Scholarship at the Turn of the Millennium*, ed. L. K. Handy. Leiden: Brill.

Negbi, O.

1974   The Continuity of the Canaanite Bronzework of the Late Bronze Age into the Early Iron Age. *Tel Aviv* 1: 159–72.

Nelson, R.

1981   *The Double Redaction of the Deuteronomistic History.* Journal for the Study of the Old Testament Supplement 18. Sheffield: Sheffield Academic Press.

Niemann, M.

1997   The Socio-Political Shadow Cast by the Biblical Solomon. Pp. 252–99 in *The Age of Solomon: Scholarship at the Turn of the Millennium*, ed. L. K. Handy. Leiden: Brill.

2000   Megiddo and Solomon: A Biblical Investigation in Relation to Archaeology. *Tel Aviv* 27: 59–72.

Porath, Y.; Yannai, E.; and Kasher, A.

1999   Archaeological Remains at Jatt. *ʿAtiqot* 37: 1–78 (Hebrew).

Singer, I.

1988–1989   The Political Status of Megiddo VIIA. *Tel Aviv* 15–16: 101–12.

Stager, L. E.

1995   The Impact of the Sea Peoples (1185–1050 B.C.E.). Pp. 332–48 in *The Archaeology of Society in the Holy Land*, ed. T. E. Levy. London: Leicester University Press.

Stern, E., et al.

1997   Tel Dor, 1994–1995: Preliminary Stratigraphic Report. *Israel Exploration Journal* 47: 29–56.

Ussishkin, D.

1985   Levels VII and VI at Tel Lachish and the End of the Late Bronze Age in Canaan. Pp. 213–30 in *Palestine in the Bronze and Iron Ages: Papers in Honour of Olga Tufnell*, ed. J. N. Tubb. London: Institute of Archaeology.

1990   Notes on Megiddo, Gezer, Ashdod, and Tel Batash in the Tenth to Ninth Centuries B.C. *Bulletin of the American Schools of Oriental Research* 277/278: 71–91.

1995   The Destruction of Megiddo at the End of the Late Bronze Age and Its Historical Significance. *Tel Aviv* 22: 240–67.

In press   Solomon's Jerusalem: The Text and the Facts on the Ground. *Tel Aviv*.

Williamson, H. G. M.

1996   Tel Jezreel and the Dynasty of Omri. *Palestine Exploration Quarterly* 128: 41–51.

Younker, R. W.

1997   Moabite Social Structure. *Biblical Archaeologist* 60: 237–48.

Remarks on Biblical Traditions and Archaeological Evidence concerning Early Israel

Amihai Mazar
Institute of Archaeology
Hebrew University, Jerusalem

Introduction

The current state of research on the history of ancient Israel includes a wide spectrum of views, ranging from extreme fundamentalism to extreme revisionism. In this paper, I shall approach the subject from an archaeological point of view and briefly try to justify a "middle-of-the-road" position.

After 150 years of biblical research, many scholars today believe that the Pentateuch and the Deuteronomistic history were written during the 7th century B.C.E. or later and were further edited during the postexilic and Hellenistic periods. The texts were cast in late Judean ideological and theological molds, and many could be defined by means of the tools of literary criticism as superb but largely fictional literature. Assuming that these conclusions are acceptable, the question I address is to what extent these biblical texts relied on and even cited earlier materials, such as the Jerusalem temple archives, ancient administrative archives, earlier Israelite historiographical texts, early poetry and prophetic literature, and folkloristic traditions, including etiologies that may have preserved cores of historical realities.

The extreme revisionists reject the existence of reliable Iron Age historical data in the biblical text and thus deny its validity for a historical reconstruction of most of the pre-exilic era (Davies 1992; Thompson 1992; 1999; Lemche 1998; for a critical review of this school of thought and a detailed bibliography, see Dever 1998; 1999). More-moderate revisionist scholars argue that, while the biblical texts were composed during the 7th century B.C.E., they have only minimal value for reconstructing the earlier periods in Israelite history, particularly those preceding the division of the monarchy. Such views have recently been expressed by, among others, Israeli biblical scholars and archaeologists—among them Finkelstein, Herzog, and Zakovitch—who call for diminished acceptance of the historical value of the biblical narratives concerning early Israel (Finkelstein 1999; Herzog 2001; Zakovitch 2001). Yet many mainstream scholars claim that, although the texts may have been written during the 7th century B.C.E., they nevertheless incorporate much early material of the kind mentioned above, which necessarily predates the time of writing and thus contains kernels of valid historical data (for example, Malamat 1983; Miller and Hayes 1986; the articles by Callaway, Lemaire, McCarter, and Sarna in Shanks 1998; Dever 2001; and many others). This statement, however, still leaves a window wide open for differing interpretations. In the following, I will try to justify such a position from an archaeological perspective.

The Settlement Period

This discussion begins with the settlement period, the first period for which biblical data can be cautiously tested against extrabiblical written documents and archaeological evidence. Such a comparison shows, in my opinion, that the biblical narratives relating to the periods of the Judges and early monarchy provide a valid general framework for Israelite history.

The great influence of Canaanite language, literature, and mythology on the biblical literature indicates continuous cultural development from the 2nd to the 1st millennium B.C.E. in ancient Israel and the incorporation of Canaanite elements into Israelite culture at a rather early stage of its history (see, for example, Cross 1973; Smith 1990). The carriers of these Canaanite literary traditions could have been surviving Canaanites who continued to inhabit the coastal and northern plains of the land of Israel, as indicated by archaeological research. These Canaanites would have been assimilated into Israel from the 10th century on, as indicated both by the archaeological evidence and in biblical passages such as 1 Kgs 9:20–21. Indeed, excavations at several sites in the northern valleys indicate the continuity of Canaanite traditions and possibly population well into the 10th century B.C.E. (Mazar 1994: 41–45). Such continuity is clearly demonstrated at Tel Reḥov in the Beth-shean Valley (Mazar 1999); and Canaanite continuity in the villages of the northern valleys has been discussed recently by Faust (2000).

Beyond these general observations, however, there are several specific points of interest that I will briefly review. These points seem to indicate that some of the biblical texts accord with early external textual and archaeological evidence and thus can hardly have been invented in the 7th century B.C.E. or later.

1. The biblical conquest narratives, and specifically the narrative in Joshua 1–11 and the list of cities in Joshua 12, recognize the existence of a Canaanite city-state system in pre-Israelite Canaan. Such knowledge of the Late Bronze Age geopolitical structure of Canaan could not be an invention of 7th-century B.C.E. authors. A continuous tradition must have existed that retained this memory from the Late Bronze Age into the Iron Age. Similarly, territorial divisions of the Late Bronze Age were retained to some extent, as reflected in the descriptions of the tribal boundaries and Solomon's districts (Na'aman 1986; however, for a different view, see more recently Na'aman 1997: 601).

2. The definition of Hazor in Josh 11:10 as "formerly the head of all those kingdoms" fits the status of Hazor in the 2nd millennium B.C.E. and could not have been invented in the 7th century B.C.E. or later. The burning of Hazor mentioned in Josh 11:11 (in contrast to all the other "conquered" cities) is supported by archaeological evidence of the tremendous conflagration that destroyed the city's Canaanite palace and temples. Yadin (1972: 200) did not hesitate to identify the conquerors as Israelites; and Ben-Tor finds no other candidates for the destroyers of Hazor than Israelites or "Proto Israelites" (Ben-Tor 1998: 465). Rather than explaining the destruction of Hazor as resulting from an Israelite conquest during the 13th century B.C.E., I would define the description in Joshua 11 as a

reflection of a long-living memory of the local inhabitants of a traumatic event that put an end to Hazor, the mightiest Late Bronze Age Canaanite city. Such memories could have been retained among the Canaanite population that remained in the country during the 12th–11th centuries and finally were assimilated into the Israelite entity of the monarchic era, with the end result that the event was attributed to Joshua in later Israelite historiography. The antiquity of the memory itself is significant, although the circumstances of the destruction of Hazor may remain elusive.

3. The network of some 250 Iron Age I settlement sites found by several survey teams in the central hill country has been the subject of extensive discussion in the literature (Stager 1985; Finkelstein 1988; the various papers in Finkelstein and Na'aman 1994). The environmental and economic background of the emergence of these settlements together with their architectural and other material culture characteristics reflect the wide-scale settlement of a people with a specific socioeconomic life-style, which in my opinion accords with premonarchic Israelite society as described in the biblical narratives. The continuity between many of these sites and later Israelite towns and villages of the monarchic era legitimizes the definition of these settlers as Israelites, as I have maintained since I excavated the site of Giloh in 1978 (Mazar 1981; 1985; 1990a), and as have many other scholars. The term "Proto-Israelites" introduced by Dever (e.g., 1992: 103; 1995: 72) and adopted by others to designate the inhabitants of these sites is in my view superfluous.

4. The biblical traditions concerning the role of the Midianites in the emergence of Israelite religion and passages mentioning Yahweh's going "forth from Se'ir" (Judg 5:4; see also Deut 33:2) may be related to "*Yhw* in the land Shasu" and the relationship between Shasu and the land of Se'ir (most likely southern Transjordan) mentioned in Egyptian documents of the 15th century B.C.E. (Redford 1992: 272–73). Cross and Stager have associated the Midianites with the archaeological finds dated to the 13th–12th centuries B.C.E. from the Hijaz and the Araba (Cross 1988; Stager 1998: 147–48). Although this equation cannot be proved, it is a tempting suggestion.

5. The appearance of Edom, Moab, and Israel in Egyptian texts of the 13th century B.C.E. is of great significance, even if these terms do not relate to settled peoples or established states (Redford 1992: 282; Kitchen 1992). The reference to Israel in the Merneptah stela has been assessed in various ways by different scholars. Recently Hasel (1998: 194–217) has convincingly suggested that this reference must have related to an important population group in Canaan; as he and others have claimed, it is tempting to identify the Israel of the Merneptah stela with the wide-scale settlement process in the hill country of Cisjordan, as well as in northern Transjordan (Gilead), which began in the late 13th century B.C.E. (see, among others, Dever 1998).

6. Several sites in these regions may provide more-specific data. ʿAi can serve as a good example. Assuming that the identification of ʿAi with et-Tell is correct, the story of its conquest in Joshua 8 can be explained in light of the archaeological evidence at the site, where an Iron Age I settlement was founded above the prominent ruins of the fortified Early Bronze Age III city. The story of the conquest of ʿAi was probably created by the Iron Age I village settlers as an etiological explanation for the massive ruins at the site (Zevit 1985). In this case, the etiology itself must have been centuries old when it was integrated into the biblical text.

7. The results of the excavations at Shiloh support the biblical traditions concerning its history, as explained convincingly by Finkelstein (in Finkelstein, Bunimovitz, and Lederman 1993: 385–89).[1]

8. The case of the Mount Ebal site is rather complicated. The line of thinking that led Zertal (1986–87) to identify the main structure at the site as the altar built by Joshua (Josh 8:30–35) recalls G. E. Wright's identification of the large *maṣṣēba* in front of the Canaanite temple at Shechem as the great stone at Shechem mentioned in Josh 24:27. Both of these suggestions have met with severe skepticism. Nevertheless, the function of the Mount Ebal site as a cult place is accepted even by some of those who reject the specific identification of the main structure as an altar (e.g., Coogan 1987; Finkelstein 1988: 82–85; Mazar 1990b: 348–50). Thus, even if Zertal's identification of the main structure at this site as an altar is not accepted, the evidence from the site may indicate that it was, indeed, a cultic site from an early phase of settlement in the hill country. Memories from the settlement period that relate to this site could have constituted the background for the traditions concerning the covenant ceremony at Mount Ebal. This tradition, however, could have been introduced into Israelite historiography in a much later period, and it should not be taken at face value, as suggested by Zertal.

9. Decades of research on Philistine culture have resulted in a picture that appears to fit the biblical concepts of the origin of the Philistines, their settlement, and the identification and nature of the major cities of the Philistine Pentapolis (for a summary, see Mazar 1990b: 300–328; for more recent treatments, see the papers by Bunimovitz, Dothan, Finkelstein, Iacovou, Karageorghis, and Sherratt in Gitin, Mazar, and Stern 1998; and the papers by Dothan, Finkelstein, Killebrew, Machinist, and Mazar in Oren 2000; see also Stager in this volume). It is inconceivable that such descriptions would have been invented in the 7th century or later.

10. Recent research in Transjordan has determined the existence of fortified settlements during the 12th and 11th centuries B.C.E. along the central plateau, from the Amman region to central Moab. The most prominent excavated examples are Tell el-ʾUmayri southwest of Amman; and Lahun, Khirbet Mudayna al-Muʿarraja, and Khirbet al-Mudayna al-ʾAliya (Routledge 2000) on the banks of the Arnon River (Wadi Mujib) and its tributaries. These new data call for a reevaluation of biblical traditions relating to Transjordan in the Iron Age I period, such as the attempt by Herr (1999), relating the finds at Tell al-ʿUmayri to biblical traditions concerning the tribe of Reuben. Similarly, the finds from the sites along the Arnon River may be related to biblical traditions concerning Moab in the Iron Age I.

11. The list of cities that were not conquered (Judg 1:27–36) accords with the archaeological finds from the cities that have been excavated: Beth-shean, Dor, Gezer, Megiddo, and possibly also Akko and Tel Keisan (the last identified as one of the cities mentioned in the Akko Valley). In all of these cities, Canaanite culture continued to thrive until the late 11th century B.C.E. (Mazar 1994: 41–45), with the exception of Taʿanach, where the

---

1. It is ironic that Finkelstein attacks this very approach in his reaction to my response to his "low chronology" (Finkelstein 1998a: 172–73). He not only uses traditional "biblical archaeology" argumentation in his summary of the excavations at Shiloh, but also biblical data concerning Jezreel as the main foundation for his "low chronology."

material culture from the early 12th century (Period I) resembles that of the central hill country "Israelite settlement" sites.[2]

In contrast to the points mentioned above, there are other instances in which disagreement between the biblical tradition and archaeology prevails. Thus, most of the conquest stories (except in the case of Hazor, as mentioned above) are either negated or cannot be corroborated by the archaeological evidence. The finds at Taʿanach preclude its inclusion among the cities that were not conquered. The Iron Age I material culture at Bethshemesh can hardly be defined as Israelite, in contrast to the biblical tradition, and Edom did not exist as a state until the 8th century B.C.E.

Apparently, the biblical texts relating to premonarchic Israel retain kernels of historical reality that were inserted into a much later literary narrative. Those points that can be confirmed by archaeology and extrabiblical texts strengthen the opinion that these kernels resulted from long-living historical memories, the transmission of traditions, and perhaps early written historiography (see above). Can a detailed history of early Israel be written, however, based on these biblical traditions? An answer to this question is beyond the scope of archaeology and the study of the few available extrabiblical epigraphic sources. The only statement that can be made is that the presence of a self-determined Israelite entity in the country from the late 13th century B.C.E. on is plausible, and that the socioeconomic status of the Israelites, as well as their spatial distribution, fit the biblical narrative. We cannot resolve all the questions of the origins of Israel and its protohistory, and we definitely cannot take the detailed stories in the Deuteronomistic history at face value.

The United Monarchy

Regarding the current debate over the historical evaluation of the United Monarchy and the rise of the Israelite states, traditional readings of the Bible expected archaeology to prove the existence of a strong, mature state with a large capital city in Jerusalem, dense urban settlement throughout the country, formal inscriptions, and art. The lack of such features led scholars such as Wightman (1990), Jamieson-Drake (1991), Niemann (1997), Finkelstein (1999), and others to minimize or deny the existence of a true Israelite state during the 10th century (for various opinions, see the volumes edited by Fritz and Davies [1997] and Handy [1997]). Indeed, the biblical texts relating to David and Solomon are definitely literary creations of the nature of national sagas, containing many fictional, ideologically-motivated stories, intended to glorify a supposed golden era in the history of Israel. Yet it is a long way from this statement to a total negation of the historicity of the United Monarchy.

Any attempt to utilize archaeology for this discussion depends on the correct dating of archaeological strata, a subject of current debate (for a summary of the traditional view, see Mazar 1990b: 368–402; for the current debate, see Finkelstein 1996; 1998a; 1999, refuted by Mazar 1997; Ben-Tor and Ben-Ami 1998; Ben-Tor 2000). According to the "low

---

2. Finkelstein (1998b) has suggested lowering the date of Taʿanach Period I to the 10th century B.C.E. However, as I have shown elsewhere (Mazar 2002: 278–79), this suggestion is based on unsound methodology. Rast's dating of Period I to the early 12th century B.C.E. (1978: 6) should be retained.

chronology" suggested by Finkelstein, the dating of strata and buildings traditionally dated to the Solomonic era, such as Megiddo IVB–VA, Hazor X, and the six-chamber gate of Gezer VIII, would be pushed forward to the 9th century, namely, to the period of the Omride dynasty. Yet the stratigraphic data from Hazor, Tel Reḥov and other sites convince me that the pottery assemblages typical of these strata began to appear during the 10th century B.C.E., and continued with very little change until the mid–9th century B.C.E. (Mazar 1999: 37–42).[3]

According to the above scenario, the United Monarchy can be described as a state in an early stage of evolution, far from being the rich and widely expanding state portrayed in the biblical narrative. Following are several comments on this issue.

1. The citadel at Tell el-Fûl, if correctly dated, reconstructed, and interpreted by the excavators (Albright and Lapp [see Graham 1981]), remains a unique feature in terms of the region and time, and perhaps could be identified as "Saul's fortress." If so, it may signify the beginning of centralized administration and public architecture among the hill country settlers. However, the archaeological data from Tell el-Fûl are full of ambiguities.[4]

2. The lack of literacy in the 10th century B.C.E. is said to prove the improbability of central administration and state documents in this period. There are even fewer inscriptions, however, dating to the 9th than to the 10th century, if the two exceptional Moabite and Aramean royal stelae erected by Mesha at Dibon and by Hazael (?) at Tel Dan are excluded. Renz (1995: 3.3–4) attributed to the 10th century B.C.E. only the Gezer inscription and three short inscriptions from Tel Batash, Tel ʿAmal, and Rosh Zayit; to these may now be added two short inscriptions from Beth-shemesh and Tel Reḥov. He attributed to the 9th century only four short ostraca from Arad (the stratigraphic contexts and chronological value of which, however, are debatable); one short inscription from Tell el-Hammah; and the inscriptions from Kuntillet ʿAjrûd, dating to approximately 800 B.C.E. Since there is a consensus concerning the existence of a developed state during the 9th century B.C.E. (at least in Northern Israel), one must ask where the inscriptions are that this state left behind? In the same vein, the lack of a significant number of inscriptions from the 10th century B.C.E. does not preclude the existence of a state during that century. The few extant short 10th-century inscriptions hint at the knowledge of writing in Israel in both the 10th and 9th centuries B.C.E. It can be assumed, therefore, that most of the documents in this period were written on perishable materials, such as parchment and papyrus.

3. Low settlement density and lack of urbanization in the 10th century have been presented as an argument for minimizing or even precluding the existence of the United Monarchy (Jamieson-Drake 1991: 48–80; Finkelstein 1999). This raises, however, meth-

---

3. C14 tests from Megiddo and Dor appear to show that Finklestein's "low chronology" is possible (with Megiddo VIA apparently dating to the early [?] 10th century B.C.E.). All these tests, however, were conducted in the same laboratory (at the Weizmann Institute), and we should wait for the results of analyses from additional laboratories before arriving at a final conclusion. In contrast, C14 testing results from Tel Dan and from Tel Reḥov hint at the validity of the traditional chronology. Much of this new material, however, is known at the time of writing only from public oral presentations. See now Gilboa and Sharon 2001; Bruins, van der Plicht, and Mazar 2003.

4. There is insufficient archaeological data from Period II at Tell el-Fûl, and the reconstruction of the fortress suggested by Graham (1981: 27, fig. 15) must therefore remain doubtful.

odological problems relating to the interpretation of surface surveys. It is difficult to assess the results of surface surveys at sites that were settled continuously for most of the Iron Age. Most of the pottery collected would come from the last occupation phases of these sites, and only stratigraphic excavation could reveal their full occupational history. Thus, calculations of the numbers of settled sites during the 10th and 9th centuries B.C.E. are open to significant errors that distort the results. Meticulous surveys and processing of the results, however, may point to a gradual increase in settlement over the entire period under discussion. Ofer (2001), who assembled and analyzed data from all the surface surveys conducted thus far in Judah, concluded that during the 10th century there were 500 acres of built-up area in Judah, with a population of around 50,000, whereas this number was three times as large in the 8th century B.C.E., on the eve of Sennacherib's invasion (with the estimated population of 150,000 then based on a coefficient of 100 persons per acre). Thus, if these numbers are acceptable for the 10th–9th centuries, Judah had a sufficient number of settlements and large enough population to justify its being regarded as a small state.

In contrast to the picture that emerges from the surveys, excavated sites in Israel and Judah, such as Beersheba, Tell Beit Mirsim, Beth-shean, Beth-shemesh, Tell el-Farʿah (North) (i.e., biblical Tirzah), Hazor, Tel Kinneret, Megiddo, Tell en-Naṣbeh (?), Tel Reḥov, and others, provide evidence of the beginnings of urbanization in the Israelite territory in the 10th century B.C.E. This was the first stage of a development that continued in subsequent centuries. This urbanization is accompanied by a significant change in material culture, characterized by the termination of Canaanite traditions in pottery production, metallurgy, and so forth, and the emergence of new traditions that continued to develop throughout the Iron Age II.

4. The lack of 10th-century finds in Jerusalem is taken by some as an argument for diminishing the historicity of biblical accounts regarding the United Monarchy of David and Solomon (Ussishkin 1997; Finkelstein 1999: 40). Yet the archaeology of Jerusalem raises considerable problems for interpreters. The dearth of finds from the 800 years between the end of the Middle Bronze Age until the 8th century B.C.E. in the City of David already raised questions and elicited a variety of interpretations. The explanations mainly relied on strong erosion and later construction activities that may have destroyed the earlier remains (see, for example, Naʾaman 1996; Knauf 2000). The archaeology of Jerusalem during these periods is, however, a case of perceiving the glass as half-full or half-empty: some focus only on the empty half, others only on the full half, and a more balanced view is needed.

Approximately half of the supposed 10th-century city lies beneath the present-day Temple Mount, which remains unknown archaeologically. The areas to the south of the Temple Mount were razed down to bedrock in many places. The "stepped stone structure" in Area G in the City of David, however, is a unique phenomenon in the archaeology of Iron Age Israel. It is an exceptionally large retaining wall of a presumably very massive building that has not been preserved. Based on pottery found below its foundations (including "collared rim" pithoi fragments and cooking pots in the Late Bronze Age tradition), and on the dwellings dated to the 9th–8th centuries B.C.E. built above this structure, the building was probably constructed sometime between the 13th and 10th centuries B.C.E. (Steiner 1994; 1998; 2001; Cahill 1998). It is highly plausible to identify this structure as the "Citadel of Zion" (מצודת ציון), which according to the biblical tradition David conquered and turned into his own citadel (2 Sam 5:7). Other areas of Shiloh's excavations of the City of David yielded pottery deposits and floor surfaces, albeit poorly preserved, from the 10th–9th centuries (De Groot and Ariel 2000: 93–94). It should be admitted that the paucity of 10th- and 9th-century finds in Jerusalem precludes describing this city as a large urban center (Tarler and Cahill 1992). Nevertheless, it cannot be claimed that the city did not exist or did not contain monumental structures (Cahill 1998). Jerusalem in the 10th century was an immature city, just as the entire United Monarchy appears to have been a state in an early stage of formation.

5. Yadin's renowned thesis concerning the finds at Gezer, Hazor, and Megiddo in relation to 1 Kgs 9:15 (Yadin 1972: 147–74) is still accepted by some and criticized by others (e.g., Wightman 1990). Most recently, Ben-Tor strongly supported this thesis in light of his excavations at Hazor (Ben-Tor 2000). This is acceptable, provided that the traditional chronology for the Iron Age II prevails (see above). The situation at Megiddo is complicated due to the few stratigraphic phases at this site, yet I tend to agree with the view that Stratum IVB–VA with its monumental palaces was founded during the Solomonic era. The attribution of the six-chamber gate to this stratum is not improbable.[5]

6. The reference to Shishak's 925 B.C.E. campaign in 1 Kgs 14:25–28 simply cannot be an invention of the 7th century B.C.E. or later; the writer had to have earlier records. Moreover, in the history of the various Egyptian military campaigns to Canaan during the Late Bronze Age, none deviated from the main routes along the coastal plain and northern valleys of Canaan. Shishak's army, however, crossed the hill country north of Jerusalem (Beth-horon and Gibeon are mentioned [Kitchen 1973: 293–300]). Therefore, there must have been a political power in the central hill country that was significant enough in the eyes of the Egyptians to justify taking such an unusual route. What else other than the Solomonic state could have been the target? Shishak's invasion seems to have been an attempt to intervene in the situation created as a consequence of Solomon's death.

---

5. Herzog, Ussishkin, Wightman, and others attribute this gate to Stratum IVA, which they date to the time of Ahab. Finkelstein also attributes this gate to Stratum IVA, but dates this city to post-Ahab times, since in his view Stratum IVB–VA should be dated to the time of Ahab. In my opinion, the gate can be attributed to Stratum IVB–VA, and thus perhaps to the Solomonic era. The following arguments are relevant. There are three gates associated with the offset-inset city wall 325, which is a rather modest wall. This situation is unparalleled at any other site in Israel. The wall abuts the upper part of the six-chamber gate as preserved. The claim that the gate had only one floor at a high level leaves inadequately explained the existence of five ashlar courses, with wooden beams between some of them, buried below this floor. Compare the situation regarding the Late Bronze Age gate of Stratum VII, which had similar ashlar courses and a floor that abutted the bottom of the lowest of these courses. A similar situation probably existed in Stratum IVB–VA, as suggested by Loud in his field diaries (Shiloh 1980) and accepted by Yadin and Shiloh. In this case, the six-chamber gate had two distinct architectural phases: the lower can be attributed to Stratum IVB–VA and the upper to Stratum IVA. The supposed lack of a city wall in Stratum IVB–VA does not necessarily imply that it had no gate, since the city was certainly defended by the outer belt of houses. Similarly, the Late Bronze Age gate at Megiddo had no associated city wall. It should be noted that according to Finkelstein's view, Megiddo during the time of Ahab (Stratum IVB–VA) had no city wall. This is highly improbable in light of the fortifications of nearby Jezreel and other Israelite cities of the 9th century B.C.E. In addition, the reference by Shalmaneser III to 2000 chariots in Ahab's army calls for dating the stables at Megiddo to the time of Ahab, and not later, as Finkelstein claims.

7. The approximately 70 sites in the Negev—some with Hebrew names, such as *ḥgr abrm* (Ḥagar Abraham) and *ḥgr ard rbt* (Ḥagar Arad Rabat)—mentioned in Shishak's list must be associated with the short-lived wave of settlement in the Negev Highlands and in the Beersheba/Arad region. These include some 50 well-planned, fortified buildings (so-called "fortresses"), the material culture of which indicates a symbiosis between Judeans and local desert dwellers (Cohen 1980; Meshel 1994; for a different view, see Finkelstein 1984). In the debate concerning the dating and interpretation of this phenomenon, I concur with Cohen and Meshel in dating these sites to the 10th century B.C.E. and associating them with the expansion of the Israelite monarchy during that period. Shishak's campaign probably aimed at putting an end to the Israelite penetration into this region.

8. The finds at Ḥorbat Rosh Zayit and its plausible identification with biblical Cabul, as suggested by Gal and Alexandre (2000), accord with the biblical story relating to the land of Cabul against the background of Phoenician-Israelite relations during the Solomonic (and probably also the post-Solomonic) era.

9. The decline of the large Philistine city of Ekron (Tel Miqne) during the 10th century (the end of Stratum IV, dated by the excavators to the first quarter of the 10th century B.C.E. [Gitin 1998: 167]), may have been a result of Israelite western expansion in the Sorek Valley during the time of the United Monarchy, as is evident at Tel Batash and Beth-shemesh. The increase in the size of Ashdod during this period may have resulted from a population movement from Ekron to Ashdod, as a consequence of Israelite pressure in the western Shephelah.

10. The absorption of Canaanite cities and villages into the Israelite sphere of influence during the 10th century can be seen at sites such as Jokneam, Megiddo, and Tel Reḥov. These cities retained their Canaanite character until the late 11th or early 10th century B.C.E. Thereafter their material culture became similar to that of other Israelite sites of the period (for the villages, see Faust 2000; for Tel Reḥov, see Mazar 1999).

11. The description of Solomon's temple is reminiscent of other second-millennium temples in the Levant, as well as the 9th–8th century temples at Tell Tainat and ʿAin Dara in northern Syria (Monson 2000), but not later structures. This description, therefore, could not have been invented in the 7th century or later.

12. The reference to the House of David on the Aramean stela from Tel Dan (and perhaps also on Mesha's stela) as the name of the Judean kingdom in the 9th century indicates that, approximately a century and a half after his reign, David was recognized throughout the region as the founder of the dynasty that ruled Judah. The role of David in Israelite ideology and historiography, therefore, cannot be a late invention.

Conclusion

It may be claimed that the biblical literary narrative distorts the true nature of the United Monarchy, but its existence cannot be denied. In evaluating this state, one should bear in mind that historical development is not linear, and history cannot be written only on the basis of socioeconomic or environmental-ecological determinism. The role of the individual personality in history should be taken into account when dealing with figures such as David and Solomon. Leaders with exceptional charisma could have created short-lived states with significant territorial expansion and military-political power. Such achievements might be beyond the capability of archaeological research to grasp. Nevertheless, if we hold to traditional chronology, archaeology can reveal much about the United Monarchy, which appears to have constituted the beginning of a new era that reached its zenith in the 9th and 8th centuries. It can be accepted that much of the biblical narrative concerning David and Solomon is fictitious. Even the descriptions of military campaigns and territorial expansion seem to be exaggerated accounts written by later authors (such as the conquests in Transjordan and Syria). Nonetheless, when Shishak invaded the Jerusalem area a few years after Solomon's death, he was probably opposing a significant state. The "deconstruction" of the United Monarchy, which has become the fashion of the day in some scholarly circles, is based in my view on unacceptable interpretations of the archaeological data. Such an approach suggests the rapid emergence in the 9th century of fully mature royal architecture and a new material culture within a short time-span of less than 50 years (Finkelstein 1996; 1998a; 1999). As explained above, in my view, this thesis is based on a debatable chronology and controversial interpretation of much archaeological data. A gradual development of Israelite statehood from the 10th to the 9th century is plausible in light of the available evidence.

To sum up, I prefer to evaluate the biblical text from a rather positivistic point of view, maintaining that it preserves data taken from early written documents and oral traditions based on a long-living common memory. These early traditions were dressed in literary, and sometimes legendary and epic, clothing and were inserted into the later Israelite historiographic narrative, with its thick theological and ideological mantle. Yet many of these traditions contain kernels of historical reality, and some of these can be examined archaeologically. By peeling off the literary, theological, and ideological layers of the texts, and by using the archaeological data intelligently and critically, the texts may be evaluated as raw material for the extraction of historical data. The results may prevent "throwing out the baby with the bathwater."

References

Ben-Tor, A.
  1998   The Fall of Canaanite Hazor: The "Who" and "When" Questions. Pp. 456–67 in *Mediterranean People in Transition: Thirteenth to Early Tenth Centuries BCE*, ed. S. Gitin, A. Mazar, and E. Stern. Jerusalem: Israel Exploration Society.
  2000   Hazor and the Chronology of Northern Israel: A Reply to Israel Finkelstein. *Bulletin of the American Schools of Oriental Research* 317: 9–16.
Ben-Tor, A., and Ben-Ami, D.
  1998   Hazor and the Archaeology of the Tenth Century B.C.E. *Israel Exploration Journal* 48: 1–37.
Bruins, H.; van der Plicht, J.; and Mazar, A.
  2003   ¹⁴C Dates from Tel Rehov: Iron Age Chronology, Pharaohs, and Hebrew Kings. *Science* 300/5617: 315–18.
Cahill, J. M.
  1998   It Is There: The Archaeological Evidence Proves It. *Biblical Archaeology Review* 24/4: 34–41.
Cohen, R.
  1980   The Iron Age Fortresses in the Central Negev. *Bulletin of the American Schools of Oriental Research* 236: 61–79.

Coogan, M. D.
1987   On Cults and Cultures: Reflections on the Interpretation of Archaeological Evidence. *Palestine Exploration Quarterly* 119: 1–8.

Cross, F. M.
1973   *Canaanite Myth and Hebrew Epic: Essays in the History of the Religion of Israel.* Cambridge: Harvard University Press.
1988   Reuben, First-Born of Jacob. *Zeitschrift für die alttestamentliche Wissenschaft* 100 (Supplement): 46–65.

Davies, P. R.
1992   *In Search of "Ancient Israel."* Journal for the Study of the Old Testament Supplement Series 148. Sheffield: Sheffield Academic Press.

De Groot, A., and Ariel, D. T.
2000   Ceramic Report. Pp. 91–154 in *Excavations of the City of David 1978–1985, V: Extramural Areas*, ed. D. T. Ariel. Qedem 40. Jerusalem: The Hebrew University.

Dever, W. G.
1991   The Late Bronze–Early Iron I Horizon in Syria–Palestine: Egyptians, Canaanites, "Sea Peoples" and Proto-Israelites. Pp. 99–110 in *The Crisis Years: The 12th Century B.C.*, ed. W. A. Ward and M. S. Joukowsky. Dubuque, Ia.: Kendall/Hunt.
1995   "Will the Real Israel Please Stand Up?" Archaeology and Israelite Historiography: Part I. *Bulletin of the American Schools of Oriental Research* 297: 61–80.
1998   Archaeology, Ideology and the Quest for "Ancient" or "Biblical Israel." *Near Eastern Archaeology* 61: 39–52.
1999   Histories and Non-histories of Ancient Israel. *Bulletin of the American Schools of Oriental Research* 316: 89–105.
2001   *What Did the Biblical Writers Know, and When Did They Know It? What Archaeology and the Bible Can Tell Us about Ancient Israel.* Grand Rapids, Mich.: Eerdmans.

Faust, A.
2000   Ethnic Complexity in Northern Israel during the Iron Age II. *Palestine Exploration Quarterly* 132: 2–27.

Finkelstein, I.
1984   The Iron Age "Fortresses" of the Negev Highlands: Sedentarization of the Nomads. *Tel Aviv* 11: 82–84.
1988   *The Archaeology of the Israelite Settlement.* Jerusalem: Israel Exploration Society.
1996   The Archaeology of the United Monarchy: An Alternative View. *Levant* 28: 177–87.
1998a   Bible Archaeology or Archaeology of Palestine in the Iron Age? A Rejoinder. *Levant* 30: 167–73.
1998b   Notes on the Stratigraphy and Chronology of Iron Age Taʿanach. *Tel Aviv* 25: 208–18.
1999   State Formation in Israel and Judah. *Near Eastern Archaeology* 62: 35–52.

Finkelstein, I.; Bunimovitz, S.; and Lederman, Z.
1993   *Shiloh. The Archaeology of a Biblical Site.* Tel Aviv: The Institute of Archaeology, Tel Aviv University.

Finkelstein, I., and Naʾaman, N. (eds.)
1994   *From Nomadism to Monarchy.* Jerusalem: Yad Izhak Ben Zvi and Israel Exploration Society.

Fritz, V., and Davies, P. R. (eds.)
1997   *The Origins of the Ancient Israelite States.* Journal for the Study of the Old Testament Supplement Series 245. Sheffield: Sheffield Academic Press.

Gal, Z., and Alexandre, Y.
2000   *Ḥorbat Rosh Zayit.* Israel Antiquities Authority Reports 8. Jerusalem: Israel Antiquities Authority.

Gilboa, A., and Sharon, I.
2001   Early Iron Age Radiometric Dates from Tel Dor: Preliminary Implications for Phoenicia and Beyond. *Radiocarbon* 43: 1343–51.

Gitin, S.
   1998   Philistia in Transition: The Tenth Century B.C.E. and Beyond. Pp. 162–83 in *Mediterranean Peoples in Transition: Thirteenth to Early Tenth Centuries BCE*, ed. S. Gitin, A. Mazar, and E. Stern. Jerusalem: Israel Exploration Society.

Gitin, S.; Mazar, A.; and Stern, E. (eds.)
   1998   *Mediterranean Peoples in Transition: Thirteenth to Early Tenth Centuries BCE*. Jerusalem: Israel Exploration Society.

Graham, J.
   1981   Chapters 3–4. Pp. 23–38 in *The Third Campaign at Tell el-Fûl: The Excavations of 1964*, ed. N. Lapp. Annual of the American Schools of Oriental Research 45. Cambridge: American Schools of Oriental Research.

Handy, L. K. (ed.)
   1997   *The Age of Solomon*. Leiden: Brill.

Hasel, M.
   1998   Domination and Resistance: Egyptian Military Activity in the *Southern Levant, 1300–1185 BC*. Leiden: Brill.

Herr, L.
   1999   Tell al-ʾUmayri and the Reubenite Hypothesis. *Eretz-Israel* 26 (Frank Moore Cross Volume): 64*–78*.

Herzog, Z.
   2001   Archaeology, Bible, and Israeli Society. Pp. 52–65 in *Bible, Archaeology and History*, ed. I. Levine and A. Mazar. Jerusalem: Yad Izhak Ben Zvi (Hebrew).

Jamieson-Drake, D. W.
   1991   *Scribes and Schools in Monarchic Judah*. Sheffield: Sheffield Academic Press.

Kitchen, K. A.
   1973   *The Third Intermediate Period in Egypt*. Warminster: Aris & Philips.
   1992   The Egyptian Evidence on Ancient Jordan. Pp. 21–34 in *Early Edom and Moab: The Beginning of the Iron Age in Southern Jordan*, ed. P. Bienkowski. Sheffield Archaeological Monographs 7. Sheffield: Collis.

Knauf, A. E.
   1998   Jerusalem in the Late Bronze and Early Iron Ages: A Proposal. *Tel Aviv* 27: 75–90.

Lemche, N. P.
   1998   *The Israelites in History and Tradition*. Louisville: Westminster John Knox.

Malamat, A.
   1983   The Proto-History of Israel: A Study in Method. Pp. 303–13 in *The Word of the Lord Shall Go Forth: Essays in Honor of David Noel Freedman in Celebration of His Sixtieth Birthday*, ed. C. L. Meyers and M. O'Connor. Winona Lake, Ind.: Eisenbrauns.

Mazar, A.
   1981   Giloh: An Early Israelite Site in the Vicinity of Jerusalem. *Israel Exploration Journal* 31: 1–36.
   1985   The Israelite Settlement in Canaan in the Light of Archaeological Excavations. Pp. 61–71 in *Biblical Archaeology Today: Proceedings of the International Congress on Biblical Archaeology (Jerusalem, April 1984)*, ed. J. Amitai. Jerusalem: Israel Exploration Society.
   1990a   Iron Age I and II Towers at Giloh and the Israelite Settlement. *Israel Exploration Journal* 40: 77–101.
   1990b   *Archaeology of the Land of the Bible (ca. 10000–586 B.C.E.)*. New York: Doubleday.
   1994   The 11th century BCE in Palestine. Pp. 39–58 in *Proceedings of the International Colloquium: Cyprus in the 11th Century B.C.*, ed. V. Karageorghis. Nicosia: Leventis Foundation.
   1997   Iron Age Chronology: A Reply to I. Finkelstein. *Levant* 29: 157–67.
   1999   The 1997–1998 Excavations at Tel Reḥov: Preliminary Report. *Israel Exploration Journal* 49: 1–42.

2002   Megiddo in the 13th–11th Centuries BCE: A Review of Some Recent Studies. Pp. 264–82 in *Studies in Memory of Aaron Kempinski*, ed. E. D. Oren and S. Aḥituv. Beersheba: Ben-Gurion University of the Negev.

Meshel, Z.
1994   The "Aharoni Fortress" near Quseima and the "Israelite Fortresses" in the Negev. *Bulletin of the American Schools of Oriental Research* 294: 36–67.

Miller, M. J., and Hayes, J. H.
1986   *A History of Ancient Israel and Judah.* Philadelphia: Westminster.

Monson, J.
2000   The New ʾAin Dara Temple. *Biblical Archaeology Review* 26/3: 20–35.

Naʾaman, N.
1986   *Borders and Districts in Biblical Historiography.* Jerusalem: Simor.
1996   The Contribution of the Amarna Letters to the Debate on Jerusalem's Political Position in the Tenth Century B.C.E. *Bulletin of the American Schools of Oriental Research* 304: 17–27.
1997   The Network of Canaanite Late Bronze Kingdoms and the City of Ashdod. *Ugarit Forschungen* 29: 599–626.

Niemann, H. M.
1997   The Socio-Political Shadow Cast by the Biblical Solomon. Pp. 252–59 in *The Age of Solomon*, ed. L. K. Handy. Leiden: Brill.

Ofer, A.
2001   The Monarchic Period in the Judean Highland: A Spatial Overview. Pp. 14–37 in *Studies in the Archaeology of the Iron Age in Israel and Jordan*, ed. A. Mazar. Journal for the Study of the Old Testament Supplement Series. Sheffield: Sheffield Academic Press.

Oren, E. D. (ed.)
2000   *The Sea Peoples and Their World: A Reassessment.* Philadelphia: The University Museum.

Rast, W. E.
1978   *Taanach I: Studies in the Iron Age Pottery.* Cambridge, Mass.: American Schools of Oriental Research.

Redford, D. B.
1992   *Egypt, Canaan and Israel in Ancient Times.* Princeton: Princeton University Press.

Renz, J.
1995   *Die Althebräischen Inschriften: Band I–III.* Darmstadt: Wissenschaftliche Buchgesellschaft.

Routledge, B.
2000   Seeing through Walls: Interpreting Iron Age I Architecture at Khirbet al-Mudayna al-ʾAliya. *Bulletin of the American Schools of Oriental Research* 319: 37–70.

Shanks, H. (ed.)
1988   *Ancient Israel.* Washington, D.C.: Biblical Archaeology Society.

Shiloh, Y.
1980   Solomon's Gate at Megiddo as Recovered by Its Excavator, R. Lamon. *Levant* 12: 69–76.

Smith, M.
1990   *The Early History of God.* San Francisco: Harper & Row.

Stager, L. E.
1985   The Archaeology of the Family in Ancient Israel. *Bulletin of the American Schools of Oriental Research* 260: 1–35.
1998   Forging an Identity: The Emergence of Ancient Israel. Pp. 123–75 in *The Oxford History of the Biblical World*, ed. M. Coogan. New York: Oxford University Press.

Steiner, M.
1994   Re-dating the Terraces of Jerusalem. *Israel Exploration Journal* 44: 13–20.
1998   It's Not There: Archaeology Proves Negative. *Biblical Archaeology Review* 24/4: 26–33.
2001   Jerusalem in the 10th and 7th centuries B.C.: From Administrative Town to Commercial City. Pp. 280–88 in *Studies in the Archaeology of the Iron Age in Israel and Jordan*, ed.

A. Mazar. Journal for the Study of the Old Testament Supplement Series. Sheffield: Sheffield Academic Press.

Tarler, D., and Cahill, J. M.
  1992   David, City of. Pp. 52–67 in vol. 2 of *The Anchor Bible Dictionary*, ed. D. N. Freedman. New York: Doubleday.
Thompson, T. L.
  1992   *Early History of the Israelite People from the Written and Archaeological Sources.* Studies in the History of the Ancient Near East 4. Leiden: Brill.
  1999   *The Mythic Past: Biblical Archaeology and the Myth of Israel.* London: Jonathan Cape.
Ussishkin, D.
  1997   Jerusalem in the Period of David and Solomon: The Archaeological Evidence. Pp. 57–58 in *New Studies on Jerusalem: Proceedings of the Third Conference*, ed. A. Faust and E. Baruch. Ramat Gan: Bar Ilan University.
Wightman, G. J.
  1990   The Myth of Solomon. *Bulletin of the American Schools of Oriental Research* 277/278: 5–22.
Yadin, Y.
  1972   *Hazor: The Head of All Those Kingdoms.* London: The British Academy.
Zakovitch, Y.
  2001   Words, Stones, Memory and Identity. Pp. 66–74 on *The Controversy over the Historicity of the Bible*, ed. L. I. Levine and A. Mazar. Jerusalem: Yad Izhak Ben Zvi and Dinur Center (Hebrew).
Zertal, A.
  1986–87   An Iron Age Cultic Site on Mount Ebal: Excavation Seasons 1982–87. *Tel Aviv* 13–14: 105–65.
Zevit, Z.
  1985   The Problem of ʿAi. *Biblical Archaeology Review* 11: 58–69.

Assyria's Expansion in the 8th and 7th Centuries and Its Long-Term Repercussions in the West

Simo Parpola

Institute for Asian and African Studies
University of Helsinki

Introduction

After a period of internal weakness and stagnation that lasted from the end of the 9th century until the middle of the 8th century B.C.E., Assyria entered a period of dynamic expansion that was to have far-reaching consequences. By the end of the 8th century, most of the Levant, eastern Anatolia, and large parts of Iran were permanently annexed to Assyria. In the 7th century, Assyria's control of the conquered territories was consolidated, and the process of expansion continued in all directions, so that by the middle of the century the Empire had reached the Aegean in the west and had absorbed Egypt in the south and the Elamite Empire in the east.[1]

This process of expansion is well documented by Assyrian sources, and its mechanisms and dynamics are on the whole well understood (Liverani 1988; 1992; Tadmor 1999; Parker 2001). The impact of Assyrian rule on the annexed territories has been investigated in several studies (e.g., Oded 1974; Eph'al 1979; Frankenstein 1979; Otzen 1979; Elat 1982; 1991; Spieckermann 1982; Gitin 1995; 1997; 1998; Lanfranchi 2000), many of which have also drawn attention to certain long-term developments set in motion by the Assyrian expansion. However, Assyria's role in affecting long-term cultural development in the territories subject to its expansion, particularly in the field of *intellectual life*, has not received the attention it deserves. In what follows I will present my personal view of the matter, focusing on the long-term consequences of the Assyrian expansion in western Anatolia and Judah. In order to address the issues at hand properly, we must first briefly consider the nature and driving forces of Assyrian imperialism, as well as the strategies and methods that it applied to achieve its goals.

The Nature of Neo-Assyrian Imperial Expansion

It is essential to keep in mind first of all that Assyria's 8th–7th-century expansion, despite its spectacular strength, was not a new phenomenon as such but rather the culmi-

---

1. Maps of Assyria usually place the western border of the Assyrian Empire at the western extremity of Cilicia (about 34° E), with the Halys River as its northern border. This is incorrect, since from the reign of Gyges (ca. 667–665) on, Lydia was an ally of Assyria, obliged to pay yearly visits to the imperial court (Tadmor and Cogan 1977; Parpola and Watanabe 1988: xviii–xix). A similar alliance between Assyria and Phrygia had already existed since the reign of Sargon II (ca. 710). In the east, Assyria extended, after the sack of Susa, as far as Parsumaš/Fars, the ruler of which, Kuraš, a former vassal of Elam, even sent his son to Nineveh as a hostage (Postgate 1989: 9; Rollinger 1999).

nation of a long process that had its roots already in the beginning of the second millennium B.C.E. and even earlier. When Assyria emerged as an independent city-state after the collapse of the Ur III Empire to which it had belonged as a province, the primary concern of its rulers appears to have been the control of the trade routes vital to the overland trade of the city (Larsen 1976; 1979). This modest strategic goal, however, soon gave way to an open claim for world dominion. The royal ideology backing this claim, which transformed the Assyrian king from a local ruler to the earthly representative of the supreme god, had been taken over directly from earlier empires (Galter 1998), as were the methods by which the imperial ambitions were furthered. Treaties, diplomacy, ruthless deployment of military force, political intimidation, indoctrination, and propaganda—essential tools of Neo-Assyrian imperialism—are all well attested already in third-millennium Mesopotamia and can therefore by no means be regarded as Assyrian innovations.

There is, however, an essential difference between the Neo-Assyrian Empire and its predecessors that accounts for the 8th–7th-century expansion—namely, the strategy of systematic economic, cultural, and ethnic integration introduced by Tiglath-pileser III in 745 B.C.E. Until then, the Empire had only a relatively limited core area under direct control of the central government, with vassal states loosely tied to the center through treaties, loyalty oaths, and royal marriages. This political structure was by its nature unstable and required constant intervention on the part of the central government; over time, it became not only impossible to expand the empire beyond certain limits, but also very difficult to maintain the areas already conquered, as demonstrated by the countless rebellions of the 9th century and the period of stagnation and shrinking in the early 8th century.[2]

The strategy introduced by Tiglath-pileser III aimed at expanding the core area by systematically reducing semi-independent vassal countries to Assyrian provinces directly controlled by the central government (Tadmor 1994: 9; cf. Garelli 1991). The reducing of a country to a province was carried out according to a standardized procedure[3] involving the utter destruction of the vassal's urban centers; massive deportations (Oded 1979); rebuilding the capital in Assyrian style; the installation of an Assyrian governor; the construction of Assyrian garrisons and forts (Parker 1997); the imposition of a uniform taxation and conscription system (Postgate 1974), imperial standards and measures (cf. Eph'al and Naveh 1993), cults (Spieckermann 1982: 322–44),[4] and a single *lingua franca*, Aramaic

---

2. On this period, see Kuhrt 1995: 482–93 and RIMA 2–3 for the sources.

3. For a typical passage in Tiglath-pileser's inscriptions reflecting the underlying procedure, see Ann 9:1–4 (Tadmor 1994: 42): "I rebuilt those cities. On top of a ruin heap which is called Humut, I established a city. I built (and) completed it from its foundation to its parapet. A palace for my royal residence I built there. I named it Kar-Aššur. I set up the weapon [i.e., a garrison] of Aššur, my lord, therein. I settled therein people of (foreign) lands, conquered by me. I imposed upon them tribute (and) I considered them as inhabitants of Assyria"; see similarly Anns 5:3–4; 10:1–4; 11:5–6; 16:4–8; 25:6–12; Summs 1:6–7; 7:36–37, and passim (omitting individual elements of the procedure). The stereotypical formulation and extraordinary frequency of such passages in Tiglath-pileser's inscriptions provides a striking contrast to the inscriptions of earlier Assyrian kings and can only be explained (despite Garelli 1991) by assuming a deliberate change in Assyria's strategy of territorial expansion.

4. Cogan (1974: 85; followed, e.g., by Frame 1997: 56) believes that "Assyria imposed no religious obligations upon its vassals." This is contradicted by Esarhaddon's Succession Treaty (VTE), in which the vassals are sworn to accept Aššur as their god and the future king as their (only) lord (see n. 13 below and the analysis of the passage in Parpola 2000b: 167). Note also Tadmor 1994: 177, 189 (Tigl. Summs 8:16–17 //

(Ephʿal 1979: 284; Garelli 1982; Tadmor 1982; Postgate 1989; Parpola 2000a: 11–12). The inhabitants of the new province became Assyrian citizens; its economy was completely reorganized in line with Assyrian commercial interests (Elat 1978; 1991; Postgate 1979; Gitin 1997; Lanfranchi 2000: 12); and the seat of the governor, a copy of the imperial court in miniature,[5] became a channel through which Assyrian culture was systematically spread to the country.

Elites as a Channel of Assyrian Cultural Influence

The drastic measures involved in the creation of new provinces were legitimized through vassal treaties that called for the total destruction of the vassal country in the event that it violated the provisions of the treaty (Parpola 1987: 161; Parpola and Watanabe 1988). From the reign of Tiglath-pileser III on, the punishments prescribed in the treaties were systematically implemented by the Assyrians—but only if the treaties had actually been broken. If the treaty was kept, the vassal would retain its formal independence. Even in this case, however, it was subject to strong and ever-increasing Assyrian influence. With the passage of time, the heavy obligations of the treaty usually resulted in an attempt to revolt and, hence, in the total annexation of the country.

Obviously, treaties were of pivotal importance to Assyria's strategy of territorial expansion, and despite the heavy obligations and terrible sanctions that came with each treaty, Assyria had no difficulty in finding new treaty partners. This was because foreign elites often needed Assyrian military or political backing to eliminate political opponents or external threats (Parpola and Watanabe 1988: xvi). Accordingly, elites were the primary target group on which the Assyrians focused their attention in their efforts to assimilate a country. Pro-Assyrian foreign elites were the best possible medium to advance Assyrian interests in a country waiting to be annexed or already annexed. For this reason, foreign ambassadors and visitors to the Assyrian capital were lavishly entertained and honored at the royal court (Postgate 1994), while exiled princes and aristocratic youths sojourning or held at the court received a thorough education in Assyrian literature, science, and ways

---

9 rev. 14–15), "A golden (statue) bearing the image of the great gods my lords and my royal image I fashioned. In the palace of Gaza I set it up and counted it among the gods of their land," and cf. p. 207 (the image of Ištar placed in Ḫadattu/Arslan Tash along with the king's own image). Similar references to royal images set up in strategic places (temples, palaces, streets, and squares of cities, even on mountaintops) throughout the Empire, not only in the provinces but in the vassal states as well, can be found throughout Assyrian royal inscriptions and royal correspondence (Cole and Machinist 1998: xiii–xv). This is clear evidence of an emperor cult imposed on vassals and citizens alike in the fashion of the late Roman and Byzantine Empires (see further Porter 1995; Winter 1997).

5. Cf. Postgate 1992: 258–59; and on the governmental palaces of Til-Barsip and Dur-Katlimmu (the best-known Assyrian provincial capitals), see Thureau-Dangin and Dunand 1936; Bunnens 1997; Radner 1998: 47–51. Note also Xenophon, *Cyropaedia* 8.6.10–14: "And *he gave orders to all satraps he sent out to imitate him in everything* that they saw him do . . . to require as many as received lands and palaces to attend at the satrap's court . . . to have the boys that were born to them educated at the local court, just as was done at the royal court. . . . 'And with you also, just as with me, let the most deserving be set in the most honourable seats. . . . Have parks, too, and keep wild animals in them. . . .' And as Cyrus then effected his organization, even so *unto this day . . . all the courts of the governors* are attended with service in the same way" (emphasis mine). It is clear, of course, that the system described here did not originate with Cyrus but ultimately went back (via the Median and Neo-Babylonian Empires) to the Neo-Assyrian Empire.

of life in general (Parpola 1972: 33–34; 1998: 328; Parpola and Watanabe 1988: xx). The over-all goal was to integrate all foreign elites as much as possible within the imperial elite and then to work on the masses through these elites.[6]

Paradoxically, Assyria's success in bringing ever new nations under its sway rested on two seemingly opposite pillars: on the one hand, *the chilling fear* that its ruthless military machine and drive to expand inspired in its opponents, and on the other hand, *the numerous benefits* it offered to those who chose to cooperate. This observation accords well with Xenophon's summary of the reasons behind the success of Achaemenid Cyrus the Great:

> He ruled over these nations, even though they did not speak the same language as he, nor one nation the same as another; for all that, he was able to cover so vast a region with the fear which he inspired, that he struck all men with terror and no one tried to withstand him; and he was able to awaken in all so lively a desire to please him, that they always wished to be guided by his will. (*Cyropaedia* 1.1.5)

Against this background we will now consider the long-term consequences of Assyria's ex-pansion in the light of the two concrete examples to which we have already alluded, Lydia and Judah.

Assyria and Lydia

The decision of Gyges ca. 665 B.C.E. to seek Assurbanipal's protection against the Cim-merian threat against Lydia provided Assyria with an excellent channel to spread its influ-ence to western Anatolia. The alliance with Assyria, which remained in effect for at least two generations, opened up a direct route of communication between Sardis and Nineveh (Burkert 1992: 14, 161)[7] that without doubt was used not only for the payment of the yearly tribute but also for commercial, military, and cultural purposes. The pro-Assyrian stance of the Lydian royal house, reflected by its genealogy, which traced its origins from Ninus and Belus (Herodotus 1.7), soon materialized in the imitation of the imperial culture and life-style. The cult of Kubaba of Carchemish was introduced to Lydia in this period (Popko 1995: 181–88; Posani 1999), as were such luxury items such as the parasol and the *kline*, among others (West 1997: 32–33).[8]

What is more important in this context, however, is that the "Assyrianization" of Lydia also directly affected the Ionian city-states of the Aegean coast, which were within Lydia's immediate sphere of influence and in lively contact with it.[9] Many scholars, in particular

---

6. Cf. n. 5 above.

7. There cannot be any doubt that the Royal Road leading from Sardis to Susa, which later served as the main artery of the Achaemenid Empire to the west (Eph'al 1983: 102–4; Dandamayev and Lukonin 1989: 107), was originally an Assyrian construction. It ran through the Assyrian heartland, following the course of the Neo-Assyrian Royal Road (Kessler 1997: 131; cf. the map in Scarre et al. 1988: 158), and its description in Herodotus 5.52–53 (cf. 8.98) accords in all details with what is known of the Neo-Assyrian royal road system.

8. On the possibility that the Lydian coinage introduced during the reign of Alyattes (ca. 600) was inspired by earlier Assyrian models, see Radner 1999: 127.

9. Note that the Lydian capital, Sardis, was only about 80 km from Smyrna and Samos, about 90 km from Ephesus, Colophon, Clazomenae, and Magnesia, and about 120 km from Miletus, Priene, and Pho-caea. According to Herodotus (1.15–17), "as soon as Gyges came to throne, he too, like others, led an army

West (1995; 1997) and Rollinger (1996), have convincingly argued in recent years that the Homeric poems were reedited in the mid–7th century B.C.E. under the influence of Akkadian literature, specifically Neo-Assyrian royal poetry and the Gilgamesh epic. The influences are such that a direct exposure to Akkadian epic poetry must be assumed (West 1997: 401; Burkert 1999: 26–31). Moreover, Abusch (2001) shows that certain structural features in the Iliad and the Odyssey imply familiarity not only with the form but also with the *esoteric content* of the late version of the Gilgamesh epic. It thus seems that the alliance with Lydia opened the gates to a strong Assyrian cultural influence on Ionia as well. In this light, it is hardly a coincidence that all the great names in late-7th-/early-6th-century Ionian philosophy come from cities in the immediate vicinity of Lydia.[10] From Lydia and Ionia, cultural influences were further transferred to mainland Greece (Burkert 1992; West 1997). One may note that Gyges dedicated numerous votive objects to Delphi (Herodotus 1.13–14) and that the late-7th-century Spartan lyric poet Alcman originally was a Lydian freed slave (Carey 1996).

However, the Greeks also received influences directly from the Assyrians. The consolidation of Assyrian control over the entire Near East created a vast market that turned out to be especially profitable for the Greeks. As Lanfranchi has shown (2000: 31), the Assyrians followed a policy that allowed foreign settlement in recently annexed Assyrian territory, but only after Assyrian control thereof had been definitively consolidated. This condition was met in the eastern Mediterranean after Sennacherib had defeated the Ionians in a naval battle and rebuilt Tarsus in Assyrian fashion in 696 B.C.E. After this date, the number of Greek commercial settlements in northern Syria and Cilicia dramatically increased, as did the number of Greek imports in the Levant and vice versa. This development brought enormous profits to the Greeks, and as a result, the initial hostility of the Greeks toward the Assyrians was soon replaced by a totally favorable attitude receptive to cultural influences from the east (Lanfranchi 2000: 32–33). Among the many cultural borrowings from Assyria in this period, one may note the Athenian governmental system of nine archons and the system of year eponyms introduced in 683 B.C.E. (Parpola 1995: 397).

Assyria and Judah

In the Levant, Judah remained a semi-independent vassal kingdom not incorporated into the Assyrian provincial system. Assyrian influence increased steadily, however,

---

into the lands of Miletus and Smyrna; and he took the city of Colophon. . . . Ardys, the son of Gyges . . . took Priene and invaded the country of Miletus. . . . Alyattes [ca. 610] took Smyrna, invaded the lands of Clazomenae . . . and laid siege to Miletus." Despite these attacks, the Lydian court continued to exert a powerful attraction for contemporary and later Ionian elites, and there were many *lydizontes* among the latter (Lanfranchi 1996: 108).

10. Thales (ca. 625–550) and his disciples Anaximander (ca. 610–548) and Anaximenes were citizens of Miletus. Pythagoras (ca. 570–494), who migrated to Italy ca. 530 BCE, was born in Samos. Xenophanes (ca. 570–480), the alleged teacher of Parmenides, was from Colophon, Heraclitus (ca. 540–490) from Ephesus, and Anaxagoras (ca. 500–428) from Clazomenae. On the indebtness of Pythagoras and other pre-Socratic philosophers to ideas from Assyria, see Halpern, in this volume; see also Parpola 1993; Kingsley 1995; 1999. Specifically, the theological notions of Xenophanes about God as "one and many," hailed by classicists as totally novel in the ancient world (Versnel 2000), can be easily traced back to the Assyrian concept of God, on which see Parpola 1997: xxi–xxvi; 2000b: 165–73.

especially during the reign of Manasseh (692–638),[11] as amply attested both in the biblical and in the archaeological record. Assyrian religious and ideological motifs appear in this period on locally manufactured seals and cult objects (Ahlström 1984; Keel and Uehlinger 1993: 327–429), and archaeological evidence indicates that the economy of Judah at least indirectly profited from the new international order created by the Assyrian overlord (Broshi 1974; Elat 1982: 246–47). Like other loyal vassals, Manasseh and his successors paid yearly tribute, participated in imperial campaigns and building projects, and, to judge from 2 Kgs 21:16, even executed anti-Assyrian elements among their own people (Weippert 1989).

However, there is a significant difference vis-à-vis Lydia in Judah's relationship with Assyria. Whereas Gyges had apparently sought Assyria's protection on his own volition, for Judah the vassalage of Assyria was from the beginning not an option but only a means to avoid total annihilation. The fate of the Northern Kingdom and the siege of Jerusalem by Sennacherib had taught Manasseh a lesson, and his primary motive in "pulling the yoke of Aššur" undoubtedly was plain *fear*, not greed.

Several scholars in recent years have pointed out remarkable parallels between Deuteronomy 13 and Neo-Assyrian treaties, especially the succession treaty of Esarhaddon (VTE; Levinson 1995; Otto 1999: 3–90; Pakkala 1999: 20–50; see also Steymans 1995a; 1995b). Significantly, the parallelism is limited to two issues: the relationship between the treaty partners (God/King vs. people) and the merciless fate of those who violate the terms of the treaty. In both cases, the subordinate party (= the people of Israel/Judah) is told to love its overlord wholeheartedly, *to the exclusion of everything else* (Deut 13:4; VTE §24),[12] the only difference being that in one case the overlord is the God of Israel, while in the other it is *the king of Assyria.*

There cannot be any doubt that, not only the king of Judah, but the ruling class of Judah as a whole was familiar with the central provisions of the treaties with Assyria, for vassal rulers were explicitly told to propagate them to their people.[13] Indeed, it can be assumed that the treaties had, figuratively speaking, "entered the intestines of their sons and daughters like bread and wine," as prescribed in VTE §72. Hence, the fact that this

---

11. This dating of the reign of Manasseh follows *The New Standard Jewish Encyclopedia* (rev. ed., 1992). Alternative dates are 693–639 (Reade 1981); 697–643 (Weippert 1989); and 698–643 (Elat 1982).

12. The Hebrew phrase *bĕkol-lēb,* "wholeheartedly," in Deut 13:4 renders the Akkadian idiom *ina gummurti libbi,* denoting the vassal's undivided loyalty toward his overlord (Stol 1993). The phrase *bĕkol-napšĕkem,* "with all your soul," in Deut 13:4 similarly corresponds to the phrase *kî napšātikunu,* "like your souls/lives" in VTE §24 (see further Otto 1999: 5, 53).

13. VTE §25: "This treaty which Esarhaddon, king of Assyria, has confirmed and concluded with you . . . *you shall speak to your sons and grandsons, your seed and your seed's seed which shall be born in the future, and give them orders as follows* [emphasis mine]: 'Guard this treaty. Do not sin against your treaty and annihilate yourselves, do not turn your land over to destruction and your people to deportation.'"

VTE §§33–34: "You and your sons to be born in the future will be bound by this oath concerning Assurbanipal . . . from this day on until what(ever) comes after this treaty. While you stand on the place of this oath, *you shall not swear this oath with your lips only but shall swear it wholeheartedly; you shall teach it to your sons to be born after this treaty* [emphasis mine]. . . . To the future and forever Aššur will be your god, and Assurbanipal, the great crown prince designate, will be your lord. May your sons and your grandsons fear him."

For epistolary evidence indicating that the entire population of the Empire (not just the elites) was familiar with the provisions of this treaty, see Parpola 1972: 30–31.

very language was chosen to formulate the laws in Deuteronomy 13, one of the core texts of Deuteronomic monolatry, has far-reaching implications. To spell it out: *in the mind of the writer of Deuteronomy 13, the God of Israel has taken the place previously occupied in the collective mind of the nation by the feared, almighty king of Assyria.* The same is implied by the paradoxical image of the Deuteronomic God, who, according to a recent analysis by Geller, "*is above all else a person*" (2000: 280 [emphasis mine]). Strikingly, the Covenant God's characteristics listed by Geller (2000: 307–8) are also central characteristics of the Assyrian king—"the very likeness of God"—as presented in Assyrian imperial propaganda (Parpola 1999: 20–21).[14] The conclusion seems inescapable that the Deuteronomic concept of God, which according to current scholarly consensus evolved in the late 7th or early 6th century B.C.E. and is basic to all later Judaism, is heavily indebted to Assyrian religion and royal ideology.

This conclusion is supported by parallel developments elsewhere within the area of the Neo-Assyrian Empire. As recently shown by Beaulieu (1997), Anu, the god of heaven of Uruk, was in post-Assyrian times transformed into a universal god through his equation with Aššur, whose cult was transferred to Uruk in the Sargonid period. The Harranian moon-god Sîn, promoted as a universal god by the Neo-Babylonian King Nabonidus, had been syncretized with Aššur already under the Assyrian Empire, possibly in order to create an imperial god more acceptable to the Aramean-speaking masses (Mayer 1998).[15] The supreme god of the Achaemenid Empire, Ahura Mazda, was likewise syncretized with Aššur, as shown by the adoption by the Achaemenid Dynasty of the winged disk of Aššur as the emblem of Ahura Mazda (Dandamayev and Lukonin 1989: 342).

It is difficult to keep these developments separate from the contemporary transformation of the Deuteronomic concept of God, particularly considering that in Ezra 1:2, Yahweh and the supreme god of the Empire are syncretized as "YHWH, the God of heaven."[16]

We do not know what would have happened if Assyria had not expanded to the shores of the Aegean and the Sea of Galilee. But it does seem that this expansion set in motion processes that would not have been possible without crucially important stimuli from Assyria. Certainly the economic, intellectual, and psychological conditions that enabled the rise of Greek civilization and led to the crystallization of the biblical image of God *were not there* before the Assyrians arrived. They were the tools and products of Assyrian statecraft and came with the Assyrian Empire.

---

14. On the Assyrian king as the image of God, see Parpola 1993: 168; Winter 1997: 374–75. On the *homoousia* of Aššur and the Assyrian king, see Parpola 2000b: 190–92, 202–5; on the king as the "son of God," see Parpola 1997: xxxvi–xliv; cf. Liverani 1979: 301, who regards Aššur as "the hypostasis of the Assyrian kingship."

15. See, e.g., van Driel 1969: 97 viii 55. Note also the prominence of Sîn beside Aššur in the names of the Neo-Assyrian kings since the reign of Sargon II.

16. Note that in contemporary cuneiform documents, both the Iranian *baga,* "God," and Yahweh are written with the logogram DINGIR.MEŠ, "gods." This spelling goes back to the Assyrian Empire, where it refers to the supreme god as "the (totality of) gods" and is well attested as a divine name (*Ilāni*), exactly comparable to the biblical *Elohim* (Parpola 1997: xxi nn. 30–31; 2000b: 172).

References

Abusch, T.
    2001   The Epic of Gilgamesh and the Homeric Epics. Pp. 1–6 in *Mythology and Mythologies: Methodological Approaches to Intercultural Influences,* ed. R. M. Whiting. Melammu Symposia 2. Helsinki: The Neo-Assyrian Text Corpus Project.

Ahlström, G. W.
    1984   An Archaeological Picture of Iron Age Religions in Ancient Palestine. *Studia Orientalia* 55: 1–31.

Beaulieu, P.-A.
    1997   The Cult of AN.SÁR/*Aššur* in Babylonia after the Fall of the Assyrian Empire. *State Archives of Assyria Bulletin* 11: 55–73.

Broshi, M.
    1974   The Expansion of Jerusalem in the Reigns of Hezekiah and Manasseh. *Israel Exploration Journal* 24: 21–26.

Bunnens, G.
    1997   Til Barsip under Assyrian Domination: A Brief Account of the Melbourne University Excavations at Tell Ahmar. Pp. 17–28 in *Assyria 1995: Proceedings of the 10th Anniversary of the Neo-Assyrian Text Corpus Project, Helsinki, September 7–11, 1995,* ed. S. Parpola and R. M. Whiting. Helsinki: The Neo-Assyrian Text Corpus Project.

Burkert, W.
    1992   The Orientalizing Revolution: Near Eastern Influence on Greek Culture in the *Early Archaic Age,* trans. M. E. Pinder and W. Burkert. Cambridge: Harvard University Press.
    1999   *Da Omero ai Magi. La tradizione orientale nella cultura greca.* Padua: Marsilio.

Carey, C.
    1996   Alcman. Pp. 55–56 in *The Oxford Classical Dictionary,* ed. S. Hornblower and A. Spawforth. 3rd ed. Oxford: Oxford University Press.

Cogan, M.
    1974   *Imperialism and Religion: Assyria, Judah and Israel in the Eighth and Seventh Century* B.C.E. Society of Biblical Literature Monograph Series 19. Missoula, Mont.: Society of Biblical Literature.

Cole, S. W., and Machinist, P.
    1998   *Letters from Priests to the Kings Esarhaddon and Assurbanipal.* State Archives of Assyria 13. Helsinki: Helsinki University Press.

Dandamayev, M. A., and Lukonin, V. G.
    1989   *The Culture and Social Institutions of Ancient Iran.* Cambridge: Cambridge University Press.

Driel, G. van
    1969   *The Cult of Aššur.* Studia Semitica Neerlandica 13. Assen: Van Gorcum.

Elat, M.
    1978   The Economic Relations of the Neo-Assyrian Empire with Egypt. *Journal of the American Oriental Society* 98: 20–34.
    1982   The Impact of Tribute and Booty on Countries and People within the Assyrian Empire. Pp. 244–51 in *Vorträge gehalten auf der 28. Rencontre Assyriologique Internationale in Wien, 6.–10. Juli 1981,* ed. H. Hirsch and H. Hunger. Archiv für Orientforschung 19. Vienna: Berger.
    1991   Phoenician Overland Trade within the Mesopotamian Empires. Pp. 21–35 in *Ah, Assyria . . . : Studies in Assyrian History and Ancient Near Eastern Historiography Presented to Hayim Tadmor,* ed. M. Cogan and I. Eph'al. Jerusalem: Magnes.

Eph'al, I.
    1979   Assyrian Dominion in Palestine. Pp. 276–89, 364–68 in vol. 4/1 of *The World History of the Jewish People,* ed. A. Malamat. Jerusalem: Massada.

1983   On Warfare and Military Control in the Ancient Near Eastern Empires. Pp. 88–106 in *History, Historiography and Interpretation: Studies in Biblical and Cuneiform Literatures*, ed. H. Tadmor and M. Weinfeld. Jerusalem: Magnes.

Eph'al, I., and Naveh, J.
1993   The Jar of the Gate. *Bulletin of the American Schools of Oriental Research* 289: 60–65.

Frame, G.
1997   The God Aššur in Babylonia. Pp. 55–64 in *Assyria 1995: Proceedings of the 10th Anniversary of the Neo-Assyrian Text Corpus Project, Helsinki, September 7–11, 1995*, ed. S. Parpola and R. M. Whiting. Helsinki: The Neo-Assyrian Text Corpus Project.

Frankenstein, S.
1979   The Phoenicians in the Far West: A Function of Neo-Assyrian Imperialism. Pp. 263–94 in *Power and Propaganda: A Symposium on Ancient Empires*, ed. M. T. Larsen. Mesopotamia 7. Copenhagen: Akademisk Forlag.

Galter, H. D.
1998   Textanalyse assyrischer Königsinschriften: Die Puzur-Aššur Dynastie. *State Archives of Assyria Bulletin* 12: 3–41.

Garelli, P.
1982   Importance et rôle des Araméens dans l'administration de l'empire assyrien. Pp. 437–47 in *Mesopotamien und seine Nachbarn: Politische und kulturelle Wechselbeziehungen im Alten Vorderasien vom 4. bis 1. Jahrtausend v. Chr.*, ed. H.-J. Nissen and J. Renger. Berlin: Reimer.
1991   The Achievement of Tiglath-pileser III: Novelty or Continuity? Pp. 46–57 in *Ah, Assyria . . . : Studies in Assyrian History and Ancient Near Eastern Historiography Presented to Hayim Tadmor*, ed. M. Cogan and I. Eph'al. Jerusalem: Magnes.

Geller, S.
2000   The God of the Covenant. Pp. 273–319 in *One God or Many? Concepts of Divinity in the Ancient World*, ed. B. N. Porter. Transactions of the Casco Bay Assyriological Institute 1. Bethesda, Md.: CDL.

Gitin, S.
1995   Tel Miqne-Ekron in the 7th Century B.C.E.: The Impact of Economic Innovation and Foreign Cultural Influences on a Neo-Assyrian Vassal City-State. Pp. 61–79 in *Recent Excavations in Israel: A View to the West*, ed. S. Gitin. Archaeological Institute of America Colloquia and Conference Papers 1. Dubuque, Iowa: Archaeological Institute of America.
1997   The Neo-Assyrian Empire and Its Western Periphery: The Levant, with a Focus on Philistine Ekron. Pp. 77–103 in *Assyria 1995: Proceedings of the 10th Anniversary of the Neo-Assyrian Text Corpus Project, Helsinki, September 7–11, 1995*, ed. S. Parpola and R. M. Whiting. Helsinki: The Neo-Assyrian Text Corpus Project.
1998   Philistia in Transition: The Tenth Century BCE and Beyond. Pp. 162–83 in *Mediterranean Peoples in Transition: Thirteenth to Early Tenth Centuries BCE*, ed. S. Gitin, A. Mazar, and E. Stern. Jerusalem: Israel Exploration Society.

Herodotus
1960   Trans. A. D. Godley. Loeb Classical Library. Cambridge: Harvard University Press.

Keel, O., and Uehlinger, C.
1993   *Göttinnen, Götter und Gottessymbole: Neue Erkenntnisse zur Religionsgeschichte Kanaans und Israels aufgrund bislang unerschlossener ikonographischer Quellen*. Questines disputatae 134. Freiburg i.B.: Herder.

Kessler, K.
1997   "Royal Roads" and Other Questions of the Neo-Assyrian Communication System. Pp. 129–36 in *Assyria 1995: Proceedings of the 10th Anniversary of the Neo-Assyrian Text Corpus Project, Helsinki, September 7–11, 1995*, ed. S. Parpola and R. M. Whiting. Helsinki: The Neo-Assyrian Text Corpus Project.

Kingsley, P.
1995   *Ancient Philosophy, Mystery and Magic: Empedocles and Pythagorean Tradition.* Oxford: Clarendon.
1999   *In the Dark Places of Wisdom: The Forgotten Origins of the Western World.* Inverness, Calif.: Golden Sufi Center.

Kuhrt, A.
1995   *The Ancient Near East c. 3000–330 BC.* 2 vols. London: Routledge.

Lanfranchi, G. B.
1996   Dinastie e tradizioni regie d'Anatolia: Frigia, Cimmeri e Lidia nelle fonti neo-assire e nell'ottica Erodotea. Pp. 89–111 in *Dall'Indo a Thule: I Greci, i Romani, gli altri*, ed. A. Aloni and L. de Finis. Trento: Università degli Studi di Trento.
2000   The Ideological and Political Impact of the Assyrian Imperial Expansion on the Greek World in the 8th and 7th Centuries BC. Pp. 7–34 in *The Heirs of Assyria*, ed. S. Aro and R. M. Whiting. Melammu Symposia 1. Helsinki: The Neo-Assyrian Text Corpus Project.

Larsen, M. T.
1976   *The Old Assyrian City-State and Its Colonies.* Mesopotamia 4. Copenhagen: Akademisk Forlag.
1979   The Tradition of Empire in Mesopotamia. Pp. 75–103 in *Power and Propaganda: A Symposium on Ancient Empires*, ed. M. T. Larsen. Mesopotamia 7. Copenhagen: Akademisk Forlag.

Levinson, B. M.
1995   "But You Shall Surely Kill Him!": The Text-Critical and Neo-Assyrian Evidence for MT Deuteronomy 13:10. Pp. 37–63 in *Bundesdokument und Gesetz: Studien zum Deuteronomium*, ed. G. Braulik. Freiburg i.B.: Herder.

Liverani, M.
1979   The Ideology of the Assyrian Empire. Pp. 297–317 in *Power and Propaganda: A Symposium on Ancient Empires*, ed. M. T. Larsen. Mesopotamia 7. Copenhagen: Akademisk Forlag.
1988   The Growth of the Assyrian Empire in the Habur/Middle Euphrates Area. *State Archives of Assyria Bulletin* 2: 81–98.
1992   *Studies on the Annals of Ashurnasirpal II. 2: Topographical Analysis.* Quaderni di Geografia Storica 4. Rome: Università di Roma "La Sapienza."

Mayer, W.
1998   Nabonids Herkunft. Pp. 245–61 in *Dubsar anta-men: Studien zur Altorientalistik. Festschrift für Willem H. Ph. Römer zur Vollendung seines 70. Lebensjahres*, ed. M. Dietrich and O. Loretz. Münster: Ugarit-Verlag.

Oded, B.
1974   The Phoenician Cities and the Assyrian Empire in the Time of Tiglath-pileser III. *Zeitschrift des Deutschen Palästina-Vereins* 90: 38–49.
1979   *Mass Deportations and Deportees in the Neo-Assyrian Empire.* Wiesbaden: Reichert.

Otto, E.
1999   Das Deuteronomium: Politische Theologie und Rechtsreform in Juda und *Assyrien*. Beihefte zur Zeitschrift für die alttestamentliche Wissenschaft 284. Berlin: de Gruyter.

Otzen, B.
1979   Israel under the Assyrians. Pp. 251–61 in *Power and Propaganda: A Symposium on Ancient Empires*, ed. M. T. Larsen. Mesopotamia 7. Copenhagen: Akademisk Forlag.

Pakkala, J.
1999   *Intolerant Monolatry in the Deuteronomistic History.* Publications of the Finnish Exegetical Society 76. Helsinki: Finnish Exegetical Society / Göttingen: Vandenhoeck & Ruprecht.

Parker, B.
1997   Garrisoning the Empire: Aspects of the Construction and Maintenance of Forts on the Assyrian Frontier. *Iraq* 59: 77–88.

2001   *The Mechanics of Empire: The Northern Frontier of Assyria as a Case Study in Imperial Dynam-ics*. Helsinki: The Neo-Assyrian Text Corpus Project.

Parpola, S.
1972   A Letter from Šamaš-šumu-ukīn to Esarhaddon. *Iraq* 34: 21–34.
1987   Neo-Assyrian Treaties from the Royal Archives of Nineveh. *Journal of Cuneiform Studies* 39: 161–89.
1993   The Assyrian Tree of Life: Tracing the Origins of Jewish Monotheism and Greek Philos-ophy. *Journal of Near Eastern Studies* 52: 161–208.
1995   The Assyrian Cabinet. Pp. 379–401 in *Vom Alten Orient zum Alten Testament: Festschrift für Wolfram Freiherrn von Soden zum 85. Geburtstag*, ed. M. Dietrich and O. Loretz. Alter Ori-ent und Altes Testament 240. Neukirchen-Vluyn: Neukirchener Verlag / Kevelaer: But-zon & Bercker.
1997   *Assyrian Prophecies*. State Archives of Assyria 10. Helsinki: Helsinki University Press.
1998   The Esoteric Meaning of the Name of Gilgamesh. Pp. 315–29 in *Intellectual Life of the An-cient Near East: Papers Presented at the 43rd Rencontre assyriologique internationale, Prague, July 1–5, 1996*, ed. J. Prosecký. Prague: Oriental Institute.
1999   Sons of God: The Ideology of Assyrian Kingship. *Archaeology Odyssey* 2/5: 16–27.
2000a   Assyrians after Assyria. *Journal of the Assyrian Academic Society* 12: 1–16.
2000b   Monotheism in Ancient Assyria. Pp. 165–209 in *One God or Many? Concepts of Divinity in the Ancient World*, ed. B. N. Porter. Transactions of the Casco Bay Assyriological Institute 1. Bethesda, Md.: CDL.

Parpola, S., and Watanabe, K.
1988   *Neo-Assyrian Treaties and Loyalty Oaths*. State Archives of Assyria 2. Helsinki: Helsinki University Press.

Popko, M.
1995   *Religions of Asia Minor*. Warsaw: Academic Publishers DIALOG.

Porter, B. N.
1995   Language, Audience and Impact in Imperial Assyria. Pp. 51–70 in *Language and Culture in the Near East*, ed. S. Izre'el and R. Drory. Israel Oriental Studies 15. Leiden: Brill.

Posani, C.
1999   *Ricerche sulla dea Kubaba*. Tesi di laurea, Dipartimento di Scienze dell'Antichità, Univer-sità degli studi di Padova.

Postgate, J. N.
1974   *Taxation and Conscription in the Assyrian Empire*. Studia Pohl: Series Maior 3. Rome: Pon-tifical Biblical Institute.
1979   The Economic Structure of the Assyrian Empire. Pp. 193–221 in *Power and Propaganda: A Symposium on Ancient Empires*, ed. M. T. Larsen. Mesopotamia 7. Copenhagen: Akade-misk Forlag.
1989   Ancient Assyria: A Multi-Racial State. *ARAM* 1: 1–10.
1992   The Land of Assur and the Yoke of Assur. *World Archaeology* 23: 247–62.
1994   Rings, Torcs, and Bracelets. Pp. 235–45 in *Beiträge zur Altorientalischen Archäologie und Al-tertumskunde: Festschrift für Barthel Hrouda zum 65. Geburtstag*, ed. P. Calmeyer et al. Wies-baden: Harrassowitz.

Radner, K.
1998   Der Gott Salmānu ("Šulmānu") und seine Beziehung zur Stadt Dur-Katlimmu. *Die Welt des Orients* 29: 33–51.
1999   Money in the Neo-Assyrian Empire. Pp. 127–57 in *Trade and Finance in Ancient Mesopota-mia: Proceedings of the First MOS Symposium (Leiden 1997)*, ed. J. G. Derksen. Leiden: Ned-erlands historisch-archaeologisch instituut te Istanbul.

Reade, J.
1981   Mesopotamian Guidelines for Biblical Chronology. *Syro-Mesopotamian Studies* 4: 1–9.

RIMA 2
   1991   A. K. Grayson. *Assyrian Rulers of the Early First Millennium BC I (1114–859 BC)*. The Royal
             Inscriptions of Mesopotamia, Assyrian Periods 2. Toronto: University of Toronto Press.
RIMA 3
   1996   A. K. Grayson. *Assyrian Rulers of the Early First Millennium BC II (858–745 BC)*. The Royal
             Inscriptions of Mesopotamia, Assyrian Periods 3. Toronto: University of Toronto Press.
Rollinger, R.
   1996   Altorientalische Motivik in der frühgriechischen Literatur am Beispiel der homerischen
             Epen: Elemente des Kampfes in der Ilias und in der altorientalischen Literatur (nebst
             Überlegungen zur Präsenz altorientalischen Wanderpriester im frühaarchaischen Griech-
             enland). Pp. 156–210 in *Wege zur Genese griechischer Identität: Die Bedeutung der früharchä-
             ischen Zeit*, ed. C. Ulf. Berlin: Akademie.
   1999   Zur Lokalisation von Parsu(m)a(š) in der Fārs und zu einigen Fragen der frühen persi-
             schen Geschichte. *Zeitschrift für Assyriologie* 89: 115–39.
Scarre, C., et al. (eds.)
   1988   *Past Worlds: The Times Atlas of Archaeology.* Verona: Times Books.
Spieckermann, H.
   1982   *Juda unter Assur in der Sargonidenzeit.* Forschungen zur Religion und Literatur des Alten
             und Neuen Testaments 129. Göttingen: Vandenhoeck & Ruprecht.
Steymans, H. U.
   1995a   *Deuteronomium 28 und die adê zur Thronfolgeregelung Asarhaddons: Segen und Fluch im Alten
             Orient und in Israel.* Orbis biblicus et orientalis 145. Fribourg: Fribourg University Press.
   1995b   Eine assyrische Vorlage für Deuteronomium 28,20–44. Pp. 119–41 in *Bundesdokument und
             Gesetz: Studien zum Deuteronomium*, ed. G. Braulik. Freiburg i.B.: Herder.
Stol, M.
   1993   Biblical Idiom in Akkadian. Pp. 246–49 in *The Tablet and the Scroll: Near Eastern Studies in
             Honor of William W. Hallo*, ed. M. E. Cohen, D. C. Snell, and D. B. Weisberg. Bethesda,
             Md.: CDL.
Tadmor, H.
   1982   The Aramaization of Assyria: Aspects of Western Impact. Pp. 449–70 in *Mesopotamien
             und seine Nachbarn: Politische und kulturelle Wechselbeziehungen im Alten Vorderasien vom 4. bis
             1. Jahrtausend v. Chr.*, ed. H.-J. Nissen and J. Renger. Berlin: Reimer.
   1994   *The Inscriptions of Tiglath-pileser III, King of Assyria: Critical Edition, with Introductions,
             Translations and Commentary.* Jerusalem: Israel Academy of Sciences and Humanities.
   1999   World Dominion: The Expanding Horizon of the Assyrian Empire. Pp. 55–62 in *Land-
             scapes: Territories, Frontiers and Horizons in the Ancient Near East.* Papers Presented to the
             XLIV Rencontre Assyriologique Internationale, *Venezia, 7–11 July 1997*, ed. L. Milano et
             al. Padua: Sargon.
Tadmor, H., and Cogan, M.
   1977   Gyges and Assurbanipal: A Study in Literary Transmission. *Orientalia* 46: 65–85.
Thureau-Dangin, F., and Dunand, M.
   1936   *Til-Barsip.* Paris: Geuthner.
Versnel, H. S.
   2000   Thrice One: Three Greek Experiments in Oneness. Pp. 79–163 in *One God or Many? Con-
             cepts of Divinity in the Ancient World*, ed. B. N. Porter. Transactions of the Casco Bay As-
             syriological Institute 1. Bethesda, Md.: CDL.
VTE
   1988   [Succession treaty of Esarhaddon] Pp. 28–58 in S. Parpola and K. Watanabe, *Neo-Assyrian
             Treaties and Loyalty Oaths.* State Archives of Assyria 2. Helsinki: Helsinki University
             Press.

Weippert, M.
1989   Manasse. Pp. 332–33 in *Reallexikon der Assyriologie und Vorderasiatischen Archäologie*, ed. D. O. Edzard et al. Berlin: de Gruyter.

West, M. L.
1995   The Date of the Iliad. *Museum Helveticum* 52: 203–19.
1997   *The East Face of Helicon: West Asiatic Elements in Greek Poetry and Myth*. Oxford: Clarendon.

Winter, I.
1997   Art in Empire: The Royal Image and the Visual Dimensions of Assyrian Ideology. Pp. 359–81 in *Assyria 1995: Proceedings of the 10th Anniversary of the Neo-Assyrian Text Corpus Project, Helsinki, September 7–11, 1995*, ed. S. Parpola and R. M. Whiting. Helsinki: The Neo-Assyrian Text Corpus Project.

Xenophon
1985   *Cyropaedia*, trans. W. Miller. Loeb Classical Library. Cambridge: Harvard University Press.

Egyptian Interventions in the Levant in Iron Age II

Kenneth A. Kitchen

School of Archaeology, Classics and Oriental Studies
University of Liverpool

Introduction

To pursue the long course of ancient Egyptian history at all accurately, through any part of its 3,000 years, it is essential to get to know closely the state of existing textual and artifactual remains from the relevant periods during that time-span, as well as to be able to grasp the *limitations* of the extant evidence and especially the *nature and extent* of the tangible gaps in that documentation (see further below).

In the earlier New Kingdom of the 18th Dynasty, Egypt briefly ruled up to the westernmost shore of the Euphrates (early 15th century B.C.E.), until Mitanni and Ḫatti pushed it back into central Syria; the Amarna episode (14th century) saw further territorial loss (e.g., Ugarit). The 19th Dynasty Ramesside kings regained no territory (13th century). In the 20th Dynasty (12th century), Ramesses III and perhaps Ramesses IV had some hold on the Canaanite western plains and Jezreel (Beth-shan); Ramesses VI (ca. 1140) is known from Megiddo and Sinai, after which there was certainly no direct Egyptian rule in Canaan. Whatever its true status, the Report of Wenamun clearly reflects the total lapse of pharaonic authority in Canaan and Phoenicia by 1080 B.C.E.

Then comes the period with which this paper is directly concerned, the Third "Intermediate" period in Egypt (21st–25th Dynasties), again (like the First and Second such periods) marked by political division of executive power and very limited deployment of wealth for monumental purposes. Practical disunity was the norm, not the exception. The 21st Dynasty Delta kings in Memphis and Tanis in effect shared power with a line of military governors (and high priests of Theban Amun) who ruled the south. The new Libyan 22nd Dynasty's founder, the astute and ambitious Shoshenq I, reimposed unity; but already during his son Osorkon I's reign, his grandson Shoshenq (II) took a royal cartouche as high priest in Thebes. A generation later, Osorkon II had to tolerate the Theban-based "king" Harsiese; and in his early years, Shoshenq III had to tolerate the rise of a collateral line of Delta kings (23rd Dynasty), to whom Thebes and the south then gave allegiance. Thereafter, during the 8th century B.C.E., Egypt in effect quietly fell to pieces: two more rulers became "kings" in Middle Egypt; a permanent "crown-princedom" ruled at Athribis (south Delta), and various Libyan "Chiefs of the Ma(shwash)" carved out their own principalities in the Delta. The result by 728 B.C.E. is clearly visible in the account of Egypt's political geography so clearly portrayed for us by Piye ("Piankhy") on his great stela celebrating his fleeting triumph in Egypt. Under the Nubian kings of the 25th Dynasty, many local rulers survived as (in effect) their vassals. Here, again, the situation is well portrayed by outsiders, in this case in the annals of Assurbanipal of Assyria.

The period of politically fragile disunity ended only when the canny Psamtek I (founder of the 26th Dynasty, from 664 B.C.E.) reunited Egypt under his personal rule and eliminated all local chiefs in favor of his own well-subordinated "civil service." Strong, fair central government brought Egypt renewed unity and prosperity, until its independence was ended by the Persian Empire under Cambyses; in the 4th century B.C.E., the 28th to 30th Dynasties could only fight off the Persian colossus briefly.

Data? Where Has It All Gone?

As mentioned in the opening paragraph, clear gaps occur in the documentation of ancient Egypt's long history. That there are gaps arises from three factors:[1] (a) the massive *destruction* and physical dissolution (by natural processes) of most data—we are but dealing with "the wrecks of Time," after all; (b) the *nonavailability* of masses of data on all places, periods, and cultures still safely locked away from us, unexcavated at the numberless ancient sites and tells of Egypt and the Near East; (c) even when documentation is copious, the ancients have only left us what interested *them*—they cannot be expected to cater to our specific and often alien demands in an epoch unforeseen by them. More pertinently, ask of antiquity a senseless (or to its peoples, irrelevant) question, and you will get a senseless answer, or (often and properly) none at all.

We need to look critically at such "gaps" to evaluate their bearing on our topic. Thus we have a mass of data for the 10–12 centuries of the Old to Middle Kingdoms (ca. 2700–1800 B.C.E.); yet not a single major historical text of any length is known from these years. Old Kingdom pharaohs, it is suspected, did not deem it necessary to address lesser beings in this way; and the gods were best served with offerings and rites, not historical reports. The royal afterlife was quite a different matter, as is proved by the presence of the "Pyramid Texts" on the king's other-worldly behalf in the pyramids from Unis onward. But an annual record of events was kept, in the first instance, for pragmatic, administrative purposes; witness the "annals" of the Palermo Stone and its fragments.[2] During the Middle Kingdom, the 12th Dynasty pharaohs used propaganda on their royal behalf in the curriculum of trainee administrators; and annals were kept, of which only the merest traces have so far been recovered to document the fact.[3]

During the New Kingdom, explicit historical sources for the pharaohs warring in the Levant are in effect limited to a variety of stelae, topographical lists, and the annals of Tuthmosis III in the 18th Dynasty; and to stelae, formal war scenes, and more lists, plus

---

1. And not from whole centuries of chronological miscalculation, as some would have it, because they cannot distinguish between accidental gaps in our present-day modern knowledge and the nonexistence of gaps in ongoing human life in antiquity (other than when periods of no human occupation occur in specific locations).

2. Well pictured in Gardiner 1961: 62, pl. 3; for a new treatment, see Wilkinson 2000.

3. Only two contiguous blocks have so far been found, reused at Memphis before the West Hall of the Temple of Ptah; they are published with translation (and earlier mentions) by Altenmüller and Moussa 1991; for the text without translation, see Malek and Quirke 1992.

the Qadesh report of Ramesses II, and war texts of Merenptah and Ramesses III. Almost all are from the more extensively preserved temples in Thebes and the south, found only rarely in Memphis and the north. That more extensive records once existed we know from brief mentions, as when Tuthmosis III says explicitly that he deposited a day-book of his campaigning in the temple of Amun at Karnak, and that he gave only extracts in the stone-carved text at Karnak (unlike in the palace day-books).[4] And the cuneiform documents add massively to the limited Egyptian sources for Egypto-Hittite relations under Ramesses II.

This brings us back to the Third "Intermediate" period, 1070–664 B.C.E., in terms of what information we have and the gaps in our knowledge. During the 21st to 25th Dynasties, the focus of political power was in the *north*, centered always upon Memphis (the nation's administrative capital), with Tanis as the gateway to western Asia and second capital during the 21st and 22nd Dynasties only (1070–715 B.C.E.). In the south, Thebes, the "holy city" of Amun, was the focus of local loyalties only and a source of division. The dry desert conditions of the south preserved all manner of artifacts (particularly in tombs), whereas in the north, with its damp mud, swampy areas, and (in the Delta) dearth of local stone, almost nothing was preserved, except hard-stone fragments (granite, etc.) of statuary and the trimmings of temple buildings; any extensive wall surfaces have long since disappeared, recycled into later structures or consumed in lime kilns. Thus, for the entire period, we have an abundance of brightly-painted mummy-cases, "Books of the Dead" on papyrus, and so on, from Thebes, but virtually no surviving historical records relating to the Levant; wars in Palestine had no relevance to a priest's afterlife. By contrast, where all the politics was centered (up north), nearly all monumental records on stone have been long since destroyed by recycling, and (unless carbonized to illegibility) papyri just do not survive in Delta mud. This is why Egypt yields almost no data on people and events in Palestine from 1070 B.C.E. onward. It is thus the height of ignorance for scholars to allege that, for example, the Hebrew "united monarchy" (and the twin monarchies down to 860 B.C.E.) did not exist merely because we have no mention of them in external sources. Except for the Siamun fragment and the imperial work of Shoshenq I at Thebes, almost no relevant documents have survived or been recovered from Egypt. And in the case of Mesopotamia, the Assyrians simply had no commemorable contact with southern Syria (or the Palestinian entities beyond) until 853 B.C.E. Thus, no records from east of the Euphrates can be expected about kingdoms in Canaan earlier than 853 B.C.E. But this does *not* "prove" that nothing existed in the westlands before then. Any such assumption is wholly naïve in these circumstances.[5]

---

4. See, for convenience, Breasted 1906: 2.164, 166, 200, §§392, 393 end, 472; for the last passage, see also Wilson 1950: 239b.

5. Biblical scholars go on and on about "no mention of Israel" between the Merenptah stela (1209 B.C.E.) and the Shalmaneser III mention (853 B.C.E.)—are they even related? But look at Assyrian references to Egypt. From Assyrian sources, we have gifts from the "king of Musri" ca. 1070 B.C.E. (Assur-bel-kala); then a 220-year gap, until soldiers of Musri are reported by Shalmaneser III in 853 B.C.E.; then another 130 years before Musri reappears in the texts of Sargon II for 722 and 720 B.C.E. If we did not have the massive stone monuments in the Nile Valley (on a scale that never existed in Israel), we might be "justified" in asking the same inane question: are these "Musris" all the same, with a common history?

Critical Survey of Historical Issues

I. Egypt and the Levant: 21st Dynasty

1. Egypt and Edom/Se'ir.   One report that relates to this period is the removal of the Edomite prince Hadad, as an infant (lit., "little boy"), to Egypt, when David of Israel sought to subdue that area by extirpating its male population (1 Kgs 11:14–22).[6] In Egypt Hadad grew up, married, and had his son weaned; then he heard of the deaths of David and Joab (cf. 1 Kgs 2:10, 28–35) and so left Egypt to reclaim his heritage. If one allowed roughly 20 years for the whole episode, Hadad would have entered Egypt approximately 990 B.C.E., under Amenemope, and have lived through the brief reign of Osochor into that of Siamun. This report contains genuine Egyptian traits and should not be dismissed lightly. Hadad's marriage to a sister of Tahpenes, the Egyptian queen, is consistent with 10th-century practices (by contrast with, e.g., the 14th century),[7] while the word Tahpenes is definitely Egyptian, consistent with this period, whether as a title ("king's wife") or a personal name.[8] Furthermore, the pharaoh's provision of "a house, food-allowance and land" for his long-stay visitor (1 Kgs 11:18) is a known Egyptian custom.[9] Recent hypercriticism of this passage by Edelman (1995: 174–83; endorsed by Ash 1999: 109–10 n. 20), denying its historicity, can be dismissed, because her "proofs" are totally spurious: (a) There could be no Edomite state in the 10th century, because Edelman knows of no "fixed structures" there at the time, only camps, cemeteries, smelting sites, and sherd-scatters. False. Organized kingship/chiefdom is not dependent on the use of fixed buildings. Edelman has overlooked much evidence to the contrary for "tented kingdoms," from both Edom and elsewhere. These include tribal rulers of Kushu (biblical Kushan)—the precursor of Edom in the 19th/18th centuries B.C.E.—including one Ya'ush, the same name that appears in Gen 36:5, 14 (*qere*), and 18.[10] Ramesses II refers often to plundering the land of Se'ir/Shasu; under Merenptah Edomites sought pasture in the eastern Delta; and Ramesses III "devastated the Se'irites, among the clans of the Shasu, (and) pillaged their tents (Semitic

---

6. A barbarism practiced down to our own time in various conflicts (in the former Yugoslavia, central Africa, etc.).

7. See below, under Siamun and Solomon's "daughter of pharaoh."

8. The simplest equivalent is the one long since proposed by Grdseloff (1947: 88–90) and refined by this writer (1996a: 274 n. 183) as *t3-ḥ(mt)-p3-nsw*, "wife of the king," that is, "queen." Here the feminine affix had long since disappeared, allowing the *m* to assimilate to the following *p*. For a similar example from the 14th century B.C.E., see Federn 1960: 33. Otherwise, as a proper name, the **T3-ḥn(t)-p3-nsw*, "she whom the king protects," suggested by Albright (1955: 32) fits the 21st Dynasty perfectly, where we find a parallel name, *T3-ḥn(t)-Dḥwty*, "she whom Thoth protects" (Ranke n.d.: 1.365:25). For a third option and further references, see Muchiki 1999: 228–29, offering **T3-(nt)-ḥ(wt)-p3-nsw*, "she of the King's House," which also has good analogues (masc. and fem.) from the New Kingdom to the Greek period.

9. Already a millennium earlier, the courtier Sinuhe was given a house, food allowance, and land on his return to court from Canaan; the yield from the land (whether for Sinuhe or Hadad) provided an income. On Sinuhe, B.286–307, see, for example, Wilson 1950: 22a. Canaanite envoys at the Egyptian court were accommodated and assigned food supplies (Epstein 1963: passim). The first Hittite princess to marry Ramesses II was assigned "ample villas [in her] name," and Ramesses II built for his bride "a fine house"(?) (see, respectively, the Marriage Stela [Kitchen 1996b: 96 at 255:5] and cuneiform letters E.21–22 [Kitchen 1999a: 149 end; for the full edition, see Edel 1994: 1.141–43; 2.222–23]).

10. See Kitchen 1992: 21–23, map 1.

ʾ*ohel*) of people and goods."[11] Thus, Edom was *not* totally empty terrain in the 13th/12th
centuries B.C.E., but was occupied from the 19th into the 12th centuries by pastoralist
tribes under chiefs—among whom a supreme chief would have been a "king" in ancient
terminology (a *ḥeqa,* "ruler," over *wrw,* "chiefs," in Egyptian terminology for foreigners).
Well beyond Edom, again in the early second millennium B.C.E., the ancestors and breth-
ren of Shamshi-Adad I of Ekallatum and Assyria came from a line of "kings that dwelt
in tents." Other "tented kingdoms" existed at the time. Such was the elusive kingdom
of Manana, being the reign of tented potentates near Kish (with its own "urban" kings)
but not in it, and hence without any archaeological remains of their own. Other examples also exist.[12]

(b) Flight into Egypt is simply a folktale motif; likewise the threefold mention of adversaries. Wrong. Real people sought help in Egypt or fled there, not just in stories. The
late-third-millennium B.C.E. relief scene of Unis of starving desert-folk implies their gain-
ing aid from Egypt.[13] A millennium later we have the aforementioned Edomites seeking
eastern Delta water and pasture under Merenptah.[14] And only two opponents of Solomon
are foreign adversaries who broke away and ultimately held their own; Jeroboam was an
internal dissident who fled to Egypt.

(c) The anonymity of Hadad's pharaoh and mother-in-law. Again, wrong (and frivo-
lous) as denoting nonhistoricity. Ramesses II married two Hittite princesses; in the ceremonial stelae dedicated to their marriages, these girls' Hittite names are never given (the
first received an Egyptian name), and their imperial father and mother also remain unnamed in the Egyptian texts.[15] The Assyrians call Shabako simply "Pharaoh of Egypt"
(Pirʾu Musri), without a name—but this does not reduce their annals to fiction.

(d) The marriage of an Egyptian princess to a foreigner. Contra Edelman and her
"facts," this *was* acceptable in the 10th/9th centuries B.C.E. (see under Siamun below).
Thus, there is no valid factual reason for denying the historicity of this incident. Irrational
and ill-informed minimalism is no substitute for hard facts.

Given the lack of Egyptian sources on the Levant throughout this period, any glean-
ings are welcome. One such is the "Moscow Literary Letter," probably a fictional composition of not later than about 1000/900 B.C.E. Its writer closes with wishing to send
his enemy off to Nahar<in>, the Euphrates (i.e., the back of beyond), to fetch (almost as
an aside) a hidden interpreter(?) "with whom he went to those of Seʿir." In other words,
at the time of composition, it was known that Seʿir had a population, and people visited
there. As Caminos has pointed out, the date of composition cannot precede 1279–1213
B.C.E., the reign of Ramesses II (the text names an Usimare-nakht; Caminos 1977: 78).
In fact, given the erratic orthography, and so on, it may, rather, have been composed in
the late 20th Dynasty; the country "was enveloped in the flames of war" seriously only
during the reign of Ramesses XI, when the Viceroy of Nubia (Panehsy) swept north
through Egypt, in conflict with Amenhotep, high priest of Amun, after approximately

---

11. See Egyptian citations in Kitchen 1992: 26–27.
12. On these early Mesopotamian data, see Wu and Dalley 1990: 159–65.
13. Scenes published in Schott 1965.
14. Papyrus Anastasi VI 51–61; for translations, see Wilson 1950: 259; Caminos 1954: 293–96.
15. For full modern translations, see Kitchen 1996b: 86–99.

1100 B.C.E. So this allusion most likely dates this document within the late 12th/11th/ 10th centuries B.C.E.[16]

   2. Siamun and the Levant.   Here we plumb new depths of hypercritical overkill. From Tanis, home base of the 21st Dynasty, there has long been known part of a triumphal relief scene showing a king—agreed to be Siamun—smiting captured foes. First of all, astonishingly, Weinstein (1998: 192–93) has dismissed this scene as showing "an unidentified king." Unidentified? Before this blundering remark is taken up by biblical scholars who may not know one hieroglyph from another, let the facts about this piece be stated clearly once and for all. In front of the king's face there appears for all to see a cartouche containing the personal name and epithet "Siamun, Beloved of Am[un]." All of the signs are legible and complete, except for loss of the second Amun's head and plumes at the top right. Numerous other intact examples of Siamun's nomen guarantee the reading absolutely. A trace of the first cartouche, adjoining at right, would have contained this king's unique and very distinctive throne name, Neterkheperre Setepenamun.[17] Second, the dating of Siamun: as amply demonstrated elsewhere (Kitchen 1996a) and summarized in excursus 1 below, this king reigned for 19 years, from 979 to 960 or 978 to 959 B.C.E., or very close to this. Third, the object held by his foe in this scene: despite much nonsense written to the contrary, this is very clearly a *crescentic* double-bladed *ax*—not a shield (Lance 1976: 216–17; Green 1978: 364), a halter (Ash 1999: 45), or still less, handcuffs (Ash 1999: 45).[18] Such a weapon in this precise form is not found in the armories of Nubia, Egypt, Libya, Syria–Palestine, Mesopotamia, or Anatolia; but doubled-bladed axes (real or ceremonial) *do* occur prominently in the Aegean cultures and in the Balkans.[19] From across the Aegean and eastern Mediterranean came the "Sea Peoples," including the Pilasti or Philistines. Therefore, whether as weapon or symbol, the ax is appropriate for the first major population group that Siamun would meet as he marched into southwest Palestine.

   The ax is clearly marked as such by a visible socket with a trace of the handle running down from it onto the now-lost lower wall surface.[20] The foe's hand is clearly visible, holding the ax awkwardly at the socket, so that he cannot wield it against the king.[21] Such a

---

16. For full publication of Papyrus Pushkin 127, see Caminos 1977. His attempts to locate *Nhr‹n›* and *n3yw-S‛r* within Egypt (pp. 33 n. 5; 68–69) do not fit the context; Wermai did not go there, but he wished others would clear off to Nahar‹in› and fetch a *tmrgn* from "those of Se‛ir." The word *tmrgn* is non-Egyptian; given the orthography of the text, it is best taken as *trgmn*, "interpreter," well known in Semitic.

17. For the original (and best) publication of this relief, see the photo in Montet 1947: pl. 9A; the small drawing often reproduced is not wholly reliable. For a selected bibliography, see Kitchen 1996a: 280–81 nn. 222–23, and 574, §506.

18. Regarding the last, handcuffs on prisoners were in fact oval, with a central slot for the prisoner's hands (Lange and Hirmer 1961: pl. 200).

19. See references, e.g., in Lance 1976: 213–14, 220 nn. 33–37; Green 1978: 364–65. The nondiscovery so far of *crescentic* axes either as weapons or symbolic standards in Philistia (so Brug 1985: 70; followed by Ash 1999: 40) is meaningless in view of the virtual lack of discovery of any weapons at all (real or ceremonial) throughout Philistia. Double-bladed axes in Canaan are cited by Schipper (1999: 26, cf. 296, Abb. 3), although his Gezer and Megiddo specimens cannot possibly be described as crescentic.

20. It cannot conceivably be a rope halter (Ash 1999: 45; his Amenhotep I scene is not a triumph scene of smiting, is irrelevant, and is misunderstood). On the contrary, bound foes in triumph scenes do hold weapons. In a scene of Tuthmosis III at Karnak, the foes brandish duck-billed axes (Lange and Hirmer 1961: pl. 136). In such scenes, foes sometimes grasp daggers by the (sheathed?) blade, as in the Shoshenq relief—grossly misread by Ash as "thin vials"! (1999: 41).

21. This refutes the errors in Giveon 1972: 143 n. 4; Ash 1999: 38.

feature is unique in the long series of triumph scenes and implicitly speaks for its commemorating a historical event. It should be remarked that, as far as can be determined, the *monumental* examples of such scenes on temple walls do seem to belong to pharaohs who had gone to war. Thus, we find such scenes of the 18th Dynasty warrior-kings, of Sethos I, Ramesses II, and Merenptah in the 19th Dynasty, and of Ramesses III and Ramesses VI in the 20th Dynasty; thereafter, only of such kings as Siamun, Shoshenq I, and Shabako/Taharqa before the Late Period. Examples in purely decorative contexts (on the sides of sacred barges, in jewelry contexts, etc.) are merely ideograms of victory in the abstract,[22] not to be confused with real records on temple walls, where triumph scenes often form the terminal scene of those showing real campaigns (19th/20th Dynasties) or substitute for them (18th Dynasty). Thus, the whole tissue of arguments against the probable historical significance of Siamun's relief can be dismissed as the special pleading it in fact is.

The other side to these decades (980–960 B.C.E.) is that they overlap with the last decade of David's reign and the first decade of Solomon's, because Solomon's reign covered, at latest, 970–930 B.C.E. (see excursus 1 below). Thus, within Solomon's first 10 years of reign, a pharaoh who seized Gezer gave it as dowry with his daughter in marriage to Solomon (1 Kgs 9:16). She stayed in the "City of David" (1 Kgs 3:1), while the Temple (for 7 years, during years 4–11) and Solomon's adjacent palace complex (for 13 years, alongside or after the Temple) were still under construction. Those 10 years overlap directly with the last decade of Siamun's reign. Hence, it is perfectly in order to recognize in Siamun the "pharaoh who smote Gezer" and who made the marriage alliance with Solomon. His war relief would confirm that (as one might expect) Gezer was not his main objective, but merely the northwestern terminus of his campaign, which spanned Philistia. The reasons for an Egypto-Israelite alliance against Philistia can only be surmised; trade might be at the root of it, if the Philistines had exploited their position by, for example, slapping excessive tolls on all goods exchanged overland between Canaan and Egypt, and even interfered with passing coastal sea traffic. But this can only be conjecture.

Objections to such a royal marriage are spurious. Despite the rather arrogant denial by, for example, Soggin (1994: 81) and Ash (1999: 117–18), the no-princesses-for-foreigners (and commoners) policy of Amenophis III belongs to New Kingdom times, almost half a millennium before Siamun and Solomon, and is not definitive for the radically changed world of the 10th century B.C.E. The Egyptian population of this time was not "strongly Libyan" (a careless quote from Taylor in Ash 1999: 117) overall; they settled only on the western Delta margins, with local chiefs across the Delta. Giving a daughter in marriage to a Libyan is giving her to a foreigner, as with princess Maatkare to Prince Osorkon (long before his accession to kingship; Ash blunders badly in stating otherwise [1999: 117 and n. 57, in which I am misquoted]). For the initial resentment of Libyan rule as foreign, note the dateline in Thebes, "Year 2, 3rd month of Akhet, 17, of the Great Chief of the Ma(sh-wash) [= Libyans], Shoshe(n)q," the name determined with the throw-stick sign for foreigner (Kitchen 1996a: 288, §242). The lack of mention of the name of the princess and the date of the marriage (Ash 1999: 113) does not prove lack of historicity; contemporary

---

22. This refutes Ash 1999: 43–44; Herihor did war, in Nubia in any case. As for Schipper 1999: 25 n. 83—the vessel of Bocchoris is a decorative minor artwork, not a temple wall.

Egyptian sources for the second Hittite marriage of Ramesses II, for example, likewise omit the names of the princess and her father, as well as the date of the event. Thus, the report of the marriage alliance in 1 Kings stands and cannot be summarily dismissed on this and other trivial excuses.[23]

3. An Overview of 21st-Dynasty Policy in the Levant.   More positively, we may now sum up. The lack of explicit, preserved documents hinders any full evaluation. In the time of Ramesses XI or of Smendes, the Assyrian king Assur-bel-kala (1074–1056 B.C.E.) could boast of receiving exotic gifts from "the king of Egypt" while campaigning in Lebanon.[24] Conversely, we have a large lapis lazuli bead (in a whole necklace of such beads) inscribed in cuneiform for the (Assyrian) grand vizier Ibashshi-ilu and his eldest daughter, found in the burial of Psusennes I (died ca. 992 or 991 B.C.E.). It might once have been part of a reciprocal gift from Assur-bel-kala (as has been argued on paleographic grounds) to the Egyptian king who had sent him gifts.[25] Thus, the outgoing Ramessides and/or incoming Tanites were disposed toward friendly relations with Near Eastern states when their interests required this.

Siamun's probable military action was limited in scope (Philistia and Gezer only), not remotely imperialistic, and possibly for economic reasons, as suggested above. The possible alliance with Solomon may likewise have had an economic motivation. There is no reason whatsoever to imagine that Siamun destroyed any of the Philistine cities; they would be much more useful as tribute-paying vassals, which was probably their status for the remaining years of his reign. What we do know from inside Egypt is that (except for Psusennes I) Siamun alone pursued an active building program at Tanis and elsewhere: a large forecourt with a colonnade at its rear and granite elements in the main Amun-temple at Tanis; and a handsome lesser temple for "Amun of the lapis lazuli" that the high priest of Ptah built in his name at Memphis.[26] Fresh wealth from such vassals would help with the cost of such enterprises. So, in the 21st Dynasty, relaxed, friendly relations with lands abroad were the rule, but limited military action was used when needful or advantageous.

---

23. Schipper (1999: 86–90) goes on at length about Libyan kings marrying off daughters differently before and after Takeloth II (to highly placed priests versus civil/military officials). But this distinction is false: they are all nonroyal commoners, priest and vizier alike. Of course, this was a policy to strengthen the royal hold over the bureaucracy. But *no* New Kingdom king used such a method. The distinction between the New Kingdom and the 21st–22nd Dynasties remains clear. What the Libyans and their 21st-Dynasty relatives did matrimonially *inside* Egypt, they could just as easily do to extend their power *outside* Egypt; so Schipper's criticisms are mistaken. His lengthy "analyses" of the biblical passages (1999: 90–107) again prove nothing whatsoever; the Hebrew texts are inherently clear in themselves, and the subjective guesswork about supposed kernels and supplements has no objective basis. One notices Schipper's total failure to consult firsthand ancient sources on how incoming foreign princesses were treated. As Solomon did for his pharaoh's daughter, so Ramesses II appears to have provided "ample villas" (first Marriage Stela) and a fine house (cuneiform letters) for his first Hittite princess. The comparison did not escape Edel (1994: 2.222), as it has done Schipper.

24. See the Annals Fragment, text 6 (Grayson 1991: 98); and compare with the "Broken Obelisk," text 7 (Grayson 1991: 103–4). Which pharaoh was involved would depend on which year of Assur-bel-kala he warred in Lebanon, but this is not clear from the surviving texts.

25. See Borger 1961: 20–22; cf. Grayson 1991: 112, text 2002. It is most improbable that a personal gift by a vizier to his daughter would reach Psusennes I simply by casual trade, as Schipper (1999: 18 n. 42) would suggest.

26. On Tanis, see the plan in Kitchen 1996a: 318, fig. 3a (central court, Si[amun]). For Memphis, see the references in Kitchen 1996a: 279 nn. 214–15.

There was no Egyptian "hegemony," except possibly for a few years under Siamun over the Philistine pentapolis. The Egyptian cultural impact on the Philistines was probably minimal (who emulates enemies?); in Israel, it would be limited to the court and ruling elite, and have no direct impact on the main rural population of Israel and Judah, as is shown by the scatter of trivia (scarab amulets, etc.) found at Iron Age II sites in Canaan, well and dutifully catalogued by Ash (1999: 75–97), especially in the more coastal areas (Ash 1999: 97), populated more by "pagans" than by the YHWH-worshiping Hebrews further inland.

II. Egypt and Israel during the 22nd (Libyan) Dynasty

1. The Campaign by Shoshenq I. Before assessing this event in its own right, we must again regretfully first clear away recently published nonsense on this topic. The recent treatments by Ash (1999: 50–56) and Schipper (1999: 119–32) show a poor level of understanding of both the sources and the event, marking not progress but a retrograde step in modern study.[27] But here, there is worse than just a step backward; there is madness in the air. Clancy (1999) would abolish everything in sight. He would suggest that (a) the Shoshenq stela from Megiddo belongs to a Shoshenq IV, not I; (b) Shoshenq I did not campaign much beyond the southwestern corner of Palestine, close to Philistia, and touched in essence neither Judah proper nor Israel (or beyond); and (c) this probably not before about 800 B.C.E.; and (d) Year 5 of Rehoboam is not historical and there was no campaign at the time, but it was invented by late Jewish visitors to Karnak who saw Shoshenq's scene, reckoned it back to Rehoboam, and so invented a "Shishak campaign" in his time, instead of around 800 B.C.E.

---

27. A few examples must suffice in each case. Ash (1999: 52) wrongly describes the text above Shoshenq's great list as "stereotypical prose"; it is in fact poetical, makes original use of traditional language, and is unique in incorporating a building text (cf. the full translation in Kitchen 1999b: 433–40 and references there). Ash's treatment of the list itself (1999: 53–55) is confused, as is that of Schipper (1999: 126–29). The latter has not fully realized that the "repetitions" of *Hagr, Negeb,* and *Hadabiyat* (1999: 128 n. 76) are nothing of the kind, but are merely the first half in each case of a double name occupying two ovals. Ash trots out the usual nonsense about Jerusalem's not being on the list (1999: 54–55). The answer is the same as always: it is either lost in one of the many lacunae of row IV, or it was not included because it surrendered without conflict (Rehoboam bought Shoshenq off). Ash is embarrassed (1999: 54 n. 166) by the probable occurrence of "Heights of David" in ovals 105/106 (in a Negev context, one may add), but he has nothing better to suggest. He pretends to be able to read hieroglyphs, but despite his say-so, there is *no* "quail chick" reading for either *w* or *o*; in these names it is the *wȝ* rope-sign. Its *w*-value as an initial sign is absolutely certain; thus its medial value may normally be the same. His further remark that the references to David (in *Beyt-Dawid*) on the Tel Dan and Mesha stelae is a place-name and not a personal name is plain wrong, of course. The phrase "House of X" denotes a kingdom (place) by reference to a dynastic *founder,* who was a *person.* There is no escaping this fact (for a full range of examples, see Kitchen 1997: 38–39, and the map on p. 37). As for Schipper, he makes no proper use of the Karnak stela (which *is* relevant). He misreads (1999: 130–31) the text of the Megiddo stela (Shoshenq I is Hedjkheperre Setepen-**re**, not -amun; and there is no "Son of Re" over the second cartouche, but either *Neb-ir-khet* or *Neb-khaʿu*). His great fuss (1999: 120–21) over the "difficulty" of synchronizing the campaign of Shoshenq I in 926/925 B.C.E. with Year 5 of Rehoboam arises because (uncritically following Donner) he insists on using the entirely outdated and erroneous chronology of Begrich and Jepsen. The problem is entirely of his own making and is imaginary. Alongside Thiele's methodologically superior work (1951/1965), we now also have that of Galil (1996), inexplicably not cited or used by Schipper (see excursus 1 below for a proper Hebrew chronology for 930–841 B.C.E.). Thus, Ash and Schipper have very little of any worth to contribute on Shoshenq I. They stand in the tradition of the nihilism shown long since by Wellhausen when he claimed that Shoshenq I might have copied his list from an older list (factually impossible).

Let us look at the facts. (a) The Megiddo stela bears beyond any doubt whatsoever the simple twin cartouches of Shoshenq I (Hedjkheperre Setepenre; Shoshenq Meri-Amun), founder of the 22nd Dynasty, author of the Karnak List and associated works, including the Year 21 Silsila stela, El-Hiba relief, and Karnak war stela. None of these monuments could possibly belong to any later king, especially the king now known as Shoshenq IV, who had the variable prenomen Hedjkheperre Setepen-amun (or -re) and the wholly distinct, long nomen Shoshenq Meri-Amun, Si-Bast, Nutjer-heq-On, all in one cartouche. No such extended second cartouche appears on the Megiddo stela or related sources.

(b) Shoshenq I's list includes a series of clear segments that are beyond rational dispute: one, in row II, 14–17, is Taʿanach/Shunem/Beth-shan/Reḥob, only possible in the Jezreel region. Another is in row II, 23–24, 26 — Gibeon/Beth-Horon/Ajalon—and another in row III, 27—a clear Megiddo, from which two series run, the second (32–39) being, north to south, Aruna/Borim/Zeyt-Padalla[28]/Yehem/x/y/Socoh/Beth-Tappua[ḥ]. More examples could be added, but these suffice to disprove the idea that Shoshenq never went beyond the southwestern edge of the Shephelah.

(c) Clancy would date Shoshenq I to approximately 800 B.C.E. simply on the say-so of a recent "crank-chronologist," Rohl (1995), whose attempts to down-date Egyptian and ancient Near Eastern chronology by 250/300 years are 100% nonsense, considering the full array of evidence we are privileged to have these days. (d) Clancy's vision of learned Jews (practising Egyptologists, but who do not know their own history) freely entering sacred Egyptian temple precincts (from which foreigners, as unclean, were normally banned), seeing the Shoshenq relief, knowing how to read it and, miraculously, how to date it, and then imagining the campaign was contemporary with an imaginary King Rehoboam they might place at that date simply beggars belief! Such visits would not be allowed; and there is no reason to credit the modest postexilic Jewish priesthood (in Jerusalem or elsewhere) with any knowledge of Egyptian hieroglyphs or former Egyptian history, or its native chronological sources. No competent person could possibly take such stuff seriously. Alas, biblical scholars all too often know no better and apparently will swallow any proposition decked out with a few notes and references (but never, of course, what the biblical writers have to say, no matter how reasonable or congruent with their own ancient world).

Again, let us return to the positive evaluation of the whole episode. On the basis of the biblical and other sources, Shoshenq I was involved in the Levant before his famous campaign, in two respects. (a) He renewed trade relations with Phoenician Byblos, which already had a 2,000-year-old history by his time; note the statue there of Shoshenq I and Abibaal, king of Byblos.[29] (b) He harbored the anti-Solomonic rebel Jeroboam during Solomon's reign, before using him as a convenient tool to disrupt the Hebrew kingdom right after Solomon's demise. Its collapse into two smaller rival kingdoms gave him his chance to subdue both without too much trouble. What is thus clear is that (i) Egyptian policy in Phoenicia was the same as always—good relations—and doubtless for the usual reason: Egypt always needed good Phoenician timber; and (ii) Shoshenq I was a new man,

---

28. That is, "Olive-Grove of Padalla," and not Ginti-Padalla ("Garden of Padalla"); the Egyptian *ḏ* reproduces the West Semitic *z*, but not *g*. The same location is doubtless intended.

29. For references, see Kitchen 1996a: 292–93 n. 283.

founder of a new dynasty, and favored a radically different policy in nearby Canaan. His actions with regard to Jeroboam imply that he viewed the Solomonic realm as a hindrance to his own possible aims for expansion, while the little Philistine pentapolis did not. The latter he could doubtless handle, if need be, as Siamun had done.[30] But the Hebrew power needed to be broken up, and he succeeded brilliantly.

But why did Shoshenq wait so long, until his Year 20 or so? Here two sets of factors can be suggested.

(a) First, internal factors. In the 21st Dynasty, Egypt had been politically divided, with the official kings ruling in the north at Memphis (Egypt's permanent capital) and Tanis (the dynastic hometown and gateway to the Levant), while Upper Egypt was, in practice, the fiefdom of a related dynasty of military governors who also doubled as high priests of Amun of Thebes and occasionally also claimed kingly status. No imperial dreams could be entertained in such circumstances; trade was a cheaper path to wealth. Shoshenq I systematically changed all this, appointing his own second son, Iuput, as the military commander and high priest for the south, installing his own nominees in some important offices, and arranging marriages of his daughters to scions of local nonroyal Theban notables (no Amenophis III snobbery here). He could thus in 10 or 15 years rebuild a united and strong state.

(b) Second, external factors. In Canaan there were three classes of power. One was the Philistine pentapolis, probably involved in trade, but not in military adventures except with its immediate Hebrew and Canaanite neighbors. Then there was a handful of residual city-states, such as the old Canaanite city at Gezer and "new" "Sea Peoples" such as the Sikils at Dor (attested also in the Wenamun report of ca. 1080 B.C.E.). Neither of these would affect Egyptian ambition, except in trade matters. But then there was a strong kingdom ruling the main areas of Canaan, with varying overlordships in Transjordan to the east and in Syria to the north, which (like Egypt) had relations with Phoenicia (Tyre). This Hebrew kingdom was rumored to be wealthy, again mainly from trade. It was a suitable prize for any Egyptian pharaoh who could deliver a swift military blow. But Egypt had never attempted anything on that scale since at least the time of Ramesses III, some 250 years before. So it seemed wiser to the canny Shoshenq to work first for the breakup of this (Solomon's) kingdom and then to await whatever seemed the best opportunity to invade, loot the rump-kingdoms, and reduce them to permanent tribute-paying vassalage. All went well, and he returned with the booty.

Immediately, Shoshenq I went on a temple-building spree, the like of which had not been seen in Egypt since the splendid days of Ramesses II himself, or even Ramesses III. At the Karnak temple in Thebes he ordered the building of a vast new colonnaded forecourt (still the largest in all Egypt), a major gateway (the "Bubastite Gate"), and a very large triumphal relief to celebrate his victory. The last was quickest built and carved, so it is essentially complete; the gate was built but the decor only begun; while the huge court and its colonnades were left unfinished and undecorated at his sudden death. This was a scheme of truly imperial dimensions. At El-Hiba a temple was also built and a beautifully

---

30. One of the few useful suggestions by Clancy (1999: 19) is that the Philistines might have aided and abetted Shoshenq I as he launched his campaign. Gaza, it should be remembered, was Egypt's usual base camp for campaigns in Palestine.

executed triumph scene carved; only tiny bits now survive. At Memphis, the capital, he added a vast forecourt to the Temple of Ptah, the twin of that at Karnak, known from his texts and Herodotus. All this cost money, lots of money; nothing like this program had been seen since Ramesses II himself. (Even at Tanis, the 21st Dynasty had built a more modest temple within its large mud-brick temple-enclosure; significantly, it was Siamun who prefaced that temple with a large court—on Philistine wealth?)

When one adds to the cost of Shoshenq I's grandiose buildings the huge but detailed expenditure of most of 400 tons of silver and gold on specific gifts to temples by his son and successor, Osorkon I, in the first four years of his reign immediately after his father's death, then one really has to ask a serious question: where did all this wealth come from? If it was not new wealth, how is it that previous kings had not already exploited this internal wealth in the service of the gods, as pharaohs were wont to do? Gradual growth from trade hardly seems a viable alternative either. Thus, if the Hebrew united monarchy had indeed amassed wealth within its central palace and Temple complex at Jerusalem, then its forced transfer to Egypt would have formed a large component of the sudden, uncharacteristic, almost obscene "lottery-style" explosion of spending by Shoshenq and Osorkon (who could still afford a solid silver coffin for his co-regent, over a generation later . . .).[31] This also explains why archaeologists will never find any Solomonic wealth at sites outside Jerusalem, nor (given the physical state of Jerusalem's ancient ruins) in Jerusalem itself; Shoshenq beat them to it. He didn't find a "cow-town," but financially he left one![32]

If Shoshenq I had reigned 31 years instead of just 21, what would have happened? (a) He would have completed his great works at Karnak and elsewhere. (b) He would have maintained his imperial image by keeping Judah and Israel in vassal status, marked by the Megiddo stela (cf. triumphal stelae of Sethos I and Ramesses II in the Levant).[33] (c) He probably would have sought to extend his power over the Aramean and Transjordanian neighbors of Judah and Israel—and over Phoenicia as well, if it did not do his bidding. The disposition of what he did at Karnak is entirely imperialistic, deliberately on a par with the surrounding works of the Ramesside and Tuthmoside kings there, and likewise at Memphis and El-Hiba in principle. His sudden death removed this threat from the Levant, and his successors clearly did not have the drive, ability, or abiding ambition to follow his path. The peculiar Zerah incident noted in Chronicles (2 Chr 14:9–15) may reflect a half-hearted attempt by Osorkon I (in whose time it occurs) to send out a general with a large (ill-trained?) force on a raid like his father's, which failed; thereafter, no other Libyan pharaoh tried his luck in this area. He did better, no doubt, in trade with Byblos, where a splendid statue of his was inscribed also by his local contemporary, King Elibaal of

---

31. For basic references, see Kitchen 1996a: 303–4, §262; on the use of ex-Solomonic gold, see Millard and Kitchen 1989: 30 and passim. For the silver coffin of Shoshenq II, see Montet 1951: 61–62, pls. 17–20.

32. This whole point is not understood by Weinstein (1998: 193 n. 11). The wealth of Late Bronze Age Syria is well illustrated by the finds (gold dishes, etc.) and texts of Ugarit; farther south, Canaan could not grow so wealthy during Egyptian overlordship. In the Iron Age I, from the later 12th century B.C.E., no great wealth would be found initially; but soon the Phoenician ports began to serve traders in the eastern Mediterranean (see already the Wenamun Report), and Levantine trade generally would begin to develop. A David would have taken over the resources of Hadadezer's short-lived imperium and drawn on Hamath as a vassal. Solomon's trading ventures cannot be peremptorily dismissed, as some would do (cf. Kitchen; Millard [vs. Miller] in Handy 1997).

33. A point noted also by Ussishkin (1990: 72–73) and duly followed by Schipper (1999: 131–32).

Byblos.[34] In short, Shoshenq I would have imposed and maintained an Egyptian "hegemony" over Canaan (and eventually even beyond); but he died without being able to realize this aim, and no successor made the same effort or (in most cases) any effort at all to re-impose Egyptian rule in the Levant.

2. The Middle and Late Libyan Kings. From the discovery of part of a third royal statue at Byblos (Dunand 1937/39: 1.115–16, no. 1741, pl. 43), it is clear that Osorkon II maintained there the same good relations as his predecessors. Except for one shadow of growing proportions, the 22nd Dynasty from then onward was content to trade with its neighbors, not to try to dominate them—a reversion to 21st-Dynasty practice, and for much the same reason. The Thebans in the south sought greater independence from the kings in Tanis and Memphis. When Pedubast I founded his own line of kings (23rd Dynasty), probably in Leontopolis, southwest of the 22nd Dynasty in Tanis/Bubastis, the Thebans eagerly dated their records by the new line and rejected Shoshenq III and the 22nd Dynasty—back to a divided regime, as in the 21st Dynasty. Thereafter other local governors and kinglets took the whole process of fission even further, until in 728 B.C.E. Egypt had four full kings, one line of permanent "heirs-apparent," and a whole series of local Libyan chiefs.[35]

The growing shadow, of course, was Assyria. Prior to 859 B.C.E., since the late 13th century B.C.E., only two kings, Tiglath-pileser I and Assur-bel-kala, had penetrated west of the Euphrates (11th/10th centuries B.C.E.),[36] until Assur-nasir-pal II in the 880s–860s B.C.E. resumed the westward march, penetrating well into northern Syria. His successor, Shalmaneser III, repeated this exploit, only to face the united opposition of most of the petty kings of the Levant in the indecisive Battle of Qarqar in 853 B.C.E. Shalmaneser lists his opponents, one being Ahab of Israel, while soldiers were sent even from Musri, in this context, from Egypt. This event occurred late in the reign of Osorkon II; a damaged alabaster presentation-vessel (for 81 hin of precious fluid) was found in the Israelite palace at Samaria.[37] Thus, it appears that Osorkon II felt obliged to send a contingent to support his Levantine neighbors, as a shield against the advance of Assyria, and had had diplomatic exchanges with Ahab to that end. In or soon after 841 B.C.E., as shown on the "Black Obelisk," Shalmaneser III received "tribute of the land of Musri" (Egypt), including exotic African animals (hippos, rhinos, elephants, monkeys, etc.).[38] Thus, Takeloth II (850–825 B.C.E.) may have sought to appease the Assyrian ruler and keep him at bay.

---

34. For references, see Kitchen 1996a: 308–9 nn. 369–70. For a recent color photo, see Yoyotte 1987: 167.

35. See Kitchen 1996a: 334ff., with an update on recent controversy on pp. xxi–xxxiv.

36. The latest edition of their texts is in Grayson 1991: 5ff. (Tiglath-pileser I), 86ff. (Assur-bel-kala).

37. Such use had long since been made of alabaster vessels with royal cartouches in the 18th and 19th Dynasties, as finds at Ugarit demonstrate. This vessel is no different, except for having a fluid measure added, and trade can be excluded in such cases. Schipper's attempt (1999: 173–78) to exclude the statues of Shoshenq I, Osorkon I, and Osorkon II from being evidence of direct Egypto-Byblite relations in favor of some mysterious trade in royal statues (after Helck and Alt) is far-fetched. What possible value could there have been in such a useless proceeding?

38. The attempt by Schipper (1999: 144–49) to avoid the clear meaning of Musri as Egypt in Shalmaneser's texts is equally weak; there was no north Syrian Musri (cf. Tadmor 1961; Röllig 1994; Kessler 1997), and since when did rhinoceroses (cf. Heimpel 1999 [Africa and India, not Syria]) and monkeys (cf. Hilzheimer 1932: 41–42) flourish as natives at any time in Syria?

For almost a century, while Assyria was engrossed in the Levant and elsewhere, Egypt could slumber and quietly fall to pieces politically. But in 728 B.C.E., Piye ("Piankhy"), king of the culturally semi-Egyptianized Nubian state of Kush, swept down the Nile to safeguard his ascendancy over Thebes, capital of his god Amun. He pursued Tefnakht I of Sais (west Delta) all the way back north to Memphis and received the obeisance of all the other kinglets and chiefs—including Osorkon IV and Iuput II, the last scions of the 22nd and 23rd Dynasties, respectively.

Barely three years later, in 726/725 B.C.E., Hoshea of Israel rebelled against Shal-maneser V of Assyria and sought help from "So, king of Egypt" (2 Kgs 17:4). No help came; Hoshea lost his throne, and Israel as a kingdom disappeared. Much fuss, inevitably, has been made over "So." But ruling in Egypt's east Delta nearest to Canaan was the 22nd Dynasty in Tanis/Bubastis; and in 725 B.C.E., the king was certainly Osorkon IV, attested in 728 B.C.E. by Piye of Kush, then as (U)shilkanni by Sargon II of Assyria in 716 B.C.E. He would also most likely have been the ruler who sent the general Re'e to support Gaza against Assyria in 720 B.C.E. Despite noisy advocacy to the contrary, "So" cannot be the town of Sais in the depths of the west Delta swamplands, 100 miles farther away, a town that never played any political role whatsoever in Levantine affairs, not even during the 26th Dynasty, which came from there—they had Memphis as the traditional capital and used Tanis for links with western Asia. The attempts to read "So" in 2 Kgs 17:4 as "Sais" are futile (as Aḥituv 1998); they require gratuitous textual emendations, and the context demands a personal name of a king. Furthermore, $S(w)^{\gamma}$ is not the proper conso-nantal frame for the town name "Sais" ($S^{\gamma}y/S^{\gamma}w$). The scholars who unwisely cite Goe-dicke's long-outdated paper (1963) on "So = Sais" (which is riddled with other, clearly factual errors) merely display their gross ignorance on the subject. There are, in contrast, many good reasons for treating "So" as a personal name and as an abbreviation of "(O)so(rkon)."[39] Contrary to assertions by some scholars, Egyptian royal names of this period do appear in abbreviated form(s), for example, Shosh for Shoshenq; and Egyptian names in the Hebrew Bible are sometimes abbreviated (e.g., Hophra for [Wa]hibre). Osor-kon IV himself appears as <U>shilkanni in Assyria, and once as Osork<on>in Egypt. Among the graffiti on the roof of the Temple of Khons at Thebes, we find a king whose nomen is written with the sign *ini* or *isi*,[40] that is, "On" or "So," depending on which is the best reading; either could be an abbreviation for Osorkon (but certainly not for any other 22nd/23rd-Dynasty name), in this case Osorkon III. It may be added that Osorkon IV is solidly attested monumentally by a sculptured block from one of his buildings (similar in style to the work of his predecessor Shoshenq V at Tanis); by an elaborate faience finger ring, almost certainly from a silver-gilt aegis (now in the Louvre); and from Piye's stela.[41] He is distinct from all other 22nd/23rd-Dynasty Osorkons by his prenomen (Akheperre Setepenamun) and by the name of his mother (or wife), Tadibast. By now, his status should be clear.

---

39. See in detail in Kitchen 1996a: 372–76, 551–52, xxxiv–xxxix.

40. For these texts, see Jacquet-Gordon 1979: 169–73 (Shoshenq VI?; Iny/Sy; cf. Kitchen 1996a: 342 n. 551).

41. For all these items, especially the block and ring, see Schneider 1985.

In terms of history, Osorkon IV can be seen first to have avoided military action in 726/725 B.C.E., because Hoshea of Samaria was too far away to become involved with him. Then in 720 B.C.E., since Gaza was much nearer to Egypt, he ventured to support Hanun of Gaza against Sargon II by sending out Reʿe with forces—but to no avail. Thus, in 716 B.C.E., with the Assyrians on his doorstep at El-Arish well along the northern Sinai coastal road, Osorkon IV finally decided to grovel his way out of possible trouble, sending a gift of 12 large horses (doubtless the best that he could muster). Thereafter, the Assyrian presence receded for over a decade, and with the Kushite king Shabako taking over Egypt in 715 B.C.E. (or soon after), Osorkon disappears. So ran the gamut of Libyan foreign policy in Egypt, from the triumphant Shoshenq I in 925 B.C.E., through the neutrality/limited action/gift-giving of Osorkon II and Takeloth II in 853–841 B.C.E., to the final groveling of Osorkon IV in 716 B.C.E. There was no Egyptian hegemony by then.

III. Egypt, Kush, and the Levant in the Late 8th–Early 6th Centuries B.C.E.

"Assyria Came Down like a Wolf on the Fold." In 712 B.C.E., Sargon II's forces moved to quell a revolt in Ashkelon, and its rebel ruler Iamani fled to Egypt and, having failed (we are told) to bribe Pirʾu of Musri ("Pharaoh of Egypt"), went south to Nubia (*Meluhha*), whose ruler (Assyr.: "king") repatriated him into Assyrian hands. As I pointed out some 30 years ago (1973: 143–44), the sole "Pharaoh" of all Egypt at the time was Shabako, not Osorkon IV (for whom the Assyrians did not exclusively use this title). Spalinger's dissenting view (1973: 100) is refuted by the firsthand evidence of documents dated by the pertinent Kushite "pharaohs" of Egypt: "Pharaoh Pi(ankh)y"; "Pharaoh Shabako"; and "Pharaoh Taharqa" (Kitchen 1996a: xlii). Because Sargon's records mention the Pirʾu of Musri also in the seventh year, 715 B.C.E. (*Annals*, lines 123–25), this could also take Shabako's rule in Egypt back to 715 B.C.E., a date for his takeover in Egypt that I long since advocated (1973: 143–44). But who is the "king of Meluhha" mentioned in the 712 B.C.E. records? Until now, we have all assumed it to be Shabako. But the recently published Tang-i Var text of Sargon II (706 B.C.E., referring back to 712 B.C.E.) names this ruler explicitly as "Shapataka," a good rendering of Shabataka (Manethonic Sebichos, our Shebitku).[42] Despite the fears of the text's first editor (Frame 1999) and commentator (Redford 1999), this does not change our chronology at all—only our knowledge of the mode of government of the vast north–south line of the Kushite/Egyptian domain. The Assyrian term *sharru* does not prove that Shebitku held full pharaonic rank in 712ff. B.C.E. Assyrian scribes describe every class of foreign potentate as *sharru*, regardless of whether they were really major kings or just town mayors (cf. Assurbanipal's lists of Delta rulers a little later). Shebitku was probably Shabako's Nubian viceroy for Shabako's entire reign, for administrative purposes, whatever title Shebitku himself actually held then.

We come now to 701 B.C.E., and the tiny phrase *melek-Kush*, "King of Kush," attached to the name of Taharqa (in 2 Kgs 19:9; Isa 37:9), a participant against Sennacherib in Palestine in that year. Despite the fact that this matter was definitively resolved

---

42. Frame 1999: especially pp. 36, 40 (line 20), 52–54; Redford 1999.

almost 30 years ago,[43] people still write nonsense about it (the two-campaign mirage, etc.).[44] I will simply reiterate the facts. The Hebrew narratives as we have them cannot predate 681 B.C.E., because they end by reporting Sennacherib's death, which happened that year, when Taharqa had been king of Egypt and Kush for 10 years already. It is nothing more than simple prolepsis, a universal usage, which Taharqa himself employs on his own stelae (Kawa IV; Kitchen 1996a: 160). He was in his twenties in 701 B.C.E., and (with a group of generals) well able to lead an army, especially into defeat! Of course, there is nothing to stop hypercritics from simply treating this tiny phrase as a later gloss if they wish, which would remain subjective and unprovable. More recently identified texts of Taharqa at Karnak do nothing whatsoever to prove that he actually warred in Palestine as king within 690–664 B.C.E. One large, broken, anonymous stela (no cartouches)[45] mentions timber from Lebanon, but this is almost always the product of trade, not war. Other fragments are purely rhetorical; Janssen long since dealt with Taharqa's spurious repute as a conqueror in late tradition (1953: 34, following Goossens 1947). There is no warrant yet for any second Sennacherib/Taharqa clash after 701 B.C.E. For the rest of Assyria's invasions of Egypt in 674ff. B.C.E. and Egypt's interventions in the Levant under the 26th Dynasty, there is little or nothing new factually. The one point worth stressing is that there was no extended Egyptian rule in the Levant then, because the Neo-Babylonian kings effectively fought off the Egyptians (albeit with an occasional defeat by them, as in 601 B.C.E.).

IV. Conclusion

I deliberately chose the term "interventions" of Egypt in the Levant to replace the hopelessly optimistic term "hegemony" used by the symposium organizers. At no time between 1100 and 580 B.C.E. did Egypt succeed in establishing a true "hegemony." Siamun may have held Philistia as vassal within the time-span of 970–960 B.C.E. Shoshenq I's triumph was short-lived (dead within a year or so of his campaign). Almost nobody else even attempted Levantine expansion, until Shebitku and Taharqa's opposition to Sennacherib failed in 701 B.C.E., and Necho II's ambitions were swiftly thwarted by Babylon.

---

43. See the full data and discussions presented in Kitchen 1996a: 158–61, 383–86, 552–59, 584–85, xxxix–xlii.

44. For examples of misunderstanding, see Shea 1985; 1999. Gallagher (1999: 221–22) has simply dismissed the matter, saying that he cannot contribute anything new and that the phrase is an anachronism; but he fails entirely to consider the facts summarized here (given in full in Kitchen 1996a). He also makes a hash of the point on prolepsis. His "Dwight D. Eisenhower, president of the United States" parody will not do. A correct parallel would be the simple phrase, "President Eisenhower"; the equivalent of his parody would have been "Lord of Both Lands, Nefertumkhure, Son of Re, Taharqa, King of Kush." But the Hebrew text does not give this, so his case fails. Shea's contention (1999: 64 n. 3) that prolepsis "does not work" is the opposite of the truth; 698 B.C.E. is *not* the proven accession date of Shebitku, and it would make nonsense of the major troop movement undertaken for him by Taharqa following his accession. Shea's appeal to Redford's (1993) "Taharqa" stela is to an anonymous monument with no royal name, in which the flood mentioned may not have occurred during the reign of Taharqa, and the captives may have been Libyan, not Levantine. Shea is completely out of touch with non-American scholarship, which is fatal in this case.

45. Published in Redford 1993; his attribution to Taharqa is possible, but over confident; other notable inundations occurred, like the one in Year 3 of Osorkon III's reign (see references in Kitchen 1996a: 342 n. 557).

Excursus 1: Chronology

It has been claimed by Ash (1999: 27–30) that the death of Solomon and the accession of Rehoboam is undatable within a 55-year time-span, 979–922 B.C.E. (variant, ca. 970–915 B.C.E.; Ash 1999: 26, 30); that Egyptian 10th–7th-century dates are unreliable; and that dead-reckoning them back from the fixed date of 664 B.C.E. (the start of the 26th Dynasty) is "impossible" (his word). These claims are spurious. These dates have *already* been successfully dead-reckoned back from 664 B.C.E., from original data, not simply Manetho (and no imaginary eclipses). In the 25th Dynasty, Taharqa reigned from 690 to 664 B.C.E. Before him, Shebitku (at 12 years; cf. Manetho if one wishes) caused Prince Taharqa to bring troops almost 2,000 miles north from Nubia in 702/701 B.C.E. for his anti-Sennacherib campaign in 701 B.C.E.; and Shabako before him reigned 14 years (13 over Egypt), from 716/715 B.C.E., being the Pir'u of Musri of 715 and 712 B.C.E. Nubian rulers were called "pharaoh" in contemporary papyri (Pharaoh Piye, Pharaoh Shabako, and Pharaoh Taharqa); Osorkon IV generally was not, as pointed out above.

Before 715 B.C.E., the 10 kings of the Libyan 22nd Dynasty reigned 227 years at an absolute minimum, 230 years at the optimal minimum—back, thus, to 945 B.C.E. (absolute minimum, 942 B.C.E.) for the accession of Shoshenq I. There is no 50-year range here, nor in Palestine. Shalmaneser III guarantees us that Ahab lived until 853 B.C.E. and that Jehu ascended the throne by 841 B.C.E.; the intervening Hebrew kings fit exactly into this interval on non-accession-dating, the system of Egypt, whence Jeroboam I came to begin his kingdom. Biblical data then begin his reign in 931/30 B.C.E. accordingly. Going back again from 841 B.C.E., the Judean kings (back to Rehoboam) fit the same time-span very closely. Note that both Thiele (1951/1965) and Galil (1996), the only serious chronologers for the Hebrew monarchy (both sidestepped by Ash [1999]), also reach this conclusion from differing and independent approaches. Shoshenq I's campaign fell late in his reign, because he commissioned his Karnak works (not just the triumph scene) in Year 21, and all except the scene were left unfinished at his sudden death. His Year 19 or 20 and Year 5 of Rehoboam would coincide very well. Ash's negative approach is false here (as often elsewhere).

References

Albright, W. F.
  1955   New Light on Early Recensions of the Hebrew Bible. *Bulletin of the American Schools of Oriental Research* 140: 27–33.
Altenmüller, H., and Moussa, A.
  1991   Die Inschrift Amenemhets II. aus dem Ptah-Tempel von Memphis: Ein Vorbericht. *Studien zur Altägyptischen Kultur* 18: 1–48, Taf. 1 and folding plate.
Ash, P.
  1999   *David, Solomon and Egypt: A Reassessment.* Journal for the Study of the Old Testament Supplement Series 297. Sheffield: Sheffield Academic Press.
Aḥituv, S.
  1998   Egypt That Isaiah Knew. Pp. 3–7 in *Jerusalem Studies in Egyptology*, ed. I. Shirun-Grumach. Ägypten und Altes Testament 40. Wiesbaden: Harrassowitz.
Borger, R.
  1961   *Einleitung in die assyrischen Königsinschriften, Erster Teil: Das zweite Jahrtausend v. Chr.* Handbuch der Orientalistik Ergänzungsband 5/1/1. Leiden: Brill.

Breasted, J. H.
    1906   *Ancient Records of Egypt*, vols. 1–4. Chicago: University of Chicago Press.
Brug, J. F.
    1985   *A Literary and Archaeological Study of the Philistines*. British Archaeological Reports International Series 265. Oxford: British Archaeological Reports.
Caminos, R. A.
    1954   *Late-Egyptian Miscellanies*. Brown Egyptological Studies 1. London: Oxford University Press (Cumberlege).
    1977   *A Tale of Woe: From a Hieratic Papyrus in the A. S. Pushkin Museum of Fine Arts in Moscow*. Oxford: Ashmolean Museum.
Clancy, F.
    1999   Shishak/Shoshenq's Travels. *Journal for the Study of the Old Testament* 86: 3–23.
Dunand, M.
    1937/39   *Les fouilles de Byblos*, part 1. Bibliothèque historique et archéologique 24. Paris: Geuthner.
Edel, E.
    1994   *Die ägyptisch-hethitische Korrespondenz aus Boghazköi in babylonischer und hethitischer Sprache I–II*. Opladen: Westdeutscher Verlag.
Edelman, D. V.
    1995   Solomon's Adversaries Hadad, Rezon and Jeroboam: A Trio of "Bad Guy" Characters Illustrating the Theology of Immediate Retribution. Pp. 166–91 in *The Pitcher Is Broken*, ed. S. W. Holloway and L. K. Handy. Journal for the Study of the Old Testament Supplement Series 190. Sheffield: Sheffield Academic Press.
Epstein, C.
    1963   A New Appraisal of Some Lines from a Long-Known Papyrus. *Journal of Egyptian Archaeology* 49: 49–56.
Federn, W.
    1960   Daḫamunzu. *Journal of Cuneiform Studies* 14: 33.
Frame, G.
    1999   The Inscription of Sargon II at Tang-i Var. *Orientalia* 68: 31–57, pls. 1–18.
Galil, G.
    1996   *The Chronology of the Kings of Israel and Judah*. Studies in the Culture and History of the Ancient Near East 9. Leiden: Brill.
Gallagher, W. R.
    1999   *Sennacherib's Campaign to Judah*. Studies in the Culture and History of the Ancient Near East 18. Leiden: Brill.
Gardiner, Sir A. H.
    1961   *Egypt of the Pharaohs*. Oxford: Clarendon.
Giveon, R.
    1972   An Egyptian Official in Gezer? *Israel Exploration Journal* 22: 143–44.
Goedicke, H.
    1963   The End of "So, King of Egypt." *Bulletin of the American Schools of Oriental Research* 171: 64–66.
Goossens, G.
    1947   Taharqa le conquérant. *Chronique d'Égypte* 22: 239–44.
Grayson, A. K.
    1991   *Assyrian Rulers of the Early First Millennium BC I (1114–859 BC)*. The Royal Inscriptions of Mesopotamia, Assyrian Periods 2. Toronto: University of Toronto Press.
Grdseloff, B.
    1947   Édôm d'après les sources égyptiennes. *Revue de l'Histoire Juive en Égypte* 1: 69–99.
Green, A. R.
    1978   Solomon and Siamun: A Synchronism between Early Dynastic Israel and the Twenty-First Dynasty of Egypt. *Journal of Biblical Literature* 97: 353–67.

Handy, L. K. (ed.)
1997   *The Age of Solomon: Scholarship at the Turn of the Millennium.* Leiden: Brill.
Heimpel, W.
1999   Nashorn. P. 185 in vol. 9, part 3/4 of *Reallexikon der Assyriologie und Vorderasiatischen Archäologie,* ed. D. O. Edzard et al. Berlin: de Gruyter.
Hilzheimer, F.
1932   Affe. Pp. 41–42 in vol. 1 of *Reallexikon der Assyriologie und Vorderasiatischen Archäologie,* ed. E. Ebeling and B. Meissner. Berlin: de Gruyter.
Jacquet-Gordon, H.
1979   Deux graffiti de l'époque libyenne sur le toit du temple de Khonsou à Karnak. Pp. 167–83 in vol. 1 of *Hommages à la mémoire de Serge Sauneron,* ed. J. Vercoutter. Cairo: Institut Français d'Archèologie Orientale.
Janssen, J. M. A.
1953   Que sait-on actuellement du Pharaon Taharqa? *Biblica* 34: 23–43.
Kessler, K.
1997   Musri I, Musri II. P. 497 in vol. 8, part 7/8 of *Reallexikon der Assyriologie und Vorderasiatischen Archäologie,* ed. D. O. Edzard et al. Berlin: de Gruyter.
Kitchen, K. A.
1973   *The Third Intermediate Period in Egypt (1100–650 BC).* 1st ed. Warminster: Aris & Phillips.
1992   The Egyptian Evidence on Ancient Jordan. Pp. 21–34 in *Early Edom and Moab: The Beginning of the Iron Age in Southern Jordan,* ed. P. Bienkowski. Sheffield Archaeological Monographs 7. Sheffield: Collis.
1996a   *The Third Intermediate Period in Egypt (1100–650 BC).* Rev. 2nd ed. Warminster: Aris & Phillips.
1996b   *Ramesside Inscriptions, Translated & Annotated: Translations,* vol. 2. Oxford: Blackwell.
1997   A Possible Mention of David in the Late Tenth Century BCE, and Deity *Dod as Dead as the Dodo? *Journal for the Study of the Old Testament* 76: 29–44.
1999a   *Ramesside Inscriptions, Translated & Annotated: Notes & Comments,* vol. 2. Oxford: Blackwell.
1999b   *Poetry of Ancient Egypt.* Documenta Mundi: Aegyptiaca 1. Jonsered: Åströms.
Lance, H. D.
1976   Solomon, Siamun and the Double-Ax. Pp. 209–23 in *Magnalia Dei: The Mighty Acts of God. Essays on the Bible and Archaeology in Memory of G. Ernest Wright,* ed. F. M. Cross, P. D. Miller, and W. E. Lemke. New York: Doubleday.
Lange, K., and Hirmer, M.
1961   *Egypt: Architecture, Sculpture, Painting.* 3rd ed. London: Phaidon.
Malek, J., and Quirke, S.
1992   Memphis, 1991: Epigraphy. *Journal of Egyptian Archaeology* 78: 13–18.
Millard, A. R., and Kitchen, K. A.
1989   Does the Bible Exaggerate King Solomon's Wealth? Where Did Solomon's Gold Go? Shishak's Military Campaign in Israel Confirmed. *Biblical Archaeology Review* 15/3: 20–34.
Montet, P.
1947   *Les constructions et le tombeau d'Osorkon II à Tanis.* La nécropole de Tanis 1. Paris: [Fouilles de Tanis, Mission Montet].
1951   *Les constructions et le tombeau de Psousennès à Tanis.* La nécropole de Tanis 2. Paris: [Fouilles de Tanis, Mission Montet].
Muchiki, Y.
1999   *Egyptian Proper Names and Loanwords in North-West Semitic.* Society of Biblical Literature Dissertation Series 173. Atlanta: Society of Biblical Literature.
Ranke, H.
n.d.   *Die ägyptischen Personnamen,* vols. 1–2. Glückstadt/Hamburg: Augustin.

Redford, D. B.
    1993   Taharqa in Western Asia and Libya. Pp. 188*–191* in *Eretz-Israel* 24 (Abraham Malamat volume), ed. S. Aḥituv and B. A. Levine. Jerusalem: Israel Exploration Society.
    1999   A Note on the Chronology of Dynasty 25 and the Inscription of Sargon II at Tang-i Var. *Orientalia* 68: 58–60.
Rohl, D. M.
    1995   *A Test of Time 1: The Bible from Myth to History.* London: Century.
Röllig, W.
    1994   Misir, Mizru, Musur, Musri III, Muzir. Pp. 264–69 in vol. 8, part 3/4 of *Reallexikon der Assyriologie und Vorderasiatischen Archäologie*, ed. D. O. Edzard et al. Berlin: de Gruyter.
Schipper, B. U.
    1999   *Israel und Ägypten in der Königszeit: Die kulturellen Kontakt von Salomo bis zum Fall Jerusalems.* Orbis Biblicus et Orientalis 170. Freiburg: Universitätsverlag.
Schneider, H. D.
    1985   A Royal Epigone of the 22nd Dynasty. Pp. 261–67, pl. 1, in vol. 2 of *Mélanges Gamal Eddin Mokhtar*, ed. P. Posener-Kriéger. Cairo: Institut Français d'Archéologie Orientale.
Schott, S.
    1965   Aufnahmen vom Hungersnotrelief aus dem Aufweg der Unaspyramide. *Revue d'Égyptologie* 17: 1–13, pls. 1–4.
Shea, W. H.
    1985   Sennacherib's Second Palestinian Campaign. *Journal of Biblical Literature* 104: 401–18.
    1999   Jerusalem under Siege: Did Sennacherib Attack Twice? *Biblical Archaeology Review* 25/6: 36–44, 64.
Soggin, J. A.
    1994   *An Introduction to the History of Israel and Judah.* Valley Forge, Pa.: Trinity.
Spalinger, A. J.
    1973   The Year 712 B.C. and Its Implications for Egyptian History. *Journal of the American Research Center in Egypt* 10: 95–101.
Tadmor, H.
    1961   Que and Musri. *Israel Exploration Journal* 11: 143–50.
Thiele, E. R.
    1951/   *The Mysterious Numbers of the Hebrew Kings.* 1st ed., Chicago: University of Chicago Press.
    1965   2nd ed., Grand Rapids: Eerdmans.
Ussishkin, D.
    1990   Notes on Megiddo, Gezer, Ashdod and Tel Batash in the Tenth to Ninth Centuries BC. *Bulletin of the American Schools of Oriental Research* 277–78: 71–91.
Weinstein, J.
    1998   Egyptian Relations with the Eastern Mediterranean World at the End of the Second Millennium BCE. Pp. 188–96 in *Mediterranean Peoples in Transition: Thirteenth to Early Tenth Centuries BCE*, ed. S. Gitin, A. Mazar, and E. Stern. Jerusalem: Israel Exploration Society.
Wilkinson, T. A. H.
    2000   *Royal Annals of Ancient Egypt: The Palermo Stone and Its Associated Fragments.* London: Kegan Paul.
Wilson, J. A.
    1950   Egyptian Historical Texts. Pp. 227–64 in *Ancient Near Eastern Texts Relating to the Old Testament*, ed. J. B. Pritchard. Princeton: Princeton University Press.
Wu, Y., and Dalley, S.
    1990   The Origins of the Manana Dynasty at Kish, and the Assyrian King List. *Iraq* 52: 159–65.
Yoyotte, J.
    1987   Tanis au temps des rois tanites et libyens. *Archéologia* 223: 30–39.

Early Achaemenid Iran: New Considerations

David Stronach
Department of Near Eastern Studies
University of California, Berkeley

In contrast to the thrust of many other papers presented at this symposium that have sought to explore questions pertaining to areas of inquiry that stand more or less directly within the purview of the W. F. Albright Institute, I would like to present—on this, the occasion of the Institute's 100th anniversary—a varied range of considerations that in one way or another may be said to bear on the emergence of two of the most consequential rulers of early Iran: Cyrus II, who ruled from 559 to 530, and Darius I, who reigned from 522 to 486.[1] In one sense, these partly novel perspectives may be said to depend on new and hitherto unsuspected links between southern Iran and southeastern Arabia in the early first millennium, and in another sense they may be said to derive from the nature of the rich contents of a tomb of the first half of the 6th century that chanced to be discovered at Arjan, in the southern highlands of Iran, some 20 years ago (fig. 1).

The Arrival of the Persians

It is perhaps necessary to begin by noting that there are markedly few sites or objects that can be used to document the early, formative phases of Achaemenid Iran's political and cultural evolution. Fifty years ago, one of the more noted authorities on early Iran, Roman Ghirshman, attempted to trace the route by which the Persians reached what he saw to be their initial southern destination in the late 8th century, namely, the vicinity of Masjid-i Suleiman and Susa (fig. 1). He then sought to document, with close reference to the location of two uninscribed tombs, the subsequent stages by which the Persians moved eastward in order to reach their ultimate homeland in Fars where, not least, the site of Pasargadae was presumed to have been founded by Cambyses, the father of Cyrus, at some date before 559 (Ghirshman 1954: 75; 1964: 129–31).

Unfortunately, virtually every signpost on this particular road map was misread. In particular, it deserves to be noted that Masjid-i Suleiman, a supposed first royal town of the Persians (Ghirshman 1964: 131), was probably not founded before the 5th century (Stronach 1974: 246; 1978: 283) and that both the rock-cut tomb of Da-u Dukhtar and the free-standing Buzpar tomb (also known as Gur-i Dokhtar), far from dating to before the accession of Cyrus II, can only be ascribed to late Achaemenid or post-Achaemenid times (Stronach 1978: 284). Furthermore, recent studies of the stoneworking techniques employed at Pasargadae have discredited the notion that any part of the site could have been

---

1. All dates are B.C.E.

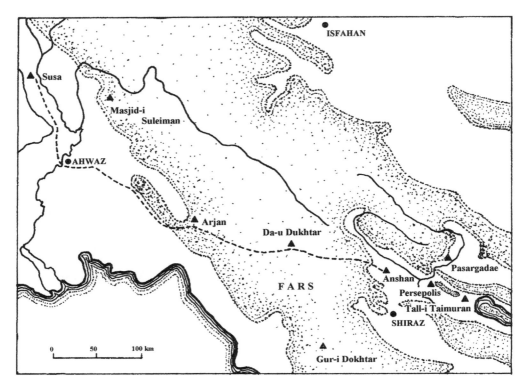

Fig. 1. Map of southwestern Iran, showing sites mentioned in the text.

founded before the reign of Cyrus; instead, it is now abundantly clear that the state-of-the-art Lydo-Ionian masonry that is a special hallmark of Cyrus's elegant capital could only have been introduced following the fall of Sardis in or close to 547 (Nylander 1970: 77–91; Stronach 1978: 22–23; and most recently, Boardman 2000: 51–65).

In more recent years, Sumner (1994) has explored a very different approach to the issue of the arrival of the Persians. In his view, the Persians could have been expected to arrive in Fars from the north or the east; and from either of these directions, they could then have been expected to penetrate, or at least reach the borders of, the historic region of Anshan—the ancient highland hub of Elamite civilization that at some point in the 6th century came to be called Parsa (from which manifestly Persian name the modern toponym for the region, Fars, is itself derived).

From the perspective of his own excavations at Tall-i Malyan—a site now known to have been the time-honored city of Anshan—and on the basis of the comprehensive surface surveys he conducted throughout the surrounding fertile region of the Marvdasht Plain, Sumner drew attention to one outstanding moment of change in the local ceramic sequence. This equates, in his estimation, with the moment in approximately 1600, when the still-nomadic Persians might well have reached "the land of Anshan." At this time, the previously ubiquitous local Kaftari pottery is supplanted by related Qaleh wares throughout the western part of the Marvdasht, while two apparently intrusive wares take over the eastern half of this broad intermontane valley. Since no known subsequent ceramic change is as dramatic or abrupt in the years leading up to the time of the foundation of the Achaemenid Empire in the mid–6th century, Sumner suggests that this must have been the specific moment at which the Persian tribes began to reach the region of Fars. The principal problem with this reconstruction is the surprisingly early date at which it would bring the Persians to their eventual homeland.[2]

In textual terms, for example, the first Persians to be mentioned in the royal annals of Assyria are those whom the Assyrians encountered in the central western Zagros in 844 (Luckenbill 1926: §581, §637; Grayson 1996: 40, 54, 60, 68, 70–71; Waters 1999: 100 n. 5). Thus, it has been possible to suppose for some time that the Persian tribes (or at least those of long-term significance that came to penetrate highland southwestern Iran) only began to make their presence felt in Fars from about 1000 onward (e.g., Miroschedji 1985: 292). This is about the same time that the city of Anshan comes to be abandoned after many centuries of continuous occupation (Carter 1994: 65), very conceivably in response to major demographic changes in the region. In this context, an unusual bridge-spouted vessel that Vanden Berghe recovered from a grave at Tall-i Taimuran and associated with an otherwise unattested "Taimuran B ware" (1959: 44, pl. 61a; see also Overlaet 1997: 9, fig. 4) has been related by Jacobs to the southward migration of the Persians at the end of the second and beginning of the first millennium (1980: 57–59). Sumner, on the other hand, is more skeptical. In his view, the Taimuran vessel, together with other "scattered and enigmatic bits of chronological evidence for the late second millennium" (including "a bridge spout found on the surface at Malyan"), are "foreign to the region" and may represent, therefore, "no more than a predictable degree of travel and trade during the late second or early first millennium B.C." (Sumner 1994: 101). For the moment, in short, there is little, if any, clear physical evidence from the archaeological record in Fars itself either to affirm or deny the possible arrival of the Persians near the beginning of the first millennium. Curiously enough, however, a measure of conceivably very relevant evidence may be available from another, decidedly unexpected quarter.

Evidence from Southeastern Arabia

In the absence of clear material evidence of the arrival of the Persians in southern Iran at any time in the first two centuries or so of the first millennium, it is now not a little intriguing to find that the adjacent Oman Peninsula (a region now more commonly referred to in the archaeological literature as southeastern Arabia [Magee 1997: 91]) evinces unmistakable indications of contact with Iran during precisely this time-frame. Thanks to recent excavations conducted at Muweilah and Rumeilah (fig. 2), it has become clear that substantial columned halls, very possibly connected to elite building traditions in northwestern and western Iran, were being constructed at both sites well before 800, and that, remarkably enough, these edifices themselves yielded bridge-spouted jars of Iranian appearance (Boucharlat and Lombard 2001: figs. 7–11; Magee 2001: fig. 12). Moreover, the possible association of such Iron Age sites with the use of underground water conduits

---

2. For still other reservations related to Sumner's postulated links between ceramic wares and ethnic groups, see Overlaet 1997: 48–49.

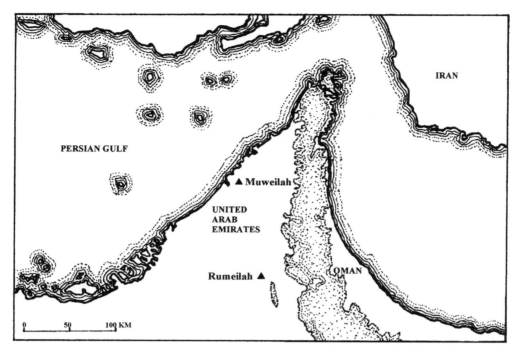

Fig. 2. Map of the Oman Peninsula, showing sites mentioned in the text.

has revived interest in the relationship between the Arabian *fallaj* and the Iranian *qanat* (and in the respective dates at which these visibly similar irrigation systems were introduced; Boucharlat and Lombard 2001: 226 n. 18).

The reason (or reasons) for these various correspondences remains uncertain. In view of various parallels between the known plans of the Arabian columned halls and the plans of a number of earlier and approximately contemporary halls in northwestern and central western Iran,[3] Magee has suggested that the columned hall at Muweilah may well reflect "the emulation of a foreign architectural form by local elites" (personal communication). At the same time, Boucharlat and Lombard are more cautious about any nonlocal origin of the "salle à poteaux" in Rumeilah I. On the one hand, they acknowledge that such a distinctive building type could have been transmitted from northwestern or western Iran to southern Iran and from there to southeastern Arabia; on the other, they do not rule out the possibility that the columned hall was separately invented in Arabia. Above all, they stress the need to associate this particular architectural form with the specific needs of local governance in the region (Boucharlat and Lombard 2001: 224, 228).

At this stage it is perhaps too early to indulge in further speculation. Nonetheless, these new discoveries in the Oman Peninsula (in a region that is separated from the south coast of Iran only by a stretch of water ca. 60 km in width) strongly suggest that further

---

3. With reference to Hasanlu, Tepe Nush-i Jan, and Godin Tepe, see, respectively, Dyson 1989: figs. 10, 17; Stronach and Roaf 1978: figs. 1, 3, pl. 3b; Young and Levine 1974: fig. 37.

work on the Iron Age in Fars could be surprisingly productive—and that such renewed research might yet throw significant light on the currently obscure nature of early Persian settlement in highland southern Iran in the first two centuries of the first millennium.

Testimony from the Early 6th Century

If we move somewhat further forward in time, Elamite inscriptions (which had ceased to be composed toward the end of the second millennium, conceivably in response to a signal shock to Middle Elamite power [Carter and Stolper 1984: 43]) are once again in evidence in the second half of the 8th century. At this juncture, in short, there was a clear revival in the fortunes of Elam. And for 100 years following the mid–8th century (until Susa fell to the Assyrians in 646), "an intimate relationship" existed "between the political histories of Mesopotamia and Elam . . . in Mesopotamian sources" (Carter and Stolper 1984: 44).

Yet, notwithstanding the renewed importance of Elam in this interval, the year 691 takes on the character of a turning point for the early Persians inasmuch as this is the last known date at which an Elamite king appears to have been in a position to summon highland auxiliaries from Fars in order to oppose the threat of Assyria. Indeed, since the auxiliaries in question are known to have included separate contingents from Anshan and Parsuash, it is tempting—even logical—to suppose that the effectively independent region of Fars already stood divided between at least two local polities by this time (Carter and Stolper 1984: 48).

One further question concerns the length of time during which this divided condition may have persisted. It could be argued (in one reconstruction) that, when Ashurbanipal obliged a certain "Kurash of Parsumash" to send his son as a hostage to Nineveh in the wake of the fall of Susa (Cameron 1936: 204), the latter ruler had already come to exercise paramount power in Susa's eastern highland hinterland, and that his royal line duly retained sole power from that early moment down to the accession of Cyrus in 559. But, as we shall see, this is not likely to represent the pattern of events.

If we seek hard evidence for the nature of the antecedents of Cyrus the Great, we must clearly begin with the testimony of this ruler's celebrated foundation cylinder, which came to light in Babylon more than 120 years ago. In one passage in this document, Cyrus can be seen to style himself as "son of Cambyses, great king, king of Anshan, grandson of Cyrus, great king, king of Anshan," and, not least, as "great-grandson of Teispes, great king, king of Anshan" (see most recently Waters 1996: 13).

Cyrus's use of the title "king of Anshan" has long puzzled modern scholars, but among the other possible reasons for the use of this dignification, it is more than possible that it represented an opportune appropriation of the eastern element in the age-old Elamite title "king of Anshan and Susa" and, as such, was selected for its intimations of millennial, legitimate rule in southwestern Iran. The alternative suggestion that Cyrus only chose to use this particular title in his foundation cylinder in order to make his antecedents more understandable to his new Babylonian subjects is, I believe, distinctly unlikely. Apart from all else, Cyrus is known to have continued to refer to Anshan in his titulary in still other Mesopotamian documents (Waters 1996: 13) at a time when a number of other

Fig. 3. Composite drawing of the collated image of the inscribed cylinder seal of Kurash, the Anshanite, son of Teispes (after Garrison and Root 1996: fig. 2a). Courtesy of M. B. Garrison, M. C. Root, and the Persepolis Seal Project; used by permission.

usages, including something like "king of the country of Parsa," would presumably have been at least as intelligible to his Mesopotamian subjects (Stronach 1978: 284 n. 15).

A further item of note in the above-cited passage from the Cyrus cylinder is the striking fact that the founder of Cyrus's royal line is given as Teispes, not Achaemenes. That this circumstance is due to something more than chance is very possibly indicated by evidence of another kind from Persepolis. In the course of the excavations conducted at the site by the Oriental Institute of the University of Chicago, a series of clay impressions came to light that permit the reconstruction of the arresting cylinder seal design shown in fig. 3. In an inscription in Elamite that simultaneously underlines both the importance that was given to Teispes and the degree of weight that the line of Cyrus would appear to have attached to the name of Anshan from the outset, the owner of the seal styles himself as "Kurash, the Anshanite, son of Teispes."

The seal design, which shows a mounted spearman in the act of defeating three opponents (fig. 3), is carved in a Neo-Elamite style appropriate to the end of the 7th century.[4] In other words, there may now be viable grounds to place the reign of the son and successor of Teispes (and, hence, the grandfather of the founder of the Achaemenid Empire) in a setting almost as late as 600, and it may be appropriate to suggest that the whole line of Cyrus only began to emerge, with Teispes as its founder figure, in the years following the Assyrian sack of Susa, when Elam ceased to exist as a major power.[5]

Not surprisingly, residual echoes of Assyria's preeminence are not hard to detect in the recently revealed contents of the above-mentioned tomb at Arjan.[6] Thus, the owner of the tomb was buried in an Assyrian-style bronze "bathtub" coffin; Curtis, who has made a close study of such coffins (1983), takes the view that the Arjan coffin (fig. 4:a)

---

4. For a date of ca. 600 B.C. based on analogies to the style of the scene that is shown in fig. 3, see especially Miroschedji 1985: 286; Potts 1999: 306.

5. In this reconstruction Teispes could have ruled from ca. 535 to ca. 515; Cyrus I from ca. 515 to ca. 590; and Cambyses I from ca. 590 to 559 (Stronach 1997a: 359; see also Miroschedji 1985: 284 n. 82).

6. For prior evaluations of the tomb and its contents see, inter alia, Tohidi and Khalilian 1982; Vallat 1984: 9; Alizadeh 1985; Vatandust 1988; Sarraf 1990; Majidzadeh 1992; Curtis 1995: 21–22; Stronach 1997b: 41; Potts 1999: 303–6.

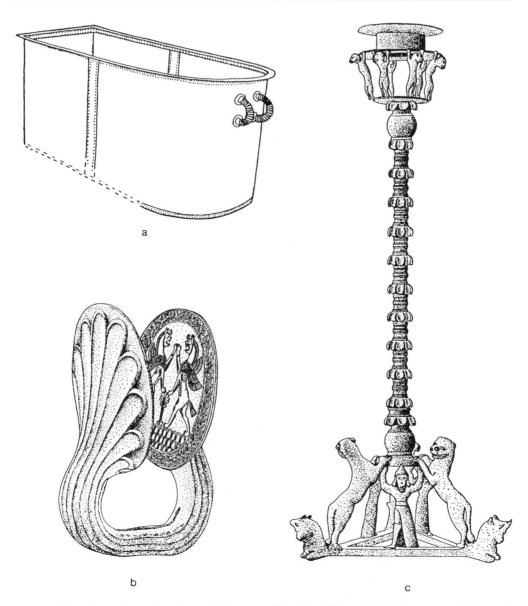

Fig. 4. Objects from the tomb at Arjan: (a) bronze coffin; (b) gold "bracelet"; (c) bronze stand (after Alizadeh 1985: figs. 2A, 3, and 4; used by permission). Not to scale.

very likely dates "from the second half of the 7th century BC or even slightly later" (Curtis 2000: 204).

In terms of Assyrian-related funerary objects from Arjan, a bronze bowl with five concentric registers of lively, incised decoration is of special note. The intricate designs include scenes of presentation, hunting, banqueting, and even date-harvesting (Majidzadeh 1992: fig. 1). But, while it is possible to detect numerous borrowings from Assyrian iconography, we can also see that Assyrian motifs were sometimes less than accurately rendered or even replaced by what would appear to have been new conventions.[7] In short, the bowl is not a stock product of an Assyrian workshop; rather, it may have been designed to meet local requirements at a moment when, following the fall of Nineveh in 612, many metalsmiths of repute were obliged to look elsewhere for sources of patronage.

Among the diverse objects from the Arjan tomb, it has to be said that, while many elements in the decoration of the Arjan bowl are notably Elamite in character (Majidzadeh 1992: 136–38), and while a group of bronze vessels from the tomb may be said to closely resemble bronze vessels from a contemporary tomb at Susa (Miroschedji 1981: fig. 40; Carter 1994: 73; Potts 1999: 303), two of the most striking objects in the corpus already appear to anticipate certain of the later characteristics of Achaemenid art.

The first, a large, ceremonial gold "bracelet" (or perhaps "icon of kingship"), 15 cm in height (fig. 4:b), which was found near the left hand of the deceased, is most remarkable for the distinctive mirror images that distinguish its opposed, disc-like finials. Each disc shows a pair of rampant, winged, leonine monsters whose pose and appearance may well descend from a type of muscular monster that was familiar to Neo-Elamite seal-cutters in the latter half of the 7th century (Amiet 1973: figs. 11–12; Potts 1999: fig. 8.7:4). It is also clear, however, that the closest analogies to the two Arjan winged creatures come from the rampant, regardant lion-griffins that adorn the elaborate sword-scabbard of Darius's personal weapon-bearer in one of the more significant early-5th-century reliefs from Persepolis (Schmidt 1953: pl. 120). The second, an elaborate bronze stand, ca. 75 cm in height (fig. 4:c), which includes three Atlas figures of decidedly Mesopotamian character (Curtis 1995: 21), also exhibits kneeling bull protomes and standing lions with their heads twisted back (or to one side), each of which looks recognizably Achaemenid in many respects.

Finally, at a time when we already seem to be dealing with a curiously hybrid Elamite-Persian world, it is far from surprising to find that the precise ethnicity of the owner of the Arjan tomb, a certain Kidin-Hutran, son of Kurlush, is less than certain. Thus, while the indubitably Elamite name Kidin-Hutran was taken by no less than three far-earlier Middle Elamite rulers (Potts 1999: table 7.5), its presence at Arjan, combined with the name Kurlush, could be said to raise more questions than it answers.

To begin with, the evident name of the single individual who occupied the tomb was written in an Elamite cuneiform script that Vallat would ascribe to the period between 646 and 539 (the year in which Cyrus occupied Babylon; Vallat 1984: 9). But since this indication of ownership appears not only on the bronze bowl (perhaps dating to ca. 600) but also on the gold "bracelet," which probably dates, at least in my view, to the second quarter of the 6th century, it is reasonable to assume that Kidin-Hutran's career overlapped a good part of the first half of the 6th century. And, since his father's name, Kurlush, could well be Iranian,[8] it seems arguable that he himself was not only Iranian but that, in answer

---

7. For example, the top of the monarch's throne exhibits a prominent pine-cone finial with its point directed upward (Majidzadeh 1992: fig. 1). In contrast, the tops of Assyrian thrones never show such finials; instead, they frequently exhibit pine-cone feet that taper in the direction of the floor (Curtis 1996: fig. 1).

8. For M. Stolper's suggestion to this effect, see Potts 1999: 295.

to certain specific political circumstances (such as the relatively western locus of his local power base), he chose to assume a prominent Elamite name.[9]

If this suggestion has any merit, it is yet another reminder of the probably fragmented nature of political power in southern Iran between approximately the mid–7th and mid–6th century. This condition was assuredly prevalent in connection with what was left of independent Elam in its twilight years (cf. Potts 1999: 301), but it is also a condition that may have applied to more of the broad uplands to the east of Arjan than is presently realized. Indeed, in trying to make sense of the history of this part of Iran in the period under review, we have to keep in mind that the adoption of one title or another, or the taking of one royal name or another, was not infrequently an opportunistic exercise.[10]

Conclusions

The foregoing remarks may serve to illustrate a number of new perspectives. Very briefly, there is now a definite prospect that the columned hall, as a potent and practical example of representational architecture, had a much more extensive diffusion throughout western Iran than was previously supposed. In particular, it now seems most unlikely that halls of this kind reached southern Iran only in the mid–6th century. If such halls were already present in the Oman Peninsula within the first two centuries of the first millennium, it is hard to imagine that Cyrus was obliged to look toward Median sites, such as Tepe Nush-i Jan and Godin Tepe, as primary models for his own columned halls. Extant local models would already have been available, we may surmise, in southwestern Iran.

Second, the remarkable combination of different cultural signifiers in the Arjan assemblage now begins to reveal how a heady mix of Elamite, Assyrian, Persian, and other broadly Iranian sources would appear to have led to the birth of something already very close to "Achaemenid art" at a time when, apparently, the stimulus of Achaemenid Persian imperial construction was not yet in place. Needless to say, this is a significant finding.

Third, the new evidence for the presence of a minor ruler—Kidin-Hutran—on the western border of Fars at a date that may well fall partly after 575 would seem to tell us either that Cyrus's forebears—that is, the "great kings, kings of Anshan," who directly preceded him—did not hold sway as far west as Arjan or that they countenanced the existence of vassal lines within their general sphere of influence at least until that date.

Last but not least, it may be fair to say that recent explorations of events in the early Achaemenid period have brought to light significant tensions between the testimony of the archaeological record and the often propagandistic nature of the available written record. In this context, it has often been supposed that Darius more than slightly embellished the standing of his line. In his apparent quest for irreproachable credentials, he chose, for example, to define Cyrus (and Cyrus's known predecessors) as a member of the Achaemenid family from which he himself was descended (Stronach 1997b: 39) and even went so far as to erect first-person inscriptions in the name of Cyrus that defined his great

---

9. Arjan is located not far to the west of the western border of Fars. In other words, this vicinity could very well have had a predominantly Elamite population at the time that Kidin-Hutran was active.

10. The inscription of Darius at Bisitun, composed ca. 520, documents for example the storied names and titles adopted by the individuals who opposed Darius's bid for the throne (Kent 1953: 116–35).

predecessor as "an Achaemenid" (Stronach 1997c: 326). On the other hand, there might now be grounds—pace the evidence from Arjan and the implications that we have just drawn from this evidence—for challenging prior assumptions about the local history of southern Iran, which were often weighted in terms of a literal reading of the overarching claims that Cyrus elected to advance on behalf of his ancestors. In sum, if Kidin-Hutran's domain stood outside the bounds of control of Cyrus's line (or if such an individual could flourish on the borders of this control in some kind of vassal status), the possibility that Darius's forebears were also in their own way kings "from long ago" (Kent 1953: 119) in one or another part of Fars—with a certain interregnum in the early to middle years of the 6th century—is no longer so difficult to entertain.

References

Alizadeh, A.
　1985　A Tomb of the Neo-Elamite Period at Arjān, near Behbahan. *Archaeologische Mitteilungen aus Iran* 18: 49–73.
Amiet, P.
　1973　La glyptique de la fin de l'Elam. *Arts Asiatiques* 28: 3–45.
Boardman, J.
　2000　*Persia and the West: An Archaeological Investigation of the Genesis of Achaemenid Art.* London: Thames & Hudson.
Boucharlat, R., and Lombard, P.
　2001　Le bâtiment G de Rumeilah (oasis d'Al Ain): Remarques sur les salles à poteaux de l'âge du Fer en Péninsule d'Oman. *Iranica Antiqua* 36: 213–38.
Cameron, G. G.
　1936　*History of Early Iran.* Chicago: University of Chicago Press.
Carter, E.
　1994　Bridging the Gap between the Elamites and the Persians in Southeastern Khuzistan. *Achaemenid History* 8: 65–95.
Carter, E., and Stolper, M. W.
　1984　*Elam: Surveys of Political History and Archaeology.* Los Angeles: University of California Press.
Curtis, J.
　1983　Late Assyrian Bronze Coffins. *Anatolian Studies* 33: 85–95.
　1995　Introduction. Pp. 15–24 in *Later Mesopotamia and Iran: Tribes and Empires, 1600–539 BC*, ed. J. Curtis. London: British Museum.
　1996　Assyrian Furniture: The Archaeological Evidence. Pp. 167–80 in *The Furniture of Western Asia: Ancient and Traditional*, ed. G. Herrmann. Mainz: von Zabern.
　2000　Animal-Headed Drinking Cups in the Late Assyrian Period. Pp. 193–213 in *Variatio Delectat: Iran und der Westen. Gedenkschrift für Peter Calmeyer*, ed. R. Dittmann et al. Münster: Ugarit-Verlag.
Dyson, R. H.
　1989　The Iron Age Architecture at Hasanlu: An Essay. *Expedition* 31/2–3: 107–27.
Garrison, M. B., and Root, M. C.
　1996　Persepolis Seal Studies: An Introduction with Provisional Concordances of Seal Numbers and Associated Documents on Fortification Tablets 1–2087. *Achaemenid History* 9: 1–41.
Ghirshman, R.
　1954　*Village perse-achéménide.* Mémoires de la Délégation (Mission) archéologique en Perse (Iran) 36. Paris: Leroux.

1964   *Persia from the Origins to Alexander the Great.* London: Thames & Hudson.

Grayson, A. K.

1996   *Assyrian Rulers of the Early First Millennium BC II (858–745 BC).* Royal Inscriptions of Mesopotamia, Assyian Periods 3. Toronto: University of Toronto Press.

Jacobs, L. K.

1980   *Darvazeh Tepe and the Iranian Highlands in the Second Millennium BC.* Ph.D. dissertation, University of Oregon, 1980.

Kent, R. G.

1953   *Old Persian: Grammar, Texts, Lexicon.* New Haven, Conn.: American Oriental Society.

Luckenbill, D. D.

1926   *Ancient Records of Assyria and Babylonia.* Vol. 1. Chicago: University of Chicago Press.

Magee, P.

1997   The Iranian Iron Age and the Chronology of Settlement in Southeastern Arabia. *Iranica Antiqua* 32: 91–108.

2001   Excavations at Muweilah 1997–2000. *Proceedings of the Seminar for Arabian Studies* 31: 115–30.

Majidzadeh, Y.

1992   The Arjan Bowl. *Iran* 30: 131–44.

Miroschedji, P. de

1981   Fouilles du chantier Ville Royale II à Suse (1975–1977): I. Les niveaux élamites. *Cahiers de la Délégation Archéologique Française en Iran* 12: 9–136.

1985   La fin de royaume d'Anšan et de Suse et la naissance de l'empire perse. *Zeitschrift für Assyriologie* 75: 266–306.

Nylander, C.

1970   *Ionians in Pasargadae: Studies in Old Persian Architecture.* Uppsala: Almqvist & Wiksells.

Overlaet, B.

1997   A Report on the 1952 and 1954/55 Soundings at Tall-i Taimuran (Fars), Iran. *Iranica Antiqua* 32: 1–51.

Potts, D. T.

1999   *The Archaeology of Elam: Formation and Transformation of an Ancient Iranian State.* Cambridge: Cambridge University Press.

Sarraf, M. R.

1990   Kiddin-Hutran's Bronze Bowl from Arjan, Behbahan. *Athar* 17: 4–61 (Persian).

Schmidt, E. F.

1953   *Persepolis I: Structures, Reliefs, Inscriptions.* Chicago: University of Chicago Press.

Stronach, D.

1974   Achaemenid Village I at Susa and the Persian Migration to Fars. *Iraq* 36: 239–48.

1978   *Pasargadae: A Report on the Excavations Conducted by the British Institute of Persian Studies from 1961 to 1963.* Oxford: Oxford University Press.

1997a   Darius at Pasargadae: A Neglected Source for the History of Early Persia. *Topoi* Supplément 1: 351–63.

1997b   Anshan and Persia: Early Achaemenid History, Art and Architecture on the Iranian Plateau. Pp. 35–53 in *Mesopotamia and Iran in the Persian Period: Conquest and Imperialism 539–331 BC,* ed. J. Curtis. London: British Museum.

1997c   On the Interpretation of the Pasargadae Inscriptions. Pp. 323–29 in *Ultra Terminum Vagari: Scitti in onore di Carl Nylander,* ed. B. Magnusson et al. Rome: Quasar.

Stronach, D., and Roaf, M.

1978   Excavations at Tepe Nush-i Jan: Part 1, A Third Interim Report. *Iran* 16: 1–11.

Sumner, W. M.

1994   Archaeological Measures of Cultural Continuity and the Arrival of the Persians in Fars. *Achaemenid History* 8: 97–105.

Tohidi, F., and Khalilian, A.
  1982   Report on the Study of the Objects from the Arjan Tomb, Behbahan. *Athar* 7/8/9: 232–86.
              [Persian]
Vallat, F.
  1984   Kidin-Hutrun et l'époch néo-élamite. *Akkadica* 37: 1–17.
Vanden Berghe, L.
  1959   *Archéologie de l'Iran ancien*. Leiden: Brill.
Vatandust, R.
  1988   A Preliminary Report of the Conservation and Technical Studies of Some of the Arjan
              Material. *Athar* 15/16: 72–116. [Persian]
Waters, M. W.
  1996   Darius and the Achaemenid Line. *The Ancient History Bulletin (Calgary)* 10/1: 11–18.
  1999   The Earliest Persians in Southwestern Iran: The Textual Evidence. *Iranian Studies* 32/1:
              99–107.
Young, T. C., and Levine, L. D.
  1974   *Excavations of the Godin Project: Second Progress Report*. Toronto: Royal Ontario Museum.

Palestine among the Empires from the 4th to the 1st Century B.C.E.: Impact and Reaction

Doron Mendels
Department of History
Hebrew University, Jerusalem

In this paper I would like to show how Palestine was viewed from the outside, that is, from the perspective of the empires of the ancient world, in the Hellenistic era.

My first point is the issue of the ideological world of empires. Although I have used the term *ideology*, I am aware that it is problematic concerning antiquity, but this question is beyond the scope of this paper. Even if one does use the term in the context of antiquity, however, it is self-evident that one does not have 19th-century ideologies in mind. In the context of this paper it is more plausible to speak of ideas, mythologies, and bodies of knowledge that arose in the courts of empires in the Hellenistic era, but that may have been influential beyond them. The concepts of empire prevalent in the literature of the Hellenistic kingdoms include, for instance, mythological figures that had become extremely popular and were even used as "precedents" for conquest and annexation. It is not coincidental that many writers of the Hellenistic period, some of whom were associated with monarchs and royal courts, invented mythological situations of imperial conquest. In Egyptian Hellenistic literature we hear about Osiris (suggesting also his Greek equivalent, Dionysus), who traveled in the eastern *oecumene* and drew the perimeter of an empire, with Egypt at its center. His conquest of the whole eastern world, including Macedonia and Greece (even more than Alexander had achieved, for Osiris took India as well), was designed as a demonstration of the legitimacy of the Ptolemies over the Alexandrinian Empire and beyond. The legends of Osiris and Sesostris—another mythological figure who already appeared in Herodotus but was adapted to the Ptolemaic scene by Hecataeus of Abdera, from whom we have this information—constituted a sort of imperial vision held by the Ptolemies (or rather, that should be attributed to court intellectuals). These were not just visions of conquest, but rather visions of a cultural mission within the visionary empire of the Ptolemies.

Another intellectual associated with Cyrene, Dionysus Scytobrachion, invented a mythological queen-hero, Myrina, who conquered a vast territory with Libya at its center, drawing a boundary line through Egypt toward Asia Minor and including parts of this region. She was more of a military conqueror than a cultural emissary. From Babylonia under the Seleucids, Berossus tells us that Nebopalassar and his son Nebuchadnezzar II

Author's note: I would like to thank Prof. B. Bar Kochva for his comments on a draft of this paper. He, however, has a different interpretation.

wielded power over Phoenicia, Coele Syria, and Egypt itself (*FGrH* 8)—the last, I suspect, being historically quite incorrect. This was, of course, wishful thinking in certain Seleucid circles that wished to be reunited with Egypt (as under the short-lived empire of Alexander). Heracles, during the period preceding the conquests of Julius Caesar, wandered about and managed affairs within a perimeter roughly coinciding with the limits of the Roman Empire of the mid–first century B.C.E. The Heracles myth was also modified from an early Hellenistic original (written by Matris of Thebes) to fit the new imperial circumstances.

One should add in this context that the Jews imitated these journeys in the *Genesis Apocryphon* (2nd century B.C.E.), but the element of conquest and cultural mission is altogether missing. It should be emphasized that *most* of the journeying of gods and heroes constituted the basic historical legitimations of Hellenistic kings, and perhaps also nourished some of the Roman generals. In these imaginary travels the land of Israel is altogether absent (except in the case of Berossus, and of course in the Jewish *Genesis Apocryphon*, which has the land of Israel at its center). In other words, in these conceptual presentations of empires in the Hellenistic and early Roman era, the land of Israel usually does not appear by name as a place conquered by world empires in the past, or for that matter, as a place that underwent a Hellenistic cultural mission (Mendels 1998: 394–419).

Judea is mentioned, however, by Hecataeus of Abdera at the beginning of the 3rd century B.C.E., as being colonized by Egypt. Hecataeus, probably a historian associated with the Ptolemaic court, writes (Diodorus Siculus, *Bibliotheca* 1.28): "The Egyptians say that a great number of colonies were spread from Egypt over all the inhabited world. To Babylon, for instance, colonists were led by Belus . . . and that of the Jews, which lies between Arabia and Syria, were founded as colonies by certain migrants from their country" (he does not even mention the name Judea). Let me also note that when historians carefully read the corpus of Jewish literature from the Hellenistic period, they may come to the conclusion that, although the land of Israel was focal in terms of theological concepts (*Jubilees* 9–11), its political position among the nations in the "real" world was not always seen as central. In Daniel 11, for instance, the land of Israel is merely a region in transition between the kings of the north and those of the south. On the other hand, the abundance of Jewish literature in comparison with the literary production in other regions may give a misleading impression about how important Palestine really was. It was, of course, culturally important; but this fact does not mean that it was acknowledged as a central place in the literature of the Hellenistic environment (Momigliano 1975).

Having said this, I turn to the real world: in the Hellenistic period, can we speak of "strategy"? Can we refer to a global policy preplanned during a long-term process of decision-making? If we think in von Clausewitz's terms, it would be quite difficult to speak of strategy as opposed to tactics in antiquity. But we should not ignore the fact that whatever happened from Alexander the Great onward on the international scene can be explained as a series of reactions and counterreactions within a political and military chain of events of communicative actions (for the political background, see Green 1990; Sartre 2001). Hence, in hindsight it looks as though there was a grand plan, some sort of overall strategy, but in reality this was not so. When we examine the chain of events from Alexander the Great to the conquest of Palestine by the Romans in 63 B.C.E. and beyond, we can easily maintain that Palestine played a certain role, as did many other territories and peoples at the time, but not necessarily a central one, as did, for instance, Greece or Egypt for both the Diadochs and the Roman Republic.

It was Alexander the Great who first conquered Palestine from an eastern power, the Persians. In contrast, he besieged Tyre for seven months, but Tyre was an important personal issue for him, since the local god Melkart, the equivalent of Heracles, Alexander the Great's ancestor and favorite god, did not want to grant him his blessing (or in other words, was not willing to acknowledge him). This is how Alexander interpreted the refusal of the Tyrians to let him into the city, which was vexing for the Macedonian king who, throughout his campaigns, needed the manifestation of receiving legitimation from local gods. He even took the very long, out-of-the-way road to the sanctuary of Ammon at Siwah on the Libyan border in order to receive the god's blessing for the conquest of Egypt. But, returning to Palestine, when Alexander arrived in Jerusalem, if the story about the peaceful reception he received from the high priest is true (Josephus, *Ant.* 11.321ff.), after settling affairs with the Samaritans, he immediately left for Egypt, which was the significant place to visit and conquer. In this respect, Alexander was the precursor of a policy that became general in the Hellenistic period, defining the secondary role of Palestine in the eyes of most rulers most of the time, until the Roman conquest. To be sure, Palestine was a land of transition from north to south, a position that granted it much value in military circles. Yet it was not recognized as a territory of central importance at many junctures during the Hellenistic era, to judge from what actually happened.

For the period of the Diadochi we have relatively few sources, but even so we receive the impression from the various Diadochi enterprises that their territorial interests during fierce fighting against each other to annex more pieces of Alexander's empire lay in other parts of the empire than Palestine. They fought over Greece and Macedonia, Asia, the Aegean, Egypt, and even Cyrene. Palestine was naturally within the scope of their targeted territories, but was not their main target. Some of the Diadochi were "goal-oriented" toward certain territories, to use Deutsch's terminology (1969: 77ff.), so that Palestine had some significance, but it was not a main object. Hence, after the Ptolemies got hold of Palestine, and even propagated the idea that it was a former colony of Egypt, they viewed it as a comfortable buffer zone guarding them against potential aggression from the Seleucids. This went on during the period in which the Ptolemies still had many possessions outside Egypt in the Aegean and Mediterranean. At this time, the 3rd century B.C.E., the Ptolemies were a power to be reckoned with, and Ptolemy II, III, and IV were powerful in international relations. Nonetheless, five of the so-called Syrian Wars between the Seleucids and the Ptolemies were fought over Palestine during the 3rd century B.C.E.

At first glance one might believe that this shows how important the land of Israel really was; a closer look reveals that neither the Seleucids nor the Ptolemies took the trouble to concentrate on Palestine and "fight it out." It is precisely these lingering wars that show that Palestine was a good economic asset to have; but it could not have been much more than that, since the Ptolemies did not show any sign of wishing to conquer the Seleucid kingdom. When they had the "will" (in von Clausewitz's terms), they could focus on a front and bring about a decisive outcome (von Clausewitz 1993: 86, §5). This is in fact what happened 80 years after the conquest of Palestine by the Ptolemies, at the battle of Raphiah (the fourth Syrian War, 217 B.C.E.).

Generally speaking, when the Hellenistic monarchs and later the Roman army wanted to fight a decisive battle, they concentrated all their forces; but such battles were few in the Hellenistic period. Von Clausewitz argues that there are only two sources for the spirit of war, and they must interact in order to create it. The first is a series of victorious wars; the second, frequent exertions of the army to the utmost limits of its strength. In most wars during the 3rd (and the 2nd) century in Palestine, the encounters were not decisive for most of the Hellenistic entities involved. The wars of attrition brought about a certain indifference among the warring parties, if the global picture is correctly seen. To fight a decisive war for a peripheral territory, however important for passage, was useless (in fact the Ptolemies did not particularly need Palestine for passage to anywhere, nor did the Seleucids; both powers could always use the sea). In Raphia in 217 B.C.E., the powers came to a certain juncture at which they wished to fight it out (after almost 100 years of inconclusive fighting). They put an enormous military force into the field (Ptolemy IV a force of 55,000 men, and Antiochus III a force of 68,000), and they made an economic effort that had repercussions later in Egypt (Galili 1999). In particular they showed, to quote von Clausewitz's terminology again, a "will" to fight a decisive battle, and it was decisive, "the biggest formal battle since Ipsus" (Green 1990: 290). Although Ptolemy gained the victory, Egypt was so weakened that one long-term result was the conquest of Palestine by the Seleucids later in the century.

While the battle of Raphia took place in Palestine, its main goal was not dominion over this territory. It was a battle over the manifestation of power between Seleucids and Ptolemies, which occurred at a certain juncture when they could fight concentratedly, without hindrance from the Macedonians or Romans. The latter were not yet on the horizon of the Near East, and in any case they were preoccupied with Hannibal's invasion. The Ptolemies and Seleucids, one should emphasize, were still at the height of their political and military power, so this battle was unavoidable. Henceforward their decline would begin and would have an impact on world politics. The battle of Raphiah was over global power politics, and Palestine was only a secondary consideration. Antiochus the Great's hopes lay elsewhere: he was in the midst of a process of regaining the east (reconquering Armenia and, in 220 B.C.E., Media Atropatene), and in 211 B.C.E. was preparing for his *anabasis* to India.

Be that as it may, Antiochus III, the Great, the conqueror of Palestine in 200 B.C.E., was of course praised by Josephus Flavius. He was benevolent to the Jews, who, according to Jewish tradition, favored his conquest of Palestine (*Ant.* 12.133). He subsequently issued the famous autonomy edict for the benefit of the Palestinian Jews. But if one examines Antiochus's policies around 200 B.C.E., one immediately sees that Palestine was a minor issue on the list of priorities of the Seleucid court. There were much more important considerations at stake at the time. I shall not go into all the details, but will only mention that Philip V, the aggressive king of Macedonia, was expanding eastward after 204 B.C.E. and conquering territory in the Aegean. This alarmed some of the Greeks, who called for Roman intervention. The rumor spread that Antiochus III and Philip V had decided to divide between them the territories of Ptolemy the IV, who had died in 204 B.C.E. In 200

B.C.E., Rome had just concluded the war with Hannibal and decided on intervention in Greece. Antiochus III's western front was vital to him, because the acquisition of Ptolemaic possessions there had become a consideration, but he also feared Philip V, with whom it seems he had a pact. Palestine was a secondary issue for Antiochus, since the land of Israel was under his sway, and he had an eye on the western territories, including Greece.

The secondary role of Palestine is also evident in the policies of Antiochus's successors, until the outbreak of the Maccabean revolt in 168 B.C.E. Before that time, the Hellenizers wished to enhance Palestine's political position in the Seleucid court, but they only partially succeeded. To make a long story short, around 200 B.C.E. there was a clear turning point in power politics, since Rome's intervention in the so-called Second Macedonian War (200–197 B.C.E.) made the world more global in terms of an international chain of events in which Palestine had a minor role. The attitude emerging from Siracide writings after the conquest of Palestine by Antiochus III reflects the unimportant and insignificant stature of Palestine in the international sphere, a position that was desirable, in this author's opinion.

After the Romans routed Philip V at Cynoscephalae in 197 B.C.E., and he withdrew from Greece in obedience to a Roman dictate, Antiochus III, like an eagle pouncing on its prey, invaded Greece in 192 B.C.E. The Romans subsequently crushed him at Magnesia in 190 B.C.E. and brought about the withdrawal of his army from the western part of Asia Minor, up to the Taurus range (the Scipios had 30,000 men and Antiochus 75,000). The Romans then fostered the rise of the kingdom of Pergamon, which in the 2nd century B.C.E. became a power to be reckoned with in the region. To continue the story of this chain of events on the international scene is beyond the scope of this paper. I would mention, however, that when in 168 B.C.E. Rome defeated the Macedonian kingdom once and for all (the Third Macedonian War), the Romans looked increasingly eastward beyond Greece and the Aegean. The triangle of Macedonia, Ptolemaic Egypt, and the Seleucids lost its fragile equilibrium. The Romans entered the vacuum, and as a first step they issued an ultimatum to Antiochus IV to leave Egypt, which he had invaded twice while they were busy with their final war against the Macedonians in 169–168 B.C.E. The ultimatum was obeyed, and on his way back to the north the Seleucid king carried out a massacre in Jerusalem. In this context, it should be emphasized that the main goal of the Seleucid king in Palestine then and later was to extract money from the Jews. But Antiochus did not linger in Palestine and immediately left for the north.

It is no coincidence that the Maccabean uprising was not a priority on the Seleucid agenda, to judge from their global policies at the time. This even comes to the fore in certain passages in the books of 1–2 Maccabees, in spite of their heavy nationalistic and Judeocentric tone. The guerrilla war of the Maccabees was not central to the global considerations of the Seleucids. Not only did they send relatively small armies, as Bar Kochva (1989) showed several years ago, but other hints can be found in the same Jewish sources. For example, the Seleucid king himself never led the army against the rebels, except for the unimportant boy Antiochus V, and Antiochus IV was more interested in the eastern front and was preparing for his *anabasis* against the Parthians, which he undertook in 165 B.C.E. In other words, the Seleucid court was in some instances unable and unwilling to cope with the flow of information coming from Palestine, sometimes through the distorted accounts of Hellenistic Jews themselves. Were it not for these Hellenists, the intervention of the Seleucids would have been even slighter than it actually was. In terms of communication, one can say that the Seleucids could not always decode what was transmitted from the "strange" Jewish community in Judea, and in any case memory was short, since the Seleucid court did not have a good system of information storage available.

The secondary position of Palestine on the global scene also becomes evident in the middle of the 2nd century B.C.E., when different pretenders to the Seleucid throne came to Palestine to fight against their sovereign (if one may use this term before Jean Bodin). As in the case of so many other pretenders in the Hellenistic and Roman Empires, their tactic was not to attack the center, but rather to operate out of a peripheral territory (Demetrius, Alexander Balas, and others, such as the pretenders who arose after Herod the Great's death, acting from peripheral regions of Palestine). Working from the periphery had many advantages, such as the fact that the flow of information from such remote regions was slow, and the ability of the central power to move an army was very limited.

The secondary political position of Palestine within the Seleucids' scale of priorities during the second half of the 2nd century B.C.E. is further emphasized by the mere fact that they were not decisive in crushing the Hasmoneans (this was not just a result of weakness). When great powers in antiquity wished to settle something decisively, they acted accordingly (Isus, Ipsus, Raphia, Pydna, Actium, etc.). Likewise the Romans, who concluded a treaty with Judas Maccabaeus in 161 B.C.E. and renewed it later, never actually supported the Hasmoneans as far as we know even when matters got very bad, either economically or militarily. To conclude the survey of the Hellenistic period, I would say that precisely the secondary position of Palestine within the Hellenistic Near East, the notion of its being a transit territory (although the sea routes were not less important at the time), the gradual decline of the Ptolemaic and Seleucid Empires, the rise of Rome, and its own indifference to Palestine all brought about the emergence of the Hasmonean state. One might note that someone like Ptolemy Lathyrus invaded Palestine not necessarily in order to hold on to it, but rather to use it as a means to return to his original territory, Egypt.

I shall now move forward to the Roman intervention, with brief mention of the Parthian invasion supporting the Hasmonean Mattathias Antigonos in 40 B.C.E. This was of course a fiasco. The Parthians did not have a real interest in Palestine, as subsequent events demonstrated. Concerning Rome's attitude towards Palestine, I would like to make a few points:

In the non-Jewish sources describing the political arena, we never hear that Palestine had a focal role in the international calculations of the Romans during the 2nd and 1st centuries B.C.E. Until 63 B.C.E. the Romans, who were already maneuvering in the Near East, did not find it important enough to become involved in local affairs. Were it not for the second delegation of the warring parties in Judea that went to Pompey in Damascus and prompted him to intervene (Josephus, *Ant.* 14.37ff.), he probably would not have done so. The Romans took action only when the parties insisted, the war between the Hasmonean brothers deteriorated, and the Romans conquered Palestine in 63 B.C.E. If one examines Roman policies from 63 B.C.E. to the rise of Herod the Great, it is evident that there was no real Roman strategy especially designed for the Near East. Roman generals in Palestine, as elsewhere in the region, acted as they saw fit in certain situations *ad rem* and *ad hoc*; one must bear in mind that these were years of great unrest in the Empire itself. At any rate, Rome did not initiate the invasion of Palestine, because at the time, 33 years before the conquest of Egypt, Palestine was peripheral.

The granting of Palestine to Herod in 40 B.C.E. by the triumvirs in Rome is described by Josephus as a central event. Those who know the whole picture of that stormy period, however, can only say that Herod was given Judea because two of the triumvirs did not care much about the region. They were happy to get rid of it and hand it over to someone who was willing to rule it, especially in view of an imminent Parthian invasion. This picture emerges from Josephus, according to whom Antonius had to instruct (*edidasken*) the senate that "it also was an advantage in their war with the Parthians that Herod should be king" (*Ant.* 14.385). From this phrase it seems that even the Parthian attack in the east was not the most acute issue on the agenda of the Roman Senate at the time. The Parthian support of Mattathias Antigonos, who was a rebel in Roman eyes, ended in a complete fiasco, since Herod conquered the whole of Palestine. But one should remember that in 40 B.C.E. Herod was more or less a fugitive who had escaped from Palestine, and he was given the territory by Rome as a personal favor, according to Josephus (*Ant.* 14.381ff.). Yet it was Herod, a client king, who enhanced the position of Palestine in the eyes of the Romans, by his strong policies and by his building projects that made it something to reckon with in the region. But Augustus does not even mention him in his *Res Gestae*. Neither does he mention the Roman victory in Palestine in 4 B.C.E. and the annexation of Archelaus's domain in 6 C.E. (Brunt 1967: 25–33).

Before concluding, I wish to emphasize that also in classical literary sources the land of Israel is presented as secondary. It suffices to consult Stern's *Greek and Latin Authors* (1976: vol. 1) to see how unimportant Palestine actually was on the international scene. At least this is the impression we gain from the surviving literary fragments. Tacitus on the Great Jewish War against Rome in 66–73 C.E. digresses in *Historiae* 5.1–13 to tell us about the Jewish people. But there is surprisingly little about Palestine as an important place within the empires that subjugated the Near East. Even Tacitus saw Palestine as a remote and peripheral place on the international political scene, one that was subdued from time to time by great empires. For him the Jews were more significant as an interesting but strange *ethnos*.

The reaction of Jewish sources is dealt with by J. J. Collins in this volume. I wish only to note that, whereas the land of Israel was central as a theological entity in that literature (for instance, the eschatological significance in the Qumranic texts), when read critically it shows what I have described above: in the reality of the international political scene, Palestine was not central at all and did not play a significant role in the international power games during most of the period.

References

Bar Kochva, B.
   1989   *Judas Maccabaeus*. Cambridge: Cambridge University Press.
Brunt, P. A.
   1967   *Res gestae divi Augusti*. London: Oxford University Press.

Clausewitz, K. von
 1993 *On War*, trans. M. Howard and P. Paret. London: Everymans.
Deutsch, K. W.
 1969 *The Nerves of Government: Models of Political Communication and Control.* New York: Free Press.
FGrH *Der Fragmente der griechischen Historiker*, ed. F. Jacoby. Berlin: Weidmann, 1926–57. Repr. Leiden: Brill, 1999.
Galili, E.
 1999 *The Battle of Raphia 217 B.C.E. Tactics, Strategy and Logistics in the Hellenistic World.* Jerusalem: Bialik (Hebrew).
Green, P.
 1990 *Alexander to Actium: The Historical Evolution of the Hellenistic Age.* Berkeley and Los Angeles: University of California Press.
Mendels, D.
 1998 *Identity, Religion and Historiography: Studies in Hellenistic History.* Sheffield: Sheffield Academic Press.
Momigliano, A.
 1975 *Alien Wisdom: The Limits of Hellenization.* Cambridge: Cambridge University Press.
Sartre, M.
 2001 *D'Alexandre à Zenobie.* Paris: Fayard.
Stern, M.
 1976 *Greek and Latin Authors on Jews and Judaism.* Jerusalem: Israel Academy of Sciences.

Part II

Religion and Distinction

Temple or "Bêt Marzeaḥ"?

Manfred Bietak

Austrian Archaeological Institute in Cairo
Department of Egyptology, University of Vienna

In the archaeological literature, buildings are often referred to as temples because they had a public function and were connected to the cultic sphere. But does this justify identifying all these buildings as temples? I shall try in this short article to challenge this simplification and to suggest alternatives that give us something to think about. In the following I shall briefly review four test cases and present a conclusion.

I. The Sacred Precinct at Tell el-Dabʿa

In the 1960s and 1970s, the remains of a sacred precinct were excavated at Tell el-Dabʿa (figs. 1–2), a site now identified as ancient Avaris (Bietak 1975), the capital of the Hyksos Dynasty.[1] The precinct dates to the period of the Late Middle Kingdom (Strata F and E/3, ca. 1700–1650 B.C.E.), shortly before the Hyksos period, but continues in use up to the end of this era. At the time of construction, it was situated at the edge of the city, which later encroached on the precinct from all sides. The inhabitants were largely of Near Eastern origin (Winkler and Wilfing 1991: 120, 139), and they were carriers of a blend of Egyptian and Syro-Palestinian Middle Bronze Age culture (Bietak 1979; 1996; 2001).

Elements of the precinct were altered over time, but this paper focuses on the situation that existed in Stratum E/3, shortly before the Hyksos period. The dominant building was the main temple (Temple III) of Near Eastern type. It had a "broad-room" (*Breithaus*)[2] sanctuary with a wide, deep niche in the south, a vestibule, a courtyard, three entrances from the north, and another from a street on the west. Some specific features point to the forecourt as Near Eastern, not Egyptian, in function. In its center is an altar for burnt offerings, probably located in the shade of trees, as the tree pits indicate. Charred acorns, probably fallen from oak trees, were found on top of the altar, preserved due to their carbonization.

The western edge of the forecourt was defined by a typical Near Eastern "broad-room" temple with bent axis, the "holy of holies" located to the left of the entrance axis. On the eastern side of this forecourt is a building that we originally defined as a house, with two rooms and an entrance hall with direct access from the altar. On the floor in the back

---

Author's note: For the primary editing of this paper, I am indebted to Adrian Melman, Vienna.

1. Although Tell el-Dabʿa is not yet finally published, overviews appear in Bietak 1991: 19–26, fig. 3; 1994: 41–42, fig. 28; 1996: 36–47, fig. 30.

2. The terminology follows the German architectural historian E. Heinrich (1982: 19–20).

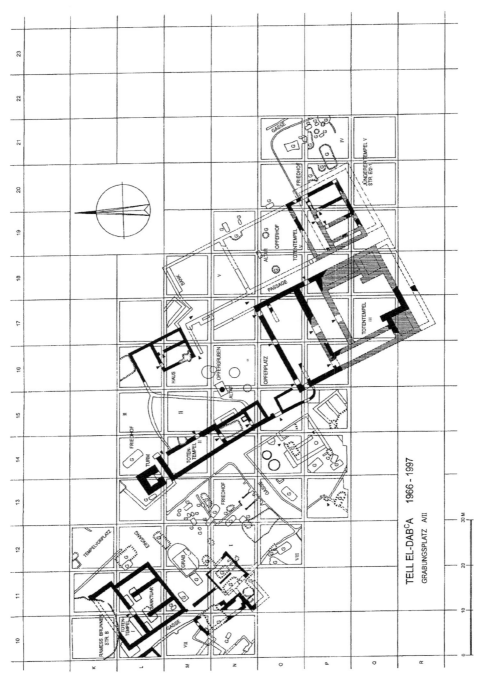

Fig. 1. The temple precinct of Tell el-Dabʿa, surrounded by cemeteries (after Bietak 1991: fig. 3 and Forstner-Müller 2001: fig. 1).

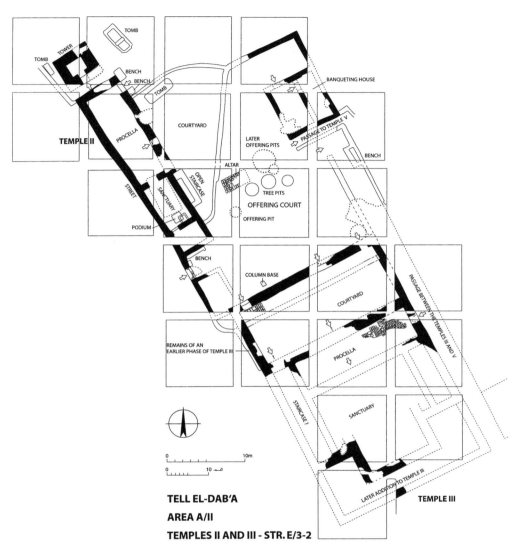

Fig. 2. Detail of the precinct of Temple III at Tell el-Dab'a (after Bietak 1996: figs. 30–31).

room, a four-handled krater with a drinking cup inside was found in situ, and farther
south, the lower part of an amphora, also with a drinking cup inside, still lying within a
hole in the ground. Nearby, also on the floor, was a large ring stand.

These appear to be the remains of ritual banquets, for which there was yet more evidence: the floor was covered with animal bones and potsherds. Similar refuse was also
found around and on top of the altar. (There, however, the animal bones were strongly cal-
cified, as they seem to have been completely charred on the altar.) This kind of pottery,
consisting of bowls in all sizes and cylindrical, neckless jars—in short, pottery specifically

for food and drink—together with sherds of amphorae and occasionally dipper juglets and quantities of charred animal bones, mainly cattle (Boessneck and von den Driesch 1992: 19–20, 25–26), were found in deep pits sunk between the altar and the house during the later Hyksos period. Müller, who evaluated the pits and refuse around the altar, came to the conclusion that they constituted the remains of ritual meals consumed in front of the temple (1996; 1998), but the house and its inventory seem to provide evidence of a different, more-secluded kind of feasting.

The house was built within the precinct of Temple III. There was, however, also access from the next precinct on the east, belonging to Temple V, which was constructed parallel to the large Temple III. Temple V also had an inner and an outer forecourt, the former with an altar for burnt offerings and several *favissae* nearby. In the northern adjoining forecourt, the floor was littered with numerous sherds and charred animal bones (Boessneck and von den Driesch 1992: 19–20). Against the northern enclosure wall, a mudbrick bench was built. The waste material from this area should again be connected to ritual meals (Bietak and Müller in press). There was also, however, a corridor leading to the forecourt of Temple III, thus providing another access to this house. It is not unreasonable to assume that it served as a banquet house for a restricted group of people, perhaps a kind of elite.

What was the function of the temple complex? The parallel precincts of Temples III and V were surrounded by cemeteries. Therefore, a funerary function seems obvious. The acorns and the tree pits give no clear indication of which deity was accommodated therein: it may have been Asherah, who is associated with trees and groves (cf. LXX = Judg 6:25, 28, 30). It is not known which deity resided in the Temple II "broad-room" and which in Temple V, next to the main temple. Because a cemetery was attached to its eastern side and because it has nearly the same plan as the mortuary chapel in Cemetery I on the west, it seems feasible that it, too, was a mortuary chapel. Near Eastern and Egyptian religious concepts obviously blended within this precinct.

The house attached to the sacred precinct of Temple III, therefore, most likely served as a place for funerary banquets at the edge of the town. In this connection, I note that, in Cemetery IX (excavated partly by Forstner-Müller in 1997) a building with two rooms was found (instead of a mortuary chapel, as in Cemetery I) that looks like an ordinary house of its time (Forstner-Müller 2001: fig. 1). However, its position suggests a different function. Could it be that it also served for funerary repasts of the owners of this cemetery? Perhaps the difference between a mortuary chapel and a funerary banquet house is not so great, as examples from Egypt may illustrate. One is reminded of the so-called "Beautiful Festival of the Valley" in western Thebes, which was a necropolis festival (Schott 1968; Graefe 1986). The families of the deceased used to visit their funerary chapels on the cliffs of the west bank and passed the days of the event feasting and drinking, sometimes (as tomb paintings reveal with malice), to excess. From what we know of this festival, it seems to have originated from a visit of the god Amun from his abode in Karnak to the goddess Hathor, the mistress of the necropolis.

One can imagine that in the syncretistic world of Tell el-Dab'a, the goddess Asherah had taken over features of Hathor and become a patroness for this sacred precinct and its enclosed cemeteries (Bietak 1996: 36–48). Because Avaris was a seaport from the Middle

Kingdom onward, not only can the presence of a fair proportion of Near Eastern population be explained in this way, but also the epithet "Asherah from the Sea."

II. The Fosse Temple at Lachish

The so-called Fosse Temple at Lachish (Tell ed-Duweir; figs. 3–4) has captured the attention of archaeologists since its discovery (Tufnell, Inge, and Harding 1940; Gittlen 1982). The presence of a shrine outside the town at the northwestern foot of the mound within the moat of the Middle Bronze Age defense system is unusual. Interpretations such as a cult place serving outsiders or Bedouin (Tufnell, Inge, and Harding 1940: 10) or even as a pottery workshop (Ottosson 1980: 86–92) have been suggested.[3] These can easily be refuted on the basis of the presence of numerous imported luxury items from Egypt, Cyprus, and the Mycenaean world more suited to an elite society. The three phases of the temple, which date roughly to the second half of the 18th and into the 19th Dynasties (ca. 1450–1200 B.C.E.), with their associated material culture, helped to establish a relative chronology for the Late Bronze Age.

Because the temple is situated outside the town and near Late Bronze Age burials (Cemeteries 100 and 200 [Tufnell 1953: pl. 125; 1958: pl. 89]),[4] it is feasible that this building could be associated with funerary activities.

Fosse Temple I is a "broad-room" temple with bent axis, oriented north–south, with the entrance in the eastern long wall and the cult niche to the left of the entrance axis in the southern wall. Temples II and III have an extraordinary plan that does not fit the common concept of Near Eastern temples: an almost square central hall with a ceiling supported by four columns containing several rows of benches arranged along the northern, eastern, and western walls. A dais and later a cult niche were built against the southern wall. The entrance via an asymmetrical entrance room is positioned west of the axis of the building, and in the south, accessible from both sides of the cult niche, is a double room.[5]

The plan has strong affinities with the Egyptian house, including orientation, the asymmetrical entrance room, the square central room with four columns, and the double room in the south (Wright 1985: 125, 129, 236). The square central room is disproportionately large, measuring about 20 × 20 Egyptian cubits.[6] This can be seen as an adaptation of the room for a special function. The emphasis on the square central room can also be

---

3. On the Fosse Temple, see also Busink 1970: 405–12; Gittlen 1982; Wimmer 1990: 1070–71; 1998: 89; Mazar 1992: 179; Ussishkin 1993: 899–900.

4. Even if only a few Late Bronze Age tombs have been found, it can be expected that a town the size of Lachish would have had, besides tombs within the town, a necropolis of considerable size situated largely undiscovered outside the town.

5. The excavators reconstructed for Temple II only one room attached to the southern wall of the central room, but the second room must have belonged to this phase, because the door in the southern wall would otherwise be meaningless (Tufnell, Inge, and Harding 1940: pl. 67).

6. At Kahun and at Tell el-Amarna, only the largest living units and houses have four-columned central rooms. There are, however, ordinary houses of the Second Intermediate period with four-columned central rooms at Elephantine (von Pilgrim 1996a: fig. 4, pl. 1a–1d; 1996b: figs. 9, 35, 48, 65, 68, 81). The central hall is not exactly square, with the 20-cubit measurement of the inner width of the hall alternating with the north–south measurement of 20 cubits including the north wall. This is a typical Egyptian practice in measuring an area for the layout of a building.

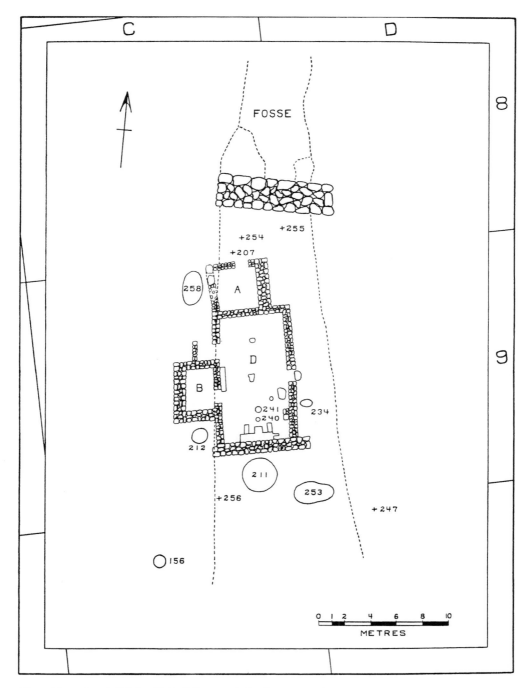

Fig. 3. Fosse Temple I (after Tufnell, Inge, and Harding 1940: pl. 66).

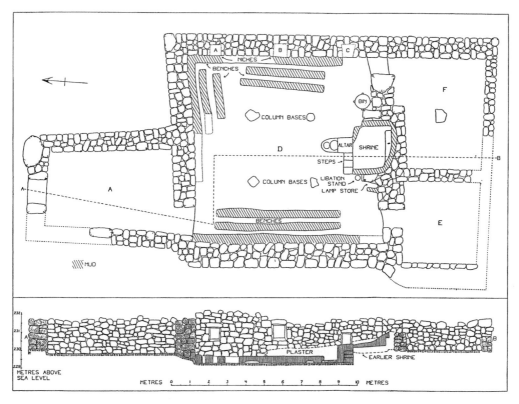

Fig. 4. Fosse Temple III (after Tufnell, Inge, and Harding 1940: pl. 68).

found in funerary architecture. In the rock tombs of the Middle and New Kingdoms in Egypt we find again and again more or less square funerary chambers with four columns, hewn out of the rock. This element and the portico are taken from domestic architecture. The central hall served as the sitting or reception room. Against its southern wall was the dais upon which the lord of the house was accommodated. In tombs, this was replaced by the cult niche, often with a statue of the owner of the tomb. Only the orientation was changed—to the west (in western cemeteries) or to the east (in eastern cemeteries, for example at Beni Hassan).

The remains within Fosse Temples I–III give a clear indication of their function (Bietak 2002). It seems that the complete inventory of the final building survived the conflagration and destruction at the end of the Late Bronze Age. During the lifespan of these so-called temples, cleanup and burial of material that had been broken or had fallen into disuse was obviously done only occasionally, after longer intervals. The functional indicators among the finds are quantities of animal bones and no fewer than 60 cooking pots, plates, bowls, drinking cups, goblets, jugs and pitchers, kraters, amphorae, and vats found distributed on the floor and benches or buried in pits. Among these were luxury items like Cypriot White Slip I and II, Base Ring I and II, and Red Lustrous wheel-made ware and

Bichrome kraters and jugs, together with Mycenaean vessels, a Mycenaean ivory pyxis, and Egyptian faience and glass vessels. The recovered remains of the inventory provide convincing evidence of food and drink typical of an elite society. Egyptian calcite vessels, normally used to hold unguents, show that members of the congregation anointed themselves for this event. The location of the temple outside the town and the proximity of the necropolis suggest that this was a place where funerary repasts were held. The cult niche in the southern wall of the main room shows that most likely a deity was venerated and invoked in connection with the ritual meals.

The affinities with the Egyptian house and tomb chapel can be explained as an influence from Egypt, where tomb chapels were places of funerary meals, not only after the burial but also during annual necropolis festivals (see above). We have evidence of a strong Egyptian influence at Lachish, particularly in the period of the 19th and 20th Dynasties. It is not impossible that this influence began in the post-Amarna period and continued thereafter, when Fosse Temples II and III were functioning.

III. The "Shrine of the Calf" at Ashkelon

A most interesting situation can be seen in the results of the excavations at Ashkelon.[7] Outside the city gate and fortification system, which was renewed several times during the MB IIA–B, was a building that already existed in the MB IIB (phase 11). The structure, set into the foot of the rampart, was situated on the track leading northwestwards to the supposed harbor. Its name derives from the discovery of a model terracotta shrine containing a silver-plated bronze figurine of a bull calf (fig. 5). The building does not look like a temple but more like a house. Small chambers (most likely storerooms) are arranged in an "L" shape around a large room. Remains within the building included an oven, animal bones, bowls, and drinking vessels, as well as amphorae and other containers for liquids—that is, evidence of food and drink. The building was surrounded by contemporary burials, thus showing much more strongly a direct relationship and association between funerary activity and funerary meals than at Lachish. The model shrine with the bull-calf figurine lends a cultic connotation to this building. Images of bulls are often associated with El or Baal, and the bull calf makes the association with Baal more likely (Stager 1991: 6–7).

IV. The Sacred Precinct of Nahariya

Situated some 100 m north of the remains of an ancient town, overlooking the sea, the sacred precinct of Nahariya (MB IIA–B) warrants special attention (see fig. 6; Yogev and Dothan 1993). Its isolated location has been explained by the presence of a spring at the site. The sanctuary seems to have been originally a High Place, a *bamah*, as ritual waste from the time before the earliest building shows. In Stratum A, a square structure (ca. 6 × 6 m), called the "Square Temple," was built next to a *bamah*, with stairs leading up from the north. If the square structure was not itself a *bamah*, it became so in Stratum B, when it

---

7. The ongoing Leon Levy Expedition is directed by L. E. Stager of Harvard University, to whom I am grateful for drawing my attention to the location of the "Shrine of the Calf" and for his encouragement and permission to write about it (see Stager 1991: 3–7).

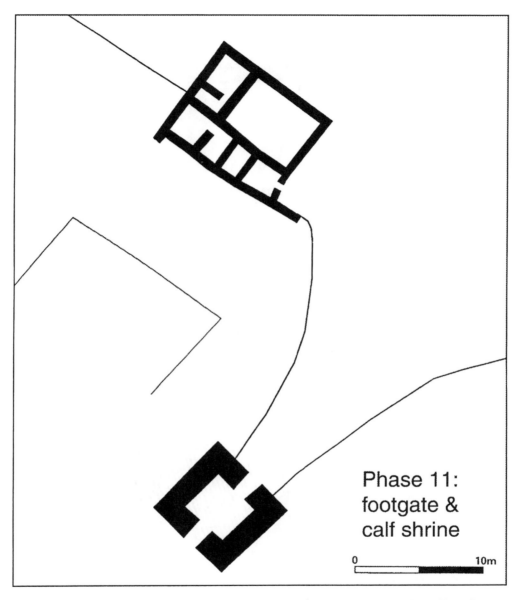

Fig. 5. The "Shrine of the Calf" at Ashkelon (courtesy of L. E. Stager, Leon Levy Expedition to Ashkelon).

was incorporated into a large High Place. The 14-m-long sides of this *bamah* were reduced in width in Stratum C. The High Place was surrounded on all sides by ritual deposits and waste.

The building of primary interest to us is a "broad-room" constructed during Stratum B north of the *bamah*, facing south. The ceiling was supported by a row of four columns. Floors 7–5 belong to this phase. In Stratum C, the building was enlarged with the addition

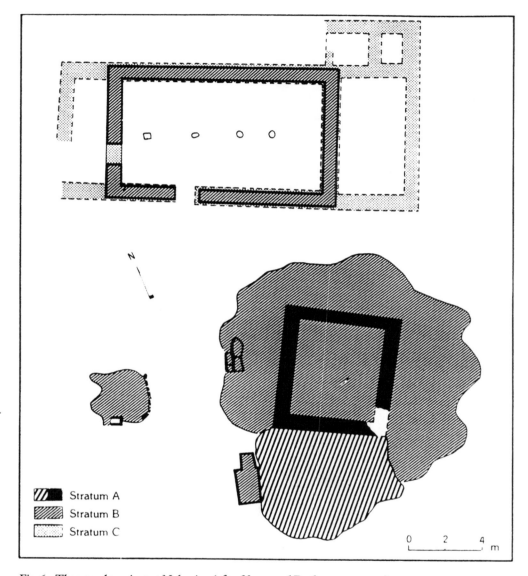

Fig. 6. The sacred precinct at Nahariya (after Yogev and Dothan 1993: 1090).

of rooms to the east and west along its narrow sides. Room 2 was used as a kitchen. The
earlier phase of the building had four distinctive floors (4–1). Little was found on these
floors other than animal bones and sherds. More refuse was found in front of the building,
including animal bones and sherds that are mainly from cooking pots.[8]

Typical votive offerings were found mainly around the *bamah*, and not in the building
itself. The majority consists of model vessels, ritual bowls with seven cups and seven-

---

8. Unfortunately, the remains from the floors and the refuse between the "broad-room" and the *bamah*
are, like most of the material, as yet unpublished.

spouted oil lamps, together with carinated bowls with a disc base, jugs, and pottery figurines of animals, some representing monkeys, which seem to demonstrate Egyptian influence. A monkey also appears as the spout of a juglet. Other such offerings included jewelry (beads and gold and silver pendants), bronze weapons, and nude female figurines. Of special interest is a stone mold for a bronze figurine of a nude deity with two horns on a high conical headdress, identified by the excavators as "Asherah of the Sea" (Yogev and Dothan 1993: 1091–92).

As can be seen from the location of the votive offerings, the real sanctuary seems to have been the commanding High Place. The "broad-room" not only lacks *ex-votos*, but also a podium or cult niche. It could have been a temple, but the other alternative may be preferable, that is, a ritual banqueting hall later attached to the *bamah*. The installation of a kitchen, the numerous cooking pots, and the animal bones would support such an explanation. Whether such an activity would be connected to funerary customs outside the town is for the moment difficult to determine; the location of the tombs is unknown and the area is covered by modern settlements. Examples of monkey figurines in Egyptian temples are often considered as remains associated with ancestor cults (Kaplony 1977: 1078–79; Dreyer 1986: 68–73). Whether this also applies to Nahariya is difficult to assess. The building, however, also could have served to house ritual meals connected with the *bamah* and its divinity, based on the find of the mold for the divine bronze figurine, most likely Asherah.

V. Conclusion

Given the above examples of archaeological evidence of places for ritual meals located outside towns or on their perimeters, in three cases in the vicinity of cemeteries (except for Nahariya, where this association is possible but thus far unsubstantiated), the conclusion that special buildings were supplied for funerary meals near the tombs is logical. In most cases the plan of the buildings are those of houses, not temples. There is some evidence that deities were included in the rituals performed in these buildings. It is interesting in this context that in two cases we seem to have some evidence of an association with Asherah.

Funerary and ritual meals are well known in Egypt, with funerary banquet and festival scenes recorded on the walls of tombs dating from the third and second millennia onward. We have literary evidence from the ancient Near East that ritual feasting was already institutionalized by the third millennium (texts from Ebla), the second millennium (texts from Ugarit), the first millennium (the Hebrew Bible and many other sources), and the Roman and Byzantine periods. The most important term for such an institution was *marzeaḥ*, including the building, *bêt marzeaḥ*.[9]

From what we know from these sources, the *marzeaḥ* was an organization, the members of which congregated for ritual feasting and drinking, sometimes to excess. The *marzeaḥ* was an institution that owned property: besides the *bêt marzeaḥ* and its furbishings, it also

---

9. For literature on *marzeaḥ*, see Eissfeldt 1969; Miller 1971; Friedman 1979–80; Pope 1981; King 1989; Lewis 1989; Bordreuil and Pardee 1990; McLaughlin 1991; and Bottéro 1993. For providing me with information on the institution of *marzeaḥ*, I would like to thank Hanan Eshel, Aren Maeir, and Irit Ziffer.

owned fields, vineyards, and other properties, the revenues from which sustained the institution. Events took place during festivals in honor of gods and were, in this case, associated with temples. There were also *marzeaḥ* funerary meals to honor the dead and console their families (Jer 16:5–9).

The ample literary evidence of the *marzeaḥ* has, to my knowledge, rarely been supported by archaeological evidence. The above-mentioned model cases would fit well with the concept of a *bêt marzeaḥ*. Other examples may soon be identified as possible archaeological counterparts and may help us to understand aspects of social life in antiquity.

References

Bietak, M.

1975   *Tell el-Dabʿa II: Der Fundort im Rahmen einer archäologisch-geographischen Untersuchung über das ägyptische Ostdelta*. Untersuchungen der Zweigstelle Kairo des Österreichischen Archäologischen Institutes 1. Vienna: Österreichischen Akademie der Wissenschaften.

1979   Avaris and Piramesse: Archaeological Exploration in the Eastern Nile Delta. *Proceedings of the British Academy, London* 65: 225–90.

1991   *Tell el-Dabʿa V: Ein Friedhofsbezirk mit Totentempel der Mittleren Bronzezeit im östlichen Nildelta*. Untersuchungen der Zweigstelle Kairo des Österreichischen Archäologischen Institutes 8. Vienna: Österreichischen Akademie der Wissenschaften.

1994   Der Sakralbezirk von Avaris. Pp. 41–46 in *Pharaonen und Fremde, Dynastien im Dunkel*. Catalogue of a special exhibition at the Historisches Museum at the City of Vienna. Vienna: Museum der Stadt Wien.

1996   *Avaris, the Capital of the Hyksos: Recent Excavations at Tell el-Dabʿa*. The First Raymond and Beverly Sackler Foundation Distinguished Lecture in Egyptology. London: British Museum.

2001   Dabʿa, Tell ed-. Pp. 351–54 in vol. 1 of *The Oxford Encyclopedia of Ancient Egypt*, ed. D. B. Redford. New York: Oxford University Press.

2002   The Function and Some Architectural Roots of the Fosse Temple at Lachish. Pp. 56–85 in *Aharon Kempinski Memorial Volume: Studies in Archaeology and Related Disciplines*, ed. E. D. Oren and S. Ahituv. Beersheba: Ben-Gurion University of the Negev.

Bietak, M., and Müller, V.

In press   *Tell el-Dabʿa: Der Sakralbezirk und die Tempel*. Untersuchungen der Zweigstelle Kairo des Österreichischen Archäologischen Institutes. Vienna: Österreichischen Akademie der Wissenschaften.

Boessneck, J., and von den Driesch, A.

1992   *Tell el-Dabʿa VII: Tiere und historische Umwelt im Nordost-Delta im 2. Jahrtausend anhand der Knochenfunde der Ausgrabungen 1975–1986*. Untersuchungen der Zweigstelle Kairo des Österreichischen Archäologischen Institutes 10. Vienna: Österreichischen Akademie der Wissenschaften.

Bordreuil, P., and Pardee, D.

1990   Le papyrus du marzeaḥ. *Semitica* 36: 49–68.

Bottéro, J.

1993   Boisson, banquet et vie sociale. Pp. 3–13 in *Drinking in Ancient Societies: History and Culture of Drinks in the Ancient Near East*. Proceedings of a Symposium Held in Rome, May 17–19, 1990, ed. L. Milano. Padova: Sargon srl.

Busink, T. A.

1970   *The Temple of Jerusalem*. Leiden: Brill.

Dreyer, G.

1986   *Elephantine VIII: Der Tempel der Satet*. Mainz: von Zabern.

Eissfeldt, O.
1969   Kultvereine in Ugarit. *Ugaritica* 6: 187–95.
Friedman, R. E.
1979–1980   The MRZḤ Tablet from Ugarit. *Maarav* 2/2: 187–205.
Forstner-Müller, I.
2001   Vorbericht der Grabung im Areal A/II in Tell el-Dabʿa 1997. *Egypt and the Levant* 11: 197–220.
Gittlen, B. M.
1982   Form and Function in the New Late Bronze Age Temple at Lachish. Pp. 67*–69* in *Eretz-Israel* 16 (Orlinski Volume), ed. B. A. Levine and A. Malamat. Jerusalem: Israel Exploration Society.
Graefe, E.
1986   Talfest. Pp. 187–89 in vol. 6 of *Lexikon der Ägyptologie*, ed. W. Helck and W. Westendorf. Wiesbaden: Harrassowitz.
Heinrich, E.
1982   *Die Tempel und Heiligtümer im Alten Mesopotamien.* Denkmäler antiker Architektur 14. Berlin: de Gruyter.
Kaplony, P.
1977   Hedjwer. Pp. 1078–80 in vol. 2 of *Lexikon der Ägyptologie*, ed. W. Helck and W. Westendorf. Wiesbaden: Harrassowitz.
King, P. J.
1989   The Marzeaḥ: Textual and Archaeological Evidence. Pp. 98*–106* in *Eretz-Israel* 20 (Yadin Volume), ed. A. Ben-Tor, J. C. Greenfield, and A. Malamat. Jerusalem: Israel Exploration Society.
Lewis, T. H.
1989   *Cults of the Dead in Ancient Israel and Ugarit.* Harvard Semitic Monographs 39. Atlanta: Scholar Press.
Mazar, A.
1992   Temples of the Middle and Late Bronze Ages and the Iron Age. Pp. 16–187 in *The Architecture of Ancient Israel: From the Prehistoric to the Persian Periods*, ed. A. Kempinski and R. Reich. Jerusalem: Israel Exploration Society.
McLaughlin, J.
1991   The Marzeaḥ at Ugarit: A Textual and Contextual Study. *Ugarit Forschungen* 23: 265–81.
Miller, P. D.
1971   The MRZḤ Text. Pp. 37–48 in *The Claremont Ras Shamra Tablets*, ed. L. R. Fisher. Analecta Orientalia 48. Rome: Pontifical Biblical Institute.
Müller, V.
1996   *Opfergruben der Mittleren Bronzezeit in Tell el-Dabʿa.* Ph.D. dissertation, University of Göttingen. [currently being revised for publication in the Tell el-Dabʿa series]
1997   Offering Deposits at Tell el-Dabʿa. Pp. 793–805 in *Proceedings of the Seventh International Congress of Egyptologists, Cambridge, 3–9 September 1995*, ed. C. J. Eyre. Orientalia Lovaniensia Analecta 82. Leuven: Peeters.
Ottosson, M.
1980   *Temples and Cult Places in Palestine.* Acta Universitatis Upsaliensis: Boreas—Uppsala Studies in Ancient Mediterranean and Near Eastern Civilizations 12. Uppsala: Almqvist & Wiksell.
Pilgrim, C. von
1996a   Elephantine im Mittleren Reich: Bemerkungen zur Wohnarchitektur in einer "gewachsenen" Stadt. Pp. 253–64 in *House and Palace in Ancient Egypt*. Proceedings of International Symposium in Cairo, April 8 to 11, 1992. Vienna: Österreichischen Akademie der Wissenschaften.

1996b   *Elephantine XVIII: Untersuchungen in einer Stadt des Mittleren Reiches und der Zweiten Zwischenzeit.* Archäologische Veröffentlichungen 91. Mainz: von Zabern.

Pope, M. H.
1981   The Cult of the Dead at Ugarit. Pp. 159–79 in *Ugarit in Retrospect: Fifty Years of Ugarit and Ugaritic*, ed. G. D. Young. Winona Lake, Ind.: Eisenbrauns.

Schott, S.
1986   *Das schöne Fest vom Wüstentale, Festbräuche einer Totenstadt.* Abhandlungen der Akademie der Wissenschaften und der Literatur in Mainz 11. Wiesbaden: Akademie der Wissenschaften und der Literatur in Mainz.

Stager, L. E.
1991   *Ashkelon Discovered.* Washington: Biblical Archaeology Society. [Collection of reprints from *Biblical Archaeology Review* 8/2–4]

Tufnell, O.
1953   *Lachish III: The Iron Age.* London: Oxford University Press.
1958   *Lachish IV: The Bronze Age.* London: Oxford University Press.

Tufnell, O.; Inge, C. H.; and Harding, G. L.
1940   *Lachisch II: The Fosse Temple.* London: Oxford University Press.

Ussishkin, D.
1993   Lachish. Pp. 897–911 in vol. 3 of *The New Encyclopedia of Archaeological Excavations in the Holy Land*, ed. E. Stern. Jerusalem: Israel Exploration Society.

Wimmer, S.
1990   Egyptian Temples in Canaan and Sinai. Pp. 1065–1106 in vol. 2 of *Studies in Egyptology Presented to Miriam Lichtheim*, ed. S. Israelit-Groll. Jerusalem: Magnes.
1998   (No) More Egyptian Temples in Canaan and Sinai. Pp. 87–123 in *Jerusalem Studies in Egyptology*, ed. I. Shirun-Grumach. Ägypten und Altes Testament 40. Wiesbaden: Harrassowitz.

Winkler, E. M., and Wilfing, H.
1991   *Tell el-Dabʿa VI: Anthropologische Untersuchungen an den Skelettresten der Kampagnen 1966– 69, 1975–80, 1985.* Untersuchungen der Zweigstelle Kairo des Österreichischen Archäologischen Institutes 9. Vienna: Österreichischen Akademie der Wissenschaften.

Wright, G. R. H.
1985   *Ancient Buildings in South Syria and Palestine.* Handbuch der Orientalistik 7/1. Leiden: Brill.

Yogev, O., and Dothan, M.
1993   Nahariya. Pp. 1088–94 in vol. 3 of *The New Encyclopedia of Archaeological Excavations in the Holy Land*, ed. E. Stern. Jerusalem: Israel Exploration Society.

Amarna and Later: Aspects of Social History

Anson F. Rainey

Department of Archaeology and Ancient Near Eastern Studies
Tel Aviv University

It is a sad paradox that the materially rich Middle Bronze Age has produced very little epigraphic evidence to help us understand the social history of this era. From the Late Bronze Age, however, when there was a considerable decline in the affluence and political status of the city-states, a relatively abundant corpus of inscriptions has been discovered. At the top of the epigraphic lists stand the Amarna Letters, 350 epistles discovered at the transitory capital of Amenhotep IV. Royal and other inscriptions from the pharaohs of the 18th and 19th Dynasties also deal with affairs in the Levant.

I. The Province Of Canaan

Geographically, the texts leave no doubt that the Egyptian administration dominated a province in the southern Levant and that this province was a well-defined entity called "Canaan." The same geopolitical situation prevailed throughout the ancient times, even up to the Roman period. The Phoenicians recognized the equation Phoenicia = Canaan, and this entity was the southern Levant, excluding the northern Syrian coast. The numismatic evidence from Beirut is decisive:

> Coins of Beirut: *l'dk' 'š bkn'n*, "Laodicea which is in Canaan," along with a Greek monogram, either ΛΑ(οδίκεια) Φ or ΒΗ(ρυτος). Other coins have *lbyrt*, "Of Beirut," also with the monogram ΛΑ Φ = Λαοδίκεια ἡ ἐν Φοινίκῃ, "Laodicea which is in Phoenicia." Thus, Phoenicia = Canaan. (Weippert 1980: 354)

Λαοδίκεια of Beirut is identified as being in Canaan, thus distinguishing it from Λαδίκεια ἐπὶ τῇ θαλάττῃ, "Laodicea on the sea" (Strabo 16.2.9), which is modern day Latakia, just 11 km south of Ras Shamra.

An Amarna letter from Alashia, written by a scribe trained in the Middle Babylonian tradition, uses the typical Middle Babylonian terminology to describe this province:

EA 36

⌈*pi*⌉-*ḫa-ti ša ki-na-'i*, "the province of Canaan." (EA 36:15; Rainey 1995–96: 111; 1996: 7–8; contra Moran 1992: 110, n. 1 p. 109; cf. *i-na ṭup-pi šu-ku-un-ma*, "put in a letter," EA 37:17)

At Alalakh in the northern Syrian kingdom of Mugish, a list of foreign mercenaries includes a Canaanite:

AT 181

Line 1—ERÍN.MEŠ LÚ.SA.GAZ EN GIŠ.TUKUL.MEŠ = *ṣābū ʿapīrū bēl kakki,* "Soldiers, *ʿapīrū,* owners of weapons," or "*ʿApīru*-soldiers, armed."
Line 9—^{I}*Šar-ni-ia* DUMU KUR *Ki-in$_4$-a-ni*^{KI}, "Šarniya, a son of the land of Canaan."
(Wiseman 1953: 71; 1954: 11)

Since a Canaanite was a foreigner at Alalakh, Canaan obviously did not extend into northern Syria. In the "Apology" of Idrimi, we find a clear-cut allusion to the town of Ammiya (in northern Lebanon), a town far south of Alalakh (and Ugarit), and located in the territory known as Canaan:

Statue of Idrimi

i-na ša-ni u$_4$-mi / an-mu-uš-ma ù a-na ma-at Ki-in-a-ni$_7$^{KI} / *al-li-ik i-na ma-at Ki-in-a-ni$_7$*^{KI} /
URU *Am-mi-ia*^{KI} *aš-bu*
The next day I went forth and came to the land of Canaan. The town of Ammiya is located in the land of Canaan. (stela of Idrimi, lines 13–28 [Smith 1949: pls. 9–10; Greenstein and Marcus 1976: 64, 67, 73–78])

The king of Mitanni knew very well that there were kings, vassals of pharaoh, in a territory called Canaan:

EA 30

a-na LUGAL.MEŠ *ša* KUR *Ki-na-a-áʾ*[*-ʾi*] / ÌR.MEŠ ŠEŠ-*ia um-ma* LUGAL-$^⌐$*ma*$^⌐$ / *a-nu-um-ma*
A-ki-ia LÚ.DUMU.KIN-*ia* / *a-na* UGU *šàr* KUR *Mi-iṣ-ri-i* ŠEŠ-*ia* / *a-na du-ul-lu-ḫi a-na kál-le-e* /
al-ta-pár-šu ma-am-ma / *lu-ú la i-na-aḫ-ḫi-is-šú* / *na-aṣ-ri-iš i-na* KUR *Mi-iṣ-ri-i* / *šu-ri-bá ù a-na*
ŠU / $^{⌐LÚ⌐}$*ḫal-*$^⌐$*zu*$^⌐$*-uḫ-li ša* KUR *Mi-iṣ-ri-i-i* / *id-*$^⌐$*na*$^⌐$*-*$^⌐$*ni*$^⌐$(?) *ḫa-mut-ta li-il-*$^⌐$*li*$^⌐$*-*$^⌐$*ik*$^⌐$ / *ù is-sú*
mi-im-ma / *i-na muḫ-ḫi-šu lu-ú la ib-bá-aš-ši*
To the kings of the land of Canaan, the servants of my brother, thus (speaks) the king: Now Akiya, my ambassador, have I sent to speed posthaste to the king of Egypt. Let no one detain him. Provide him with safe entry to Egypt and hand him over to the fortress commander of Egypt. Let him go on quickly and may there not be any pitfall in his way.
(Artzi 1975; Moran 1992: 100)

The ruler of Babylon also understood this situation perfectly:

EA 8:25

[KUR *K*]*i-na-áʾ-ʾi* KUR-*ka ù* $^⌐$LUGAL$^⌐$.ME[*š-ša* ÌR-*ka*]
[The land of C]anaan is your land and [its] king[s are your servants]. (Moran 1992: 16)

EA 9:19–21

i-na Ku-ri-gal-zu a-bi-ia ki-na-ʾa$_4$-ayyu-ú ga-ab-bi-šu-nu / *a-na mu-uḫ-ḫi-šu il$_5$-ta-ap-ru-ni*
um-ma-a a-na qa-an-ni KUR / $^⌐$*ku*$^⌐$*-*$^⌐$*uš*$^⌐$*-da-am-ma i na-ba-al-ki-ta-am-ma* / [*it-t*]*i-ka i ni-ša-ki-in*
In <the time of> Kurigalzu, my ancestor, all the Canaanites wrote here to him saying: "C[om]e to the border of the country so we can revolt and we can become allied [wit]h you." (Moran 1992: 18–19 nn. 4–5; CAD Q 81b; N/1 17a; Š/1 157a)

Officials in the Egyptian administration bore titles pertaining to their duties in the province of Canaan:

EA 367:7–8
ᴵḪa-an-ni DUMU *ᴵMa-i-re-ia* / LÚ.PA.TÙR *ša* LUGAL *i-na* KUR *Ki-na-á'-'ì*
Ḫanni, the son of Maireya, the stable overseer of the king in Canaan.

Furthermore, the local rulers themselves make reference to their status as vassals of Egypt:

EA 137:75–76
šum-ma qa-al LUGAL *a-na* URU.KI / *gáb-bi* DIDLI.URU.KI KUR *Ki-na-á'-ni ia-nu a-ʳnaˈ ša-šu*
If the king keeps silent concerning the city, none of the towns of Canaan will be his.

An Egyptian message to the ruler of Tyre takes cognizance of his position at an important intelligence-gathering post on the Lebanese coast. From his place *in Canaan* he is ordered to report all the news that has come his way.

EA 151:49–67
LUGAL *be-li-ia iš-ta-pár a-na ia*[*-š*]*ì* / *ša ta-aš-me iš-tu* KUR *Ki-na-á'-na* / *ù šu-pur a-na ia-ši* /
šàr KUR *Da-nu-na* BA.UG₇ / *ù ša-ar-ra* ŠEŠ*-šu* / *a-na* EGIR*-šu ù pa-aš-ḫa-at* / KUR*-šu ù* É *šàr* URU
*Ú-ga-ri-it*ᴷᴵ / *i-ku-ul i-ša-tu₄ mi-ši-ʳilˈ-šu* / *i-kúl ù mi-ši-<il>-šu ia-nu* / *ù* LÚ.MEŠ ERÍN KUR
Ḫa-at-ti ia-nu / *ᴵE-ta-ga-ma pa-wu-ri* / URU *Qí-id-ši ù* / *ᴵA-zi-ra nu-kúr-tu₄* / *it-ti*
ᴵBir₅-ia-wa-zi / *nu-kúr-tu₄* / *a-ta-mur ḫa-ba-li* / *ᴵZi-im-re-da* / *e-nu-ma ip-ḫu-ur* / GIŠ.MÁ.MEŠ
ERÍN.MEŠ *iš-tu* URU.DIDLI.ḪÁ *ᴵA-zi-ʳraˈ* / *a-na muḫ-ḫi-ia*
The king, my lord has written to me: "That which you have heard *from Canaan*, send to me"; the king of the land of Danuna is dead and his brother became king afterwards and his land is at peace; fire destroyed the palace of the king of Ugarit; it destroyed half of it and half of it not; but the Hittite army is not there; Etakkama, the ruler of Kedesh and Aziru are at war—it is with Biryawaza that they are at war; I have experienced the brutalities of Zimredda when he assembled the ships (and) troops from the cities of Aziru against me. (Rainey 1964; 1996: 8–11; Mangano 1990: 176–77; Moran 1992: 238–39 nn. 4–6; contra Lemche 1996, 1998)

Attempts to distort the meaning of this passage (Lemche 1998) in order to prove that "Canaan" could also refer to northern Syria (Ugarit) and even Cilicia (Danuna) are based on ignorance of Levantine geography and Akkadian semantics. See an exact parallel to the phrase cited above:

Taanach Text 1:15–18
ù a-wa-ta₅ ʳmiˈ-ʳimˈ-ʳmaˈ / *ša ti-iš-mé* / *iš-tu aš-ra-nu-um* / *šu-upˈ-ra-am it-<ti>-i*[*a*]
And whatever word that you have heard from there, send (in writing) to me. (Rainey 1977: 41, 43–44)

Also:

EA 145:23–26 from Sidon
a-wa-at-mi / *ti-iš-te₉-mé iš-tu aš-ra-ʳnuˈ-ʳumˈ* / *tú-te-ra-am a-na ia-a-ti*
The word that you have been hearing from there, send to me. (Mangano 1990: 176–77; Moran 1992: 232 n. 6)

Lemche's attempt to introduce EA 147:66–69 into the discussion completely misses the point. The request to Abimilki for news *from Canaan* represents a standard syntagma used by the scribes when a senior official requested information from a junior. The syntagma begins with an imperative and refers to the place where the recipient is located. EA 147:66–69 is not such a syntagma.

Ethnicity and nationality were also alive and well in the Late Bronze Age. Just ask any Egyptian!

EA 109:44–46
pa-na-nu da-ga-li-ma / ⌐LÚ⌐ KUR *Mi-iṣ-ri ù in₄-<na>-ab-tu* / ⌐LUGAL⌐.MEŠ KUR *Ki-na-áʾ-ni iš-tu pa-n[i-šu]*
Formerly, seeing a man of Egypt, then the kings of Canaan fled bef[ore him].

The administrative texts from Ugarit, like those from Alalakh, also use ethnicons to designate foreigners at Ugarit; for example:

KTU 4.96 (= RS 11.840; Rainey 1963)
(03)	*aryn . adddy*	ʾAriyannu, an Ashdodite
(06)	*nʿmn . mṣry*	Naʿmānu, an Egyptian
(07)	*yʿl . knʿny*	Yaʿilu, a Canaanite

KTU 4.230 (= UT 1089 = RS 16.341)
| (03) | *kd . l aṯr[y]m* | A jar for the Assyrians |
| (07) | *kd . l . mṣrym* | A jar for the Egyptians |

KTU 4.14 9 (= UT 1090 = RS 15.039)
| (04) | *kd l ḫty* | A jar for the Hittite |

As at Alalakh, a Canaanite is a foreigner at Ugarit. This is not to say that such "ethnicons" had a direct relation to one's DNA. The Egyptian listed above had a Semitic name, and the Ashdodite a Hurrian name. But every person had his own self-definition, which was recognized by his peers.

II. Society

The texts give a fair picture of most levels of society, at least the main ones. Local city-states in Canaan were much smaller that the territorial states of Ugarit or Mugish. They were ruled by a "king" whom the Egyptians called *ḫazananu*, "mayor."

Local Leadership

The local government was essentially an oligarchy. The chief responsibility was on the shoulders of the designated (usually dynastic) ruler, but in the absence of an official political chief executive, the council of "elders" would take charge. Two examples of such a situation are the following:

EA 100:1–4
ṭup-pí an-nu-ú ṭup-pí / URU *Ir-qa-ta a-na šàr-ri* / EN-*nu um-ma* URU *Ir-qa-ta ù* LÚ.MEŠ *ši-b<u>-ti-ši*
This tablet is the tablet of the city of ʿIrqata to the king our lord; thus (spoke) the city of ʿIrqata and its el<ders>. (Albright 1946: 23; Moran 1992: 173 n. 1)

EA 59:1–2

a-na šàr KUR-*ti*₄ *Mi-iṣ-ri be-li-ni / um-ma* DUMU.MEŠ URU *Tù-ni-ip*^KI LÚ^ÌR-*ka-ma*

To the king of the land of Egypt, our lord, thus (spoke) the sons (= citizens) of Tunip your servant.

These societies were in no sense "democracies," but oligarchies. The members of the council were the upper-class landowners, the "noblemen."

Maryannu

The "chariot warrior," whose status is best illustrated in the texts from Alalakh and Ugarit (Rainey 1965: 19–21), was to be found at each Levantine state, although the term *maryannu* is rarely used. However, there is a unique instance of this technical term in one of the Byblos texts:

EA 107:41–45

ù / ⌈*id*⌉-*na-ni* 30 *ta-pal /* [A]NŠE.KUR.RA *qa-du* GIŠ.GIGIR.MEŠ */* [*i*]-*ba-šu* LÚ.MEŠ ŠÌR (= KEŠDA) / ⌈*mar*⌉-*ia-nu-ma a-na ia-ši / ù ia-nu* ANŠE.KUR.RA / *a*-⌈*na*⌉ *ia-ši*

So give me thirty pairs of [ho]rses with chariots; I have *maryannu* warriors but I don't have horses. (Rainey 1989–90: 60; cf. Moran 1950: 166; 1992: 305 n. 3; 306–7 n. 2)

The ideogram ŠÌR (= KEŠDA) clearly is being used here as a designation for *maryannu*. It appears in a parallel text in which the Sumerian vocalization is given in a gloss (contra Liverani 1997), instead of the Akkadian (Indo-Ḫurrian) translation:

EA 108:13–17

la-qú ANŠE.KUR.RA.MEŠ */ šàr-ri ù* GIŠ.GIGIR.MEŠ *ù / na-ad-nu* LÚ.MEŠ ŠÌR \ *ši-ir-ma / ù* LÚ.MEŠ *wi-i-ma a-na / >a-na<* KUR *šu<-ba>-ri*

They took horses of the king and chariots and they gave chariot warriors and foot soldiers to the land of Su<ba>ru. (Moran 1992: 182 n. 3; cf. EA 109:40)

Ḫupšu

The Alalakh and Ugarit texts make it clear that this class of people was far down on the social ladder (Rainey 1965: 25). They were the yeoman farmers who tilled the soil for the wealthy landowners, but in times of stress, they could not be trusted.

EA 112:10–13

iš-tu ma-an-ni i-na-ṣa-ru-na / iš-tu na-ak-ri-ia / ù iš-tu LÚ.MEŠ *ḫu-up-ši-ia / mi-nu yi-na-ṣí-na-an-ni*

From whom should I be on guard? From my enemies? And from my yeoman farmers, who will protect me? (cf. Moran 1950: 169; 1992: 186)

EA 125:25–30

ù ia-nu ŠE.IM.ḪÁ */ a*-⌈*na*⌉ *a-ka*-⌈*li*⌉-*ia / ù* LÚ.MEŠ ⌈*ḫu*⌉-*up-ši / pa-aṭ-ru a*-[*na*] URU.MEŠ */ a-šar i-ba*-⌈*ši*⌉ ŠE.IM.⌈ḪÁ⌉ */ a-na a-ka-li-šu-nu*

And there is no grain for me to eat so my free men have departed to towns where there is grain for them to eat.

There can be no question of comparing the Amarna ḫupšu with the status offered by Saul to the slayer of Goliath.

1 Sam 17:25

וַיֹּאמֶר אִישׁ יִשְׂרָאֵל הַרְאִיתֶם הָאִישׁ הָעֹלֶה הַזֶּה כִּי לְחָרֵף אֶת־יִשְׂרָאֵל עֹלֶה וְהָיָה הָאִישׁ אֲשֶׁר־יַכֶּנּוּ יַעְשְׁרֶנּוּ
הַמֶּלֶךְ עֹשֶׁר גָּדוֹל וְאֶת־בִּתּוֹ יִתֶּן־לוֹ וְאֵת בֵּית אָבִיו יַעֲשֶׂה חָפְשִׁי בְּיִשְׂרָאֵל:

And the men of Israel said, "Have you seen this man who has come up? Because it is to revile Israel that he has come up. The king will enrich the man who smites him with great wealth, and his daugher he will give to him, and he will raise his father's house to free status."

To be sure, both words, ḫupšu and ḫōpeš are built on the *qutl* form of the same root, but their semantic connotations are entirely different. Albright made the equation between the ḫupšu and ḫōpšî (Albright 1924; 1926) and he was followed by Pedersen (1926). Gray had added the Ugaritic ḫpt̲ troops to the equation, claiming that they were "a class set apart for military service and, as such, enjoying certain privileges which are usually associated with the feudal system" (Gray 1952: 54–55). It is abundantly clear, however, that the ḫupšū were not one of the higher classes of society (Mendelsohn 1941; 1955). The same equation is accepted and elaborated on by Loretz (1984: 252–63). As I have pointed out before (Rainey 1975: 103–4; 1987: 541), there is really no reason for associating these two terms. This entire syndrome—an equation between an Amarna term, ḫupšu, with a biblical nisbe, ḫopšî—is related to the similar and equally invalid equation of ʿapîru with Hebrew ʿibrî, which I will deal with below.

ʿApîru

The only linguistic equation for this term that warrants consideration is offered by Borger—that is, that ʿapîru is the cognate of Syriac ʿăpîr, "dusty" (Borger 1958: 131). All the syllabic orthographies of this social designation show a vowel after the second radical. One never finds *ʿapru. This can only mean that one of the vowels is long, either ʿâpiru or ʿapîru. The most likely of the two is certainly ʿapîru. All other proposals are based on wishful thinking and/or faulty linguistic reasoning. The attempt to equate ʿapîr with ʿibrî is just as unreasonable as trying to equate pairs of words such as the following:

חפיר	≠	חבר
שפיר	≠	שבר
עפיר	≠	עבר

Note that all of these pairs have the same first consonant and the final radical is *reš*. The second radical is *pe* in one and *beth* in the other. The same absurd mental gymnastics would be required to assume that any word in the right column is cognate to its partner in the left column. But somehow wishful thinkers tend to ignore the linguistic realities.

As is well known, the ʿapîru (West Semitic term) and its ideographic Sumerian reflex, SA.GAZ (sometimes just GAZ in the Amarna texts), are documented through 800 years of history, from Ur III down to the Egyptian 20th Dynasty. They are never mentioned as pastoralists, and the preserved personal names of people bearing this designation do not come from a single linguistic group. There are Semites, Ḥurrians, and others. They never belong to tribes. They may worship various deities. Geographically they are known from east of the Tigris, to Anatolia, to Egypt—in short, throughout the ancient Near East. There is absolutely nothing to suggest an equation with the biblical Hebrews.

On the other hand, they are also not to be equated with "revolting peasants" throwing off the yoke of their feudal Canaanite overlords. The passage that might suggest this in fact says quite the opposite:

EA 288:43–44
a-mur ¹*Zi-im-re-da* URU *L[a-k]i-si*^KI *ig-gi-ú-šu* ÌR.MEŠ *ip-šu a-na* LÚ.MEŠ ⸢*ḫa*⸣-⸢*pí*⸣-⸢*ri*⸣
Behold, as for Zimredda (of) Lachish, they smote him, viz. servants that have joined the *ʿapîru* men. (Ebeling 1915: 1546; Moran 1992: 332 n. 10)

These "servants/slaves" included the brother of the ruler of Lachish, who actually succeeded Zimredda as city ruler of Lachish. The "servants" were those who were supposed to be loyal to Egypt, while the *ʿapîru* were people who had behaved disloyally toward pharaoh.

Neither did the documented *ʿapîru* want to escape to the mountains in order to "retribalize." On the contrary, they wanted to find a place in the good old Late Bronze Age feudal social structure. Usually their best option, as males with military training, was to become mercenaries. Sometimes they signed on with a charismatic adventurer such as Labʾayu of Shechem or ʿAbdi-Ashirta of Amurru or Idrimi of Alalakh. But they were also hired by the Egyptian authorities. They formed part of the Egyptian "foreign legion." A local ruler who had responsibilities as a district overseer for pharaoh had such troops under his command:

EA 195:24–32—Biryawaza, Comissioner of Kômidi, to Pharaoh Amenhotep IV or to Tutankhamon
a-nu-ma a-na-ku qa-du / ERÍN.MEŠ-*ia ù* GIŠ.GIGIR.MEŠ-*ia* / *ù qa-du* ŠEŠ-*ia* / *ù qa-du* LÚ.MEŠ SA.GAZ.MEŠ-*ia* / *ù qa-du* LÚ.MEŠ *šu-te-ia* / *a-na pa-ni* ERÍN.MEŠ *pí-ṭá-te* / *a-di a-šar yi-la-ku* / ¹LUGAL *be-li-ia*
Now, I, with my infantry and my chariotry and with my colleagues and with my *ʿapîrû* and with my *Sutû* (will be) at the head of the troops to wherever the king, my lord, shall go. (Rainey 1995: 490)

In fact, Biryawaza had hired mercenaries, who surely were outcasts from the urban city-state society, alongside a unit of nomadic warriors, the *Sutû*. Incidentally, this shows that nomadic mercenaries were never confused with urbanized *ʿapîru*.

The Egyptian government also recruited *ʿapîru* mercenaries for service in the foreign legion at bases in Cush (Sudan). The following letter from Kâmid el-Lôz deals with just this:

KL 69:277:5–11—Pharaoh to Ruler of Damascus
ša-ni-tam šu-bi-la-an-ni / LÚ.MEŠ SA.GAZ.ZA *a-bu-ur-ra* / *ša aš-pu-ra-ku* UGU-*šu-nu* / *um-ma-a a-na-an-din-šu-nu-ti* / *i-na* URU.ḪÁ KUR *Ka-a-ša* / *a-na a-ša-bi i-na lìb-bi-*⸢*šu*⸣ / ⸢*ki*⸣-*mu-ú ša aḫ-ta-bat-šu-nu-*⸢*ti*⸣

Furthermore, send me the *ʿapîru* men of the west(?) concerning which I wrote to you, saying, "I will cause them to dwell in the towns of Cush in place of those whom I carried off." (Cochavi-Rainey 1988: 42*–43*; cf. Edzard 1970: 55–60)

Cushite mercenaries, in turn, were often stationed in Canaan (cf. EA 287:33–37).

In this light, we must understand the references to *ʿapîru* in Egypt, for example:

Pap. Leiden 349:14–15

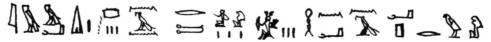

imy dỉ ỉty nȝ n rmt mšʿ ḥnʿ nȝ ʿprw
Cause to be given the grain of the army personnel with the *ʿapîru*.
(Greenberg 1955: 56–57)

These *ʿapîru* men are receiving rations alongside troops of the regular army. Both groups are engaged in some public project. There is no reason whatever to equate such *ʿapîru* with the Hebrews in Egypt—not socially, historically, and especially not linguistically.

III. Towns and Texts

There is finally a postmodernist quotation with which I can agree: "there is no archaeological record as such, only fragmented material traces of the past" (Hamilakkis 1999: 60). Archaeologists have to accept the fact that archaeological remains are the result of purely random processes of preservation. The absence of a stratum for some particular period does not necessarily mean that the site was not occupied at that time, especially when there is strong epigraphic evidence to the contrary.

The ancient city of Byblos is a case in point. Nearly 70 Amarna Letters were written there and sent to Egypt. They make it clear that this important commercial export city had a palace and at least one temple, all filled with riches.

EA 137 from Beirut, concerning Byblos
ú-ul ia-qú-ul₁₁-mi LUGAL *be-li iš-tu* / URU-li^KI *šum-ma ma-gal ma-ad* / KÚ.BABBAR GUŠKIN *a-na lìb-bi-ši a-na* É DINGIR.MEŠ-*ši* / *ma-ad mi-im-mu*
May the king, my lord, not neglect the city (Byblos), since there is very much silver and gold in it; in its temple there is much property.

But the excavations found no Amarna Age stratum at Byblos; from the Crusader and Roman periods, they went directly into the Middle Bronze Age. It is said that the excavator failed to recognize some elements of Late Bronze Age remains. If so, this was probably due, not only to the poor methods used by the excavator, but also to the badly disturbed state of whatever Late Bronze Age strata had been there. There is also the possibility that a portion of the tell, perhaps with its royal palace, has been eroded away by the action of the sea (as in the case of a large portion of Tel Michal on the coast north of Tel Aviv). Furthermore, the Tale of Wenamon attests to a major seaport there with a palace and a temple at Byblos in the 11th century B.C.E., but no 11th-century stratum was found. The Aḥîrôm funerary inscription, the Yəḥîmilk building inscription, the ʾAbîbaʿl inscription (on the base of a Shishak statue), and the ʾElîbaʿl inscription (on a statue of Osorkon I) all attest to a rich occupation at Byblos in the 10th century B.C.E., but neither is there a stratum from the 10th century. The epigraphic evidence is conclusive: Byblos was a thriving city with major buildings during the 14th, 11th, and 10th/9th centuries. The absence of stratified archaeological remains from those periods is indeed regrettable, but not determinative for the occupational history of the site.

Naʾaman (1996) has made the same point with regard to Jerusalem. There are six Amarna Letters from ʿAbdi-Ḫeba, the ruler of the city, that point to a well-established dynastic center:

EA 287 from Jerusalem

a-mur a-na-ku la-a ᴸᵁ*a-bi-ia* / *ù la-a* ᴹᴵ*ú-mi-ia* \ *ša-ak-na-ni* / *i-na aš-ri an-ni-e* / *zu-ru-úʾšàr-ri* ᴷᴬᴸ.ᴳᴬ / *ú-še-ri-ba-an-ni a-na* É ᴸᵁ*a-bi-ia*

Look, as for me, it was not my father and it was not my mother who put me in this place; the strong arm of the king installed me in my father's house.

The Amarna Letters from Jerusalem are themselves archaeological finds. Their written contents are weighty testimony that cannot be gainsaid. It is hardly credible that the town existed only in proximity to the Gihon Spring. It is inconceivable that anyone would settle down below and leave the present "Temple Mount" unoccupied. That latter is a hill that dominates the entire ridge. No settlement below it would be safe unless it were secured by substantial fortification on the hill above. The fact that bedrock is presently exposed on the "Temple Mount" is no obstacle.

Years ago Albright noted concerning Râs el-Kharrûbah:

Dr. Bergman's suggestion that the traces of occupation before the exile are not sufficiently numerous to warrant our locating Anathoth here, is unnecessary. . . . It is hard to overestimate the effect of more than two thousand years of denudation on such exposed summits, bearing the ruins of unwalled villages, at the top of the watershed ridge in central Palestine. (Albright 1936: 6)

Although the subsequent excavations conducted by Biran (formerly Bergman) have shown (Biran 1985) that a more likely candidate for the 7th-century site of Anathoth was at Deir es-Sîd, Albright's general observation holds true. Today we can add the evidence from el-Jîb, Tell en-Naṣbeh, Tell el-Fûl, Ramat Raḥel, and Khirbet Rabûd. At all these sites, bedrock is exposed or near the surface at the center of the tell. And we might add the ancient tell of Bethehem upon which the Church of the Nativity stands; the sacred cave shows that bedrock would have been exposed on top of the mound. The Herodian engineers simply did not leave any previous remains when they built the giant temple platform in Jerusalem. Hadrian, the Moslems, and the Crusaders also must have radically changed the inner surface of the platform.

As with Byblos, the Jerusalem Amarna Letters attest to a Late Bronze city. Certain obviously authentic passages in the early chapters of the book of Kings also validate the presence of a capital city with a palace and temple in the 10th century B.C.E. (Naʾaman 1997). But that is a topic for some other occasion.

IV. Pastoralists

When Norman Gottwald first presented his thesis about the "revolting peasant theory" at the Society of Biblical Literature meeting in 1979, I thought that the whole issue would blow over within two years. I sadly underestimated the naïveté of so much of biblical scholarship. The theory, consciously or unconsciously, was adopted by many field archaeologists. One of the first to give support to the view that the new Iron I settlements in the Cisjordan highlands were established by the Canaanites from the western coastal areas was Callaway:

> My conclusion in the light of these discussions is that the Iron I villagers at Ai had their background in Canaanite culture and religion and that this can be documented extensively with artifacts which have their parallels at lowland and coastal sites. (Callaway 1987: 96–97)

Today, Callaway's view, which was widely accepted, is totally unnecessary (Franken 1975: 336; Finkelstein and Na'aman 1994: 10; Franken and London 1995). Recently, van der Steen has provided us with a series of articles that clarify the situation (1995; 1996; 1999). First, there is plenty of evidence that the occupants of Transjordan, even the pastoralists, were fully aware of the Late Bronze ceramic and other cultural traditions (van der Steen 1996). If the new settlers in the Iron I Hill Country sites in Cisjordan came from Transjordan, their pottery would be expected to reflect the Late Bronze traditions. Furthermore, the bedouin of Transjordan, especially in the Jordan Valley during the 19th century c.e., provide many illuminating parallels for ancient pastoralists in the process of sedentarization (van der Steen 1995; 1999). Today it is in vogue to seek anthropological theories to explain ancient societies; now van der Steen has given us real anthropology: analogies from bedouin life in the same ecological niche as the ancient Iron I settlers. Her studies make it abundantly clear that the best "model" for the transition from the Late Bronze to the Iron I is that of Transjordanian pastoralists and small farmers who moved from east to west, via the Jordan Valley, because of ecological stress.

The evidence for this ecological stress is assembled and ably discussed by Stiebing (1989: 167–87). His objection to a desert origin for the Israelites may be mitigated by the recognition that the pastoralists inhabited the steppe, which, incidentally, is the correct translation of the Semitic *madbaru/miḏbār*. The same ecological stress (decreasing rainfall, declining productivity) throughout the eastern Mediterranean and the Near East brought the Libyans into the Egyptian delta, the Phrygians into Anatolia, the Aramaeans into Syria and Mesopotamia, not to mention the "Sea Peoples" into the Levant (also headed toward the delta, but via an eastern route along the coast of Syria/Canaan).

Israeli scholars who grew up during the 1970s knew the Jordan Valley as a modern military border; in their scholarship, the Jordan Valley remained a psychological border. In order to find an origin for the newly settled pastoralists at the end of the Late Bronze and beginning of the Iron Age, Finkelstein resorted to virtually "invisible" pastoralists who were in the Hill Country during the Late Bronze Age without leaving a trace (Finkelstein 1988: 343–44). However, some of his evidence (e.g., the shrine at the Amman airport) comes from Transjordan. Bunimovitz converts the Cisjordan Hill Country into a "frontier" to which people in distress migrated from the coastal plains (1994: 193–202). The reality—that pastoralists on the Transjordanian steppe, the real frontier, were always living in symbiosis with the sedentary population of Cisjordan and that pastoralists in the Syrian steppe lived in symbiosis with the sedentary population of the Lebanese Beqaʿ (and even the Lebanese coastal towns)—needs to be emphasized anew. The Sutû/Shasu were always there, and they continually appear in the texts. Some time ago Stager noted that there would not have been enough Canaanite peasants to populate all the new Iron I settlements that sprang up:

> Given the low aggregate of the Late Bronze Age population throughout Canaan, it appears unlikely that the peasantry, even if they had all "revolted," could have been large enough to account for the total Iron Age village population. (Stager 1985b: 84)

He also described the process of the "settlement," which van der Steen has so admirably expounded in detail, as follows:

> So long as the Late Bronze markets and exchange networks were still operating, the sheep-goat pastoralists would have found specialization in animal husbandry a worthwhile occupation. However, with the decline of these economic systems in many parts of Canaan in the late thirteenth to early twelfth centuries B.C.E. . . . the "pastoralist" sector, engaged in herding and huckstering, may also have found it advantageous to shift toward different subsistence strategies, such as farming with some stock raising. (Stager 1985b: 85; cf. Rainey 1989: 92)

There are Egyptian epigraphic testimonies to this process, specially texts from the 19th Dynasty. The graphic Karnak reliefs depicting Seti I's campaign to Canaan focus on the disruption caused by the Shasu pastoralists.

> The foe belonging to the Shasu are plotting rebellion. Their chiefs are gathered together, waiting *on the mountain ridges* of Kharru. They have begun clamoring and quarreling, one of them killing his fellow. They have no regard for the laws of the palace. (Kitchen 1970: I:9:3–8)

> The desolation which the mighty arm of Pharaoh . . . wrought among the foe belonging to the Shosu—from the fortress of Sillû to the Canaan. (Kitchen 1970: I:9:8–12)

It must be borne in mind that Kharru (or Khurru) was a synonym for Canaan in 19th-Dynasty texts.

The age-old need for pastoralists to seek relief during times of drought by immigrating to the Egyptian delta is illustrated by an entry in Papyrus Anastasi VI:

> We have completed the transfer of the Shasu tribes of Edom (*ʾá-du-ma*) past the fortress "Merneptah-ḥotep-ḥer-Maʿat . . ." which is in Ṣəku (= Succo[th]), to the pools (sic!) of Per-Atum (= Pithom) of "Merneptah-ḥotep-ḥer-Maʿat . . . ," which are in Ṣəku (= Succo[th]), in order to keep them alive and in order to keep their cattle alive.
>
> (lines 51–57 [Gardiner 1937: 76–77])

The terms "Edom" (*ʾá-du-ma*) and Mt. Seir need not refer to the mountains east of the ʿArabah. They were often applied to the highlands of the modern-day Negev (wrongly called)—for example, 1 Chr 4:42; Num 20:14ff.; Josh 15:21.

It may also be just a curiosity, but among the "lands" of the Shasu in a list from temples of the 18th and 19th Dynasties, the following reference appears:

Amara West No. 97 = Soleb 4A2

𓈉 𓆓 𓃀 𓏤𓏤 𓅓 𓆑𓋴

T3 š3sw Ya-h-wə
The land of the Shasu, Yahwə.

Is this a reference to Yahweh? No one knows. But it is interesting to note that in the very ancient and archaic poem called "The Song of Deborah," we find:

Judg 5:4

יְהוָה בְּצֵאתְךָ מִשֵּׂעִיר בְּצַעְדְּךָ מִשְּׂדֵה אֱדוֹם אֶרֶץ רָעָשָׁה גַּם־שָׁמַיִם נָטָפוּ גַּם־עָבִים נָתְפוּ מָיִם

Yahweh, when you went out from Seir, when you marched from the region of Edom, the earth trembled, and the heavens poured, the clouds indeed poured water.

Perhaps it is only a coincidence, but the most ancient literary tradition we have associated Yahweh with an area that can quite possibly be equated with a territory occupied by Shasu pastoralists.

Poem in the Merneptah Stela

In conclusion, the early reference to Israel in Egyptian texts must be considered. The passage in the Merneptah stela describing that pharaoh's campaign in Canaan can be seen to have a definite literary structure (Rainey 1992; see diagram, top of p. 181). The composer has chosen four geographical entities to represent the success of the campaign—three city-states and one socioethnic group. These may not have been all the enemies encountered during the campaign.

Yurco's research (1978; 1986; 1990; 1991; 1997) has shown that Merneptah also commissioned wall reliefs depicting his Canaanite victories on the outer face of the western wall enclosing the "Cour de Cachett" at Karnak. Three cities are shown, the preserved name of one of them being Ashkelon. There was surely a fourth city, to provide symmetry, which has largely been destroyed by the loss of at least three courses over most of the wall's length (Rainey 1999; 2001). However, Yurco has insisted that this fourth scene must depict a battle in the open field, in which the defeated enemies are identical to the socioethnic group mentioned in the poem.

Yurco's interpretation is nullified by four major errors in judgement on his part, as follows:

1. The assumption that there must be exact correspondence between the reliefs and the victory poem. Quite the contrary is the case. Thutmose III left his annals with the description of the conquest of Megiddo inside the Karnak temple; but his stelae, for example the stela found at Gebel Barkal, provide other details about the battle. Seti I, Merneptah's grandfather, recorded his first military campaign on the northern wall of the hypostyle hall of the Karnak temple; but the important details on the action in the Beth-shean Valley during the same campaign are ignored on the temple wall. For the conflict in the Beth-shean Valley and its resolution we are dependent on the victory stela of Seti I found there.

The Great Ones are prostrate, saying "Peace" (*ša-la-ma*);
Not one raises his head among the Nine Bows;
    Plundered is Theḥenu, Khatti is at *peace*;
        Canaan is plundered with every evil;
            Ashkelon ( ) is conquered;
            Gezer ( ) is seized;
            Yanuʿam ( ) is made non-existent;
            Israel ( ) is laid waste, his seed is no more;
        Kharu has become a widow because of Egypt;
    All lands together are at *peace*;
Any who roamed have been subdued.
                                    (Kitchen 1970: IV:19:1–8)

2. The assumption that one is required to read the reliefs starting from Ashkelon on the lower right and continue clockwise to the two on the left and then to the scene above Ashkelon (which he thus equates with the clash with Israel as on the stela). It has been pointed out that Yurco's "precedent" is highly questionable (Huddleston 1991).

3. The assumption that three towns, the depictions of which have survived on the relief, are (clockwise) Ashkelon, Gezer, and Yanuʿam. It is more likely that the scene of Pharaoh attacking a city on foot, instead of charging with his chariot, is to be equated with Yanuʿam. Yanuʿam was located in Transjordan, probably on a branch of the Yarmuk River (Naʾaman 1991).

4. The assumption that soldiers using chariots in open warfare can be equated with the socioethnic element mentioned in the poem on the stela and defined by the determinative . Anyone conversant with the status of the chariot warriors in the Late Bronze Age Levant (as in the texts from Alalakh and Ugarit [Rainey 1965]) and the concomitant expenses of maintaining the horses and the equipment would realize that Yurco's identification is impossible. This point alone should have been sufficient to rule out any identification of Israel on the stela with the Canaanite soldiers and their chariots on the relief.

The above illustration shows that the figures in the scene (Yurco's no. 4) are not only dressed as typical Canaanite soldiers, but also are using battle chariots. Yurco and Stager (1985a: 61*) have made some rather ineffectual attempts to explain how a socioethnic group (tribal or village) could have possessed such expensive and sophisticated a weapon as the battle chariot. If these soldiers, dressed as Canaanites, are using chariots, they cannot be equated with the socioethnic group demarcated by the determinative (𓏤𓀀𓏥).

In fact, soldiers like those in scene no. 4, dressed in typical Canaanite array, are to be seen fighting in the open country below Ashkelon. The caption reads:

> The wretched town which his majesty seized when it was rebellious, Ashkelon. (Kitchen 1970: II:2)

The horses are in such disarray that the chariot is obviously that of a fleeing enemy, but Stager nevertheless makes an attempt to assign the chariots to the Egyptians.

The upper left scene (Yurco's no. 3) also has Canaanite soldiers fighting in the open country beneath it:

The fleeing horseman and the prostrate Canaanites leave no doubt that these are vanquished enemy troops. We would suggest, contra Yurco, that this unnamed city is probably Gezer, the second city mentioned in the victory poem. Pharaoh is attacking it in his chariot, suggesting that both this town and Ashkelon were situated in the open plain.

The scene in the lower left (Yurco's no. 2) is also not without its Canaanite soldiers in open country:

Here, Pharaoh is attacking the city on foot, suggesting that it is located in rough country. As mentioned above, we suggest that this town may be equated with the Yanuʿam of the victory stela, since that town must have been somewhere in northern Transjordan, according to the Amarna texts (Naʾaman 1977). A site along the Yarmuk drainage system, such as Tell esh-Shihâb (Naʾaman 1977: 169), would be eminently suitable. Canaanite soldiers are falling beneath the feet of pharaoh.

Finally, we must note that the soldiers in Yurco's no. 4 are on about the fourth course below the top course (which bears the cartouche of Ramesses II):

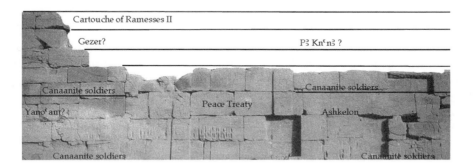

It is far more likely that Yurco's no. 4 also depicted the conquest of a city; this would give symmetry to the reliefs. We would suggest that this fourth city might have been *P3 Knʿn3*, as in Seti I's reliefs on the north wall of Karnak. Yurco has argued that there is no room for another city in scene no. 4 (1990: 33), but a comparison with no. 3 reveals that: (1) the two scenes are about the same width; (2) the horses of pharaoh are at the same scale; and (3) there is just enough room for another city to the left of the horses. In any case, even if this fourth scene (actually meant to be the first) showed Pharaoh attacking enemy troops only, it can hardly represent members of a tribal or village society such as the group called Israel in the victory stela (Rainey 1989: 92–93; 1992; 1999).

The supposedly most-convincing arguments for interpreting these soldiers as fighters from the socioethnic group thus seem to be groundless.

On the other hand, Merenptah's same wall reliefs depict Shasu prisoners being led back to Egypt (as in Seti I's relief). Yurco does not see how to fit them into the correlation with the victory poem. The answer is quite simple. The Shasu can be equated with the socioethnic group in the victory poem (see photo, bottom of p. 183: Shasu prisoners being marched back to Egypt; Yurco's no. 7). In any case, the intelligence officer on Merneptah's staff kept accurate records of every enemy encountered during the campaign. If the victory poem is meant to express a geographic order, then the progress from Ashkelon (on the southern coast) to Gezer to Yanuʿam (in Transjordan) may indicate the the socioethnic group was encountered east of the Jordan Rift Valley. Whether in Bashan or in Gilead is impossible to say, but whatever the venue, the intelligence officer made it clear that Pharaoh's army had fought with a socioethnic group somewhere in Canaan, and its name was Israel.

References

Albright, W. F.
  1924   Canaanite Ḥofšî, "Free," in the Amarna Tablets. *Journal of the Palestine Oriental Society* 4: 169–70.
  1926   Canaanite Ḫapši and Hebrew Ḫofšî Again. *Journal of the Palestine Oriental Society* 6: 106–8.
  1936   Additional Note to Bergman: Soundings at the Supposed Site of Old Testament Anathoth. *Bulletin of the American Schools of Oriental Research* 62: 25–26.
  1946   Cuneiform Material for Egyptian Prosopography. *Journal of Near Eastern Studies* 5: 7–25.
Artzi, P.
  1975   El Amarna Document No. 30. Pp. 1–7 in *Actes du XXIXᵉ Congrès international des Orientalistes, 1973*. Paris: l'Asiathèque.
Biran, A.
  1985   On the Identification of Anathoth. Pp. 209–14 in *Eretz-Israel* 18 (Nahman Avigad volume), ed. B. Mazar and Y. Yadin. Jerusalem: Israel Exploration Society (Hebrew).
Borger, R.
  1958   Das Problem der ʿapīru (Ḫabiru). *Zeitschrift des Deutschen Palästina-Vereins* 74: 121–32.
Bunimovitz, S.
  1994   Socio-Political Transformations in the Central Hill Country in the Late Bronze–Iron I Transition. Pp. 179–202 in *From Nomadism to Monarchy: Archaeological and Historical Aspects of Early Israel*, ed. I. Finkelstein and N. Naʾaman. Jerusalem: Yad Izhak Ben-Zvi and Israel Exploration Society.
CAD
  1956–   *The Assyrian Dictionary of the Oriental Institute of the University of Chicago*. Chicago: The Oriental Institute.
Callaway, J. A.
  1987   Ai (et-Tell): Problem Site for Biblical Archaeologists. Pp. 87–99 in *Archaeology and Biblical Interpretation: Essays in Memory of D. Glenn Rose*, ed. L. G. Perdue, L. E. Toombs, and G. L. Johnson. Atlanta: John Knox.
Cochavi-Rainey, Z.
  1988   *The Akkadian Texts Written by Egyptian Scribes in the 14th–13th Centuries B.C.E.* Ph.D. dissertation, Tel Aviv University (Hebrew).

Ebeling, E.
  1915   Glossar. Pp. 1358–1583 in *Die El-Amarna-Tafeln*, ed. J. A. Knudtzon, O. Weber, and E. Ebeling. Vorderasiatische Bibliothek 2. Leipzig: Hinrichs. [reprinted, Aalen: Zeller, 1964]

Edzard, D. O.
  1970   Die Tontafeln von Kāmid el-Lōz. Pp. 55–62 and pls. 10–14 in *Kamid el-Loz—Kumidi*, ed. D. O. Edzard et al. Bonn: Habelt.

Finkelstein, I.
  1988   *The Archaeology of the Israelite Settlement*. Jerusalem: Israel Exploration Society.

Finkelstein, I., and Naʾaman, N.
  1994   Introduction: From Nomadism to Monarchy—The State of Research in 1992. Pp. 9–17 in *From Nomadism to Monarchy: Archaeological and Historical Aspects of Early Israel*, ed. I. Finkelstein and N. Naʾaman. Jerusalem: Yad Izhak Ben-Zvi and Israel Exploration Society.

Franken, H. J.
  1975   Palestine in the Time of the Nineteenth Dynasty: (b) Archaeological Evidence. Pp. 331–37 in *The Middle East and the Aegean Region c. 1380–1000 b.c.* Vol. 2/2 of *Cambridge Ancient History*. 3rd ed. Cambridge: Cambridge University Press.

Franken, H. J., and London, G.
  1995   Why Painted Pottery Disappered at the End of the Second Millennium bce. *Biblical Archaeologist* 58/4: 214–22.

Gardiner, A. H.
  1937   *Late Egyptian Miscellanies*. Bibliotheca Ägyptiaca 7. Brussels: Édition de la Fondation égyptologique Reine Elisabeth.

Gray, J.
  1952   Feudalism in Ugarit and Early Israel. *Zeitschrift für die Alttestamentliche Wissenschaft* 64: 49–55.

Greenberg, M.
  1955   *The Ḫab/piru*. New Haven, Conn.: American Oriental Society.

Greenstein, E. L., and Marcus, D.
  1996   The Akkadian Inscription of Idrimi. *The Journal of the Ancient Near Eastern Society of Columbia University* 8: 59–96.

Hamilakkis, Y.
  1999   La trahison des archéologues? Archaeological Practice as Intellectual Activity in Postmodernity. *Journal of Mediterranean Archaeology* 12/1: 60–79.

Huddleston, J. R.
  1991   Merenptah's Revenge: The "Israel Stela" and Its Modern Interpreters. Paper Presented on 23 November at the Annual Meeting of the American Academy of Religion and Society of Biblical Literature, Kansas City, 23–26 November.

Kitchen, K. A.
  1970   *Ramesside Inscriptions, Historical and Biographical*. Oxford: Blackwell.

Lemche, N. P.
  1996   Where Should We look for Canaan? A Reply to Nadav Naʾaman. *Ugarit-Forschungen* 28: 767–72.
  1998   Greater Canaan: The Implications of a Correct Reading of EA 151:49–67. *Bulletin of the American Schools of Oriental Research* 310: 19–24.

Liverani, M.
  1997   The Shirma-People Are Back. *Nouvelles Assyriologiques Brèves et Utilitaires* 4: 123.

Loretz, O.
  1984   *Habiru-Hebräer: Eine sozio-linguistiche Studie über die Herkunft des Gentiliziums ʿibrî zum Appellativum* ḫabiru. Beiheft zur Zeitschrift für die alttestamentliche Wissenschaft 160. Berlin: de Gruyter.

Mangano, M. J.
    1990   *Rhetorical Content in the Amarna Correspondence from the Levant.* Ph.D. dissertation, He-
            brew Union College.
Mendelsohn, I.
    1941   The Canaanite Term for "Free Proletarian." *Bulletin of the American Schools of Oriental
            Research* 83: 36–39.
    1955   New Light on the Ḫupšu. *Bulletin of the American Schools of Oriental Research* 139: 9–11.
Moran, W. L.
    1950   *A Syntactical Study of the Dialect of Byblos as Reflected in the Amarna Tablets.* Ph.D. disserta-
            tion, Johns Hopkins University.
    1992   *The Amarna Letters.* Baltimore: Johns Hopkins University Press.
Naʾaman, N.
    1977   Yenoʿam. *Tel Aviv* 4: 166–77.
    1996   The Contribution of the Amarna Letters to the Debate on Jerusalem's Political Position
            in the Tenth Century B.C.E. *Bulletin of the American Schools of Oriental Research* 304: 17–27.
    1997   Cow Town or Royal Capital? Evidence for Iron Age Jerusalem. *Biblical Archaeology Re-
            view* 23/4: 43–47, 67.
Pedersen, J.
    1926   Note on Hebrew Ḥofšī. *Journal of the Palestine Oriental Society* 6: 103–5.
Rainey, A. F.
    1963   A Canaanite at Ugarit. *Israel Exploration Journal* 13: 43–45.
    1964   Ugarit and the Canaanites Again. *Israel Exploration Journal* 14: 101.
    1965   The Military Personnel of Ugarit. *Journal of Near Eastern Studies* 24: 17–27.
    1975   Institutions: Family, Civil and Military. Pp. 69–107 in vol. 2 of *Ras Shamra Parallels*,
            ed. L. R. Fisher. Analecta Orientalia 50. Rome: Pontifical Biblical Institute.
    1977   Verbal Usages in the Taanach Texts. *Israel Oriental Studies* 7: 33–64.
    1987   Review of O. Loretz, *Habiru-Hebräer: Eine sozio-linguistiche Studie über die Herkunft des
            Gentiliziums ʿibrî zum Appellativum* ḫabiru (Beiheft zur Zeitschrift für die alttestament-
            liche Wissenschaft 160; Berlin: de Gruyter, 1984). *Journal of the American Oriental Society*
            101: 539–41.
    1989   Biblical Archaeology Yesterday (and Today). Review of *Biblical Archaeology Today: Pro-
            ceedings of the International Congress on Biblical Archaeology, Jerusalem, April, 1984*, ed. J. Ami-
            tai (Jerusalem: Israel Exploration Society, 1985). *Bulletin of the American Schools of Oriental
            Research* 273: 87–96.
    1989–90 A New Translation of the Amarna Letters—after 100 Years. Review of W. L. Moran, *Les
            lettres d'el-Amarna: Correspondance diplomatique du pharaon* (avec la collaboration de V. Haas
            et G. Wilhelmm, traduction française de D. Colon et H. Cazelles; Paris: Cerf, 1987). *Ar-
            chiv für Orientforschung* 36–37: 56–75.
    1992   Anson F. Rainey Replies. *Biblical Archaeology Review* 18/2: 73–74.
    1995   Unruly Elements in Late Bronze Canaanite Society. Pp. 481–96 in *Pomegranates and
            Golden Bells: Studies in Biblical, Jewish, and Near Eastern Ritual, Law, and Literature in Honor
            of Jacob Milgrom*, ed. D. P. Wright, D. N. Freedman, and A. Hurvitz. Winona Lake, Ind.:
            Eisenbrauns.
    1995–96 A New English Translation of the Amarna Letters. *Archiv für Orientforschung* 43–43: 109–
            21.
    1996   Who Is a Canaanite? A Review of the Textual Evidence. *Bulletin of the American Schools of
            Oriental Research* 304: 1–15.
    1999   Merenptah's Wall Reliefs. Paper Presented at the Annual Meeting of the American
            Schools of Oriental Research, Boston, Mass., 18–20 November.
    2001   Israel in Merneptah's Inscription and Reliefs. *Israel Exploration Journal* 51: 57–75.

Smith, S.
1949   *The Statue of Idri-mi*. Occasional Publications of the British Institute of Archaeology at Ankara 1. London: The British Institute of Archaeology at Ankara.

Stager, L. E.
1985a   Merenptah, Israel and Sea Peoples: New Light on an Old Releif. Pp. 56*–64* in *Eretz-Israel* 18 (Nahman Avigad volume), ed. B. Mazar and Y. Yadin. Jerusalem: Israel Exploration Society.
1985b   Respondents. Pp. 83–87 in *Biblical Archaeology Today: Proceedings of the International Congress on Biblical Archaeology, Jerusalem, April, 1984*, ed. J. Amitai. Jerusalem: Israel Exploration Society.

Steen, E. van der
1995   Aspects of Nomadism and Settlement in the Central Jordan Valley. *Palestine Exploration Quarterly* 127: 141–58.
1996   The Central East Jordan Valley in the Late Bronze and Early Iron Ages. *Bulletin of the American Schools of Oriental Research* 302: 51–74.
1999   Survival and Adaptation: Life East of the Jordan in the Transition from the Late Bronze Age to the Early Iron Age. *Palestine Exploration Quarterly* 131: 176–91.

Stiebing, W. H.
1989   *Out of the Desert? Archaeology and the Exodus/Conquest Narratives*. Buffalo, N.Y.: Prometheus.

Weippert, M.
1980   Kanaan. Pp. 352–55 in vol. 5 of *Reallexikon der Assyriologie und vorderasiatischen Archäologie*, ed. D. O. Edzard. Berlin: de Gruyter.

Wiseman, D. J.
1953   *The Alalakh Tablets*. Occasional Publications of the British Institute of Archaeology at Ankara 2. London: The British Institute of Archaeology at Ankara.
1954   Supplementary Copies of Alalakh Tablets. *Journal of Cuneiform Studies* 8: 1–30.

Yurco, F.
1978   Merenptah's Palestinian Campaign. *Society for the Study of Egyptian Antiquities Journal* 8: 70.
1986   Merenptah's Canaanite Campaign. *Journal of the American Research Center in Egypt* 23: 189–215.
1990   3,200-Year-Old Picture of Israelites Found in Egypt. *Biblical Archaeology Review* 16/5: 20–38.
1991   Frank J. Yurco's Response. *Biblical Archaeology Review* 17/6: 61.
1997   Merenptah's Canaanite Campaign and Israel's Origins. Pp. 27–55 in *Exodus: The Egyptian Evidence*, ed. E. S. Frerichs and L. H. Lesko. Winona Lake, Ind.: Eisenbrauns.

The Aegean and the Orient: Cultic Interactions

Trude Dothan

Institute of Archaeology
Hebrew University, Jerusalem

This paper presents in brief several architectural features and material culture elements with cultic connotations associated with the initial settlement of the Sea Peoples in Philistia that reflect their Aegean origins, as we find more and more pieces to add to the mosaic. The material culture and architecture found in the Philistine settlements show that these settlers tried to recreate their familiar Aegean milieu in their new environment, bringing with them not the artifacts, but the know-how, traditions, and artisans. In terms of artifacts, this is most strikingly apparent in the locally-made Mycenaean IIIC:1b pottery, both elegant tableware and coarse ware, the zoomorphic terra-cottas (predominantly bulls), anthropomorphic figurines (such as the "Ashdoda" and mourning figurines), pinched clay loomweights in the Aegean tradition, and a wealth of special finds, including luxury items. As for architecture, although domestic architecture is less well known, the well-planned public and cultic buildings at these sites strongly reflect architectural elements from Cyprus and the Aegean, such as the megaron plan, freestanding features such as the rectangular and round hearths, and, in particular, the use of combinations of features: hearths, bathtubs, benches, pillars, stelae, and *bamot*. The gastronomic preferences the new settlers brought with them are also evident in the sharp increase in the number of pig and cattle bones found in the Philistine occupation strata, suggesting the introduction of pork and beef in place of goat and mutton (Hesse 1986: 23).[1]

The excavations of the cities of the Philistine Pentapolis (fig. 1) are bringing a growing body of new evidence to light, enabling us to form a broader and more detailed picture of Philistine culture. The identification of three of the five cities has now been established by the excavated data: Ashdod (M. Dothan and Freedman 1967; M. Dothan 1971; 1993; M. Dothan and Porath 1982; 1993),[2] Ashkelon (Stager 1991; 1993;

Author's note: I would like to thank Tami Nahmias for her assistance in the research for this paper and Edna Sachar for her meticulous work in preparing and editing the manuscript. The architectural graphics are by J. Rosenberg. The Tel Miqne-Ekron drawings are by Sarah Halbreich and Marina Zeltser, and the photos by Ilan Sztulman.

1. Other evidence that may be pertinent in this regard are the dog remains found in Iron I deposits in Field IV at Ekron, several of which bore cut marks. These finds (see also n. 18 below) seem to parallel the canid skeletal remains in Philistine deposits at Ashkelon, where two puppies were found in pots, as well as the bones of adult canids bearing cut marks (information based on an e-mail report by Brian Hesse, Miqne faunal analyst, March 16, 2001).

2. The long-term excavations at Ashdod were directed by Moshe Dothan, Department of Archaeology, Haifa University. The sixth volume of the Ashdod final report series was prepared for publication by David Ben-Shlomo of the Hebrew University (M. Dothan and Ben-Shlomo in press).

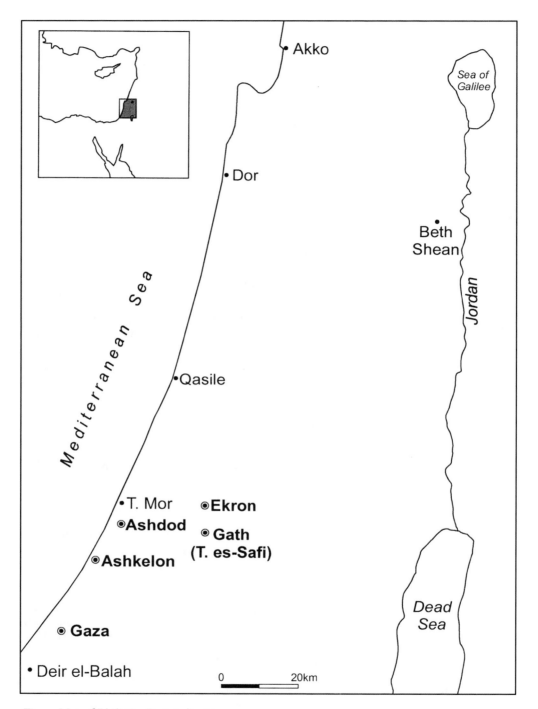

Fig. 1. Map of Philistine Pentapolis cities.

1998),[3] and Ekron (T. Dothan 1990; T. Dothan and Gitin 1990; 1993; 1997; Gitin 1990).[4] The identification of Tel Miqne with Ekron was incontrovertibly confirmed by the remarkable find during the final excavation season of a royal dedicatory inscription dated to the beginning of the 7th century B.C.E. The inscription includes the names of Ekron and its rulers, two of whom are also documented as kings of Ekron in extrabiblical texts (Gitin, Dothan, and Naveh 1997). While Gaza, like Ashdod and Ashkelon, retains its ancient name, the remains of the Philistine city lie beneath modern Gaza and are yet to be excavated. Thus, with the confirmation of Tel Miqne as Ekron, four of the five cities of the Philistine Pentapolis have been identified. As for the fifth city—Gath—Tell es-Safi has long been considered a candidate for identification as this city, and the results of the new excavations being conducted at the site already strongly support this probability (Maeir 2001; Maeir and Ehrlich 2001).[5]

The following discussion focuses on the architectural features and material culture from the initial settlement of the Sea Peoples in Philistia, with particular emphasis on those indicative of their western origins, as reflected on Cyprus and in the Aegean. The growing corpus of relevant material from the excavated cities of the Philistine Pentapolis, together with slightly later evidence from the Philistine settlement and temples at Tell Qasile (Mazar 1980; 1985a; 1986; 1989) and other "Sea Peoples" sites (such as the Sikil occupation at Tel Dor [Stern 2000]), provide a rich source of data and the potential for comparing and integrating this information.

The interpretation of a building or room as cultic in nature is based on the presence of components of cultic praxis. Thus, the proximity and configuration of these components are taken as indications of a cultic function (Renfrew 1985: 25–26). In the initial settlement in Philistia, however, these components are not necessarily found in recognized characteristic configurations or within a single cultic area, as they may be in the later phases of settlement, when they become more cohesive (Gilmour 1995). The development from the establishment to the crystallization of cultic places and their continuity can be traced over time. Nevertheless, the combinations of isolated components found in Philistia, many of them reflecting Aegean and Cypriote origins, show the interchange of culture, with the new settlers both introducing elements foreign to Canaan in their desire to retain their Aegean milieu and incorporating elements from local Canaanite culture. Research into these cultic interactions is on the verge of a breakthrough, with more and more indications of parallels of western origin (T. Dothan 1998a; 1998b; 2000; 2002). This is only the beginning of the exciting new possibilities of where the evidence may lead,

---

3. The ongoing long-term excavations at Ashkelon are directed by Lawrence E. Stager of Harvard University, to whom I am very grateful for sharing and discussing with me information relating to some of the issues raised in this paper.

4. The Tel Miqne–Ekron Excavation and Publications Project is directed by the author and S. Gitin, W. F. Albright Institute of Archaeological Research, Jerusalem. The field archaeologists during the project's 1981–96 excavation phase were: Field I—Ann Killebrew, Bruce MacKay, Mark Meehl; Field III—Barry Gittlen; Field IV—Yosef Garfinkel, Steven Ortiz; Field X—Neal Bierling.

5. The Tell es-Safi/Gath Archaeological Project is directed by Aren Maeir (Institute of Archaeology, Martin [Szusz] Department of Land of Israel Studies, Bar Ilan University), with co-director Carl Ehrlich (Division of Humanities, York University).

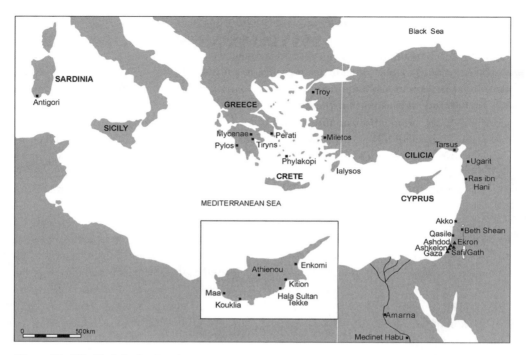

Fig. 2. The World of the Sea Peoples.

adding more detail to and broadening the picture of this period, which is made all the more complex by population dislocations and the lack of written evidence.

The origins of the various elements found in Philistia illustrating cultic interactions between the Aegean and the Orient, both in terms of artifacts and architectural features, can be seen at various key sites, such as Mycenae, Pylos and Tiryns in Greece, Phylakopi on Melos, Ialysos on Rhodes, Kastelli-Khania and Vronda-Kavousi on Crete, and particularly at Enkomi, Kition, Maa-Palaeokastro and Alassa on Cyprus, the bridgehead to the Orient (fig. 2).[6] Furthermore, these material culture elements and architectural features can now also be traced from their initial appearance in Philistia through the stages of their internal development and continuity in the course of the 12th and 11th centuries B.C.E.[7]

The evidence from Ekron comes from buildings with cultic connotations associated with the initial phase of Philistine settlement in the 12th century B.C.E. and its subsequent development (fig. 3). The cultic nature of these buildings and rooms is indicated by the combination of architectural characteristics and/or features in association with objects and other finds. Furthermore, the continuity of the presence of such special features and finds in a given area is typical of the reuse of sanctified places over time (see below).

---

6. I would like to express my gratitude to my friend and colleague Vassos Karageorghis, Director of the Anastasios G. Levantis Foundation in Nicosia, with whom I have had extensive discussions regarding the subjects raised in this paper.

7. The evidence presented below from Ashdod, Ashkelon, and Ekron is based on both published data and on material in the process of being prepared for publication.

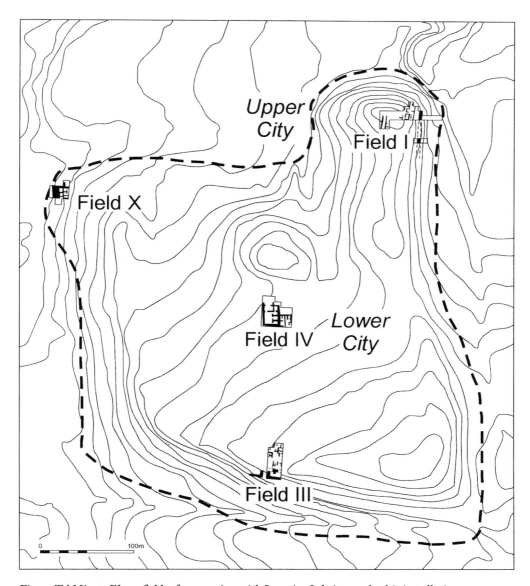

Fig. 3. Tel Miqne–Ekron fields of excavation with Iron Age I shrines and cultic installations.

In the heart of the city, in Field IV—"downtown Ekron"—a series of shrines and monumental buildings were excavated. These show a continuity of cultic-related function from the initial phase of settlement in Stratum VII, the early 12th century B.C.E.—built directly on top of the destruction of the abandoned Middle Bronze Age settlement—through each successive Iron Age I phase. The first phase, Stratum VIIB, is represented by one-room Building 357. Later, in Stratum VIIA, another room, Building 352, was built to the south (fig. 4), and over time, the area became densely populated, with the Stratum VII rooms incorporated into a large building complex in Stratum VI (12th/11th century

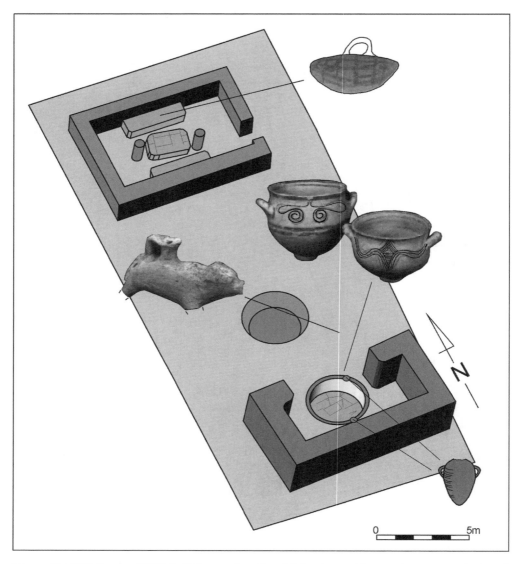

Fig. 4. Field IV, Stratum VIIB Building 357 (north), with benches and freestanding rectangular hearth flanked by two pillars, showing findspots of Stratum VIIB Aegean-type bull vessel and Mycenaean IIIC:1b bowl with antithetic spiral decoration, and Stratum VIIA Building 352, with silo (south), showing findspots of Stratum VIIA Mycenaean IIIC:1b bowl with antithetic tongue decoration and two storage jars. Also shown is the findspot of the Stratum VIB askos.

B.C.E.). A dramatic change occurred in Stratum V (first half of 11th century B.C.E.), when Philistine Temple Building 350 was constructed on top of the Stratum VI structures. This monumental building incorporates new architectural elements and installations, such as a megaron-style entrance, round pebbled hearth, and *bamah*. These and the associated objects show the consolidation and continuity of Aegean traditions, while continuing to

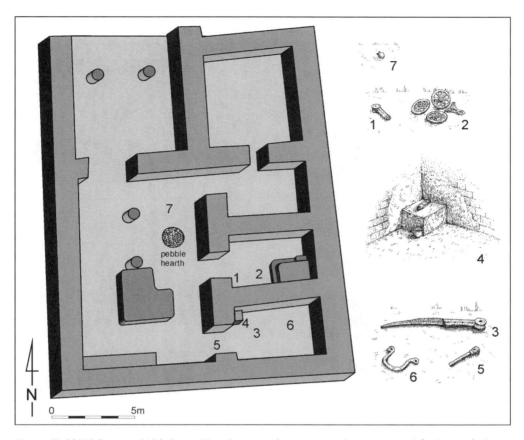

Fig. 5. Field IV, Stratum V Philistine Temple 350 with megaron-style entrance and findspots of objects: 1: ivory knife handle; 2: miniature bronze wheels and corner of frame; 3: iron knife; 4: iron bar; 5: bronze linchpin; 6: bronze looped handle; 7: bronze bud-shaped pendant.

incorporate Canaanite features (fig. 5). The basic plan of the area continued through Stratum IV (second half of the 11th century B.C.E.), with some modifications (fig. 6), until its destruction and abandonment at the end of the 11th / early 10th century B.C.E.

These superimposed sanctuaries demonstrate that, once sanctified, a given area continued to be considered sacred. The area in this case was continually cleaned, developed, and reused, and there is no evidence of destruction until the final destruction of the building in Stratum IVA. There is also evidence of the transference and reuse of "heirloom" luxury objects, such as a pair of ivory earplugs, one of which was found in Stratum V and one in Stratum IV, and the limestone baboon statuette found in a Stratum IVA cache (see fig. 6), with its inscribed base found in Stratum V. Interestingly, after an occupation gap of ca. 250 years, the 7th-century B.C.E. royal temple complex, in which the Ekron dedicatory inscription was found, was built in the same vicinity, with several earlier round stone pillar bases reused in its construction, again suggesting the continuity in the sacred nature of the location (Gitin, Dothan, and Naveh 1997).

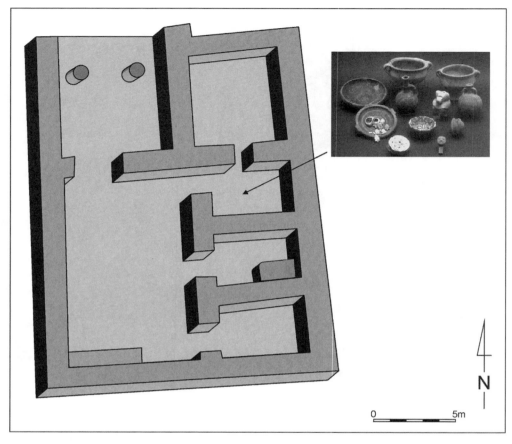

Fig. 6. Stratum IVA Temple 350, with cache of votive objects.

The special nature of the core Stratum VII buildings is indicated by the construction techniques, architectural features, installations, and artifacts. In the original single-room building, a rectangular hearth with pillars and benches in different configurations appears from Stratum VIIB through Stratum VIA (fig. 4). The Stratum VII pottery is locally-made Mycenaean IIIC:1b Monochrome, a continuing reflection of these types of vessels known from the Aegean world (figs. 4, 7). Also of great significance are the finds of locally-made zoomorphic vessels associated with these and other shrines. These include a bull in a "flying gallop" stance, reminiscent of Aegean bull vessels, from Stratum VIIB and an intact (except for the broken handle) miniature bird askos found on a Stratum VIB bench (both in Field IV; see fig. 4), as well as a Mycenaean IIIC:1b terra-cotta hedgehog (see fig. 16) found in Field X (see below for further details on these objects).

Most significant is the appearance in Stratum VII of the single freestanding hearth as a central feature in a communal room, which has clear parallels on Cyprus (for a detailed discussion and references, see Karageorghis 1998; 2000). These raised rectangular hearths are made of mudbrick and clay and paved with pebbles and, in some instances, sherds.

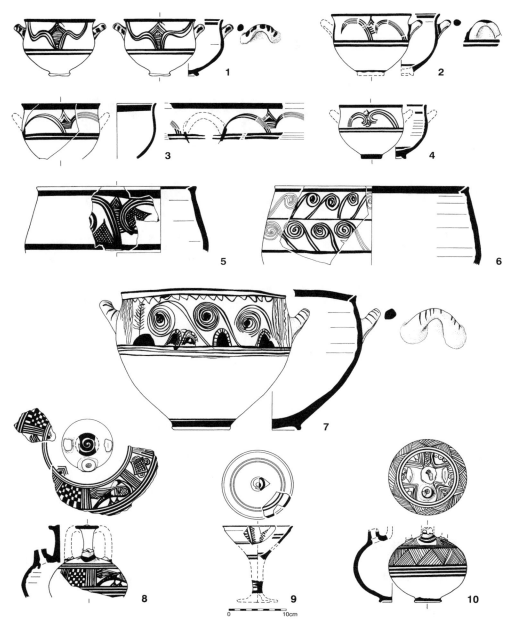

Fig. 7. Mycenaean IIIC:1b Monochrome pottery from Strata VII (nos. 1–7, 9) and VIB (nos. 8, 10).

The technique of paving hearths and other surfaces with sherds relates to Cyprus and the Aegean (for example, at Athienou [Ben-Tor 1983: 11–12], Enkomi [Dikaios 1969: vol. 3a, pls. 20:1–2, 4; 33:5], and Tiryns [Kilian 1979: 385; 1981a: 162; 1982: 401]) and is not indigenous to Canaan. This technique also appears in rectangular hearths at Ashdod (M. Dothan and

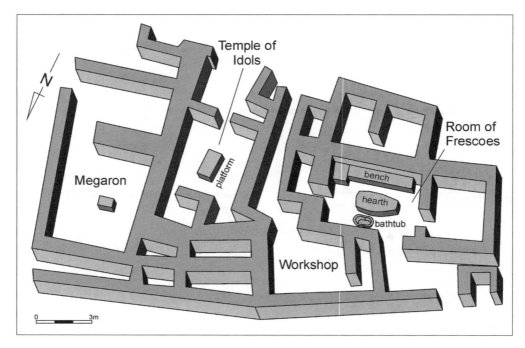

Fig. 8. Cultic area at Mycenae with shrines, including the Temple of Idols and the Room of Frescoes containing a hearth, bench, and bathtub (after Taylour 1970: fig. 1; French 1981: 42, fig. 1).

Porath 1993: 54–55), Ashkelon (Stager 1987: 68), and Tell Qasile (Mazar 1986: 3–6). Equally significantly, in addition to this type of hearth, the combination of features in such cultic rooms (for example, the pillars flanking the hearth and the benches, as well as the associated objects) is also not in the Canaanite tradition. These rooms have parallels, inter alia, at Enkomi, one of the major cities on Cyprus, with its prevalence of large, free-standing square hearths (Dikaios 1969: 1.107, 112–13, 175–76; vol. 3b, pls. 254, 273, among others), and Mycenae (Taylour 1970: fig. 1; French 1981: 42, fig. 1) (see fig. 8 here). A variant of this hearth—a "keyhole" hearth—as a central feature was found at Tell Qasile XII (Mazar 1986: 3–4, fig. 2) and Enkomi (Dikaios 1969: vol. 3a, pl. 41:2). While pebbled surfaces were used in the rectangular hearths, their appearance is more prominent in the round hearths. The sherd and pebble surfacing no doubt served for heat retention and convection.

An important feature that in Philistia is thus far unique to Ekron is the round, pebbled hearth. This type of hearth already appears in various configurations and sizes in the early phases of settlement in Strata VII/VI—for example, the 13 such hearths excavated in a Field I open activity area in Stratum VI (T. Dothan and Gitin 1997: 31).[8] Furthermore, the large domestic Building Complex 404 in Field III included 15 small, round, pebbled hearths in Stratum VI, and the Stratum VIA surface of one of these hearths also yielded a chalice and a complete Philistine-style bull-shaped zoomorphic vessel (information based on a written communication from B. M. Gittlen, July 19, 2001).

8. Another 12 such hearths were found in the same area in Stratum V (T. Dothan and Gitin 1997: 31).

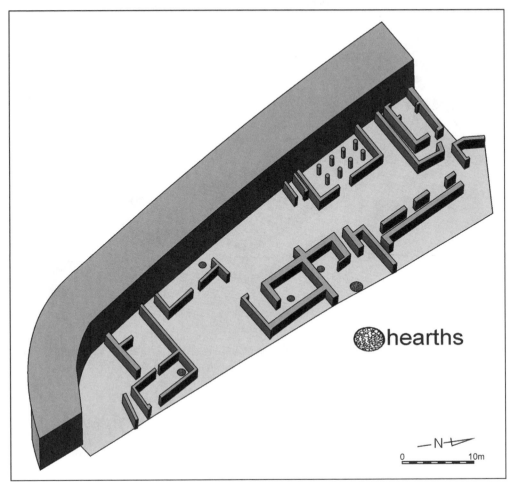

Fig. 9. Tiryns lower citadel units with hearths (after Kilian 1981b: 51, Abb. 2; 55, Abb. 8).

As a central feature in a clearly defined cultic context, however, this type of hearth appears only in Stratum V. In Field IV, in the large central hall of Philistine Temple Building 350, with its impressive megaron-style entrance, a number of superimposed hearths were excavated (see fig. 5). These features echo the tradition of the hearths that appear as a central feature in the megarons of the palaces at Mycenae (Mylonas 1966: 55–56, 60), Tiryns (Kilian 1980; 1982: 401, Room 123), and Pylos (Blegen and Rawson 1966: 85–87), among others. Another strong link is to the lower citadel of Tiryns, where a similar type of round pebbled hearth (some also lined with sherds) was found in popular shrines with diverse architectural ground plans, which may reflect facets of Mycenaean traditions (Kilian 1981b: 51, Abb. 2; 55, Abb. 8) (see fig. 9 here). Also noteworthy is that, after the destruction of the upper citadel palace at Tiryns, the megaron room was rebuilt on a smaller scale, and the associated pottery is distinctly Mycenaean IIIC:1b. These finds indicate post-palatial

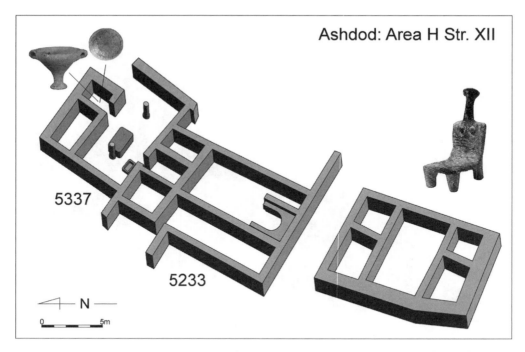

Fig. 10. Large-scale Iron I complex at Ashdod, Area H, with gold disc and kylix found in Building 5337, also showing Stratum XI "Ashdoda" figurine (after M. Dothan and Ben-Shlomo in press: plan II.3).

period settlement, not only in the lower city, but also on the acropolis (J. Maran, personal communication). [9]

Important examples of architectural elements and combinations of architectural features and other finds reflecting Aegean traditions come from Philistine Ashdod. In Area H, a large-scale 12th-century B.C.E. architectural complex with special characteristics was excavated in Stratum XIII/XII, the early phases of Philistine settlement (M. Dothan 1993: 97–98) (see fig. 10 here). The structure included rebuilt and reused Late Bronze Age walls in some places, and was constructed directly on the remains of the Late Bronze Age Canaanite city (M. Dothan 1993; M. Dothan and Ben-Shlomo in press). [10]

The southernmost unit of the complex includes an apsidal structure within Building 5233, possibly in a courtyard, for which there are no parallels in Philistia. [11] The apsidal

---

9. I am grateful to Professor Joseph Maran of the University of Heidelberg for sharing with me information on the features of these shrines from both the lower and upper citadels and his insights into the post-palatial, Mycenaean IIIC period at Tiryns. Another point of interest that he mentions is that, in some cases, "silos" were also used as hearths.

10. The following presentation of the material from Ashdod is based on M. Dothan and Ben-Shlomo in press.

11. The apsidal plan, known in the Neolithic period, disappears and then reappears for a relatively short time as special buildings in the 12th-century Aegean, only to disappear again for centuries thereafter, apparently never becoming an integral part of an evolving architectural tradition.

structures that appear in Aegean in the 12th/11th century may have a cultic function. These buildings, however, in contrast to the Ashdod example, are freestanding—for example, at Lefkandi, where holes for wooden stilts (that were not preserved) were found around the structure (Ainian 1997: figs. 82–89). At Ashdod, the fill inside the apsidal structure yielded Mycenaean IIIC:1b pottery, including kalathos fragments (M. Dothan and Ben-Shlomo in press: pl. III.21:1–3).

The northernmost unit, Building 5337, contained a hall with a raised rectangular hearth and two pillars. The building yielded Mycenaean IIIC:1b and Philistine Bichrome pottery and special finds, including fragments of "Ashdoda"-type figurines, bird bowls, and beads. The northeastern room contained a mudbrick bench, possibly a *bamah*, and yielded Philistine pottery and a wealth of special finds: two gold discs decorated in the Aegean style (probably used as covers for sword pommels), a faience amulet and miniature bowls, beads, decorated ivories, and a miniature Mycenaean IIIC:1b kylix (see fig. 10). A similar bench was excavated at the same level in the northwestern room, which produced Mycenaean IIIC:1b bowls and Philistine Bichrome pottery, and the special finds included fragments of a fenestrated pottery stand; a bird rattle; a complete, very elaborately decorated Philistine beer jug; a square ivory plaque; a rosette-shaped ivory button and other ivories; and bronze objects. The architectural plan of this building, including a large central hall flanked by several rooms, is typical of the buildings at Philistine Ashdod and appears in the same stratum in Area G (M. Dothan and Porath 1993: 70–73, plan 11 on p. 69). Similar architectural plans found in 12th-century Greece suggest an Aegean origin—for example, the plan of House G at Asine, which includes a hall (Room XXXII) containing two pillars, a bench, and associated finds of a cultic nature, interpreted as a sanctuary (Hägg 1981: especially figs. 1–2). The special houses found in the ongoing excavations at Panagia, outside the walls of Mycenae, are a close parallel. One of these houses, which includes a large room with a rectangular hearth as a central feature and two pillars (fig. 11), is strikingly similar to Building 5337 at Ashdod and the Stratum VII buildings in Field IV at Ekron (fig. 4). It is dated slightly earlier than the Ashdod complex, but continues in use into the 12th century B.C.E. (Shear 1987: 29–30, figs. 4–5, House II).[12]

A seated "Ashdoda" figurine attributed to Stratum XI was also found in the vicinity of the Ashdod Area H complex (see fig. 10).[13] A cult stand featuring musicians as well as other vessels that suggest a cultic function were found in this area in Stratum X, following the destruction of Stratum XI, probably at the end of the 11th century. This appears to be another good example of the continuity of the use of previously sanctified places for cultic praxis.

The special nature of these buildings in terms of their size, architecture, and associated finds suggests an official building or perhaps a wealthy residence, in part with a cultic function, within a sophisticated society. The entire complex, however, did not function as

12. The ongoing excavations at Panagia are revealing more and more buildings and rooms with such features, which seem to indicate domestic cult areas (Kim Shelton, assistant to the director of the excavations at Mycenae, personal communication).

13. For a recent study on the Aegean background of the "Ashdoda" figurine and its interpretation, see Yasur-Landau 2001.

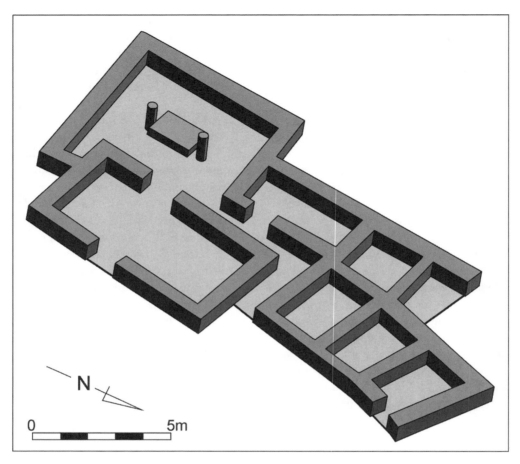

Fig. 11. One of the special houses at Panagia, with rectangular hearth and two flanking pillars (after Shear 1987: figs. 4–5).

a shrine, unlike the well-defined sanctuaries at Ekron and the Philistine temples at Tell Qasile (Mazar 1980; 1985a; 1985b; 1986; 2000: 215–19).

A breakthrough in research on cultic connections between Philistia, Cyprus, and the Aegean came with the recent finds of several bathtubs at Philistine Pentapolis sites, and, in particular, the configuration of these and other features and objects in communal rooms. One terra-cotta bathtub (larnax) was excavated in the large "elite" architectural unit on the upper tel at Ashdod, Area G, in Stratum XII (M. Dothan and Porath 1993: 72, plan 11 on p. 69, pl. 22:2). The Mycenaean IIIC:1b pottery found in this building comes from the early phase of Philistine settlement, and the large communal room of the unit, the megaron, contained a terra-cotta bathtub in close proximity to a freestanding rectangular hearth (fig. 12). The building is defined as communal on the basis of the architecture, features, and finds with cultic connotations, including the head of a bull from a large zoomorphic libation vessel found in the larnax and an ivory fan handle found in Room 4145 (M. Dothan and Porath 1993: fig. 38:1) (see fig. 12 here). Given its megaron plan and other finds, the room does not have the appearance of a bathroom, as is supported by the paral-

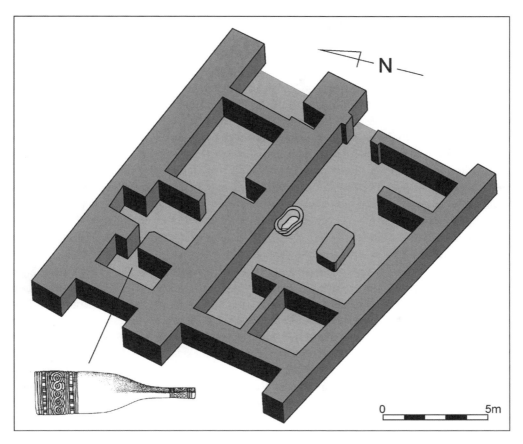

Fig. 12. Ashdod Area G Stratum XII building with bathtub and hearth and ivory fan handle (after M. Dothan and Porath 1993: plan 10).

lels presented below, and probably served for purification, with the hearth used as part of the ritual.

The Ashdod bathtub has close parallels among the many terra-cotta bathtubs known from Cyprus, found in a variety of configurations in both sanctuaries and bathrooms (the entire Cypriote corpus with parallels has been discussed by Karageorghis [2000]). At Mycenae, a terra-cotta bathtub was found in a clear-cut cultic context on the western slope: one complex in this cultic area includes the "Temple of Idols," with a platform and numerous terra-cotta figurines, and the "Room of Frescoes," with an "oval" hearth in the center and a bathtub, platform, and benches (Taylour 1970; French 1981) (see fig. 8 here). The associated paraphernalia leaves no doubt that this is a cultic building.[14] Also of interest is the fragment of a terra-cotta bathtub found at Tell Qasile in the initial Philistine settlement of Strata XII–XI (A. Mazar, personal communication).

14. Another close parallel for the Ashdod bathtub comes from Pylos, where a beautifully decorated bathtub, which also has a step, was found. In this case, however, the bathtub was in a bathroom adjacent to the throneroom of the palace (Blegen and Rawson 1966: 186–89).

Another aspect of the cultic area on the western slope at Mycenae that is pertinent to our discussion is that it is comprised of a series of shrines, rather than a large, well-planned monumental building (fig. 8). As mentioned above, a similar phenomenon existed in the lower citadel at Tiryns (Kilian 1981b: 51, Abb. 2; 55, Abb. 8) (see fig. 9 here). The features and character of such shrines are more akin to and connected with those dated to the early phases of Philistine settlement at Ekron. The most complete and unequivocal examples of Philistine temples are at Tell Qasile, on the periphery of Philistia, attributed to a slightly later date than the earliest shrines/cultic rooms at Ekron and Ashdod. Tell Qasile follows a different settlement pattern, and the initial Mycenaean IIIC:1b phase typical of the Philistine Pentapolis cities is absent. The first occupation phase at Tell Qasile is represented by Philistine Bichrome pottery (T. Dothan 1982; Mazar 1985b; 2000: 215–19).

Another exciting development is represented by the three limestone bathtubs recently excavated in various configurations of features and finds at Ekron and Ashkelon. On the Acropolis at Ekron, in Field I, when the area of the deep sondage was expanded, a room was exposed that contained a bench, a freestanding square hearth in the center, and a limestone bathtub adjacent to the wall, together with Mycenaean IIIC:1b pottery. This room was part of a larger, well-built, Stratum VII complex associated with the initial phase of Philistine settlement in the 12th century B.C.E. (fig. 13). The bathtub, found in situ, had evidently been exposed to a destruction fire. A similar limestone bathtub was found in a large room in Stratum VIA Building 353 in Field IV, also dated to the early phases of Philistine settlement, adjacent to a rectangular raised hearth with an associated monolith in the center of the large room (fig. 14). This bathtub is approximately 1 m wide and 60 cm deep, with an opening to allow the water to run out. These configurations of features in a large room, although the finds in and of themselves do not indicate its function, are characteristic of a communal/assembly room containing elements that appear to fulfill a role in purification and/or other rituals.

A well-preserved, elaborate limestone bathtub was excavated at Ashkelon in the 1999 season in a large room that also contained a hearth.[15] The bathtub is well crafted and has four rectangular projections that served as handles below the rim. In the reconstruction based on Stager's data and the photographs, the bathtub in this case stood in the corner of the large room (fig. 15). It apparently was subsequently reused, but its initial use belongs to the early stages of Philistine settlement at Ashkelon. The Ashkelon example also illustrates the phenomenon of communal purification or ritual areas characterized by the presence of bathtubs and hearths in large rooms, in many cases associated with special finds.

In reexamining the Ashdod material in light of the limestone bathtubs from Ekron and Ashkelon, we noted that fragments of another possible example, most reminiscent of the Ashkelon bathtub, may have been found at Ashdod as well. This installation was found in secondary use embedded in the L. 4123 Stratum XII floor, in the complex to the north of the hall in which the clay bathtub was found (M. Dothan and Porath 1993: 72–73). According to the excavators, "A number of worked limestone fragments, probably related to this unit, were found nearby" (M. Dothan and Porath 1993: 73).

---

15. I wish to thank L. E. Stager for permission to include the Ashkelon bathtub in this paper and J. Rosenberg for his assistance in providing the stratigraphic and spatial information.

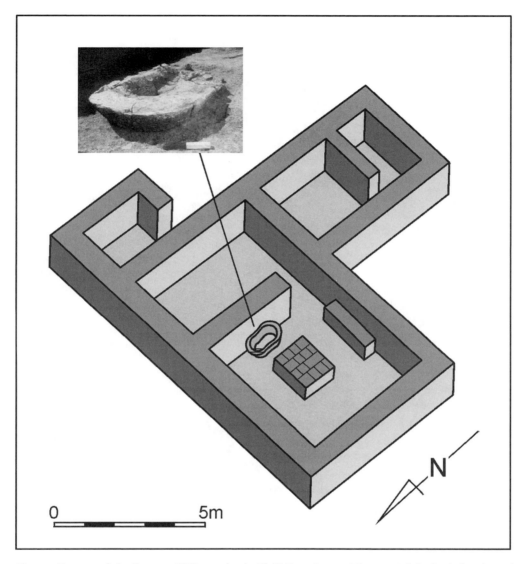

Fig. 13. Room 1 of the Stratum VII complex in Field I sondage at Ekron, with bathtub, bench, and platform.

The parallels of limestone bathtubs from Cyprus include three examples from Enkomi (Dikaios 1969: 1.107, 141; Courtois 1992: 151; Karageorghis 2000: 266–744), one of which is strikingly similar to the Ashkelon bathtub. It was found in what was interpreted as a bathroom in the large ashlar building complex, "Bâtiment 18" (Courtois 1992: 151), but this interpretation is not necessarily correct (Karageorghis 2000: 260). In any event, the ritual aspect of the bathtub may be illustrated by the presence of a limestone bathtub that did not serve as a coffin in a tomb at Palaepaphos-*Skales* (Karageorghis 2000: 272). In general, the presence of bathtubs, mainly made of terra-cotta but also of limestone, in

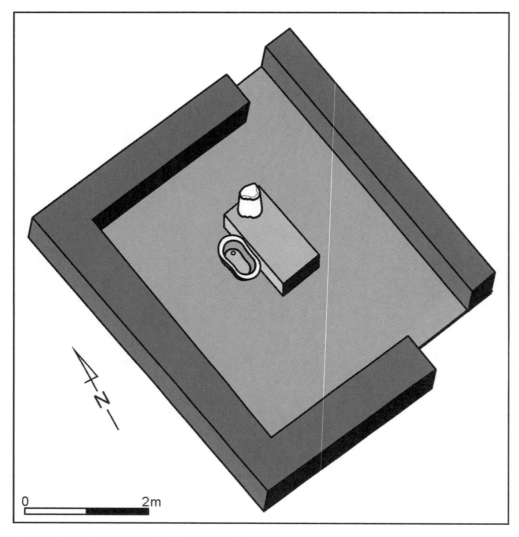

Fig. 14. Ekron Stratum VI Building 353 in Field IV, with raised rectangular hearth, monolith, and bathtub.

clear cultic contexts, burials, and bathrooms, and in association with hearths, stone pillars, and benches, became increasingly common on 12th-century B.C.E. Cyprus (Karageorghis 2000). Although this is uncharted territory, it appears that, in Philistia, the presence of bathtubs in well-defined rooms containing hearths and other features and finds with cultic connotations certainly seems to indicate their use in purification rituals.

At Ekron, there are several other examples of configurations of architectural features and finds in buildings and rooms that illustrate cultic connotations and connections to Cyprus and the Aegean. A good example comes from Field X, where a series of rooms adjacent to the fortifications on the western periphery of the site yielded special finds

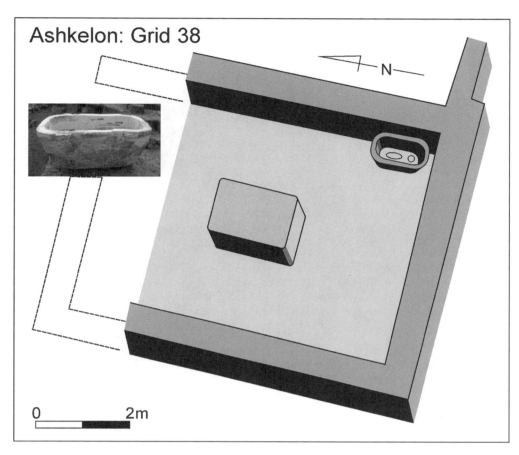

Fig. 15. Ashkelon Grid 38 room with bathtub and rectangular hearth.

from the initial settlement phase (fig. 16). One of the rooms contained a *bamah* and one a foundation deposit of a Mycenaean IIIC:1b krater and lamp beneath the wall. Another room produced an assemblage of decorated Mycenaean IIIC:1b vessels from the initial phase of the settlement, including a beautiful terra-cotta hedgehog—a libation vessel— locally made in the characteristic Mycenaean IIIC:1b style, ware, and decoration (T. Dothan 1998b; Ben-Shlomo in press a; in press b) (see fig. 16 here).[16] Parallels for hedgehog terra-cottas are extremely common in the repertoire of Mycenaean IIIB cultic vessels, appearing mainly in cult centers as imports into the Levant. Interestingly, the hedgehog from Ekron is the only Mycenaean IIIC vessel of this type found to date. These are well known as libation vessels in the Aegean, Cyprus, and Ugarit. Another recent find is a small libation vessel, a bird askos, well known in the Mycenaean pottery repertoire; it is hand-

16. The assemblage of zoomorphic terra-cottas and figurines from Tel Miqne–Ekron is being studied and prepared for publication by David Ben-Shlomo, Ph.D. Candidate, Hebrew University. The as-yet-unpublished material mentioned below appears in Ben-Shlomo in press a; in press b.

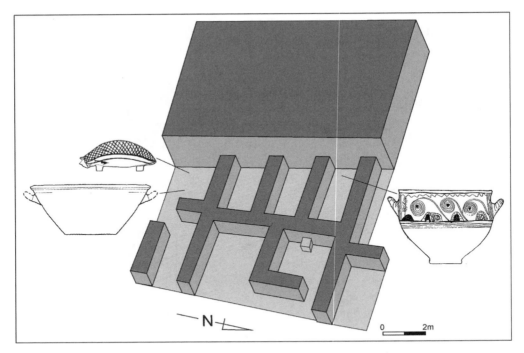

Fig. 16. Ekron Field X rooms adjacent to fortifications, with terra-cotta hedgehog, kalathos, large krater, and bamah.

made, using the same distinctly Aegean folding-over technique as the hedgehog vessel. The bird askos (see fig. 4) was found in the Stratum VIB cultic room in Field IV. These vessels are Aegean in origin, where they are found in burials as well as cultic contexts, but locally made. The Mycenaean IIIC miniature bull figurines from the initial phase of settlement in Field I—exact, locally-made replicas of the Mycenaean IIIC originals—are also of great significance. These objects no doubt played an important role in burial and cult practices.

A recent exact parallel for the lion rhyton found at the entrance to a Stratum V shrine in Field I at Ekron (fig. 17) comes from Tell es-Safi/Gath (Maeir and Ehrlich 2001: 29). These cultic objects are well attested in Philistia (including a large assemblage found in a *favissa* at Tell Qasile [Mazar 1980; 1985a]), as well as in the Aegean (T. Dothan 1982: 229–34). The incised scapulae, found embedded in the white plaster floor of this shrine at Ekron (see fig. 17), has parallels in Philistia at Ashkelon and at Sikil Dor and other "Sea Peoples" sites, and their analogies on Cyprus, at Kition and Enkomi in particular (e.g., in the shrine of the "Ingot God"), are well known (Webb 1986).

To review briefly a few other special finds that demonstrate cultic connections (T. Dothan 2002):[17] Stratum V (11th-century B.C.E.) Philistine Temple Building 350 yielded an

17. Details of the finds mentioned below and their parallels have recently been published in English in T. Dothan 2002.

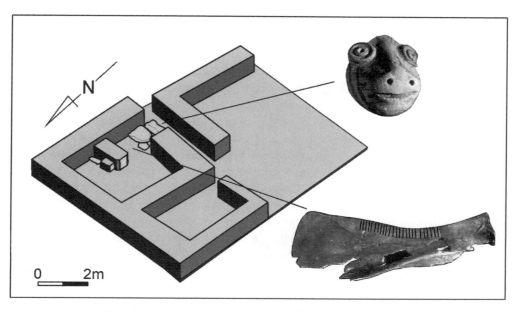

Fig. 17. Ekron Field I Stratum V shrine complex, Locus no. INE 3024, with bamah, rhyton, and incised ivory scapula.

iron knife with an ivory handle and bronze rivets, and a second worked ivory handle with traces of an iron blade, both found in association with *bamot*; a double-headed bronze linchpin; and three miniature wheels, the fragment of a frame corner, and a bud-shaped pendant (see fig. 5), all made of cast bronze, which can be reconstructed as a cultic wheeled stand. These stands are reminiscent of the biblical descriptions of the *mechonot* in the Temple of Solomon and parallels are well known on Cyprus. The linchpin (see fig. 5), too, is stylistically linked to Cyprus, by association with Aegean elements in Cypriote bronze work. Two additional ivory knife-handles, one with traces of an iron blade, were found at Ekron, in Fields III and I.[18] Similar knives come from a number of sites in Israel, including Tell Qasile (Mazar 1985a: 6–8, fig. 2) and two from Sikil Dor (E. Stern, personal communication). The implications of finding such objects in shrines are extremely important. These iron artifacts are rare and are linked to Cyprus and the Aegean. They were transmitted, in my opinion, from west to east, and not the other way around.

This examination and reevaluation of the available corpus provides a better understanding of the complex picture of cultic interactions. Clearly, as mentioned above, this is not a case of complete cultic units, together with their assemblages, being transferred from the west but of the traditions and know-how that the "Sea Peoples" brought with

18. The complete remains of a puppy, buried with its disarticulated head placed between its legs, were found in close proximity to the findspot of the ivory knife-handle, suggesting a possible connection to cult practice. The evidence suggests that the animal, almost certainly a dog, *Canis familiaris*, was not skinned before burial, and was approximately 4–6 months of age at death. No cut marks were found on the bone surfaces (information based on an e-mail report by Brian Hesse, Miqne faunal analyst, March 16, 2001; see also n. 1 above).

them and implanted in their new environment in Canaan. This interpretation is also suggested by the cessation of maritime trade in Iron Age I, which, together with the apparent disappearance of script (although documents may have been written on perishable materials), led to its appellation as the "Dark Age" in the Aegean and the Levant. The architectural features and finds with cultic connotations from Philistia can be isolated and integrated to expand our understanding of influences transmitted from the Aegean to Cyprus and to the Levant. Thus, we can further develop our picture of the flourishing new urban centers in Philistia, showing the emergence of a new entity, the substratum of which was rooted in the Aegean tradition, that adapted to the new environment in Canaan and adopted facets of Canaanite culture. A variety of features with cultic connotations illustrate this phenomenon: the architecture of public buildings with relatively large communal halls and incorporated megaron plans, and the configurations of features such as hearths, *bamot*, bathtubs, pillars, and benches and their associated pottery and special finds, including terra-cotta figurines, zoomorphic vessels, bronze and iron objects, incised scapulae, ivory artifacts, and luxury objects, among others. All these components, incorporated within the overall picture, characterize the highly sophisticated urban civilization of Iron Age I in the cities of the Philistine Pentapolis. I hope that the new material presented above provides an indication of the exciting possibilities for further research.

References

Ainian, A. M.

    1997   *From Rulers' Dwellings to Temples: Architecture, Religion and Society in Early Iron Age Greece 1000–700 BC*. Studies in Mediterranean Archaeology 121. Jonsered: Åströms.

Ben-Shlomo, D.

    In press a   Zoomorphic Terracottas from Tel Miqne-Ekron: Religious and Secular Aspects. In *Proceedings of the Third International Congress on the Archaeology of the Near East, Paris, April 15–19, 2002*, ed. J. Margueron, P. de Miroschedji, and J.-P. Thalmann. Winona Lake, Ind.: Eisenbrauns.

    In press b   *Iron Age Zoomorphic Vessels, Kernoi, and Figurines from Tel Miqne-Ekron*. Ekron Limited Edition Series. Jerusalem: W. F. Albright Institute of Archaeological Research.

Ben-Tor, A.

    1983   Stratigraphy and Architecture. Pp. 3–24 in *Excavations at Athienou, Cyprus, 1971–1972*, by T. Dothan and A. Ben-Tor. Qedem 16. Jerusalem: Hebrew University.

Blegen, C. W., and Rawson, M.

    1966   *The Palace of Nestor at Pylos in Western Messenia* I:1. Princeton: Princeton University Press.

Courtois, J. C.

    1992   Une baignoire monolithe en calcaire du Bronze Récent à Enkomi. Pp. 151–54 in *Studies in Honour of Vassos Karageorghis*, ed. G. C. Ioannides. Nicosia: Society for Cypriot Studies.

Dikaios, P.

    1969   *Enkomi Excavations 1948–1958*. Vols. 1, 3a, and 3b. Mainz: von Zabern.

Dothan, M.

    1971   *Ashdod II–III*. ʿAtiqot 9–10. Jerusalem: Department of Antiquities and Museums.

    1993   Ashdod. Pp. 93–102 in vol. 1 of *The New Encyclopedia of Archaeological Excavations in the Holy Land*, ed. E. Stern. Jerusalem: Israel Exploration Society.

Dothan, M., and Ben-Shlomo, D.
In press *Ashdod VI: Excavations of Areas H–K. The Fourth and Fifth Seasons of Excavation 1968–69.*
         ʿAtiqot. Jerusalem: Israel Antiquities Authority.
Dothan, M., and Freedman, D. N.
1967 *Ashdod I.* ʿAtiqot 7. Jerusalem: Department of Antiquities and Museums.
Dothan, M., and Porath, Y.
1982 *Ashdod IV.* ʿAtiqot 15. Jerusalem: Department of Antiquities and Museums.
1993 *Ashdod V.* ʿAtiqot 23. Jerusalem: Israel Antiquities Authority.
Dothan, T.
1982 *The Philistines and Their Material Culture.* Jerusalem: Israel Exploration Society.
1990 Ekron of the Philistines, Part I: Where They Came From, How They Settled Down and
         the Places They Worshipped In. *Biblical Archaeology Review* 16/1: 27–36.
1998a Initial Philistine Settlement: From Migration to Coexistence. Pp. 48–61 in *Mediterranean
         Peoples in Transition: Thirteenth to Early Tenth Centuries BCE*, ed. S. Gitin, A. Mazar, and
         E. Stern. Jerusalem: Israel Exploration Society.
1998b The Pottery. Pp. 20–51 in N. Bierling, *Tel Miqne-Ekron: Report on the 1995–1996 Excava-
         tions in Field XNW*, ed. S. Gitin. Ekron Limited Edition Series 7. Jerusalem: W. F. Albright
         Institute of Archaeological Research / Hebrew University.
2000 Reflections on the Initial Phase of Philistine Settlement. Pp. 145–58 in *The Sea Peoples and
         Their World: A Reassessment*, ed. E. D. Oren. University Museum Monograph 108. Phila-
         delphia: University of Pennsylvania Press.
2002 Bronze and Iron Objects with Cultic Connotations from Philistine Temple Building 350
         at Ekron. *Israel Exploration Journal* 52: 1–27.
Dothan, T., and Gitin, S.
1990 Ekron of the Philistines. *Biblical Archaeology Review* 16/1: 20–26.
1993 Ekron. Pp. 1051–59 in vol. 3 of *The New Encyclopedia of Archaeological Excavations in the
         Holy Land*, ed. E. Stern. Jerusalem: Israel Exploration Society.
1997 Tel Miqne. Pp. 30–35 in vol. 4 of *The Oxford Encyclopedia of Archaeology in the Near East*,
         ed. E. M. Meyers. New York: Oxford University Press.
French, E. B.
1981 Cult Places at Mycenae. Pp. 41–48 in *Sanctuaries and Cults in the Aegean Bronze Age*,
         ed. R. Hägg and N. Marinatos. Stockholm: Åströms.
Gilmour, G.
1995 *The Archaeology of Cult in the Southern Levant in the Early Iron Age: An Analytical and Com-
         parative Approach.* D.Phil. dissertation, University of Oxford.
Gitin, S.
1990 Ekron of the Philistines, Part II: Olive-Oil Suppliers to the World. *Biblical Archaeology
         Review* 16/2: 32–42.
Gitin, S.; Dothan, T.; and Naveh, J.
1997 A Royal Dedicatory Inscription from Ekron. *Israel Exploration Journal* 47: 1–16.
Hägg, R.
1981 The House Sanctuary at Asine Revisted. Pp. 91–94 in *Sanctuaries and Cults in the Aegean
         Bronze Age*, ed. R. Hägg and N. Marinatos. Stockholm: Åströms.
Hesse, B.
1986 Animal Use at Tel Miqne-Ekron in the Bronze Age and Iron Age. *Bulletin of the American
         Schools of Oriental Research* 264: 17–27.
Karageorghis, V.
1998 Hearths and Bathtubs in Cyprus: A "Sea Peoples'" Innovation? Pp. 276–82 in *Mediterra-
         nean Peoples in Transition: Thirteenth to Early Tenth Centuries BCE*, ed. S. Gitin, A. Mazar, and
         E. Stern. Jerusalem: Israel Exploration Society.

2000   Cultural Innovation in Cyprus Relating to the Sea Peoples. Pp. 255–79 in *The Sea Peoples and Their World: A Reassessment*, ed. E. D. Oren. University Museum Monograph 108. Philadelphia: University of Pennsylvania Press.

Kilian, K.
1979   Ausgrabungen in Tiryns 1977. *Archäologischer Anzeiger* 1: 379–447.
1980   Zum Ende de mykenischen Epoche in der Argolis. *Des Römisch-Germanischen Zentralmuseums Mainz* 27: 166–95.
1981a   Ausgrabungen in Tiryns 1978. *Archäologischer Anzeiger* 2: 149–256.
1981b   Zeugnisse Mykenischer Kultausübung in Tiryns. Pp. 49–58 in *Sanctuaries and Cults in the Aegean Bronze Age*, ed. R. Hägg and N. Marinatos. Stockholm: Åströms.
1982   Ausgrabungen in Tiryns 1980. *Archäologischer Anzeiger* 3: 393–466.

Maeir, A. M.
2001   The Philistine Culture in Transformation: A Current Perspective Based on the Results of the First Seasons of Excavations at Tell es-Safi/Gath. Pp. 111–29 in *Settlement, Civilization and Culture: Proceedings of the Conference in Memory of David Alon*, ed. A. M. Maeir and E. Baruch. Ramat Gan: Bar Ilan University (Hebrew).

Maeir, A. M., and Ehrlich, C. S.
2001   Excavating Philistine Gath: Have We Found Goliath's Hometown? *Biblical Archaeology Review* 27/6: 22–31.

Mazar, A.
1980   *Excavations at Tell Qasile, Part One*. Qedem 12. Jerusalem: Hebrew University.
1985a   *Excavations at Tell Qasile, Part Two*. Qedem 20. Jerusalem: Hebrew University.
1985b   The Emergence of the Philistine Culture. *Israel Exploration Journal* 35: 95–107.
1986   Excavations at Tell Qasile, 1982–1984: Preliminary Report. *Israel Exploration Journal* 36/1–2: 1–15.
1989   Comments on the Nature of the Relations between Cyprus and Palestine during the 12th–11th Centuries B.C. Pp. 94–103 in *The* Civilisations of the Aegean and Their Diffusion in Cyprus and the *Eastern Mediterranean, 2000–600 B.C.*, ed. V. Karageorghis. Larnaca: Pierides Foundation.
2000   The Temples and Cult of the Philistines. Pp. 213–32 in *The Sea Peoples and Their World: A Reassessment*, ed. E. D. Oren. University Museum Monograph 108. Philadelphia: University of Pennsylvania Press.

Mylonas, G. E.
1966   *Mycenae and the Mycenaean Age*. Princeton: Princeton University Press.

Renfrew, C.
1985   *The Archaeology of Cult: The Sanctuary at Phylakopi*. London: British School of Archaeology at Athens.

Shear, I. M.
1987   *The Panagia Houses at Mycenae*. University Museum Monographs 68. Philadelphia: University of Pennsylvania Press.

Stager, L. E.
1987   Notes and News. *Israel Exploration Journal* 37: 68–70.
1991   When Canaanites and Philistines Ruled Ashkelon. *Biblical Archaeology Review* 17/2: 24–43.
1993   Ashkelon. Pp. 103–12 in vol. 1 of *The New Encyclopedia of Archaeological Excavations in the Holy Land*, ed. E. Stern. Jerusalem: Israel Exploration Society.
1998   Forging an Identity: The Emergence of Ancient Israel. Pp. 123–75 in *The Oxford History of the Biblical World*, ed. M. D. Coogan. New York: Oxford University Press.

Stern, E.
2000   The Settlement of the Sea Peoples in Northern Israel. Pp. 197–212 in *The Sea Peoples and Their World: A Reassessment*, ed. E. D. Oren. University Museum Monographs 108. Philadelphia: University of Pennsylvania Press.

Taylour, W.
   1970   New Light on Mycenaean Religion. *Antiquity* 44: 270–80.
Webb, J. M.
   1986   The Incised Scapulae. Pp. 326–27 in *Kition V*, ed. V. Karageorghis. Nicosia: Department
            of Antiquities.
Yasur-Landau, A.
   2001   The Mother(s) of All Philistines? Aegean Enthroned Deities of the 12th–11th Century in
            Philistia. Pp. 329–43 in *Potnia: Deities in the Aegean Bronze Age*, ed. R. Laffineur and
            R. Hägg. Aegaeum 22. Liège: Université de Liège.

The Cult of Astarte in Cyprus

Vassos Karageorghis
Foundation Anastasios G. Leventis
Nicosia

The cult of a "goddess" of fertility was deeply rooted in Cyprus from the prehistoric period to the end of antiquity. The symbolism of the idea of fertility, both male and female but particularly female, had already begun in the Chalcolithic period, in the fourth millennium B.C.E. Nude female figures, often pregnant or about to give birth, holding their breasts or touching their genitalia, ithyphallic male figures or phallic symbols, and figures combining both male and female genitalia are all frequently represented, both in terra-cotta and in stone. It is obvious that we cannot assert with certainty that during the Chalcolithic period the prehistoric Cypriots had already conceived the idea of a divinity. This may also be true for the Early and Middle Bronze Ages and even the early part of the Late Bronze Age, when the symbolism of the idea of fertility often appears in the form of a nude woman holding an infant. It is true that no real sanctuaries have so far been discovered dating to these early periods and, therefore, we know little about the actual cult; the few models of sanctuaries that have survived do not offer a precise notion of the cult (for a general discussion, see J. Karageorghis 1977: 7–69; Bonnet 1996: 69–86).

The picture changes after the middle of the Late Bronze Age. No doubt rural sanctuaries existed throughout the prehistoric period, one of which has been excavated at Ayios Iacovos dating to the early part of the Late Bronze Age, but these may have been simple sacred enclosures, within which ritual performances took place. Actual temples, to use a term usually applied to sacred structures of later periods that appear as monumental structures, are known from about 1200 B.C.E. or soon thereafter. At Enkomi, on the east coast of Cyprus, we have temples dedicated to a male god of fertility, symbolized by the bull, but at Palaepaphos on the west coast and at Kition on the southeast coast, these temples may have been dedicated to a female divinity. I say "may," because few symbols have been found that could indicate with certainty the identification of the divinity who was worshiped. I base my suggestion of a female divinity on their presence during later periods. While at both Palaepaphos and Kition the temples are associated with "horns of consecration," a religious symbol of Aegean (Cretan) origin, this may not represent decisive support for a male divinity. "Horns of consecration" also appear at the more modest cult place of Myrtou-Pigadhes, near the northwestern coast (for a general survey, see V. Karageorghis 1982: 92–106).

Whereas the sanctuaries of the earlier periods may have been cult places for both male and female "divinities," or rather, divinities of fertility characterized variously by male and female symbols, during the later part of the Late Bronze Age it appears that there were distinct divinities, but we do not know their names. At Enkomi, in the two main temples, we have cult statues of the divinities, a bronze male wearing a horned helmet, and another bronze male, fully armed, standing on a base in the form of an oxhide ingot (V. Karageorghis 1982: 100–104).

The social structure and economic evolution of the island, based on the production of copper, but also on agrarian production, may have dictated the iconography and general character of the new religious symbols. At Enkomi, the two main cult places are associated with skulls of oxen, probably worn as masks during religious rituals. But at the same time, they have distinct cult statues of specific anthropomorphic gods: a Horned God (a god of the shepherds and farmers) and the Ingot God (associated with the production of copper) respectively, the two pillars of the economy, agrarian and industrial. It is interesting that there is, at the same time, a female divinity associated with copper production, represented by the traditional nude female figure holding her breasts, but now standing on a base in the form of an oxhide ingot, making a pair with the Ingot God.

It is quite possible that the worship of both took place in the same sanctuary (as in the case of Enkomi, in the sanctuary of the Horned God) and that the distinction of separate cult places for male and female divinities may be a later phenomenon. More Late Bronze Age sanctuaries must be excavated before we can be in a position to pronounce a firm opinion.

If the Cypriot economy around 1200 B.C.E. and even before was based on the production of and trade in copper, which was exported from the harbors of the main urban centers of the south and east coasts, the male elite of these harbor towns may have preferred to place their wealth and power under the protection of a male divinity, but they could not in any way ignore the deeply rooted power of the traditional female divinity. It has been suggested that the fully armed Ingot God may represent the protector of the copper mines of Cyprus, whereas the corresponding female divinity may symbolize the fertility of the copper mines (Catling 1971; see also Knapp 1996, with relevant bibliography).

It may be argued that one aspect of the male god, especially the god of farmers and shepherds, known also as Apollo Keraeates or Apollo Alasiotas, may have been influenced by newcomers to Cyprus from the Aegean, particularly Arcadia, but the female divinity, both in religious conception and in iconography, has deep roots on the island.

The cult place of the Ingot God at Enkomi may have also sheltered a female divinity during the first half of the 11th century B.C.E., judging from the terra-cotta figurines, both male and female, found at the site. The female ones show the strong influence of the newly arrived goddess from the Aegean, namely from Crete, known as the goddess with uplifted arms. Apart from her attitude, the other specific characteristics are a tiara around her head, spots on her cheeks, bulging eyes, and a long necklace with a pendant. Her resemblance to the representations of the corresponding Cretan goddess is striking (cf. V. Karageorghis 1993a: 58–61, with previous bibliography).

Very little is known of the gods and goddesses worshiped in Cyprus during the Dark Ages, but we may say with certainty that the goddess with uplifted arms was universally accepted. Her cylindrical, wheel-made body, however, as it appears on examples found at Amathus dated to the 11th century B.C.E., or others from a later period (8th–7th centuries B.C.E.), was not at all within the Cypriot tradition, which favored the nude female goddess. The Cypriots, however, had adopted the Cretan goddess and assimilated her with their own nude fertility goddess. It is therefore not surprising to see this Cretan goddess adapted to the Cypriot taste.

We first see the nude female goddess with uplifted arms on embossed plaques from Lapithos Tomb 417, dating to the late 11th century B.C.E. This type of the goddess, wearing a tiara, may constitute a Cypriot adaptation of the Cretan goddess, but it may also be an iconographic variant of the Syrian type of the Late Bronze Age, with arms stretched downwards or bent upwards to hold flowers. Such gold plaques, decorated with a nude female figure with arms bent upwards, continue to appear in tombs of the Cypro-Geometric and Cypro-Archaic I periods, especially in places that were famous as cult places in honor of Astarte, such as Amathus, Palaepaphos, and Tamassos. Sometimes they hold their breasts; very rarely, they are draped (see discussion in V. Karageorghis 1986; see also J. Karageorghis 1977: 153–60; Washbourne 1999: 168).

The examples on the wall-brackets of the Hadjiprodromou Collection and in the Louvre, respectively, decorated in the style of Bichrome III pottery and dated to the end of the 9th century B.C.E. or approximately 800 B.C.E., show the goddess in relief, nude, but otherwise with the attitude and facial features of the Cretan goddess. She is also associated with a bull protome, the traditional religious symbol of fertility. In other cases, the goddess with uplifted arms is associated with the snake, also a traditional religious symbol of Cyprus, connected with fertility and death (V. Karageorghis 1993a: 90–91, with bibliography).

On bronze discs found in Tomb 79 at Salamis, dating to ca. 700 B.C.E., we see the nude female goddess in the attitude of a *Potnia Theron*, standing on the back of two lions and holding lions in her hands. We know that the lion was the favorite animal of the goddess of fertility and power, as seen in Near Eastern representations of Cybele and Ishtar. She is frequently associated with the goddess Hathor, imitating her hairstyle. The goddess Ishtar is also the protector of horses; hence these representations on horse gear (J. Karageorghis 1977: 161–64).

Nude female figures with uplifted arms appear also in relief on two small limestone boxes, which may date to the Cypro-Geometric III period. The female figure is shown within a rectangular frame, probably illustrating a temple or a tomb (J. Karageorghis 1977: 152–53; Washbourne 1999: 172–73).

Although we cannot yet be sure of the name of the goddess represented on the two wall-brackets and the gold plaques mentioned above, it is quite possible that the radical change shown by the nude appearance of the goddess may be due to Phoenician influence. The earlier representation on the Lapithos plaque may have an iconographic rather than a cultic significance. We know that by the end of the 9th century B.C.E., the Phoenicians had arrived at Kition on the southeast coast, and there they built a large temple on the foundations of the abandoned Late Bronze Age temple. They dedicated the temple to their own goddess, Astarte, who by that time, during the reign of King Ethbaal, had become their official goddess and was carried to all the places they inhabited or colonized.

Whether or not the Great Temple I at Kition is dedicated to Astarte, as epigraphic evidence may suggest (although this is not universally accepted), the Phoenician influence on the cult of the goddess worshiped in the temple is clear. The Phoenician inscription engraved on a Red Slip Phoenician bowl found on the earliest floor of the temple, destroyed by fire soon after 800 B.C.E., speaks of a certain ML (obviously a Phoenician), who went to Kition from Tamassos, known for its copper mines, which must have attracted the newly arrived Phoenicians. At Kition, in the temple of Astarte, he offered a sacrifice for himself and for his family; he cut his hair, placed it in that bowl and dedicated it to Astarte, a custom known from the Phoenician world until late antiquity (V. Karageorghis 1982: 123–27; see also 1998; Bonnet 1996: 70–74).

We may imagine that similar adaptations may have occurred at Palaepaphos, in the monumental temple of the goddess. Although the type of the Cretan goddess with uplifted arms continued into the 8th century B.C.E., as seen in terra-cotta figurines from this site, other terra-cotta figurines of a slightly later date clearly show Levantine influences — for example, one with a nose-ring (V. Karageorghis 1993b: 98). The general type of the Cretan goddess, with upraised arms and wearing a high flat tiara, however, persists in the region of Palaepaphos, particularly at Yeroskipou (the ancient Ierokepis mentioned by Strabo, the name meaning "the town of the sacred garden"). The Levantine and particularly Phoenician character of the cult in Palaepaphos, even outside the limits of the Great Temple, is well known from sculptures found among the debris of the so-called "siege mound" erected by the Persians near the city wall at the time of the revolt against them in 499 B.C.E. These include limestone *naïskoi* of a Phoenician type, as they are known in the Punic world (Maier 1984: 21). It is interesting that an inscription of the 3rd century B.C.E., found at the site of the Great Temple, refers to the goddess as Astarte *Paphia* (Masson and Sznycer 1972: 81–86).

The epithet of the goddess, *Paphia*, introduces us to the world of Homer. In the *Odyssey*, Homer refers to the adventures of the goddess (for him Aphrodite) on Mount Olympus, when she was caught red-handed in her love affair with the god of war, Ares, and her subsequent flight in shame to Paphos, where she had a temple and a fragrant altar. It is unlikely that Homer refers to the Late Bronze Age temple that was built in approximately 1200 B.C.E., but more likely he knew the later temple, which had become famous throughout the eastern Mediterranean. Homer must have associated it with the rest of his "Orientalia," which included ivory thrones and beds and silver vases of fine Sidonian workmanship. For him and the rest of the Greeks, the goddess was *Paphia* or *Kypris*, the Goddess of Cyprus, thus adding to her exotic, eastern character. For the Cypriots, however, she was known only as *Wanassa* (our Lady). For Hesiod, the goddess has numerous Near Eastern qualities, as seen in the poet's recording of her birth. She is the daughter of a sky-god, as indeed was the Near Eastern goddess Ishtar (for a general discussion, see J. Karageorghis 1984; Bonnet 1996: 75–81; Washbourne 1999: 163–64).

It is unfortunate that we know little about the cult of the Great Goddess at Amathus, on the south coast of Cyprus (for a general survey, see Hermary 1988; see also Bonnet 1996: 81–84). But already in the Cypro-Geometric III period (850–750 B.C.E.), side by side with the goddess with uplifted arms, as she appears on some gold plaques decorated in repoussé, we have the representation of the head of the Egyptian goddess Hathor, no doubt imported from Egypt by the Phoenicians. The cult of Hathor continues at Amathus in the 7th, 6th, and 5th centuries B.C.E., as we see in vase painting and sculpture. It has been suggested that the Eteocypriot name of this goddess was "Anat," a suggestion supported by epigraphic evidence (e.g., on the stone vase from Amathus now in the Louvre), thus providing another Phoenician connection of the cult of this goddess. Next to this female divinity, the Amathusians worshiped a male Horned God, not unlike the Phoenician-Egyptian god Bes, whose iconography is quite rich at Amathus in later periods. The colossal stone vase that was found on top of the Acropolis of Amathus (now in the Louvre), dating to the Cypro-Archaic period (7th century B.C.E.), was no doubt associated with the cult of a fertility goddess. It served, like a second fragmentary vase found in the same spot during recent excavations, for lustral purifications, recalling the "Sea of Bronze" of the Solomonic temple (Hermary and Schmid 1996: 110–16; Aupert 1996: 35).

The site of Amathus has also yielded a limestone throne supported by sphinxes on either side. Such thrones are known in the Phoenician world in association with Astarte (Hermary 1981: 67–68). In this respect we should also mention the terra-cotta figurine from the sanctuary of Ayia Irini, representing a woman seated on a throne, again supported by sphinxes, and the ivory throne from Salamis Tomb 79, also adorned with a sphinx.

The nude female goddess holding her breasts is quite frequent in the coroplastic art of Amathus of the 6th century B.C.E., known mainly from tombs. She appears side by side with the survival of the goddess with uplifted arms mentioned above. On the magnificent stone sarcophagus, no doubt destined for a king, found in the necropolis of Amathus (now in the Metropolitan Museum of Art in New York), dating to the early years of the 5th century B.C.E., the goddess is prominently represented, together with the god Bes (Tatton-Brown 1981).

This funerary aspect of the Cypriot nude goddess is also Near Eastern (Washbourne 1999). It is connected with the goddess Inanna or Ishtar, who descends to the underworld to cause the rebirth of the dead. Thus, in the underworld, she exercises her powers as a goddess of fertility and regeneration, in the same way that, among the living, she was the sacred prostitute, the goddess of fertility. It is not surprising, therefore, to find her in association with funerary monuments. In tombs at Amathus, numerous terra-cotta figurines have been found illustrating the goddess either nude, holding her breasts, or draped. Worshipers of the goddess are also numerous, appearing as terra-cotta figurines of musicians playing the tambourine or the lyre (V. Karageorghis 1987). Another symbol of Astarte, found mainly at Amathus in association with nude female figurines, as well as on the miniature clay *naïskoi* with the image of the goddess inside them (anthropomorphic or aniconic), is the crescent or disc and crescent, well known in Near Eastern iconography as a symbol of Astarte (V. Karageorghis 1996: 57–67).

By the end of the Classical period, under strong Greek influence, this goddess worshiped at Amathus becomes *Kypria* (the Cypriot), as seen in an inscription, a dedication by the last king of Amathus, Androkles (Aupert 1996: 51–52).

That the introduction of the cult of Astarte to Cyprus was due to the Phoenicians is not only iconographically attested, but also mentioned in ancient Greek literature. Herodotus (1.105.2–3) mentions that the cult of Aphrodite-Astarte was introduced to Cyprus from Ashkelon. According to Pausanias (1.14.7), the cult of Aphrodite was initiated by the Assyrians, and thereafter adopted by the Paphians and the Phoenicians of Ashkelon. Herodotus (1.199.1–5) records sacred prostitution on Cyprus, known also from Babylon.

In conclusion, the notion of Aphrodite, goddess of love and beauty, is a Greek conception. On Cyprus, she is a goddess of fertility, deeply rooted in the island's remote past. With the arrival of the Greeks at the end of the Late Bronze Age, she undergoes certain iconographic changes, but her role remains the same. This role is strengthened under the influence of the Phoenicians, whose goddess Astarte finds a proper atmosphere in the religious traditions of Cyprus. Her iconography is dominant for nearly three centuries, from the 8th through the 6th centuries B.C.E. She is shown as a nude female figure holding her breasts, the type of the Phoenician Astarte. She is represented on funerary monuments, and her terra-cotta figurines are placed in tombs, symbolizing the goddess who ensures the rebirth of the dead. Among the living, she is worshiped as the sacred prostitute, the goddess of fertility. The association of Aphrodite-Astarte with Cyprus was well known in the Greek world. The invention of the mold made the transfer of artistic ideas much easier, and the type of Astarte was widespread throughout the Mediterranean, mainly through the Phoenicians. During the Classical and Hellenistic periods, the notion of the goddess on Cyprus, both from the religious and the iconographical point of view, underwent serious changes under strong Greek influence. Of the old fertility goddess, only her nudity remains, a nudity associated with beauty rather than fertility.

References

Aupert, P.
    1996   Histoire de la ville et du royaume. Pp. 18–69 in *Guide d'Amathonte*, ed. P. Aupert. Athens: École Française d'Athènes and Leventis Foundation.

Bonnet, C.
    1996   *Astarté: Dossier documentaire et perspectives historiques.* Rome: Consiglio nazionale della ricerche.

Catling, H. W.
    1971   A Cypriot Bronze Statuette in the Bomform Collection. Pp. 15–32 in *Alašia I*, ed. C. F. A. Schaeffer. Paris: Mission Archéologique d'Alašia.

Hermary, A.
    1981   *Amathonte II. Testimonia 2: La Sculpture.* Paris: Éditions A.D.P.F. and École Française d'Athènes.
    1988   Le culte d'Aphrodite à Amathonte. *Report of the Department of Antiquities, Cyprus* 1988: 101–9.

Hermary, A., and Schmid, M.
    1996   Le sanctuaire d'Aphrodite. Pp. 110–72 in *Guide d'Amathonte*, ed. P. Aupert. Athens: École Française d'Athènes and Leventis Foundation.

Karageorghis, J.
    1977   *La Grande Déesse de Chypre et son culte à travers l'iconographie de l'époque néolithique au IVème s.a.C.* Lyon: Maison de l'Orient.
    1984   Mythology and Cult. Pp. 358–75 in *Paphos: History and Archaeology*, ed. F. G. Maier and V. Karageorghis. Nicosia: Leventis Foundation.

Karageorghis, V.
    1982   *Cyprus: From the Stone Age to the Romans.* London: Thames and Hudson.
    1986   Tiarae of Gold from Cyprus. Pp. 129–32 in *Insight through Images: Studies in Honor of Edith Porada*, ed. M. Kelly-Buccellati. Malibu, Calif.: Undena.
    1987   The Terracottas. Pp. 1–46 in vol. 3 of V. Karageorghis and A. Hermary, *La Nécropole d'Amathonte. Tombes 113–367.* Études Chypriotes 9. Nicosia: Leventis Foundation.

1993a   *The Coroplastic Art of Ancient Cyprus II: Late Cypriote II–Cypro-Geometric III.* Nicosia: Leventis Foundation.

1993b   *The Coroplastic Art of Ancient Cyprus III: The Cypro-Archaic Period. Large and Medium Size Sculpture.* Nicosia: Leventis Foundation.

1996   *The Coroplastic Art of Ancient Cyprus VI: The Cypro-Archaic Period. Monsters, Animals and Miscellanea.* Nicosia: Leventis Foundation.

1998   Astarte at Kition. Pp. 105–8 in *Archäologische Studien in Kontaktzonen der antiken Welt*, ed. R. Roller and K. Schmidt. Göttingen: Vandenhoeck & Ruprecht.

Knapp, A. B.

1996   The Bronze Age Economy of Cyprus: Ritual, Ideology and the Sacred Landscape. Pp. 71–106 in *The Development of the Cypriot Economy from the Prehistoric Period to the Present Day*, ed. V. Karageorghis and D. Michaelides. Nicosia: University of Cyprus and Bank of Cyprus.

Maier, F. G.

1984   *Alt-Paphos auf Zypern: Ausgrabungen zur Geschichte von Stadt und Heiligtum, 1966–1984.* Mainz: von Zabern.

Masson, O., and Sznycer, M.

1972   *Recherches sur le Phéniciens à Chypre.* Paris: Droz.

Tatton-Brown, V.

1981   Le sarcophage d'Amathonte. Pp. 74–83 in *Amathonte II. Testimonia 2: La Sculpture*, by A. Hermary. Paris: Éditions A.D.P.F. and École Française d'Athènes.

Washbourne, R.

1999   Aphrodite *Parakyptousa*, "The Woman in the Window": The Cypriot Astarte-Aphrodite's Fertility Role in Sacred Prostitution and Rebirth. *Report of the Department of Antiquities, Cyprus* 1999: 163–77.

False Dichotomies in Descriptions of Israelite Religion: A Problem, Its Origin, and a Proposed Solution

Ziony Zevit
University of Judaism
Los Angeles, California

Introduction

Despite attacks on Albright's legacy, expressions of umbrage, protests, and disclaimers, and despite all the clever avoidance strategies practiced during the past two decades, the "biblical archaeology" and "archaeological bibliology" paradigms remain intact.[1] Both are necessary for comprehending Israel's ancient history and for achieving insights into its culture, under which term I include its religion. Consequently, biblicists focusing on Israelite religion require archaeology to clarify *realia* and physical contexts; Iron Age archaeologists working with cultic artifacts or sites (in Cisjordan and Transjordan) require bibliology to clarify nonmaterialistic aspects of finds, such as their social and cultural contexts.[2]

The interest of some biblicists and archaeologists in phenomena loosely identified as "Israelite popular religion" over the last fifteen years reflects an attempt to make sense of one-half century of accumulated parallels between Ugaritic and other ancient Near Eastern literatures and the Bible, as well as an attempt to synthesize information about Middle and Late Bronze and Iron Age cultic structures and artifacts with data derived from the Bible. This development follows trends in general history that focus on groups rather than on individuals and that incorporate insights and adopt terminology from the social sciences when creating descriptive, explicatory narratives.

As a consequence, new narratives and discussions at academic meetings borrow and adapt vocabulary from general history and the social sciences to label different phenomena, a borrowing that results in a shared vocabulary but not always in clarity. Different

---

Author's note: The word *dichotomies* in the title refers to the division of a general category into two mutually exclusive branches on the basis of a particular criterion.

1. *Biblical archaeology*, in this juxtaposition of terms, refers to the part of archaeology that engages the Bible in some way when interpreting finds; *archaeological bibliology* refers to the part of biblical research that engages archaeology in some way when interpreting texts or text-related problems. Since the objectives of archaeology and bibliology differ, the respective discussions may treat similar materials differently; but no matter from which perspective data are analyzed, practitioners of each discipline should have a reasonably sophisticated comprehension of what the auxiliary discipline involves.

2. The theological presuppositions of all extant biblical narratives in their original *Sitzen im Leben* and their function in historical or contemporary *Nachleben* compel all biblicists to engage them as religious in some way.

writers employ the same key words but with different meanings. Therefore, although they often appear to address the same topic, in actuality they do not.

This essay addresses one set of words. It aims (1) to isolate the problem of the way that language used to describe some religious phenomena misinforms; (2) to indicate the problem's source by clarifying the reasons that some common descriptors used in formal and informal discussion of Israelite religion lack a historical referent; and (3) to propose a way that the problem may be avoided. Although primarily an analysis of terminology, this essay bears on how we perceive, conceive, analyze, and present data bearing on religious and cultic matters.[3]

The Problem

In the introduction to *Asherah and the Cult of Yahweh in Israel*, Olyan lists the questions for which his study is the intended response. Among them is the following: "Was her worship an element only of popular religion, as many scholars believe, or an aspect of the official cult, or both?" (1988: xiii). After working through material available to him, Olyan concludes that "Asherah and her cult symbol were legitimate not only in popular Yahwism, but in the official cult as well. The evidence of the Hebrew Bible alone suggests strongly that Asherah and the asherah were considered legitimate in the state cult, both of the north and south, in Jerusalem, Samaria and Bethel, and probably in very conservative circles" (1988: 74).

Although Olyan's question distinguishes between "popular religion" and "official cult," his conclusion lumps "state cult" and the undisclosed religion of "very conservative circles" with "official cult." Throughout his discussion, Olyan presupposes a consensus that comprehends these distinctions. But even as he adopts dichotomous terms to describe subsets of cult, he inquires whether the particular worship that seems to have been a distinctive criterion of one belongs to both subsets. If so, the terms are useless.

In *Under Every Green Tree: Popular Religion in Sixth-Century Judah*, Ackerman (1992) decries what she identifies as the misuse of the term "popular religion." Commonly viewed from an elitist position, it has negative connotations and is characterized as the religion of the "teeming masses, the uneducated, the lower classes, the rustics, the unsophisticated, the simple, the *Volk*." She calls this an oversimplification, pointing out that the beliefs of the king may be those of the commoner, and the "temple may as likely contain 'popular' religion as the . . . *bāmôt*."

"What then," she asks rhetorically, "is popular religion?" She responds: "It is . . . easier to say what it is not: it is not the religion usually presented to us as normative in the Bible. . . . it is not the religion of the Deuteronomistic school, the priests, or the prophets."[4]

---

3. Although dichotomous pairs, such as popular and elite, official or royal, do occur in published studies of Israelite religion, they do so with less frequency than I suspected at first, even in popular presentations such as those published in *Biblical Archaeology Review*. The terms do cluster, however, in focused collections of studies, such as Miller, Hanson, and McBride (eds.) 1987. For a survey, see Berlinerblau 1996: 17–22 and 1999: 153–55 (Berlinerblau's 1999 essay was written prior to the publication of his book in 1996, which cites it as "forthcoming").

4. The technique of negative definition is also used by Kamioka (1993) in describing an element of Iranian folk religion, the belief in the *imamzade*, local numens addressed for many minutiae of daily life, often

Ackerman observes that, since the religion of these three excluded groups came to be viewed as normative, popular religion from a normative standpoint is about losers who "probably held the majority and represented the mainstream in their day" (1992: 1–2).

After rejecting one common characterization of popular religion, Ackerman redefines it by exclusion, not inclusion: popular religion in ancient Israel, the religion of the majority, is defined as what is left after the religion of three minority groups is removed (1992: 216–17).[5] (This is akin to defining "Democrats" in the American body politic as what remains after all registered Republicans are removed.)

Consideration of how "popular religion" is employed by Olyan and Ackerman, both trained in the same institution at the same time, indicates that the usages are incompatible. Olyan contrasts popular religion with official and state cult; his may be considered a political dichotomy. Ackerman ostensibly rejects the political—seeing no contrast between official and state religion on the one hand and popular religion on the other, as Olyan has it—in favor of a quasi-social dichotomy—that is, the number of adherents. Her use of the terms "minority," "majority," and "suppression," however, reintroduces political conceptions in a somewhat more volatile way. Although each writer is consistent, the lack of congruence between the referents of their common vocabulary renders some of their analytical conclusions about the topic incompatible.[6]

Tsumura (1993) writes in a manner that appears to bridge the gap of definitional incompatibility: "It is not always easy to distinguish between the official religion and popular religious beliefs in society. Many aspects of the popular religion do appear in the official religious cults, while many traces of the official cults can be recognized in popular religious traditions" (1993: 40). Fifteen pages later he writes:

> While "the sun worship" was *officially* introduced to ancient Israel by Manasseh in the seventh century, in the *popular* phase of the religious life it seems to have existed in Canaan from the earliest time.... While the "official" religion of Yahwism prohibited such Canaanite religious cults, in "popular" religion they continued to be practiced. In Israel, where only one God was supposed to be worshipped in the *official* cult, Baal Astarte, Anath and Asherah as well as the solar deity continued to be worshipped in the *popular* religion evoking condemnation from the Prophets. (1993: 55; italics and quotation marks in original)

For Tsumura, "official" has to do with what is going on in the Jerusalem temple; everything else is "popular." Manasseh's innovations metamorphose, as a matter of definition, from "popular" into "official." But Tsumura's expression, "official religion of Yahwism,"

---

involving difficult and tragic circumstances, when the faithful feel it inappropriate to say "*Allahu akbar.*" He writes: "It is impossible . . . to define popular belief in general. . . . It can be better and safely defined in a negative manner: It is not the official Islam . . . whose activities primarily center on and in mosques and are largely administered by the clergy. It usually functions and can operate without having an essential relationship with either mosques or clergy" (1993: 135–36).

5. The contents of the excluded religion are left undetermined, but whatever they were, the religion of priestly/Deuteronomistic/prophetic groups later "suppressed" that of the majority and "won."

6. I selected the works of Olyan and Ackerman because both are highly regarded, important contributions to the ongoing discussion of Israelite religion that have withstood criticism and aged well. The point I am discussing does not bear on the main focus of either work.

beclouds the almost clear dichotomy. On the one hand, it attaches a normative element to "official" religion not discussed by Olyan but rejected explicitly by Ackerman; on the other, it contradicts his own usage of the adjective "official," since what he may consider "official Yahwism" seems not to have had any "official" *Sitz im Leben* during most of the First Temple period. Finally, it is unclear from what he writes whether the prophets (by which term I assume he refers to the literary prophets of the Hebrew Bible) are identified with official or state religion in its normative mode, or whether they are off to the side in an undefined limbo.

Why this terminological confusion? Is it simply a matter of independent-minded people playing with semantics in the manner of Humpty-Dumpty in Lewis Carroll's *Through the Looking Glass*, who reported to Alice, "When I use a word it means just what I choose it to mean—neither more nor less"? Berlinerblau, who has dedicated several recent studies to this issue, points out that, although religiologists and biblicists share a sense that "popular religion" has to do with the man in the street, the term is "conceptually ambiguous," and no consensus exists about its meaning (1996: 19).[7]

The Source of the Problem

Vrijhof (1979) provides significant insights (1) illustrating the terminological chaos; (2) explaining how, when, and why it developed; and (3) recommending what could be done to remedy the situation. Vrijhof studied 18 essays dealing with the "official" and "popular" in world religions and discerned that distinctions between the two were explained variously by different authors. These differences fall into five somewhat overlapping categories:

1. practices endorsed by an authoritative body versus those not so endorsed;
2. codified, established, conceptualized and institutionalized religions versus those not so treated;
3. religions prescribed and controlled by institutions versus those not prescribed and controlled;
4. groups constituting formal associations in which official bodies play a role versus culturally embedded practices controlled by local communities; and
5. elite versus mass. (Vrijhof 1979: 669–73)

These comprehensions all focus on authority in matters of determining, codifying, and interpreting doctrines and praxis; on specialized knowledge that underlies this authority; and on elites either linked to the state, with its coercive power, or possessing such power on their own. Focusing on the essays that yielded the official-popular dichotomy best, Vrijhof keenly observes: "These descriptions refer especially to the institutionalized and codified Christian religion in the western world. Thus, the historical and cultural conditioning of the official and popular religion theme becomes apparent" (1979: 674).

The origin of the distinction lies in the relationship of the Western Church to the indigenous religions of Europe during and after the Middle Ages. Initially, the two were in

---

7. Despite the niggling definitional problem, even dichotomous terminology is preferable to the theological, value-laden terminology employed by the biblical writers themselves, which is sometimes reflected in terms such as "foreign worship" or "Canaanite religion."

competition; but when the Church grew in power and authority through its connections with leading social groups of the emerging nation-states, indigenous religions were denigrated and held to be primitive superstitions, and attempts were made to suppress them. As Christianity spread, archaic elements that persisted in folk culture came to be considered marginal and abnormal (Vrijhof 1979: 675). Alston, a scholar of English religious history, explains the dichotomy as due to tensions arising between the Church defined as ecclesiastical hierarchy and the Church defined as community of faithful believers, between the religion of the learned and that of the unlearned, between a conservative elite that constituted a minority and an active laity that concerned itself with doctrine, as well as with the influence of what she calls "ancient peasant fears" (Alston 1993: 1–4).

The scholars in Vrijhof's analysis who had the most difficulty with the terms and found it necessary either to augment them with other expressions or to define them very broadly were those studying religions with histories and organizations that differed considerably from Western Christianity—namely Hinduism, Buddhism, African religions, and Islam. Since the implicit bias of the "official-popular" dichotomous pair restricted its usefulness, Vrijhof explored the potential of adjectives such as "normative, folk, alternative, operative, lived, common religion," and even "center-periphery" in order to propose a terminology applicable to religion universally. He finally settled on "official" and "non-official" as functional concepts applicable to all religions in all social and historical contexts.

Vrijhof suggests that the term "official religion" should refer to that about which decisions had been considered necessary. Deciders would have been individuals or bodies deemed authorized. Such religion would be recognized, normative, and valid, and would be supported by those accepting the authority of the authorizers. Other people might not have accepted the deciders or authorizers, may not have known about them, or may have been indifferent to them, in which case the religion of the second group would be "non-official" religion (1979: 686–91). Paradoxically, such non-official religion might look exactly like the official, or might be in conflict with it.[8]

Vrijhof's proposed resolution of the terminological issues does not achieve its objective. It simply digitizes the dichotomies and so presents an impression of scientific precision.[9] Its theoretical semantic neatness is belied by data. It conceives of an original "official" religion with which the other related forms are in some sort of relationship. It does not spell out, however, the implication of a scenario in which a group involved with "non-official" religion generates an authorizing body so that there are two or more competing official religions, as in the case of Roman Catholicism and Orthodox traditions, or in the case of Protestant Christianity and Mormonism. Moreover, it does not contribute to discussions of religions in cultures that, as a consequence of their historical

---

8. In addition, Vrijhof retains the term "popular religion." Within the context of "official" religion, he suggests that "popular" would refer to local styles of religion.

9. The word *digitize* refers to the coding of information, as in binary numerals with ones and zeros, to indicate the presence or absence of a feature. Digitation, used in mathematics and electronics, has proved itself an informing descriptive device in phonology and anthropology, and has the advantage of providing order, or at least the semblance of order, when employed in systems of classification. Rosch noted its adoption as a feature of categorization by American social scientists attempting to make their work more scientific (1975: 179). It was introduced into religiology by Saler (1993: 12–17).

development, did not experience and hence do not recognize the phenomenon of an over-arching "official" religion.[10]

Chinese religion consists of several religions with no authoritative institutions; both contemporary Judaism and contemporary Islam have various authoritative bodies, not all of which recognize the authority of the others. For Rabbinic Judaism, this circumstance is encapsulated in a statement attributed to R. Elazar ben Azariah. Expositing on the words *baʿălê ʾăsuppôt* in Eccl 12:11, which were taken to mean "masters of assembly," R. Elazar said, "these are the disciples of the wise that sit in assembly after assembly busying themselves in Torah. Some declare ritually impure and others ritually pure; some prohibit and others permit, [some declare unfit] and some declare fit" (*b. Ḥagigah* 3b).[11]

Vrijhof's solution, along with the solutions of others attempting terminological realignment, have not met with success, and the old terminology endures despite its recognized faults.[12] Why?

In an intellectual *tour de force* entitled *Conceptualizing Religion*, Saler (1993), a cultural anthropologist, suggests that the situation persists because the very concept of "religion" is a category within Western thought that conceives it as a component of an even larger category, that of "culture." As a concept in Western culture, information about and attitudes toward religion are absorbed by those growing up within the culture, participating in religious activities, and/or reading about them. People studying religion—religiologists, anthropologists, archaeologists, and biblicists—no matter what their personal beliefs, practices, and attitudes and, even if they are not involved with a distinctly Western religion and/or are not trained in the West, work within academic paradigms informed by these categories and communicate to people similarly informed. Consequently, it is through this culture that comprehends religion in Christian categories that all religions are viewed (Saler 1993: 8–10, 212–13, 227–28).[13] In this context, scholars find it necessary and convenient to translate the foreign and exotic into the familiar and common, despite the disforming and misinforming nature of the procrustean fit.[14] In short, the old terminology endures because of intellectual inertia.

---

10. As a rule of thumb, I posit that, (a) where religious bodies evolved an implicit understanding that the role of their religion was not only to be in the world but to change it; (b) when such bodies evolved a vertical organization; and (c) where this was accompanied by a practical missionary tendency—then centralization and officialization could occur. In the absence of one or more of the necessary conditions, it did not occur.

11. The *Baraita* continues, indicating in a most Derridian way that competing and conflicting views are all reflections of the single revelation.

12. The comment of Francis Bacon (d. 1626) in *Novum Organum*, §38, comes to mind: "The idols and false notions which are now in possession of the human understanding, and have taken deep root therein, not only beset men's minds that truth can hardly find entrance, but even after entrance obtained, they will again in the very instauration of the sciences meet and trouble us, unless men being forewarned of the danger fortify themselves as far as may be against their assaults."

13. Saler cites one study that indicates that many academics associated with the American Academy of Religion and its affiliates are either committed mainly to Christianity or have had significant educational experiences informed by such a commitment, and a second study that charges some of them with insinuating theology into religious studies (Saler 1993: 3). The first study is Pals 1990; the second is Weibe 1990.

14. Saler's own solution to the ethnocentric situation is two-pronged. First, scholars should learn the history of the ideas and institutions in their own culture that they discern in other cultures; second, they should use the key conceptual terminology of the studied foreign culture in describing that culture and for the purpose of cross-cultural comparison (Saler 1993: 263–64).

Scholars comfortably at home in non-Western, polytheistic cultures employ the terms, but not as dichotomies. For example, in a study of Japanese popular religion, Miyata (1993) equates "popular belief" with what "can be seen in the average Japanese person's everyday life." For Miyata, the category "average person" includes individuals with vague attitudes toward religion, not necessarily believers or followers of Buddhism or Shinto, but people who share patterns of belief and practices that include shrines, spirits, small gods, and amulets (Miyata 1993: 16–22).[15] Miyata conceives of the popular religion as an undefined base consisting of unscripted cultural givens that define the ethos. (According to him, formally organized religions in Japan as different as Shinto and Buddhism attract adherents because they emphasize certain of these underlying features.) Similarly, Hitoshi understands folk religion as that which "arises from within daily life and reflects aspects of . . . the daily lives of ordinary people, in contrast to world religions such as Christianity, Islam, and Buddhism" (1996: 120). For these researchers, the terms "popular" and "folk" address matters of social location and sociology on the one hand, and common cultural elements on the other (compare what is identified as Vrijhof's fourth category above). Furthermore, in their respective studies, both Miyata and Hitoshi illustrate that folk religion undergoes historical development and change just as the centralized, formally organized, and structured religions do.

Let us take a more complicated example. Different Judaisms have been identified as functioning in Late Antiquity, among which are Rabbinic, Pharisaic, Sadducean, Essenic, Qumranic, and Samaritan, as well as Jewish-Christianity. These groups could be classified according to geographical dispersion, political aspirations, political power, and ideologies.[16] Nothing in this balkanized distribution can be identified as "official." Nevertheless, it is possible to isolate features shared by most (but not all) of these groups, as well as by the overwhelming majority of Jews at the time who did not belong to any group. This congeries of features constitutes what may be called "common Judaism": concern for and loyalty to the temple (when it stood); for purity (however expressed); for piety expressed through prayer and common worship; for Sabbath observance (however defined); and for consumption of "proper" food and drink (Sanders 1992: 47–303).[17] The groups may be

---

15. Tato Takahama, a journalist, describes Japan as a nominally religious country and reports that 84% of Japanese say they observe both Shintoism and Buddhism (*Los Angeles Times*, May 19, 2000: B9). Apropos Saler's observations, Miyata writes: "In recent times we have had the Western general concept of god in our head, but Japanese gods are beings that do not have clear statues or images. And so, whenever we use the expression *kami* in Japanese, we have a problem. I personally do not write the Chinese character for *kami* but use *katakana*. This is one way of expressing the difference between the Western and Japanese concepts of god" (1993: 18).

16. Compare with Boccaccini, who distinguishes two major ideological streams that cut through some of the groups: Zadokite, a ritualistic priestly one; and Enochic, a mystical theosophic one. These streams gave rise to different social and political constellations of people (1998: 11–17, 165–96).

17. In an earlier work, Sanders (1977) provided a list of ideas that may have characterized this common Judaism: God chose Israel, gave the Torah, and promised election if Israel obeyed the covenant. There is reward and punishment along with opportunities for repentance so that people can rejoin the covenant community when they have disobeyed or fallen short of covenant requirements. People in the covenant community will be saved (cf. 1977: 422). The specific comprehensions of these generalized beliefs differed from group to group, so that although two could have espoused the same statement, each would have comprehended it differently, even to the extent that the interpretation in one group could exclude the other from the covenant and salvation.

seen as organized embodiments of particular tendencies or developments within common Judaism.

Even though the Jewish context was not polytheistic, the connections or relationships between common Judaism and its unique instantiations in Late Antiquity are comparable—but hardly identical—to those between the contemporary popular religion and the more organized religions practiced by the Japanese. It was certainly more like what is attested in contemporary Japan than like what went on in medieval Europe.

Recognizing that the social organization of Israel in Early Antiquity differed from that of the Jews in Late Antiquity provides a solution to the problem.

A Solution to the Problem

Israelite society, according to data in the Hebrew Bible, organized itself by groups of related individuals living in proximity to each other as *bātê ʾāb*, "father's houses," generally understood as extended families; *mišpāḥôt*, "clans," groupings of *bātê ʾāb*, and *šĕbāṭîm*, "tribes," (in)formal confederations of *mišpāḥôt*.[18] Josh 7:13–14, a sixth-century B.C.E. text, presents the nested social hierarchy as follows: *ʿām*, "public/people"; *šēbeṭ*, "tribe"; *mišpāḥâ*, "clan"; *bayit*, "house/extended family"; *geber*, "individual male."

At each level, relatedness was expressed in terms of genealogical descent. Although at each level, degrees of consanguinity most likely correlated with geographical proximity, father's houses or clans could cluster in small individual sites or occupy smaller or larger villages or share towns and villages with others from different clans, even clans from different tribes. A range of biblical texts drawn from both narrative and legal genres dated to different periods during the Iron Age II indicate that Israelite writers described cultic activities occurring at each level of social organization, as follows.

Individual.   Abraham's offering of Isaac (Gen 22:3–10) and Jephthah's offering of his daughter (Judg 11:34–40) were individual acts (whether or not Jephthah's daughter was actually dispatched). Manasseh and others caused their children to pass through fire (2 Kgs 21:6; and the king of Moab sacrificed his son [2 Kgs 3:26–27]). Mic 6:6–7 describes a series of individual offerings that Israelites are represented as having proposed, among which are calves, rams, goats, oil, and firstborn children. According to Deut 17:2–5 and 29:17, individuals could engage in private cultic activities, while according to priestly legislation, individuals had private cultic obligations (Leviticus 1–4).[19]

Noting the frequency with which biblical narratives represent characters as praying spontaneously, Greenberg attempts to describe the conceptual world within which individual Israelites, men and women, kings and commoners, composed and offered spontaneous prayers (1983: 1–57).[20] His work has opened a door to an understanding of private piety.

---

18. The most recent discussion of these terms with an extensive bibliography is presented in Faust 2000: 29–30.

19. Van der Toorn considers the descriptions of family in the pentateuchal narratives and concludes that "the Elohistic narratives show that the terms and concepts of family religion were familiar to an Israelite audience of the eighth century" (1996: 255–65).

20. Greenberg's work is particularly important because the individual piety that he isolates is described casually across a wide range of genres originating in different periods, suggesting that it was more common than not.

Father's House. The shrine of Micah in the hill country of Ephraim was a proprietary shrine of one family (Judg 17:5–13); Elkanah went to Shiloh regularly with his nuclear family (1 Sam 1:3); Deut 13:7–8 conjectures anti-Yahwistic incitement occurring when one is recruited by a full brother, son, daughter, wife, or *rēʿa*, a close relative, all members of the father's house.[21]

Clan. Danites forced a Levite-Priest to become their tribal priest, a priest for a *šēbeṭ ûlĕmišpāḥâ*, a "tribe-clan" (Judg 18:19); David's absence from Saul's table is explained as due to his participating in a *zebaḥ mišpāḥâ*, a "clan sacrifice" (1 Sam 20:6, 29); Deut 29:17 lists the *mišpāḥâ* as a social unit that, as a unit, can trespass the covenant; Lev 20:5 holds an *ʾîš*, an "individual," and his *mišpāḥâ*, "clan," culpable if the individual participates in the Molek cult.[22]

Tribe. Reubenites, Gadites, and Transjordanian Manassites build a large altar that in the narrative is reasonably construed by other tribes as intended for cultic purposes (Josh 22:10–29); Deut 29:17 lists the *šēbeṭ* as a social unit that, as a unit, can trespass the covenant.

People/Public. Saul made an offering on behalf of a collection of tribes identified as an *ʿām* (1 Sam 13:8–9), a nonspecific term for related folk; see also, for example, Gen 34:16; Ruth 1:5.[23]

Other social units involved in cultic observances were *mantic communities* (Deut 13:2–3), such as those that formed around Samuel, Elijah, and Elisha or that Deuteronomy conjectured might form around an idolatrous mantic (Deut 13:2–3) or even an individual *ʿîr*, "city" (Deut 13:13–16). The religion of these communities cut across or rather through the above-mentioned consanguine groups.[24]

At one and the same time, an individual belonged to different, nested, social groupings, each of which had cultic celebrations and obligations. In addition, individuals could

---

21. Judg 18:14 indicates that Micah's domicile consisted of a cluster of structures, *bātîm*. Faust's research indicates that rural houses were, as a rule, larger than urban ones, that they contained almost twice as many internal room divisions, and that they often had a second courtyard. He explains them as homes of extended families (2000: 19–20).

22. The context addresses the culpability of the clan and a supraclan group, the *ʿam hāʾāreṣ*, but not the father's house. Perhaps because of the call for execution, the immediate family was relieved from carrying out sentence.

23. Ostensibly, rulings in Leviticus regarding *ḥaṭṭāʾt* (purification) offerings are incongruent with this pattern of organization. They progress from the anointed priest (Lev 4:3) to all the congregation of Israel (Lev 4:13), who would be represented in the offering by *ziqnê hāʿēdâ*, "the elders of the congregation" (Lev 4:15), to the *nāśîʾ*, "tribal leader/ruler" (Lev 4:22), and finally to any individual (Lev 4:27). The ordering appears to skip the *mišpāḥâ* as a unit, despite the fact that the elders of the congregation are clan leaders as well as leaders of their individual *bêt ʾāb*, "father's house." Since the elders are clan leaders, and the *nāśîʾ* is most likely to be identified with the *nāśîʾ bêt ʾāb*, "leader of the father's house" (Num 3:24, 30, 35 from the tribe of Levi and Num 25:14 from Simeon) and the title *rōʾš bêt ʾāb*, "head of the father's house" (in Num 7:2; 36:1), I consider it reasonable to allow that the elders were in themselves leaders/heads of father's houses. The terminology in Leviticus 4 reflects their position vis-à-vis the larger group represented. Because the text of Leviticus 4 implies that, as units, they could become liable to purification offerings, it is therefore indicating that, at certain times and under certain circumstances, clans and father's houses functioned independently of other similar units.

24. Villages may have been occupied by consanguine groups. Ophrah, Gideon's home, is represented as having been occupied by a single clan, the Abiezrites (cf. Judg 6:27, 34 and 8:32) and Nob, a town of perhaps 160 people, by a single, priestly *bêt ʾāb* (1 Sam 22:16–19).

belong to different cultic communities that had their own unique celebrations. In the case of the former, he or she participated in the cult as a member of a father's house and/or clan and/or tribe; in the case of the latter, he or she was an individual joining others in a community whose sole raison d'être was religiocultic. In the case of the former, the group was primary, and the individual a derivative of the group; in the case of the latter, the individual was primary, the group being a derivative of the individuals.

Underlying both organizational patterns was some minimal Israelitish *koiné*, of credo and praxis, similar to the "common Judaism" of Late Antiquity. It may have consisted of acknowledging YHWH somehow in (at least regionally) conventionalized word and normalized offerings. Insofar as there is no reason to assume that cultic observances at the level of the father's house were less formal, regulated, or tradition-bound than at the poly-tribal level, and because there is no reason to assume any significant difference in formality between the observances of consanguine groups and those of affiliations of unrelated individuals, the digitized dichotomies simply do not apply. Their words lack a social or ideological referent in the culture of ancient Israel.[25] They mislead.

There was no state or elite or official or popular religion in ancient Israel. There was a political body that we may label "state"; there were social and economic elites; there were sacerdotal and royal officials; there was a populace; and there was the so-called "man in the street." But data do not support the proposition that a particular type of pattern of credo or praxis may be associated with them.[26]

This conclusion engages archaeology only when archaeologists move into historical interpretations of the sociocultic setting of cultic data. Following are some well known examples:

At Tell el-Far'ah (North), identified as Tirzah, Locus 439, a room in House 440 of Stratum VIIb, dated to the beginning of the 9th century, contained fragments of a model shrine. This can be treated as evidence of the religion of a small *bêt 'āb* or even of individuals within the family, not as an example of domestic/house cults, and discussed in the

---

25. Priestly material, generally taken as reflecting practice at the central shrine in Jerusalem, describes and prescribes fairly well-choreographed rituals. I speculate that the looseness of social connectedness between individuals in Jerusalem, even though most belonged to the same *šēbeṭ* or *'ām*, is what necessitated formal descriptions defining the duties and obligations of all anonymous role-players in ritual acts. At the level of *bêt 'āb* or *mišpāḥâ*, where connectedness was tight and people were not anonymous, rituals may have been more individualistic — compare school or family traditions — but not less formal.

26. Van der Toorn, who accepts a nested, sociological model of Israelite religion, assigns a role to state religion after the rise of the monarchy. Under Saul, YHWH became a national deity because his cult was that of the military. The unifying force of the military and the development of a state religion precipitated the "invention" of a national identity and a cult with YHWH as its deity. The complex relationship was expressed through the "charter myth" of the Exodus (van der Toorn 1996: 271–81, 287–306, 315). Using examples from Saul (cf. 1 Sam 28:3, 9), but primarily from the Omrides, he argues that the state religion could be manipulative and coercive, attempting to suppress elements of family religion (1996: 317–20, 328–34). The case of Saul's attempted suppression of necromancy is exceptional, even as the narrative describes it as a failed policy. The medium at 'Endor is described as being suspicious of strangers soliciting her services, not of neighbors. The Omrides, particularly Jezebel, persecuted prophets for personal reasons. The Deuteronomistic historian describes her pogrom as a reaction to Elijah's slaughter of the Baal prophets at Mt. Carmel. Van der Toorn's work implicitly suggests a weak-state-religion versus family-religion dichotomy, which is then complicated by the Yahweh Alone movement and the mass exiles that necessitated a redefinition of Israelite identity. The crossover into this ideologically-driven movement is justified, but beyond the self-imposed limits of my study.

context of whatever other cult-like finds were found in the structure, such as a figurine body of a nursing woman and the head of a horse figurine (Chambon 1984: 136–39).

At Megiddo, an array of incense stands, burners, and two small altars was found tucked in the southwest corner of Locus 2081, possibly the forecourt of a large building from Stratum VA–IVB1, conventionally dated to the 10th century (Loud 1948: 45–46). The formal arrangement of the artifacts in a corner of the locus, on the one hand, and the absence of benches for displaying artifacts, on the other, suggest that the location was not designed originally for cultic use (as was, for example, Cult Room 49 at Lachish). Physically, the cult corner could only have accommodated two or three people in addition to the artifacts. At Megiddo, then, this array can also be treated as evidence of the religion of a *bêt ʾāb*.

The Bull Site in northern Manasseh, an Iron Age I site of the 12th century, could accommodate a large group of people within its perimeter (Mazar 1982: 32–36; 1983: 34–40). Its location suggests that it was built by and for the needs of a local population that journeyed to the site. The size of the boulders used in constructing the lower courses of the perimeter walls—boulders not currently in evidence in the immediate vicinity—indicates that the enclosure was built at a great expenditure of energy, involving many people and draft animals. It can be associated with some cultic practices of a *mišpāḥâ* whose individual *bātê ʾāb* lived in villages close by.[27]

Both the cult complex at Dan known from archaeology (Biran 1982: 15–43) and the Jerusalem temple known from texts can be considered urban, tribal shrines.[28] This does not preclude their being used also by individuals or consanguine groups from other tribes. Both appear to have been open to members of the *ʿām* and home to a range of practices that included those in the *koinē* as well as others. The fact that both were very large and elaborate, benefiting from royal patronage, does not indicate that what went on in their precincts differed appreciably in essence from what went on elsewhere, or that it was more official or sanctioned.[29]

Because the corpus of places such as these where religion was practiced is small and their number statistically irrelevant, generalizations about them remain tentative. Under such circumstances, I suggest that it is productive to describe both the sites and Israelite religion as expressions of known ancient social realities. This is preferable to describing them in dichotomous terms, lacking social referents in the ancient culture. The terms are semantic shadows cast on the walls of our conceptual universe by the faith-flames of medieval Europe. It is time to turn on the lights.

---

27. If typical, more such enclosures with telltale signs of cultic use should be found. I speculate that more than one *mišpāḥâ* could have used the same enclosure for certain events and that at certain locations considered particularly propitious, different *mišpāḥôt* might have built their own enclosures.

28. The reigning monarch in Jerusalem was legitimated in his position by tribal authorities. He was essentially the chief elder of his tribe; his kingdom encompassed primarily *mišpāḥôt* of his tribe; and the temple—despite whatever claims were exerted on its behalf—was until the destruction of the Northern Kingdom in 721 B.C.E. primarily the main, but not the exclusive, shrine of his own tribe. (Although the Arad temple is an archaeologically unique find, I do not grant that it was unique as an institution in preexilic Judah during the time that it functioned.)

29. In some cases, the direction of authority may have flowed from the cult centers that sanctioned the legitimacy of the kings (cf. Zevit 1985: 61, 64–65).

References

Ackerman, S.
   1992   *Under Every Green Tree: Popular Religion in Sixth-Century Judah.* Harvard Semitic Monographs 46. Atlanta: Scholars Press.

Alston, M.
   1993   *Faith and Fire: Popular and Unpopular Religion 1350–1600.* London: Hambledon.

Berlinerblau, J.
   1996   *The Vow and "Popular Religious Groups" of Ancient Israel: A Philological and Sociological Inquiry.* Journal for the Study of the Old Testament Supplement Series 210. Sheffield: Sheffield Academic Press.

   1999   Preliminary Remarks for the Sociological Study of Israelite "Official Religion." Pp. 153–70 in *Ki Baruch Hu: Ancient Near Eastern, Biblical, and Judaic Studies in Honor of Baruch A. Levine,* ed. R. Chazan, W. W. Hallo, and L. H. Schiffman. Winona Lake, Ind.: Eisenbrauns.

Biran, A.
   1982   The Temenos at Dan. *Eretz-Israel* 16 (Orlinsky Volume): 15–43.

Boccaccini, G.
   1998   *Beyond the Essene Hypothesis: The Parting of the Ways between Qumran and Enochic Judaism.* Grand Rapids, Mich.: Eerdmans.

Chambon, A.
   1984   *Tell el-Farʿah I: L'âge du Fer.* Paris: Éditions Recherche sur les Civilisations.

Faust, A.
   2000   The Rural Community in Ancient Israel during Iron Age II. *Bulletin of the American Schools of Oriental Research* 317: 17–39.

Greenberg, M.
   1983   *Biblical Prose Prayer as a Window to the Popular Religion of Ancient Israel.* Berkeley: University of California Press.

Hitoshi, M.
   1996   Rethinking Japanese Folk Religion: A Study of Kumano Shugen. Pp. 120–34 in *Religion in Japan: Arrows to Heaven and Earth,* ed. P. F. Kornicki and I. J. McMullen. Cambridge: Cambridge University Press.

Kamioka, K.
   1993   Some Aspects of Modern Iranian Popular Belief. Pp. 135–71 in *Official Cult and Popular Religion in the Ancient Near East: Papers of the First Colloquium on the Ancient Near East—The City and Its Life, Held in the Middle Eastern Cultural Center in Japan (Mitaka, Tokyo), March 20–22, 1992,* ed. E. Matsushima. Heidelberg: Universitätsverlag C. Winter.

Loud, G.
   1948   *Megiddo II: Seasons of 1935–39.* Oriental Institute Publication 62. Chicago: Oriental Institute.

Mazar, A.
   1982   The "Bull Site": An Iron Age I Open Cult Place. *Bulletin of the American Schools of Oriental Research* 247: 27–42.

   1983   Bronze Bull Found in Israelite "High Place" from the Time of the Judges. *Biblical Archaeology Review* 9/5: 34–40.

Miller, P. D.; Hanson, P. D.; and McBride, S. D. (eds.)
   1987   *Ancient Israelite Religion: Essays in Honor of Frank Moore Cross.* Philadelphia: Westminster.

Miyata, N.
   1993   *Kami* and *Hotoke* in Japanese Popular Belief. Pp. 16–30 in *Official Cult and Popular Religion in the Ancient Near East: Papers of the First Colloquium on the Ancient Near East—The City and Its Life, Held in the Middle Eastern Cultural Center in Japan (Mitaka, Tokyo), March 20–22, 1992,* ed. E. Matsushima. Heidelberg: Universitätsverlag C. Winter.

Olyan, S. M.
    1988   *Asherah and the Cult of Yahweh in Israel.* Society of Biblical Literature Monograph Series 34. Atlanta: Scholars Press.
Pals, D. L.
    1990   Autonomy, Legitimacy, and the Study of Religion. *Religion* 20: 1–16.
Rosch, E.
    1975   Universals and Cultural Specifics in Human Categorization. Pp. 177–206 in *Cross-Cultural Perspectives on Learning,* ed. R. Brislin et al. New York: Sage.
Saler, B.
    1993   *Conceptualizing Religion: Immanent Anthropologists, Transcendent Natives, and Unbounded Categories.* Studies in the History of Religions/Numen Book Series 56. Leiden: Brill.
Sanders, E. P.
    1977   *Paul and Palestinian Judaism.* London: SCM.
    1992   *Judaism Practice and Belief 63 BCE–66 BCE.* London: SCM.
Tsumura, D. T.
    1993   The Interpretation of the Ugaritic Funerary Text KTU 1.161. Pp. 40–55 in *Official Cult and Popular Religion in the Ancient Near East: Papers of the First Colloquium on the Ancient Near East—The City and Its Life, Held in the Middle Eastern Cultural Center in Japan (Mitaka, Tokyo), March 20–22, 1992,* ed. E. Matsushima. Heidelberg: Universitätsverlag C. Winter.
Van der Toorn, K.
    1996   *Family Religion in Babylonia, Syria, and Israel: Continuity and Change in the Forms of Religious Life.* Leiden: Brill.
Vrijhof, P. H.
    1979   Conclusion. Pp. 668–99 in *Official and Popular Religion: Analysis of a Theme for Religious Studies,* ed. P. H. Vrijhof and J. Waardenburg. The Hague: Mouton.
Weibe, D.
    1990   Disciplinary Aims, Boundary Conditions and the Academic Study of Religion: Comments on Pals and Dawson. *Religion* 20: 17–29.
Zevit, Z.
    1985   Deuteronomistic Historiography in I Ki 11–II Ki 17 and the Reinvestiture of the Israelite Cult. *Journal for the Study of the Old Testament* 32: 57–73.

Mesopotamian Imperialism and Israelite Religion: A Case Study from the Second Isaiah

Peter Machinist

Department of Near Eastern Languages and Civilizations
Harvard University

Introduction

The Neo-Assyrian and Neo-Babylonian Empires were the most imposing of their day, and in gauging their impact on the states and peoples under and around them, modern scholarship has understandably expended much effort on their most obvious manifestations in warfare, politics, the economy, and monumental architecture. But there was a cultural dimension also, as in all imperial situations, and while this has been less well highlighted because more elusive in its evidence, in recent years it has claimed increasing recognition and discussion. A particular concern here has been religion, not only that of the emperors and their courts and priestly establishments, but the effect of this imperial religion, and the imperial presence more generally, on the beliefs and practices of the smaller states and peoples. Of the latter, Israel and Judah have emerged as a most challenging set of cases, because they appear to offer, through the Hebrew Bible and archaeological sources, the fullest opportunity to examine this imperial impact from the side of the subjects, not simply the emperors.

Scholarship on this imperial impact as it affected Israelite and Judean religion has taught us to see it in a wide variety of forms. The issue, indeed, was joined three decades ago when McKay (1973), and independently and more substantially Cogan (1974), argued that coercive religious policies played only a very limited role in the governance of the Neo-Assyrian Empire. Their position was, in the nature of things, contested by others—most prominently Spieckermann (1982)—as they had contested their predecessors; and the debate continues, with Cogan (1993) weighing in with a thoughtful reply to his critics and Holloway (1992; 2002) reviewing in a massive way the whole issue anew. My own sense is that Cogan's and McKay's position—Cogan here offering the more substantial and searching analysis—has not been essentially refuted (Machinist 1992: 75–76). But at the least, it is fair to say, they have made it clear that the imperial impact on the culture and religion of its subjects more often worked subtly and indirectly than broadly and forcibly.

In this paper, I propose to take up just such an instance of indirect impact, which was, as I hope to show, no less significant for its indirectness. The matter concerns not Israel and Judah in their homelands, but Judah in Babylonian exile—thus, the first half of the 6th century B.C.E. The focus is on one of the major religious thinkers of that community, the anonymous prophet labeled in modern studies, *faute de mieux*, the Second or Deutero-Isaiah, whose work, by broad current agreement, is contained at minimum in

237

chaps. 40–55 of the book of Isaiah (for surveys, see, e.g., Whybray 1983; Seitz 1991: especially pp. 1–35; Clifford 1992).

Biblical scholarship of the last two centuries has come to see that Second Isaiah is important for several reasons: (1) for the development of Israelite religious ideas, especially the concept of deity; (2) for the transformation of older literary forms and language in Israel and their integration in new ways; and (3) as a crucial witness to the reorganization of imperial power in the Near East in the mid–6th century B.C.E., from the Neo-Babylonian Empire to that of the Achaemenid Persians beginning with Cyrus II. Much in the cultural and sociopolitical history of biblical Israel, in other words, reaches a major watershed in the period of the Second Isaiah, and the realization of this by modern scholars is matched only by the difficulty they still confront in achieving a consensus on how precisely the prophet reflects this divide in his work.

I want to look here at one aspect of the divide as it involves Second Isaiah's treatment of the concept of deity. That treatment is manifest especially in two kinds of literary material: the prophet's denunciation of the images of gods in the world around him as so much nonsensical idol-making (especially Isa 44:9–20), and, in what will be our central preoccupation, his use of trial speeches presented as coming from the Israelite god, Yahweh, which accuse or challenge those perceived to be Yahweh's opponents. We will begin with the definition of these trial speeches as a literary group. We shall then move to the question of their historical context and significance: more precisely, to what could have motivated the appearance of these texts in the Second Isaiah and the appearance of such related utterances as his denunciations of divine images.

The Trial Speeches as a Literary Group

It was German form-critical scholarship that isolated and undertook the fundamental description of the "trial speeches," the *Gerichtsreden*, in a line of work that began with Gressmann's pioneering analysis (1914) and reached a notable point in the 1960s as part of Westermann's wider examination of prophetic speech (1960; 1964: especially pp. 134–44; 1969: 17–19 and passim; cf. Richter 1981: 95–98). Later refinements have come in the studies of Schoors (1973: 176–245), Melugin (1976: 45–63), Spykerboer (1976), Merendino (1981), Wilson (1986: 23–128), and others.

Westermann's work, extended especially by Schoors, reestablished the basic definition of the trial texts as speeches put into the mouth of the god Yahweh that present legal challenges—the legal character evident in the argumentative tone and particularly in the pervasive appearance of what look like legal terms, for example, *šāpaṭ* (judge [43:26]), *mišpāṭ* (decision [41:1]), *ʿaṣūmôt* (pleas [41:21]), *qārab* (bring to court [41:1, 21]), *ṣādaq* (be vindicated [43:9, 26; 45:25]), and *rîb* (lawsuit, accusation [41:21]). Within this basic definition, as Schoors forcefully recognized (1973: especially pp. 239–45; see also Melugin 1976: 45–63), two types of speeches could be isolated. The first has Yahweh speaking against Israel for its sins. As distinct from such statements in earlier prophets, those in the Second Isaiah do not present a divine judgment on Israel that will take place in the future but, rather, aim to justify a past judgment or punishment—one that Israel had already experienced in the form of exile. Schoors and others (Schoors 1973: 189–207, 239; e.g., Westermann 1969:

17, 108–14, 130–33, 223–25) have found at least two instances of this Yahweh-against-Israel type: in 43:22–28 (the most complete) and in 50:1–3, with 42:18–25 perhaps a third example (Schoors 1973: 201–7 and, in part, Westermann 1969: 17, 109; contra Melugin 1976: 41–43). The second type of trial speech has become the more well known in biblical scholarship, and the Second Isaiah texts reckoned to exhibit it number at least five: 41:1–5, 41:21–29, 43:8–13, 44:6–8, and 45:20–25. This second type has Yahweh speaking against foreign nations and their gods, challenging them, especially the gods, to appear and prove that they are deities. The litmus test is whether these gods can show what events of the past (*rī'šōnôt* [41:22, 43:9]; *mē'āz, miqqedem* [45:21]) they successfully predicted (and directed) or what of the present–future (*habbā'ôt* [41:22]; [*ha*]*'ōtiyyôt* [41:23, 44:7]; *'aḥărît* [41:22]) they may yet foretell and bring to pass. Yahweh then claims that only He can do these things, sometimes pointing to the calling of Cyrus as deliverer as at least part of the events involved (41:2, 25 [not explicit]). As a result, He argues, He alone is God; the other so-called deities are "nothing" (*mē'ayin* [41:24], *'ayin* [by correction,[1] 41:29]), their deeds "nothing" (*mē'āpa'* [41:24]; *'epes* [41:29]), and their images "unformed wind" (*rûaḥ wā-tōhu* [41:29]);[2] or, in a frequent refrain with variant forms, "I am the first and the last; besides Me there is no other" (41:4; 43:10–11 [cf. 13]; 44:6, 8; 45:21–22). To this whole demonstration by Yahweh can be added an appeal to Israel as witnesses (43:10, 12; 44:8), as opposed to the other nations, which cannot bring their witnesses when Yahweh challenges them to do so (43:9).

From this literary analysis, it would seem clear that we are dealing with a particular kind of spoken legal argument in the Second Isaiah. But the clarity is not what it seems. In the first place, of the five texts representing the second type—Yahweh against the foreign nations/gods—none exhibits all the features described. In addition, there is some debate about the number of textual examples for this same group (whether more than five) and about the precise limits of three of the five texts that have been commonly accepted— 41:1–5 or 1–4; 43:8–13 or 9–13; and 44:6–8 or 6–8 + a conclusion in 21–22, with 9–20 thus regarded as a secondary insertion (e.g., Schoors 1973: 208, 212–13, 223–24, 232–33). Third, other literary formulas that have been identified in the Second Isaiah corpus can appear in the trial texts. Of these formulas, the most prominent is the so-called "self-praise," in which Yahweh identifies himself and affirms his nature and authority; it appears, at least in traces, in 41:1–5 (4b), 41:8–13 (10bβ–13), 44:6–8 (6b–7, thus practically all of this speech!), and 45:20–25 (21b and perhaps also the first half of this verse, 21a).[3] Fourth, the features of the trial speeches that we have described are not all exclusive to them but can be found

---

1. See, e.g., Blenkinsopp 2002: 204–5 note o, noting that *'ayin* is the reading in the large Isaiah manuscript from Qumran, 1QIsa[a]. On the other hand, Baltzer (2001: 122 ad 29) wishes to retain MT *'āwen*, "evil."

2. Other occurrences of this phrase are in Gen 1:2, arguably the *locus classicus*, and Jer 4:23; cf. Isa 34:11. The occurrence in Genesis 1 is particularly important, because it is only one of many connections between this priestly account of creation and Second Isaiah, as made clear by Weinfeld 1967–68.

3. This divine "self-praise" was first noted by Gressmann (1914: 286–92) and labeled by him as *Selbstprädikation*. Gressmann found it in the Second Isaiah particularly in oracles expressing salvation from Yahweh. Among later treatments, building on, but nuancing Gressmann's characterization in various respects, are Dion 1967; Zimmerli 1969: 29–34 (in a broader study of *Selbstprädikation* elsewhere in the Hebrew Bible); Schoors 1973: 8–9 and chap. II (on the salvation oracle more generally); Weippert 2001: especially pp. 42–49, who differentiates between *Selbstvorstellung*, in which the formula begins "I am + divine name," and *Selbstprädikation*, which has "I am + divine epithet."

elsewhere in Second Isaiah: so the description of foreign nations as *gôyîm* (nations) and *ʾiyyîm* (islands/coastlands);[4] the characterization of other gods as senseless non-deities;[5] the reference to the predictions of the *rîʾšōnôt/mēʾāz/miqqedem* (former/from then/from before) and the *bāʾôt/ʾōtiyyôt/ʾaḥărît/ḥădāšāh/ḥadāšôt* (coming/end/new);[6] the self-praise by Yahweh;[7] and the use of rhetorical questions designed to challenge the power of foreign gods.[8] Finally, one should note another literary category, advocated by H. Gunkel, J. Begrich, C. Westermann (with modifications), and others, that overlaps our trial speeches in a number of features. This is the "disputation" (in German, depending on the particular characterization, *Disputation*, *Streitgespräch*, or *Bestreitung*), which has been discussed for other prophetic passages as well (for reviews of research, see Schoors 1973: 188–89, 245–95; Richter 1981: 95–96; Graffy 1984: 10–15). Yet even the criterion advanced as a principal distinction between the disputations and our trial speeches—that disputations are conducted by the prophet and the trial speeches by Yahweh—does not always obtain. Thus, within the disputation of 40:12–31 (the boundaries of which do not command complete scholarly agreement; Graffy 1984: 10–14, 86–91), v. 25 has Yahweh speaking.[9]

The problems that we have been discussing do not, in the end, invalidate the recognition of the trial speech in the Second Isaiah. For there still remains, particularly for the Yahweh-against-the-nations/gods type, the common group of features that we have observed. But the problems do suggest that we cannot be too rigid in our definition of this speech, too eager to embrace the label *genre* for it.[10] What we have, I submit, are certain themes and language scattered throughout the Second Isaiah text, a number of them legal, more particularly courtroom-like. In the present layout of the text, these crystallize at certain points into speeches of Yahweh, some against Israel, others against foreign nations and their gods, and then dissolve, with the elements reappearing in

---

4. In the trial speeches against foreign nations/gods in 41:2, 5; 43:9; and 45:20; and elsewhere in Second Isaiah in 40:15, 17; 42:4, 6, 10; 45:1; 49:1, 6, 22; 51:5; 52:10, 15; and 54:3.

5. In the trial speeches against foreign nations/gods in 41:24, 29; and elsewhere in Second Isaiah in 40:19–20; 42:17; 44:9–20; 46:1–2, 6–7; and 48:5.

6.

	Trial speeches against foreign nations/gods	*Elsewhere in Second Isaiah*
rîʾšōnôt	41:22; 43:9	42:9; 43:18; 46:9; 48:3
mēʾāz	44:8; 45:21	48:3, 5, 7, 8
miqqedem	45:21	46:10
bāʾôt	41:22	— — —
ʾōtiyyôt	41:23; 44:7	45:11
ʾaḥărît	41:22	46:10; 47:7
ḥădāšāh/ ḥadāšôt	— — —	42:9; 43:19; 48:6

7. For the occurrences in the trial speeches against foreign nations/gods, see the main text above; for elsewhere in Second Isaiah, see 42:6, 8; 43:3, 11, 13; 44:24; 45:5–7, 18; 46:9; 48:12; and perhaps 52:6.

8. In the trial speeches against foreign nations/gods in 41:1; 43:9; 44:7–8; 45:21; and elsewhere in Second Isaiah in 40:12–14, 18, 25; 42:24; 46:5; 48:14; and perhaps 50:8–9; 51:9–10.

9. As Graffy (1984: 6) points out, L. Koehler at an early stage of the scholarly discussion identified as *Streitgespräch* what seem actually to be trial speeches. For one example of the disagreement, see the main text above on 42:18–25 and the opinions there of Schoors, Westermann, and Melugin.

10. See Spykerboer 1976: 109, who refers to his teacher, A. S. van der Woude, as one who "questions the existence of a separate literary genre of the trial speech, without denying the presence of elements which are taken from court proceedings."

similar or different combinations elsewhere in the text. The trial speeches, in this analysis, are thus not isolated units in the Second Isaiah, but serve to focus, at various moments,[11] major themes of the prophetic text as a whole: the impotence, indeed non-existence, of other gods, especially those of Babylonia; and the corresponding sovereign, indeed unique, power and omniscience of Yahweh, the God of Israel.

The Historical Background of the Trial Speeches

Whether specific genre or a looser collection of elements, we must ask now where the trial speech, its rhetorical form and content, came from: on what was the Second Isaiah drawing? Modern study has isolated, first, an inner biblical background (e.g., Melugin 1976: 58–63). Among the features involved is the lawsuit or *rîb* (Nielsen 1978; Ringgren 1990; Bovati 1994: 30–166). Like the Second Isaiah trial speeches, the *rîb* is a speech of legal accusation by Yahweh, and where it occurs, largely in the prophetic literature, it also seems to come in two types: a speech against Israel, with likewise a statement of accusation and announcement of punishment (one oft-cited example is Mic 6:1–8, although the punishment comes in the following vv. 9–16); and a speech against other nations, also with accusation and punishment (for example, Amos 1–2). Yet the *rîb* against Israel puts the punishment in the future and thus as a warning; it does not describe it as past, as in the Second Isaiah speeches. As for the *rîb* against other nations, perhaps in the end it should not be considered a *rîb* but only something related, since it does not appear to be molded as a lawsuit and lacks the label of *rîb*. In any case, it focuses on nations, never also on their gods whom it challenges to justify themselves, as in the Second Isaiah. Put otherwise, the trial speeches against the nations and gods in the Second Isaiah, even if they share some of the legal rhetoric of the earlier *rîbôt*, are more like cross-examination speeches of

---

11. Other units, such as the Servant speeches, perform a similar function. It must be recognized, however, that there is far from any consensus on the organization of the text of the Second Isaiah: the discussion varies between those who see the text as a loose(r) collection of independent but related poetic utterances, perhaps within a framework set by a prologue (40:1–11) and epilogue (55:6–11), and those who see a systematic, sequential structure to the whole; see, e.g., the survey and analysis of Melugin (1976) and, for a recent proposal of a sequential structure in the form of a drama, Baltzer 2001. The discussion of organization, of course, is also affected by the boundaries set for the text; and here again, there is no consensus about whether Second Isaiah comprises just chaps. 40–55 or includes also 34–35 and/or 56–66, or, indeed, how 40–55 are to be connected with the rest of the book of Isaiah overall. Finally, it must be stated that there is no consensus about the compositional history of the text: whether it is the work of a single author, either the prophet himself or a disciple amanuensis who has taken down and perhaps edited his words, or the result of several stages of editing, from the original prophet/amanuensis, who would have experienced the Babylonian Exile and probably its end as brought about by Cyrus's conquest of Nabonidus, through later disciples, who would have certainly lived beyond the Exile. My own sense, as suggested in the main text above, is that there is enough of a body of recurrent themes and language to give chaps. 40–55 a real conceptual unity, such as would result from a single author or an author with a close disciple or disciples. On the other hand, it is entirely possible that these chapters do show some chronological development that moves from the last stages of Nabonidus's reign through the Persian conquest—with many scholars marking a major change between chaps. 40–48, which contain the trial speeches against foreign nations/gods, and 49–55. For the latest review and examination, see Blenkinsopp 2002: 42–81, who argues for "a relatively high level of coherence and unity in style and substance, more so in the first part (40–48) than in the second (49–55)" (2002: 80); cf. Weippert 2001: 35–36.

challenge instead of the final summation or sentencing speeches that the *ríbôt* appear to resemble. As Nielsen puts it: "No crime has taken place which demands sentencing; it is only the truth of a statement which is to be evaluated" (1978: 68).

If the *ríbôt* do not provide a perfect precedent, the gaps may be filled in, at least in part, by other biblical texts, although it must be admitted that many of these texts are difficult to date and consequently to relate chronologically to the Second Isaiah. One gap is the assertion of Yahweh as uniquely God. Its prominence in the trial speeches as well as in other parts of the Second Isaiah makes its absence from the *ríbôt* all the more glaring. But it does turn up in other biblical texts, representing different literary forms. The most familiar example is the Song of Moses, Deuteronomy 32, which does appear to precede Second Isaiah, being preexilic and perhaps even early monarchic in date.[12] Verse 39 reads: "See now that I, even I, am He; and there is no god besides Me. I kill and I give life; I wound and I heal; and there is none that can deliver out of My hand." The echo in the trial speech in Isa 43:13 is striking: "I am God, and also henceforth I am He; there is none that can deliver out of My hand" (the identical Hebrew: *wě'ên miyyādî maṣṣîl*). Yet however close the two texts look, the recognition elsewhere in the Song of Moses of the existence of other gods (32:8, 12, 16) suggests that the Song did not understand the statement "I am God, etc." in the evidently monotheistic way that Second Isaiah intends.

A second motif of the Isaianic trial speeches that is not in the *ríbôt* per se is the confrontation with foreign gods, to challenge their worth as gods. This is obviously complementary to the first motif asserting Yahweh's uniqueness and, like it, occurs in other biblical texts of varying literary form (Preuss 1971). One example is 1 Kings 18, which demonstrates through a contest on Mt. Carmel between Elijah and the prophets of Baʿal that Yahweh, not Baʿal, is the real god, since only He is able to act, and act forcefully, in response to His human worshipers (cf. Melugin 1976: 58–60, who also emphasizes the differences from Second Isaiah). A similar contest is hinted at in Judges 6, a narrative that brings together a complex of elements, wherein the Israelite Gideon sacrifices to Yahweh and successfully elicits a response from one of his messengers, but then cuts down with impunity, indeed with no divine response, the altar of Baʿal belonging to his father and the adjacent Asherah symbol. Or, as a third example, one may point to Psalm 82, in which Yahweh accuses the deities in His council of failing to act justly, especially toward vulnerable humans, and so punishes them by demoting them all to mortal status, leaving only Himself as God. These three texts obviously parallel Yahweh's challenges to the gods in the Isaianic speeches, and while they are not arranged rhetorically as a *ríb*, the fact that they involve contests of judgment and may even use the term suggests that they come from the same or a related ambience (see Preuss 1971: 70, 72, 114). Whether they furnish chronological precedents to Second Isaiah, however, is uncertain, although not incon-

---

12. To be sure, the date of the Song of Moses remains the subject of debate, as Nelson notes in a recent brief review (2002: 369). However, from the serious and, in my view, compelling discussion of Tigay (1996: 510–13), it appears that the Song is older than almost all of the rest of the book of Deuteronomy and thus obviously preexilic and quite possibly earlier, even significantly earlier, than the beginning of so-called classical prophecy in the mid–8th century B.C.E. Tigay, it should be observed, does not commit himself to a precise date.

ceivable.[13] In any case, precedent or not, these three texts, as well as other examples that may be adduced (see Preuss 1971: 53–55, 74–80, 159–63), not only resemble the Isaianic speeches but also significantly differ from them, for they exhibit no speeches of cross-examination, which turn on the issue of predicting and accomplishing "former" and "latter" things and allow Yahweh His self-praise as the one and only deity. One may note, to be sure, that the Mt. Carmel contest concludes with a proclamation that "Yahweh, He is God" (1 Kgs 18:39; cf. v. 24); yet, however close this appears to statements in the Isaianic speeches (such as 43:13 translated above), it is praise by others, not by Yahweh Himself.

---

13. Judges 6, as generally recognized, belongs to the core material of the book of Judges, which, in turn, is part of the Deuteronomistic History, the latter apparently going through several stages in its composition, with its basic form set in preexilic times no later than Josiah of Judah in the latter part of the 7th century B.C.E. (e.g., Mayes 1985: 10–34; McKenzie 1991: especially pp. 1–19, 147–50). As part of the core of Judges, then, Judges 6 (and probably the related 7–9) should belong in the basic, preexilic stage of the Deuteronomistic History, all the more so because the chapter can easily fit into a preexilic historical context (e.g., Mayes 1985: 26–27, 32–33) and does not betray any real indications of exilic events or interests.

As for 1 Kgs 18:21–39, it too is part of the Deuteronomistic History, but its place in the development of the History and its date are more controversial. In particular, scholars have argued over whether 18:21–39 is composite, showing both an earlier, pre-Deuteronomic and thus preexilic form, and later Deuteronomic additions that could have been carried into the Exile (e.g., Jones 1984: 311–13; Würthwein 1984: 215–20); or whether it is essentially unitary, in which case it could have been taken over by the Deuteronomic historian in his initial composition of the History, thus in preexilic times, or added later, in exilic times (e.g., McKenzie 1991: 81–87; Cogan 2001: 445–46 n. 1). Interwoven with this issue of literary coherence is a thematic one, concerning the depiction of Yahweh. For some interpreters, Yahweh's victory as "God" in 18:39 is presented not merely as a success over Ba⁶al but as an assertion of His unique status as deity, thus as a monotheistic issue that can belong only in the period and ambience of the Second Isaiah (Albertz 1994: 153–54, 318–19 n. 54). Others have looked at the passage more locally as a religiopolitical contest with Ba⁶al and his human entourage, as manifested at Mt. Carmel, and so have found a place for the text in preexilic times (so Šanda, with whom McKenzie [1991: 87–88 n. 12] seems inclined to agree), even in the 9th-century B.C.E. struggle with the Omrides in Northern Israel (White 1997). My own solution is something in between (cf. partly Würthwein 1984: 217–19): 1 Kgs 18:21–39 originally referred to a more localized contest of power between Yahweh and Ba⁶al, thus in a preexilic setting, but in the course of transmission through the exilic redaction of the Deuteronomistic History, this contest came to be seen more explicitly as a justification of Yahweh's unique qualification as deity; one may compare the depiction of Yahweh versus Chemosh in the narrative of Jephthah's war with the Ammonites (Judges 11).

In turning, finally, to Psalm 82, we encounter a text having no clear historical reference, with the result that exegetes vary widely in dating it, from preexilic to postexilic times (see the survey in Jüngling 1969: 78–79), or simply abstain from any date (e.g., Miller 1986: 122). Some have sought to argue, not unlike in the case of 1 Kgs 18:21–39, that the psalm must be dated to the period of Second Isaiah, because its conception of Yahweh's sovereignty closely overlaps the prophet's ideas (e.g., Jüngling 1969: 79–80). But one could just as well argue that, while the psalm points in the direction of Second Isaiah's monotheism, it is not quite there yet, since it still knows the world of the heavenly court, even as it shows the elimination of that court over and against texts that maintain it and talk about its function, such as Deut 4:19 and 32:8–9 (the latter read with the Old Greek and a Qumran manuscript [e.g., Nelson 2002: 367c]). Psalm 82, therefore, looks intermediate in conception between Deuteronomy and Second Isaiah, as indeed many have supposed (e.g., Tsevat 1969–70: especially pp. 123–25, 133–34). Yet one cannot confidently infer that the psalm was actually composed between these two other texts, let alone exactly when the date of composition was (cf. Miller 1986: 122). On the one hand, given the pervasiveness and longevity of the conception of the heavenly court, which continues well after the entire biblical canon was established, one cannot be sure whether it was Deuteronomy—or indeed what text, if any—that the author of Psalm 82 was reacting against. On the other hand, even if the psalm's view of deity appears conceptually prior to that in Second Isaiah, this does not absolutely require that the psalmist lived before the prophet; he could have been a contemporary or even a successor, representing just a different, albeit less radical, way of looking at deity.

In sum, an inspection of the inner biblical background permits us to identify some of the elements on which Second Isaiah probably drew for his trial speeches, both those against Israel and those against foreign nations and their gods. But there is nothing in that background that encapsulates and explains everything the prophet has done with this material, particularly with the speeches against nations and gods. This conclusion, it must be observed, does not stand alone and isolated in modern scholarly discussion. Clifford, for example, following, to be sure, a somewhat different line from that taken here, ends with even less background to point to from other biblical/Israelite traditions:

> Exactly where in Israel's traditions Second Isaiah found the inspiration for the trial scene is not known. It seems too elaborate to be a transposition from the day-to-day "trial in the gate." The contest between Yahweh and the other deities, and between Israel and the nations, is so central to the scene as to suggest that the prophet designed the scene chiefly to display these contrasts. It seems not to have arisen from a real life situation. (Clifford 1984: 90)

Extrabiblical Context

The question is whether we must stop here and remain perplexed, as Clifford apparently is, about the context or impetus for these trial speeches, especially those against nations and gods. Put another way, insofar as there was a background for these speeches, is it to be found only in innerbiblical/Israelite traditions or can we consider also—note the "also" here, not "instead"—external circumstances and cultural traditions? To answer this question, we must clarify the time and place in which the prophet functioned. Unfortunately, the text of the Second Isaiah does not give us a neat and precise description—there is no introductory rubric, for instance, as in other prophetic books—yet we are not without clues. The first is the orientation of the prophet, which exhibits a strong sense of looking within his exilic community in Babylon and then outward to a return to the Judean homeland (Isa 46:1–2; 47; 48:20; 49:8–12; 51:9–11; 52:11–12; see Clifford 1992: 492). But occasionally, it must be admitted, we appear to be in Judah, looking out to those returning to it (43:5–6; Blenkinsopp 2002: 222, cf. pp. 103–4). The second clue is the prophet's reference to the coming conquest by the Achaemenid Cyrus II of the lands within some part of which the prophet is residing (44:28; 45:1–7; cf. 41:2–3). As has frequently been remarked, this is the only concrete historical figure and event mentioned by the prophet; it should be noted, however, that Cyrus's Babylonian conquest is always described in the future—never, apparently, as an event already concluded. Finally, there are the range and depth of the prophet's acquaintance with Babylonia, particularly Babylonian culture, evident in such features as the lampooning of the two principal Babylonian gods of the Neo-Babylonian period, Marduk and his son, Nabu, and the movements of their cult images (46:1–2; see further below); the description of the construction of divine images, showing knowledge of general ancient Near Eastern, and particularly Mesopotamian, practice (44:9–20; also 40:19–20; 41:7; 46:6–7; see Williamson 1986; Eph'al 1986–89; Berlejung 1998: especially pp. 369–91; Dick 1999: especially pp. 24–30; Vanderhooft 1999: 172–75; Albani 2000: 181–83); the references to divination, which can best be understood as Mesopotamian/Babylonian (e.g., 47:9–13; see below); and the language of Babylonian and, more broadly, Mesopotamian royal inscriptions (e.g., 42:6–7; 43:1; see Paul 1968, with bibliography).[14] Taken alone, each of these three clues—orientation, Cyrus, and Babylonian/ Mesopotamian features—may be ambiguous in terms of situating the context of the prophet's activity. But when they are combined, as they should be, since they all interweave with one another in the text, particularly in the first major unit of chaps. 40–48,[15] the clues yield a reasonably clear and definite picture of the historical context. The center of it is the Babylonian Exile, under the Neo-Babylonian dynasty, where Second Isaiah, it can now be proposed, spent some crucial part of his career, being active in the reign of the last Neo-Babylonian king, Nabonidus, before, and especially shortly before, Nabonidus and his kingdom were conquered by Cyrus in 539 B.C.E. Yet verses such as 43:5–6 make it entirely possible that our prophet, and/or some of his close disciples, lived through the actual conquest, not remaining in Babylonia, but able to make the return to Judah, whence they could view the return of other exiles.[16]

Given this setting and the Babylonian acquaintance it reflects, we are encouraged to ask: can the setting offer any help in explaining Second Isaiah's use of trial speeches and other polemic against foreign gods and for Yahweh as deity uniquely? The positive answer that is often given is something like this: we should imagine the prophet preaching to his fellow Judeans in the Babylonian Exile and warning this dispirited people against the temptations of their alien environment—that is, against the conclusion that the God of Israel is weak or at least has failed them, and that the Babylonian gods, with their cosmic powers, rule (e.g., Koch 1984: 127, 131–33; Blenkinsopp 1996: 187–89). But while this context makes sense (cf. Isa 48:5), it is often described in a general way that is not focused on specific details of Babylonian history and culture in the period of Judean exile. So expressed, therefore, the context is inadequate to explain and to provide a matrix for the particular intensity and language of Second Isaiah's trial speeches and related rhetoric,

---

14. A Mesopotamian background has also been posited for the divine "self-praise" in Second Isaiah. Starting with Gressmann, who first discussed this "self-praise" in the prophet, this feature has been derived from Mesopotamian oracles—or as these may now be mostly characterized, prophecies—to the gods Ištar and Nabu, which come from the Neo-Assyrian kings of the 7th century B.C.E. (1914: 289–90). Dion (1967) reviewed the issue and extended the search for Mesopotamian antecedents back to late-third-millennium B.C.E. Sumerian literature. On the other hand, while these affinities have been acknowledged, the specific historical dependence on them by Second Isaiah has been questioned in the light of parallels elsewhere in the ancient Near East and the lack of a clear chain of transmission from the Neo-Assyrian texts to Second Isaiah, a century afterward; see most recently Weippert 2001: especially pp. 57–58, who suggests that what was involved was a more general ancient Near Eastern literary/theological convention, of which Second Isaiah and the Neo-Assyrian prophecies were particular manifestations.

15. On the coherence of chaps. 40–48, see n. 11 above.

16. Such a two-phased setting makes better sense of the evidence in chaps. 40–55 than an insistence on only a Babylonian or Judean locale for Second Isaiah. The Babylonian locale remains, it appears, the majority position among scholars, and is even slightly favored in the recent assessment by Blenkinsopp (2002: 102–4), who, however, moves back and forth in discussing the features of both options. On the other hand, there have been some recent efforts to argue for a Judean/Palestinian setting; for example, Barstad 1987; 1994; 1997; with a review of and reaction to the last by Clifford (1999). Also for Judah is Baltzer (2001: 30–33 and passim), who proposes additionally an unusually late date for chaps. 40–55, namely, in the latter 5th century B.C.E., overlapping the activity of Nehemiah. As the argument of the present paper indicates, I do not accept Baltzer's date and setting, although I recognize the stimulation afforded by a number of his observations.

with their unprecedented mode of deflation of foreign deities and nations and exaltation of Yahweh.

Can we thus go further and locate a situation within the exilic Babylonian environment that would have provided the bed for such polemic? I believe we can, and it involves the last Neo-Babylonian, indeed, the last Babylonian king, Nabonidus (556–539 B.C.E.), whose reign and conquest by Cyrus, as we have seen, are implicitly marked out by the text of the Second Isaiah as the very period of the prophet's activity. One of the leitmotifs of Nabonidus's reign is the conflicts between the king and various of his elites, especially the priesthood of the national god, Marduk, centered in the Esagila, Marduk's principal sanctuary complex in the capital city of Babylon. The chronological dimension of these conflicts was laid out by Tadmor in a groundbreaking article (1965); this chronology was then refined and the nature of the conflicts more elaborately discussed by Beaulieu in his 1986 Yale University dissertation (revised and published in book form in 1989). For our concerns, one aspect of these conflicts is particularly instructive: Nabonidus's promotion of the moon-god Sin to chief god of the realm, a promotion carried out at the expense of the status of Marduk and his entourage, including his divine son, Nabu.

As Tadmor and especially Beaulieu have made clear, this promotion moves through three stages. In the first, comprising Years 1–3 of Nabonidus's reign (556–553 B.C.E.), Sin becomes an ever more prominent member of the pantheon, although Marduk's prominence and authority are still recognized. The second stage covers the next ten years, 4–13 (553–542 B.C.E.), during which Nabonidus sojourns at the northern Arabian oasis of Teima and the governance of Babylon and Babylonia is left in the hands of his son and regent, Bel-šar-uṣur (= biblical Belshazzar).[17] The latter, it appears, goes back to a focus on Marduk, presumably under the pressure of that god's priestly establishment. The third and final stage spans the last four years of Nabonidus's reign, Years 14–17 (542–539 B.C.E.), from his return from Teima to Babylon and active rule of the realm until his conquest by Cyrus. In this period, the promotion, indeed exaltation, of Sin reaches its most dramatic level, resulting virtually in a unique position for the moon-god, although Marduk, it appears, is still allowed recognition.[18]

The changes in these three stages, as Tadmor (1965) and Beaulieu (1989) have shown, can be tracked most clearly in the royal inscriptions, both of Nabonidus and of Bel-šar-uṣur. In particular, the final stage can be described not only from Nabonidus's inscriptions, especially his stelae discovered at Harran (Schaudig 2001: 486–513) and a chronicle-

---

17. See Tadmor 1965: 356–57, 362–63; he regarded it as significant that the ancient sources do not mention Bel-šar-uṣur (Belshazzar) as being involved in the construction of Sin's temple, the Ehulhul, and he implied but did not make explicit that this absence indicates a retreat on Bel-šar-uṣur's part from Nabonidus's developing program for the exaltation of Sin. The idea of a retreat was subsequently made explicit and convincingly elaborated on by Beaulieu (1989: especially pp. 5–54, 62–64).

18. So in the Babylonian Chronicle (Grayson 1975a: 109: iii 5–8), which mentions Bel's (Marduk's) participation in the New Year's festival resumed by Nabonidus in Year 17 of his reign, after his return from Teima. This apparent attention to Marduk by Nabonidus and his subsequent attention to the images of other gods he brought into Babylon (Grayson 1975a: 109: iii 9–12; Beaulieu 1993) are not surprising. There is no indication that they reflect a sudden abandonment or repentance by the king in his final days, faced with the oncoming Persian army of Cyrus, of the favor he had been showing to Sin (as suggested by Goldstein [2002: 115]). Rather, we have here a traditional acknowledgment of the Babylonian pantheon, over which, however, Sin was now to reign supreme.

like text (Schaudig 2001: 590–95), but also from the texts of Nabonidus's opponents, specifically the so-called Persian Verse Account (Schaudig 2001: 563–78), the Cyrus Cylinder (Schaudig 2001: 550–56, especially lines 1–19), and the Babylonian Dynastic Prophecy (Grayson 1975b: 32–33, II 11–16).

Despite (or, rather, behind) the opposing views of these two sets of texts, they share five major points in common:

1. Nabonidus establishes a new, and in some ways unprecedented, cult for the god Sin, whom he identifies as his personal god and celebrates for his ability to put him on the throne. As Nabonidus formulates it, Sin is the *ilu/ilāni ša ilāni*, "the god(s) of the gods," which, in Beaulieu's apt judgment, is "probably the highest epithet ever given to a god in the Mesopotamian tradition" (1989: 62; also 1993: 254–55; for the text, see Schaudig 2001: 351–52: I 29, II 5; p. 495: III 40 n. 708). And what has been accomplished, says the king, is "the great miracle of Sin (*epišti* ᵈ*Sîn rabîti*) that none of the (other) gods and goddesses knew (how to achieve), that has not happened to the country from the days of old, that the people of the country have <not> observed nor written down on clay tablets to be preserved for eternity" (Schaudig 2001: 487, 496: I 1–5). This same innovation is also acknowledged, even if castigated, by the anti-Nabonidus Persian Verse Account: "[against the will of the g]ods he (= Nabonidus) would perform an unholy action . . . he created something without substance. [A god whom ear]lier no one had (ever) seen in the land . . . he put on a podium/sockel" (Schaudig 2001: 566, 573: I 20′–23′; the first restoration as in A. L. Oppenheim apud Pritchard 1969: 313a). And while the innovation per se does not appear to be castigated in the extant text of the Cyrus Cylinder, the latter does refer to Nabonidus's removal of the Marduk cult: "Worship of Marduk, the king of the gods, he extirpated from its center [= i.e., of Esagila, Marduk's sanctuary in Babylon]" (Schaudig 2001: 551–52, 554:7).

2. Nabonidus's veneration of Sin involves also (re)building a sanctuary for him, the Ehulhul, in the northern Syrian city of Harran. The command to do so, reports Nabonidus, came to him from the god in a dream: "Rebuild speedily Ehulhul, the temple of Sin in Harran, and I will hand over to you all the countries" (Schaudig 2001: 488, 496:10–14). The enterprise is condemned, in turn, in the Persian Verse Account, which makes Nabonidus blaspheme, "I will make a sanctuary (= Ehulhul) with an appearance that is a replica of the Temple (= Esagila of Marduk)."[19] As a result, asserts the Verse Account, Nabonidus's work was an "abomination, a work of unholiness" (Schaudig 2001: 568, 574: II 17′). This charge, that Nabonidus was intent on replacing the primacy of Marduk and his chief shrine with that of Sin and his Ehulhul, is made even more explicit in the Cyrus Cylinder (Schaudig

---

19. The understanding of this line in Akkadian has been debated. I follow the reading in Schaudig 2001: 567, 574: II 6′, with a copy on p. 760, Abb. 41: *a-na* É.KUR ÈŠ *tam-ši-lu si-mat lu-me-šil*; my translation, however, diverges a bit from Schaudig's, which is: "Dem Heiligtum (= Esangil) will ich einen Tempel gleich an Zier zur Seite stellen." The advantage of this reading is that it brings the charge against Nabonidus presented here—that he is replacing the Esagila of Marduk by the Ehulhul of Sin—into line with the same sentiments expressed later in the Verse Account and in the Cyrus Cylinder, as noted above. An alternative reading of the line, which would work equally well palaeographically but does not yield the same exact convergence of sentiment, is proposed by W. G. Lambert and adopted in *CAD* M/1 356b, 4a, s.v. *mašālu*, as well as by Beaulieu 1989: 206 n. 43: *a-na é-kur ap-tú ù si-kur lu-me-šil*, "I will make the window and locks (= of the Ehulhul) similar to (those of) the Ekur (= the temple of Enlil in Nippur)."

2001: 551, 554:5). Later in the Verse Account, we are told, indeed, that Nabonidus had only hatred for Esagila and announced that Sin had taken over Esagila and put on it his sacred symbol, the moon crescent, in place of Marduk's spade (Schaudig 2001: 570, 577: V 16′–22′).

3. The New Year's festival, known in the Neo-Babylonian period as *zagmukku* or *akītu*,[20] in which Marduk along with his son Nabu is the chief divine actor, ceases to be celebrated while Nabonidus is in Teima and is resumed only upon his return to Babylon in the last four years of his reign. The Persian Verse Account, in its criticism of Nabonidus, connects this cessation with the king's exaltation of Sin and Sin's cult (Schaudig 2001: 567, 574: II 4′–11′), while the Cyrus Cylinder speaks of Nabonidus's instituting "inappropriate rituals" for "Ur and the other sacred sites" and "interrupt[ing] in a spiteful way the regular offerings" (Schaudig 2001: 551, 554:5–7). Nabonidus, for his part, comes to the issue of blasphemy as well, but turns it in a different direction, emphasizing in his Harran stela his need to go to the Teima area, because the citizens of his Babylonian cities "sinned against his (= Sin's) great divinity, doing evil and committing sacrilege . . . they neglected his (!; literally, "their") rites, and they blabbed lies and untruths" (Schaudig 2001: 488, 497: I 16–17, 19–20). In Nabonidus's view, therefore, the people's failure to recognize the exaltation of Sin is a "sin" (*ḫīṭu*) (Beaulieu 1989: 64–65); and this parallels, in turn, the charge of "abomination" (*ikkibu*) that the king's opponents hurl against him for this very exaltation.

4. In the last year of his reign, after his return from Teima and in reaction to the news of the Persian Cyrus's advance into Babylonia, Nabonidus gathers the images of the Babylonian gods and goddesses from their primary sanctuaries in Babylonia and has them removed to the capital, Babylon. The gathering and removal are not mentioned in the extant royal inscriptions of Nabonidus but are recorded in various archival documents of the king's officials, as described by Beaulieu (1989: 220–24; 1993). They, as well as the gods that were not removed, are also noted in the Babylonian Chronicle (Grayson 1975a: 109: iii 8–12) and, very critically again, as a sacrilegious act in the Verse Account (Schaudig 2001: 571, 577: V 28′ff.) and the Cyrus Cylinder (Schaudig 2001: 552, 554–55:9–10). In turn, the Chronicle, Verse Account, and Cyrus Cylinder all emphasize that Cyrus, upon conquering Babylon, moved immediately to reverse these actions and restore the deities to their proper homes (Grayson 1975a: 110:21–22; Schaudig 2001: 572, 578: VI 12′–17′; 553–54, 556:32–35).

5. Connected with the above four features is a certain emphasis on Nabonidus's claim to special knowledge of the cultural traditions of the realm, above that of ordinary mortals, indeed god-like. This knowledge is particularly of the heavens and its gods, as well as the divinatory arts related thereto. Thus, in a chronicle text with epic-like features from Nabonidus's circle, the king describes the discovery by his scribes and at his direction of various important objects from the Mesopotamian past. Among these are tablets of the great astronomical series, Enuma Anu Enlil, which as the chronicle narrates it "no one

---

20. Before the first millennium B.C.E., the two labels evidently do not always coincide in usage and reference to the same festival, namely, of the New Year. *Zagmukku*, a Sumerian loan in Akkadian, is strictly the term marking the "boundary of the year" and thus the New Year; *akītu* is the term for a ceremony bound up with one or both equinoxes, in the spring and fall. For a recent brief review, see Bidmead 2002: 41–43.

(that is, especially the experts around the king) understood without his (= Nabonidus's) telling (him)" (Schaudig 2001: 591, 593: III 5', following Machinist and Tadmor 1993: 149). In the Persian Verse Account, on the other hand, the king's special knowledge, also reckoned as focused on astronomy, is understood as the highest hubris: "(It was) he (who) stood up in the assembly (of his courtiers and experts) to praise hi[mself], (saying), 'I am wise, I know, I have seen (what is) hi[dden]. . . . The god Ilteri (see below, conclusion; n. 33) has given me revelations; he ha[s shown me] everything. As for (the astronomical series) u₄.sakar ᵈAnum ᵈEn.líl.la, which Adapa (= the first of the primeval sages) compiled, I surpass it in all wisdo[m]'" (Schaudig 2001: 569–70, 576: V 8'–13'). This astronomical series, to which the Verse Account has Nabonidus refer, evidently did not exist; the Verse Account seems to have made it up on the basis of the well-known series Enuma Anu Enlil, as a way of poking fun at the scholarship that Nabonidus boasts about. In other words, Nabonidus's scholarship is declared to be just so much pseudoerudition, pure hokum. It is also, for the Verse Account, a dangerous blasphemy against the gods, and to confirm the point the Account goes on, as we have seen, to claim that Nabonidus was able to use his hokum to deceive "the assembled experts" (*puḫur mārē ummāni*) into believing that the divine symbol of the moon crescent had appeared on the Esagila temple of Marduk, signifying that this most important shrine belonged in reality to the moon-god, Sin (Schaudig 2001: 570, 577: V 19'–22'; see also Machinist and Tadmor 1993: especially pp. 146–50; Schaudig 2002: especially pp. 622–25).

In sum, the five points we have discussed, most dramatically the last on special knowledge, reveal a close relationship in theme and language between the texts of Nabonidus and the texts in conflict with them. At issue here, clearly, is not simply a literary relationship; it is a real-life situation of polemics and counterpolemics during Nabonidus's reign, particularly in his later years, after his return from Teima, pitting, as many scholars have recognized,[21] Nabonidus and his circle of "Sin-ners" against those opposed to his policies, centered among the "Marduk-ers," particularly the Marduk priestly establishment in the capital of Babylon that comes to be enlisted by the eventual conqueror of Nabonidus, Cyrus II. Three features of this controversy deserve emphasis.

First, it is "a characteristically scribal conflict, between two groups which know each other and share in much of the same culture." In it, furthermore, "one cannot fail to recognize that Nabonidus steps forward as a scribal intellectual in his own right" (Machinist and Tadmor 1993: 150).[22] Second, while the controversy concerns issues of cult and its proper handling, underlying it is the more basic issue of the nature and conception of deity itself, and human access to and knowledge of this. To be sure, this issue must be coaxed out of the surviving sources, because, as Beaulieu has rightly remarked (1989: 43), no text survives from Nabonidus's circle explaining Sin's exaltation on the order, say, of Enuma Eliš, which was composed earlier to explain and justify Marduk's. We have, in

---

21. For example, Beaulieu 1989: especially pp. 62–65, 203–19; Machinist and Tadmor 1993; Hallo and Simpson 1998: 147. In favor of diminishing, if not eliminating, the significance of these religious/cultural polemics for understanding the history of the period are Kuhrt (1990: especially pp. 135–46) and Weisberg (1997: especially p. 555). Against such a view, see in brief Machinist and Tadmor 1993: 150 n. 34.

22. For further discussion of scribal traditions as they concern Nabonidus and his period, see, e.g., Beaulieu 1989: especially pp. 138–43; 1994; Winter 2000; Schaudig 2002. The latest and most profound analysis is Michalowski 2003.

short, no theologoumenon from Nabonidus about Sin. Yet the phrases we have encountered in Nabonidus's inscriptions acclaiming the *episti Sîn rabîti*, Sin as *ilu/ilāni ša ilāni*, and the like, plus the reactions in the Cyrus Cylinder and especially the Verse Account—all do speak very much not only to the question of which deity is to be preeminent but of what preeminence means. To put matters in another way, even if the promotion of Sin can be placed typologically as the latest in a long Mesopotamian history of divine exaltations (Inanna/Istar, Marduk, Assur, and others; Beaulieu 1989: 43), it is still an unusual, even unique episode, *at least as it has survived to us*, because of the intensity of its expression and the vigor of the counterattack. The third and last feature is that this counterattack, although it is attested in texts (the Verse Account and especially the Cyrus Cylinder) that date only after Cyrus's defeat of Nabonidus in 539 b.c.e., must have begun before then. For the very retreat from Nabonidus's program to exalt Sin during the ten years of his absence in Teima and of his son Bel-šar-uṣur's regency in Babylonia and the concomitant return to Marduk in Babylonia at that time—these together show clearly that the opposition to Sin must have been rather strong well before Cyrus arrived. Cyrus, therefore, capitalized on this anti-Nabonidus opposition; he did not initiate it (Machinist and Tadmor 1993: 150 n. 34).

Nabonidus and His Opposition, and the Second Isaiah

The controversy in Babylonia that we have been examining should not appear utterly strange, if we now return to the writing of the Second Isaiah, especially to his "trial speeches." Let us look again, therefore, at the principal features of these speeches and of other passages in the prophet in the light of the Nabonidus materials.

1. The trial/courtroom setting of the speeches, one must admit, is not directly found in the Nabonidus texts, whether pro- or anti-. But we are reminded of that setting, it may be proposed, by the picture of Nabonidus talking to his assembly of scholars, and the argumentative character of what he says there and of what is said back to him.

2. Beyond this argumentative setting alone, it is the issues being asserted and demonstrated within it—the propositions for and against deities and their powers of accomplishment—that bring Nabonidus and Second Isaiah together. These issues, on the one hand, are negative. Thus, we hear Nabonidus condemning those opposed to Sin as sinful (Harran stela), while his opponents reject his god Sin, statue, and cult as a monstrosity, as something undivine (Verse Account and Cyrus Cylinder). And as we hear this polemical exchange, we can also hear an echo in the Second Isaiah: in his utter rejection, in the trial speeches and the idol parodies, of the other gods and the supposed physical images of them as idiotic, powerless, and undivine.

3. Conversely, one may recall Nabonidus's assertion that only Sin of all deities could act to bring about an event without precedent in Mesopotamian history (the *epišti* ^{d}*Sîn rabîti*). While the relevant inscriptions do not fully describe this event, they do make clear that it includes Sin awarding kingship to Nabonidus and the fact that the latter is a most unlikely candidate, since he is "the lonely one, who has nobody, in whose (literally: in my) heart was no thought of kingship" (Schaudig 2001: 487–88, 496: I 8–9). From such an assertion, it would appear, it is not a long leap to statements in the Isaianic trial speeches in which Yahweh alone acts to bring "this new thing," namely, to give world dominion to the

non-Judean Cyrus, by allowing him to defeat and conquer Babylonia—the Babylonia, it turns out, of Nabonidus. The "newness" of this thing is epitomized by what Second Isaiah says, outside of the trial speeches, that Yahweh has granted Cyrus—namely, the titles of "my shepherd" (*rōʿî*) (44:28) and "anointed" (*māšîaḥ*) (45:1)—the latter, in fact, unprecedented in the biblical corpus for a foreigner.[23]

4. Connected with Nabonidus's elevation of Sin, as we have seen, is a demotion in status and power of the other Babylonian deities, specifically the otherwise leading member of the pantheon, Marduk. We have just such a demotion in Second Isaiah, in 46:1–2, which focuses not only on Marduk, calling him Bel (this being his usual title in first-millennium B.C.E. Babylonia), but also on his son, Nabu, here in the Hebrew form, Nebo. The reference to Nabu is no accident; rather, it reflects the fact, well documented in Mesopotamian sources, of the increasing prominence of that deity—a prominence, indeed, that by the Neo-Babylonian period had reached a kind of rivalry with that of his father (Pomponio 1998: especially pp. 17, 20–21; Millard 1999; Michel 2001). In the Isaianic verses, the two gods appear in paired cola accompanied by parallel verbs: Bel described as "bowing down" (*kāraʿ*) and Nebo as "stooping, almost doubled over" (*qōrēs*).[24] The pejorative meaning of these two verbs is reinforced in the following clauses, which describe the images of these two gods ("their idols," *ʿăṣabbêhem*), carried into captivity by animals that are wearily loaded down with them, the gods themselves being unable to do anything about it.

All of this language, it has been widely recognized, is not simply pejorative, but parodic; parodic of what, however, is the problem. At the least, it appears that some kind of movement, some journey, of the images of Marduk and Nabu is at stake. Commentators have proposed, in the main, two possible journeys—or some combination of these—that could be the object of the parody (e.g., Westermann 1969: 178–80; Vanderhooft 1999: 175–80; Blenkinsopp 2002: 266–68). The first is a cultic processional, most likely of the *zagmukku/akītu* (New Year's) festival at Babylon, in which in the Neo-Babylonian period, as we have seen, Marduk and Nabu were the main divine actors: the statue of Nabu being taken on a journey from its primary home in the city of Borsippa to the capital in Babylon to join Marduk in his principal sanctuary, Esagila, for the occasion (M. E. Cohen 1993: 437–41). As Second Isaiah would present this festival, then, the movement is not a proud one in a resplendent wagon to celebrate the *zagmukku/akītu*, but a journey of despair, pulled by weary animals into exile at the hands of the conquerors of Babylonia. An alternative view of the parody in Isa 46:1–2 involves a specific defensive action recorded of Nabonidus as he prepared to face Cyrus's invasion. This action, as noted above, entailed the gathering by Nabonidus of all the images of the Babylonian gods from their various

---

23. The other title, "shepherd" (*rōʿeh*), is, of course, in cognate forms a common term for ruler in other ancient Near Eastern and non–Near Eastern cultures. In the Hebrew Bible, however, it is mostly reserved for Israel and Judah, whether in the singular or the plural. In fact, aside from the reference to Cyrus, it seems to occur for foreigners only in one other place in the Bible, namely, in Nah 3:18, where, in the plural, it does not actually apply to the king himself, who is explicitly differentiated from it, but to his officials, in parallel with the term "noble" (*ʾaddîr*). (Cf. Greenberg 1997: 708, although he believes that the reference in Nahum is "to the entire political leadership [kings, counselors, officials, magistrates . . .].")

24. This verb is a hapax legomenon in the Hebrew Bible. To clarify its meaning here, one should look not only to the parallel verb *kāraʿ* but to two nouns occurring in the Bible that are built on the same root as *qōrēs*: *qeres*, "hook," and *qarsōl*, "ankle"; see, e.g., North 1967: 163 ad 1.

primary sanctuaries throughout Babylonia and their transfer to the capital in Babylon, presumably for safekeeping and to provide the capital with increased divine protection. In this view, then, Second Isaiah would be saying that Nabonidus's action resulted not in the expected protection but only in exile, when Cyrus conquered Babylon and took the divine statues away. Alternatively, the prophet could be saying that Nabonidus's transfer was itself not an act of homage to the gods but of blasphemy, by exiling them from their rightful places.

It must be admitted that both views of the parody in 46:1–2—a cultic > *akītu* processional at Babylon or the gathering of the gods there—have their difficulties. The principal stumbling block[25] is the statement in v. 2 that these views are trying to explain—namely, the prediction that the statues of Bel and Nebo will be exiled. This was evidently not borne out by the historical reality. For as we have seen, the Babylonian Chronicle, the Verse Account, and the Cyrus Cylinder tell us that when Cyrus conquered Babylon and Babylonia, the statues of all the Babylonian gods were returned at Cyrus's command from Babylon to their original and proper Babylonian sanctuaries. The notice about this return cannot be explained, or explained merely, as an ideological fabrication to make Cyrus look good: it describes an action too specific, widespread, and thus well known to have been made out of whole cloth and comports too well with the impression that all the relevant sources give us of Cyrus's trying to undermine Nabonidus from within by recruiting his opponents, such as the Marduk priesthood, and presenting himself as the legitimate Babylonian king. Moreover, it has a clear parallel, as Beaulieu notes (1993: 243), in the action of an earlier, Neo-Assyrian king, Sargon II, against his opponent, the Chaldean king Merodach-baladan II. Therefore, if Second Isaiah's prediction about the exile of the divine statues is to have any historical credibility, it should probably be accounted for in one of two ways: either it would have to have been uttered before Cyrus's actual conquest of Babylon, reflecting the expectation based on past Mesopotamian history that the victims' divine images would be removed, deported, and/or destroyed by the conqueror;[26] or, if uttered during or after the conquest, the prediction would have represented a Judean view of what Cyrus accomplished—namely, that he did, vis-à-vis Nabonidus's previous ingathering of the images, "exile" them from Babylon. However the matter is decided, at the least it does look as if the treatment of Marduk and Nabu in Second Isaiah 46:1–2 can easily be understood as a response to activities in the period of Nabonidus.

5. We should consider, finally, the emphasis in the Nabonidus texts on special knowledge: knowledge of divine traditions and the heavens, including divination, which is understood to confer a special power on the king that those around him (and this includes, in the anti-Nabonidus texts, even the primeval sages) do not possess. In the Second Isaiah,

---

25. There are other difficulties as well. For example, if we accept the second view of the parody, that Second Isaiah is referring to Nabonidus's gathering of the divine images to Babylon, the fact is that the king would not have had to gather the image of Marduk, since it was already in the city. And even the image of Nabu may not have been involved, since the Babylonian Chronicle observes that the gods of certain cities, namely, of Borsippa, Cuthah, and Sippar, did not enter Babylon at this time (Grayson 1975a: 109: iii 11)—the principal god of Borsippa was Nabu.

26. Recent reviews of this practice, which could also be expressed literarily/theologically as the abandonment by a god(s) of the place and the human community that he/she had patronized, are Kutsko 2000: 103–23, 157–69; Holloway 2002: 121–51. An important earlier analysis was by Cogan 1974: 9–41, 119–21. As these discussions show, the majority of attestations of spoliation are Neo-Assyrian.

the situation is, to be sure, not set up in quite the same way, but the emphasis on Nabonidus's claim to special divine knowledge cannot fail to recall the criterion by which the prophet distinguishes Yahweh, especially in the trial speeches, but also elsewhere: Yahweh is the only one who knows and determines the past and its activities (*rī'šōnôt*) and the present–future (*bā'ôt, 'aḥărît, 'ōtiyyôt*). Particularly relevant to the Nabonidus context, it may be suggested, is the fact that the Hebrew terms in Isaiah's formulations appear to refer not only to the events themselves that Yahweh controls but to the divine "signs" of these events that He "announces" (*higgîd*) and "makes heard" (*hišmî'a*) (e.g., 42:9)—signs that only special experts, gifted prophets such as Isaiah, can discern and interpret.

These signs and the capacity to make sense of them also have a negative turn in the Second Isaiah, in passages other than the trial speeches. Thus, they correspond to the vilification of Nabonidus's special knowledge by his critics as idiotic fantasy and utter blasphemy. Two sets of passages in Second Isaiah are at issue here. The first comes in Isa 47:8 and 10 against Babylon, which is personified as a woman and pilloried for her boast "I am, and there is no one besides me." It is, of course, a boast about power that is presented as the worst sort of hubris, because it is meant to contrast with the assertion in the Isaianic trial speeches of Yahweh himself that "I am the first and I am the last, and besides Me there is no god" (44:6).[27] The second set of passages in the Second Isaiah comprises in particular 44:25 and 47:9–13, describing the skills of divination and witchcraft practiced by the Babylonians, which Yahweh frustrates and so shows up as foolish. Such descriptions and various of the terms for them cited by the prophet—"(ominous) signs" (*'ōtôt*), "sorceries" (*kĕšāpîm*), "prognosticators" (*qōsĕmîm*), and "wise men" (*ḥăkāmîm*)—are not new or unique to the Second Isaiah; they appear in other, and sometimes earlier, biblical texts, most prominently, Deut 18:10–11.[28] This does not mean, of course, that their appearance in the Second Isaiah is historically nugatory, all the more so as divination figured as a critical force in the Babylonian, specifically Nabonidus, environment in which the prophet lived. The probability is that the prophet has drawn on traditional Israelite materials reflecting encounters with divinatory practices from earlier times to make sense of his present moment. And this probability appears to be strengthened by two features of his description that seem to be new, even as they are intimately linked to Babylonian practices, including those of the Nabonidus period: the emphasis on astronomical divination (47:13), and the apparent mention of the *bārû*, the most widely attested of the Mesopotamian divination experts (44:25).[29]

---

27. Cf. also Isa 41:4; 43:10–11; 45:5–6. One may also compare Zeph 2:15, as Vanderhooft notes (1999: 182), where a boast in the same language is put in the mouth of Nineveh, here functioning as a metaphor for imperial Assyria, just as Babylon functions in Second Isaiah as a metaphor for Assyria's successor, imperial Babylonia.

28. For discussions of divination and other forms of magic in the Hebrew Bible, see, e.g., Kuemmerlin-McLean 1992, and, more elaborately, Cryer 1994: 229–332. The particular technical terms that occur may be studied ad loc. in the volumes of the *TWAT.*

29. On Nabonidus and divination, see Schaudig 2002: 625–27. For the Babylonian nature of the Second Isaiah passages, Vanderhooft 1999: 182–87 and Albani 2000: 102–22 should be consulted. The identification of the *bārû* in Isa 44:25 was apparently first made by Haupt (1900: 57–58, 68 n. 39), who suggested emending the MT reading there, *baddîm*, "liars," to *bārîm*, "*bārû*-diviners." The latter nicely fits the context, which otherwise deals with "prognosticators" (*qōsĕmîm*), but it has not always been accepted (see, e.g., Baltzer 2001: 214 n. 42).

Conclusion

The five areas of correspondence we have been discussing between Nabonidus and the Second Isaiah, it must be conceded, do not make a perfect fit. Put another way, in the known evidence no "smoking gun" has turned up so far—no clinching connection between these two historical figures and the sources for each. For example, we find no explicit mention of Nabonidus and his Sin debate in the Second Isaiah, nor any trial speech as such in the Nabonidus materials, pitting Sin against the other Babylonian deities. Furthermore, the five correspondences, taken individually, involve, as we have seen, phenomena that are not in every instance exclusive to Nabonidus and Second Isaiah but can occur in other periods and sources both from the Mesopotamian and from the Israelite sides.

Yet these five areas should not be taken individually but are, for Nabonidus and Second Isaiah, respectively, intertwined complexes; and the Nabonidus complex corresponds as a complex to that of the Second Isaiah. So considered, the relationship appears close enough, detailed enough, and extensive enough to give us pause—all the more so because it is a relationship between two figures and their pronouncements and activities in the same time and place. What we have then, it may be suggested, is not the influence of a precise literary genre from Babylonia upon the trial speeches and other utterances of the Second Isaiah. It is, rather, the influence of a group of ideas and the kind of pointed, passionate language used to express them that were part of the pressing issues of the day among the Babylonian elites. Second Isaiah, it is proposed, heard these ideas and their expressions and was aware of at least something of the intense debates and tensions they entailed. They became, thus, an important stimulus to him to rethink and rearticulate the traditions of his own community, living now in exile and facing the arrival of Cyrus, about their God Yahweh. And the process took form, for the prophet, especially in the trial speeches, for which he also drew, as we have seen, on some earlier Israelite literary traditions.

We may describe the phenomenon as the influence of a certain Babylonian *Zeitgeist* on the Second Isaiah—something, in short, that was not coerced or perhaps even direct, but was no less substantial and impelling for that. What strengthens the connection is that the *Zeitgeist* was not merely the province of a tiny ruling clique and counterclique in Nabonidus's world. For, as the cycle of Daniel stories shows, especially chaps. 2–5 of the biblical book of Daniel and the *Prayer of Nabonidus* (4Q242) from Qumran, knowledge of the religiopolitical debates in the Nabonidus world spread well beyond the participants involved.[30] Admittedly, these Danielic texts are to be dated to well after Nabonidus, but they clearly reflect sources that reach back to his reign, and there is no reason to deny that the spread of the "news" could have occurred early—at least by the time of Cyrus's victory in Babylonia, as the pro-Marduk opponents of Nabonidus sought to disseminate their views, build up their support, and eradicate any traces of Nabonidus's legitimacy.

---

30. For a recent survey of the Qumran Danielic texts, see Flint 2001; for recent studies of the Mesopotamian elements in the biblical Daniel 1–6, see Paul 2001; van der Toorn 2001. The survival of the memory of Nabonidus is examined in Sack 1982; 1983.

Certainly, there was no impregnable barrier between the Judean exiles and the Babylonian culture and politics in which they lived. To be sure, the modest evidence we have on social organization does not place the exiled Judeans at the centers of action and decision-making in the Babylonian realm, fully integrated into Babylonian society: there is no record of them as, say, government officials, such as a few became in the subsequent Achaemenid period of Babylonia (Zadok 2002: 27–45, 55–56, 58–63). Rather, they, like other exiled communities, appear regularly grouped together by kinship and their home townships, and settled especially in rural parts of Babylonia (see especially Eph'al 1978; 1983a; 1983b; also Vanderhooft 2003: 219–23, 234). On the other hand, there is no evidence that these settlements were completely closed ghettos, isolated by a systematic policy of persecution by the Babylonian authorities.[31] Various of them were situated near or on canals with easy access to Babylonian towns and cities (Zadok 2002: 52–53). And some could be found in the larger cities themselves: so for the Egyptians, in Babylon, Uruk, Sippar, and Borsippa (Eph'al 1978: 76–80); and for the Judeans, in Nippur, Babylon, and in the vicinity of Borsippa and Uruk (Zadok 1979: 34–35, 38–40; 2002: 27–28). The most interesting case here is that of the exiled Judean king, Jehoiachin. In Neo-Babylonian and biblical sources — the former from the reign of Nebuchadnezzar II in or about 592 B.C.E., the latter describing his successor, Awel-Marduk (biblical Evil-Merodach), ca. 562 B.C.E. — Jehoiachin is depicted as being quartered with his family, retainers/officials, and others in Babylon. There, as the Neo-Babylonian texts reveal (Weidner 1939: especially pp. 925–28), they received rations from the royal palace administration in Babylon, as did various other exiled groups. Thirty years later, according to the biblical source (2 Kgs 25:27–30), Jehoiachin was released from prison by Awel-Marduk (why and when he was put there go unnoticed), was shown favor by Awel-Marduk, and was given the seat of honor at the Babylonian king's table, above those of the other (exiled) kings there, where he ate daily. It may be that the terms of Jehoiachin's release have been exaggerated by the author of Kings. But at the least, it is clear, the notices in Kings and the Neo-Babylonian ration lists indicate that there was contact between Jehoiachin and other exiled rulers, along with their varied associates, and the Babylonian court in the capital city of Babylon.

Babylonian contact is also evident in the naming practices of the exiled Judeans (see especially Zadok 1979: 7–35, 38–43; 2002: 10–19, 27–28, 55–63; Demsky 1999). Admittedly, it is impossible to recognize all of these Judeans by name, and we must be careful not to extrapolate too much from the names that we can recognize concerning Judean beliefs

---

31. See, in brief, Oded 1995: 209, contra Wilkie 1951. Of course, this is not to deny that ill-feeling and even gestures of independence on the part of the Judean exiles occurred (e.g., Psalm 137; Jeremiah 29), suggesting that the exilic situation was not always received as a happy one and could occasionally have seen tough Babylonian measures to make sure that the exiles posed no "security" problems. We do have one example, to be sure, of what looks like Babylonian persecution. It is in Daniel 3 and concerns the three Judean youths that Nebuchadnezzar put into the furnace for refusing to worship the Babylonian gods. But this story is clearly legendary, designed as a tale of faith in the superiority of Yahweh, whom Nebuchadnezzar eventually acknowledges. It has no basis in the attested cuneiform evidence of Nebuchadnezzar II. And even at the time of Nabonidus, who may be the figure lying behind Nebuchadnezzar in this tale, the polemics and counterpolemics that we have discussed did not evidently lead to an active proscription of worship of gods other than Sin. These other gods were, after all, never formally denied by Nabonidus in his official texts, even in the later Harran stelae that emphatically exalt Sin; indeed, he took their images into Babylon in the end, as we have seen.

and behaviors in exile. Still, it is significant that among the recognizable names are some that are Babylonian, over against the bulk, which are native Judean and so exhibit the element *Yahweh* or some other distinctive Judean cultural feature. These Babylonian names were borne, noticeably, by some of the Judean leaders (e.g., Sheshbazzar [=?] Shenazzar, and Zerubbabel), who were most likely assigned them by the Babylonian authorities (e.g., Zadok 2002: 57). But such names were not restricted to the leadership (Avigad 1965: 228–30, pl. 40E) and thus were not always imposed externally. Indeed, the fact that children of the Babylonian name-bearers can appear with native Judean names and the children of native Judean-named parents can appear with Babylonian names suggests that name-giving was not some kind of mindless exercise. This is all the more so, if Bickerman is correct in identifying a shift in onomastic patterns within the Babylonian Judean community in the latter half of the 5th century B.C.E. (1978; approved by Zadok 1979: 84–86), thus a century after the Achaemenid conquest of Babylonia. The bulk of this evidence comes from Nippur and shows a new prominence of Yahwistic names, bespeaking, in Bickerman's view, a new interest in ancestral Israelite/Judean ties, which was not unconnected to a significant return of Judeans from Babylonia to Judah under Ezra at this time.

The Babylonian exilic evidence that we have briefly examined—settlement patterns, the case of Jehoiachin, and personal names—is, to reiterate, meager: wholly inadequate to provide a substantive picture of Babylonian/Judean relationships. The difficulties, in turn, are compounded by the fact that neither the Bible nor any other source describes precisely where Second Isaiah lived in Babylonia and what his social setting was. Nonetheless, our evidence is sufficient to show that the Judean exiles, and so Isaiah, were not isolated from the world of their Babylonian masters, indeed could have been exposed to a variety of its facets, social, economic, political, and cultural. When this is added to the clear indication that the polemics of Nabonidus's reign did make their way into biblical tradition, the evidence does provide a context in which the Nabonidus *Zeitgeist* could have influenced our prophet.

If this is accepted, then one final observation emerges as significant. It is that Second Isaiah's reaction to the *Zeitgeist* does not appear to have expressed itself in a choice between the Babylonian king and his opponents. On the one hand, as we have seen, the divine patrons of the opponents, Marduk/Bel and Nabu/Nebo, are treated rather witheringly by Isaiah (46:1–2). As for Nabonidus's favorite, the lunar Sin, this deity is frankly much less clearly in evidence in our prophet, and that may be an indication that, for Isaiah, Nabonidus's time had already passed. Yet significantly, whatever the prophet might be understood to offer us about Sin also looks critical: note his remark in 47:13 about those wearisome Babylonian diviners "who at the new moons (*ḥŏdošîm*) predict (lit., 'make known') what shall befall you (= Babylon)"; they are powerless, says Isaiah, to save Babylon or themselves from the coming disaster.[32] Or as one other possibility, consider

---

32. It is unlikely that "new moons" here is simply a neutral calendrical indication, because that would not explain why divination is said to be performed at this time. Furthermore, the preceding, parallel part of the verse speaks clearly of types of astronomical observation and divination: of "those who cut up the heavens and those who gaze at/have visions of the stars." Since the astronomical bodies were not merely physical phenomena, but also manifestations of the gods, it makes sense to associate "new moons" here with the lunar deity, Sin (cf. the recent discussion of this verse in Albani 2000: 107–12).

the prophet's condemnation of Babylon in 47:11: "disaster shall come upon you; you do not know its *šaḥar* (*šaḥrāh*)." To be sure, this verse is rather difficult, but Vanderhooft has made a most interesting, although he admits speculative, suggestion about it (1999: 185–86). It is that *šaḥar* may be the rendering of the Aramaic name of the moon-god, Śahr, which in Akkadian was rendered Šēru/i, Tēri, and Iltehri/Iltēr/Iltēri—Iltēri occurring, as we have seen, in the Verse Account directed against Nabonidus.[33] The sense, then, could be that Babylon, meaning its rulers and particularly its intellectual elite, does not know how to save itself from the coming disaster, because it cannot understand and deal with the moon-god that is in some way connected with that disaster. On this interpretation, Isaiah is perhaps granting some recognition to the moon-god, but it is in the polemical context of arguing that the Babylonians know nothing about this deity and his powers — surely, thus, a slap against Nabonidus's claims.[34] The point in all of this is clear: however

33. Śahr is a deity whose worship included Arabia. The major early discussion of this deity, as Vanderhooft notes and uses, is in Lewy 1945–46: 425–33; for a recent update, see Lipiński 2000: 620–23. Vanderhooft's suggestion that *šaḥrāh* be identified as Śahr has been favorably received by Albani (2000: 109). Its plausibility rests not only on its fit within the context of Second Isaiah but on the phonology of *šaḥrāh*, more specifically its first two consonants, *šîn* and *ḥēt*. The contextual fit has been touched on above in the main text. As for the phonological issue, in Aramaic alphabetic script, the god Śahr always appears as *ś* (i.e., the grapheme *šin/śîn*) *hr* (e.g., Cross 1986: 390–91; Lipiński 2000: 621). The Akkadian renderings *šēru/i, tēri, tēr,* and *tehri* (the last two only as part of *iltēri/iltehri*) are found in Neo-Assyrian and Neo-Babylonian sources; they represent a variation in the initial consonant between *š* and *t*, while the second consonant is a guttural that appears as *ḥ* or *ʿ*, or is replaced by *ē* (Fales 1978: especially p. 95). As for the Akkadian *iltēr/iltēri/iltehri*, this is of uncertain analysis: it could be a compound, *il(u) Tēr/Tēri/Tehri*, "the god who is manifest as Tēr/Tehr (= Śahr)" (so Lewy 1945–46: 428–29), or the *il + t* could be a graphemic representation of the initial sibilant, and thus the word would simply be understood as "Tēr/Tehr (= Śahr)" (so Fales 1978, comparing forms for Šamaš and Šagab). If we put these Akkadian renderings together with the Aramaic alphabetic form, it would appear that the underlying Aramaic consonants being represented here are *śhr*, wherein *ś* could be rendered in Akkadian as *š, t,* and perhaps, if Fales is correct, as *il-t* (e.g., Fales 1978: especially p. 91 with other references).

The question, then, is whether *šaḥrāh* in Isa 47:11 can fit into this phonological scheme. That appears difficult if *šaḥrāh* is to be considered a linguistic reflex of the Aramaic divine name, as Vanderhooft's suggestion supposes, since then we would expect the Hebrew to be the same as the Aramaic, viz., *śahrāh*. In fact, a form of the word for "moon" with exactly this rendering of the consonants occurs elsewhere in the Bible, namely, as the diminutive *śahărōn* (only in the plural *śahărōnîm*) in Judg 8:21, 26, and (1) Isa 3:18; it appears to mean, following Lipiński 2000: 622, "little moon," that is, "an amulet or pendentive with the symbol of the Moon-god" (see also, e.g., BDB 962a, s.v.). Lipiński has proposed another biblical occurrence as well, in Song 7:3, where the form is *sahar* and the meaning, for Lipiński, is "moon," that is, the deity (2000: 622; cf. Pope 1977: 618–19 with other references). To be sure, the initial consonant of this form is *samek*, not *šîn* as in *śahărōnîm* in Judges and (1) Isaiah, but this is not a problem, since the interchange of *šîn* and *samek* is well attested in Biblical and later Hebrew (e.g., Joüon and Muraoka 1991: 28–29 m).

Does all of this mean that we should reject on phonological grounds the equation of *šaḥrāh* in (2) Isa 47:11 with Aramaic Śahr? (Lipiński 2000: 620–23 does not include our Isaiah verse in his discussion of biblical occurrences.) That is not necessary, if we assume that *šaḥrāh* here is somehow influenced by the Akkadian renderings of the Aramaic name, *šēru, iltehri* (although no *šeḥru* is attested), instead of directly by the Aramaic.

34. For other interpretive possibilities concerning Isa 47:11, see Vanderhooft 1999: 185. Among these, the most likely to me and the one that I had earlier endorsed (Machinist 1991: 205), as Vanderhooft notes—he too finds it attractive, though in a somewhat different form—is the suggestion by J. D. Michaelis (see Driver 1935: 400, who, incorrectly, objects to it). It is to read MT *šaḥrāh*, not as a noun with 3rd-fem. sing. suffix, but as an infinitive construct with that same suffix, cognate to Arabic *saḥara*; the meaning would then be "to enchant it (away)." This infinitive could be understood as *qal*, in which case a slight emendation of the MT to *šaḥărāh* would be needed (cf. Blenkinsopp 2002: 277a). But perhaps it would be better construed as a *piel* (see *HAL* 4.1359b–1360a, 2), for in that case the MT *šaḥrāh* could remain, as a

fascinated by the debate over Sin, Marduk, and the other gods, Second Isaiah in the end stands back from it, able to use and transform it with startling creativity in the trial speeches and other oracles, drawing on his ability as a literatus both in his native Israelite and in Babylonian tradition. We may understand the prophet, thus, to be saying: a pox on all these Babylonian houses, those of the "Sin-ers" and those of the "Marduk-ers"; for their squabbles serve only to reveal that it is Yahweh, the God of Israel, who alone predicts and interprets, determines, creates, and controls events—who alone is God.[35]

variant of the expected *šaḥărāh*, and it would correspond with *kappĕrāh*, the *piel* infinitive construct with 3rd-fem. sing. suffix in the following parallel stich (see *HAL* 4.1359b–1360a, 2). Whether as *qal* or *piel*, the sense would be the same: to criticize the Babylonians for not being able to "enchant away" the coming disaster. So taken, *šaḥrāh* would fit well in the context, since in the following v. 12, the Babylonian magicians and diviners are explicitly disparaged. Michaelis's "enchanted" interpretation, therefore, continues to attract me but not at the expense of Vanderhooft's intriguing suggestion.

35. The connection between Nabonidus and his activities concerning Sin and Second Isaiah has also been made by Albani (2000: especially pp. 102–22). It is referred to as well, in briefer form, by S. Cohen and Hurowitz (1999: 290 n. 33), although their overall focus is on the related text of Jer 10:3 in the light of Mesopotamian sources, including those of Nabonidus. I became aware of both of these studies only after I had completed the essential work on the present paper; and while this paper overlaps with some of their observations and conclusions, its argument and format are framed differently.

References

Albani, M.
    2000   *Der eine Gott und die himmlischen Heerschaften.* Arbeiten zur Bibel und ihrer Geschichte 1. Leipzig: Evangelische Verlagsanstalt.

Albertz, R.
    1994   *A History of Israelite Religion in the Old Testament Period*, vol. 1: *From the Beginnings to the End of the Monarchy.* The Old Testament Library. Louisville: Westminster John Knox.

Avigad, N.
    1965   Seals of Exiles. *Israel Exploration Journal* 15: 222–32, pl. 40 B–F.

Baltzer, K.
    2001   *Deutero-Isaiah: A Commentary on Isaiah 40–55.* Hermeneia. Minneapolis: Fortress.

Barstad, H. M.
    1987   On the So-Called Babylonian Literary Influence in Second Isaiah. *Scandinavian Journal of the Old Testament* 2: 90–110.
    1994   Akkadian "Loan-Words" in Isaiah 40–55—And the Question of Babylonian Origin of Deutero-Isaiah. Pp. 36–48 in *Text and Theology: Studies in Honour of Professor Dr. Theol. Magne Saebø Presented on the Occasion of His 65th Birthday*, ed. A. Tangberg. Oslo: Verbum.
    1997   *The Babylonian Captivity of the Book of Isaiah: "Exilic" Judah and the Provenance of Isaiah 40–55.* Institute for Comparative Research in Human Culture Series B/CII. Oslo: Novus.

BDB
    1953   *A Hebrew and English Lexicon of the Old Testament*, ed. F. Brown, S. R. Driver, and C. A. Briggs (reprinted with corrections). Oxford: Clarendon.

Beaulieu, P.-A.
    1989   *The Reign of Nabonidus, King of Babylon 556–539 B.C.* Yale Near Eastern Researches 10. New Haven: Yale University Press.
    1993   An Episode in the Fall of Babylon to the Persians. *Journal of Near Eastern Studies* 52: 241–61.

1994   Antiquarianism and the Concern for the Past in the Neo-Babylonian Period. *Bulletin of the Canadian Society for Mesopotamian Studies* 28: 37–42.

Berlejung, A.
1998   *Die Theologie der Bilder.* Orbis Biblicus et Orientalis 162. Freiburg: Universitätsverlag / Göttingen: Vandenhoeck & Ruprecht.

Bickerman, E. J.
1978   The Generation of Ezra and Nehemiah. *Proceedings of the American Academy for Jewish Research* 45: 1–28.

Bidmead, J.
2002   *The Akītu Festival: Religious Continuity and Royal Legitimation in Mesopotamia.* Gorgias Dissertations: Near Eastern Studies 2. Piscataway, N.J.: Gorgias.

Blenkinsopp, J.
1996   *A History of Prophecy in Israel.* Revised and enlarged ed. Louisville: Westminster John Knox.
2002   *Isaiah 40–55.* The Anchor Bible 19. New York: Doubleday.

Bovati, P.
1994   *Re-establishing Justice: Legal Terms, Concepts and Procedures in the Hebrew Bible.* Journal for the Study of the Old Testament Supplement Series 105. Sheffield: JSOT Press.

CAD M/i
1977   *The Assyrian Dictionary of the Oriental Institute of the University of Chicago* M/i, ed. M. Civil et al. Chicago: Oriental Institute.

Clifford, R. J.
1984   *Fair Spoken and Persuading: An Interpretation of Second Isaiah.* New York: Paulist.
1992   Isaiah, Book of (Second Isaiah). Pp. 490–501 in vol. 3 of *The Anchor Bible Dictionary*, ed. D. N. Freedman. New York: Doubleday.
1999   Review of Hans M. Barstad, *The Babylonian Captivity of the Book of Isaiah: "Exilic" Judah and the Provenance of Isaiah 40–55* (Oslo: Novus, 1997). *Biblica* 80: 131–34.

Cogan, M.
1974   *Imperialism and Religion: Assyria, Judah and Israel in the Eighth and Seventh Centuries* B.C.E. Society of Biblical Literature Monograph Series 19. Missoula, Mont.: Scholars Press.
1993   Judah under Assyrian Hegemony: A Reexamination of *Imperialism and Religion. Journal of Biblical Literature* 112: 403–14.
2001   *1 Kings.* The Anchor Bible 10. New York: Doubleday.

Cohen, M. E.
1993   *The Cultic Calendars of the Ancient Near East.* Bethesda, Md.: CDL.

Cohen, S., and Hurowitz, V. A.
1999   חקות העמים הבל הוא (Jer 10:3) in Light of Akkadian *Parṣu* and *Zāqīqu* Referring to Cult Statues. *Jewish Quarterly Review* 89/3–4: 277–90.

Cross, F. M.
1986   A New Aramaic Stele from Taymāʾ. *Catholic Biblical Quarterly* 48: 387–94.

Cryer, F. H.
1994   *Divination in Ancient Israel and Its Near Eastern Environment: A Socio-Historical Investigation.* Journal for the Study of the Old Testament Supplement Series 142. Sheffield: Sheffield Academic Press.

Demsky, A.
1999   Double Names in the Babylonian Exile and the Identity of Sheshbazzar. Pp. 23–40 in vol. 2 of *These Are the Names: Studies in Jewish Onomastics*, ed. A. Demsky. Ramat Gan: Bar-Ilan University.

Dick, M. B.
1999   Prophetic Parodies of Making the Cult Image. Pp. 1–53 in *Born in Heaven, Made on Earth: The Making of the Cult Image in the Ancient Near East*, ed. M. B. Dick. Winona Lake, Ind.: Eisenbrauns.

Dion, H.-M.
1967 Le genre littéraire sumérien de l'"hymne à soi-même" et quelques passages du Deutéro-Isaie. *Revue Biblique* 74: 215–34.

Driver, G. R.
1935 Linguistic and Textual Problems: Isaiah XL–LXVI. *Journal of Theological Studies* 36: 396–406.

Eph‘al, I.
1978 The Western Minorities in Babylonia in the 6th–5th Centuries B.C.: Maintenance and Cohesion. *Orientalia* 47: 74–90.
1983a The Babylonian Exile. Pp. 17–27, 256–58 in *Return to Zion: The Persian Period*, ed. H. Tadmor. The History of the People of Israel Series 1. Jerusalem: Pele/Am Oved (Hebrew).
1983b On the Political and Social Organization of the Jews in Babylonian Exile. Pp. 106–12 in *Zeitschrift der Deutschen Morgenländischen Gesellschaft Supplement V. XXI. Deutscher Orientalistentag vom 24. bis 29. März 1980 in Berlin. Ausgewählte Vorträge*, ed. F. Steppat. Wiesbaden: Steiner.
1986–89 On the Linguistic and Cultural Background of Deutero-Isaiah. *Shnaton* 10: 31–35, xi–xii (Hebrew with English summary).

Fales, F. M.
1978 A Cuneiform Correspondence to Alphabetic ש in West Semitic Names of the I Millennium B.C. *Orientalia* 47: 91–98.

Flint, P. W.
2001 The Daniel Tradition at Qumran. Pp. 329–67 in vol. 2 of *The Book of Daniel: Composition and Reception*, ed. J. J. Collins and P. W. Flint. Leiden: Brill.

Goldstein, J.
2002 *Peoples of an Almighty God: Competing Religions in the Ancient World*. The Anchor Bible Reference Library. New York: Doubleday.

Graffy, A.
1984 *A Prophet Confronts His People: The Disputation Speech in the Prophets*. Analecta Biblica 104. Rome: Pontifical Biblical Institute.

Grayson, A. K.
1975a *Assyrian and Babylonian Chronicles*. Texts from Cuneiform Sources 5. Locust Valley, N.Y.: Augustin.
1975b *Babylonian Historical-Literary Texts*. Toronto Semitic Texts and Studies. Toronto: University of Toronto Press.

Greenberg, M.
1997 *Ezekiel 21–37*. The Anchor Bible 22A. New York: Doubleday.

Gressmann, H.
1914 Die literarische Analyse Deuterojesajas. *Zeitschrift für die alttestamentliche Wissenschaft* 34: 254–97.

HAL
1967–96 *Hebräisches und Aramäisches Lexikon zum Alten Testament*, ed. L. Koehler et al. Vols. 1–5 and *Supplementband*. Leiden: Brill.

Hallo, W. W., and Simpson, W. K.
1998 *The Ancient Near East: A History*. 2nd ed. Fort Worth: Harcourt Brace.

Haupt, P.
1900 Babylonian Elements in the Levitic Ritual. *Journal of Biblical Literature* 19: 55–81.

Holloway, S. W.
1992 *The Case for Assyrian Religious Influence in Israel and Judah: Inference and Evidence*. 3 vols. Ph.D. dissertation, University of Chicago Divinity School.
2002 *Aššur is King! Aššur is King! Religion in the Exercise of Power in the Neo-Assyrian Empire*. Culture and History of the Ancient Near East 10. Leiden: Brill.

Jones, G. H.

  1984   *1 and 2 Kings*. Vol. 2. New Century Bible Commentary. Grand Rapids: Eerdmans.

Joüon, P.

  1991   *A Grammar of Biblical Hebrew* I. *Part One: Orthography and Phonetics; Part Two: Morphology*. Trans. and rev. T. Muraoka. Subsidia Biblica 14/1. Rome: Pontifical Biblical Institute.

Jüngling, H.-W.

  1969   *Der Tod der Götter: Eine Untersuchung zu Psalm 82*. Stuttgarter Bibelstudien 38. Stuttgart: Katholisches Bibelwerk.

Koch, K.

  1984   *The Prophets 2: The Babylonian and Persian Periods*. Philadelphia: Fortress.

Kuemmerlin-McLean, J. K.

  1992   Magic (Old Testament). Pp. 468–71 in vol. 4 of *The Anchor Bible Dictionary*, ed. D. N. Freedman. New York: Doubleday.

Kuhrt, A.

  1990   Nabonidus and the Babylonian Priesthood. Pp. 119–55 in *Pagan Priests: Religion and Power in the Ancient World*, ed. M. Beard and J. North. London: Duckworth.

Kutsko, J. F.

  2000   *Between Heaven and Earth: Divine Presence and Absence in the Book of Ezekiel*. Biblical and Judaic Studies from the University of California, San Diego 7. Winona Lake, Ind.: Eisenbrauns.

Lewy, J.

  1945–46   The Late Assyro-Babylonian Cult of the Moon and Its Culmination at the Time of Nabonidus. *Hebrew Union College Annual* 19: 405–89.

Lipiński, E.

  2000   *The Aramaeans: Their Ancient History, Culture, Religion*. Orientalia Lovaniensia Analecta 100. Leuven: Peeters.

Machinist, P.

  1991   The Question of Distinctiveness in Ancient Israel: An Essay. Pp. 196–212 in *Ah, Assyria . . . : Studies in Assyrian History and Ancient Near Eastern Historiography Presented to Hayim Tadmor*, ed. M. Cogan and I. Eph'al. Scripta Hierosolymitana 33. Jerusalem: Magnes.

  1992   Palestine, Administration of (Assyro-Babylonian). Pp. 69–81 in vol. 5 of *The Anchor Bible Dictionary*, ed. D. N. Freedman. New York: Doubleday.

Machinist, P., and Tadmor, H.

  1993   Heavenly Wisdom. Pp. 146–51 in *The Tablet and the Scroll: Near Eastern Studies in Honor of William W. Hallo*, ed. M. E. Cohen, D. Snell, and D. Weisberg. Bethesda, Md.: CDL.

Mayes, A. D. H.

  1985   *Judges*. Old Testament Guides. Sheffield: JSOT Press.

McKay, J.

  1973   *Religion in Judah under the Assyrians*. Studies in Biblical Theology Second Series 26. London: SCM.

McKenzie, S. L.

  1991   *The Trouble with Kings: The Composition of the Book of Kings in the Deuteronomistic History*. Vetus Testamentum Supplements 42. Leiden: Brill.

Melugin, R. F.

  1976   *The Formation of Isaiah 40–55*. Beiheft zur Zeitschrift für die alttestamentliche Wissenschaft 141. Berlin: de Gruyter.

Merendino, R. P.

  1981   *Der Erste und der Letzte: Eine Untersuchung von Jes 40–48*. Vetus Testamentum Supplements 31. Leiden: Brill.

Michalowski, P.
  2003   The Doors of the Past. Pp. 136*–52* in *Eretz-Izrael* 27 (Hayim and Miriam Tadmor Volume), ed. I. Eph'al, A. Ben-Tor, and P. Machinist. Jerusalem: Israel Exploration Society.
Michel, C.
  2001   Nabû. Pp. 552–54 in *Dictionnaire de la civilisation mésopotamienne*, ed. F. Joannes. Paris: Laffont.
Millard, A. R.
  1999   Nabu, נבו. Pp. 607–10 in *Dictionary of Deities and Demons in the Bible*, ed. K. van der Toorn, B. Becking, and P. W. van der Horst. 2nd ed. Leiden: Brill.
Miller, P. D., Jr.
  1986   *Interpreting the Psalms*. Philadelphia: Fortress.
Nelson, R. D.
  2002   *Deuteronomy*. Old Testament Library. Louisville: Westminster John Knox.
Nielsen, K.
  1978   *Yahweh as Prosecutor and Judge*. Journal for the Study of the Old Testament Supplement Series 9. Sheffield: University of Sheffield.
North, C. R.
  1967   *The Second Isaiah: Introduction, Translation and Commentary to Chapters XL–LV.* Oxford: Clarendon.
Oded, B.
  1995   Observations on the Israelite/Judaean Exiles in Mesopotamia during the Eighth–Seventh Centuries BCE. Pp. 205–12 in *Immigration and Emigration within the Ancient Near East: Festschrift E. Lipiński*, ed. K. van Lerberghe and A. Schoors. Orientalia Lovaniensia Analecta 65. Leuven: Peeters.
Paul, S. M.
  1968   Deutero-Isaiah and Cuneiform Royal Inscriptions. *Journal of the American Oriental Society* 88: 180–86.
  2001   The Mesopotamian Background of Daniel 1–6. Pp. 55–68 in vol. 1 of *The Book of Daniel: Composition and Reception*, ed. J. J. Collins and P. W. Flint. Leiden: Brill.
Pomponio, F.
  1998   Nabû, A. Philologisch. Pp. 16–24 in vol. 9 of *Reallexikon der Assyriologie und Vorderasiatischen Archäologie*, ed. D. O. Edzard. Berlin: de Gruyter.
Pope, M. H.
  1977   *Song of Songs*. The Anchor Bible 7C. Garden City, N.Y.: Doubleday.
Preuss, H. D.
  1971   *Verspottung fremder Religionen im Alten Testament*. Beiträge zur Wissenschaft vom Alten und Neuen Testament 5/12. Stuttgart: Kohlhammer.
Pritchard, J. B., ed.
  1969   *Ancient Near Eastern Texts Relating to the Old Testament*. 3rd ed. Princeton: Princeton University Press.
Richter, A.
  1981   Hauptlinien der Deuterojesaja-Forschung von 1964–1979. Pp. 89–123 in *Sprache und Struktur der Prophetie Deuterojesajas*, by C. Westermann. Calwer Theologische Monographien A/11. Stuttgart: Calwer.
Ringgren, H.
  1990   ריב *rîb*. Pp. 496–50 in vol. 7/3–5 of *TWAT*.
Sack, R. H.
  1982   Nebuchadnezzar and Nabonidus in Folklore and History. *Mesopotamia* 17: 67–131.
  1983   The Nabonidus Legend. *Revue d'Assyriologie* 77: 59–67.
Schaudig, H.
  2001   *Die Inschriften Nabonids von Babylon und Kyros des Grossen samt den in ihrem Umfeld entstandenen Tendenzinschriften: Textausgabe und Grammatik*. Alter Orient und Altes Testament 256. Münster: Ugarit-Verlag.

2002 Nabonid, der "Gelehrte auf dem Königsthron." Omina, Synkretismen und die Ausdeutung von Tempel- und Götternamen als Mittel zur Wahrheitsfindung spätbabylonischer Religionspolitik. Pp. 619–45 in *Ex Mesopotamia et Syria Lux: Festschrift für Manfried Dietrich zu seinem 65. Geburtstag*, ed. O. Loretz, K. A. Metzler, and H. Schaudig. Alter Orient und Altes Testament 281. Münster: Ugarit-Verlag.

Schoors, A.
1973 *I Am God Your Saviour: A Form-Critical Study of the Main Genres in Is. XL–LV*. Vetus Testamentum Supplements 24. Leiden: Brill.

Seitz, C. R.
1991 *Zion's Final Destiny*. Minneapolis: Fortress.

Spieckermann, H.
1982 *Juda unter Assur in der Sargonidenzeit*. Forschungen zur Religion und Literatur des Alten und Neuen Testaments 129. Göttingen: Vandenhoeck & Ruprecht.

Spykerboer, H. C.
1976 *The Structure and Composition of Deutero-Isaiah, With Special Reference to the Polemics against Idolatry*. Th.D. dissertation, Rijksuniversiteit te Groningen.

Tadmor, H.
1965 The Inscriptions of Nabunaid: Historical Arrangement. Pp. 351–63 in *Studies in Honor of Benno Landsberger on His Seventy-Fifth Birthday April 21, 1965*, ed. H. G. Güterbock and T. Jacobsen. Assyriological Studies 16. Chicago: University of Chicago Press.

TWAT
1970– *Theologisches Wörterbuch zum Alten Testament*, ed. G. J. Botterweck, H. Ringgren, and H.-J. Fabry. Stuttgart: Kohlhammer.

Tigay, J. H.
1996 *Deuteronomy*. The JPS Torah Commentary. Philadelphia: Jewish Publication Society.

Toorn, K. van der
2001 Scholars at the Oriental Court: The Figure of Daniel against Its Mesopotamian Background. Pp. 37–54 in vol. 1 of *The Book of Daniel: Composition and Reception*, ed. J. J. Collins and P. W. Flint. Leiden: Brill.

Tsevat, M.
1969–70 God and the Gods in Assembly: An Interpretation of Psalm 82. *Hebrew Union College Annual* 40–41: 123–37.

Vanderhooft, D. S.
1999 *The Neo-Babylonian Empire and Babylon in the Latter Prophets*. Harvard Semitic Museum Monographs 59. Atlanta: Scholars Press.
2003 New Evidence Pertaining to the Transition from Neo-Babylonian to Achaemenid Administration in Palestine. Pp. 219–35 in *Yahwism after the Exile*, ed. R. Albertz and B. Becking. Studies in Theology and Religion 5. Assen: Van Gorcum.

Weidner, E. F.
1939 Jojachin, König von Juda, in babylonischen Keilschrifttexten. Pp. 923–35 and pls. 1–5 in vol. 2 of *Mélanges syriens offerts à Monsieur René Dussaud*. Bibliothèque archéologique et historique 30. Paris: Geuthner.

Weinfeld, M.
1967–68 God the Creator in Gen. I and in the Prophecy of Second Isaiah. *Tarbiz* 37: 105–32, i–ii. [Hebrew with English summary]

Weippert, M.
2001 "Ich bin Jahwe"—"Ich bin Istar von Arbela": Deuterojesaja im Lichte der neuassyrischen Prophetie. Pp. 31–59 in *Prophetie und Psalmen: Festschrift für Klaus Seybold zum 65. Geburtstag*, ed. B. Huwyler, H.-P. Mathys, and B. Weber. Alter Orient und Altes Testament 280. Münster: Ugarit-Verlag.

Weisberg, D. B.
  1997   Polytheism and Politics: Some Comments on Nabonidus' Foreign Policy. Pp. 547–56 in *Crossing Boundaries and Linking Horizons: Studies in Honor of Michael C. Astour on His 80th Birthday*, ed. G. D. Young, M. W. Chavalas, and R. E. Averbeck. Bethesda, Md.: CDL.

Westermann, C.
  1960   *Grundformen prophetischer Rede*. Beiträge zur evangelischen Theologie. Theologische Abhandlungen 31. Munich: Chr. Kaiser.
  1964   Sprache und Struktur der Prophetie Deuterojesajas. Pp. 92–170 in *Forschung am Alten Testament: Gesammelte Studien*. Theologische Bücherei: Altes Testament 24. Munich: Chr. Kaiser.
  1969   *Isaiah 40–66*. The Old Testament Library. Philadelphia: Westminster.

White, M. C.
  1997   *The Elijah Legends and Jehu's Coup*. Brown Judaic Studies 311. Atlanta: Scholars Press.

Whybray, R. N.
  1983   *The Second Isaiah*. Old Testament Guides. Sheffield: JSOT Press.

Wilkie, J. M.
  1951   Nabonidus and the Later Jewish Exiles. *Journal of Theological Studies* n.s. 2: 36–44.

Williamson, H. G. M.
  1986   Isaiah 40, 20: A Case of Not Seeing the Wood for the Trees. *Biblica* 67: 1–20.

Wilson, A.
  1986   *The Nations in Deutero-Isaiah: A Study on Composition and Structure*. Ancient Near Eastern Texts and Studies 1. Lewiston, N.Y.: Edwin Mellen.

Winter, I. J.
  2000   Babylonian Archeologists of The(ir) Mesopotamian Past. Pp. 1785–98 and figs. 1–3 in vol. 2 of *Proceedings of the First International Congress on the Archaeology of the Ancient Near East: Rome, May 18th–23rd, 1998*, ed. P. Matthiae et al. Rome: Università degli Studi di Roma, "La Sapienza."

Würthwein, E.
  1984   *Die Bücher der Könige 2: 1. Kön. 17–2. Kön. 25*. Das Alte Testament Deutsch 11/2. Göttingen: Vandenhoeck & Ruprecht.

Zadok, R.
  1979   *The Jews in Babylonia during the Chaldean and Achaemenian Periods according to the Babylonian Sources*. Studies in the History of the Jewish People and the Land of Israel Monograph Series 3. Haifa: University of Haifa Press.
  2002   *The Earliest Diaspora: Israelites and Judeans in Pre-Hellenistic Mesopotamia*. Publications of the Diaspora Research Institute 151. Tel Aviv: Tel Aviv University Press.

Zimmerli, W.
  1963   Ich bin Yahwe. Pp. 11–40 in *Gottes Offenbarung: Gesammelte Aufsätze zum Alten Testament*. Theologische Bücherei: Altes Testament 19. Munich: Chr. Kaiser. (Original publication, 1953.)

When the Heavens Darkened: Yahweh, El, and the Divine Astral Family in Iron Age II Judah

Mark S. Smith

Skirball Department of Hebrew and Judaic Studies
New York University

Introduction

For over three decades, a debate has ensued over the background of astral religion in Iron II Judah. Two monographs in the early 1970s set the stage for the debate. In his important monograph published in 1973, *Religion in Judah under the Assyrians*, McKay argued that the astral religion of "the sun, moon and the stars," denounced in a number of biblical texts (e.g., Deut 4:19, 17:3), reflected an indigenous West Semitic traditional worship and not exclusively an importation under Neo-Assyrian influence. McKay cites a range of sources, including some references to the sun and the moon as deities in the Ugaritic texts (1973: 38, 51). He reconstructs a scenario involving "the reappearance of old Canaanite cults" in the time of Manasseh along with the possibility of Neo-Assyrian influence on astral cult (1973: 27, 71).

The following year witnessed the publication of Cogan's well-argued and better-documented case for essentially the same view, entitled *Imperialism and Religion* (1974). Cogan's study includes a close examination of Akkadian texts that suggest latitude in matters of local worship, contrary to the negative reputation attributed by scholars to the Neo-Assyrian Empire's policies. Apart from the "chariots of the sun" mentioned in 2 Kgs 23:11, Cogan sees little clear Neo-Assyrian influence on Judean astral cult (1974: 86–88). Instead, he tends to view astral cults as "outgrowths of local traditions, popularly rooted" (1974: 86). Echoing W. F. Albright, Cogan's monograph also offers a deep appreciation of the Aramean-Assyrian ensemble of influences that was more subtle than imperial imposition.

In retrospect, it is surprising to see that, in discussing the Queen of Heaven (Jeremiah 7 and 44), Cogan made little use of the *kawwānîm*, "the cakes," dedicated to her cult. It is difficult to ignore the Akkadian background of this word, as Held (1982) would later emphasize. In the Bible, one does see a few features that sound Neo-Assyrian, and one might be inclined to add the cult of the Tammuz (Ezekiel 8) or the references to *mazzālôt* (2 Kgs 23:5) / *mazzārôt* (Job 38:22). These disparate phenomena, however, hardly require a theory of Neo-Assyrian imposition, only influence. Indeed, later research would suggest that factors of trade and economic influence could be expected to play significant roles in the Neo-Assyrian *imperium* along with political administration (Frankenstein 1979; for the application of this model to Philistine Ekron, see Gitin 1989; 1992: 46*; 1995). In sum, Cogan's contributions seemed to close the question of Neo-Assyrian cultic imposition on Iron II Judah (see also Cogan 1993).

The early 1980s witnessed a reopening of the discussion. In his 1982 book, *Juda unter Assur in der Sargonidenzeit*, Spieckermann suggests Neo-Assyrian imposition of religious policy and practice on Iron II Judah, including the cult of Ishtar under the guise of the Queen of Heaven, a Neo-Assyrian astral cult in the form of the sun, the moon, and "the hosts of heaven," including the horses and the chariots of the sun (1982: 212–21). He also argues for Neo-Assyrian influence in the form of various religious practices in Judah, including oracles and exstipicy; observation of the heavens and astronomical omens; observation of times and calendar; prayer and ritual; and female prophecy (Spieckermann 1982: 236–306). All in all, a maximal case. Spieckermann even sees local temples, including the Jerusalem temple, as instruments of Neo-Assyrian religious imposition (1982: 306).

Spieckermann's case, however, suffers from claims that seem exaggerated, given the low level of explicit support from written sources. When the biblical sources' authors wish to identify Mesopotamian influence, they seem to show no difficulty in "naming names" of foreign deities, whether they be Sakkut and Kaiwan in Amos 5, the Tammuz in Ezekiel 8, or the string of Mesopotamian deities in 2 Kings 17. Even the one exception perhaps undermines Spieckermann's case. The title "Queen of Heaven" is, in Spieckermann's formulation (1982: 212), a "chiffre," a cipher for Ishtar, but that this figure was influenced by the cult of Ishtar is to be deduced only by the further evidence of her *kawwānîm* and not from the goddess's title itself. Moreover, this evidence hardly precludes an indigenous goddess lying behind the title, only to be identified secondarily with Ishtar and revered in the Mesopotamian fashion of *kawwānîm* offerings (Ackerman 1992: 28). Some scholars would go further by raising critical questions about the Mesopotamian background of these offerings or Mesopotamian influence on the goddess's cult (for example, Olyan 1987: 173). By the same token, the biblical term does seem to be an Akkadian loanword, which would point in the direction of some Neo-Assyrian influence (Held 1982).

In a short study published in 1985, entitled *Solare Elemente im Jahwesglauben des Alten Testaments*, Stähli ventures to show the old solar religion lying behind later Jewish mosaics with astral elements in synagogues such as Beth Alpha. While the issue of zodiacs in synagogues was Stähli's initial concern, his study, however short, introduced a wide variety of textual evidence into the discussion, suggesting a broad background of solar elements in traditional Israelite religion. These included biblical passages, such as Mal 3:20 and Psalm 84, as well as place-names and personal names with the elements of *šemeš* and *ḥeres*. Stähli's work does not take up the question of Neo-Assyrian influence, but its general approach clearly supports the position of McKay and Cogan. Studies on solar religion in the 1990s built on Stähli's work: these include Taylor's 1993 book, *Yahweh and the Sun* (based on his 1989 dissertation), and a 1990 article by this author. Taylor uses a wide array of evidence from both texts and material culture to suggest no Neo-Assyrian influence on any religious feature, including "the horses of the sun." Just as Spieckermann pushed the evidence hard in one direction, Taylor's work tacked hard back in the other direction. Taylor's work clearly enjoys the virtue of assuming that features criticized in the Bible need not be viewed as "pagan" or non-Israelite, a notion found in earlier works on the subject. In retrospect, one can see that, since Taylor was attempting simply to establish solar Yah-wism, his treatment did not consider the possible varieties of solar Yahwism or astral Yah-wism. The evidence now calls for a diachronic analysis that distinguishes between and examines the Iron I and II evidence, not to mention the Persian period material. In re-engaging the basic debate, Holloway (1992) examines yet a wider array of Neo-Assyrian textual and artifactual evidence, as well as the standard Judean material. He cautiously hews to the older view of McKay and Cogan, while noting some gaps in evidence.

The discussion changed little until the newer thrust of iconographic inquiry by Keel and Uehlinger. In their well-known 1992 tome translated into English in 1998 under the title *Gods, Goddesses, and Images of God in Ancient Israel,* the coauthors give comfort to the position of Spieckermann. The value of this work, besides its rightly heralded focus on often neglected iconography, is to show the theoretically possible coherence between the iconographic and written records. While avoiding claims of Neo-Assyrian imposition of cult, Keel and Uehlinger (1998: 286) nicely marshal pictorial evidence for a larger mélange of influences unleashed by the imperial changes marked by the Neo-Assyrian advance in the west. For the coauthors, the significant increase in astral cults in Judah, with their astral figurations of divine symbols, resulted from Assyro-Aramean influence following in the wake of the Neo-Assyrian imperial presence, although there were older astral ele-ments in Israelite religion (1998: 318). Keel and Uehlinger conclude: "The predominance of astral symbolism, accompanied by the decline in importance of the mediating, numi-nous protective powers, is probably connected to a growing need for a more direct rela-tionship with the eternal orders, a need that was in conflict with the concurrent revival of the old 'Canaanite' traditions" (1998: 318).

Keel and Uehlinger's work marks a completion in the shift of the terms of the debate. The discussion in the 1970s was pitched largely as an argument over Neo-Assyrian impe-rial imposition, although Cogan's work opened the door to what was an increasing trend in Holloway and then in Keel and Uehlinger, namely, the issue of more complex cultural influences in the wake of changes brought about by Neo-Assyrian *imperium*. This change in the terms of the debate is highy valuable, as researchers appeal to more complex models of change and influence. What is also evident from this review of the literature is how the scope of the lines of discussion, as well as the evidence under consideration, shapes the scope of analytical perspectives and conclusions. We may admire—justifiably—the range of textual evidence addressed by Holloway (1992) for the Iron II period or the range of iconographic resources marshaled by Keel and Uehlinger (1998). Indeed, one great advan-tage of the latter work is its longitudinal perspective, reaching from the Middle Bronze IIB period through the end of the Iron Age.

Yet, perhaps inevitably, in any given discussion, one resource slips through the cracks. The evidence in this case, specifically West Semitic textual evidence for the Late Bronze Age, when wedded to the already acknowledged and analyzed Iron Age textual evidence, would suggest a perspective quite at odds with the final conclusion in Keel and Uehlinger's remarks cited above. Specifically, one may take issue with Keel and Uehlinger's contrast between the new influx under the Neo-Assyrian *imperium*—which I do not question as such—and what they call "a need that was in conflict with the concurrent revival of the old 'Canaanite' traditions" (1998: 318). I would ask whether astralization was consonant with older West Semitic astral cult, including the older indigenous astral deities. Indeed, astral deities may have been part of the old West Semitic religious traditions, and these were always present, not revived as such. One may wonder if Keel and Uehlinger's reading of the evidence (including citations of biblical evidence) reinscribes the biblical traditions' own suppression of the older West Semitic astral religion.

Finally, the most recent entry into the discussion of West Semitic astral religion should be noted. Theuer (2000) addresses the history of lunar devotion in Syro-Palestinian religion, noting the Ugaritic evidence for the moon-god, as well an increase in lunar cult in Iron II Judah under Assyro-Aramean influence, in particular due to the moon cult of Haran. The approach taken in this work appears largely consistent with the model advocated in this paper.

With these issues as background, I wish to discuss some aspects of astral religion in West Semitic religion. My discussion proceeds in four brief parts: (1) El's astral family in the Ugaritic texts; (2) mythological allusions to astral religion in Israelite texts; (3) signs of displacement of astral religion in the Ugaritic texts; and (4) El and Yahweh in ancient Israel and the displacement of astral religion in Judah.

1. El's Astral Family in the Ugaritic Texts

In general, it may be said that the notion of the family serves as a basic feature (over and above the language of divine council) in developing a cohesive vision of religious reality. In Wyatt's apt formulation: "The image of the one family is a classic instance of systematic theology at work" (1992: 429). The immense importance that the patrimonial household holds for understanding both human and divine society in the Ugaritic texts has been underscored in a lucid discussion by Schloen (1995). At the end of his lengthy treatment of the patrimonial household in Ugarit, Schloen turns to the question of its mythology:

> Although little mention has so far been made of the well-known mythological texts from Ugarit, it is worth considering here briefly the structure of authority that is revealed in them. Of course, myths are often murky refractions rather than direct reflections of mundane social realities, but it is striking that a concern for the preservation of the patrilineage is prominent in the Epics of Keret and Aqhat. Furthermore, the household of the gods themselves has the appearance of a typical Near Eastern joint family, complete with rivalries among adult sons and daughters. In the Baal Cycle, a major theme is Baal's desire for a house of his own—as the eldest son and heir he is restless and unhappy under the direct supervision of the aging patriarch, El. The acquisition of his own house does not mean, however, that Baal is totally independent of El or wants to be his rival; indeed, his true rivals are members of his own generation—favorites of El such as Yamm and Mot who want to displace him as heir. (Schloen 1995: 399)

Here Schloen lays out the basic social paradigm for understanding the Ugaritic pantheon as a whole. The pantheon is a large multifamily or joint household headed by a patriarch with several competing sons. While older studies of Ugaritic religion and literature have recognized the language of the family in Ugaritic myths, its social background has perhaps not been equally appreciated. Since Schloen barely applies his own insight into the divine family (apart from CAT 1.12 and 1.23), the following discussion largely follows his lead in detailing the applicability of the patrimonial household to the presentation of divinity in Ugaritic texts (for details, see Smith 2001: 54–66, 67–80).

The four tiers of the pantheon correspond to different tiers of the divine household: the top two are occupied by the divine parents and their children, while the bottom two consist of deities working in the divine household (Smith 1984). El is the father of the deities and humanity. Accordingly, El's capacity as ruler of the pantheon is expressive of his function as patriarch of the family. His wife Athirat (biblical Asherah) is considered the mother of the deities and humanity. El and Athirat are the divine royal parents of the pantheon, and the dominant deities are generally regarded as their royal children. Beneath the family members is a third tier, the esteemed craftsman Kothar wa-Hasis, who serves the family. The fourth or lowest tier involves servant-gods, including messengers or what readers are accustomed to recognizing as angels. This household is the divine version of the royal household. Hence, the language of monarchy and family is fully integrated in the presentation of the divine family.

Beyond this general four-tier structure, it would appear that this family at times is understood as astral in character. This notion seems to be reflected in one text (CAT 1.101.3–5), which evidently lists "the assembly of the stars" in parallelism with "the sons of El":

which the sons of El do not know (?) . . .	[ ]*ḥ dlydʿ bn ʾil*
the assembly of the stars . . .	[ ]*pḥr kbbm*
the circle of those of heaven . . .	[ ]*dr dt šmm*

The evidence in this text is shaky, however, given the broken nature of the lines in question. Accordingly, the case that El's family is astral will require support from texts that mention El and astral deities. Many astral figures are worthy of consideration in this regard: Shahar and Shalim; Yarih; Shapshu, Athtar and Athtart; and Resheph.

A. Shahar, "Dawn," and Shalim, "Dusk," are El's two sons, according to CAT 1.23.

B. The moon-god Yarih is evidently identified as *nʿmn* [*ʾi*]*lm*, "the favorite of El," in CAT 1.24.25 (Theuer 2000). In 1.92.14–16, Athtart's hunt provides meat for El and Yarih, presumably as a member of the head god's household. Yarih participates in the meal in El's house in 1.114 (Keel 1998: 85 n. 13).

C. The sun-goddess Shapshu serves as El's special messenger according to CAT 1.6 VI. It should be noted further that the stars (*kbkbm knm*) are generally grouped after her in 1.23.54 (cf. *bt ʾilm kbkbm* in 1.43.2–3). Note also the blessing in 1.102.26–27 paralleling the sun and moon with El: *lymt špš wyrḫ wnʿmt šnt ʾil*. From these texts, it might be suggested that the sun, moon, and stars belong to El's family.

D. Athtar and Athtart seem also to belong to El's family, although in different texts. The Baal Cycle indicates that Athtar, unlike Baal, belongs to the family of El and Athirat (1.6 I). Athtart likewise seems to belong to El's family (see 1.92.14–16 and 1.114.10).

E. Resheph may be an astral figure. Dahood (1958: 86–87) and Fulco (1976: 38–40) have argued for the astralization of Resheph at Ugarit, based on the astronomical omen text, CAT 1.78: *bṯt ym ḥdṯ ḫyr ʿrbt špš tǵrh ršp*, "on day six (?) of the new moon (in the month) of Ḥyr, the Sun went down, with Resheph (= Mars?) as her gate-keeeper" (see

Fulco 1976: 39–40; for the text and interpretation, see also de Jong and van Soldt 1987–88; Pardee and Swerdlow 1993). If the identification of Resheph with Mars is correct, then the text provides evidence for the astral character of the god. However, this identification is not assured. It may be noted perhaps in support of Resheph's astral character that 1.107.40 pairs him with Yarih. Yet, it also remains unclear if Resheph belongs specifically to El's family.

Beyond the textual evidence we might appeal further to the iconographic record. Keel and Uehlinger have argued for a lunar presentation of El on a cylinder seal from Beth-shean (1998: 312; see also Keel 1998: 44). Brody has drawn attention to the astral features of Athirat's iconography as well (1998: 27). By the same token, the textual evidence for the astral character of El and Athirat is admittedly minimal. This paucity of information may be due to the fact that the family of El and Athirat was displaced by the Ugaritic cult of the storm-god Baal, who does not belong to that family, a point to which we will return shortly. In sum, it may be suggested with all due caution that the sun, moon, and stars were especially associated with El in West Semitic religion during the Late Bronze Age.

2. *Astral Religion in Israelite Texts*

The later religion of Israel may have known a cult of El that included a minimum number of these astral deities. Limits on the scope of this paper prevent a full-scale examination of the pertinent material, but some well-known biblical texts may illustrate the situation. El's astral family may underlie the divine question posed to Job in 38:6–7:

Who set its cornerstone
when the morning stars sang together
and all the divine beings [*bĕnê ʾĕlōhîm*] shouted for joy?

In the verse, Yahweh the creator-god (like old El?) asks Job if he was present when Yahweh set the cornerstone of the world's foundations, an ancient event celebrated by the divine beings, here specified as stars. In this passage, the morning stars are clearly parallel to *bĕnê ʾĕlōhîm*, and on the basis of this verse, Oldenburg (1970) connects the astral bodies with El. The god's astral association apparently lies behind the polemic in Isa 14:13 against the king of Babylon, who attempts to ascend into heaven and exalt his throne "above the stars of El" (*mimmaʿal lĕkôkĕbê-ʾēl*); it should be noted that Shahar is mentioned in the previous verse. The astral dimension of such a polemic against a foreign king perhaps lived on in the polemics directed against Antiochus IV Epiphanes in Dan 8:9–11: the "little horn" grew "even to the host of heaven" and cast some of them down.

Although they are not explicitly connected with El or Yahweh in Israelite religion, Sha-har and Shalim seem to continue. As mentioned above, Shahar is known from biblical literature by allusion to the myth of Shahar ben Helal, the fallen star (Isa 14:12). Shahar also appears as an element in Hebrew proper names. Shalim is attested sporadically in biblical literature, including in the form of proper names such as *ʾăbîšālōm* and those with *šlm* as the theophoric element in inscriptions from Arad, En-gedi, and Lachish (Tigay 1987: 164, 166). Given their earlier and later attestation as deities, the sun and moon also probably continued as deities at this stage.

As part of his identification with El, Yahweh continued the association with astral deities in the form of the "host of heaven," as noted by Halpern (1987: 94, 98; 1991: 81, 83–84) and Taylor (1993: 105–6, 258). According to this notion, Yahweh would appear as the great monarch over all his subjects, conceptualized at times as astral bodies. Taylor points to passages such as 1 Kgs 22:19 and Zeph 1:5 as evidence for the association of the host of heaven with the cult of Yahweh. 2 Kgs 21:5 mentions Manasseh's construction of "altars for all the host of heaven in the two courts in the house of Yahweh." Another text possibly associating the sun and moon as part of Yahweh's military host (or at least as subservient to Yahweh) is Josh 10:12. Joseph's dream, with the sun, moon, and stars bowing down to him in Gen 37:9, would also make good sense in this milieu (Lipiński 1995: 1449). All in all, these texts suffice to indicate popular Yahwistic astral devotion and belief. What is particularly important about the reference to the host of heaven with Yahweh in 1 Kgs 22:19 — if this text presupposes an astral notion of this heavenly host — is its date prior to the Neo-Assyrian *imperium*. Finally, it may be noted that Keel and Uehlinger have adduced a number of 7th-century seals depicting Yahweh possibly as "the celestial/lunar El" (1998: 312).

Perhaps as the last phase in the "career" of astral divinities in Israelite religion, biblical texts (e.g., Deut 4:19, 17:3) criticize astral deities within the cult of Yahweh under the rubric of the "sun, moon, and the stars." It is possible that the criticism represented by these prohibitions derived from a perceived threat of Neo-Assyrian astral cult during the Iron II period, but this does not diminish the indigenous character of the cultic devotion to the sun, moon, and stars.

3. Displacement of Astral Religion in the Ugaritic Texts

Let us return to the Ugaritic situation: the astral background of El's family versus Baal as a storm-god may lie at the root of Baal's status as an outsider to this family. This outsider status is expressed through the family metaphor in CAT 1.24.25–26, where the moon-god Yarih is called the "brother-in-law of Baal." The family metaphor can be extended to include outsider figures by use of the concept of a divine marriage between an insider deity and an outsider deity. Baal's own title, *bn dgn*, "son of Dagan" (CAT 1.2 I 19; 1.5 V 23–24), apparently points to his separate paternity from the rest of the divine family. Yet Baal can stereotypically refer to El as his father, since El is generically regarded as the father of the pantheon. When it appears that Baal is about to be permanently knocked out of the running as divine king, Athtar emerges as the nominee of El and Asherah for the throne.

If Athtar, unlike Baal, is an astral figure and full-fledged son of El, his conflict with Baal in the Baal Cycle may provide some insight into Baal and the divine family. The Ugaritic texts, as well as the most proximate comparative evidence from Emar, would suggest that Athtar was an astral deity who was considered a major warrior figure and associated with forms of precipitation other than the storm (Smith 1995). It has been suggested, for example, that Athtar was considered a god of irrigated soil because the Arabic noun cognate with his name bears this meaning (Gaster 1977: 128); other alternatives for Athtar at Ugarit, such as representing dew-fall, may be possible. The narratives of CAT 1.2 III and

1.6 I 63 stress that Athtar is not powerful enough to be king. In the Ugaritic texts, Athtar is rendered a weak god, perhaps a historical reflection of his cult's demise, perhaps at the hands of Baal's cult, as Caquot argues (1958: 55). Both were warrior-gods, but Baal was the divine patron of the Ugaritic dynasty. The geographical distribution of the cults of Baal and Athtar may clarify their status. The historical cult of Athtar may have been generally restricted to inland areas. Apart from the Ugaritic texts, there is no clear evidence for the cult of Athtar on the coast. As far as I am aware, Athtar receives no mention in Amarna letters from coastal sites, Egyptian sources mentioning West Semitic deities, the Bible, or Philo of Byblos; and the single Phoenician attestation is debatable (Smith 1995). In contrast, the cult of Baal is at home on the coast, which receives substantial rainfall. At Ugarit, for example, the rains occur over seven or eight months and exceed 800 mm a year. In contrast, at many of the inland locales where Athtar is attested, either dry farming or natural irrigation was practiced. It might be argued, then, that in the environment of Ugarit the god of the coastal storm would naturally supplant the god of lesser precipitation. Unfortunately, it is impossible to ground any further speculation regarding Baal and the family of El, but the picture we are left with involves a contrast between the astral family of El and Baal's role as warrior storm-god.

4. El and Yahweh in Ancient Israel and the Displacement of Astral Religion in Judah

The eventual identification of Yahweh and El within Israel perhaps had ramifications for the continuation of other deities as well. It has been argued that Asherah became the consort of Yahweh as a result of his identification with El (Olyan 1988). The history of astral deities in ancient Israel may have been affected by the identification of El and Yahweh. Perhaps originally associated with El, these astral deities became part of the divine assembly subordinate to Yahweh, and then the storm imagery associated with Yahweh came to dominate Israelite religious discourse, perhaps to the displacement of astral language. If El was the original god of Israel, then how did Yahweh come to be the chief god of Israel and identified with El? One may posit three hypothetical developments, not necessarily discrete in time or geography (for details, see van der Toorn 1996: 236–86; Smith 2001: 135–48):

A. El was the original god of early Israel. As noted by scholars, the name Israel would point to the first stage, as would some biblical references to El as a separate figure from the god who would emerge as Israel's national god (Genesis 49; Psalm 82).

B. El was the head of an early Israelite pantheon, with Yahweh as its warrior-god. Texts that mention both El and Yahweh, but not as the same figure (Genesis 49; Numbers 23–24; Psalm 82), suggest an early accommodation of the two in some early form of Israelite polytheism. If Psalm 82 reflects an early model of an Israelite polytheistic assembly, then El would have been its head, with the warrior Yahweh as a member of the second tier. Yet the same psalm also uses familial language: the other gods are said to be the "sons of the Most High." Accordingly, Yahweh might have been earlier understood as one of these sons.

C. El and Yahweh were identified as a single god. If El was the original god of Israel, then his merger with Yahweh took place at different rates in different parts of ancient

Israel. Many scholars place Judges 5 in the premonarchic period, and perhaps the cult of Yahweh spread further into the highlands of Israel in this period, infiltrating cult sites of El and accommodating to their El theologies. The references to El in Numbers 23–24 and perhaps in Job (5:17, 6:4, etc.) appear to be further indications of a separate survival of El's cult in Transjordan. Beyond this rather vaguely defined pattern of distribution, it is difficult to be more specific. Perhaps, then, as part of this identification, the storm-god Yahweh assimilates the astral mythology of El. By the same token, this astral mythology takes a back place to the more dominant imagery of the storm associated with the Israelite national god.

If the general outlines of this development hold some measure of validity, then one should suspect, following McKay (1973) and Cogan (1974), that astral religion in Iron II Judah did not involve imperial imposition; instead, it involved a long-standing indigenous practice, with some further Neo-Assyrian influence. Indeed, the political prestige and economic empire of the Neo-Assyrian *imperium* would suggest some indications of influence. Therefore, perhaps Cogan, as opposed to Taylor, is correct in seeing Neo-Assyrian influence behind "the horses of the sun" in 2 Kgs 23:11 (see also Keel and Uehlinger 1998: 158). By posing the discussion in these terms, one may suggest that some monarchs and people in Iron II Judah wedded traditional practices with newer Neo-Assyrian analogues. Indeed, one might well suspect that the appeal of things Neo-Assyrian lay not only in their prestige, but also in their capacity to be conformed to traditional Judean features. Such a model offers the most economical explanation for interpreting the Queen of Heaven with her *kawwānîm*, and it provides a suitable model for the apparent increase in astral representation in Iron II Judah (for iconography of Ishtar in the west, see Ornan 2001; for further pertinent archaeological evidence, see King and Stager 2001: 350). Neo-Assyrian influence then may hardly have been in conflict with older religious devotion. This situation was not unique to Iron II Judah; a similar situation, the cult of indigenous deities, survived at Philistine Ekron despite its vassal status (Gitin and Cogan 1999: 201–2). In Judah, what Keel and Uehlinger call its "old 'Canaanite' practices" may not have needed any revival. Instead, the extant evidence permits the conclusion that such practices were fully functional and not in opposition to Neo-Assyrian influence.

Conclusion

I would close with an afterthought that raises a highly speculative set of questions for both Iron I and Iron II religion in Israel. At present, the distribution of the evidence currently available may steer scholars to compare El or Baal with Yahweh and away from the very small hint that I would note here comparing the profiles of astral Athtar and Yahweh. Both gods of relatively arid zones, Athtar and Yahweh could have shared a set of characteristics more proximate than Baal and Yahweh, as is commonly supposed. Yahweh was originally a god in southern Edom (possibly in northwestern Saudi Arabia), as known by the biblical names of Edom, Midian, Teman, Paran, and Sinai (van der Toorn 1996: 281–86; Smith 2001: 135–48). This general area for old Yahwistic cult is attested not only in the Bible (Deut 33:2; Judg 5:4–5; Ps 68:9, 18; Hab 3:3) but also in inscriptional sources. Inscriptional evidence from Kuntillet ʿAjrûd also attests to "Yahweh of Teman." Indeed, the movement of Yahweh's cult from the southern climes of Edom/Sinai/Teman, vestigially attested in the above-cited poetic sources, could comport with a secondary assimilation of Yahweh to Baal, hence a massive coastal storm-god, just as Yahweh was secondarily assimilated at highland cult sites of El, such as Shechem, Shiloh, and Bethel (for details, see Smith 2001: 140–41). One might even take the extraordinary step of using Ginsberg's (1938) reading of Psalm 29 as originally a hymn to Baal, rewritten for Yahweh, as suggestive of this development.

This approach would suggest the following speculative theoretical possibilities for the field to consider: (1) at Ugarit, El's astral family was displaced by the cult of Baal; and (2) correspondingly in Israel, Yahweh was originally not a storm-god but a deity whose desert (and astral?) character may have been displaced by the coastal and highland religion of the storm-god presented early in biblical tradition as Israel's emerging national god. In other words, if the conflict between Baal and Athtar in the Ugaritic texts was paralleled later by a conflict between Baal and Yahweh, then the resolution of this religious conflict in the form of attributing coastal storm imagery to Yahweh might have obscured the profile that Yahweh could have shared with a figure such as Athtar, including any astral association. In conclusion, Iron II Judah witnessed a general development, and then displacement, of old traditional religious features. This dislocation, in the form of biblical criticisms of astral deities, may have obscured not only astral religion in general, but also the possible astral features of Yahweh; and in turn, this Iron II displacement has perhaps been reinscribed in modern scholarly accounts. These final comments are offered less with the conviction that they hold certitude and more with the hope that they might contribute toward further efforts to scrutinize the record of ancient Israelite religion. In the end, it does seem evident that many biblical sources reflect secondary developments in Israelite religion generally and in the history of Yahweh's profile specifically. As a result, scholarly investigation of Israelite religion must reckon with the distinct possibility that the original profile of the biblical god, at least in part, may be irretrievably lost.

References

Ackerman, S.
    1992   *Under Every Green Tree: Popular Religion in Sixth-Century Judah*. Harvard Semitic Monographs 46. Atlanta: Scholars Press.

Brody, A. J.
    1998   *"Each Man Cried Out to His God": The Specialized Religion of Canaanite and Phoenician Seafarers*. Harvard Semitic Monographs 58. Atlanta: Scholars Press.

Caquot, A.
    1958   Le dieu ʿAthtar et les textes de Ras Shamra. *Syria* 35: 45–60.

CAT
    1995   *The Cuneiform Alphabetic Texts from Ugarit, Ras ibn Hani and Other Places*, ed. M. Dietrich, O. Loretz, and J. Sanmartín. Abhandlungen zur Literatur Alt-Syriens-Palästinas und Mesopotamiens 8. Münster: Ugarit-Verlag. [KTU 2nd ed.]

Cogan, M.
    1974   *Imperialism and Religion: Assyria, Judah and Israel in the Eighth and Seventh Centuries B.C.E.* Society of Biblical Literature Monographs 19. Missoula, Mont.: Scholars Press.

    1993   Judah under Assyrian Hegemony: A Reexamination of *Imperialism and Religion*. *Journal of Biblical Literature* 112: 403–14.

Dahood, M. J.
 1958 Ancient Semitic Deities in Syria and Palestine. Pp. 65–94 in *Le antiche divinità semitiche*, ed. S. Moscati. Studi semitici 1. Rome: Centro di studi semitici.

Frankenstein, S.
 1979 The Phoenicians in the Far West: A Function of Neo-Assyrian Imperialism. Pp. 269–91 in *Power and Propaganda*, ed. M. T. Larsen. Copenhagen: Akademisk Forlag.

Fulco, W. J.
 1976 *The Canaanite God Rešep*. American Oriental Series Essay 8. New Haven, Conn.: American Oriental Society.

Gaster, T. H.
 1977 *Thespis: Ritual, Myth, and Drama in the Ancient Near East*. New York: Norton.

Ginsberg, H. L.
 1938 A Phoenician Hymn in the Psalter. Pp. 472–76 in *Atti del XIX Congresso Internazionale degli Orientalisti, Roma, 23–29 Settembre, 1935-XIII*. Rome: Tipografia del Senato.

Gitin, S.
 1989 Tel Miqne-Ekron: A Type Site for the Inner Coastal Plain in the Iron II Period. Pp. 23–58 in *Recent Excavations in Israel: Studies in Iron Age Archaeology*, ed. S. Gitin and W. G. Dever. Annual of the American Schools of Oriental Research 49. Winona Lake, Ind.: Eisenbrauns.

 1992 New Incense Altars from Ekron: Context, Typology and Function. Pp. 43*–49* in *Eretz-Israel* 23 (Avraham Biran volume), ed. E. Stern and T. Levi. Jerusalem: Israel Exploration Society.

 1995 Tel Miqne-Ekron in the 7th Century B.C.E.: The Impact of Economic Innovation and Foreign Cultural Influences on a Neo-Assyrian Vassal City-State. Pp. 61–79 in *Recent Excavations in Israel: A View to the West. Reports on Kabri, Nami, Miqne-Ekron, Dor and Ashkelon*, ed. S. Gitin. Archaeological Institute of America Colloquia and Conference Papers 1. Dubuque, Ia.: Archaeological Institute of America.

Gitin, S., and Cogan, M.
 1999 A New Type of Dedicatory Inscription from Ekron. *Israel Exploration Journal* 49: 193–202.

Held, M.
 1982 Studies in Biblical Lexicography in the Light of Akkadian. Pp. 76–85 in *Eretz-Israel* 16 (Harry M. Orlinsky volume), ed. B. A. Levine and A. Malamat. Jerusalem: Israel Exploration Society.

Halpern, B.
 1987 "Brisker Pipes than Poetry": The Development of Israelite Monotheism. Pp. 77–115 in *Judaic Perspectives on Ancient Israel*, ed. J. Neusner, B. A. Levine, and E. S. Frerichs. Philadelphia: Fortress.

 1991 Jerusalem and the Lineages in the Seventh Century BCE: Kinship and the Rise of Individual Moral Liability. Pp. 11–107 in *Law and Ideology in Monarchic Israel*, ed. B. Halpern and D. W. Hobson. Journal for the Study of the Old Testament Supplements 124. Sheffield: Sheffield Academic Press.

Holloway, S. W.
 1992 *The Case for Assyrian Religious Influence in Israel and Judah: Inference and Evidence*. Vol. 1. Ph.D. dissertation, University of Chicago.

Jong, T. de, and van Soldt, W. H.
 1987–88 Redating an Early Solar Eclipse Record (KTU 1.78): Implications for the Ugaritic Calendar and for the Secular Accelerations of the Earth and the Moon. *Jaarbericht van het Vooraziatisch-Egyptisch Gezelschap (Genootschap) Ex Oriente Lux* 30: 65–77.

Keel, O.
   1998   *Goddesses and Trees, New Moon, and Yahweh: Ancient Near Eastern Art and the Hebrew Bible.*
           Journal for the Study of the Old Testament Supplements 261. Sheffield: Sheffield Aca-
           demic Press.
Keel, O., and Uehlinger, C.
   1998   *Gods, Goddesses, and Images of God in Ancient Israel,* trans. T. H. Trapp. Minneapolis:
           Fortress.
King, P. J., and Stager, L. E.
   2001   *Life in Biblical Israel.* Library of Ancient Israel. Louisville: Westminster John Knox.
Lipiński, E.
   1995   Shemesh. Pp. 1445–52 in *Dictionary of Deities and Demons in the Bible,* ed. K. van der Toorn,
           B. Becking, and P. W. van der Horst. Leiden: Brill. [*DDD*]
McKay, J. W.
   1973   *Religion in Judah under the Assyrians.* Studies in Biblical Theology 2/26. Naperville, Ill.:
           Allenson.
Oldenburg, U.
   1970   Above the Stars of El: El in South Arabic Religion. *Zeitschrift für die alttestamentliche Wis-
           senschaft* 82: 187–208.
Olyan, S. M.
   1987   Some Observations concerning the Identity of the Queen of Heaven. *Ugarit-Forschungen*
           19: 161–74.
   1988   *Asherah and the Cult of Yahweh.* Society of Biblical Literature Monographs 34. Atlanta:
           Scholars Press.
Ornan, T.
   2001   Istar as Depicted on Finds from Israel. Pp. 235–56 in *Studies in the Archaeology of the Iron
           Age in Israel and Jordan,* ed. A. Mazar. Journal for the Study of the Old Testament Supple-
           ments 331. Sheffield: Sheffield Academic Press.
Pardee, D., and Swerdlow, N.
   1993   Not the Earliest Solar Eclipse. *Nature* 363: 406.
Schloen, J. D.
   1995   *The Patrimonial Household in the Kingdom of Ugarit: A Weberian Analysis of Ancient Near
           Eastern Society.* Ph.D. dissertation, Harvard University.
Smith, M. S.
   1984   Divine Travel as a Token of Divine Rank. *Ugarit-Forschungen* 16: 397.
   1990   The Near Eastern Background of Solar Language for Yahweh. *Journal of Biblical Litera-
           ture* 109: 29–39.
   1995   The God Athtar in the Ancient Near East and His Place in KTU 1.6 I. Pp. 627–40 in
           *Solving Riddles and Untying Knots: Biblical, Epigraphic, and Semitic Studies in Honor of Jonas
           C. Greenfield,* ed. Z. Zevit, S. Gitin, and M. Sokoloff. Winona Lake, Ind.: Eisenbrauns.
   2001   *The Origins of Biblical Monotheism: Israel's Polytheistic Background and the Ugaritic Texts.* Ox-
           ford: Oxford University Press.
Spieckermann, H.
   1982   *Juda unter Assur in der Sargonidenzeit.* Forschungen zur Religion und Literatur des Alten
           und Neuen Testaments 129. Göttingen: Vandenhoeck & Ruprecht.
Stähli, H. P.
   1985   *Solare Elemente im Jahwesglauben des Alten Testaments.* Orbis Biblicus et Orientalis 66.
           Freiburg: Universitätsverlag.
Taylor, J. G.
   1993   *Yahweh and the Sun: Biblical and Archaeological Evidence for Sun Worship in Ancient Israel.*
           Journal for the Study of the Old Testament Supplements 111. Sheffield: Sheffield Aca-
           demic Press.

Theuer, G.

 2000   *Der Mondgott in den Religionen Syrien-Palästinas unter besonderer Berücksichtigung von KTU 1.24.* Orbis Biblicus et Orientalis 173. Freiburg: Universitätsverlag.

Toorn, K. van der

 1996   *Family Religion in Babylonia, Syria and Israel: Continuity and Change in the Forms of Religious Life.* Studies in the History and Culture of the Ancient Near East 7. Leiden: Brill.

Wyatt, N.

 1992   Baal, Dagan, and Fred: A Rejoinder. *Ugarit-Forschungen* 24: 428–30.

Israelite and Philistine Cult and the
Archaeological Record in Iron Age II:
The "Smoking Gun" Phenomenon

Seymour Gitin
W. F. Albright Institute of Archaeological Research
Jerusalem

Religious practices of ancient Israel and its neighbors have been a major focus of archaeological research in this country since the early part of the last century. In their classic treatments of the subject, May (1935), Albright (1956), and de Vaux (1965), among others, relied heavily on archaeological evidence interpreted within the broader context of ancient Near Eastern cultic tradition. In some cases, archaeological data were also employed to test the authenticity of biblical religious practices. For example, since the 1920s, the four-horned altars found in Iron Age II Israelite archaeological contexts, which fit the description of the four-horned incense altars in the Hebrew Bible, have been used by some scholars to demonstrate the validity of the practice of burning incense as cited in the biblical text. This paralleling of text and artifact provided support for the early dating of the Priestly (P) code, to which such practices are ascribed in the Bible (Wiener 1927: 1–22). It also was used to refute the claim that the burning of incense and other biblical cultic activities did not represent authentic early Israelite religious practice, but were only introduced in the postbiblical period (Wiener 1927: 23–31).[1]

Recently, however, a more comprehensive approach to the use of archaeological data in the study of biblical religious practice has shifted the emphasis from the limited agenda of drawing parallels between artifacts and text descriptions of cultic praxis to one that is more issue oriented. This has been primarily the result of the impact of a greatly expanded Iron Age II archaeological record with dramatic new finds that highlight the unique character of Israelite and Philistine religious practice.

An example of this new issue-oriented agenda that has drastically affected our understanding of the early development of monotheism is the controversy over whether or not a goddess was worshiped alongside Yahweh, perhaps as his consort. What initiated this widely discussed issue was the inscription uncovered by Dever during the 1967 salvage excavations of an 8th–7th century Judean bench tomb at Khirbet el-Qôm (1970: 159). Lemaire (1977: 599), Naveh (1979: 28), and others read one phrase of this inscription as

---

Author's note: The plans in figs. 1 and 6 are by J. Rosenberg; the artist's rendition in fig. 2 is by Balage Balogh; the photo in fig. 3 is by Z. Radovan; the drawing of the figurine in fig. 4 is by M. Zeltzer, of the inscriptions in figs. 5, 7a, 7b, 8a, and 8b are by A. Yardeni, and of the altars in fig. 9 are by E. Cohen, S. Halbreich, and M. Zeltzer.

1. For a fuller discussion of this issue, see Gitin 1989: 53*, 58*.

"Yahweh and his Asherah."[2] Further fuel was added to this discussion in the mid-1970s, when Meshel's excavations at Kuntillet ʿAjrûd, a caravanserai in Sinai dated to the first half of the 8th century B.C.E., produced paintings and inscriptions on two large storage jars. A line in one inscription ends with the words "to Yahweh of Samaria and his Asherah" (Meshel 1978: above pl. 9). For decades, the interpretation of "Yahweh and his Asherah" in the Khirbet el-Qôm and Kuntillet ʿAjrûd inscriptions has generated a lively debate over the monotheistic and polytheistic aspects of ancient Israelite religion, resulting in an extensive literature, in which a number of scholars have offered different interpretations of the word *asherah* as signifying a goddess, a cult object symbolizing the deity, or the consort of Yahweh.[3] This debate over the interpretation and the role of Asherah has far-reaching implications not only for understanding monotheism in early Israelite religion but also for the study of Philistine religion. Two storage-jar inscriptions from Tel Miqne–Ekron that read "dedicated to [or for] Asherat," found in Temple Auxiliary Building 654, indicate that this goddess was also worshiped by the Philistines (Gitin 1993: 251–54). It is logical to assume that the contents of the storage jars on which these inscriptions were found were intended for a goddess and not for her symbol—for example, a pole.

Another example of a more issue-oriented agenda is the question of whether or not monolatry existed in the religion of preexilic Israel; that is, whether or not other gods were recognized but not necessarily worshiped, as in polytheism. This question was examined in a groundbreaking study by Tigay (1986), who analyzed more than 1,200 Israelite and Judean personal names and their theophoric, that is, Yahwistic, and non-Yahwistic elements that are documented in Iron Age II inscriptions. Assuming that this type of data would reflect the Israelite religious worship system, Tigay concludes "that the evidence currently available makes it very difficult to suppose that many Israelites worshipped gods other than YHWH" (1986: 41). This conclusion is significant in and of itself, despite the innate bias in Tigay's sample created by the "accidental nature of the epigraphic discoveries" (Millard 1991: 225). What is most pertinent to the current discussion, however, is Tigay's pioneering effort in using the empirical method based on the archaeological record, which has both broadened and enhanced the discussion of Israelite religion.

These two examples demonstrate how an expanded archaeological record has helped to advance the development of an issue-oriented approach to the study of the religion of ancient Israel. Until recently, however, the use of archaeological evidence has been limited mostly to epigraphic evidence, and only to the inscriptions and ostraca that are generally considered relevant to the primary arena of discussion—that is, the literature of biblical scholarship.

This situation, however, has begun to change, albeit only to a limited extent, as some text scholars have come to use archaeological material culture as a source of evidence upon which to base the discussion of a wide range of cultic issues. In the past decade, for instance, aniconism has developed into a major concern of students of ancient Israelite religion, primarily due to the publication of Mettinger's in-depth study (1995). Aniconism involves the visual representation of a deity without pictorial, human, or animal images, as opposed to idolatry, with the deity seen as an object with a divine image or symbol.

---

2. A reappraisal of the evidence appears in Dever 1999.
3. For the most up-to-date discussion, see Zevit 2001: 400–405.

Mettinger, an Old Testament scholar, assembled the archaeological evidence of aniconic cult objects, mostly represented by *maṣṣebot,* that is, standing stones, or pillars, often referred to as *betyls,* "houses of gods," like the Hebrew *bêt-ēl* (Mettinger 1995: 35, 111). Two of his conclusions have greatly expanded the parameters of the debate on the use of cultic objects in biblical ritual, both developed largely on the basis of groups of standing stones from dozens of prehistorics sites documented and excavated by Avner in the Sinai and the Negev (Avner 1993: 166–81). For Mettinger, this material demonstrates that aniconism had a history of thousands of years, indicating a long local tradition, which, he suggests, was valid until the end of the 8th century B.C.E., prior to the reign of the Judean King Hezekiah. From this, Mettinger further concludes that the prohibitions in the Bible against the worship of *maṣṣebot,* for example, must therefore be a late phenomenon (1995: 25–26). In support of his suggestion that the long tradition of aniconism lasted through most of the Iron Age, he brings the evidence of *maṣṣebot* from Arad, Dan, and many other sites (1995: 135–90).

By establishing the deep roots of aniconism in early West Semitic cultic tradition, which continue through the Iron Age, Mettinger (1997: 197) has also provided new evidence to address the claims of the "minimalist school" regarding the lateness of Israelite cultic praxis. His rebuttal of the claim that the origins of Israelite religious traditions are to be found, not as indicated in the Bible, but much later—perhaps as late as the Hellenistic period—adds another dimension to Mettinger's use of the archaeological record and further extends his impact on the study of ancient Israelite religion. Although Mettinger's presentation and methodology have been challenged by some scholars, who raise questions about his uneven and incomplete discussion (e.g., Lewis 1998: 36), this does not diminish the significance of his research.

The archaeological data in support of aniconism also demonstrate a dichotomy that is basic to another major issue regarding ancient Israelite religion: that is, whether different cultic systems coexisted in the biblical period. Mettinger's "material aniconism," defined as employing symbols like *maṣṣebot* (1995: 24), seems to have been practiced in peripheral areas, in the villages and countryside of Judah (1995: 143–91). This must have occurred concurrently with the practice of "empty space aniconism" in Jerusalem, represented by the use of the cherubim throne in the Solomonic Temple, which held no idol or image of a deity (Mettinger 1995: 139). Thus, two different cultic systems were employed at the same time, the evidence of which could just as easily be used to indicate the presence of "official" and "folk" or of "centralized" and "decentralized" worship systems.[4]

Another indication that text scholars are referring increasingly to material culture can be seen in the use of iconographic data. The best example is the work of the "Fribourg school" led by Keel and Uehlinger (1998). Their main goal is to show that iconographic evidence, based on a sample of 8,500 stamp seals, including a large number that are contemporaneous with the biblical period, represents an authentic witness to cultic practice (1998: 10). In the process, they also discuss a wide range of other iconographic artifacts, including figurines, plaques, and inscribed objects. The growing impact of iconographic

---

4. Evidence of such a dual worship system is attested at Ekron by the disparate character and diffuse distribution of four-horned incense altars as opposed to the central location of the Ekron sanctuary and its assumed priestly support system (Gitin 2002: 113–14).

data is also well represented in a volume edited by van der Toorn (1997), which provides an extensive treatment of archaeological evidence as it applies to the study of the role of the divine image in the biblical world. It includes seminal studies by biblical and other text scholars on, inter alia, Yahweh's cult statue (Niehr 1997), anthropomorphic cult statuary (Uehlinger 1997), and aniconism (Hendel 1997). Perhaps the most extensive treatment of archaeological cultic data by a biblical scholar is Zevit's tour de force (2001), in which Zevit relates the direct archaeological witness of cultic inscriptions, architecture, installations, and artifacts such as incense altars to the biblical text.

Although the above examples indicate the growing awareness of text scholars of the value of material culture for the study of Israelite religion, archaeological evidence has not yet had a significant impact on the field of biblical and religious studies. The anepigraphic data—that is, the architecture, installations, altars, statuary, figurines, chalices, astragali, bones, seeds, and so on—which constitute 99% of the archaeological record are, with but a few exceptions, rarely considered by biblical scholars. Current biblical scholarship for the most part has not integrated archaeological evidence into its examination of religious practices, turning its attention instead to the study of form and literary criticism. This reaction can partly be attributed to a reaction to the overemphasis on biblical archaeology in the pre– and post–World War II period, when Albright and his students dominated biblical scholarship.[5] Also, the new direction that archaeology has taken in recent years, with its emphasis on a more anthropological, theory-based approach and the publication of more technical reports, has tended to take the "story" out of history and consequently has produced little of interest for text scholars and historians. To some degree, the negative attitude of biblical scholars toward archaeology has also been prompted by the position of the minimalist school, which all but denies archaeology a role in understanding the past. The minimalists' position that only documents contemporary with the biblical period can be used to write the history of that period, while they deny the existence of such documents, places them squarely in the camp of postmodernist philosophy, which maintains that true history cannot be written; only an impression of what history was can be written. This certainly denies archaeology any role in defining ancient Israelite and Philistine cult.[6]

While these are contributing factors, perhaps the main reason for the lack of a broader acceptance of the archaeological record by text scholars is the perceived failure of biblical archaeology to deliver a "smoking gun." Archaeologists and biblical scholars alike recognize this lack of decisive confirmation—that is, the absence of a direct witness or proof of cultic activity. For example, in a comprehensive and pragmatic evaluation of the archaeological data relating to early Israelite cult, Dever concludes that "while the 'external evidence' of archaeology may have enhanced our perception of the value of the biblical sources for understanding both Israelite history and theology, it has not proportionally given us an independent and direct witness to the ancient cult" (1987: 217). Thus, he acknowledges an inherent weakness in the archaeological evidence, namely, its speculative character and, by implication, its inability to convince biblical or other text scholars

---

5. An analysis of the impact of the approach of Albright and his students on biblical studies appears in Gitin 2003.

6. For the most recent review of the minimalist literature, see Dever 2001: 23–52.

to consider material culture as a reliable source for their study of the religion of ancient Israel. From the point of view of biblical scholars, Freedman puts the case as follows in an evaluation of the impact of Albright's scholarship: the lack of a "smoking gun," that is, a decisive confirmation of or confrontation with specific biblical events, is the reason that archaeological evidence carries no real weight in the discussion of biblical cultic practices (1989: 40).

The "smoking gun" is undoubtedly an essential criterion for evaluating and authenticating biblical religious practice. Considering it the only criterion, however, in effect eliminates the category of evidence of visible religion—that is, facts in context. Such facts, including the epigraphic and iconographic evidence cited above, would also be contemporary with and provide a direct link to the physical and cultural environment in which cultic objects are found and thus serve as an authentic witness to biblical cult. They also would reflect the ancient context more closely than a document, which may have been committed to writing hundreds of years after the fact and/or edited with a cultural tendenz. Considering the "smoking gun" as the only valid criterion would also deny another relevant category of evidence created when there is a convergence of the texts and the material culture data, especially when extrabiblical sources can be directly related to artifacts in situ.

The somewhat negative view of archaeology held by the current generation of biblical scholars, which has drastically limited the study of Israelite religion, has not yet affected the study of Philistine cult, for which reliable archaeological data first began to appear only in the 1970s, with the excavations at Ashdod (M. Dothan 1993) and Tell Qasile (Mazar 1993). Consequently, Philistine cultic practice became a subject of serious archaeological study only in the last one and one-half decades of the 20th century. By then, the Albright Institute / Hebrew University's joint excavation project at Tel Miqne–Ekron, directed by T. Dothan and S. Gitin, had produced a sufficient mass of data to form the basis for a well-documented study of Philistine cultic practice for both the Iron I and Iron II periods.[7] My essay addresses the late Iron II evidence—that is, from the 7th century B.C.E. city of the late Philistine period.

Ekron (Tel Miqne), founded in the 12th century B.C.E. by the "Sea Peoples"/Philistines as one of five capital cities, achieved the zenith of its physical and economic growth during the 7th century B.C.E., during the last chapter of its history. In this period, Ekron became an international commercial entrepôt, as it developed into the largest industrial center for the production of olive oil known to date in the ancient Near East, and the excavations of the city yielded a wide variety of epigraphic and anepigraphic cultic assemblages.[8] This evidence, which includes three prime categories of data—a "smoking gun," artifacts in contexts, and a convergence of texts and material culture—for the most part came from the sanctuary in the west wing of Temple Complex 650 and from the adjacent Temple Auxiliary Building 654 in the elite zone.

---

7. The major Iron I cultic features at Ekron are discussed in T. Dothan's essay in this volume. The major Iron II cultic evidence has previously been published in a number of special studies, including Gitin 1989; 1993; 2002; Gitin, Dothan, and Naveh 1997; Gitin and Cogan 1999.

8. For the latest reports on the Tel Miqne–Ekron excavations, see T. Dothan and Gitin 1993; Gitin, Dothan, and Naveh 1997.

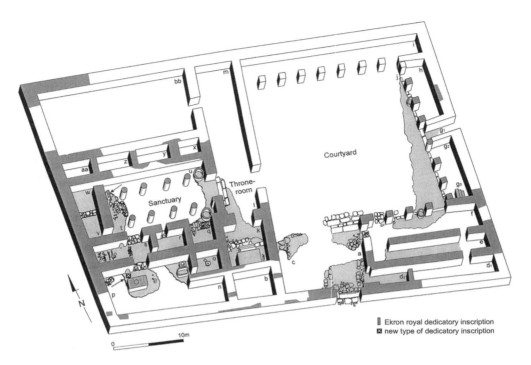

Fig. 1. Tel Miqne–Ekron: Plan of Temple Complex 650, Field IV, Strata IC–IB, 7th century B.C.E. *(revised version of plan published in Gitin and Cogan 1999: 195).*

The monumental Temple Complex 650 (ca. 57 × 43 m) is one of the largest such buildings excavated in Israel (fig. 1). Its plan, unique in the Levant, is based on a Neo-Assyrian architectural design concept, with three primary components: an east wing composed of a large, square-shaped, open courtyard (fig. 1: room j) with rooms built around it; a long, narrow, rectangular-shaped throne room or reception hall in the center (fig. 1: rooms k, l, m), which at one end had a platform or throne with steps leading up to it (fig. 1: room k); and a large west wing with a temple (fig. 1: rooms n–bb). As in Neo-Assyrian-type monumental buildings, the throne room served as a buffer between the east and west wings (Gitin, Dothan, and Naveh 1997: 3–7). The most important architectural feature of Temple Complex 650 and the main component of its west wing is the rectangular-shaped temple with a monumental stepped-stone threshold (fig. 2). The hall of the temple was lined with two parallel rows of four column bases (fig. 1: room u). A raised cella stood at the far end (fig. 1: room t), behind which were two storage areas (fig. 1: rooms v, w), and there were eleven rooms on three sides of the building (fig. 1: rooms n–s, x–aa). The plan of the pillared temple reflects a Phoenician design, paralleled, for example, in the Astarte temple at Kition on Cyprus (Karageorghis 1974: 24–25).

The excavations of the temple or pillared sanctuary of Temple Complex 650 produced the "smoking gun," namely, the Ekron royal dedicatory inscription (fig. 3). It is the most important artifact uncovered in the 14 excavation seasons at the site and one of the most significant finds excavated in Israel in the 20th century (Gitin, Dothan, and Naveh

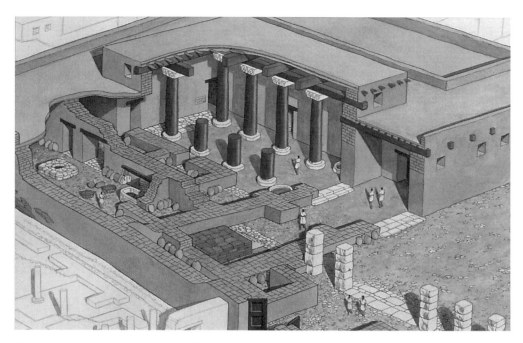

Fig. 2. Artist's rendition of temple/pillared sanctuary within Temple Complex 650.

Fig. 3. Ekron royal dedicatory inscription.

1997: 1). The inscription, incised on a block of limestone weighing more 150 kg, is complete, and contains 5 lines and 72 letters. It reads: "The temple which he built, *ʾkys* [Achish, Ikausu] son of Padi, son of *Ysd*, son of Ada, son of Yaʿir, ruler of Ekron, for *Ptgyh* his lady. May she bless him, and protect him and prolong his days, and bless his land" (Gitin, Dothan, and Naveh 1997: 9–10).[9]

Combining the attributes of both a "smoking gun" and an artifact in context, the inscription is an authentic witness of Philistine cult. The Philistine (Aegean) character of the inscription is attested by the non-Semitic name of the king, Ikausu, who, according to the inscription, built the temple in which the inscription was found. The name *Ikausu* is related to the word *Achaean*, meaning "Greek," which accords with the generally held view that the Philistines came from the Aegean (Gitin, Dothan, and Naveh 1997: 11); its Hebrew version, Achish, occurs as the name of a Philistine king in the Bible (Naveh 1998). Furthermore, the name of the city ruled by Ikausu is given as Ekron, which is known from the Bible as one of the capitals of the Philistine pentapolis (1 Sam 6:17). It also appears in the Neo-Assyrian Annals in the context of Assyria's relations with the city-states of *Palastu* (Philistia; Pritchard 1969: 287–88, 291, 294). As for cultic activity, this is evident from the fact that the inscription was found in a temple, defined as such architecturally, that contained cultic installations and objects. The Philistine character of that cultic practice is indicated by the non-Semitic name of the goddess, *Ptgyh*, to whom Ikausu dedicates the temple. *Ptgyh* has been associated with the sanctuary at Delphi known as Pytho, the shrine of Gaia, the Mycenaean mother-goddess (Schäfer-Lichtenberger 2000), which fits well with the Aegean origins of the Philistines. Phoenician or West Semitic traditions are also reflected in the inscription's language and formulaic blessings (Gitin, Dothan, and Naveh 1997: 11–15).

The inscription is also a prime example of the convergence of artifact and text, providing an indisputable chronological correlation that dates the inscription and the construction of the sanctuary in which it was found to the first quarter of the 7th century. Two of the five names of city's rulers mentioned in the inscription—Padi and Ikausu—appear in the Neo-Assyrian Annals as kings of *ʾamqar(r)ūna*, that is, Ekron, an Assyrian vassal city-state in the 7th century B.C.E. (Gitin 1995: 62). Padi is known from the Annals of Sennacherib in the context of the Assyrian king's 701 B.C.E. campaign, at the end of which he gave the towns of the defeated Judean King Hezekiah to Padi and others (Pritchard 1969: 287–88). Padi is also cited in a docket dated to 699 B.C.E., according to which he delivered a light talent of silver to Sennacherib (Fales and Postgate 1995: 21–22). lkausu is listed as one of the 12 coastal kings who transported building materials to Nineveh for the palace of Esarhaddon (680–669 B.C.E.), and his name also appears in a list of kings who participated in Ashurbanipal's first campaign against Egypt in 667 B.C.E. (Pritchard 1969: 291, 294). The final phase of the Ekron temple is dated by the massive destruction layer that sealed the inscription and the cella of the sanctuary in which it was found, which is attributed to the Neo-Babylonian King Nebuchadnezzar's campaign to Philistia in 604 B.C.E. (Gitin 1998: 276 n. 2). The stratigraphic certainty of the inscription found in situ in a securely defined

---

9. Italics indicate that the pronunciation of a name is uncertain; the reading of the name Achish is based on its occurrence in the Hebrew Bible and of Ikausu in the Assyrian texts.

Fig. 4. Phoenician-type female figurine found in the pillared sanctuary of Temple Complex 650.

archaeological context within a datable destruction level is the clinching piece of evidence that confirms the inscription's "smoking gun" and artifact-in-context attributes.

Late-7th-century Ekron also produced other cultic artifacts in context sealed by the 604 B.C.E. destruction debris. Among the main examples are a figurine, several inscriptions, and a number of four-horned incense altars, which further expand the profile of late Philistine cult. Because these examples also represent foreign cultural traits, they demonstrate the extent to which such influences were adopted by and absorbed into the Philistine worship system, and are therefore a good measure of how far the process of acculturation had progressed by the 7th century B.C.E.

One of the most important of the anepigraphic artifacts, found in the cella of the temple (fig. 1: room t), is a Phoenician-type female figurine (fig. 4). It is the only figurine known to have been found in a temple or other independently defined cultic context in the Levant, and could possibly represent the image of the goddess of the temple. Similar figurines have been found throughout the Mediterranean basin, for example at Carthage, Motya, and Tharros (Acquaro 1988: 623, nos. 234–35; Ciasca 1988: 358, 363), and on Cyprus (Gjerstad 1937: pl. 203:3).

Fig. 5. New type of dedicatory inscription from Ekron (facsimile drawing).

Another example is the new type of dedicatory inscription represented by two words incised on the side of a storage jar (fig. 5) found in one of the southern side rooms of the temple (fig. 1: room p). The cultic character of the room is defined by its unique assemblage of cultic installations and artifacts. These include, among others, the only olive oil installation found in situ outside the olive oil industrial zone (fig. 1: room p), which was probably used to produce sacred oil for temple rituals, and three ivory pieces, apparently parts of a large Egyptian musical instrument often depicted in scenes of temple worship (Gitin and Cogan 1999: 196). The inscription reads *lbʿl wlpdy*, "for Baʿal and for Padi," that is, "for god and king." Baʿal, known in the Bible as the chief adversary of Yahweh, was the fertility- and storm-god in the Canaanite and Phoenician pantheons (Gitin and Cogan 1999: 196–97). Padi, as mentioned above, was a king of Ekron. The "for god and king" formula itself emulates the Assryian phraseology "to revere god and king," indicating the responsibility of a citizen to pay cultic taxes and to perform crown services (Gitin and Cogan 1999: 197–98). This inscription adds to our knowledge of Philistine cultic praxis by providing evidence that the West Semitic deity, Baʿal, was one of the gods in the Philistine

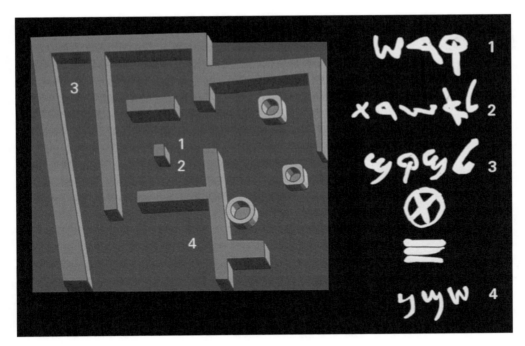

Fig. 6. Ekron, Field IV Temple Auxiliary Building 654.

pantheon and by implying the existence of a Philistine priesthood to which cultic taxes were paid.

Equally significant storage-jar inscriptions written in ink, which are also cultic artifacts in context, came from Temple Auxiliary Building 654 (fig. 6), located in a complex of auxiliary buildings immediately south of Temple Complex 650. One of the inscriptions was composed of two words, *qdš* on one side of the jar (fig. 7a) and *l'srt* on the other (fig. 7b), that is, "dedicated to [or for] Asherat," showing, as mentioned above, that the West Semitic or Canaanite goddess Asherat was worshiped at Ekron (Zevit 2001: 402). The spelling and the writing of the goddess's name are Phoenician (Gitin 1993: 250, 257 n. 37). Another inscription includes the word *lmkm* (fig. 8a), which in Phoenician and occasionally in Biblical Hebrew means "for the shrine" (Levine 1997: 248; Vanderhooft 1999: 628–30). The same vessel bears the sign of a *tet*, which may indicate that the contents of the jar were set aside as a tithe. Under the sign are three horizontal lines, representing 30 units in the Phoenician numbering system (Gitin 1993: 251) (fig. 8b).[10] This inscription indicates that there was a shrine or temple at Ekron to which offerings were brought, as well as supporting the existence of a priesthood, as suggested by the *lb'l wlpdy* inscription.

One of the dominant cultic artifacts at Ekron is the four-horned incense altar, 6 of which were found in the Temple Auxiliary buildings in the elite zone, 2 each in Buildings

---

10. Other inscriptions contain additional occurrences of *qdš* and *l'šrt*, as well as the word *šmn*, "olive oil" (Gitin 1993: 250, 252).

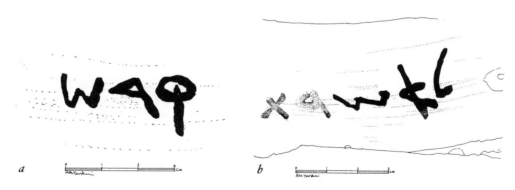

Fig. 7. a. qdš *inscription; b.* l'šrt *inscription.*

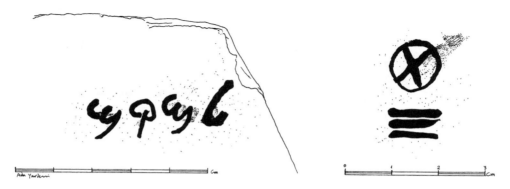

Fig. 8. a. lmqm *inscription; b. inscription of* ṭet *and three horizontal lines.*

651, 653, and 654. Another 2 came from the domestic zone and 9 from the olive oil industrial zone (Gitin 2002: 113). The disparate locations of these 17 altars in all of the city's occupation zones (Gitin 2002: 114) demonstrate that, whatever their function, it could have been performed virtually anywhere—at home, at work, or in a cultic setting. Thus, the placement of the altars indicates their role in some form of decentralized worship system. The fact that 12 of them were portable further supports their function as an appurtenance of decentralized worship (Gitin 2002: 113–14) (fig. 9). This is in stark contrast to the centralized worship indicated by the pillared sanctuary in Temple Complex 650, the royal dedicatory inscription, and the inscription "for the shrine." No doubt, this dual worship system was a result of Ekron's exposure to multiple ethnic cultic traditions when it became an international olive-oil production center in the 7th century B.C.E. Further analysis of the type and location of these altars and other cultic features, some of them discussed above, constituted the basis for identifying five examples of coexistence and duality in the cultic practices at 7th-century Ekron. These include private and public worship in religious and secular areas, the portability and fixed character of acts of religious

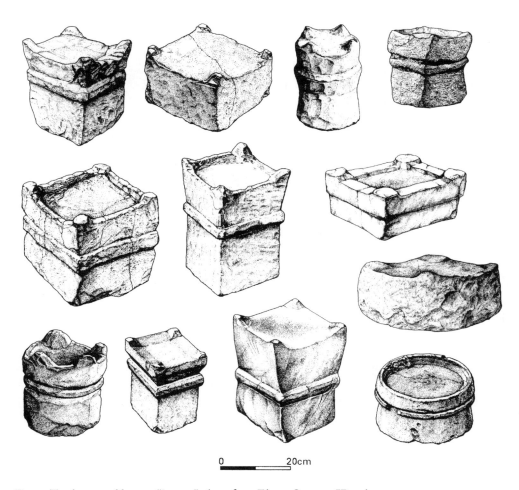

Fig. 9. Twelve portable stone "incense" altars from Ekron, Stratum IB, 7th century B.C.E.

worship, centralized and decentralized systems of worship, and local and foreign traditions in religious practices (for a detailed discussion, see Gitin 2002: 113–17).

Even this cursory review of the cultic evidence from 7th-century Ekron demonstrates the value of archaeological data in determining the existence and character of late Philistine religious practice. The Ekron data show that, while Philistine cultic practice in the 7th century remains Philistine in context, it was considerably influenced by contact with foreign cultic practices. The result is a highly acculturated, multifaceted worship system, at the core of which was a central place of worship, that is, a temple, with a priestly support system, including tithing. The king who built the temple considered himself Greek, and the goddess to whom he dedicated the temple was Greek, both reflecting the Aegean origin of the Philistines. The language, writing, and formula of the temple dedication show strong Phoenician influences, as does the temple architecture, while the building complex that houses the temple has Neo-Assyrian architectural characteristics. Parallel to this centralized worship system, a decentralized worship system existed that involved the burning of incense, which, based on the find spots of the four-horned incense altars, apparently took place everywhere except in the temple. In addition to *Ptgyh*, the god and goddess worshiped were Baʿal and Asherat, reflecting both the Phoenician and West Semitic pantheons, while the figurine image of the goddess found in the temple is Phoenician.

These insights into late Philistine religious practice are based on undeniably reliable archaeological evidence. Whether or not such data ultimately will have an impact on the larger fields of Bible and ancient history depends on the willingness of scholars in these disciplines to accept the Ekron data as relevant. The main stumbling block to achieving this goal is not the lack of a "smoking gun" or other kinds of credible evidence, as has been claimed is the case for Israelite religious practice, but the bias that has formed over the past 50 years as a result of the negative reaction to Biblical Archaeology. It does not matter by what name this field of archaeology is called—the Archaeology of Ancient Israel or Syro-Palestinian Archaeology—most biblical scholars and historians have tended for a variety of reasons to disregard the archaeological data it produces. In so doing, they are oblivious to the fact that archaeology today is based on empirical evidence and without due consideration are willing to "throw the baby out with the bathwater." This perception has handicapped many text scholars and skewed their view of ancient cultic practices, because they disregard the relevant material culture data in the archaeological record.

If the Ekron data is approached with an open mind by biblical scholars and historians, it could initiate a new relationship with archaeologists in which material culture remains would be accepted as a valuable tool, not only in deciphering Philistine cultic praxis, but also in dealing with other issues relating to the history of Canaan, ancient Israel, and their neighbors.

References

Acquaro, E.
    1988   Catalogue. Pp. 581–754 in *The Phoenicians*, ed. S. Moscati. Milan: Bompiani.
Albright, W. F.
    1956   *Archaeology and the Religion of Israel.* 4th ed. Baltimore: Johns Hopkins University Press.
Avner, U.
    1993   Mazzebot Sites in the Negev and Sinai and Their Significance. Pp. 161–81 in *Biblical Archaeology Today 1990: Proceedings of the Second International Congress on Biblical Archaeology, Jerusalem*, ed. A. Biran and J. Aviram. Jerusalem: Israel Exploration Society.
Ciasca, A.
    1988   Masks and Protomes. Pp. 354–69 in *The Phoenicians*, ed. S. Moscati. Milan: Bompiani.
Dever, W. G.
    1970   Iron Age Epigraphic Material from Khirbet el-Kom. *Hebrew Union College Annual* 40–41: 139–204.
    1987   The Contribution of Archaeology to the Study of Canaanite and Early Israelite Religion. Pp. 209–47 in *Ancient Israelite Religion: Essays in Honor of Frank Cross*, ed. P. D. Miller, P. D. Hanson, and S. D. McBride. Philadelphia: Fortress.

1999 Archaeology and the Ancient Israelite Cult: How the Kh. El-Qôm and Kuntillet ʿAjrûd ʿAsherah' Texts Have Changed the Picture. Pp. 9*–15* in *Eretz-Israel* 26 (Frank Moore Cross Volume), ed. B. A. Levine et al. Jerusalem: Israel Exploration Society.

2001 *What Did the Biblical Writers Know and When Did They Know It?: What Archaeology Can Tell Us about the Reality of Ancient Israel.* Grand Rapids, Mich.: Eerdmans.

Dothan, M.

1993 Ashdod. Pp. 93–102 in vol. 1 of *The New Encyclopedia of Archaeological Excavations in the Holy Land*, ed. E. Stern. Jerusalem: Israel Exploration Society.

Dothan, T., and Gitin S.

1993 Ekron. Pp. 1051–59 in vol. 3 of *The New Encyclopedia of Archaeological Excavations in the Holy Land*, ed. E. Stern. Jerusalem: Israel Exploration Society.

Fales, F. M., and Postgate, J. N.

1995 *Imperial Administrative Records II: Provincial Administration and Taxation.* State Archives of Assyria 11. Helsinki: Helsinki University Press.

Freedman, D. N.

1989 William F. Albright in Memoriam. Pp. 33–44 in *The Scholarship of William Foxwell Albright: An Appraisal*, ed. G. W. Van Beek. Atlanta: Scholars Press.

Gitin, S.

1989 Incense Altars from Ekron, Israel and Judah: Context and Typology. Pp. 52*–67* in *Eretz-Israel* 20 (Yigael Yadin Memorial Volume), ed. A. Ben-Tor, J. C. Greenfield, and A. Malamat. Jerusalem: Israel Exploration Society.

1993 Seventh Century B.C.E. Cultic Elements at Ekron. Pp. 248–58 in *Biblical Archaeology Today, 1990: Proceedings of the Second International Congress on Biblical Archaeology, Jerusalem*, ed. A. Biran and J. Aviram. Jerusalem: Israel Exploration Society.

1995 Tel Miqne–Ekron in the 7th Century B.C.E.: The Impact of Economic Influences on a Neo-Assyrian Vassal City-State. Pp. 61–79 in *Recent Excavations in Israel: A View to the West*, ed. S. Gitin. Archaeological Institute of America Colloquia and Conference Papers 1. Dubuque, Ia.: Kendall/Hunt.

1998 The Philistines in the Prophetic Texts: An Archaeological Perspective. Pp. 273–90 in *ḤESED VE-EMET: Studies in Honor of Ernest S. Frerichs*, ed. J. Magness and S. Gitin. Brown Judaic Studies 320. Atlanta: Scholars Press.

2002 The Four-Horned Altar and Sacred Space: An Archaeological Perspective. Pp. 95–123 in *Sacred Time, Sacred Place: Archaeology and the Religion of Israel*, ed. B. M. Gittlen. Winona Lake, Ind.: Eisenbrauns.

2003 The House That Albright Built. *Near Eastern Archaeology* 65/1: 5–10.

Gitin, S., and Cogan, M.

1999 A New Type of Dedicatory Inscription from Ekron. *Israel Exploration Journal* 49/3–4: 193–202.

Gitin, S.; Dothan, T.; and Naveh, J.

1997 A Royal Dedicatory Inscription from Ekron. *Israel Exploration Journal* 47/1–2: 1–16.

Gjerstad, E.

1937 *The Swedish Cyprus Expedition 1927–1931, III: Plates.* Stockholm: Petterson.

Hendel, R. S.

1997 Aniconism and Anthropomorphism in Ancient Israel. Pp. 205–28 in *The* Image and the Book: Iconic Cults, Aniconism, and the Rise of Book *Religion in Israel and the Ancient Near East*, ed. K. van der Toorn. Leuven: Peeters.

Karageorghis, V.

1974 Kition: Mycenaean and Phoenician. *Proceedings of the British Academy* 59: 1–27.

Keel, O., and Uehlinger, C.

1998 *Gods, Goddesses, and Images of God.* Minneapolis: Fortress.

Lemaire, A.

1977 Les Inscriptions de Khirbet el-Qôm et Ashérah de Yhwh. *Revue Biblique* 84: 597–608.

Levine, B. A.

1997   The Next Phase in Jewish Religion: The Land of the Israel and Sacred Space. Pp. 245–57
         in *Tehillah le-Moshe: Biblical and Judaic Studies in Honor of Moshe Greenberg*, ed. M. Cogan,
         B. L. Eichler and J. H. Tigay. Winona Lake, Ind.: Eisenbrauns.

Lewis, T. J.

1998   Divine Images and Aniconism in Ancient Israel. *Journal of the American Oriental Society*
         118/1: 36–53.

May, H. G.

1935   *Material Remains of the Megiddo Cult*. Chicago: Oriental Institute of the University of
         Chicago.

Mazar, A.

1993   Qasile, Tell. Pp. 1204–12 in vol. 4 of *The New Encyclopedia of Archaeological Excavations in
         the Holy Land*, ed. E. Stern. Jerusalem: Israel Exploration Society.

Meshel, Z.

1978   *Kuntillet ʿAjrud: A Religious Centre from the Time of the Judaean Monarchy on the Border of Si-
         nai*. Israel Museum Catalogue 175. Jerusalem: Israel Museum.

Mettinger, T. N. D.

1995   *No Graven Image?: Israelite Aniconism in Its Ancient Near Eastern Context*. Stockholm: Alm-
         qvist & Wiksell.

1997   Israelite Aniconism: Developments and Origins. Pp. 173–204 in *The Image and the Book:
         Iconic Cults, Aniconism, and the Rise of Book Religion in Israel and the Ancient Near East*, ed.
         K. van der Toorn. Leuven: Peeters.

Millard, A.

1991   Review of J. H. Tigay, *You Shall Have No Other Gods: Israelite Religion in the Light of Hebrew
         Inscriptions* (Atlanta: Scholars Press, 1986). *Israel Exploration Journal* 41/1–3: 224–26.

Naveh, J.

1979   Graffiti and Dedications. *Bulletin of the American Schools of Oriental Research* 235: 27–30.

1998   Achish-Ikausu in the Light of the Ekron Dedication. *Bulletin of the American Schools of
         Oriental Research* 310: 35–38.

Niehr, H.

1997   In Search of Yʜᴡʜ's Cult Statue in the First Temple. Pp. 73–96 in *The Image and the Book:
         Iconic Cults, Aniconism, and the Rise of Book Religion in Israel and the Ancient Near East*, ed.
         K. van der Toorn. Leuven: Peeters.

Pritchard, J. B., ed.

1969   *Ancient Near Eastern Texts Relating to the Old Testament*. 3rd ed. Princeton: Princeton Uni-
         versity Press.

Schäfer-Lichtenberger, C.

2000   The Goddess of Ekron and the Religious-Cultural Background of the Philistines. *Israel
         Exploration Journal* 50/1–2: 82–91.

Tigay, J. H.

1986   *You Shall Have No Other Gods: Israelite Religion in the Light of Hebrew Inscriptions*. Atlanta:
         Scholars Press.

Toorn, K. van der

1997   *The Image and the Book: Iconic Cults, Aniconism, and the Rise of Book Religion in Israel and the
         Ancient Near East*. Leuven: Peeters.

Uehlinger, C.

1997   Anthropomorphic Cult Statuary in Iron Age Palestine and the Search for Yahweh's Cult
         Images. Pp. 97–155 in *The Image and the Book: Iconic Cults, Aniconism, and the Rise of Book
         Religion in Israel and the Ancient Near East*, ed. K. van der Toorn. Leuven: Peeters.

Vanderhooft, D.

1999   Dwelling beneath the Sacred Place: A Proposal for Reading 2 Samuel 7:10. *Journal of Bib-
         lical Literature* 118: 628–30.

Vaux, R. de
   1965   *Ancient Israel II: Religious Institutions.* New York: McGraw Hill.
Wiener, H. M.
   1927   *The Altars of the Old Testament.* Leipzig: Hinrichs.
Zevit, Z.
   2001   *The Religions of Ancient Israel.* London: Continuum.

Phoenician Cult Expressions in the Persian Period

Edouard Lipiński
Department of Oriental Studies
Catholic University of Leuven

Introduction

Phoenicia was not a centralized country with a single recognized capital, like Judah or Samaria. It was, like Greece, a congeries of city-states that had never been amalgamated into a single political entity and clung fondly to the idea of separate independence, or at least civic autonomy. In the Persian period, besides the cities of Phoenicia proper, from Rās al-Basiṭ in the extreme north to the Naḥal Soreq in the south, there were Phoenician royal cities on the island of Cyprus, while the former colonies in the western Mediterranean basin were by then completely independent from the mother-cities in the Levant. The political history of these various Phoenician entities, and even their religious practices and beliefs, cannot be reduced easily to common patterns. Although the names of some of the Phoenician deities appear in various periods and in several areas, this should not prevent us from being cautious, the more so as the cult is a reality quite different from the pantheon. The cult is a system of rites and ceremonies with reference to the worship of a deity or of the dead. The Phoenicians worshiped their gods, like most other ancient peoples, with prayer, hymns of praise, sacrifices, processions, and votive offerings. Each temple had its festival times when worshipers flocked to it, and its gods were honored with prolonged services and sacrifices on a larger scale than ordinary. Burial ceremonies were performed on burial grounds, at least; but excavated cemeteries show a great diversity of practices that certainly existed in temple rituals and private forms of cult as well.

At any rate, we must distinguish among the successive stages of Phoenician religion and also look for particular sources of information on this subject in the different areas where Phoenician presence or influence is well attested. Let us consider a few examples of cult practices on the coastal strip from the Nahr ad-Dāmūr in the north to the Naḥal Soreq in the south, as well as in the inland settlements of this region. This is still a large area of more than 200 km north–south as the crow flies, and it contains sites such as Sidon, Sarepta, Kharayeb, Tyre, Umm al-ʿAmed, Achzib, Akko, ʿAtlīt, Dor, Makmish (Tel Michal), and Jaffa, as well as Kāmid el-Lōz, Tell Keisan, Ramat Hanadiv, Miṣpe Yammim, and Eliachin.

Our main sources for the Persian period are tombs and *favissae*. The few dedicatory inscriptions are not very informative and we do not have any liturgical texts, sacred laws, or mythological compositions, except for the work that Philo of Byblos, in the 1st or 2nd century C.E., compiled with respect to the "origins" of his countrymen and attributed to Sanchuniathan. Almost half a millennium separates the end of the Persian period from Philo's "Phoenician History." Therefore, the value of its remaining fragments for our purposes seems to me only slight, independent of Philo's rationalizing interpretation of his sources.

I. Burial Practices

Two of the lengthiest Phoenician documents from the Persian period are the inscriptions engraved on the sarcophagi of Tabnit I and Eshmunazor II, kings of Sidon in the first part of the 5th century B.C.E.[1] The main purpose of both inscriptions was to curse the desecrator who disturbed the resting place of the departed kings. Both kings were buried in Egyptian fashion, and Tabnit's body was certainly embalmed (Hamdy Bey and Reinach 1892: 103). Embalming and burying in an Egyptian sarcophagus certainly imply ritual ceremonies to which the corpse and the finished mummy were subjected. We have no information about the Phoenician ritual, and therefore do not know whether a ceremony comparable to the Egyptian "Opening of the Mouth" was performed on the mummy in order to give it life and enable it to receive the *ba* and *ka* souls.[2] This complex ceremony was accompanied in Egypt by food offerings, libations, and incense burning, as shown, for example, on a vignette of the papyrus of Hu-nefer with the text of the Book of the Dead.[3] It is at least very likely, as we shall see, that in Phoenicia, there was a funerary farewell banquet in which the dead person was supposed to take part.

The body of the woman buried in Sidonian sarcophagus no. 17, discovered under the so-called Tomb of Mourning Women, also was mummified, as shown by fragments of linen bands found inside the coffin. She was wearing an oval golden fillet on her head, and a large golden ring lay to her left (Hamdy Bey and Reinach 1892: 82–83, figs. 32–33). The grave was undisturbed and did not contain any artifacts aimed at accompanying the deceased in another world. This was also the case with the sarcophagus of Tabnit I and most likely of Eshmunazor II,[4] thus confirming the statement in the inscriptions that no riches were deposited in the coffin. Their absence was certainly not motivated by the sheer apprehension of exposing the body to violation. It had to reflect a particular conception of life after death and resulted from an established burial ritual and cult of the dead. The same conception probably underlies the burial practice attested in the cemetery of Makmish, dating to the 5th–4th centuries B.C.E., where most of the 20 graves excavated by Avigad in 1958–60 did not contain any burial offerings. The fact that the covers were still intact seems to indicate that they were not robbed.[5]

A careful analysis of the burial contents of the 92 graves from the Persian period uncovered at Kāmid el-Lōz, in the southern Beqaʿ Valley, provides further elements connected with the cult of the dead (Hachmann and Penner 1999). The site lies at the end of the shortest route from Sidon to the Beqaʿ Valley and can thus be related to Sidonian burial practices. When dealing with burial contents it is important, in general, to distinguish

---

1. *KAI*: nos. 13–14 = *TSSI III*: nos. 27–28. Photographs of these monuments can be found in Lipiński (ed.) 1992: 328, fig. 129; 434, fig. 161.

2. The basic edition of the ritual remains the one Otto 1961.

3. This vignette is reproduced in *ANEP* 1969: 210, fig. 640.

4. At least de Luynes (1856) does not mention any burial contents.

5. Only succinct preliminary reports on these excavations have been published by Avigad (1960; 1961). See also Avigad 1993, as well as Stern 1982: 72.

between two categories of objects. First, there are items belonging to the dress of the dead, such as personal jewelry, toggle-pins, fibulae, rings, chains, bracelets, and also amulets, and objects that were constantly used by the deceased in everyday life, such as mirrors, combs, cosmetic palettes, small implements of various kinds, and also weapons, if the deceased was a military man. Second, there are furnishings for use in another world, including food and drink. The only items from Kāmid el-Lōz clearly belonging to the latter category are the coins found in nine of the graves, generally in a place suggesting that they were inserted initially in the mouth of the corpse (Hachmann and Penner 1999: 177–78, 228). There is little doubt that this practice parallels the Greek "Charon's obol" (Hachmann and Penner 1999: 178–79).[6] Charon's duty was to ferry over the Styx and Acheron the shades of the deceased who had duly received the rites of burial, in payment for which service he received an obol, which had been placed in the mouth of the dead.

This product of popular belief cannot antedate the creation of coinage and should thus be considered an innovation of the Persian period. However, its origin cannot be Greek, although the description of Charon and his boat by Lucian of Samosata (Harmon 1915: 395–447) corresponds to their representation on Greek *lekythoi* with black figures on white background as early as the 6th century B.C.E. (Mavleev 1986). In fact, Charon as boatman parallels the function of Urshanabi, the boatman of Utnapishtim in the Gilgamesh Epic.[7] Urshanabi ferried Gilgamesh over "the waters of death" to the land of Utnapishtim, where Utnapishtim was enjoying everlasting life. As for the coin, it may just be an innovative form of older means of payment, possibly a cock. This hypothesis would explain why the cock appears in Punic funerary iconography (Lipiński 1995: 383, and further references there; Longerstay 1995: 215–16)[8] and why the skeleton of a fowl was found in Tomb 1 of Kāmid el-Lōz near the head of the dead (Hachmann and Penner 1999: 179).[9]

The ritual practice of "Charon's obol" is apparently attested also in the ʿAtlit tombs that contained silver coins (Johns 1932), generally of Sidonian or Tyrian type, but their exact location in the grave is not specified in the archaeological report, although drawings indicate the places of other objects found in the tombs. Fourth-century silver coins from Tyre were also found in two tombs at Makmish (Herzog 1980: 140; Stern 1982: 72; Avigad 1993: 934) and most likely should be explained in the same way. The examples can be multiplied easily, but disturbed graves and the lack of precision in some archaeological reports do not help in interpreting this phenomenon in particular instances.

Besides the coins, other items uncovered in the graves at Kāmid el-Lōz seem to be related to the burial ritual. This probably applies in the case of the bronze bowls or phials

---

6. The linguistic connections proposed by Hachmann and Penner (1999) are very problematic, but Charon's oriental origin has been recognized by De Ruyt (1934: 236–42). His name is very similar to that of Horon, a West Semitic god of the underworld, as pointed out in Lipiński 1968: 220 n. 4. However, Horon has not appeared thus far as a boatman, but the presence of his cult in the coastal areas of Beth-Ḥoron and Yamnia is an interesting fact. Later oriental parallels of "Charon's obol" are referred to in Oettel 2000: 110–11.

7. Epic of Gilgamesh tablet X. No opinion is expressed regarding this striking analogy in Dräger 1997.

8. A late reflection of the ritual function of the cock may be seen in the 4th-century C.E. marble mosaic from Nabeul, which represents two cocks picking up golden coins from a jar. A good reproduction can be found in the catalogue *Carthage* 1995: 259; see also *30 ans* 1986: 172, no. III.25.

9. Oettel suggests that small bells served a similar function (2000: 112–17).

found in 13 graves (Hachmann and Penner 1999: 226–27; cf. pp. 100–137), which is very similar to the one represented at Sidon in the Tomb of the Satrap, the reliefs of which bring to light not only the activities of an unknown king, but also some rites of the burial ceremony. One scene depicts a veiled woman seated in front of a young servant holding a jug and filling a horn presented by a man resting on a *kline*, with the bowl in his left hand (Hamdy Bey and Reinach 1892: 43ff., pl. 21; Kleemann 1958: 120–25, pls. 13–17). This is probably the dead king who takes part in the farewell ceremony in the presence of his veiled wife (Hamdy Bey and Reinach 1892: 194).[10] The phials belonging to the deceased, who was supposed to have participated in the burial ritual, were placed in the tomb next to the head of the dead after the ceremony (Hachmann and Penner 1999: 227).

Kāmid el-Lōz is only one of many sites where this practice is attested. For example, a similar bronze bowl dating to the 6th–5th centuries B.C.E. was found intact at the eastern end of Tomb 183 at Makmish. This location indicates a place near the head of the dead, since a skeleton lying on its back with its head to the east was found in nearby Tomb 181 (Herzog, Negbi, and Moshkovitz 1978: 118). Bowls have been found in many tombs of the Persian period and have been studied at length, but rarely has attention been paid to their exact location inside the grave and to their possible ritual function.

The inscriptions of Tabnit I and of Eshmunazor II seem to indicate that only quietness and rest were expected in life in the other world, while wealthy Phoenicians' care for the preservation of their bodies after death implies a belief that death was not the end of everything and that ensuring a quiet existence in "the house of eternity" was important enough to admit of cursing anyone who might disturb their corpses. No burial offerings were required, since the dead did not need them in the afterworld. However, this conception was not universal among the Phoenicians, as shown by other burials with rich funerary offerings, including vessels and lamps. A particular question is raised by the cremation burials found along the Phoenician coast, although hardly at all after the early 6th century B.C.E., with one exception. The custom of burning the human body, eventually with funerary gifts and some personal possessions of the deceased, does not seem therefore to have been a common mortuary practice among Phoenicians in the period and the area we are surveying.

II. Dedicatory Figurines

Other aspects of Phoenician ritual are revealed by figurines found by archaeologists in *favissae* or repository pits of sanctuaries. In most cases, they are the sole evidence of temples, since actual building remains are very rare, and when they have been discovered, sometimes they have not been investigated, as in the case of the shrine constructed of well-hewn stones at Eliachin (*Hadashot Arkheologiyot* 14 [1965]: 10; cf. 17 [1966]: 13; see also Kamlah 1999: 170–72)[11] and dedicated in the Persian period to the

---

10. The distinction made by Kleemann between the intention of the person who ordered the sarcophagus and its actual realization as a funerary banquet is not convincing (1958: 155–56).

11. A sanctuary from the Persian period was also found at Makmish, but only brief preliminary reports have been published (see above, n. 5).

Arabian god Ashtarum.[12] On the other hand, the poorly preserved rectangular building uncovered near the great *favissa* of Kharayeb, approximately 15 km north of Tyre, has been investigated twice, the second time in 1969–70, when it was identified as a sanctuary originally dating to the Persian period but rebuilt in Ptolemaic times (Kaoukabani 1973). The *favissa* yielded more than 1,100 figurines belonging to the period from the end of the 4th century B.C.E. through the late 1st century B.C.E., thus postdating the Achaemenid times, mainly exhibiting Hellenistic types (Chéhab 1951–52; 1953–54).[13] Another sanctuary from the Persian period was excavated at Mişpe Yammim, 4 km southwest of Safed in Upper Galilee. However, no *favissa* was found, and the small Egyptian bronzes discovered at the site point rather to a shrine devoted to the worship of Egyptian deities, although a short Phoenician inscription there was dedicated to Astarte by ʿAkbōr, son of Bod-Eshmun (Frankel 1997; Frankel and Ventura 1998; Kamlah 1999: 164–70, 172–90).[14]

Terra-cotta figurines placed in sanctuaries by worshipers were removed after a lapse of time and buried in a nearby pit in order to make room for new offerings. This practice is comparable to a certain extent with the Jewish custom of storing books or ritual objects that were no longer deemed fit for use in the *genizah* of a synagogue. In most cases, the figurines seem to have been broken deliberately before being thrown into the *favissa*, very likely because their presence in the sanctuary had made them sacred and thus unfit for profane use. But there may have been another, purely lucrative, reason for this: the broken figurines could not be reused, and the believers had to buy new ones to be deposited in the shrine as visible signs of their devotion.

What is interesting for the historian of religions are the types of clay figurines and statuettes found in the *favissae*, because they may reflect a particular supplication of the worshiper to the deity. Among the oriental-style figurines from the Persian period found at Tel Dor in 1980 are three female figurines, all expressing the desire to have a child or being related to childbirth, namely: (1) a nude woman supporting her breasts, as Isis does to feed Horus the Child; (2) a pregnant woman with her hands on her belly, the so-called *dea Tyria gravida*; and (3) a woman cradling her baby or holding a swaddled baby with only its head peeking out (Stern 1994: 165–67).[15] A somewhat larger and apparently older child is carried in its mother's arms on a relatively well-preserved terra-cotta from a *favissa* discovered at Tell Şippor, east of Ashkelon.[16] These figurines were presented to the deity by women applying for help or thanking the deity in an expressive way. The frequently recurring motif of the seated pregnant woman is perhaps the most significant, and

---

12. This is known from the inscribed offerings published by Deutsch and Heltzer (1994: 69–89, nos. 33–39). The shrine was close to a cemetery, which yielded "a number of ancient coins, fibulae, arrowheads, and gold, silver and bronze jewellery" (Deutsch and Heltzer 1994: 69).

13. One of the figurines, no. 1130, an unusual one, is not a terra-cotta but a limestone statuette and bears a Phoenician inscription that de Vaux (1956) proposed reading as *kšmʿ qlm ybrkm*, "because he heard their voice; may he bless them." Since only the last letters, *nm*, of line 1 are preserved, the name of the deity is unknown. See also Chéhab 1955; Magnanini 1973: 41, no. 11:1.

14. The site corresponds to Ğebel al-ʾArbaʿin. The name of the dedicator must be read as ʿkbr instead of ʿkbw, and one should read further *š pʿl* instead of *ʾpʿl*, as corrected by Weippert (1999).

15. Fragments of similar female figurines have been found at Apollonia-Arsuf (Roll and Tal 1999: 192–93).

16. The small mound was excavated in 1963 and many terra-cotta and limestone figurines were found in a *favissa* dating to the Persian period (Biran and Negbi 1964: 400, pl. 20b).

despite its designation as *dea Tyria gravida*, does not necessarily portray a goddess.[17] These figurines were popular not only along the Phoenician coast, but also on Cyprus and in the Punic settlements of the western Mediterranean.[18] They are usually hollow, molded in the front and plain in the back, and represent pregnant women veiled and clothed; they wear a skirt reaching to their ankles, and their headdress drapes down to their shoulders. A crude example from Tel Mevorakh differs in that it is solid, is hand-made, portrays the woman nude, and indicates the details of the chair by means of etching (Stern 1978: 41–42, fig. 11:1, pl. 42:3). These features do not suggest that this particular statuette had a different meaning.

The proposed interpretation of these figurines might, however, be challenged by the very fine specimen found in a tomb at Achzib (Prausnitz 1960).[19] On the other hand, the motif may simply point to maternal death in childbirth, in consequence of which the statuette was placed in the burial next to the corpse of the deceased young woman. A similar explanation would fit the terra-cotta figurine of a seated woman with a small child found in the tomb of a woman buried at Kition/Larnaka in the 6th century B.C.E. (Clerc et al. 1976: 244, fig. 25, and bibliography p. 289 n. 414).[20] At any rate, a clear distinction should be made between the Phoenician-style figurines of seated young pregnant women and the Greek-style statuettes of enthroned elderly females sometimes found in Palestine (Stern 1982: fig. 289:3–4).

Mothers, not goddesses, are portrayed also by the figurines representing a woman holding a child on her shoulder or in her arms (Stern 1982: 171, 272 nn. 58–59; 1995: 443–45, nos. 8–10). Such votive offerings may record a ceremony of thanksgiving on the part of the mother shortly after the birth of her child or her ritual cleansing in the sanctuary after childbirth, as prescribed in Leviticus 12. This practice is referred to in various treatises of the Mishnah and is echoed in the presentation of Mary and the child Jesus at the Temple according to the Gospel of Luke (2:22–24).

A few iconographic details, however, have to be examined, especially in relation to the somewhat different types represented by the 400 terra-cotta figurines from the shipwreck off Shavei-Zion. They date to the 5th century B.C.E., as indicated by the storage jars found with the figurines. These "were cast in molds and represent a female figure standing on a pedestal; her right arm is raised in a gesture of blessing, and her left arm resting on her belly or between her breasts. In some figurines a little child clings to the female figure" (Linder 1993: 30*; see also 1973a; 1973b). The gesture of blessing is the attitude of the worshiper standing in front of the enthroned deity. It appears, for instance, on the stela of

---

17. Contrary to the opinion of Winter (1983: 370–72); Stern (1999: 253–54); cf. Brandl (2000: 197–98), among others. Many examples are listed in Pritchard 1988: 50–52 and Brandl 2000: 195–96. See also Culican 1969, reprinted in Culican 1986; Pritchard 1975: 35–37, 39–40. A very well-preserved specimen is in the collection of the Hecht Museum in Haifa (Raban and Stieglitz 1993: 20*, 33).

18. Two very fine specimens from Carthage are in the collection of the Bardo Museum in Tunis; see *Carthage* 1995: 102, where they are dated erroneously to the 8th century B.C.E., but were found in tombs dating to the 6th–5th centuries B.C.E. Both probably had been imported from the Levant (cf. Ferjaoui 1992: 78–79, pls. 10–11).

19. A similar statuette, said to come from Achzib, belonged to the collection of Randel Harris and is preserved at Woodbrooke College, Birmingham. It was published by Lambert (1970: 50–51, fig. 6).

20. The same statuette is reproduced in Lipiński (ed.) 1992: 248, fig. 197. A similar explanation would fit the above-mentioned, well-preserved statuettes from cemeteries at Carthage (see n. 18 above).

Yehawmilk, king of Byblos in the 5th century B.C.E. (*ANEP*: 165, no. 47), and very likely corresponds to the biblical phrase *barūk 'adōnāy*, "blessed be the Lord." This gesture does not denote a deity, especially when the figure is standing. The figurine's left arm resting on the belly or between the breasts indicates that a felicitous pregnancy or ample milk for the baby in the period immediately after birth were requested from the deity. In other words, the position of the hand indicates the place on the body where divine intervention and blessing are requested. The worshiping woman thus identifies herself with the figurine, which is deposited in the sanctuary.

A particular question is raised by the so-called "Sign of Tannit" and by the dolphin that appear in relief on the pedestal of some figurines from the above-mentioned shipwreck, exceptionally in their center, on the belly (Stern 1982: 170, fig. 291; Raban and Stieglitz 1993: 43; see also van Gils 1990: frontispiece, nos. 7–8, 11, 13). The presence of the "Sign of Tannit" does not prove that the figurines represent the goddess Tannit. Despite its name, the "Sign of Tannit" has a wider scope and derives from the Egyptian *ankh* sign (Lipiński 1995: 206–15, with earlier literature; see also Bertrandy 1993), as confirmed by some of the Shavei-Zion representations of the symbol without the horizontal base-line. As in Egypt, it is a symbol of life and fertility, the use of which perfectly suits female figurines expressing the hope of begetting a child. As for the dolphin, which often appears in Phoenician iconography (Bertrandy and Sznycer 1987: 71, with references), it cannot function in this case as a conductor of the dead to Hades, as in Greek mythology. The statement of Jewish sages that "dolphins reproduce like human beings" (*b. Bekorot* 8a), rather, suggests that the dolphin, a well-known creature since ancient times to all who knew the sea, was seen as a symbol of maternity. Seafarers noticed, no doubt, that the female, which brings forth a single offspring at a time, was a devoted parent and this may have been the origin of the symbol.

Dolphins appear as symbols also on a Neopunic shrine at Thuburbo Maius in Tunisia, dating to the 2nd or 1st century B.C.E. and dedicated to Demeter, called "Mother" in some Greek texts (Lipiński 1995: 375–76). These scattered indications at least favor the proposed interpretation of the dolphin on the Shavei-Zion terra-cottas. No divine symbols appear on the Dor figurines, and this should also prevent us from interpreting them too quickly as representations of the fertility goddess or the Mother Goddess. The female figurines in question functioned to invoke "sympathetic magical powers" in order to beget a child or to guarantee the survival of an infant. Thus they may also be regarded as the mute prayers of women coming to the sanctuary, as did Hannah in 1 Samuel, either to pray to beget or guarantee the survival of a child, or to thank the deity for the blessing.

There is also a type of figurine portraying a bearded male with a large mustache. Earlier specimens show him wearing the *atef*-crown of Osiris (Stern 1982: 166, fig. 283; Gubel 1987: 86, pl. 16, no. 38; Avigad 1993: 933; Brandl 2000: 197, 205 nn. 29–30), later replaced by flat-topped round headgear (Stern 1982: 165, nos. 40–41; 1994: 166–67; Brandl 2000: 197),[21] which occurs frequently on Phoenician reliefs of the Persian and Hellenistic periods and represents the typical Phoenician headdress of the time (Maes 1991: 213, figs. 1–3, 7). The two types represent the same personage, as shown in particular by the gesture of clasping

---

21. One head of each type was found at Apollonia-Arsuf (Roll and Tal 1999: 190–91).

the beard with the right hand. Despite the *atef*-crown, these figurines do not represent the Egyptian god Osiris, who is never pictured with a beard and a mustache, but they must evoke the "childless" father, as was Osiris before his death in the Egyptian divine triad of Osiris, Isis, and Horus, who were well known also in Phoenicia (Lemaire 1986: 93–97). As for the gesture of clasping the beard, it recalls a sentence from several Mari letters sent by Shamshi-Addu to his son Yasmah-Addu: "Are you not yet a man? Is there no beard at your chin?" (*ARM I*: nos. 61:10; 73:44; 108:7; 113:8). Even if the figurines initially represented a deity, perhaps Dagon, the fertility and corn god, their significance should parallel that of the female statuettes. This means that they are the mute prayers of adult men asking for a son. The presence of these offerings in the sanctuary had to remind the deity continuously of the meaning of the worshiper's prayer. Once the deity had given ear to the prayers, the figurines could be removed.

We shall not enter here into a discussion of the Greek type of figurine found at Tel Dor in two *favissae* in 1980 and 1982 and in some other areas. This is an intricate question, because the original meaning of a type of figurative artifact and its function in a somewhat different cultural context do not need to coincide. However, there is one exception, the so-called Temple-Boy figurines, which generally exhibit the boy's sex in an intentional way (Beer 1994).[22]

The current explanation of these figurines is that they represent boys dedicated by their parents to serve in the sanctuary, again recalling the biblical account of Hannah and Samuel. Although the name "Temple-Boy" originates from this interpretation, it does not explain why the sex of the boy is usually shown in a prominent way. Another explanation, even less credible, is that these figurines are representations of Pataikos or of Horus Harpocrates, Horus the Child. Pataikos, however, is not a small child, but a dwarf, and he is usually characterized by the narrow-fitting cap of Ptah and by a large collar (Arav and Bernett 1997: 203ff., with further literature). As for Harpocrates, who never wears clothes, several iconographical traits distinguish him from the Temple-Boy. The view identifying the latter with Horus the Child can be accepted only in the case of figurines showing characteristic features of Harpocrates, represented with his finger on his lips, a symbol of childhood, and, more importantly, with a large lock of hair falling on his right shoulder (Schoske and Wildung 1993: nos. 18–31).

Several marble statuettes of the Temple-Boy have been found in Eshmun's sanctuary at Bostan esh-Sheikh near Sidon (Stucky 1993), one with a princely dedication to the god Eshmun (*TSSI III*: no. 29; Parrot, Chéhab, and Moscati 1975: fig. 132). There is little doubt that these are votive offerings placed in the sanctuary of a healing deity, at a sacred spring, where ritual ablutions or baths were supposed to heal children or to strengthen the boy's fertility, possibly in connection with the circumcision rite. Similar statuettes found in other sanctuaries also aimed at placing the child under divine protection and probably had an established ritual function. In fact, wherever circumcision is performed as a traditional rite, it is regarded as of the profoundest religious significance. Its importance in ancient Israel and Judah is evident from the repeated contemptuous references to the

---

22. Beer's monograph (1994) deals especially with Cypriote and related material. Temple-Boy figurines are known also in the Punic world, for example, at Kerkouane in Tunisia, dated to the 4th century B.C.E. (Fantar 1991: 60).

Philistines as "uncircumcised," and the same qualification seems to have been used in Phoenician-speaking areas, at least if the savage people called γοριλλας in Hanno's *Periplus* 18 were globally stigmatized as *ʿōrilīm, "uncircumcised." Further speculation about possible connections between circumcision, purificatory washing, and dedication of Temple-Boy statuettes to a deity are unwarranted given the present extent of our knowledge.

Conclusion

The study of cult expressions may be hampered by the practice of some art historians who study iconographic items in a speculative way, without considering whenever possible the immediate archaeological context in which they were found. It can also be jeopardized by the tendency to identify various kinds of figurative items with divinities. Figurines are thus described as "Astarte pregnant," "Astarte carrying her child," or "Horus the Child." These appellations are often not justified and fail to explain why sanctuary attendants were not afraid of breaking divine figurines deliberately before throwing them into *favissae*. A careful description and analysis of the objects are absolute prerequisites, but wider comparative studies are necessary as well. And some objects, like apotropaic masks for example, can be used in various contexts—in burials, in sanctuaries, and in private houses. Inscriptions may be helpful, unless their meaning is distorted by the same tendency to find divine names where places, objects, or verbal forms are meant.

References

ANEP
1969   J. B. Pritchard, *The Ancient Near East in Pictures Relating to the Old Testament.* 2nd ed. Princeton: Princeton University Press.

Arav, R., and Bernett, M.
1997   An Egyptian Figurine of Pataikos at Bethsaida. *Israel Exploration Journal* 47: 198–213.

ARM I
1946   G. Dossin, *Archives royales de Mari*, vol. 1: *Lettres.* Textes cunéiformes du Louvre 22. Paris: Geuthner.
1950   G. Dossin, *Archives royales de Mari*, vol. 1: *Correspondance de Šamši-Addu et de ses fils, transcrite et traduite.* Paris: Imprimerie Nationale/Geuthner.

Avigad, N.
1960   Excavations at Makmish, 1958: Preliminary Report. *Israel Exploration Journal* 10: 90–96.
1961   Excavations at Makmish, 1960: Preliminary Report. *Israel Exploration Journal* 11: 97–100.
1993   Makmish. Pp. 932–34 in vol. 3 of *The New Encyclopedia of Archaeological Excavations in the Holy Land*, ed. E. Stern. Jerusalem: Israel Exploration Society.

Beer, C.
1994   *Temple-Boys—A Study of Cypriote Votive Sculpture, Part 1: Catalogue.* Studies in Mediterranean Archaeology 113. Gothenburg: Åström.

Bertrandy, F.
1993   Les représentations du "Signe de Tanit" sur les stèles votives de Constantine, IIIᵉ–Iᵉʳ siècles avant J.-C. *Rivista di Studi Fenici* 21: 3–28.

Bertrandy, F., and Sznycer, M.
1987   *Les stèles puniques de Constantine.* Notes et documents des Musées de France 14. Paris: Réunion des musées nationaux.

Biran, A., and Negbi, O.
  1964   Tell Ṣippor. *Revue Biblique* 71: 399–400, pls. 20a–b.
Brandl, B.
  2000   Various Finds from Iron Age II and the Persian Period (Eighth–Fourth Centuries B.C.E.).
           Pp. 187–210 in *Ramat Hanadiv Excavations: Final Report of the 1984–1998 Seasons*, by
           Y. Hirschfeld. Jerusalem: Israel Exploration Society.
Carthage
  1995   *Carthage, l'histoire, sa trace et son écho*. Paris: Association Française d'Action Artistique.
Chéhab, M.
  1951–52 *Les terres cuites de Kharayeb: Texte*. Bulletin du Musée de Beyrouth 10. Paris: Maisonneuve.
  1953–54 *Les terres cuites de Kharayeb: Planches*. Bulletin du Musée de Beyrouth 11. Paris: Maison-
           neuve.
  1955   Inscription phénicienne de Kharayeb. *Bulletin du Musée de Beyrouth* 12: 45–46.
Clerc, G., et al.
  1976   *Fouilles de Kition*, vol. 2: *Objets égyptiens et égyptisants*. Nicosia: Department of Antiquities
           of Cyprus.
Culican, W.
  1969   Dea Tyria Gravida. *Australian Journal of Biblical Archaeology* 1/2: 35–50.
  1986   *Opera selecta*. Gothenburg: Åström.
De Ruyt, F.
  1934   *Charun, démon étrusque de la mort*. Études de philologie, d'archéologie et d'histoire anci-
           enne 1. Brussels: Institut historique belge de Rome.
Deutsch, R., and Heltzer, M.
  1994   *Forty New Ancient West Semitic Inscriptions*. Tel Aviv: Archaeological Center.
Dräger, P.
  1997   Charon (1). Cols. 1107–08 in vol. 2 of *Der Neue Pauly*. Stuttgart: Metzler.
Fantar, M. H.
  1991   *Carthage: Les lettres et les arts*. Tunis: Alif.
Ferjaoui, A.
  1992   *Recherches sur les relations entre l'Orient phénicien et Carthage*. Études et recherches 17.
           Carthage: Beït al-Hikma.
Frankel, R.
  1997   The Sanctuary from the Persian Period at Mount Miṣpe Yamim. *Qadmoniot* 30: 46–53 and
           frontispiece (Hebrew).
Frankel, R., and Ventura, R.
  1998   The Miṣpe Yamim Bronzes. *Bulletin of the American Schools of Oriental Research* 311: 39–55.
Gils, H. van
  1990   *Godinnen van de vruchtbaarheid langs de libanese kust*. Middelburg: Pzem Galerie.
Gubel, E.
  1987   *Phoenician Furniture*. Studia Phoenicia 7. Leuven: Peeters.
Hachmann, R., and Penner, S.
  1999   *Kāmid el-Lōz 3: Der eisenzeitliche Friedhof und seine kulturelle Umwelt*. Saarbrücker Beiträge
           zur Altertumskunde 21. Bonn: Habelt.
Hamdy Bey, O., and Reinach, T.
  1892   *Une nécropole royale à Sidon: Fouilles de Hamdy Bey*. Paris: Leroux.
Harmon, A. M.
  1915   *Lucian II*. London: Heinemann.
Herzog, Z. (ed.)
  1980   Excavations at Tel Michal, 1978–1979. *Tel Aviv* 7: 111–51.
Herzog, Z.; Negbi, O.; and Moshkovitz, S.
  1978   Excavations at Tel Michal, 1977. *Tel Aviv* 5: 99–135.

Johns, C. N.
1932   Excavations at ʿAtlit (1930–31). *Quarterly of the Department of Antiquities in Palestine* 2: 41–104, pls. 13–37.
KAI
1964–66   H. Donner and W. Röllig, *Kanaanäische und aramäische Inschriften.* 3 vols. Wiesbaden: Harrassowitz.
Kamlah, J.
1999   Zwei nordpalästinische "Heiligtümer" der persischen Zeit und ihre epigraphischen Funde. *Zeitschrift des Deutschen Palästina-Vereins* 115: 163–90.
Kaoukabani, B.
1973   Rapport préliminaire sur les fouilles de Kharayeb, 1969–1970. *Bulletin du Musée de Beyrouth* 26: 41–59.
Kleemann, I.
1958   *Der Satrapen-Sarkophag aus Sidon.* Istanbuler Forschunger 20. Berlin: Deutsches archäologisches Institut.
Lambert, W. G.
1970   Objects Inscribed and Uninscribed. *Archiv für Orientforschung* 23: 46–51.
Lemaire, A.
1986   Divinités égyptiennes dans l'onomastique phénicienne. Pp. 87–98 in *Religio Phoenicia*, ed. C. Bonnet, E. Lipiński, and P. Marchetti. Studia Phoenicia 4. Namur: Société des Études Classiques.
Linder, E.
1973a   A Cargo of Phoenician-Punic Figurines. *Archaeology* 26: 182–87.
1973b   A Cargo of Figurines of the Persian Period Discovered in the Sea off Shavei Zion. *Qadmoniot* 6: 27–29 (Hebrew).
1993   The Shavei-Zion Figurines. Pp. 29*–31* in *Phoenicians on the Northern Coast of Israel in the Biblical Period*, ed. A. Raban and R. R. Stieglitz. Haifa: Hecht Museum.
Lipiński, E.
1968   *La royauté de Yahwé dans la poésie et le culte de l'ancien Israël.* 2nd ed. Verhandelingen van de Koninklijke Vlaamse Academie voor Wetenschappen, Letteren en Schone Kunsten van België: Klasse der Letteren 55. Brussels: Paleis der Academiën.
1995   *Dieux et déesses de l'univers phénicien et punique.* Studia Phoenicia 14 = Orientalia Lovaniensia Analecta 64. Leuven: Peeters.
Lipiński, E. (ed.)
1992   *Dictionnaire de la civilisation phénicienne et punique.* Turnhout: Brepols.
Longerstay, M.
1995   Les représentations picturales de mausolées dans les haouanet du nord-ouest de la Tunisie. Pp. 210–19 in vol. 2 of *Actes du IIIᵉ Congrès international des Études phéniciennes et puniques*, ed. M. H. Fantar and M. Ghaki. Tunis: Institut National du Patrimoine.
Luynes, A. de
1856   *Mémoire sur le sarcophage et l'inscription funéraire d'Eshmunazar, roi de Sidon.* Paris: Imprimerie Royale.
Maes, A.
1991   Le costume phénicien des stèles d'Umm el-ʿAmed. Pp. 209–30 in *Phoenicia and the Bible*, ed. E. Lipiński. Studia Phoenicia 11 = Orientalia Lovaniensia Analecta 44. Leuven: Peeters / Departement Oriëntalistiek.
Magnanini, P.
1973   *Le iscrizioni fenicie dell'Oriente.* Roma: Istituto di Studi del Vicino Oriente.
Mavleev, E.
1986   Charon. Pp. 225–36 in vol. 3/2 of *Lexicon Iconographicum Mythologiae Classicae.* Zurich: Artemis.

Oettel, A.
2000   Charonspfenning und Totenglöckschen: Zur Symbolik von Münzen und Glöckschen. *Altorientalische Forschungen* 27: 106–20.

Otto, E.
1961   *Das ägyptische Mundöffnung Ritual: Text und Kommentar.* 2 vols. Ägyptologische Abhandlungen 3. Wiesbaden: Harrassowitz.

Parrot, A.; Chéhab, M. H.; and Moscati, S.
1975   *Les Phéniciens—L'expansion phénicienne: Carthage.* L'univers des formes. Paris: Gallimard.

Prausnitz, M.
1960   Akhziv. *Revue Biblique* 67: 398, pl. 25b.

Pritchard, J. B.
1975   *Sarepta.* Philadelphia: University of Pennsylvania Press.
1988   *Sarepta,* vol. 4: *The Objects from Area II, X.* Beirut: Université Libanaise.

Raban, A., and Stieglitz, R. R. (eds.)
1993   *Phoenicians on the Northern Coast of Israel in the Biblical Period.* Haifa: Hecht Museum.

Roll, I., and Tal, O. (eds.)
1999   *Apollonia-Arsuf. Final Report of the Excavations I. The Persian and Hellenistic Periods.* Tel Aviv: Tel Aviv University Press.

Stern, E.
1978   *Excavations at Tel Mevorakh,* vol. 1. Qedem 9. Jerusalem: Hebrew University.
1982   *Material Culture of the Land of the Bible in the Persian Period: 538–332 B.C.* Warminster: Aris & Phillips.
1994   *Dor, Ruler of the Seas.* Jerusalem: Israel Exploration Society.
1995   *Excavations at Dor: Final Report IB. Areas A and C: The Finds.* Qedem Reports 2. Jerusalem: Hebrew University / Israel Exploration Society.
1999   Religion in Palestine in the Assyrian and Persian Periods. Pp. 245–55 in *The Crisis of Israelite Religion: Transformation of Religious Tradition in Exilic and Post-Exilic Times,* ed. B. Becking and M. C. A. Korpel. Leiden: Brill.

Schoske, S., and Wildung, D.
1993   *Gott und Götter im Alten Ägypten.* 2nd ed. Mainz: von Zabern.

Stucky, R. A.
1993   *Die Skulpturen aus dem Eschmun-Heiligtum bei Sidon: Griechische, römische, kyprische und phönizische Statuen und Reliefs vom 6. Jahrhundert v. Chr. bis zum 3. Jahrhundert nach Chr.* Basel: Vereinigung der Freunde antiker Kunst.

30 ans
1986   *30 ans au service du Patrimoine: XXVIII centenaire de Carthage.* Tunis: Institut National d'Archéologie et d'Art.

TSSI III
1982   J. C. L. Gibson, *Textbook of Syrian Semitic Inscriptions,* vol. 3: *Phoenician Inscriptions.* Oxford: Clarendon.

Vaux, R. de
1956   Review of M. Chéhab, *Les terres cuites de Kharayeb. Revue Biblique* 63: 306.

Weippert, M.
1999   Eine phönizische Inschrift aus Galiläa. *Zeitschrift des Deutschen Palästina-Vereins* 115: 191–200.

Winter, U.
1983   *Frau und Göttin.* Orbis Biblicus et Orientalis 53. Freiburg: Universitätsverlag.

The Phoenician Source of Palestinian Cults
at the End of the Iron Age

Ephraim Stern
Institute of Archaeology
Hebrew University, Jerusalem

During the period of the Monarchy, there were seven nations in Palestine. An eighth nation—the Arameans of the land of Geshur, who had lived on the northeastern border of Israel—had been deported by the Assyrians in 732 B.C.E. and never returned. The seven nations are, from north to south: the Phoenicians located along the northern coast; the Israelites in the Galilee and the province of Samaria; the Philistines centered in their four city-states of Ashdod, Ashkelon, Ekron, and Gaza; three in eastern Jordan (the Ammonites, the Moabites, and the Edomites); and, finally, the Judeans.

In the Iron Age, each of these seven nations had its own independent cult, consisting of the worship of a pair of major deities. Each of the male gods of these cults had a distinct name, of which most, but not all, are mentioned in the biblical sources. The chief deity of the Arameans was Haddad; of the Phoenicians, Ba'al; of the Philistines, Dagan and also Ba'al; of the Ammonites, Milcom; of the Moabites, Chemosh; of the Edomites, Qos; and of the Israelites and the Judeans, Yahweh.[1] It is interesting to observe that for all, including the Philistines, Israelites, and Judeans, the chief female deity was Astart, or Asherah.

It is well known by now that each of these nations created the images of its gods in a different form from that of the others. By the later part of the Monarchic period, the representations of the different deities had been clearly consolidated, and it is easy for an experienced archaeologist or specialist in ancient art to attribute a particular figurine to a Phoenician, Philistine or even Judean cult at first glance. At the same time, one of the strange results of the study of the various cult objects is that, despite the differences in deities and cults, there is also a considerable unity. Except for the differing images of their gods, the various nations used similar cult objects: the same types of incense altars made of stone or clay, bronze and clay censers, cult stands and incense burners, chalices, goblets, and bronze and ivory wands adorned with pomegranates, and so on. Cult vessels of one deity, for example from the sanctuary at Arad, could readily be placed in the service of another, as described in the famous stela of Mesha, the king of Moab, who delivered the vessels of Yahweh taken from the conquered Judean city of Nebo to the temple of Chemosh (Suder 1984: 93–95; Dearman 1989).

The purpose of this short essay is to show that the cults practiced in Palestine during the Iron Age by six of the nations settled there—the Israelites, Judeans, Philistines,

---

1. On these deities, see the relevant entries in van der Toorn, Becking, and van der Hoorst 1999; see also Stern 2001: passim.

Ammonites, Moabites, and Edomites—were almost one and the same, and that all stemmed from the cult of the Phoenicians, thus continuing the older Canaanite tradition. In the following I shall try to demonstrate this hypothesis by comparing two of these cults: the Phoenician and the Judean.

I. *The Phoenician Cult*

The number of excavated Phoenician sanctuaries is surprisingly small; even smaller are those dating to the Iron Age. The Phoenician sanctuaries along the Phoenician and Palestinian coast are mostly from the Persian period. Of the sanctuaries dating to the Iron Age, those found at Kition on Cyprus are the most well known (Karageorghis 1976), but will not be discussed in this paper.

The only Iron Age sanctuary found to date at Sarepta (Pritchard 1975) is Temple 1, uncovered in the potters' quarter, above which a Persian period sanctuary had been built. According to the excavators, Temple 1 is a rectangular structure (2.5 × 6.5 m), with a floor made of hard-packed lime cement, and was oriented east–west. Along the walls were plastered benches. The most interesting element was a built table attached to the western wall, probably for votives. The three sides of the table were coated with lime. In front of it was a large ashlar stone. A square (40 × 40 cm) depression in the floor attests to the presence of another element, perhaps a stela or an incense altar, which is missing. Near the table, a few cult objects were found, such as clay figurines, clay masks, ivory carvings, medallions, and lamps (Pritchard 1975: 13–40).

The plan of the two sanctuaries is notable, since even in this late period, it still preserves the old Canaanite tradition. It is almost identical to Late Bronze Age Canaanite temples such as the "Fosse Temple" at Lachish, the temple at Tel Mevorakh, some of the Beth-Shean temples, and many others. These sanctuaries are even related to some earlier Middle Bronze Age temples, such as the one at Nahariyah (Pritchard 1975: 13–40).

In recent years, a few small prayer chapels have also been found, consisting of one room. These, too, follow an old Canaanite concept, as seen in the Area C temple at Hazor (Yadin 1972: 69–74). This room usually contained the sculpture of a god or goddess, or sometimes a row of stone stelae. Chapels of this type have been found at a number of other sites, for example, one at the foot of Tel Michal (dating to the 10th century B.C.E.)[2] and others close to the Tel Dan city gate (Biran 1996: 55–58). Many more chapels were found in the Phoenician settlements along the coast as well as overseas, and recently also in various Judean fortresses, such as Ḥorvat Radum (Beit-Arieh 1993), Vered Jericho (Eitan 1986: 30–34), Meẓad Michmash (Riklin 1994), and in the Aramean town of Bethsaida (Arav 1999: 81–88), among others (see below).

We have some biblical and Greek sources on cultic practices in the Phoenician sanctuaries. Among the Phoenician written sources, all found in excavations, we have several inscriptions, of which the majority come from the Persian period. The longest is an ostracon found at Akko, probably at the site of a sanctuary. This is an order issued on the city's authority to the guild of metal workers to present to the person appointed as the

---

2. I would like to thank the excavator, Prof. Z. Herzog of Tel Aviv University, for this information.

head of the sanctuary a precious metal basin, as well as a number of additional metal objects, some made of gold or silver. A few of the object names are Greek, but written in Phoenician script (M. Dothan 1985).

A similar inscription, but somewhat earlier, was incised on a red-burnished bowl found in one of the Phoenician temples at Kition (Temple I, dated 850–800 B.C.E.). In this inscription, we are told about a citizen of the city of Tamassos on Cyprus who came to the Kition temple to present an offering of his hair, which was cut and placed in a bowl dedicated to Astart. An additional testimony to this tradition is in another Phoenician inscription recently found at Kition that lists some of the accounts of the Astart temple at the site. Among the sanctuary's employees are "the sacred barbers," who perhaps performed the ceremony. In the same inscription, a number of other functionaries of the temple are mentioned, such as scribes, metalworkers, the police, and the children, among others (Coote 1975).

There are extensive lists of cultic objects, especially in the Phoenician inscriptions from Kition, which include dozens of metal objects, mostly made of copper. The list of "Tariffs" found at Marseilles in France, which probably originated in one of the nearby Punic colonies and was associated with the temple of "Baʿal-Zaphon," included the prices of the various animals brought to the temple (Cooke 1903: 112–22). It resembles similar biblical lists. Additional details can be found in the many Punic inscriptions on stone stelas that deal with similar subjects (Cooke 1903: 123–58).

The evidence collected as far as the western Mediterranean is the same as the evidence of the cult practiced by the Phoenicians along their own and the Palestinian coast, as well as that from Cyprus and the western colonies.

II. The Nature of the Phoenician Cult, Its Symbols, and Its Remains

Generally, the archaeological finds are composed of two major types of figurines that appear simultaneously in all assemblages: an adult male, represented as a king sitting on a throne or standing or as a warrior on a horse; and a female goddess, depicted either as a ruling queen sitting on a throne or as a fertility goddess holding her breasts or in the shape of pregnant woman or a woman nursing a small child.

This is consistent with Moscati's observation that the Phoenician cult was composed of

> a triad of deities: a protective god of the city, a goddess, often his wife or companion who symbolizes the fertile earth; and a young god somehow connected with the goddess (usually her son), whose resurrection expresses the annual cycle of vegetation. Within these limits, the names and functions of the gods vary, and the fluidity of this pantheon, where the common name often prevails over the proper name, and the function over the personality, is characteristic. Another characteristic of the Phoenician triad is the flexibility from town to town. (Moscati 1978: 7)

The major archaeological sources for the study of the Phoenician religion are the hundreds of dedicatory inscriptions found along the coasts of both the eastern and western Mediterranean, in which, as a rule, the names of a pair of gods are mentioned: a male god and a goddess. If additional names appear, these are duplicate names or two names of the same god—for example, Ba‘al-Melqart, Ba‘al-Eshmun, Ba‘alat-Geval, Ashtoreth-Tanit, Tanit-Pane-Ba‘al, and others. Only rarely does an inscription mention the name of an additional deity, and these are usually names of ancient gods that were preserved from the remote past, such as Shadrap or Shamash (Stern 2001: 71–87).

The male god is Ba‘al, and this name became a regular component in hundreds of Phoenician personal names, including those of kings and high officials of the various Phoenician city-states—for example, Eliba‘al, Adoniba‘al, Itenba‘al, Ba‘alnatan, Ba‘alsaleah, and so forth (Stern 2001: 71–87). This tradition also became common among the Israelites, Judeans, Philistines, Moabites, Edomites, and Ammonites—each group incorporating its own god's name.

Secondary titles were often added to the name Ba‘al, intended to emphasize his important position in the divine hierarchy or to distinguish a particular attrribute of the many he possessed, such as the title "Ba‘al Shamaim" ("Ba‘al of Heaven"), written on a papyrus sent in 604 B.C.E. from Ashkelon or Ekron to the king of Egypt (Porten 1981), or "Ba‘al Shmem" mentioned in ostraca found at Tel Michal (Rainey 1989: 381) and Tel Jemmeh (Izre'el 1999: 197–200).

More than a few of the Ba‘al titles, however, are connected with geographical regions or features, sometimes denoting his ownership of certain territories, such as sacred mountains—"Ba‘al Zaphon" or "Ba‘al Lebanon," and perhaps also "Ba‘al Carmel"—but mainly his role as the chief deity of the various Phoenician cities and colonies. In these cases, a separate name was added for each site: at Sidon, he is "Ba‘al Sidon" or "Ba‘al Eshmun"; at Tyre, "Ba‘al Tyre" or "Ba‘al Melqart"; at Geval (Byblos), "Ba‘al Geval"; and at Carthage, "Ba‘al Hamman" (Stern 2001: 71–87).

The territorial significance of these Ba‘als is indicated by the archaeological finds from Palestine. According to our written sources, both Phoenician and Greek, the coastal region of Palestine was divided between Tyre and Sidon, and some ostraca from the Sharon Plain that are connected with Sidon, such as those from Dor and Apollonia, mention the name of Eshmun, "Ba‘al of Sidon" (Roll and Tal 1999: 197–200). A Phoenician building inscription from Jaffa describes the erection there of a temple to "Ba‘al Eshmun" (Condor 1892), and an ostracon from Nebi Yunis (near Ashdod) tells us about the establishment in that location of a sanctuary dedicated to the "Ba‘al of Tyre" (Cross 1964).

Territorial ownership like that of Ba‘al was also attributed to the deities of the other nations of Palestine, each with its particular god, including the one worshiped in the cult of Israel and Judah. For the last we may point to the inscription found at Kuntillet ‘Ajrud in which the names "Yahweh of Samaria and his Asherah" and "Yahweh of Teman and his Asherah" are mentioned (Meshel 1979: 28–29; Emerton 1982; Dever 1984; McCarter 1987: 138–39, 143–44), or "Yahweh, the god of Jerusalem," in the Beit Lei inscription (Naveh 1963: 81–92; Cross 1970) (see below).

In addition to geographical and city names, Ba‘al also had many titles to glorify him— for example, "adon" (lord), "adir" (mighty), and "ha-melekh" or "molekh" (the king)—of which numerous examples are found among the Phoenician and Punic inscriptions (Bisi 1967: passim). These titles, too, were used by all the other Palestinian nations.

The same applies to Ba'al's consort Ashtoret (Astart), whose name appears in many Phoenician proper names of both males (e.g., Ebed [servant of]-Astart) and females (e.g., Em [mother of]-Astart, Bat [daughter of]-Astart, Amath [servant of]-Astart, Han [the beauty of]-Astart, etc.). Territorial ownership was also attributed to the goddess, as supported by excavation finds of inscriptions bearing the names "Astart of Lebanon," "Ba'alat-Geval," "Ba'alat Tyre," or "Astart Sidon" (Slousch 1942: 8, no. 5, line 3; 156, no. 137, line 1).

Astart often appears in conjunction with the name of her consort: for example, in "Astart, the name of Ba'al," "Astart, the wife of Ba'al," "Astart, the face of ('Arst) Baal," or "Tanit, the face of (Pane) Baal"; or, in Moab, as "Ishtar-Chemosh" (Cooke 1903: 1, inscription no. 1, line 17). She also bears some of the honorary titles usually attributed to the gods, such as "to rabat (lady) to Astart" (Bisi 1967: passim).

It should be added that in the late Iron Age, especially in its later part when the consolidation of relations with Egypt took place, we find a strong Egyptian influence on Phoenician cult in particular and on the other Palestinian cults in general, such as the penetration of Egyptian motifs into the Phoenician cult, as had occurred previously in Canaanite cult. An example of the introduction of Egyptian deity figures into the local cult is the appearance of the goddess Isis as Ba'alat-Geval in the stela of Yehaumilk, king of Byblos (Moscati [ed.] 1988: 305). The incorporation of the figure of the Egyptian god Osiris was also common among the Phoenicians. This phenomenon is reflected in the Egyptian lists of Phoenician names, which often included Egyptian deities—for example, "Ebed-Ibsat" (servant of the Egyptian goddess Bestet), "Ebed-Osiri" (Osiris), and "Ebed-Ptah." On occasion, the goddess Isis is mentioned in Phoenician inscriptions by her full name, as a goddess per se, to whom one should pray (Slousch 1942: 39, no. 22:B, line 1; 124, no. 107, line 2). This custom is also reflected in the common use of Egyptian-made figurines or the local imitations that have been found among all the Palestinian nations of the period, which adopted them from the Phoenicians.

Among the Phoenician cult objects, the most common finds are the clay figurines. These are discussed in detail, since in this case too, all the Palestinian nations, including the Judeans, adopted the Phoenician example (see below).

The figurines characteristic of the Phoenicians are mainly female. From the Iron Age, we find the "bell-shaped" figurines—that is, figurines with hollow, round, wheel-made bodies. Their heads are molded and attached to the bodies by means of a tang. The goddess is usually depicted nude, supporting her breasts with both hands. In addition to the "bell" form, she is characterized by a long "Phoenician wig," the hair falling to her shoulders. This wig is different from the short Judean wig (Stern 2001: compare 81, fig. I.42, with 206, fig. I.87). At the end of the Iron Age, the appearance of the figurines changes and they are usually made using a new technique brought from Greece, as a hollow figurine with the front molded and the back smoothed. Even the features of the figurine are changed: the majority of the late figurines depict women either supporting their breasts or in an advanced stage of pregnancy (with one hand placed on the belly). A smaller number portrays women taking care of a young male child, nursing him, playing with him on their knees, or carrying him on their shoulder (Stern 2001: 496–97, figs. III.27–III.28). There are usually no inscriptions to help us identify the deities represented, but a few figurines recovered in an underwater excavation near Shavei Zion, which closely resemble the figurines discussed above, include the insignia of the goddess "Tanit, Pane-Ba'al," or a dolphin, another of her emblems (Stern 2001: 78, fig. I.40). As noted above, in the Sarepta dedicatory inscription, Tanit and Astarte are one and the same goddess.

A separate group of Iron Age Phoenician clay figurines consists of mainly female figures playing various musical instruments. Most of these "bell-shaped" figurines were made using the common Phoenician technique, their heads covered with long "Egyptian" wigs, but instead of the usual position—hands supporting the breasts, a hand on the belly, or nursing an infant—they are playing one of four musical instruments: a frame-drum, tambourine, lyre, or double-flute. These four instruments are very common in the figurines found at the Phoenician sites of Sarepta, Achzib (mainly in tombs), Akko, Tell Keisan, Shiqmona, Tel Megadim, and Dor, as well as at those along the eastern coast of the Mediterranean, on Cyprus, and in the Punic colonies (see, for example, Stern 2001: 81, fig. I.42). This "orchestra" was also a favored motif on Phoenician ivories, where the musicians appear as a group or individually, as well as on decorated Phoenician metal bowls (for example, Markoe 1984: 252–53, Bowl Cy 6; 316, Bowl G 3; 328, Bowl G 8) and Phoenician and Israelite seals (Stern 2001: 81).

This Phoenician "orchestra" also has Canaanite prototypes. They appear as ordinary clay figurines or as decorations on metal or clay cult stands. The most important of these is the "musicians stand" found at Ashdod (T. Dothan 1982: 250, pl. 33), which depicts the entire quartet, like the above-mentioned ivories and metal bowls. There can be no doubt that this "orchestra," like the other Phoenician cult components, was introduced into all the Israelite and Judean sanctuaries, as well as those of the other local cults (cf. 1 Sam 10:5, "thou shalt meet a company of prophets coming down from the high-place with a psaltery, tarbet, pipe, and harp before them").

Figurines of musicians with the same four instruments were also found in Israel (at Dan, Hazor, Beth-Shean, Taanach, and Tirzah), Judah, Philistia, and all the kingdoms of Transjordan, as were figurines depicting male musicians—for example, a tambourine player at Tel 'Ira in Judah, a harp player at Philistine Ashdod, and a double-flute player at Edomite Tel Malḥata (Stern 2001: 266–87, figs. I.115–I.116).

The third group of female figurines, at this stage peculiar to the Phoenicians (found at Achzib and at various sites on Cyprus and in the Punic world), depicts women engaged in everyday activities. Thus far, figurines of women washing themselves in a bath and kneading loaves of bread on a table are known (Prausnitz 1993: 34, photo top left; Stern 2001: 82, fig. I.43). It is not clear whether these figurines represent cultic activities, as do the musicians, or regular daily work.

It should also be mentioned that female figurines were not only made of clay. There are a few figurines made of ivory or bone (from Achzib, Dor, and Sarepta [e.g., Pritchard 1975: fig. 43:1]), some identical to the clay figurines. Figurines made of metal also occur, usually attached to metal stands, and the same figures also frequently appear on Iron Age seals and seal-impressions (Stern 2001: 499–501, figs. III.30–III.31).

Another noteworthy aspect is the mutual identification that existed between the Phoenician mother-goddess Astart and the Egyptian Isis. It is quite common for the Phoenician Astart to appear in the Phoenician glyptic in the form of the Egyptian deity, and but for the accompanying inscriptions, we would not be able to differentiate between the two. One example is the above-mentioned Phoenician Baʿalat-Geval on the Yehaumilk stela, who is depicted as Isis (Moscati [ed.] 1988: 305), and there are many others of figurines and amulets of the Egyptian goddess found in Phoenician temples and *favissae* at Palestinian sites such as Atlit, Dor, Tel Michal, Ashkelon, and elsewhere (Stern 2001: 490–510).

Male figurines are relatively rare, and apart from the musicians, among the many Phoenician clay types only one male figure appears, the "horseman." This figurine must represent the warrior-god. Horsemen of the Phoenician type, riding large, decorated horses of a specific rendering have been uncovered in the tombs and houses excavated at Achzib, Kabri, Tel Keisan, Akko, Megiddo, Dothan, Tel Megadim, Shiqmona, and Dor (Stern 2001: 84, fig. I.44). The horsemen have long faces and noses; they wear pointed helmets reminiscent of that of the Egyptian god Osiris and should be regarded as depictions of gods. Similar figurines, in large quantities, are well known also from Syro-Phoenician coastal sites, as well as Cyprus (Karageorghis 1993: pls. 29–30). All should be interpreted as the "fighting Baʿal" (Stern 2001: 84, fig. I.44).

The only other male Phoenician figurine comes from one of the temples at Sarepta, where a head was found with a round "turban" (Pritchard 1975: fig. 42:3) of the type common among male figurines of the other Palestinian nations, for example, the Judeans and the Ammonites (see below).

It should be noted that the Phoenician figurines, like other figurines of the period, were painted in strong colors, mainly red and black, emphasizing the details of the faces, both of the humans and of the horses.

III. Comparison of the Phoenician Cult to the Judean Cult

On the basis of recent archaeological finds, we may assume that, in Judah, many sanctuaries dedicated to the Judean god were established at various sites. Such a sanctuary was called "the House of Yahweh." The most important and central of these was, no doubt, the sanctuary on the Temple Mount in Jerusalem. The Old Testament itself testifies to the existence of additional sanctuaries at Dan, Bethel, Shiloh, and Beersheba (1 Sam 1:24, 2 Kgs 23:15–20, Amos 8:14).

A complete Judean sanctuary was excavated by Aharoni in the fortress at Arad (1968; see also Ussishkin 1988). This temple may serve as an exemplar for all the Judean temples and sanctuaries of the period. The Arad sanctuary had three parts—an *ulam*, a *heichal*, and a *debir*—and was oriented east–west. From the central unit, the *heichal*, three steps led up to the holy of holies, which was a raised platform. One of its *maṣṣebot* was found in the destruction level, and another two embedded in the wall of the holy of holies that were not in use in the sanctuary's final phase. On the third step, two limestone incense altars were found, with the remains of burned material on their upper surfaces, probably incense. In the courtyard was a large altar (2.5 × 2.3 m), built of clay bricks and unhewn stones and covered with a thick layer of plaster. According to Aharoni, the plan of the structure and its contents supported the conclusion that it was "a Yahwistic-Judean temple" (1968: 25).

In addition to the sanctuary at Arad, cultic installations have been excavated at other Judean fortresses, for example, the cultic platforms with a number of steps leading up to them close to the gates of the fortresses at ʿUza and Radum near Arad (Beit-Arieh and Cresson 1991; Beit-Arieh 1993). Another *bamah* was reported near the gate of the Judean fortress at Beersheba, where a large, four-horned, stone altar was also found (Yadin 1976). A similar installation, identified by the excavator as a cultic *bamah*, was found at the Judean fortress of Vered Jericho (Eitan 1986: 30–34). Several stone steps found near the gate of the fortress at Meẓad Michmash on the kingdom's northern border were also interpreted as leading to a sacred platform or *bamah* (Riklin 1994: 69–70). These finds support Aharoni's assumption that almost all the border fortresses of the Judean kingdom had cultic centers (Stern 2001: 201–3). It should also be mentioned that numerous figurines, altars, and other types of cultic objects were recovered from many of these fortresses.

It may be assumed that there was a sanctuary dedicated to Yahweh also at Lachish, the second most important city in Judah, since the Lachish relief at Nineveh depicts a pair of large cultic stands among the spoils of war removed by Sennacherib's soldiers when they sacked the city (Ussishkin 1982: 84–85, fig. 69). These stands are of the same type as the smaller examples found at many of the Judean sites.

It should be added that the establishment of sanctuaries dedicated to Yahweh in settlements outside Jerusalem was a regular custom: for example, the famous cultic site at Kuntillet Ajrud, dating to the end of the 9th century B.C.E., dedicated to "Yahweh of Samaria and his Asherah" or "Yahweh of Teman and his Asherah" (see above). Another sanctuary is mentioned in the even-earlier Mesha stela, in which the Moabite king claims to have taken the vessels of Yahweh from the city of Nebo and laid them before Chemosh (see above). This implies that there was also a sanctuary dedicated to Yahweh in the Judean city of Nebo before it was plundered by the Moabites.

The "House of Yahweh" is indeed mentioned in many inscriptions of the period, for example, the Arad ostracon that reads, "he is in the House of Yahweh" (Aharoni 1981: text 18:9–10; Renz 1995: 382–84). A more-recently published Judean ostracon reads, "Pursuant to the order to you of Ashyahu the king to give by the hand of Zecharyahu silver of Tarshish to the house of Yahweh, three shekels" (Bordreuil, Israel, and Pardee 1996: 46).[3] Furthermore, an inscription on a small ivory pomegranate reads, according to Avigad's translation, "Sacred to the priest of the house of Yahweh" (1989).

The phrase "House of Yahweh" that appears in the two above-mentioned ostraca led their publishers to believe that they alluded to the temple in Jerusalem. However, if one takes into consideration all the currently available information, it is doubtful whether this assumption is necessary. A "House of Yahweh" may have been located in any settlement in Judah or in any area settled by Judeans.

In this regard, we should add that ostraca from the sanctuary at Arad itself mention the names of two well-known priestly families, Mermot and Pashur, who probably served in the local "House of Yahweh." Generally, the posts of the priests serving in the Yahweh sanctuaries were passed down within families through the generations, from father to son, and only seldom were they appointed by the ruler. There are a few seals in which the title *kohen* ("priest") is added to the name. One example is "Ianan the son of Helqiah the

---

3. On this inscription, see also Becking 1998; Berlejung and Schule 1998.

priest," who may have been a high priest in Jerusalem (Elayi 1987). A seal dating to the end of the Israelite kingdom mentions an Israelite priest active in the Yahwistic temple at Dor: "Belonging to Zechario the priest of Dor" (Avigad 1975; cf. "Amaziah, the priest of Bethel" in Amos 7:10). There is also the seal of "Miqnayahu, servant of Yahweh," which means that Miqnayahu served in one of the many Yahwistic temples (Avigad 1997: 59–60 nn. 27–29). From this data it may be concluded that a person bearing the title of priest could serve in any of the country's temples.

Furthermore, evidence found in the various archaeological excavations in Judah points to the frequent use of Yahweh as a component of Judean names. According to Millard, the dominance of this element in clear: of approximately 1,200 personal names on seals and ostraca, 557 are compounded with *yhwh*, 77 with *'l*, and only 35 with the names of other deities (1998: 114–15). The many occurrences of the name Yahweh in the ostraca of Lachish and Arad, as well as other Judean sites, are noteworthy (Tigay 1986: 47–63), and the name also appears in oaths and blessings: for example, "I have blessed you to Yahweh," "May Yahweh let hear my lord tidings of peace," "May Yahweh bless you in peace," "May Yahweh give my lord pleasant tidings," and "May Yahweh give you prosperous tidings" (Torczyner et al. 1938; Aharoni 1981).

Yet another inscription from Judah dating to the same period mentions the names of the divine couple worshiped by the local population—Yahweh and Asherah. This corresponds to the occurrence of these names in the inscriptions in the early Israelite sanctuary at Kuntillet Ajrud and the worship of these deities by the Israelites at the time. The inscription was found in a tomb at Khirbet el-Qôm in the central hill country of Hebron (perhaps to be identified with biblical Makkedah). The inscription reads: "Blessed will be Ariyahu to Yahweh and his Asherah" (Dever 1969–70: 158–69, 200–201; Lemaire 1977). At the nearby site of Beth Loya, a Judean tomb inscription was found that mentions Yahweh as the lord of Jerusalem and the mountains of Judah (Naveh 1963: 84).

Another type of cultic object unique to the Judeans appears frequently—hundreds of both female and male figurines. Cultic practice in Judah is represented by a rich assemblage of finds, whether imitations of foreign types (either Egyptian or Phoenician) or figurines of local Judean origin, in the form of the deities of Yahweh and Asherah. The figurines are dated from the late 8th through the beginning of the 6th centuries B.C.E. and are distributed throughout Judah: from the Benjamin region in the north, at Bethel, Tell en-Naṣbeh, Gibeon, Ramot, and Moṣa, to Jerusalem, Ramat Raḥel, Beth-Zur, and Khirbet Rabud on the mountain ridge, to Jericho and En-Gedi in the east, and to Gezer, Beth-Shemesh, Batash, Azekah, Tell Judeideh, Tel 'Erani, Tel Ḥalif, Lachish, Tell Beit Mirsim, and other sites in the west. In the southern part of Judah, they were found at Beersheba, Tel Masos, Tel 'Ira, Aroer, and Arad. They were found in both large settlements and small fortresses, such as Khirbet Abu Tuwein; in short, throughout Judah (see pertinent entries in Stern [ed.] 1993).

In Judah, as in the other Iron Age kingdoms, most of the figurines are female, and they belong to the type known as pillar figurines. The type has mold-made heads that all have a similar expression and appear somewhat stylized. The body is usually solid and hand-made, in the shape of a small column, to which exaggerated breasts supported by the hands were added (Stern 2001: 206, fig. I.87; see also Kletter 1996). This type of figurine is usually identified with Astart, the fertility goddess. The deity is sometimes depicted playing a tambourine or holding a dove—the traditional emblem of Astart in all periods. Such figurines seldom occur with a hollow, round body, made in the Phoenician style of "bell-shaped" figurines (see above), and even more rarely on the impressed flat plaques that represent similar figures (Moscati [ed.] 1988: 347).

Another popular type is represented by the Astart figurines with "pinched" heads, sometimes called "bird-head figurines." On these, the head is handmade, like the body, not fashioned by pressing it against a mold. These figurines also portray a standing female supporting her breasts with one or both hands.

Like the Phoenician figurines, those from Judah were painted in strong colors: red, black, and white. The paint is completely preserved on a few of the figurines, which show that the color was used to emphasize the eyes and hair in particular, and sometimes jewelry was added around the neck. The best examples come from the City of David in Jerusalem (Gilbert-Peretz 1996). Astart figurines made of different materials, such as ivory and bone, have also been found in Judah (for example, Barnett 1982: pl. 20:C). As mentioned above, the extensive distribution of the Astart figurines shows that this cult was practiced throughout the kingdom. In his comprehensive study of the Judean pillar figurines (JPFs), Kletter writes:

> If we adopt the heartland of Judah concept [i.e., Judah within the borders described above—E.S.], then 822 JPFs (ca. 96%) were found within this area. This number is so high, that there is only one possible conclusion: the JPFs are Judean figurines, found in the kingdom of Judah. (1996: 45)

It should also be noted that, of the 822 figurines found in Judah, no fewer than 405(!) came from Jerusalem itself. They were found either in the City of David, in the excavations conducted by Kenyon, Shiloh, and B. and E. Mazar, or in the upper city, in those conducted by Avigad and others.[4] Since Kletter's study (1996), many more figurines, female and male alike, have been published, some found only a short distance away from the Temple Mount itself (Gilbert-Peretz 1996).

The male figurines, although found by the dozen at all the sites in Judah enumerated above, including Gibeon and Jerusalem, are not well represented in the literature. Now that we have some results and statistical data from the cults practiced in other parts of the country—namely, by the Phoenicians, Ammonites, Edomites, and Philistines—it seems that their male deities are also significantly represented among the cultic finds. In this respect, as well, Judah did not differ from its neighbors.

Like the Phoenician male figurines, those from Judah appear in two forms: the more complete figurines are of horsemen, representing the warrior-god, which occurs in the cults of all the other nations in the country (cf. Isa 13:4, "the lord of hosts is mustering a host of war"). The Judean horseman figurines are stylistically unique: their heads are sometimes made the in the "pinched" form of the "bird-head figurines," in the same manner as the heads of some of the Judean Astart figurines (see above). The horse also has a very characteristic head—long and cut straight at its end—which has no analogy among

---

4. See Pritchard 1943; Holland 1975; 1977; Nadelman 1989; Gilbert-Peretz 1996; Kletter 1996.

the horseman figurines of the other nations. The bodies of the Judean horsemen and horses are solid and handmade.

The second type of Judean male figurine has a head crowned with a round "turban." This type is rare and only a few dozen heads have been found. The "turban" closely resembles those worn by the Judeans depicted as leaving the city on the Lachish relief (Ussishkin 1982: 84–85, fig. 69). Identical "turbans" appear on some of the Israelite male figurines dating to the Assyrian era from Megiddo (May 1935: pl. 33: M4553), as well as on a number of Ammonite stone sculptures (Stern 2001: 250, fig. I.103). If we compare the Judean male figurines to the more complete Ammonite examples, it seems that they, too, should be reconstructed with their hands beside the body or one hand raised in blessing.

Which Judean deities are represented by these clay figurines? We can only guess. They might represent one of the foreign deities whose cult was also practiced in Jerusalem, perhaps the Phoenician Baʿal. It is also possible, however, that they are pagan representations of the Judean nation's god, Yahweh, and his consort, Astart or Asherah, since these figurines—as we have seen—are uniquely Judean. The combination of the archaeological finds—namely, the occurrence of the names Yahweh and his Asherah/Astart in ostraca and other Judean written sources and the fact that many of the clay figurines are typical of Judah alone—leads us to the inevitable conclusion that between the foreign pagan practices and the pure monotheism of the Judeans, a cult existed that may be called "Yahwistic paganism." The material presented above mainly belongs to this mixed cult. It includes the remains of sanctuaries, *bamot* (open sacred high places), together with altars, figurines, and vessels that were used in the sanctuaries. With regard to the use of these artifacts, there is hardly any difference between their function in the Judean cult and in the cult of the Phoenicians, except in the name of the nation's chief god. This cult was very common in Jerusalem and the rest of Judah throughout the period, until the destruction of the monarchy.

References

Aharoni, Y.
   1968   Arad: Its Inscriptions and Temple. *Biblical Archaeologist* 31/1: 2–32.
   1981   *Arad Inscriptions.* Jerusalem: Israel Exploration Society.
Arav, R.
   1999   Bethsaida. *Qadmoniot* 118: 78–91 (Hebrew).
Avigad, N.
   1975   The Priest of Dor. *Israel Exploration Journal* 25: 101–5.
   1989   The Inscribed Pomegranate from the "House of the Lord." *Israel Museum Journal* 8: 7–16.
   1997   *Corpus of West Semitic Stamp Seals*, rev. and completed by B. Sass. Jerusalem: Israel Academy of Sciences and Humanities.
Barnett, R. D.
   1982   *Ancient Ivories in the Middle East.* Qedem 14. Jerusalem: Hebrew University.
Becking, B.
   1998   Does a Recently Published Paleo-Hebrew Inscription Refer to the Solomonic Temple? *Biblische Notizen* 92: 5–11.
Beit-Arieh, I.
   1993   Ḥorvat Radum. Pp. 1254–55 in vol. 4 of *The New Encyclopedia of Archaeological Excavations in the Holy Land*, ed. E. Stern. Jerusalem: Israel Exploration Society.

Beit-Arieh, I., and Cresson, B. C.

1991   Ḥorvat ʿUza: A Fortified Outpost on the Eastern Negev Border. *Biblical Archaeologist* 54/3: 126–35.

Berlejung, A., and Schule, A.

1998   Erwägungen zu den neuen Ostraka aus der Sammlung Moussaief. *Zeitschrift für Alt Hebraistik* 10: 68–73.

Biran, A.

1996   High Places at the Gates of Dan? Pp. 55–58 in *Eretz-Israel* 25 (Joseph Aviram volume), ed. A. Biran et al. Jerusalem: Israel Exploration Society (Hebrew).

Bisi, A. M.

1967   *Le Stele Puniche*. Rome: Istituto di Studi del Vicino Oriente.

Bordreuil, P.; Israel, F.; and Pardee, D.

1996   Deux ostraca paléo-hébreux de la Collection Sh. Moussaïeff. *Semitica* 46: 49–76, pls. 7–8.

Condor, C. R.

1892   The Prayer of Ben Abdas on the Dedication of the Temple of Joppa. *Palestine Exploration Fund Quarterly Statement* 24: 170–74.

Cooke, G. A.

1903   *A Text-Book of North Semitic Inscriptions*. Oxford: Oxford University Press.

Coote, R. B.

1975   The Kition Bowl. *Bulletin of the American Schools of Oriental Research* 220: 47–50.

Cross, F. M.

1964   An Ostracon from Nebi Yunis. *Israel Exploration Journal* 14: 185–86.

1970   The Cave Inscriptions from Khirbet Beit Lei. Pp. 299–306 in *Near Eastern Archaeology in the Twentieth Century*, ed. J. A. Sanders. New York: Doubleday.

Dearman, A. (ed.)

1989   *Studies in the Mesha Inscriptions and Moab*. Atlanta: Scholars Press.

Dever, W. G.

1969–70   Iron Age Epigraphic Material from the Area of Khirbet El-Kôm. *Hebrew Union College Annual* 40–41: 139–204.

1984   Asherah, Consort of Yahweh? New Evidence from Kuntillet ʿAjrud. *Bulletin of the American Schools of Oriental Research* 255: 21–37.

Dothan, M.

1985   A Phoenician Inscription from ʿAkko. *Israel Exploration Journal* 35: 81–94.

Dothan, T.

1982   *The Philistines and Their Material Culture*. New Haven: Yale University Press.

Eitan, A.

1986   BAR Interviews Avraham Eitan: Israel Antiquities Director Confronts Problems and Controversies. *Biblical Archaeology Review* 12/4: 30–38.

Elayi, J.

1987   Name of Deuteronomy's Author Found on Sealing. *Biblical Archaeology Review* 13/5: 54–56.

Emerton, J. A.

1982   New Light on Religion: The Implications of the Inscriptions from Kuntillet ʿAjrud. *Zeitschrift für die Alttestamentliche Wissenschaft* 1982: 2–20.

Gilbert-Peretz, D.

1996   Ceramic Figurines. Pp. 29–41 in vol. 4 of *Excavations at the City of David, 1978–1985*, ed. D. T. Ariel and A. De Groot. Qedem 35. Jerusalem: Hebrew University.

Holland, T. A.

1975   *A Typological and Archaeological Study of Human and Animal Representations in the Plastic Art of Palestine during the Iron Age*. D.Phil. dissertation, Oxford University Press.

1977   A Study of Palestinian Iron Age Baked Clay Figurines with Special Reference to Jerusalem: Cave 1. *Levant* 9: 121–55.

Izre'el, S.
  1999   Three Phoenician Inscriptions on Clay Vessels. Pp. 197–204 in vol. 1 of *Apollonia-Arsuf*, ed. I. Roll and O. Tal. Tel Aviv: Tel Aviv University Press.
Karageorghis, V.
  1976   *Kition: Mycenaean and Phoenician Discoveries in Cyprus*. London: Thames & Hudson.
  1993   *The Coroplastic Art of Ancient Cyprus II: The Cypro-Archaic Period. Large and Medium Size Sculpture*. Nicosia: Leventis Foundation.
Kletter, R.
  1996   *The Judean Pillar-Figurines and the Archaeology of Asherah*. British Archaeological Reports International Series 636. Oxford: Archaeological and Historical Associates.
Lemaire, A.
  1977   Les Inscriptions de Khirbet el-Qôm et l'Ashéra de YHWH. *Revue Biblique* 84: 595–608.
Markoe, O.
  1984   *Phoenician Bronze and Silver Bowls from Cyprus and the Mediterranean*. Berkeley: University of California Press.
May, H. G.
  1935   *Material Remains of the Megiddo Cult*. Chicago: University of Chicago Press.
McCarter, P. K.
  1987   Aspects of the Religion of the Israelite Monarchy: Biblical and Epigraphic Data. Pp. 137–55 in *Ancient Israelite Religion: Essays in Honor of Frank Moore Cross*, ed. P. D. Miller, P. D. Hanson, and S. D. McBride. Philadelphia: Fortress.
Meshel, Z.
  1979   Did Yahweh Have a Consort? The New Religious Inscriptions from the Sinai. *Biblical Archaeology Review* 5/2: 24–35.
Millard, A.
  1998   The History of Israel against the Background of Ancient Near Eastern Religious History. Pp. 101–17 in *From Ancient Sites of Israel: Essays on Archaeology, History and Theology in Memory of A. Saarisalo*, ed. T. Eskola and E. Junkkaala. Helsinki: Theological Institute of Finland.
Moscati, S.
  1978   *The World of the Phoenicians*. London: Weidenfeld & Nicolson.
Moscati, S. (ed.)
  1988   *The Phoenicians*. Rome: Bompiani.
Nadelman, Y.
  1989   Appendix A: Iron Age II Clay Figurine Fragments from the Excavations. Pp. 123–27 in E. Mazar and B. Mazar, *Excavations in the South of the Temple Mount: The Ophel of Biblical Jerusalem*. Qedem 29. Jerusalem: Hebrew University.
Naveh, J.
  1963   Old Hebrew Inscriptions in a Burial Cave. *Israel Exploration Journal* 13: 74–92.
Porten, B.
  1981   The Identity of King Adon. *Biblical Archaeologist* 44/1: 36–52.
Prausnitz, M. W.
  1993   Achzib. Pp. 32–35 in vol. 1 of *The New Encyclopedia of Archaeological Excavations in the Holy Land*, ed. E. Stern. Jerusalem: Israel Exploration Society.
Pritchard, J. B.
  1943   *Palestinian Figurines in Relation to Certain Goddesses Known through Literature*. New Haven, Conn.: American Oriental Society.
  1975   *Sarepta: A Preliminary Report on the Iron Age*. Philadelphia: University Museum, University of Pennsylvania.
Rainey, A. F.
  1989   The "Lord of Heaven" at Tel Michal. P. 381–82 in *Excavations at Tel Michal, Israel*, ed. Z. Herzog, G. Rapp, and O. Negbi. Minneapolis: University of Minnesota Press.

Renz, J.
  1995   *Die Althebräischen Inschriften.* Vol. 1 of J. Renz and W. Röllig, *Handbuch der Althebräischen Epigraphik.* Darmstadt: Wissenschaftliche Buchgesellschaft.
Riklin, S.
  1994   The Fortress of Michmash on the Northeastern Boundary of the Judean Desert. *Judea and Samaria Research Studies* 4: 69–79 (Hebrew).
Roll, I., and Tal, O. (eds.)
  1999   *Apollonia-Arsuf.* Tel Aviv: Tel Aviv University Press.
Slousch, N.
  1942   *Treasures of Phoenician Inscriptions.* Jerusalem: Bialik Institute (Hebrew).
Stern, E.
  2001   *Archaeology of the Land of the Bible II: The Assyrian, Babylonian, and Persian Periods (732–332 B.C.E.).* New York: Doubleday.
Stern, E. (ed.)
  1993   *The New Encyclopedia of Archaeological Excavations in the Holy Land.* Jerusalem: Israel Exploration Society.
Suder, R. W.
  1984   *Hebrew Inscriptions: A Classified Bibliography.* Selinsgrove, Pa.: Susquehanna University Press.
Tigay, J. H.
  1986   *You Shall Have No Other Gods: Israelite Religion in the Light of Hebrew Inscriptions.* Harvard Semitic Studies 31. Atlanta: Scholars Press.
Toorn, K. van der; Becking, B.; and van der Hoorst, P. W. (eds.)
  1999   *Dictionary of Deities and Demons in the Bible.* Leiden: Brill. [*DDD*]
Torczyner, H., et al.
  1938   *Lachish I: The Lachish Letters.* London: Oxford University Press.
Ussishkin, D.
  1982   *The Conquest of Lachish by Sennacherib.* Tel Aviv: Tel Aviv University Press.
  1988   The Date of the Judaean Shrine at Arad. *Israel Exploration Journal* 38: 142–57.
Yadin, Y.
  1972   *Hazor: The Schweich Lectures 1970.* London: Oxford University Press.
  1976   Beer-Sheba: The High Place Destroyed by Josiah. *Bulletin of the American Schools of Oriental Research* 222: 5–17.

Late Israelite Astronomies and the Early Greeks

Baruch Halpern

Departments of History, Classics and Ancient Mediterranean Studies,
Religious Studies and Social Thought
Pennsylvania State University

I. Israel's Priestly Astronomies and Their Milesian Counterparts

In 585 B.C.E., a Milesian sent shockwaves through the Hellenistic world by predicting a solar eclipse.[1] No Greek could explain Thales's accomplishment for 200 years.

In the late 7th century B.C.E., a Jerusalem priest (P) produced a cosmology, Genesis 1.[2] Both there and in Ezekiel 1, earth and sky were enclosed beneath a two-dimensional vault. Behind the vault, below the god, Yahweh, was water. Above the water was fire, emanating from Yahweh. The stars were membranes in this celestial vault, admitting the fire and water from above into the biosphere. Lightning, comets, and meteors were temporary rifts in the vault. The vault's rotation produced the regularities of the celestial cycle.

Ezekiel's more elaborate description has been taken as fantasy. His vault consists of ice, crystalline. Above it are thunder and the heavenly fire, which courses down through the vault, refracted like the rainbow, to the constellations in the shape of cherubim. The constellations are marked by stars ("eyes") on these griffins' bodies, and on wheels below them.[3] These wheels, and wheels within them, are fixed relative to one another.

---

1. Section 1 of this essay summarizes an initial publication, which contains fuller documentation and argument. The interpretation was inspired by a course in Assyrian astronomy taught at the University of Heidelberg's Institut für Assyriologie by Erlend Gehlken in 1999, which I attended thanks to my student Kay Joe Petzold, and was first made explicit in the spring semester, 1999, at the Hochschule für Jüdische Studien, Heidelberg.

2. This was the author of the P source. For the sources of the Pentateuch, see Friedman 1985. Friedman dates P to the late 8th or early 7th century. However, as the following discussion shows, P cannot much antedate the 6th century. Instead, P is in dialogue with Deuteronomy and Jeremiah. While P's date is highly disputed, the philological evidence assembled by Hurvitz (1982; 2000) indicates that it antedates Ezekiel. Further, references to P in Jeremiah (605–580 B.C.E.) ensure that it was written before the 6th century, as Friedman has observed (1981: 72–76). In addition, the representation of foreign names in P does not permit one to set it back further than the 7th century (Halpern 2001: chap. 3). P's astronomy also fits far better in the period toward the end of the 7th or start of the 6th century than earlier or later. I believe that P is best understood as a rival to Dtn at almost the same time as the latter, in which sense Engnell's (1969) D-work :: P-work contrast was on the right track, in part. While the author of the Josianic edition of DtrH, therefore, justified his vantage point by appeal to a revised history of the nation, *after the time of the canonical national epic*, JE (which was certainly written down by the late 8th century or at least considerably earlier than P, based on phonological evidence), the author of P *rewrote the mythic epic* to justify his own. The incentive to create a JED and a JEP was to show that each of the two competing versions conformed to the tradition that it in fact was deliberately subverting! P's strategy suggests that DtrH had usurped the more compelling choice.

3. This is why Ezekiel uses the term "eye" ('yn) to mean "appearance" with greater frequency than any other source, however one construes the meaning of the term in P (Leviticus 13). The usual terms for "appearance" involve other roots altogether—r'h, dmh, t'r, ṣlm, and so on.

The internal wheels represent the objects, such as the inner planets, that from a geocentric perspective rotate around the solar wheel.

Like P's understanding of the sky, Ezekiel's presupposes the regularity of astral and atmospheric phenomena. Two mid-6th-century B.C.E. Milesian naturalists concur with their conceptions. The earlier, Anaximander, posits an eternal cosmic fire. However, moisture, which evaporated from earth's primordial muck, forms a vault concealing the fire from view. The fire acts on the moisture; the evaporation creates wind; wind causes the moisture, or cloud, to rotate. The stars are holes in the cloud, like standing waves in rapids, caused by the wind; irregular astral and atmospheric phenomena are caused by sudden gusts.

Anaximander's three or four wheels of fire, with cloud-rims that reveal the fire in spots, resemble the four wheels in Ezekiel's vision. Their number reflects the conviction that astral orbits are multiple—for fixed stars, sun and outer planets, inner planets, and perhaps the zodiacal constellations. The fire outside the heavenly vault of moisture is the fire of Ezekiel and Genesis 1. And the appeal to the fire as the agent of creation—it created the evaporation that caused clouds and wind—probably approximates what Ezekiel had in mind.

Shortly after Anaximander, Anaximenes suggested that the stars were pegged to "the crystalline," the vault of heaven, like nails. The vault rotated, carrying the stars with it. The stars were two-dimensional, like leaves, a shape borne aloft by air. The sun was lowest, presumably because it provided heat. Further, the heavens wound like a turban around one's head: the paths of the stars crossed over one another, confounding observers. Anaximenes hypothesized that the stars originated from the wind's effect on the primordial waters; the same view probably underlies Genesis 1. Further, his vault rotates as a whole, as in Genesis 1. Thus, in large measure, Anaximander and Ezekiel coincide, and Anaximenes and P coincide.

The coincidence of Jerusalemite and Milesian views in the 7th through mid–6th centuries B.C.E. has a genetic explanation. In the mid–8th century, Babylonian astronomers began compiling daily diaries of heavenly phenomena. They had long known that lunar eclipses could only occur at the full moon, solar eclipses at the new moon. In Sargon II's time, these astronomers were incorporated into the service of an Assyrian realm reaching into the Mediterranean. Nor did it take them long to discover the periodicity of lunar eclipses. By the end of the century, they were undertaking to predict solar eclipses, and would do so with increasing success.

Assyrians conceived the sky as a two-dimensional surface. This assumption programed the Western astronomies reviewed above. Indeed, Anaximenes places the earth equidistant from all points of the crystalline. This is the basis of his argument that it is suspended on air. Anaximenes understands the heavens as a hemisphere, supported on the air like the earth at their center.

From Thales to Anaximenes, Milesian astronomies reflect Assyrian and Babylonian influences. The same holds for P and Ezekiel, and, as argued below, other figures both in Judah and in Ionia. The commonality suggests a mechanism for the transfer, which is explored below. By sharing the results of celestial observation, Assyria and Babylon introduced the notion of the predictability of the sky into Judah and Greece, precipitating profound theological turmoil, since the independence of the gods was suddenly called into question. Even eclipses were mechanical.

The Western revolution facilitated by Mesopotamian astronomy has its roots in the 8th century B.C.E. At that time, Mesopotamian glyptic shifted away from anthropomorphic representation toward using symbols of gods, which became dominant in Neo-Babylonian art (Ornan 1993a). Whether West Semitic or Mesopotamian in origin,[4] the shift toward nonfigurative iconography is paralleled in 7th-century Syria and Transjordan, where the trend was toward astral symbols. In Judah, starting in the 8th century, the transition was toward aniconic seals, although rare seals with figures also moved from solar to lunar and astral imagery in the 7th century.[5]

Against the background of international developments and particularly the socialization of astronomical knowledge during these centuries, the change in art probably had multiple significations, not all mutually exclusive. On the one hand, it expressed the elevation of astral gods. Prescinding from iconic invocation of the high (solar) god in favor of more proximate subordinates may, however, reflect deference to the god's special pertinence to the king, or even local subordination to an international or universal overlord. Or perhaps it celebrated the heavens' regulation, the divine natural order.

Deuteronomy, the Josianic edition of Kings, Zephaniah, and Jeremiah (as well as P and Ezekiel, obliquely) first introduce the term "the host of heaven." Their assault on "the host of heaven" coincides with the introduction of the terms "heavens of the heavens" in Deuteronomy and Kings and "pitched [as a tent] the heavens" in Jeremiah and Ezekiel. That is, in the late 7th century, a new idea of the sky arrived in Jerusalem. The skies were limited by the plate, or vault, restricting access to the heavens of the heavens—the sky above the terrestrial sky.[6] The stars were membranes, holes, in the vault. The presence of such language in literature from Josiah's court—and the resistance to assault on the host in concessive sources, such as P and Ezekiel—indicate that the producers of royal literature had not only deployed the astral theories of the Mesopotamian center, but were in addition squabbling over their implications. How far these theories penetrated and how they were appropriated, both in Judah and in Ionia, is the subject of the next sections of this discussion.

II. Astronomy in Jeremiah and Xenophanes

Judahite astronomies, like those of P and Ezekiel and, indeed, Jeremiah and others are occult, not explicit. Whether this represents a defensive strategy, concealing iconoclastic treatments of the heavens from broad audiences, is unsure. However, Near Eastern writing is often intended for a bifurcated audience of insiders and outsiders. The effect on outsiders is supposed to be different from that on insiders (Halpern 2001: chap. 5C). This is why it is so often anonymous: the authorship is communal, shared among the

---

4. See Mettinger 1995; cf. Ornan 1993b; Hendel 1997. The two modes of representation probably coexisted for millennia, and almost certainly from the onset of scribal literacy (in Mesopotamia, for example, the scribal sign for the sky god, An, was a star).

5. For the date of the transition, see Uehlinger 1993: 284–86; for the transition itself, see Keel and Uehlinger 1992: 327–429.

6. This is why Ezekiel (1:1) can say, "the heavens were opened": the visible sky is a fabric, like a tent.

insiders. Even in texts with authorial attribution, the same principle often applies, so that, for example, Ezekiel's assumptions about the sky and its constellations are encoded into rather than espoused by his vocation narrative. Examination of the consequences of Assyrian proselytization in the 7th–6th centuries B.C.E. consequently requires attention to implicit assumptions or cryptic elements in biblical texts. These relate astronomy to theology, extending the earlier cosmologies described above in ways resembling their extension in Ionia.

The rejection of the astral gods in 7th-century Jerusalem entailed a reinterpretation of Yahweh's Host. Late in the century, P writes in Gen 2:1:

> The heaven and the earth were completed, and all their Host.

Here, the Host is singular, and represents all created things. P identifies Yahweh's Hosts, plural, specifically as Israel (Exod 12:40–42):

> So it was, at the end of thirty years and four hundred years, that in the middle of this very day, all the hosts of Yahweh went forth from the land of Egypt. It is a night of commemoration to Yahweh, to their having been brought forth from the land of Egypt . . . for all the sons of Israel for their generations.

But the Host's desacralization went farther. Jeremiah 10 and Deuteronomy 4, around 600 B.C.E., extend it.[7]

Deut 4:6–11 claims that the nations see Yahweh's laws as Israel's incomparable wisdom. No great nation has gods as "close" as Yahweh is to Israel. The Israelites saw, *with their own eyes*:[8]

> Yahweh spoke to you from the midst of the fire, you hearing the sound of the words, but not seeing an image, only a sound.

Yahweh provided the tablets of the covenant.[9] Moses stresses that they saw no image at Horeb, lest they fashion images of any sort, male or female, bird, animal, or fish (4:13–18),

---

7. A post-exilic dating of Jeremiah 10, based on its resemblance to Deutero-Isaiah, is refuted by Sommer 1998; see further Halpern 1998a. The view that Deuteronomy 4 is postexilic is also based on its similarity to Deutero-Isaiah's theology, but as Sommer shows, Deutero-Isaiah was influenced by Jeremiah 10, and the likelihood is that Deuteronomy 4, which is closely related to Jeremiah 10, constituted another of the influences on Jeremiah. For the dating of Deuteronomy 4, see Friedman 1981. Note that the characterization of Yahweh in Jeremiah 10 is picked up again in Jeremiah 51, indicating that it is earlier than that collection; Jeremiah 50–51 is a prophecy against Babylon, repeatedly invoking proto-Isaiah, but except in an added verse, 51:28, calqued from 51:27, it evinces no knowledge of events after 539 B.C.E. Similarly, the vocabulary of Jeremiah 10 is purely Jeremianic, including terms such as *hebel*, not employed for this purpose in Deutero-Isaiah; neither does Deuteronomy 4 resemble Deutero-Isaiah. Finally, the frontal assault on astral divination is not an element in Deutero-Isaiah, where it is merely mocked in 47:13: it is not a concern of the late 6th, but of the late 7th century B.C.E.

8. Note that he reminds them of how Horeb burned unto the heart of the heavens, with darkness, cloud, and dark cloud (*ʿrpl*): the epiphany is fire surrounded by dark cloud, moisture that contains it. The emphasis on eyewitness testimony handed down through the generations is particularly ironic in an archaizing pseudepigraph, yet central to its purpose.

9. And instructed Moses in the law for Canaan (Deut 4:12). That is, Deuteronomy is presented as the supplement to the J decalogue of Exodus 34, and as an elaboration of the Covenant Code in E, when in fact it deliberately revises both. The contrast to Ezekiel's and Jeremiah's views of JE, treated below, is important.

and, coordinate with this,

> lest you lift up your eyes to the heavens, and see the sun and the moon and the stars, all
> the host of the heavens, and stampede[10] and prostrate yourself to them and serve them,
> which Yhwh your god distributed to all the peoples under all the heavens; whereas, *you*,
> Yahweh took, and brought you forth from the iron furnace, from Egypt, to be a people
> to him, an ancestral lot as on this day.[11]

The conclusion renews the emphasis on avoiding iconography, "for Yahweh your god is
consuming *fire*" (4:23–24): Yahweh *is* fire in Deuteronomy (and these images are meaningful). He, not the stars, is the fire behind the vault of the heavens.

This text equates the stars with icons. The argument that icons are of human manufacture (4:28) traces its pedigree through Isaiah (2:8); our passage adds that they distort reality—that Yahweh has no image, a theology shared with Jeremiah.[12] The stars are not
Israel's special province, but are universal. Unlike Yahweh, who is *near to Israel*, immanent,
sublunary, the stars are *distant*, disinterested. In the same vein, Deuteronomy banishes all
mantic arts other than direct aural revelation by Yahweh (18:8–22).

Jer 10:2 likewise pairs icons with star-gazing:

> Don't learn the way of the nations, nor be panicked by the signs of the heavens, for the
> nations are panicked by them.

The stars, statutes, and statues[13] of the nations are illusion (*hebel*), manufactured items
(Jer 10:2–9). Yahweh is the *real* (*'mt*) living god; causing earthquakes; the one who established the world (*tbl*) *with his wisdom, and with his insight* pitched the heavens; at the sound
of whose putting water in the heavens (thunder), mists rise up from the ends of the earth;

---

10. *ndḥ*: the term appears with the meaning "to be impelled from the true path" in Deut 4:19; 13:6, 11,
14; 30:17; Jer 23:2; 30:17; 2 Kgs 17:21 Qre (probably incorrectly). It is a standard term for the act of exile in
Jeremiah (8:3; 16:15; 23:3, 8; 24:9; 27:10, 15; 29:14, 18; 30:17; 32:37; 40:12; 43:5; 46:28; 49:5, 36; 50:17) and Deuteronomy (30:1, 4 > Neh 1:9; also Deut 22:1), and also appears in portions of Isaiah (16:3–4; 27:13) and Ezekiel (4:13; 34:4, 16; in dialogue with Jeremiah), in Joel 2:20; Ps 5:11; Dan 9:7; 2 Chr 21:11, and, with a slightly
different meaning, in Micah 4:6 = Zeph 3:19; Isa 13:14; Deut 22:1. The *Hiphil* appears to mean "to cause to
stampede." The term is characteristic of Deuteronomy and Jeremiah only, and is certainly not derived
there from post-exilic sources.

11. Deut 4:19–20. This represents a reinterpretation of Deut 32:8–9 (and also Mic 4:5, "all the nations
go, each in the name of its own god") to imply that the nations all follow the same, equally meaningless,
gods, namely, those they think are reflected in the stars (see below).

12. Ezekiel, by contrast, attributes a fire-like image to the deity that assumes a quasi-human shape (as
in 1:13, 26–27).

13. *ḥqwt*: Jeremiah uses this term relating to the astral bodies in 31:35; 33:25 and to time in 5:4. Only in
the narrative account in Jer 44:10, 23 is the feminine plural used in referring to Yahweh's statutes, in the
vein of Leviticus (P), Num 9:3 (P), Deuteronomy, 1 and 2 Kings, Ezekiel, Gen 26:5, 2 Sam 22:23 = Ps 18:23;
89:32, and, in a single instance only in Chronicles, taken from a source in 1 Kings: 2 Chr 7:19. The feminine
singular appears only in P texts. Jer 5:22 uses the masculine singular again in a cosmogonic context, as Jer
31:36 uses the masculine plural form. The narrative in Jer 32:11 uses the masculine singular form in a legal
context. In sum, the usage in Jeremiah relates this term to the natural world, and the main referent is the
stars. It is noteworthy that the term never occurs in Deutero-Isaiah. However, because the term means
both "statutes" and "inscriptions," it represents a pun on the stars, as *šiṭir šamê*, "writings of the heavens."
The intertextual reference is to Deut 4:5ff., which opens with the statement on Yahweh's statutes as
Israel's wisdom. Yahweh wrote his statutes in the sky as well as on the tablets of the commandments.

who makes lightning into rain, causing the wind to go forth from his treasure houses (10:10–13; 51:15–19). The *real* god lifts water with thunder, and the evaporation causes lightning, which causes rain; the lightning and moisture cause wind. Unlike the lifeless ("windless") gods of the foolish peoples, this is Israel's proprietary god (10:14–16).

Jeremiah's immanent god ("am I a god from nearby, and not a god from afar?" [Jer 23:23]) is thus like P's and Deutero-Isaiah's. Although he is immobile, he causes locomotion, which P, at least, defines as life. Conversely, it is central to the gods (or primary causes) of Thales, Anaximenes, and Heracleitus that they themselves are in motion. Xenophanes' disciples, however, explicitly deny the possibility of such motion. On the stars, Thales represents a traditional view. P maintains that the stars circulate only with the heavens. This is assumed by Anaximander and Ezekiel, and stressed by Anaximenes.

As Hippolytus notes, the traditional view was that the celestial bodies circle the earth. This assumption implied the existence of an underworld, which is absent from the texts described above. The repudiation of the underworld and afterlife transformed the culture of the 7th–6th centuries B.C.E. Too radical to persist, its doctrinal residue nevertheless programmed later cosmology. The Milesian recourse was to deny the three-dimensionality of the stars. This overture, anticipated by Jeremiah, resonates in Heracleitus and Xenophanes, and in Trito-Isaiah. The sun and planets as orbs would return with a vengeance in the 5th century, and they remained important in other theologies throughout the ancient Near East in later centuries. But the reduction of celestial phenomena to two dimensions, with another reality behind them, from Deuteronomy, Jeremiah, and P onward, revolutionized and secularized cosmology, begetting a cosmos that was Newtonian, regular, and susceptible to scientific understanding.

The connections between Jeremiah and Deutero-Isaiah, on the one hand, and radical cosmologies in 6th-century Ionia, on the other, are central to understanding Assyrian and Babylonian influences in the West. There are hints about the connections: Jeremiah 10 and Deutero-Isaiah deploy satire against iconography; one pre-Socratic joins them.

Xenophanes mocks icons as well as anthropomorphism and divine immorality in Homer and Hesiod.[14] The resemblance is to P and Jeremiah, both of whom minimize

---

14. Germane in this context are the following fragments and testimonia: Diogenes Laertius 9.20; Aristotle, *Rhet.* B23 1399b 5; B26 1400b 5; Timon fr 59 = Sext. Emp., *Pyr.* 1.224; Diogenes 9.18; Athenaeus 11.462c 19–22; and especially DK frags. 11–12, 14–16, 23.

DK frag. 15. Clem., *Strom.* 5.110: "But if cattle [and horses] and lions had hands, or could draw with hands and fashion artworks as do men, then horses would draw images of gods like horses, cattle images of gods like cattle, and they would draw bodies according to the frame that [each] has."

DK frag. 16. Clem., *Strom.* 7.22: "And Ethiopians [say that their own gods are] flat-nosed (*simos*, concave) and black (-haired?), while Thracians (say theirs are) light-eyed and red-haired."

The principle is summarized in DK frag. 23. Clem., *Strom.* 5.109, the start of a key sequence: "One god, greatest among gods and men, not like mortals in bodily frame or thought."

The protest is carried into anthropomorphism in general, as Clement continues:

DK frag. 14. Clem., *Strom.* 5.109: "But the mortals believe (hold) the gods to have been born, to have their (mortals') own clothing, and voice and (bodily) frame."

And Sextus reports in DK frag. 11. Sext., *Math.* 9 193 (also DK frag. 12. Sext., *Math.* 1 289): "All those things, Homer and Hesiod attributed to the gods, which among men are a disgrace and a failing, to steal, to commit adultery, and to trick/defraud one another."

The view is confirmed by a retort concerning the power of the dead attributed by Plutarch to Hieron: Plutarch, *Reg. apophth.* (Sayings of Kings and Commanders) 175c: "To Xenophanes the Colophonian, when

anthropomorphism.[15] Deuteronomy's stress on god's disembodiment (4:12) is also a theme taken up by Xenophanes. He takes Homer and Hesiod to task for not realizing that "god" is an absolute, not relative, quantity. Related is the rejection of JE in Deuteronomy, P, Jeremiah, and Ezekiel—a rejection of anthropomorphism, the ancestral cult, and, principally, tradition.

Like Hosea, and especially Jeremiah, Xenophanes insists that the gods are manifestations of something more basic, the one, greatest being. Aristotle in particular makes it clear that Xenophanes defined both "god" and earth as "unbounded" spatially and temporally.[16] Furthermore, Xenophanes' god is all intellect: he perceives and knows as a whole, does not move,[17] and moves the world by force of mind,[18] as P's creator does by fiat. Xenophanes' astral theory was strongly influenced by Thales's prediction of the solar eclipse of 585.[19] Xenophanes, in Weberian terms, inhabited a "disenchanted" world.

Xenophanes characterizes celestial phenomena as ephemeral, misleading, illusory. Dust carried skyward by evaporation combusts, creating stars, which coalesce into suns. Where there is no water, the resultant sun vanishes. Suns are repeatedly created and extinguished. Heraclitus follows Xenophanes in saying that "the sun is new every day."

---

he said he could barely keep two servants, he (DK Hieron) said, 'Yet Homer, whom you disparage, keeps more than a myriad as a dead man.'"

15. On the "finger of god" in the mouth of Egypt's prestidigitators, see Exod 8:15; see also Exod 31:18 = Deut 9:10, in a work that denies that Yahweh has any form (see below); further anthropomorphism in P tends toward the most hackneyed expressions only, for example, Exod 7:4–5.

16. See Aristotle, *On the Heavens* 2.13 294a 21 (where Empedocles criticizes Xenophanes for thinking that what cannot be seen is like what can be seen, that is, for extrapolating from the known rather than the unknown!); *Rhetoric* B23 1399b 5, where, with Aeschylus (*Supplices* 96–103), Aristotle applies to the many gods the argument Xenophanes almost certainly applied to the One; compare with *Metaphysics* A5 986b 18, where Aristotle has Xenophanes fail to address the topic of whether the prime cause and/or the constituent matter of the universe is the One. There is uniform agreement between our ancient synthesizers and epitomizers and the extant fragments of Xenophanes' discourse that he was the first figure surviving into the Greek philosophical tradition who maintained the Oneness of the cosmos, and particularly of god. So Aristotle, *Metaphysics* A5 986b 18; Cicero, *Acad. Pr.* 2.118; less so Plato, *Sophist* 242cd. Gibbon remarks in connection with Stoicism, "as it was impossible for them to conceive the creation of matter, the workman in the Stoic philosophy was not sufficiently distinguished from the work; whilst, on the contrary, the spiritual God of Plato and his disciples resembled an idea rather than a substance" (n.d.: 27). Xenophanes fell into neither trap, standing, as it were, ahead of the bifurcation. The ancients counted Parmenides and Empedocles and the entire Eleatic school as his successors. But they tended either to elaborate or to reject particular elements of his system of thought (as is implied in Aristotle, *Metaphysics* A5 986b 8–34).

17. Diogenes Laertius 9.19–20; Aristotle, *Metaphysics* A5 986b 18; Simpl., *in Phys.* 22, 22ff.; Hippol., *Haer.* 1.14, 1ff.; Cicero, *Acad.* 2.118; d n deor 1.11.28: Pseudo-Galen, *On Philosophical History* 7 (DK 604 17); Timon fr 59 Sext. Emp., *Pyr.* 1.223; Timon fr 60 Sext. Emp., *Pyr.* 1.224; Diogenes Laertius 9.18; Theodoret 4.5 from Aetius D 284 not; Galen, *Commentary on the Hippocratic Treatise on Nature* (in Hippocr D nat hom) 15.25k; Aetius 2.4.11; DK frags. 23, Clem., *Strom.* 5.109; 24, Sext. *Math.* 9.144 (Diog 9.18ff. has similar); 25, Simpl., *in Phys.* 23.19; 26, Simpl., *in Phys.* 23.10.

18. See especially DK frag. 25. In Xenophanes' universe, there is no intellection without perception (especially frag. 18, but also frags. 24–25, 34–36; Philo, *Prov.* 2.39; Hippol., *Haer.* 1.14.5–6; Sext. Emp., *Math.* 7.14; and the various natural scientific observations).

19. Along with Herodotus (1.74) and Heraclitus (DK 22 B 38), Xenophanes was highly impressed by the prediction (see DK 21 B 19).

Jeremiah calls the stars *hebel*, vapors, phantoms.[20] Deutero-Isaiah, in a related vein, speaks of multiple "suns" and of permanent illumination by Yahweh as replacing the ephemeral sun and moon.[21] Jeremiah describes Yahweh as "the source of living waters," and the rising of water into the sky for lightning as the essence of creation. He and Xenophanes have transcendent gods that are immanent, near, inside the biosphere.[22]

In this combination of views, Xenophanes is unique on the Greek side and Jeremiah alone on the Israelite.

One Jeremianic complex deserves closer attention: ancestral devotion to "bootless" non-gods and "(the) baal" (2:8, 11), characterized as vapors (2:5), made the ancestors into vapors (2:5). Jeremiah (2:13) summarizes:

> For my people have done two bad things: (1) they abandoned the source of living waters (*mĕqôr mayîm ḥayyîm*) to (2) hew for themselves cisterns, broken cisterns that do not hold water.

In a second passage, Jeremiah extends the metaphor. The extramural high place with altars and *asherim* by leafy trees will be despoiled (17:2–3), and the man who trusts in man will live in drought (17:5–6); the man who trusts in Yahweh will flourish like a leafy tree, never fearing drought, always producing fruit. Yahweh's anger is fire, his beneficence water. The continuation there adds:

> O, Israel's reservoir (*miqwe*), Yahweh! All who abandon you will dry up (or, blanch: *ybšw*), and will be reckoned (lit.: written) as those turning into the Earth,[23] for they have abandoned the source of living waters, Yahweh.

Jeremiah contrasts the Edenic park terraces of the high places with the true nourishment of the faithful. Yahweh is the "source of living water." "Living" water is ground water,[24] which excludes foreign rivers, the Nile and Euphrates (Jer 2:18). Apostates from the true waters are as those reverting to their state as earth:[25] they "dry up," like the primordial

---

20. Jer 10:2; cf. the invocation of "statutes" in 31:35–36, in which Yahweh is "he who installs the sun for daily light, the statutes (= engravings) of the moon and stars for light at night, who quiets the sea that its waves murmur." In 15:9, Jeremiah uses the stars as a metaphor: "the progenetrix of seven is anguished, her soul expires, her sun sets while it is still daytime. . . ." Why the mother of seven and the setting of the sun? The image is that of the planets, the Pleiades (Hebrew *kîmâ*), or both. The mother of seven is the Israelite (high) goddess whom Jeremiah rejects. Thus *šeqer* in Jeremiah is "mere appearance." For the Heraclitan fragment, see DK 22 B 6; for the image of the Pleiades in the company of the sun and moon found at 7th-century B.C.E. Ekron, see Gitin 1995: 71, fig. 4.14.

21. Isa 54:12, with the permanent illumination in a new heaven and earth (60:19–20; 65:17; 66:22). The new heaven and earth are the rebuilt Temple of Jerusalem, and the direct illumination by Yahweh in place of the impermanent sun and moon reflects unmediated access from the Temple to the region originally beyond the vault of the heavens. Whether the suns of Isa 54:12 are astral or architectural is disputed, as is its relation to Ps 84:12.

22. The clearest statement of this principle in Jeremiah is in 23:24: "Do I not fill the heavens and the earth?" Note further Deut 4:7 and Jeremiah's extension of it in 23:23. Jeremiah's god, like Xenophanes', is infinite.

23. Read with 4QJer^a, *wswry b'rṣ yktbw*; on the first term, see Jer 2:21, as well as 17:13 Qere. Compare the inscription of the sin of Judah in 17:1, to which this line returns.

24. It can sit in a well (Gen 26:19, J). For the term, see Gen 26:19, J; Lev 14:5, 6, 50–51, 52; 15:13; Num 19:17; Deut 4:10; Jer 2:13; 17:13; Zech 14:8; Cant 4:15.

25. Compare J in Gen 3:19. The J passage is a divine pronouncement to humans that they came from earth and revert to it. While it is not the point of this paper to trace differences in various Israelite

mud in Xenophanes' later cosmology, and this dessication is the nature of death. The reason is that they "trust in man," a reference that may include the ancestors.

Also pertinent is Jeremiah's image of the deities for whom Israel abandoned Yahweh— namely, broken cisterns that do not hold water. The reference is twofold. On the one hand, it calls to mind subterranean tombs, not intended to retain water. On the other, Jeremiah refers to "the land of the living," a term he shares with other sources, including Ezekiel.[26] This contrasts with the underworld, because consignment there ends the memory of a man, or, in the metaphor, of a tree.

Admittedly, this is close exegesis. But the context is definitive. Chthonic objectification of other gods cannot have been lost on Jeremiah's colleagues. Moreover, the image of the broken cisterns is supplemented in Jer 31:37. The context features some of Jeremiah's more innovative speculation: Yahweh's rejection of ancestral moral liability (31:29–30), the inscription of a new covenant into the hearts of the remnant (31:31–34), and the assurance that Israel's nationhood will be as enduring as the natural law of the alternation of the luminaries, of the shining of the sun, moon and stars, and of the movement of the sea. After 31:37, Jeremiah continues:

> Behold, days are coming, says Yahweh, when the city will be rebuilt for Yahweh. . . .[27] *And the offal, and all the terraces* (šdmwt) *up to the Kidron Brook, up to the Corner of the Horse Gate to the east, will be sacred to Yahweh; it will not be torn up nor destroyed again forever.* (31:38–40)

The offal, terraces, and Kidron call to mind Josiah's reform report. So, too, does the Horse Gate to the east, namely, the direction of the sun's rising (Jeremiah employs the term connected with that rising, *mizraḥ*); the Horse Gate was probably located somewhere in the vicinity of the present Lion's Gate. This is the region Josiah disturbed, and used as a ground of profanation. It must be where the horses dedicated to the sun were situated before the Reform. Jeremiah is making the extraordinary claim that Jerusalem's burial grounds will be purified—just the opposite of Josiah's intentions.

A statement on the processual regularity of the luminaries and the sea leads to Jer 31:37:

> Could the heavens be measured, upward, could the foundations of the earth be plumbed, downward, I too would reject all the seed of Israel because of all they have done.[28]

---

cosmologies, examining them helps to situate Jeremiah and later texts, such as Job (as 7:21; 14:7–22), in related trajectories. J regards humanity and all animals as the products of a mixture of earth with Yahweh's breath, which is the animating force. In Greek terms, the equivalence would be earth and wind (*pneuma*) or air. Enuma Elish, by contrast, traces man to earth mixed with divine blood, something that does not translate as readily into the later elements of the Greek philosophical tradition. P regards animate beings as having the wind or inspiration of god, and to be mobile as a result.

26. Jer 11:19, with occurrences in Isa 38:11; 53:8 (cut off from); Jer 11:19 (cut off, as a tree, so that his name is no longer mentioned); Ezek 26:20; 32:23–27, 32; Pss 27:13; 52:7; (?56:14; 116:9, lands of the living); 124:3; 142:6; Job 28:13 (33:30). Descent of the living to Sheol appears in Num 16:30, 33; Ps 55:16; Prov 1:12.

27. ". . . from the Tower of Hananel to the Corner Gate. And the measuring tape will go forth again before it, to the Hill of Gareb, and around to Goah." On Gareb, see only 2 Sam 23:38, an Ithrite officer. The LXX reads the succeeding segment of the verse as "it will be surrounded with precious stones."

28. The LXX seems to read *yrmw* for MT *ymdw*, and perhaps to emend *yḥqrw*. It understands Yahweh to be saying, "Could the heavens be raised (higher) into the air, the foundations of earth be lowered below . . . ?" The translator imposed his own cosmology onto Jeremiah's words.

This does not necessarily mean that the heavens extend infinitely upward and the earth infinitely downward. However, the heavens do not surround the earth and the earth's underside cannot be reached; that is, the stars do not circulate beneath the earth. It is a consequence of that inference—the extension of the known into the unknown—that there can be no netherworld. Xenophanes, going further still, alleges that the earth stretches infinitely, both in extension and in depth. Xenophanes also denies the reality of afterlife. In general, then, Jeremiah's language reflects an assault on ancestral worship.

Jeremiah's most explicit concern is astral deities.[29] While his Yahweh is "the source of living waters" and a "reservoir," "the baals" are "broken cisterns, that do not hold water." The implication is that the host, the stars, were membranes through which the heavenly waters flowed into the biosphere—broken cisterns. Jeremiah's immeasurable heavens and earth may or may not have been infinite. Jeremiah does speak of stars as inscriptions; and he does employ the phrase "pitched the heavens."[30] But his doctrine foreshadows Xenophanes' view that the stars are ephemeral. For Jeremiah, the stars are illusory in the sense that they are at best two-dimensional holes, not three-dimensional independent objects. Xenophanes amplifies and concretizes the implication.

Not coincidentally, Xenophanes denies the possibility of divination; he is the only classical thinker, with the possible exception of Epicurus, to take this stance. It coincides with the rejection of astrology and divination in Deuteronomy and Jeremiah, and of divination in Deutero-Isaiah. It also coincides with the view that astral circulation is determined, and that there is no underworld. Denial of an afterlife relates directly to the denial of divination in societies reliant on necromancy. Jeremiah, too, denies the possibility of direct human knowledge of god's presence: "Who has stood in the council of god and seen and heard his word?" (23:18). There is no council, he implies. Divination comes from within. Deutero-Isaiah maintains that only Yahweh himself can predict the future.

One biblical passage coincides almost directly with Xenophanes, namely, Isa 40:28: Yahweh is an eternal god, creating the farthest reaches of the earth.[31] He does not tire ($yy\'p$), nor does he weary himself ($yg\'$), there is no searching out his intellect.

---

29. As in Jer 7:18; 8:2; 10:2; 19:13; 44; from 19:13, it follows that 32:29 belongs to the same category.

30. For the stars as heavenly writing, see Jer 10:3; 31:35; 33:25; similarly, Job 38:33. Deuteronomy 4 shares the Jeremianic view and probably represents its inspiration. For "pitched the heavens," a leitmotif in Deutero-Isaiah (as in 40:22; 42:5; 44:24; 45:12; 51:13, 16), see Jer 10:12; 51:15. Note the "four extremities of the heavens" in Jer 49:36, although this does not necessarily imply limitations, because Deutero-Isaiah, who seems to posit an infinite earth, speaks of Yahweh as creating the earth's extremities.

31. *Qṣwt h'rṣ*. The term *qṣh* means the edge or side, used regularly in P's account of the construction of the Tabernacle (Exod 25:18–19; 26:4, 28; 27:4; 28:7, 23–26; 36:11, 33; 37:7, 8; 38:5; 39:4, 16–19), in the description of the Temple adyton (1 Kgs 6:24), and for the end of a stick in Ezek 15:4; Judg 6:21; 1 Sam 14:27, 43. Its use with "of the people" in Gen 19:4; 47:2; Num 22:41; 1 Kgs 12:31; 13:33; 2 Kgs 17:32; Judg 18:2 (Jer 51:31?); and Ezek 25:9 is more general, the meaning being, from some of the people. Job 26:14 speaks of the ends of god's way, as though they were in fact the merest beginnings, the tip of it (including pacifying Sea-Rahab and puncturing the slithering snake in the heaven, Drago). Similar is Balak's counsel to Balaam that from a certain vantage point he will see only the tip (*qṣh*) of Israel, not all of it, in Num 23:13. The ends of the heavens appear in Deut 4:32 (from the first things, from the time Yahweh created man on the earth, from the ends of the heavens to the end of the heavens, has ever such a thing been?, representing the temporal and spatial extent of human reality); 30:4 (quoted in Neh 1:9); Jer 49:36 (the four edges); Ps 19:7 (and the heavens, namely the stars, address the end of *tbl* in 19:5). Isa 13:5 mentions "from a distant land, from the end of the heavens" (cf. Isa 5:26, "the end of the earth"). The idea in 1 Kings 8 that even the highest

Xenophanes' version is:

But aloof from exertion (*apaneuthe ponoio*) by the imagination of the intellect (*noou phreni*) he sets all things in motion.[32]

This is arguably a logical consequence of transcendental monotheism, and it has an antecedent in Jeremiah 10 (above). But the resemblance, as well as the relation to, Genesis 1 is eerie. This is evidence that the conversation was international.

Xenophanes' god cannot be localized, because he is ubiquitous and infinite temporally[33] and spatially.[34] The exegetical tradition confirms this—Aeschylus, Euripides, and later texts explain why there could not be more than one such god; if god is everywhere, no other such god could be there.[35] The other ancient Near Eastern god who is not localized is the god of Jeremiah, and perhaps Deuteronomy.[36]

Because his god is infinite, Xenophanes rejects theogony: those who claim that gods can be born are as blasphemous as those who say that gods can die.[37] The only previous Mediterranean traditions without a theogony are Israelite, specifically in the combination of JE, and in D, P, Jeremiah, and Deutero-Isaiah. Since Hezekiah's men codified JE, we ought not to expect Isaiah or Micah to provide evidence of a theogony.[38] Conversely,

---

heavens, the heavens of the heavens, cannot contain Yahweh implies that the god is the only infinite in that theology. The end(s) of the earth appears in Deut 28:49, "a distant nation from the edge of the earth"; Isa 5:26, summoning a nation from the end of the earth (cf. Isa 13:5, "the end of the heavens"); 26:15; 40:28; 41:5, 9 (*ll'ṣyly*, where he gathered Israelites from); 42:10 (likewise); 43:6 (likewise); 48:20 (likewise); 49:6 (Israel as the light to the nations, to the end of the earth); 62:11 (Yahweh made it known to the end of the earth). Except for the reference to their creation, the ends of the earth in Isaiah are always the most distant peoples, not the land itself. In Jeremiah, (*m*)*qṣh h'rṣ* appears in 10:13 = 51:16, the region from which Yahweh raises mists (> Ps 135:7); and in 12:12; 25:31, 33, where the reference is in fact as in Deut 13:8; 28:64, to the edges of Canaan (see physical boundary below). "End of the earth" also occurs in Ps 46:10; 48:11; 61:3 ("from the end of the earth I call on you"); 65:6. Prov 17:24 may contain a pun on *ksyl*, "fool," and "Orion": the eyes of the fool/stars of Orion are on the end of the earth. The term denotes a physical boundary in Gen 23:9; 47:21 (from the edge of the territory of Egypt unto its edge); Exod 13:20; 16:35; 19:12; Num 11:1; 20:16; 22:36; 33:6, 37; 34:3 (Deut 13:8 + 28:64 ["from the edge of the land to the edge of the land," i.e., Canaan = Jer 12:12; 25:31, 33]); Josh 3:8, 15; 4:19; 13:27; 15:1–2, 5, 8, 21; 18:15–16, 19; 1 Sam 9:27; 14:2; 2 Kgs 7:5, 8; Isa 7:3, 18; Ezek 25:9; 48:1; Ruth 3:7. The term limits time in Gen 8:3; Deut 14:28; Josh 3:2; 9:16; 2 Sam 24:8; 1 Kgs 9:10; 2 Kgs 8:3; 18:10; Ezek 3:16; 39:1. In Isa 56:11, the term seems to be purely metaphorical.

32. *Kradainein*: "shakes, agitates"; or "wields." Simpl., *in Phys.* 22, 22ff.; DK frag. 25; cf. frag. 24.

33. See especially DK frag. 26 and Diogenes Laertius 9.19; see also Arist., *de Melliso, Xenophane, Gorgia* (ed. Bekker and Brandis), p. 977a, 14.2, 8; Simpl., *in Phys.* 22.4–5; Hippol., *Haer.* 1.14.2; Cicero, *Acad.* 2.118; Theodoret 4.5; Aetius 2.4.11.

34. Simpl., *in Phys.* 22.5, 9; Cicero, *Academ.* 2.118; d n deor 1.11.28; Aetius 2.24.9; Aristotle, *On the Heavens* 2.13 294a 21 = DK frag. 28; the earth is infinite in the following: (Ps) Plut., *Str.* 4 (Eusebius, *Praep. ev.* 1.8.4.D.580); Aetius 3.9.4; 2.11.12; Cicero, *Prior Academics* 2.39.122; Hippol., *Haer.* 1.14.3.

35. See especially Arist., *de Melliso Xenophane Gorgia* (ed. Bekker and Brandis), pp. 977ab, 978ab, 979a; Simpl., *in Phys.* 22.22.1–9; Hippol., *Haer.* 1.13.2; Cicero, *Nat. d.* 1.11.28; it turns out that string theory now invalidates the assumption underlying the syllogism.

36. One could argue as to whether Deuteronomy's later partisans shared this view ("even the heavens cannot contain you" in 1 Kgs 8:27, a text from the Josianic or Hezekian edition of Kings).

37. Diogenes Laertius 9.19; Arist., *de Melliso Xenophane Gorgia* (ed. Bekker and Brandis), p. 977a 14.2, 8; Simpl., *in Phys.* 22.4–5; Hippol., *Haer.* 1.14.2; Cicero, *Acad.* 2.118; Theodoret 4.5; Aetius 2.4.11.

38. The Psalter, although full of cosmogony, some of it involving a theomachy, exhibits very little theogony except in the form of references to the "sons of El." It has been filtered through the sifter of Hezekiah's court. The older materials, such as Psalm 68, are those that do not address cosmogony.

later philosophers, and later Israelites, did incorporate forms of theogonies into their cosmologies.[39]

Related is Xenophanes' treatment of the dead. One should not mourn gods, he claims, nor worship mortals. This view derives from the implications of earlier astronomies, and its extrapolation explains why the earth stretches infinitely downward in Xenophanes, and cannot be plumbed in Jeremiah. Xenophanes and, implicitly, Jeremiah reject what is uncertain in favor of what is real: they extend the earth downward, rather than positing a realm of the gods below the earth. They can do so because the heavens turn as a whole, with the stars not circulating under the earth. The effect is to reduce the number of the gods, which no longer includes the stars.

Jerusalem holds the line on this issue. Ezekiel holds out hope for a resurrection, rescuing the tradition represented by entombment near high places and by tomb offerings. But Josianic reform repudiates afterlife by being the first one in history to systematically desecrate the graves of one's own people (see III below). The repudiation of afterlife is taken up, as noted, in Jeremiah, and a group among the Israelite elite embrace it for some time. Job positively denies afterlife: a tree has hope, but, though all the water of the sea be spilled out, a man will not revive (14:16–20).

The Greeks, however, rebelled. Heraclitus followed Xenophanes in an absence of a cosmogony or a theogony, as well as on the evanescence of the sun. But, ever conservative, he insisted on an immortal afterlife.[40] Later, no one agreed that the earth was unbounded in depth or breadth, because, starting with Parmenides and the Saros cycle that developed during the 6th–5th centuries, the earth became spherical, the moon reflected the light of the sun, and already in Empedocles, eclipses were being explained correctly. From the 5th century on, the earth undeniably had an underside.

III. *The State Assault on the Ancestors*

The denial of an afterlife or of ancestral power was most firmly rooted in Judah, principally by virtue of the state's attempt to forge a national, rather than local, identity. It is here that one sees the implications of the new cosmologies acted out in practice.

Judah was ripe for such a development. The first inroad against the ancestors comes in Amos's prophecy against the funerary society (*marzēaḥ*). Later, Isaiah denies the effectiveness of ancestral protection against Assyria and consigns the participants in the funerary cult to the underworld.[41] Isaiah ridicules necromancy and petitions for ancestral intercession:

> Wrap up the document; seal the oracle among my students. I await Yahweh, who is hiding his face from the house of Jacob, and I wish for him. . . . But should they say to you,

---

39. Israelites do so, especially in apocalyptic literature, in positing the generation of divine beings, sons of "God," demons and so on, rather than in the postulation of successive generations of divine rulers.

40. See especially DK 22 B 25–27, 62–63, among others.

41. Amos 6:1–10; Isaiah 28, especially vv. 14–20; 5:11–15; cf. Jer 16:5–7. Note further Isa 14:9–11, where uninterred ancestors have biers of maggots and shrouds of worms; 14:18–20, where even the living lament when an Assyrian king (Sargon II, or predictively, Sennacherib), who, claiming kingship in Babylon, devastated the region, and is denied a formal burial and funerary celebration. On Isaiah 28, see Halpern 1986.

"Seek the spirits, and the mediums, who chirp and murmur. Should a people not seek its gods, on behalf of the living, (seek) the dead?" To (written) oracle and document (they should seek). (Isa 8:16–20)[42]

The life of those who do not seek the oracle is dimness, like the underworld (8:17–22). Isaiah repeatedly suggests the impotence of the ancestors.

This rejection of tradition coincided with a shift in funerary practice in the country-side. After Hezekiah's revolt against Assyria, interment in tombs containing multiple family units or clan sections gave way to the construction of tombs designed for individual households. Hezekian policy seems to have been geared toward marginalizing the kinship system, of which the ancestral cult was an important symbolic expression, and the lineage tombs an even more important object of attachment (Halpern 1991).

Hezekiah's policy was intensified in Josiah's reforms. In Bethel, Josiah exhumed bones from a cemetery on a hill facing the Bethel altar, sparing only the grave of the man of god who had predicted his actions:[43]

the altar that was in Bethel . . . and the high place, he tore down, and he burned the high place, crushed it to ash, and burned an asherah-icon. Now Josiah turned and saw the graves that were there on the hill, and he sent and took the bones from the graves and burned them on the altar, and defiled it. (2 Kgs 23:15–16)

The man of God's oracle was:

Altar . . . a son will be born to David's house, Josiah is his name, and he will sacrifice upon you the priests of the high places who make offerings on you, and the bones of humans they will burn on you. (1 Kgs 13:2)

The local prophet adds that Josiah will do the same to all high places in Samaria (1 Kgs 13:32).

Since 1 Kgs 13:2 was written in light of Josiah's actions, 2 Kgs 23:16 must fulfill the prophecy that priests and bones would be sacrificed. Even the diction in 1 Kgs 13:2 implies sacrifice of the dead—one never "sacrifices" *bones*, only animals or people. But by mentioning both priests *and* bones, 13:2 misleads the reader to expect human sacrifice.

At other towns in Samaria:

Likewise all the high-place temples that were in the towns of Samaria, which the kings of Israel donated in order to anger (Yahweh), Josiah removed. And he did to them all the deeds that he did in Bethel. And he *sacrificed all the priests of the high places who were there on the(ir) altars, and burned the bones of humans on them*. (2 Kgs 23:19–20)[44]

The double sacrifice of priests and human bones corresponds to 1 Kgs 13:2; the sacrifice in Samaria's towns corresponds to 1 Kgs 13:32—the verses fulfilling the oracles beginning and

---

42. The reference is to their preparation in 8:16. For denial of the value of necromancy or of ancestral intercession, see, in addition to Isa 8:19, also Isa 19:3 and 29:4.

43. The protagonist of the story in 1 Kings 13 is modeled on Amos (Halpern 1988: 248–54).

44. Following for the most part the Lucianic readings (in parentheses).

ending 1 Kings 13 enclose Josiah's actions in the North.[45] The diction also gives the impression that Josiah sacrificed live priests, yet careful reading discloses that he disinterred all the priests that he "sacrificed." The treatment of priests in Judah—they are not killed, but are awarded a Temple prebend—indicates how he addressed the living. This disparity between rhetoric and reality again confirms the authenticity of the account and its contemporaneity with that king: were the account later, it would not employ mere ambiguity to deceive the reader. These are the tools, the linguistic technologies, of royal inscriptions.[46]

The account of Josiah's Northern reforms discloses that elite cemeteries, with marked tombs, lay in sight of high places.[47] Barrick (1992) has shown that high places were often constructed and intramural;[48] some, however, were extramural.[49] The location of cemeteries in sight of the (extramural?) high places suggests hope for preference in the hereafter; specifically, the inhumations probably involved public commemoration at the high

---

45. 2 Kgs 23:15, 19. The placement of the seemingly more radical act at the end of the 2 Kings 23 Reform Account has parallels, for example, in 2 Samuel 8, the list of David's conquests. The author's idea—and no doubt this technique was taught in school ("Advanced Royal Inscriptions"), with 2 Samuel 8 used as a paradigm—was that placing a strong statement at the end of the recitation would leave the reader with an exaggerated impression of the king's achievements (Halpern 2001: part 3).

46. In this case, they are deployed not on a monument, but in historiography, with a reach that extends clear back to the book of Deuteronomy. Were the material invented late and in a vacuum of information about the Iron Age, unambiguous lies would have been adjudged more serviceable. In Samuel–Kings, these tools are applied to sculpt the regnal accounts of David, Solomon, Hezekiah, and possibly Jehoshaphat. Conversely, about David's youthful career, sheer, unqualified lies abound.

47. The text claims that the Northern cemeteries are those of the priests of the high places. The sources place us in an unfortunate position with regard to the Northern priesthood. On the one hand, it is clear that there were Levitic, or specialist, elements in priestly service there, not least at Dan (Judg 18:30). On the other hand, Kings claims that only non-Levites were ordained. Not unnaturally, many scholars, including this writer, have dismissed this as a mere canard. And yet, even the most sustained polemic may in fact invoke genuine differences between states or cultures.

48. See further, for the indubitable argument that high places were architectural in character, Barrick 1980; 1996.

49. Outside of 2 Kings 23, see Halpern 1996: 298–99 nn. 20–21, as well as Solomon's high places. For the association of high places with cemeteries or the dead, note the commemoration of the burial locations of the "minor judges," which probably reflect shrines; see van der Toorn 1996: 206–35, and 239–41, 244–45, 253–71 for their occasional extramurality (e.g., Rachel's tomb; the oak of Tabor/Deborah; Abraham's altar east of Bethel, and perhaps that at "the sacred place of Shechem"). Note that family tombs are often "in" towns (e.g., in Judg 8:32; 10:2, 5; 12:7, 10, 12, 15; 1 Sam 10:2). Kish's family tomb is reportedly in Zela (2 Sam 21:14) or Zela of the Clan (Josh 18:28), but possibly merely on a hillside (as in 2 Sam 16:13). David's men bury Abner *in Hebron*, with a procession to the tomb (2 Sam 3:31–32). In 2 Sam 4:12, they bury the head of Ishbaal in the tomb of Abner *in Hebron*, and in 2 Sam 2:32, they bury Asahel "in the tomb of his father *'šr byt lḥm*." If this denotes "which is at Bethlehem" (relative + unmodified locative GN), do these texts imply intramural inhumation? Bethlehem is circumvallated (hence the heroes' breaching of the Philistine camp to reach the *gate* of Bethlehem in 2 Sam 23:13–17). Yet there is no archaeological evidence of intramural inhumation in the Israelite period, but substantial evidence of extramural inhumation. Thus, the evidence favors the burials' being in the territory, rather than within the walls, of the town. The same might apply in the case of some high places, even though, as Barrick (1992) observes, these are consistently said to be "in" towns. Note, however, the locution regarding Abraham's location "in Hebron," when he builds his altar there in Gen 13:18; see the altar west of Bethel in 12:8–9; 13:3–4 or at the oracular oak of Shechem in 12:6–7. Whether or not state shrines were ever extramural, therefore, clan shrines may consistently have been, which would explain the dearth of shrines in settlements as well as phenomena such as the Bull Site and Mt. Ebal. The lumping together of state and clan shrines as illegitimate is a function of Deuteronomistic ideology in the Josianic era only.

place. There is textual and archaeological evidence of such a connection at Jerusalem: an elite necropolis for individuals and nuclear families is situated across the Kidron, Jerusalem's ancient boundary, at the foot of the Mount of Olives and Jebel Baṭin al-Hawa (Ussishkin 1993). 2 Sam 15:30–32 locates a shrine atop Olivet, facing Jerusalem. Solomon's shrines also face Jerusalem, from the south of Har Hammashḥit.[50] David's precinct was within sight of the elite necropolis.

Josiah's desecrated priestly graves simultaneously defiled sanctuaries (2 Kgs 23:15) and punished the dead; hence the unnamed man of god is exempted. In other towns, Josiah sacrificed all the priests of the high places who were there on the(ir) altars, *and* burned the bones of humans on them (2 Kgs 23:20). The double description of the action both insinuates the sacrifice of living priests and expresses the valences of punishing acolytes and defiling shrines. The acolytes were probably identified as priests by virtue of their interment in sight of the sacred precinct.

The posthumous vengeance on priests does not just profane Israel's *bāmôt*, but all who officiate at them. Filling Solomon's high places with bones (2 Kgs 23:14) defiles them permanently, like the Northern high places.[51] Scattering the ash of the asherah-icon over graves profanes the icon. Regarding Judah, however, the text conceals where the bones come from. It does not explain how Josiah defiles the Topheth (23:10) or the rural high places (23:8). He dismantles, but does not defile, the high places outside Jerusalem's gates (23:8).[52] And the text does not mention bones until 23:14, so that readers, having encountering earlier references to action in Judah, miss the implication even in connection with Solomon's *bāmôt* of tomb desecration.[53]

---

50. Today, Har Hammashḥit is sometimes identified with Jebel Baṭin al-Hawa (cf. Cogan and Tadmor 1988: 289). But for the Iron Age, both this hill and some part of the Mount of Olives constitute plausible candidates. If Solomon's high places were on Olivet, or on the east side of Baṭin al-Hawa, facing the town, as the text says, and to the right of the hill as regarded from the town, they too had a direct view of the necropolis.

51. In contrast to the Second Temple period, unclean meat could not be employed for this purpose in the Iron Age. The filling of the sanctuaries defeats the efficacy of rituals to purify Israelites from contact with the dead (for this observation, I am indebted to my friend Gary Knoppers). Note, however, the limitation of priestly mourning to the nuclear family (Lev 21:1–5, 10–11; Ezek 44:25; see also Num 6:6).

52. *Ntṣ*. Yadin's identification of the altar inside the gate at Beersheba with a "high place of the gates" is absolutely emblematic of how archaeologists err in the identification of artifact with text. Yadin did not examine the usage, which clearly indicates that the high places in question were outside the gates, and specifically outside a particular Jerusalem gate (a double gate system; see Halpern 1998c). The altar inside the fortification wall at Beersheba functions as a civic, state shrine. The distinction between intramural and extramural shrines was crucial in the world view of the ancient Israelites and of Hezekiah's reformers.

53. The single case in which Josiah moves bones in Judah—as distinct from scattering ash on graves— is eloquent in its implications. Only Solomon's high places and the sanctuaries of Samaria have more than one form of destruction visited upon them. The other heterodox installations are torn down, burned, and defiled, without details being furnished. The priests royally installed in Judah's high places are not killed or disinterred, merely cashiered and awarded a Temple prebend. We might infer, then, that Josiah treated the high places that he explicitly identified with foreign gods, of the sort that Micah identifies in his famous couplet (4:5: "all the peoples go each in its own god's name"; compare Deut 32:8–9 with 4Q LXX), with a combination of disinterment—played diminuendo in Judah—and defilement with human remains. This implies that the Solomonic and Northern high places are treated in the text as especially alien, especially offensive, to Josiah's cult. And this explains why 2 Kings 23 addresses Solomon's high places at the end of the account of the reform in Judah and just before the reform in Samaria. These are transitional both in precipitating the schism in 1 Kings 11 and in Josiah's remedying its causes (Halpern 1988: 154–55, 174–75, 220–28, 248–54; Knoppers 1993: 187–91). The Northern high places, of course, are in the theology

Although the fact is often overlooked, Kings also identifies the priesthoods of the North as central to Jeroboam's sin. True, 1 Kgs 12:30 reports that the calves entice the people "to go before" them. But Jeroboam's crimes continue: he made *bāmôt*-temples[54] and appointed non-Levitic priests.[55] 1 Kgs 13:33–34 refers to this last point alone. The priests are the moral fulcrum of the condemnation of Israel after the Solomonic schism.

---

of Josiah's court ideologues one of the causes of the Assyrian exile. This in turn raises the question of the organization of the reform account. Regarding Judah, the movement is complex. The first unit is the Temple itself, but this is not separable from the baals, the astral gods, attributed to the countryside—so the two come together. The asherah of the Temple is the next subject, and it is not altogether separable from the Temple itself and, therefore, does not lead to massive measures of contamination. Then come the priests and high places of the towns and of Jerusalem, the former dealt with rather humanely, the latter with an indeterminate defilement. The final movement equates iconoclasm in Jerusalem with the profaning of the Topheth and of the Solomonic high places. The principle of organization seems to be an escalating degree of offensiveness.

Josiah's strewing of the asherah's ashes over graves is not his solution for the asherah-icons of Solomon's high places or Bethel (23:15). The ash of the kings' altars, for example, goes into the Kidron Brook (23:12), as do the goods donated to the host at the Temple (23:4).

Consideration of this action, however, produces new backlighting for the text. In 23:4, Josiah incinerates the vessels of the host on the *šadmôt* of Kidron. The Targum, followed by the medieval commentators and by Stager (1982), takes it to mean the floor by the wadi, that is, the agricultural terrace—*mîšôr* (Stager extends the meaning to include architectural terraces). Yet Jer 31:40 associates the *šĕdēmôt* with the city of Jerusalem rather than the wilderness side of the Kidron, and associates the valley floor with corpses and offal (*dešen*, the term used in 1 Kings 13 to prefigure the human bone desecration), no more to be torn up. Admittedly, the Mot in *šĕdēmôt* may have no more significance than the sin in syncretism. The removal of the ash to Bethel is a bit odd, since all other ash is locally disposed of, and one wonders if Rashi is not right to read "to an impure place" rather than the place-name. This may be the chapel house of the high place. The other ash disposed of in Jerusalem is that of the altars of former kings (23:12), and it is again removed to the Kidron Brook. The Kidron is also the place to which goods donated to the host are removed (23:4). This regular disposal at the Kidron may be connected with the grave sites there, as in Jeremiah. And the association of the Kidron with the graves in 23:6 comes early enough in the account at least to inform our understanding of what happens to the altars' ash.

This possible association of the Kidron with interments cannot be proved. But the scattering of the asherah-icon's ash on the graves leads to another question. In implementing a policy of disinterment, is Josiah merely punishing the dead priests and defiling the sanctuary, or is he additionally making some statement about the ancestors?

54. 1 Kgs 12:31–32; read "houses," plural, with the LXX, as in 1 Kgs 13:32. As Barrick (1992) stresses, these are temples or at least shrines located at the *bāmôt*. However, note the peculiar wording on the Mesha Moabite stone of "making" *bāmôt*: this appears in three of eight occurrences in Kings, in one of four occurrences (Ezekiel versus Jeremiah) in the prophets, and in two of four in Chronicles. "Making" is used much less frequently with "house" than "building" in Kings; except in 1 Kgs 7:8 (where the LXX omits and where the OG has a variant reading), and in the making of *bāmôt* shrines, it is only applied to the metaphorical use of "house" for "dynasty" (as also in Exod 1:21). Similarly, towns are built, not "made." However, at least in the account of Solomon's reign, the architectural elements of buildings are "made." It is difficult to figure out what to make of "making" *bāmôt* and *bāmôt*-houses (shrines). However, the Moabite stone may provide some guidance: in line 3, Mesha reports that *w'ś hbmt z't lkmš*, whereas in line 27 he relates that *'nk bnty bt bmt ky hrs h'*. The latter may be either a town name or a shrine at Aroer. But the contrast in usage suggests that "making" *bāmôt* involves dedicating or preparing them for sacrifice, whereas "building" them refers to the construction of the actual building in which ritual meals might take place.

55. The sense of 1 Kgs 12:31–33 is that Jeroboam constructed multiple shrines, appointed priests for all of them, and then inaugurated the new cultic regimen with a sacrifice at the Bethel altar. Thus, at the end of v. 32, in the accusative nominal phrase "the priests of the *bāmôt* that he made," it is impossible to determine whether the verb in the relative clause refers to priests, *bāmôt*, or both.

The punishment of dead Northern priests is justified by an assertion of continuity in priestly tradition after the loss of the calves to Assyria. 2 Kgs 17:24–41 relates the instruction of the Assyrian transplants, establishing continuity between Jeroboam's cult and the cult that Josiah destroyed. 2 Kgs 17:29 claims that the transplants reused the old high places, and v. 32 claims that they "made priests" "from their *qāṣôt*"—the *qāṣôt* and the unusual expression "to make a priest" echo Jeroboam's actions. The Northern priests and devotees of Josiah's time are identified as closely as possible with Jeroboam's; *and* vv. 34 and 41 take us to Josiah's time in the narrative universe to reinforce the point. In sum, Josiah undoes the causes of Israel's schism and fall. In the absence of the calves, *only* the priests and precincts of the North remained for expurgation.

This is the earliest text in which a king celebrates desecrating domestic tombs. Slightly earlier, Asshurbanipal shattered, instead of capturing, Elamite gods[56] and uprooted shrines. He also demolished royal tombs.[57] Still, Asshurbanipal was dealing with incorrigible rebels. The Judahite variation, typically, directed this response inward, as it also directed Assyrian treaty provisions into the nuclear family (see especially Deuteronomy 13 [Dion 1991; Halpern 1991]). Josiah's account, too, spotlights the bones' effect on places, not the disinterment. Still, Josiah's actions shatter the tradition. In the last movement of the reform, Josiah suppresses Judah's necromancers.[58]

The Jerusalem Topheth that Josiah defiled (2 Kgs 23:10) was probably also part of the ancestral complex. There, fathers rather than specialists sacrificed children. After Josiah's death, Jeremiah discusses the Topheth.[59] He complains (7:30–31) that Judah introduced *šiqqûṣîm* into the Temple; that Yahweh never demanded infanticide, a refrain he repeats;

---

56. For the earlier revolts, see Rassam, *Annals* 3.35ff.; 4.1ff.; 5.21–40; for shattering images, 5.119 (BIWA 52 A V 119 F IV 61). It is noteworthy that even Shushinak, the Elamite god who determines fate, "the work of whose divinity no one sees" (A 6.30–32), and who dwells apart or perhaps in obscurity (*ina puzrati*), is liable to deportation and is thus presumably iconically represented.

57. The text is cited in Barrick 2000:

> I wasted, destroyed, exposed to the sun
> the tombs of their earlier and recent kings,
> who did not fear Asshur and Ishtar, my lords,
> who perturbed the kings, my fathers.
> To the land of Asshur I took their bones.
> I imposed sleeplessness on their spirits;
> I let them thirst for ancestral offerings and water libations.

> kimāhi šarrānīšunu mahrūti arkūti
> la pālihūti ᵈAššur u ᵈIštar bēlēya (variants here)
> munarriṭū šarrāni ābēya
> appul aqqur ukallim ᵈšamši
> esmētišunu alqa ana māt ᵈAššur
> eṭimmēšunu la ṣalālu ēmid
> kispī nāq mê uṣammešunūti

Annals 6.70–76 (Streck, Asb); BIWA 55 A VI 70 F V 49–A VI 76 F V 54 (F is missing A VI 75–76); 241 F V 49–54 (tr). Note also A II 115–118. For the condemnation of the spirits to no rest, see 1 Sam 28:15.

58. And the *teraphim* used in necromancy, as van der Toorn (1996) stipulates. It is not coincidental that Rachel, whose tomb was the object of a cult, probably one of intercession (Jer 31:15), is associated with the successful theft of Laban's *teraphim*.

59. In his Temple sermon, as in Jer 26:1; chap. 26 is the narrative version of chap. 7.

and later claims that infanticide is apostasy, which is a rhetorical trope. His remedy (7:32ff.) is to strew offal on the Topheth.[60] The text concludes:

> They will exhume the bones of the kings of Judah and the bones of its officials and the bones of the priests and the bones of the prophets and the bones of the inhabitants of Jerusalem from their tombs. And they will spread them out before the sun and the moon and all the host of the heavens, whom they loved, and whom they served, and after whom they went, and whom they sought. They will not be placed in tombs for burial, and they will not be interred, but will be detritus on the surface of the earth. (Jer 8:1–2)[61]

In a parallel passage, Jeremiah claims that the kings and people alienated the Topheth to nontraditional gods (19:1–13, especially vv. 11–13).[62] He castigates them (19:5) for building the high places of the baal (7:31, *bāmôt* of the Topheth) and for infanticide, of which Yahweh never dreamed. The indictment is: (1) worshipers claim to sacrifice to Yahweh; (2) Yahweh never enjoined human sacrifice; and (3) the worshipers were really sacrificing to new gods.[63] This reversal of the traditional understanding, flatly contradicted in Mic 6:6–7, also involves rereading Genesis 22.[64] It leads directly to Jeremiah's rejection of JE as a scribal forgery (Jer 8:8–9).[65]

Some time after 609 B.C.E., Jeremiah could predict universal exhumation of all devotees of astral deities. The dead would be punished. Their bones would defile the Topheth. The dual valence of the disinterment and profanation mirrors the presentation of Josiah's

---

60. The contrast being to Rizpah's protection of the Saulides. Note that Jeremiah's claim that there will be burials in the Topheth for want of room elsewhere does not explain the failure to inter remains there.

61. The last is one of Jeremiah's pet expressions: 8:2; 9:21; 16:4; 25:33 (but not in the later materials). Elsewhere it occurs only in 2 Kgs 9:37, which is probably Jeremiah's point of departure, and in Ps 83:11. On *'sp*, "to prepare for burial," note that it is a stage secondary to the mourning of death in Jer 25:33. Introduction of the corpse into the tomb is the likely referent, with burial representing the sealing of the tomb and some attendant ritual of separation (for more on the vocabulary of death, see Halpern and Vanderhooft 1991: 179–244).

62. At this point, Jeremiah returns to the subject of the Topheth outside the "Potsherd Gate." He promises evil against Jerusalem that will make the ears ring, a motif associated with the condemnation of Manasseh, probably afterward. He condemns the Judahites for filling it with the blood of innocents (another phrase associated with Manasseh in Kings).

63. The renaming of the site follows in 7:32, and it is where, in 19:7, the corpses of Judah will again be exposed. "I'll feed you," he continues (19:9), "your sons' flesh and your daughters' flesh" and each other's, in siege conditions. Then he repeats that there will be burials in the Topheth, for lack of room elsewhere—in other words, emergency mass graves. He plans to make the whole town like a Topheth (19:12–13) for burning incense to the astral gods and pouring libations out to other gods. This remark inverts Isaiah's wonderful suggestion that the town would become a Topheth for those who assail it. Aside from 2 Kgs 23:10; Jer 7:31–32; and 19:6, 11–13; Isa 30:33 is the only biblical text to mention the precinct by name.

64. And of texts in J, such as Exod 34:20; such a reinterpretation occurs in P, where the Levites become substitutes for offerings of the firstborn.

65. The *trmyt* and regression of 8:4ff. refer back to the accusations and condemnations of 7:1–8:4. Ezekiel likewise refers to JE as a fraud, but as one authentically perpetrated by Yahweh rather than the scribes (Ezek 20:25). This, too, comes in immediate juxtaposition to the sacrifice of the firstborn in Ezek 20:26, where the verb *h'byr* is used to denote the sacrifice. Ezek 20:5 echoes Exod 6:3, 7, and the sequence in Ezekiel 20 presupposes a giving of the law at Sinai, then a second exhortation to obey it on the plain of Moab. Because Ezekiel here repeatedly echoes P, it is likeliest that he was following that text, or P plus Deuteronomy. Getting rid of JE was clearly an important part of the reformist agenda after Josiah's reign.

deeds. Were the other gods, to whom libations were poured, also ancestral?[66] Were the astral gods identified with the ancestors, since Israel was to be as numerous as the stars? Jeremiah's diatribe (cf. 32:34–35) indicates that Josiah did not strew corpses on the Topheth or raid the Silwan necropolis. In Judah, he used bones to defile, not to punish past trespasses. This suggests a certain unwillingness to disinter Judahites.

This unwillingness, masked by the text, is regularly missed by readers.[67] The text insinuates that disinterment was not a policy in Judah. And yet, the author of the reform report

---

66. The libation ritual also attaches to astral and sky gods, and Jeremiah's qualification in 19:4, "other gods, whom they did not know, neither they nor their fathers nor the kings of Judah," suggests an exclusion of the ancestors from this address.

67. Two other texts describe Josiah's innovation. As is well known, the Chronicler backloads of all Josiah's lustrative reforms into his 12th year, reserving year 18 for the covenant and Passover only.

> In year twelve he began to purify Judah and Jerusalem from the high places and the asherim and the icons and the *massēkôt* [molten images or plating on the other icons]. And they ripped down [*nts*, D] before him the altars of the baals, and the [unidentified cult objects — *ḥammānîm* — seemingly in the position of the *maṣṣēbâ*] that were above them he felled [*gd‘*], and the asherim, and the icons and the *massēkôt* he shattered and crushed [*dqq*, C] and hurled [*zrq* in Kings versus *šlk* in Chronicles] onto the surface of the graves of those who sacrificed to them. The bones of priests he burned on their altars, and he purified Judah and Jerusalem, and the towns of Manasseh and Ephraim and Simeon all the way to Naphtali, in their ruins all about. He ripped down [*nts*, D] the altars and the asherim, and the icons he chopped up to crush, and all the *ḥammānîm* he felled [*gd‘*] in all the land of Israel. (2 Chr 34:3–7)

(The *ḥammānîm* appear in Isa 17:8; Lev 26:30; Ezek 6:4, 6; Isa 27:9; 2 Chr 14:4; and, with the meaning "altar" or "chapel," in Nabatean and at Palmyra. These objects, as well as high places and multiple sanctuaries, are legitimate in the P text, as the context indicates. Ezekiel reinterprets the P curse formula to imply that they were illegitimate.) The Chronicles text homogenizes Josiah's treatment of Judah with that of Israel, which is probably something like the impression the author of Kings wanted to create. It extends the scattering of the ash of the asherah-icon to embrace the other items it takes to have been expunged early, and interprets the graves of the people in 2 Kgs 23:6 as those of votaries (probably under Jeremiah's influence). The Chronicler could justify his interpretation by claiming that the altars, *ḥammānîm*, icons, and molten items were what 2 Kgs 23:4 says Josiah cast into the Kidron from the Temple nave, that is, dedications to the astral gods (the Chronicler would claim that the asherah-icon and the astral cult with the Asherah of Yahweh were identical). Chronicles also extends the exhumation of priests to embrace Judah, again because of Jeremiah's prophecy for the Topheth. But one cannot be certain from the text whether the burned human bones come from above or below the ground. Jeremiah exerts a remarkable influence on Chronicles, which sometimes understands his words, on the basis of the intentional implication of the text, to have antedated Josiah's death (for the influence of Jeremiah on Chronicles, see Halpern 1998a; 1998b). This interpretation tells us a good deal about the effect of the text on an early reader. The later reader goes further. In *Ant.* 10.50, Josephus determines that Josiah's reforms began when the boy was 12, taking 2 Chr 34:3 or its original *Vorlage* in Kings (lost because of haplography from year 8 to year 18) to report a year of Josiah's life rather than of his reign. Josephus probably derived this inference by comparing Josiah's seeking of Yahweh in year 8 (2 Chr 34:3) with Josiah's accession at the age of 8 (34:1). Josephus accepts, as do the medieval harmonizers, the story of Manasseh's reform (2 Chr 33:12–16). He concludes that Josiah was able to reform because his predecessors' follies no longer held (Chronicles introduces the reform to explain Manasseh's longevity). Josephus alleges that as a 12–year-old, the young Josiah demolished groves, altars, and dedications to foreign gods all over Jerusalem and Judah (*Ant.* 10.52). In his 18th regnal year, after finding the book, he ejected the vessels that had been placed in the Temple as dedications to foreign gods (10.65). This is a brilliant qualification: accepting the assertion of Chronicles that Manasseh purged the Temple, Josephus deduces that Manasseh inadvertently failed to expunge the secondary accumulation of goods for illicit gods. Josephus also has Josiah execute non-Aaronide priests of the idols, as the context (10.66) makes clear, all over Judah and Jerusalem. Josephus follows the Chronicler's interpretation, in other words, about the application of Josiah's purge to Judah, but moves some of it to Josiah's 18th year. The Chronicler had the reform of year 12 embrace Israelite territory, but Josephus felt that the

wished to imply that it was.[68]

Altogether, the text asks us to infer that: (1) Josiah killed priests of the cults; (2) he disinterred corpses to defile the high places; and (3) the disinterred were priests, sacrificed posthumously for sacrificing illegitimately. Yet Josiah neither killed nor disinterred any priests in Judah. The victims' status, too, may have been deduced from their location in order to salve the opposition—both personal and principled—that a policy of desecrating graves would arouse. Even this plea applies only to the North. The resistance to desecra-

---

source meant that Judah was reformed in year 12 and Israel in year 18 of Josiah's life. The Chronicler infers the sacrifice of the priests of Judah's high places from the treatment of the North in Kings. Josephus makes it unambiguous by explicitly including killings. Probably Josephus found this interpretation to be confirmed by the fact that Jeremiah predicted it (Jeremiah, again, being misdated to before the reform). But Josephus confines the explicit actions of 2 Kgs 23:4–20 to year 18. Some of this, all the same, he must read in the pluperfect. Thus, the removal of the asherah from the Temple (23:6) and possibly the houses where women wove for the asherah (23:7) may belong to year 12 of Josiah's reform. More certainly, the defilement of the high places in 23:8 does belong to year 12, and possibly even the destructive action in 23:13 against Solomon's high places. Less clear is how Josephus understood the ingathering of the rural priests in 2 Kgs 23:8a, 9. He clearly associates the elimination of the horses and the altars in 2 Kgs 23:11–12 (*Ant.* 10.69) with year 18, and also consigns the killing of Judah's priests to the end of his account of the reform in Judah (10.65), just before the similar actions in Israel (10.66). In so doing, Josephus mirrors the placement of the account of the Solomonic high places at just before the campaign in Israel in Kings. In sending Josiah north, Josephus combines Kings (in providing details about Bethel) and Chronicles (in identifying further searches in the north [2 Chr 34:33], before Passover), his rendition of which follows Chronicles. Overall, Josephus's account reflects considerable critical acumen. In Kings, again, the profanation of Solomon's high places with human bones is followed by Josiah's Northern activity. Chronicles and Josephus show that the sequence implied to sympathetic readers that Josiah killed the priests of illicit shrines in Judah. Josephus, of course, is also harmonizing Chronicles with Kings. The Chronicler's notice of a reform in year 18 of "all the lands belonging to the Israelites" (2 Chr 34:33) leads him to relate Kings's last reform measures in Judah to the same stage as the killing of the priests. All the same, where Josephus elects to discover a shift in the tense of his source narrative is instructive: between 2 Kgs 23:8–9—the ingathering of the priests, but also the destruction of the high places, which he clearly places in year 12—and 2 Kgs 23:11—the elimination of the horses and chariots of the sun, which he clearly associates with year 18. Between the two—and year 18 is the year in which Josephus believes priests to have been killed—falls 2 Kgs 23:10, the verse about the Topheth, which, again, was validated and dated for him historically by Jeremiah's words. Taking his cue from the combination of Josiah's desecration of the site and Jeremiah's description of it, the latter stemming from the treatment of the North by Josiah, at least as reported in Kings, Josephus concludes that what falls after 23:10 all belongs to year 18 and is homogeneous with what he takes to be the report about Israel, namely, that living priests were sacrificed (or, in Chronicles, dead ones exhumed). In other words, Josephus concludes that 2 Kgs 23:5–9, framed as it is with a humane treatment of the priests of the high places, is given as background to the much more radical reform of year 18 introduced in 23:4, the narrative of which must pick up at 23:10. Or we could say that Josephus was guided by the inclusio between 23:5 and 23:9, or indeed the seeming epanalepsis, in the use of the verb, "to cashier," in 23:4 and 23:11.

68. As an aside, consider a modern case of tomb desecration—H. H. Kitchener's destruction of the Mahdi's tomb. The repugnance that Churchill characterizes as Christian and progressive was not shared by Kitchener or, publicly at least, by Lord Cromer; and it is arguable that these officials were thinking in terms of retribution for Chinese Gordon's dismemberment. But Churchill's outrage, which was expurgated after the first printing of *The River War*, is instructive. Concern with Mahdism probably played a role in the British colonial administration. It is not at all out of court that a similar thought process motivated Josiah and Jeremiah, the hereafter being connected to the high place. And yet, they must also have been restrained in some significant measure both by a natural repugnance of the sort that flows from Churchill's pen, and by the even more virulent repugnance of the local populations. See the excerpts from Churchill 1899 in the appendix at the end of this paper.

tion was stronger in Judah, where the indigenous population was partly in place[69] and was an important royal constituency.[70]

What does it mean that our text creates the impression that Josiah was more radical than he in fact was? The first implication is that the audience was the wing of the Josianic coalition most disapproving of the ancestral cult and rural priesthoods. This conclusion contradicts the consensus that DtrH was the work of a disenfranchised Levitic faction. The second implication is that our authors shared Jeremiah's views on the matter. Exhumation even in Samaria was radical, and it confirmed to the elite that the dead were, after all, powerless, as Isaiah had argued. This also became their guiding doctrine, such that the distinctively Judahite repudiation of afterlife[71] pervades Deuteronomistic literature, although not the book of Deuteronomy. How this party set out to change culture and the degree of its success makes for an interesting story. The difference between the party and the book of Deuteronomy, let alone between the party and the sources of the Former Prophets, indicates that the party as we know it took ideological shape well after the writing of the book, or that a purge of moderates occurred before Josiah's reform.

The strategy employed in Kings to relate Josiah's desecrations dictates that, were we insensitive to the depth of Israelite ancestral veneration, we would understand Josiah's disinterments not as desecration, but as activity aimed at the pollution of other cults, just as the graves are used as a polluting acid bed for the asherah. Some hints of the process are tantalizing. In Josiah's period, the phrase "the living god" assumes prominence (2 Kgs 19:4, 16; Isa 37:4, 17; Deut 5:3; Jer 10:10; 23:26, *'ĕlōhîm ḥayyîm*, with a precursor in Hos 2:1, *'ēl ḥāy*, and possibly 1 Sam 17:36). The polemic is indirect, yet the phrase seems to imply Yahweh's superiority to dead gods and that the most pervasive of these are the ancestors (as in Isa 8:19; 1 Sam 28:13).[72]

Similarly, by the late 7th century, the Hebrew Bible stigmatizes all other gods as "foreign." This includes the gods in Yahweh's suite, the baals and asherahs that are the host of heaven.[73] Foreign gods (*'ĕlohê nēkār*), and other gods (*'ĕlōhîm 'ăḥērîm*) are identified with

---

69. For the history of the population and settlement in Judah in the 7th century, see Halpern 1991, and archaeologically, Ofer 1993.

70. In much the same way today, in central Pennsylvania in the U.S.A., for example, when multiple churches with small memberships consolidate, those with cemeteries are least likely to close. They often survive on the part-time assistance of a clergyman from a neighboring institution. And the attachment of cemeteries to churches is also connected with concerns for communal continuity and for the welfare of the ancestors in the afterlife.

71. In the book of Job (as 14:18–22) and, as Gary Knoppers reminds me, in Ecclesiastes. No comparable doctrine is preserved elsewhere in the Semitic world.

72. See further van der Toorn 1996: 206–65. Typically, the locution is understood to contrast Yahweh with the dying and rising gods of neighboring cultural spheres, especially the Egyptian and Hellenic. However, after the 13th century, no evidence for the phenomenon occurs in the West Semitic pantheon; and the reference to Tammuz in Ezek 8:14 is an isolated one to a Mesopotamian deity. Rather, the implications of the phrase probably come by derivation from the oath formula "as Yahweh lives" and the acclamation formula "may the King live" (for the oath formula, see Kreuzer 1983; on the royal acclamation, see Halpern 1981: chap. 5).

73. Although in a partitive sense, it is possible that the host are the stars and the baals, and *ashtarot* either the planets or the planets and the constellations. However, the usage tends to be plastic, so that Jeremiah's "baal," for example, seems to include the ancestors, as detailed above.

the host and with the baal(s).[74] The Rephaim present a similar case. In biblical and Ugaritic poetry, the Rephaim are ancestral figures, possibly of elite groups. In 7th-century prose works, however, the Rephaim are a native group of Canaanites that was supplanted by Israel (Talmon 1983). The ancestors, like the baals and the high places, are identified with the aborigines. Deuteronomy 2 introduces the usage repeatedly, in a conscious conceit. It affirms that, whatever the name of a local population at the time of Israel's advent in Canaan,[75] all were Rephaim—that is, members of an overarching ethnic group, like the concept of Hebrews in J's ethnography, or, indeed, P's, which covers divers political units. The results are comparable to the European "Christianization" of Madagascar in the 18th–19th centuries: as the British assailed the ancestral cult, the islanders developed the idea that the ancestors were really aborigines displaced by more appealing modern inhabitants. Some desecration of ancestral shrines resulted (Berg 1973).

Although Deuteronomy limits ancestral devotions, it preserves the concept of a kinship network.[76] P conforms to this world view in presenting systematic national genealogies, but also evinces a converse principle by furnishing a single funerary shrine of the patriarchs (Genesis 23; 25:9; 35:27–29; 49:30; 50:13). P propagates the Josianic view that the dead pollute the state cult (as in Lev 21:1–4, 11; 22:4; Num 6:6, 9; 19:11–18; cf. Hag 2:13). The view arose late, since only starting with Manasseh were royal interments divorced from the Temple (Ezek 47:3 [Halpern and Vanderhooft 1991: 194–96]).[77] But P expected that a national tomb site away from Jerusalem would centralize the elite ancestral cult. The patriarchs would insinuate themselves into the domestic cult, a result visible in later biblical and Jewish liturgy. The contrast is to Isaiah's diminution and Jeremiah's dismissal of

---

74. For the character of the usage, with "baal" as a collective noun denoting a class of gods or possibly all classes of gods, see Halpern 1993.

75. It takes the local names from Genesis 14: Deuteronomy's historical recitation, as is well known, was written on the basis of the JE material in the Pentateuch. There does seem to be some contact with P, but it is not of a sort that enables us to determine whether the phenomenon reflects a dependence of D on P or the use of shared oral exegesis. The references to Genesis 14 are part of the intellectual and argumentative structure of Deuteronomy 2, itself integral to the book. The implication would seem to be that Genesis 14 was a part of JE before the writing of Deuteronomy.

76. The observation stems from D. S. Vanderhooft, who treats the related issue of kinship in P in his M.A. thesis (1991). This must have to do with the coalition politics of the era. Note that Deuteronomy and DtrH never trace Abraham from a particular town: he is referred to only as an Aramean in Deut 26:5 and as hailing from "across the River" in Josh 24:3 (for "the River" as referring to the Euphrates only from the 7th century on, see Halpern 2001: chap. 14). Why J locates Abraham in Harran is unclear, but P's Babylonian affinities may reflect Hezekiah's or Josiah's alliances. For the restrictions on ancestral connections, note Deut 14:1–2; 18:10–14; 26:14. The limitations on mourning in Deuteronomy and P (Lev 21:5) relate to contemporary as well as older practice: Mic 1:16; 4:14; Isa 3:24 15:2; 22:12; Jer 16:6; 41:5; 48:37; Ezek 7:18; 27:31; Amos 6; 8:10; Isaiah 28. This is mocked in 1 Kgs 18:28 as well. The echoing of Deut 14:1, *htgdd* and *qrh*, in Jer 16:6 (cf. also 5:7; 47:5) is clearly conscious and direct, so that the implication of the text may be more complex than a surface examination suggests. This is particularly interesting in that sumptuary laws become a staple of classical legislation beginning in the mid–5th century at the latest: in the equation governing the speed of cultural transmission (the velocity of the idea multiplied by the capacity of the means of communication and by the inverse of the resistance in the particular sphere of custom), this is immediately after the publication of Deuteronomy. Among formal texts, it was, after all, law-codes that traveled fastest when collectors wanted them; and with them, but more slowly, followed interpretation, such as Jeremiah's. Notably, bilateral citizenship also is introduced almost simultaneously in Judah and Athens.

77. The shifts in interment practice reflect the attack on the ancestral cult (Halpern 1991: 71–77), so it is unlikely that Manasseh and his successors were moving toward the Temple rather than away from it.

the power of the ancestral spirits, and to Hezekiah's and Josiah's policy. P's tomb concept co-opts the cult, on the same principle as the nationalization of elite ancestry in traditional China.

It is possible that Jerusalem would have launched or did launch its attack on the ancestral cult without the impetus of astronomical advances. But Jeremiah and P, at least, representatives of the fiercest phases of that assault, incorporated the new astronomy into their ideological arsenal. It not only was compatible with the rejection of tradition, but accelerated it, in Judah as well as in Ionia.

IV. The Mechanisms of the Transfer

Assyrian astronomical scholarship on lunar eclipses kick-started cosmological revisionism. It lay behind Thales's prediction of the solar eclipse. The same source propelled Israelite innovations. Among these in the 8th century were the literary prophets' *Sprachkritik*; the removal of astral imagery from the Jerusalem Temple, starting with Ahaz; and perhaps the invocation of Seraphim rather than Cherubim in Isaiah's call narrative.[78]

The center remained conservative, and the whole Near East experienced an excess of archaism because increased cultural commerce created a need to reassert local identities. On the peripheries, however, Assyria's program of domination and exploitation impelled intellectual accommodation and created opportunities for implementing new insights in policy: it was on the most far-flung peripheries that evidence of these comes to light.[79] The Babylonian assumption that the stars were on a curved plane relative to the earth underlies the theorizing of Anaximander, Ezekiel, and P. The same concept was amended by Anaximenes and attacked by Xenophanes, but was not discarded in Greek thought until the 5th century, by Empedocles and Anaxagoras. This led to the Hipparchan cosmos, materially like our own. The innovation spread from Mesopotamia. Still, the affected elites maintained contact with one another, as the dialogue of Xenophanes and the Judahite elites and of 5th-century Athens and Jerusalem shows.

What of the 7th-century shift in glyptic, from solar to stellar iconography (Keel and Uehlinger 1992: 335–39)?[80] Glyptic is drawn from a common elite, public fund of motifs. But this is hardly an elite revolt against court-sanctioned "monotheism." The court would punish iconography that defied its impositions. In addition, if 8th-century royal Judahite *lmlk* seals feature solar scarabs, 7th-century glyptic rosettes can be taken as substitutes for starbursts. And the names of the courtiers are monotheistic. The epigraphic seals that increasingly dominate 7th-century Judah also express elite ideology by avoiding visual symbolism. If luni-stellar iconography reflected militant polytheism, then aniconism would

---

78. On the astral connections of the Seraphim, see Morenz and Schorch 1997, who link the Cherub, by contrast, with the wind. The question of why Isaiah invokes Seraphim, not Cherubim, was posed to me by Hayim Tadmor in a conversation in 1984; the choice is certainly freighted theologically and may also have to do with Hezekiah's elimination of the snake-icon, Nehushtan.

79. In Judah in the 7th century; in Ionia in the 6th century; in Babylon, in a way, in the 6th century; and in Persia from the 5th century on (but with the sun above, not below, the great fire).

80. At this time, too, personal names shed all elements of divine names other than Yahweh or epithets unambiguously pertaining to Yahweh.

reflect its monotheistic counterpart, the innovation against which the crescent moon is directed. But such open conflict among the elite is rare in the authoritarian court life of the ancient Near East. Furthermore, on the reverse of some aniconic stamp seals imagery *still* appears. The impression might be aniconic, but the seal is not. The shift toward stellar iconography was part of a process that led to ideological aniconism.

Judahite avoidance of solar-disk iconography increased the distance between iconic reference and Yahweh. But solar iconography might affirm the puissance of celestial bodies. Lunar eclipses took place semiannually, whether they were seen or not. Solar eclipses also exhibited regularity, but their exact periodicity was more difficult to stipulate. Solar iconography was ambiguous, but its absence was not. Luni-stellar iconography proclaimed that all celestial phenomena were predictable, determined by the greater intelligence behind the vault or, for Jeremiah and Xenophanes, permeating the cosmos. The dominance of aniconic seals by 600 B.C.E. comes together with the latter world view, although it also reflects an increasing emphasis on literacy (Keel and Uehlinger 1992: 406–25; see Halpern 1991: 79–91 for the view that it also reflected increasing abstraction and literacy in Judahite society). Late Western stellar iconography may have had a theological valence with this development.[81] Was elite astral worship in Judah reconceived as an expression of monotheistic devotion?

One point of the foregoing treatment is that the job of deciphering texts from the 7th century onward involves awareness of categories in surrounding cultures. For example, P's light is not just visual but tactile—fire. P's wind, and Jeremiah's, is air as well, just as the pre-Socratics' air is wind. Jeremiah's terms *hebel* and *šeqer*, usually related to deceit, equate to doxographic *phainomēnē*, "(mere) appearance." Xenophanes' view of the stars and planets as deceptive is related. The world was closely intertwined semantically as well as economically (e.g., Dever 1995; Gitin 1995). It may be that Xenophanes was responding as much to Jeremiah as to his Ionian predecessors.

But this is no accident. The denial of astral signification in Israel and Greece reflects the calculated recruitment of peripheral elites from the Mesopotamian center. Although tradition reasserted itself, its rejection was the scarlet thread. Assyria had an interest, and Babylon after it, in the evisceration of traditional local symbol systems. Elite hostages, like Ezekiel, were natural targets; so also were travelers and fellow-travelers. Nor were Assyria and its successors the only parties engaged in recruitment. Egypt also played the

---

81. The rejection of the old iconography, as by Josiah, Ahaz, and in part Hezekiah, was itself a product of a Bauhaus critique. Thus, the stars could be pictured as lacking the significance that the sun held in the earlier glyptic tradition. Even in 7th-century Judah, figurines continue to be well represented archaeologically in households at every site still excavated (Kletter 1996; on their distribution and its implications, see Holladay 1987; for an overall discussion, see Dever 1969–70; see also Dever 1982; 1983; 1984; 1987; 1990; 1994a; Olyan 1988). But among the elite, the insistence that the symbol should represent *itself*, not something else, had taken hold—a view first urged in the 8th century by Amos and Hosea (Halpern 1987; see also Dever 1994b). Thus, in the 7th century, stars on seals represented themselves, as being insignificant except in pointing to a more distant divinity. Possibly to some of the elite they remained all that they were before—symbols of the divine (like Sin in Babylon). Thus, some parties apparently thought that the world was as it always had been, with a shift of emphasis to the stars. In that case, our internal Judahite documents, the Jeremiahs and Ezekiels, in effect represented occult literature until after the exile, much as one assumes the early Milesians and other Ionians did. But this is far from sure, just a possibility for consideration.

game, affording Ionian travelers, and no doubt Judahites, unparalleled access to its temples. Hecateus allegedly was impressed by the 360 generations of ancestors he was shown in an Egyptian temple, versus his own 10 or 15 generations (were the Egyptian "ancestors" *ushabtis*?). Xenophanes and Heraclitus both reputedly repudiated Egyptian ancestral worship on the spot.[82] Herodotus visited both Babylon and Egypt, in an era of Persian involvement in mainland Greek politics.

The travelers in question were ambassadors and potential moles at home. The disclosure to Thales that an eclipse was in the works did not take place in a vacuum. This is also why Ionian philosophers so frequently ended up as advisers to tyrants. Assyria shared secrets with potential agents on the peripheries, which would never have been revealed in Mesopotamia itself; it thus inducted the agent and gave him a "leg up" at home. And it was Mesopotamia that won out in Ionia: Nabonidus, or more likely Nebuchadrezzar, was a mediator in the Lydian war of 585 B.C.E.; the Babylonians continued Assyrian policy in Ionia as in Judah, where Jeremiah was a recruit. In this sense, Western culture is the deep penetration agent of Assyrian imperial ambitions: Assyria advanced an elite international culture, promoting monism for a unified world. Its aim was to manufacture a postnationalist ecumene in which local nativism was abated. Every empire attempts, some more successfully than others, to hoodwink vassals into thinking that peace rather than war, accommodation rather than aggression, is in their best interests.

No such new ideas came to the fore at the center. Esarhaddon and Asshurbanipal were more traditionally sanctimonious than their predecessors. Their Babylonian successors went to extremes in archaizing. In the case of Judah, at least, the new culture was presented in the same light, as archaism rather than innovation. But the archaizing required pseudepigraphic support, in the form of Deuteronomy and perhaps P.

The astronomies described above were circumscribed chronologically. They were tenable only during one chronological window of opportunity. By the early 5th century, when contacts between Jerusalem and Athens exploded, eclipses were predictable. The identification of the earth's shadow on the moon revealed that the earth was spherical. It showed that the earth could be interposed between sun and moon. This invalidated the radical view that the earth was infinite, rather than limited and spherical.

The chronological implications are profound. Deutero-Isaiah depends heavily on Jeremiah (Sommer 1998). Yet the Heraclitan view of astronomy that Deutero-Isaiah reflects could not possibly date from the mid–5th century. Even assuming, against overwhelming probabilities, that Deutero-Isaiah is a forgery, one could not in good faith place the text after 450 B.C.E. All this means that the cosmologies expressed in P, Deuteronomy, Jeremiah, and so on must antedate 500 B.C.E. and postdate 700 B.C.E.

Postexilic Judah remained in close contact with Greece. But the cosmological upheavals of the 7th and 6th centuries were in large measure responses to stimuli originating in the 8th century. When the pre-Socratics transmitted Near Eastern culture to the West, they were in dialogue with the last of the great Israelite prophets of the 7th and 6th centuries B.C.E.

---

82. DK 21 A 13; 22 B 127. DK regards the latter as a false attribution. The oldest version of the report on Xenophanes, however, relates the story with regard to Elea.

Appendix: Excerpts from Churchill, The River War *(1899, 2 vols.)*

On the Occupation of Omdurman (2.175–76)

. . . the Sirdar rode steadily onward through the confusion, the stench, and the danger, until he reached the Mahdi's tomb.

Here a shocking accident occurred. The open space in front of the mausoleum was filled with troops, when suddenly a shell screamed overhead and burst close to the General and his Staff. All looked up in blank amazement, and when two more shells followed in quick succession everyone hurried from the square in excitement and alarm. But Mr. Hubert Howard, who had dismounted and was standing in an adjacent doorway, was killed by a fourth shell before he could follow. The two guns which had been left outside the town had suddenly opened fire on their attractive target. Apparently their orders, which directed them to shell the tomb under certain circumstances, justify their action; nor does it seem that any blame attaches to the officer in command, who had received his instructions personally from Sir H. Kitchener.

On the Memorial Service for Gordon (2.205)

More than thirteen years had passed since the decapitated trunk of the Imperial Envoy had been insulted by the Arab mob. The lonely man had perished; but his memory had proved a spell to draw his countrymen through many miles and many dangers, that they might do him honour and clear their own, and near his unknown grave, on the scene of his famous death, might pay the only tributes of respect and affection which lie within the power of men, however strongly they be banded together, however well they may be armed.

On a Visit to the Mahdi's Tomb (2.211–15)

From the Khalifa's house I repaired to the Mahdi's Tomb. The reader's mind is possibly familiar with its shape and architecture. It was much damaged by the shell-fire. The apex of the conical dome had been cut off. One of the small cupolas was completely destroyed. The dome itself had one enormous and several smaller holes smashed in it; the bright sunlight streamed through these and displayed the interior. Everything was wrecked. Still, it was possible to distinguish the painted brass railings round the actual sarcophagus, and the stone beneath which the body presumably lay. This place had been for more than ten years the most sacred and holy thing that the people of the Soudan knew. Their miserable lives had perhaps been brightened, perhaps in some way ennobled, by the contemplation of something which they did not quite understand, but which they believed exerted a protecting influence. It had gratified that instinctive desire for the mystic which all human creatures possess, and which is perhaps the strongest reason for believing in a progressive destiny and a future state. By Sir H. Kitchener's orders the Tomb had been profaned and razed to the ground. The corpse of the Mahdi was dug up. The head was separated from the body, and, to quote the official explanation, 'preserved for future disposal'—a phrase which must in this case be understood to mean that it was passed from hand to hand till it reached Cairo. Here it remained, an interesting trophy, until the affair came to the ears of Lord Cromer, who ordered it to be immediately reinterred at the Nile. Such was the chivalry of the conquerors!

Whatever misfortunes the life of Mohammed Ahmed may have caused, he was a man of considerable nobility of character, a priest, a soldier, and a patriot. He won great battles; he stimulated and revived religion. He founded an empire. To some extent he reformed the public morals. Indirectly, by making slaves into soldiers, he diminished slavery. It is impossible for any impartial person to read the testimony of such men as Slatin and Ohrwalder without feeling that the only gentle influence, the only humane element in the hard Mohammedan State, emanated from this famous rebel. The Greek missionary [Ohrwalder] writes of 'his unruffled smile, pleasant manners, generosity, and equable temperament.' When the Christian priests, having refused to accept the Koran, were assailed by the soldiers and the mob and threatened with immediate death, it was the Mahdi who, 'seeing them in danger, turned back and ordered them to walk in front of his camel for protection.' When Slatin went to report the death of the unhappy French adventurer Olivier Pain, the Mahdi 'took it to heart much more than the Khalifa, said several sympathetic words, and read the prayers for the dead.' To many of his prisoners he showed kindness, all the more remarkable by comparison with his surroundings and with the treatment which he would have received had fortune failed him. To some he gave employment; to others a little money from the Beit-al-Mal, or a little food from his own plate. To all he spoke with dignity and patience. Thus he lived; and when he died in the enjoyment of unquestioned power, he was bewailed by the army he had led to victory and by the people he had freed from the yoke of the 'Turks.'

It may be worth while to examine the arguments of those who seek to justify the demolition of the Tomb. Their very enumeration betrays a confusion of thought which suggests insincerity. Some say that the people of the Soudan no longer believed in the Mahdi and cared nothing for the destruction of a fallen idol, and that therefore the matter was of little consequence. Others contend on the same side of the argument that so great was the Mahdi's influence, and so powerful was his memory, that though his successor had been overthrown his tomb would have become a place of pilgrimage, and that the conquering Power did not dare allow such an element of fanaticism to disturb their rule. The contradiction is apparent. But either argument is absurd without the contradiction. If the people of the Soudan cared no more for the Mahdi, then it was an act of Vandalism and folly to destroy the only fine building which might attract the traveller and interest the historian. It is a gloomy augury for the future of the Soudan that the first action of its civilised conquerors and present rulers should have been to level the one pinnacle which rose above the mud houses. If, on the other hand, the people of the Soudan still venerated the memory of the Mahdi—and more than 50,000 had fought hard only a week before to assert their respect and belief—then I shall not hesitate to declare that to destroy what was sacred and holy to them was a wicked act, of which the true Christian, no less than the philosopher, must express abhorrence.

No man who holds by the splendid traditions of the old Liberal party, no man who is in sympathy with the aspirations of Progressive Toryism, can consistently consent to such behaviour. It will also be condemned by quite a different school of thought, by the wise public servants who administer the Indian Empire. It is an actual offence against the Indian Penal Code to insult the religion of any person; nor is it a valid plea that the culprit thought the said religion 'false.' When Sir Bindon Blood had forced the Tanga Pass and invaded Buner, one of his first acts was to permit his Mohammedan soldiers to visit the Tomb of the Akhund of Swat, who had stirred the tribes into revolt and caused the Umbeyla campaign of 1863. It is because respect is always shown to all shades of religious feeling in India by the dominant race, that our rule is accepted by the mass of the people. If the Soudan is to be administered on principles the reverse of those which have been successful in India, and if such conduct is to be characteristic of its Government, then it would be better if Gordon had never given his life nor Kitchener won his victories.

[At this point, the editor, Col. F. Rhodes, inserts a notice of his disagreement with the author and his agreement with Cromer that the destruction of the tomb and removal of the body were necessary and justifiable, although he does feel that the manner of the desecration and disinterment was awkward.]

References

Barrick, W. B.
  1980   What Do We Really Know about High Places? *Svensk Exegetisk Årsbok* 45: 50–57.
  1992   High Place. Pp. 196–200 in vol. 3 of *The Anchor Bible Dictionary*, ed. D. N. Freedman. New York: Doubleday.
  1996   On the Meaning of *bêt hab-bāmôt* and *bātê hab-bāmôt* and the Composition of the King's History. *Journal of Biblical Literature* 115: 621–42.
  2000   Burning Bones at Bethel: A Closer Look at 2 Kings 23, 16a. *Scandinavian Journal of the Old Testament* 14: 3–16.
Berg, G. M.
  1973   *Historical Traditions and the Foundations of the Monarchy in Imerina.* Ph.D. dissertation, University of California at Berkeley.
Bekker, I., and Brandis, C. A.
  1831–70   *Aristotelis opera.* Berlin: Reimer.
BIWA
  1996   R. Borger, *Beiträge zum Inscriftenwerk Assurbanipals.* Wiesbaden: Harrassowitz.
Churchill, W. L. S. C.
  1899   *The River War.* 2 Vols. London: Longmans, Green.
Cogan, M., and Tadmor, H.
  1988   *II Kings.* Anchor Bible 11. Garden City, N.Y.: Doubleday.

Dever, W. G.

1969–70 Iron Age Epigraphic Material from the Area of Khirbet el-Kom. *Hebrew Union College Annual* 40–41: 139–204.

1982 Recent Archaeological Confirmation of the Cult of Asherah in Ancient Israel. *Hebrew Studies* 23: 37–43.

1983 Material Remains and the Cult in Ancient Israel: An Essay in Archaeological Systematics. Pp. 571–87 in *The Word of the Lord Shall Go Forth: Essays in Honor of David Noel Freedman in Celebration of His Sixtieth Birthday,* ed. C. L. Meyers and M. O'Connor. Winona Lake, Ind.: Eisenbrauns.

1984 Asherah, Consort of Jahweh? New Evidence from Kuntillet ʿAjrud. *Bulletin of the American Schools of Oriental Research* 255: 21–37.

1987 The Contribution of Archaeology to the Study of Canaanite and Early Israelite Religion. Pp. 209–47 in *Ancient Israelite Religion: Essays in Honor of Frank Moore Cross,* ed. P. D. Miller, P. D. Hanson, and S. D. McBride. Philadelphia: Fortress.

1990 *Recent Archaeological Discoveries and Biblical Research.* Seattle: University of Washington Press.

1994a Ancient Israelite Religion: How to Reconcile the Differing Textual and Artifactual Portraits. Pp. 105–25 in *Ein Gott allein?* ed. W. Dietrich and M. A. Klopfenstein. Orbis Biblicus et Orientalis 139. Freiburg: University of Freiburg Press.

1994b The Silence of the Text: An Archaeological Commentary on 2 Kings 23. Pp. 143–68 in *Scripture and Other Artifacts: Essays on the Bible and Archaeology in Honor of Philip J. King,* ed. M. D. Coogan et al. Louisville: Westminster John Knox.

1995 Orienting the Study of Trade in Near Eastern Archaeology. Pp. 111–19 in *Recent Excavations in Israel. A View to the West: Reports on Kabri, Nami, Miqne-Ekron, Dor, and Ashkelon,* ed. S. Gitin. Archaeological Institute of America Colloquia and Conference Papers 1. Dubuque, Ia.: Kendall/Hunt.

Dion, P. E.

1991 Deuteronomy 13: The Suppression of Alien Religious Propaganda during the Late Monarchical Era. Pp. 147–216 in *Law and Ideology in Monarchic Israel,* ed. B. Halpern and D. W. Hobson. Journal for the Study of the Old Testament Supplements 124. Sheffield: JSOT Press.

DK H. Diels, *Die Fragmente der Vorsokratiker,* ed. W. Kranz. 10th ed. 3 vols. Berlin: Weidmann, 1961.

Engnell, I.

1969 *A Rigid Scrutiny.* Nashville: Vanderbilt University.

Friedman, R. E.

1981 *The Exile and Biblical Narrative.* Harvard Semitic Monographs 25. Chico, Calif.: Scholars Press.

1985 *Who Wrote the Bible?* New York: Simon and Schuster.

Gibbon, E.

n.d. *The Decline and Fall of the Roman Empire.* New York: Modern Library.

Gitin, S.

1995 Tel Miqne-Ekron in the 7th Century B.C.E.: The Impact of Economic Innovation and Foreign Cultural Influences on a Neo-Assyrian Vassal City-State. Pp. 61–79 in *Recent Excavations in Israel. A View to the West: Reports on Kabri, Nami, Miqne-Ekron, Dor, and Ashkelon,* ed. S. Gitin. Archaeological Institute of America Colloquia and Conference Papers 1. Dubuque, Ia.: Kendall/Hunt.

Halpern, B.

1981 *The Constitution of the Monarchy in Israel.* Harvard Semitic Monographs 25. Chico, Calif.: Scholars Press.

1986 The Excremental Vision: The Doomed Priests of Doom in Isaiah 28. *Hebrew Annual Review* 10: 109–21.

1987   "Brisker Pipes Than Poetry": The Development of Israelite Monotheism. Pp. 77–115 in *Judaic Perspectives on Ancient Israel* (H. L. Ginsberg festschrift), ed. J. Neusner, B. A. Levine, and E. S. Frerichs. Philadelphia: Fortress.

1988   *The First Historians: The Hebrew Bible and History.* San Francisco: Harper & Row.

1991   Jerusalem and the Lineages in the Seventh Century BCE: Kinship and the Rise of Individual Moral Liability. Pp. 11–107 in *Law and Ideology in Monarchic Israel*, ed. B. Halpern and D. W. Hobson. Journal for the Study of the Old Testament Supplements 124. Sheffield: JSOT Press.

1993   The Baal (and the Asherah) in Seventh-Century Judah: Yhwh's Retainers Retired. Pp. 115–54 in *Konsequente Traditionsgeschichte: Festschrift für Klaus Baltzer zum 65. Geburtstag*, ed. R. Bartelmus, T. Krüger, and H. Utzschneider. Orbis Biblicus et Orientalis 126. Fribourg: University of Fribourg Press.

1996   "Sybil, or the Two Nations?": Alienation, Archaism, and the Elite Redefinition of Traditional Culture in Judah in the 8th–7th Centuries BCE. Pp. 291–338 in *The Study of the Ancient Near East in the Twenty-First Century: The William Foxwell Albright Centennial Conference*, ed. J. S. Cooper and G. M. Schwartz. Winona Lake, Ind.: Eisenbrauns.

1998a   The New Names of Isaiah 62:4: Jeremiah's Reception in the Restoration and the Politics of "Third Isaiah." *Journal of Biblical Literature* 117: 623–43.

1998b   Why Manasseh Is Blamed for the Babylonian Exile. *Vetus Testamentum* 48: 1–42.

1998c   The Death of Eli and the Israelite Gate. Pp. 52*–63* in *Eretz-Israel* 26 (Frank Moore Cross volume), ed. B.A. Levine et al. Jerusalem: Israel Exploration Society.

2001   *David's Secret Demons: Messiah, Murderer, Traitor, King.* Grand Rapids, Mich.: Eerdmans.

In press   The Assyrian Astronomy of Genesis 1 and the Birth of Milesian Philosophy. In *Eretz-Israel* 27 (Hayim and Miriam Tadmor volume), ed. I. Eph'al, A. Ben-Tor, and P. Machinist. Jerusalem: Israel Exploration Society.

Halpern, B., and Vanderhooft, D. S.

1991   The Editions of Kings in the 7th–6th Centuries B.C.E. *Hebrew Union College Annual* 62: 179–244.

Hendel, R. S.

1997   Aniconism and Anthropomorphism in Ancient Israel. Pp. 205–28 in *The Image and the Book: Iconic Cults, Aniconism, and the Rise of Book Religion in Israel and the Ancient Near East*, ed. K. van der Toorn. Leuven: Peeters.

Holladay, J. S.

1987   Religion in Israel and Judah under the Monarch: An Explicitly Archaeological Approach. Pp. 249–99 in *Ancient Israelite Religion: Essays in Honor of Frank Moore Cross*, ed. P. D. Miller, P. D. Hanson, and S. D. McBride. Philadelphia: Fortress.

Hurvitz, A.

1982   *A Linguistic Study of the Relationship between the Priestly Source and the Book of Ezekiel.* Cahiers de la Revue Biblique 20. Paris: Gabalda.

2000   Once Again: The Linguistic Profile of the Priestly Material in the Pentateuch and Its Historical Age. A Response to J. Blenkinsopp. *Zeitschrift für die alttestamentliche Wissenschaft* 112: 180–91.

Keel, O., and Uehlinger, C.

1992   *Göttinnen, Götter und Gottessymbole: Neue Erkenntnisse zur Religionsgeschichte Kanaans und Israels aufgrund bislang unerschlossener ikonographischer Quellen.* Quaestiones Disputatae 134. Freiburg: Herder.

Kletter, R.

1996   *The Judean Pillar-Figurines and the Archaeology of Asherah.* British Archaeological Reports International Series 636. Oxford: Tempus Reparatum.

Knoppers, G.

1993   *Two Kingdoms under God: The Deuteronomistic History of Solomon and the Dual Monarchies, 1: The Reign of Solomon and the Rise of Jeroboam.* Harvard Semitic Monographs 52. Atlanta: Scholars Press.

Kreuzer, S.
   1983   *Der lebendige Gott*. Beiträge zur Wissenschaft des Alten und Neuen Testaments 6/16. Stuttgart: Kohlhammer.
Mettinger, T. N. D.
   1995   *No Graven Image? Israelite Aniconism in Its Ancient Near Eastern Context*. Stockholm: Almqvist & Wiksell.
Morenz, L. D., and Schorch, S.
   1997   Der Seraph in der Hebräischen Bibel und in Altägypten. *Orientalia* 66: 365–86.
Ofer, A.
   1993   *The Highland of Judah during the Biblical Period*. Ph.D. dissertation, Tel Aviv University.
Olyan, S. M.
   1988   *Asherah and the Cult of Yahweh in Israel*. Society of Biblical Literature Monographs 34. Atlanta: Scholars Press.
Ornan, T.
   1993a   The Transition from Figured to Non-Figured Representation in First Millennium Mesopotamian Glyptic. Pp. 39–56 in *Seals and Sealings in the Ancient Near East*, ed. J. Goodnick Westenholz. Jerusalem: Bible Land Museum.
   1993b   The Mesopotamian Influence on West Semitic Inscribed Seals: A Preference for the Depiction of Mortals. Pp. 52–73 in *Studies in the Iconography of Northwest Semitic Inscribed Seals*, ed. B. Sass and C. Uehlinger. Orbis Biblicus et Orientalis 125. Fribourg: University of Fribourg Press.
Sommer, B.
   1998   *A Prophet Reads Scripture: Allusion in Isaiah 40–66*. Stanford: Stanford University Press.
Stager, L. E.
   1982   The Archaeology of the East Slope of Jerusalem and the Terraces of the Kidron. *Journal of Near Eastern Studies* 41: 111–21.
Streck, M.
   1916   *Assurpanipal und die letzten assyrischen Könige bis zum Untergang Niniveh's*. Leipzig: Hinmels.
Talmon, S.
   1983   Biblical *Repā'im* and Ugaritic *Rpu/i(m)*. *Hebrew Annual Review* 7: 235–49.
Toorn, K. van der
   1996   *Family Religion in Babylonia, Syria and Israel*. Studies in the History of the Ancient Near East 7. Leiden: Brill.
Uehlinger, C.
   1993   Northwest Semitic Inscribed Seals, Iconography and Syro-Palestinian Religions of Iron Age II: Some Afterthoughts and Conclusions. Pp. 257–88 in *Studies in the Iconography of Northwest Semitic Inscribed Seals*, ed. B. Sass and C. Uehlinger. Orbis Biblicus et Orientalis 125. Fribourg: University of Fribourg Press.
Ussishkin, D.
   1993   *The Village of Silwan: The Necropolis from the Period of the Judean Kingdom*. Jerusalem: Israel Exploration Society.
Vanderhooft, D. S.
   1991   *Kinship Organization in Ancient Israel*. M.A. thesis, York University.

The Jewish World and the Coming of Rome

John J. Collins
Divinity School, Yale University

In 1 Maccabees 8 we are told that, after the defeat of Nicanor in 161 B.C.E., "Judas heard of the fame of the Romans, that they were very strong and were well disposed toward all who made an alliance with them, and that they pledged friendship to those who came to them and that they were very strong" (1 Macc 8:1–2). Accordingly, he dispatched Eupolemus, whose father had negotiated Jewish rights with Antiochus III, to Rome "to establish friendship and alliance." According to 1 Maccabees, the Romans responded by making an alliance with the Jews that required each party to come to the aid of the other in case of war. Thus began the fateful relationship of Rome and the Jews. It was initiated by the Jews, with a view to freeing themselves from the yoke of the Greeks. In time, the yoke of Rome would prove far heavier than anything imposed by the Seleucids and result in destruction on a scale comparable to that wrought by the Assyrians and Babylonians. Rome, the erstwhile supposed protector, eventually became the archetypical enemy of the Jews.

The alleged treaty between Rome and Judas Maccabee had little significance in its time, and some have questioned whether it was a formal treaty at all (e.g., Sherwin-White 1984: 70–79; see also Gruen 1984: 745–51). Judas was killed shortly after the embassy to Rome; treaties normally lapsed with the death of the ruler with whom they were made and Judas was not even formally a ruler of the Jewish people. Nearly 20 years later, Jonathan Maccabee sent ambassadors to Rome to confirm and renew their friendship (1 Macc 12:1–4). Again, the Romans responded positively, but they took no action when Jonathan was kidnapped and murdered by the usurper Tryphon. When Simon Maccabee assumed the high priesthood, he too sent ambassadors to Rome, with a gift of a golden shield (1 Macc 14:24). But again, Rome took no action when Simon was murdered, and promises of aid were similarly empty when John Hyrcanus was attacked by Antiochus VII Sidetes. Hyrcanus appealed for help again later in his reign when he was attacked by Antiochus IX. This time a *senatus consultum* ordering Antiochus to desist seems to have had the desired effect (Smallwood 1976: 10). As Gruen has observed, the Roman responses to these Jewish advances "expressed no more than polite courtesies" (1984: 746–47), but they allowed the Jews to view Rome as a benevolent power that might provide a useful counterweight to the Seleucids. The Romans had crushed Antiochus the Great and were the "Kittim" who had humiliated Antiochus Epiphanes in Egypt, as noted in the book of Daniel 11. And yet the Jews were not unaware of the potentially detrimental aspects of the exercise of Roman power. The same passage in 1 Maccabees that reports the embassy of Judas notes that the Romans crushed Antiochus the Great and imposed heavy tribute on his heirs, and that they had plundered and enslaved the Greeks. But, it adds, "with their friends and those who rely on them they have kept friendship" (1 Macc 8:12).

I. Pompey

The first serious intervention of Rome in Judea came almost a century after the embassy of Judas Maccabee. The context was a civil war between the Hasmonean brothers Aristobulus II and Hyrcanus II. The Roman general Pompey, having defeated Mithridates in 66 B.C.E., sent his lieutenant Scaurus to Syria. Both Aristobulus and Hyrcanus pleaded for his support. Aristobulus sent a lavish grapevine of gold, worth 500 talents, to Pompey, in hope of winning his favor. Subsequently, three Jewish delegations appeared before Pompey in Damascus—one from Aristobulus, one from Hyrcanus, and one from the Jewish people that was critical of both. Pompey deferred his decision, but when Aristobulus impatiently withdrew, the Roman general marched against him. Aristobulus surrendered, but he was unable to deliver Jerusalem to Pompey. There the followers of Hyrcanus opened the gates to the Romans, but the followers of Aristobulus entrenched themselves on the Temple Mount, and a siege ensued. The siege lasted three months and ended in a blood-bath in which some 12,000 Jews were said to have died, including priests at the altar. Pompey, notoriously, entered the Holy of Holies, where only the high priest was allowed to go, but he left the Temple treasure untouched. His treatment of Jerusalem was severe. He had the leaders of the resistance executed and imposed a tribute. Hyrcanus was left as high priest without royal title. Aristobulus was forced to walk before Pompey's chariot in the celebration of his triumph in Rome. Thousands of Jews were deported to Rome as slaves, where they eventually were set free and swelled the ranks of the city's Jewish community (Josephus, *Ant.* 14.1–79; *J.W.* 1.120–58; Schuerer 1973: 1.233–42).

One Jewish reaction to Pompey's invasion is recorded in the *Psalms of Solomon*: "Foreign nations went up to your altar; in pride they trampled it with their sandals" (*Pss. Sol.* 2:2). The defilement was just punishment for the defilement of Jerusalem by its inhabitants, not least by the Hasmonean rulers. But the assassination of Pompey in Egypt in 48 B.C.E. is also viewed as divine punishment for the arrogance of the Roman general: "He did not consider that he was a man, nor did he consider the end. He said, I will be lord of land and sea and he did not recognize that God was great" (*Pss. Sol.* 2:28–29).

We might compare this view of Rome to Isaiah's view of Assyria, the "rod of Yahweh's anger," which would itself be punished for its excess. Another reaction is found in the *Pesher on Habakkuk* in the Dead Sea Scrolls, which identified the Romans, or "Kittim," with "the Chaldeans, a cruel and determined people," of whom the prophet spoke. The pesherist is clearly impressed by their power—"fear and dread of them are on all peoples" (1QpHab iii 4)—but he has no illusions about their moral character—"all their thoughts are to do evil, and with cunning and treachery they behave towards all the nations. . . . All of them come to use violence . . . to devour all the nations, like an eagle, insatiable." The pesher goes on to note that "they gather their wealth with all their loot like fish of the sea" (vi 1). Yet it also affirms that God will not destroy his nation at the hand of the peoples, but will place the judgment over all the peoples in the hand of his chosen ones (v 3–4).

II. Herod

Rome, however, was to have a more-lasting impact on Judea than Assyria had. In the following years the Jews would get the flavor of Roman rule in the east (Schuerer 1973: 1.245–46). Aulus Gabinius, who had been a legate of Pompey, was assigned control of Syria in 57–55 B.C.E. and had to put down an uprising by Alexander, son of Aristobulus. Gabinius was frequently denounced by Cicero for corruption and extortion, and he was eventually convicted of extortion in Rome. His successor, Crassus, appropriated the Temple treasury and also stripped gold from the Temple building to support his campaign against the Parthians. This provoked another abortive revolt, led by one Pitholaos, which resulted in the enslavement of more Jewish prisoners-of-war. During the civil war between Pompey and Caesar, Aristobulus and his son Alexander were put to death by supporters of Pompey. When Caesar gained control of Palestine, he enhanced the status of the High Priest Hyrcanus, but he essentially renewed the settlement that had been imposed by Pompey. Most significantly, he awarded Roman citizenship to the Idumean Antipater in recognition of services rendered and gave him responsibility for supervision of taxation (Smallwood 1976: 39). Antipater's son Herod would rule Judea for most of the remainder of the century as a client king of Rome.

Herod's rule was arguably the most brilliant that Jerusalem had seen since the legendary Solomon, whom Herod emulated in his Temple building project (Shalit 1969; Schuerer 1973: 1.287–329; Richardson 1996). Like Solomon, Herod was liberal in his support of pagan temples, although he confined them to the non-Jewish cities in his kingdom. His building projects undoubtedly brought a measure of splendor to Palestine (Roller 1998). Whether, or how far, these projects were supported by heavy taxation is disputed. Applebaum argues that they were, and he points to Josephus's statement that Herod spent more than he could afford (Josephus, *Ant.* 16.154–56; Applebaum 1976: 654–66). Against this, however, it has been pointed out that Herod had many sources of income besides taxation. He controlled trade routes, and he had income from royal estates such as Jericho and from copper mines on Cyprus, which he leased from Augustus. The harbor he constructed at Caesarea was a boon to trade in Palestine, and his building projects provided much employment.[1]

There is no doubt that some people prospered during Herod's reign, but the fate of the general populace is less clear. Herod is credited with reducing taxes by one-third in 20 B.C.E. and by a one-quarter in 14 B.C.E. (Josephus, *Ant.* 15.365–67, 16.64; Schuerer 1973: 1.315) and with providing relief with his own funds in time of famine (Josephus, *Ant.* 15.299–316). But that tax relief was needed and that the famine occurred suggest that the situation of the common people was precarious. In any case, Herod was widely reviled by the end of his reign. In part, his disrepute was due to the incessant palace intrigue and blood-letting and in part it arose from religious resentment of the symbols of paganism that abounded during his reign. Shortly before his death, two teachers, Judas and Matthias, incited people to tear down a golden eagle from the Temple gate. Herod had the leaders burned alive (Josephus, *Ant.* 17.149–67; *J.W.* 1.647–55). Such action could only increase popular resentment. That some resentment was also due to economic issues is shown by the demands of the populace after his death: reduction of taxes; abolition of duties; and release of prisoners (*J.W.* 2.4). According to Josephus, Jewish delegates besought Rome to rid them of Herodian rule and assume direct control, "for he had tortured not only the persons of his subjects, but also their cities; and while he crippled the towns in his own dominion, he embellished those of other nations, lavishing the lifeblood of Judaea on

---

1. All of this is acknowledged by Applebaum; see also the discussion in Sanders 1992: 164.

foreign communities. In place of their ancient prosperity and ancestral laws, he had sunk the nation to poverty and the last degree of iniquity" (*J.W.* 2.84–93). Of course, this diatribe was not an objective assessment of the situation. It entailed a romantic view of the past and resentment of Herod's expenditures on Gentile cities. But it certainly was not the voice of a contented populace.

III. The First Century C.E.

Herod ruled at the pleasure of Rome, as he well knew. His death was followed by rebellion, which was put down harshly by Varus, the governor of Syria (Josephus, *Ant.* 17.206–323; *J.W.* 2.1–100; Schuerer 1973: 1.330–35). Herod's son Archelaus was installed as ethnarch, but he was deposed after two years because of Jewish and Samaritan complaints. Judea was then annexed as a prefectorial province. The client kingship would be restored briefly under Claudius, with Agrippa I as king (41–44; D. R. Schwartz 1990).[2] Thereafter, it would revert to provincial status, ruled by Roman procurators. After two decades of turbulence under the procurators, Judea would erupt in revolt (Schuerer 1973: 1.330–483; Smallwood 1976: 144–292; McLaren 1991: 80–187; Paltiel 1991). There was a roughly parallel development in the Egyptian Diaspora, where Roman rule was also welcomed at first, but the situation of the Jews gradually deteriorated. In Egypt, the catastrophic revolt came a little later, in the early second century, under Trajan (for the classic account of this history, see Tcherikover and Fuks 1957–64: 1–111; see also Smallwood 1976: 220–55; Modrzejewski 1995).

What caused this deterioration in Jewish affairs under Roman rule? Inevitably, we are dependent on the account of Josephus, whose reliability is often open to question, and who must be read critically (S. Schwartz 1990; McLaren 1998). Goodman distinguishes five major explanations for the conflict between the Jews and Rome, all based on Josephus's work: the incompetence of the Roman governors, the oppressiveness of Roman rule, Jewish religious susceptibilities, class tensions, and quarrels with local Gentiles (1987: 7–14; cf. McLaren 1998: 150–58). He adds another factor: the division within the Jewish ruling class and the failure of that class to fulfill its role as mediator between Rome and the Jewish people. While all of these factors deserve serious consideration, I will focus here on the two that seem to me most fundamental: Jewish religious susceptibilities and the oppressiveness of Roman rule. Many of the other issues—the incompetence of the governors, class division, tensions within the ruling class, and even friction with the local Gentiles—were, I believe, grounded in, or at least exacerbated by, the pressures created by Roman rule.

IV. Jewish Religious Sensibilities

Josephus lays much of the blame for the conflict on the so-called "fourth philosophy," which resisted Roman rule for religious reasons.[3] After the deposition of Archelaus, we are told, "a Galilean named Judas incited his countrymen to revolt, upbraiding them as cowards for consenting to pay tribute to the Romans and tolerating mortal masters" (*J.W.*

---

2. On the fortunes of Herod's descendants, see Kokkinos 1998.
3. See especially Hengel 1989.

2.118). This "philosophy," according to Josephus, "filled the body politic immediately with tumult, also planting the seeds of those troubles which subsequently overtook it" (*Ant.* 18.9). The sentiments attributed to Judas are repeated later by Eleazar, the commander of Masada: "A long time ago, brave comrades, we firmly resolved to be subject neither to the Romans nor to any other person, but only to God, for only he is the true and lawful Lord of men" (*J.W.* 7.323). The sentiment is an old one: compare the misgivings about the introduction of the monarchy in Israel in 1 Sam 8:7: "They have not rejected you but have rejected me from being king over them." It is undoubtedly true that many of the flashpoints of conflict involved religious issues—the incident over the golden eagle at the end of Herod's reign, the introduction of Roman insignia into Jerusalem under Pontius Pilate, and the demand that a statue of Caligula be placed in the Jerusalem Temple. There was a tradition of Jewish resistance to foreign rule, dating back to the Maccabean revolt, and this tradition had always entailed religious zeal (Farmer 1956). Moreover, Jewish religion was exceptional in the ancient world in its exclusiveness and in its sensitivity to iconic representations. This exclusiveness, no doubt, was difficult for some pagans to comprehend, and it often occasioned conflict.[4]

Yet religious differences can hardly be placed at the root of the conflict with Rome. Roman policy (like that of the Greeks and Persians before) generally affirmed the right of people to live according to their ancestral laws. This right was granted to Greek cities, as well as to Jewish communities: "Whatever laws, whatever right, whatever custom existed . . . the same laws and the same right and the same custom shall exist" (a sample inscription cited by Pucci ben Zeev 1998: 461; see also 1998: 413–14).[5] The reason was simply that it was the easiest way to keep peace. This policy often worked to the benefit of Jews, as it guaranteed their rights even in Greek cities. Allowances were made for Jewish sensibilities: notably, exemption from military service, permission to send offerings to the Temple in Jerusalem, and permission to offer sacrifices for the emperor instead of worshiping him. Of course, other people, too, offered sacrifices on behalf of emperors, and some emperors (Augustus, Tiberius, and Claudius) sometimes refused divine honors offered by eastern peoples (Pucci ben Zeev 1998: 476–77). The emperor cult was not monolithic, at least in the first century, and each community was free to honor the emperor in its own way. There were occasional lapses in Roman tolerance in this matter—notably in Caligula's demand that his statue be worshiped—but the exceptions prove the rule. Even after the destruction of Jerusalem, we find that Titus refused the request of the people of Antioch that the Jews be expelled from their city and insisted that their rights remain as they were before (Josephus, *J.W.* 7.100–111).

Moreover, few Jews are likely to have held to the philosophy that submission to human masters was incompatible with the rule of God. The Scriptures provided numerous injunctions to the contrary. Jeremiah had affirmed that the kingship of Nebuchadnezzar was granted by God and that all people should obey him (Jer 27:6–11). Josephus had the Jewish delegation that requested direct Roman rule instead of the ethnarchy of Archelaus promise that "the Jews would then show that, calumniated though they now were as

---

4. Brunt argues that Jewish religion was the peculiar factor that distinguished the situation in Judea from other parts of the empire (1990: 528). On Roman perceptions of the Jews, see Noethlichs 1996: 44–69.

5. On the extent and limits of Roman tolerance, see also Noethlichs 1996: 27–43.

factious and always at war, they knew how to obey equitable rulers" (*J.W.* 2.92). In fact, Jewish resistance to Roman rule was sporadic and was triggered by other factors in addition to opposition to foreign rule as such. This is not to deny that most Jews would have regarded foreign rule as ultimately unacceptable and would have hoped for eventual restoration of native rule. But this was not always a matter of great urgency, and for some upper-class Jews Roman rule was probably quite beneficial for the present.

In this regard, it is interesting to note that Rome plays a very limited role in the Dead Sea Scrolls, which constitute our main corpus of Jewish documents from the land of Israel around the turn of the era (Lichtenberger 1996). (It may be that most of the Scrolls were written before the arrival of Pompey; but it is clear that some, at least, date after that time.) Rome is never mentioned by name in the Scrolls and only one Roman is mentioned by name—Pompey's lieutenant, Aemilius Scaurus, in 4Q324a, a calendrical text. The "Kittim" in the pesher on Habakkuk are clearly to be identified as the Romans, as we have already seen. It is generally assumed that the "Kittim" are also the Romans in the *War Rule*, although it is possible that the "Kittim" of Asshur and the "Kittim" in Egypt, in 1QM 1, were originally references to the Seleucids and the Ptolemies (Collins 1997: 106–7). The "Kittim" in the *War Rule* are the eschatological enemy, the opponents in the final war, but what is perhaps most striking about their portrayal in this text is the lack of specific information about them. They are simply "the other"—no more defined than Gog from the land of Magog in Ezekiel, or the somewhat garbled Gog and Magog in the book of Revelation. Such texts bespeak a general hostility to the Gentile world that is deeply rooted in biblical traditions about the Day of the Lord. For the Qumran sect, as for Judas the Galilean, foreign rule was ultimately unacceptable as such, and its destruction was assured. Unlike Judas, however, the Qumranites were resolved not to requite evil to anyone until the Day of Wrath, and so they must have reconciled themselves to Roman rule until the time was right, a time that they may have believed to have come in 66 C.E.

The relatively restrained rhetoric of the Scrolls with regard to Rome may be contrasted with the bitter outpourings in the apocalyptic writings after 70 C.E. (Charlesworth 1985). In *4 Ezra* 12 the messianic lion reproves the Romans, who are represented by an eagle: "He will denounce them for their ungodliness and for their wickedness, and will display before them their contemptuous dealings." The fifth *Sibylline Oracle*, written perhaps a little later, around the time of the Diaspora revolt (115–17 C.E.), is more vindictive: "Alas, city of the Latin land, unclean in all things, maenad, rejoicing in vipers, as a widow you will sit by the banks and the river Tiber will weep for you, its consort. You have a murderous heart and impious spirit" (*Sib. Or.* 5:168–71). Most eloquent of all is the Book of Revelation, in which Rome is portrayed as the whore of Babylon. All of these portrayals, however, were written after the destruction of Jerusalem. No doubt, negative feelings about Rome had built up over the first century and ran high on the eve of the revolt. But the animosity reflected in the apocalyptic texts is not simply a rejection of Roman rule in principle, but is a reaction to a century of misrule and oppression.

V. Roman Oppression

In fact, while Jewish relations with Rome had their distinctive character, which was colored by religion, they were not atypical of relations between Rome and other subject peoples: in the words of Dyson, "one of the most persistent phenomena related to the extension of Roman conquest and control in the Western Empire was the sudden, widespread native revolt" (1971: 239). Dyson discusses five major examples—in Britain, Gaul, Germany, and Pannonia-Dalmatia. We know of these revolts primarily from Roman sources, but where we get glimpses of their motivation a fairly consistent pattern emerges. Native peoples resented Roman depredation and the erosion of their traditional way of life. Disregard for native religion was sometimes a factor. In Britain, for example, the Romans attacked and desecrated a Druid center off the coast of Wales (Dyson 1971: 260). A relatively early formulation of native reactions to Rome is attributed to Mithridates of Pontus, in an attempt to enlist the support of the Parthians: "For the Romans have never had but one reason for making war on all nations, peoples and kings—an insatiable desire for power and wealth" (Sallust, *Epistulae et Orationes* VI, Epistula Mithridatis).[6]

An oracle preserved in *Sibylline Oracles* Book 3, sometimes associated with the campaign of Mithridates (Geffcken 1902: 8; Kippenberg 1983: 45) and sometimes with that of Cleopatra (Tarn 1932; Collins 1974: 57–61), expresses an easterner's desire for revenge and reflects the typical grievances of the conquered peoples against Rome:

> However much wealth Rome received from tribute-bearing Asia,
> Asia will receive three times that much again
> From Rome and will repay her deadly arrogance to her.
> Whatever number from Asia served the house of Italians
> Twenty times that number of Italians will be serfs
> In Asia, in poverty, and they will be liable to pay ten-thousand fold.
>   (*Sib. Or.* 3:350–55)[7]

It is surely significant that the initial rebellion of Judas of Galilee was sparked by a census for the purpose of introducing a poll-tax (Smallwood 1976: 150–53). Other rebellions against Rome were ignited by the introduction of regular tax assessment, in Gaul in 12 B.C.E. and in Cilicia in 36 C.E. (Goodman 1987: 11 n. 38). There is an ongoing debate as to whether taxation in Roman Judea was excessive. On the one hand, Applebaum, for example, has argued that the Jewish peasantry was "crushed with merciless executions under Pompey and his successors and no less under Herod" (1976: 661–62). On the other, Sanders has argued that Rome took local conditions into account, and that taxation was not especially oppressive before the revolt, although the tax imposed by Vespasian was admittedly punitive (1992: 157–61). Sanders's argument, however, is largely a relative one—the burden on people in other parts of the empire was just as heavy. Indeed. And it sometimes led to revolts, even if not on the same scale as that in Judea. What may have seemed like reasonable, moderate taxation to the Romans did not necessarily seem so to those who paid the tax. Julius Caesar had granted Judea certain exemptions, from tribute in the seventh year and from the requirement of billeting troops (Josephus, *Ant.* 14.202–10). Nonetheless, Tacitus records a complaint against the tax burden in 17 C.E. (*Ann.* 2.42). Pontius Pilate took money from the Temple treasury to pay for an aqueduct, admittedly a worthy cause (Josephus, *Ant.* 18.60; *J.W.* 2.175). The procurator Florus confiscated Temple

---

6. See further Fuchs 1938: 16–17.
7. Collins 1983: 370. On resistance to Roman rule, see further MacMullan 1966.

funds for "the imperial service" (*J.W.* 2.293). There was a general increase in Roman taxation under Nero and an extraordinary levy under the procurator Albinus in the early sixties (*J.W.* 2.273). Even Sanders admits that in the end, "the people were hard pressed" (1992: 168). The phenomenon of brigandage throughout this period, but especially in the years before the revolt, is most readily explained against a background of economic hardship. It should also be noted that there was famine in Judea under Herod, who famously provided relief from his own funds, and again under Claudius, when relief was provided by Queen Helena of Adiabene (Josephus, *Ant.* 20.101). Moreover, there was more at stake than the simple ability to pay. Taxation by a foreign power had implications for status, and symbolic significance. The resentment of the *laographia*, or poll-tax, by the Jews of Alexandria seems to have been largely a matter of status, vis-à-vis the Alexandrian Greeks.

By all accounts, Roman rule in Judea became more oppressive after the reannexation of the province under Claudius (Paltiel 1991: 261–301). The procurators who followed the brief reign of Agrippa I were not impressive people. Even if we view Josephus's account of their maladministration with some suspicion, we must note that Tacitus wrote that Felix "practised every kind of cruelty and lust, wielding the power of a king with all the instincts of a slave" (*Hist.* 5.9), while his statement that the patience of the Jews lasted until Gessius Florus (*Hist.* 5.10) accords with the view of Josephus that Florus was the last straw. But the problem lay deeper than the personalities of the procurators. In the increasingly centralized Roman system, procurators lacked authority, and they often had little experience and low social standing. One—Felix—was an ex-slave. The governor of Syria could intervene at any time in Judean affairs. The combination of exacting imperial demands and poor administration created the pressure that exacerbated other problems, such as social divisions.

The Romans, of course, did not view themselves as oppressive. On the contrary, they prided themselves on their humanity and justice.[8] Roman law, when properly administered, was perhaps the main cultural legacy of the empire. But by definition, the interests of Rome came first, and policy was directed to the advancement of the wealth and power of the empire. The glory of the empire was enhanced by the construction of cities and buildings. The archaeological remains brought to light in recent years show the splendor of Herod's constructions at Caesarea and elsewhere and, indeed, the luxury of the wealthier residents of Jerusalem (Avigad 1980; Levine 1998: 48–51). Yet the Jewish experience of Roman rule is all too vividly symbolized by the story of Herod's Temple. This was a splendid project that enhanced the glory of Jerusalem and of Judaism. It provided employment in Jerusalem for decades and was finally completed a few years before the revolt. Less than a decade later, there was scarcely left of it a stone upon a stone. The prosperity that attended Roman rule for a time, at least among the upper class, was swept away in the brutal suppression of the revolt. The Jewish experience was ultimately similar to that of the Gauls, Germans, and other peoples brought under the yoke of Rome. I can think of no better articulation of that experience than the indictment of Rome attributed to the Briton Calgacus by the Roman historian Tacitus:

---

8. See the speech attributed to Titus in Josephus, *J.W.* 6.333–36, where he ironically suggests that the Jews were driven to revolt by Roman *philanthropia*.

These plunderers of the world, after exhausting the land by their devastations are rifling the ocean: stimulated by avarice, if their enemy be rich; by ambition, if poor; unsatiated by the East and by the West; the only people who behold wealth and indigence with equal avidity. To ravage, to slaughter, to usurp under false titles, they call empire; and when they make a desert, they call it peace. (*Agricola* 30)

References

Applebaum, S.
  1976   Economic Life in Palestine. Pp. 631–700 in *The Jewish People in the First Century*, ed. S. Safrai and M. Stern. Compendia Rerum Judaiscarum ad Novum Testamentum 1/2. Philadelphia: Fortress.

Avigad, N.
  1980   *Discovering Jerusalem*. Jerusalem: Shikmona.

Brunt, P. A.
  1990   *Roman Imperial Themes*. Oxford: Clarendon.

Charlesworth, J. H.
  1985   The Triumphant Majority as Seen by a Dwindled Minority: The Outsider according to the Insider of the Jewish Apocalypses. Pp. 285–315 in *"To See Ourselves as Others See Us": Christians, Jews, Others in Late Antiquity*, ed. J. Neusner and E. S. Frerichs. Chico, Calif.: Scholars Press.

Collins, J. J.
  1974   *The Sibylline Oracles of Egyptian Judaism*. Society of Biblical Literature Dissertation Series 13. Missoula, Mont.: Scholars Press.
  1983   The Sibylline Oracles. Pp. 317–472 in vol. 1 of *The Old Testament Pseudepigrapha*, ed. J. H. Charlesworth. New York: Doubleday.
  1997   *Apocalypticism in the Dead Sea Scrolls*. London: Routledge.

Dyson, S. L.
  1971   Native Revolts in the Roman Empire. *Historia* 20: 239–74.

Farmer, W. R.
  1956   *Maccabees, Zealots and Josephus: An Inquiry into Jewish Nationalism in the Greco-Roman Period*. New York: Columbia University.

Fuchs, H.
  1938   *Der Geistige Widerstand gegen Rom in der antiken Welt*. Berlin: de Gruyter.

Geffcken, J.
  1902   *Komposition und Entstehungszeit der Oracula Sibyllina*. Leipzig: Hinrichs.

Goodman, M.
  1987   *The Ruling Class of Judaea*. Cambridge: Cambridge University Press.

Gruen, E. R.
  1984   *The Hellenistic World and the Coming of Rome*. Berkeley: University of California Press.

Hengel, M.
  1989   *The Zealots: Investigations into the Jewish Freedom Movement in the Period from Herod I until 70 A.D.* Edinburgh: T. & T. Clark.

Kippenberg, H. G.
  1983   Dann wird der Orient Herrschen und der Okzident Dienen. Pp. 40–48 in *Spiegel und Gleichnis: Festschrift für Jacob Taubes*, ed. N. W. Bolz and W. Hübner. Würzburg: Königshausen & Neumann.

Kokkinos, N.
  1998   *The Herodian Dynasty*. Sheffield: Sheffield Academic Press.

Levine, L.
  1998   *Judaism and Hellenism in Antiquity: Conflict or Confluence?* Seattle: University of Washington Press.

Lichtenberger, H.
　1996　Das Rombild in den Texten von Qumran. Pp. 221–31 in *Qumranstudien*, ed. H.-J. Fabry. Göttingen: Vandenhoeck & Ruprecht.

MacMullan, R.
　1966　*Enemies of the Roman Order*. Cambridge: Harvard University Press.

McLaren, J. S.
　1991　*Power and Politics in Palestine: The Jews and the Governing of Their Land, 100 BC–AD 70*. Sheffield: Sheffield Academic Press.
　1998　*Turbulent Times? Josephus and Scholarship on Judaea in the First Century CE*. Journal for the Study of the Pseudepigrapha Supplement 29. Sheffield: Sheffield Academic Press.

Modrzejewski, J. M.
　1995　*The Jews of Egypt: From Rameses II to Emperor Hadrian*. Princeton: Princeton University Press.

Noethlichs, K. L.
　1996　*Das Judentum und der römische Staat: Minderheitenpolitik im antiken Rom*. Darmstadt: Wissenschaftliche Buchgesellschaft.

Paltiel, E.
　1991　*Vassals and Rebels in the Roman Empire: Julio-Claudian Policies in Judaea and the Kingdoms of the East*. Brussels: Latomus.

Pucci ben Zeev, M.
　1998　*Jewish Rights in the Roman World*. Texte und Studien zum antiken Judentum 74. Tübingen: Mohr.

Richardson, P.
　1996　*Herod: King of the Jews and Friend of the Romans*. Columbia: University of South Carolina Press.

Roller, D.
　1998　*The Building Program of Herod the Great*. Berkeley: University of California Press.

Sanders, E. P.
　1992　*Judaism: Practice and Belief, 63 BCE–66 CE*. Philadelphia: Trinity.

Schuerer, E.
　1973　*The History of the Jewish People in the Age of Jesus Christ*, rev. G. Vermes and F. Millar. Edinburgh: T. & T. Clark.

Schwartz, D. R.
　1990　*Agrippa I: The Last King of Judaea*. Tübingen: Mohr.

Schwartz, S.
　1990　*Josephus and Judaean Politics*. Leiden: Brill.

Shalit, A.
　1969　*König Herodes: Der Mann und sein Werk*. Berlin: de Gruyter.

Sherwin-White, A. N.
　1984　*Roman Foreign Policy in the East: 168 B.C. to A.D. 1*. Norman: University of Oklahoma Press.

Smallwood, E. M.
　1976　*The Jews under Roman Rule*. Leiden: Brill.

Tarn, W. W.
　1932　Alexander Helios and the Golden Age. *Journal of Roman Studies* 22: 135–59.

Tcherikover, V., and Fuks, A. (eds.)
　1957–64　*Corpus Papyrorum Judaicarum*. Cambridge: Harvard University Press.

Helios and the Zodiac Cycle in Ancient Palestinian Synagogues

Jodi Magness
Department of Religious Studies
University of North Carolina at Chapel Hill

Introduction

A panel containing the figure of Helios surrounded by a zodiac cycle and personifications of the four seasons was discovered in the mosaic floors of seven ancient synagogues in Palestine: at Hammath Tiberias, Beth Alpha, Naʿaran, Khirbet Susiya, Husifa, Yafia, and Sepphoris. All seven examples repeat the same basic composition, with the circle of the zodiac inscribed in a square and the four seasons in the corners (Hachlili 1988: 301–8; Roussin 1997: 83–84; Kühnel 2000). In addition, a Hebrew inscription in the floor of the synagogue at En-gedi lists the 12 signs of the zodiac, followed by the 12 Hebrew months (Barag, Porat, and Netzer 1981: 118; Levine 1981). At Hammath Tiberias, Beth Alpha, Naʿaran, and Sepphoris, where the medallion in the center of the zodiac cycle was still preserved, it contained a depiction of Helios in his chariot (in the case of Sepphoris, an aniconic Helios [Weiss and Netzer 1996: 28, 35–36; Weiss 2000a: 58; 2000b: 22–23]). Scholars have suggested that this panel represents a kind of liturgical calendar, or that it had magical, cosmic, or astrological significance. Why did some Palestinian Jewish congregations place the figure of the Greco-Roman sun god in a central position in their synagogues? In this paper, I suggest that Helios and the zodiac cycle should be understood in part within the context of two contemporary and possibly related phenomena: the rise of Christianity; and the strengthening of the Jewish priestly class in Late Antique Palestine. I begin by examining the synagogue at Hammath Tiberias, which is decorated with the earliest datable example of this composition (Dothan 1983: 48).

I. Hammath Tiberias

In his 1961–65 excavations at the site, Dothan uncovered the remains of four superimposed synagogue buildings. According to Dothan, the earliest synagogue, of Stratum IIb, was constructed during the first half of the 3rd century (ca. 230)[1] (1983: 26, 66–67). He suggests that this synagogue was destroyed in the earthquake of 306, and that the subsequent

Author's note: I wish to thank Hanan Eshel, Bar-Ilan University; Kenneth G. Holum, University of Maryland; Paul V. M. Flesher, University of Wyoming; and Karen C. Britt, Indiana University, for their comments on my paper. I would also like to thank David Amit, Israel Antiquities Authority, for bringing to my attention the possible connection with the rise of the priestly class. I am grateful to the Israel Exploration Society for their permission to reproduce the illustrations in figs. 1 and 2.

1. All dates refer to the Common Era, unless otherwise noted.

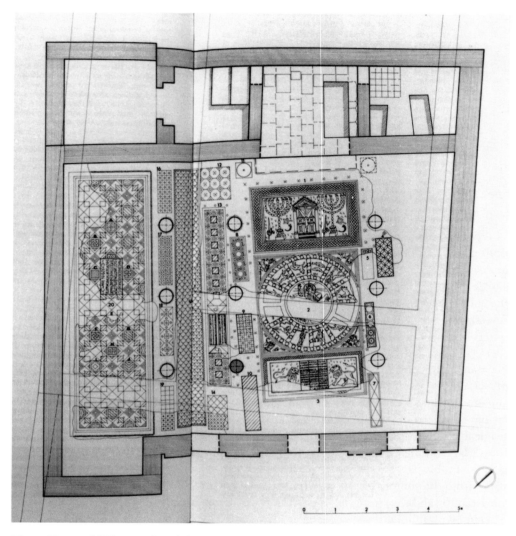

Fig. 1. Hammath Tiberias: plan of the Stratum IIa synagogue (from Dothan 1983: 34–35).

Stratum IIa synagogue was constructed during the first quarter of the 4th century (1983: 66–67) (see fig. 1). This building, which he calls the "Synagogue of Severos," has a mosaic floor decorated with Helios and the zodiac cycle (1983: 57, 67; see fig. 2). On the basis of the pottery and the coins (the latest dated to 395), Dothan places the end of the use of this synagogue in the late 4th or early 5th century (1983: 64, 66) and suggests that it was destroyed in the earthquake of 419 (2000: 12). According to Dothan, the next synagogue (of Stratum Ib) was erected immediately after the earthquake and was completed by 423 (2000: 12). The layout of the Stratum Ib synagogue is completely different from the broadhouse of Stratum IIa. It has a basilical plan, with three rows of columns creating aisles that encircled the nave on the north, east, and west sides, and an interior apse on the

Fig. 2. Hammath Tiberias: the nave mosaics in the Stratum IIa synagogue (from Dothan 1983: pls. 10–11).

south (Dothan 2000: 12–18). The hall was paved with polychrome mosaics depicting floral and animal designs (Dothan 2000: 33–34). According to Dothan, the Stratum Ib synagogue was damaged in the first half of the 7th century, that is, at the beginning of the Umayyad period, and was then rebuilt along similar lines in Stratum Ia. The Stratum Ia synagogue remained in use until it was destroyed in the mid–8th century, perhaps by an earthquake (1981: 68–69; 1993: 577; 2000: 93; but according to 2000: 37, the Stratum Ib synagogue was destroyed in the mid–8th century).

An analysis of the published evidence suggests that Dothan's chronology for all of these buildings, which is based largely on the numismatic evidence, is too early.[2] He seems to have associated at least some of the coins with certain strata based on the coins' dates instead of on their archaeological context: "The earliest coin in Stratum II is of Julia Maesa from Caesarea Paneas (220). Chronologically, this coin precedes the coins of Elagabalus, Gordianus, Alexander Severus, and other emperors of the 3rd century found in this stratum. *It may be assumed* that they originated in the early synagogue (IIb)" (1983: 64, emphasis mine). Most of the 4th-century coins come from a treasury (L52) in the Stratum IIa synagogue. This consisted of a cist sunk into the western side of the raised platform (presumably for the Torah shrine) at the end of the nave. The latest identifiable coin was of Valentianus II (383). While most of the 31 small bronze coins from this locus were too worn to be identifiable, according to the report, "in shape and size, however, they seem to be attributable to Roman Imperial Coinage of the 4th–5th centuries; as we have identified among them only early 5th century coins, it seems probable that those which are too worn are also from the beginning of the 5th century" (Rahmani and Sharabani 1983: 74). Dothan concludes that these coins provide an early-5th-century terminus post quem for the end of the Stratum IIa synagogue (1983: 65–66).

In addition to these coins, many oil lamp fragments were found on the floor of L52. They include lamps with a bow-shaped nozzle, a type associated with Beit Nattif. The type ranges from the second half of the 3rd century to the 5th century (Dothan 1983: 65, fig. 5:A–B; pl. 24:2, 6).[3] The circular shape of the body and size of the filling hole of some of the lamps point to a similar or slightly earlier date (Dothan 1983: 65, fig. 5:F–G, J). Although the northern type oil lamps with impressed or incised decoration have traditionally been dated from the 3rd to the mid–4th century, recent evidence suggests that they are either later or that they continued into the 5th century and perhaps later (Magness 2001: 12 n. 15).

The illustrated pottery from Stratum II includes Galilean bowls and local cooking pots (Dothan 1983: 63, fig. 4:A–L, N–O). Some examples of the latest variant of Galilean

---

2. Because the pottery and coins from the synagogues of Strata IIb and IIa are published without providing contexts (that is, without locus numbers or a description of what was found above or below the floor levels), it is difficult to determine the precise dates of these buildings. In addition, although the locus numbers and stratum assignments of the pottery and lamps are provided for the Stratum Ib and Stratum Ia synagogues, there are no clean Stratum Ib loci. In other words, all of this material either comes from mixed Stratum Ib and Ia contexts or from Stratum Ia contexts (Dothan 2000: 123–29). There is also no indication as to whether the material comes from above or below the floor levels.

3. Because there are no descriptions of the illustrated pottery, it is impossible to determine whether some of the other fragments, such as the multinozzled lamps, also represent this type (Magness and Avni 1998: 94–95).

bowls were "found in Loci 106 and 107, immediately below the flagstone floor of Stratum Ib" (Dothan 1983: 62–63, fig. 4:A, D, G; cf. Adan-Bayewitz 1993: 103–9, Kefar Ḥananya Form 1E, dated mid–3rd century to early 5th century). According to Adan-Bayewitz, this variant was common from the 4th to early 5th centuries (1993: 107; cf. Magness 2001: 37 n. 109 for the suggestion that these local types are currently dated too early). There are also two Late Roman "C" (Phocean Red Slip) Ware Form 3 bowls (one of which is nearly complete), dating from the mid–5th to the mid–6th centuries (Dothan 1983: 63, fig. 4:M, P; pl. 23:4).[4]

The presence of Late Roman "C" Form 3 bowls indicates that the use of the Stratum IIa synagogue continued beyond the mid–5th century. This is confirmed by the condition of the early-5th-century coins from L52 (perhaps including specimens from later in the 5th century), which were too worn to be read, indicating that they were in circulation for some time before being deposited. This evidence suggests that the Stratum IIa synagogue was occupied at least until the third quarter of the 5th century.

Dothan dates the construction of the synagogue immediately above that of Stratum IIa (that is, the Stratum Ib synagogue, which was the first one with a basilical plan) to the years 420–23, and its destruction to the first half of the 7th century (2000: 93; see also above). This chronology, however, is not supported by the ceramic and numismatic evidence.[5]

Unfortunately, all of the pottery and coins published from Stratum Ib come from mixed Strata Ib–Ia contexts; none of this material is assigned to Stratum Ib alone. The earliest ceramic type illustrated from Strata Ib–Ia contexts is a Fine Byzantine Ware bowl of mid–6th- to 7th-century date (Johnson 2000: 61–62, no. 71).[6] The other types represented in Strata Ib–Ia contexts include 8th- to 9th-century red-painted ware and glazed pottery of the 9th century and later. There are also buff ("Mefjer") ware vessels, a type that did not appear in Palestine before the second half of the 8th century. One buff ware jug from "the end of Stratum Ib" is inscribed with a text comprising Hebrew characters with a mixture of Arabic, Aramaic, and Hebrew elements (Dothan 2000: 102–3). The oil lamps from Strata Ib–Ia contexts are of the channel-nozzle type, with a range of the 7th to 10th centuries, although the high knob or tongue handle is characteristic of the 8th to 10th centuries.[7] The coins are consistent with the ceramic evidence: those from Strata Ib–Ia

---

4. These are misidentified as African Red Slip Ware; according to Dothan, these bowls "are probably from Stratum IIa" (1983: 62). For this type, see Hayes 1972: 329–38; these bowls do not represent the earliest variants of this form. There are also two stamped Late Roman Red Ware fragments, including an African Red Slip Ware bowl stamped with a fringed concentric circle motif of the late 4th to the third quarter of the 5th century (Dothan 1983: 63, fig. 4:Q–R; pl. 23:6–7; cf. Hayes 1972: 237, type 36, fig. 40).

5. The same observation was made by B. L. Johnson, who published the pottery and coins from the later synagogues and edited the report: "although the date proposed by Prof. Dothan for Synagogue Ib appears reasonable from the historical and political point of view, it is not supported by the datable artifacts found at the site" (Dothan 2000: 93).

6. The only other 6th- to 7th-century type illustrated is an Egyptian Red Slip Ware bowl fragment from a Stratum Ia context (Johnson 2000: 61).

7. For the buff wares from Strata Ib–Ia contexts, see Johnson 2000: 54–61, nos. 2, 4, 6, 8–9, 12, 15, 17, 22, 26, 29, 32–35, 44, 53, 58–62, 69; for the red-painted wares from these contexts, see Johnson 2000: 65–67, nos. 90–93; and for the glazed wares, Johnson 2000: 69–71, nos. 110, 112, 114. For the dating of these types, see Magness 1994; Avissar 1996: 75–82, 155–63; Magness 1997a; Sauer and Magness 1997. For the oil lamps from Strata Ib–Ia contexts, see Johnson 2000: 75–82, nos. 1, 3, 6, 8, 10–11, 13, 15, 18–19, 30–31, 33; and

contexts range in date from Justin II (571–72) to the Abbasid period.[8] To summarize, the earliest coins from Strata Ib–Ia contexts are from the reign of Justin II, while the earliest ceramic type (the single FBW Form 1B bowl) dates from the mid–6th to 7th century. Thus the ceramic and numismatic evidence provides a late-6th- to 7th-century terminus post quem for the construction of the Stratum Ib synagogue. The inscribed buff ware jug associated with this synagogue, as well as the other pottery and coins, indicate that it remained in use until the second half of the 8th century or later. According to Dothan, the Stratum Ib synagogue immediately succeeded that of Stratum IIa (2000: 12). However, the apparent absence of ceramic types and coins suggests that there was a gap or period of abandonment between the end of Stratum IIa and the beginning of Stratum Ib. Based on the available evidence, this gap can be dated roughly from the late 5th to the late 6th century.

Is it possible to determine when the Stratum IIa synagogue was built? According to Dothan, this synagogue was constructed immediately after its predecessor in Stratum IIb went out of use. He dates the Stratum IIb synagogue on the basis of the 3rd-century coins and pottery found in the fills of Stratum II: "The coins of Elagabalus (218–22 C.E.) provide a terminus post quem for the synagogue's construction, while the two coins of Alexander Severus (222–35 C.E.) seem to indicate the actual period of building" (1983: 66). These coins would, of course, provide a 3rd-century terminus post quem for the construction of the Stratum IIb synagogue.

Dothan cites two Greek inscriptions in support of an early-4th-century construction date for the Stratum IIa synagogue. The first, in a panel at the entrance to the nave, reads: "Sever[os], disciple of the most illustrious Patriarchs fulfilled (it). Blessings upon him. Amen" (Dothan 1983: 55). The second inscription, located in a panel to the west of the nave, reads: "Severos, disciple of the most illustrious Patriarchs completed (it). Blessings on him and on Ioullos the supervisor" (Dothan 1983: 60). Dothan notes that "most illustrious" (Greek *lamprotaton patriarchon*; Latin *vir clarissimus*) was the title given to the Patriarch in the Theodosian Code of 392. This was the third highest rank among the Roman officials, and meant that the Patriarch belonged to the senatorial class. In 396–97, the Patriarch still belonged to the senatorial class, but his title was *illustris* (*endoxotatos*), which began to be used at the time instead of, or perhaps in addition to, *clarissimus*. The Patriarch Gamaliel VI was called *vir spectabilis* in 404, and the senatorial rank was withdrawn altogether by Theodosius II in 415 (Dothan 1983: 58). If these inscriptions refer to the Patriarchate of the House of Hillel, they were executed before 396–97.[9] Based on the

---

for the dating of these lamps, Magness 1993: 255–58; Sauer and Magness 1997: 478–79. The glazed cooking pan from Strata Ib–Ia illustrated in Johnson (2000: 68–69, no. 104) dates from the second half of the 9th to the 10th century (Avissar 1996: 139–41, type 13). For a close (uninscribed) Islamic-period parallel for the inscribed buff ware jug, see Magness 1992: 165–66, fig. 12:20.

8. Amitai-Preiss 2000: 95–99, nos. 1 (a coin of Justin II, dated 571–72, from L54), 8 (a Byzantine or Byzantine-Arab coin from L54), 16 (an Umayyad coin from L54), 21 (an Umayyad coin from L10), 22 (an Umayyad coin from L10), 23 (an Umayyad coin from L12/2), 25 (an Umayyad coin from L54), 41 (an Abbasid coin from L14), 42 (an Abbasid coin, dated 815–911, from L8), 43 (an Abbasid coin from L14), 45 (an Abbasid coin from L54), and 49 (an Abbasid coin from L10).

9. Dothan notes that the title *lamprotatos* is mentioned three times in two Jewish inscriptions of the 5th to 6th centuries from Palestine, and that patriarchs are mentioned in three Jewish inscriptions, including one reference to a synagogue official. He maintains that these "minor patriarchs" served as the heads of Jewish communities in various locales (Dothan 1983: 59).

assumption that the Patriarch must have been invested with the title *lamprotatos* during the reign of Diocletian or Constantine I, Dothan dates the construction of the Stratum IIa synagogue to this period and concludes that the inscriptions mentioning the "most illustrious Patriarchs" refer to Gamaliel IV or Judah III (1983: 58–59). However, since we know that the Patriarch held the title *lamprotatos* in 392, there is no reason that this mosaic floor, and with it the Stratum IIa synagogue, should not be dated to the late 4th century.[10] This is consistent with the fact that the scale pattern decorating part of the mosaic floor is not attested at Antioch before the 5th century or in Palestine before the second half of the 4th century (Dothan 1983: 52).[11] The synagogue was thus in use at least until the third quarter of the 5th century. This chronology accords well with the ceramic and numismatic evidence. The earliest synagogue (Stratum IIb) should therefore be dated to the 4th instead of the 3rd century.

II. The Priestly Class

I have suggested elsewhere (Magness 2001) that the archaeological evidence indicates that the Galilean-type synagogues at Gush Ḥalav and Capernaum were established no earlier than the second half of the 5th century and the first half of the 6th century, respectively. At Khirbet Shemaʿ, there is evidence for only one synagogue building, apparently constructed in the late 4th or early 5th century (Magness 1997b). As we have seen, the earliest example of a synagogue mosaic decorated with Helios and the zodiac cycle (at Hammath Tiberias) dates to the late 4th century. I believe that the chronology of each synagogue building must be evaluated independently. However, the cumulative body of evidence indicates that the traditional typology of ancient Palestinian synagogues must be revised. Although the institution of the synagogue had developed much earlier, the buildings that housed these gatherings developed a monumental architectural style and distinctive types of decoration only in the course of the 4th century, especially during its latter part.[12] I propose that the rise of monumental synagogue architecture and art at this time was primarily due to two possibly related factors: (1) the influence of, and perhaps competition with, contemporary Christianity; and (2) the strengthening of the priestly class in Palestinian Jewish society.

During the 4th century (and especially its latter part), monumental churches began to be constructed in Palestine and other parts of the Roman world. The similarities and differences between the layout and decoration of these churches and contemporary Palestinian synagogues are well known. Certain motifs in Jewish art developed in tandem with, or perhaps in response to, those used in contemporary Christian art. However, the rise of

---

10. Goodman points out that only from the mid–4th century and later do we have evidence of a Patriarch achieving the status of a *clarissimus*, and that the Patriarch's power peaked in the late 380s. He therefore concludes that the Hammath Tiberias inscriptions should be dated to the later 4th century (1992: 130 n. 11). Levine notes that the Patriarchate reached the peak of its prestige and power shortly before its disappearance around 425 (1999: 94, 97). Based on stylistic considerations, Talgam suggests that the Stratum IIa synagogue at Hammath Tiberias should be dated to the second half of the 4th century (2000: 100).

11. One of the three Palestinian examples cited by Dothan is in the southern aisle of Constantine's Church of the Nativity in Bethlehem. However, Avi-Yonah notes that, since this floor is at a higher level than the original floor, it must represent a 5th-century repaving (1993: 206).

12. Here I refer only to Palestine; the case of the synagogue at Dura Europos indicates that the Diaspora must be considered independently.

monumental synagogue architecture and art in Palestine also seems to be connected with the strengthening of the priestly class at the time, a phenomenon that may be connected to the emergence of Christianity and its clergy (Irshai 1998: 115; Levine 2000a: 500). As Levine notes, "Many, if not most, priests continued to remain a separate and distinct entity throughout late antiquity. Organized into twenty-four priestly courses scattered throughout Judaea for centuries prior to the loss of Jerusalem, they appear to have retained this framework even afterward" (2000a: 492; see also Fraade 1991: 73: "In fact, several kinds of evidence suggest that priestly status, and perhaps authority, continued to be a factor in Jewish communal life long after 70 C.E."). During the 4th and 5th centuries, the priestly class became increasingly prominent, filling the void left by the abolition of the Patriarchate and the decline of the sages (Irshai 1998: 115–16; Yahalom 1999: 113; 2000: 90).[13] The recurring motif of the priestly courses in *piyyutim* and in synagogue inscriptions attests to the rise of the priestly class, which was centered in Galilee after the Bar-Kokhba Revolt (Miller 1984: 131; Yahalom 1999: 107).[14] The priestly courses provided a reference connecting the priestly families of Galilee with the Jerusalem Temple (Irshai 1998: 115–17; Yahalom 1999: 107–8).

A number of scholars note the tension that existed between the priestly class and the sages, whose main institution was the Beth Midrash (e.g., Fine 1997: 57–58; Yahalom 1999: 111–13; 2000: 89).[15] The rabbis apparently exercised little influence over and had limited involvement in ancient Palestinian synagogues (Levine 1992). Levine notes that, whereas other functionaries of ancient synagogues, including priests, are mentioned by the Church Fathers and in the Theodosian code, sages are not (2000a: 443).[16] Priests are also mentioned as donors in synagogue inscriptions from Naʿaran, Eshtemoa, Khirbet Susiya, and Sepphoris (Fine 1997: 88; Levine 2000a: 494). This evidence suggests that priests were involved in, and perhaps exercised some control over, ancient Palestinian synagogues, as opposed to the sages, who were apparently involved mainly as teachers, preachers, and adjudicants of Halakhic matters (Levine 1992: 208–11). As Rutgers states, "In Late Roman and Byzantine Palestine, descendants of priests continued to make a mark on society in

13. Although in this paper I do not differentiate between the members of "the priestly class," I realize that this was a stratified rather than a monolithic group. Some priests were rabbis, and not all priests belonged to the aristocracy (Miller 1999: 559). I am grateful to Stuart Miller for bringing this reference to my attention.

14. Yahalom refers to a Hellenized, intellectual "priestly elite" whose center was in Sepphoris (1999: 110, 113; 2000: 90).

15. For the sages, the sanctity of the Beth Midrash was greater than that of the synagogue (Levine 1992: 203 ["the primary social, intellectual, and religious setting of the rabbis in late antiquity was the *bet midrash*"]; Fine 1997: 68–69; Baumgarten 1999: 79). For more on the tensions between the priests and sages, see Fraade 1991: 92 ("the rabbinic sages claimed . . . roles that were formerly assigned to the priesthood") and 118 ("the implicit argument [by the rabbis] that Torah study is the superior successor to the Temple rites"); Irshai 1998: 115; Swartz 1999: 104–9. Similarly, Schwartz argues against "a Rabbinizing approach to synagogue art" (2000: 166–68). See also Levine 1989: 171: "It is quite probable that one group within the Galilean aristocracy with which the sages came into conflict was the priestly families"; and p. 172: "Rabbinic literature tends either to ignore the priests and everything related to them, or to refer to them disparagingly." However, Levine also notes that "priests were amply represented among the sages throughout much of the Talmudic period" (2000a: 492; see also Miller 1999: 559).

16. On the other hand, Levine notes that no priests are named among the many synagogue officials mentioned in edicts from the end of the 4th century (in contrast to the situation among the Samaritans; Levine 2000a: 495). Could this perhaps be because most or all priestly influence in Palestinian synagogues postdates the 4th century?

general and on the synagogue in particular" (1999: 196).[17] Part of this problem appears to be chronological, since by the turn of the 5th century, the sages are no longer mentioned as a definable group (Levine 2000a: 531).[18]

The issue of chronology raises the question of the relevance of rabbinic sources with regard to ancient Palestinian synagogues. The Tannaitic or Amoraic sources cited by scholars in relation to ancient Palestinian synagogues antedate the buildings (at least those decorated with Helios and the zodiac cycle). Levine notes the problem of using chronologically or geographically disparate rabbinic sources for the study of ancient synagogues (2000a: 567). In addition, the interpretation of many passages and their relevance with regard to synagogue buildings is disputed. Interestingly, the Jerusalem Talmud (which was completed by the early 5th century) and later Aggadic *midrashim* are "infinitely richer" in material relating to synagogues than 2nd-century Tannaitic sources (Levine 1992: 208, although rabbinic involvement in synagogue activities still appears sporadic and limited in scope; for the "synagogization" of the Temple in post-Amoraic sources, see 1997: 88). And, whereas the status of the Jewish aristocracy improved considerably by the late 3rd and early 4th centuries, that of the sages had clearly deteriorated (Levine 1989: 173). At the same time, the application of Temple terminology and forms to synagogues and the conceptualization of synagogues as "small temples" increased dramatically (Fine 1997: 81–82, 93; Talgam 2000: 105). Similarly, the centrality of prayer within the synagogue was expanded during the Amoraic period, becoming equal in significance to Torah study (Fine 1997: 85).

Fine notes that the application of Temple terminology and forms increased in the course of Late Antiquity (1997: 81). This was expressed in various ways, including the conceptualization of synagogues as "small temples," with furniture recalling that of the Temple (including the Torah shrine cast in the mold of the Ark of the Covenant, the menorahs, and the incense shovels; Fine 1997: 79–87; on p. 92 he notes that, "while the Tannaim were concerned that synagogues could become too much like the Temple, the Amoraim and those who followed them were not").

It is also evident in the increased use of Temple themes in liturgical contexts, perhaps best expressed in the appearance of *piyyutim* (Fine 1997: 87). In fact, the earliest *paytan* (liturgical poet) known to us by name is Yose ben Yose, a priest active in the 5th century (Yahalom 1999: 65). Priestly themes are prominent in the collections of *piyyutim* that follow the order of the weekly scripture readings. *Piyyutim* recited on the Sabbath and festival mornings were called *qerovot*, from the language of sacrifice. Fine notes that the *paytan* took on the role of the priest offering the "sacrifice" on behalf of the community through his recitation (1997: 88; see also Yahalom 1999: 64–92; Levine 2000a: 552). It is therefore

---

17. As opposed to the Diaspora, where priests were never a force to be reckoned with (Rutgers 1999: 196); see also Levine (2000a: 499), "The importance of the priests themselves for the recitation of these blessings is preserved in Palestinian practice, but not in Babylonian."

18. Cohen (1981–82) lists 50 instances in which "rabbis" are mentioned in Palestinian inscriptions. Most of these come from the catacombs at Beth She'arim and antedate the 5th century. Of the remainder, no. 8 comes from a Beth Midrash; and nos. 9 (Rama, between Akko and Safed), 10 (Sepphoris), 11 (Hammath Gader), 42 (Beth Alpha), 48 (Na'aran), 54 (En-gedi), and 57 (Susiya) are associated with synagogues. Cohen concludes that we cannot securely identify any of these epigraphical rabbis with figures known from Talmudic texts, and not all rabbis in antiquity were Talmudic rabbis — it could be used as an honorific title. Even if all of these were Talmudic rabbis, they did not exercise control over ancient synagogues.

not surprising that many of the *paytanim* known from Late Antiquity were priests (Irshai 1998: 117). The fact that many *piyyutim* deal with Temple issues and the priestly courses may be due in part to the priestly lineage of so many synagogue *paytanim* (Irshai 1998: 117; Yahalom 1999: 108; Levine 2000a: 499–500). The impetus for composing such poetry might have come from priestly circles wishing to maintain the memory of the Temple and, indirectly, their own standing in the community (Yahalom 1999: 112; Levine 2000a: 555). Some scholars have suggested that the appearance of *piyyutim* also reflects the influence of the Christian liturgy.[19] The development of ancient synagogues in Palestine paralleled (and perhaps developed in response to) contemporary trends in Christianity, including the rise in monumental architecture and art, priests, and liturgy.

The priestly courses (or watches) in the Temple are a common theme in the late antique *piyyutim* (Yahalom 1999: 107). The priests were divided into 24 courses, designated by the names of the heads of the priestly families enumerated in 1 Chr 24:7–18. The division into courses enabled all of the priests to participate in the Temple service, as each course would take its weekly turn officiating (Miller 1984: 62 n. 1). Numerous *piyyutim* list the 24 courses and their homes in the Galilee. Most were concentrated in the Beit Netofa Valley in Lower Galilee and in the Tiberias area, although priests lived in other parts of Palestine as well (Irshai 1998: 116, noting that, despite questions regarding the historical accuracy of the locations listed, the courses attest to the strengthening of the priestly class, especially in the Galilee). Synagogue inscriptions listing the courses have been found at Caesarea, Ashkelon, Reḥov, and in the area of Nazareth (Fine 1997: 88).[20] The plaques listing the priestly courses affixed to the walls of synagogues and the references to the courses in *piyyutim* reflect the prominence of priests within the liturgical setting of the synagogue. The liturgy of the synagogue service often highlighted elements of earlier Temple worship, with which priests were identified (Irshai 1998: 116; Yahalom 1999: 108; Levine 2000a: 496). Priests were accorded priority in the Torah-reading ceremony and during the ʿAmidah service, with the recitation of the priestly blessing (Levine 2000a: 497–98).

III. Iconography

In my view, the iconography of mosaic floors decorated with Helios and the zodiac cycle was intended to recall the Jerusalem Temple and therefore reflects priestly interests. In his discussions of this composition, Foerster makes the following points:

---

19. See Irshai 1998: 117; Schwartz 2000: 176: "This development may be seen as the institutionalization, perhaps under the impact of a similar development among Christians, of the practice of liturgical improvisation that prevailed in some Palestinian synagogues." Schwartz also notes the striking formal resemblance of some *piyyutim* to the *kontakion*, a type of Christian liturgical poetry written in Greek and introduced at the same time as the *piyyutim* (2000: 177). See also Levine 2000a: 530, 553; on p. 426, however, he points out that "This pattern of locally based authority [in synagogues] is somewhat similar to that found in pagan life and stands in contrast to that typical of Christianity, where the concentration of power in a dominant ecclesiastical framework tended to homogenize patterns of leadership."

20. See also Avi-Yonah 1964: 53: "When the persecution [instituted by Hadrian] came to an end (*ca.* AD 140) the Jewish remnant was reorganized in Galilee; the survivors of the priestly courses were transferred there and settled in various towns and villages, from ʿAithalu in the north to Beth-Yerah in the south." A possible plaque comes from Kissufim, and the longest and most complete fragment comes from Yemen (Levine 2000a: 496).

1. Helios and the zodiac cycle were intended to be a visual depiction and celebration of God's creation, the universe (Foerster 1985: 383; 1987: 225). Helios thus represents the sun, surrounded by the signs of the zodiac and the seasons representing the heavens and the cycle of the year (1985: 382, 387).

2. These images were also intended to evoke the Temple, for example, the signs of the zodiac = the 12 tribes = the 12 vessels in the Temple = the 12 gems on the breastplate of the High Priest (1987: 230).

3. These images corresponded with the liturgy in the synagogues; the *piyyutim* were a verbal expression of the images that surrounded the worshipers in the synagogues (1987: 231). Similarly, Fine suggests that the synagogue mosaic at Sepphoris should be interpreted primarily in relation to the liturgy (Fine 1999: 229; for liturgical interpretations of the Dura Europos synagogue paintings, see Kraeling 1956: 92, 346).

Foerster concludes that the Helios and zodiac cycle were intended to represent and celebrate the order of God's universe (1985: 388; see also Weiss and Netzer 1996: 35).

Although I agree with Foerster's points, I believe that the underlying motivation for this composition reflected priestly concerns. In his discussion of the Caesarea inscription, Avi-Yonah notes that the priestly courses are one of the central themes of the *piyyutim* composed by Palestinian *paytanim* (1964: 50, 53–54; on p. 50 noting that "it is a fact that the poets who composed the *qeroboth* [liturgical poems] dealing with the 24 courses were all connected with the land of Israel. This confirms the assumption that this custom originated in a country where the memory of the priestly villages was kept alive from local topographical knowledge"). However, the priestly courses were also connected with the calendar, since each served twice a year in the Temple, for a total of 48 courses.

Avi-Yonah notes that this connection is attested in the Dead Sea Scrolls, not surprising in light of the priestly orientation of the sect. The sectarians used a 364-day solar calendar consisting of 52 weeks per year (Avi-Yonah 1964: 55; see VanderKam 1994: 376 for evidence that, at Qumran, the 364-day calendar was the basis of the periods of service of the priestly groups).[21] Avi-Yonah concludes that the zodiac cycle in synagogue mosaics should be understood as a visual representation of the priestly courses and the calendar year (1964: 56; see also Vitto 1995: 295: "The painted inscriptions containing the names of the months and the list of the 'twenty-four priestly courses' [at Rehov] may correspond to the zodiac on the mosaic floors [of other synagogues]"). Like many of the *piyyutim*, the zodiac cycle refers to the priestly courses and, by way of extension, to the service in the Jerusalem Temple.[22]

In the Dead Sea Scrolls, the word *ḥodesh* apparently designates the beginning of the month (and not the new moon; VanderKam 1998: 111: "For the Qumran calendars it is the full moon that marks the inception of the new month"). This term seems to correspond

---

21. For recent discussions of the Qumran calendar, see VanderKam 1994; 1998; Beckwith 1996; Glessmer 1999: 227, 240–52, who refers to it as a 364-Day Calendar Tradition, instead of as a solar calendar.

22. Contra Roussin, who argues that "the fact that in most of the preserved zodiac pavements most of the seasons and months do not correspond also makes calendrical interpretation unlikely" (1997: 89). Talgam, however, supports the idea that Helios and the zodiac cycle "served both as a zodiac and a calendar" (2000: 104).

with the signs of the zodiac in the synagogue mosaics, while the four seasons (*tekufot*) indicate the cardinal points of the year and the seasons dependent on them. In the scrolls, these terms apparently derive from an ancient priestly calendar used for liturgical ceremonies that was preserved and preferred by the sectarians (Elior 1995: 30–33; VanderKam 1998: 116; Glessmer 1999: 226, 230, 232; for a different opinion, see Beckwith 1996: 101–13; for calendars of priestly courses from Qumran, see VanderKam 1994: 380; Beckwith 1996: 151; Vermes 1998: 335–62). VanderKam's discussion of calendrical scrolls from Qumran highlights the priestly interests in the Temple cult that are common to these scrolls and the zodiac cycles in synagogues:

> The solar calendar is the one according to which the religious holidays are dated, and dating sacred festivals is one of the central uses to which the calendar was applied. Not only is the expanded list of holidays coordinated with the 364-day system; the priestly courses are also an integral part of the calendar documents. By incorporating the dates of sabbaths and festivals and the periods of service for the priestly courses into their system for measuring time, the cultic and theological concerns of the authors come to expression. The calendars are, with few exceptions, oriented towards worship. In the case of the priestly divisions, it seems as if the covenanters worked with this institution because they anticipated a return to the Jerusalem sanctuary and to service it according to what they believed was the divine will. The group seemed to have been confident that their exile from the temple was only temporary. The calendars, with their unalterable rhythms, also expressed the theological or philosophical conviction that the courses of the luminaries and the cycles of festivals and priestly duties operated in a cosmic harmony imposed upon them by the creator God himself. The liturgical and theological emphases of the Qumran calendars betray a heavy influence from priests and priestly traditions. (VanderKam 1998: 112)[23]

Sectarian writings indicate that the sun was considered to be the source of light/good, as opposed to darkness/evil. A liturgical work (4Q395) proclaims that "He created darkness [and l]ight is His, and in His dwelling is the most perfect light, and all gloominess ceases before Him. It is not for Himself the distinction between light and darkness, for He has distinguished them for the sons of man: light during the day by means of the sun; (and during the) night (by means of) moon and stars" (Vermes 1998: 383).[24] This sort of outlook might be what led Josephus to conclude that the Essenes offered prayers to the

---

23. See also M. Albani, quoted in VanderKam 1998: 74: "The basic idea of the calendrical arrangement represented in the 4QMishmarot texts is the concept of a correspondence between heaven and earth, according to which the circuits of the stars and the cycles of the priestly courses have a common origin. This universalizing of the temple cult to the farthest horizon of the creation naturally could have sprung only from the theological interests of priestly circles." Elior notes that the sectarians probably preferred the solar over the lunar calendar because it was possible to determine in advance the dates of festivals (such as Shavuʿot) that are not otherwise set by the Torah (1995: 29).

24. Other examples are: "And when the sun rises the firmament of heaven ... they shall bless" (Vermes 1998: 370); "... who hast created the morning as a sign to reveal the dominion of the light as the boundary of the daytime.... For the light is good" (Vermes 1998: 373). Other writings found at Qumran, such as *1 Enoch* and the book of *Jubilees*, attest to the connection between the sun and the calendar (Beckwith 1996: 136; for example, *Jub.* 2:9, "And God appointed the sun to be a great sign on the earth for days and for Sabbaths and for months and for feasts and for years and for weeks of years and for jubilees and for all seasons of the years").

sun (*J.W.* 2.128–29; Goodman in press). The passage from 4Q395 recalls the synagogue mosaics, in which Helios is flanked by the moon and stars (that is, the heavenly bodies that provide light at night).[25] In the solar calendar of Qumran, the year (and hence, Creation) began on Wednesday instead of Sunday. The rationalization for this was that the heavenly luminaries were not placed in the sky until the fourth day of the week (Beckwith 1996: 103). Goodman notes that, by Late Antiquity, the sun had become the symbol of monotheism, not only among pagans, but also among Christians and probably Jews. He therefore suggests that the figure of Helios in the synagogue mosaics actually represented the God of Israel (Goodman in press).[26]

The figure of Helios thus represents the sun in the center of the universe (or, according to Goodman [in press], the God of Israel) and alludes to the solar calendar. Many other images decorating the mosaic floors of ancient Palestinian synagogues apparently refer to the Temple cult as well. The gabled structure flanked by menorahs in the uppermost panel of these mosaics is usually understood as representing the Torah shrine in synagogues. However, the Torah shrine itself and the ritual objects surrounding it—including the menorah, lulav and ethrog, shofar, and certainly the incense shovel—were modeled after or intended to recall festivals and sacrifices in the Jerusalem Temple (Hachlili 1988: 236–85; Branham 1992: 387–89; Fine 1997: 112–21; Kühnel 2000: 34, noting that the intent was to depict "the future Temple that is to be restored as the natural successor and cultic synthesis of the Tabernacle in the desert and the Temple in Jerusalem").[27] Some of the figured scenes in these synagogues, such as the binding of Isaac depicted at Beth Alpha and Sepphoris, clearly refer to the Temple cult and sacrifices.[28] Not surprisingly, the most detailed and explicit Temple iconography found to date in a Palestinian synagogue comes from Sepphoris, which was the center of a priestly community (Miller 1984; Yahalom 1999: 108–10; 2000: 89–90; for a priest mentioned as a donor in the Sepphoris synagogue, see Levine 2000a: 494). In addition to Helios and the zodiac cycle, as well as a representation

---

25. VanderKam suggests that the term *duk* mentioned in the *mishmarot* texts from Qumran denotes a moon that is near the new crescent (1994: 382). Could it be that this element is represented by the crescent moon flanking the figure of Helios in the synagogue mosaics at Hammath Tiberias, Sepphoris, and Beth Alpha?

26. I am grateful to Martin Goodman for his permission to mention this suggestion, presented in his forthcoming paper. Mathews's observation that the term *pantokrator* corresponds with the Hebrew term referring to "the Lord God of Hosts" (1995: XI, 14–15) lends support to Goodman's suggestion.

27. The wheels depicted on the Capernaum relief indicate, in my opinion, that these rectangular structures with pitched roofs and double paneled doors were intended to represent the Ark of the Tabernacle, rather than a portable Torah shrine on wheels (e.g., Hachlili 1988: 219–20, fig. 57, describing the object in the Capernaum relief as a "wheeled Ark"; or Kohl and Watzinger 1975: 193–95, suggesting that it was a Roman *carruca*, or carriage, for transporting the members of the house of Rabbi Judah ha-Nasi; for another interpretation, see Sukenik 1934: 17–18 n. 2). The Ark of the Tabernacle is depicted on wheels in one of the panels in the Dura Europos synagogue (Kraeling 1956: pl. 56).

28. For a discussion of this theme, see Yahalom 1999: 108–10; E. Kessler 2000. In the Sepphoris mosaic, Abraham and Isaac were apparently depicted barefoot, as indicated by the two pairs of upturned shoes beneath the tree in the pertinent panel. According to Weiss and Netzer, since this detail is not mentioned in the biblical account, it must reflect a lost *midrash* (1996: 30–31; see also Weiss 2000b: 27–28). However, Yahalom suggests that it reflects the influence of priestly groups at Sepphoris that wished to keep alive the memory of the service in the Jerusalem Temple, which was performed barefoot (1999: 110; 2000: 84–85, "the practice [of removing shoes during prayer] was [possibly] connected to members of the priestly line, for whom the gestural allusion to the Temple service was particularly important").

of the Torah shrine flanked by menorahs and ritual objects, the images in this floor include Aaron before the Tabernacle, the binding of Isaac, and panels depicting cultic objects from the Temple (including a basket of firstfruits, the table for the showbread, a lamb, a jar of oil, and a container of flour; Weiss and Netzer 1996; Fine 1999: 232–33; Weiss 2000b; for the aniconic Helios, see Mack 1998). Some of the non-Temple imagery in synagogue mosaics, such as Daniel in the lion's den, apparently refers to the liturgy and prayer service (Fine 1997: 125).

IV. The Relationship to Christianity

Many of the biblical scenes represented in synagogue mosaics were also used in contemporary Christian art (such as the binding of Isaac, Daniel in the lion's den, Noah's ark, and the visitation to Abraham of the three angels announcing Isaac's birth; Fine 1997: 124; Jensen 2000; H. L. Kessler 2000; Talgam 2000). As Fine states, "Significantly, the only distinctively Jewish contents that can be identified in the Sepphoris mosaic are the Torah shrine panel and the images of vessels from the Temple cult. In fact, without the menorahs and the Hebrew and Jewish Aramaic inscriptions, the synagogue floor might be mistaken for a church mosaic!" (Fine 1999: 232). I believe that this reflects the fact that, in Palestine, monumental synagogue architecture and art (and perhaps also the strengthening of the priestly class/synagogue hierarchy and the liturgy in ancient synagogues) developed together with or in response to the rise of Christianity (H. L. Kessler 2000: 72). As Branham notes, Christian sources reveal a fascination with and desire to claim the sanctity associated with the destroyed Temple, as well as an attempt to sever the institution of the synagogue from its Jewish ancestry (1992: 387). Many of the biblical passages represented in the Dura Europos synagogue are among those central to Jewish/Christian polemics (Weitzmann and Kessler 1990: 179). The strengthening of the priestly class, the development of a synagogue liturgy, and the rise of monumental synagogue architecture and art should be viewed against this struggle between Jews and Christians over the claim to the Temple traditions (for the rise of a synagogue hierarchy, including epigraphic and literary references to the priest or *hieros*, see Branham 1992: 386–87 n. 63). This appears to have led to the development of a concept of "Temple space" within the synagogue walls (Branham 1992: 387).

Ancient synagogues became the locus of priestly memorialization of Temple liturgy and the symbolic recreation of Temple space through certain physical actions (Branham 1992: 391). Jews and Christians appropriated each other's visual language and symbols in their attempts to lay claim to the Temple. Thus, Branham notes, "Although chancel arrangements in churches and synagogues correspond to unanalogous liturgical activities . . . the division of synagogue interior spaces may have signaled comparable implications of hierarchy and sacrality" (1992: 386). In synagogues, the chancel area memorialized an area ascribed to Temple space and the priestly class that once officiated there (Branham 1992: 387).[29] This is illustrated by an inscribed synagogue chancel screen from Ashkelon with a reference to the priestly courses (Goodenough 1953: 220–21; Branham 1992: 387).

---

29. For a more recent study of chancel screens in synagogues, see Habas 2000. Habas rejects Branham's interpretation on the grounds that the rabbinic sources do not attest to any segregation between the congregation and office-holders in synagogues (2000: 129). She fails to take into account, however, that most if not all rabbinic sources antedate the appearance of chancel screens in synagogues.

Branham notes that a mosaic floor panel behind the chancel screen of the late-6th-century chapel of the Theotokos at Mount Nebo appears to depict the Jerusalem Temple, flanked by bulls and gazelles (1992: 381; see also Piccirillo 1993: 151, no. 200; Talgam 2000: 107). The Greek inscription above it reads, "Then they shall lay calves upon thy altar." This passage from Psalm 51 identifies the bulls represented in the mosaic as sacrificial animals and was part of the 4th-century Greek liturgy in Jerusalem. Repeated three times by the priest after offerings had been placed on the altar, it recalled the liturgy of the Jerusalem Temple (Branham 1992: 381–82). Foerster points out the similarities between apparent depictions of the facade of the Jerusalem Temple in the mosaic floors of the synagogue at Khirbet Susiya and the chapel of the Priest John at Mount Nebo (1990: 546–47; see also Gutman, Yeivin, and Netzer 1981: 125; Piccirillo 1993: 175, no. 228; Fine 1997: 120; Talgam 2000: 107–8). Dedicatory inscriptions found in other mosaics indicate that early Christians considered the church to be a temple (Talgam 2000: 105).

As mentioned above, Foerster (1985; 1987) suggests that Helios and the zodiac cycle should be understood as:

1. a visual depiction and celebration of God's creation, the universe;
2. an evocation of the Jerusalem Temple; and
3. a reflection of the liturgy and *piyyutim* recited in the synagogues.

These points closely correspond with the three systems of interpretation that Demus (1964) describes as underlying the decoration of Byzantine churches:

1. The Byzantine church is an image of the Cosmos, symbolizing heaven, paradise (or the Holy Land), and the terrestrial world in an ordered hierarchy, descending from the sphere of the cupolas, which represent heaven, to the earthly zone of the lower parts.
2. The building is conceived as the image of the places sanctified by Christ's earthly life.
3. The church is an image of the festival cycle as laid down in the liturgy, and the icons are arranged in accordance with the liturgical sequence of the ecclesiastical festivals (Demus 1964: 15–16). Thus, the third interpretation is based on the calendar of the Christian year.

More recently, Mathews has noted that the narrative scenes in the vaulted zone below Byzantine church domes are noncalendrical in order, and therefore he suggests that they are a narrative set in the life of Christ. In addition, he argues that the narrative scenes do not refer to specific places in the Holy Land, but rather, that the sanctuary of the church represents the entire Holy Land at once (1995: XII, 15–17). Although he rejects the idea that these scenes depict a cycle of liturgical festivals, Mathews concludes that "the narrative subjects also reinforce the liturgical action" (1995: XII, 17).

The parallels between the system of decoration in Middle Byzantine churches and the late-4th- to 6th-century synagogue mosaics discussed here are striking. This is because elements of the Middle Byzantine decorative system evolved centuries before its crystallization in the late 9th century and thereafter (Demus 1964: 11, 45–50; see also Vitto 1995:

299). Few wall and ceiling mosaics of the early Byzantine period have survived in the churches of the Christian East (Vitto 1995: 288–89). We know, however, that the dome and upper walls of the church of St. Sergius at Gaza were decorated with a monumental mosaic cycle representing the life of Christ in 18 scenes. Although no physical remains survive, Choricius's detailed description indicates that this church was built and decorated prior to 536 (Krautheimer 1979: 266).[30] Early Byzantine sources indicate that such decorative programs were not uncommon. For example, in the 5th century, Nilus of Sinai advised a correspondent to "fill the holy church on both sides with pictures from the Old and the New Testaments, executed by an excellent painter" (Mathews 1995: XII, 15–16, with references to other sources). I propose that the arrangement of Helios and the zodiac cycle in ancient Palestinian synagogues corresponded spatially with the figured programs in churches. One of the most striking and consistent features of Helios and the zodiac cycle is the placement of this composition in the center of the nave. Why did these Jewish congregations place a circular design in the center of a rectilinear building covered by wooden beams that supported a pitched, tiled roof?

As some scholars have noted, such circular compositions originated in ceiling decorations that were copied onto floors. The Helios and zodiac cycle therefore represented the celestial sphere or "Dome of Heaven" (Lehmann 1945: 9, noting in relation to the mosaic at Beth Alpha that "these heavenly floor mosaics, more or less reflect ceiling decoration"; Foerster 1985: 380, 383; Roussin 1997: 84). In my opinion, Helios and the zodiac cycle were meant to be "read" three-dimensionally, like the interior decoration of a church, representing the celestial sphere or Dome of Heaven. Helios, symbolizing the sun (and perhaps God?) and alluding to the solar calendar, was literally conceived of as dominating the building from the top of the dome. His figure fills the circular medallion that corresponds with the large opening ("oculus") in the center of domed structures, such as Hadrian's Pantheon or the octagonal room in Nero's Domus Aurea in Rome, through which the sun

---

30. For Choricus's description, see Mango 1986: 60–68. Mango summarizes this description as follows: "St. Sergius' was a domed building with a square central bay, reduced by squinches to an octagon. The pictorial decoration was very elaborate: in the apse the Virgin Mary, attended by the patron saint and the founder of the church; in the vaults a lengthy New Testament cycle comprising at least twenty-four separate scenes, with particular emphasis on the miracles of Christ; in the drum of the dome the Prophets" (1986: 55).

Talgam notes that, whereas sacred themes and Jewish symbols decorate synagogue floors, the mosaics on the floors of churches generally have secular motifs (2000: 93–94). On the other hand, the fact that a law issued in 427 forbade the placing of Christ's image on the ground indicates that floor mosaics with his image must have existed (Vitto 1995: 299; Goodman in press). The vault mosaic of the sanctuary in the 6th-century church of S. Vitale in Ravenna shows a lamb in the center of a starry sky. The mosaic in the vault of the mausoleum of Galla Placidia depicts a cross in the center of a starry sky (Mathews 1993: 145–53). Mathews (1993; 1995: XI) disagrees with the interpretation of the Dome of Heaven suggested by Lehmann. For the identification of Helios as Sol Invictus, see Dothan 1983: 39–43; Goodman in press. In an e-mail communication of 9 November 2000, K. C. Britt pointed out to me the parallels between Helios and the zodiac cycle in synagogues and the dome decoration of the Orthodox and Arian baptisteries in Ravenna. As Mathews notes, these baptisteries "contain the best preserved Early Christian dome decoration" (1993: 155), dating to 458 and to the first half of the 6th century, respectively (Mathews 1993: 132, 162). The scene of the baptism of Christ that occupies the "oculus" of both domes is encircled by the 12 apostles (perhaps paralleling the signs of the zodiac, which refer to the priestly courses). In the Orthodox baptistry, the zone immediately below this is decorated with ritual objects, such as thrones, altars, and open books. I am grateful to Britt for sharing her observations with me.

was visible. The figure of Christ Pantokrator occupies this space in Middle Byzantine churches (Demus 1964: 17–21; Mathews 1995: XII, 17). Below and surrounding Helios are the signs of the zodiac (*ḥodashim*), with the four seasons (*tekufot*) in the "spandrels." The Temple imagery (that is, the panel with the Ark of the Tabernacle/Torah shrine flanked by menorahs and ritual objects) and the figured panels with biblical scenes were located in the "earthly zones" below the celestial area in the dome. Other scholars have read this decorative program as progressing forward from the bottom of the mosaic (that is, beginning at the entrance to the nave).[31]

Helios and the zodiac cycle are part of a mosaic program that represented, in two dimensions, a three-dimensional view of the universe: the sun (or God) in the Dome of Heaven, above the earthly Temple (represented by the cultic furniture), and scenes of sacrifice or prayer. In my opinion, this program represents a Jewish response to the decorative schemes of contemporary Christian churches (H. L. Kessler 2000: 72). The Jewish-Christian struggle over the claim to the Temple was part of a larger debate over salvation and redemption. For Christians, Jesus was a substitute for the sacrifices offered in the Temple and the means by which they were offered salvation and atonement for their sins. For this reason, iconography associated with Jesus, sacrifices, and salvation (such as lambs, peacocks, and symbols of the eucharist) dominates early Christian iconography. Naturally, these images also had liturgical significance, since participation in the church services provided worshipers with the means to salvation.[32]

Because Jews rejected Jesus as a substitute for the Temple sacrifices, Temple imagery and allusions to the solar calendar associated with the Temple festivals were selected for the synagogue mosaics. Perhaps the priestly class arose not only in response to the rise of a church hierarchy, but because of the Jewish need to counter the Christian claim that Jesus was the substitute for the Temple sacrifices. For Jews, Jesus did not supersede or replace the Temple sacrifices, which would one day be reinstituted. In the interim, prayer in synagogues (not the acceptance of Jesus as the Christ) took the place of sacrifices. The prayers and sacrifices were directed to God (not Christ) in the heavens above. Although the different interpretations proposed by Foerster and others are valid, I believe that the underlying motivation for this decorative program was Temple-oriented. The menorah

---

31. For example Roussin, who discussed this in relation to *Sepher Ha-Razim*: "The lowest level represents the earthly realm, the Helios-in-zodiac panel in the center represents the celestial sphere, and in the highest sphere is the Torah Shrine panel" (1997: 93). Goodenough interpreted these panels as representing a progression from purgation, the first step in mysticism (e.g., the binding of Isaac), to the illumination of the heavens, the second step in mysticism (Helios and the zodiac cycle), to unification, the third stage of mysticism ("the implements of the revealed cult of Judaism"; 1988: 170–71). At the same time, the sequence of panels can be understood in relation to the liturgy conducted within the synagogue, with the depiction of the Ark of the Tabernacle/Torah shrine in the mosaic in front of the actual Torah shrine, at the top of the nave.

32. H. L. Kessler states that "the difference between Jewish and Christian use of shared imagery is most emphatic in the representations of the Tabernacle. As Weiss and Netzer have argued, the Tabernacle and sacrifice at Sepphoris allude to God's promise of redemption and return, that is, to Jewish confidence that the Temple would be rebuilt. In the Christian chapels, the same symbols asserted the very opposite, the Christian belief that the Jewish liturgy of blood sacrifices had been superseded by Christ's crucifixion and the new sacrifice of the Eucharist" (Weiss and Netzer 2000: 70). This is why the motifs used in synagogue mosaics contain a clear narrative element, whereas all historical references were eliminated in the decoration of early Christian churches (H. L. Kessler 2000: 71; see also Talgam 2000: 103).

became the preferred Jewish symbol because it evoked the Temple cult, the focus of Jewish salvation, as opposed to the Christian cross, which symbolized Jesus' sacrifice (for the menorah and the connection of some of the synagogue images with salvation, see Fine 1997: 117–20, 124; Levine 2000b).[33]

The association of the Helios and zodiac cycle with the Jewish solar calendar and, by way of extension, with the Temple cult explains why this composition was never used in the decorative programs of contemporary Christian churches (contrary to the opinion that this was due to Christian opposition to astrology; see, for example, Mathews 1995: XI, 15).[34] Mathews notes that the figure of Christ Pantokrator represented in the domes of Middle Byzantine churches holds the Gospel in his left hand and raises his right hand in blessing. The space under the dome (and in front of the chancel screen) was where the liturgy was performed and the worshiper encountered the divine (Mathews 1995: XII, 17–18). The first half of this liturgy was an instruction in divine revelation. According to Mathews, "It is certainly significant that the invariable attribute of the Pantokrator is his Gospel book, for the solemn procession of the Gospel with candles and incense, the Little or First Entrance, is dramatically the high point of the first half of the liturgy, and it takes place directly beneath the dome. Furthermore, the reading of the Gospel that follows, which is the climax of the instruction, is performed by the deacon on the step before the bema underneath the dome" (1995: XII, 18).

In contrast, the Torah-reading ceremony was a central focus of the liturgy in Late Antique synagogues (Levine 2000a: 545). This ceremony had its origins in the period before the destruction of the Second Temple (Levine 2000a: 506). Surely the prominent position given to the Ark of the Tabernacle in synagogue mosaics (in the uppermost panel at the end of the nave) was intended as a response to the Christian claim that the Gospels (New Testament) superseded the Hebrew Bible (Old Testament). Thus, whereas the Gospels were one focus of the liturgy and iconography in churches, the Torah was given a prominent position in the decorative scheme and liturgy of synagogues. By modeling the Torah shrine in synagogues after the Ark of the Tabernacle, Jews were not only laying claim to the Hebrew Bible/Old Testament as their own but were illustrating the authority of the ancient Jewish Law over the new Christian one (Jensen describes the manner in which the Christian clergy and theologians treated the Hebrew Bible as "a kind of literary despoliation" [2000: 71]).

The appearance of Helios and the zodiac cycle in synagogues might also represent a Jewish response to fact that the church calendar began to replace the Roman civil calendar among the Christian population at this time (Irshai 1998: 115).[35] Irshai notes an

---

33. Weiss and Netzer emphasize the eschatological message of the theme of redemption (1996; Weiss 2000a; 2000b; see also Talgam 2000: 107–9). Weiss also states that the Sepphoris mosaic reflects Talmudic influence instead of sources within priestly circles (2000b: 28–30). However, it is equally possible that this literature preserves the memory of the same traditions depicted in the mosaics (such as the blowing of trumpets during the daily sacrifice). Either way, in my opinion, the Sepphoris mosaic program is clearly Temple- (and sacrifice-) oriented.

34. On the other hand, Christ was sometimes depicted as Sol Invictus, and sun and light were prominent elements in early Christian iconography (Dothan 1983: 41–42; Jensen 2000: 42–43).

35. See also Talgam, reviving an earlier suggestion (by A. G. Sternberg) connecting the first appearance of Helios and the zodiac cycle (at Hammath Tiberias) with Hillel II's publication of the rules for fixing the calendar (Talgam 2000: 101).

increase in messianic or eschatalogical expectations among both the Jewish and Christian populations of Palestine in the 5th and 6th centuries (1998: 117). The cyclical and regular nature of the solar calendar made it possible to calculate the dates of important events, both past and future—including the arrival of the Messiah (Elior 1995: 35; Beckwith 1996: 106–7, 217–75). The figure of Helios/the sun is prominent in Hekhalot and Merkavah literature, as well as in *Sepher Ha-Razim* (the Book of Mysteries). Although their sources and date of composition are disputed, there is no doubt that the mystical-poetical works known collectively as Hekhalot and Merkavah literature were popular in Palestine during Late Antiquity (Elior 1997: 217–18).[36] These works describe heavenly *hekhalot* (where the heavens are essentially a temple containing a varying number of shrines) composed of firmaments, angels, chariots, legions, hosts, and other wondrous phenomena and beings (Elior 1997: 220–21, 227). Elior attributes the emergence of this literature to the need to create a new spiritual world after the destruction of the Second Temple, especially among certain priestly circles (1997: 222–24), and states that "The authors of this literature were inspired directly by priestly tradition and belonged to circles whose concern was to preserve and consolidate a visionary and ritual tradition associated mythopoetically with the Temple service" (Elior 1997: 226).

The influence of earlier apocryphal literature, the Qumran writings, and the books of Enoch is evident in the Hekhalot and Merkavah literature (Elior 1997: 224–25). Enoch, who was the 7th antediluvian forefather, was one of the central figures in Jewish and Christian apocalyptic literature from the 2nd century B.C.E. to 3rd century C.E. (Nickelsburg 2000). Because he was the 7th forefather and lived for 365 years, Enoch became associated with the reckoning and transmission of the solar calendar (and is well represented in the Qumran literature; Elior 1995: 36; Beckwith 1996: 93–94; Reeves 2000: 249). In the Hekhalot literature, Enoch, a human being, was transformed into Metraton, an angelic priest who served in the supernal shrines and instructed the "descenders to the Merkavah" in the secrets of the heavenly Temple and the angelic service (Elior 1997: 228–30).

Enoch is one of the 13 ancestors of the world (from the genealogy in 1 Chr 1:1–4) listed at the beginning of the lengthy inscription in the mosaic floor of the En-gedi synagogue. These are followed by the names of the signs of the zodiac (Levine 1981: 140). According to Elior, the ancestors named in this inscription (especially Enoch) were responsible for the transmission of the secrets of creation and the universe, including the solar calendar, to future generations (Elior 1995: 37 n. 18). There is thus a connection between the names of the 13 ancestors and the signs of the zodiac in this inscription, as well as an expression of messianic expectations. Because Enoch's death is not described in the biblical account (Gen 5:24 simply states that "then he was no more, because God took him"), traditions developed in Jewish pseudepigraphical literature of the Second Temple period regarding his access to heavenly mysteries (Reeves 2000).[37] Enoch's ability to interpret the heavenly

---

36. For the connection between the oldest Hebrew Merkavah texts preserved at Qumran and the later Hekhalot and Merkavah literature, see Baumgarten 1988.

37. The mystical expressions in the Hekhalot literature from the 4th century on were apparently an outgrowth of earlier Jewish apocalypticism (Wolfson 2000). Chariot speculation and a cosmology that divides the heavens into seven successive firmaments are common elements of these traditions. Because *Sepher Ha-Razim* includes prayers offered to Helios, some scholars have connected the synagogue mosaics with a stream of mystical Judaism (for example, Goodenough 1988: 158; Roussin 1997: 93; for an English

signs (astronomy/astrology) meant that he could also predict the future (Elior 1995: 38). In contrast, the Tannaim advocated the use of the lunar calendar, and Enoch is either not mentioned or is presented in a negative light in rabbinic sources (Elior 1995: 38). Thus, Helios and the zodiac cycle not only allude to the solar calendar and reflect priestly interests in the Temple cult, but also express Jewish messianic or eschatalogical expectations.[38] These expectations apparently developed at the same time as or perhaps in response to eschatalogical hopes among the contemporary Christian population.

V. Galilean-Type Synagogues

If Galilean-type synagogues such as those at Gush Ḥalav and Capernaum were contemporary with those at Beth Alpha and Hammath Tiberias (Magness 2001), why do they have such different architectural styles, and why do the Galilean-type synagogues lack decorated mosaic floors? In my opinion, Galilean-type synagogues reflect the architectural traditions of Syria to the north. Still, how do we account for the fact that these synagogues lack the explicit Temple iconography found in the mosaic floors decorated with Helios and the zodiac cycle? According to Levine's map, only 4 of the 24 priestly courses were located in Upper Galilee during the Talmudic period and the rest were in Lower Galilee (Levine 1989: 175; from east to west, the 4 were at Safed, Meiron, Mafsheta, and Beth Hovaya). Other evidence of the priestly presence in Palestine comes from inscriptions referring to the priestly courses in ancient synagogues, references to priests as donors in synagogue inscriptions, and synagogues with mosaic floors decorated with Helios and the zodiac cycle (all of these discussed above). Inscriptions from ancient synagogues referring to the priestly courses have been found at Caesarea, Ashkelon, Reḥov, and in the area of Nazareth. Priests are mentioned as donors in synagogue inscriptions from Naᶜaran, Eshtamoa, Khirbet Susiya, and Sepphoris.

---

translation of *Sepher Ha-Razim*, see Morgan 1983). For priestly connections with Hekhalot literature, see Elior 1995: 40 n. 23; 1997: 222–24.

38. In this context, the following passage from the *Qerovah* of Yannai for Numbers 8 is worth quoting (from Schwartz 2000: 179):

> [the heavenly bodies (identified here with the angels)] arise at night/to declare Your faith by night/trembling like slaves before You/those who are made according to Your plan/who run alongside the wheels of Your chariot/who face the surfaces of Your throne/but see not the likeness of Your face/but rather the luster of the light of Your face/surrounded by snow and fire/and its wheels [of the divine chariot] are burning fire/and a river of fire is drawn out before it/from which they [the angels/heavenly bodies] are created/and through which they pass/but their light avails You not/for it was You who lit the lamps/You who make the lights/ who create the heavenly bodies/who bring forth the constellations/who spread out the stars/ who light the light of the sun/who cause to shine the luster of the moon/which runs to the light of the sun/who cause the sun to shine/and Mercury to scintillate/who set Venus in its place/who correct the moon-star/who illuminate the light of Jupiter/who enrich the splendor of Saturn/who make red the light of Mars/and all of these are lamps in the heavens/and You wished to light lamps on earth/like . . . the appearance of the tent of heaven/was made the likeness . . . [of the Temple?].

The images decorating the interiors of churches and synagogues were not only used as "propaganda" tools and accompanied the liturgy, but served to educate the illiterate members of the congregation. Thus, although few contemporary Jews could understand the *piyyutim*, which were composed in an obscure and allusive style (Schwartz 2000: 177), the images evoked in the poems were illustrated in the mosaics.

Finally, synagogues with mosaic floors decorated with Helios and the zodiac cycle have been found at Beth Alpha, Naʿaran, Khirbet Susiya, Husifa (on Mount Carmel, southeast of Haifa), Yafia (near Nazareth), and Sepphoris (plus the inscription in the synagogue at En-gedi). All these sites are located in the area extending from Lower Galilee to the south (including the coastal region and Judea). In other words, there is little evidence of priestly presence and activity in Upper Galilee and the Golan. Conversely, the only Galilean-type synagogues attested at sites with evidence of a priestly presence are at Meiron and Arbel. This means that nearly all the Galilean-type synagogues were built outside the area of known priestly activity and presence. This might explain why they lack the explicit Temple iconography found in synagogues decorated with Helios and the zodiac cycle, as well as references to the priestly courses.[39] Perhaps there were also differences in the liturgy conducted in these synagogues, if we assume that Helios and the zodiac cycle were connected with the *piyyutim* and other elements of the service.

Although the Galilean-type synagogues therefore seem to reflect less (or less-explicit) priestly influence than those decorated with Helios and the zodiac cycle, they are not completely devoid of Temple imagery; for example, their carved reliefs include menorahs and other Jewish ritual objects (and the apparent depiction of the wheeled Ark of the Tabernacle at Capernaum mentioned above [Hachlili 1988: 219–20]). In addition, I believe that the buildings were either modeled after, or at least were intended to evoke, the Jerusalem Temple. The earliest surviving depictions of the Jerusalem Temple, after its destruction, appear on the coins of the Bar-Kokhba Revolt. The building is represented with a flat roof and four columns along or in front of the facade. An arched element of disputed identity appears in the center of the facade, between the two inner columns (for example, Yadin 1971: 25). Thus, unlike classical Greek and Roman temples, which had moderately pitched and tiled roofs, the Second Temple seems to have had a flat roof.

Another depiction of the facade of the Jerusalem Temple is painted above the niche for the Torah shrine in the 3rd-century synagogue at Dura Europos (Kraeling 1956: pl. 16). As on the Bar-Kokhba coins, this building has a flat roof and four columns in front of the facade, but the arched element in the center of the facade clearly consists of double doors with a conch shell above. The flat roof could either be understood as deriving from the authentic tradition/recollection of the Jerusalem Temple, or as reflecting the fact that buildings in the local architectural tradition (at Dura Europos) had flat roofs (Kraeling 1956: 15, 29). In the mosaic floor of the synagogue at Khirbet Susiya, the facade of the Temple has four columns in front (see references above). The conch shell above the two paneled doors in the center of the facade between the two inner columns probably represents the Tabernacle inside the Temple. This element is similar to the Dura Europos painting, and perhaps to the disputed element on the Bar-Kokhba coins. However, this depiction of the Temple differs from the earlier examples in that it has a pitched and tiled roof over its center. It therefore represents a basilica with a clerestory, not a building with a flat roof. In other words, by the time this mosaic was laid, the Jews of Khirbet

---

39. One possible exception is a relief from the synagogue at Chorazin, which is usually described as a Medusa head (Hachlili 1988: 219, pl. 46). H. Eshel believes that it might represent the sun (personal communication).

Susiya envisioned the Jerusalem Temple as a basilical structure, rather than as a building with a flat roof.

Similarly, in the chapel of the Priest John at Mount Nebo (see references above), the facade of the Jerusalem Temple is depicted with four columns along the front, a conch shell above an inscription in the center, and a pitched, tiled roof covering the entire building (that is, as a basilical structure with two-story high aisles). I disagree with Fine that "the architectural form of late antique synagogues was . . . drawn from the basilica and not from the Temple" (1997: 93). Technically, of course, this is true; *we* know that the Jerusalem Temple was not a basilica, but these depictions indicate that the Jews and Christians of Late Antique Palestine envisaged it as such. In fact, the exteriors of many synagogues (including and perhaps especially Galilean and Golan types) appear consciously to reflect this architectural arrangement. For example, the main facade of the synagogue at Capernaum is divided into three sections by four pilasters, which frame the doors (for an illustration, see Hachlili 1988: 163, fig. 11). The central door and the huge arched window above echo the depiction of the Tabernacle between the two inner columns. The roof, of course, is pitched and tiled.

The representation of the Temple as a basilica with a clerestory in the mosaic at Khirbet Susiya is even more closely paralleled by synagogues with a "Syrian" gable (compare Gutman, Yeivin, and Netzer 1981: 125; and Hachlili 1988: 10). A similar arrangement, but without the arched window, can be seen at Hammath Tiberias, where the facade of the Stratum IIa synagogue was pierced by three doors (with the central doorway larger than the others), framed by four pilasters (Dothan 1983: 69). Although the Galilean-type synagogues lack the explicit Temple-oriented iconographic mosaic program with Helios and the zodiac cycle, the arrangement of their facades and monumental size must have been intended to imitate, or at least evoke, the Jerusalem Temple (as well as to compete with contemporary churches in the region, also laying claim to the Temple heritage).

References

Adan-Bayewitz, D.
    1993   *Common Pottery in Roman Galilee: A Study of Local Trade.* Ramat-Gan: Bar-Ilan University.
Amitai-Preiss, N.
    2000   Byzantine and Medieval Coins from the Synagogue of Hammath Tiberias. Pp. 95–101 in *Hammath Tiberias II: Late Synagogues,* by M. Dothan. Jerusalem: Israel Exploration Society.
Avissar, M.
    1996   The Medieval Pottery. Pp. 75–172 in *Yoqneʿam I: The Late Periods,* by A. Ben-Tor, M. Avissar, and Y. Portugali. Qedem Reports 3. Jerusalem: Hebrew University.
Avi-Yonah, M.
    1964   The Caesarea Inscription of the Twenty-Four Priestly Courses. Pp. 46–57 in *The Teacher's Yoke: Studies in Memory of Henry Trantham,* ed. E. J. Vardaman and J. L. Garrett, Jr. Waco, Tex.: Baylor University Press.
    1993   Bethlehem: The Church of the Nativity. Pp. 205–8 in *The New Encyclopedia of Archaeological Excavations in the Holy Land,* ed. E. Stern. Jerusalem: Israel Exploration Society.
Barag, D.; Porat, Y.; and Netzer, E.
    1981   The Synagogue at ʿEn-Gedi. Pp. 116–19 in *Ancient Synagogues Revealed,* ed. L. I. Levine. Jerusalem: Israel Exploration Society.

Baumgarten, J. M.
    1988   The Qumran Sabbath Shirot and Rabbinic Merkabah Traditions. *Revue de Qumran* 13: 199–213.
    1999   Art in the Synagogue: Some Talmudic Views. Pp. 71–86 in *Jews, Christians, and Polytheists in the Ancient Synagogue*, ed. S. Fine. New York: Routledge.

Beckwith, R. T.
    1996   *Calendar and Chronology, Jewish and Christian: Biblical, Intertestamental and Patristic Studies.* Leiden: Brill.

Branham, J. R.
    1992   Sacred Space under Erasure in Ancient Synagogues and Early Churches. *Art Bulletin* 74: 375–94.

Cohen, S. J. D.
    1981–82   Epigraphical Rabbis. *The Jewish Quarterly Review* 72: 1–17.

Demus, O.
    1964   *Byzantine Mosaic Decoration: Aspects of Monumental Art in Byzantium.* Boston: Boston Book and Art Shop.

Dothan, M.
    1981   The Synagogue at Hammath-Tiberias. Pp. 63–69 in *Ancient Synagogues Revealed*, ed. L. I. Levine. Jerusalem: Israel Exploration Society.
    1983   *Hammath Tiberias I: Early Synagogues and the Hellenistic and Roman Remains.* Jerusalem: Israel Exploration Society.
    1993   Hammath-Tiberias. Pp. 573–77 in *The New Encyclopedia of Archaeological Excavations in the Holy Land*, ed. E. Stern. Jerusalem: Israel Exploration Society.
    2000   *Hammath Tiberias II: Late Synagogues.* Jerusalem: Israel Exploration Society.

Elior, R.
    1995   The Jewish Calendar and Mystic Time. Pp. 22–42 in *The Hebrew Calendar*, by U. Simon and R. Elior. Jerusalem: The Presidential Residence (Hebrew).
    1997   From Earthly Temple to Heavenly Shrines. *Jewish Studies Quarterly* 4: 217–67.

Fine, S.
    1997   *This Holy Place: On the Sanctity of the Synagogue during the Greco-Roman Period.* Notre Dame, Ind.: University of Notre Dame.
    1999   Art and the Liturgical Context of the Sepphoris Synagogue Mosaic. Pp. 227–37 in *Galilee through the Centuries: Confluence of Cultures*, ed. E. M. Meyers. Duke Judaic Studies 1. Winona Lake, Ind.: Eisenbrauns.

Fraade, S. D.
    1991   *From Tradition to Commentary: Torah and Its Interpretation in the Midrash Sifre to Deuteronomy.* Albany: State University of New York.

Foerster, G.
    1985   Representations of the Zodiac in Ancient Synagogues and Their Iconographic Sources. *Eretz-Israel* 18 (Avigad Volume): 380–91.
    1987   The Zodiac in Ancient Synagogues and Its Place in Jewish Thought and Literature. *Eretz-Israel* 19 (Avi-Yonah Volume): 225–34.
    1990   Allegorical and Symbolic Motifs with Christian Significance from Mosaic Pavements of Sixth-Century Palestinian Synagogues. Pp. 545–52 in *Christian Archaeology in the Holy Land: New Discoveries. Essays in Honor of Virgilio C. Corbo*, ed. G. C. Bottini, L. Di Segni, and E. Alliata. Jerusalem: Studium Biblicum Franciscanum.

Glessmer, U.
    1999   Calendars in the Dead Sea Scrolls. Pp. 213–78 in vol. 2 of *The Dead Sea Scrolls after Fifty Years: A Comprehensive Assessment*, ed. P. W. Flint and J. C. VanderKam. Leiden: Brill.

Goodenough, E. R.
    1953   *Jewish Symbols in the Greco-Roman Period*, vol. 1. New York: Pantheon.
    1988   *Jewish Symbols in the Greco-Roman Period.* Abridged ed. Princeton: Princeton University Press.

Goodman, M.
  1992   The Roman State and the Jewish Patriarch in the Third Century. Pp. 127–39 in *The Galilee in Late Antiquity*, ed. L. I. Levine. New York: Jewish Theological Seminary of America.
  In press The Jewish Image of God in Late Antiquity.
Gutman, S.; Yeivin, Z.; and Netzer, E.
  1981   Excavations in the Synagogue at Horvat Susiya. Pp. 123–28 in *Ancient Synagogues Revealed*, ed. L. I. Levine. Jerusalem: Israel Exploration Society.
Habas, L.
  2000   The *Bema* and Chancel Screen in Synagogues and Their Origin. Pp. 111–30 in *From Dura to Sepphoris: Studies in Jewish Art and Society in Late Antiquity*, ed. L. I. Levine and Z. Weiss. Journal of Roman Archaeology Supplementary Studies 40. Portsmouth, R.I.: Journal of Roman Archaeology.
Hachlili, R.
  1988   *Ancient Jewish Art and Archaeology in the Land of Israel*. Leiden: Brill.
Hayes, J. W.
  1972   *Late Roman Pottery*. London: British School at Rome.
Irshai, O.
  1998   The Byzantine Period. Pp. 94–133 in *Israel: Land, People, State. A Nation and Its Homeland*, ed. A. Shinan. Jerusalem: Yad Izhak Ben-Zvi (Hebrew).
Jensen, R. M.
  2000   *Understanding Early Christian Art*. New York: Routledge.
Johnson, B. L.
  2000   Pottery and Lamps. Pp. 54–83 in *Hammath Tiberias II: Late Synagogues*, by M. Dothan. Jerusalem: Israel Exploration Society.
Kessler, E.
  2000   The ʿAqedah in Early Synagogue Art. Pp. 73–81 in *From Dura to Sepphoris: Studies in Jewish Art and Society in Late Antiquity*, ed. L. I. Levine and Z. Weiss. Journal of Roman Archaeology Supplementary Series 40. Portsmouth, R.I.: Journal of Roman Archaeology.
Kessler, H. L.
  2000   The Sepphoris Mosaic and Christian Art. Pp. 64–72 in *From Dura to Sepphoris: Studies in Jewish Art and Society in Late Antiquity*, ed. L. I. Levine and Z. Weiss. Journal of Roman Archaeology Supplementary Series 40. Portsmouth, R.I.: Journal of Roman Archaeology.
Kohl, H., and Watzinger, C.
  1975   *Antike Synagogen in Galilaea*. Osnabruk: Otto Zeller.
Kraeling, C. H.
  1956   *The Excavations at Dura-Europos Conducted by Yale University and the French Academy of Inscriptions and Letters, Final Report VIII, Part I: The Synagogue*. New Haven: Yale University Press.
Krautheimer, R.
  1979   *Early Christian and Byzantine Architecture*. New York: Penguin.
Kühnel, B.
  2000   The Synagogue Floor Mosaic in Sepphoris: Between Paganism and Christianity. Pp. 31–43 in *From Dura to Sepphoris: Studies in Jewish Art and Society in Late Antiquity*, ed. L. I. Levine and Z. Weiss. Journal of Roman Archaeology Supplementary Series 40. Portsmouth, R.I.: Journal of Roman Archaeology.
Lehmann, K.
  1945   The Dome of Heaven. *Art Bulletin* 27: 1–27.
Levine, L. I.
  1981   The Inscription in the ʿEn Gedi Synagogue. Pp. 140–45 in *Ancient Synagogues Revealed*, ed. L. I. Levine. Jerusalem: Israel Exploration Society.
  1989   *The Rabbinic Class of Roman Palestine in Late Antiquity*. Jerusalem: Yad Izhak Ben-Zvi.

1992   The Sages and the Synagogue in Late Antiquity: The Evidence of the Galilee. Pp. 201–22 in *The Galilee in Late Antiquity*, ed. L. I. Levine. New York: Jewish Theological Seminary of America.

1999   The Patriarchate and the Ancient Synagogue. Pp. 87–100 in *Jews, Christians, and Polytheists in the Ancient Synagogue*, ed. S. Fine. New York: Routledge.

2000a   *The Ancient Synagogue: The First Thousand Years.* New Haven: Yale University Press.

2000b   The History and Significance of the Menorah in Antiquity. Pp. 131–53 in *From Dura to Sepphoris: Studies in Jewish Art and Society in Late Antiquity*, ed. L. I. Levine and Z. Weiss. Journal of Roman Archaeology Supplementary Series 40. Portsmouth, R.I.: Journal of Roman Archaeology.

Mack, H.
1998   The Unique Character of the Zippori Synagogue Mosaic and Eretz Israel Midrashim. *Cathedra* 88: 39–56 (Hebrew).

Magness, J.
1992   The Byzantine and Islamic Poterry [*sic*] from Areas A2 and G. Pp. 164–69 in *Excavations at the City of David 1978–1985, Directed by Yigal Shiloh III: Stratigraphical, Environmental, and Other Reports*, ed. A. de Groot and D. T. Ariel. Qedem 33. Jerusalem: Hebrew University.

1993   *Jerusalem Ceramic Chronology circa 200–800 C.E.* Sheffield: Sheffield Academic Press.

1994   The Dating of the Black Ceramic Bowl with a Depiction of the Torah Shrine from Nabratein. *Levant* 26: 199–206.

1997a   The Chronology of Capernaum in the Early Islamic Period. *Journal of the American Oriental Society* 117: 481–86.

1997b   Synagogue Typology and Earthquake Chronology at Khirbet Shemaʿ, Israel. *Journal of Field Archaeology* 24: 211–20.

2001   The Question of the Synagogue: The Problem of Typology. Pp. 1–48 in *Judaism in Late Antiquity*, vol. 4/3: *Where We Stand: Issues and Debates in Ancient Judaism—The Special Problem of the Synagogue*, ed. A. J. Avery-Peck and J. Neusner. Leiden: Brill.

Magness, J., and Avni, G.
1998   Jews and Christians in a Late Roman Cemetery at Beth Guvrin. Pp. 87–114 in *Religious and Ethnic Communities in Late Roman Palestine*, ed. H. Lapin. College Park, Md.: University Press of Maryland.

Mango, C.
1986   *The Art of the Byzantine Empire, 312–1453.* Toronto: University of Toronto Press.

Mathews, T. F.
1993   *The Clash of Gods: A Reinterpretation of Early Christian Art.* Princeton: Princeton University Press.

1995   *Art and Architecture in Byzantium and Armenia.* Brookfield, Vt.: Ashgate.

Miller, S. S.
1984   *Studies in the History and Traditions of Sepphoris.* Leiden: Brill.

1999   Those Cantankerous Sepphoreans Revisited. Pp. 543–73 in *Ki Baruch Hu: Ancient Near Eastern, Biblical, and Judaic Studies in Honor of Baruch A. Levine*, ed. R. Chazan, W. W. Hallo, and L. H. Schiffman. Winona Lake, Ind.: Eisenbrauns.

Morgan, M. A.
1983   *Sepher Ha-Razim, The Book of the Mysteries.* Chico, Calif.: Scholars Press.

Nickelsburg, G. E.
2000   Enoch, Books of. Pp. 249–53 in *Encyclopedia of the Dead Sea Scrolls*, ed. L. H. Schiffman and J. C. VanderKam. New York: Oxford University Press.

Piccirillo, M.
1993   *The Mosaics of Jordan.* Amman: American Center of Oriental Research.

Rahmani, L. Y., and Sharabani, M.
  1983   Appendix: Catalogue of Coins. Pp. 71–74 in *Hammath Tiberias I: Early Synagogues and the Hellenistic and Roman Remains*, by M. Dothan. Jerusalem: Israel Exploration Society.
Reeves, J. C.
  2000   Enoch. P. 249 in *Encyclopedia of the Dead Sea Scrolls*, ed. L. H. Schiffman and J. C. VanderKam. New York: Oxford University Press.
Roussin, L. A.
  1997   The Zodiac in Synagogue Decoration. Pp. 83–96 in *Archaeology and the Galilee: Texts and Contexts in the Graeco-Roman and Byzantine Periods*, ed. D. R. Edwards and C. T. McCollough. Atlanta: Scholars Press.
Rutgers, L. V.
  1999   Incense Shovels at Sepphoris? Pp. 177–98 in *Galilee through the Centuries: Confluence of Cultures*, ed. E. M. Meyers. Duke Judaic Studies Series 1. Winona Lake, Ind.: Eisenbrauns.
Sauer, J. A., and Magness, J.
  1997   Ceramics: Ceramics of the Islamic Period. Pp. 475–79 in vol. 1 of *The Oxford Encyclopedia of Archaeology in the Near East*, ed. E. M. Meyers. New York: Oxford University Press.
Sukenik, E. L.
  1934   *Ancient Synagogues in Palestine and Greece*. London: British Academy.
Schwartz, S.
  2000   On the Program and Reception of the Synagogue Mosaics. Pp. 165–81 in *From Dura to Sepphoris: Studies in Jewish Art and Society in Late Antiquity*, ed. L. I. Levine and Z. Weiss. Journal of Roman Archaeology Supplementary Series 40. Portsmouth, R.I.: Journal of Roman Archaeology.
Swartz, M. D.
  1999   Sage, Priest, and Poet: Typologies of Religious Leadership in the Ancient Synagogue. Pp. 101–17 in *Jews, Christians, and Polytheists in the Ancient Synagogue*, ed. S. Fine. New York: Routledge.
Talgam, R.
  2000   Similarities and Differences between Synagogue and Church Mosaics in Palestine during the Byzantine and Umayyad Periods. Pp. 93–110 in *From Dura to Sepphoris: Studies in Jewish Art and Society in Late Antiquity*, ed. L. I. Levine and Z. Weiss. Journal of Roman Archaeology Supplementary Series 40. Portsmouth, R.I.: Journal of Roman Archaeology.
VanderKam, J. C.
  1994   Calendrical Texts and the Origins of the Dead Sea Scroll Community. Pp. 371–88 in *Methods of Investigation of the Dead Sea Scrolls and the Khirbet Qumran Site: Present Realities and Future Prospects*, ed. M. O. Wise et al. New York: New York Academy of Sciences.
  1998   *Calendars in the Dead Sea Scrolls: Measuring Time*. New York: Routledge.
Vermes, G.
  1998   *The Complete Dead Sea Scrolls in English*. New York: Penguin.
Vitto, F.
  1995   The Interior Decoration of Palestinian Churches and Synagogues. Pp. 283–300 in *Bosphorus: Essays in Honour of Cyril Mango*, ed. S. Efthymiadis, C. Rapp, and D. Tsougarakis. Amsterdam: Adolf M. Hakkert.
Weiss, Z.
  2000a   The Sepphoris Synagogue Mosaic. *Biblical Archaeology Review* 26: 48–61, 70.
  2000b   The Sepphoris Synagogue Mosaic and the Role of Talmudic Literature in Its Iconographical Study. Pp. 15–30 in *From Dura to Sepphoris: Studies in Jewish Art and Society in Late Antiquity*, ed. L. I. Levine and Z. Weiss. Journal of Roman Archaeology Supplementary Series 40. Portsmouth, R.I.: Journal of Roman Archaeology.
Weiss, Z., and Netzer, E.
  1996   *Promise and Redemption: A Synagogue Mosaic from Sepphoris*. Jerusalem: Israel Museum.

Weitzmann, K., and Kessler, H. L.

1990   *The Frescoes of the Dura Synagogue and Christian Art.* Washington, D.C.: Dumbarton Oaks.

Wolfson, E. R.

2000   Heikhalot Literature. Pp. 349–50 in *Encyclopedia of the Dead Sea Scrolls*, ed. L. H. Schiffman and J. C. VanderKam. New York: Oxford University Press.

Yadin, Y.

1971   *Bar-Kokhba: The Rediscovery of the Legendary Hero of the Last Jewish Revolt against Imperial Rome.* London: Weidenfeld and Nicolson.

Yahalom, J.

1999   *Poetry and Society in Jewish Galilee of Late Antiquity.* Tel Aviv: Hakibbutz Hameuchad (Hebrew).

2000   The Sepphoris Synagogue Mosaic and Its Story. Pp. 83–91 in *From Dura to Sepphoris: Studies in Jewish Art and Society in Late Antiquity*, ed. L. I. Levine and Z. Weiss. Journal of Roman Archaeology Supplementary Series 40. Portsmouth, R.I.: Journal of Roman Archaeology.

Part III

The History of the Family:
Continuity and Change

Nine Months among the Peasants in the Palestinian Highlands: An Anthropological Perspective on Local Religion in the Early Iron Age

Karel van der Toorn
Faculty of Humanities
University of Amsterdam

Introduction

What follows is more in the nature of a dream report than in the style of a scholarly study. On the basis of the available evidence and the secondary literature—a selection of which is presented at the end of this paper—I have speculated on what it would have been like to spend nine months in an early Israelite village in the highlands. A dream offered itself as a possible setting for this piece of fiction—for fiction it is, even though it attempts to get as close to the historical reality as the data and imagination allow. A scholar-of-religion-turned-anthropologist, I would spend nine months in a hamlet in the central Hill Country, enough to get at least an idea of the inhabitants' customs and beliefs.

I

The village that would be *my* village for the nine months was situated on the western slope of a hill. It overlooked a narrow valley, closed in by other hills to the west and the north. Beginning at the level of the village, a series of terraces ran some 30 meters down to the valley. A small path at the other end of the village led up to the hilltop; a 30-minute walk would take you to a series of cave tombs on the hillside facing a platform of tamped earth, with an open-air fireplace and a roofed structure lined with two benches of stone opposite each other. You only had to climb 10 more meters to reach the top of the hill, which gave you a view of the next valley. On a clear day—and most days were clear—you could see four other settlements, much like our own, isolated dots in the landscape.

Our village was small. It consisted of about 20 houses, built in groups of three or four, six compounds placed in such a way as to form a circle around an open space, in the center of which was a huge oak. During the day this area served as a cattle-pen; at night, the goats and sheep would be taken into the houses. The houses themselves followed a straight-forward design. You would enter through an open courtyard; immediately to the right was a roofed gallery where the cattle were kept. To your left might be another roofed space used for the storage of food and various implements. The sleeping quarters were at the back of the house, one rectangular room, dark but for the light from one or two narrow square windows. This is where the entire family would sleep, although in the heat of the summer they might make their beds on the roof. A roofed upper story was exceptional. It was my luck to be adopted, so to speak, by the family of Elḥanan, the village chief, whose house boasted a second-story room. He offered it to me as a guest room and allowed me to stay there for the full nine months. I came to look upon his family as my own.

Family was important to these people, as I soon found out. In fact, "family" was the single concept used to express the relations between the inhabitants of the village. They were all relatives. Individual houses were dwellings for what we could call nuclear families: a couple, their two or three children, and sometimes an elderly relative or a stranger who had chanced upon the village, such as myself. In the three houses adjacent to Elḥanan's lived his two brothers with their families, and one was used by his parents and their un-married daughter, a woman in her late thirties. The situation in the other compounds was similar. Three—in one case, four—generations of one family lived in close proximity to one another. The six family groups of the village were all kin; they referred to each other as "flesh-and-blood" and constituted what they called a *mišpāḥâ*, a term that in my anthro-pological jargon I would render as "clan." The more general term *ʿam*, "people," was often used in the same fashion.

I admit I had a hard time finding out the precise relationship between the villagers; in fact, I am not sure that they all were related, in the biological sense of the term. But they did claim descent from a common ancestor. This man, one Elyachin, had given his name to the village. People called it Ramat-Yachin, "Hill of Yachin." He was supposedly one of those buried on the hillside, a half-hour's walk from the village.

Family relations beyond the confines of the village were vague and of little practical consequence in daily life. There was a general belief that the inhabitants of the four vil-lages on the other side of the hill were "brothers," that is to say, related in one way or another. The main advantage of this idea—perhaps a fiction—that I could discover was that it extended the choice of marriage partners.

My first acquaintance with the villagers had left me with the impression that the prin-cipal division of the community was between the various family compounds. Each com-pound seemed a tightly-knit group whose members combined their efforts in farming and cattle-breeding. The compound cultivated a common piece of land on the terraces; and when the boys took the sheep to graze in the outlying fields, the families would pool their animals.

After a few days I came to realize, however, that another division, less obvious but nonetheless profound, ran through the village; this was the division of gender. Men and women lived in almost separate worlds. Being a man, I would find it hard to get in touch with the village women. Early in the morning nearly all the men would leave the village, most of them to work in the fields, some to take care of the herds. Apart from the older men, whose age or poor health kept them home, only one or two stayed behind to protect the women and children. During my stay this proved an unnecessary precaution, since no foreigners with evil intentions cared to pay us a visit. Those left as guardians would do menial chores, plastering the roofs of their houses, repairing farming tools, and the like. The other men were away all day, only returning toward sunset. At that time everybody went home for an early evening meal. I would join Elḥanan and his son. Eating was done separately, too. Except for special occasions, there was no such a thing as a family dinner. The men would sit down to eat in the courtyard, while the women remained in the back of the house. Theirs was a world almost impossible to penetrate. Most of what I know about the life of the women in the village I have gathered from glimpses and rare conversations with Elḥanan's wife.

The principal way to meet the village women was to go to the well, where they would go in groups in the course of the morning. Such behavior for a man, however, was rather suspicious. At times some of the young men would sneak away from the group to watch the girls at the well. The older men knew such things happened because of having done the same in their youth, and they would usually turn a blind eye toward the curious lads; but no youngster would dare to make such escapades a habit. The only occasions when men and women would mingle more or less freely were the harvest days and the wine festival.

The sense of seclusion was reinforced by the measures taken in connection with women during their menstruation. Menstruating women were not allowed to be in the vicinity of men; they were forbidden even to prepare food. Usually they would withdraw, in groups of three or four, to a separate shed on the outskirts of the village. Men made jokes about the custom, saying that gossip was running high; but they would never disrupt the intimacy of the women.

II

In the evening, when the cattle had been brought in, the central open space of the village (what we might call a "common") served as a meeting ground for the men. A fire was lit, and, seated on stones near the oak tree, the men waited for the stars to appear, exchanging small talk and telling each other stories.

It was during these evening gatherings that I developed a notion of the ideas that the highland peasants entertained about the world that surrounded them. Since I had come to study their religion, I was especially eager to follow up on conversation topics that had to do with their beliefs. Religion was hardly on the minds of these men, however. They did not even have a word for it. They did hold certain beliefs about the supernatural, but these were rarely discussed. There was a common, mostly tacit, understanding that the land they lived on was made and governed by El, a word that simply means "god" but was used as a proper name. This belief elicited little enthusiasm from my hosts, much less devotion. The deity they most frequently referred to was Baal, held to be responsible for the growth of the crops and the fertility of the cattle. Baal means "lord," and at first I took it as an epithet of El. The villagers located both of them in the sky, or said they lived on a mountain in the north; when asked about the shape of these gods, they came up with contradictory information: some said they looked like giants, others said they were heavenly bulls, while yet others combined the two notions, saying they were giants riding bulls. The two seemed indistinguishable, but it turned out that El and Baal were really two separate gods. Baal was the lord, and more particularly, the lord of the village; El was a dim deity by comparison. A god named "Yahweh" was unknown to the villagers, although a visiting divine once mentioned him as the deity worshiped in some settlements to the south.

One of the men possessed an image of Baal, which he volunteered to show me. It turned out that he kept it in the corner of his sleeping room: a miniature bull of terra-cotta, standing in the opening of what looked like a stable or a shrine, also made of terra-cotta. It had been in the possession of his family for three generations, originally brought back as a souvenir from a visit to a temple. He told me he sometimes prayed to it for rain and good crops. As I pressed him with questions, he shrugged his shoulders and ventured that it mattered little whether you prayed to an image or not: Baal could also hear you from the sky.

In general, the men were not forthcoming with details on their religion. When I would bring up the subject, their reactions were brief, to the point of being impolite. How about the sun and the moon, I wanted to know, were they not gods too? Sure, they were gods alright; everybody knew that. But it did not occur to my informants to specify their particular field of activity, apart from the obvious fact that they were the "lamps of heaven." In the end I had to resign myself to the idea that the villagers had a religion, but that it was more a religion of action than of speculation. Nor did the village have a resident religious specialist who might possess a superior knowledge of the tenets informing religious practice. In what follows I shall therefore necessarily restrict myself to a description of the rituals that I witnessed. Their deeper meaning is a matter for others to discover.

As in most peasant communities, in Ramat-Yachin there were cyclical rites and rites performed at times of crises, big or small. Three cycles marked the rhythm of the life of the village: the cycle of the natural day; the cycle of the month; and the cycle of the agricultural year. There were corresponding daily, monthly, and annual rites.

Most daily rites were unobtrusive, and it took some time before I recognized them as such. Greeting is a good example. The first thing people would do when they awoke was to wash their hands and face, go out to the inner courtyard, and curtsy, touching their nose or their forehead with their right hand. The gesture, performed with the person facing east, was obviously addressed to the sun. A similar rite of greeting was performed at the appearance of the lunar disk. No particular fervor was implied by this practice: it was a matter of recognizing the universe in which the villagers lived. Greeting or blessing (another translation of the same term) was indeed an act of affirmation, also in the social realm. In the course of the morning, people would greet each other by bringing their hand to their face and wishing each other well; to meet someone without greeting him was considered an affront. The interdependence of the villagers was such that no one would lightly omit a greeting. Although they used religious phrases ("El be with you"—"And with you, too"), the significance is comparable to our "Good to see you"—"Good to see to you, too": an affirmation of membership in the community. Etiquette requires that greetings be soft-spoken, almost murmured; it also prescribes a subtle order of initiative: the senior men respond to the greetings of the junior men, husband responds to wife, parents to their children.

One greeting that I have not mentioned is the one directed to the family ancestors, performed at the entrance of the back room. Elḥanan, being the head of his compound, had three small wooden statuettes located near the doorpost; just in front of them was a wick-lamp, which burned all night, to be put out only at the break of day, usually by the woman of the household. The statuettes were referred to as *teraphim* or "gods" (*elohim*) and represented or symbolized different generations of the family ancestors. They varied in size from 20 to 40 cm (4–8 in.); roughly carved, their upper end was in the shape of a head.

The men greeted them twice a day: in the morning, as they left the sleeping room, and in the evening, as they went back in. Their greeting was in fact a brief prayer of thanksgiving in the morning and for protection in the evening. The principal function ascribed to these ancestors was indeed to protect. At the same time, however, they embodied the essence or the identity of the family. I recall when I first came to Elḥanan's house, my host took me to these figurines as a kind of introduction. As long as I stayed under his roof, I was part of his family, and I should therefore acknowledge his ancestors and be acknowledged by them. Neither the shape nor the weight of the statuettes was an obstacle to their being carried around, but they were rarely taken to other places inside or outside the house. I can think of only one time, when Elḥanan's son was quite ill, that his mother transported the figurines to his bedside. Other than that, throughout my stay, the ancestors were not moved from the door.

III

The sun had barely begun to warm the day when the men would leave for the fields. We would walk in silence, but once we set to work, songs would fill the air. They were rhythmic, monotonous songs with many repetitions, recalling feats of hunting, exceptional harvests, or the strange habits of foreigners. One man would intone a line and the others would respond in an antiphony that could last for hours. Religious songs were rare, although the lyrics did recognize unusual events as acts of God. The first meal of the day, taken just before noon, was preceded by hand-washing and a short prayer uttered by one of the family heads—a formula of praise to El, Baal, and the ancestors. The men spoke little while they ate. Afterward they withdrew, mostly alone, to the shade of a tree and lay down for one and one-half hours. It was presumed to be dangerous to work in the early afternoon; the sun might strike you or a demon might catch you. As the worst heat subsided, work continued for another two hours. Then we headed home to the village for the evening meal. It followed more or less the same routine that the first meal did. The best part of the day came after the meal, however, when the men would gather in a circle around the fire. Until darkness descended they discussed the events of the day, made weather forecasts, recited stories of the past, or played at riddles.

Religious topics were rare, as I have noted—with one exception. The men loved to tell each other dreams. Their dreams were perhaps not religious in the strict sense of the term, but many of them involved actors from another world, be they gods, demons, or ghosts. It was as though the excitement of the night had to make up for the dullness of the day. These men enjoyed an intimacy with the other world that one would not expect in people of so practical a bent of mind. As I came to discover, however, the discussion of dreams was their way of expressing their inner life. You must realize that these people were hardly ever alone, nor would they speak about their feelings—to such an extent that you might believe they simply did not have them. They were always together and seemed to live on the surface. Only asleep were they alone, and dreams were the outlet for their feelings. Feelings of desire, guilt, ambition, jealousy, love, and hatred assumed the shape of visitors from beyond, commanding them to do things and involving them in strange adventures.

Let me cite a typical example. One evening as we were sitting in a circle, some on stones, others with their back against the great oak, yet others simply sprawled on the ground, Bekor, a cousin of Elḥanan's, signaled for silence—"I had a dream I want you to hear." The others looked at him, curious about what was to come. "In my dream I was walking up to the tombs, when I heard a voice behind my back. It was a strange voice, unlike anyone I know, high-pitched and almost shrieking. 'Do not turn,' said the voice, 'for you will not be able to see me. Your forefathers sent me, for they are displeased with you. You love the living more than the dead.' I was dumbfounded. How could he say such a thing? You know I have always been faithful in paying respect to the ancestors. As I turned around to ask for an explanation, I saw the shape of a huge man. No sooner had I opened my mouth than he vanished. Struck by a sudden sadness I continued the road to the hill-top. As I approached the tombs, I saw an old man sitting at the roadside, head between his hands, crying like a child. I stepped up to him and recognized my grandfather, blessed be his memory. I reached out to touch his shoulder. At my touch he shrank, and before my very eyes he turned into an infant. A stone was lying nearby. I took it and killed the baby on the spot. Strange as it seems, I felt in a glorious mood. I ran back home and kissed my wife. She knew everything that had happened, without my telling her. We embraced—I was still dreaming—and the next moment I woke up." The others, who knew that Bekor had lost a baby boy the year before, kept silent. I dared not speak either. Later, however, I confessed my bewilderment to Elḥanan. "How can he be happy about such a nightmare," I asked. "If we want to live," Elḥanan explained, "we must kill our dead. Bekor loved that little son of his so much that he had to kill him. He is free now."

Several months later, as my stay among the highlanders drew to an end, it was clear that Bekor's wife was pregnant again. "When the gods call upon a child to join them," said Elḥanan, and I understood he was speaking about the ancestors, "they will also give a replacement. But first you must kill the child." Who knows how the human mind works? Perhaps Bekor and his wife had to come to terms with their grief before she could conceive again.

IV

The day was different for the women. They rose before the men to prepare the meal their husbands and sons would take with them. After the men's departure, the daily routine of grinding began. Most households possessed a hand-mill, a simple tool consisting of two stones: a larger lower stone and a smaller upper "rider." Women from the same compound would often team up to distract themselves from the monotony of grinding with talk and song. The flour is used to prepare a dark type of bread in the shape of circular cakes; unleavened, it is the principal ingredient of every meal. Olives, figs, dates, fruits, and vegetables (especially leeks and onions) come with the bread, and the main drink is goat's milk, although they also produce wine and some beer. While the preparation of food would seem to be a rather mundane task, the women put an almost religious zeal into it. Most of them take particular pride in preparing dishes that look attractive; the monotony of the diet is counterbalanced, so to speak, by the presentation: the cakes of bread are decorated with incised stars and crescents, and a plate of fruit is arrayed in geometrical patterns. Their culinary art pleases the eye more than the palate.

A practice that would almost pass unnoticed is the custom always to put aside a small part of the food in a separate basket. This is not to be eaten, but to be given to the ancestors, present in the *teraphim*. The pouring out of some liquid, usually water, seemed to be optional but frequent. I am tempted to call it a daily ceremony, but it is done so naturally and as a matter of course that the word "ceremony" seems exaggerated. Nor does this small rite trigger particular demonstrations of devotion. The ancestors, invisible but for their symbols, are part of the world of the peasants. The women take care of them as they do of the rest of the family. The word "offering" may also evoke the wrong associations: it is really food, given for the sustenance of beings one does not see but who are nonetheless very much present.

Much of the afternoon and the early evening are spent spinning and weaving. Whereas the washing of clothes is done by both men and women, spinning and weaving are considered exclusively female chores, so much so that the spindle whorl is like a symbol of womanhood. The main products of weaving are clothes and carpets; the material is thick and rugged, but what it lacks in comfort is made up for by the simple beauty of the decorations woven into the fabric. These decorations have a special significance: not only do they provide aesthetic pleasure, they also serve as an identity marker for the villagers. In the course of my stay, I came across various people from other villages, and each village had its own decoration pattern. Once you became aware of this, there was no need to ask people where they came from: their garments answered the question before it was asked.

One of the first things you notice as you enter the village is its smells: the smell of burning wood, the smell of cooking, and, especially in the evenings, the smell of incense. Most homes have at least one incense burner. The perfume it releases is meant to drive away, or to smother, other less-pleasant odors. The peasants are indeed remarkably sensitive to smells, a trait not to be confused with a care for hygiene. They will wash only once every week or two, preferring instead to sit close to the incense burner and fumigate themselves. They also apply body lotion, some sweetened olive oil, not merely as a protection against the sun (certainly not a luxury under these skies), but also for its perfume. But in addition to the social motive, the burning of incense has a religious dimension. Performed in the private quarters of the house, that is, the sleeping room, it is thought to please the gods as well.

These gods are the ancestors and the invisible spirits of the village, but the women think most of the goddesses of fertility and lactation. I mention them in passing, but to the peasant women these goddesses, represented by roughly carved wooden statuettes, are of paramount importance. El and Baal are the all-important gods, of course, but they are the gods with whom the men are concerned; their territory lies beyond the house. In the domestic realm, the goddesses prevail. Known as Asherah and Astarte (both are proper names but are also used as generic designations of their statuettes), they play a large role in the lives of the women. It is they who grant conception and protection during pregnancy, assure a safe delivery, provide young mothers with milk, and watch over the health of infants. The sleeping room is their proper sanctuary, their natural habitat, so to speak. In a world that makes little distinction between love, sex, and fertility, it is not unnatural that the devotion of women should focus on such goddesses. Their lives depend on them.

V

The cycle of the lunar month has two stages, marked by the full moon at mid-month and the new moon at its end. The full moon is the occasion for a holiday. The men remain in the village and spend the day working on their houses, sharpening their tools, and talking with the other men. Mid-month is also a day for weddings; people are at leisure to celebrate, and the full moon is believed to enhance the chances of conception. Women enjoy a day off, too. It is customary to spend much of the preceding day preparing the meals for the day of the full moon. Family visits, also to and from other villages, are typically planned for mid-month. There is little religious activity; the day is foremost a social event.

Twice during my stay the village received a visit on the day of the full moon from a wandering divine, called a "man of God." He stayed overnight with one of the families, and by day he sat in the shade of the great oak on the common. People had been expecting him and came to him for advice on a variety of matters. He was especially popular with the women. Pregnant women asked about the sex and appearance of their future babies, whether they would have twins, and the significance of whatever physical discomfort they might be feeling. Other women asked about the likelihood of future pregnancy, the health of their children, the whereabouts of a lost object, or their chances of winning the affection of a lover. Although the men of the village did not swarm to the divine as the women did, they treated him with respect, and were not averse to consulting him themselves. They would want to know about means to increase the fertility of their flocks or what they should plant next year. The "man of God" had traits of a pastor, practitioner, and prophet. People paid for his services with a fee, usually items of food or clothing, sometimes an earring or another ornament.

On one occasion the divine was asked to give his opinion on a case that involved a whole family. This was the family of Oreb, who lived with his wife and two children in the house of his widowed mother, together with his unmarried sister. It was no secret in the village that Oreb's wife Rebecca and his sister Tamar were not the greatest of friends. They avoided each other's company, if they could help it. Rebecca's demeanor was withdrawn; in the company of other women she would hardly speak. Tamar, on the other hand, was a chatterbox; "better a leaking roof than a garrulous wife," the men would say, commenting on her spinsterhood. Tamar had spread word that Rebecca was a sorceress. She claimed that the woman was trying to poison her own husband (who, indeed, frequently complained about abdominal pain). In the village, Tamar's insinuations were met with a shrug of the shoulders, but they did have an effect on Rebecca. She was growing thin and always had a worried look on her face. Moreover, her mother-in-law did not seem impervious to the accusations.

Oreb had decided to resolve the case by bringing it to the "man of God," at the risk of exposing his family to disgrace, because many other villagers witnessed the session. Oreb explained the situation and asked for a verdict about the guilt of his wife. The divine listened to the story, asked a few questions, and proceeded to prepare what seemed to be a strange elixir. He asked for water from the well, had it put into a goblet, scraped some sand from the floor of Oreb's sleeping room and put it in too, and produced a rectangle of donkey hide, a reed pen, and ink. Watched by the villagers, he wrote some words on the skin. Nobody in the village knew how to read or write; the very act of writing seemed a feat of magic to them. The divine read aloud the curses he had written, dipped the hide into the goblet, and took it out when the ink had mixed with the liquid. He made both Rebecca and Tamar stand up to proclaim their innocence. The women did so, but when the man then gave them the cup to drink, Tamar refused. "Why should I expose myself to a curse on account of that witch," she cried. Oreb urged her to drink, but she was not to be persuaded. "Say no more, woman," said the divine, "and leave your sister in peace." The face of Rebecca, who had taken a few sips, broke into an expression of relief. The liquid had been bitter, but the outcome was sweet. From that day on, Tamar did not dare to speak evil of her sister-in-law. She had been put to shame and was shunned by the rest of the villagers. I rarely saw her afterward.

By comparison with the day of the full moon, the occasion of the new moon is more important. For the one or two days that the moon is invisible, all work is suspended. At the transition of one moon to the next, of one month to the next, all the men of the village aged 12 and over go for a meal to the sacred area opposite the cave tombs. At the *bāmâ*, as the villagers call the platform and adjacent structure, the men enjoy a banquet in the vicinity of (and, I am tempted to say, in the company of) the ancestors. Elḥanan acts as the master of ceremonies. This is the one time in the month when the villagers eat meat. It is usually Elḥanan who provides one or two sheep and has them slaughtered near the altar as an act of devotion and munificence. As the butcher cuts off the head of the animal, its blood is collected in an earthen pot. The master of ceremonies takes the pot and, putting his thumb into the tepid liquid, marks the earlobe of all participants with a simple streak. Then he goes to the altar, puts some blood on it as well, then goes over to the tombs and smears some blood above the entrances. The idea is that of a community by blood, uniting the men of the village, their ancestors, and Baal. What is left of the blood is poured on the ground.

In the next stage of the proceedings, the animal is burned on the altar. One piece is left for the deity, but the bulk is divided among the men, and more or less symbolic portions are brought to the graves. Community and kinship are the commanding concepts of the ritual. One might call it a celebration of community and kinship, but it would perhaps be more to the point to say that the ritual creates and confirms kinship ties among the participants. To partake of the meal is to be part of the community. The fact that I, as a visitor, was allowed to join in the festivities signified that for all practical purposes I was accepted as a member of the group, enjoying the protection of its god and ancestors.

Although the ritual might be viewed as a rite of fraternization, it would be misguided to think of it as an equalizer, blurring the distinctions of age and authority in a general mood of cheerfulness. Cheerful the ritual certainly is, with little of the austere solemnity that can make our religious ceremonies so gloomy. The atmosphere is much like that at the American Thanksgiving celebration. There is food and drink in abundance and the mood is one of banter and comradeship. Yet in a subtle but unmistakable way, the ceremony confirms and in a sense legitimizes the traditional division of roles and responsibilities. The most obvious division of roles, of course, is that between men and women. Women never participate; although they may have been born into the village, they remain outsiders to the community of god, the ancestors, and the male adults. Or to put it more mildly, they belong to that community by virtue of their ties, either by blood or marriage, to the men. They participate in the second degree, so to speak. There is also a division of roles among the men. If Elḥanan provides the food and takes the lead in the ceremony, it shows that he is the chief of the village. His authority has the approval of the ancestors and god, because he mediates between them and the other men. The distribution of the meat follows a fixed pattern along the lines of rank and authority. Only when all the heads of the families have received their share are the rest of the men given theirs.

Apart from a few formulas of presentation spoken by Elḥanan as he sacrifices the sheep and distributes its meat (a kind of greeting or blessing of Baal and the ancestors), the ritual is a sequence of simple acts performed in accordance with an unwritten code of etiquette. The liturgy, if this term can be used, is unemphatic and might pass for being spontaneous. As the meal progresses, the mood becomes more and more ebullient, bordering at times on a loss of propriety. The feast lasts into the evening, and although the village is just a half-hour's walk away, everybody stays for the night. We sleep in and around the *bāmâ*, making our way back only the following morning. The next evening, the first appearance of the new moon crescent is greeted with shouts of joy by men and women alike. Then the new moon festivities are over, and everything returns to normal.

VI

The rituals of the annual cycle have little connection with sun or moon but follow the rhythm of the seasons and the phases of agricultural and pastoral activities. When I first came to the village of Ramat-Yachin, it was late January. The nights were cold, and by day the temperature rarely rose above 15 degrees Celsius. There were occasional bouts of rain, which forced us to stay indoors. Most days were dry, however, and the men of the village would plow their fields and plant; the wheat and barley had already been sown, but legumes and vegetables were planted in January and February.

Toward the middle of March, the weather changed. Almost overnight spring arrived. The hills changed color to green; amidst the grass and trees there erupted a sudden bloom of wild flowers, such as anemones, cyclamens, lilies, daffodils, mandrakes, and orchids. Spring was brief, giving way about two months later to the first heat of summer. But, however transitory spring might be, it was, especially at its outset, a magical time. The villagers spent most of the day outdoors; the men went to the meadows to cut grass, later to be used as fodder for the cattle; the woman went out in groups of two or three to collect fragrant herbs, which they would use for cooking; and the children went out to play on the common, between the houses, and among the trees just outside our hamlet. It was also the time for the goats and sheep to be taken out. Left in the care of some of the boys, they would graze on the hillside meadows around the village. The air was soft and promising, filled with the smell of growing things.

The onset of spring was marked by a ceremony that was largely celebrated separately by the family compounds, yet all at the same time. On the first full moon of the season, the family heads went up to the *bāmâ* near the hilltop, each bringing a young lamb. Other family members, many of them children, joined them in their half-hour walk to the sacred place. The lambs, none of them older than a year, were slaughtered, and the blood was collected in vessels. Back home, the blood was smeared on the doorposts of the houses; it possessed virtue to ward off demons, the men said, and tonight, the first full moon of spring, a death-dealing demon would prowl about the houses of the village. The severed heads of the lambs were left to be burned on the altar of the *bāmâ*, but the rest of the animal was wrapped in a piece of cloth and taken back home.

There the families gathered at the house of the family leader for a special supper that would last well into the night. In the front yard of the house, the lamb was roasted, the family seated in a circle around the fire. The women seasoned the animal with herbs, and unleavened cakes were served with the meat. It was the custom to dip the meat in a strong and rather bitter sauce before eating it. Unlike the regular meals, this one was delicious. The lamb was soft, the sauce pungent, and the mood festive. Outside, demons might lurk in the air; within, the wick-lamps burned peacefully and the embers of the fire spread a warm glow. The new year was beginning. Tomorrow the small cattle would be taken to graze outside, after months of seclusion, the newborn animals for the first time in their life. The women would give their homes a proper cleaning; everybody and everything made a fresh start.

A few weeks later, by mid-April, shortly after the late rains, the harvest season began. For about six or seven weeks the men went out to the terraced fields to reap first the barley, then the wheat. Everything was gathered in baskets and carried to the village at the end of the day. There was something of a contest among the men as to who would gather the first sheaf. The winner took it to the village and paraded it as a trophy among the villagers, who greeted it as the symbol of the harvest to come. There was joy and relief; the first sheaf announced that Baal did not withhold his blessing and that there would be food for the months to come.

This sheaf was kept apart from the rest of the harvest and taken to the *bāmâ* at the first celebration of the new moon. On this occasion the usual ritual was preceded by a ceremony in which the village chief, my host Elḥanan, lifted the sheaf of corn above his head and, facing the altar, moved it from left to right as if to show the invisible powers above and around that their gift had been received. No fervent prayers were spoken, and there was no show of devotion. But, while the ceremony might strike onlookers as a tepid performance, the participants derived comfort from its regularity. The very fact that it could be performed, just as in preceding years, strengthened their belief that they lived in a world of order and of mutual goodwill between Baal, the dead, and the living. Such thoughts were never spoken out loud, nor did they need to be. The ritual, performed as a pious duty, spoke for itself to the participants; they did not ask for its meaning, nor did they care to talk about it.

The new moon ceremonies offered but a brief respite from the labors of harvest. For days on end the men went to their fields to gather the wheat and barley, collect it in baskets, and store it in the barns next to their fields. The end of the harvest inaugurated the period of threshing and winnowing. The transition between activities did not pass unnoticed: whereas the reapers would return to the village at the end of the day's work, the threshers tended to spend the night outdoors, close to the threshing floor. By the end of May, when the harvesting had come to an end, the nights were warm enough to sleep outside; the temperature rarely dropped below 15 degrees Celsius. But the temperature was not the reason that the men passed their nights next to the threshing floors. It was in part to protect the produce from being stolen and, more importantly perhaps, because it was a time of celebration over the finished harvest, and the men liked to sleep close to the yield of their fields, much as children might cling to their presents on the night of their birthday.

Since there was a good deal of merry-making and intoxication with drink, moreover, staying the night was also the practical thing to do. Thus, as the fire grew dimmer and the conversation faded, the men withdrew to their fields to a shelter contrived for the occasion and, wrapped in their mantles, fell asleep. On one or two occasions I noticed female company; there was nothing like an orgy going on, but some girls took advantage of the cover of night and the drowsiness of the other men to spend a few hours in the company of a loved one. They had left without a trace before dawn. Allusive remarks the next morning proved that it was not a figment of my imagination, however.

The happy days following the harvest led to another event that would break the monotony of daily life in the village. Just before the summer heat settled over the Hill Country, the sheep were taken to be sheared in another town, located a full day's walk away. Elḥanan allowed me to go with the two men who led the flock, knowing that this was precisely the kind of thing I was curious to see. He instructed me to keep a close eye on the proceedings, to make sure that the wool was properly collected and marked by the name of the sheep's owners. The different families of the village each had their own sheep, recognizable as such by a sign branded on the animal's ear. Since they were not present at the shearing themselves, it was a matter of trust that their portion of the wool would not be diminished. My presence would be helpful.

Early in the morning we left the village with a flock of about 120 sheep. I had never before been more than an hour's walk from the village, and this was my first chance to see the Hill Country beyond the surroundings of Ramat-Yachin. We walked at a leisurely pace on a narrow path on the mountain ridge in a northerly direction; six hours later we took a path that branched off to the west to make our way to Beer-Zuph, our final destination. Unlike Ramat-Yachin, this town was surrounded by a wall. As we approached the gate, the bleating of other flocks rose to greet us. The narrow streets were filled with sheep. By comparison with the quiet of our own village, this was a town bustling with people, activity, and noise. I was at a loss, but my companions knew their way around. The sheep were taken to a corral, and we went to the inn for dinner and a night's rest.

The establishment we went to was built abutting the city wall, which served as its back wall. A small rectangular window in our second-story room allowed a view of the last slopes of the hills, a riverbed, and the beginnings of a plain beyond. The place was run by a woman in her forties; she saw it as her duty, apparently, to provide her guests with all the comforts that she could offer. When we had finished our meal, drinks were served, and the woman inquired whether she should send up girls for the night. I declined, but the other men accepted. Some duties have their reward, one of them observed. I understood that the distinctions between bar, inn, and brothel were spurious here. The next morning my companions were in excellent spirits. The town was in a festive mood over the sheep-shearing, and they participated in the enjoyment.

Summer is not as grim in the hills as it is on the plains or in the Jordan Valley, but the heat can be quite suffocating. Especially in the morning, before the western wind reaches us, the hot air weighs on us like a blanket and slows down our movements. The dew can be heavy but brings little relief: it evaporates quickly as the sun rises. When the clouds of mist have disappeared, the hills meet the eye, covered in a variety of brown, ochre, red, gray, and yellow. The village lies languidly under the clear skies. The dogs and the birds make little sound. Dust hangs in the air where people or animals move. Later in the morning, as the steady breeze returns some life to the village, people go out to the orchards and vineyards on the gentle slope just above the settlement. All through summer the fruit harvest continues: it reaches a climax by August, when almost the entire population is engaged in the picking of grapes. Whereas the harvest of cereals is left mainly to the men, the summer harvest brings out the women and children as well.

Summer's biggest event is the wine festival, as people call it. It comes as an outburst of joy after a long period of dullness. The festivities take place around mid-September and last for seven days. A few days before the celebration, two men make the rounds of the hamlets to invite their kinsmen, as they are regarded, to join in the frolic. Their call does not go unheeded: for the period of the festival, the population of Ramat-Yachin triples. At no other time of the year is there such a large gathering of people. In the weeks preceding the festival, the grapes are collected and trodden in the winepresses, the latter activity accompanied by a good deal of rhythmic and rather monotonous singing. The fresh juice is collected into jars. The winemakers seal the jars with clay, mark them with a tag, and store them in a kind of cellar cut into the rock. The day before the new moon, one jar is opened, and the new wine is poured into much smaller terra-cotta decanters.

A religious ceremony opens the festival. In the late afternoon of the first day, all the men gather for the offering of the new wine to Baal and the ancestors. All the men of the village take a decanter and, along with the male visitors, go up in procession to the cult place near the hilltop. As they leave the village, the women form a throng and sing to the sound of flutes and clapping. I could not make out all of the lyrics, but I remember a few lines: "Here is the wine, the wine of the turning of the year, wine that gladdens the heart of god and man; juice that delights and heals aching bones; sap of the vine that goes down the gullet and mounts to the head; blood of the gods that inspires men with courage, and reddens the cheeks of bashful girls." Halfway to the sanctuary, the women return, laughing and giggling, back to the village to prepare for the next day.

The men proceeded to celebrate at the *bāmâ*. Elḥanan took his flask, went to the altar, spoke a benediction, and poured half of the liquid on the ground. The other men followed his example, after which the group made its way to the cave tombs. Libations were made and benedictions murmured, until Elḥanan gave the sign to go back to the *bāmâ*. The men seated themselves in circles around him and Elḥanan motioned for silence. This was the first and only time I would hear him give something amounting to a speech at a ritual. His tone of voice was a pitch higher than usual, and the words he chose sounded strangely solemn. He spoke of the blessing of the harvest; the year had been good: there was sufficient grain for the months to come, and the yield of the vineyards had been exceptionally plentiful. Baal had proved, Elḥanan said, that he still ruled the land; the ancestors, who nourished the soil, had been favorable. The past few months had been dry and dead; Baal had sojourned in the world below, staying with the ancestors, leaving the land a playground for Death, his adversary. Life had been drained from grasses and plants, the flocks had been

listless, and joy had abandoned the inhabitants of the hills. But now Baal had returned and
had brought the ancestors with him. He showed his presence in the new wine, reinvigorating all those who drink it. Death had been defeated; Baal reigned supreme. In a few weeks'
time he would shower his rains upon them, preparing the fields for a new sowing. The
coming year would be even better than the last one: the flocks would multiply, women
would hold new children on their laps, and the efforts of the men would bear fruit. As
Elḥanan spoke about the future, his words had the quality of an incantation. The audience
responded now with shouts, now with whispers.

When Elḥanan reached the end of his peroration, the men rose to their feet. Lightly
swaying, they raised their voices for a song in which several of the phrases that Elḥanan
had used were repeated. The theme of a struggle between Baal and Death, which I had
taken for a poetic description of the succession of the seasons, was apparently part of traditional mythology. The song took it up and elaborated on it, magnifying Baal for his victory over his foes. The song signaled the end of the solemn part of the ceremony. It was
followed by a general toast and mutual congratulations. The libations had not exhausted
the wine; there was enough left for the men to drink their fill.

VII

If the anthropologist stays long enough, he or she will get a fair idea of the cycles of
daily, monthly, and annual rites of the highland peasants. Acquiring knowledge of the
gamut of religious action in response to a crisis, as well as such events as the passage to
puberty or marriage, is in large measure fortuitous. No one died while I was at Ramat-
Yachin; for all the importance of the ancestor cult to the villagers, I am unable to tell how
they conducted a burial. Comparative anthropology suggests that one of the most common occasions for noncyclical ritual action is illness. During the time of my stay—nine
months compressed into one dream—I witnessed only two cases of illness that called for
measures that had a religious side to them.

Most diseases in the village were suffered in silence. Bowel disorders, due no doubt to
unhealthy water and a general lack of hygiene, were endemic; headaches and bouts of
fever seemed to be frequent as well. But these and similar ailments belonged to the normal pattern of life. People complained, but attached no particular significance to them.
When Elḥanan's youngest son fell ill, however, things were very different.

The boy was in his fourth year and had just been weaned. His illness came unexpect-
edly, as most illnesses do. The transition from lactation to a solid food diet had been an
occasion for a small celebration, because it is regarded by the villagers as the transition
from infancy to childhood; and, since infant mortality is high, those who survive their first
three years are expected to live. But Yair, as the boy was called, seemed to contradict these
expectations. The lively child that he had been changed into a silent boy lying listlessly in
a corner of the backroom. His skin felt warm, and his eyes grew languid; his food remained untouched and water was the only thing he ingested. At first his parents hoped for
a passing disease but, when Yair's illness did not leave him, they became more worried
each day. The women of the family compound took turns keeping watch over the sick
child; they had taken the images of the ancestors and put them at his bedside; the various
goddess statuettes they possessed were similarly brought to the boy. Night and day, the

penetrating sound of laments and murmured prayers was heard. Elḥanan kept his composure, but is was clear from the look in his eyes that fear was gnawing at him. Two weeks after the onset of the illness, he saddled a donkey, took four silver earrings, and went to find the "man of God" to persuade him to come and look at the child. Three days later he was back, accompanied by the divine.

The man, whom I knew from his earlier visits to the village, seemed to know everything there was to know about the condition of the child. He hardly glanced at Yair. Instead of treating the child, he ordered a meeting of the family heads of the village. Late in the afternoon, at Elḥanan's summons, they assembled under the oak on the village common. Seated in a semicircle, the six men faced the divine as he waited for silence to settle. The other men of the village, myself included, stood in a group behind them. Although we did not take part in the deliberations, we were witnesses to every word that was spoken; should anyone conceal the truth or tell a lie, we would know. The "man of God" spoke first of the reason for his coming and this meeting: he described the history of Yair's illness, emphasized Elḥanan's prominence in the community, and urged that the present misfortune was not the misfortune of one family only but of the whole village. The men responded with nods; these were apparently familiar themes.

Then the divine launched into the diagnosis of the disease. The boy suffered, he said, not on account of his own guilt—what could be the guilt of a four-year old?—but for the sin of the community. If Yair was being dragged away to the realm of the dead, it meant that the ancestors held a grudge against the village. They were asking for their due. At these words, Elḥanan asked for permission to speak. Addressing the elders as much as the divine, he observed that the prescribed sacrifices had been dutifully offered. He swore that the village had kept the covenant with Baal and the ancestors. The "man of God" accepted his statement. "The dead are dissatisfied," he said, "because of a vow that has been left unfulfilled. One of you has made a promise and failed to keep it. Go home now, consult with your heart, consult with your kinsmen, and come back tomorrow morning."

Early the next morning the proceedings continued as though there had been no interruption. After repeating the conclusion of the day before, the divine admonished the elders to come forth with a confession. They should honor the gods by speaking the truth. As the divine spoke, they darted glances at each other, each impatient to see who would break the silence. But no one said a word. The divine took his time; his eyes rested on each of the six elders, trying to decipher the unspoken language of their faces and movements. Ten minutes passed with no other sound than the call of a bird or the yelp of a dog. Finally, the "man of God" produced a leather pouch containing four polished stones, two black and two white. Since the elders refused to speak, El would speak on their behalf. One by one he summoned them to come forward, and each time his hand went into the pouch, took out two stones, and let them drop to the ground. Two white stones stood for innocence, two black for guilt, and one white and one black meant undecided.

Four of the family heads were cleared, two received the combination of black and white. They were to step forward once again. But before the divine could repeat the procedure, one of them broke out in a stammer. "It is my daughter-in-law," he said in a plaintive voice. "She took a vow and kept it hidden from my son. He did not know, nor did I. But I swear I shall pay."

The face of the divine showed no trace of emotion. "How much?" he simply asked.

When the man told him that she had promised three goats for the birth of a son, the elder was ordered to sacrifice three goats that evening. Moreover, he should indemnify Elḥanan for the costs of the divine, and give half the yield of his vineyard to be drunk at next year's wine festival. The man did not argue. A murmur of release went through the audience. "Always the women," whispered my neighbor. Such was clearly the general feeling. Vows were popular with the women of Ramat-Yachin, as I noticed on more than one occasion. But since they often lacked their own means of payment, it was the husband and his family who would bear the consequences. Many a vow of a desperate wife would bring despair to her husband; vows were trouble.

As for Yair, he soon recovered. Sheer coincidence? I do not know. What I do know is that the intervention of the divine brought about a complete change of atmosphere. Elḥanan harbored no doubts about the recovery of his son, and the women turned cheerful within the hour. There was a sense of relief that may have touched the boy as well. And I cannot exclude the fact that the "man of God" left Elḥanan with instructions for medication, which may have been more effective than the sacrifice of three goats.

The second case of illness that I am aware of occurred in the late summer, not long before I left the village. It concerned the wife of one of the younger men. I had seen her before on only one or two occasions, but her illness rendered her conspicuous to the entire community. She was suffering from a skin disease that tainted her hands and face with ugly white spots. The rest of her body she kept covered as much as she could, but I imagine it must have been no pretty sight either. No one knew for sure for how long the illness had been going on, but things had evidently reached a point at which her disease could no longer be concealed. Physically speaking, her life was not in danger; socially, however, her affliction amounted to a death sentence. There was no need for a divine to be consulted, for every villager knew what her condition meant. The woman was stricken with a curse. What she had done to deserve this did not matter: this was a curse that could not be lifted through human agency. She had been repudiated by the gods and turned into a spectacle that filled every villager with disgust. Her husband had no recourse but to send her away, for as long as her illness lasted, she was impurity itself. The mere sight of her might transmit that impurity to others; she had to leave the village.

The elders decided that a hut should be built outside the village, at a distance of about one-half mile. There she must stay as long as her affliction lasted. The head of her family compound raised no protest; the case was unambiguous, and no other solution would do. The construction of the hut took no longer than a day. When the structure was finished, the woman left the village and withdrew to what would be her living quarters for the rest of my stay and probably well beyond. She was not left to die. Every morning her mother-in-law could be seen leaving the village with a small supply of food: she would leave the basket at a respectable distance from the hut and return with the empty basket from the previous day. What became of the diseased woman afterwards, I am unable to say, but I confess I fear the worst, because there is no life outside the village. Not only would she live unprotected, but she would be alone. In Ramat-Yachin no one is ever alone; it is a condition the villagers do not know. Introspection, which requires at least mental withdrawal, is foreign to them. They breathe in unison with their human surroundings; how they would survive outside that community is hard to imagine.

Impurity does not call for healing but cleansing. After the departure of the woman the "man of God" was called upon to perform the necessary purifications. The clothes of the woman were burned, her house was fumigated, and lustrations were made all over the village. The rite was concluded by the divine's making a round, torch in hand, along the perimeter of Ramat-Yachin. The invisible stain had been removed. Would the husband, divorced from his wife because of disease, later remarry? Possibly. But I would not be around to see it; my stay was rapidly coming to a close.

Conclusion

Nine months among the peasants of the Palestinian Highlands — it was just a dream, informed by a tiresome amount of reading. I could have decided to keep the dream to myself, and present you instead with an enumeration of the data that any reconstruction of local religion (a term that covers both domestic and village religion) must take into account. Such data are few and familiar to most of you. What would you gain thereby? The dissembled bones of a skeleton, at best. Let these bones live! This is why I stepped outside the confines of a strictly scholarly treatment and allowed myself to attempt to add flesh and blood to the data. The reality was no doubt different, but perhaps not entirely different, from my dream.

Selected Literature

Ahlstrom, G. W.
  1986   *Who Were the Israelites?* Winona Lake, Ind.: Eisenbrauns.
Albertz, R.
  1978   *Persönliche Frömmigkeit und offizielle Religion.* Calwer Theologische Monographien 9. Stuttgart: Calwer.
  1992   *Religionsgeschichte Israels in alttestamentlicher Zeit.* Vols. 1–2. Göttingen: Vandenhoeck & Ruprecht.
Albright, W. F.
  1957   The High Place in Ancient Palestine. Pp. 242–58 in *Volume du Congrès de Strasbourg 1956*, ed. E. Jacob. Vetus Testamentum Supplements 4. Leiden: Brill.
Beck, P.
  1990   A Note on the "Schematic Statues" from the Stelae Temple at Hazor. *Tel Aviv* 17: 91–95.
Bird, P. A.
  1997   *Missing Persons and Mistaken Identities: Women and Gender in Ancient Israel.* Minneapolis: Fortress.
Borowski, O.
  1987   *Agriculture in Iron Age Israel.* Winona Lake, Ind.: Eisenbrauns.
Cross, F. M.
  1998   Kinship and Covenant in Ancient Israel. Pp. 3–21 in *From Epic to Canon: History and Literature in Ancient Israel.* Baltimore: Johns Hopkins University Press.
Dever, W. G.
  1987   The Contribution of Archaeology to the Study of Canaanite and Early Israelite Religion. Pp. 209–47 in *Ancient Israelite Religion*, ed. P. D. Miller, P. D. Hanson, and S. D. McBride. Philadelphia: Fortress.
Frick, F. S.
  1989   Ecology, Agriculture, and Patterns of Settlement. Pp. 67–93 in *The World of Ancient Israel*, ed. R. E. Clements. Cambridge: Cambridge University Press.

Geus, C. H. J. de
  1983   Agrarian Communities in Biblical Times: 12th to 10th Centuries B.C.E. *Recueils de la So-*
          ciété Jean Bodin 41/2: 207–37.
Lewis, T. J.
  1989   *Cults of the Dead in Ancient Israel and Ugarit.* Harvard Semitic Monographs 39. Atlanta:
          Scholars Press.
Loretz, O.
  1992   Die Teraphim als "Ahnen-Götter-Figur(in)en" im Lichte der Texte aus Nuzi, Emar und
          Ugarit. *Ugarit-Forschungen* 24: 133–78.
McNutt, P. M.
  1999   *Reconstructing the Society of Ancient Israel.* Library of Ancient Israel. London: Westminster
          John Knox.
Meyers, C.
  1988   *Discovering Eve: Ancient Israelite Women in Context.* New York: Oxford University Press.
Moor, J. J. C. de
  1972   *New Year with Canaanites and Israelites.* Vols. 1–2. Kampen: Kok.
Rouillard, H., and Tropper, J.
  1987   TRPYM, rituels de guérison et culte des ancêtres d'après 1 Samuel XIX 11–17 et les
          textes parallèles d'Assur et de Nuzi. *Vetus Testamentum* 37: 340–61.
Smith, G. A.
  1966   *The Historical Geography of the Holy Land.* New York: Harper & Row.
Stager, L. E.
  1985   The Archaeology of the Family in Ancient Israel. *Bulletin of the American Schools of Orien-*
          tal Research 260: 1–35.
Toorn, K. van der
  1996   *Family Religion in Babylonia, Syria and Israel: Continuity and Change in the Forms of Religious*
          Life. Studies in the History and Culture of the Ancient Near East 7. Leiden: Brill.
Vaux, R. de
  1976   *Les institutions de l'Ancien Testament.* Vols. 1–2. Paris: Cerf.
Winter, U.
  1983   *Frau und Göttin: Exegetische und ikonographische Studien zum weiblichen Gottesbild im Alten*
          Israel und in dessen Umwelt. Orbis Biblicus et Orientalis 53. Fribourg: Universitätsverlag.

Building Identity:
The Four-Room House and the Israelite Mind

Shlomo Bunimovitz

Institute of Archaeology, Tel Aviv University
Ramat Aviv

Avraham Faust

Department of the Land of Israel Studies
Bar-Ilan University, Ramat Gan

Introduction

During the late 1920s, three singular houses of strikingly similar design were found by the Pacific School of Religion's Expedition to Tell en-Naṣbeh. When the first was excavated in the campaign of 1927, it was promptly interpreted as a temple, and the director, Professor W. F. Badé, held a church service in its ruins (Wright 1978: 149). The enthusiasm about interpreting these and similar buildings with monolithic structural pillars as temples, which were considered to be associated with *maṣṣeboth*, quickly evaporated (e.g., Broshi 1987: 21). Today, hundreds of such buildings are known, referred to by the generic name of the "four-room house," after their basic plan. They are spread all over the country and are considered the most typical domestic building in ancient Israel during the Iron Age. As such, the four-room house with its subtypes—the three- and the five-room house—has been the subject of numerous studies devoted to its origins, architecture, and the ethnic affiliation of its inhabitants (e.g., Shiloh 1970; 1973; Wright 1978; Braemer 1982; Stager 1985; Holladay 1992; 1997; Netzer 1992). The prototype of the building seems to appear at the beginning of the Iron Age I, and the house reached its mature form toward the end of this period. It dominated the architecture of Iron Age II and completely disappeared with the Babylonian Exile. Some scholars believe that the four-room house crystallized from the presedentary nomad's tent (Fritz 1977a; 1977b; Kempinski 1978; Herzog 1984: 75–77), while others seek its roots in Late Bronze Age Canaanite architecture, especially in the region of the Shephelah (e.g., Mazar 1985: 66–68; Callaway 1987; Givon 1999).

The high popularity of the four-room house was explained first and foremost in terms of its close association with the Israelites. The idea of the four-room house as *the* Israelite house was best expressed by the late Y. Shiloh, one of the progenitors of this idea: "In the light of the connection between the distribution of this type and the borders of Israelite settlement, and in the light of its period of use and architectural characteristics, it would seem that the four-room house is an original Israelite concept" (1970: 180).

Surprisingly, neither Shiloh nor any other early proponent of the direct correlation between the four-room house and the Israelites suggested a satisfactory answer to the most basic question: why was *this* type of building so popular among the Israelites? It is only recently that an explanation for this puzzle has begun to be formulated, mainly along the lines of a functional interpretation. The functional analysis of daily life within the four-room house, best exemplified by the seminal studies of Stager (1985) and Holladay (1992; 1997), is based first and foremost on ethnographic and ethnoarchaeological data. It is worth noting in passing that, thus far, virtually no systematic research on functionality and synthesis of the *archaeological* finds from the many excavated four-room houses has been presented in the professional literature. The exemplary analysis of household activities at Beersheba by Singer-Avitz (1996) is an important exception testifying to the unfortunate rule. In any event, the ethnographic analogies to the four-room house have led to a consensus regarding its functional success. As clearly maintained by Stager,

> The pillared house takes its form not from some desert nostalgia monumentalized in stone and mudbrick, but from a living tradition. It was first and foremost a successful adaptation to farm life: the ground floor had space allocated for food processing, small craft production, stabling, and storage; the second floor was suitable for dining, sleeping, and other activities.... Its longevity attests to its continuing suitability not only to the environment ... but also for the socioeconomic unit housed in it—for the most part, rural families who farmed and raised livestock. (Stager 1985: 17)

Holladay's conclusions, almost echoing Stager's, are also worth quoting:

> From the time of its emergence in force until its demise at the end of the Iron II Age, the economic function of the "Israelite House" seems to have been centered upon requirements for storage and stabling, functions for which it was ideally suited.... Furthermore, its durability as preferred house type, lasting over 600 years throughout all the diverse environmental regions of Israel and Judah, even stretching down into the wilderness settlements in the central Negeb ..., testifies that it was an extremely successful design for the common—probably landowning—peasant. (Holladay 1992: 316)

While the functional analysis of the four-room house with its interesting conclusions about the suitability of the building to the peasants' daily life in ancient Israel is highly compelling, it seems to us that it is still far from conveying the full story of the structure's exceptional dominance as an architectural form during the Iron Age, and beyond this, as a cultural phenomenon.

I. A Functional Design?

As noted above, the prevalent explanation for the dominance of the four-room house during the Iron Age emphasizes its supposedly high suitability for peasant life. Already three decades ago, however, Shiloh noticed that the four-room plan defines a great variety of Iron Age II buildings, from the common private dwelling found at every Israelite site to monumental buildings such as the citadel of Hazor in the north or the main building at Tell el-Kheleifeh in the south (fig. 1). He reasonably concluded that "the four-room plan was thus used as a *standard plan for buildings of very different function* within the Israelite city" (Shiloh 1970: 190, emphasis added). This conclusion can be further expanded today to include many examples of the four-room plan and its subtypes ranging through all the

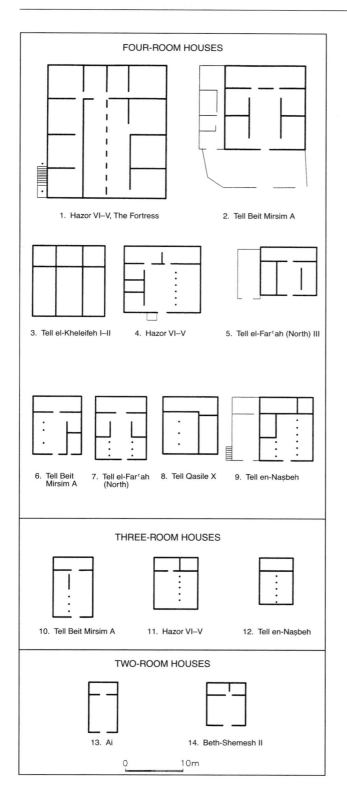

Fig. 1. Four-, three-, and two-room house typology (adapted from Ben-Tor 1992: 331, fig. 9.24).

levels of Iron Age II settlement hierarchy, from isolated farms and hamlets to the main urban centers. Moreover, although we still lack detailed functional analyses of all these buildings, it is evident from their contents that they served a great variety of functions: residences for single soldiers (Singer-Avitz 1996), nuclear and extended family dwellings (Stager 1985; Faust 1999a; 2000), administrative buildings (Branigan 1966; Shiloh 1970; 1973), etc. Amazingly enough, all these diverse functions were carried out within the same basic architectural plan. This "astonishing rigidity in concept," as Fritz aptly put it (1995: 142), also had astonishing durability—almost 600 years—as noted by Holladay and others. Apparently, one cannot ignore the fact that the four-room house, which seems to appear concurrently with the ethnogenesis of Israel in Iron Age I, completely disappeared with the demise of the kingdom of Judah. If the raison d'être of this structure lies only in its functional suitability for peasant life, why did the peasants in ancient Israel not continue to use it in the aftermath of the Babylonian destruction and exile through the Persian period and thereafter?

Notably, the basic plan of the four-room house was also used in the rock-cut family tombs prevalent in Judah during the later part of the Iron Age II (Mazar 1976: 4 n. 9; Barkai 1994; 1999). Going beyond the reasonable observation that the tombs imitate the houses of the deceased, we should bear in mind that the same four-room plan was applied to simple tombs in peripheral towns, as well as to the luxurious and elaborate burial complexes of the monarchical elite in Jerusalem. In short, function seems only a partial explanation for the dominance and durability of the four-room house and layout during the Iron Age II. Evidently, this unique phenomenon in the architectural history of ancient Israel requires a more comprehensive explanation, based on both social and cognitive approaches to the subject.

II. Distribution

Relying on the spatial and temporal distribution of the four-room house, Shiloh (1970; 1973), Wright (1978), and Holladay (1992; 1997), among many others, argued for a close relationship between the house and the Israelites. Other scholars opposed this idea, pointing to examples of four-room houses outside Israelite territory (e.g., Ibrahim 1975; Ahlström 1993: 339–40; Finkelstein 1996: 204–5). First and foremost, it should be emphasized that most of these examples (e.g., at ʿAfula, Tel Qiri, Tell Keisan, and Sahab) lack the typical characteristics of the four-room house. In some cases, the houses do have four rooms, but their configuration is completely different from that of the four-room house; in others, pillars were used, but again, the overall architectural plan bears no similarity to the four-room house (there seems to be some confusion between four-room houses and pillared buildings; see, e.g., Ibrahim 1975). Second, the examples of "real" four-room houses outside the supposed Israelite territory mainly date to the Iron Age I (e.g., Kautz 1981; Daviau 1999: 132), prior to the final crystallization of ethnic groups in the region (see below). Finally, some of these houses may actually have been located within "Israelite territory" (e.g., Ji 1995; 1997; Herr 2000: 178). The examples of "real" four-room houses outside "Israelite territory" are therefore very few indeed, and should be explained as representing ephemeral use by non-Israelites or by Israelites living in non-Israelite regions.

In light of the above, we shall attempt to confirm the original hypothesis about the relationship between the four-room house and the Israelites by demonstrating that this house plan and its subtypes can be related to the Israelite mind. Moreover, we propose that, while conceived by the Israelite mind and practiced in daily life, the four-room plan reflexively structured that very mind.

III. Purity and Space Syntax

The first scholar to suggest that both the rough correspondence between the distribution of the four-room house and the areas settled by the Israelites and its high popularity throughout most of the Iron Age have to do with the ideological/cognitive realm was M. Weinfeld (see Netzer 1992: 199 n. 24). More than a decade ago, he tentatively, albeit insightfully, commented that the house plan might have resulted from the Israelite tribes' way of life, namely, facilitating the separation between purity and impurity, such as the avoidance of a woman during menstruation. Indeed, on examining the four-room plan one can immediately recognize its greatest merit, which is maximal privacy. Once the central space of the building, whether an open or roofed courtyard was entered, each of the rooms could be entered directly without going through adjacent spaces.

Interestingly, other dwelling structures in ancient Israel during the Bronze and Iron Ages seem to lack this special quality. These important, albeit intuitive, observations can be confirmed today by the more formal procedure known as access analysis. Following the work of Hillier and Hanson (1984; see also Banning and Byrd 1989; Foster 1989; Blanton 1994: 24–37) concerning the social logic of space, researchers can analyze and compare different building plans for their *space syntax*. This term refers to the spatial configuration within a built structure and the hierarchy of accessibility or passage from one room to another. The social meaning of space syntax is the possible contact of a building's inhabitants with strangers, as well as contact among themselves. Different syntaxes, therefore, hint at different systems or codes of social and cultural relations. When properly analyzed, the syntax of the four-room house and its subtypes turns out to be conspicuously different from those of other house types known in ancient Israel (fig. 2). While the other house types express hierarchy and restricted access or movement within the house (in this regard, see also Banning and Byrd 1989: 156; Brown 1990: 103), the four-room house indicates the opposite: easy and direct access to each room. If matters of purity were crucial in the conduct of Israelite daily life, the unique plan of the four-room house more than facilitated it. Since each room could be entered directly from the central space without passing through other rooms, purity could be strictly maintained even if an "unclean" person resided in the house. Notably, unlike in other ancient Near Eastern societies, most of the biblical purity laws (those of P) do not require menstruating women to leave the house (Milgrom 1991: 952–53).[1] Menstruating women, therefore, were allowed to remain within

---

1. While there is almost a consensus regarding the dating of some of the laws to the Iron Age (those of D), the dating of P is debatable. Apparently, most scholars believe that P was written during the Persian period (e.g., Eissfeldt 1965: 207–8; Rofé 1994; see also Wenham 1979: 9–11). Recently, however, there is a tendency to date P to the exilic period and to maintain that some, or even most, of its content is earlier in

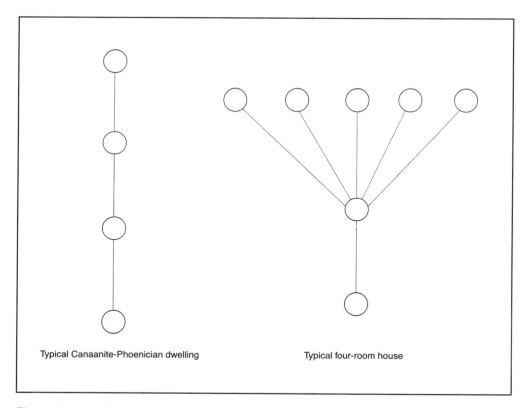

Typical Canaanite-Phoenician dwelling   Typical four-room house

Fig. 2. Access analysis comparison of typical four-room houses and Canaanite-Phoenician dwellings.

the house, but given the restrictions imposed on them by the purity laws, it is reasonable to assume that they spent some of their time in a separate room. The plan of the four-room house seems suitable for such a practice. As discussed below, the possible connection between the four-room plan and specific ethnic behavior, such as that related to purity/impurity laws, may hint that the plan was adapted or developed to accommodate this behavior. Another possibility is that the laws (conducts of behavior) were structured by the house plan.

IV. Ideology

An even more intriguing implication of access analysis of the four-room house is the correspondence between its nonhierarchical configuration and the "democratic" or egalitarian ethos of Israelite society.

---

origin (e.g., Clines 1993: 580). This suffices to allow us to refer to P in our discussion, but it is even more important and relevant that a growing number of scholars studying the Pentateuch (and/or P) date P on various grounds to the Iron Age (e.g., Hurvitz 1974; Weinfeld 1979: 28–33; Wenham 1979: 13; Friedman 1987; Milgrom 1991: 12–13; Schwartz 1999: 32–33). Furthermore, as claimed below, it is not necessarily the laws that shaped the four-room house, but possibly the other way around. No less plausible is a dialectic relationship between the two.

Relying on a cross-cultural sample of houses and households, Blanton (1994: 64) has recently demonstrated that large households with more families display a complex and hierarchically structured arrangement of living and sleeping spaces reflecting their complex social structure. This is often manifested as a hierarchical grading of accessibility and structural depth of spaces within the house related to generational and in some cases gender-based status distinctions (or both). These are houses in which special living/sleeping areas are frequently set aside for married children, as opposed to the ad hoc sleeping arrangements or shared sleeping spaces often seen in societies with simpler houses. Since four-room houses, especially in the rural sector and at the elite/well-to-do level, usually contain multiple rooms created by the division of the four main rooms, it is clear that established arrangements for space usage were part and parcel of daily life within these houses. Yet, as mentioned above, the four-room plan lacks "depth" or access hierarchy and expresses a more egalitarian spirit than the contemporaneous or previous house plans in ancient Israel, as well as many contemporary ethnographic examples.

Biblical scholars have long emphasized the democratic and egalitarian character of Israelite society as portrayed by the biblical narratives (e.g., Wolf 1947; Gordis 1971; Speiser 1971: 284). Mendenhall's (1962) and Gottwald's (1979) treatments of this subject as part of their social hypotheses concerning the origins of the Israelites and their establishment of a "new society" raised the question of social reality versus social ideology. Since anthropology teaches us that "equality is a social impossibility" and that "there is no such thing as a society composed of exactly equal members," to quote Fried (1967: 27–28), Lemche's perception, according to which "instead of speaking of egalitarian societies it would be more appropriate to speak of societies which are dominated by an egalitarian ideology" (1985: 223), is surely appropriate. In the case of Israelite society, to quote Lemche once again, "this would allow for the fact that a society whose ideology is egalitarian need not in fact *be* egalitarian" (1985: 223; in fact, Lemche doubts the existence of egalitarian ideology in Israelite society [1985: 277, 407]). While the Bible reflects an egalitarian *ethos*, daily life in Iron Age Israel must have been very different in social terms. Ethnoarchaeology has shown that material culture is not a direct reflection of behavior, since ideology, symbolism, and religious ideas interfere between them (e.g., Hodder 1982b). In some societies, for example, simple burials reflect a social ideal of egalitarianism that is not effectively put into practice in everyday life (Huntington and Metcalf 1979: 122; Trigger 1989: 348). The four-room house with its "egalitarian" plan seems to have been in line with Israelite ideology and social perception more than other house plans, and thus was enthusiastically adopted as the main type of building. As we shall see below, this has nothing to do with the fact that there were small and large houses, poor and rich. Interestingly, when one moves from the single building plan to examine the overall settlement system, a similar ideology is revealed. In studying biblical terminology describing Israelite spatial organization, Portugali came to the conclusion that Israelite spatial perception reflects "a collective mental map of a tribal, egalitarian and non-hierarchical society" (1999: 72).

V. Nonverbal Communication

It is widely accepted that houses are part of a society's system of nonverbal communication (Blanton 1994: 24–37). There are two main categories of messages communicated by the material environment of the house. In the first, named "canonical" (Blanton 1994: 8ff.), what is communicated largely pertains to the meaning of enduring symbols reflecting mutually-held concepts of people participating in a common cultural system. Typically, symbolic communication through the medium of the dwelling involves the creation of a built environment that manifests social divisions based on gender, generation, and rank, linked to cosmological schemes that express categorical oppositions like order/disorder, elite/nonelite, and purity/danger. In these instances, the house as habitus is a medium of communication primarily among the occupants of the house itself, providing a material frame that structures not only day-to-day interactions, but also the more infrequent formal household rituals. In this sense, the form of the house embodies taxonomic principles specific to a cultural system; by living in the house, its occupants are constantly made aware of these principles, which are thus inculcated and reinforced.

The house can also serve as a channel of nonverbal communication that transmits messages from its occupants to others outside. In this second category of messages, called "indexical" (Blanton 1994: 8ff.), information is communicated concerning the current status of a household, expressed in terms of variables such as wealth or social status. While the canonical messages lie primarily within the inner parts of the house, the indexical communicative role of the house involves its more public areas and elements that provide information about costliness and taste to outsiders.

In the case of the four-room house, the inner structure with its supposedly egalitarian ethos seems to bear a canonical message essential for the structuring of Israelite society and thus for the continuity of the ethos itself. In addition, it is important to bear in mind that building a house according to the traditional code of a society communicates a social message—"we're part of the community"—and enhances the coherence of that community. However, inextricably intertwined with the message of uniformity are messages of difference. As Faust showed in his recent doctoral dissertation (1999b) on the social structure of Israelite society in the 8th and 7th centuries B.C.E., the existence of a variety of three-, four-, and even five-room houses exhibiting marked differences in affluence indicates that the houses communicated indexical messages related to social variables.

VI. Order and Dominance

Undoubtedly, the most puzzling issue concerning the four-room plan is its ubiquitousness. As emphasized above, the functional interpretation falls short of explaining the fact that this plan was applied not only to peasants' dwellings but also to public buildings outside the rural sphere. One may suspect, therefore, that behind this extraordinary cultural phenomenon again lay cognitive aspects.

According to Douglas (1966), many of the biblical laws, mainly those related to holiness are actually about order. In an insightful analysis of the "Abominations of Leviticus," as well as certain passages in Deuteronomy, she developed the idea that holiness is exemplified by wholeness and completeness. Many of the laws—covering all aspects of life, from war to sexual behavior and from social conduct to dietary rules—are related to sets of precepts stemming from this basic principle. All of these precepts embrace the idea of holiness as order and of confusion as sin. Holiness requires completeness in a social context—an important enterprise, once begun, must not be left incomplete. Holiness requires that individuals conform to the class to which they belong, and that different classes of things not be confused. To be holy is to be whole, to be one; holiness is unity, integrity, perfection of the individual and of the kind. Hybrids and other confusions are abominations.[2]

In light of this ideology, the astonishing dominance of the four-room plan on almost all levels of Israelite architectural design becomes intelligible. If the Israelites were deeply engaged with unity and "order" as a negation of separateness and confusion, then these concepts must have percolated through all spheres of daily life, including material culture. Thus, it can be surmised that, once the four-room house took shape and was formalized as *the* container and embodiment of the Israelite lifestyle and symbolic "order," it became the "right" house type and, hence, its great popularity. Building according to other architectural schemes must have been considered a deviation from the norm and possibly a violation of the holy "order."

VII. The Four-Room House and Israelite Ethnicity

Returning full circle to Shiloh's original contention that the four-room house should be considered the "Israelite house," the insights gained by our cognitive approach delineate the possible route by which this type of building became synonymous with the Israelite ethnic group.

It seems that at the beginning of Iron Age I, the embryonic versions of the four-room house and its more humble subtypes were but options among a variety of available house plans. Accordingly, the popularity of the house was still limited, barely hinting at its forthcoming ubiquity. It is certainly possible that at this stage function played a role in the evolution of the building's plan, but one should not forget that for many generations Canaanite peasants seem to have managed quite well utilizing other types of dwellings. In any event, during the later part of Iron Age I, the well known form of the house crystallized and became dominant, mainly in the central Hill Country. Here we must reiterate that the few "real" examples of the four-room house recorded outside this region did not outlast the Iron I. The handful of genuine four-room houses found outside the core region of the prototype are but a minor offshoot of its main distribution, emphasizing the existence of the core area.

Apparently, it is in this very phase of Israelite ethnogenesis that Israelite ideology and cognitive doctrines shaped (and were shaped by) the final form of the house. At this point, the house began to reflect Israelite ethnic behavior: egalitarian ethos, privacy, seclusion of the impure, and so on, perhaps becoming an ethnic marker. Following Barth (1969) and others (e.g., Kamp and Yoffee 1980: 96; Hodder 1982a; McGuire 1982: 160; Emberling 1997: 299; Jones 1997: 113), we are well aware today that material culture should not be simply equated with ethnicity. However, in the process of the self-identification of any

---

2. Douglas subsequently changed her opinion, suggesting other considerations in the classification of pure and impure creatures (e.g., 1993: 17). This was part of a broader transformation in her views (Fardon 1999: 185–205). It is beyond the scope of this paper to discuss in detail Douglas's ideas, but her initial interpretation seems to be more in line with the reality of ancient Israelite society (see also Milgrom 1991: 728). In any event, it should be noted that she still stresses the importance of "order."

human group vis-à-vis other groups, certain aspects of material culture may reflect ethnic behavior or may even be deliberately chosen to communicate ethnicity. Internally, the four-room house successfully negotiated Israelite values and way of life, as demonstrated by its growing popularity. Moreover, because of the "order" perception of the Israelites, the four-room layout soon became the normative and dominant building plan throughout Israelite territory for more than half a millennium. Whether it was deliberately chosen at the end of Iron I as an ethnic marker for external identity negotiation or gradually attained this rubric cannot be determined. Yet evidently during the later part of the Iron Age I and throughout the Iron Age II, the four-room plan must be considered predominantly Israelite, although others might have sporadically used this type of dwelling.

While conceived by the Israelite mind concurrently with the Israelite ethnogenesis, for many generations the four-room house actually structured Israelite identity and enhanced Israelite ethnic coherence. The Assyrian and Babylonian mass destructions of the kingdoms of Israel and Judah, as well as the exile of the majority of their populations in the closing years of the Iron Age, violently eliminated the *raison d'être* of that omnipresent ethnic symbol. Together with its progenitors and maintainers, it exited the historical stage, leaving us only hints with which we may try to decipher its social and cognitive meaning for ancient Israelite society. Hopefully, this paper has brought us closer to this aim.

References

Ahlström, G. W.
   1993   *The History of Ancient Palestine from the Palaeolithic Period to Alexander's Conquest.* Sheffield: Sheffield Academic Press.
Banning, E. B., and Byrd, B. F.
   1989   Alternative Approaches for Exploring Levantine Neolithic Architecture. *Paléorient* 15: 154–60.
Barkai, G.
   1994   Burial Caves and Burial Practices in Judah in the Iron Age. Pp. 96–164 in *Graves and Burial Practices in Israel in the Ancient Period*, ed. I. Singer. Jerusalem: Yad Izhak Ben-Zvi (Hebrew).
   1999   Burial Caves and Dwellings in Judah during Iron Age II: Sociological Aspects. Pp. 96–102 in *Material Culture, Society and Ideology: New Directions in the Archaeology of the Land of Israel*, ed. A. Faust and A. Maeir. Ramat Gan: Bar-Ilan University (Hebrew).
Barth, F. (ed.)
   1969   *Ethnic Groups and Boundaries.* Boston: Little, Brown.
Ben-Tor, A. (ed.)
   1992   *The Archaeology of Ancient Israel.* New Haven: Yale University Press.
Blanton, R. E.
   1994   *Houses and Households: A Comparative Study.* New York: Plenum.
Braemer, F.
   1982   *L'architecture domestique du Levant à l'âge du Fer.* Paris: Éditions Recherche sur les civilisations.
Branigan, K.
   1966   The Four Room Buildings of Tell en-Naṣbeh. *Israel Exploration Journal* 16: 206–9.
Broshi, M.
   1987   Religion, Ideology, and Politics and Their Impact on Palestinian Archaeology. *Israel Museum Journal* 6: 17–32.

Brown, F. E.
1990   Comment on Chapman: Some Cautionary Notes on the Application of Spatial Measures to Prehistoric Settlements. Pp. 93–109 in *The Social Archaeology of Houses*, ed. R. Samson. Edinburgh: Edinburgh University Press.

Callaway, J. A.
1987   Ai (et-Tell): Problem Site for Biblical Archaeologists. Pp. 87–99 in *Archaeology and Biblical Interpretation: Essays in Memory of D. Glenn Rose*, ed. L. G. Perdue, L. E. Toombs, and G. L. Johnson. Atlanta: John Knox.

Clines, D. J. A.
1993   Pentateuch. Pp. 579–82 in *The Oxford Companion to the Bible*, ed. B. M. Metzger and M. D. Coogan. Oxford: Oxford University Press.

Daviau, P. M. M.
1999   Domestic Architecture in Iron Age Ammon: Building Materials, Construction Techniques, and Room Arrangement. Pp. 113–36 in *Ancient Ammon*, ed. B. MacDonald and R. W. Younker. Leiden: Brill.

Douglas, M.
1966   *Purity and Danger: An Analysis of the Concept of Pollution and Taboo*. London: Routledge and Kegan Paul.
1993   The Forbidden Animals in Leviticus. *Journal for the Study of the Old Testament* 59: 3–23.

Eissfeldt, O.
1965   *The Old Testament: An Introduction*. Oxford: Blackwell.

Emberling, G.
1997   Ethnicity in Complex Societies: Archaeological Perspectives. *Journal of Archaeological Research* 5: 295–344.

Fardon, R.
1999   *Mary Douglas: An Intellectual Biography*. London: Routledge.

Faust, A.
1999a   Differences in Family Structure between Cities and Villages in Iron Age II. *Tel Aviv* 26: 233–52.
1999b   The Social Structure of the Israelite Society during the 8th–7th Centuries B.C.E. according to the Archaeological Evidence. Ph.D. dissertation, Bar-Ilan University (Hebrew).
2000   The Rural Community in Ancient Israel during the Iron Age II. *Bulletin of the American Schools of Oriental Research* 318: 17–39.

Finkelstein, I.
1996   Ethnicity and the Origin of the Iron Age I Settlers in the Highlands of Canaan: Can the Real Israel Stand Up? *Biblical Archaeologist* 59: 198–212.

Foster, S. M.
1989   Analysis of Spatial Patterns in Buildings (Access Analysis) as an Insight into Social Structure: Examples from the Scottish Atlantic Iron Age. *Antiquity* 63: 40–50.

Fried, M. H.
1967   *The Evolution of Political Society*. New York: Random House.

Friedman, R. E.
1987   *Who Wrote the Bible?* New York: Summit.

Fritz, V.
1977a   Bestimmung und Herkunft des Pfeinlerhauses in Israel. *Zeitschrift des Deutchen Palästina-Vereins* 93: 30–45.
1977b   *Tempel und Zeit*. Neukirchen-Vluyn: Neukirchener Verlag.
1995   *The City in Ancient Israel*. Sheffield: Sheffield Academic Press.

Givon, S.
1999   The Three-Roomed House from Tel Harassim, Israel. *Levant* 31: 173–77.

Gordis, R.
    1971   Primitive Democracy in Ancient Israel. Pp. 45–60 in *Poets, Prophets and Sages: Essays in Biblical Interpretation*. Bloomington: University of Indiana Press.
Gottwald, N. K.
    1979   *The Tribes of Yahweh*. New York: Orbis.
Herr, L. G.
    2000   The Settlement and Fortification of Tell al-ʿUmayri in Jordan during the LB/Iron I Transition. Pp. 167–79 in *The Archaeology of Jordan and Beyond: Essays in Honor of James A. Sauer*, ed. L. E. Stager, J. A. Greene, and M. D. Coogan. Studies in the Archaeology and History of the Levant 1. Winona Lake, Ind.: Eisenbrauns.
Herzog, Z.
    1984   *Beer-Sheba II: The Early Iron Age Settlements*. Tel Aviv: Tel Aviv University Press.
Hillier, B., and Hanson, J.
    1984   *The Social Logic of Space*. Cambridge: Cambridge University Press.
Hodder, I.
    1982a   *Symbols in Action*. Cambridge: Cambridge University Press.
    1982b   *The Present Past*. London: Batsford.
Holladay, J. S., Jr.
    1992   House, Israelite. Pp. 308–18 in vol. 3 of *The Anchor Bible Dictionary*, ed. D. N. Freedman. New York: Doubleday.
    1997   Four-Room House. Pp. 337–41 in vol. 2 of *The Oxford Encyclopedia of Archaeology in the Near East*, ed. E. M. Meyers. New York: Oxford University Press.
Huntington, R., and Metcalf, P.
    1979   *Celebrations of Death: The Anthropology of Mortuary Ritual*. Cambridge: Cambridge University Press.
Hurvitz, A.
    1974   The Evidence of Language in Dating the Priestly Code. *Revue Biblique* 81: 24–56.
Ibrahim, M. M.
    1975   Third Season of Excavation at Sahab, 1975 (Preliminary Report). *Annual of the Department of Antiquities of Jordan* 20: 69–82.
Ji, C. H. C.
    1995   The Iron I in Central and Northern Transjordan: An Interim Summary of Archaeological Data. *Palestine Exploration Quarterly* 127: 122–40.
    1997   A Note on the Iron Age Four-Room House in Palestine. *Orientalia* 66: 387–413.
Jones, S.
    1997   *The Archaeology of Ethnicity*. London: Routledge.
Kautz, J. R.
    1981   Tracking the Ancient Moabites. *Biblical Archaeologist* 44: 27–35.
Kamp, K., and Yoffee, N.
    1980   Ethnicity in Western Asia during the Early Second Millennium B.C.: Archaeological Assemblages and Ethnoarchaeological Prospectives. *Bulletin of the American Schools of Oriental Research* 237: 85–104.
Kempinski, A.
    1978   Tel Masos. *Expedition* 20/4: 29–37.
Lemche, N. P.
    1985   *Early Israel*. Leiden: Brill.
Mazar, A.
    1976   Iron Age Burial Caves North of the Damascus Gate, Jerusalem. *Israel Exploration Journal* 26: 1–8.
    1985   The Israelite Settlement in Canaan in the Light of Archaeological Excavations. Pp. 61–71 in *Biblical Archaeology Today: Proceedings of the International Congress on Biblical Archaeology, Jerusalem, April 1984*, ed. J. Amitai. Jerusalem: Israel Exploration Society.

McGuire, R. H.
  1982   The Study of Ethnicity in Historical Archaeology. *Journal of Anthropological Archaeology* 1: 159–78.
Mendenhall, G. E.
  1962   The Hebrew Conquest of Palestine. *Biblical Archaeologist* 25: 66–87.
Milgrom, J.
  1991   *Leviticus 1–16.* Anchor Bible 3. New York: Doubleday.
Netzer, E.
  1992   Domestic Architecture in the Iron Age. Pp. 193–201 in *The Architecture of Ancient Israel from the Prehistoric to the Persian Period,* ed. A. Kempinski and R. Reich. Jerusalem: Israel Exploration Society.
Portugali, Y.
  1999   *Space, Time and Society in Ancient Eretz Israel,* Part 1: *Social Morphology.* Tel Aviv: The Open University of Israel (Hebrew).
Rofé, A.
  1994   *Introduction to the Composition of the Pentateuch.* Jerusalem: Academon (Hebrew).
Schwartz, B. J.
  1999   *The Holiness Legislation: Studies in the Priestly Code.* Jerusalem: Magnes (Hebrew).
Shiloh, Y.
  1970   The Four-Room House: Its Situation and Function in the Israelite City. *Israel Exploration Journal* 20: 180–90.
  1973   The Four-Room House: The Israelite Type-House? Pp. 277–85 in *Eretz-Israel* 11 (I. Dunayevsky Memorial Volume), ed. N. Avigad et al. Jerusalem: Israel Exploration Society (Hebrew).
Singer-Avitz, L.
  1996   Household Activities at Beersheba. Pp. 166–74 in *Eretz-Israel* 25 (Joseph Aviram Volume), ed. A. Biran et al. Jerusalem: Israel Exploration Society (Hebrew).
Speiser, E. A.
  1971   The Manner of the Kings. Pp. 280–87 in *The World History of the Jewish People: Judges,* ed. B. Mazar. Jerusalem: Massada.
Stager, L. E.
  1985   The Archaeology of the Family in Ancient Israel. *Bulletin of the American Schools of Oriental Research* 260: 1–35.
Trigger, B. G.
  1989   *A History of Archaeological Thought.* Cambridge: Cambridge University Press.
Weinfeld, M.
  1979   Literary Creativity. Pp. 27–70 in *The World History of the Jewish People. The Age of the Monarchies: Culture and Society,* ed. A. Malamat. Jerusalem: Massada.
Wenham, G. J.
  1979   *The Book of Leviticus.* The New International Commentary on the Old Testament. London: Hodder and Stoughton.
Wolf, C. U.
  1947   Traces of Primitive Democracy in Ancient Israel. *Journal of Near Eastern Studies* 6: 98–108.
Wright, G. E.
  1978   A Characteristic North Israelite House. Pp. 149–54 in *Archaeology in the Levant: Essays for Kathleen Kenyon,* ed. R. Moorey and P. Parr. Warminster: Aris & Phllips.

Material Remains and Social Relations:
Women's Culture in Agrarian Households of the Iron Age

Carol Meyers

Department of Religion, Duke University
Durham, North Carolina

1. Introduction

The American writer Harriet Beecher Stowe, most famous for her novel *Uncle Tom's Cabin*, was also, along with her father and husband (both were scholars and clergymen) a serious student of the Bible and of the "new" biblical criticism that reached American shores early in the 19th century. She had a particular interest in biblical women, and in the introduction to her little-known book, *Women in Sacred History* (1874), she makes two comments that seem prescient of what will be discussed below. She envisions the land of Canaan as divided into homesteads, each ruled by "family governance," with "the family as the central part of the state," and she refers to the married Israelite woman as the "coequal queen of the home." These comments suggest two things: the primacy of the household in agrarian life; and the importance of the woman's role in the household.

Both features are, theoretically, aspects of the social and economic organization of any society and as such are susceptible to examination in the material cultural record of that society. Inspired by Stowe's comments, as well as by the request of the organizers of this symposium that I present a paper on women's lives in relation to the household economy, I will consider the following:

- The concept of the household, with its artifactual and architectural components
- The interpretation of households as configurations of gendered space
- Two examples of gendered activities and activity areas, as components of women's culture
- Implications of women's activities for social relations

The chronological focus of this study is intentionally loose. Unlike most archaeological enterprises in Israel, which are overwhelmingly dominated by diachronic agendas, that is, by the interest in identifying continuity and change over time in the archaeological record, this study of the agrarian household is fundamentally synchronic. It assumes some commonality in the economic functions and social dynamics of productive domestic units in virtually all agrarian communities — both small rural villages or hamlets (Faust 2000) and walled villages and towns — throughout the Iron Age.[1] The relative stability of the

---

1. Agrarian communities include settlements called *ʿārîm* in the Hebrew Bible. In the Iron Age, many of these "cities" did not have the functions and features associated with the urban life of their Bronze Age predecessors; most had no public buildings and were little more than walled towns inhabited by farming families who worked the surrounding land (Frick 1997; Fritz 1997). Given this distinction between walled

varied ecosystems of Israel and Judah and the persistence of kinship-based structures meant a continuity of fundamental economic processes throughout that period. A system of mixed peasant agriculture (Holladay 1995: 386; cf. Hopkins 1985; Stager 1985)—basically the plow-assisted cultivation of cereal crops, along with varying amounts of viticulture, arboriculture, and the keeping of small animals—was carried out for hundreds of years in decentralized settlements scattered throughout the Judean and Israelite heartland. Peasant economies based in producing and consuming households began in Iron I and persisted throughout the period of the monarchies (Holladay 1995: 392–93).[2] The vast majority of Iron II settlements, despite the impression to the contrary created by the relative imbalance of traditional archaeological concentration on the relatively fewer and densely settled urban sites, were agricultural and rural, not urban (McNutt 1999: 152, 168).

The focus in this paper is thus on the agricultural class of the Iron Age, which constituted the majority of the population, rather than on the urban elites, even though these elites produced most of the monumental architecture and sumptuary goods as well as the ethnohistorical sources (viz., the biblical record) that have long attracted researchers. More specifically, I will examine the household, in which the primary functions of any society take place (Sharer and Ashmore 1987: 439).

2. Households

An examination of *households* entails recognition of their organizational, material, and social complexity. As has long been understood by social anthropologists, arriving at a definition of a household that is universal across cultures is virtually impossible. However, certain features of households in premodern societies can be identified. For one thing, households are not the same as families; these are distinct, albeit overlapping, social phenomena (Bender 1967: 495; Wilk and Netting 1984: 3). Similarly, households are not simply domiciles—structural configurations that constitute abodes for certain groups of people. Rather, a household is a built environment consisting of not only persons and their "hardware" (their material culture, including their domicile and all its associated installations and artifacts) but also their activities and other aspects of their daily lives (Rapoport 1994: 461). The household is thus fundamental to human society because it is the level at which premodern social groups articulate directly with the environment in order to survive. To put it another way, the household is a *strategy*, participating in and utilizing material culture, to meet the productive and reproductive needs of humans (Wilk and Rathje 1982: 618). It is based on an economic premise, going back to Polanyi (1944: 53), that people produce for their own sake and/or for that of the group of which they are a part (Henshaw 1999: 79).

---

towns and true urban centers, it is likely that only a tiny minority of people in agricultural societies lived in truly urban settings (Lenski 1984: 199–200). The common translation of the Hebrew *'îr* as "city" is misleading in this respect. Note that the Hebrew *mibṣārîm* ("fortified towns") is the most frequent specification of *'îr*. These terms and other designations for settlements are discussed in Levine 1999.

2. Holladay's judgment (1995; cf. 1992) is based in part on the persistence of the basic architectural unit (the four-room house and its variations), devised or adapted for small agrarian units, successfully exploiting the difficult highland environment.

Three elements of the household emerge from this understanding of its socioeconomic complexity. First, it is a social, or demographic, unit comprised of varying configurations of affinals and consanguinals; and it may sometimes include unrelated servants or sojourners. Also, as a demographic unit, it encompasses reproductive functions. Second, it has material components, which makes it susceptible to archaeological investigation. These components are the dwelling itself and the items of material culture—artifacts— that enable its inhabitants to satisfy their physical, social, and also their spiritual or ideological needs. The third element is the behavioral, that is, the set of activities carried out in the household context in order to meet the needs of its residents. The household is thus the most important locus of economic production and social interaction in traditional societies.

Studying the household provides the opportunity to understand the way people organize their economic and, just as importantly, social relations (Whitridge 1998: 2). For several decades now, anthropologists have done this by explicitly practicing "household archaeology," a micro-scale investigation of the activities and spatial organization of the built environment. By analyzing the structure itself and its associated material remains, the major economic features of a household can be recovered. Then, using the artifactual and architectural record as the main data base, one can infer relations of production and consumption, of diverse tasks and divided task performance, and of associated ideologies (Steadman 1996: 54, 63). In short, the investigation of households offers the promise of providing information available in no other way about human behavior in past societies.

Analyzing the social context of material culture is difficult, and even risky, because of the complex interpretive processes necessary to move from physical remains to hypotheses about social relations; but it is a worthwhile venture that all too few archaeologists working in the historical periods have been willing to undertake. The existence of written documents from the Bronze and Iron Ages has given us the sense, probably false in many ways, that we have access to more direct and reliable sources of information about the past than the "mute stones" themselves. Furthermore, the information in those written records, the Hebrew Bible in particular, has seduced us into using archaeology to trace large-scale social and political processes without paying much attention to small-scale social and political processes. We have let the agendas of the texts set the agendas of our digs. We have been concerned with ethnicities and kingdoms, not with individual family groups. The "state" or "city-state" or "tribe" has been reckoned the primary social structure,[3] when in reality the *household*, as the basic unit of production and reproduction, is the primary socioeconomic unit of society and should be acknowledged as the social and economic center of any settlement.

We should learn from prehistorians that a wealth of information about a society is possible were we to take more often a bottom→top perspective instead of the top→down perspective that has dominated Syro-Palestinian archaeology. We need to take advantage of the ubiquity and abundance of households and of their surviving material components—structures and artifacts—in order to learn more about life in the Iron Age as it

---

3. Ironically, Gottwald's analysis of early Israel, with its explicit use of social-science methods and models, nonetheless depicts the tribe as the "primary structure," with the extended family as "tertiary" (1979: 237–92).

was experienced by most of the population and not just the leadership classes. Too often the objects and buildings we excavate are disembodied; their meanings are expressed in typological and relative constructs, rather than as reflections of the way people organized and valued their activities and thus their interactions with each other. Among other things, therefore, the synchronic analysis of households—difficult as it may be—provides a window into the lives of the people, both women and men, in the societies that we study. And, because it can situate architecture and artifact assemblages within an economic and social context (Lawrence 1999: 121–23), household archaeology can also thereby explore the gendered relations of production.

3. *Households and Gendered Space*

Household archaeology must de facto address gender issues. Gender is an aspect of every society. We must resist the tendency to equate human behavior with the behavior of males; we must "identify or assert the presence of the activities of women" (Conkey and Gero 1997: 414–15), some of which can be differentiated from the activities of men in the archaeological record. The division of labor by gender has long been recognized and recorded by social scientists, who recognize that gender is a prominent feature in the allocation of responsibilities for subsistence tasks in even the simplest societies (Kent 1990b: 148; Costin 1996: 112). Thus, gender-specific activity areas exist in the built environments of all but the least complex societies (Sweely 1999: 164), and the study of households as settings for activity systems necessarily examines gendered behavior.

The activity areas in a household can be conceptualized in two ways. First, discrete household activities are performed in "gendered space." In every household, from antiquity to the present, there are certain loci used predominantly for task performance by one gender rather than the other (Kent 1984: 2; Sweely 1999: 164).[4] This does not necessarily involve fully segregated space, with no crossover of gendered activity. Rather, *common* space in agrarian households is typically used differently by women and by men, sequentially or in overlapping temporal units depending on the time of day, the season of the year, and the nature of the tasks to be done (Bourdieu 1973: 99; Steadman 1996: 65; Whitridge 1998: 2).[5]

Second, household space, especially in its gendered aspects, is "social space," a term that describes the interplay of ground area (physical space) with the social relationships of the people using that space (Chernoff 1999: 7, 9; cf. Rapoport 1994: 480). Many, if not all, of the productive tasks in agrarian systems in an environment such as the highlands of

---

4. These divisions are not necessarily absolute—that is, women and men may sometimes, to greater or lesser degrees, perform tasks associated primarily with the other gender—but they are usually powerful enough to produce a cognitive association of certain domestic spaces with one gender rather than the other. Even in "liberated" Euro-American households, kitchens and garages tend to be gender-specific activity areas and, consequently, are perceived differently by the male and female occupants of the household (Kent 1990a: 6).

5. The variety of gendered functions in a single space means cognitive differences in the way such space is perceived and experienced by women and men (Ardener 1993: 19; Steadman 1996: 65). The fact that the household is called *bêt 'ēm* ("mother's household") rather than *bêt 'āb* ("father's household") in biblical texts dealing with women's experience is probably rooted in the way Iron Age women and men differently perceived the household (Meyers 1991a).

ancient Israel would have involved group labor, whether the tasks were characterized by simple simultaneity (several people doing the same thing at the same time) or complex simultaneity (different tasks performed by several people at the same time).[6] That several females from the same or nearby households typically carry out productive tasks together (Sweely 1999: 163) thus has implications for understanding social relations.

4. Gendered Activities/Activity Areas

Identifying gendered social space is a project that has received very little attention in traditional Syro-Palestinian archaeology. Thus, such a project can be helped enormously, in terms of method and content, by the veritable explosion in the past few decades of research on gender in premodern societies conducted by prehistorians and anthropologists. That research has challenged the way archaeology is practiced and presented, and the way its data are interpreted (Conkey and Gero 1997: 413). Although we are not always aware of it, archaeology is a "highly constructed form of knowledge-seeking" (Roberts 1993: 18), and its interpretive processes can serve various research agendas. In Syro-Palestinian archaeology, for example, publications tend to illustrate ceramic and artifactual materials in stylistic groupings rather than in locus groups (Daviau 1993: 26–27). This publication strategy reflects the diachronic goals of the excavators: to illumine change over time in correlation with sociopolitical history. As a result, determining the precise find spots of objects in relation to each other and to their architectural context is often difficult, if not impossible. Yet recovering the spatial distribution of artifacts and ceramics is essential for the reconstruction of room function (i.e., activity areas), as opposed to room configuration (i.e., architectural identity).

Gendered archaeology, or the archaeology of gender, must therefore redefine archaeological agendas in order to recover, organize, and interpret data in ways that can illumine past gendered behavior (Wright 1996a: 3).[7] Valuable data have undoubtedly been lost because of excavation and record-keeping techniques (Steadman 1996: 76), as well as publication strategies, which have not been sensitive to the possibilities of recovering the

---

6. These analytical distinctions set forth by Wilk and Rathje (1982: 622–23) two decades ago are still operative in the interpretive strategies of anthropologists and archaeologists seeking to describe the household, estimate its size, and predict its articulation with surrounding residential or kinship groups. Larger households and strongly interconnected household groups are, in some ways, strategies to solve simultaneous labor requirements for the production and processing of diverse agro-products or to deal with land scarcity when the population increases (Wilk and Rathje 1982: 621; Wilk and Netting 1984: 7; Steadman 1996: 56). Iron Age households would have been variable in size and makeup, tending toward such large, or extended, family groupings. Faust (2000) has made the case for complex families in Iron Age rural communities. Even Holladay's claim that the nuclear family was the basic social and domestic unit is modified by the inclusion of unrelated servants in that group, by the realization that the nuclear family is part of a segmentary structure with the extended family as the next level of complexity, and by the suggestion that certain activity areas (especially female ones) were probably used jointly by the extended family (Holladay 1995: 387–89; see also the discussion in Meyers 1997a: 13–19).

7. The archaeology of gender is often also a feminist project, in that it must grapple with the biases in the contemporary world and in academia that have precluded the recovery of material culture in ways that inform the inquiry into gendered behavior. Although elitist biases are being addressed in Syro-Palestinian archaeology, androcentric tendencies in both data recovery and interpretation are not yet being redressed in significant ways (see the discussion in Meyers 1997b).

gendered production of archaeological materials. Yet attempts can be made to salvage some such information from past projects, and future projects can be made more gender-friendly in their field work and publications.

The claim that archaeology can produce information useful for the reconstruction of gendered household activities is tested here by examining two examples of productive activities visible in the archaeological record. If these can be identified as female-gender specific, they can be probed for knowledge about the relationships in which they are embedded, that is, women's culture. Establishing gender specificity for an activity means taking the artifacts or artifact assemblages used in that activity, which are not intrinsically gender articulate, and establishing whether they were used predominantly or exclusively by one gender or the other. Then, using the spatial distribution of such objects or assemblages, household activity areas can be identified according to gender (Steadman 1996: 63) and interrogated for information about human behavior, hierarchies, and power differentials.

Can we really be sure about who—females or males—used specific artifacts? In order to resist imposing gender identities on artifacts from outside the experiential world of the Iron Age people we are studying, we can apply various interpretive strategies. Prehistorians practicing gendered archaeology have pioneered in identifying specific ways in which the gendered use of artifacts can be determined (e.g., Gero and Conkey 1991; Wright [ed.] 1996; Nelson 1997). Such gender-attribution procedures utilize three major sources: *ethnography, ethnohistory,* and *iconography* (Costin 1996: 117–20). All of these sources are often used in interpreting the data produced by Syro-Palestinian archaeology.[8] Studies of Iron Age dwellings and their various functions (Stager 1985; Holladay 1992; 1997), for example, have been heavily dependent on several classic ethnographic studies of Iranian villages (Watson 1979; Kramer 1982). When attributing gender to household activities, the direct observation of human behavior is especially important in helping to determine, at the very least, the range of possibilities (Rapoport 1994: 480; Costin 1996: 121).

A. Food Preparation: Grains into Bread

Making bread is one of the most common of all food preparation activities, and archaeological remains establish the household as its setting.[9] Although grinding-stones and other artifacts used in transforming grains into finished loaves are not always found in situ, not always published in ways that allow their spatial locations to be retrieved, and may not ever be published at all, even the minimal artifactual data suggest that bread was produced in individual households in Iron Age settlements. At ʿIzbet Ṣarṭah, for example, the 13 grinding-stones of Strata II–IV (late 11th–early 10th centuries B.C.E.) were evenly distributed, with 1–3 in every four-room building unit and none found outside living areas

---

8. Ethnographic data used analogically to interpret archaeological remains, or ethnoarchaeology, is often challenged by those who question the value of using recent behavior patterns for interpreting ancient cultures. When used with caution and, if possible, in conjunction with other sources, ethnographic information can be invaluable, particularly if one uses data from the same geographic region, where there is the possibility of some cultural continuity. Even cross-cultural data from other geographic regions should be considered, especially if the ecosystems are similar (see the discussions in Carter 1997; Meyers 1997b: 276–78).

9. For a fuller discussion of bread production in Iron Age Israel, see Meyers in press.

(Finkelstein 1986: 93–94). In addition, remains of baking ovens, or *tabun*s, sometimes more than one, are found in virtually all households. In House 75 in the western quarter of Beersheba, to give just one of many possible examples, an oven was found with grinding-stones and cooking vessels beside it (Beit-Arieh 1973: 33, pl. 67). Also, each of the units identified as serving extended families (that is, households) in the Iron II villages de-scribed by Faust (2000) apparently had grinding tools and baking installations.[10] Clearly, whether in the courtyard space (Mazar 1992: 488) and/or in an area of the main room of a four-room house, many of the complex and time-consuming series of operations needed to make cereal crops edible (Meyers 1997a: 25; 1998: 253–54) took place in the household. Moreover, the presence of several grinding-stones in individual household units suggests that several people would have been processing grain at the same time.

The gender attribution of these processes can be established with reasonable certainty. First, *ethnographic* evidence from the contemporary Middle East as well as from global cross-cultural studies indicates that food preparation tasks, and those involving cereals in particular, are almost always performed by women. In the landmark analysis of data from the Human Relations Area Files (HRAF), collected on 185 societies worldwide judged to be representative of human labor patterns (Murdock and White 1969), 50 technological activities were arranged according to the ratio of male and female participation, begin-ning with those mostly associated with men and ending with those in which women pre-dominate (Murdock and Provost 1973). Food preparation in general appears in 49th place and the preparation of vegetal food in 50th place—they are the technological activities most strongly associated with women and are dominated by men in only 3 or 4 of the 185 societies represented (Murdock and Provost 1973: tables 1, 5). Many studies of individual societies corroborate these findings and also indicate another important feature about grain-processing tasks: such tedious activities are often performed in gendered work groups, in which women of one household and even of neighboring households gather to-gether to grind, knead, and bake (Friedl 1991: 208; Sweely 1999: 168). Ethnographic evi-dence from regions close to Syria–Palestine (e.g., Kramer 1979; Watson 1979) invariably show women controlling the production of bread and other food-stuffs. Similarly, Pales-tinian ethnographic data collected in the late 1970s reveal female control of the artifacts of bread-production and the associated space (Hirschfeld 1996).

Iron Age *ethnohistorical* information from Syria–Palestine accords with the ethno-graphic materials. Texts show some gender variability in several other food preparation tasks, but the references to steps in the grain-to-bread sequence uniformly mention women.[11] Furthermore, these sources often seem to indicate collective grinding or baking task performance. Mesopotamian sources also attest to the fact that women spent much time grinding grain and baking bread; millstones might even be a part of a woman's dowry

---

10. A. Faust, personal communication, 1 May 2000.

11. See Lev 26:26; 1 Sam 8:13, 28:24; Eccl 12:3; Jer 7:18; and cf. Isa 27:11. Discussions of some of these passages can be found in Meyers 2000d (which examines Lev 26:26 and how it depicts women not only as bread-bakers but as those who allocate portions); 2000a (which considers 1 Sam 8:13 and its reference to female bakers as specialists in the upper levels of the political hierarchy in ways often reserved for men in traditional societies); 2000g (which suggests that the reference in Eccl 12:3 to "women who grind" is a pars pro toto designation of the role of women in converting grain to bread); and 2000e (which sees Isa 27:11 as a reference to women's responsibility for gathering wood and building fires to bake bread).

(Harris 1992: 949). Egyptian sources likewise suggest that women of all social classes were associated with a variety of household technologies, especially those associated with baking (Robins 1993: 100–102, 117–19, 126).

Finally, late Iron Age *iconographic* sources depict women, and not men, grinding or kneading, often in pairs or larger groups. A clay model from Achzib, dating to the 6th century B.C.E., depicts a female figure bending over a bread-trough and kneading dough (Pritchard [ed.] 1954: 152). A plethora of such genre scenes showing women grinding or kneading, perhaps inspired by Levantine coroplasts, have been recovered on Cyprus, some depicting women working at this task in tandem (Karageorghis 1998: fig. 24; pls. 29:9–10; 30:1–2, 4–5, 6–8). Similar figural appear in ancient Greece; and a Boetian terracotta showing women kneading dough in a communal trough led the excavators of Tel Dor to interpret an installation in an Iron I context as a bread-kneading trough (Stern et al. 1997: 52–56, figs. 10–12). Iconographic data (tomb models and wall paintings) from ancient Egypt also suggest that bread production was "one of the few activities usually involving women" in elite households as well as those of workers (Robins 1993: 102, 118).

Taken together, these sources make the attribution of bread production to women reasonably certain. The areas in Iron Age households in which bread was produced thus functioned as female space, at least during the hours—perhaps as many as two per day (Bossen 1989; Meyers 1998: 254)—devoted to bread production. Many other food-processing activities were probably also women's tasks and were carried out in proximity to the grain-to-bread area, thereby creating an overall female activity area for many of the daylight hours in Iron Age households. The implications of this female use of space for the production of bread, the communal nature of this productive task, and the very fact that this basic household function was controlled by women will be considered below.

B. *Textile Production: Spinning, Sewing, and Weaving*

Scant remains of textiles themselves have been recovered from archaeological deposits. However, some of the implements used in the production of cloth and clothing—spindle whorls, needles, and loom weights—provide the hard data for considering spinning, sewing, and weaving as gendered activities. Unfortunately, perhaps even more than for grain-processing implements, the location of the tools of textile production are not easily, if at all, recoverable from many excavation reports. A study carried out in early 1990s attempted with little success to identify the find spots of spindle whorls and loom weights in the publications of Iron II sites (Meyers 1991b[12]). There are exceptions, however. For example, at Tell es-Saʿidiyeh, in each of five different Stratum V (8th century B.C.E.) buildings, groups of loom weights were recovered, usually in the main (pillared) room. They were aligned in such a way as to suggest that they were in situ, dropped from a horizontal beam (Pritchard 1985: 35–38; figs. 73–75, 87–89). All the excavated dwellings of this period and the preceding two Iron Age strata were identified as small domestic units in which, among other activities, weaving apparently took place on a house-by-house basis (Pritchard 1985: 78).

---

12. The then-graduate-student Karla Bohmbach who assisted in the study reported that "it's shocking the amount and kind of information that is left out [about loom weights and spindle whorls]."

Weaving in discrete households is not the only discernible pattern. Other data suggest that, at least in the Late Iron Age (8th–7th centuries B.C.E.), weaving may have been conducted in specialized workshops, at sites in the Shephelah and Beth-shean Valley, in order to supply Assyrian tribute demands for fine fabrics (Browning 1988). Clearly, more careful recovery and more nuanced studies of the location and concentration of spindle whorls and needles, in addition to loom weights, are necessary before the various facets and types of thread and cloth production, whether linen, cotton, and/or wool, can be determined. Still, the evidence of textile production in households for household use and perhaps also for tribute, trade, or communal use, is substantial. The gender attribution of textile production can be established, again using several kinds of evidence.

Ethnographic data reveal a remarkably strong division of labor in craft production (Costin 1996: 121). The HRAF materials show loom-weaving to be a woman's activity in 84%, and spinning in 87%, of the societies in which they occur (Murdock and Provost 1973: table 1; Costin 1996: table 4.1). In the few societies in which both women and men work in textiles, they tend to have specialized technological niches—men may be fullers or shearers, for example, while women spin, weave, and embroider (Wright 1996b: 98). This overall division of labor in textile production apparently is consistent across class lines and is found for work performed in both households and workshops. The latter point is important because it suggests that even if some Iron II textile production was "industrial," it still may have been a female enterprise. The distribution of women and men as textile artisans across cultures suggests that men have a dominant role in such activities mainly in societies quite different from that of Iron Age Syria–Palestine: in horticultural societies, in which much of women's labor is devoted to the production of foodstuffs; and in large-scale agroindustrial societies that produce export-quality cloth, although even then, men do not control all of the technologies (Schneider and Weiner 1986: 181).

Ethnohistorical materials likewise indicate that weaving was done by women. Mesopotamian texts provide evidence that women were organized in workshops to produce materials for trade (Veenhof 1972: 195; Wright 1996b). Indeed, the production of cloth and clothing was probably women's work in the ancient Near East from the Neolithic period through the Iron Age (Barber 1997; Nemet-Nejat 1999: 106–7). Egyptian texts provide similar information. A papyrus from the late Middle Kingdom, for example, lists the occupations of 29 women—20 of them connected with weaving (Hayes 1955: 105). In the late-13th-century B.C.E. Story of Two Brothers, the wife of Anubis tries to seduce his brother Bata with the promise of making fine clothes (Pritchard [ed.] 1955: 24). In Egyptian peasant households and also in those of the elite, weaving was a female activity (Robins 1993: 35, 64, 95, 110). Ethnohistorical records from Syria–Palestine provide similar information. In Ugaritic literature, the goddess Athirat is said to have worked with "a mighty spindle" as well as a cooking pot (Smith 1997: 122). Iron Age biblical texts mention "weaving women" and "skilled women" who produce fabrics of colored yarns and linen and also of goat hair.[13] Note that these biblical references to women imply that they worked in

---

13. 2 Kgs 23:7 and Exod 35:25–26, 36:6 (see the discussion of these passages in Meyers 2000c and 2000b, respectively). Note also the reference to Delilah's skill with the loom in Judg 16:13–14. The specification of females in these passages does not preclude the possibility that males were weavers, as they may have been in certain state-sponsored workshops (see Isa 19:9, which refers to wage-earning textile workers in Egypt).

groups. Furthermore, these women were considered artisans or skilled designers, designations consonant with the high level of textiles produced in Syria–Palestine in the Iron Age (Sheffer 1995: 545–50).

Iconographic evidence relevant to cloth production is apparently nonexistent from Syria–Palestine, but images of women as weavers and spinners do appear in representational art from other ancient Near Eastern societies, for example, a stone relief of uncertain date from Susa depicting an upper-class woman spinning wool (Pritchard [ed.] 1954: fig. 144). Most graphic evidence for weaving as a gendered activity comes from Egyptian models and tomb scenes (e.g., Pritchard [ed.] 1954: figs. 142–43), which frequently depict women as the personnel involved in textile manufacture (Robins 1993: 103), especially in the production of linen cloth (Barber 1997: 192).

5. *Discussion: Implications of Gendered Activities for Sociopolitical Relations*

Because at least two household activities in Iron Age households can be strongly linked with women, certain Iron Age household areas can be identified as women's social space. To understand the full implications of this identification, several obstacles must be overcome, perhaps the most significant being present-mindedness. Assumptions about the meaning and value of women's household activities cannot be based on our experiences in contemporary middle-class Western culture (Nelson 1997: 13–21, 88). This is most salient in the tacit appraisal of what is masculine as inherently powerful and/or prestigious, with women's activities considered supportive and secondary, thereby being trivialized and marginalized.

Such negative evaluations of women's work are rooted in the identification of women with the home in Western ideologies in the last two centuries (Lawrence 1999: 121), which in turn is the result of the removal of significant economic processes from the household as part of the industrial revolution. Because women's unpaid tasks came to be seen as simply housekeeping chores, the economic value and concomitant social power and prestige of premodern women's household labor tended to become obscured (Meyers 1999a: 154–58). The conventional wisdom that saw women as passive and powerless in virtually all premodern societies is now recognized to be deeply flawed. In reality, women's productive activities in premodern societies had major economic value (Brumfiel 1991: 224–25). Newer studies of traditional societies show that women's household economic roles, in both subsistence tasks and craft production, functioned in ways that contest our often unexamined but persistent notions of female dependency and patriarchal dominance. The work patterns and authority structures in premodern societies meant that daily life was rarely hierarchical along gendered lines.

Another related and equally powerful obstacle to reaching an emic perspective on Iron Age or any other ancient culture is the public-private dichotomy. This analytical construction, which also stems from the modern experience in industrialized societies, posits the public (political and economic activities and institutions) and the private (family or domestic life) as separate domains. Popular several decades ago in assessing women's roles in traditional societies (e.g., Rosaldo 1974; Sanday 1974), the private-public binary as a useful analytical framework is no longer accepted (Sharistanian 1987; Helly and Reverby 1992; cf. Rosaldo 1980; Meyers 1988: 32–33, 175–76). A more integrated approach now recognizes that in premodern societies the "public" and "private" are overlapping domains. The notion of a dichotomy between the two does *not* reflect reality. Rather, *all* activities in the household are significant for *both* the private and the public realm—the domestic *is* political and the private *is* public (Hegland 1991: 216–18, 228–29).[14] The economic activities and concomitant social relations of an Iron Age household would not have been separate from larger domains, including political alliances (cf. Yanagisako 1979: 191; Hendon 1996: 47).

Women's productive activities, carried out in the gendered spaces of Iron Age households, were dynamic elements in the social and political fabric of their communities. As ethnographic research has shown, gender-associated artifacts signify gender-associated economic activities, which in turn have implications for gender-linked power. Traditional Western approaches to power tend to focus on formal institutions of power and authority, whereas informal power relations in traditional societies are the concomitants of the control of productive activities (Sweely 1999: 155–56) and are just as important as, if not more important than, formal relations of power.

Thus we can infer that power accrued to women in Iron Age agrarian communities because of their control of certain productive tasks. This would certainly have been true for bread-making. The virtual exclusivity of women as producers and distributors of any fundamental nutritional source of a society, which cannot be obtained in any other way, is an indicator of female power (Counihan 1998: 2, 4). A similar evaluation can be made about cloth production, especially because of the technological skill required for all its discrete operations. Cross-cultural studies of women's weaving indicate that "weaving women" exercise power because of their skills and also because of the economic value of the objects they produce. This is so whether or not they have direct control over the thread they spin or the cloth they weave or the garments they sew (Brumfiel 1991: 225; Sweely 1999: 165). But Iron Age women, according to at least one ethnohistorical source, *did* engage in marketing as well as making textiles.[15] Considerable power accrues to such women.

Another critical aspect of female power linked to economic tasks is derived from the fact that grain-processing (grinding, kneading, baking bread) and textile production (spinning, weaving, sewing) involved women working in groups. Whether the work took place in households, in communal workshops, or even (as was probably the case for weaving at certain times of the year) in shady outdoor space beyond the settlement perimeter, women gathered together to perform these labor-intensive tasks. The presence of female work groups, whether for food-processing or crafts production, signals the existence of women's networks. Gendered household activity areas were thus social spaces, in which

---

14. This is true even today in Third World countries, where the state does not always reach into peasant households in rural areas. Politics in the communities comprising such households are conducted through kin relationships. Observations not long ago in Aliabad in Iran revealed that "personal and domestic relations were also public and political relations" (Hegland 1991: 215).

15. Proverbs 31 indicates the role of a female household manager in securing (buying?) wool and flax (v. 13), spinning thread (v. 14), making clothing (vv. 22, 24 and perhaps v. 21), and marketing the garments she produces (vv. 24 and 18). Although Proverbs probably received its final editing in the late 6th century B.C.E. (the Persian period), its materials are largely from the Iron Age II (Fontaine 1988: 495). Scholars are divided as to whether the acrostic poem in chap. 31 is pre- or postexilic.

women shared with each other certain kinds of knowledge and experienced certain kinds of interaction.

The sharing of knowledge relating to a particular trade, craft, or service is hardly a trivial matter. Textile production, especially in terms of the expertise required, was a quasi-professional enterprise involving knowledge of techniques, substances, equipment, guidelines, and other production factors (Meyers 1999a: 161–62, 165). That women gathered, however sporadically, to engage in the serial or simultaneous operations of cloth and clothing manufacture meant that those experienced in the craft passed on their skills and knowledge to younger artisans. This mentoring role entailed female leadership and the opportunity for women to experience status and prestige.

In addition, women working together for textile production would have developed a sense of solidarity,[16] which also would have been a significant factor in the more informal networks of women who gathered in one household or another to carry out the often tedious tasks of food production. Whether kneading dough together in a communal trough or working side-by-side with differing foodstuffs, women sharing productive social space meant that they had access to social knowledge as well as technical knowledge. They knew each other and thus each other's families; and this sphere of relationships, which a woman began to build as soon as she married and entered her husband's household, meant that women had information otherwise unavailable to men that was critical for forging political connections, solving economic problems such as the differential need for field labor among households, and assisting with difficulties such as illness or death in individual households (Meyers 1999a: 176–77, 182–83; cf. Ardener 1993: 9; Sirman 1995). These informal alliances among women are designated in Iron Age ethnohistorical texts as *šĕkēnôt* or by several feminine forms of the verb *rʿh*, all signifying female cohorts (Meyers 1999b; 2000f).

Such women's groups were hardly casual affairs, even though they may represent a more diffuse and thus more elusive form of female power than the more visible power in male social groups. Indeed, especially in societies with limited material and labor resources, such women's networks contribute to the viability of the community as a whole.[17] Women's networks may have constituted the informal but important mediating group that forged households into larger "kin groups," or *mišpāḥôt*, that functioned as "protective association[s] of families" by extending mutual social, economic, and military aid (Gottwald 1979: 257–67; cf. Lamphere 1993: 70). Indeed, not only because of their group labor but also because of their marital and consanguinal ties, women were better positioned than men to mediate such relations.[18]

16. The sense of intimacy among women engaged together in labor-intensive textile work was recently replicated in a project in experimental archaeology. In producing fabrics and sewing garments that would reproduce the "fashion" of Minoan women, the women working together on the project experienced a sense of connection to each other and even to ancient Minoan seamstresses (Jones 2000: 38).

17. Evidence of the importance of women's groups comes from ethnographic information about traditional societies (e.g., Strathern 1972; March and Taqqu 1986; Marcus 1992; Zonabend 1996). It is interesting to note that, even in developed societies, the often unrecognized bonds among women have now been heralded as important factors in social and political life (e.g., Smith-Rosenberg 1975; Evans 1989; Lambert 1995).

18. Women married into one household while still maintaining links with their natal households. They therefore had structural links with two descent groups, whereas men had such a link only with their own lineage (Meyers 1999a: 171–72).

Forged and maintained in female household social space, women's groups empowered Iron Age women as social actors in the larger community and contributed in important ways to the complexity and richness of their daily lives. Furthermore, just as craft-oriented women's groups entailed the leadership of certain women, so too the formation of a web of interconnecting kin and neighbor relationships through the social work space of households meant differentiation in female social roles according to age, experience, family status, or other such variables. Thus, these female-gendered groups would have had their own structures and hierarchies, however shifting and informal they may have been.

Acknowledging the hierarchical ordering of women's groups (Lamphere 1993: 71) means contesting the conventional wisdom about male dominance in pervasive hierarchical structures affecting all domains of human interaction in premodern societies. Because the household in Iron Age settlements was the primary unit of society, and because women had significant power in household social spaces, it may be better to consider the gendered spheres of these settlements as complementary rather than hierarchical. The social organization of Iron Age settlements is thus better understood as heterarchical rather than hierarchical (Meyers 2002). The concept of "heterarchy" was first introduced by anthropologists as an alternative to the central-place model in analyzing settlement patterns (Crumley 1979; 1987). It has since attracted widespread interest among researchers unhappy with the failure of evolutionary models to fit with archaeological data (Ehrenreich, Crumley, and Levy 1995). The concept of heterarchy as an organizational structure in which "each element possesses the potential of being unranked (relative to other elements) or ranked in a number of different ways depending on systemic requirements" (Crumley 1979: 144) allows for systems to be perceived as related to each other laterally rather than vertically.

Heterarchy is particularly suitable to accommodate the variability, context, and fluctuation of social relations in peasant societies (Levy 1995: 47). Women's activities are subsystems in such a conceptualization, each with their own patterns of rankings, privileges, and statuses, with some women exercising meaningful leadership and dominance vis-à-vis other women in the system. Women's systems, along with those of men, can be understood as constituent systems of a heterarchical complexity. Situating gendered activity within heterarchical structures is an especially useful model to account for and acknowledge significant aspects of women's culture in the Iron Age.

Harriet Beecher Stowe may have had it right. She borrowed the term "homesteads" from American pioneer history, thereby acknowledging the economic primacy of the household. And she called women "queens," an inappropriate term to be sure, but one that nonetheless signifies what this study in household archaeology has shown—that women had power in their own stratified structures and that daily life in Iron Age agrarian settlements entailed more complex roles for all individuals than might otherwise be imagined. The lives of women, as producers of essential foods and fabrics, would have been replete with intricate and subtle opportunities for contributing to household and communal well-being.

References

Ardener, S.
1993   Ground Rules and Social Maps for Women: An Introduction. Pp. 1–30 in *Women and Space: Ground Rules and Social Maps*, ed. S. Ardener. Cross-Cultural Perspectives on Women 5. Providence: Berg.

Barber, E. J. W.
1997   Textiles of the Neolithic through Iron Ages. Pp. 191–95 in vol. 5 of *The Oxford Encyclopedia of Archaeology in the Near East*, ed. E. M. Meyers. New York: Oxford University Press.

Bender, D. R.
1967   A Refinement of the Concept of Household: Families, Co-Residence, and Domestic Functions. *American Anthropologist* 69: 493–504.

Beit-Arieh, I.
1973   The Western Quarter. Pp. 31–37 in *Beer-sheba I: Excavations at Tel Beer-sheba, 1969–1971 Seasons*, ed. Y. Aharoni. Tel Aviv: Tel Aviv University Press.

Bossen, L.
1989   Women and Economic Institutions. Pp. 318–50 in *Economic Anthropology*, ed. S. Plottner. Stanford, Calif.: Stanford University Press.

Bourdieu, P.
1973   The Berber House. Pp. 98–110 in *Rules and Meanings*, ed. M. Douglas. Hammondsworth: Penguin.

Browning, D. S., Jr.
1988   *The Textile Industry of Iron Age Timnah and Its Regional and Socioeconomic Contexts: A Literary and Artifactual Analysis*. Ph.D. dissertation, Southwestern Baptist Theological Seminary.

Brumfiel, E. M.
1991   Weaving and Cooking: Women's Production in Aztec Mexico. Pp. 224–51 in *Engendering Archaeology: Women and Prehistory*, ed. J. M. Gero and M. W. Conkey. Oxford: Blackwell.

Carter, C. E.
1997   Ethnoarchaeology. Pp. 280–84 in vol. 2 of *The Oxford Encyclopedia of Archaeology in the Near East*, ed. E. M. Meyers. New York: Oxford University Press.

Chernoff, M.
1999   Gender, Family and Farming in Turkish Agricultural Villages: Multiple Perspectives on the Past. Paper presented at the American Schools of Oriental Research Annual Meeting, Cambridge, Mass.

Conkey, M. W., and Gero, J. M.
1997   Program to Practice: Gender to Feminism in Archaeology. *Annual Review of Anthropology* 26: 411–37.

Costin, C. L.
1996   Exploring the Relationship between Gender and Craft in Complex Societies: Methodological and Theoretical Issues of Gender Attribution. Pp. 111–40 in *Gender and Archaeology*, ed. R. P. Wright. Philadelphia: University of Pennsylvania Press.

Counihan, C. M.
1998   Introduction—Food and Gender: Identity and Power. Pp. 1–10 in *Food and Gender: Identity and Power*, ed. C. M. Counihan and S. L. Kaplan. Food in History and Culture 1. Amsterdam: Harwood Academic.

Crumley, C.
1979   Three Locational Models: An Epistemological Assessment of Anthropology and Archaeology. Pp. 141–73 in *Advances in Archaeological Method*, ed. M. B. Schiffer. New York: Academic Press.

1987　A Dialectical Critique of Hierarchy. Pp. 155–59 in *Power Relations and State Formation*, ed. T. C. Patterson and C. W. Gailey. Washington, D.C.: Anthropological Association of America.

Daviau, P. M. M.
1993　*Houses and Their Furnishings in Bronze Age Palestine.* Journal for the Study of the Old Testament / American Schools of Oriental Research Monograph Series 8. Sheffield: Sheffield Academic Press.

Ehrenreich, R. M.; Crumley, C. L.; and Levy, J. E. (eds.)
1995　*Heterarchy and the Analysis of Complex Societies.* Archaeological Papers of the American Anthropological Association 6. Arlington, Va.: American Anthropological Association.

Evans, S. M.
1989　*Born for Liberty: A History of Women in America.* New York: Free Press/Macmillan.

Faust, A.
2000　The Rural Community in Ancient Israel during Iron Age II. *Bulletin of the American Schools of Oriental Research* 317: 17–39.

Finkelstein, I.
1986　*ʿIzbet Ṣarṭah: An Early Iron Age Site near Rosh Haʿayin, Israel.* British Archaeological Reports International Series 299. Oxford: B.A.R.

Fontaine, C. R.
1988　Proverbs. Pp. 495–517 in *Harper's Bible Commentary*, ed. J. L. Mays. San Francisco: Harper & Row.

Frick, F. S.
1997　Cities: An Overview. Pp. 14–19 in vol. 2 of *The Oxford Encyclopedia of Archaeology in the Near East*, ed. E. M. Meyers. New York: Oxford University Press.

Friedl, E.
1991　The Dynamics of Women's Spheres of Action in Rural Iran. Pp. 195–214 in *Women in Middle Eastern History: Shifting Boundaries in Sex and Gender*, ed. N. R. Keddie and B. Baron. New Haven: Yale University Press.

Fritz, V.
1997　Cities of the Bronze and Iron Ages. Pp. 19–25 in vol. 2 of *The Oxford Encyclopedia of Archaeology in the Near East*, ed. E. M. Meyers. New York: Oxford University Press.

Gero, J. M., and Conkey, M. W. (eds.)
1991　*Engendering Archaeology: Women and Prehistory.* Oxford: Blackwell.

Gottwald, N. K.
1979　*The Tribes of Yahweh: A Sociology of the Religion of Liberated Israel, 1250–1050 B.C.E.* Maryknoll, N.Y.: Orbis.

Harris, R.
1992　Women: Mesopotamia. Pp. 947–51 in vol. 6 of *The Anchor Bible Dictionary*, ed. D. N. Freedman. New York: Doubleday.

Hayes, W. C.
1955　*A Papyrus of the Late Middle Kingdom in the Brooklyn Museum.* New York: Brooklyn Museum.

Hegland, M. E.
1991　Political Roles of Aliabad Women: The Public-Private Dichotomy Transcended. Pp. 215–30 in *Women in Middle Eastern History: Shifting Boundaries in Sex and Gender*, ed. N. R. Keddie and B. Baron. New Haven: Yale University Press.

Helly, D. O., and Reverby, S. (eds.)
1992　*Gendered Domains: Rethinking Public and Private in Women's History.* Ithaca, N.Y.: Cornell University Press.

Hendon, J. A.
1996　Archaeological Approaches to the Organization of Domestic Labor: Household Practice and Domestic Relations. *Annual Review of Anthropology* 25: 45–61.

Henshaw, A.
  1999   Location and Appropriation in the Arctic: An Integrative Zooarchaeological Approach
          to Historic Innuit Household Economies. *Journal of Anthropological Archaeology* 18: 79–
          118.
Hirschfeld, Y.
  1996   The Traditional Palestinian House: Results of a Survey in the Hebron Hills. Pp. 109–215
          in *The Palestinian Dwelling in the Roman-Byzantine Period*, by Y. Hirschfeld. Studium Bibli-
          cum Franciscanum Collectio Minor 34. Jerusalem: Franciscan Printing Press / Israel Ex-
          ploration Society.
Holladay, J. S., Jr.
  1992   House, Israelite. Pp. 308–18 in vol. 3 of *The Anchor Bible Dictionary*, ed. D. N. Freedman.
          New York: Doubleday.
  1995   The Kingdoms of Israel and Judah: Political and Economic Centralization in the Iron II
          A–B (ca. 1000–750 B.C.E.). Pp. 368–98, 586–90 in *The Archaeology of Society in the Holy
          Land*, ed. T. E. Levy. New York: Facts on File.
  1997   Syro-Palestinian Houses. Pp. 94–114 in vol. 3 of *The Oxford Encyclopedia of Archaeology in
          the Near East*, ed. E. M. Meyers. New York: Oxford University Press.
Hopkins, D. C.
  1985   *The Highlands of Canaan: Agricultural Life in the Early Iron Age.* The Social World of Bibli-
          cal Antiquity Series 3. Sheffield: Almond.
Jones, B. R.
  2000   Revealing Minoan Fashions: Cretan Styles Regain Center Stage. *Archaeology* 53: 36–41.
Karageorghis, V.
  1998   *The Coroplastic Art of Ancient Cyprus V. The Cypro-Archaic Period: Small Female Figurines, A.
          Handmade/Wheelmade Figurines.* Nicosia: Leventis Foundation.
Kent, S.
  1984   *Analyzing Activity Areas: An Ethnoarchaeological Study of the Use of Space.* Albuquerque:
          University of New Mexico Press.
  1990a   Activity Areas and Architecture: An Interdisciplinary View of the Relationship between
          Use of Space and Domestic Built Environments. Pp. 1–8 in *Domestic Architecture and the
          Use of Space: An Interdisciplinary Cross-Cultural Study*, ed. S. Kent. Cambridge: Cambridge
          University Press.
  1990b   A Cross-Cultural Study of Segmentation, Architecture, and the Use of Space. Pp. 127–
          52 in *Domestic Architecture and the Use of Space: An Interdisciplinary Cross-Cultural Study*,
          ed. S. Kent. Cambridge: Cambridge University Press.
Kramer, C.
  1979   An Archaeological View of a Contemporary Kurdish Village: Domestic Architecture,
          Household Size, and Wealth. Pp. 139–63 in *Ethnoarchaeology: Implications of Ethnography
          for Archaeology*, ed. C. Kramer. New York: Columbia University Press.
  1982   *Village Ethnoarchaeology: Rural Iran in Archaeological Perspective.* New York: Academic
          Press.
Lambert, C.
  1995   Leadership in a New Key. *Harvard Magazine* 97: 28–33.
Lamphere, L.
  1993   The Domestic Sphere of Women and the Public Sphere of Men: The Strengths and Lim-
          itations of an Anthropological Dichotomy. Pp. 67–77 in *Gender in Cross-Cultural Perspec-
          tive*, ed. C. B. Brettel and C. F. Sargent. Englewood Cliffs, N.J.: Prentice Hall.
Lawrence, S.
  1999   Towards a Feminist Archaeology of Households: Gender and Household Structure
          in the Australian Goldfields. Pp. 121–41 in *The Archaeology of Household Activities*, ed.
          P. M. Allison. London: Routledge.

Lenski, G.
  1984   *Power and Privilege: A Theory of Social Stratification.* 2nd ed. Chapel Hill, N.C.: University
          of North Carolina Press.
Levy, J. E.
  1995   Heterarchy in Bronze Age Denmark: Settlement Pattern, Gender, and Ritual. Pp. 41–53
          in *Heterarchy and the Analysis of Complex Societies*, ed. R. M. Ehrenreich, C. L. Crumley,
          and J. E. Levy. Archaeological Papers of the American Anthropological Association 6.
          Arlington, Va.: American Anthropological Association.
Levine, B. A.
  1999   The Biblical "Town" as Reality and Typology: Evaluating Biblical References to Towns
          and Their Functions. Pp. 421–53 in vol. 2 of *Urbanization and Land Ownership in the Ancient
          Near East*, ed. M. Hudson and B. A. Levine. Cambridge, Mass.: Peabody Museum of
          Archaeology and Ethnology, Harvard University.
March, K. S., and Taqqu, R. L.
  1986   *Women's Informal Associations in Developing Countries.* Women in Cross-Cultural Perspec-
          tive. Boulder, Colo.: Westview.
Marcus, J.
  1992   *A World of Difference: Islam and Gender Hierarchy in Turkey.* London: Allen and Unwin.
Mazar, A.
  1992   *Archaeology of the Land of the Bible: 10,000–586 B.C.E.* New York: Doubleday.
McNutt, P. M.
  1999   *Reconstructing the Society of Ancient Israel.* Library of Ancient Israel. Louisville: Westmin-
          ster John Knox.
Meyers, C.
  1988   *Discovering Eve: Ancient Israelite Women in Context.* New York: Oxford University Press.
  1991a   "To Her Mother's House": Considering a Counterpart to the Israelite *Bêt 'āb*. Pp. 39–51,
          304–7 in *The Bible and the Politics of Exegesis: Essays in Honor of Norman K. Gottwald on His
          Sixty-Fifth Birthday*, ed. D. Jobling, P. L. Day, and G. T. Sheppard. New York: Pilgrim.
  1991b   Women and Weaving: The Archaeology of Textile Production as It Relates to Gender in
          Iron II Israel. Unpublished project report, Duke University Research Council.
  1997a   The Family in Early Israel. Pp. 1–47 in *Families in Ancient Israel*, by L. G. Perdue, J. Blen-
          kinsopp, J. J. Collins, and C. Meyers. Louisville: Westminster John Knox.
  1997b   Recovering Objects, Re-visioning Subjects: Archaeology and Feminist Biblical Study.
          Pp. 270–84 in *A Feminist Companion to Reading the Bible: Approaches, Methods and Strategies*,
          ed. A. Brenner and C. Fontaine. Sheffield: Sheffield Academic Press.
  1998   Everyday Life of Women in the Period of the Hebrew Bible. Pp. 251–59 in *The Women's
          Bible Commentary* (expanded edition), ed. C. A. Newsom and S. H. Ringe. Louisville:
          Westminster John Knox.
  1999a   Guilds and Gatherings: Women's Groups in Ancient Israel. Pp. 154–84 in *Realia Dei: Es-
          says in Archaeolgy and Biblical Interpretation in Honor of Edward F. Campbell, Jr.*, ed. P. M.
          Williams Jr. and T. Hiebert. Atlanta: Scholars Press.
  1999b   "Women of the Neighborhood" (Ruth 4.17): Informal Female Networks in Ancient Is-
          rael. Pp. 110–27 in *Ruth and Esther*. A Feminist Companion to the Bible, ed. A. Brenner.
          Second Series 3. Sheffield: Sheffield Academic Press.
  2000a–g a: Daughters as Perfumers, Cooks, and Bakers (1 Sam 8:13). P. 255; b: Skilled Women (and
          Men) (Exod 35:25–26; 36:6). Pp. 201–02; c: Weaving Women (2 Kgs 23:7). P. 278;
          d: Women as Bread-Bakers (Lev 26:26). Pp. 213–14; e: Women Making a Fire (Isa 27:11).
          Pp. 320–21; f: Women of the Neighborhood (Ruth 4:17). P. 254; g: Women Who Grind
          (Eccl 12:3). P. 310 in *Women in Scripture: A Dictionary of Named and Unnamed Women in the
          Hebrew Bible, the Apocryphal/Deuterocanonical Books, and the New Testament*, ed. C. Meyers,
          T. Craven, and R. S. Kraemer. Boston: Houghton Mifflin.

2002   *Tribes* and Tribulations: Retheorizing Earliest "Israel." Pp.35–45 in *Tracking 'The Tribes of Yahweh': On the Trail of a Classic*, ed. R. Boer. Journal for the Study of the Old Testament Supplement 351. New York and London: Sheffield Academic Press.

In press   From Field Crop to Food: Attributing Gender and Meaning to Bread Production in Iron Age Israel. In *The Archaeology of Difference: Gender, Ethnicity, Class, and the "Other" in Antiquity: Studies in Honor of Eric M. Meyers*, ed. D. R. Edwards and C. T. McCollough.

Murdock, G. P., and Provost, C.
1973   Factors in the Division of Labor by Sex: A Cross-Cultural Analysis. *Ethnology* 12: 203–25.

Murdock, G. P., and White, D. R.
1969   Standard Cross-Cultural Sample. *Ethnology* 8: 329–69.

Nelson, S. M.
1997   *Gender in Archaeology: Analyzing Power and Prestige*. Walnut Creek, Calif.: AltaMira.

Nemet-Nejat, K. R.
1999   Women in Ancient Mesopotamia. Pp. 85–114 in *Women's Roles in Ancient Civilization: A Reference Guide*, ed. B. Vivante. Westport, Conn.: Greenwood.

Polanyi, K.
1944   *The Great Transformation*. Boston: Beacon.

Pritchard, J. B.
1985   *Tell es-Saʿidiyeh: Excavations on the Tell, 1964–66*. Philadelphia: University of Pennsylvania Press.

Pritchard, J. B. (ed.)
1954   *The Ancient Near East in Pictures Relating to the Old Testament*. Princeton: Princeton University Press.

1955   *Ancient Near Eastern Texts Relating to the Old Testament*. Princeton: Princeton University Press.

Rapoport, A.
1994   Spatial Organization and the Built Environment. Pp. 460–502 in *Companion Encyclopedia of Anthropology*, ed. T. Ingold. London: Routledge.

Roberts, C.
1993   A Critical Approach to Gender as a Category of Analysis in Archaeology. Pp. 16–21 in *Women in Archaeology: A Feminist Critique*, ed. H. du Cros and L. Smith. Canberra: Australian National University Press.

Robins, G.
1993   *Women in Ancient Egypt*. Cambridge: Harvard University Press.

Rosaldo, M. Z.
1974   Women, Culture, and Society: A Theoretical Overview. Pp. 17–42 in *Women, Culture, and Society*, ed. M. Z. Rosaldo and L. Lamphere. Stanford, Calif.: Stanford University Press.

1980   The Use and Abuse of Anthropology: Reflections on Feminism and Cross-Cultural Understanding. *Signs* 5: 389–417.

Sanday, P. R.
1974   Female Status in the Public Domain. Pp. 189–206 in *Women, Culture, and Society*, ed. M. Z. Rosaldo and L. Lamphere. Stanford, Calif.: Stanford University Press.

Schneider, J., and Weiner, A. B.
1986   Cloth and the Organization of Human Experience. *Current Anthropology* 27: 178–84.

Sharer, R. J., and Ashmore, W.
1987   *Archaeology: Discovering Our Past*. Mountain View, Calif.: Mayfield.

Sharistanian, T. (ed.)
1987   *Beyond the Public/Private Dichotomy: Contemporary Perspectives on Women's Lives*. Contributions to Women's Studies 78. Westport, Conn.: Greenwood.

Sheffer, A.
　1995　Needlework and Sewing in Israel from Prehistoric Times to the Roman Period. Pp. 527–59 in *Fortunate the Eyes That See: Essays in Honor of David Noel Freedman in Celebration of His Seventieth Birthday*, ed. A. B. Beck et al. Grand Rapids, Mich.: Eerdmans.

Sirman, N.
　1995　Friend or Foe? Forging Alliances with Other Women in a Village of Western Turkey. Pp. 199–218 in *Women in Modern Turkish Society: A Reader*, ed. S. Tekeli. London: Zed.

Smith, M. S. (trans.)
　1997　The Baal Cycle. Pp. 81–180 in *Ugaritic Narrative Poetry*, ed. S. B. Parker. Society of Biblical Literature Writings from the Ancient World 9. Atlanta: Scholars Press.

Smith-Rosenberg, C.
　1975　The Female World of Love and Ritual: Relations between Women in Nineteenth-Century America. *Signs* 1: 1–29.

Stager, L. E.
　1985　The Archaeology of the Family in Ancient Israel. *Bulletin of the American Schools of Oriental Research* 260: 1–35.

Steadman, S. R.
　1996　Recent Research in the Archaeology of Architecture: Beyond the Foundations. *Journal of Archaeological Research* 4: 51–93.

Stern, E., et al.
　1997　Tel Dor, 1994–1995: Preliminary Stratigraphic Report. *Israel Exploration Journal* 47: 29–56.

Stowe, H. B.
　1874　*Women in Sacred History: A Series of Sketches*. New York: Ford.

Strathern, M.
　1972　*Women in Between: Female Roles in a Male World*. Seminar Studies in Anthropology 2. London and New York: Seminar.

Sweely, T. L.
　1999　Gender, Space, People, and Power at Cerén, El Salvador. Pp. 155–71 in *Manifesting Power: Gender and the Interpretation of Power in Archaeology*, ed. T. L. Sweely. London: Routledge.

Veenhof, K. R.
　1972　*Aspects of Old Assyrian Trade and Its Terminology*. Leiden: Brill.

Watson, P. J.
　1979　*Archaeological Ethnography in Western Iran*. Viking Fund Publications in Archaeology 57. Tucson: Wenner-Gren Foundation for Anthropological Research / University of Arizona.

Whitridge, P.
　1998　Gender, Labor, and the Divisions of Space in Thule Society. Paper (revised) presented at the 30th Annual Meeting of the Canadian Archaeological Association, Saskatoon, 1997.

Wilk, R. R., and Netting, R. McC.
　1984　Households: Changing Forms and Functions. Pp. 1–28 in *Households: Comparative and Historical Studies of the Domestic Group*, ed. R. McC. Netting, R. R. Wilk, and E. J. Arnould. Berkeley, Calif.: University of California Press.

Wilk, R. R., and Rathje, W. L.
　1982　Household Archaeology. *American Behavioral Scientist* 25: 617–39.

Wright, R. P.
　1996a　Introduction: Gendered Ways of Knowing in Archaeology. Pp. 1–19 in *Gender and Archaeology*, ed. R. P. Wright. Philadelphia: University of Pennsylvania Press.
　1996b　Technology, Gender, and Class: Worlds of Difference in Ur III Mesopotamia. Pp. 79–110 in *Gender and Archaeology*, ed. R. P. Wright. Philadelphia: University of Pennsylvania Press.

Wright, R. P. (ed.)
    1996   *Gender and Archaeology.* Philadelphia: University of Pennsylvania Press.
Yanagisako, S. J.
    1979   Family and Household: The Analysis of Domestic Groups. *Annual Review of Anthropology* 8: 161–205.
Zonabend, F.
    1996   An Anthropological Perspective on Kinship and the Family. Pp. 25–39 in vol. 1 of *Distant Worlds, Ancient Worlds: A History of the Family*, ed. A. Burguière et al. Trans. S. H. Tenison, R. Morris, and A. Wilson. Cambridge, Mass.: Belknap.

The Clan-Based Economy of Biblical Israel

Baruch A. Levine

Department of Bible and Ancient Near Eastern Studies
New York University

Introduction

Much has been said about kinship as a dominant feature of the Israelite societies, north and south, of biblical times. The clan, or "sib," as it has been called, was the salient socioeconomic realization of kinship in biblical Israel. One's status, rights, prerogatives, and obligations of all sorts are based on one's affiliation as a member of a family or clan; in other words, they are based on who one's relatives are and who one's forebears were, primarily consanguineously (blood-related), but at times also affinally (related by marriage). When kinship is operative, the larger society is usually configured as a network of kinship groups of various circumferences, and even the nation, in its totality, may be regarded as a single encompassing kinship group. Lineage is the defining diachronic feature of kinship groups, and at least a decided preference for clan endogamy is the defining synchronic feature. The patriarchal narratives of the book of Genesis provide a significant illustration of the kinship principle, because they relate how brides were sought from the ancestral clan back in Haran (Genesis 24; 28–29).

It has been recognized that there is a fictive, or metaphorical, aspect to some of the expressions of kinship in biblical literature, and furthermore, that not every aspect of Israelite societies can be explained in terms of kinship. Yet there are many areas in which real kinship was operative. As an example of contrasts, consider the following: the reference to the Israelite people (*benê Yiśrā'ēl*) collectively as one of the *mišpāḥôt*, "clans, sibs, extended families," of the earth strikes us as figurative in Amos 3:1–2, where the prophet imputes collective responsibility to the entire nation and its leaders:

> Heed this oracle that Yahweh has spoken regarding you, O people of Israel;
> regarding the entire clan (*mišpāḥâ*) that I brought up from the land of Egypt:
> only you have I acknowledged of all the clans of the earth (*mišpeḥôt hā'adāmâ*).
> This is why I shall call you to account for all your iniquities.

However, other uses of the term *mišpāḥâ* in more discrete frames of reference is surely realistic. The most prominent is the economic context, in which the term relates to land ownership or land tenure in a predominantly agrarian economy; or, as some prefer, in a dimorphic economy, in which pastoral pursuits also produce wealth and goods. There is nothing fictive about the basic role of kinship in biblical legislation governing the inheritance of land, the restriction of its alienation outside the clan, and the pledging of land to debt. Certain narratives involving the disposition of clan property also exhibit a strong element of realism, and the same could be said for biblical prophecy and wisdom in their references to property and wealth.

I. Methodology

Before attempting to describe the clan economy of ancient Israel as we know it, we must clarify a methodological principle: one could (and many do) attempt to explain the economy of biblical societies in terms of traditional tribal, or clannish, patterns of social and political organization—that is, to identify kinship as the organizing social principle, and economic policy as its result. It would be preferable, however, to reverse the priority and explain the predominance of kinship groupings in terms of the economic policies and objectives that they served and abetted. Such kinship patterns, however they originated, persisted because they were suitable to agrarian societies; they were effective in structuring production and consumption. It would be inaccurate, therefore, to view economic policy, in the first instance, as merely the consequence of a set kinship pattern.

It is important to note that the study of ancient economies has generally lagged behind other disciplines, such as archaeology and history, literary-textual study and linguistics, sociology, anthropology, politics, and, especially, when speaking of the Hebrew Bible, the field of religion. This lag is even more observable in any comparison of Western scholarship with Soviet scholarship, which, especially since World War II and mainly for political reasons, focused on economic agendas in the study of ancient societies. The picture is rapidly changing as Western scholars begin to realize the extent of their neglect of these very agendas.

II. The Nature of the Evidence for Biblical Israel

Let me begin by discussing the nature of the available evidence on the clan-based economy of biblical societies, and in so doing, emphasize the severe limitations of this evidence. Generally speaking, we lack external written evidence for the biblical period, which would have to be in the form of Hebrew epigraphy, of which very little has been discovered until now. As a consequence, we are almost totally reliant on the biblical record and on comparative materials from neighboring, and even somewhat distant, lands. Given this situation, the problem becomes one of evaluating the realism of the biblical record; and this is a very subtle scholarly enterprise, since there are considerable inconsistencies and even disagreements within the Bible itself. There is no escaping the need to deal with the literary history of diverse biblical texts through source criticism, although most archaeologists and many of those who currently adduce social models for biblical Israel tend to disregard this caveat.

Material culture must also be studied with a view toward arriving at certain conclusions about society and economy, and indeed archaeologists are of late showing greater interest in the economic implications of their discoveries, although there is a long way to go to affect a proper synthesis. To observe just how the clan operated as a productive and marketing unit, we would need reliable methods for estimating not only population density in local areas, but the sizes of farms and groves under cultivation. We should be able to map agricultural and horticultural patterns on the ground, and to know more about both urban and village life and the demographic intersections of the clan with administrative bureaucracies in population centers. Finally, we should know more about marketing. A new study by Schloen, entitled *The House of the Father as Fact and Symbol* (2001), which synthesizes extensive archaeological, economic, and textual evidence from Ugarit and other areas of the ancient Near East, is of great help in addressing these and related problems. Schloen employs social theory in the process, which, together with an impressive comparative reach, renders his work exceedingly relevant to a realistic understanding of the role of clan-based units in ancient Israel.

III. Biblical Terminology and Historical Reality

Bêt ʾāb as Clan

We begin by offering the judgment that as far as biblical kinship terminology is concerned, *ʿam*, "patrilineal kinship group," *mišpāḥâ*, "clan, sib," *bêt ʾāb*, "patrilineal 'house,'" and *ʾelep*, "clan," represent more-realistic categories for investigation than "tribe," Hebrew *šēbeṭ* and *maṭṭeh*. It is not that there were no tribes in ancient Israel, but rather that the textual sources on the subject of tribes are somewhat confusing and at times exhibit a degree of artificiality. Furthermore, some of the names of the tribes, the etymologies of which often elude us, are more likely to be names of regions and territories in the first instance, rather than eponyms or social groupings. Was *Yehûdâ* (Judah) in the first instance the name of a person or family, or of a region of Canaan? According to Mic 5:1, the inhabitants of Bethlehem of the district of Ephrath are "the youngest (= least) of the clans of Judah" (*ṣāʿîr liheyôt beʾalpê Yehûdâ*), suggesting that Judah was the name of a region, in which other towns and their resident clans were more notable than Bethlehem. This is, after all, the point of the prophecy.

The evidence bearing on clan terminology is less ambiguous. A West Semitic cognate of Hebrew *bêt ʾāb* (*bīt abi*) occurs in the royal inscription of Idrimi, the ruler of Aleppo around the middle of the second millennium B.C.E. (Kempinsky and Naʾaman 1973). Hebrew *ʾelep* is matched by a Ugaritic cognate, *ulp* (*KTU²* 1.40), and the root *š-p-ḥ*, from which Hebrew *mišpāḥâ* (and *šipḥâ*, "family slave"?) also occurs in Ugaritic, in clear family contexts (*KTU²* 1.16). The term *ʿam* (variant *ḥam*) has cognates in most of the Semitic languages, and the most convincing demonstration of its kinship matrix lies in the fact that it also means "paternal uncle, kinsman" (Koehler and Baumgartner 1983: 791–94).

Although we do not have clear and consistent definitions of these socioeconomic units, we are able to define the biblical *mišpāḥâ* maximally as an extended family, often spanning three generations and usually including cousins and uncles, and perhaps others as well. Most of what we know in this regard is in the nature of inferential evidence, coming from what I would classify as late biblical texts, priestly sources such as Leviticus 18 and 20 on marriage and incest; Leviticus 21 on the funerary restriction of priestly families; and Numbers 27 and 36 on inheritance. One could also factor in the somewhat earlier Levirate law of Deuteronomy 25 and its reflex, the story of Ruth. It must be recognized, however, that the reader cannot ascertain from the relevant texts just how extended or how limited the projected *mišpāḥâ* was in each case.

The term *bêt ʾāb* in its early usage is patrilocal, not merely patrilineal, and it is predicated on ownership of a shared clan residence or residences (the strict sense of the term *bayit*), along with shared, arable land often attached or adjacent. Whatever we may conclude about the currency of matriarchal clans in biblical Israel, and there is some evidence of such, it is doubtful whether the construction *bêt ʾimmî*, "my mother's house" (Cant 3:4; 8:2), is a genuine counterpart of *bêt ʾābî*. More likely, it merely refers to the home of the young woman; it is where she brings her beloved, and in Cant 3:4, *bêt ʾimmî* is parallel with *ḥeder hôrātî*, "the chamber of my parent."

It occurs to me that the West Semitic *bêt ʾāb* correlates with what has been termed the "institutional household," a socioeconomic unit of great antiquity, operative most prominently in southern Mesopotamia and elsewhere. It is a socioeconomic structure better accommodated to city-state networks than to centralized kingdoms. This unit, usually referred to in Greek as *ôikos*, has been recently discussed by Lamberg-Karlovsky, who describes the institutional household as follows:

> The household may be defined as a residential group that forms a social as well as an economic unit of production and consumption. Members of the household consisted of kin and clients providing voluntary labor. (Lamberg-Karlovsky 1999: 168)

Lamberg-Karlovsky goes on to dispute the often-held notion that such units as the institutional household, which is based on status, inevitably gave way to governmental bureaucracies based on merit, insisting that in fact they not only antedated such centralized structures in many areas of the ancient Near East, but continued to operate fully long after the bureaucracies established their hold. As he puts it:

> It is important to recognize that throughout the vast majority of Near Eastern antiquity the private household remained the primary focus of economic activity. (Lamberg-Karlovsky 1999: 183)

Bêt ʾab as Land-Owner

Whereas the term *mišpāḥâ* is purely relational, or lineage-based, and does not of itself establish whether ownership of land is involved, one would normally apply the term *bêt ʾāb* to a kinship group that did indeed own land on which it resided, as noted above. This is brought out rather subtly by the incident reported in Genesis 31 concerning the daughters of Laban, Rachel and Leah. As is often the case, variations on the theme define the limits of the theme, and this applies with respect to the biblical *naḥalâ*. After Jacob's flocks experience miraculous increment, Jacob decides on immediate flight to Canaan and summons his wives out to the countryside where the flocks are gathered. His two wives have the following to say to him:

> Do we still retain an estate share (*ḥēleq wenaḥalâ*) in our patrilineal "house" (*bĕbêt ʾābînû*)? Have we not been regarded as outsiders (*nokriyyôt*) by him, for he has sold us out! Moreover, he has surely eaten up our silver! So it is that all of the wealth that God has extricated from our father (surely) belongs to us and to our sons. Now, then, all that God has commanded you, do! (Gen 31:14–16)

By way of explanation—we have translated the ambiguous *bêt ʾābînû* as the *terminus technicus* "in our *bêt ʾāb*," in view of the immediate context. By leaving home with their husband, who took all his accumulated flocks with him, Laban's daughters had angered their father to the point of disowning them. We are to understand that at the time of their marriage Laban would have given his daughters silver in place of the usual *naḥalâ*, consisting of clan-owned land, because they were following their husband to another country. However, because of the conflict between Jacob and Laban, Rachel and Leah were dealt out of their *naḥalâ*, so that all of their wealth ended up consisting of the flocks that Jacob had spirited away from Laban's grasp. Rachel and Leah, if they had entertained any qualms about how Jacob had gained control of the flocks, were now free of these qualms and eager to own the flocks. As for the term *ʾelep*, it is harder to define specifically, especially since it is homonymous with the word for "thousand." As a socioeconomic term, Hebrew *ʾelep* represents an extension of the meaning "bull, ox," thus meaning initially "the clan perceived as herd," thereby reflecting a pastoral economy. The Ugaritic evidence, recently investigated by Shedletsky and Levine (1999), correlates well with the biblical, showing how *ʾelep/ulp* came to designate other than kinship groupings as well.

Premonarchic and Monarchic Clan Traditions

To illustrate our judgment that there is more discrete biblical information about clans than there is about tribes, I will compare two sets of biblical traditions. Traditions that relate that the tribes of Israel were allotted territories in the Promised Land at the time of a unified original settlement of the entire land of Canaan are probably less realistic than the Caleb traditions, for example, that relate how a hero was granted a territory in the Judean Hills as a reward for his role in the conquest of that region of the land. This is partially because the Caleb traditions reflect the known practice of royal grants. Thus Joshua, acting in *loco regis*, was said to have granted to this uniquely loyal head of a clan, Caleb, perhaps only secondarily affiliated as a Judean, a sizable territory, some of which Caleb proceeded to grant to his daughter on the occasion of her marriage to a younger conquering hero (Joshua 15; Judges 1). Also note that, in an early biblical source, Judg 17:7, *Yehûdâ* (Judah) is termed a *mišpāḥâ*, not a tribe. This is not the only instance in which the terminology overlaps.

It is important to emphasize that land owned by the *mišpāḥâ* (or the *bêt ʾāb* or *ʾelep*) was private only in the sense that it did not belong collectively to the tribe as a whole, to the realm in the office of the king, or to a temple or town. This land was not individually owned, however, and was not free from clan obligations and restrictions regarding its alienation (Levine 1996). The David stories in the books of Samuel refer to royal grants of land as a means of generating this kind of nonpublic property. A cycle of such stories centers on a steward named Ziba, a man of large family and considerable wealth (2 Samuel 9; 16; 19). In 1 Sam 22:7–8, Saul taunts some of his fellow Benjaminites who had sided with David, as follows:

> Hear me, sons of Benjamin! Will the son of Jesse indeed grant all of you fields and vineyards; will he appoint all of you commanders of thousands and commanders of hundreds? Is this why you have all conspired against me?

There is a similar allusion to royal grants in the words of two insurgents against Moses, whose roles are often modeled after those of a king, in Num 16:14:

> You have not yet brought us to a land flowing with milk and sap, or granted us fields or vineyards as our domain (*naḥalâ*).

The other aspect of the subject, royal attempts to expropriate clan-owned land, is also instructive. The most famous case is that of Naboth of Jezreel in his encounter with Ahab and his queen, Jezebel, as related in 1 Kings 21. The story seems to be predicated on the right of a landowner to refuse to sell to the king his "ancestral estate" (in Hebrew *naḥalāt ʾābôt*). Reference to *ʾābôt* holds the clue, and it tells us that clan land was involved. The king of Israel could not simply expropriate such property because he craved it; he had to resort to subterfuge. Yet the prophet Samuel cautions the people regarding the perils of having a king:

> He will confiscate your fields and your best vineyards and olive trees so as to grant them to his courtiers, and he will exact a tithe of your grain and vineyards and give that to his personal guards and courtiers. (1 Sam 8:14–15)

These cases may be classified as inferential evidence because they focus on the rights of the heads of families to their land. In the first instance, land belonged to the head of the family, who could allocate it to his sons and daughters under circumscribed conditions. The conclusion of the 1 Sam 8:14–15 statement refers to the right of a king to impose taxes. The above sources are suggestively monarchic in their configuration, and they illustrate the characteristic conflicts between the prerogatives of royal authority and the rights of families and clans. When the institutional households of a city-state polity came under the hegemony of a more centralized royal authority, there was inevitable tension. Some of this tension is reflected in the sparse Hebrew epigraphy that has come to light, in which estate managers and others complain of tax collectors, magistrates, and administrative/military officials, such as the *śar*. The Lachish and Arad ostraca provide ample evidence of such tension.

A good deal of the information available on the clan in biblical times comes from literature purporting to represent the premonarchic period of Israelite history. Much depends, therefore, on our judgments as to the authenticity of biblical traditions on the so-called tribal confederation of early Israel, as well as those regarding the role of the clan in this context. For example, when Gideon doubts his capacity to lead an army against the Midianites, he expresses himself as follows:

> With what can I rescue Israel? Behold, my clan (*ʾelep*) is the poorest in Manasseh, and I am the youngest in my patrilineal "house" (*bêt ʾābî*). (Judg 6:15)

It is risky to attempt to squeeze socioeconomic information out of this single statement. Here Manasseh could represent either the name of a tribe or of a region, or both. Yet one could take this statement as an indication that the clan participated as a unit in military ventures and bore its own costs; and furthermore, that the leading family of the clan had first access to its wealth. There was a hierarchy of families within the clan, just as there was, presumably, a hierarchy of clans within the tribe (note the reference to *śar hāʾelep*, "commander of the clan," in 1 Sam 17:18). In 1 Sam 9:21, Saul characterizes his own inferior status in terms similar to those used by Gideon. The prophet Samuel tells Saul that he needn't worry about the lost asses, because he and his *bêt 'āb* are about to come into possession of great wealth. Saul at first doesn't understand what the prophet means and replies:

> I am only a Benjaminite, from the smallest of the Israelite tribes, and my *mišpāḥâ* is the least of all the *mišpāḥôt* of the tribe of Benjamin, so why have you said these things to me?

As we have seen, the early material in the book of Judges, to the extent that we are able to isolate it textually, gives the impression of being realistic regarding the role of the clan. The Song of Deborah speaks of the *'ammāmîm*, "clans," of Benjamin, *'ammāmîm* being a diminutive form of the term *'am*, which essentially designates a kinship group of consanguineal relatives. When the Israelites are collectively designated *'am* by extension, the clear intent is to adduce patrilineal kinship for the entire nation. No matter how fictive or metaphorical the usage of *'am* becomes, the original matrix continues to peer through. Thus a study of the term *'am hā'āreṣ* in such contexts as Abraham's purchase of land in Canaan indicates that patrilineal clans are envisioned as owning such lands and that it is up to these heads of clans to approve sales. Similarly, Joseph, after confiscating the produce of the fat years, ends up redistributing it to the Egyptian *'am hā'āreṣ*, namely, the land-owning clans. There is a degree of humor in the fact that biblical narrators assume that other societies are managed in the same way as theirs.

The Song of Deborah also mentions the Machirite clan, well known in the Transjordanian traditions. It is also true, of course, that the same Song of Deborah mentions many names elsewhere known as designating tribes, although most would agree that in the statement "Gilead is settled in Transjordan," the ballad's author is transparently using the name of a known region as an eponym. This probably applies as well to other names occurring in the Song of Deborah. Although the social portrait of premonarchic Israel in Judges is a mixed bag, it is possible to state that it endorses the realism of the clan as a basic unit of society. Mention should be made of a clan celebration called *zebaḥ mišpāḥâ*, "the sacred meal of the clan" (1 Sam 20:20). Jonathan makes excuses for David's absence at a New Moon feast hosted by Saul, saying that David told him he was returning home to Bethlehem for such an occasion to see "my kinsmen" (*'eḥḥay*).

Postexilic Clan Fragmentation

It is probably reasonable to assume that the clan continued to serve as the basic economic unit in biblical societies throughout the First Temple period and that clans still owned most of the arable land in common, either within a larger tribal framework or, as suggested above, within an administrative, regional districting system. The clan system seems to have broken down to a degree in the postexilic period, when the individual landowner comes into prominence. This conclusion is based on the stated relationships and duties among members of the same clan toward one another, leading us to reiterate that most of the legal sources on the role of the *mišpāḥâ* and the attendant obligations of clan members are preserved in Torah literature, and at that, in the priestly strata of this corpus. The limited historical indicators present in the historical books are absent from Torah literature, and we are on uncertain ground even in determining whether a given legal or narrative source in the Torah is pre- or postexilic, much less in establishing its precise *Sitz im Leben*.

It is my view, based on independent considerations, that the priestly strata of Torah literature were composed in the postexilic, Achaemenid period and in curious ways reflect the fragmenting of the clan, against the background, still visible in these late sources, of the earlier monarchic periods of preexilic history.

In contrast, an old practice still operative in postexilic times was the sacred duty to restore the blood of a murdered clan relative. There is a remarkable episode reported in 2 Samuel 14 that is relevant to this point. In a melodramatic ruse, a disguised woman entraps King David with a tale of fratricide and clan retaliation. The entire scene is intended to bring home to David the consequences of his continuing refusal to allow the return of his seditious son, Absalom. Following is what the woman has to say:

> Verily, I am a widowed woman, my husband having died. Your servant had two sons who did combat in the field, and there was none to keep them apart, so that one struck the other and killed him. And behold, the entire *mišpāḥâ* rose up against your servant, saying: "Hand over the fratricide and let us put him to death in place of the life of his brother whom he killed." Thus they would eliminate the heir, as well, and extinguish my estate that remained, not affording my husband a surviving name on the face of the earth. (2 Sam 14:5b–7)

If Jeremiah 32 is truly near exilic in provenience and not a later insertion, we have inferential evidence of the duty of a *dôd*, an uncle or perhaps cousin, to redeem the land of his relative that had been pledged to debt. The report is replete with legal terminology, indicating that the practice of clan redemption of mortgaged land was a reality.

A study of debt in biblical Israel once again focuses our attention on the primacy of arable land in the biblical economies. With the exception of debt incurred by craftsmen or merchants, virtually all debt was land related. Landowners would borrow seasonally to acquire seed and implements and to pay laborers, and they hoped to repay their indebtedness after the harvest. A bad harvest, or natural disasters and the effects of war, would often make repayment impossible, leading to indenture and the loss of clan land by foreclosure.

When I say that the clan was fragmented in the postexilic period, I am thinking of the abolition of the sabbatical moratorium on debt and indenture, a change in the law introduced in Leviticus 25 and echoed in Leviticus 27. This change worked in favor of the individual creditor against the interests of the clan. Note the curious provision in Lev 25:47 that the duty to come to the aid of a clan relative facing foreclosure obtained only in cases in which land had been mortgaged to non-Israelites. Otherwise, if he had the resources or if a *gōʾēl* was willing to act as redeemer, he was guaranteed the right to redeem the forfeited land. If not, he had to await the Jubilee, which he might never live to see. Yet one so fortunate as to be able to return to his *ʾaḥuzzâ* would also be returning to his *mišpāḥâ* (Lev 25:10), the people who owned, or had owned, the *ʾaḥuzzâ*. Also noteworthy is the introduction of relationship terms that are not reflective, even fictively, of clan identity. The most notable of these is *ʿamît*, which could very well be rendered "fellow citizen" (namely, a person encountered in daily life), a term that occurs only in the priestly sources of Leviticus and in Zech 13:7, at the tail end of Second Zechariah. We thus observe indications of three successive phases in the economic role of the clan in biblical literature: (1) the premonarchic phase; (2) the monarchic phase; and (3) the post-exilic, imperial phase. Of these, the Persian imperial phase offers the best chance of reconstruction. If only we had biblical information on marketing and trade on the part of the clan . . . but there is little that can be discerned. It is realistic, in most cases, to assume that the functional, productive unit was also the marketing unit.

Conclusion

It would be wrong to overemphasize the economic role of the clan to the neglect of the economic role of the government, in all its manifestations. The role of temples must also be factored in. Much of the epigraphic evidence that survives is more informative about these societal structures simply because it was produced by such agencies in the first place. The Bible's interest in kinship, clan, and land ownership is understandable, however, in terms of its own agendas, which were primarily social and religious, in affirming the peoplehood of Israel and its common history and destiny in the land. The most prominent feature of biblical traditions in this regard is the primacy of patrilineage in establishing ownership of land. The major variable in the equation is political development, which brought the land owned by families and clans (and maybe tribes) under ever-increasing governmental control. Yet it would be a mistake to underestimate the power of real kinship, or to fail to appreciate the strength of the kinship metaphor applied to all of Israel. If the most powerful affinal metaphor in biblical literature is marital infidelity, the most powerful consanguineal metaphor is the kinship of the clan.

References

Kempinsky, A., and Na'aman, N.
  1973   The Idrimi Inscription Reconsidered. Pp. 211–20 in *Excavations and Studies: Essays in Honor of Professor Shemuel Yeivin*, ed. Y. Aharoni. Ramat Aviv: Tel Aviv University.
Koehler, L., and Baumgartner, W.
  1983   *Hebräisches und Aramäisches Lexikon zum Alten Testament* 3. Leiden: Brill.
KTU²
  1995   *The Cuneiform Alphabetic Texts from Ugarit* (*KTU* 2nd ed.), by M. Dietrich, O. Loretz, and J. Sanmartín. Münster: Ugarit Verlag.
Lamberg-Karlovsky, C. C.
  1999   Households, Land Tenure, and Communications Systems in the 6th–4th Millennia of Greater Mesopotamia. Pp. 167–201 in *Urbanization and Land Ownership in the Ancient Near East*, ed. M. Hudson and B. A. Levine. Cambridge, Mass.: Peabody Museum.
Levine, B. A.
  1996   Farewell to the Ancient Near East: Evaluating Biblical References to Ownership of Land in Comparative Perspective. Pp. 223–46 in *Privatization in the Ancient Near East and Classical World*, ed. M. Hudson and B. A. Levine. Cambridge, Mass.: Peabody Museum.
Schloen, J. D.
  2001   *The House of the Father as Fact and Symbol: Patrimonialism in Ugarit and the Ancient Near East.* Studies in the Archaeology and History of the Levant 2. Winona Lake, Ind.: Eisenbrauns.
Shedletsky, L., and Levine, B. A.
  1999   The *mšr* of the Sons and Daughters of Ugarit (KTU 1.40). *Revue Biblique* 100: 321–45.

At Home with the Goddess

Susan Ackerman

Department of Religion, Dartmouth College
Hanover, New Hampshire

For most English speakers, the word "home," although it can mean a dwelling of any sort, typically has more intimate and familial connotations: "home" is the residence that houses our closest relatives and where we keep our most important possessions; the shelter that serves us as a refuge and that can even offer us happiness and love; the place, according to Robert Frost's almost hackneyed description, "where, when you have to go there, they have to take you in" (1995: 43). Biblical Hebrew has no precise analog; *bayit*, "house," comes closest, especially in those passages (592 according to the count in Brown, Driver, and Briggs 1980: 109b) where *bayit* describes a "household" or "family." However, unlike the English "home," *bayit* was commonly used by the ancient Israelites to refer also to houses that were not private family residences: for example, the temple or "house" of Yahweh in Jerusalem or the palace or "house" of the king.

In this paper, on domestic goddess worship, I propose to take my cue from this Hebrew usage and survey our evidence for goddess worship both in private family domiciles and in more public "homes," such as Yahweh's Jerusalem temple, and also Yahweh's Northern Kingdom shrines and the royal palaces of Jerusalem and Samaria. I undertake this multidimensional review because I believe that there are some continuities worth considering between our evidence for goddess worship in temple and palace locations, on the one hand, and in private, familial settings, on the other. Thus, after discussing, respectively, temple-based goddess worship, goddess worship in royal palaces, and goddess cults in private homes, I will conclude with some remarks on the interrelationship between the three.

I. At Home with the Goddess in the Temple

For students of ancient Israelite religion, the 1975–76 discoveries at the northeastern Sinai site of Kuntillet ʿAjrûd, of inscriptions and also perhaps iconography that paired the Israelite god Yahweh with "his *ʾăšērâ*," were nothing less than astonishing (Meshel and Meyers 1976; Meshel 1976; 1978a; 1978b; 1979). But I have come to think that equally astonishing was the way in which those discoveries caused both archaeologists and biblical scholars to return to and rethink data that were already in our possession. For archaeologists, this primarily meant returning to the 8th-century B.C.E. inscription that Dever had published from the Judean site of Khirbet el-Qôm (1969–70) and rereading that inscription so that it, too, contained a reference to Yahweh and "his *ʾăšērâ*" (Lemaire 1977; 1984a; 1984b; Dever 1982: 40; 1983: 570, 583 n. 17; 1984: 22). For biblical scholars, the process of reevaluation required returning to the biblical text and rethinking the significance of the 40 some occurrences of the term *ʾăšērâ* (and the related terms *ʾăšērîm* and *ʾăšērôt*) found within the Hebrew Bible's pages. More specifically, biblical scholars found themselves reassessing whether the biblical descriptions of cult activities involving the term *ʾăšērâ*—descriptions that had generally been taken as evidence of foreign and therefore heterodox beliefs and practices that had been imported into Israel—might instead signify that, at least for some ancient Israelites, during at least some points in Israelite history, worship involving this *ʾăšērâ* was a perfectly appropriate part of the Yahwistic cult. Especially relevant to this section of the paper are biblical passages that might suggest that worship involving this *ʾăšērâ* was for some ancient Israelites, during at least some points in ancient Israelite history, a perfectly appropriate part of the Yahwistic *temple* cult.

Before turning to these texts, however, I shall comment on the translation of Hebrew *ʾăšērâ*. As is well known, there is no consensus among scholars on this matter. For example, while many students of the Kuntillet ʿAjrûd and Khirbet el-Qôm materials have argued that the description of Yahweh's *ʾăšērâ* in these inscriptions is to be taken as a reference to Yahweh alongside his goddess consort, Asherah, others—concerned about the grammatical improbability of a pronominal suffix on a proper name ("his *ʾăšērâ*")— have insisted that *ʾăšērâ* in the inscriptions must be taken as a common noun. But a common noun with what meaning? "Shrine," as originally proposed by Lipiński (1972)? "The female aspect of Yahweh," reified and given a separate identity, as suggested by both Miller (1986: 246) and McCarter (1987: 149)? A cult object called the *ʾăšērâ*, which is the meaning of the term *ʾăšērâ* that is found most frequently in the Hebrew Bible? My own preference is for either the first or fourth of these alternatives: to understand Yahweh's *ʾăšērâ* at ʿAjrûd and el-Qôm either as a reference to Yahweh's goddess consort Asherah or to the cult object known from the Hebrew Bible as the *ʾăšērâ*. I would also follow the biblical witness in describing this cult object as an image that was in the shape of a stylized wooden pole or tree. Deut 16:21 mentions "planting" (*nāṭaʿ*) the *ʾăšērâ*; elsewhere in the Hebrew Bible, the cult object is "made" (*ʿāśâ*), "built" (*bānâ*), "stood up" (*ʿāmad*), or "erected" (*hiṣṣîb*). When destroyed, the *ʾăšērâ* is "burned" (*bīʿēr* or *śārap*), "cut down" (*kārat*), "hewn down" (*gādaʿ*), "uprooted" (*nātaš*), or "broken" (*šibbēr*).[1]

Moreover, while we have to acknowledge that the image of the sacred tree is ubiquitous in Semitic art, and thus admit that it is often difficult to identify such trees with one particular god or goddess, it is nevertheless the case that our West Semitic evidence more often than not argues for the association of sacred trees with the Canaanite mother goddess Asherah. Hestrin (1987a; 1987b) has advanced perhaps the most persuasive arguments in support of this position in her descriptions of (1) the late-13th-century Lachish Ewer; (2) the several Late Bronze Age gold and electrum pendants depicting a naked female that come from Ugarit and other sites in the northern Levant; and (3) the 10th-century Taʿanach cult stand. Regarding the ewer, Hestrin points out the way in which it pairs sacred tree iconography with a dedicatory inscription to Elat, an epithet of Asherah well known from both Ugaritic and Phoenician sources. Regarding the gold and electrum pen-

---

1. The LXX, moreover, most commonly translates the Hebrew *ʾăšērâ* as *alsos*, "grove," and twice as *dendra*, "trees," and the Latin similarly reads *lucus*, "grove," or *nemus*, "wood," "grove," for Hebrew *ʾăšērâ*.

dants, she argues that because many of the images found on them—especially lions, snakes, and the female figure's Hathor headdress—are frequently associated with Asherah,[2] we should conclude that the pendants are depictions of that goddess and should further understand that the stylized branch or tree often etched in the figure's navel is a representation of Asherah's sacred tree. Regarding the Taʿanach cult stand, Hestrin suggests that the nude female of the bottom register is Asherah, given that this figure is flanked by the lions characteristically associated with the goddess, and that in Register 3, therefore, where we again have the flanking lions, we should also read the central figure as a representation of Asherah, although this time depicted in the form of the sacred tree.[3]

Not to belabor the obvious, but what all these data suggest to me, and I believe to the majority of commentators, is that the ancient Israelites understood the term *ʾăšērâ* both as a proper name, the name of the Canaanite mother goddess Asherah, and as a common noun designating an object in the shape of a wooden pole or tree that represented the goddess Asherah in the cult.[4] Indeed, I believe that the ancient Israelites would have made little differentiation between these two meanings, which is to say that in ancient Israelite religion, the cult symbol of the goddess would have readily been perceived as the goddess herself. As Day has pointed out (1992: 486a), the strategy of designating a cult object by the name of the deity it represents is attested elsewhere in West Semitic religion: thus Philo of Byblos reports that the Phoenicians "consecrated steles and staves" in the names of their deities (Eusebius, *Praeparatio Evangelica* 1.9.29 [Attridge and Oden 1981: 33]). Within Israelite religion, we can compare the ancient Israelite understanding of Yahweh's primary symbol in the League cult and in the Jerusalem temple, the ark, in order to see how close the relationship was between cult object and deity. Num 10:35–36, the so-called "Song of the Ark," illustrates perfectly the simultaneity of symbol and god in Israelite imagination: "Whenever *the ark* set out, Moses said, 'Arise, O *Yahweh*'"; similarly, "when *it* [the ark] rested, he [Moses] said, 'Return, O *Yahweh*.'" Note, too, 1 Kgs 12:28, where Jeroboam is described as identifying cult symbols with the deity the symbols represent when he says of the bull *images* of Dan and Bethel that they are "your *gods*, O Israel, who brought you out of Egypt." We would expect that the *ʾăšērâ*, the cult symbol, and Asherah, the goddess, would also have been understood by the ancient Israelites as essentially one and the same.[5] I noted above that I would favor a translation of the phrase "Yahweh's *ʾăšērâ*" in the Kuntillet ʿAjrûd and Khirbet el-Qôm inscriptions that *either* took the reference to be to Yahweh's goddess consort Asherah *or* to the cult object known from the Hebrew Bible as the *ʾăšērâ*. But it would perhaps be a little more

---

2. On Asherah's association with lions, see, e.g., *CAT* 1.3.5.37; 1.4.1.8; 1.4.2.25–26 (Dietrich, Loretz, and Sanmartín 1995), where the children of Asherah are called her "pride of lions," *šbrt ary*. On the goddess's association with snakes, see, e.g., *KAI* 89 (Donner and Röllig 1962), a Punic devotional tablet on which Asherah bears the epithet *ḥwt*, which may mean "serpent," cognate with Old Aramaic *ḥwh* (Sefire I, A, 31 = *KAI* 222; Donner and Röllig 1962), later Aramaic *ḥiwâ*, *ḥiwyāʾ*, *ḥewyāʾ*, and Arabic *ḥayya*.

3. Oden has further proposed that the caduceus imagery associated in a later period with Phoenician-Punic Tannit, whom he identifies primarily with Asherah, had its origins in a depiction of a date palm tree that, over time, became increasingly stylized and abstracted (1977: 149–55).

4. Cf. Smith 1990: 80–94; see also the useful survey of scholarly positions found in Day 1986: 398–404.

5. See similarly the discussion in Olyan 1988: 31–32 regarding bull iconography in Near Eastern religion and the ability of this iconography to function as both the symbol of deity and the deity himself (Baal Haddu, El, Yahweh).

accurate for me to suggest that my preference is for *both/and*, taking the meanings "Asherah the goddess" and "*ʾăšērâ* the cult object" to be embedded in one another.

It is Olyan (1988), writing in the light of the Kuntillet ʿAjrûd and Khirbet el-Qôm discoveries, who has most persuasively and thoroughly argued for the presence of the cult object of the *ʾăšērâ* in Yahweh's Jerusalem temple. Olyan in particular points out the fact that each of Judah's reformer kings, Asa, Hezekiah, and Josiah, is said to have removed an *ʾăšērâ* image from Jerusalem, which suggests to him that in times other than these moments of reformation—that is, throughout most of the 9th, 8th, and 7th centuries B.C.E.—Asherah's cult object stood uncontested in Yahweh's *cult city* of Jerusalem. We are, moreover, explicitly told that the 7th-century Jerusalem *ʾăšērâ*, the one that Josiah removed, stood in Yahweh's *temple* in Jerusalem (2 Kgs 23:6); we are also told in 2 Kgs 23:4 and 7 that the temple furnishings of Josiah's day included vessels made for Asherah and that the temple held within its walls houses[6] in which women wove garments[7] for Asherah (which I, along with most commentators, take to mean that these women wove clothing that would have been draped over a cult statue dedicated to the goddess Asherah).[8] This evidence of Asherah's presence in the 7th-century temple of Josiah's day leads Olyan to suggest (1988: 9), and I agree, that the 8th-century *ʾăšērâ* Hezekiah is said to have removed from Jerusalem also stood in Yahweh's temple (2 Kgs 18:4). I have similarly argued elsewhere (1993: 390; 1998: 144) that the 9th-century *ʾăšērâ* Asa destroyed stood in Yahweh's temple, and this because that *ʾăšērâ* was said to have been made by Asa's queen mother Maʿacah (1 Kgs 15:13), and where would Maʿacah, as a member of the royal court, most naturally place her *ʾăšērâ* but in the temple that was immediately proximate to the family's palace? Thus, while our evidence for the 9th and 8th centuries is not as conclusive as it is for the 7th, the data still suggest that at several points during the Iron II period, Yahweh shared his "home" in Jerusalem with the goddess Asherah.

In general, the biblical record, given its Judahite bias and perspective, tells us comparatively little about religious practices in Israel's Northern Kingdom, which means that we can say comparatively less about Asherah's presence at Yahweh's two Northern "homes" of Dan and Bethel. Only for Bethel do we have any specific evidence, and that only for the 7th century, 100 years after the fall of the Northern Kingdom. Thus, 2 Kgs 23:15 reports that the Southern king Josiah, in the zealousness of his reforms, crossed the old Northern–Southern boundary line to destroy the *ʾăšērâ* that stood in the Bethel sanctuary. Still, Olyan (1988: 6–9) has again led the way in suggesting that Asherah worship was, for many, an accepted part of the Yahwism of the Northern Kingdom throughout its existence and that an *ʾăšērâ* image would therefore have been expected at Yahweh's Northern temples.

---

6. The LXX reads *oikon* (singular).

7. Reading *battîm*, cognate with Arabic *batt*, "woven garment," for the MT *bāttîm*, the plural of *bayit*, "house," as originally proposed by Šanda (1912: 344; pointed out by Day 1986: 407) and by Driver (1936: 107; pointed out by Gray 1964: 664 note b, and by Cogan and Tadmor 1988: 286). This revocalization is supported by the Lucianic recension of the LXX, which reads *stolas*, "garment, robe."

8. The practice of clothing cult statues is known from the Bible (Jer 10:9; Ezek 16:18) (Gressmann 1924: 325–26, pointed out by Cogan and Tadmor 1988: 286). It is also attested elsewhere in the Semitic and eastern Mediterranean worlds (Oppenheim 1949, as again pointed out by Cogan and Tadmor 1988: 286). It is finally interesting to note that among the archaeological discoveries found at Kuntillet ʿAjrûd were many textile fragments (Meshel 1978b; Dever 1984: 29), perhaps because textiles were somehow associated with the cult activities at this site.

He notes particularly the way that Yahweh worship seems paired with Asherah worship in the Northern capital city of Samaria, as is suggested first by the Kuntillet ʿAjrûd inscription dedicated to "Yahweh of Samaria and his *ʾăšērâ*," and second by the fact that the zealous Yahwistic reformer king of the North, Jehu, allowed the *ʾăšērâ* that had previously been erected by King Ahab in Samaria to remain standing, despite Jehu's pains otherwise to remove all non-Yahwistic imagery from the Northern cult. Indeed, Olyan uses the Kuntillet ʿAjrûd evocation of "Yahweh of Samaria" to buttress older theories that argue for the presence of a Yahwistic shrine in Samaria (even though one is never mentioned explicitly in the biblical text); in his words, "the inscriptions mentioning Yahweh *šōmĕrôn* ['Yahweh of Samaria'] now make it clear that a Yahwistic sanctuary existed in Samaria." He then adds, ". . . and . . . the asherah stood in it" (1988: 35). If Olyan is correct, then Samaria offers, along with Jerusalem and Bethel, yet another example of Yahweh in his temple, "at home with the goddess."

II. At Home with the Goddess in the Palace

I have already mentioned briefly the biblical text that most clearly locates goddess worship in the royal palace in Jerusalem, namely, 1 Kgs 15:13 (paralleled by 2 Chr 15:16), which describes how Maʿacah, the queen mother or *gĕbîrâ* of King Asa (913–873 B.C.E.), was removed from her position by the king because "*ʿāśĕtâ mipleṣet lāʾăšērâ*," which I would translate as "she made an abominable image for Asherah [the goddess]" or, alternatively, as "she made an abominable image of the asherah [the cult image]."[9] In my opinion, the second translation is less satisfactory, since the reading "she made an abominable image of the asherah [the cult image]" borders on the nonsensical: what does it mean, after all, to make an image of an image?[10] Yet whichever of the two translations is preferred, I would nevertheless maintain, as above, that the sense is still the same. Maʿacah made a stylized wooden pole or tree that symbolized the Canaanite mother goddess Asherah and was consecrated to her worship.

Asa, in deposing Maʿacah from her position as queen mother, clearly indicates that he does not see the *ʾăšērâ* image or the worship of Asherah more generally as appropriate within the royal cult, and his biblical biographers agree, lauding him as one who was "faithful to Yahweh all of his days" (1 Kgs 15:14, paralleled in 2 Chr 15:17). Many modern

---

9. The specifics of the translation have been debated because the definite article prefixed to *ʾăšērâ* can be taken to preclude the understanding of *ʾăšērâ* as a proper name. But this argument is not conclusive, because the definite article can be explained as appellative, as it is elsewhere in Deuteronomistic prose (Judg 2:11, 13; 3:7; 10:6). Indeed, the Chronicler (2 Chr 15:16), by transposing the two words in question in order to read *ʿāśĕtâ lāʾăšērâ mipleṣet*, which can only be translated "she made for Asherah an abominable image," clearly suggests that his Deuteronomistic antecedent intended *ʾăšērâ* to be read as a proper name. A second problem, the meaning of *mipleṣet*, which occurs only in 1 Kgs 15:13 and in the Chronicles parallel, is more easily addressed: the root meaning of *plṣ*, "to shudder," readily suggests that this verb's nominal form should mean something like "a thing to be shuddered at"; "a horrid thing"; or, as here, "an abominable image."

10. Note, in fact, that elsewhere in Deuteronomistic prose, when *ʾăšērâ*, the image, is referred to, the noun *ʾăšērâ* typically stands alone without *mipleṣet* or a similar modifier: e.g., 1 Kgs 16:33, *wayyaʿaś ʾaḥāb ʾet-hāʾăšērâ*, "and Ahab made the asherah" (note the similar use of *ʿśh*, "to make," in both this passage and 1 Kgs 15:13, while contrasting the treatment of *ʾăšērâ* as object). I understand 2 Kgs 21:7, *pesel hāʾăšērâ*, in the same way as I have analyzed 1 Kgs 15:13 and thus would translate it as "an image of Asherah."

commentators have also followed suit, arguing that Maʿacah's worship of Asherah was a foreign and therefore heterodox element introduced by her into the Jerusalem court (e.g., Ahlström 1963: 59, 61 [who cites Albright 1946: 157–59 and Yeivin 1953: 162–64]; Spanier 1994: 194; cf. Ackroyd 1983: 255). The crucial piece of evidence that most of these commentators adduce is Maʿacah's presumed foreign ancestry, since she was apparently the granddaughter of another Maʿacah, who was brought from the court of King Talmai of Geshur to be married to King David (2 Sam 3:3, paralleled in 1 Chr 3:2). But just as we can no longer presume that the worship of Asherah was foreign to Yahwism in general, we can no longer presume it was foreign to the royal cult in particular. Indeed, given the fact that Asherah worship may have been incorporated into the temple cult of Jerusalem at several points during the Iron II period, and given that the Jerusalem temple cult and the Jerusalem royal cult were integrally linked (through both geographical proximity and ideological confession), we might well suppose that Asherah worship would be as integrated into the religion of the palace as it was integrated into the religion of the temple.

In fact, I have elsewhere argued that there are compelling reasons why a queen mother like Maʿacah would devote herself to the worship of Asherah within the Jerusalem court (Ackerman 1993; 1998: 142–54). This would be because of the well-known Jerusalem royal ideology that conceived of the king as the metaphorical son of Yahweh (for example, in Ps 89:27–28 [English vv. 26–27], where the king cries out to Yahweh, "You are my father, my God and the rock of my salvation," and Yahweh replies, "I surely will make him my firstborn, the highest of the kings of the earth"). What I have suggested is that if we pair this notion of metaphorical sonship with the notion that at least at several points during the 9th, 8th, and 7th centuries B.C.E. Yahweh's cult in Jerusalem incorporated the worship of his goddess consort Asherah, then we might well suppose that just as Yahweh was understood as the metaphorical father of the Jerusalemite king, so Asherah the consort would likewise have been understood as the king's metaphorical mother. And would it thus not follow that the king's actual mother, his queen mother, would associate herself with the cult of this metaphorical mother, the goddess Asherah, as Maʿacah does? Indeed, is it not likely that the queen mother, as the human counterpart of the king's goddess mother, even represents Asherah in the Jerusalem court?

In the Northern Kingdom, the office of queen mother is not nearly as well represented as the office of queen mother in the South; thus, of the 18 queen mothers whose names are preserved in the Hebrew Bible from the period of the divided monarchy, 17 come from the Southern Kingdom of Judah. To me, this evidence stands in support of the hypothesis I have just proposed: that there is something about the Southern royal ideology of metaphorical sonship that necessitates an important role in the court for the Southern queen mother, whereas the ideology of a more charismatic kingship that Alt long ago described for the North does not entail a position of great consequence for the Northern queen mother (1951). I would suggest, moreover, that it cannot be coincidence that the one woman assigned the title "queen mother" in the North—Jezebel—held this office during a period in the history of the Northern Kingdom when Northern kingship most closely resembled the institution of kingship in the South. For example, the Northern monarchy of Jezebel's day operated according to the more typically Southern principle of dynastic succession rather than adhering to a charismatic model; this so-called Omride dynasty conceived of its capital city of Samaria much as an analog to the Southern capital city of Jerusalem; and Omride policies establishing foreign alliances cemented by foreign marriages mimicked similar alliances in the South. I would also not regard it as coincidence that Jezebel, in addition to being the one Northern woman said to hold the more typically Southern office of queen mother, is the one royal woman of the Northern Kingdom said to be associated with the worship of Asherah.

In short, what I am suggesting in general terms is that a certain ideology of monarchy—an ideology based on dynastic succession, where the king is understood as the metaphorical son of Yahweh—drives a certain understanding of the role of the queen mother in the royal court, an understanding that conceives of the queen mother as associated with the cult of Yahweh's consort Asherah, devoting herself to the worship of the goddess and even functioning as Asherah's earthly representative in the palace. More specifically, in Jezebel's case, I am arguing that the prevailing consensus of a generation ago is wrong and that the worship of Asherah that the Hebrew Bible associates with Jezebel is not to be taken as evidence of a foreign and therefore heterodox cult that Jezebel brings with her from her Phoenician homeland. Rather, the Asherah worship associated with Jezebel was appropriately adopted by her within the context of the Southern-style monarchy instituted in the Northern Kingdom by her father-in-law, Omri. In a palace conceived of in this particular way, members of the royal court—and especially the king's mother—are comfortably "at home with the goddess."

III. At Home with the Goddess in Private Family Residences

There are two major bodies of evidence that address the question of goddess worship in noncultic and nonroyal "homes," that is, in the private homes of non-elite Israelites. These are first the biblical texts in Jeremiah 7 and 44 that allude to families among Judah's population in the late 7th and early 6th centuries B.C.E. that worshiped a goddess known by the epithet "Queen of Heaven," and second the numerous so-called "pillar" figurines, commonly taken to be images of goddesses, that have been found by archaeologists in Iron II domestic contexts. Two questions about these two bodies of evidence particularly interest me. One, do they indicate a cult of Asherah located in non-elite domestic contexts that is cognate with the temple- and palace-centered cults of Asherah that seem to be attested, especially in Judah, at points during the 9th, 8th, and 7th centuries B.C.E.? Two, is there any basis for the often-assumed correlation between family-based goddess worship and women's religious activities?

In the case of the two Jeremiah passages that allude to the worship of the Queen of Heaven, my answer to my first question must be "no"; I do not believe the goddess called the "Queen of Heaven" is Asherah. Rather, I would identify the "Queen of Heaven" as a composite deity who incorporates elements of West Semitic Astarte and East Semitic Ishtar (Ackerman 1989; 1992: 5–35). Both Astarte and Ishtar, associated with the planet Venus, embody the astral characteristics that the epithet "Queen of *Heaven*" implies; in extrabiblical sources both are called by the title "Lady of Heaven," which is obviously closely related to the Hebrew Bible's "Queen of Heaven" epithet;[11] and both are associated with agricultural fertility, as is Jeremiah's "Queen of Heaven" according to Jer 44:17–18 (in which the Queen's devotees report to Jeremiah that when they worshiped the Queen of Heaven they had "plenty of food and it went well with us," but when they neglected her cult they were "consumed . . . by famine").[12] Both Astarte and Ishtar, in addition, have associations with war, as may the Queen of Heaven (the people report to Jeremiah that to leave off her worship means not only to be consumed by famine but also by the sword [Jer 44:18]).[13] Also, both the cult of Astarte and of Ishtar have as a crucial element the offering of cakes, as does, according to Jer 7:18 and 44:19, the cult of the Queen of Heaven.[14] Ishtar, moreover, is often explicitly called in Akkadian by the precise epithet "Queen of Heaven," and *kawwānîm*, the Hebrew term used to describe the cakes said to be baked as an offering for the Queen (Jer 7:19; 44:19), is usually taken by lexicographers as a loan word from Akkadian *kamānu*, which generically means "cake" but is often more specifically used to refer to cakes baked in honor of Ishtar (Ackerman 1992: 30–31). To be sure, some of these parallels can also be cited with regard to the goddess Asherah. She, too, for example, can be called "Lady" and "Queen"; she, too, can be associated with fertility; and her cult, too, surely could include offering cakes (as could the cults of most, if not all, ancient Near Eastern deities). But Asherah, although she can be addressed as "Queen" or "Lady," does not possess the astral characteristics that the title "Queen of *Heaven*" implies; her associations with fertility concern more human fecundity than the kind of agricultural bounty that seems to be associated with the cult of the Queen of Heaven; and nowhere, to my knowledge, is the Ishtar-related vocabulary

---

11. For the title "Lady of Heaven" used for Astarte, see from New Kingdom Egypt a stone bowl dated to Horemheb's reign (XVIIIth Dynasty), on which Astarte is called "Lady of Heaven" (Redford 1973: 37); a stela from Memphis dating from the time of Merneptah, which refers to Astarte as "Lady of Heaven, Mistress of all the Gods" (Petrie 1909: 19); and a stela of Pharaoh Siptah from Abu Simbel, dating to the end of the XIXth Dynasty, which names Astarte "Lady of Heaven" (Maspero 1909: 131–32). For this title used for Ishtar, see Thureau-Dangin 1910: 61; Kramer 1963: 153; Edzard 1965: 81; Falkenstein 1966: 78–79; Helck 1971: 73; Held 1982: 80 n. 24.

12. In Biblical Hebrew the noun *'aštārôt*, derived from the divine name *'aštart*, means "issue, progeny" and refers specifically to the bounteous issue or progeny of the flocks. The ancient identification of Mesopotamian Ishtar with the storehouse likewise demonstrates that goddess's associations with agricultural bounty.

13. The stela of Merneptah from Memphis (above n. 11), which identifies Astarte as "Lady of Heaven," depicts the goddess with a shield and spear. Other Egyptian representations of Astarte show her on horseback carrying weapons of war (Leclant 1960: passim). Egyptian texts from both the second and first millennia also describe Astarte as a war goddess. Thutmose IV (XVIIIth Dynasty) is described as being mighty in the chariot like Astarte (Pritchard 1969: 250a n. 16). Astarte is called a shield to Pharaoh Ramesses III (Pritchard 1969: 250a n. 18) and a part of a 13th-century king's war chariot (Pritchard 1969: 250a n. 17). In the second millennium she carries the epithet "Lady of Combat" (Leclant 1960: 25); a Ptolemaic text describes her as "Astarte, Mistress of Horses, Lady of the Chariot" (Leclant 1960: 54–58; Pritchard 1969: 250a n. 16). In the Canaanite realm Astarte acts as a war goddess in concert with Ḥoran in Ugaritic mythology (*CAT* 1.2.1.7–8; 1.16.6.54–57 [Dietrich, Loretz, and Sanmartín 1995]). Herrmann has pointed out that the obverse of *PRU* 5, 1 (19.39) also describes Astarte as a war goddess (1969: 7–16). Ishtar's associations with war, especially during the Akkadian period, are so well known that one example suffices: her epithet as "the Lady of the Battle and of the Fight" in the Code of Hammurapi (Col. 50 [Rs. 27] 92–93).

14. Regarding Astarte, see the Kition Tariff inscription, which lists the monthly expenditures for the temple of Astarte at Kition, line 10: *l'pm // 'š'p 'yt ṭn' ḥlt lmlkt*, "for the two bakers who baked the basket of cakes for the Queen [i.e., for Queen Astarte]" (as translated by Peckham 1968: 305–6).

of *kamānu/kawwānîm* used to describe cakes offered as a part of Asherah's cult. Thus the cult of the "Queen of Heaven," while a fascinating example concerning family-based goddess worship (and an example to which I will return below), cannot be taken as an example of family-based *Asherah* worship in Iron II Israel, cognate with the Asherah worship that I have previously located in temple and palace.[15]

Establishing the identity of the pillar figurines so commonly found in Iron II domestic contexts is an extremely complex (and contested) matter. On one side of the debate, we find, for example, Meyers, who argues that because images of deities are typically made of precious metals or stones and because such images normally exhibit some symbols of divine identity (e.g., divine headdresses, divine garb, a typical deific pose, or an attached object typically associated with deity), we cannot take the rather plain and humble pillar figurines and related terra-cottas as goddess images (1988: 161–63). Rather, according to Meyers, they represent votive objects used within household religion to express the quest for female fecundity (1988: 162). The converse position, of course, holds that the figures do represent a goddess, and the identification most commonly proposed is Asherah. Hestrin, for example, suggests that because the pillar and breasts are made by hand (versus the head, which could either be shaped by hand or made in a mold), we should take the pillar and breasts as the more significant parts of the figure and should see both as symbolizing Asherah, the pillar representing the trunk of Asherah's sacred tree and the breasts the life-giving and nurturing attributes of the mother goddess (Hestrin 1987a: 222).

Dever arrives at the same conclusion, although by a somewhat different route, arguing that the discovery of the Kuntillet ʿAjrûd and Khirbet el-Qôm inscriptions, when coupled with the kinds of reassessments of the biblical text I have previously described, point to a worship of Asherah that is so widespread in Israel that the pillar figurines most logically should be taken as a part of this goddess's cult (Dever 1990: 158). In their exhaustive study, *Gods, Goddesses, and Images of God in Ancient Israel*, Keel and Uehlinger (1998) likewise identify the subject of the pillar figurines as the goddess Asherah, although in this case it is because they see continuities between the pillar figurines and what they call the "Branch Goddess" representations of Asherah from the Bronze Age, and also because they feel that the El-like character described for Yahweh, especially in Judah, would most naturally be associated with El's Canaanite consort Asherah (1998: 335). For my part, I find these authors' reminder that the pillar figurines are predominantly attested in Judah to be of particular importance, given that the evidence for Asherah worship we have already surveyed may suggest that the goddess's cult is somewhat more prevalent in Judah than in Israel, especially the goddess's cult as practiced within the royal palace. Still, whatever evidence one takes as primary, I think it is generally fair to say that the majority position would accept the identification of the pillar figurines with Asherah and thus see in them a rich body of evidence suggesting many non-elite Israelites "at home with the goddess."

And so to my second question: is there any basis for the correlation that is often assumed between the worship of the goddess Asherah in a familial context and women's religious activities? My response would be a nuanced "yes." Certainly, as I see it, we cannot

---

15. Note that I do presume here, contrary to some commentators, that the goddesses we know of as distinct beings from earlier Canaanite sources, most notably from the Late Bronze Age archives of Ugarit, remain distinct in the Iron II period (see Olyan 1988: 19–40; cf. Dever 1984: 28–29).

speak of Asherah worship in the private, family-based context as the *exclusive* province of ancient Israelite women. Although, as I have earlier argued, they concern a different goddess, the Jeremiah materials regarding the worship of the Queen of Heaven nonetheless strike me as significant here, since according to these portrayals of family-based goddess worship, the whole family—or at least the whole nuclear family—is involved: "the *children* gather wood, the *fathers* kindle fire, and the *women* knead dough to make cakes for the Queen of Heaven" (Jer 7:18). Still, despite this depiction of the whole family's involvement, I think that it is fair to say that the women's contribution—the actual making of the offering cakes—is the most religiously significant, and thus it is reasonable to see these women as somehow *especially* involved in the goddess's worship. Indeed, in the polemic against the Queen of Heaven cult in Jeremiah 44, Jeremiah seems to make exactly this point, since it is *women* who are specifically identified in Jer 44:19 as those who have "burned incense to the Queen of Heaven and poured out libations to her . . . and made for her cakes in her image," and it is thus *women*, in the culmination of Jeremiah's fulminations (44:25), who are singled out for the prophet's special scorn.

Meyers, moreover, has pointed out that it only makes sense that women would be especially associated with rituals like libation offerings and the making of offering cakes within the household sphere; this "because in the household context the female controlled food preparation" (1988: 163). To be sure, Meyers is not writing specifically of *goddess* worship here, but more generically about household cult activities. Nevertheless, if we do reconstruct an Israelite domestic environment in which Asherah worship was present, then Meyers's comments about the crucial role that women would play in any household cult should be evidence for their crucial role in the cult of Asherah. I also believe that some of the data I mentioned earlier regarding the role of women in Asherah worship in Yahweh's Jerusalem temple and in the royal court, especially the Judahite royal court, are relevant. With regard to the role of women in Asherah worship in Yahweh's Jerusalem temple, recall the report of 2 Kgs 23:7 that, at least in the 7th century B.C.E., there were women housed within the temple compound who wove garments to be draped over the goddess's cult statue. Surely these women were not the *sole* devotees of Asherah within the temple cult, because it must have been the temple's male priesthood that oversaw the erecting of the cult icon of the *'ăšērâ* in the temple in the first place and that assumed the responsibility for filling the goddess's cult vessels—mentioned in 2 Kgs 23:4— with offerings. As with the worship of the Queen of Heaven described in Jeremiah, we cannot speak of Asherah worship in the Jerusalem temple as the *exclusive* province of women. Yet we can still note that women seemed to play an *especially significant* role in the goddess's cult. Indeed, the description in 2 Kgs 23:7 of women within the temple compound who weave garments for Asherah is the *only* text in the entire Hebrew Bible that describes an actual cultic role for women within the temple's ritual life.

Likewise, the *only* biblical text that mentions explicitly the ritual life of ancient Israelite queen mothers is the text in 1 Kgs 15:13 that describes Maʿacah's devotions regarding Asherah. Again, we cannot claim from this that Asherah worship in the royal court was the *exclusive* province of women; rather, the fact that the Southern king Manasseh and the Northern king Ahab are each said to have erected an *'ăšērâ* in his capital city suggests that royal men, too, could be Asherah devotees. Still, Asherah worship, as I have argued, does seem to have been *especially important* to royal women, the queen mothers of Judah in particular. And hence my nuanced "yes" in answer to my question regarding women's role in the worship of the goddess Asherah in a private, family-based context: over and over, it seems to me, our evidence suggests that goddess worship does have a special place in women's religious lives, both generally (as in the case of the Queen of Heaven), and concerning Asherah worship in particular (as in the cases of the women weaving in Yahweh's temple and of the queen mother's cultic activities).

IV. Conclusions: At Home with the Goddess in Ancient Israelite Religion

Let me end by teasing out some more general implications that I think are embedded in the above discussion of the role of women in the family-based, royal, and temple worship of Asherah, namely, implications regarding the nature of the phenomenon we often call Israelite "popular" religion. My concern here is particularly with those who would see the term "popular religion" as connoting the religious beliefs and practices of the populace writ large, and who, moreover, would see the religious beliefs and practices of this populace writ large as somehow standing in opposition to those of the religious elite, whose religious traditions are represented within the state and temple cult. My arguments here, however, suggest that Asherah worship—which is frequently described using this rubric of "popular religion"—is hardly restricted to the non-elite. Indeed, I have proposed that at least one aspect of Asherah worship, the special role of women within Asherah's cult, is best understood by seeing a close interrelationship between the Asherah cult as it was practiced in the temple, as it was practiced in the palace, and as it was practiced in private Israelite households. "Popular religion," at least in this one case, needs to be understood as transcending any elite versus non-elite divide; rather, the divide here seems to be between a significant cross section of the Israelite population on the one hand, and on the other hand certain biblical authors (especially the prophets Isaiah, Jeremiah, and Micah and the spokespersons of the Deuteronomistic school) who regard the worship of Asherah in Israel as wrong. Again, Jeremiah's descriptions of the worship of the "Queen of Heaven" provide a useful analogy, because at one point those accused by Jeremiah of devoting themselves to the Queen respond by claiming that Jeremiah represents a minoritarian point of view when compared to those across the spectrum of the population—"we, our ancestors, our kings, and our princes" (Jer 44:17)—who engaged in the Queen's worship.

In short, however uneasy at least some spokespersons of the biblical point of view may have found themselves when confronted with Israelite worship of Asherah, I believe that our evidence increasingly suggests that, during at least some points in Israelite history, a significant cross section of the population—temple personnel, royal personnel, and non-elite Israelites, especially women—found themselves comfortably "at home with the goddess."

References

Ackerman, S.

1989   "And the Women Knead Dough": The Worship of the Queen of Heaven in Sixth-Century Judah. Pp. 109–24 in *Gender and Difference in Ancient Israel*, ed. P. L. Day. Minneapolis: Fortress.

1992   *Under Every Green Tree: Popular Religion in Sixth-Century Judah*. Harvard Semitic Monographs 46. Atlanta: Scholars Press.

1993   The Queen Mother and the Cult in Ancient Israel. *Journal of Biblical Literature* 112: 385–401.

1998   *Warrior, Dancer, Seductress, Queen: Women in Judges and Biblical Israel*. Anchor Bible Reference Library. New York: Doubleday.

Ackroyd, P. R.

1983   Goddesses, Women and Jezebel. Pp. 245–59 in *Images of Women in Antiquity*, ed. A. Cameron and A. Kuhrt. London: Croom Helm.

Ahlström, G. W.

1963   *Aspects of Syncretism in Israelite Religion*. Horae Soederblomianae 5. Lund: C.W.K. Gleerup.

Albright, W. F.

1946   *Archaeology and the Religion of Israel*. 2nd ed. Baltimore: Johns Hopkins University Press.

Alt, A.

1951   Das Königtum in der Reichen Israel und Juda. *Vetus Testamentum* 1: 2–22.

Attridge, H. W., and Oden, R. A.

1981   *Philo of Byblos: The Phoenician History. Introduction, Critical Text, Translation, Notes*. Catholic Biblical Quarterly Monograph Series 9. Washington, D.C.: Catholic Biblical Association.

Brown, F.; Driver, S. R.; and Briggs, C. A.

1980   *Hebrew and English Lexicon of the Old Testament, with an Appendix Containing the Biblical Aramaic*. Oxford: Clarendon.

Cogan, M., and Tadmor, H.

1988   *II Kings*. Anchor Bible 11. Garden City, N.Y.: Doubleday.

Day, J.

1986   Asherah in the Hebrew Bible and in Northwest Semitic Literature. *Journal of Biblical Literature* 105: 385–408.

1992   Asherah. Pp. 483b–487a in vol. 1 of *The Anchor Bible Dictionary*, ed. D. N. Freedman. New York: Doubleday.

Dever, W. G.

1969–70   Iron Age Epigraphic Material from the Area of Khirbet el-Kôm. *Hebrew Union College Annual* 40/41: 158–89.

1982   Recent Archaeological Confirmation of the Cult of Asherah in Ancient Israel. *Hebrew Studies* 23: 37–43.

1983   Material Remains and the Cult in Ancient Israel: An Essay in Archaeological Systematics. Pp. 571–87 in *The Word of the Lord Shall Go Forth: Essays in Honor of David Noel Freedman in Celebration of His Sixtieth Birthday*, ed. C. L. Meyers and M. O'Connor. Winona Lake, Ind.: Eisenbrauns.

1984   Asherah, Consort of Yahweh? New Evidence from Kuntillet ʿAjrûd. *Bulletin of the American Schools of Oriental Research* 255: 21–37.

1990   *Recent Archaeological Discoveries and Biblical Research*. Seattle: University of Washington Press.

Dietrich, M.; Loretz, O.; and Sanmartín, J.

1995   *The Cuneiform Alphabetic Texts from Ugarit, Ras Ibn Hani and Other Places*. Münster: Ugarit-Verlag.

Donner, H., and Röllig, W.
 1962   *Kanaanäische und aramäische Inschriften*, vols. 1–3. Wiesbaden: Harrassowitz.
Driver, G. R.
 1936   Supposed Arabisms in the Old Testament. *Journal of Biblical Literature* 55: 101–20.
Edzard, O.
 1965   Inanna, Ištar. Pp. 17–139 in *Wörterbuch der Mythologie*, ed. H. W. Haussig. Stuttgart: Klett.
Falkenstein, A.
 1966   *Einleitung*. Vol. 1 of *Die Inschriften Gudeas von Lagas*. Analecta orientalia 30. Rome: Pontifical Biblical Institute.
Frost, R.
 1995   The Death of the Hired Man. Pp. 40–45 in *Collected Poems, Prose, and Plays*. The Library of America 81. New York: Library of America.
Gray, J.
 1964   *I and II Kings*. Old Testament Library. London: SCM.
Gressmann, H.
 1924   Josia und das Deuteronomium. *Zeitschrift für die Alttestamentliche Wissenschaft* 44: 313–37.
Helck, W.
 1971   *Betrachtungen zur grossen Göttin und den ihr verbundenen Gottheiten*. Religion und Kultur der alten Mittelmeerwelt in Parallelforschungen 2. Munich: Oldenbourg.
Held, M.
 1982   Studies in Biblical Lexicography. Pp. 76–85 in *Eretz Israel* 16 (Harry M. Orlinsky volume), ed. B. A. Levine and A. Malamat. Jerusalem: Israel Exploration Society (Hebrew).
Herrmann, W.
 1969   Astart. *Mitteilungen des Instituts für Orientforschung* 15: 6–55.
Hestrin, R.
 1987a   The Lachish Ewer and the ʾAsherah. *Israel Exploration Journal* 37: 212–23.
 1987b   The Cult Stand from Taʿanach and Its Religious Background. Pp. 61–77 in *Phoenicia and the East Mediterranean in the First Millennium B.C.*, ed. E. Lipiński. Studia Phoenicia 5; Orientalia lovaniensia analecta 23. Leuven: Peeters.
Keel, O., and Uehlinger, C.
 1998   *Gods, Goddesses, and Images of God in Ancient Israel*. Minneapolis: Fortress.
Kramer, S. N.
 1963   *The Sumerians: Their History, Culture, and Character*. Chicago: University of Chicago Press.
Leclant, J.
 1960   Astarté à cheval d'après les représentations égyptiennes. *Syria* 37: 1–67.
Lemaire, A.
 1977   Les inscriptions de Khirbet el-Qôm et l'Ashérah de Yhwh. *Revue Biblique* 84: 597–608.
 1984a   Date et origine des inscriptiones hébraïques et phéniciennes de Kuntillet ʿAjrud. *Studi epigraphici e linguistici* 1: 131–43.
 1984b   Who or What Was Yahweh's Asherah? *Biblical Archaeology Review* 10/6: 42–51.
Lipiński, E.
 1972   The Goddess Aṯirat in Ancient Arabia, in Babylon, and in Ugarit. *Orientalia lovaniensia analecta* 3: 101–19.
McCarter, P. K.
 1987   Aspects of the Religion of the Israelite Monarchy: Biblical and Epigraphic Data. Pp. 137–55 in *Ancient Israelite Religion: Essays in Honor of Frank Moore Cross*, ed. P. D. Miller, P. D. Hanson, and S. D. McBride. Philadelphia: Fortress.
Maspero, M. G.
 1909   Notes de Voyage. *Annales du Service des antiquités de l'Égypte* 10: 131–44.
Meshel, Z.
 1976   Kuntillet ʿAjrûd: An Israelite Site from the Monarchical Period on the Sinai Border. *Qadmoniot* 9: 118–24 (Hebrew).

1978a   Kuntillet 'Ajrûd: An Israelite Religious Center in Northern Sinai. *Expedition* 20: 50–54.
1978b   *Kuntillet 'Ajrûd: A Religious Center from the Time of the Judean Monarchy.* Israel Museum Catalogue 175. Jerusalem: Israel Museum.
1979   Did Yahweh Have a Consort? The New Religious Inscriptions from Sinai. *Biblical Archaeology Review* 5/2: 24–35.

Meshel, Z., and Meyers, C.
1976   The Name of God in the Wilderness of Zin. *Biblical Archaeologist* 39: 6–10.

Meyers, C.
1988   *Discovering Eve: Ancient Israelite Women in Context.* New York: Oxford University Press.

Miller, P. D.
1986   The Absence of the Goddess in Israelite Religion. *Hebrew Annual Review* 10: 239–48.

Oden, R. A.
1977   *Studies in Lucian's De Syria Dea.* Harvard Semitic Monographs 15. Missoula, Mont.: Scholars Press.

Olyan, S. M.
1988   *Asherah and the Cult of Yahweh in Israel.* Society of Biblical Literature Monograph Series 34. Atlanta: Scholars Press.

Oppenheim, A. L.
1949   The Golden Garments of the Gods. *Journal of Near Eastern Studies* 8: 172–93.

Peckham, J. B.
1968   Notes on a Fifth-Century Phoenician Inscription from Kition, Cyprus (*CIS* 86). *Orientalia* 37: 304–24.

Petrie, W. M. F.
1909   *Memphis* I. London: School of Archaeology in Egypt/Quaritch.

Pritchard, J. B. (ed.)
1969   *Ancient Near Eastern Texts Relating to the Old Testament.* 3rd ed. Princeton: Princeton University Press.

Redford, D. B.
1973   New Light on the Asiatic Campaigning of Horemheb. *Bulletin of the American Schools of Oriental Research* 211: 36–49.

Šanda, A.
1912   *Die Bucher der Könige*, vol. 2. Münster: Aschendorff.

Smith, M. S.
1990   *The Early History of God: Yahweh and the Other Deities in Israel.* San Francisco: Harper & Row.

Spanier, K.
1994   The Queen Mother in the Judaean Royal Court: Maacah—A Case Study. Pp. 186–95 in *A Feminist Companion to Samuel and Kings*, ed. A. Brenner. The Feminist Companion to the Bible 5. Sheffield: Sheffield Academic Press.

Thureau-Dangin, F.
1910   *Lettres et Contrats.* Paris: Geuthner.

Yeivin, S.
1953   Social, Religious, and Cultural Trends in Judaism under the Davidic Dynasty. *Vetus Testamentum* 3: 149–66.

The Family in Persian Period Judah: Some Textual Reflections

H. G. M. Williamson
Christ Church
University of Oxford

In recent years there have been some impressive attempts to offer synthetic descriptions of what can be said about the nature and understanding of the family in postexilic Judah. Some have striven for a comprehensive presentation of all the possible sources of information (e.g., Collins 1997), some have concentrated on particular biblical texts (e.g., Fechter 1998), some have limited their analysis to the definition of terms (e.g., Scharbert 1982; Weinberg 1992: 49–61), and others have focused on particular topics, such as the impact of Persian imperial policy on the nature and role of the family in Judean society (e.g., Hoglund 1992, especially pp. 226–40).

At the risk of being exorcised as a ghost from the banquet, I believe it is necessary to enter some words of caution into what seems at first sight to be a steady accumulation of solidly based advances in knowledge, drawing as they do on the results of interdisciplinary research. Although we shall see later that there are indeed some positive things to be said about our subject on the basis of the textual evidence, it is perhaps more important at the present juncture to emphasize and come firmly to terms with the limitations of the available evidence. Unless we constantly bear this in mind, there is a danger that theories that rely upon the combination of imperfectly understood data from various sources will end up distorting one or another of the pillars on which they rest. The failure to appreciate this by the first wave of biblical archaeologists has long been accepted by the archaeological community. It is not, perhaps, inappropriate for a textual scholar to make the mirror-image point that the same can be said about the use of literary sources. The following are only the chief factors that need to be borne in mind.

First, however rich their contribution to other matters, written sources from outside the Hebrew Bible itself cannot be used as primary data for our purpose. Two major collections of papyri are often appealed to in this connection, but they can at best serve only in a secondary capacity. On the one hand, the Babatha archive and similar related Aramaic texts from the Dead Sea region are far too late to be used without severe reservation (for the details of publication, still in progress, see Collins 1997: 152). Apart from the inevitable internal development in law and custom that is likely to have taken place over the some 500 years separating these documents from our period, careful attention should

---

Author's note: All scripture in this essay is cited according to the Hebrew chapter and verse divisions.

also be paid to the possible impact of Hellenistic and Roman practice on Jewish society, as well as influence from the neighboring Nabatean peoples. On the other hand, while the Elephantine and related papyri do not suffer from this chronological discrepancy, the peculiar circumstances of the Jewish colony in Upper Egypt must also be considered. The origins of the community remain uncertain, but there would be general agreement that in many respects their culture reflects that of preexilic Judah (or even Israel). Specific instruction had to be sent, for instance, in the matter of recent innovations regarding the correct celebration of the festival of unleavened bread (and probably Passover). It would thus be dangerous to cite their practices as evidence if we are particularly concerned with tracing postexilic developments. In addition, although we learn much about family law as practised in the colony from the (sometimes extensive) archives relating to the family affairs of certain prominent women, such as Mibtaḥiah, Tapmut, and Yehoishma (Porten 1968; Eskenazi 1992), there is a strong likelihood that this was influenced by Egyptian conventions (not least since Egyptians were variously directly involved). The history of the laws of the community are complex and seem to show influence from a variety of non-Judean backgrounds (Yaron 1961; Muffs 1968). It would therefore be a mistake of method to cite them first and foremost for evidence of practice in Judah. Points of comparison may, of course, legitimately be sought, but this very enterprise demands prior and independent knowledge of the situation in Judah, and for this the biblical texts alone provide the primary evidence.

Second, then, with regard to the biblical texts themselves, there are several factors to be considered. These are so well known that it would hardly be worth itemizing them were it not for the fact that they are all too easily sidelined as soon as scholars move into descriptive mode. There are first of all the familiar problems of dating, which are immediately the despair of colleagues in other branches of ancient Near Eastern studies; there is sometimes a feeling that this argument is being brought out like a rabbit from a hat in order to promote a novel hypothesis or to sideline some uncomfortable pieces of data. The problem, however, will not go away for the simple reason that the books of the Bible are quite unlike most other artifacts that have been unearthed by archaeologists. They have not reached us firsthand, like an ostracon or a papyrus, but have survived solely because of their value as part of a developing community that has preserved them as living texts, with the result that the earliest complete exemplars are early Medieval. And even the partial testimony of the Dead Sea Scrolls brings us to a period long after the one with which we are concerned, and to a time when the agreed text, although not yet fixed, was becoming more stable. During the Persian period, however, matters were in a far greater state of flux, with consequences for historical reconstruction, even of a relatively conservative nature such as I myself favor, that complicate their use.

Take, for example, the so-called priestly portions of the Pentateuch, which are of fundamental importance for the definition of terms, such as בית אבות, or the understanding of the nature of the extended family on the basis of the table of kindred in Leviticus 18. In the first place, the majority view remains that this material is of postexilic date, and so at first sight might be considered of primary importance for our subject. There is, however, a significant and vocal minority that maintains a preexilic date, which immediately complicates matters. But in fact, the situation is far worse, for on the one hand, even those who date the material late generally agree that it contains reflections of earlier material, while on the other, those who date it earlier would agree that it maintained its influence later on. So of which period, if either, does it reflect the social reality? Not dissimilar difficulties confront the use of parts of the wisdom literature, which in many ways are directly relevant to the understanding of the family (cf. Camp 1985), to say nothing of the prophetic books, in which the history of redaction is clear for all to see. That these are not artificially contrived problems may be seen in considering the case of Chronicles, in which the history of the preexilic period is retold in the postexilic period, so that it is frequently difficult to disentangle what is earlier from what is later. The recent attempt by Fechter (1998), promisingly entitled *Die Familie in der Nachexilszeit*, to deal with precisely these problems tackles a small group of varied texts (Joshua 7; 1 Samuel 10; Leviticus 18; Ruth; Mic 7:1–7) and subjects them to minute literary-critical analysis in order to demonstrate the nature of the contribution of their postexilic redactors and so to gain an understanding of their views about the family. While the aim is laudable and the work of a high standard, the inevitably hypothetical nature of the results remains. Clearly what is lacking is an attempt to correlate the results with texts of agreed Persian period provenance, such as Ezra–Nehemiah and the postexilic prophets. It might be supposed that these should be the starting point for all such investigations.

Even when we turn our attention to these, however, our problems are not at an end. There is no need to dwell upon the obvious and well-known fact that most historiography is ideological in nature and that its testimony is, from a modern standpoint, partial and one-sided, a fact that remains even if, as I have argued elsewhere (1985), the sources are reasonably reliable in what they affirm; this is a general consideration with which historians have long had to deal. Rather, the major problem for our present purposes is that in some matters central to the consideration of family law in this period the texts speak not of the norm, but rather of particular and extraordinary events. This is clearest with regard to Ezra's infamous dissolution of so-called mixed marriages, a topic that continues to receive more attention than any other within our brief (see, for instance, several of the contributions in Eskenazi and Richards 1994). And while we are on the topic of divorce, the other contemporary passage that apparently refers to it, Mal 2:10–16, is textually so difficult (for a full survey of opinions, see Hugenberger 1994) that, while each commentator forms his or her own opinion regarding its significance, it would clearly be hazardous in the extreme to base any conclusion centrally upon it. Thus, the commentator who is interested in social history rather than the haphazard witness of sporadic particular events has to learn to interrogate the sources for what they assume and presuppose, rather than necessarily for what they relate on the surface.

Bearing all these negative caveats firmly in mind, let me turn in the balance of this paper to what may be said positively about the family in Persian period Judah, based exclusively on the textual evidence. The picture turns out to be considerably more mixed than some recent surveys have suggested.

In the first place, there seems little reason to doubt that, throughout the period for which we have evidence (roughly the first half of the Persian period), the position of many individuals in the community was defined by their genealogical affiliation. "Family," therefore, was in some sense, yet to be defined, a central building block of society.

The evidence for this statement comes from several different directions. First, on the occasions on which we have what appears to be a formal definition of the constituent members of the community or a part thereof, it invariably includes a major element categorized by genealogical association (see especially the lists in Ezra 2/Nehemiah 7; Ezra 8:3–14; Neh 11:4–20). Second, the negative point is made that there were some who "could not prove their families or their descent, whether they belonged to Israel" (Ezra 2:59), and we note that these included both lay and priestly groups. Finally, during the economic crisis confronting Nehemiah (Neh 5:1–13), it was to the sense of family solidarity that he appealed, based apparently on the ancient kinship-based customs of redemption (Vogt 1966: 108–17; Blenkinsopp 1988: 258–59).

Within the totality of "Israel" as a single community, it is widely agreed that the major social subdivision at the time was the so-called "fathers' house" (בית אבות), a term that has been variously understood and therefore needs some unpacking. To the extent that one may speak of a consensus of opinion on the matter, it would be something along the following lines. In the preexilic period, Israel was divided socially into three decreasing-sized units — the tribe (שבט or מטה), the clan or kin group (משפחה, a word for which it is difficult to find a fully satisfactory English equivalent; cf. Gottwald's "protective association of extended families" [1979: 315]), and the "father's house" (בית אב), an extended family living together in a single locality, even if not in a single building (Stager 1985).[1] In the postexilic period, however, the term משפחה drops out of use, to all intents and purposes, and is replaced by בית אבות (plural), which is thought to be a direct continuation of the earlier בית אב, albeit increased in size. The question of whether any terminology then arose to replace what was previously the smallest social unit is not addressed.

Since our present concern is with textual reflections, it is important to attend carefully to the evidence of the texts and not to impose tidy patterns upon them too quickly. Of the many points that could be advanced in consequence, let the following serve initially as representative.

In the first place, there need certainly be no objection to the possibility that significant terms descriptive of social realities may have changed their meaning in the course of time to reflect historical developments. The example of the "people of the land" (עם הארץ) is a well-known case in point that cannot be denied (see most recently Willi 1995: 11–17, 30–33, with further literature), even if the evidence from the early postexilic prophets (who constitute our most reliable source of contemporary data) suggests that the shift did not coincide with the period of the exile, but must rather have come later (Hag 2:4; Zech 7:5).

On the other hand, there is considerable doubt as to whether the tidy picture outlined above does full justice to the evidence for the preexilic period, which is the necessary starting point for documenting subsequent development. Without necessarily overpressing the point, there is sufficient evidence of variety in the use of the key terminology to suggest both that there may well have been (as we should expect) development within that extended period itself, so that it would be hazardous to lump everything together as descriptive of the situation at the time of the exile, and that the terminology is used

---

1. Although they do not agree among themselves on many matters, the standard discussions of these divisions include Andersen 1969; de Geus 1976: 133–50; Gottwald 1979: 237–341; Lemche 1985: 245–85; Martin 1989; Wright 1990: 48–55; Bendor 1996; van der Toorn 1996: 183–205; Blenkinsopp 1997. For some preliminary remarks on the difficulties involved, see Rogerson 1978: 86–101.

either somewhat freely and/or in an idealized fashion, so that to proceed straight from one selection of the textual evidence to a description of the reality on the ground may be premature (see, e.g., C. Meyers 1988: 122–38).

The usual threefold division summarized above is most clearly expressed in some of the lists in Numbers, starting with the very first chapter (see especially Gray 1903: 4–5). This at once introduces the difficulties that (a) the material is priestly, so that its application to the preexilic period is at least contentious, and (b) the book of Numbers itself sometimes seems to equate בית אב with other units, such as the tribe (e.g., Num 17:17; for other examples of the "promiscuous" use of the relevant terminology, see, for instance, Amos 3:1; 1 Chr 24:6; cf. Smith 1989: 101–2; Bendor 1996: 75–77; van der Toorn 1996: 194–205). Next, support for the usual view as expressed in Numbers is usually sought in such passages as Joshua 7, in which Achan is found by a system of lot-casting from tribe to clan and so on. Unfortunately, the vital phrase בית אב does not occur here; rather, the movement at its first listing is from tribe to clan to house (unqualified; v. 14) and at its second listing from tribe (v. 16) to clan to "men" (גברים, v. 17), who are then brought out, each according to his "house" (בית, v. 18), and Achan is unmasked. Most commentators immediately make the assumption that "house" and "father's house" are identical (as explicitly, for instance, Bendor 1996: 54; Blenkinsopp 1997: 50–51). A more natural assumption would be rather to correlate the "father's house" with the גברים of this passage (although this is no more than conjecture, of course) and to regard it as comprising a number of house(hold)s, which the continuation of the passage (v. 24) would suggest comprised a nuclear family with its appurtenances. Interestingly, in the otherwise closely comparable passage in 1 Sam 10:20–21, the movement is straight from tribe to clan to individual, so that again there is no mention of the "father's house."

The conclusion that the house(hold) and the father's house should not immediately be equated, although this is almost universally assumed, has been forcefully maintained by Cowling (1988), in an article apparently unknown to Fechter (1998). It has been said that Cowling's arguments "do not seem particularly persuasive" (Blenkinsopp 1997: 93), but since they are based on the analysis of particular texts rather than on an over-hasty attempt at neat synthesis, they perhaps deserve better treatment in a discussion such as this. A particular point that Cowling rightly stresses is that not every occurrence of the collocation of "house" and "father" should immediately be identified with a "father's house" in the technical sense, since בית is an ambiguous word, which can refer, for instance, either to a physical structure or to a group of related people. This becomes important in a discussion of the much-disputed question of whether the primary social unit was a nuclear or an extended family (cf. Lemche 1985: 245–90; Bendor 1996: 121–28). In favor of the former, for instance, attention is frequently drawn to Judg 14:19, with its reference to Samson's "father's house," which, according to the preceding context, seems to have comprised merely his father, mother, and himself. A moment's common-sense consideration of the context, however, reveals that "house" in this case refers to the physical structure inhabited by his parents (following a verb of motion, ויעל) and thus has nothing directly to do with "father's house" as a technical term.

In fact, the most promising passage for understanding the extended family is, by common consent, Leviticus 18. Porter (1967), in particular, building on the earlier analysis of Elliger (1955), used the table of forbidden unions in vv. 6–18 to help define the extent of a family living together as a unit. Indeed, he provocatively went so far as to assert that such living together is most suitable to a tent encampment and that the passage therefore reflects a time "before the national religion had made its influence dominant . . . when as yet there was no such entity as 'Israel'" (Porter 1967: 8–9). A problem for this approach, however, that has long been noted is the omission from the list of a man's daughter and full sister, and appeals to the possibility of textual losses to account for this are not convincing. This fact is used by Rattray (1987) first negatively, to argue that the table cannot be dealing with "membership in a patrilineage or household constituency" (1987: 541), and second positively, to suggest that there is a hidden reference to the nuclear family in the phrase כל־שאר בשרו, "anyone near of kin," in v. 6 (which, on the basis of Lev 21:2–3, would have included any of father, mother, son, daughter, brother, and unmarried sister), and that the full list then goes on to define others in the wider family who are also excluded. (Rattray's explanation for the inclusion of the mother in the list, initially unexpected in her view, has been improved on by Hartley [1992: 287–89].) This attractive approach suggests that the nuclear/extended family debate may have been too polarized, or in other words, that there was an awareness of both concepts in ancient Israel and that both reflected certain social realities (Faust 1999). Again, the natural consequence of this observation would be to align the two with the distinction already observed between a "house(hold)" and a "father's house." The former would have been based on a nuclear family (itself somewhat larger in principle than in modern parlance), but would also have been capable of including other residents such as servants, Levites, resident aliens (as laborers, perhaps), and so on (Micah's "house" in Judges 17–18 is routinely cited in evidence). It was the only social unit that was capable in principle of including the total population (hence its importance in Joshua 7), so that in practical terms it could not be defined by consanguinity alone. The "father's house," by contrast, would have been a more genuine extended family, not necessarily living together physically, but with a sufficiently identifiable sense of relatedness to prevent marriage within the otherwise endogamous "clan."

Finally, the point needs to be emphasized that most discussions of these terms are undertaken in the context of attempts to understand the nature of Israelite society in its earliest premonarchic form, with allowance made for all the uncertainties that are raised for the use of texts in relation to this period. Indeed, the picture that emerges from these terms, however understood in detail, is clearly most suited to a society that is not strongly centralized. Nevertheless, however much it may be agreed that grassroots Israel was socially conservative, so that these terms would have persisted in use under the Monarchy and even retained something of their original significance,[2] it can hardly be denied that several hundred years of monarchy and its attendant structures must have had a significant impact, especially in the later Judean period, under the pressure of the strongly centralizing tendencies of Hezekiah and Josiah (Hopkins 1983; Blenkinsopp 1997: 85–92). Moreover, it is widely agreed that the practical reality behind the use of kinship models was closely related to the preservation of land (Wright 1990; see notably the "ancestral inheritance," נחלת אבתי, of 1 Kgs 21:3). The pressure to persist with the system would

---

2. This is stressed by Bendor (1996), with some justification, but he perhaps underplays the fact that the evidence from the prophets of the continuation of the structure also attests to the extent to which it came under serious threat.

therefore have diminished to some extent with increasing urbanization (see especially Faust 1999), the development of a more complex economy, and the increase in the number of families that developed specialized crafts and skills not directly dependent on land. Certainly, the use of these terms in their technical sense decreases markedly in the texts referring primarily to the period of the late monarchy, and it is highly probable that, by this time, place of residence (i.e., a collection of households rather than the בית אב) would have been the major practical social entity (see especially Andersen 1969).

Extensive as these reflections on the preexilic situation have been, they are necessary if we are to make any advance regarding the difficulties that the actual texts from the Persian period raise in connection with the consensus view outlined above of the importance of the family at the time. Let me mention three such difficulties to indicate the nature of the problem.

First, in the lists of Ezra 2/Nehemiah 7 and Nehemiah 3, alongside those who are certainly identified by some sort of genealogical association (and Ezra 2:59/Neh 7:61 indicates that it is reasonable to subsume this within the system of the בית אבות), there are also a good number of those who are listed geographically on the basis of their place of domicile. How are these to be accounted for in the standard view?

Second, the leadership of the community during the first half of the Persian period for which we have evidence is less uniform than an exclusive focus on the system of fathers' houses might lead us to expect. The anticipated pattern is certainly consistently applied in Ezra. In common with other parts of the Hebrew Bible, the leaders of these associations are referred to as "heads," and these indeed feature in our texts, as expected (e.g., Ezra 1:5; 2:68; 3:12; 4:2–3; 8:1; 10:16. Neh 8:13 may be taken together with the Ezra material). Interestingly, however, they never occur in the first-person Nehemiah material. On the basis of Ezra 3:12, it might be thought that "elders" was an alternative title for the same group, but the context suggests that זקנים there literally means old men (those who still remembered the first temple); it is therefore uncertain whether the (Aramaic) word "elders" of Ezra 5:5, 9 and 6:7–8, 14 refers to the same group of leaders, although 5:10 hints that it probably does. Similarly, שרים occurs in Ezra 8:29 (and cf. 10:5) in what seems to be an identical sense, in which case the unqualified use of the term in 9:1 probably reflects the same, although in 9:2 these leaders are joined by an otherwise unidentified group of סגנים. Finally, as far as the Ezra material is concerned, we have "princes and elders" in 10:8 and "princes" and "elders of every city" in 10:14, again all acting in a capacity similar to the "heads of fathers' houses" in v. 16. This looks very much, therefore, as though we are dealing with a single system of leadership for which, with the isolated exception of סגנים, the terms "heads," "elders," and "princes" (שרים) were to all intents and purposes interchangeable (cf. Vogt 1966: 103–5).

The picture in the Nehemiah Memoir itself could not be more different. The complete absence of this type of terminology has already been noted.[3] Instead, we find such terms as סגנים (in 2:16; 4:8, 13; 7:5; 13:11) and חרים (in 2:16; 4:8, 13; 6:17; 7:5; 13:17). Furthermore, Nehemiah returns to dividing the people by משפחה (4:7), which, as we have seen, is

---

3. The only exception is בית אבי in Neh 1:6. This is traditional language, however, as is clear both from its use in a prayer and from the fact that the older singular form is used against the otherwise universal plural for the postexilic period.

unprecedented, while as motivation for self-defense he lists "your brothers, your sons, your daughters, your wives and your house[hold?]s" (4:8), terminology that again sounds like a return to an earlier state of affairs, as described above. Finally, Nehemiah apparently has a considerable body of personal retainers, his נערים (chaps. 4–5, passim; 13:19), and 4:16–17 suggests that there were other prominent citizens in a similar situation. While this might loosely be associated with the older "household" system, it suggests that there was a considerable element in the population whose loyalty was directed other than by family considerations as usually understood.

The material in the book of Nehemiah that does not belong to the first-person account is mixed. On the one hand, the older terminology continues in 11:13, 16 and 12:12, 22–23. Neh 10:1, 15; 11:1, 3; and 12:46 are comparable. On the other hand, however, we find new titles, or new uses of older terms, also intruding. In chap. 3, which was probably not first penned by Nehemiah, but may well have been included in his account, there are many references to an elaborate system of district governors (the word is שר, but its connotation is clearly quite distinct from that in Ezra;[4] the same applies to the first-person account in Neh 4:10 and 7:2[5]), as well as one mention of "nobles" (אדירים) in 3:5. It is also worth noting at this point that several groups are listed by guild (3:8, 31–32), suggesting a different system of association from the purely genealogical, while the unprecedented reference to Shallum "and his daughters" (3:12) has rightly attracted comment recently as standing out from anything that had gone before (Eskenazi 1992: 39–40; none of the possible examples she mentions that might adumbrate this in Ezra seems so clear or convincing). The word אדירים then recurs in 10:30, while פקיד is a new term that appears in 11:9, 14, 22; 12:42, and נגד occurs once, in 11:11. This mixture of the new and the old might well be explained as the result of a conservative group's gradually coming to terms with a newly developed situation.

Third, reference should again be made to the outcry of the people in Nehemiah 5. Three groups seem to be complaining of varying degrees of economic hardship in vv. 2–5 (for a discussion, see Williamson 1985: 236–39, with further literature), and the terms in which they do so (referring to wives, sons, daughters, and their land-holdings) do not seem to extend beyond the nuclear family or household. They appeal to the whole of the community as being of the same "flesh" (v. 5), and Nehemiah's response assumes the same with its language of brotherhood (vv. 7–8), although again the leaders are termed חרים and סגנים (v. 7). Where, we might ask, are the "fathers' houses" with their "heads"? If they have replaced the משפחה, as in the consensus view, this is the very point at which they should

---

4. Demsky (1983) has made a case that פלך does not refer to a "district," as is usually supposed, but to "corvée labor." Even if he is right, the use of שר in this connection would still be markedly different from what is found in Ezra. The problem with Demsky's view is that he relies on cuneiform texts of the Neo-Assyrian period, whereas in texts from the Persian period *pilku* normally means "region, district" (cf. *AHW* 863).

5. The occurrences in Neh 12:31–32 are less straightforward. "The princes of Judah" may (although do not necessarily) imply a style of leadership closer to that seen in Ezra, and this apparently in the first-person account. From a literary point of view, however, the description of the dedication of the wall was almost certainly assembled from more than one source (Williamson 1985: 369–71), so that there can be no certainty whether the use of שר here reflects Nehemiah's inconsistent use of terminology or that of other material in the book of Nehemiah, which, as we have already seen, often continues the usage characteristic of Ezra.

be most prominent, whereas in fact nothing seems to come between the small family and the community as a whole (קהל in v. 13; קהלה in v. 7, however, is probably not a term for the community).

None of these three points seems to me to be adequately explained by proposals that lump the whole of Persian period Judah together under a single sociological model: for example, that imperial policy dictated that the whole population was treated as a collection of agnatic groups of "father's houses" in order to determine a new system of land tenure as imperial domain (e.g., Hoglund 1992). Nor do I see how they can all be subsumed within a proposed "citizen-temple community," which encompassed only part of the population of the province (e.g., Weinberg 1992); the evidence from Nehemiah, which according to this theory is supposed to reflect only that community, is simply too different in its outlook to accommodate under this heading (against the "citizen-temple community" as a whole, see Bedford 1991; Williamson 1998; Carter 1999: 294–307).[6] Clearly, a fresh proposal is called for that is both sensitive to the different literary styles and genres in these books and bears in mind the possibility of historical development during the period under consideration.

In sketching the outlines of such a proposal (space limitations preclude more), we may begin by noticing that the unqualified use of the "fathers' house" terminology relates primarily to the situation in Babylon and to those who returned from there when they are considered a separate group. This is clear, for instance, in Ezra 1:5 and 8:1–14, both of which are set in Babylon, while in 4:2–3, the context established by v. 1 as well as the conclusion of v. 3 suggest that the same sort of group is involved. There is good reason to believe that this reflects historical reality. It has often been observed that the loss of other foci of social cohesion among the exiled Judeans is likely to have led to an increased emphasis on ethnicity as a means of preserving a sense of communal identity (e.g., Smith 1989; 1991). Whether real or fictional, the "father's house" seems an obvious size of unit on which to have fastened, since it is unlikely that larger units, such as the "clan," would have survived intact. It must be remembered, however, that both in origin and theoretically in continuation, these associations were inextricably bound up with land tenure by way of family inheritance, and it was this, no doubt, that allowed the institution to be fluid and flexible in the preexilic period in the way that our sources suggest (Hopkins 1985: 251–61). As families grew and split in the natural course of events, either dividing the inheritance or developing new territory, so the "father's house" would change to reflect the identity of its new heads (cf. Bendor 1996). In exile, however, this organic process would have come to an abrupt halt; the identity of the "father's house" would have become, as it were, frozen. As an inevitable consequence, not only would its membership have grown in size over time by the natural process of family development, but the ancestor after whom it was named at the point of exile would have become increasingly remote from the current generation.

---

6. It should also be noted at this point that while, with Clines (1990), full allowance must be made for the possibility that Nehemiah distorted his account of events in order to further his own agenda, the evidence sketched above is not part of his personal program, but derives from what he merely assumes as background, and therefore is likely to be reliable.

This, I suggest, may help to account for the change from the singular בית אב to the plural בית אבות, which, it should be empasized, not only means a plurality of father's houses (as Scharbert [1982] rightly insists it can), but can also refer to a single "house" with a plurality of fathers (as Fechter [1998: 214] rightly emphasizes on the basis of Exod 12:3). The change of terminology need not, therefore, be regarded as indicating a complete lack of continuity between the pre- and postexilic periods, with the two institutions being totally unrelated to one another (Smith 1989: 102), but may be more plausibly ascribed to a fully intelligible development on the basis of radically changed historical circumstances. By the time of the return, therefore, we find that the groups of those who returned were parts of larger associations than those that had gone into exile, and that the term to describe them had evolved accordingly. Finally on this point, just as we saw that previously more than biological relations were included within particular households, so the same is likely to have continued. The development of genealogies to reflect relationships wider than those based on consanguinity alone is too well known to require discussion (e.g., Wilson 1977).

The next point to consider, however, is that the lists that reflect the situation of the community back in the land are precisely those that include more than "fathers' houses" alone, and justice must be done to this frequently ignored fact. This is not in doubt with regard to Nehemiah 3, so that attention must initially focus on the so-called *golah* list of Ezra 2/Nehemiah 7. While the introduction to this list suggests that it is made up entirely of those who returned from Babylon, there are strong indications that it must have been drawn up, at the very least, once the return had been accomplished. Both the start and the conclusion of the list already refer to the people settling in their towns and villages, and this finds further support in the presence in office already of the Tirshatha and the note on contributions to the work of the temple (Ezra 2:63, 68–69/ Neh 7:65, 70–72).

The date and purpose of this list have been much discussed, and I have sought elsewhere to argue that the evidence points to a setting soon after the first period of return(s) (Williamson 1985: 28–32). To summarize the main points, we may note the following. (1) Among those who were excluded from the priesthood because they could not prove their pedigree was the family of Hakkoz (Ezra 2:61/Neh 7:63), but by the time of Ezra (Ezra 8:33) and again of Nehemiah (Neh 3:4, 21), they appear to have been reinstated. (2) The registration of those without genealogical record according to the (obscure) Babylonian places from which they came (Ezra 2:59/Neh 7:61) only makes sense within a period shortly after their return. (3) The list presupposes a date when there was as yet no "priest with Urim and Thummim" (Ezra 2:63/Neh 7:65). In the postexilic period, this was clearly a reference to the high priest (cf. Exod 28:30; Lev 8:8; Num 27:21), in which role Jeshua was certainly active from 520 B.C.E. onward. (4) The presentation of the minor cultic officials in the second half of the list reflects an earlier situation in the development of their position than elsewhere in Ezra and Nehemiah, as well as Chronicles (for full details, see Gese 1963; Williamson 1979). (5) The use of the gold drachma (Ezra 2:69/Neh 7:69) probably antedates the introduction of the daric by Darius (Williamson 1977: 123–25). (6) The distribution of the population is not what one would expect had the list been drawn up as late as Nehemiah's time (Sellin 1932: 89).

As far as the reason for the compilation of the list is concerned, no more convincing proposal has been advanced than that of Galling (1964; see also Schultz 1980). Galling points to the need posed by Tattenai's inquiry at the time of the rebuilding of the temple (Ezra 5:10) for a list of all who were covered by Cyrus's permission to return from exile and to rebuild the temple. This, at least, is concrete evidence of the need for such a list at the appropriate date, and it also helps to explain the otherwise peculiar inclusion of burden-bearing animals (Ezra 2:66–67/Neh 7:68).

As we have already seen, the elements in the list that identify groups according to their fathers' houses are likely to refer to those who had recently returned from Babylon. Conversely, however, the groups identified by place of domicile cannot be so easily accommodated within this scheme, and the obvious solution is to assume that they refer to those who had remained in the land throughout the time of the exile but who still felt themselves sufficiently related by ties of blood, social orientation, and religion to join and be accepted by those returning to rebuild the temple (Japhet 1983; and surprisingly, since it does not otherwise fit his overall theory, this is also accepted by Weinberg [1992: 132]). That such groups were included in the operation is explicitly mentioned in Ezra 6:21, and the theory gains support from the observation that a high proportion of the places listed are in Benjamite territory, and indeed only two (of a total of 22) are located south of Jerusalem (Blenkinsopp 1988: 86–87); this, of course, reflects what is known of the areas where settlement primarily continued during the exile, even if recent data have led to the modification of some earlier generalizations about this (Carter 1999: 233–48; Lipschits 1999).

That the identification of such groups should be by place of residence is to be expected on the basis of what has been seen above regarding the development of social structures in the late preexilic period. For reasons already stated, locality had by that time become the major focus for self-identity in practical terms, and it was suggested that this could best be understood as a collection of households. Of course, it is difficult to say how much disruption the transfer to Babylonian authority caused for these rural areas, although Lipschits (1999) notes significantly that, as far as the territory of Benjamin was concerned, settlement continued in the major centers, while declining drastically in more isolated regions. The lists may, therefore, simply reflect a continuation of what had already developed earlier, but if there were significant forcible shifts in population in the region under the Babylonians, the links to place rather than kindred are likely to have been even further emphasized.

My proposal, then, is that the social structure of early Persian period Judah was more mixed than has generally been thought, representing within the single community elements whose social orientation was based on the developed "fathers' house," as well as elements who continued to reckon themselves by households grouped according to locality. In other words, we should beware of attempts to impose a single understanding or definition of the family on the community in this period; the mixed experiences of the component parts of the community appear to have had a sociological reflex for some considerable time to come. There is no evidence from such contemporary sources as Haggai and Zechariah 1–8 that there was any particular polarization at the time, and the inner-communal divisions reflected in the later chapters of uncertain date in Isaiah are based upon quite other considerations. The textual expressions of the sharpest polarization in

Ezra–Nehemiah are, in my opinion, written much later and reflect circumstances that had developed long after the social realities had changed in major and significant ways. The question of settlement patterns based on recent archaeological surveys is, of course, of great importance (summarized in Milevski 1996–97; Carter 1999), and attempts should certainly continue to compare their results with those of the texts; but this lies outside my brief, and in any case should, as already stressed, follow independent analysis of the separate sources of data.

The effect of the passage of time together with inevitable developments brought about by living together in a relatively circumscribed territory and by the continuing impact of imperial requirements such as taxation are bound to have led toward a leveling out of these differences. That Ezra's perception, based upon his Babylonian background, remained rooted in the "fathers' house" model is only to be expected, and it is likely that this would have continued as a theoretical construct, at least, among the more conservative elements, such as we find in what I have argued are priestly sources in the book of Nehemiah (1999). As has already become clear, however, revised lay perceptions are vividly seen in the first-person account of Nehemiah, and this would have been accentuated by the fact that he was primarily involved in the practical business of administration. Here, the basic unit of society seems to be predominantly the nuclear family, engaged in either agriculture or crafts, with no intermediate groupings for practical purposes between it and the population as a whole. The leadership, too, is no longer termed according to familial structures (of course, we have no way of knowing whether these continued to play a part behind the scenes), but implies a combination of regional authority and social hierarchy. Where, as in chap. 4, Nehemiah appeals to religious values to support his program, he does so in the typically lay manner of drawing a general analogy between the present situation and some well-known stories from his people's national history (Kellermann 1967: 18). His language, which in this chapter seems to hark back to older paradigms, is thus influenced by his rhetorical purpose at that point, and should not be used to draw far-reaching conclusions regarding the contemporary reality. For this, we must focus, rather, on what he simply takes for granted in the bulk of his narrative, and as we have seen, this points firmly toward a developed and less-religiously-based form of social organization than had previously prevailed.

Finally, while there is no reason to doubt that this was largely the result of the inevitable change over time of a community coming to terms with a radically new set of externally imposed circumstances, the possibility also exists that it may have been hastened by a change in administrative structures at or shortly before the time of Nehemiah's governorship. Some, of course, may wish to associate this with Alt's theory that Judah became a province separate from Samaria only at this time (1934). Although this theory continues to attract some support (e.g., Stern 1971, modified slightly in 1984; McEvenue 1981; Weinberg 1992: 135–37), it is being increasingly abandoned, correctly, in my opinion, in the light of new epigraphical data, as well as the revisiting of the textual evidence (see, for example, Avigad 1976; E. M. Meyers 1985; 1987; Williamson 1988; Lemaire 1990; Hoglund 1992: 69–86). Despite this, there remains evidence of administrative developments of a rather different kind. Kreissig (1973) and Kippenberg (1978) have in their different ways drawn attention to the economic and social pressures that may have contributed to these developments, while Hoglund (1992) has well documented the external political stimuli that could have served as a catalyst (see also E. M. Meyers 1987). Willi (1995), too, has observed the extent to which the texts point to the significant change in the use of social terminology coming later in the Persian period rather than at its inception. A possible reflex of all this may be seen in neighboring Samaria, with the appointment of Sanballat as the first in a quasi-dynastic line of governors. On the assumption that the debacle in Ezra 4:7–23 should be dated to this time, the appointment of Nehemiah could well be interpreted along similar lines. Whether this can be supported by extratextual evidence, however (see provisionally Carter 1999: 116–17, with fuller documentation throughout the book; and Willi 1995: 34–39, who reminds us that there remain epigraphical developments to be explained), and if so, what its impact on the structure of the family may have been, is a question that goes beyond the limits prescribed for the present paper.

References

AHW
      W. von Soden, *Akkadisches Handwörterbuch*. Wiesbaden: Harrassowitz, 1969–76.

Alt, A.
  1934   Die Rolle Samarias bei der Entstehung des Judentums. Pp. 5–28 in *Festschrift Otto Procksch zum 60. Geburtstag*. Leipzig: Deichert and Hinrichs. Reprinted pp. 316–37 in vol. 2 of *Kleine Schriften zur Geschichte des Volkes Israel*. Munich: Beck, 1953.

Andersen, F. I.
  1969   Israelite Kinship Terminology and Social Structure. *Bible Translator* 20: 29–39.

Avigad, N.
  1976   *Bullae and Seals from a Post-Exilic Judean Archive*. Qedem 4. Jerusalem: Institute of Archaeology, Hebrew University.

Bedford, P. R.
  1991   On Models and Texts: A Response to Blenkinsopp and Petersen. Pp. 154–62 in *Second Temple Studies, 1. Persian Period*, ed. P. R. Davies. Journal for the Study of the Old Testament Supplement Series 117. Sheffield: Sheffield Academic Press.

Bendor, S.
  1996   *The Social Structure of Ancient Israel: The Institution of the Family (beit 'ab) from the Settlement to the End of the Monarchy*. Jerusalem Biblical Studies 7. Jerusalem: Simor.

Blenkinsopp, J.
  1988   *Ezra–Nehemiah: A Commentary*. Old Testament Library. London: SCM.
  1997   The Family in First Temple Israel. Pp. 48–103 in *Families in Ancient Israel*, ed. L. G. Perdue et al. Louisville: Westminster John Knox.

Camp, C. V.
  1985   *Wisdom and the Feminine in the Book of Proverbs*. Bible and Literature Series 11. Sheffield: Almond.

Carter, C. E.
  1999   *The Emergence of Yehud in the Persian Period: A Social and Demographic Study*. Journal for the Study of the Old Testament Supplement Series 294. Sheffield: Sheffield Academic Press.

Clines, D. J. A.
  1990   The Nehemiah Memoir: The Perils of Autobiography. Pp. 124–64 in *What Does Eve Do to Help? and Other Readerly Questions to the Old Testament*. Journal for the Study of the Old Testament Supplement Series 94. Sheffield: Sheffield Academic Press.

Collins, J. J.
  1997   Marriage, Divorce, and Family in Second Temple Judaism. Pp. 104–62 in *Families in Ancient Israel*, ed. L. G. Perdue et al. Louisville: Westminster John Knox.
Cowling, G.
  1988   The Biblical Household. Pp. 179–92 in *"Wünschet Jerusalem Frieden": Collected Communications to the XIIth Congress of the International Organization for the Study of the Old Testament, Jerusalem 1986*, ed. M. Augustin and K.-D. Schunck. Frankfurt am Main: Lang.
Demsky, A.
  1983   *Pelekh* in Nehemiah 3. *Israel Exploration Journal* 33: 242–44.
Elliger, K.
  1955   Das Gesetz Leviticus 18. *Zeitschrift für die Alttestamentliche Wissenschaft* 67: 1–25.
Eskenazi, T. C.
  1992   Out from the Shadows: Biblical Women in the Postexilic Era. *Journal for the Study of the Old Testament* 54: 25–43.
Eskenazi, T. C., and Richards, K. H. (eds.)
  1994   *Second Temple Studies, 2: Temple and Community in the Persian Period.* Journal for the Study of the Old Testament Supplement Series 175. Sheffield: Sheffield Academic Press.
Faust, A.
  1999   Differences in Family Structure between Cities and Villages in Iron Age II. *Tel Aviv* 26: 233–52.
Fechter, F.
  1998   *Die Familie in der Nachexilszeit: Untersuchungen zur Bedeutung der Verwandtschaft in ausgewählten Texten des Alten Testaments.* Beihefte zur Zeitschrift für die Alttestamentliche Wissenschaft 264. Berlin: de Gruyter.
Galling, K.
  1964   Die Liste der aus dem Exil Heimgekehrten. Pp. 89–108 in *Studien zur Geschichte Israels im persischen Zeitalter.* Tübingen: Mohr (Siebeck).
Gese, H.
  1963   Zur Geschichte der Kultsänger am zweiten Tempel. Pp. 222–34 in *Abraham Unser Vater: Festschrift für Otto Michel*, ed. O. Betz, M. Hengel, and P. Schmidt. Leiden: Brill. Reprinted pp. 147–58 in H. Gese, *Vom Sinai zum Zion: Alttestamentliche Beiträge zur biblischen Theologie.* Munich: Kaiser, 1974.
Geus, C. H. J. de
  1976   *The Tribes of Israel: An Investigation into Some of the Presuppositions of Martin Noth's Amphictyony Hypothesis.* Studia Semitica Neerlandica 18. Assen/Amsterdam: Van Gorcum.
Gottwald, N. K.
  1979   *The Tribes of Yahweh: A Sociology of the Religion of Liberated Israel 1250–1050 B.C.E.* London: SCM.
Gray, G. B.
  1903   *A Critical and Exegetical Commentary on Numbers.* International Critical Commentary. Edinburgh: T. & T. Clark.
Hartley, J. E.
  1992   *Leviticus.* Word Biblical Commentary 4. Dallas: Word.
Hoglund, K. G.
  1992   *Achaemenid Imperial Administration in Syria–Palestine and the Missions of Ezra and Nehemiah.* Society of Biblical Literature Dissertation Series 125. Atlanta: Scholars Press.
Hopkins, D. C.
  1983   The Dynamics of Agriculture in Monarchical Israel. Pp. 177–202 in *Society of Biblical Literature 1983: Seminar Papers*, ed. K. H. Richards. Society of Biblical Literature Seminar Papers 2. Chico, Calif.: Scholars Press.
  1985   *The Highlands of Canaan: Agricultural Life in the Early Iron Age.* The Social World of Biblical Antiquity 3. Sheffield: JSOT Press.

Hugenberger, G. P.

1994   *Marriage as a Covenant: A Study of Biblical Law and Ethics Governing Marriage Developed from the Perspective of Malachi.* Vetus Testamentum Supplements 52. Leiden: Brill.

Japhet, S.

1983   People and Land in the Restoration Period. Pp. 103–25 in *Das Land Israel in biblischer Zeit,* ed. G. Strecker. Göttingen: Vandenhoeck & Ruprecht.

Kellermann, U.

1967   *Nehemia: Quellen, Überlieferung und Geschichte.* Beihefte zur Zeitschrift für die Alttestamentliche Wissenschaft 102. Berlin: Alfred Töpelmann.

Kippenberg, H. G.

1978   *Religion und Klassenbildung im antiken Judäa: Eine religionssoziologische Studie zum Verhältnis von Tradition und gesellschaftlicher Entwicklung.* Studien zur Umwelt des Neuen Testaments 14. Göttingen: Vandenhoeck & Ruprecht.

Kreissig, H.

1973   *Die sozialökonomische Situation in Juda zur Achämenidenzeit.* Schriften zur Geschichte und Kultur des alten Orients 7. Berlin: Akademie.

Lemaire, A.

1990   Populations et territoires de la Palestine à l'époque perse. *Transeuphratène* 3: 31–74.

Lemche, N. P.

1985   *Early Israel: Anthropological and Historical Studies on the Israelite Society before the Monarchy.* Vetus Testamentum Supplements 37. Leiden: Brill.

Lipschits, O.

1999   The History of the Benjamin Region under Babylonian Rule. *Tel Aviv* 26: 155–90.

Martin, J. D.

1989   Israel as a Tribal Society. Pp. 95–117 in *The World of Ancient Israel: Sociological, Anthropological and Political Perspectives,* ed. R. E. Clements. Cambridge: Cambridge University Press.

McEvenue, S. E.

1981   The Political Structure in Judah from Cyrus to Nehemiah. *Catholic Biblical Quarterly* 43: 353–64.

Meyers, C.

1988   *Discovering Eve: Ancient Israelite Women in Context.* New York: Oxford University Press.

Meyers, E. M.

1985   The Shelomith Seal and the Judean Restoration: Some Additional Considerations. Pp. 33*–38* in *Eretz-Israel* 18 (Nahman Avigad volume), ed. B. Mazar and Y. Yadin. Jerusalem: Israel Exploration Society.

1987   The Persian Period and the Judean Restoration: From Zerubbabel to Nehemiah. Pp. 509–21 in *Ancient Israelite Religion: Essays in Honor of Frank Moore Cross,* ed. P. D. Miller, P. D. Hanson, and S. D. McBride. Philadelphia: Fortress.

Milevski, I.

1996–97   Settlement Patterns in Northern Judah during the Achaemenid Period, According to the Hill Country of Benjamin and Jerusalem Surveys. *Bulletin of the Anglo-Israel Archaeological Society* 15: 7–29.

Muffs, Y.

1968   *Studies in the Aramaic Legal Papyri from Elephantine.* Studia et Documenta ad Iura Orientis Antiqui Pertinentia 8. Leiden: Brill.

Porten, B.

1968   *Archives from Elephantine: The Life of an Ancient Jewish Military Colony.* Berkeley: University of California Press.

Porter, J. R.

1967   *The Extended Family in the Old Testament.* Occasional Papers in Social and Economic Administration 6. London: Edutext.

Rattray, S.
    1987   Marriage Rules, Kinship Terms and Family Structure in the Bible. Pp. 537–44 in *Society of Biblical Literature 1987: Seminar Papers*, ed. K. H. Richards. Society of Biblical Literature Seminar Papers 26. Atlanta: Scholars Press.
Rogerson, J.
    1978   *Anthropology and the Old Testament*. Oxford: Blackwell.
Scharbert, J.
    1982   *Bēyt ʾāb* als soziologische Grösse im Alten Testament. Pp. 213–37 in *Von Kanaan bis Kerala: Festschrift für Prof. Mag. Dr. Dr. J. P. M. van der Ploeg O.P. zur Vollendung des siebzigsten Lebensjahres am 4. Juli 1979*, ed. W. C. Delsman et al. Alter Orient und Altes Testament 211. Neukirchen-Vluyn: Neukirchener Verlag / Kevelaer: Butzon & Bercker.
Schultz, C.
    1980   The Political Tensions Reflected in Ezra–Nehemiah. Pp. 221–44 in *Scripture in Context: Essays on the Comparative Method*, ed. C. D. Evans, W. W. Hallo, and J. B. White. Pittsburgh: Pickwick.
Sellin, E.
    1932   *Geschichte des israelitisch-jüdischen Volkes 2: Vom babylonischen Exil bis zu Alexander dem Grossen*. Leipzig: Quelle & Meyer.
Smith, D. L.
    1989   *The Religion of the Landless: The Social Context of the Babylonian Exile*. Bloomington, Ind.: Meyer-Stone.
    1991   The Politics of Ezra: Sociological Indicators of Postexilic Judaean Society. Pp. 73–97 in *Second Temple Studies, 1: Persian Period*, ed. P. R. Davies. Journal for the Study of the Old Testament Supplement 117. Sheffield: Sheffield Academic Press.
Stager, L. E.
    1985   The Archaeology of the Family. *Bulletin of the American Schools of Oriental Research* 260: 1–35.
Stern, E.
    1971   Seal-Impressions in the Achaemenid Style in the Province of Judah. *Bulletin of the American Schools of Oriental Research* 202: 6–16.
    1984   The Persian Empire and the Political and Social History of Palestine in the Persian Period. Pp. 70–87 in *Introduction: The Persian Period*, ed. W. D. Davies and L. Finkelstein. Vol. 1 of *The Cambridge History of Judaism*. Cambridge: Cambridge University Press.
Toorn, K. van der
    1996   *Family Religion in Babylonia, Syria and Israel: Continuity and Change in the Forms of Religious Life*. Studies in the History and Culture of the Ancient Near East 7. Leiden: Brill.
Vogt, H. C. M.
    1966   *Studie zur nachexilischen Gemeinde in Esra–Nehemia*. Werl: Dietrich-Coelde.
Weinberg, J.
    1992   *The Citizen-Temple Community*. Journal for the Study of the Old Testament Supplement Series 151. Sheffield: Sheffield Academic Press.
Willi, T.
    1995   *Juda—Jehud—Israel: Studien zum Selbstverständnis des Judentums in persischer Zeit*. Forschungen zum Alten Testament 12. Tübingen: Mohr (Siebeck).
Williamson, H. G. M.
    1977   Eschatology in Chronicles. *Tyndale Bulletin* 28: 115–54.
    1979   The Origins of the Twenty-Four Priestly Courses: A Study of I Chronicles xxiii–xxvii. Pp. 251–68 in *Studies in the Historical Books of the Old Testament*, ed. J. A. Emerton. Vetus Testamentum Supplements 30. Leiden: Brill.
    1985   *Ezra, Nehemiah*. Word Biblical Commentary 16. Waco, Tex.: Word.
    1988   The Governors of Judah under the Persians. *Tyndale Bulletin* 39: 59–82.

1998   Judah and the Jews. Pp. 145–63 in *Studies in Persian History: Essays in Memory of David M. Lewis*, ed. M. Brosius and A. Kuhrt. Achaemenid History 11. Leiden: Nederlands Instituut voor het Nabije Oosten.

1999   The Belief System of the Book of Nehemiah. Pp. 276–87 in *The Crisis of Israelite Religion: Transformation of Religious Tradition in Exilic and Post-Exilic Times*, ed. B. Becking and M. C. A. Korpel. Oudtestamentische Studiën 42. Leiden: Brill.

Wilson, R. R.

1977   *Genealogy and History in the Biblical World*. Yale Near Eastern Researches 7. New Haven: Yale University Press.

Wright, C. J. H.

1990   *God's People in God's Land: Family, Land, and Property in the Old Testament*. Grand Rapids: Eerdmans.

Yaron, R.

1961   *Introduction to the Law of the Aramaic Papyri*. Oxford: Clarendon.

Roman-Period Houses from the Galilee: Domestic Architecture and Gendered Spaces

Eric M. Meyers

Department of Religion, Duke University
Durham, North Carolina

My thinking about domestic space, gender, and household activities has been shaped by a number of factors. First and foremost has been the maturation of the field of Women's Studies in general and its application to the field of archaeology in particular (Kent 1990; Allison 1999). Classical scholars and archaeologists working in New World contexts have for some time considered the data deriving from domestic space from a variety of new perspectives that take into account the dominant social mores governing gender in traditional societies, often drawing on material from ethnoarchaeology to make their points (McKee 1999). Over-reliance on male-produced or -edited documents has had an especially negative influence on classical archaeology, since these documents presuppose a strict separation between the male sector of a domicile, the *andron*, and a separate women's quarter (Goldberg 1999: 142). Drawing also on data inferred from Athenian vase paintings, classicists identified the *andron* as the place where men attended *symposia*.

Such a rigid separation of domestic space by gender has had the result of raising the level of interest in the quest to determine the women's sector or rooms known as the *gunaikonitis* (or "place for women"). One of the major consequences of focusing on such questions has been to view Athenian households as "places of integration, where individuals who were separated by gender distinctions, as well as by sex and family and class, negotiated norms and space" (Goldberg 1999: 143). In the classical Greek world it turns out that it was the courtyard that became the chief site of such integration (Jameson 1990: 179). Because the courtyard is such a central feature of the Syro-Palestinian house in the Roman period, the Athenian analogy is very helpful in better understanding the situation in the Jewish world.

Examining the domestic space of Athenian houses, Goldberg has noted (1999: 145, fig. 9.2) that it was Walker (1983: 87) who first observed that the gendered division of household space was the organizing architectural principle of the ancient Greek house. Despite the fact that Greek literature and vase paintings separate space into male and female sectors or domains, Goldberg shows that the courtyard in every circumstance partakes of both genders and of their associated activities from time to time. Hence, she concludes that Walker's work is flawed and has justly been criticized as being too rigid in respect to delineating gendered spaces. Thus, for example, in the Greek world almost no rooms in any excavated context have produced a preponderance of what might be called women's

objects (e.g., mirrors, jewelry, etc.). Also, loomweights have been found in only a few localized contexts (Jameson 1990: 186), suggesting that the looms were portable, just as were
items of furniture. Hirschfeld's ethnographic data included in his important work *The Palestinian Dwelling* (1995: 217ff.) substantially confirm this aspect of flexibility in respect to
various spatial components of a house, although I will challenge his interpretation of
some of the literary data when it comes to matters of gender.

Hence, Goldberg concludes (1999: 150) that in Greek society women were not kept in
strict isolation in women's quarters, as many had previously assumed to be the case. Moreover, Goldberg notes that therefore the older view of separate gender domains based on
both literary sources and vase paintings is flawed (1999: 142, 147). In truth, vase paintings,
when looked at once again in light of recent studies of gender, may be reinterpreted to
suggest the absence of fixed space for each gender. Such observations have also led to a
conclusion that is quite relevant to the Syro-Palestinian region, namely, that the house is
an organization of physical space that varies over time. Insofar as most furnishings were
portable in Greece and Palestine, individual rooms and the courtyard itself could change
function at different times. Thus, these sorts of considerations may be utilized in our
assessment of domestic and gendered space in the Jewish setting of the Galilee.

A basic question underlying our inquiry about the house in Roman period Jewish
Galilee is whether or not the physical domiciles reflect the construction of gender that
one encounters in rabbinic texts. Since houses were frequently modified over time, we
should not think of domestic space in static terms. As the place in which the extended
family lived, the house was ever changing to accommodate new individuals and realities.
Yet if we were to inquire why the rabbis called the husband in a household *ba'al-ha-bayit*,
"master of the house," we would begin to get a sense of the dominance of the male in the
general ideological schema of the times. Also, domestic space when considered apart
from archaeology has usually been taken to be part of the private as opposed to public
domain (Wegner 1988; Peskowitz 1993: 26), a designation that would identify most of the
activities of the household as being female or as being in the domain of women. In order
to dispel this still-dominant public/private dichotomy, with its specific connotations of
gender and its disposition to view work and status as something that resides outside the
home (Wallace-Hadrill 1988), let me begin by presenting the evidence from ancient
Meiron Insula I (fig. 1). According to Hirschfeld's nomenclature, the houses there are a
development of the simple house and characteristic of private domiciles in rural areas
(1995: 30–31).

What is so interesting at Meiron from the point of view of gender considerations is the
combination of work activities together with other activities of production and sustenance that may all be associated with this insula. In the larger residence, we find on the
ground floor an eight-room configuration that opens onto a courtyard (Meyers, Strange,
and Meyers 1981; see fig. 1). The nature of the debris in this area suggests the existence of
an upper story that doubtless functioned as sleeping quarters, very similar to the situation
in the Old City of Jerusalem to this day. The size of the residence suggests a family or extended family of some means. Room E, which contained a stone workbench and an iron-
handled bronze planer, was identified by the excavators as a cooperage that produced
wooden crates or barrels, possibly for the Galilean trade in olives or olive oil (fig. 2). The

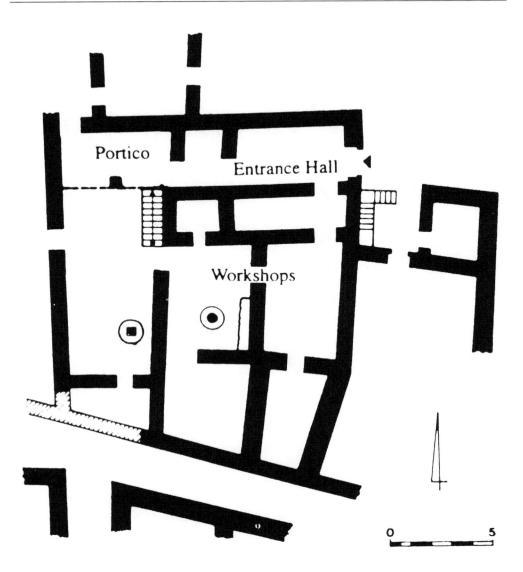

Fig. 1. Meiron Insula I.

adjacent room D was also identified as a workspace, and room A was utilized as a passage-way to the courtyard. Rooms F and C contained stone grinders necessary for the produc-tion of food (fig. 2). In addition, food grinders and bone and bronze needles were found in the courtyard, suggesting that food production and sewing took place there. The pres-ence of a private *miqveh* off the courtyard should also be mentioned, apparently used by members of the family. In all, the building represents 180 m² of space, including the 5 × 7 m courtyard west of the house (figs. 1–2).

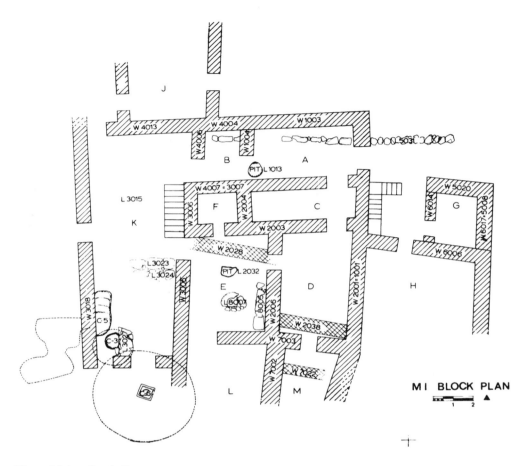

Fig. 2. Meiron Insula I.

The implication of the Meiron residence for our presentation is quite clear: the interior of the house does not represent private space as distinct from work space. Rather, a variety of work was carried out there, consisting of food production, textile work, and carpentry. The notion of public/private dichotomy simply cannot characterize this space, where all manner of household, family, and everyday activities were carried on. Although inscriptional support is lacking for husbands and wives working together, the organization of space suggests such a possibility, as well as the involvement of family members in a variety of household tasks (Peskowitz 1993: 32). Indeed, at the Meiron residence it is difficult even to determine where one dwelling ends and another begins, much less determine how all the rooms were meant to interconnect (Meyers and Meyers 1982–83: 32). The house, whether in a village, town, or city, was rarely if ever isolated but was rather a place of "dynamic arrangements, of access and exclusion, opening and closing, enclosing and disclosing, that shifted and varied with the time of day, the activity undertaken, the season of the year, relations between persons occupying or passing through, mechanisms of exchange and commerce, and so forth" (Baker 1997: 65).

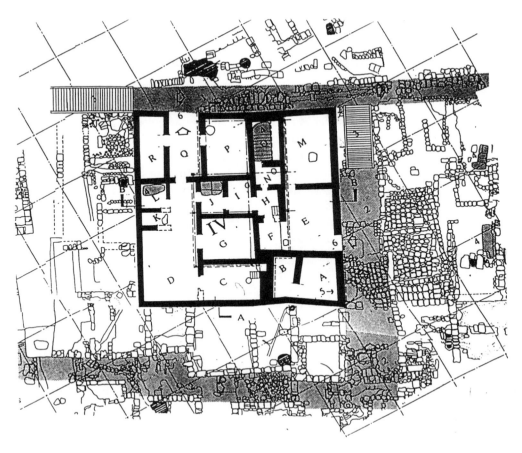

Fig. 3. Sepphoris House Insula IV.

It is precisely this sense of fluidity that allows us to view domestic space and some of the material from areas on the western acropolis at Sepphoris with new insight. This examination excludes the elaborate peristyle courtyard house or mansion with the Dionysos mosaic, which may have served some public function as a guest house near the theater. Another possibility is that it could have been the domicile of one of Sepphoris's urban aristocracy, most likely Jewish, since it is so close to the "Jewish Quarter" on the western acropolis. The relatively few such peristyle houses of this sort found in Palestine led Hirschfeld to conclude that "this negative finding suggests that the penetration of Hellenistic-Roman traditions—at least in private construction—was limited" (1995: 290). More typical of Jewish Galilee are the ones that we have already examined at Meiron, with shops, the complex house, or the courtyard house such as we find in Insula IV at Sepphoris (fig. 3).

One of the few criticisms we may direct at Hirschfeld is that his otherwise commendable study of the house presupposes the existence of privacy, whether in describing the courtyard as "a convenient barrier between the public and private domains," or in characterizing the simple or complex house as offering "greater privacy" (1995: 21–22). But, as we have already noted, it is very difficult to ascertain the true nature of the relationships that obtained among the residents of any particular domicile. Courtyards, in particular, permit of multiple connections with neighbors and of multiple relationships among the people residing within the domicile. Hirschfeld states it this way: "Maintaining the privacy of the courtyard was apparently as important in the Roman-Byzantine period as it was in traditional Palestinian culture. In fact, the Jewish sources define the various types of courtyards according to the degree of privacy they provided" (1995: 272). But, to restate the position with which we concur, some courtyards "may serve as spaces for privacy while others are common space used by dwellings as an extension of household space, but hardly as a means of affording privacy" (Baker 1997: 159). In a topographical situation such as the one at Meiron, which is steeply sloped, several of the courtyards up-slope clearly could be observed from the upper slope, and even the lower rooftop of the lower house could serve as public space for the neighbors above (Meyers, Strange, and Meyers 1981: 55–61).

The Sepphoris house in Insula IV is also known as Area 84.1 and is briefly described in the Sepphoris exhibition catalogue (Nagy et al. 1996: 41–45) (see fig. 4). This domicile is situated along the northern ridge of the westernmost residential area and is built alongside a very well-preserved east–west roadway that connects the entire area with the area on the peak of the acropolis near the theater and Dionysos mansion. In the Roman period, this house underwent numerous renovations, and parts of it may have taken shape originally in the Hellenistic period (fig. 3). Two *miqva'ot* have been identified in the structure; the earlier, dating to the Early Roman period (end of the Second Temple period), is labeled L on the ground plan. It certainly continued in use until ca. 300 C.E., and it may have been used into the 4th century as well. A much larger and more-elaborate *miqveh*, identified as O on the plan, had by the 4th century clearly been sealed over and the space put to other use. For several centuries the domicile had two ritual baths in simultaneous use, both located near water cisterns.

The main entrance to the house, from ca. 70–363 C.E., labeled Q, provides immediate access to the east–west roadway. Room R, just to the west as one enters facing south, doubtless provided easy storage for goods and supplies and possibly quarters for pack animals, such as a donkey, which might have carried the materials from the eastern market in the lower city, a fairly lengthy walk with heavy supplies. The small room K that might have served to collect water from the rooftops has a collection basin in its center. The main focal point of this section of the house, however, is the large unroofed courtyard D in the southwest corner. It is important to note that the courtyard is well situated with respect to the main northern entryway to the domicile (Q) and that the adjoining room to the east, room C, has a cistern and ample space for storage of work tools and cool storage for food supplies; a similar case may be made for room G, which yielded a number of spindle whorls. Slightly to the north are rooms J and I: room J has a small stepped pool, either for washing vessels or purifying glass or metal ones; and room I contains interlocking cisterns that were converted in the Middle Roman period to underground storage. Also, abutting the east–west roadway is a very large storage area, room P, which had the greatest number of spindle whorls and items of personal adornment, as well as extensive underground stor-

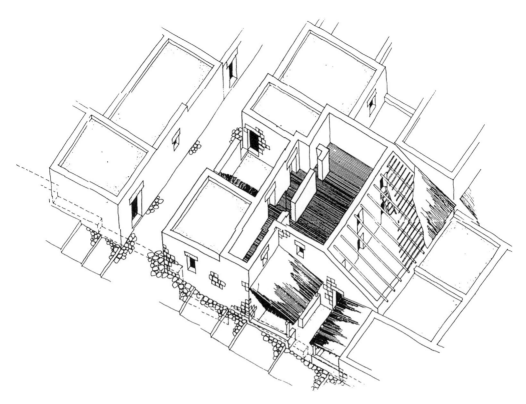

Fig. 4. Isometric reconstruction of Sepphoris House Insula IV.

age space for olives, olive oil, wine, etc. This lower section of the house probably had a second story above units G, F, H, I, J, N, O, and P, no doubt residential private spaces such as we had at Meiron Insula I, hence the preservation of extensive items of personal use and adornment, spindle whorls, toggle pins, and hair pins.

Because so much of the area within the house was not sealed from above, except for the cisterns and underground chambers, it is difficult to do a definitive distribution chart of small finds and pottery types that might help us better understand room function and possible associations with gender. Before considering these matters further, let me point out a distinctive corpus of evidence in the Sepphoris house under consideration (84.1). First there is the corpus of chalk or stone vessels that date to the Early Roman period and probably to the pre-70 C.E. era, similar to those found in Jerusalem and elsewhere in the Galilee (Cahill 1992; Deines 1993; Magen 1994). The vessels are clearly related to the issue of ritual purity and are found in virtually all early Roman loci on the western acropolis. In the context of 84.1, however, we may clearly relate these vessels to the two *miqva'ot* and possible smaller immersion pools for vessels already noted.

Of special note too are the 50 fragments and whole examples of round and rectangular incense shovels found in 84.1, more than have been found in any other location at Sepphoris, where other excavations have also noted their presence (Rutgers 1999: 191).

All of these are ceramic, which make them a unique corpus, since all other known examples are bronze, although the Mishnah mentions ceramic examples (*Kelim* 2.3, 7). Many similar types are depicted in ancient Jewish art. Their chronological range spans the Middle–Late Roman period; they appear to be slightly later than the chalk vessels, but most others are used throughout the Middle Roman period, at least up to ca. 300 C.E. and probably until 363 C.E. Because of their similarity to the incense shovels in Jewish art, Rutgers (1999: 178–83) has related the rectangular examples (fig. 5) to the priestly *maḥtah* that was used in the Temple service; the oval ones (fig. 6) he has related to the *patera*, such as were found in the Bar Kochba caves (Yadin 1963: 46–63).

There is something quite enigmatic, however, about the incense shovels from Sepphoris: none of them appears ever to have been used. There is no trace of burning or residue, yet there is no doubt that they are what they are—incense shovels. Rutgers concludes that, since incense is associated with priestly function in the Temple and matters of purity, the shovels are indicative of a priestly presence, a social reality that we know well from rabbinic references (1999: 192–96). But the suggestion that they were intended not to be used is something with which I am very uncomfortable, so I would suggest alternatively that they possibly were used to hold sweet-smelling dried plants, a kind of potpourri, or were intended for burning scented oil, which would not leave any trace, or for containing a mixture of resin, spices, and herbs.[1] Such a hypothesis would allow for indications of a priestly identity and hence the existence of an elite class at Sepphoris, which goes well with the evidence for what might be considered extreme concern with ritual purity and a concomitant concern for keeping the air inside a very large house fresh with mild scent.

The array of artifacts from the rooms and spaces in and around the courtyard suggests a variety of domestic activities: grinders for food preparation, bone needles for sewing, toggle pins for clothing, loom weights, and so on. The lower space of 84.1 is thus analogous to the Meiron lower insula (fig. 1). What is new is that, similar to the priestly house in Jerusalem, the installation and accoutrements associated with ritual purity—*miqva'ot* and stone vessels—are found in abundance along with the later incense shovels. This is perhaps indicative of a priestly element in residence during and after the destruction of the Temple in 70 C.E., no doubt an influential and wealthy group that could well have had an impact on the Sepphorean citizenry in adopting a pro-Roman stance in 68 C.E.

---

1. I have conferred with a number of paleobotanists and geologists who have suggested that a non-functional interpretation is highly unlikely. Annette Green, head of the Fragrance Foundation in New York City and author of numerous articles on the subject, informs me that the use of dry fumigants to provide scent for households was very common in antiquity and that the list of plants and spices is quite long. While not denying the priestly association that Rutgers has made, we may suggest that the use of fumigants in incense shovels was as much a reflection of social standing and class as it was of religious background, especially since both the vessel and the fumigants would have cost a not-inconsiderable sum of money. C. L. Meyers has dealt with the possible use of incense in Iron Age period cup-and-saucers from nearby Tel 'Ein Zippori (1998: 34–37). She concludes that the burning of incense or fumigants could well have occurred in domestic contexts as opposed to cultic, and that the use of imported resins, "often mixed with herbs or spices from fumigation was somewhat more restricted for economic reasons. But even so, the notion that burning incense could mean only the burning of the costly fruit of trees or shrubs of South Arabia or West Africa must be rejected" (1998: 36). This suggestion accords well with what I have proposed here in regard to the ceramic priestly shovels at Sepphoris. Where we do not find incense shovels that have been used with burned material, it is quite possible that fumigants were burned on other types of vessels, such as plates or even on cupped broken sherds.

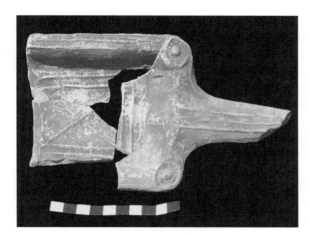

Fig. 5. Rectangular incense shovel.

Fig. 6. Oval incense shovels.

(E. M. Meyers 1999: 109–22). For the priests of the Second Temple, what mattered most was the status quo and preserving the Temple service. Subsequently, when they dispersed to new centers after 70 C.E., such as to Sepphoris, they became part of the Galilean aristocracy (Levine 1989: 171).

There is one possible inference to be drawn from some of the data, which has already been mentioned but needs to be questioned—namely, that maintaining privacy was a major aspect of the courtyard house (Hirschfeld 1995: 272; Baker 1997: 159). The situation of courtyard D in Area 84.1 at Sepphoris (fig. 3) hardly was a zone of privacy; rather, it could only have been the hub of a variety of activities that were carried out by the extended family that inhabited this household. Hirschfeld, however, does not take the notion of privacy to the extreme of declaring that one section of the house was for women and another for men; he suggests only that men were normally thought to be active in the courtyard closer to the roadway, while the women concentrated their activities close to the inner courtyard (1995: 49; see also Baker 1997: 161). Had Hirschfeld had access to the Sepphoris material, the only other spaces that might have qualified for such an interpretation would have been rooms M or E in the older, northeast wing of the household (fig. 3). Since the roadway that runs just north of 84.1 is virtually intact to this day in its ancient configuration, it is plain to see that room M is contiguous with it. Similarly, the excavators have concluded that another ancient walkway or a crossroad that divided insulae would have been located just east of rooms M and E, where a modern walkway for tourists may be placed (no. 3), with no. 2 representing bedrock, with occasional cut stones still in place from the Early Roman road that was reused in the Byzantine period. In Hirschfeld's privacy scheme, we would have to conclude that only women utilized courtyard D, a suggestion that cannot be supported by the data.

If one were to examine rabbinic literature systematically, a strong case for locating women in all sorts of diverse spatial contexts can be made, inside and outside the home, and men and women were involved with fieldwork, production of goods, and moving about in towns, villages, and urban environments. If we may assume the presence of a significant priestly segment of society at Sepphoris, and especially in connection within domicile 84.1, then we must also be prepared to say that in an environment that took ritual purity matters very seriously, women and men necessarily had to have had numerous contacts (not physical) during their daily activities. In the built environment of ancient Galilee, it is virtually impossible to construct a scenario whereby men and women could have avoided each other either at home or outside the home. Even Meiron is mentioned in the list of priestly courses as the location of the clan of Yehoiariv. And we have observed the number and variety of work activities conducted in Meiron Insula I; there the *miqveh*, however, was located off the courtyard, which would have facilitated its use by men and women in the compound.

There is no doubt that the urban environment of Sepphoris has contributed to the upscale nature of the households uncovered there, similar in fact to those uncovered in Jerusalem near the Temple. Hence, while we can say that 84.1 is larger and more elaborate than the Meiron insula and offers a greater possibility of privacy in regard to the availability of several *miqva'ot* in the household, we cannot infer from the data that the range of activities carried out at home was fewer or limited solely to women. I have not posited the size of the Sepphoris house because the eastern side is not as well preserved as the western side, the latter of which had an upper story. Assuming that the east was one story high only, since it is built on bedrock and is much higher upslope, 84.1 by the Middle Roman period is nearly double the size of the Meiron I household, that is, ca. 300 m², which probably accommodated more than 20 individuals. In Jewish practice, brides were transferred from their father's home to that of the groom, along with elderly parents, aunts, uncles, and children, so that the number in a household could soar quite quickly.

While the full shape of 84.1 in the Early Roman period is not known, because so many portions of the western sector go back to that era, it is possible that two households and/ or homes were combined in the mid–2nd century to create a much larger unit of space, so that each half of the larger unit may have been comparable in size to Meiron Insula I in the pre-70 C.E. era. In any case, the suggestion of Guijarro (1999: 60–61) that the average size of the 1st-century family household in Galilee was four seems much too low, especially in view of the practice of sons' bringing their wives home with them. If I am correct in assuming that two houses and households may have existed side by side in late Second Temple times but were combined in the space occupied by 84.1 from ca. 135 to 363 C.E., each half in the earlier setting would have had ample water storage space, at least one *miqveh*, and a courtyard, and each would have bordered on one or more streets or alleyways that constituted important activity areas for residents. Such places were areas where various people met and congregated, both men and women—not to mention at nearby water areas as well. What the implications were for the families when the two units were possibly combined into one is difficult to say. But these priestly families, as aristocratic as they might have been and as committed as they were to high standards of ritual purity, were pretty much obliged to do a considerable rate of work activity at home, whether it be food preparation or the manufacture of textiles. The nearby pedestrian traffic along the adjoining walk and roadways assured both men and women of easy access to markets, shops, fields, reservoirs, and so on—all likely places for regular contacts like these, just as at home.

As a result of our consideration of domestic space at ancient Meiron and Sepphoris, and in light of parallels from the classical world, I have concluded that it is difficult to defend any notion that Jewish houses and households were areas of confinement or concealment for women. Although women were advised and even required by rabbinic norms and practice to go out to the marketplace and streets in modest demeanor and dress, the archaeology of domestic space and town or urban life require a much greater flexibility of understanding. Rigid rabbinic constructions of gender that masculinize Torah study and feminize women at home, to oversimplify matters, were a way of legitimizing the rabbinic reconstruction of Judaism without the Temple; and in so doing the rabbis created a myth of women left at home, denied access to the world, and devoid of knowledge that did not concern the household or children. But the changing world order that shaped Roman-period Judaism led ultimately to an alternative ordering of society that only archaeology can help us to reveal and locate within the social fabric. Even for buildings from among the priestly circles of Sepphoris, a consideration of domestic spaces and the built environment enables us to picture a world giving way to the growing open-market economy and to the by-products of growing urbanization and the encroachment of Hellenization. Such processes ultimately led to a greater participation of women in the full range of social and professional activities, which in the Diaspora communities are perhaps to be observed with greater clarity (Brooten 1982).

References

Allison, P. A. (ed.)
   1999   *The Archaeology of Household Activities.* London: Routledge.

Baker, C. M.
1997   *Rebuilding the House of Israel: Gendered Bodies and Domestic Politics in Roman Jewish Galilee c. 135–300 CE.* Ph.D. dissertation, Duke University.

Brooten, B.
1982   *Women Leaders in Ancient Synagogue.* Chico, Calif.: Scholars Press.

Cahill, J. M.
1992   Chalk Vessel Assemblages of the Persian/Hellenistic and Early Roman Periods. Pp. 190–271 in *Excavations at the City of David 1978–1985 Directed by Y. Shiloh III: Stratigraphical, Environmental, and Other Reports*, ed. D. T. Ariel and A. De Groot. Qedem 33. Jerusalem: Hebrew University.

Deines, R.
1993   *Jüdische Steingefässe und pharisäische Frommigheit: Ein archäeologisch-historischer Beitrag zum Verständnis von Joh. 2, 6 und der jüdischen Reinheitshalacha zur Zeit Jesu.* Tübingen: Mohr.

Goldberg, M. Y.
1999   Spatial and Behavioral Negotiation in Classical Athenian City Houses. Pp. 142–61 in *The Archaeology of Household Activities*, ed. P. A. Allison. London: Routledge.

Guijarro, S.
1999   The Family in First-Century Galilee. Pp. 42–65 in *Constructing Early Christian Families: Family as Social Reality and Metaphor*, ed. H. Moxnes. London: Routledge.

Hirschfeld, Y.
1995   *The Palestinian Dwelling in the Roman-Byzantine Period.* Jerusalem: Franciscan Printing Press and Israel Exploration Society.

Jameson, M.
1990   Domestic Space in the Greek City-State. Pp. 92–113 in *Domestic Architecture and the Use of Space: An Interdisciplinary Cross-Cultural Study*, ed. S. Kent. Cambridge: Cambridge University Press.

Kent, S.
1990   Activity Areas and Architecture: An Interdisciplinary View of the Relationship between Use of Space and Domestic Built Environments. Pp. 1–8 in *Domestic Architecture and the Use of Space: An Interdisciplinary Cross-Cultural Study*, ed. S. Kent. Cambridge: Cambridge University Press.

Levine, L. I.
1989   *The Rabbinic Class of Roman Palestine in Late Antiquity.* Jerusalem: Yad Izhak Ben-Zvi.

Magen, Y.
1994   *"Purity Broke Out in Israel": Stone Vessels in the Late Second Temple Period.* The Reuben and Edith Hecht Museum Catalogue 9. Haifa: University of Haifa.

McKee, B. R.
1999   Household Archaeology and Cultural Formation Processes: Examples from the Cerén Site, El Salvador. Pp. 30–42 in *The Archaeology of Household Activities*, ed. P. A. Allison. London: Routledge.

Meyers, C. L.
1998   Fumes, Flames or Fluids? Reframing the Cup-and-Bowl Question. Pp. 30–39 in *Boundaries of the Ancient Near Eastern World: A Tribute to Cyrus Gordon*, ed. M. Lubetski. C. Gottlieb, and S. Keller. Journal for the Study of the Old Testament Supplement Series 273. Sheffield: Sheffield Academic Press.

Meyers, E. M.
1999   Sepphoris on the Eve of the Great Revolt (67–68 C.E.): Archaeology and Josephus. Pp. 109–22 in *Galilee through the Centuries: Confluence of Cultures*, ed. E. M. Meyers. Winona Lake, Ind.: Eisenbrauns.

Meyers, E. M., and Meyers, C. L.
   1982–83   Talumudic Village Life in the Galilean Highlands. *Bulletin of the Anglo-Israel Archaeological Society* 1982–83: 32–36.
Meyers, E. M.; Strange, J. F.; and Meyers, C. L.
   1981   *Excavations at Ancient Meiron.* Cambridge, Mass.: American Schools of Oriental Research.
Nagy, R. M., et al. (eds.)
   1996   *Sepphoris in Galilee: Crosscurrents of Culture.* Raleigh, N.C.: Museum of Art.
Peskowitz, M.
   1993   "Family/ies" in Antiquity: Evidence from Tannaitic Literature and Roman Galilean Architecture. Pp. 9–38 in *The Jewish Family in Antiquity*, ed. S. J. D. Cohen. Atlanta: Scholars Press.
Rutgers, L. V.
   1999   Incense Shovels at Sepphoris? Pp. 177–98 in *Galilee through the Centuries: Confluence of Cultures*, ed. E. M. Meyers. Winona Lake, Ind.: Eisenbrauns.
Walker, S.
   1983   Women and Housing in Classical Greece. Pp. 81–91 in *Images of Women in Antiquity*, ed. A. Cameron and A. Kurht. London: Routledge and Kegan Paul.
Wallace-Hadrill, A.
   1988   The Social Structure of the Roman House. *Papers of the British School at Rome* 56: 43–97.
Wegner, J. R.
   1988   *Chattel or Person? The Status of Women in the Mishnah.* Oxford: Oxford University Press.
Yadin, Y.
   1963   *Finds from the Bar Kochba Period in the Cave of Letters.* Jerusalem: Israel Exploration Society.

Apocryphal Women: From Fiction to (Arti)fact

Amy-Jill Levine
Divinity School and Graduate Department of Religion
Vanderbilt University, Nashville, Tennessee

I. History's Remains

The Deuterocanonical Texts / Old Testament Apocrypha, women's history, feminist studies, and archaeology all suffer from an academic stigma, whether in the undergraduate classroom or the seminary hall. The Apocrypha, and especially the novellas, remain neglected in scholarship for several reasons: the religious prioritizing of the canons of synagogue and Protestant Christianity over the Deuterocanonical documents and the academic prioritizing of history and theology over fiction, of stories of men and war over stories of women and seduction, and so on. Although today there are increasing numbers of publications on the novellas—Brenner's edited collection, *A Feminist Companion to Esther, Judith and Susanna* (1995); Wills's *Jewish Novel in the Ancient World* (1995); Moore's Anchor Bible commentary on Tobit (1996); Spolsky's edited volume, *The Judgment of Susanna: Authority and Witness* (1996), among others—they remain minor voices, rarely assigned in the classroom, rarely cited in articles, and even more rarely invoked from pulpits. Their primary dialogue partners are in fact most often disciplines outside of religious studies, Judaica, or biblical studies; they converse with Classics, women's studies, and sometimes feminist and narrative theory. A new trend, or rather the revival of the old *Forschungsberichte*, appears to be the next stage for work on the Hebrew Bible's Apocryphal novellas: the tracing of a character across time and culture, as in Stoker's work on Judith (1998) and in several of the articles in the Spolsky collection (1996). Still, scholars of the novellas have yet to enter into any sustained dialogue with questions of material culture or archaeology.

Women's history and feminist studies are similarly problematic. True, the concerns of these disciplines are more integrated into curricula today than they were a generation ago, and many if not most students of religion have a passing familiarity with at least the *Frauenfrage*. The Lady Eve and her first runner-up in the "Women of the Hebrew Bible" contest, Lady Wisdom, often receive attention, as do, in the Christian canon, Pauline injunctions and household codes (whether apologetically, polemically, or historically), as well as anyone named "Mary." However, the secondary sources most popular in biblical studies classrooms are those that address the literary depictions of female characters, not the real lives of real women. For the Old Testament/Tanach/Hebrew Bible, the works of Mieke Bal, Cheryl Exum, and Phyllis Trible are more likely to be cited in the classroom and remembered by the student than archaeological reports. Even from archaeologists in the field, such as Carol Meyers, the major point students outside the archaeological discipline retain from her work is, I suspect, the revisionist translation of Genesis 3—again, literature prevails over material culture.

Worse, in the graduate classroom—as women's history continues its relationship to feminist theory—the focus is shifting from women to gender, and the study of gender, it appears, means first the interrogation of "the male" or "the masculine" and, occasionally, challenges to this normative construct via newer approaches such as "Queer Theory." We today know more about gender construction in the Judean royal court, Hellenistic society, and Christian Rome than we do, I suspect, about real women doing real things.

In a similar way, the cultural appropriation of history has a firmer hold over the contemporary imagination than the artifacts of history itself. Thus, students as well as the general public are more apt to remember Renaissance paintings than ancient mosaics (archaeologists would do well to have their findings, such as the mosaic from Sepphoris, the "Mona Lisa of the Galilee" [Meyers, Netzer, and Meyers 1987], mass-produced for display on dorm- or living-room walls).

This preference for appropriation and reformulation over the "real" or the "historical" finds its own institutional corollary. With the rise of globalization in the academy, social location-based reading has become increasingly popular. Especially when conjoined with a literary-critical perspective, in which one interprets autobiographically and "in front of" the text rather than historically and so "behind" it, this approach erases interest in—indeed, erases the need for—any historical grounding. The situation is the logical extension of the entirely justified critiques of traditional historical criticism that feminists and others continue to pose. Certainly scholars did (and some still do) adopt a completely objectivist stance, rather than recognize how their own presuppositions and interests drove both their questions and many of their conclusions. The extreme form of this reaction, often justified by appeal to reader-response or post-colonial method, begins from the contemporary, immediate experiences of the interpreters; readers consequently ignore (they do not need) information on, say, Hasmonean expansionism or Roman imperialism. History is the first loser; material culture and archaeology never entered the race. For all that objectivist history is at best an ideal, it nevertheless is the case that parts of the past can be recovered, and that archaeologists can derive interpretations that are firmly grounded.

Scholarly and cultural interests conjoin in yet another way to remove attention from the Hellenistic period. Just as the Apocryphal novellas are marginalized, given the priorities already noted, so too the period in which they were likely composed—in early and mid–Hellenistic Palestine—is at best less interesting than, for example, Iron Age sites or Herodian remains. The former offer more data with potential relationship to famous images and figures from the biblical text; the latter contributes, for better or ill, to the ever-popular life-of-Jesus approach. I wonder if, as well, the Hasmonean period (the likely time of the composition of the book of Judith) may suffer also from what those in the U.S. might call "political incorrectness"; Jewish expansionistic policies, Jewish military exploits, Jewish assimilation, and so forth, are not subjects particularly dear to the liberal college student, let alone professor.

Confirming the role of these various ideological divisions in creating a disconnection between Deuterocanonical novels and archaeological investigation is professional training. Literary critics are not often trained in archaeology, and I suspect many if not most lack even an interest in it. Problems are inevitable when the student of the Bible attempts to integrate matters of material culture, determined via archaeological discovery, with the literary text. In too many cases, the problems are resolved by dismissing the archaeological record entirely. For scholarship on texts such as the Apocryphal novellas—that is, for fictional literature—the case has to be made that archaeological investigation and insights into material culture are even relevant pursuits.[1] Since the texts have been approached disconnected from archaeological study for so long, the need for this study is not self-evident.

Finally complicating the relationship of art to artifact are the recent discoveries related to the rabbinic period. The Mishnah does not reflect the realia of Jewish life in Palestine; it constructs a world of its own that only later was itself brought into being. Archaeology thus to a great extent tells us that the Mishnah is fiction, an ideal world constructed by the rabbis; thus, the Mishnah can substantially continue to be studied as it had been in the past—completely divorced from interest in, or knowledge of, the real people who composed it, their neighbors, and their wives.[2] This is not to say that there is no progress, as those familiar with the Albright Institute well know, in integrating questions of material culture with analysis of literary texts. Moreover, such integration may become increasingly prominent as the archaeological discipline shifts from a focus on treasure troves and the ever-popular biblical "proof" to the hows and whys of the lives of common men and women. It will likely be through this focus that (real) women will resurface on the scholarly radar. With the conjoining of analysis of the literary text with a deeper understanding of the material culture in which it was produced and originally preserved—the data are available; the problem is that they are not arranged in such a way as to make them useful to the literary critic (S. White Crawford, personal communication)—both disciplines benefit, as do the their practitioners.

II. *Questions in the Dirt*

I do not know why the symposium organizers chose specifically to address the topic of women in the Apocrypha,[3] but it stimulated my interest and provoked a sufficient number of questions for me to find this an insightful move and a wonderful invitation.

Was the concern of the organizing committee that "women" be included? Surely the topic would be addressed by others.[4] Nevertheless, the Apocryphal focus insists on the topic. Was it to include reference to the Apocrypha, a collection too often ignored? If so, good again. Or could it have been so that students of the Apocryphal novellas—Judith,

---

1. The conjoining of biblical studies with a focus on the realia of people's lives is not entirely absent from scholarly pursuit: the new collection edited by Kraemer and D'Angelo (1999) offers some detail on the lives of real women, as does the volume by Balch and Osiek (1998). The sister volume of the latter, by Perdue et al. (1998), is similarly attuned to material culture and archaeological investigation. In this volume, however, as might be expected, the very detailed article on Second Temple Judaism by John Collins has little to offer the student of the women in the Old Testament Apocryphal novellas.

2. For an archaeologically informed reading of this material, see Peskowitz 1997.

3. My own situation at the time of the symposium (i.e., recuperating from open-heart surgery [another form of archaeological investigation]) prevented my asking this question.

4. It would do my heart good to know that this was the case!

Susanna, Tobit, Greek Esther—and the context of Hellenism in which they took shape might be able to learn from and contribute to the work of archaeology? If so, and this is my hope, terrific.

Thus, this paper seeks to begin a discussion on the terms by which communication between the literature-based and culturally informed researcher and the field archaeologist can be facilitated. The goal is to enrich our knowledge about the representations of Jewish women in the Hellenistic period and, if possible, of their real sisters.

Problem One: The Fictional Text

Unlike the Deuteronomic history, which at least portends a basis in fact, and unlike the stories of Jesus (Gospels) and by Jesus (parables), which evoke a setting at least partially recognizable as reality-based, the novellas have long been recognized as fiction. To use them as a basis for historical investigation, let alone material culture, would be tantamount to using the modern "bodice ripper" as a key into life in Saxon England (if there were in fact bodices in Saxon England) or, for that matter, using Heliodorus's *Ethiopian Story* to learn about Greek life in North Africa. Analysis must be much more nuanced.[5]

Even fictional texts yield historical insight, as the recent explosion of ideological criticism vocally insists. Culturally, the Apocryphal novellas, preserved if not originally composed in Greek, testify to the impact Hellenism had on Jewish self-identity. No longer do most scholars look to 5th-century Babylon (Susanna) or Persia (Esther), let alone post-exilic "Assyria" (Tobit), for the origins of these volumes; they fit as redacted if not composed in light of Hellenism and as having a strong tie to if not actual composition in Palestine. Furthermore, motifs in the novels are, if not particular to, at least strongly indicative of late Hellenistic society: the development of an entrepreneurial class with its concerns for brokerage, patron-client relationships, and increase in the honor/shame mechanism (which provides internal control in the face of outside pressures), as well as an attendant rise in the literacy rate. Recently, Ilan (1999: chap. 4) has argued that Esther, Judith, and Susanna may have served as propaganda for the reign of the Hasmonean queen, Salome Alexandra (Selamzion).[6]

The very existence of these texts opens a variety of material-culture questions. How were the texts copied, on what, by whom, and for whom? How were they distributed? To how large an audience? And where were they read—in elite homes? In what sort of rooms? Did mosaics provide a means of envisioning Susanna's garden, or Susanna herself?

Of the various Apocryphal women, Judith has received the greatest amount of attention in relation to dating and setting. Torrey (1899) already located Bethulia in Shechemite

---

5. Wills 1995: 3 (see also pp. 26–27, 55) speaks of "the creation of invented worlds which are nevertheless like our own." Thus, Susanna, for example, purports to be an account of Jewish life in Babylon. Yet, unlike most prophetic books, as well as the rest of the Danielic corpus, Susanna does not name the reigning monarch or indicate the year from the time of the exile. Generically, it conforms to the modern category of historical romance: the setting appears familiar, but it is more artistic projection than historical precision. It is we readers who may choose to read the text as history or as fantasy. For the reading of Susanna according to the terms of modern romance genre, see Levine 1998.

6. This chapter in Ilan 1999, "'And Who Knows Whether You Have Not Come to Dominion for a Time like This?' (Esther 4:14): *Esther, Judith* and *Susanna* as Propaganda for Shelamzion's Queenship," is one of the few in this excellent volume that is not dependent on nonliterary sources.

territory, and to date, this thesis remains intact (see also Stummer 1947). Can we go further? Few have dared, no doubt because of lack of controls. Indeed, Wright's article on Judith, published in an ASOR volume (1999), ranges from Neolithic skull cults to Guatemala and Borneo, but does not invoke anything discovered by an ASOR archaeologist.

The argument that Bethulia is located in Shechemite (i.e., Samaritan) territory is now generally accepted: it appears best to fit the story's topography and, probably of greater weight, the story of Judith evokes the account of Shechem in Genesis 34. Bethulia is usually taken to be cognate to the Hebrew *betulah*, "virgin"; thus Judith, the descendant of Simeon, protects the "virgin" that her ancestor avenged (viz., Dinah, in Genesis 34).

This in turn permits the dating of the text to sometime in the late 2nd or early 1st century B.C.E., when Samaritan territory came under Jerusalem's authority following the campaigns of John Hyrcanus (for a good summary, see Wright 1999: 208). Narrowing the geography further, Torrey argued that the text's frequent (and apparently unnecessary) references to Dothan suggest this to be the place of authorship (1945: 91). Might we go beyond these general markers? For example, have we any evidence that the numerous stories of decapitation popular in the Hellenistic period (from the excesses of the Bacchae to the death of Orpheus to the defeat of Crassus [Wright 1999: 209–10]) were popularized in mosaics or performed in theaters? Granting Wright's point that *betulah* may have some connection to "[the temple of] the virgin," that is, Anat (Wright 1999: 222), perhaps studies of Judith would be enhanced by juxtaposing the text with the Anat myth and cult. What then do we know of this cult's vestiges in late Hellenism (e.g., its association with Athena)?

There is also a practical aspect to these questions: should archaeologists find any of these materials, to what extent would our studies be advanced? Would we read the texts differently? Would we interpret the remains otherwise? When dealing with a fictional text, what benefit do literary critic and historian gain from archaeology, and vice versa?

Problem Two: The Women

Susanna, the book of Tobit's Anna, Sarah, and Edna, Judith and her maid, and Greek Esther, along with the widow of 2 and 4 Maccabees, are both fictional figures and cultural codes. As characters, they help to drive the plots of their respective narratives. As cultural codes, they symbolize (either partially or wholly) the covenant community and reveal through dialogue and action its fears and hopes. Classical literature can trace the representations of women's bodies and their metonymic connections to land and state through such images as woman-as-field (more precisely, furrow), woman-as-vase, and so on (DuBois 1988: 129). Correlation of these changes materially and chronologically with developments in agriculture, innovation in oven design and placement, aesthetic shifts in vase-painting, and other documentable transformations in material culture allow fiction and artifact to become mutually informative.

Similar shifts in the presentation of women's bodies appear in the Jewish-Hellenistic texts, and these changes appropriately correspond to the changing experiences of the people relative to their land, nation, and traditions. The Jewish-Hellenistic narrative corpus depicts women who recapitulate and then outstrip (often literally) the metaphoric potentials of their biblical and classical sisters. Like their Hebrew and Hellenic counterparts, the women of the Apocrypha serve as signs for their nation; like them, they are threatened with humiliation, rape, and death. However, unlike their biblical and classical sisters, the women of the Jewish novels are not compromised, and the community is never fully broken.[7]

What might this change in the "woman-as-symbol-of-covenant-community" indicate? For example, is the Apocrypha's interest in the threat to but protection of women's bodies supported by a change in domestic architecture (something also hinted at by Sirach's paranoia)? Might the Apocrypha's comparatively greater interest, compared to the Tanach, in women's toilettes (Judith, Susanna, Greek Esther) indicate a culture in which these matters were increasingly part of the market? Specifically, might Hasmonean-based investigation yield increasing numbers of, or changes in, women's toiletry items: makeup cases, perfume flasks, combs, or mirrors? Are there increases to or changes in artistic depictions of women, with perhaps a new focus on the female body?

Finally, might the dominant women characters signal an increasing concentration of wealth or influence in the hands of women? Might one expect to find a proportionally higher percentage of women's seals, for example, during the Ptolemaic, Seleucid, or Hasmonean periods? Are there any gender-based remains from Salome Alexandra's projects?

Alternatively, does the greater focus on women in Jewish texts relate to a comparatively greater role for women in society? Archaeologists have definitively shown that the earlier views of women in Mediterranean cultures—walled up in women's quarters, uneducated, having no religious life, forbidden to speak to men, and so forth—do not fit the evidence (Peskowitz 1997; Ilan 1999). Indeed, these are projections based on select texts both Jewish and pagan, and often, for the Hasmonean and Herodian periods, driven by a Christian apologetic that seeks to portray Jesus as a liberator of women (who, in this scenario, clearly needed liberation). Thus, the increasing prominence of women in the public sphere might be mutually implied in the literature.

Problem Three: House and Garden

The Apocryphal novellas depict the "Better Homes and Gardens" of Hellenistic Judaism: no self-respecting house would be without an inhabitable second story or rooftop—there Judith can commune with her "Lord"; there, Tobit's Sarah retreats in her contemplation of suicide. Are these architectural notices matched by realia; are they evocations of earlier stories (e.g., the second floor of the widow of Zarephath or the widow of Shunem, Bathsheba's bathing place, Daniel's upper chamber); or are they projections by the authors of what "rich people" are supposed to have? Are these novellistic architectural observations attempts by the authors at verisimilitude (worthy of Cecil B. DeMille's set designers) in order to conjure up a past time, reflections of contemporary wealthy homes, or some standard trope, the origins of which are now lost? To take a modern analogy: mining an Apocryphal novella, especially one back-dated such as Tobit, for evidence of the Hellenistic period is tantamount to recreating the lifestyle (not the

---

7. For detailed discussion of the way in which the cultural shifts are marked by representations of the bodies of women, see Levine 1997.

values; this is actually easier) of a 21st-century woman by reading a novel she wrote about Arthurian England.

Nevertheless, perhaps the architectural interests of the novellas, interests that are extensive, can be supported by Hasmonean, or more generally, Hellenistic sites: were homes in Hellenistic Palestine equipped for multigenerational families? How many rooms would be typical in the home of a merchant such as Raguel (at least three, aside from a food preparation area, are suggested)? Since the families of Tobias and Anna are not depicted as among the most wealthy, does the text suggest changes in private family architecture for the entrepreneurial class? Are we to envision separate homes rather than insulae? Do these people have neighbors or is the text projecting an ideal of privacy for a culture that lacks it? Put most crassly: what evidence have we for two-story homes in Hasmonean Palestine?

The home of Raguel and Edna, Tobias's in-laws, raises additional questions: what evidence, if any, is there of private cemeteries (given that Raguel's backyard appears to resemble that of Norman Bates), in addition to if not instead of cave burials? Do Tobit's own burial practices—find a corpse, bury it wherever (?)—match any find on Palestinian soil? We might appeal to the cemeteries at Qumran and elsewhere, but how would we even know of private spaces (save for a serendipitous find)? To what extent would a private burial be possible, given at least some concern in Palestine for corpse contamination. As for cave burials, how typical is Judith's interment in her husband's plot? Where might such private plots be located?

The same questions apply to gardens: Susanna's garden—actually, her husband's garden—matches Judith's rooftop: it is her (semi)private, personal (women's) space. Again, questions: is there evidence from the Persian, Ptolemaic, Seleucid, or Hasmonean periods of private gardens in the Palestinian region? Were they walled? Did they contain trees? What grew in them? Is Susanna's *paradeisos* more than evocative of the Garden of Eden or the Garden in the Song of Songs? Were gardens becoming increasingly common among the entrepreneurial class or was the pleasure garden the possession only of the most elite?

What, too, of baths? Judith bathes; Esther virtually marinates; and Susanna—although never actually depicted in a tub—intends a bath. *Jub.* 33:2–9 and *T. Reub.* 3:10–13 both employ the trope of the seductive naked bather in their depiction of Bilhah. The former text (33:2) reads: "And Reuben saw Bilhah, the attendant of Rachel [and] his father's concubine, washing in the water privately, and he desired her." The *Testament* extends the parallel by including a condemnation of the woman herself: "Do not devote your attention to a woman's looks, nor live with a woman who is already married, nor become involved in affairs with women. For if I had not seen Bilhah bathing in a sheltered place, I would not have fallen into this great lawless act. For so absorbed were my senses by her naked femininity that I was not able to sleep until I had performed this revolting act . . ." (*T. Reub.* 3:10–13).[8] Does the bath then undergo any evolution in Ptolemaic, Seleucid, or Hasmonean settings? Is there any connection between the private bath and the *mikveh* (ritual bathing, even in the case of Judith, is not clearly depicted in these texts)? What are the

---

8. For additional discussion of this scene in Susanna, see Levine 1995.

processes by which private baths would collect water, aside from rainfall? How elite is the imagery?

Problem Four: Religious Practice

Women in the Apocryphal novellas are overtly pious: they all pray; several fast; Susanna and Judith are instructed in Torah, even as Tobit learned from his grandmother; Greek Esther, unlike her Hebrew counterpart, is pious in the extreme. But has this religious practice any material basis? Inscriptions found in the diaspora concerning the "mother of the synagogue" or "priestess" would match nicely the Apocrypha's depictions of women's religiosity, but what, if any, material attestation do we have for women's religious involvement in Palestine?

III. More Questions

This paper cannot end with a "conclusion" per se; its concerns about the mutual interpretation of Apocryphal women and material culture remain open questions. I do not know how I would read the texts differently had I access to contemporaneous remains; indeed, I do not know if such archaeological discoveries would even help me to determine more clearly the time in which the texts were written. Nor do I know what knowledge of these novellas contributes to archaeologists in terms of their professional work.

In the case of the Apocryphal/Deuterocanonical texts, external confirmation or lack of it is not an issue. Thus the genre of the novellas distinguishes these texts from the Mishnah or the New Testament in terms of the import of archaeology. The matching of archaeology with the Mishnah is essential, in that the Mishnah purports to be normative—and for centuries has been taken as such—for Jews. The material culture makes clear that the rabbinic text is prescriptive, not descriptive. Archaeology also substantially enhances studies of Christian origins: understanding how Roman power manifested itself through construction, coinage, art, etc. enriches interpretation of the metaphors used by, travels undertaken by, and pressures exerted upon this nascent group.

We have yet to see *how* or even *if* the archaeology of Hellenistic Palestine will transform our understanding of the Apocryphal/Deuterocanonical novellas. It is my suspicion that there is a way and a possibility for transformation of understanding; one cannot have been a student of Eric and Carol Meyers and not expect archaeological investigation to yield usable information. Perhaps by the Albright/ASOR's next centennial, we'll have our answers.

References

Balch, D., and Osiek, L.
  1998   *Families in the New Testament.* Louisville: Westminster/John Knox.
Brenner, A. (ed.)
  1995   *A Feminist Companion to Esther, Judith and Susanna.* Feminist Companion to the Bible 7. Sheffield: Sheffield Academic Press.
DuBois, P.
  1988   *Sowing the Body: Psychoanalysis and Ancient Representations of Women.* Chicago: University of Chicago Press.

Ilan, T.
 1999   *Integrating Women into Second Temple History.* Tübingen: Mohr [Siebeck].
Kraemer, R., and D'Angelo, M. R. (eds.)
 1999   *Women and Christian Origins.* Oxford: Oxford University Press.
Levine, A.-J.
 1995   "Hemmed in on All Sides": Jews and Women in the Book of Susanna. Pp. 175–90 in *Social Location and Biblical Interpretation in the United States,* ed. F. F. Segovia and M. A. Tolbert. Vol. 1 of *Reading from This Place.* Minneapolis: Fortress.

 1997   Threatened Bodies: Women, Apocrypha, Colonialism. Bilgray lecture at the University of Arizona, Tucson.

 1998   Bodies up for Grabs: Susanna Awash in Feminist Biblical Criticism. Paper presented to the Feminism and Literary Criticism Group of the Canadian Society for Biblical Studies.
Meyers, E. M.; Netzer, E.; and Meyers, C.
 1987   Artistry in Stone: The Mosaics of Sepphoris. *Biblical Archaeologist* 50/4: 223–31.
Moore, C.
 1996   *Tobit: A New Translation with Introduction and Commentary.* Anchor Bible 40A. New York: Doubleday.
Perdue, L., et al.
 1998   *Families in Ancient Israel.* Louisville: Westminster/John Knox.
Peskowitz, M. B.
 1997   *Spinning Fantasies: Rabbis, Gender, and History.* Berkeley: University of California Press.
Spolsky, E. (ed.)
 1996   *The Judgment of Susanna: Authority and Witness.* Early Judaism and Its Literature 11. Atlanta: Scholars Press.
Stoker, M.
 1998   *Judith: Woman Warrior.* New Haven: Yale University Press.
Stummer, F.
 1947   *Geographie des Buches Judith.* Bibelwissenschaftliche Reihe 3. Stuttgart: Katholisches Bibelwerk.
Torrey, C. C.
 1899   The Site of Bethulia. *Journal of the American Oriental Society* 20: 160–72.

 1945   *The Apocryphal Literature.* New Haven: Yale University Press.
Wills, L.
 1995   *The Jewish Novel in the Ancient World.* Ithaca, N.Y.: Cornell University Press.
Wright, G. R. H.
 1999   The Head Huntress of the Highlands. Pp. 203–34 in *Archaeology, History and Culture in Palestine and the Near East: Essays in Memory of Albert Glock,* ed. T. Kapitan. American Schools of Oriental Research Books 3. Atlanta: Scholars Press.

Part IV

Closing Remarks

Syro-Palestinian and Biblical Archaeology: Into the Next Millennium

William G. Dever
Department of Near Eastern Studies
University of Arizona

Introduction

The discipline of Syro-Palestinian archaeology and its popular offshoot "Biblical Archaeology" began almost exactly a century ago; and both have been intimately connected with the American Schools of Oriental Research and its Jerusalem branch, now the W. F. Albright Institute of Archaeological Research, the centennial of which we are celebrating in this symposium.

I shall try to contribute to this celebration by addressing what I consider to be several key issues as we enter our second century.

I. General Considerations: "Coming of Age"

In several "state-of-the art" analyses over the past 30 years, I have used the metaphor of "coming of age" to describe how our branch of archaeology has gradually matured, finally becoming largely independent from its venerable parents, ancient Near Eastern and biblical studies.[1] This growth has been accompanied by heated controversy, much of it simply the venting of emotions, since we are dealing with the Bible and the Holy Land. Nevertheless, there is a general consensus today that Syro-Palestinian archaeology—or, if you wish, the archaeology of Israel, Jordan, and the Palestinian Authority—has become a mature, autonomous, secular, and professional academic discipline.[2] The old-style, amateur "Biblical Archaeology" is long dead; its obituary has been written by myself and others, and no one really mourns its passing.

A. Integrating the New Technology

What then remains on our agenda for the *full* self-realization for our discipline? The major challenge now, I would argue, is to integrate all the diverse and complex new technologies in fieldwork and analysis of data into a unified approach to what is, after all, the fundamental intellectual challenge of archaeology: the explication of culture and cultural change over long time-spans. By this, I do not mean the misguided search for "universal laws of the cultural process" that characterized the scientific pretensions of the "New

---

1. Cf. Dever 1985; 1989; 1992; 1993a; 2000a. These works include full references to the other literature.
2. See n. 1 above and the literature cited in these publications. A renewed critical discussion of terminology is long overdue, but there is virtually nothing published worth citing.

Archaeology" of the 1970s–1980s and hastened its demise.[3] I envision, rather, a return to more traditional, regional "culture histories"—but this time with vastly more sophisticated methods and a wealth of new, factual information about a real past.

The newer archaeological technologies that have been pioneered in the past two or three decades—some of them even in our rather parochial branch—are too well known to need detailing here. By now, most archaeologists know how to develop research designs; how to dig and record carefully; how to observe complex stratigraphic phenomena; how to retrieve a wide variety of both artifactual and environmental data; and how to exploit field and laboratory analyses from many of the natural sciences. Among the most recent and promising innovations, however, I would single out more precise Carbon 14 dating methods; improved neutron activation sourcing of clays for ceramic manufacture; use-wear analysis of artifacts; Geographical Information Systems (GIS) methods for aerial mapping and detailed reconstructions of the ancient landscape; and computer-aided, three-dimensional spatial modeling of artifact clusters, now available the same day, right in the field.[4] These and many other new technologies have absolutely transformed the typical archaeological project in Israel or Jordan, as I am painfully aware when I visit a dig these days and compare it with Gezer in the 1960s, which we thought at the time very *avant garde*. The new technologies are complex, enormously expensive, and in some case still highly experimental; but they are here to stay, and they have enormous potential.

B. *The Problem of Publication*

What shall we do with all the exciting new information about the past of this region that newer technologies have brought to light? One answer might be: publish it. Yet the very mass and variety of data we now possess, plus the temptation to go back to the field for more of what we know we could learn, make publication ever more complex, time-consuming, and expensive. It is no secret that our failure to keep up in publication has now become scandalous, as admitted by many authorities in two volumes of essays edited and published recently by our *bête noir*, Hershel Shanks.[5] Some have suggested a moratorium on fieldwork for several years, but this is scarcely realistic. It may be that all of us will simply have to devote a far larger proportion of budget and staff to the workup of the excavated materials. And sponsoring institutions must take full responsibility for actual publication costs, even if these may lie down the road for many years. We archaeologists need to develop a conscience about publication: to excavate without publishing in full and in appropriate places is not merely irresponsible, it is immoral. And until published, there are no "archaeological data," no "facts," only bits and pieces of disjointed information, most of it simply impressions in the archaeologists' mind, fading with each passing year.[6]

---

3. The classic statement was P. J. Watson, LeBlanc, and Redman's 1971 publication. For how completely we have repudiated the notion of "cultural laws," see almost any of the references in nn. 5 and 10 below.

4. A convenient summary can be found in several of the essays in Drinkard, Mattingly, and Miller 1988.

5. See the essays in H. Shanks 1996; 1999.

6. Virtually the only treatment of archaeological epistemology in our field is Dever 1993a; 1994; 1997a; but see also Bunimovitz 1995; Faust and Maeir 1999 for the growing interest (and sophistication) of younger Israeli archaeologists. On epistemology in the larger world of archaeology, see several basic works of "postprocessualists" or "cognitive" archaeologists, one of whose major emphases is on archaeological

If ours is ever to become a truly empirical science, the database with which we purport to work must be made available to both our professional colleagues and to the general public.

C. *Developing Appropriate Theory: Or How Do We Know What We Think We Know?*

It is widely acknowledged that our branch of archaeology has been pragmatic from the beginning and has always been theoretically impoverished compared to other branches of worldwide archaeology, particularly prehistory and New World archaeology. Some have even prided themselves on this, even though it obviously isolates us in the backwaters, rather than placing us in the mainstream. That must change, if Syro-Palestinian archaeology is ever really going to come of age. And by "theory" I do not mean, of course, mere speculation (which we all decry, but engage in constantly and usually naïvely), but rather a body of explicit interpretive principles that serve to guide research. Without such principles, archaeological excavation is little better than treasure-hunting and the presentation of the results nothing but journalism. If we cannot articulate our methodology, we do not really know what we are doing; and what we claim to know is mostly an illusion.[7]

The "New Archaeology" has come and gone almost without notice in our little branch of archaeology, except for the introduction of some multidisciplinary approaches. This is a pity, for in spite of its many deficiencies, the "New Archaeology" *was* essentially a clarion call for *theory-building* (as Binford put it), but it fell on deaf ears in our circles.[8] The result is that Syro-Palestinian archaeologists, despite some *rapprochement* with the field of anthropology in recent years, are still dismissed by our colleagues as parochial, naïve, and incapable of contributing anything to the advance of archaeology as a discipline. Again, some of our more Neanderthal colleagues ridicule any desire to be in the mainstream, but they are terribly wrong. We who work in this part of the world have an unparalleled database, one that stretches over at least a million years and encompasses a vast array of data from hundreds of sites. Ancient Palestine should provide a brilliant "case-study" in the analysis of the rise of complex society, with much to teach our colleagues in archaeology elsewhere in the world.[9]

II. *The Postprocessual Challenge*

Whatever opportunities we may have missed in the past, the appearance of "postprocessual" archaeology on the horizon in the 1990s presents us with a theoretical challenge

---

"meaning" and how it is derived or generated; for example, Tilley 1990 (ed.); 1991; 1993; M. Shanks and Tilley 1987; and most recently several essays reprinted in Whitley 1998 (ed.) (especially those by Clarkson; Flannery and Marcus; Peebles; M. Shanks and Hodder; Whitley). Many of the essays in Yoffee and Sherratt 1993, while not ostensibly by "postprocessualists," address the general issue of theory (and the lack thereof) in a provocative manner.

7. See references in n. 6 above; any epistemological framework is obviously dependent on a body of general theory.

8. Cf. Binford 1977; but his explicit call for theory-building goes back to his earliest publications, e.g., 1962. P. J. Watson, LeBlanc, and Redman (1971) and virtually all their followers based their "revolution" on a new *theoretical* framework for archaeology. Cf. also references in nn. 6 above and 10 below.

9. An example is Joffe 1993, a University of Arizona dissertation that typifies the more deliberately anthropological and cross-cultural approach that our program has espoused.

that we cannot ignore. Some leading theoreticians in the general field expressed misgivings about the "New Archaeology" already in the mid-1970s, such as John Fritz and Kent Flannery, and even used the term "cognitive archaeology." Mark Leone, originally a processualist but later associated with a Marxist-materialist approach, addressed the question of "the archaeology of mind" as early as 1982, as did Alison Wylie in several publications in 1982–85. Bruce Trigger, who had never been a true convert to the "New Archaeology," raised crucial theoretical questions in 1984 (as well as in *A History of Archaeological Thought* [1989]).[10]

It was Ian Hodder, however, who deliberately set out the early agenda of postprocessual archaeology in the 1980s, especially in his influential book, *Reading the Past: Current Approaches to Interpretation in Archaeology* (1986). Hodder has remained the leading spokesman of the movement, in part I think because of his willingness to engage in dialogue and to modify his own position. He had originally moved from structuralism to poststructuralism, then to what he often calls "cognitive" or "contextual archaeology."[11] Other leading proponents of postprocessual archaeology in the 1980s and early 1990s were, in Britain, Michael Shanks and Christopher Tilley and, in the United States, Timothy Earle and Robert Preucel (cf. the latter's edited volume *Processual and Postprocessual Archaeologies: Multiple Ways of Knowing the Past* [1991]).[12]

By the late 1980s, postprocessualism was being hotly debated in journals such as *American Antiquity* and *Current Anthropology*, as well as making an appearance in two massive histories of archaeological thought by Bruce Trigger (1989) and C. C. Lamberg-Karlovsky, ed. (1989). A series of essays edited by David Whitley, *Reader in Archaeological Theory: Post-processual and Cognitive Approaches* (1998), makes it clear, I think, that postprocessual archaeology is now the *dominant* approach among Americanists. And a similar trend in Britain is clear from reports of the proceedings of such symposia as those of the "Theoretical Archaeological Group."[13]

Because postprocessualism is deliberately eclectic, attempting to avoid becoming a new orthodoxy, it is notoriously difficult to define, at least as a "school." There are, however, a number of consistent distinctions in the approach that postprocessualists tend to take.[14] (1) First, there is the generally reactionary character of the movement, as noted above, with its skepticism regarding all "positivist" presuppositions. (2) There is an overriding emphasis on culture, not simply as "adaptation to the natural environment," but in the larger sociocultural sense of what Hodder calls "contextual" archaeology. (3) Postpro-

---

10. For these authors and general bibliography on "postprocessualism," see Flannery 1973; Fritz 1978; Leone 1982; Wylie 1982; 1985; Trigger 1984; 1989; Kohl 1985; Hodder 1986; 1987 (ed.); 1999; Earle and Preucel 1987; Leone, Potter, and Shackel 1987; M. Shanks and Tilley 1987; Patterson 1989; Lamberg-Karlovsky 1989; R. Watson 1990; Tilley 1990 (ed.); 1991; 1993; Bintliffe 1991 (ed.); Preucel 1991 (ed.); 1995; Flannery and Marcus 1993; Yoffee and Sherratt 1993; Renfrew and Zubrow 1994; Ucko 1995; Preucel and Hodder 1996; Hodder et al. 1997; Whitley 1998 (ed.); VanPool and VanPool 1999. Note that the essays in Whitley 1998 (ed.), except for that of Whitley himself, are reprints of articles published between 1986 and 1998 (e.g., Flannery and Marcus 1993, above).

11. Cf. Hodder 1986: 118–46; 1987 (ed.); and more recently, Flannery and Marcus 1993 (= 1998).

12. See references in n. 10 above.

13. The papers in Yoffee and Sherratt, for instance, originated in a symposium of this group (1993: 2); see also Bintliffe 1991.

14. The most recent and perhaps the best summary is Whitley 1998.

cessualists disavow nomothetic, determinist explanations of cultural change, since they are unobtainable, preferring more limited or "probabilistic" explanations. (4) Postprocessualism is concerned with fundamental epistemological questions—with *hermeneutics*—in keeping with its partly postmodernist origins. As "interpretive archaeology," it seeks to form a systematic body of genuine knowledge about the past, not pseudoscientific but humanistic and archaeologically derived. (5) Postprocessualism's understanding of history is strongly in the "idealist" tradition of historians such as R. G. Collingwood and others. As Hodder puts it, "to study history is to try to get at purpose and thought," at "the inside of events" (1986: 90–97, especially 91). This approach to the past, deliberately emphasizing the subjective mental processes of both actor and observer, has given the movement one of its much-misunderstood labels—the "archaeology of mind" or simply "cognitive archaeology." (6) In keeping with several of the above emphases, postprocessualism is concerned with establishing the "meaning of things," events as well as material culture remains, eschewing, however, both the determinist notion that meaning is external and functionalist and the relativist notion that all assignments of meanings are equally valid. In particular, postmodernists have used the metaphor of "reading," that is, of interpreting material culture remains much in the same way as one would read texts, the other primary source for history-writing. Hodder, for instance, has spoken of the "language, grammar, and syntax" of artifacts—again, hermeneutical principles. This approach explains another common term for postprocessualism—*contextual*—which Hodder uses sometimes in wordplay as "con-text," that is, artifacts *with* texts.[15]

For those of us in Near Eastern and Syro-Palestinian archaeology, it seems to me that the first lesson we can learn from the relatively rapid collapse of the much-vaunted "New" or processual archaeology of the 1970s–1980s is that there is no single "right" way of doing archaeology (although there are many wrong ways). Second, while archaeology is inevitably "materialist" and must remain close to fieldwork, deep in the dirt, we cannot bury our theoretical heads like ostriches. *Theory*—seeking to interpret the "meaning of things"—is fundamental to all that we do, at least if it is to remain of any value in a world that considers itself "postmodern."

Turning, however, to specifics, let me evaluate some aspects of postprocessualism that would seem to be particularly congenial to most Syro-Palestinian (and "biblical") archaeologists—that is, promising general trends in postprocessual archaeology from which we can profit.

First, postprocessualism's sweeping rejection of the vulgar materialism and the functionalist-determinist obsession of much of the "New Archaeology" is like a breath of fresh air! Most of us remained more idealistic all along, more committed to the role of ideology—of art, symbol, aesthetics, religion, and human decision-making—in culture and cultural change. Now we can hold up our heads again as unabashed *humanists*, no longer in fear of being dismissed as Luddites.

Second, the recent attempt to "read" material culture like texts and the concomitant cognition of the centrality of hermeneutics ought to find an immediate and enthusiastic response from us. Most of us, whether from a biblical, classical, or ancient Near Eastern

---

15. See n. 11 above.

background, take the importance of historical texts and the need for competence in read-ing ancient texts for granted (as for hermeneutics, some of us were raised on that!). And it is not coincidental, as I have recently shown elsewhere (1997a), that an "archaeological hermeneutic," when fully developed, will parallel almost exactly the development of the various hermeneutical "schools" in biblical criticism over the past century. It really is pos-sible, indeed necessary, to "read" material culture remains as we do the biblical texts, for instance—alongside of, sometimes complementary to, often contradictory to, but always interpreted by means of virtually the *same* hermeneutical principles. The consequence of this revolution in method is that archaeology will no longer be "mute," as biblicists often claim, but will speak with a powerful voice. Already archaeology has become a primary source for rewriting the history of ancient Israel from its earliest origins to the develop-ment of religion and cult.[16] (We archaeologists are the *real* "revisionist" historians.) The deliberate and systematic adoption of some of postprocessualism's eclectic, common-sense interpretive methods and emphases can only enhance the much-needed dialogue between biblical scholars and archaeologists, a dialogue that the reductionist, jargon-ridden "New Archaeology" frustrated for 20 years.

Third, postprocessualism's social consciousness—its willingness to be culturally and even politically involved—complements the sense of professional responsibility and moral standards that many of us never abandoned in pursuit of scientism. Whether we came from a specifically biblical background or were simply committed to the defense of the now much-beleaguered Western cultural tradition, we believed that there were truths to be discovered in the study of the past by honest seekers, truths that could enlighten and enrich our common human experience, and also mistakes from which we could profit in seeking to build a more just society. Such a view is not naïve positivism; but it *is* moral optimism and courage, infinitely preferable in my view (2000b) to the cyn-ical and impotent relativism of the postmodernist piffle in vogue today in so many of the social and behavioral sciences. Postprocessualism shows us that archaeology is not just an antiquarian pursuit, but a socially relevant humanistic discipline that can justify itself in a world of diminishing resources, competing cultural claims, and impersonal super-technologies that hold out false utopias. Archaeology, firmly anchored in a knowable past, can guard against cruel futurist illusions.

Finally, postprocessualism's refurbishing of history-writing as a major goal of archaeol-ogy is enormously encouraging. Some of us, after all, never gave up on being historians, whether of ancient Palestine or Israel. And now history is once again a respectable enter-prise—and one with vastly expanded horizons, almost inexhaustible new data, and far more sophisticated models.

III. The Future of Our Particular Discipline: "Who Owns the Past?"

It is commonplace today to refer to archaeological sites and artifacts as "cultural prop-erties." But *whose* properties? And what are the *legitimate uses* of our knowledge of the

---

16. See, for example, Dever 1997b; 1997c; cf. Finkelstein and Silberman 2001 for a larger-scale approach, but also the review in Dever 2001b.

past? Here we confront the problem of our own inevitable modern ideologies in all reconstructions of the past, of "cultural values" that we ourselves create and that shape us in turn, often unconsciously.

A. *Archaeology, Nationalism, and Cultural Heritage*

In a recent collection of essays entitled *Archaeology under Fire: Nationalism, Politics and Heritage in the Eastern Mediterranean and Middle East* (Meskell 1999), the chapter on the archaeology of our region, by the well-known writer Neil Silberman, is entitled "Whose Game Is It Anyway? The Political and Social Transformations of American Biblical Archaeology" (1999). The first part of the title is a paraphrase from a piece I wrote several years ago, in which I highlighted several ominous trends in America that cast some doubt upon the survival of the discipline (1995). But Silberman knew very well that, in remarking that "we [American archaeologists] are . . . often reduced to the role of spectators at a game that *we* invented" (Dever 1995: 52), I was being ironic, calling attention to the ascendancy of the national schools in the Middle East and the corresponding decline in the foreign schools.

The point is that archaeology is not a game; and if it becomes one, it will turn out to be deadly. In the past few years, some Israelis and many Palestinians are using archaeology to play the game of "who was here first"—and therefore has exclusive claims to the land. The discussion has already caused a furor, especially since Zeev Herzog's innocent-sounding but inflammatory remarks in the *Ha'aretz Magazine* (1999). Dragging politics into archaeology, which some of us have battled against for a lifetime, perverts the discipline. The study of the past may pose such questions as national identity, but it cannot answer them.

Who "owns" the past? *Only those who attempt to appropriate it on its own terms, for whatever timeless and universal lessons it may have to teach us.* And if our reconstruction of the past is too biased by our own modern concerns, then it may become a monstrous caricature that can only lead us into nationalist nightmares and unimaginable tragedies. The last people to abuse archaeology thus were Europe's fascists and Nazis. Such extremism may be unthinkable here, but there is a danger nonetheless in this politically-charged region. Vigilance is in order. We must seek to construct and tolerate "multiple pasts," none of them perfect reflections of reality. Of course, postmodernists have argued all along that all claims to knowledge are but "social constructs" and that the reading of ancient texts in particular (and artifacts are also "texts") is always political and tends to result in a "metanarrative" that must be resisted. Now I loathe postmodernism with all my heart and soul, but its advocates have a point here. "Metanarratives" *can* be perverse.

One form that the discussion of nationalism in archaeology currently takes is framed in terms of whether or not one can discern ethnicity in the archaeological record. Many archaeologists are basically skeptical. Thus Israel Finkelstein, who in the late 1980s authored a ground-breaking book entitled *The Archaeology of the Israelite Settlement* (1988), now argues that there are no recognizable "Israelites" in the archaeological record of the 12th–11th centuries B.C.E. (1996). Unfortunately, this unfounded skepticism plays right into the hands of a circle of minimalist biblical scholars calling themselves "revisionists," some of whom in my judgment are closet anti-Semites (Dever 1999b). Yet the issue of "ethnicity" has become fundamental. Sian Jones, in *The Archaeology of Ethnicity*, quotes Olivier and Coudart (1995: 365) as follows:

> The crucial theoretical question of archaeology today is that of national identity, or more specifically that of the relationship archaeology enjoys with the construction (or the fabrication) of *collective* identities. (Jones 1997: 1)

Note: the "fabrication" of ethnicity. A people's concept of themselves is fictional, that is, it has no objective reality and can only lead to "cultural imperialism." Like other postmodern social theorists, Jones advocates a "nonjudgmental," "multicultural," "relativist," "politically correct" archaeology (1997). I find this absurd and as tediously ideological as that of the ideologues whom the postmodernists delight in exposing. In my view it is possible, and indeed legitimate, for Israelis, Jordanians, and Palestinians to identify with the past peoples and cultures of this land, their predecessors, *without* falling into blind chauvinism. And if the general public does not resonate in some sense with the cultural heritage of the past in this region, local archaeology will become an increasingly unsupportable luxury, eclipsed by the pressing needs of modern development.

A final aspect of this topic concerns the proliferation of local museums, the reconstruction of archaeological sites, and the development of national parks as a way of promoting a certain cultural "message" (propaganda, if you wish) through archaeological media. This is now common all over the world, especially as archaeologically-oriented tourism expands. Suddenly archaeology is *big business* — and it also provides a convenient platform for disseminating a particular cultural self-image, especially in the so-called Holy Land. But is this really the image that archaeologists themselves wish to convey? In many cases, it is not. A recent visit to Tel Dan and then to Bethsaida convinced me that I had stumbled into the Bible Belt in the American South — biblical labels everywhere. Archaeology is indeed a powerful educational tool, and it must be if it is to survive; but it is easily subverted by being packaged for commercial and pedagogical uses. Archaeological sites and museums have become classrooms; let us be fully aware of what we are teaching.[17]

B. Archaeology, History-Writing, and the Bible

The "New Archaeology" rather pompously considered itself "explicitly scientific," repudiating history-writing as an impossible, even illegitimate goal of archaeology. But today's postprocessual approaches have brought us back full circle to archaeology as a basically historical discipline. Archaeology may be considered simply "writing history from *things*" (to borrow the title of a recent book edited by Lubar and Kingery [1993]). As argued above, we must learn to "read" artifacts with the same hermeneutical principles as those used in interpreting texts. Both constitute encoded, symbolic messages about the past.

In the case of our quest for an "ancient" or "biblical Israel," I would argue that archaeological data now take precedence over texts as a primary source for history-writing. Yet

---

17. This point was first forcibly made by M. Shanks and Tilley (1987). But virtually every subsequent "postprocessualist" has taken up the theme, as most recently Hodder (1999). And, of course, that is the thrust of the essays (including Silberman's) in Meskell 1999.

the biblical "revisionists" reject the very possibility of such an Israel ever having existed. The Hebrew Bible is "pious fiction," a collection of fantastic stories, not from the Iron Age, but rather stemming from Judaism's identity crisis in the Hellenistic period. There was no "ancient" or "biblical Israel." As one of the "revisionists" put it recently, the Hebrew Bible is simply "the original Zionist myth" (Lemche 1998: 129). I have recently described all this as "pseudo-sophisticated Bible bashing," attributing it to the sort of postmodernist nonsense that passes for scholarship these days (1999b: 64). Yet until very recently most biblical scholars and virtually all archaeologists have ignored the threat that the "revisionists" pose, namely that of "erasing biblical history," as Baruch Halpern has put it (1995).

Archaeologists *in particular* should be responding, if for no other reason than the fact that nearly every resort of the "revisionists" to archaeology is a gross caricature. Take, for instance, Thomas Thompson's most recent book, *The Mythic Past: Biblical Archaeology and the Myth of Ancient Israel* (1999). Thompson cites absolutely no real archaeological data, and his attack on archaeology in general resurrects as his whipping boy an amateur style of "biblical archaeology" that has been dead for at least 25 years. As for "myth," the only myth in this case is that Thompson is an honest scholar. On the dust jacket of his book, however, there are quotations full of lavish praise from both biblical scholars and archaeologists.[18] Have we taken leave of our senses?

Yet the biblical "revisionists" and other minimalists—including Israel's "post-Zionists" and "new historians"—are right about one thing: in all our disciplines, today we face a far-reaching historiographical challenge, which some anthropologists have recently termed "a crisis of representation" (Marcus and Fischer 1986: 7–16). How do we describe the phenomena that we claim to understand; and can we, in fact, really know anything about an "objective past out there," in our case, the past of this region? This epistemological crisis has gravely affected all the social sciences in an age of postpositivist philosophies, of "creeping skepticism" as a putative historical method. As for archaeology, if it cannot write *some* kind of history, it will be reduced to mere antiquarianism.

Elsewhere (1997d) I have suggested that archaeology can contribute to the necessary *multiple* ways of knowing the past by explicitly embracing the kind of history-writing for which it is uniquely equipped. This would be a sort of "natural history" or the history of *material culture* in its broadest ecological context, akin to *la longue durée* of the *annales* historians. This approach would leave "political history"—the history of ideas—largely to textual specialists, and concentrate instead on the history of environmental changes, subsistence, technology, demography, settlement types and patterns, social structure, art and aesthetics, and international relations. Modern archaeology produces a wealth of information on all of these topics, most of them barely mentioned in ancient texts, such as the Hebrew Bible.

In setting themselves to such tasks, archaeologists would become partners in an exciting and immensely productive dialogue about the past, and especially the past of Israel and its neighbors (the theme of this symposium). Unfortunately, up until now we see little but tiresome monologues: biblical scholars myopically fixated on their texts,

---

18. See further the review of Thompson's book in Dever 1999b. For full references to "revisionism" in general, as well as my critiques of it, see Dever 1998; 1999b; 2000a; 2001a.

archaeologists with their heads buried in the ground, as usual. Halpern, one of the few biblical scholars to take archaeology seriously, has described these "two monologues" eloquently (1997). The isolation of the two disciplines has always been characteristic of Israeli scholarship and institutions, to their detriment, I believe. And now in the post-Albrightian era in Europe and America, we confront a generation of biblical scholars who are so caught up in the "Bible as literature," in new literary criticism, feminist hermeneutics, liberation theology, and other fads that they are oblivious to the historical dimensions of the Hebrew Bible and its enduring message. Archaeology might bring us back to earth, if anyone out there were interested. Yet I am rather pessimistic.

In my many travels all over North America, I have become convinced that Syro-Palestinian archaeology as a discipline may survive only in the few conservative Christian circles in which the Bible, for better or worse, is still taken seriously and there are institutional commitments of people and resources. In other private institutions, and especially in state universities, administrations are simply not interested in what we archaeologists do.

In *popular* circles, to be sure, there is still a gratifying interest, as witness the large crowds at lectures and the frequent media coverage. But none of this translates into what we need: money for excavation and research, or the most pressing need, jobs for young people. Despite the resentment I may incur, I must state that the professional discipline of Syro-Palestinian archaeology in Europe and America is moribund today. "Biblical archaeology," as a sort of amateur pursuit, may survive; but this is not adequate to support a discipline. We face an ironic dilemma. Having bravely left parents and home in the biblical world a generation ago to seek our fortune in the larger world of anthropology and social science, we may have to come crawling back. But would we "secularists" be *welcome* now?

This may appear to be a peculiarly American dilemma, given our long history of the confusion of archaeology with biblical studies. But even in Israel, which has historically taken a very different approach, there are clear signs that the Bible is now becoming a key issue. Finkelstein (1998) has branded Mazar a "Bible archaeologist" (and, by implication, me and others as well). And with Herzog's (1999) pulling the supposedly biblical and archaeological underpinnings out from under the perception of many Israelis that theirs is a real past in the land, the Israeli general public has become involved. (Of course, the media have spread alarmist stories of this controversy all over the world.) Having thrown the Bible and theology out the back door 30 years ago, some of us are dismayed to find it now being dragged in the front door. We seem to have come full circle: somehow, the "biblical connection" will have to be confronted and defined all over again. An old war-horse now, I gladly leave this battle to the next generation.

IV. ASOR and the Albright Institute in the Next Millennium

Having surveyed the general field thus far, I ask that you not think me provincial if I conclude by referring more specifically to the American institutions whose centennial we celebrate in this symposium. After all, their future is closely bound up with the fortunes of the larger discipline.

ASOR, the American Schools of Oriental Research, now faces the consequences of the growing isolation of archaeology from biblical studies outlined above. It no longer meets annually in conjunction with the Society of Biblical Literature, one of its venerable parents a century ago. While there are professional advantages, many deplore the lost opportunities for dialogue. The name of the journal, the *Biblical Archaeologist*, has been changed to *Near Eastern Archaeology*, which signifies the search for a new audience. Much of the role of mainstreaming Syro-Palestinian archaeology, in which ASOR should have played a major part, has in fact been usurped by the Biblical Archaeology Society headed by Hershel Shanks and its journal, the *Biblical Archaeology Review*. Some even suggest that ASOR is an institution that has become obsolete. Yet ASOR in some ways remains viable; it has raised large sums of money, has reorganized itself, and has managed at least to survive into its second century. Perhaps it is simply ASOR's role as "parent" of the three overseas institutes in Jerusalem, Amman, and Cyprus that is waning, leaving ASOR itself to manage only the annual meetings, the fellowships, and some of the publications.

The Jerusalem school, the W. F. Albright Institute of Archaeological Research, has been particularly successful. This is driven home to me when I compare the floundering, nearly bankrupt Institute I left in 1975 with the vibrant, thriving Institute today, under the exemplary leadership of the Director since 1980, Seymour Gitin. My prescription for the future? Keep up the good work! Of course, this will require constantly expanding financial support, as well as far-sighted policies of the Board of Trustees. And the Albright, now the dominant foreign school in Jerusalem, must continually reshape its role in and contribution to the archaeology of Israel, its host country. My major concern is that, with the Tel Miqne-Ekron, Sepphoris, and Ashkelon digs coming to an end, we need new American projects with both Israelis and Palestinians, preferably begun by younger archaeologists of the next generation. And perhaps we should envision another long-running joint American-Israeli project. All told, our second century in Jerusalem looks bright. (I leave comments on the future of the Amman and Cyprus institutes to the scholars who are participating in the celebrations held there.)

Conclusion

William Foxwell Albright and the first archaeological excavation in Palestine (that conducted by Petrie at Tell el-Hesi) were both ten years old when ASOR was founded in 1900 and the Jerusalem school was established. We have come a long way in our first century. But we are now at a critical juncture. The Albrightian era is over, and with its passing, the easy alliance of archaeology and biblical studies has disappeared (Dever 1993b). Syro-Palestinian archaeology has come of age as a secular, highly specialized, professional academic discipline. Yet its further progress is hampered by financial constraints, Middle Eastern politics, unresolved epistemological issues, and what I would call a historiographical failure of nerve. Let us hope that all of these may be only "growing pains."

Archaeology by definition looks backward at the past. But it can also look optimistically toward the future, because it is only as we understand the human past that we *have* any future as a species. *'Ad me'a ve-'esrîm*—until at least another 120 years, and much longer.

References

Binford, L. R.
  1962   Archaeology as Anthropology. *American Antiquity* 28: 217–25.
  1977   *For Theory Building in Archaeology.* New York: Academic.
Bintliffe, J. L.
  1991   Post-modernism, Rhetoric and Scholasticism of TAG: The Current State of British Archaeological Theory. *Antiquity* 65: 274–78.
Bintliffe, J. L. (ed.)
  1991   *The Annales School and Archaeology.* Leicester: Leicester University Press.
Bunimovitz, S.
  1995   How Mute Stones Speak: Interpreting What We Dig Up. *Biblical Archaeology Review* 21/2: 58–67, 96–100.
Clarkson, P. B.
  1998   Archaeological Imaginings: Contextualization of Images. Pp. 119–30 in *Reader in Archaeological Theory: Post-processual and Cognitive Approaches*, ed. D. S. Whitley. London: Routledge.
Dever, W. G.
  1985   Syro-Palestinian and Biblical Archaeology. Pp. 31–74 in *The Hebrew Bible and Its Modern Interpreters*, ed. D. A. Knight and G. M. Tucker. Philadelphia: Fortress.
  1989   Archaeology in Israel Today: A Summation and Critique. Pp. 143–52 in *Recent Excavations in Israel: Studies in Iron Age Archaeology*, ed. S. Gitin and W. G. Dever. Annual of the American Schools of Oriental Research 49. Winona Lake, Ind.: Eisenbrauns.
  1992   Archaeology: Syro-Palestinian and Biblical. Pp. 354–67 in vol. 1 of *The Anchor Bible Dictionary*, ed. D. N. Freedman. New York: Doubleday.
  1993a   Biblical Archaeology: Death and Rebirth? Pp. 706–22 in *Proceedings of the Second International Congress on Biblical Archaeology, Jerusalem, June 1990*, ed. A. Biran and J. Aviram. Jerusalem: Israel Exploration Society.
  1993b   What Remains of the House That Albright Built? *Biblical Archaeologist* 56/1: 25–35.
  1994   Archaeology, Texts, and History-Writing: Toward an Epistemology. Pp. 105–17 in *Uncovering Ancient Stones: Essays in Memory of H. Neil Richardson*, ed. L. M. Hopfe. Winona Lake, Ind.: Eisenbrauns.
  1995   The Death of a Discipline? *Biblical Archaeology Review* 21/5: 50–55, 70.
  1997a   On Listening to the Texts—And the Artifacts. Pp. 1–23 in *The Echoes of Many Texts: Reflections on Jewish and Christian Traditions: Essays in Honor of Lou H. Silberman*, ed. W. G. Dever and J. E. Wright. Atlanta: Scholars Press.
  1997b   New Archaeological Data and Hypotheses on the Origins of Israel. Pp. 20–50 in *Archaeology and Biblical Interpretation*, ed. J. R. Bartlett. London: Routledge.
  1997c   Folk Religion in Early Israel: Did Yahweh Have a Consort? Pp. 27–56 in *Aspects of Monotheism: How God Is One*, ed. H. Shanks and J. Meinhardt. Washington, D.C.: Biblical Archaeology Society.
  1997d   Philology, Theology, and Archaeology: What Kind of History Do We Want, and What Is Possible? Pp. 290–310 in *The Archaeology of Israel: Constructing the Past, Interpreting the Present*, ed. N. A. Silberman and D. Small. Journal for the Study of the Old Testament Supplements 237. Sheffield: Sheffield Academic Press.
  1998   Archaeology, Ideology, and the Quest for an "Ancient" or "Biblical" Israel. *Near Eastern Archaeology* 61/1: 39–52.
  1999a   Histories and Nonhistories of Ancient Israel. *Bulletin of the American Schools of Oriental Research* 316: 89–105.
  1999b   Review of T. L. Thompson, *The Mythic Past: Biblical Archaeology and the Myth of Israel* (New York: Basic Books, 1999). *Biblical Archaeology Review* 23/5: 64–65.

2000a   Biblical and Syro-Palestinian Archaeology: A State-of-the-Art Assessment at the Turn of the Millennium. *Currents in Research: Biblical Studies* 8: 91–116.

2000b   Save Us from Postmodern Malarkey. *Biblical Archaeology Review* 26/2: 28–35, 68.

2001a   *What Did the Biblical Writers Know, and When Did They Know It? Archaeology and the Reality of Ancient Israel.* Grand Rapids: Eerdmans.

2001b   Excavating the Hebrew Bible, or Burying It Again? *Bulletin of the American Schools of Oriental Research* 322: 67–77.

Drinkard, J. F.; Mattingly, G. L.; and Miller, J. M. (eds.)

1988   *Benchmarks in Time and Culture: An Introduction to Palestinian Archaeology.* Atlanta: Scholars Press.

Earle, T. K., and Preucel, R. W.

1987   Processual Archaeology and the Radical Critique. *Current Anthropology* 28: 501–38.

Faust, A., and Maeir, A. (eds.)

1999   *Material Culture, Society and Ideology: New Directions in the Archaeology of the Land of Israel.* Ramat-Gan: Bar-Ilan University (Hebrew).

Finkelstein, I.

1988   *The Archaeology of the Israelite Settlement.* Jerusalem: Israel Exploration Society.

1996   Ethnicity and Origin of the Iron I Settlers in the Highlands of Canaan: Can the Real Israel Stand Up? *Biblical Archaeologist* 59: 198–212.

1998   Bible Archaeology or Archaeology of Palestine in the Iron Age? *Levant* 30: 167–74.

Finkelstein, I., and Silberman, N. A.

2001   *The Bible Unearthed: Archaeology's New Vision of Ancient Israel and the Origin of Its Sacred Texts.* New York: Free Press.

Flannery, K. V.

1973   Archaeology with a Capital S. Pp. 47–58 in *Research and Theory in Current Archaeology*, ed. C. L. Redman. New York: Wiley.

Flannery, K. V., and Marcus, E. J.

1993   Cognitive Archaeology. *Cambridge Archaeological Journal* 3: 260–70.

1998   Cognitive Archaeology. Pp. 35–48 in *Reader in Archaeological Theory: Post-processual and Cognitive Approaches*, ed. D. S. Whitley. London: Routledge.

Fritz, J.

1978   Paleopsychology Today: Ideational Systems and Human Adaptation in Prehistory. Pp. 37–59 in *Social Archaeology: Beyond Subsistence and Dating*, ed. C. L. Redman et al. New York: Academic.

Halpern, B.

1995   Erasing History: The Minimalist Assault on Ancient Israel. *Bible Review* 11/6: 26–35, 47.

1997   Text and Artifact: Two Monologues? Pp. 311–41 in *The Archaeology of Israel: Constructing the Past, Interpreting the Present*, ed. N. A. Silberman and D. Small. Journal for the Study of the Old Testament Supplements 237. Sheffield: Sheffield Academic Press.

Herzog, Z.

1999   Deconstructing the Walls of Jericho. *Ha'aretz—Weekend Magazine*, October 29: 6–8.

Hodder, I.

1986   *Reading the Past: Current Approaches to Interpretation in Archaeology.* Cambridge: Cambridge University Press.

1999   *The Archaeological Process: An Introduction.* Oxford: Blackwell.

Hodder, I. (ed.)

1987   *The Archaeology of Contextual Meanings.* Cambridge: Cambridge University Press.

Hodder, I., et al.

1997   *Interpreting Archaeology: Finding Meaning in the Past.* London: Routledge.

Joffe, A. H.

1993   *Settlement and Society in the Early Bronze Age I–II Southern Levant: Complementarity and Contradiction in a Small-Scale Complex Society.* Sheffield: Sheffield Academic Press.

Jones, S.
   1997   *The Archaeology of Ethnicity.* London: Routledge.
Kohl, P. K.
   1985   Symbolic Cognitive Archaeology: A New Loss of Innocence. *Dialectical Anthropology* 9:
             105–17.
Lamberg-Karlovsky, C. C. (ed.)
   1989   *Archaeological Thought in America.* Cambridge: Cambridge University Press.
Lemche, N. P.
   1998   *The Israelites in History and Tradition.* Louisville: Westminster John Knox.
Leone, M. P.
   1982   Some Opinions about Recovering Mind. *American Antiquity* 47/4: 742–60.
Leone, M. P.; Potter, P.; and Shackel, P.
   1987   Toward a Critical Archaeology. *Current Anthropology* 29: 283–302.
Lubar, S., and Kingery, W. D. (eds.)
   1993   *History from Things: Essays on Material Culture.* Washington: Smithsonian Institution.
Marcus, G. E., and Fischer, M. M. J.
   1986   *Anthropology as Cultural Critique: An Experimental Moment in the Human Sciences.* Chicago:
             University of Chicago Press.
Meskell, L. (ed.)
   1999   *Archaeology under Fire: Nationalism, Politics and Heritage in the Eastern Mediterranean and
             Middle East.* London: Routledge.
Olivier, L., and Coudart, A.
   1995   French Tradition and the Central Place of History in the Human Sciences: Preamble to
             a Dialogue between Robinson Crusoe and His Man Friday. Pp. 363–81 in *Theory in Ar-
             chaeology: A World Perspective,* ed. P. J. Ucko. London: Routledge.
Patterson, T. C.
   1989   History and the Postprocessual Archaeologies. *Man* 24: 555–66.
Peebles, C. S.
   1998   Annalistes, Hermeneutics and Positivists: Squaring Circles or Dissolving Problems.
             Pp. 183–97 in *Reader in Archaeological Theory: Post-processual and Cognitive Approaches,*
             ed. D. S. Whitley. London: Routledge.
Preucel, R. W.
   1995   The Postprocessual Condition. *Journal of Anthropological Archaeology* 3/2: 147–75.
Preucel, R. W. (ed.)
   1991   *Processual and Postprocessual Archaeologies: Multiple Ways of Knowing the Past.* Carbondale,
             Ill. Southern Illinois University Press.
Preucel, R. W., and Hodder, I. (eds.)
   1996   *Contemporary Archaeology in Theory.* Oxford: Blackwell.
Renfrew, A. C., and Zubrow, E.
   1994   *The Ancient Mind: Elements of Cognitive Archaeology.* Cambridge: Cambridge University
             Press.
Shanks, H. (ed.)
   1996   *Archaeology's Publication Problem* 1. Washington: Biblical Archaeology Society.
   1999   *Archaeology's Publication Problem* 2. Washington: Biblical Archaeology Society.
Shanks, M., and Hodder, I.
   1998   Processual, Postprocessual and Interpretive Archaeologies. Pp. 69–95 in *Reader in
             Archaeological Theory: Post-processual and Cognitive Approaches,* ed. D. S. Whitley. London:
             Routledge.
Shanks, M., and Tilley, C.
   1987   *Re-constructing Archaeology: Theory and Practice.* Cambridge: Cambridge University Press.

Silberman, N. A.
   1999   Whose Game Is It Anyway? The Political and Social Transformations of American Biblical Archaeology. Pp. 175–88 in *Archaeology under Fire: Nationalism, Politics and Heritage in the Eastern Mediterranean and Middle East*, ed. L. Meskell. London: Routledge.

Thompson, T. L.
   1999   *The Mythic Past: Biblical Archaeology and the Myth of Ancient Israel.* New York: Basic Books.

Tilley, C.
   1991   *Material Culture and Text: The Art of Ambiguity.* London: Routledge.
   1993   *Interpretive Archaeology.* Oxford: Berg.

Tilley, C. (ed.)
   1990   *Reading Material Culture.* Oxford: Blackwell.

Trigger, B. G.
   1984   Archaeology at the Crossroads: What's New? *Annual Review of Anthropology* 13: 275–300.
   1989   *A History of Archaeological Thought.* Cambridge: Cambridge University Press.

Ucko, P. J. (ed.)
   1995   *Theory in Archaeology: A World Perspective.* London: Routledge.

VanPool, C. S., and VanPool, T. L.
   1999   The Scientific Nature of Postprocessualism. *American Antiquity* 64/1: 33–53.

Watson, P. J.; LeBlanc, S. A.; and Redman, C. L.
   1971   *Explanation in Archaeology: An Explicitly Scientific Approach.* New York: Columbia University Press.

Watson, R.
   1990   Oxymandis, King of Kings: Post-processual Radical Archaeology as Critique. *American Antiquity* 55: 573–89.

Whitley, D. S.
   1998   New Approaches to Old Problems: Archaeology in Search of an Ever Elusive Past. Pp. 1–28 in *Reader in Archaeological Theory: Post-Processual and Cognitive Approaches*, ed. D. S. Whitley. London: Routledge.

Whitley, D. S. (ed.)
   1998   *Reader in Archaeological Theory: Post-processual and Cognitive Approaches.* London: Routledge.

Wylie, A. W.
   1982   Epistemological Issues Raised by a Structuralist Archaeology. Pp. 39–46 in *Symbolic and Structural Archaeology*, ed. I. Hodder. Cambridge: Cambridge University Press.
   1985   The Reaction against Analogy. Pp. 63–111 in *Advances in Archaeological Method and Theory*, ed. M. B. Schliffer. New York: Academic.

Yoffee, N., and Sherratt, A. (eds.)
   1993   *Archaeological Theory: Who Sets the Agenda?* Cambridge: Cambridge University Press.

Special Public Lecture

Jerusalem as a Royal and Cultic Center in the 10th–8th Centuries B.C.E.

David Ussishkin
Institute of Archaeology
Tel Aviv University

The first archaeological investigations in Jerusalem took place in February 1851, when the French traveler de Saulcy conducted his study of monumental tombs (1854). Ever since, for nearly 150 years, archaeological investigations—namely, scholarly excavations, salvage work, and surveys—have continued, to the present day. There is no other cardinal site in the Holy Land that has so intensively been investigated. After such a long time-span of field work, we can allow ourselves—nay, we are even obliged—to evaluate the available factual evidence and use it to reconstruct the history and character of the biblical city. This I propose to do in brief in the present paper, limiting myself to a period of three centuries, from the reign of Solomon to the reign of Hezekiah.

The biblical text is the sole written source describing King Solomon's glorious reign and his capital Jerusalem. It presents Jerusalem of the time as a large and rich city, befitting its role as the capital of a great and prosperous kingdom and king. We are told that Solomon expanded the small town or citadel that he inherited from David, known as the "Stronghold of Zion" or "City of David," and incorporated the Temple Mount into the enlarged city. There he built a large royal palace (1 Kgs 7:1–12) and a magnificent temple next to it. We are also told that Solomon blocked the "breaches of the city of David" (1 Kgs 11:27) and surrounded it with a city wall (1 Kgs 9:15), and also built a *millo*, apparently a structure or structures based on construction fills (1 Kgs 9:15, 24; 11:27). The text emphasizes the luxury and extravagance of all that the king did and desired to build in Jerusalem (1 Kgs 9:19), the best expression of which is presented in the story of the visit of the queen of Sheba in 1 Kgs 10:4–5: "And when the queen of Sheba had seen all Solomon's wisdom, and the house that he had built, and the meat of his table, and the seating of his servants, and the attendance of his ministers, and their apparel, and his cup bearers, and his ascent by which he went up unto the house of the Lord, *there was no more breath in her.*"

When we turn to the archaeological evidence, the following picture emerges. Settlement in Jerusalem began in the Early Bronze Age on the eastern side of the southeast hill, that is, the City of David, to the south of the Temple Mount (fig. 1). The settlement was founded in this area due to the presence of the Gihon Spring, its main source of water.

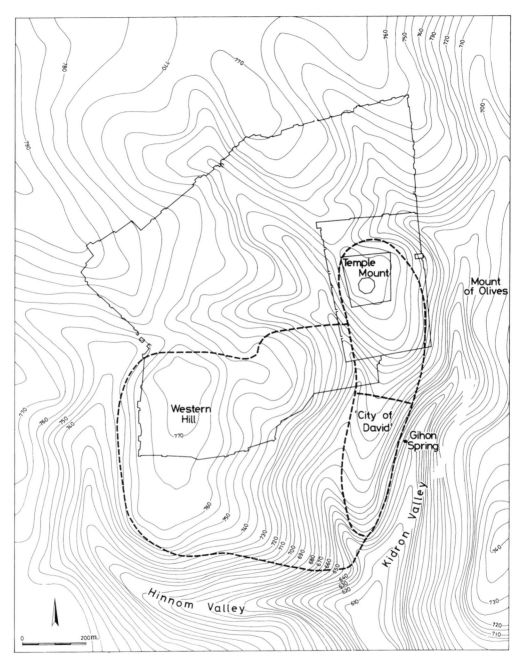

Fig. 1. Map of Jerusalem in the First Temple period.

Jerusalem became an important settlement in the later part of the Middle Bronze Age, when it was surrounded by a massive city wall, which was studied on the eastern slope of the City of David by Kenyon (1974: 76–97) and Shiloh (1984: 12, 26). The Gihon Spring was also protected by a massive tower, recently excavated by Reich and Shukron (1999). It appears that the tunnel leading to the spring, known as Warren's Shaft, also dates to this period.

The archaeological data regarding the long period that followed, that is, from the end of the Middle Bronze Age until the 8th-century city, discussed below, are rather scant and problematic. This important chapter in the history and archaeology of Jerusalem was recently the subject of several studies (Na'aman 1996; Cahill 1998; Steiner 1998). Jerusalem was not abandoned, and there are remains of some human activity and settlement on the eastern slope of the City of David, in the area above the Gihon Spring, throughout this period.

Of particular interest is the enigmatic and unique "stepped stone structure," a kind of retaining wall supporting the steep rocky slope above the spring (Shiloh 1984: 15–17). The structure was used and rebuilt for many generations. Shiloh (1984: 17), Cahill and Tarler (1993), and Steiner (1993; 1994) have attempted to determine its exact date on the basis of the pottery in the fills. It seems that this structure, or parts thereof, dates to the end of the Bronze Age and continued in use until the Second Temple period. Its original function is unclear, and no remains were found on the summit above it. At this point we cannot determine whether it was the retaining wall of a fortress or whether it had some other function.

Beyond this, we have small amounts of pottery, some remains of flimsy walls and floors (Cahill 1998), and, for the Late Bronze Age, also a few tombs outside the city proper, one of them very large (Saller 1964).

When evaluating the pottery from this settlement, we have to remember that the chronology of the pottery of this period in general is problematic and controversial. The pottery chronology was determined on the basis of sites located in the valleys and in the Shephelah, and we have very little secure data from the hills of Judea and Samaria. The main chronological pivots are the pottery assemblages from Level VI at Lachish, the last Canaanite city, destroyed by a terrible fire in the third quarter of the 12th century (Ussishkin 1985), and from Level III at Lachish, destroyed in 701 B.C.E. (Ussishkin 1977). The chronology of the pottery between these two dates is problematic: one scholar may attribute pottery to the 12th century, while another dates the same piece to the 11th century B.C.E. (on these chronological problems, see recently Finkelstein 1995; 1996; A. Mazar 1997).

As long as the pottery found in Jerusalem by Kenyon and Shiloh remains largely unpublished, it is difficult to discuss its exact dating. But we need not dwell here on this complex question. We can safely assume that settlement above the Gihon Spring existed between the 16th and 8th centuries B.C.E., possibly with some breaks in occupation during this long time-span.

Focusing on the period of the United Monarchy, the available archaeological evidence, when evaluated independently, indicates that a settlement, apparently limited in size and importance, existed in the City of David, in the area above the Gihon Spring. When we attempt to interpret this evidence, we find that the archaeologists are divided in their approach into two distinct groups. I would call the first "the followers of William Foxwell Albright" and the second "the followers of Hercule Poirot."

Albright established the scientific basis for the archaeology of Palestine in the biblical period (e.g., Albright 1960). He accepted biblical history from the age of the Patriarchs onward as the basis for understanding the material culture of the country, and in fact divided the archaeological periods accordingly. The archaeological data (which were poor and partial when he started his archaeological work in the 1920s) were "fitted" into the historical framework based in the main on biblical history. This method can be compared to a jigsaw puzzle, in which each individual piece is fitted separately into a general basic framework, with the aim of eventually achieving a complete picture.

The impact of Albright's work and method was enormous, and in fact his school of thought largely dominates the present-day archaeology of Palestine. His most prominent followers in Israel were Yigael Yadin and Yohanan Aharoni, and the excellent school of archaeology at the Hebrew University of Jerusalem, my alma mater, is the main pivot of Albrightian thought in Israel today. In the United States, G. Ernest Wright was one of Albright's principal disciples, and his students, William G. Dever, Lawrence E. Stager, and many others, whose archaeological concepts were crystallized in the excavations of ancient Shechem and Gezer, actively continue this line of thought today.

Returning to Solomonic Jerusalem, we see that Shiloh (1984: 27), A. Mazar (1990: 375–79), and Shanks (1995: 47–79, especially the figure on pp. 74–75), to mention but a few who have written on biblical Jerusalem in recent times, adopted a clear-cut Albrightian view in their interpretation of the evidence. They assumed that the Solomonic city was a magnificent capital, protected by a massive city wall, densely populated, and crowned by a large royal palace and temple. Into this picture, which they accept as fact, the real finds uncovered in the field are fitted like pieces of a jigsaw puzzle. In other words, they conclude that the city at the time was as described in the biblical text but that, for one reason or another, only some poor finds were uncovered on the slope above the Gihon Spring, although these fit well into the general picture.

On the other hand, there is the second group of archaeologists, unfortunately smaller in number than the former, that I have labeled on previous occasions "the radicals." My colleague Israel Finkelstein resented this title; hence, I shall nickname the group "the followers of Hercule Poirot." Monsieur Poirot, the famous eccentric sleuth with the curled moustache, the literary creation of Agatha Christie, always put the onus of his work on the objective analysis of the factual data. This was the starting point of his investigations in all his cases. The same principle applies to a proper approach to archaeological evaluation. The starting point of the archaeologist should be the data collected on the ground and its objective and unbiased evaluation. Had Hercule Poirot been an archaeologist, he undoubtedly would have done the same, following his rule, expounded in *Death on the Nile*, that "it is always well to proceed with order and method."

According to this school of thought, the above principle applies to biblical archaeology in general and to the case of Solomonic Jerusalem in particular. From the point of view of the archaeologist, what counts first and foremost are the archaeological data, rather than the biblical text. We can add that it is much easier now to evaluate independently the archaeological evidence than it was in Albright's time, when much less was known and understood. When studying Solomonic Jerusalem using this approach, however, we observe that the extant remains indicate the existence of a small settlement, rather than a large magnificent capital. For the following four disturbing reasons, it seems that this is the realistic archaeological picture that will not be radically changed in the future.

1. *The Fortifications.*   Two systems of fortifications have been excavated in Jerusalem, one dating to the Middle Bronze Age and the other to the 8th century B.C.E. and later (see below). On the eastern slope of the City of David, these two walls were parallel to one another and even partly superimposed. There are no fortifications dating to the long time-span between the periods of use of these two walls. Kenyon (1974: 130–44) suggested that the Middle Bronze Age wall continued in use thereafter and was later replaced by another wall that has not been found, so that the city was protected continuously by a city wall until the 8th century. This suggestion, however, lacks a sufficient factual basis and cannot be accepted. It thus seems clear that the settlement that existed in Jerusalem in the 10th century B.C.E. was not surrounded by a city wall.

2. *The Gihon Spring.*   The Gihon Spring was the most crucial point in the ancient city. The City of David was chosen in the Early Bronze Age as the area to be settled due to the location of the Gihon Spring, the settlement's main source of water at least until the 8th century B.C.E. The recent excavations by Reich and Shukron showed much activity near the spring—massive fortifications, as well as tunnels and water systems from the MB II and then in the later part of the Iron Age (Reich and Shukron 1999; Shanks 1999). They observed no signs of human activity from the period of the United Monarchy, a clear indication of how insignificant the settlement of the City of David was at the time.

3. *The Question of Pottery.*   Pottery vessels usually have a short life-span and then break. These pottery sherds do not decay and are not swept away, remaining in the debris of the site. Assuming that a large settlement existed in Jerusalem in the 10th century, with its focal point on the Temple Mount, we would expect to have found, collected, and identified many thousands of contemporaneous pottery sherds in the debris throughout the area, in particular around the Temple Mount. But this is not the case. Moreover, in the vast areas exposed by Benjamin Mazar to the west and south of the Temple Mount, very few pottery sherds of the 10th–9th centuries were identified (e.g., E. Mazar and B. Mazar 1989). As mentioned above, scholars are divided on the chronology of the pottery of this period, but since very little was found here in any event, the complex questions of pottery chronology are irrelevant to our discussion.

4. *Future Excavations.*   In all similar cases, we are used to hearing the argument that, while not much evidence was found, future excavations will uncover more. Although so many excavations and surveys have been carried out in Jerusalem, new discoveries can still be made, as shown recently by Reich and Shukron in the Gihon Spring excavations (Reich and Shukron 1999; Shanks 1999). However, the weight of all the field work conducted thus far in Jerusalem is such that it is very doubtful that a new discovery here or there will change the overall picture.

This is the archaeological interpretation that the professional archaeologist of the "Hercule Poirot" school presents for the evaluation of historians and biblical scholars.

The first eminent scholar to have taken up the challenge was Na'aman (1996). On the basis of the archaeological evidence, he defined 10th-century Jerusalem as a "highland stronghold," and the kingdom of Judah in the late 10th–9th centuries B.C.E. as a "peripheral small and powerless kingdom" (Na'aman 1996: 24).

Turning to the next stage in the history of Jerusalem, we see that a large settlement existed in the 8th–7th centuries B.C.E., when Jerusalem was the capital of the Judean kingdom, which was destroyed in 587/6 B.C.E. by the Babylonian army of Nebuchadnezzar. During this period, Jerusalem expanded in size, becoming a metropolis, the central city in Judah. It encompassed the entire City of David, the Temple Mount, and the western hill, now the Jewish Quarter of the Old City. The city was heavily fortified. Massive city walls were uncovered by Kenyon (1974: 144–47), Shiloh (1984: 28), and E. Mazar (E. Mazar and B. Mazar 1989) along the eastern slope of the City of David, and lower walls were recently excavated in this area by Reich and Shukron (Shanks 1999). Even stronger fortifications were discovered by Avigad on the western hill (1983: 23–60). Complex water systems, tunnels, and pools had been cut into the rock or constructed (Ussishkin 1995). There are indications that a royal park, "the king's garden," a smaller imitation of the royal parks of Nineveh, was located near the lower edge of the City of David (Ussishkin 1995: 300–303).

The conclusion that this large city already existed in the 8th century B.C.E. is based on the pottery, which is similar to that of Level III at Lachish, the city destroyed by Sennacherib in 701 B.C.E. Of particular interest in the Lachish Level III pottery are the many stamped royal Judean storage jars, known as *lmlk* storage jars (Ussishkin 1977). These were apparently produced by the government of Hezekiah in the context of the preparations for the Assyrian invasion (Na'aman 1979). Hundreds of stamped handles of such storage jars have been found throughout Jerusalem (catalogued by Gabriel Barkay [see Vaughn 1999]). The Lachish Level III type pottery and the *lmlk* storage jars show that Jerusalem had already reached its larger dimensions by the end of the 8th century B.C.E.

This large city, however, may well have developed earlier, in the course of the 8th century or even in the later part of the 9th century B.C.E. Many Judean towns were already extensively settled in the 9th century, if not earlier. Significantly, by this time, a massively fortified city had been built at Lachish, designated Level IV. Can we accept the conclusion that Jerusalem, the capital, was smaller and poorer compared with Lachish, as well as with other towns in Judah? Alternatively, should we take this as an indication that the great metropolis was in fact founded and had begun to develop already in the 9th century? I would opt for the second alternative, assuming that an in-depth study of the Jerusalem pottery reveals a large number of sherds of the Lachish Level IV type, which at Lachish precedes the Level III type pottery mentioned above.

At this point, I will turn to the royal acropolis of Jerusalem, built on the Temple Mount, which was the focus and heart of the biblical city. Unfortunately, there are no available archaeological data regarding the compound and its buildings. In our studies, we rely on topographical data, the biblical text, and comparable archaeological material. Therefore, on this particular issue, "the followers of Albright" and "the followers of Hercule Poirot" proceed hand in hand, all scholars being equally frustrated that no proper investigation can be carried out on the Temple Mount.

In reconstructing the appearance of the royal compound, all scholars agree that it was smaller than the later Herodian compound, the shape of which is preserved to the present day. Many graphic reconstructions (e.g., A. Mazar 1990: 418, fig. 10.8) depict the outlines of the rectangular Herodian compound with the smaller Iron Age compound marked by curving lines inside (a similar reconstruction is presented in fig. 1).

On the other hand, other scholars, among them Père Vincent, Kenyon (1974: 111–14, fig. 22), and, more recently, Ritmeyer (1992), believe that the Herodian walls follow, at least in part, the lines of the Iron Age walls, and hence the walls of the earlier compound were straight rather than curved. Wightman (1993: 29–31) compared the Solomonic compound with that of Omride Samaria, also reconstructing its walls in straight lines.

I would like to develop these lines of thought, as follows: We can assume that the royal compound of the kings of the House of David in Jerusalem was based in plan and character on the same model as the royal Omride compounds at Samaria (Crowfoot, Kenyon, and Sukenik 1942) and Jezreel (Ussishkin and Woodhead 1997: 11, fig. 4). These compounds have much in common, thus representing a crystallized model and concept. At both Samaria and Jezreel, the compound was founded on the summit of a hill, with bedrock constituting much of the surface. In both places, the compound is rectangular, surrounded by a casemate wall. Large amounts of soil and debris were dumped against the casemate walls as construction fills, turning the enclosed area into a podium, its surface almost horizontal. At Samaria, several buildings were found inside the compound, which also had large open courtyards. The excavations barely touched the inside of the compound at Jezreel, but it seems to have had similar open spaces.

Three sides of the rectangular compound at Jezreel were protected by a deep, rock-cut moat. Because the fourth side faced a steep slope, there was no need for such a moat. In Jerusalem, the Temple Mount was surrounded on three sides by a steep slope, but on the northwestern side, it was connected by a topographical saddle to the hill running farther to the north. This constituted the topographical weak point in the defense of the Temple Mount. It seems quite possible, as suggested already by Wilson and Warren (1871: 13) and recently advocated by Ottosson (1989) and Oredsson (2000: 92–95), that a moat was cut into the rock across the saddle in the First Temple period.

If the above reconstruction is correct, it would mean that the Herodian architects adopted for the new compound a plan similar to that of the Iron Age, although much larger in scale and grandeur. Furthermore, Fortress Antonia was built especially to protect the northwestern corner of the compound. There was, however, one basic difference: the later compound did not contain a royal palace.

Turning to the buildings in the Davidic compound—our sole source being the biblical text—we find that it contained a royal palace and a temple. In later periods the temple gained in importance, while the palace was almost forgotten. At the time of its construction, however, the royal palace was undoubtedly the main edifice in the compound. This palace, briefly described in 1 Kings 7, was much larger than the temple: we are informed that it took 13 years to build the palace, but only seven to build the temple. The palace contained a ceremonial wing with a large, magnificent throne room, almost certainly based on the model of the Syrian *bīt-ḫilāni* palace type; residential wings; and "the house

of the Forest of Lebanon"—probably the royal treasury—which was as big as the temple
(Ussishkin 1973). The palace complex was enclosed within its own large courtyard.

Assuming that the temple stood on the summit of the hill, where the Dome of the
Rock is presently situated, all scholars reconstruct the royal palace to the south of the
temple, where the ground is lower (e.g., Galling 1937: 411; Wightman 1993: 31, fig. 9). This
reconstruction is based on several indications in the biblical text that one had to ascend
from the palace to the temple, and—more importantly—on the description of the construction of the city walls of Jerusalem in Neh 3:25–29; 12:37 (Avi-Yonah 1954; Tsafrir 1977;
Eshel 2000). The descriptions of Nehemiah's wall and its relationship to the palace can,
however, be interpreted in different ways.

In my view, we have to consider the possibility that the palace stood on lower ground
to the north of the temple, an area spacious enough to accommodate such a large complex. This suggestion is based on the principle location of many rulers' palaces of this
period. In many cities, we find the acropolis built at the edge of the city, and the ruler's
palace built at the edge of the acropolis or the city, for example, at Hittite Ḫattusha;
Canaanite Ugarit and Megiddo; Aramean Gozan; and Assyrian Calah, Nineveh, Dur-
Sharukin, Til Barsib, and Megiddo. There are, of course, other cases, notably Israelite
Samaria and Neo-Hittite Sam'al-Zincirli, in which the acropolis was located in the middle
of the city, but in both of these cities, the royal palace was also located at the edge of
the acropolis.

If located to the north of the temple, the royal palace of Jerusalem would have been
ideally situated: the royal acropolis was at the northeastern edge of the city and the palace
at the northern end of the acropolis, adjacent to the edge of the fortified city. This is undoubtedly the place where, in 701 B.C.E., the Assyrian general Rab-shakeh stood in front
of the camp of the Assyrian army, facing the city wall, and challenged Hezekiah in his own
palace (Ussishkin 1979; 1995).

Finally, we must evaluate the position of the royal acropolis vis-à-vis the city. As shown
above, the location and character of the acropolis accord beautifully with the large metropolis in the 8th century as we know it. But what was there in the earlier periods? Knauf
(2000) recently suggested that the cultic and secular center of both the Late Bronze and
Israelite cities was on the Temple Mount, but there are no textual or archaeological indications to support this theory. The "followers of Albright" suggest that the royal acropolis
was built by Solomon as an extension of the city, but as discussed above, this concept does
not correspond to the archaeological evidence.

If we accept the view advocated by the "followers of Hercule Poirot" that the Jebusite
and 10th-century Israelite settlements were limited to the central part of the City of
David, we are in fact faced with three alternative possibilities. None of these alternatives
is based on archaeological evidence, but merely on the interpretation and evaluation of
the biblical text and on historical interpretation. The first possibility is that the royal
acropolis was built as a separate entity by Solomon, as described in the biblical text, and
was incorporated into the expanding city at a later date. The second is that, as suggested
by Na'aman (1996: 23), Solomon built a temple on the Temple Mount, "though on a much
smaller scale than the one built in the late monarchical period"; the same may apply, perhaps, to a modest version of the adjacent secular palace. The third alternative is that the

royal acropolis was built as described in the biblical text, but in a later period, when the so-called "highland stronghold" became a large city.

The question of the royal acropolis of Jerusalem ends this brief paper. The complex questions raised here warrant further discussion in depth, which I hope to present in a future paper.

References

Albright, W. F.
  1960   *The Archaeology of Palestine*. Rev. ed. London: Penguin.
Avigad, N.
  1983   *Discovering Jerusalem*. Nashville: Thomas Nelson.
Avi-Yonah, M.
  1954   The Walls of Nehemiah: A Minimalist View. *Israel Exploration Journal* 4: 239–48.
Cahill, J.
  1998   It Is There, the Archaeological Evidence Proves It. *Biblical Archaeology Review* 24/4: 34–41.
Cahill, J. M., and Tarler, D.
  1993   Response to Margreet Steiner—The Jebusite Ramp of Jerusalem: The Evidence from the Macalister, Kenyon and Shiloh Excavations. Pp. 625–26 in *Biblical Archaeology Today, 1990: Proceedings of the Second International Congress on Biblical Archaeology*, ed. A. Biran and J. Aviram. Jerusalem: Israel Exploration Society and Israel Academy of Sciences and Humanities.
Crowfoot, J. W.; Kenyon, K. M.; and Sukenik, E. L.
  1942   *The Buildings at Samaria*. London: Palestine Exploration Fund.
Eshel, H.
  2000   Jerusalem under Persian Rule: The City's Layout and the Historical Background. Pp. 327–43 in *The History of Jerusalem: The Biblical Period*, ed. S. Aḥituv and A. Mazar. Jerusalem: Yad Izhak Ben-Zvi (Hebrew).
Finkelstein, I.
  1995   The Date of the Settlement of the Philistines in Canaan. *Tel Aviv* 22: 213–39.
  1996   The Archaeology of the United Monarchy: An Alternative View. *Levant* 28: 177–87.
Galling, K.
  1937   *Biblisches Reallexikon*. Tübingen: Mohr.
Kenyon, K. M.
  1974   *Digging Up Jerusalem*. London: Ernest Benn.
Knauf, E. A.
  2000   Jerusalem in the Late Bronze and Early Iron Ages: A Proposal. *Tel Aviv* 27: 75–90.
Mazar, A.
  1990   *Archaeology of the Land of the Bible: 10,000–586 B.C.E.* New York: Doubleday.
  1997   Iron Age Chronology: A Reply to I. Finkelstein. *Levant* 29: 157–67.
Mazar, E., and Mazar, B.
  1989   *Excavations in the South of the Temple Mount: The Ophel of Biblical Jerusalem*. Qedem 29. Jerusalem: Institute of Archaeology, Hebrew University.
Na'aman, N.
  1979   Sennacherib's Campaign in Judah and the Date of the *lmlk* Stamps. *Vetus Testamentum* 29: 61–81.
  1996   The Contribution of the Amarna Letters to the Debate on Jerusalem's Political Position in the Tenth Century B.C.E. *Bulletin of the American Schools of Oriental Research* 304: 17–27.
Oredsson, D.
  2000   *Moats in Ancient Palestine*. Old Testament Series 48. Stockholm: Almqvist and Wiksell.

Ottosson, M.
  1989   Topography and City Planning with Special Reference to Jerusalem. *Tidsskrift for Teologi og Kirke* 4: 263–70.
Reich, R., and Shukron, E.
  1999   Light at the End of the Tunnel. *Biblical Archaeology Review* 25/1: 22–33, 72.
Ritmeyer, L.
  1992   Locating the Original Temple Mount. *Biblical Archaeology Review* 18/2: 24–45.
Saller, S. J.
  1964   *The Jebusite Burial Place.* Part 2 of *The Excavations at Dominus Flevit (Mount Olivet, Jerusalem).* Studium Biblicum Franciscanum 13. Jerusalem: Franciscan Press.
Saulcy, F. de
  1854   *A Narrative of a Journey Round the Dead Sea and in the Bible Lands; in 1850 and 1851.* Vol. 2. London: Richard Bentley.
Shanks, H.
  1995   *Jerusalem: An Archaeological Biography.* New York: Random.
  1999   Everything You Ever Knew about Jerusalem Is Wrong (Well, Almost). *Biblical Archaeology Review* 25/6: 20–29.
Shiloh, Y.
  1984   *Excavations at the City of David I, 1978–1982: Interim Report of the First Five Seasons.* Qedem 19. Jerusalem: Institute of Archaeology, Hebrew University.
Steiner, M. L.
  1993   The Jebusite Ramp of Jerusalem: The Evidence from the Macalister, Kenyon and Shiloh Excavations. Pp. 585–88 in *Biblical Archaeology Today, 1990: Proceedings of the Second International Congress on Biblical Archaeology,* ed. A. Biran and J. Aviram. Jerusalem: Israel Exploration Society and Israel Academy of Sciences and Humanities.
  1994   Re-dating the Terraces of Jerusalem. *Israel Exploration Journal* 44: 13–20.
  1998   It's Not There: Archaeology Proves a Negative. *Biblical Archaeology Review* 24/4: 26–33.
Tsafrir, Y.
  1977   The Walls of Jerusalem in Nehemiah's Time. *Cathedra* 4: 31–42 (Hebrew).
Ussishkin, D.
  1973   King Solomon's Palaces. *The Biblical Archaeologist* 36: 78–105.
  1977   The Destruction of Lachish by Sennacherib and the Dating of the Royal Judean Storage Jars. *Tel Aviv* 4: 28–60.
  1979   The "Camp of the Assyrians" in Jerusalem. *Israel Exploration Journal* 29: 137–42.
  1985   Levels VII and VI at Tel Lachish and the End of the Late Bronze Age in Canaan. Pp. 213–30 in *Palestine in the Bronze and Iron Ages: Papers in Honour of Olga Tufnell,* ed. J. N. Tubb. London: Institute of Archaeology.
  1995   The Water Systems of Jerusalem during Hezekiah's Reign. Pp. 289–307 in *Meilsteinen: Festgabe für Herbert Donner,* ed. M. Weippert and S. Timm. Wiesbaden: Harrassowitz.
Ussishkin, D., and Woodhead, J.
  1997   Excavations at Tel Jezreel 1994–1996: Third Preliminary Report. *Tel Aviv* 24: 6–72.
Vaughn, A. G.
  1999   *Theology, History, and Archaeology in the Chronicler's Account of Hezekiah.* Archaeology and Biblical Studies 4. Atlanta: Society of Biblical Literature.
Wightman, G. J.
  1993   *The Walls of Jerusalem from the Canaanites to the Mamluks.* Mediterranean Archaeology Supplement 4. Sydney: University of Sydney.
Wilson, C., and Warren, C.
  1871   *The Recovery of Jerusalem: A Narrative of Exploration and Discovery in the City and the Holy Land.* London: Richard Bentley.

Discussions

———

Part I
Historical and Political Landscape: The Levant and Beyond

Palace Economies in the Late Bronze Age and
The Dark Age That Never Was (Iron Age I)

Michal Artzy and Joe D. Seger (Chairs/Respondents)

Vassos Karageorghis: It is rare that I agree with Susan Sherratt, and this time I do! In conformity with what she has told us about the Cypriote activity in trade with the west, I would add that this may explain the fact that all the copper ingots found in Sardinia up to now are of Cypriote origin, although Sardinia produces copper. The Cypriotes, if they were no longer interested in copper, would sell their main product at any price to Sardinians. So this may explain the enigma of why there is so much Cypriote copper in the central Mediterranean.

Susan Sherratt: I agree that it's quite pointless to try to look for any sort of rationality in this trade. They were going round and round selling whatever they could wherever they could. It does make sense of the ingots in Sardinia, particularly if one then sees them as ingots rather than copper. This was the de-commodification of copper—that these things were actually traveling as ingots and being acquired by Sardinians as ingots rather than as copper, and in that sense, they were status symbols.

Anson Rainey: I'd like to address a question to Prof. Muhly about Anatolia. Regarding the destruction of the Hittite Empire, he depicts it as being destroyed by a warrior class. Does this mean that the Phrygians have now lost their right to ethnic identity? I didn't hear him mention this term at all. Where do they come in?

James Muhly: I had a section in the paper on ethnic identity, which I cut out because it was way over time. As far as I'm concerned, associating Phrygians with *Buckelkeramik* is just another example of the old pots and peoples equation, which I would like to get away from. I think it's one of the things that has bedeviled the study of Early Bronze Age archaeology all over the Mediterranean world. We are so obsessed with identifying a style of pottery with a particular ethnic group that we become much more interested not in what was being made and what was being done, but who was doing it. I would like to move away from putting an ethnic identity on everything. Patricia Bikai pointed out some time ago that it was often very difficult to distinguish between Cypriote and Phoenician pottery in the Skales cemetery, and I think the implication of this is that maybe these identifications are really not that important.

Aren Maeir: Two short comments. One to Dr. Caubet: an additional important aspect of the continuity between Late Bronze and Iron I is the linguistic substrata, such as the Aramean substrata, for example, seen at Emar, and the so-called possible harbingers of Phoenician substrata seen at Ugarit. This would be the ethnic linguistic continuity between the Late Bronze Age and the Iron Age, as you were hinting archaeologically.

My main question, though, is to Susan Sherratt, about the so-called Philistine trade. If, in fact, there was such intense trade with Philistia, and even if it was not in pots, from the mid–12th to the late 11th century, Philistine culture developed in its very own and separate trajectory. It was not influenced by Cypriote, Phoenician, and Aegean pottery until the middle to end of the 11th century. I'm not saying that it didn't start from those traditions, but it lost them and went on its own track for a while. That makes it quite difficult for those knives that you point to with the Urnfield parallels. The ivory handles, if anything, may have influenced the metal handles with the circles and not the opposite.

Susan Sherratt: Just to finish off the point about the iron knives, I don't think you can make the chronology of that work at all, saying that the kind of knives that are being produced around the Alpine region and in Italy are influenced by iron knives with ivory handles. It just wouldn't work. It makes no sense whatsoever, and in fact, at this stage, the iron knives did not get as far west as Italy. A few of them reached the Aegean, but they didn't actually manage to get further than that. And on pots, I would disagree with you, because, as Prof. Dothan has several times pointed out, you see a development, for instance, within the so-called Philistine Monochrome, the so-called Mycenaean IIIC:1, at Tel Miqne itself. You can see a development, which parallels what is also happening in Cyprus between the end of the 13th century and sometime in the later part of the 12th century, before Philistine Bichrome develops.

Eliezer Oren: However much I like Cypriote archaeology (and I really admire Cypriote archaeologists, of course), I am somewhat uneasy about the Cypro-centricity expressed here, especially as regards metal production, in terms of monopolizing metal production all over the ancient world. One should really take more seriously the very active metallurgical activity here, particularly in Canaan. Probably many of the objects that have been designated as Cypriote by, of course, typological standards, end up being what I would call Egypto-Canaanite metals.

The Dynamics of Statehood (Iron Age II)

Amnon Ben-Tor (Chair/Respondent): A word to Ami Mazar, with whom I agree almost one hundred percent. There is only one thing—which he keeps repeating—and before it becomes the "truth," I would like to comment on it. Ami says, "Ben-Tor does not hesitate in identifying the destroyers of Hazor as having been the Israelites." I have said repeatedly that the early Israelites should not be ruled out automatically, as is so often the case. Every other agent of destruction—other Canaanite cities, Egyptians, Sea Peoples—is kosher, except the only one explicitly mentioned as having destroyed Hazor, just because this information comes from the Bible. All I ask is that the Israelites should be kept as a possibility, especially since Ami himself told us, and I quote, "The settlement pattern fits the early Israelite society as described in the biblical narrative" and "Israel must have been an important population group in Canaan, and in the Gilead, a similar network of settlements appears to have existed." Given all this, and there is more, all I ask is: let's give the Israelites the benefit of the doubt. Whether they were early Israelites, proto-Israelites, or whatever you like, let's at least give them a chance of having had something to do with the destruction of Canaanite Hazor.

Last, but not least, while there is not enough time for a complete response to my good friend Israel Finkelstein, allow me a short anecdote. There was a group of people sitting around and one of them asked, "Do you want to hear a nice story?" So they said, "Yes." So he says, "I was once working on a boat on the high seas, and we were sitting on the deck and there was a huge wave that threw me overboard and I was completely naked. As I was fighting for my life, I was attacked by an enormous shark. So I took out a knife from my pocket and I killed the shark." So somebody said, "How is that possible? You were naked a minute ago." So he says, "Aha! You don't want a nice story, you want to have an argument." Well, I want to have an argument.

We had a wonderful picture drawn about the new Canaan. It is a nice picture, broadly painted, but facts and data, as we just heard, are also, sometimes, to be taken into consideration. As an example, I would like to comment on only one issue, even though I have a feeling of *déjà vu*, or *déjà entendu*, and also *déjà répondu*. A lot was made of the statement, as though there was a continuity of the population. Everything today has to do with continuity—maybe this is the modern fad—and there is no real break around 1200. Agreed, there is a continuity, periods are not cut off from each other like slices of salami. But, I quote from Finkelstein's paper, "David Ilan has recently shown that most of the small Late Bronze Age sites around Hazor continued to be settled in Iron I and the sites indicate a clear demographic and cultural continuity." And we also heard a lot about the stability of the rural settlement. Let us see what David Ilan's study really shows—and, let me add, also a recent study published by Yosef Stepansky—about the Hula Valley.

First of all, absolutely nothing can be said about sites that have not been excavated. Try and see for a minute what could we say about Hazor, where we know there was an interruption, without Hazor's excavation. We would clearly be able to say that the settlement continued without any disruption. Let's see the excavated sites. Of the 41 sites David Ilan worked on in the Hula region, and the sites in the southern Hula discussed by Stepansky, only two were excavated: Tell Wawiyat and Tel Anafa. At the former, nothing is known about the Late Bronze Age settlement, whether it was destroyed or not, while at the latter, Tel Anafa, the relevant remains are, and I quote from David Ilan, "an LB/Iron I transitional phase." No clear Iron I architectural remains were reported, only pottery sherds. As for the other 39 sites in the region, there are only 10—that is, less than 25 percent overall—in which the relevant periods, LB and Iron I, are represented by sherds. Of these, 6 are defined as "ephemeral camps," one—Abel Bet-Maʿacha—is defined as a "first-order site with architecture," and the 3 remaining are Hazor, characterized by a sharp settlement disruption, Tel Anafa, where there is no information with regard to the nature of the transition between the two periods, and Tel Dan, where an ash layer was observed between Level VII, the latest LB stratum, and Level VI, the earliest Iron I stratum.

I quote the excavator of Tel Dan, Avraham Biran: "There can be no doubt with regard to the profound difference in the nature of settlement and its material culture between the settlement of Iron I and the latest LB settlement." With regard to who was who in the region, let me again quote Ilan's study: "The post–Late Bronze Age settlement in the region involved local groups of agriculturalists, nomadic pastoralists, newcomers with village urban backgrounds from the south, and people with coastal origins." There is, thus, no shred of evidence—if you wish, no sherd of archaeological evidence—for the claimed continuity of settlement and clear demographic and cultural continuity in Iron I. Therefore, it seems to me that there is also no need to go along with Finkelstein's claim, and I quote again: "The basis for the archaeological structure built in the 1920s is nonexistent, and we are therefore free to look at the finds free of bias." Not everything we inherited from our predecessors is, by definition, wrong. To constantly enlarge our database, yes; to explore new insights, yes; to expand our knowledge without bias, yes; to disregard, to discard and substitute, no.

Jacob Milgrom (Professor Emeritus, Biblical Studies, University of California): I refer only and specifically to an archaeological fact, one that I am surprised that Dr. Finkelstein omitted entirely: namely, the matter of pig bones, that is, the total absence of pig bones in Iron Age I in the central highlands, as compared with the existence of pig bones in the coastal region, at Tel Batash, Tel Miqne, and Ashkelon. Today we are certain, by virtue of the pottery, that these are Philistine settlements. And so you have this sharp, clear distinction, which is something that does not exist in the ancient Near East at all, except as we see from the biblical record. I certainly would like to hear Dr. Finkelstein address this fact directly.

Simi Shavel (Graduate Student, Department of Bible, Hebrew University): I want to address a comment also to Dr. Finkelstein about using the Deuteronomistic ideology to dismiss the entire biblical record, not from the archaeological side, which Amihai Mazar spoke about, but from the literary side. Precisely because of the Deuteronomist's strong identifiable ideology, you can recognize texts, which he must have imported, that existed before he wrote. He didn't create them wholesale out of broadcloth. There are three examples. First is David, the best for the Deuteronomist, and the stories of 2 Samuel, which really don't present the best. Second, King Manasseh lasts for 52 years, which, in the Deuteronomistic ideology, is a little bit of a problem. There is a dissonance regarding how the worst possible king could have had the longest reign, so much so that the Chronicler invents a reason to explain it: he repented, so God allowed him to continue so long. Third, Jeroboam is evaluated by the Deuteronomist as being the absolute worst king of the North, and yet, the extent of his reach goes all the way to Mevoh Hamat, which, of course, recalls David. This leads to the second thing in your favor. None of this is to say that these texts are historical—simply that they predate the Deuteronomist. The David tradition, and that coincidence of Mevoh Hamat, perhaps are a combination of traditions from the North, from the monarchical period, however long it existed, and specifically, of the reign of Hezekiah, because Hezekiah is viewed as a messianic person who will unite the North and the South. So between Jeroboam, a successful king, and Hezekiah, who will unite, there may be other traditions that also were associated later with the figure of David.

Anson Rainey: Rather than getting into this debate, I would just like to point something out. We haven't yet demythologized Shishak, so Shishak is a marvelous paradigm for David. His people, the Lybians, arrived in the Delta by a series of violent and nonviolent immigrations during the 12th and 11th centuries. When they became strong enough as an ethnic element in the Delta, their leading warrior chieftain established a new dynasty. One of the first things he must have done—and I am sorry that Prof. Kitchen didn't bring the picture of Shishak's statue from Byblos, which is on the base of a throne where Shishak is sitting, and there is also a Phoenician inscription on it—in his new political role was to establish economic and political relations with Byblos, with whom he never waged a war. This is obviously an act of peace and friendship. By the same token, people have asked, what about this fragment at Megiddo? Would he have set up a victory stela? Is it a victory stela? I don't think it is. It's a fact that in the early years of his reign, he also sent a statue, maybe more than one, to establish friendly economic and political relations with the United Monarchy, which controlled Megiddo. Therefore, should we take the Shishak fragment out of our consideration of whether the city was destroyed or not, in which stratum, and so forth? Of course, sadly enough, it was found out of context.

Kenneth Kitchen: First, Shishak gained the throne through being linked to the royal family of the 21st Dynasty and the ruling people of Memphis. It's a dynastic matter, not an ethnic one. Second, he had to spend 10 or 20 years first reuniting Egypt. During this stage, Egypt was two kingdoms in one: a lot to do in internal politics before he could do anything—so statues from Byblos, yes. Shosenq I, Osorkon I, and Osorkon II: that's a steady relationship. It may or may not have taken place early, it could have taken place later. A victory stela is not the sort of thing you give when you're having a peaceful relationship. It's like the Ramesside stela at Nahr el-Kelb and so on. I don't think you can take it out, but thank you very much for your contribution.

Israel Finkelstein: On Megiddo VI, Tim Harrison's study is extremely important, because it has to do with methodology and that, really, is something I have to explain. We—David Ussishkin, Baruch Halpern, and I—have been excavating at Megiddo since 1994. We've excavated two areas with remains from Stratum VIA. We already have, from the Megiddo expedition of the 1920s and 1930s and from our own excavations, huge assemblages of pottery, with assemblages of intact vessels from Stratum VIA. I suppose that we are speaking of about 500 vessels unearthed so far, and not even a single Philistine vessel in the assemblage. Area CC, which is now being published by Tim Harrison, was excavated in the 1920s and was declared by the excavators, the University of Chicago team, a mess—not by me, but by the excavators themselves. So I think that when we have evidence from their own excavations and from our own excavations of the same areas that they declared to be a mess, we have to be very careful with their information.

To my dear friend Amnon, about continuity, we don't share the same views about how to interpret certain information. Indeed, the material from the Hula Valley can be interpreted in more than one way. However, when you look at the Jezreel Valley, for instance, and you see information both from excavations such as the ones that I mentioned and from surveys, I think that the overall picture is quite clear. By the way, I believe that if we had had to analyze survey material from Hazor without excavations, only from surveys, the picture that we today in the year 2000 would have presented would have been of some sort of a Late Bronze break and then recovery, not really continuation. It's a matter of how to look at the data.

Now to Jacob Milgrom's question about pig bones, I suppose that you quoted me, so what can I say? I agree with you fully about the pig bones. Indeed, the pig bones, a matter first put forward by Larry Stager, but which I elaborated on later in a special article, is one of the most important elements that we have today for some sort of—what would I call it?—identity of the Iron I people in the highlands. However, we have to be very careful with the way that we interpret this evidence on pig bones, because it can be interpreted in more than one way against the background of the animosity with the lowlands people and so on. I don't want to go too much into it. Indeed, the evidence is there, but there is more than one way to interpret it.

My final comment is on the Deuteronomistic historian. Indeed, there is no doubt that the Deuteronomistic historian or historians of the 7th century used earlier material, and I bring more evidence to the items that were presented to us before. For example, the description of the early days of David in the southern hill country and in the Shephelah is a description that cannot be described against the background of 7th-century Judah. So, definitely, we have in this case earlier material, which must go back at least to the early 8th century. I have to give you some good news in order to let you take a break now with some positive feelings, so let me just say, as the excavator of Shiloh, that Shiloh was a major site in Iron I in the highlands, so we are speaking about the 11th century and, possibly, according to my recent views, the 10th century, but not later than the 10th century. Even if Iron I goes to the 10th century, there was nothing there, or almost nothing there, in the 9th and 8th centuries B.C.E. The meaning is that the centrality of Shiloh in the narrative, the way we see it in the Deuteronomistic history, must have been taken from some sort of early tradition. It couldn't have been a display of any reality of late monarchic Judah as such. So, definitely, there were early materials in the Deuteronomistic history; there is no doubt about it.

Imperial Interventions
(The Persian, Hellenistic, and Roman Periods)

Moshe Kochavi (Chair/Respondent): Although this is not my time period, as I am more of a biblical archaeologist, still, I have a comment. It was very interesting to hear that a person can talk about tribes migrating, coming into a new country, and making their own kingdom there, and nobody opposes it!

Part II
Religion and Distinction

Shadow-Boxing the Canaanites (The Late Bronze Age)

Aren Maeir (Chair/Respondent): I'd like to note that, in light of the new Canaan that we heard of yesterday, it's good to hear some nice ideas about the old Canaan. I would first like to talk about Prof. Bietak's lecture. His idea is fascinating, and I think it may help us explain, not only his temple, but possibly other temples as well—for example, the Amman, the Mevorakh, and the Ashkelon temples, and so on. I must say that the only functional problem I have with the explanation of the Lachish temple as a place where they sat is the size of the benches—it would be rather hard to put your feet in between them if you sat down. They are very, very small. You can strengthen the possible case for the relationship between the *marzeaḥ* temple and the *marzeaḥ* ritual, based on the evidence from the temple. The one slide I have to show is of the well-known jar, the ewer, from Lachish, which has the inscription *Matan shai le-rabbati Elat*, translated as, *Matan* (a personal name), a gift to my lady *Elat*. By the way, if you want biblical archaeology, I would say that Matan is *rav-marzeaḥ* of this temple, and maybe he's like the Matan, the priest of Baʿal, from the Atalyah story. Elat, at Ugarit, is clearly the consort of El, and El is the most important god in the *marziḥu* ritual at Ugarit. For example, I quote a short passage from KTU 1:114, using Wyatt's recent translation: "El summoned his drinking companions. El took his seat in his feasting house. He drank wine to satiety, new wine until intoxication. El went off to his house. He stumbled off towards his dwelling. *Thakumanu* and *Shunama* supported him. A creeping monster approached him with horns and tail. He floundered in his faeces and urine." Talk about a bad hangover! An additional possibility, which strengthens this case, again comes from Ugarit—that is, the well-known Rhyton temple, which was discovered and published not long ago. The excavators already pointed to the very clear architectural parallels between that temple and the Fosse temple, and, if you look at the plan, they are very, very similar. It has even been suggested by Yon that this is a place where *marziḥu* rituals were conducted. And if you add, for example, the famous small sitting statue, which is identified with El, this again can strengthen his case. Thus, there may be a very strong case for arguing for the connection of the *marzeaḥ* ritual and the Lachish Fosse temple. Thus, if I may say, Prof. Bietak, a man of Qemet, so to speak, on a visit to the land of Kharu, seems to have opened up a very interesting window toward understanding Late Bronze Canaanite cult practices.

Regarding Prof. Rainey's lecture, although there is no doubt that Canaan was a clearly defined geographical entity in the Late Bronze Age (and Ugaritians did not consider themselves Canaanites), there are close similarities in the material culture, despite regional differences. Thus, and I'm sure Prof. Rainey agrees with me on this, although one should not define them within the same ethnic group, let us not forget that they do belong to the same cultural milieu, somewhat like the cultural and ethnic relationships between later Phoenicians and Israelites. Finally, I was wondering: if slaying Goliath can turn you into a *Hophshi* (whatever way one interprets it), does digging his grandchildren also count? Yes, I am the excavator of Gath!

Vassos Karageorghis: I found Prof. Bietak's interpretation of the Fosse Temple at Lachish very attractive. I would like to mention, however, that this form of sanctuary was common in the whole of the eastern Mediterranean during the Late Bronze Age. I have in mind the temples at Kition and Enkomi, which are almost duplicates of the Lachish temple. By the way, Mr. Chairman, with regard to the benches, at least at Enkomi and Kition, we interpret them as places where one puts offerings.

Aren Maeir: That's the standard interpretation.

Vassos Karageorghis: Yes, one does not sit. Well, may I suggest another interpretation, or an alternative interpretation? At Enkomi, we have a sanctuary outside the city wall, near a gate. I don't know if the Fosse Temple is outside the gate, perhaps not; but at Enkomi at least, and elsewhere in the eastern Mediterranean and in the Aegean, we interpret these sanctuaries outside the perimeter of a city as sanctuaries where ceremonies took place every year, when the god or goddess was invoked into the city. So, instead of looking outside for the cemetery, you look inside for the ceremonial entrance of the god or the patron god or goddess every year into the city.

William Dever: Just two quick comments. This is one of those rare occasions on which I am delighted to agree with my colleague Manfred Bietak. As for the Merneptah stela, I just came from the second meeting of the International Congress on the Archaeology of the Ancient Near East in Copenhagen, and Thompson and I read papers—not surprisingly, against each other—in a workshop on revisionism. You might be interested in Thompson's explanation of the reference to the Israelites in the Merneptah stela. He argues that this term with a gentilic ending refers to an eponymous ancestor of the whole population of the land of Hurru and he implies that, more or less by accident, the scribe made up the name Israel to refer to that Late Bronze Age population. It has nothing whatsoever to do with our biblical Israel. This is an example of what we encounter everywhere today in place of scholarship—fashionable nonsense.

Annie Caubet: To come back to Prof. Bietak's interpretation, I would agree that most of the material culture of the Levant in the Late Bronze Age is very Egyptianizing. However, the architectural characteristics of the Fosse Temple and of many other temples of the same type, which have been found in an area much larger than Canaan—Ugarit, of course (whether or not it's Canaan is another question) and Cyprus—I believe are not Egyptian. This is because the main characteristic of the Fosse temple and the Rhyton temple, and the same is true of the temple at Enkomi, is that its hall is not pillared. Its asymmetrical, protruding side room, whether it's an entrance or something behind the cella, is another problem. But it's completely asymmetrical, and I think that this disaccords completely with the very regular, symmetrical, complex construction of both the temple and the houses in Egypt. Otherwise, I agree with you. The significance and the possible funerary meaning, in addition to the *marzeaḥ*, are quite interesting.

Manfred Bietak: Well, we heard some most interesting suggestions and comments on this lecture of mine, and I am most grateful for and interested in them. However, regarding the Enkomi example, at Lachish the temple was not at the entrance. It was far to the north of the entrance. It was really in a very isolated position with respect to the town entrance, and it was in the direct vicinity of two cemeteries. Therefore, the idea of associating this is appealing, and I think that in no time, we shall find many more parallels. Commenting on the suggestion of Annie Caubet, I pointed out the difference between the Fosse temple and Egyptian temples. The Fosse temple has, indeed, especially with the asymmetrical entrance and the square room, elements of an Egyptian house type. We have seen in the lecture of Eliezer Oren that the Egyptian house also had its entrance into governmental residences in the Near East, so it was not foreign to this world. I am, therefore, not surprised to have similar temples, so-called temples, perhaps they are not temples, somewhere else. Nevertheless, thank you very much for the suggestions. Michal Artzy has also informed me that at Tel Nami, she has a very similar temple, again in the vicinity of a cemetery. At Tel Mevorakh, there is another one, which shares similar features, also in the vicinity of a cemetery. Perhaps we will know more after further study of this subject.

Anson Rainey: The issue of Callaway, I have labeled properly "obsolete consensus." This was Joseph Callaway's opinion, after digging at Ai and Radanna, about the material culture of the early Iron Age sites that sprang up in the hill country. My conclusion in light of these discussions is that the Iron I villagers at Ai had their background in Canaanite culture and religion and that this can be documented extensively with artifacts—not with texts, with artifacts—that have parallels at lowland and coastal sites. Now, this is a chance to give a good plug for a marvelous young lady who is at the cutting edge of modern research, Eveline van der Steen, because I think she's turned the world upside down. Of course, there are reminiscences of Canaanite culture in the early Iron Age villages that sprang up suddenly in the hill country areas, but modern research in Transjordan has shown that the people over there were thoroughly versed in Canaanite culture. Finkelstein had to invent some invisible pastoralists in the Late Bronze Age, who could then settle down and form all these settlements. He and our colleague Bunimovitz grew up in the 1970s, when the Jordan Valley was a military border, and for them it was a psychological barrier. They couldn't recognize that things were going on in Transjordan that would help to illuminate our problems. Once I saw the work of McGovern in the Buqeiah, I realized that pastoralist groups had Canaanite pottery and imports and all sorts of things, and I realized that that was no obstacle to the direction. But Eveline also brings us some ethnoarchaeology. These young people want ethnoarchaeology—she's got it, in the Bedouin of the 19th century. She explains how they used to make the rounds from the market at Amman and at Salt and Nablus, back and forth, back and forth, across the Jordan Valley. For my young colleagues, the Jordan Valley was a link fence; in reality, it was a living link between Transjordan and the hills of Samaria and Galilee and elsewhere. Therefore, today, I think there's no reason to doubt it—in fact, even Larry Stager said there are not enough Canaanites to go around to man these sites. I think that the ecological stress that brought the Lybians to the Delta, the Arameans to Mesopotamia and Syria, and the Phrygians to Anatolia, also brought the Transjordanian pastoralists to the hills of Cisjordan.

Emerging Forms and Practices (Iron Age I)

Shalom Paul (Chair/Respondent): I would like to take the opportunity, as the Chair, to present three specific questions to the presenters. First, to Trude Dothan: after your wonderful presentation of the Aegean imprints upon the sites you have studied, I would like to know, do these Aegean imprints totally outweigh the non-Mycenaean elements that have been found? In other words, what is the proportion between Aegean and non-Aegean elements at Philistine sites?

Vassos Karageorghis, I would like to make a point for your consideration. You have shown the movement of Astarte to Cyprus and, of course, in the first millennium, Astarte is known throughout the entire Mediterranean basin. However, it is very interesting that in the second millennium, especially in the Ugaritic texts, Astarte is almost a non-entity. The chief goddess there is Anat. When we come to the first millennium, Astarte takes over and Anat only appears in the two site names of Anatot in the Bible. We also have Shamgar ben-Anat, but Anat seems almost to disappear, at least from our textual evidence. Later, however, we get an Aramaic synchronization, Athar/Athargartes, in which

Anat and Astarte have been combined. My question is whether or not this epigraphic documentation can in any way be correlated with your iconographic material, in which at the very end you saw possibly a recurrence of Anat after Astarte had been present for some hundreds of years. So, Astarte and Anat, iconographically, would very well correlate with what we have in the epigraphic evidence.

Ziony Zevit, I think it was significant that you brought to bear the problematics of semantics and analyzed the various terms that scholars have proffered for a distinction, and then, of course, your rejection of them all. As for your conclusion that an individual can probably belong to different cultic communities and, therefore, digitilized dichotomies do not apply, my question is: does that mean that as an individual he will have one set of cultic obligations, as a member of a *bêt-ʾāb* probably another, and as a member of a *mišpāḥâ* maybe a third? Can they not, in turn, be in conflict with one another?

Trude Dothan: Well, it is a very good question, but it's not a one-minute question. What I presented here is the tip of the iceberg of the material we have. And what we are doing, really, is gathering together information from all the excavations that are relevant and trying to identify the objects and the assemblages. What we are working on is very difficult material. We don't have standing shrines and standing temples; rather, we are dealing with difficult material that we have to interpret. As for Canaanite cities, both Ekron and Ashkelon were destroyed, but not everything vanished when the Philistines settled there. Canaanites were definitely part of Philistine Ekron and Ashkelon. I see Israel Finkelstein, so I wouldn't call them Neo-Canaanites—but whatever Canaanites continued.

Vassos Karageorghis: On Cyprus, we have no evidence of a name for the female goddess of the second millennium B.C.E. And even in the first millennium, the first appearance of a name for a goddess is in the early 8th century B.C.E. on a Phoenician inscription. It was during the late Classical period that the Cypriotes started giving a name to their goddesses—Aphrodite, or Astarte Paphia, or Paphia—probably under the influence of Homer. So all these names that you have in Near Eastern documents simply do not apply to the Cypriotes. For them, she was a goddess of fertility.

Ziony Zevit: The answer is yes. Our academic culture tries to put everything into neat packages, so things are clear. But the fact of the matter is that, in real life, things are not clear. If I had to pass on which religion (in an official sense of the monotheistic religions) is most monotheistic, I would say it's Islam, in the purity of its expressions. But the question is a different one. Are Muslims, in their actual practices, always monotheistic? That is to say, once the same Muslim goes out from one place and then goes home, and there are cults of saints and *hamseh*s on doors, there is something else going on. And in Judaism and Christianity, this becomes even more complex. So, that's the way it is, and I think that's the way it may have been in the past. We're better off functioning with an awareness of social context, rather than functioning essentially as Medieval churchmen, in analyzing ancient Israel.

The Formative Period of State Religion (Iron Age II)

Mordechai Cogan (Chair/Respondent): It has been almost 30 years since my first engagement with the question of the influence of the Assyrian Empire on the cultic life of its subjects. As noted by our speakers, that initial probe into the cuneiform and biblical textual evidence prompted a number of studies of the material finds, as well as a broad-ened reinvestigation of the text corpus. When the textual work seemed to have reached a stand-off on the matter of imperial imposition, the discussion refocused on the question of cultural impact. Rather than argue again what I have presented a number of times in print, I think it might be useful to record a couple of methodological considerations that should be *aleph-bet* in our work, but are not always sufficiently addressed.

1. *The perspectives of our witnesses and their respective ideological positions.* Assyrian royal inscriptions present the Assyrian monarch's justification to the gods for his behavior in war and victory. The often-stereotyped descriptions found in these writings are as close as we are likely to get to an official statement of the rules of governance of conquered lands. But at the same time, we should keep in mind that these press releases had a very circum-scribed audience, and their correlation with life in the towns and villages of the far-flung empire seems unknowable. For the complementary picture of the daily operation of the empire, the administrative records and correspondence are our best source. But here, too, the formalities of reportage cover up popular dealings.

Of an entirely different order is the Hebrew Bible, and the sections relevant to our in-quiry—the scribal and prophetic compositions of the 8th–6th centuries. Theirs is didac-tic writing, teaching the lessons of reward and punishment as meted out by Israel's God to his chosen people. And though these texts contain descriptions of popular cultic behav-ior, and sometimes even "popular by-words," the depictions have most likely been skewed for polemical effect. As for Assyria, here too the polemics of Israel's prophets run high. At times the great king is the staff of Yahweh's anger; at others he is promised a bitter end for his excessive arrogance. Thus, it is difficult to imagine that one could recover a picture of reality in Israel and Judah solely from the Bible.

2. *Models and historical depth.* It should not be expected that a single coherent policy was in effect in all areas of the ancient Near East throughout its century-long domination by Assyria. Many researchers tend to view societies as operating according to predeter-mined, undeviating models, as if hard-and-fast rules determined under what circum-stances an area was annexed to the empire, after which fixed procedures were set in motion. Explanations of this sort, besides imposing modern anthropological conceits on the ancients, deprives life of its dynamic element, of the ad hoc, of the new and the inno-vative. Moreover, individual approaches and solutions to problems of empire-building and maintenance can be identified among the Sargonite kings, and no one pattern fits all circumstances. For example, governing the western peripheries, namely, Egypt and Pales-tine, was not the same as controlling areas that were part of the Mesopotamian heartland, Babylonia, and its near neighbor, Elam.

These two caveats should warn the historian away from easy solutions derived from the textual sources. To his aid in filling in further pieces in the mosaic of life in ancient Israel comes the material evidence recovered by archaeology. The archaeological artifact is itself a text that calls for explication. And here, too, the interpretive tendency is toward coordi-nation and confirmation—the "smoking gun." With a spade in one hand and the Bible in the other, we search for the cornerstone of Solomon's Temple. But archaeology contrib-utes what texts can never give us—a glimpse into the unrecorded, unfiltered life.

Thus, for example, the debate over the goddess Asherah and her role in Israel's cult has been changed forever by the finds at Ajrud. The work of Dothan and Gitin at Ekron has put a new face on Philistine cult that we lacked due to the disputatious account in 1 Samuel 4–6. Freed from its status as handmaid to the Bible, archaeology can speak as an untrammeled witness, if the archaeologists do not get themselves caught up in theoretical models. Taking these strictures into consideration (and I admit that in imperialism and religion, I too was ready to compartmentalize Assyrian imperial policy into neat categories), I still contend that neither in the Assyrian corpora nor in the Bible is there any explicit reference to the imposition of Assyrian cults or to interference in native cults. As Mark Smith has aptly remarked, when foreign cults are present, the Bible has no problem in identifying the source of what is considered a threat to Israel's God. Assyrian gods are not hiding behind Canaanite and Aramean names.

The Assyrian scribes, for their part, tell us just how far conformity went. In areas made over into Assyria, exiles were expected to behave like Assyrians; but beyond tax payments to palace and temple, the former ways of their subjects continued undisturbed. Even more so with regard to vassal kingdoms—the polytheistic empire had an unrepressive stance and, therefore, did not impose itself. Thus, the view that the appearance of astral motifs in late Judah represents the blossoming of contemporary Assyrian-Aramean fashion upon "traditional religious features" has much to speak for it.

Karel van der Toorn: I have a question for Peter Machinist. It was a very interesting suggestion you made. I was wondering about the social place, the social position, of the author of Second Isaiah. You said the struggle was really between the scribal schools in Babylonia, so how would an Israelite, a Judahite in Babylon, know about this? Was he part of that milieu?

Peter Machinist: Thank you, a very good question. I had only a moment at the end to allude to it. First, I would say, just to recapitulate, this debate within the Nabonidus circle eventually got into some kind of broader perspective, as witnessed by the book of Daniel, the Qumran Danielic material, and Herodotus. When that happened, of course, is the issue, but it would seem to me that one could easily make a case for this dispersal occurring certainly by the time of Cyrus, and maybe even earlier. So, the question is, what kind of level are we talking about? Obviously, in a certain respect, I cannot answer this. I don't know what Isaiah had for breakfast or what his daily walking routine was. We are not told where he lived in Babylonia, as we are with Ezekiel, for example. The interesting comment that 2 Kings 25 has its confirmation in the famous Weidner tablets—that the exiled King Jehoachim and his court somehow lived at the Babylonian court in Babylon and then were freed from house arrest—suggests that there was some access for so-called exilic groups. Prof. Israel Ephʿal, of course, has investigated as much as one can of this process. So I think that there was some kind of limited access, but I don't know. How much of what Isaiah was concerned with permeated the broader community of exiles is again a question, and I would be very cautious here also, in light of what my colleagues have said today about equating all levels of social intercourse. But I don't think we ought to assume that things were as compartmentalized as we sometimes do. Even the Assyrian royal inscriptions got out—in terms of the physical manifestation of their stelae—into corners of the empire and, as I tried to explore some years ago, did some echoes of that kind of language get into the first Isaiah? Let's hope we'll find a few "smoking guns" in this regard.

Shalom Paul: Peter, it's very interesting, I also was going to ask a similar question and wanted to phrase it a bit differently. First, I am very happy that you also see the Babylonian milieu of our anonymous prophet, unlike a fellow scholar whose book shortly will be coming out. My question is: need one posit an internal scribal theological debate between the Siners and the Mardukers, based on the knowledge of our prophet? We can adequately explain the entire scene by the exiles living in this foreign area, with the tremendous impact of the cult upon them, and the prophets denouncing and vilifying this in order not to have them attracted to the cult found there. In addition, I'd like to bring in another piece of evidence. In Isaiah 44, we have a description of idol-making, which, of course, he is denouncing. And it has been seen that it is a very odd description, because it starts with the final product and then goes back—that is, then he goes into the forest to look for a tree, and then he opens the Yellow Pages to find a metallurgist—and the question is why? Now, the *mīs pî* ceremony, which was already seen years ago by Thorkild Jacobsen, is finally published, and this is exactly the way in which the Mesopotamians described their own idol-making. They did start from the final product and they worked back, for reasons that obviously you know. This means that the prophet did have intimate knowledge of the entire ceremony, and this ceremony is in no way related to a debate between the cult of Sin and the cult of Marduk. It is, I would say, making light and making a fiasco of all that is taking place—which the exiles saw, but they had no intimate knowledge of the elite circles.

Peter Machinist: To Prof. Paul, one of the great contributors to this discussion, I would say two things. On the one hand, there is a broader range of knowledge in this prophet about matters Babylonian, among them the issue of making images. It's not confined to Isaiah, of course—you also have it in chapter 10 of Jeremiah, although Isaiah's materials are much fuller and more specific. Eph'al, for example, in an article some years ago in *Shnaton*, took the matter so far as to suggest that there may even have been an echo of a particular inscription of Ashur-Etil-ilāni in one of the passages, I think in Isaiah 40, about idol-making.

So, on the one hand, there are these bodies of material in Isaiah that could have merged into anybody's cognizance in the area. It's interesting, by the way, that the key part of the *mīs pî* is not mentioned, and it's critical—mainly the actual washing of the mouth—that this isn't mentioned in either the Jeremiah or the Isaiah text.

In the other part, which I was always particularly interested in, there is an intensive focus in this prophet on the issue of the nature of deity. And it's a polemical focus, which is laid out in the manner that I tried to describe. This is not something that occurs everywhere, although there are bits and pieces that are found in other parts of the Bible, again, as I tried to point to. But the intensity and the comprehensiveness of the discussion of what deity is, and the polemic about one kind of candidate for deity over against another—this suggests to me that there is something more specific in the background of Isaiah that he is reacting to, and that's what I was trying to discover. But again, "smoking guns" or no "smoking guns."

Kathryn Slanski (Lecturer, Department of Archaeology and Ancient Near Eastern Studies, Tel Aviv University): I can't help but think, when you're talking about the trial speeches in Second Isaiah, that this is precisely the same language, the same ideology, and the same philosophy of the process of divination in Babylonia—a person goes to the gods for a decision. It's even here on the Haran stela, when Nabonidus is talking: "Then my good fortune was found again in the victims used for the decisions of the diviner." It seems to me that this supports what you're saying about this greater sort of cultural knowledge that the writer of Isaiah has come into contact with among the Babylonian literati.

Peter Machinist: You're absolutely right. The divination part of this is critical and it's played on, among other things, in terms of special knowledge. On the one hand, Nabonidus is praised, and on the other hand, he's vilified for this. Within the Isaianic corpus, God is the author of this divinitory knowledge. The prophet has access to it, and the Babylonians are vilified for their way of going about it.

Cult—Coast and Interior (The Persian Period)

Eilat Mazar (Chair/Respondent): With your permission, I wish to respond briefly about the one cosmological icon that is connected to all three lectures that we have heard, and that is the sun disc. Prof. Lipiński correctly paid attention to the fact that some of the Phoenicians are buried without their personal goods or any precious goods. From excavations in Tyre and Achziv in Iron Age II, starting in the 10th century B.C.E., this phenomenon is characteristic only of the practice of adult cremations, mainly in the cemeteries that we can recognize as the original *tophet* sites. These burials, without their personal belongings, stand in contrast to the dozens of inhumations in family tombs, all with personal belongings. I think that, from this point of view, we have to continue our search for understanding the appearance or nonappearance of personal goods or precious goods with Phoenician burials in the Persian period.

It is important also to mention in this connection that on the majority of the stelae at the *tophet* site of Achziv, the simple circle appears as the only symbol, probably representing Ba'al Shamem. It seems that the burials without personal belongings are somehow closely connected to that one god. Prof. Stern suggested that the Phoenician cult concept influenced the other nations around them. In this connection, it is important to mention the special Phoenician phenomenon of worshiping a chief god, which we infer both from the sun disc symbol appearing alone on the stelae and from Sanchuniathon, the Phoenician priest, who described the only lord of heaven, Ba'al Shamem, as the god of the sun. It seems to me that this symbol presents a certain stage in the development of the Phoenician monotheistic concept.

Romans, Jews, and Christians

Jerome Murphy-O'Connor (Chair/Respondent): We thank Jodi Magness and John Collins for two very stimulating lectures. They have left me with perhaps more questions than convictions, and so I would like to start the ball rolling in the discussion by asking each of them a question. John, I was struck by the difference between the northern coast of the Mediterranean and the southern coast. There were just as many Jews in the provinces of Asia, Macedonia, Achaia, and, of course, in Italy itself, as there were in the southern provinces of Cyvenica, Egypt, and Syria. Yet in the southern provinces, you have violent rebellions that are directed not against Rome but against their non-Jewish countrymen. The only militarily active armed rebellion directed explicitly against Rome was, of course, here in Judea and Galilee. So why this difference? Because Roman law, Roman attitudes, Roman officials must have been pretty much the same north of the Mediterranean as south of the Mediterranean.

So, while John is thinking about that . . . Jodi, I was very impressed by the argument that synagogues, especially the very decorated southern Galilean synagogues, were perhaps created in competition with monumental Christian structures. And so, the question really has two parts. First, what does that say: that Jews and Christians were able to build monumental public buildings, which were very definite religious statements, apparently in perfect harmony one with the other? And second: where did they get the tradition of mosaic art? Did they draw on the same pool? Did the same craftsmen work for Jews and for Christians?

John Collins: Thank you, Jerry, for asking such a nice narrow, specific question! One can say that the reason you have direct conflict with Rome in Judea is obvious, because here is a case where you have a Jewish people and direct rule from Rome. Now, you have conflict with the Gentiles in Caesarea, but in Judea, these are the two powers that come in contact with each other.

Concerning the situation in the diaspora, the only situation where I am aware of extensive evidence is Egypt. Presumably, we didn't have revolts, say in Asia Minor, but we really know very little about what was going on in those communities. Now, the story in Egypt, of course, is fascinating. I have written on it before, and so I was tempted in fact to do that—it would have saved me a little time here—but it was old history, and it had to do with the complex relations of the Greek community with the Romans. As I understand that situation, the pressure there again came with taxes. It's the *laographia* that, contrary to what some people have argued in recent years, we really don't have the evidence for. I mean, we have for various *laographia*s, but not for the poll tax in this particular form, before Augustus.

Then you get a competition for status between the Alexandrine Jews and the Alexandrine Greeks. The Alexandrine Greeks have their own turbulent history. That's the conflict that produced the initial conflict, and then that situation, as Shimon Applebaum showed, was complicated greatly by the influx of refugees from Judea after 70 C.E., and a general deterioration in Roman attitudes toward the Jews at that point. So, that's a long way short of giving a very good answer to your question, but I'm afraid it's the best I can do for the moment.

Jodi Magness: I don't know if I can answer your questions either and, actually, I'm going to evade the first one and try to answer the second one. The first one is not an archaeological question, it's more of a historical and social-history question, and I really don't feel qualified to answer it. I have to say that a lot of these buildings have been misdated because of historical preconceptions. I would rather present the archaeological evidence and then let others who are more qualified in terms of social history try and place it within the proper context. So, that's my evasion of your first question.

And to the second question, I have a rather mixed answer. The zodiac helios motifs, as many other scholars have shown, including Gideon Foerster, is of course unique to

Palestinian synagogues. It's not found in contemporary churches. We know sometimes who the workmen were, or we have a good idea. In the case of the Hammath-Tiberias mosaic, there are strong similarities with Antioch and the schools in the area. The mosaic floor at Beth Alpha is actually signed by a couple of local workmen—Marianos and his son Hanina—so sometimes we know. I guess that it would be a mixture—that they could have been local workmen, Jewish or not Jewish, or perhaps, in the case of a place like Hammath-Tiberias, people who were brought in—that is, hired from or at least had some training outside the local area. There is actually a tradition of mosaic floor decoration that is common to the area from Madaba, Transjordan, which is very rich in mosaics, that sort of spills over onto this side of the Jordan Valley.

Unidentified person: Many years ago, I was a volunteer on a dig where the archaeologist uncovered the 6th-century mosaic floor of the synagogue at Maʿon. I tried to research it, and what I understand is that the 6th century in the Gaza Strip was a very cultured period and that this mosaic floor is very similar to Christian mosaic floors in the Gaza Strip. Could they have been made in the same workshop in Gaza?

Jodi Magness: Yes, you're right. I didn't go into the other kinds of mosaic floors or include that in my answer to Dr. Murphy-O'Connor, but there is, in fact, apparently a group of buildings that includes both churches and synagogues, which have these medallions filled with animals or plants that are common in the southern part of the country and are thought to originate in a Gaza workshop or a series of workshops in the Gaza area. This has been discussed by a number of scholars—Asher Ovadiah and Rachel Hachlili, among others.

Simo Parpola: I have a question for John Collins. Being an Assyriologist, I'm not really competent in this matter, but I happened to hear a lecture by my colleague Mayer-Opificius on the very same issue about which you have been speaking today. He suggested that the problem with the revolts of the Jews might have lain in the fact that the Roman soldiers that were employed by the administration there were not really Roman at all, but that local levies from other parts of the Levant were used for that purpose. These quasi- or pseudo-Roman soldiers purposely provoked the Jews—that is to say, the blame for the conflict really lay with the Romans, or Roman administration, in choosing these kinds of soldiers. What do you think about this suggestion?

John Collins: I don't know the facts of the matter, but I'm pretty sure that there was an element of that, and I think it fits with the point I was making, which also follows on what Doron Mendels was saying yesterday about the Greek period. From the viewpoint of the Roman Empire, this was the boondocks, and you don't send your brightest and best to Judea. You just send people to whom you are beholden for one reason or another, and you want to post them as far from Rome as you can get them; and equally, it's kind of like riff-raff, whatever, you put them in the army to deal with them. Now, you know very few enough exceptions to that, but I think it's that kind of imperial neglect. In some ways, the Romans were very exact and demanding. The first thing they did when they annexed a province was to take a census. They had to make sure they were not missing anybody on the taxes. But they didn't really put a whole lot of quality effort into administration. And that, in fact, deteriorated as the century went on.

Part III
The History of the Family: Continuity and Change

Units and Cultural Unities (Iron Age I)

Dan Bahat (Chair/Respondent): The first lecture, by Karel van der Toorn, was quite refreshing. Recent reports on archaeological excavations are so full of tables of numbers that the spirit is missing. You, however, brought a lot of spirit to archaeology, although many of the details you referred to were not certain, such as the sudden appearance of certain gods, and your exhibition of a phenomenon of all kinds of libations.

As for the second presentation, by Bunimovitz and Faust, on the four-room house, it is a very difficult subject. I am afraid that I cannot agree with everything you said. First of all, the four-room house shows itself for the first time not in typical Israelite areas. It appears mostly on the Coastal Plain, such as at Tell Qasile, among other sites. The problem is that we don't really know the source of the four-room house. The late Yigal Shiloh did not succeed in showing it, and we didn't see it today. The other thing is that, when we speak about the four-room house, we speak about so many variants. If it were so Israelite, we would expect to see it a lot in Judah. If we take, for example, a site such as Tell Beit Mirsim, Stratum A, the latest stratum, which should have produced, according to your lecture, the culmination of this form, we find the two-room house, we find the columned house, and we also have the three-room house. If the design and function of the four-room house relates to the laws of purity, other systems could also have related to those laws, such as the central courtyard house. It is not just the four-room plan that could demonstrate your thesis. As for your argument that the four-room plan disappears in 586 B.C.E., many other things also disappeared—many types of pottery and features such as city plans, and so on. Some tombs did continue to use the four-room plan, but tomb styles are usually very traditional. Generally speaking, basing the plan of a house on the needs of more spiritual matters such as purity is a very interesting idea, but I'm not sure that it works with the four-room house. It came suddenly; it left suddenly. You see it actually as a public building in many ways; it's not so much a private building. The private building would be three rooms, two rooms, a columned house. If you put all this into the four-room house, then you would be right, but I am afraid that is not the case.

Manfred Bietak: I have two questions. First is the proof that the four-room house had a second floor. A staircase is not proof, because a staircase may lead to a roof. I think it's very important to have proof that the four-room house had a second floor. Second, the Chicago expedition in Egypt unearthed the remains of a workmen's quarter, workmen's housing, constructed in wattle and daub, in the temple precinct of Aya and Horemheb. It matched the four-room house perfectly, even the disposition of columns on one side and not on the other. These workmen's quarters can be dated most likely to the time of Ramses IV, in the second half of the 12th century, but could even be as late as the beginning of the 21st Dynasty. But the most likely option is Ramses IV, because these workmen were employed to pull down the temple of Aya and Horemheb, and we know that in the time of

Ramses III, many prisoners-of-war were brought into Egypt. In theory, the inhabitants of these quarters could have been proto-Israelites. I have pointed out this four-room house in this Theban area in an article in the Avraham Biran festschrift and also elsewhere. But I was very reluctant to attribute it to the Israelites. It's possible, but I would like to know how sure we can be that these were Israelites; or perhaps there was another ethnic group involved that was related to the proto-Israelites. Is it so clear that this four-room house should be attributed to Israelites? If so, this would be fantastic.

Uzi Avner (Aravah Institute): Two comments about the four-room house. One is that Israel Finkelstein has published in quite a few places his opinion that its origin was a Bedouin tent. This, in my opinion, is totally impossible, for one basic reason: the desert of the Negev and Sinai is full of remains of tents—there are thousands of them—in tent camps. Each one contains between 5 and 25, or sometimes even more, tents that are obviously circular. Some of these tent camps are dated to one period, which is, let's say, the late Neolithic/Chalcolithic—this is the beginning—let's say the fifth millennium B.C.E. Some of them are much later, and at least until the Mamluk period, we still see the circular tents and very rarely square or rectangular ones. It is quite a question when and under what circumstances the large, rectangular Bedouin tent appeared, but in any case, it must be very late—during the last centuries or so, not earlier. So, this could not be the basis or the origin of the four-room house. Second, Benno Rothenberg excavated a building in the Timnah Valley, which, although he did not identify it as such, could be called either a four-room house or a proto-four-room house, with all the necessary elements such as monoliths with filled stone masonry in between. The plan is correct: it is not only very orthogonal, but a little rounded and twisted. This building is dated to the 13th century B.C.E., which is quite early compared with others in Israel and also in Jordan. Another building like this, but much more orthogonal and quite large—12 m × 12 m—is in the Uvdah Valley. I excavated it only in a probe. The pottery parallels the three main types found at Timnah, so we are still speaking about the 13th–12th centuries B.C.E. Also at earlier sites, of the fourth–third millennia B.C.E., we see ground plans that are very close to the four-room house. It is quite possible (there is a lot of work still to do on this) that the origin of the four-room house somehow lies in the desert.

Eric Meyers: I want to address comments to the dynamic duo here [Bunimovitz and Faust—eds.]. The matter of purity in the four-room house, I think, requires a more convincing explanation. I would like to have further elaboration. It is not clear at all that in early Israel the purity laws would be relevant. The question of the sudden disappearance of the four-room house in the 6th century is also enigmatic, especially when the Second Temple period itself would be a period when there would be a much more compelling reason for the laws of purity to be reflected in architecture. Why this sudden disappearance? Why, in the "Return," in the Persian period, might you not then find one, two, a couple of four-room houses somewhere?

William Dever: A couple of comments regarding Karel van der Toorn's paper. How refreshing to get away from the attempt to reconstruct early Israelite theology, and talk about real life. That's what archaeologists can do. We ought to do more of it. Religion is not just about words. And, regarding the paper by Avraham Faust and Shlomo Bunimovitz: a wonderful application of Hodder's "Archaeology of Mind," which is, again, so exciting, even if somewhat speculative. I only wish our minimalist colleagues at Sheffield and Copenhagen could have heard this. There are no early Israelites, but they built wonderful houses.

Eilon Shiloh (Professor Emeritus, Anthropology, University of South Florida): I just want to say a word in favor of ethnoarchaeology. It's a real challenge to get out there and try to go beyond mere cataloguing, and I would venture to say that at the next Albright/ASOR bicentennial symposium, many sections will be devoted to ethnoarchaeology.

Anson Rainey: There are two considerations I have in mind that are always to some degree in conflict when you build a house. One of them is light, and the other is temperature control. And it seems to me that this design of house is very useful in providing opportunities for compromises in both directions. On the one hand, when you have this long, internal courtyard, you can provide access to light for the rooms all around. At the same time, if you're building this in the hill country, where you need to keep warm in the winter, it provides practical ways of closing up and confining yourselves to, say, the back rooms and other places. You can also build fires, even in the central courtyard, for doing your daily work. But if you're building a house in Beersheba, you need a way to try to stay cool. This is also possible. When they built the new city of Arad, they did a lot of work on this, how to make walkways and sidewalks so that people would not be overly exposed to the sun. So, just from the purely technical point of view, this particular plan provides opportunities for variation, while maintaining an overall architectural layout.

Now, Bunimovitz and Faust mentioned Lily Singer-Avitz's study of Beersheba. As I pointed out to her, one of her four-room houses was really not a four-room house. I had excavated one wing of it myself, over against the city wall, and she hadn't noticed that it was divided into another three-unit house. But there, all the families living around the periphery, apparently of lower rank, had three-unit houses: a courtyard, a covered area, and a casemate room. I have excavated what I believe is an elite house in Beersheba, Building 32 (right next door, Itzhaq Beit-Arieh excavated another), but in this particular place, there is no way you could bring animals into the center of the city and into that house. There is no room for them. So, I don't believe the plan was initiated to be a house for peasants. It has various functions, but I would look at it that way.

Avraham Faust: I'll start with one point that emerged in several comments. We referred to all subtypes of the four-room, the four-space house—including the two-, three-, four-, and five-roomed variations that share all the attributes we refer to in the paper—including houses at Tell Beit Mirsim and other places. For example, you mentioned the courtyard house, which you said could share some of the attributes too, but the point is that most courtyard houses from the Middle Bronze or Late Bronze Age do not. Most of them, to use the access-analysis term, have some depth. At least at some point, after you enter the courtyard, you go into another room, and then you can go into another room, which is deeper inside. So it's not the same. One of the major characteristics of the four-room house—which applies to most of them, at least the large ones—is its complexity. Nevertheless, if you look at, let's say, the nearly two hundred plans I've seen, you can hardly find a single house where you need to enter one room in order to get to another. You can enter all of the rooms from the courtyard. And this is not the same in the courtyard house of the Middle Bronze or Late Bronze or later periods.

You also mentioned other architectural changes in the 6th century B.C.E. Maybe the changes in the structure of the society, some population changes and other internal changes in the same population, caused and brought about those changes as well.

Dan Bahat: So, now, why not in tombs, as you yourself pointed out?

Avraham Faust: It happens in tombs, but I don't know of any tomb of this type that was built after the 6th century. In a few of them, there was continuous use in the 6th century, but that's all. They were not built later.

As for the purity laws, it is true that in the Second Temple period, especially in the late Second Temple period, this issue was much more developed, but the point is that the four-room house is not the only plan affected by purity laws or other influences. It's one option. Other ways could have been developed, or probably were developed, to keep these laws. The point is that the four-room house enables this, unlike most other structures in the Bronze and Iron Ages. Later, other methods of keeping these laws or rituals could be found, probably were found. About the viability or the functionality of the house—well, it is true; but still, all those merits existed or could have existed after the 6th century. The climate didn't change, and still this house disappeared. So the reason that it was so popular cannot be because it was so functional. It could be used in all types of environment, but people lived in those types of environment later and they didn't keep the house.

As for the house in Egypt, it's difficult for me to comment on a single house. But it could be that this house in Egypt belonged to another group, not necessarily Israelite, which is also an option even later. We did not suggest that any time you see a four-room house, you see an Israelite family. But Israelites used and lived in four-room houses. To rephrase it differently, if you find a site with no four-room houses, I think you can question whether the inhabitants were Israelites. But you can't go all the way to the opposite and say that, any time you find a single four-room house, it means that the inhabitants were Israelites. We can only say that it was suitable for the Israelite way of life. I don't think there is anything we can add. Generally, scholars do not agree on whether there was a second floor, but again, we don't have anything more to contribute on this issue other than what we wrote in our paper.

Household Economy (Iron Age II)

J. Edward Wright (Chair/Respondent)

Mark Smith: My comment is for both Susan Ackerman and Carol Meyers. If you need a model for the production carried out by women that has to do with both food and weaving, you have nothing better to look at than a passage of Asherah doing exactly these chores in KTU 1.4, column 2 or 3. The interesting thing about this passage, though, is that she's not in the house; she's by the water, by the sea.

Simo Parpola: I don't want to miss this opportunity first of all to compliment Susan Ackerman on your paper and to point out that there is very important evidence from Assyria that corroborates much of what you said. Asherah corresponds to the Assyrian goddess Mullissu, who is an aspect of Ishtar and combines many of the features of Asherah that you discussed in your paper. She's the queen of heaven, she's the consort of the supreme god, Ashur, and she is also represented in the form of a sacred tree, a totem symbol. I just wanted to briefly refer to this fact, and if you are interested, you will find much more in my book on Assyrian prophecies that was published a couple of years ago.

James Muhly: I just want to make a comment on the discussion about popular religion that's gone on here for the past few days. About 40 years ago, the great Swedish classical scholar, Martin Nilsson, published a book called *Greek Folk Religion*. He dealt with exactly the problems that we are dealing with here, and I highly recommend his book to anyone dealing with this problem of official state cult versus so-called popular religion.

Tallay Ornan (Curator of Western Asiatic Antiquities, Israel Museum): I just want to add a short comment on the fascinating presentation of Susan Ackerman. I would like to shift the discussion from Asherah to her consort, and I would say that such a presentation actually reinforces our notion that we cannot speak of pure monotheism any more or monotheism at all before the exilic period.

Jacob Milgrom (Professor Emeritus, Biblical Studies, University of California): As usual, I'm not going to neglect Baruch Levine. There is no one else in the entire discipline of ours who has stimulated me more than Baruch with regard to my dealing with the priestly material. I would like to comment that in the priestly material, there is a distinction between the *bêt 'āb* and the *bêt 'ābôt*. *Bêt 'ābôt* is often synonymous with the *mišpāḥâ*, with the clan, but the *bêt 'āb* seems to be the real power base, or the most important familial structure, and it probably means the nuclear family, the *bêt 'āb*. So, I wonder how that fits into your differentiation of the various groups that might have been the most important group in the entire structure of the Israelite people.

Baruch Levine: It used to be much more vital, you know, when we argued with each other. More was at stake. Now, we're both senior statesmen, we can talk about this in a very friendly way. No, there's a great deal of subtlety about the usage, and I have discussed this—to put in a plug—in the second volume of the *Numbers* commentary, which will be out any day, in the Anchor Bible series. To try to trace the usage of *bêt 'āb* to *bêt 'ābôt*, which I feel is a subsequent pluralization—more in the idiom of later Biblical Hebrew, you know, where you pluralize the object of the genitive construction, so it's *bêt 'ābôt*, not *batê 'ābôt*, but *bêt 'ābôt*—there is a great deal of subtlety and it is very difficult at times to ascertain what's involved. For the most part (and I've checked this, because George Buchanan Grey gave the same interpretation as you have, believing that *bêt 'āb* was a smaller unit), I think that in most cases—the breakdown as we have it, let's say, in Numbers 3 and so forth, for the Levitical tribe—the *bêt 'āb* is a larger group. The original *bêt 'āb* is a much larger group than just the *bayit*, from which it has to be distinguished. The term for the nuclear family is *bayit*, and Raymond Westbrook and others have written some interesting works on this subject.

Jacob Milgrom: Then I withdraw my comment until I read your commentary.

William Dever: This session has dealt wonderfully well with the question of what it was really like to live in ancient Israel. Needless to say, I resonate with my former colleague Susan Ackerman's paper, but I have a comment for Carol Meyers, again, in an attempt to get at this question. I just came from the Second International Congress on the Archaeology of the Ancient Near East in Copenhagen, and we had a field trip one day to an experimental center, a Viking center in northern Denmark; there, a group of a dozen graduate students in archaeology are living year-round at a Viking site. They have felled trees in the forest with Iron Age tools, they have adzed the logs and built a house, and have thatched it with straw from grain they grew in the fields. They are wearing Viking clothes, they are cooking meat that they themselves butcher in pots over an open fire, and they're living under sheepskins. These students have been living there for the last three years, through the cold Danish winters. They are really struggling to understand what it was like. Now, I think we should build an Iron Age house and equip it with the proper furnishings, and I think that young people should live there, but not me.

Jacob Milgrom: On the matter of the destitution of the Israelite family as found in Leviticus 25, you have to keep in mind that, as long as the ancestral land is not sold completely, there is a *gô'ēl*, there is a provision for redemption. It's only when they lose the land and enter into, sink to the level of, slavery that suddenly there's a disappearance. But my own feeling, or the suggestion I throw out to you, is that, in this particular case, they don't become slaves; they become day laborers. They are laborers, and the assumption is in such a case that redemption does not apply. They are expected to get enough funds ultimately to redeem themselves. If not, of course, there is the jubilee, which will redeem them. But specifically, the redeemer only comes into play when there is the loss of land or the loss of a person, because he becomes an indebted person to a non-Israelite. Only in such cases is there really a redeemer.

Carol Meyers: I wanted first to respond to what Mark Smith said—I didn't read the footnotes of my paper, but what you referred to is in a footnote. The fact that she's doing this in an exterior space is also quite resonant with the kinds of things I found ethnographically, that the household is not just within the four-room house. It can be outside, outdoor space and courtyard space, where actually women probably did gather, at least at certain times of the year, to weave together.

I'd also like to say, with respect to what Bill described regarding experimental archaeology, that, in terms of weaving, there are some women who have tried to replicate Minoan garments by getting together and copying the fabrics that they see in the paintings. One of the comments—it was totally an aside in the report of how they made these garments—is that sitting together for hours doing this needlework created solidarity and brought a kind of intimacy, where they shared certain things.

The third thing I want to say is not in response to any question. With regard to the discussion of the *bêt 'āb*, I am reminded that at least four times in the Bible there are references to *bêt 'ēm*, and there are also indirect references to that. I think that, from the interior perspective of the household and the kind of activities that went on there, many of which were controlled by women, we shouldn't forget that, while it's not in terms of lineage a *bêt 'ēm*, in terms of productive activities it might in fact be so.

Gabriel Barkay (Lecturer, Jerusalem University College): I would like first to express my gratitude for the description of the wide role of Asherah in Israelite and Judahite society. Still, I have some questions. In the catalog of West Semitic seals that was published by the late Prof. Nahman Avigad, and in many other seals and in biblical and extrabiblical sources, we have many hundreds of names. As far as I remember, none of these proper names is connected with Asherah. On the other hand, we have hundreds of names that are Yahwistic, Yahwistic names both for males and for females.

Susan Ackerman: That's an excellent point and, of course, names are a very important body of evidence. I would remind us, though—and I'm primarily a biblical scholar, so I'm going to speak from biblical evidence—that in the Bible, certain people who are identified as being worshipers of Asherah or worshipers even of Ba'al, nevertheless gave their children good Yahwistic names. Ahab and Jezebel are the prime example; Athaliah in Judah is another such example. Especially in the case of the Asherah names, I have to say I am just not particularly bothered if Asherah is worshiped in conjunction with Yahweh, rather than instead of Yahweh. Then it's perfectly fine to give your children nice Yahwistic names, yet, at the same time, have a functioning Asherah cult.

Uzi Avner (Aravah Institute): Two notes about earlier occurrences of the Asherah goddess. In the late Neolithic burial ground of Eilat, I excavated a nicely built installation, with the remains of a Juniper tree inside, a tree-trunk, 30 cm high and 14 cm wide. It was dated by ^{14}C to about 5000 B.C.E. and clearly represents Asherah remains. There are four other remains from different periods that were suggested to be related to Asherah in the Near East. This is the earliest and the best preserved and, I think, the most obvious. Also, its connection with burial, although it is a symbol of fertility, is quite well understood. Another point is that in the Uvdah Valley, I excavated two shrines with broad *maṣṣebot*. Various papers and lectures have presented the distinction between a narrow, tall *maṣṣebah* and the broad, shorter one. The broad, shorter one, quite logically, represents a goddess. On the two *maṣṣebot* I excavated, which stand alone, not in a group, I found grinding stones. I saw these as part of the equipment of the shrine, left there to prepare flour in order to make dough for cakes for the queen of heaven. This custom has parallels in the *Kamannu* in the Akkadian culture, as well as in the Hittite and Egyptian cultures, and here we have remains dated by ^{14}C to the very early sixth millennium B.C.E.

Susan Sherratt: Just a quick remark to Carol Meyers. The osteological study of skeletal material is another entry into detecting gender-related occupations. I'm thinking particularly of activities such as grinding corn, which, if you are doing it for several hours a day in the same position and with the same repetitive movement, does terrible things to your feet, knees, and lower back, and this has been documented at Tell Abu-Hureira, as far as I understand. Also—and it may be that I'm from the wrong side of the Atlantic and therefore have a rather more jaundiced view—but I do have problems in seeing that women's engagement in economically significant work automatically translates into any form of wider social status. After all, if you think of it, most of the work that most women do nowadays is indeed economically significant—everything ranging from looking after children to producing garments in sweatshops, preparing food, typing other people's letters and organizing their lives for them, primary-school teaching, nursing, and so on—it is in the wider sense economically significant, but as far as I can see, it confers very little status, very little power, and men still run the show.

Trude Dothan: To Carol Meyers, this is not a question, just a small reminder about the very everyday function of the so-called spinning or twining bowls that we find in large numbers in our excavations in the Late Bronze and Iron Ages, as well as in Egypt. It's very interesting to see the interaction of workshops of this type. As for men and women, in this case—I don't know if I'm a feminist or not, I'm not clear about it yet—but I do know that in the Egyptian wall paintings we definitely have men and women doing the same work.

Families, Houses, and Homes
(The Persian, Hellenistic, and Roman Periods)

Sidnie White Crawford (Chair/Respondent): As for Amy-Jill (A-J) Levine's paper, one thing struck me—that was also brought out very well by Carol Meyers—when A-J asks archaeological questions about the Hellenistic period: I'm sure that the data are there but are not arranged in such a way that makes it easy for these answers immediately to come to mind. For example, when she asks the question about private cemeteries and in-ground inhumation, of course, I immediately thought of Qumran and various other cemeteries that have been found. But I didn't know, off the top of my head, whether any of these cemeteries were associated with private dwellings or whether they were only associated with larger groupings, be they the community at Qumran or other villages. Also, A-J raises valid questions about the relationship of fictional writing, which of course becomes much more prevalent in this period, to realia on the ground. How much can we assume is real? I found her questions even more complicated than she suggests, because if you look at, for example, the book of Tobit, which was originally composed in Aramaic, possibly in Palestine—although some would argue in the diaspora—it still is supposedly set in the Assyrian Empire in Nineveh. To a certain extent at least, it is trying to reach some kind of historical verisimilitude, if only with its names. So, it's not a picture of Hellenistic Palestine; it doesn't mean to be, although you can probably glean some information from it. I think A-J's questions led me to more questions, rather than answers.

Ziony Zevit: This question is directed to Eric Meyers, but it's also directed to Sidnie White Crawford in light of a comment that she made on A-J's paper. I'm going to go on the assumption that Palestinian compositions reflect Palestinian realia, even if the setting is foreign, in the same way that European art represents the Holy Land in European dress. The question that I'm asking is the following: you made the point that what we learn about the Tannaitic period on the basis of the excavations at Zippori gives us a very different picture of what's going on in life than comes through Tannaitic, primarily, I guess, Halakhic sources. The material discussed by A-J seems to go in a similar direction. I'm not aware that the patterns of piety and so forth, and burial practices that were referred to, are addressed or at least alluded to in Tannaitic sources. Nothing came to mind, and I'd like to know if you could comment on and perhaps amplify the archaeological comments in A-J's paper and the rabbinic aspects in your own work.

Eric Meyers: What comes to mind about A-J's paper—and she is another Duke University Ph.D.—is that Jason's tomb is a Hellenistic tomb right here in Jerusalem. So you do have material that would illuminate wealthy landed families in Jerusalem from the Hellenistic period. Also, there would be realia to go along with a lot of A-J's comments, but it would take a bit of searching. To elaborate a bit on my comments and answer you more directly, I think what archaeology is doing is giving you a picture of women being much more involved, as they were in the Iron Age, in a whole variety of activities. This is true not only at Sepphoris but at many other sites, such as Khirbet Kana, and other Jewish sites in the Galilee, such as Bethsaida. At Sepphoris, with its concentration of rabbinic authority, there was a leading community where, presumably, the Mishnah was edited, redacted, and promulgated. The realia show you in a convincing fashion that the notion that women are confined here and there in certain kinds of spaces is not true. I don't think the spaces in domiciles lend themselves to what we call the narrative of privacy that you get from the Mishnah.

Similarly, we have public baths at Sepphoris, and by the 2nd/3rd century, by the time the theater is up and going and public baths appear, you may even have for the *hoi polloi* a public collection of *miqva'ot*, since not everybody is living up on the acropolis. My colleague Jonathan Reed is digging down the slope to step down the tel, to see if getting off the top into the suburbs is going to give a different picture of a less elitist way of life. I'm not saying that it allows us to paint a really clear picture, but if you take the diaspora situation, and A-J has also referred to some of the inscriptional evidence that we have there, which is extensive in Bernadette Brooten's collection, you have evidence of women doing this and that in all these Jewish communities.

I know some people have disputed whether these are honorific titles or actual working jobs within the Jewish community, but let's say that Brooten was correct and others who have followed her are correct. Then I believe the real proof lies somewhere in between, and Melissa Aubin, who did her dissertation on magic, found that the production of magical amulets was, as the textile industry, pretty much dominated by women. So they had a status role within what we were calling this morning popular religion—that, or non-Tannaitic, non-rabbinic sorts of activities within the religious sphere that really would give them an entirely different kind of status about which we would know nothing, if we had only the Mishnah. And there are dozens and dozens of these amulets that are published, and this seems to be pretty much a domain of women and very important at that.

James Muhly: Since we're into ethnography today, I'd like to point out that in the 17th, 18th, and 19th centuries—that is, early modern or traditional Greece—people lived in enclosed courtyard houses. There's no evidence of any kind of segregation of the sexes, and there is very little sense of privacy. In fact, the Greek language does not even have a word for privacy.

Peter Machinist: I direct my question particularly to Eric Meyers, although it relates to something that a variety of people have commented on. The interpenetration of public and private, or work and private, that you and others have talked about leads me essentially to rephrase Jim Muhly's question. What is the very sense of the terms *private* and *public*? Did these terms cease to have any meaning, in the archaeological context that you have, over against at least some of the texts, particularly Halakhic, where they may still carry that meaning? I wondered if Eric could respond about the meaning of these categories.

Eric Meyers: Clearly, in the archaeological context, they mean less and less. That was the main point of my presentation. As for what they mean in reality, I think we might have to turn to Jim Muhly's suggestion of looking at the ethnography, although Yizhar Hirschfeld's otherwise wonderful book superimposes the rabbinic mind-set on his ethnography. Some of that is implicit in the West Bank villages that he studied, which are largely Muslim, I suppose—a largely Muslim population in traditional settings. So, I think that was one of the reasons that the ethnographic data he collected from this area have not been as helpful as we would like them to be. I don't know. This is a tough question, and

I'm not sure we're able to determine zones of privacy. One of the problems is that we can't reconstruct these houses from bottom to roof. This is a huge challenge, when things are preserved one–two meters or less, to get up to a second story, and then get in all of the little alleyways and the light sources. It's very difficult to do this. So when you do an axiometric drawing, just putting in a window when you don't have it is problematic, whether it's an Iron Age four-room house or a Roman domicile such as the one I showed you. It's very, very problematic, and that's one of the reasons we're all struggling with this.

Jodi Magness: Eric, I enjoyed your paper and I am happy to see you trying to identify the functions of rooms on the basis of the materials found in them, which is a very good approach. You started out by looking at parallels from the Classical world, and I wondered, since you started with Classical Athens, whether it might not be helpful to look at contemporary material from Pompei and Herculanium, which is of course contemporaneous in terms of the society. It's much more appropriate. The furniture is still preserved in the rooms, so we have a good idea of what many of the rooms were used for. Houses at Herculanium, at least, are preserved to their second story, and a lot of work has been done recently on these houses by Andrew Wallace-Hadrill and others.

Eric Meyers: Thank you, and I do quote him. That's very helpful, but it's a long way from Rome to Jerusalem, despite the importance of that evidence, as we know.

Charles Harris (former Chair, ASOR Board of Trustees): I did not want this session to end without ASOR in its official way (and I'm speaking for P. E. MacAllister, our Chairman, who cannot be here because of the illness of his wife) expressing our thanks to these two people in particular, sitting in the front row here, Seymour Gitin and Lydie Shufro, and all of their colleagues, who have done so much to make this a remarkable birthday celebration for ASOR/Albright.

Special Public Lectures

David Ussishkin: Jerusalem as a Royal and Cultic Center in the 10th–8th Centuries B.C.E.
W. G. Dever: Did God Have a Consort? Archaeology and "Popular" Religion in Ancient Israel [1]

Lydie T. Shufro (Chair)

Amnon Ben-Tor: I have a question addressed to Hercule Poirot [referring to Ussishkin's lecture—eds.]. As he advocates, we should start with the facts. He quotes Nadav Na'aman but, actually, what Nadav Na'aman says is the very opposite. What about Jerusalem in the Amarna period, which happens to be a very, very important site, as we know not from the Bible, but from an "objective" source—the Amarna archive. Where is that city? And Bill, what about Hazor XI?

David Ussishkin: Well, we are moving to the Amarna period. Amarna period Jerusalem is known from the texts, and certainly it was a capital of some sort, but the actual remains on the site are very small and very dull, and they show that the city of the

---

1. Not included in the volume.

Amarna period was indeed very poor and dull. This is not the only case. If you investigate other cases—not all of them, but some of them—you will see the same picture. Take Giza, for example. The only remains at Giza are of a big outer wall, which, according to Hercule Poirot, dates to the Iron Age. So, Giza is mentioned in the Amarna texts as a big place but there are, in fact, hardly any remains. The same applies to Shechem, the same applies to Megiddo, the same applies in fact to Lachish, where there is hardly any organized settlement. So obviously, at this time, the cities or the towns, the settlements, were much smaller than they appear from the texts, and this applies also to Jerusalem.

William Dever: Actually, that wasn't Amnon Ben-Tor—that was Israel Finkelstein who asked that question! Just kidding. Amnon wants to know why I didn't mention the hoard from Stratum XI at Hazor, which Yadin had dated to the 12th century and to a kind of Israelite squatter occupation after the destruction of the lower city. There is a small jar in which some silver items were found, including an axe-head and, in particular, a male figurine. Now, if we were sure that was Israelite, this would be a very important piece of evidence for the earliest Israelite religion, and it would be in the Canaanite tradition. My problem is that the male figurine is precisely of the Late Bronze Age type, and I have always thought it was a kind of hoard or a carry-over from the 13th century, found in the destruction material by the squatters, so I didn't follow Yadin's interpretation. But if one were to do that, then that would be a very important datum for early Israelite religion. And the Canaanite connection wouldn't bother me; I would expect it.

Uzi Avner (Aravah Institute): One comment on Bill's lecture, about the two Bes figures from Ajrud. In many articles, including at least four that I remember by Dever himself, these figures are presented, as they were on the projection screen just now; but here there is a mistake that many scholars fall into. The right-hand figure, in our view, has a restoration made by the person who drew it. Actually, in the original, you do not see any remains of, any indication of, a tail or a penis. On the other hand, the right figure, which is a smaller one, has a breast, and, therefore, it should be a male and a female. Not only this, in many cases of pairs of *maṣṣebot*, the right one, in our view, is smaller and usually broader than the other one. So, in both cases, I believe that we see a male and a female. If you look at this pair in this way, you see a male with the mask of a calf, shall we say, and a female with the mask of a cow, and then it corresponds to the inscription above, to the second line of the inscription, Yahweh and his Asherah. This way, the inscription also makes better sense in connection with the drawing.

William Dever: That certainly is a possible interpretation. Mordechai Gilula and others have argued that, indeed, you have in the two Bes-like figurines a male and a female, Yahweh and his consort. I don't agree. Bes can be portrayed as either a male or a female, so the appearance of one figure with breasts and the other apparently with a penis is not really a problem. Bes is popular in the Judean cult, but scholars disagree passionately about the interpretation of those two figures. And I should mention that not everybody agrees with me that the seated, half-nude female figure is Asherah. I published that already 15 years ago. Some are convinced; others are not. The late Pirhiya Beck, for instance, was not convinced at all. When dealing with pictographic representations, even when we have a text, it's very difficult. It's also obvious that the figures are drawn by one hand on this jar and the text by another. Nevertheless, whoever did the one saw the other and fit them together somewhere in his head. We can easily describe religious practice on the basis of the material remains of the cult. It's very difficult to be sure about belief.

Hershel Shanks (Editor, *Biblical Archaeology Review*): Prof. Ussishkin, I was curious why you allowed yourself to speculate concerning the palace of Solomon and the temple, when there is absolutely no evidence for it. Why didn't you conclude simply that there was no palace and there was no temple in the time of Solomon?

David Ussishkin: Well, how to answer your question? I can't explain my methodological approach from the beginning. The point is, and I said it quite clearly, I'm an archaeologist and I feel I am a technician. I'm a man of material culture; I go to the ground, I see what there is, and I try to combine all this evidence, first, as the basis for everything. I don't say that there is no text, or the text doesn't have importance, or that we don't read, or we've stopped reading the text. The written text certainly exists and certainly has its importance and, of course, the great importance and value of the biblical text is known. I don't have to praise it here. What I am saying is that when an archaeologist comes to study the archaeological material, the material in his hand, his starting point should be the archaeological evidence. He should see what is on the ground, what are the possibilities on the ground, and from that, he should proceed and continue to other spheres, to the written sphere. Now, regarding the Temple Mount, we also, as archaeologists, start from the archaeological material, but we have only the topographical data, and comparisons to other sites. We only know what happens there later. But this is our starting point, and from this we continue to the text. But we certainly don't ignore the text; the text is very important—but it is not our starting point, that's all.

Israel Finkelstein: I would like to respond to both Amnon Ben-Tor and Hershel Shanks, and to add another dimension to what we have just heard from David Ussishkin. The el-Amarna situation is exactly what we need to remember when we come to reconstruct Jerusalem of the 10th or the 9th century. That is to say, for the Amarna period, for the 14th century—maybe for the 13th century, but definitely for the 14th century—we have historical evidence and, at the site, we have a few Late Bronze sherds spread here and there—not much more than that. For the 10th and 9th centuries, we have the sherds and we have possibly also the text, Hershel. So here we have almost a comparable situation, and that is the reason why I would argue that in the 10th and the 9th centuries, we still have, not only in Jerusalem but in the southern hill country, an Amarna situation. I wouldn't say that there was no Davidic dynasty and I wouldn't say that there were no Davidic kings, and I wouldn't deny the historicity of David and Solomon, but we are still in an Amarna situation. And to support that, I would just like to remind the audience that we also have to look at the situation in the southern hill country, for which we have quite a lot of information from both excavations and surveys. And what we see until the 8th century is basically negative—that is to say, for the southern hill country (from Jerusalem to the south, including Hebron)—and that most of the sites (Beth Zur and other sites excavated in the south, quite a lot of them) show strong evidence from the 8th century onward. They show very little evidence, if at all, for Iron I and early Iron II. Moreover, if we look at the surveys, we see that the real boom in the southern highlands comes in the 8th century. The meaning is that the evidence from Jerusalem and the evidence from the southern hill country go together.

Kenneth Kitchen: "Fools rush in where angels fear to tread"! Now, I'm not a dirt archaeologist; I have no right to speak. But I put before everyone this simple fact: If you go and look at the archaeological reports issued by our good colleagues who do the archaeology, in most cases (because of money, time, opportunity), nine-tenths of a site is never dealt with. We are looking at traces when we hear all these reports. It's very suspicious to me that, at all these sites, the Amarna period is so poor, when Pharaoh gets some sort of wealth from them. There is more to a site than is ever dug. In the case of Jerusalem, of course, the place is a wreck, so much has been rubbled over. The beautiful huge compound of Herod masks everything on that site. Bill Dever wanted a permit and didn't get it. Unless someone does, we can't even find it. Bedrock comes up, that's perfectly right, our lecturers have talked about that. In Hattusas that was mentioned: look at the plans there of the great Hittite capital. The bedrock comes up so high that some of the buildings can only be dotted in by the excavators as presumably being there, but they're still gone. They can't find them; they never will. Negative evidence of that kind. When we haven't dug 90 percent of the site, 95 percent of the site, it's a little premature to draw conclusions.

And these great surveys that have been done in Israel in the last 10 or 20 years are extremely valuable, but a survey without digs is not enough. Also, when the digs are 5 percent or 10 percent of a site, in most cases, they can't necessarily give us the whole picture. Let us be careful. Also, it is very interesting—the idea about the palace's being on the north rather than on the south side—but let's not be too schematic. Not all palaces are always built in the same place. Big empires don't need huge capitals. I don't think the Bible says that the City of David is a huge capital. It's merely a dynastic center named after him, to which a temple and palace were added. Thutmose I and Thutmose III of Egypt were the greatest conquerors that Egypt ever had, but Thebes in their day was very small. It wasn't the great thing you see today when you go to Egypt. Karak then was a small temple, the Thutmose section in front of it—not the temple one-quarter of a mile long that the tourist sees today. Don't equate power with bulk of building. It doesn't always fit, not even in Egypt. That's just a caveat. I've enjoyed the whole presentation. There's a lot for all of us to think about. Do take care, however; don't base too much on the *leonem ex ungue*. You can sometimes restore the lion from just a little claw, but unless you've got more of it, you may not know enough about the lion.

Appendix I

Opening of the Israel Museum Exhibit
Thundering on High:
Images of the Canaanite Storm God
in Honor of the Albright/ASOR Centennial

Greetings

James S. Snyder, Director, Israel Museum

It is a pleasure to welcome our guests on the occasion of the Albright/ASOR Centennial Symposium in Jerusalem, and a special pleasure always to welcome guests to the Israel Museum, as the host venue and an honorary sponsor of the symposium.

The Archaeology Wing of the Israel Museum, which holds the most comprehensive display of treasures of the archaeology of the ancient Holy Land, regards as a highest priority its deep commitment to the connection between archaeological excavation and research and the restoration, presentation, and interpretation of the material culture of ancient Israel. Here, we work hand in hand with archaeological researchers engaged in the field, upholding the highest standards, in exactly the manner in which the Albright Institute has worked for the past one hundred years.

Throughout our galleries are numerous examples of artifacts unearthed from a host of excavations involving Albright/ASOR scholars—from Ashkelon to Caesarea to Ekron, where I had my own first Holy Land archaeological experience, with Sy Gitin and Trude Dothan, the directors of the Ekron excavation project, on my first day as Director of the Museum in 1996. And, before proceeding to our business of the moment, I would like to congratulate the Albright Institute and the American Schools of Oriental Research on their first one hundred years and to recognize Sy Gitin, Director of the Albright Institute, and Lydie Shufro, Chair of the Organizing Committee, for arranging this symposium.

It is now my pleasure to offer an example of our work in progress together, on this occasion of the opening of the exhibition "Thundering on High: Images of the Canaanite Storm God," organized by Ossi Misch-Brandl, our curator of the Chalcolithic period and Bronze Age.

Among the many Canaanite deities, the storm god was preeminent, and his story evolved over many periods and in many archaeological forms—in literary texts on tablets, seals, and reliefs, and in statuettes. The presentation of his story here is indeed the result of work in the field, research, restoration, and interpretation and is exemplary of the collaborative enterprise of archaeology in the field and in the museum.

I want to close by acknowledging Ossi Misch-Brandl's excellent accomplishment—together with the supportive collaboration that her achievement here represents. I invite Ossi to introduce the exhibition to you, before inviting all of our guests to enjoy the exhibition and the evening.

Osnat Misch-Brandl, Curator
Chalcolithic Period and Bronze Age, Israel Museum

Dear Friends: I am delighted that this symposium is taking place here at the Israel Museum. The fact that such a significant international event is being held here in the most important archaeological museum in Israel could not be more appropriate, as I am sure you will agree.

A year ago, when we received the proposed program for the Albright/ASOR symposium, the sessions offered on Religion and Distinction attracted my attention. For a long time, I had been collecting material for an exhibition on the subject of cult and religion in Canaan. Such an exhibition, of course, could not have been prepared in a year, and, therefore, I had to concentrate on a single theme. What could be better than "Thundering on High," an exhibition devoted to Ba'al—the Storm God—a young, virile, and powerful deity, the protector and main fertility divinity of the Canaanite pantheon.

The main focus of the exhibition is the finds discovered in the Orthostat Temple at Hazor. This temple, dating to the Middle and the Late Bronze Age, was excavated by the late Professor Yigael Yadin during the 1950s and is the only sanctuary found in Israel that we know was dedicated to the god Ba'al. While the Ba'al temple at Ugarit was identified by an inscription, the Hazor temple was related to the deity on the basis of the discovery of a unique, three-dimensional statue of the god standing on a bull. The object, which is on exhibit here, was exquisitely restored by Ruta Yekutiel of the Israel Museum laboratory.

Most of the exhibits on display were excavated at various sites throughout Israel and have kindly been lent to us by the Israel Antiquities Authority. Special thanks go to H'san and the Hazor Museum. Other objects were lent to us by the Eretz-Israel Museum in Tel Aviv, the Hecht Museum in Haifa, the Bible Lands Museum in Jerusalem, and the Moussaieff family of Herzliya. Thank you all.

I am grateful to all the people involved in the preparation of the exhibition: Bella Gershovich, my colleague, who covered for me whenever necessary, and it happened often; and Dorit Ben-Simhon, the designer, who successfully rose to the challenge of incorporating a temporary exhibition into the permanent display. My appreciation also goes to the editors, Nancy Benovitz and Tami Michaeli; to Penina Arad for her wonderful drawings; to Menahem Amin and Maurice Lasry, who installed the exhibits; and to the staff in the various laboratories for their assistance.

Finally, to all my colleagues of the Bronfman Archaeology Wing of the museum, especially to the Chief Curator, Sylvia Rosenberg, to Ornit Ilan, and to Miriam Tadmor, thank you.

And last, thanks to all of you, dear guests, for attending this opening, and I wish you all a successful and interesting symposium.

Appendix II

Greetings Presented at the Israel Exploration Society Reception on Behalf of the Archaeological Institutions in Israel Held at the Israel Museum

Joseph Aviram

Greetings

It is a great achievement that, after 100 years, Albright/ASOR is still alive and well, active, successful, expanding its activities, and celebrating its centennial here and in America. Many institutions have disappeared from view over the past 100 years, and we congratulate Albright/ASOR on its continued vitality.

Participants in the Albright/ASOR Centennial Symposium, honored guests, it is a great privilege for me to present greetings at this festive gathering, on behalf of the Israel Exploration Society and all the Israeli archaeological institutions that have members on the IES Board of Directors or Council. The IES, where I have worked for some 60 years, that is, since 1940, is rightly regarded as the younger sister of ASOR, since it was founded in large part because of ASOR, 14 years after ASOR was established. A group of well-known individuals decided that it was not right that only foreign expeditions, led by ASOR, the Palestine Exploration Fund, and the École Biblique, should conduct research concerning this country and that we, the residents here, should not "tend our own vineyard." They, therefore, founded our Society, calling it the Jewish Palestine Exploration Society. They were not yet properly organized when World War I broke out, and all activities ceased, to be renewed in 1920, during British Mandatory rule. For the past 80 years, relations between our Society and ASOR have been cordial, due, in large measure, to the personalities who stood at the helm of ASOR, such as William Foxwell Albright, Nelson Glueck, G. Ernest Wright, Frank Moore Cross, Phillip King, Bill Dever, Joe Seger, and many others. The close relationship and cooperation we have today with the Albright Institute and its Director, Sy Gitin, goes without saying.

Prior to the establishment of the State of Israel, the Israel Exploration Society was the only local body involved in archaeology. Since the 1950s and 1960s, institutes and departments of archaeology have been established at universities throughout the country. Prior to 1949, there was but a handful of local archaeologists. Today, there are several hundred, and the number of archaeological excavations to date far exceeds what one would have imagined possible.

We thought it appropriate on this festive occasion to invite three of the pioneers of archaeological and biblical research to present their greetings. The first is Dr. Avraham Biran, President of the IES and an ASOR Fellow in the 1930s. The second is a member of the Executive Committee of the IES, Prof. Abraham Malamat, who was associated with ASOR in the 1940s. The third is Prof. Trude Dothan, the co-director of the Tel Miqne–Ekron excavations, an Albright Fellow during the 1980s and 1990s.

I hope that in the coming century Albright/ASOR will continue their blessed activities and expand and flourish. To conclude, I would like to announce that our Society, together with the Albright Institute, has decided on a joint project that will benefit all of the archaeologists in Israel and in neighboring countries, as well as students and archaeologists worldwide. This project involves the preparation and publication of a comprehensive volume concerning the ancient pottery of Israel. Nearly 35 years have passed since the publication of Ruth Amiran's *Ancient Pottery of the Holy Land*. It has long been out of print and is much in need of updating, as a result of the hundreds of excavations that have been conducted since it was written. The Dorot Foundation has already agreed to support this project, and we hope that additional funding will follow.

I wish you all an interesting and fruitful symposium in the coming days.

Avraham Biran

ASOR, Jerusalem, in the 1930s

There is always a risk in letting an old-timer such as myself recall that prehistoric period of the 1930s, when I was the ASOR Thayer Fellow, the "good old days." While at that time the American Schools of Oriental Research in Jerusalem boasted such giants as Petrie, Albright, Fisher, and Glueck, it could not compare to today's Albright Institute, under its able director, Dr. Seymour Gitin, with its quarter-of-a-million dollars in grants and fellowships and a galaxy of scholars and students.

Way back in 1935, the Thayer Fellowship had no funds. It was only thanks to Albright, who, in his consideration and kindness, asked me to assist him in preparing his Holy Land Atlas, that it was possible for me to keep body and soul together. Still, those were indeed wonderful days — traveling the length and breadth of the country with the Bible as a guide and learned scholars to lead us through inscrutable sites.

I do not know whether the students today gather for tea in the garden, but for us, those afternoons were highlights of our stay, when we met such luminaries as Père Vincent, Albrecht Alt, L. A. Meyer, Speiser, and Sukenik.

I shall always be grateful to the Schools for setting me on the path I followed, and to Albright, who sent me on my very first dig and urged me to prepare the results of my excavation and identification of the site for publication. Indeed, he published my article in *BASOR*, alongside his article suggesting a different identification!

Today, we justly bask in the glory of the Albright Institute and the other branches of the American Schools of Oriental Research. I recall the time when Ernest Wright thought of moving the School away from Jerusalem, and I urged him not to do so. Can we imagine Jerusalem without the Albright, or the Albright not in Jerusalem?

May the School continue to flourish in fulfilling the promise of its early founders. As the oldest living Thayer Fellow and on behalf of the Israel Exploration Society and the Nelson Glueck School of Biblical Archaeology, which bears the name of the director of the American Schools in 1936, heartiest congratulations and best wishes.

Abraham Malamat

ASOR, Jerusalem, in the 1940s

First, let me state that I had no formal association with ASOR: from 1941 to 1946/7, I had only an informal connection, using the facilities of the ASOR (Albright) premises and, above all, its library. My motivation in making use of these facilities was to be able to expand my research perspective beyond Palestine, an option not available at the Hebrew University in 1941. At the time, ancient Near Eastern studies were not represented at the Hebrew University, the closest subjects offered being Cassuto's Ugarit and Torzcyner's (Tur-Sinai's) Semitic philology courses. Mazar was not yet teaching at the University.

I do not remember exactly how I became acquainted with ASOR, but around that time, I registered as a student at the Dominican monastery of the École Biblique, a neighbor of the ASOR facility. The area between the two institutions was still not built up and was very rocky. At the École, I undertook formal studies under Père de Vaux, Père Abel, and Père Tournay, and I visited ASOR regularly, at least twice a week, for some five years.

The route from my home to both institutions led through Me'a She'arim, the Ultra-Orthodox quarter in Jerusalem. I would frequently go to ASOR on a Friday evening, the holy day, and one Friday evening I was surrounded by a group of youngsters in Me'a She'arim, who jumped on me, particularly because I was not wearing a hat and was carrying a schoolbag full of books. To protect myself, I blurted out that I was going to "the American *schul*" (the Yiddish word for synagogue), thinking that if they understood this to be a synagogue, they would be appeased. Thus, the American School became a "*schul*" for me for the next several years.

The Secretary of the School at the time was Mrs. Ina Pomerantz, and on my first visit, she introduced me to a tall gentleman, who started to speak to me in fluent Hebrew. This was the exceptional Morton Smith, a Fellow at ASOR, who told me he was in the final stages of writing his dissertation on the New Testament and Rabbinics. One of his supervisors was Prof. Schwabe. I learned later that Morton Smith had several private Hebrew teachers: one for Biblical Hebrew and another for Mishnaic Hebrew. To give you an idea of his linguistic talents—one day, on entering the library, he noticed the dust on the shelves and said in Hebrew, *Ha'avadim ve-hashfakhot lo ba'u haboker lenakot.* Morton Smith was the first Gentile to write a dissertation at the Hebrew University.

In the few minutes at my disposal, I shall mention the different personalities who visited the School, rather than the studies carried out there. While the premises were quite empty, one regular visitor was Aage Schmid, a Dane, who had an *idée fixe* that the Holy Ark was to be found at Shiloh, despite the fact that the Bible places it elsewhere, and he dug there for several years. There was also Prof. Pick from Hungary, who carried out comparative research on Akkadian and Talmudic sources. Most prominent was Prof. Paul Kraus, professor of Arabic at el-Azhar University, Cairo, and an acquaintance of King Farouk of Egypt. Another impressive personality stormed the school every few years. He came from his excavations in Jordan, and you can certainly guess who it was: the famous Nelson Glueck, adventurous, like Lawrence of Arabia, but with more archaeological skill.

There were occasional visitors to the School from Jerusalem, such as Prof. H. J. Polotsky, the renowned Egyptologist, and J. L. Magnes, a good friend of the School, whose American in-laws supported both the School and the Hebrew University. Ironically, it was at the School rather than at the Hebrew University that I met Yigael Sukenik (later Yadin) for the first time, since he had already finished his studies at the Hebrew University. His motivation, too, in coming to the School was to use the library's collection in ancient Near Eastern studies. We sat for hours poring over this material and became close friends. Suddenly one day, in 1946, he approached me in the ASOR library and asked me if I would take over his Rockefeller Museum guided tours. He remarked that he had to leave everything and would not visit the School any more. I was puzzled as to why he would drop everything, including his half-finished dissertation, and he gave me a mysterious answer. Six months later, I learned that Ben-Gurion had appointed him to the High Command of the newly established Israel Defence Forces, and later, as you all know, he became Chief-of-Staff.

All in all, the 1940s marked a decline in the School and its activities, and it was a leisurely period of tranquility in Jerusalem that allowed us to concentrate on our work, although one must remember that these were the troubled times of the Second World War and its aftermath.

Trude Dothan

The Albright in the 1980s and 1990s

In a city like Jerusalem, it is particularly refreshing and stimulating to have a place like the Albright, not only for its contributions to the understanding of archaeology and the past, but as a model for us all. It is a place where people from all over the world come together for an open and friendly exchange of ideas and information, and a neutral meeting ground for Israelis and Palestinians. Today, the more than 50 Fellows include a wide spectrum of scholars: American, Palestinian, Israeli, British, Canadian, German, French, Swedish, Polish, Hungarian, Czech, Slovak, and Korean. It is a veritable United Nations. Sometimes, I think that Polish is the *lingua franca* there.

It is also a center of intensive activity. Apart from catering to the resident Fellows, the Albright sponsors a wide range of lectures, seminars, workshops, and field trips to 130 sites in Israel and others parts of the Middle East. Then there is the five-star monthly dinner prepared by Hisham, after which the guest of honor is expansive in opening up and sharing with us his or her life and work, and much more. It is not only fun but informative. It helps you to understand the person behind the scholarship and his or her particular point of view and is always followed by a lively discussion.

For the past 20 years, I have been closely associated with the Albright through my work with Sy Gitin, as together we excavated Tel Miqne, Ekron of the Philistines—myself as an "early Philistine" and Sy as a "late Philistine." Sy: dynamic Director of the Albright, colleague, and friend. . . . I am not quite sure how he does it, but he does, and he remains intensely involved with his research on the 7th-century B.C.E. Philistines and the Neo-Assyrian Empire. We are working on the publication of the Ekron excavations with a wonderful team at the Albright and the Hebrew University, while envisaging and preparing for an exhibition on the Sea Peoples, the Philistines, within the walls of this museum. And at the same time, Sy remains the moving spirit in all the intricate and time-consuming affairs of the Albright, which make it the most prominent of the American Schools of Oriental Research, and ready for the future.

Seymour Gitin

Response

On behalf of the Albright Institute and ASOR, I wish to thank the Israel Exploration Society and Joseph Aviram for organizing this wonderful reception. We also deeply appreciate Joseph's strong support over the years for ASOR's many research and excavation projects. He was especially helpful to Trude and myself when we began the excavations at Tel Miqne–Ekron in 1981. I am also very pleased that the IES and the Albright are jointly sponsoring the publication of the *Ancient Pottery of Israel and Its Neighbors* volume. This will be a most exciting challenge, and I look forward to working with Joseph on the project.

Also on behalf of Albright/ASOR, I would like to thank the Israel Museum and its Director, James Snyder, for allowing us to hold our symposium at this wonderful venue, and Osnat Misch-Brandl for organizing the Museum's exhibition, "Thundering on High: Images of the Canaanite Storm God," in honor of our centennial.

Avraham Biran, I want to assure you that the Albright Fellows still gather every afternoon for tea. This has remained a hallowed Albright/ASOR tradition. You will be pleased to learn that the routine has changed somewhat since Lady Petrie's time. Today, everyone is allowed two cookies and two lumps of sugar. I have also learned something new this afternoon: when Avraham Biran was the ASOR Thayer Fellow in Jerusalem in 1936, there were no funds for a stipend. Avraham, I know that Joe Seger, the current ASOR president, who is in the audience today, will want to rectify that situation and retroactively grant you a stipend with interest for the last 65 years!

Abraham Malamat has also taught me something new. For years, I suspected that there was something different, something strange, about the Albright. Now I know what it is. The Albright is "the American *schul*."

I also want to thank Trude for her kind words. I look forward to continuing the cooperative effort between the Albright and the Hebrew University and the early publication of the results of our joint excavation project at Tel Miqne–Ekron.

And to all of you who are participating in this symposium, from far and near, thank you for helping to make the Albright/ASOR centennial celebration such a success.

Indexes

Index of Authors

Index of Scripture

New Testament

Luke
   2:22–24   302

Deuterocanonical Literature

1 Maccabees
   8:1   353
   8:12   353
   12:1   353
   14:24 353
4 Ezra
   12   358

Jubilees
   2:9   374
   9–11   146
   33:2   507
Psalms of Solomon
   2:2   354
   2:28–29   354

Sibylline Oracles
   3   359
   3:350   359
   5:168–71   358
Testament of Reuben
   3:10   507
   3:10–13   507

Index of Ancient Texts